THE PICTURE ANNUAL

covering films of 1988

1989

CineBooks

CineBooks, Inc.
Evanston, Illinois, 1989

C000318644

President: Anita L. Werling; **Editorial Director:** William Leahy; **Senior Writers:** James J. Mulay, Daniel Curran; **Senior Editor:** Jeffrey H. Wallenfeldt; **Editor:** Jenny Mueller; **Research Director:** William C. Clogston; **Associate Editors:** Jeannette Hori, Jennifer Howe, Michaela Tuohy.

Business Manager: Jack Medor; **Assistants:** Bernie Gregoryk, Lena Hicks; **Advertising Manager:** Craig Carter.

Contributors: Linda Aleahmad, David Almquist, John Barnes, John Bertelsen, Meredith Babeaux Brucker, Constance R. Buckley, David Bushman, David Christman, Anton V. Condino, James Cordes, Charles Epstein, Robert Farhi, Sam Frank, Kevin Gillogly, Tom Hinckley, Christina Hoffman, Jane Ike, Mark R. Johnson, Valerie Kaufman, Jeff Kerwin, Chuck Krusling, Thomas Mills, Gary Milo, Barbara J. Mitchell, Diane L. Nickelberg, David Noh, Fred James Nuccio, Adrienne Onofri, Mark Pavia, Phil Pantone, Mark Protosevich, Maia Rodman, Bob Satuloff, Daniel Schackman, Michael Theobald, Marlon West.

Editorial & Sales Offices
CINEBOOKS
990 Grove Street
Evanston, Illinois 60201

Copyright © 1989, CINEBOOKS, INC.

ISBN: 0-933997-21-3

CINEBOOKS, INC. is a McPhersons's Publishing Company

Printed in the United States
First Edition

1   2   3   4   5   6   7   8   9   10

PREFACE

The 1989 Motion Picture Annual provides a detailed chronicle of the films released in the United States in 1988. It was a pretty good year. Once again Hollywood set a new box office record, grossing $4.4 billion domestically, a figure 4 percent above last year's record of $4.25 billion. While the business seems to be in sound financial shape, the real news is that within the glut of mainstream product, several gems managed to emerge. The major releases seemed to swing to extremes: When they were good, they were very good (WHO FRAMED ROGER RABBIT?, BIRD, DEAD RINGERS, RAIN MAN, BIG), and when they were bad, they were very bad (LAST RITES, HEARTBREAK HOTEL, FRESH HORSES, COCKTAIL).

Perhaps the biggest stories of the year were the protests over several major Hollywood releases. The first to make the national news was the controversy over COLORS, Dennis Hooper's film about Los Angeles gang warfare. Civic leaders, social activists, and even the Guardian Angels came out against the film, calling it glorification of gang violence and urged that it be banned nationwide. There was genuine concern over potential violence at theaters where the film played —and there were a few incidents—but nothing as dire as what was predicted.

The hoopla over COLORS, however, was nothing compared to what happened over the summer as Martin Scorsese's long-awaited THE LAST TEMPTATION OF CHRIST neared release. Incited by what they perceived as an outright snub against the Christian community, fundamentalist Christians rose up and attacked the film while it was still in post-production, decrying its allegedly blasphemous content on the basis of a 10-year-old screenplay. Amid the accusations of "Christian-bashing," there was an unmistakable strain of anti-Semitism running through one of the protests when Christians gathered in front of the home of Lew Wasserman, the chairman of Universal Pictures' parent company, MCA, Inc. and staged a mock flagellation of Jesus Christ. While debate raged, Universal sought to quell the controversy by releasing the film several weeks ahead of schedule so that the public could decide for itself. Although a few theater chains refused to book the film, THE LAST TEMPTATION OF CHRIST played in several theaters in major markets and sold out nearly every show in the first few weeks—a result, no doubt, of all the protests.

The year ended with a controversy as well, when the much-ballyhooed and critically praised Alan Parker film MISSISSIPPI BURNING received a harsh backlash from historians and civil rights activists who charged the film distorted history. While director Parker remained virtually mum on the subject, Gene Hackman, the film's star, was thrown to the wolves with an appearance on ABC's "Nightline," where he found himself practically apologizing for his participation in the film.

There was little controversy, however, over the excellence of the most successful film of the year, Robert Zemeckis' ground-breaking tribute to animation, WHO FRAMED ROGER RABBIT?. Rarely have art and commerce blended as beautifully as in this film, which has already become a classic of Hollywood movie-making. WHO FRAMED ROGER RABBIT? heralded the triumphant return of animation, and was followed by the successful release of Don Bluth's THE LAND BEFORE TIME and Disney's OLIVER AND COMPANY. Once again, cartoons were big box office.

Some stunning technological advances were made in 1988, most notably WHO FRAMED ROGER RABBIT?'s flawless integration of live-action and animation, and the pioneering split-screen techniques that allowed Jeremy Irons to act opposite himself in David Cronenberg's chilling DEAD RINGERS. Unfortunately, the techniques were so specialized and expensive that they now are being applied mainly to soft-drink commercials, with Roger Rabbit appearing for Diet-Coke and Michael J. Fox with a twin for Pepsi.

Speaking of twins, Hollywood was obsessed with them in 1988 and several films dealing with duplicates were released. DEAD RINGERS was the best of the lot, while the concept was played for laughs by Bette Midler and Lily Tomlin in BIG BUSINESS and Arnold Schwarzenegger and Danny DeVito in TWINS. In low-budget land, Judy and Audrey Landers were featured in DEADLY TWINS.

Men becoming boys again was an even more prominent theme. While the trail was blazed in 1987 with LIKE FATHER, LIKE SON, the brunt of the like-concept movies hit in 1988 with VICE VERSA, 18 AGAIN!, and BIG. Luckily, BIG was so good that it nearly made up for the execrable efforts that preceded it.

Baseball movies—which have rarely done well—were in vogue this year, with the surprise success BULL DURHAM hitting a home run at the box office, while Sayles' EIGHT MEN OUT hit a single, and the direct-to-video TRADING HEARTS struck out (the strangely titled BAT 21 *was not* a baseball film, and 1989 will see at least one hold-over from the baseball fad, SHOELESS JOE).

1988 also saw the once-dominant macho action film take a slide at the box office with Sylvester Stallone in RAMBO III and Arnold Schwarzenegger in RED HEAT attracting much less money than anticipated. If strong silent types fared poorly, they were successfully replaced by less cartoonish action heroes such as Robert DeNiro in MIDNIGHT RUN and Bruce Willis in DIE HARD.

The screens were pockmarked with sequels—more than ever and worse than usual: ANGEL III, ARTHUR II, BIG TOP PEE WEE, BRADDOCK: MISSING IN ACTION III, CADDYSHACK II, CRITTERS II, COCOON: THE RETURN, CROCODILE DUNDEE II, THE DEAD POOL (DIRTY HARRY 5), DEATHSTALKER II, ERNEST SAVES CHRISTMAS, FRIDAY THE 13TH PART VII, GHOULIES II, HALLOWEEN IV, HELLBOUND: HELLRAISER II, HOWLING IV, IRON EAGLE II, IT'S ALIVE III, L.A. CRACKDOWN II, THE NEW ADVENTURES OF PIPPI LONGSTOCKING, NIGHTMARE ON ELM STREET 4, PHANTASM II, POLICE ACADEMY 5, POLTERGEIST III, RAMBO III, RETURN OF THE KILLER TOMATOES, RETURN OF THE LIVING DEAD

PART II, A RETURN TO SALEM'S LOT, RETURN TO SNOWY RIVER: PART II, SHORT CIRCUIT 2, and SLEEPAWAY CAMP 2.

A heavy crop of remakes was harvested as well, with THE BLOB, D.O.A., AND GOD CREATED WOMAN, NOT OF THIS EARTH, SWITCHING CHANNELS (which was a remake of HIS GIRL FRIDAY, which was a remake of THE FRONT PAGE), and DIRTY ROTTEN SCOUNDRELS (a remake of BEDTIME STORY) all flopping at the box office—and some would argue that Walter Hill's RED HEAT was a remake of his previous 48 HRS., and that the George Lucas-produced WILLOW was a remake of his STAR WARS.

Surprisingly, foreign-language films made a comeback this year, with AU REVOIR, LES ENFANTS, BABETTE'S FEAST, WINGS OF DESIRE, WOMEN ON THE VERGE OF A NERVOUS BREAKDOWN, and SALAAM BOMBAY doing respectable business—contradicting conventional wisdom that subtitled films simply won't play in the U.S. anymore.

With few exceptions, however, most of the best films of the year didn't succeed financially. Alain Resnais' MELO, Cronenberg's DEAD RINGERS, Robert Frank and Rudy Wurlitzer's CANDY MOUNTAIN, George Romero's MONKEY SHINES, Francis Ford Coppola's TUCKER: THE MAN AND HIS DREAM, Clint Eastwood's BIRD, Alan Rudolph's THE MODERNS, Erick Rohmer's BOYFRIENDS AND GIRLFRIENDS, Jean-Luc Godard's KING LEAR, Chris Menges' A WORLD APART, and Tenghiz Abuladze's REPENTANCE, all did poorly at the box office.

With **The 1989 Motion Picture Annual** you can make informed viewing choices—whether theatrically, on home video, or cable television. Chronicling nearly every picture released in the U.S. this past year, including scores of direct-to-video releases, we have attempted to provide the reader with the most complete reference tool to the films of 1988. Naturally, it is necessary to limit the scope of such publications, so we have omitted documentaries, re-releases, shorts, concert and performance films, and made-for-cable movies.

In addition to the Film Reviews, **The 1989 Motion Picture Annual** also includes sections on People to Watch, profiles of young actors, writers and directors who made impressive debuts last year; Obituaries, tributes to industry veterans who passed away in 1988; and Awards, listings of the nominees and winners of Academy Awards, as well as honors bestowed by the film critics in Los Angeles and New York, the British Film Institute, and others.

Every effort has been made to provide the reader with as much information about each film as possible. In gathering such information as cast, character names, production credits, and running times, sources often conflict. CineBooks has made a concerted effort to assure the reliability of our information, but invariably mistakes will be made and we apologize for any that may have slipped past.

For those interested in both US *and* foreign film releases world-wide in 1988, we direct your attention to our **The Motion Picture Guide 1989 Annual,** a hardcover publication which includes more than 1500 film entries, People to Watch, more obituaries, an international awards round-up and an extensive index.

We welcome and appreciate the comments and suggestions of our readers so that future editions of **The Motion Picture Annual** may be even more useful.

Table of Contents

FILMS BY STAR RATING

All films reviewed in this annual are listed below by their star, ratings. The star ratings indicate:
*****: masterpiece; ****: excellent; ***: good; **: fair; *: poor; zero: not worth a glance.

*****

BOYFRIENDS AND GIRLFRIENDS
MELO
WHO FRAMED ROGER RABBIT
WINGS OF DESIRE

****

ANOTHER WOMAN
BIRD
CANDY MOUNTAIN
DEAD RINGERS
FRANTIC
HEAT AND SUNLIGHT
KING LEAR
LAST TEMPTATION OF CHRIST, THE
LITTLE DORRIT
MODERNS, THE
MONKEY SHINES: AN EXPERIMENT IN FEAR
REPENTANCE
SOMEONE TO LOVE
TUCKER: THE MAN AND HIS DREAM
WEDDING IN GALILEE
WELCOME IN VIENNA
WHEN THE WIND BLOWS
WORLD APART, A

***1/2

ALICE
ANGUISH
BAGDAD CAFE
BEAST, THE
BEETLEJUICE
BIG
BILOXI BLUES
BULL DURHAM
COLOR OF DESTINY, THE
COP
CRY IN THE DARK, A
DA
DANGEROUS LIAISONS
D.O.A.
DRAGON CHOW
FISH CALLED WANDA, A
FULL MOON IN BLUE WATER
HAIRSPRAY
HIGH SEASON
LADY IN WHITE
LAND BEFORE TIME, THE
MASS IS ENDED, THE
MIDNIGHT RUN
PUNCHLINE
RAIN MAN
SALOME'S LAST DANCE
SHAME
SHY PEOPLE
STAND AND DELIVER
STORMY MONDAY
TALK RADIO
TAXING WOMAN, A
THEY LIVE
THINGS CHANGE
WORKING GIRL
ZELLY AND ME

***

ACCIDENTAL TOURIST, THE
APPOINTMENT WITH DEATH
BABETTE'S FEAST
BAT 21
BEATRICE
BLOB, THE
CHOCOLATE WAR, THE
CITY OF BLOOD
CLEAN AND SOBER
COLORS
CROSSING DELANCEY

DEAD POOL, THE
DIE HARD
DOMINICK AND EUGENE
EIGHT MEN OUT
END OF THE LINE
FRIENDSHIP'S DEATH
GORILLAS IN THE MIST
HALLOWEEN IV: THE RETURN OF MICHAEL MYERS
HOUSE ON CARROLL STREET, THE
I'M GONNA GIT YOU SUCKA
JACK'S BACK
LATE SUMMER BLUES
LONELY PASSION OF JUDITH HEARNE, THE
MADAME SOUSATZKA
MANIFESTO
MARRIED TO THE MOB
MILES FROM HOME
MURDER ONE
NIGHT IN THE LIFE OF JIMMY REARDON, A
PATTI ROCKS
PROMISED LAND
PULSE
RED HEAT
RUNNING ON EMPTY
SALAAM BOMBAY
SALSA
SERPENT AND THE RAINBOW, THE
SHOOT TO KILL
TOKYO POP
TRAVELLING NORTH
UNDER SATAN'S SUN
WHITE OF THE EYE

**1/2

ABOVE THE LAW
ACCUSED, THE
ALOHA SUMMER
AU REVOIR LES ENFANTS
BETRAYED
BIG TOP PEE-WEE
BORDER HEAT
BRAIN DAMAGE
BRIGHT LIGHTS, BIG CITY
BUSTER
CASUAL SEX?
CHILD'S PLAY
COCOON: THE RETURN
COMING TO AMERICA
COUCH TRIP, THE
DIRTY ROTTEN SCOUNDRELS
DUDES
ERNEST SAVES CHRISTMAS
EVERYBODY'S ALL-AMERICAN
FIVE CORNERS
GRAND HIGHWAY, THE
HANDFUL OF DUST, A
HANNA'S WAR
ILLEGALLY YOURS
IT'S ALIVE III: ISLAND OF THE ALIVE
JOURNEY TO SPIRIT ISLAND
LAIR OF THE WHITE WORM, THE
LIGHTHORSEMEN, THE
LITTLE NIKITA
MILAGRO BEANFIELD WAR, THE
MYSTIC PIZZA
NAKED GUN, THE
NIGHTMARE ON ELM STREET 4: THE DREAM MASTER, A
OLIVER & COMPANY
PASS THE AMMO
PATTY HEARST
PENITENT, THE
PERMANENT RECORD
PRISON
RETURN TO SALEM'S LOT, A
RIKKY AND PETE
SHAKEDOWN
SPIKE OF BENSONHURST
SWITCHING CHANNELS

TEQUILA SUNRISE
TORCH SONG TRILOGY
UNBEARABLE LIGHTNESS OF BEING, THE
VICE VERSA
WHITE MISCHIEF
WITHOUT A CLUE
YEAR MY VOICE BROKE, THE

**

ALIEN NATION
AMERICAN GOTHIC
ARIA
ASSAULT OF THE KILLER BIMBOS
BAD DREAMS
BANDITS
BIG BUSINESS
BLOODSPORT
CALL ME
CONSUMING PASSIONS
CRITTERS 2: THE MAIN COURSE
CROCODILE   DUNDEE II
DADDY'S BOYS
DECEIVERS, THE
DISTANT THUNDER
ELVIRA: MISTRESS OF THE DARK
FURTHER ADVENTURES OF TENNESSEE BUCK, THE
GHOST TOWN
GOOD MOTHER, THE
HELL COMES TO FROGTOWN
HELLBOUND: HELLRAISER II
HERO AND THE TERROR
HIGH SPIRITS
HOWLING IV: THE ORIGINAL NIGHTMARE
JAILBIRD ROCK
LASER MAN, THE
LETHAL OBSESSION
LIGHT YEARS
MEMORIES OF ME
MIDNIGHT CROSSING
MISFIT BRIGADE, THE
MISSISSIPPI BURNING
MR. NORTH
MOON OVER PARADOR
NEW ADVENTURES OF PIPPI LONGSTOCKING, THE
NEW LIFE, A
NIGHT ZOO
1969
NOT SINCE CASANOVA
OFF LIMITS
PHANTASM II
PLATOON LEADER
POUND PUPPIES AND THE LEGEND OF BIG PAW
PUMPKINHEAD
RENT-A-COP
RETURN OF THE LIVING DEAD PART II
RIDERS OF THE STORM
SATURDAY NIGHT AT THE PALACE
SCARECROWS
SHE'S HAVING A BABY
SILENT ASSASSINS
SISTER SISTER
SPLIT DECISIONS
STAR SLAMMER: THE ESCAPE
SWEET HEART'S DANCE
TALKING TO STRANGERS
TIGER'S TALE, A
TRACK 29
TWINS
WILLOW
WIZARD OF LONELINESS, THE
WORLD GONE WILD
YOUNG GUNS

*1/2

ACTION JACKSON
BEAT, THE

BIG BLUE, THE
BOOST, THE
CELLAR DWELLER
CLARA'S HEART
DEAD MAN WALKING
FAR NORTH
FUNNY FARM
JUDGMENT IN BERLIN
JULIA AND JULIA
KILLER KLOWNS FROM OUTER SPACE
MANIAC COP
MASQUERADE
PASCALI'S ISLAND
POLTERGEIST III
PRESIDIO, THE
RAMBO III
SCHOOL DAZE
SCROOGED
'68
SLAUGHTERHOUSE
STICKY FINGERS
SUMMER STORY, A
TAPEHEADS
TOUGHER THAN LEATHER
TRAXX
TWO MOON JUNCTION
WRONG GUYS, THE

*

ANGEL 3: THE FINAL CHAPTER
APPRENTICE TO MURDER
ARTHUR 2 ON THE ROCKS
BEACHES
BLACKOUT
BLUE IGUANA, THE
BRADDOCK: MISSING IN ACTION III
CADDYSHACK II
COCKTAIL
DEAD HEAT
DEADLY DREAMS
DRACULA'S WIDOW
DRIFTER, THE
18 AGAIN!
FOR KEEPS
GHOULIES II
GREAT OUTDOORS, THE
HEARTBREAK HOTEL
HOT TO TROT
IRON EAGLE II
IT COULDN'T HAPPEN HERE
KANDYLAND
KANSAS
LAST RITES
LICENSE TO DRIVE
MAN OUTSIDE
MOVING
MY STEPMOTHER IS AN ALIEN
NOT OF THIS EARTH
POLICE ACADEMY 5: ASSIGNMENT MIAMI
  BEACH
PRIMAL SCREAM
REMOTE CONTROL
RESCUE, THE
RETRIBUTION
SATISFACTION
SCAVENGERS
SEVENTH SIGN, THE
SHORT CIRCUIT 2
SLAUGHTERHOUSE ROCK
STARS AND BARS
STEALING HOME
SUICIDE CLUB, THE
SUNSET
TAFFIN
TELEPHONE, THE
TIME OF DESTINY, A
UNHOLY, THE
VERNE MILLER
YOU CAN'T HURRY LOVE

zero

AND GOD CREATED WOMAN
BERSERKER
BULLETPROOF
DEADLY TWINS

FRANKENSTEIN GENERAL HOSPITAL
FRESH HORSES
FRIDAY THE 13TH PART VII--THE NEW
  BLOOD
GALACTIC GIGOLO
INVISIBLE KID, THE
JOHNNY BE GOOD
NEW YORK'S FINEST
RED HEAT
RENTED LIPS
R.O.T.O.R.
SEVEN HOURS TO JUDGEMENT
SLEEPAWAY CAMP 2: UNHAPPY CAMPERS
UNINVITED, THE

FILMS BY PARENTAL RECOMMENDATION (PR)

All films reviewed in this annual are listed below by the parental recommendation (PR) given to the film. The PR ratings indicate the following: AA: Good for children; A: Acceptable for children; C: Cautionary; O: Objectionable for children.

AA
JOURNEY TO SPIRIT ISLAND
LAND BEFORE TIME, THE
OLIVER & COMPANY
POUND PUPPIES AND THE LEGEND OF BIG PAW
WILLOW

A
BABETTE'S FEAST
BIG BLUE, THE
BIG TOP PEE-WEE
BOYFRIENDS AND GIRLFRIENDS
COCOON: THE RETURN
ERNEST SAVES CHRISTMAS
FRIENDSHIP'S DEATH
ILLEGALLY YOURS
JUDGMENT IN BERLIN
LITTLE DORRIT
MELO
MR. NORTH
NEW ADVENTURES OF PIPPI LONGSTOCK-ING, THE
SHORT CIRCUIT 2
SOMEONE TO LOVE
STAND AND DELIVER
SWITCHING CHANNELS
TUCKER: THE MAN AND HIS DREAM
TWINS
WHO FRAMED ROGER RABBIT
WRONG GUYS, THE
ZELLY AND ME

A-C
APPOINTMENT WITH DEATH
AU REVOIR LES ENFANTS
BIG
DA
END OF THE LINE
FOR KEEPS
FRANTIC
GREAT OUTDOORS, THE
HAIRSPRAY
KING LEAR
LIGHTHORSEMEN, THE
LITTLE NIKITA
MADAME SOUSATZKA
PERMANENT RECORD
RESCUE, THE
VICE VERSA
WITHOUT A CLUE

C
ALOHA SUMMER
ANOTHER WOMAN
APPRENTICE TO MURDER
ARTHUR 2 ON THE ROCKS
BANDITS
BEACHES
BEETLEJUICE
BIG BUSINESS
CADDYSHACK II
CANDY MOUNTAIN
CHOCOLATE WAR, THE
CLARA'S HEART
CRITTERS 2: THE MAIN COURSE
CROCODILE DUNDEE II
CROSSING DELANCEY
CRY IN THE DARK, A
DIRTY ROTTEN SCOUNDRELS
DOMINICK AND EUGENE
DRAGON CHOW
18 AGAIN!
ELVIRA: MISTRESS OF THE DARK
FAR NORTH
FRESH HORSES
FUNNY FARM
GORILLAS IN THE MIST
HANDFUL OF DUST, A
HEARTBREAK HOTEL

HIGH SPIRITS
HOT TO TROT
HOUSE ON CARROLL STREET, THE
INVISIBLE KID, THE
IRON EAGLE II
LADY IN WHITE
LATE SUMMER BLUES
LIGHT YEARS
MAN OUTSIDE
MASS IS ENDED, THE
MEMORIES OF ME
MILAGRO BEANFIELD WAR, THE
MILES FROM HOME
MOON OVER PARADOR
MY STEPMOTHER IS AN ALIEN
NEW LIFE, A
1969
POLICE ACADEMY 5: ASSIGNMENT MIAMI BEACH
PULSE
PUNCHLINE
REMOTE CONTROL
RENT-A-COP
REPENTANCE
RUNNING ON EMPTY
SALSA
SATURDAY NIGHT AT THE PALACE
SCAVENGERS
SCROOGED
SEVENTH SIGN, THE
SPIKE OF BENSONHURST
STEALING HOME
STICKY FINGERS
SUICIDE CLUB, THE
SUNSET
TAFFIN
TELEPHONE, THE
THINGS CHANGE
TIME OF DESTINY, A
TRAVELLING NORTH
WHEN THE WIND BLOWS
WINGS OF DESIRE
WIZARD OF LONELINESS, THE
YEAR MY VOICE BROKE, THE

C-O
ACCIDENTAL TOURIST, THE
BAGDAD CAFE
BEAT, THE
BILOXI BLUES
BIRD
BUSTER
COLOR OF DESTINY, THE
D.O.A.
EIGHT MEN OUT
EVERYBODY'S ALL-AMERICAN
FISH CALLED WANDA, A
GHOST TOWN
GHOULIES II
HANNA'S WAR
HIGH SEASON
IT COULDN'T HAPPEN HERE
JULIA AND JULIA
KANSAS
KILLER KLOWNS FROM OUTER SPACE
NAKED GUN, THE
PASCALI'S ISLAND
PENITENT, THE
POLTERGEIST III
PRESIDIO, THE
RAIN MAN
SATISFACTION
SHE'S HAVING A BABY
STARS AND BARS
SUMMER STORY, A
SWEET HEART'S DANCE
TAXING WOMAN, A
TIGER'S TALE, A
UNDER SATAN'S SUN
WORLD APART, A

O
ABOVE THE LAW
ACCUSED, THE
ACTION JACKSON
ALICE
ALIEN NATION
AMERICAN GOTHIC
AND GOD CREATED WOMAN
ANGEL 3: THE FINAL CHAPTER
ANGUISH
ARIA
ASSAULT OF THE KILLER BIMBOS
BAD DREAMS
BAT 21
BEAST, THE
BEATRICE
BERSERKER
BETRAYED
BLACKOUT
BLOB, THE
BLOODSPORT
BLUE IGUANA, THE
BOOST, THE
BORDER HEAT
BRADDOCK: MISSING IN ACTION III
BRAIN DAMAGE
BRIGHT LIGHTS, BIG CITY
BULL DURHAM
BULLETPROOF
CALL ME
CASUAL SEX?
CELLAR DWELLER
CHILD'S PLAY
CITY OF BLOOD
CLEAN AND SOBER
COCKTAIL
COLORS
COMING TO AMERICA
CONSUMING PASSIONS
COP
COUCH TRIP, THE
DADDY'S BOYS
DANGEROUS LIAISONS
DEAD HEAT
DEAD MAN WALKING
DEAD POOL, THE
DEAD RINGERS
DEADLY DREAMS
DEADLY TWINS
DECEIVERS, THE
DIE HARD
DISTANT THUNDER
DRACULA'S WIDOW
DRIFTER, THE
DUDES
FIVE CORNERS
FRANKENSTEIN GENERAL HOSPITAL
FRIDAY THE 13TH PART VII--THE NEW BLOOD
FULL MOON IN BLUE WATER
FURTHER ADVENTURES OF TENNESSEE BUCK, THE
GALACTIC GIGOLO
GOOD MOTHER, THE
GRAND HIGHWAY, THE
HALLOWEEN IV: THE RETURN OF MICHAEL MYERS
HEAT AND SUNLIGHT
HELL COMES TO FROGTOWN
HELLBOUND: HELLRAISER II
HERO AND THE TERROR
HOWLING IV: THE ORIGINAL NIGHTMARE
I'M GONNA GIT YOU SUCKA
IT'S ALIVE III: ISLAND OF THE ALIVE
JACK'S BACK
JAILBIRD ROCK
JOHNNY BE GOOD
KANDYLAND
LAIR OF THE WHITE WORM, THE
LASER MAN, THE
LAST RITES
LAST TEMPTATION OF CHRIST, THE

FILMS BY GENRE

All the films included in this annual are listed below by the genre best suited to the film. Those films which can be classified by more than one genre are listed under each of the genres in which they fit. For example, the comedy/drama LITTLE DORRIT is listed under both of those genres.

ACTION
ABOVE THE LAW
ACTION JACKSON
ANGEL 3: THE FINAL CHAPTER
ARIZONA HEAT
BLOODSPORT
BORN TO RACE
BRADDOCK: MISSING IN AC-
TION III
BULLETPROOF
CAPTIVE RAGE
CRIME ZONE
DEAD MAN WALKING
DEATH CHASE
DIE HARD
FEAR
HOLLYWOOD COP
IRON EAGLE II
LONE RUNNER, THE
MESSENGER OF DEATH
ORDER OF THE BLACK EAGLE
OUTLAW FORCE
PRESIDIO, THE
RAMBO III
RED HEAT
RED HEAT
RENT-A-COP
RESCUE, THE
ROLLING VENGEANCE
SHAKEDOWN
SILENT ASSASSINS
SKELETON COAST
TAFFIN
TERMINAL ENTRY
TERROR SQUAD
TOUGHER THAN LEATHER
TRAXX
WAR
WHITE GHOST
WORLD GONE WILD

ADVENTURE
BIG BLUE, THE
BULLETPROOF
CROCODILE   DUNDEE II
CRYSTALSTONE
DARK AGE
DEATHSTALKER II
DECEIVERS, THE
FURTHER ADVENTURES OF
TENNESSEE BUCK, THE
ORDER OF THE BLACK EAGLE
RESCUE, THE
SCAVENGERS
SKELETON COAST
VIBES

ANIMATION
BRAVESTARR
LAND BEFORE TIME, THE
LIGHT YEARS
OLIVER & COMPANY
POUND PUPPIES AND THE LEG-
END OF BIG PAW
WHEN THE WIND BLOWS
WHO FRAMED ROGER RABBIT

BIOGRAPHY
BIRD
PATTY HEARST
TUCKER: THE MAN AND HIS
DREAM
VERNE MILLER
WORLD APART, A

CHILDREN'S
CRYSTALSTONE
ERNEST SAVES CHRISTMAS

LAND BEFORE TIME, THE
NEW ADVENTURES OF PIPPI
LONGSTOCKING, THE
OLIVER & COMPANY
POUND PUPPIES AND THE LEG-
END OF BIG PAW
PURPLE PEOPLE EATER, THE

COMEDY
ACCIDENTAL TOURIST, THE
ALOHA SUMMER
AMERICAN SCREAM, THE
ANOTHER CHANCE
ARTHUR 2 ON THE ROCKS
ASSAULT OF THE KILLER BIM-
BOS
BAGDAD CAFE
BEACH BALLS
BEETLEJUICE
BIG
BIG BUSINESS
BIG TOP PEE-WEE
BILOXI BLUES
BLUE IGUANA, THE
BLUE MOVIES
BOYFRIENDS AND GIRL-
FRIENDS
BULL DURHAM
BUSTER
CADDYSHACK II
CASUAL SEX?
COCOON: THE RETURN
COMING TO AMERICA
COMPUTER BEACH PARTY
CONSUMING PASSIONS
COUCH TRIP, THE
CROCODILE   DUNDEE II
CROSSING DELANCEY
DANGEROUS CURVES
DEAD HEAT
DIRTY ROTTEN SCOUNDRELS
DR. HACKENSTEIN
18 AGAIN!
ELVIRA: MISTRESS OF THE
DARK
ERNEST SAVES CHRISTMAS
FAR NORTH
FEDS
FISH CALLED WANDA, A
FIVE CORNERS
FOR KEEPS
FRANKENSTEIN GENERAL
HOSPITAL
FULL MOON IN BLUE WATER
FUNNY FARM
GALACTIC GIGOLO
GLITCH
GREAT OUTDOORS, THE
HAIRSPRAY
HIGH SEASON
HIGH SPIRITS
HOLLYWOOD CHAINSAW
HOOKERS
HOME REMEDY
HOT TO TROT
I HATE ACTORS
I MARRIED A VAMPIRE
ILLEGALLY YOURS
I'M GONNA GIT YOU SUCKA
INVISIBLE KID, THE
IT TAKES TWO
JOHNNY BE GOOD
LASER MAN, THE
LICENSE TO DRIVE
LITTLE DORRIT
MAC AND ME
MANIFESTO
MARRIED TO THE MOB

MASS IS ENDED, THE
MEMORIES OF ME
MIDNIGHT RUN
MILAGRO BEANFIELD WAR,
THE
MR. NORTH
MOON OVER PARADOR
MORGAN'S CAKE
MOVING
MY BEST FRIEND IS A VAM-
PIRE
MY STEPMOTHER IS AN ALIEN
MYSTIC PIZZA
NAKED GUN, THE
NEW LIFE, A
NEW YORK'S FINEST
NIGHT BEFORE, THE
NIGHT IN THE LIFE OF JIMMY
REARDON, A
NOT OF THIS EARTH
NOT SINCE CASANOVA
PARAMEDICS
PASS THE AMMO
PATTI ROCKS
POLICE ACADEMY 5: ASSIGN-
MENT MIAMI BEACH
PUNCHLINE
RENT-A-COP
RENTED LIPS
RETURN OF THE KILLER TO-
MATOES
RETURN OF THE LIVING DEAD
PART II
RICKY 1
RIDERS OF THE STORM
RIKKY AND PETE
SALOME'S LAST DANCE
SCHOOL DAZE
SCROOGED
SENIOR WEEK
SEXPOT
SHE'S HAVING A BABY
SHORT CIRCUIT 2
SLIME CITY
SOMEONE TO LOVE
SORORITY BABES IN THE
SLIMEBALL BOWL-O-RAMA
SPIKE OF BENSONHURST
STAR SLAMMER: THE ESCAPE
STARS AND BARS
STICKY FINGERS
STUDENT AFFAIRS
SWEET HEART'S DANCE
SWITCHING CHANNELS
TAPEHEADS
TAXING WOMAN, A
TELEPHONE, THE
THINGS CHANGE
THINKIN' BIG
TIGER'S TALE, A
TIN STAR VOID
TOKYO POP
TRADING HEARTS
TRAXX
TWINS
VIBES
VICE VERSA
WHO FRAMED ROGER RABBIT
WITHOUT A CLUE
WIZARD OF SPEED AND TIME,
THE
WRONG GUYS, THE
YOU CAN'T HURRY LOVE

CRIME
ARIZONA HEAT
ASSAULT OF THE KILLER BIM-
BOS

BANDITS
BLUE IGUANA, THE
BORDER HEAT
BUSTER
COLORS
CRIME ZONE
DADDY'S BOYS
DANCE OR DIE
DEAD POOL, THE
DEADLY TWINS
DIRTY ROTTEN SCOUNDRELS
FISH CALLED WANDA, A
HERO AND THE TERROR
KANSAS
KILLING GAME, THE
L.A. CRACKDOWN
L.A. CRACKDOWN II
LETHAL OBSESSION
MARRIED TO THE MOB
MIDNIGHT RUN
MURDER ONE
NIGHT ZOO
SAIGON COMMANDOS
SHAKEDOWN
SHOOT TO KILL
STORMY MONDAY
TAKE TWO
THINGS CHANGE
THRILLKILL
TIN STAR VOID
UNDERACHIEVERS, THE
VAMPIRE AT MIDNIGHT
VERNE MILLER
WORKING GIRL

DANCE
DANCE OR DIE
ILLUSORY THOUGHTS

DOCU-DRAMA
CRY IN THE DARK, A

DRAMA
ACCIDENTAL TOURIST, THE
ACCUSED, THE
ALOHA SUMMER
AND GOD CREATED WOMAN
ANOTHER WOMAN
ASTONISHED
AU REVOIR LES ENFANTS
BABETTE'S FEAST
BAGDAD CAFE
BEACHES
BEAT, THE
BILOXI BLUES
BODY BEAT
BOOST, THE
BOYFRIENDS AND GIRL-
FRIENDS
BRIGHT LIGHTS, BIG CITY
CANDY MOUNTAIN
CHOCOLATE WAR, THE
CLARA'S HEART
CLEAN AND SOBER
COCKTAIL
COLOR OF DESTINY, THE
COMPUTER BEACH PARTY
DA
DANGEROUS LIAISONS
DISTANT THUNDER
DOMINICK AND EUGENE
DON'T MESS WITH MY SISTER!
DRAGON CHOW
END OF THE LINE
FAMILY VIEWING
FAR NORTH
FIVE CORNERS
FOR KEEPS
FRESH HORSES

THE MOTION PICTURE ANNUAL

1989

Film
Reviews

A

ABOVE THE LAW**½   (1988) 99m WB c

Steven Seagal *(Nico Toscani)*, Pam Grier *(Delores Jackson)*, Henry Silva *(Zagon)*, Ron Dean *(Lukich)*, Daniel Faraldo *(Salvano)*, Sharon Stone *(Sara Toscani)*, Nicholas Kusenko *(Agent Neeley)*, Joe V. Greco *(Father Gennaro)*, Chelcie Ross *(Nelson Fox)*, Thalmus Rasulala *(Deputy Superintendent Crowder)*, Jack Wallace *(Uncle Branca)*, Joseph Kosala *(Lt. Strozah)*, John Drummond *(TV Reporter)*, Ronnie Barron *(CIA Bartender)*, Miguel Nino *(Chi Chi)*, Metta Davis *(Rosa Toscani)*, Gene Barge *(Detective Henderson)*, Danny Goldring *(Zagon's Aide)*, Mike James *(Officer O'Hara)*, India Cooper *(Sanctuary Nun)*, Gregory Alan-Williams *(Agent Halloran)*, Henry Godinez *(Father Tomasino)*, Joe D. Lauck *(Senator Harrison)*, Michelle Hoard *(Lucy)*, Christopher Peditto *(Pimp)*, Rafael Gonzalez *(Abandano)*, Nydia Rodriguez-Terracina *(Bomb Woman)*, Cheryl Hamada *(Watanabe)*, Ralph Foody *(Federal Clerk)*, Vince Viverito *(Giuseppe)*, Alex Ross *(Luigi)*, Toni Fleming *(Grandma Zingaro)*, Gene Hartline, Tom Milanovich, Dan Janecek, Michael Rooker *(Men in Bar)*, Patrick Gorman, Lee de Broux, Gary Goldman *(CIA Interrogators)*, Le Tuan *(Interpreter)*, Dennis Phun, April Tran *(Asian Prisoners)*, Chantara Nop *(Cambodian Irregular)*, Al Rasho *(Grocery Owner)*, Mike Coglianese *(Branca's Bodyguard)*, Sandy Holt *(Hostess)*, Mike Nakayama *(NEC Show Rep)*, Zaid Farid *(Street Dude)*, Juan Ramirez *(Machete Man)*, Mario Nieves *(Man with Gun)*, Terry Stewart *(Machete Man's Buddy)*, Lisa Tejero *(Refugee Woman)*, Chris Karchmar *(Refugee Man)*, Clare Peck *(Judge Alspaugh)*.

As Ronald Reagan's "morning in America" approaches dusk and the country begins to swing from the right back to the center, a new set of national values has begun to manifest itself in our popular entertainment. In 1985 the jingoistic RAMBO was the action film of choice; in 1988 we have the decidedly left-wing ABOVE THE LAW. Although the rabble-rousing title seems to indicate that it is star Steve Seagal who is "above the law," the title actually refers to CIA covert operations—operations of which this film is highly critical. The film begins as the voice of Seagal informs us how, as a young Italian-American child, he became fascinated with martial arts. When old enough, he traveled to Japan to study aikido (the most challenging of the martial arts). After years of intense training he graduated to sixth-degree black belt status and then became the first white man to open an aikido school in Tokyo. At a party at the American embassy in Tokyo, Seagal was approached by the CIA and recruited for duty during the Vietnam War (this, according to the film's publicity, is nearly all autobiographical, although Seagal refuses to discuss his CIA connections. In Cambodia the upstanding Seagal runs afoul of evil CIA interrogator Silva, a man who likes to drug his victims, then hack off their limbs until they talk. Although Seagal is inclined to kill Silva, he is dissuaded by fellow agent Kusenko. Disillusioned, Seagal quits the CIA and becomes a Chicago cop. Twenty years later, Seagal is a respected detective with a tough black female partner, Grier. He is also a devoted husband and father whose family ties to the Mafia are always a source of tension with his fellow officers. When what Seagal and Grier thought was to be a South American drug deal turns out to be the sale of plastic explosives, Seagal begins to suspect his old buddies at the CIA. Seagal then learns that his parish priest is hiding Salvadoran refugees in the church basement, but shortly thereafter the priest is killed in an explosion during Sunday mass. Grier discovers that one of the parishioners killed in the blast was an aide to the head of the Senate Foreign Relations Committee, which is currently investigating charges of drug running by the CIA to fund a covert invasion of Nicaragua. Seagal deduces that the bomb was really meant to kill the senator's aide and not the parish priest. He then learns that one of the refugees, a young Salvadoran priest, has proof that the CIA intends to assassinate the crusading senator if he blows the whistle on their covert operations. But by the time Seagal pieces the puzzle together, the priest has vanished and is being tortured by none other than Seagal's old nemesis Silva. Late one night Seagal gets a phone call his former CIA partner, Kusenko, telling him to lay off the case or his family will suffer. Seagal refuses and soon the CIA arrests him at his home and makes veiled threats on his family. Suspended by the police department, Seagal calls in his Mafia-connected relatives to protect his wife and child while he goes after the CIA with both barrels. After several attempts on his life and the wounding of Grier, Seagal finally manages to catch up with Silva and foils the CIA assassination attempt by single-handedly killing the five-man hit squad. In the end, the heroic Seagal agrees to testify against the CIA before the Senate Foreign Relations Committee.

Although there is an inherent contradiction in having a self-righteous hero preach against the immorality of the CIA while running around brutally violating the civil rights of scores of others, ABOVE THE LAW is an exciting, well-crafted actioner with a surprising difference: it is the first mainstream American action film of the 1980s to openly criticize current US foreign policy. The explicit discussion of long-rumored CIA/contra drug dealing is, frankly, shocking considering that the film was shot and released while Ronald Reagan was still in the White House. ABOVE THE LAW could be the initial entry in a string of post-Reagan mainstream entertainments that represent a national disillusionment with a once wildly popular administration—a situation similar to the rash of antigovernment conspiracy films that were released on the heels of Watergate. That ABOVE THE LAW was a big hit at the box office seems to indicate mass acceptance of the possibility of CIA drug-running by the wary American public. While the film may be a bit dogmatic and wear its politics on its sleeve, at least it is a liberal alternative to the right-wing fantasies that have dominated the box office in the Reagan era.

Left-wing politics aside, director Andrew Davis delivers what is really required here: a slam-bang action film with some stunning scenes of mayhem and violence. This is Seagal's big debut as an action hero and he makes an impressive splash. Tall, lean, and soft-spoken, he is more reminiscent of Clint Eastwood than the muscle-bound Stallone-Schwarzenegger automatons, and plays the part of loving family man convincingly. As was director Davis' style in the Chuck Norris film CODE OF SILENCE, the martial arts moves are kept to a minimum and are flashy and impressive when need be. The rest of the cast is a typically solid stable of supporting characters—many of them Chicago actors—with the gorgeous Pam Grier making a welcome return to the screen after several minuscule supporting roles. Taking a character that could have been a cliche, Grier turns her role into something special—a vibrant, confident, intelligent woman who is the equal of any man and commands respect. Her easy on-screen rapport with Seagal does much to humanize her character. Seagal's scenes with Grier are much more effective in this respect than the brief and clumsy domestic passages between husband and wife (played badly by Sharon Stone). Director Davis, a Chicago native, has a great eye for locations and avoids the tired panoramic lakefront vistas that every director who shoots in the Windy City exploits. There is no Wrigley Field here, no museums, no Lake Shore Drive, just street-level Chicago neighborhoods that convey a sense of time, place, and community little seen on American screens. Although the political speeches may become somewhat overbearing and the narrative unnecessarily complicated, ABOVE THE LAW is a worthy and unusual entry into the action film genre of the 1980s. *(Graphic violence, profanity.)*

p, Steven Seagal, Andrew Davis; d, Andrew Davis; w, Steven Pressfield, Ronald Shusett, Andrew Davis (based on a story by Andrew Davis, Steven Seagal); ph, Robert Steadman (Technicolor); ed, Michael Brown; m, David M. Frank; prod d, Maher Ahmad; art d, Ned Parsons; set d, Bill Arnold, Ed McDonald; spec eff, Art Brewer, Leo Solis; ch, Steven Seagal; makeup, Rodger Jacobs.

Action   Cas.   (PR:O MPAA:R)

ABSOLUTION †   (1988) 105m Trans World c

Richard Burton *(Father Goddard)*, Dominic Guard *(Benji)*, Dai Bradley *(Arthur)*, Billy Connolly *(Blakey)*, Andrew Keir *(Headmaster)*, Willoughby Gray *(Brigadier Walsh)*, Preston Lockwood *(Father Hibbert)*, James Ottaway *(Father Mathews)*, Brook Williams *(Father Clarence)*, Jon Plowman *(Father Piers)*, Robin Soans *(Father Henryson)*, Trevor Martin *(Mr. Gladstone)*, Sharon Duce *(Louella)*, Brian Glover, Dan Meaden *(Policemen)*, Hilary Mason *(Miss Froggatt)*, Hilda Fenemore *(Mrs. Haskins)*, Robert Addie *(Cawley)*, Kevin Hart *(Peterson)*, Philip Leake *(Gregory)*, Michael Crompton *(O'Dowd)*, Andrew Boxer, Richard Willis, Michael Parkhouse, Richard Kates, Martyn Hesford, Clive Gehle, Charles Rigby, Michael Bell, Martin Stringer, Francis Fry, Julian Firth, Tim Short *(Other Boys)*.

Filmed back in 1979 but left on the shelf due to "legal matters," this thriller written by Anthony Shaffer (THE WICKER MAN) and starring Richard Burton was finally given a limited release in selected markets in 1988 before going to home video. Continuing his obsession with stifled sexuality, screenwriter Shaffer presents a Catholic boy's school presided over by uptight priest Burton—a place where repressed homosexual desires are at a boiling point. The pious, humorless Burton runs the school with an iron fist, but he does have a favorite student, the bright and handsome Guard. Guard is also admired by a fellow student, the lame, greasy, nerdy Bradley, who follows Guard around like a lost puppy. Trouble arises, however, when an amoral drifter (Connolly) takes up residence in the nearby woods. Guard is intrigued by the stranger and befriends him, thrilling to his romantic tales of the open road. Burton is outraged by the outsider and moves to have him forced off the land. In retaliation, Guard and Connolly devise a scheme to break Burton: Guard will confess to having committed a murder, and Burton—whose vows prevent him from revealing what he has heard in confessional—will be powerless to do anything about it. The prank has the desired effect and Burton begins to slip into madness.

Written in the early 1970s, ABSOLUTION was reportedly a pet project of Burton's and he worked hard to get the film made, taking just a fraction of his usual salary. Unfortunately, legal hassles between coproducers Elliott Kastner and Danny O'Donovan prevented the film's distribution. Nine years after its completion Trans World Entertainment released the film, but Burton, who died in 1984, didn't live to see it.

p, Elliott Kastner, Danny O'Donovan; d, Anthony Page; w, Anthony Shaffer; ph, John Coquillon; ed, John Victor Smith; m, Stanley Myers, Billy Connolly; prod d, Natasha Kroll; set d, Terry Parr; cos, Anne Gainsford; makeup, Freddy Williamson.

Thriller   Cas.   (PR:NR MPAA:R)

ACCIDENTAL TOURIST, THE***   (1988) 121m WB c

William Hurt *(Macon Leary)*, Kathleen Turner *(Sarah Leary)*, Geena Davis *(Muriel Pritchett)*, Amy Wright *(Rose)*, Bill Pullman *(Julian)*, Robert Gorman *(Alexander*

Pritchett), David Ogden Stiers *(Porter Leary),* Ed Begley, Jr. *(Charles Leary),* Bradley Mott *(Mr. Loomis),* Seth Granger *(Ethan),* Amanda Houck *(Debbie),* Caroline Houck *(Dorrie),* London Nelson *(Caroline),* Gregory Gouyer *(Paris Boy),* W.H. Brown *(Morgue Detective),* Donald Neal *(Morgue Detective),* Peggy Converse *(Mrs. Barrett),* Maureen Kerrigan *(Laura Canfield),* Jacob Kasdan *(Scott Canfield),* Paul Williamson *(London Hotel Manager),* Walter Sparrow *(Hot Dog Vendor),* Todd Adelman *(Macon's Doctor),* Meg Kasdan *(Receptionist),* David Combs *(Minister),* Jonathan Kasdan *(Boy At Doctor's Office),* Thomas Paolucci *(Taunting Boy),* Neana N. Collins *(Taunting Girl),* Roland Riallot *(Paris Cab Driver),* Boone Narr *(Stunt Person),* Audrey R. Rapoport *(Girl On Plane),* Bud *(Edward the Dog).*

The film adaptation of Anne Tyler's novel hinges on William Hurt's magnificently understated performance as Macon Leary, a "Baltimore man" who writes travel guides for businessmen who hate to travel. With a winged armchair as his symbol (armchair travelers long to travel; traveling armchairs long to stay at home), Hurt provides tips that allow his readers to shield themselves from the unfamiliarity of foreign environments. His occupation is symbolically telling, as Hurt has gone through life insulated from feeling, carefully orchestrating his world so that the unpredictable chaos of intense emotion doesn't intrude upon his ordered but pessimistic existence. As the story begins, Hurt's wife, Turner (who sizzled with Hurt in Kasdan's BODY HEAT), leaves him, unable to endure his continued emotional sterility in the face of their 12-year-old son's murder during the robbery of a fast food restaurant a year earlier. Hurt reacts to her departure by trying bring even more off-the-wall order to his life, but his interior existence and dreams are dominated by the tremendous sense of loss he feels, but has been unable to express, for his son. When he breaks his leg, Hurt moves in with his oddball middle-aged sister (Wright), who arranges the kitchen cabinets alphabetically, and his equally eccentric brothers (Begley and Stiers) in the house they grew up in. Because his son's Welsh corgi has become a disciplinary problem, Hurt is forced to call upon the dog-training services of Davis, a long-legged, vibrant divorcee who has been trying to become a part of Hurt's life. During their training sessions, Davis' quirky, ingenuous charm begins to penetrate Hurt's adamant standoffishness, and, almost before he knows what's happening, Hurt is cohabiting with Davis and her anemic but adorable young son (Gorman) in their less-than-modest home. While Hurt's brothers can't understand why he's taken up with "this Muriel person," his sister falls in love with and marries his publisher, Pullman, a swinging single who longs for the ultratraditional lifestyle that Wright offers. At their wedding, Hurt encounters Turner, and it isn't long before she begins telephoning him, moves into their old house, and asks him to come back to her. He does, but when he has to go to Paris to update one of his books, Davis follows him, though he fends off her attempts at reconciliation. When Hurt is immobilized by his trick back, Turner also comes to Paris to take care of him and to celebrate a second honeymoon. She knows that Davis is there, but Hurt explains that she has come on her own; then, after a night of contemplation and a touching explanation to Turner, he chooses to return to the States with Davis, embracing his newfound appreciation of life.

Although he has been forced to eliminate some characters and telescope some events, Kasdan (THE BIG CHILL; SILVERADO) has remained true to the spirit of Tyler's National Book Critics Circle Award-winning novel, preserving much of her wonderful dialog and humor, and providing a suitable cinematic interpretation of Macon Leary's interior life. Working with cinematographer John Bailey, Kasdan visually evokes the intimate examination of Hurt's psyche with an abundance of close-ups, and his insular existence is frequently conveyed through the use of an anamorphic camera process that creates a shallow depth of field, leaving backgrounds indistinct. Some of the books funnier moments have disappeared in Kasdan's screenplay, but his treatment of Hurt's strange family—sold by the excellent performances of Amy Wright, David Ogden Stiers, and Ed Begley, Jr.—is nearly as satisfying as the book's and the rendering of their esoteric card game, Vaccination, is even more hilarious than Tyler's description. Kasdan has also expanded Kathleen Turner's role for the film, and she responds with a capable performance that presents a Sarah who is little more hollow at her center than her print equivalent. As the other important woman in Hurt's life, Geena Davis (THE FLY; BEETLEJUICE) skillfully captures all of Muriel's quirkiness and insouciance, but, significantly, never conveys the soulfulness that steals Macon's heart in the novel—the simple turning of Muriel's head that he finds so pregnant with meaning and heart-piercing. Hurt and Davis unquestionably have a chemistry between them in the film's lighter moments, but the absence of this more profound bond works against the film's overall effect. It is difficult, however, to find anything wrong with Hurt's assured performance, as he manages to be appropriately passive and tortured, communicating the pessimism and caution of Macon's painful worldview in the way he carries his shoulders and squints his eyes. Hurt's performance is one of minute gestures and almost imperceptible changes in character, so that his liberation from emotional exile has the impact of a moonshot, and his outstanding work is only rivaled by that of Bud, the amazingly expressive Welsh corgi that "plays" Edward.

THE ACCIDENTAL TOURIST came to the screen as a result of the interest shown by actor John Malkovich (DANGEROUS LIAISONS; MAKING MR. RIGHT) and Phyllis Carlyle, who read a prepublication version of Tyler's novel and persuaded Warner Bros. to secure the rights to it. Frank Galati was then chosen to adapt the novel, but after Malkovich, who was to executive produce, was forced by other commitments to leave the project, Kasdan decided to completely rewrite Galati's screenplay. A great admirer of Tyler and the novel, Kasdan wrote six drafts of the script before he felt confident enough to send it to the author for her approval. Tyler, for her part, liked the screenplay enough to chauffeur Kasdan around Baltimore when he came to scout locations, showing him the real-life places where events in the novel occur. Although devotees of Tyler may not be wholly satisfied by Kasdan's film, it is nonetheless a reverent, funny, touching adaptation of a book that has brought much pleasure to many readers. *(Adult situations.)*

p, Lawrence Kasdan, Charles Okun, Michael Grillo; d, Lawrence Kasdan; w,

Frank Galati, Lawrence Kasdan (based on a novel by Anne Tyler); ph, John Bailey (Technicolor); ed, Carol Littleton; m, John Williams; m/l, Frankie Adams, Wilbur Jones; prod d, Bo Welch; art d, Tom Duffield, Cricket Rowland; set d, Paul Sonski, Nick Navarro, Ann Harris; cos, Ruth Myers; makeup, Leonard Engelman.

Comedy/Drama   (PR:C-O MPAA:PG)

ACCUSED, THE✶✶½   (1988) 110m PAR c

Kelly McGillis *(Kathryn Murphy),* Jodie Foster *(Sarah Tobias),* Bernie Coulson *(Kenneth Joyce),* Ann Hearn *(Sally Frazer),* Steve Antin *(Bob Joiner),* Tom O'Brien *(Larry),* Allan Lysell *(Asst. D.A. Al Massi),* Leo Rossi *(Cliff Albrecht),* Carmen Argenziano *(Paul Rudolph),* Terry David Mulligan *(Det. Duncan),* Woody Brown *(Danny Rudkin),* Peter Van Norden *(Ted Paulson).*

Little more than a graphic television movie, THE ACCUSED is structured like so many "Disease of the Week" treatments. In this overstated melodrama, however, the "disease" is a societal one, and all too widespread—the belief that the rape victim is a promiscuous woman who somehow "asked for it." Perfectly honorable in their intentions, the makers of THE ACCUSED are more concerned with social statement than with filmmaking. The story, which bears some resemblance to a much-publicized 1983 incident in Massachusetts, centers on the rape of a sexy young woman, played by Jodie Foster, who lives life in the fast lane. She lives in a trailer park, smokes pot, drinks too much, and dresses sluttishly. One evening she walks into a blue-collar bar after having argued with her live-in lover. Wearing a mini-skirt and a revealing top, she bumps and grinds in the bar's back room to a song on the juke box. Before long, one of the men has set her atop a pinball machine and has begun to rape her. Another takes his turn, and then a third—each rapist encouraged by a group of crass, cheering macho animals. Foster gets her chance to escape and runs from the bar, screaming and crying. After a very clinical hospital examination, Foster is approached by McGillis, an assistant DA who takes her case. When McGillis learns that her client is less than respectable and has a police record that includes a drug bust, she realizes that her case is a weak one. Rather than put Foster on the stand, McGillis strikes a deal with the attorneys for the three rapists. They are sentenced to two-to-five years' imprisonment on a lesser, nonsexual charge, with parole likely in nine months. Foster knows she has been victimized by a judicial system prejudiced against the underclass. Enraged, she barges into a quaint yuppie dinner at McGillis' apartment and tells the assistant DA just how worthless she really is. With guilt gnawing away at her, McGillis devises a new strategy—to put the cheering onlookers on trial for "criminal solicitation." Since the cheering patrons made the rape possible and encouraged others to rape, McGillis believes she can put them away and, in the process, make sure the three previously convicted men serve their full five-year terms. McGillis' star witness is a college frat boy, Coulson, whose best friend was one of the rapists. Coulson, who watched the rape, did so silently, which may be immoral but is not a crime. He not only gives the jury a clear description of the rape, but identifies those who encouraged the others to participate. When the jury returns from its deliberation, it names all three defendants guilty.

THE ACCUSED effectively condemns society's view of rape as a nonviolent crime in which most victims get what they deserve. Director Jonathan Kaplan (HEART LIKE A WHEEL, PROJECT X) and screenwriter Tom Topor (whose Richard Dreyfus-Barbra Streisand vehicle NUTS shows numerous parallels with this picture) purposely paint Foster's character as a slut in order to strengthen their argument. No matter how provocatively she was dressed or how erotically she danced, no one can leave this film believing that Foster wanted to be gang raped on a pinball machine in a public place with an audience. She may have wanted to find a man to take her home, or maybe even out to his car, but she surely did not "ask" to be raped. Kaplan and Topor take great pains to compare the onlookers' actions to those of a crowd watching spectator sports. The main characters go to a hockey game and cheer at the frequent fights; bar patrons watch boxing and are entertained by the flurry of exchanged punches. Their reactions to these violent, macho sports are no different than the cheers of the group that egged on the rapists.

The filmmakers' views are without doubt noble ones, touching issues that are rarely—if ever—explored on film, and nothing in THE ACCUSED is overtly exploitative. (Efforts to create drama where there isn't any—finding and confronting witnesses, putting McGillis' job on the line—seem cheap attempts to engage the audience.) Even the obligatory rape flashback, which occurs during Coulson's courtroom testimony, makes its point without being offensive. However, as a film judged by the criteria of the medium—art, entertainment, craftsmanship—THE ACCUSED is a conventional, predictable, lightweight picture that lacks insight, character, and energy. The script plays on an audience's outrage by giving us the usual scenes (the callous boy friend, the unloving mother, and the self-serving attorneys)—as the filmmakers stack the deck in their favor, just in case the audience isn't already moved by the gross indignities heaped upon the rape victim. (In the event we don't already feel terrible that Foster was gang raped, we're reminded that her mom doesn't care about her.) The audience never gets a chance to think for itself as it is constantly led along by the filmmakers, and THE ACCUSED only works as well as it does because of Jodie Foster and Kelly McGillis, who share a powerful on-screen bond. McGillis, whose role is less showy than her costar's, is wholly believable as the heretofore uncaring assistant DA. Foster, however, is the real guts behind the film. She charges forward into the frame with explosive energy, carrying the dead weight of the script like a ball and chain. Foster, who also refused to sink in the mire of her previous film, STEALING HOME, turns in a very special performance, proving once again that she has far too much talent to let weak filmmaking bring her down. Like this year's BETRAYED, THE ACCUSED wears the skin of a powerful social issue, but is ultimately hollow in its lack of guts. Unfortunately, lack of guts beneath a semblance of controversy seems par for the course in Hollywood these days. *(Adult situations, sexual situations, violence, profanity, nudity, substance abuse.)*

p, Stanley R. Jaffe, Sherry Lansing; d, Jonathan Kaplan; w, Tom Topor; ph, Ralf D. Bode (Alpha Cine Services Color); ed, Jerry Greenberg, O. Nicholas Brown; m, Brad Fiedel; prod d, Richard Kent Wilcox; art d, Sheila Haley.

Drama   **Cas.**   **(PR:O MPAA:R)**

ACTION JACKSON*½   (1988) 96m Lorimar c

Carl Weathers (Jericho "Action" Jackson), Craig T. Nelson (Peter Dellaplane), Vanity (Sydney Ash), Sharon Stone (Patrice Dellaplane), Thomas F. Wilson (Officer Kornblau), Bill Duke (Capt. Armbruster), Robert Davi (Tony Moretti), Jack Thibeau (Detective Kotterwell), Roger Aaron Brown (Officer Lack), Stan Foster (Albert), Mary Ellen Trainor (Secretary), Ed O'Ross (Stringer), Bob Minor (Gamble), David Glen Eisley (Thaw), Dennis Hayden (Shaker), Brian Libby (Marlin), David Efron (Birch), Alonzo Brown (Big Lady With Purse), Diana James (Hooker), Matt Landers, Thomas Wagner (Desk Sergeants), Deidre Conrad (Policewoman), Bill Burton, Sr. (Policeman), Preston Hanson (Master of Ceremonies), Ivor Barry (Stuffy Old Guy), Al Leong (Dellaplane's Chauffeur), John Lyons, Glenn Wilder, Steve Vandeman (Yacht Guards), Michael McManus (Grantham), De'voreaux White (Clovis), Melissa Prophet (Newscaster), Prince A. Hughes (Edd), Jim Haynie (Morty Morton), Edgar Small (Raymond Foss), James Lew (Martial Arts Instructor), Nicholas Worth (Cartier), Chino "Fats" Williams (Kid Sable), Chris Broughton (Pickpocket), Charles Meshack (Poolroom Bartender), Miguel Nunez, Branscombe Richmond, Richard Duran (Poolroom Thugs), The Knudsen Brothers (Streetsingers), Armelia McQueen (Dee), Sonny Landham (Mr. Quick), Sue Lentini (VW Driver), Kenneth Belsky (Red Devil Bartender), Frank McCarthy (Oliver O'Rooney), Ronnie Carol (Party Guest).

Superb stunts, fine photography, and a singular performance by actress-singer Vanity make ACTION JACKSON a good example of a movie that is less than the sum of its parts. The film opens as a union attorney and his secretary are working late in a high-rise Detroit office. Suddenly, five men crash into the office, killing the secretary and blasting the lawyer with a weapon that turns him into a ball of flames. The five, who come to be known as "The Invisible Men," then disappear. Next we see Weathers at the Detroit Police Department, and quickly learn that he is something of a rebel, with little taste for rules and regulations. He's now a sergeant, but was a lieutenant until he was busted after making the mistake of arresting the son of the wealthy and highly influential Nelson. Nelson is to be honored as "Businessman of the Year" at a banquet that evening, and Weathers, much to the maverick cop's dismay, is assigned to attend as the department representative. As Nelson makes his acceptance speech, Weathers strikes up a conversation with gorgeous blonde Stone, telling her he doesn't much like the man at the podium. He later learns that Stone is Nelson's wife. Over the next few days, The Invisible Men strike again, killing two more union officials. After the second murder, Stone overhears one of her husband's employees implicate himself in the murder. She tries to tell Nelson about what she has heard, but when he ignores her she goes to Weathers with the information. When she tells Nelson of her meeting with Weathers, he kills her and has her body dumped in Weathers' apartment. Now Weathers must hide out, doing so in the apartment of Nelson's drug-addicted girl friend, Vanity. Though he's on the run, Weathers is able to learn that The Invisible Men work for Nelson, who is intent on taking control of the union because it will make him the most powerful man in the city. Weathers is able to foil this plan, kills Nelson in a ferocious battle at the film's conclusion, and finally goes off with Vanity, who has miraculously kicked her drug habit for a happy ending.

What ACTION JACKSON lacks, more than anything else, is credibility. Ludicrous plot twists, unexplained motives, and absurd coincidences combine to make the film laughable—even for the action genre, in which plots are notoriously thin. Craig T. Nelson's character is thoroughly reprehensible (not only do we see him kill Stone, but we learn that he also murdered his first wife and his business partner, and plans to murder his son), and perhaps because his role is so overdrawn, the actor goes way over the top in his portrayal. On the plus side, the muscular and poised Carl Weathers makes an attractive hero, more than a little reminiscent of Richard Roundtree's Shaft character from the 1970s. As for Vanity, she shows the potential to be a real movie star. She's already known for her beauty and sex appeal, but in ACTION JACKSON she reveals that she can act as well, a considerable accomplishment given her cliched and underwritten role. One hopes that both Vanity and Weathers will go on to find more suitable films in which to display their considerable talents. Songs include "He Turned Me Out" (Lemel Humes, Mary Lee Kortes, performed by The Pointer Sisters), "Action Jackson" (Bernadette Cooper, performed by Madame X), "Vesti La Giubba" (Leoncavallo, performed by Mario Del Monaco), "Faraway Eyes" (Sue Ann Carwell, Jesse Johnson, performed by Vanity), "Protect and Serve" (Stevie Salas, Pee Wee Jam, M.C. Jam, performed by West Coast Posse), "Undress" (Teresa Laws, Kim Cage, Jerri Hubbard, Vanity, performed by Vanity), "Keeping Good Loving" (Kathy Sledge, Kae Williams, Jr., performed by Sister Sledge), "Lovers' Celebration" (Randy Muller, performed by Skyy), "Funky Broadway" (Arlester Christian, performed by Wilson Pickett), "That'll Be the Day" (Buddy Holly, Jerry Allison, Norman Petty, performed by The Knudsen Brothers), "Shotgun" (Autry DeWalt, performed by Vanity, David Koz), "For the Love of Money" (Anthony Jackson, Leon Huff, Kenneth Gamble, performed by Levert). (Graphic violence, nudity, sexual situations, excessive profanity.)

p, Joel Silver; d, Craig R. Baxley; w, Robert Reneau; ph, Matthew F. Leonetti (Metrocolor); ed, Mark Helfrich; m, Herbie Hancock, Michael Kamen; md, Jackie Krost; m/l, Lemel Humes, Mary Lee Kortes, Ruggiero Leoncavallo, Bernadette Cooper, Jesse Johnson, Sue Ann Carwell, Stevie Salas, Pee Wee Jam, M.C. Jam, Kae Williams, Jr., Kathy Sledge, Teresa Laws, Kim Cage, Jerri Hubbard, Vanity, Randy Muller, Arlester Christian, Norman Petty, Buddy Holly, Jerry Allison, Autry DeWalt, Kenneth Gamble, Leon Huff, Anthony Jackson; art d, Virginia

Randolph; set d, Phil M. Leonard; spec eff, Al Di Sarro; cos, Marilyn Vance-Straker; ch, Paula Abdul; stunts, Jophery Brown; makeup, Scott H. Eddo.

Action   **Cas.**   **(PR:O MPAA:R)**

ALICE***½   (1988, Switz./Brit./Ger.) 85m Condor-Hessisches Rudfunk-SRG/Film Four c

Kristyna Kohoutova (Alice), Camilla Power (Voice of Alice).

The nonsensical writings of Lewis Carroll have been favorites of Surrealists ever since such luminaries as Louis Aragon and Andre Breton first sang their praises, but it has taken Jan Svankmajer, a member of the Prague Surrealist group, to bring Carroll's Alice's Adventures in Wonderland alive in a film that expresses the degree of fear and perversity contained in the Victorian mathematician's original prose. By combining live action and puppet animation, Svankmajer, in his first feature film after a career of directing shorts, has created a truly marvelous depiction of Alice's world. Beginning as Alice, played by the preteen Kohoutova, sits near a brook while her older sister ignores her and flips through a book, the film then cuts to a tight close-up of Alice's lips, saying: "Alice thought to herself, 'Now, you will see a film . . . for children . . . perhaps.'" Next, in her playroom, she tosses pebbles into an overflowing coffee cup. The room is filled with toys, stuffed animals, and playing cards. A sound is heard from across the room, where, inside a glass case, a stuffed rabbit is stirring, pulling his paws loose from the artificial wilderness of the exhibit's floor. Nails protrude from the rabbit's front paw; the beast savagely chews them off, then, as sawdust pours from an open wound on its chest, the rabbit smashes through the glass case and exits the bedroom. Alice follows. The rabbit reaches a wooden desk in the middle of a vast, rocky wasteland, climbs in and disappears. Alice does the same, although, because of her size, it takes considerably more effort. Once in Wonderland, she spots the rabbit eating a meal of sawdust. As Alice's visual adventure in the strange and unknown recesses of her imagination continues, she finds that she is able to change size (the small Alice is "played" by an animated doll puppet) by eating cookies or drinking ink, or that she can change the sizes of other things by biting into a bit of wooden mushroom. Things are not what they seem here. Stuck in a room from which she is too large to escape through its tiny door (yes, after she has eaten a cookie), Alice sheds a roomful of tears. Pouring out like waterfalls, the tears rise to her chin level. Next, out of nowhere, a rat wearing a blue velvet suit swims by, dragging a treasure chest. Dripping wet, the rat climbs atop the shocked Alice's head, for it is the only "land" in sight. He drives two stakes into her skull, prepares a meal, readies a campfire, and then sets it ablaze. Alice promptly dunks her head under the ocean of tears and douses the flames. After finally becoming the proper size (for the room, that is), Alice (as puppet) is washed into the rabbit's garden by the flow of tears. When the rabbit mistakes Alice for his assistant and asks her to fetch him a pair of scissors, Alice explores his dollhouse-sized home. After finding another cookie, Alice grows to human size again and becomes confined to a very small (depending on how you look at it) bedroom. Unable to leave, she fends off an attack by the angry rabbit, who calls upon a grotesque army of assistants—small birds and lizards, with skeletal heads and feet and stuffed bodies. They chase her and finally lure her into a vat of mysterious liquids, turning her into a large, shell-like doll. Imprisoned in a storeroom, the human Alice claws her way out from the inside of the shell, and, after encountering a number of oddities that include a living piece of raw meat, finds the key (hidden in a sardine tin) that unlocks the door. She enters three more rooms—one full of living, wormlike socks that bore holes through the wooden floor; a second in which a fly-gulping frog tends to a crying baby that, held by Alice, turns into a squealing pig; and a third in which the Mad Hatter and the March Hare incessantly drink tea and butter pocket watches. Finally, Alice comes across the King and Queen of Hearts, who, of course, threaten everyone with the dreaded command, "Off with their heads." Alice plays a game of croquet with the Queen and is subsequently brought to trial. Refusing to admit her guilt, Alice wakes up. In her bedroom, the "characters" of her story are scattered about. All seems to be in order, except for the glass exhibition case, which is still missing its rabbit.

Viewers who go to see ALICE—which received a limited theatrical release in New York and Chicago and its US premiere at the San Francisco Film Festival—expecting the safe entertainment of Paramount's 1933 adaptation, the sweetness of the 1951 Disney version, or the narrative logic of 1984's DREAM CHILD are likely to be more than a little surprised and perhaps somewhat disturbed by Svankmajer's treatment. There is nothing safe or cute about this Wonderland, in which raw meat (through live-action animation using a real piece of meat) may slither out of a pot or a sharp tack may unexpectedly turn up in a fingerful of marmalade. This Wonderland is a dangerous one, filled with images of death and violence—all imagined by the sweet little Alice, dressed ever-so-nicely in a lace dress, white stockings, and black patent leather shoes. If many have been content to paint Alice's imagination as a relatively benign, merely "curious" dreamland, Svankmajer, a self-described militant Surrealist, leans towards the nightmarish in his depiction. Very little that happens to Alice here is even remotely pleasant. Wonderland is a world of cruelty in which the little girl has her arm gouged by a hacksaw, has a stake driven into her skull, is attacked by an army of skeletons, and discovers a container full of cockroaches. Nothing is safe in Wonderland, not even the velvet-jacketed rat who camps atop Alice's head—later he is glimpsed with his neck broken by a mousetrap.

In true Surrealist spirit, Svankmajer keeps the line between dream and reality ambiguous. Throughout the film, he keeps us from forgetting that this is Alice's dream by cutting to a close-up of Alice's lips. As she speaks (in a hopelessly poor dubbing job), she refers to herself as the storyteller, and all the character's voices are her own. Just as the character of Alice—whom she "plays" in her imagined film—is a part of the dreaming Alice's self, so too are the White Rabbit, the March Hare, the Mad Hatter, and the Queen of Hearts, and all of Wonderland's depravity, violence, and grotesqueness is a product of her own imagination. It is this aspect of Alice's adventures (made clearer by Svankmajer's consistent, almost rhythmic, use of the shot of Alice's lips) that makes Svankmajer's adaptation so disturbing. It is less a film of fantasy than a photographic record of a child's imagination, a documentary of the unfettered marvelous. *(Violence.)*

p, Peter-Christian Fueter; d, Jan Svankmajer; w, Jan Svankmajer (based on *Alice's Adventures in Wonderland* by Lewis Carroll); ph, Svatopluk Maly (Eastmancolor); ed, Marie Zemanova; art d, Eva Svankmerova, Jiri Blaha; set d, Jan Svankmajer; anim, Bedrich Glaser.

Fantasy   **(PR:O MPAA:NR)**

ALIEN FROM L.A. †   (1988) 87m Golan-Globus/Cannon c

Kathy Ireland *(Wanda Saknussemm)*, Thom Matthews *(Charmin)*, Don Michael Paul *(Robbie)*, Linda Kerridge *(Auntie Pearl/Freki)*, Richard Haines *(Professor Arnold Saknussemm)*, William R. Moses *(Guten "Gus" Edway)*, Janie du Plessis *(Gen. Rykov/Shank)*, Russel Savadier *(Loki)*, Simon Poland *(Consol Triton Crassus/Mailman)*, Lochner de Kock *(Professor Paddy Mahoney)*, Deep Roy *(Mambino)*, Christian Andrews *(Brick Bardo)*, Paul Jacobs *(Dr. Madagasin)*, Fats Bookholane *(Lord Over)*.

The title stranger is model Kathy Ireland, who plays a mousy Valley girl whose dull and boring life changes when she heads to Africa to locate her explorer father. Both of them fall into a pit and find themselves in a lost city somewhere in the center of the Earth, populated by totalitarian descendants of space aliens. Directed by Albert Pyun (RADIOACTIVE DREAMS; DOWN TWISTED) this is yet another Cannon entry that got zilch from the distribution department.

p, Menahem Golan, Yoram Globus; d, Albert Pyun; w, Debra Ricci, Regina Davis, Albert Pyun; ph, Tom Fraser (TVC color); ed, Daniel Loewenthal; m, James Saad, Tony Riparetti, Simon LeGassick, Jim Andron; prod d, Pamela Warner; spec eff, John Hartigan; cos, Birgitta Bjerke; stunts, Solly Marx.

Science Fiction   **Cas.**   **(PR:NR MPAA:PG)**

ALIEN NATION**   (1988) 94m FOX c

James Caan *(Matthew Sykes)*, Mandy Patinkin *(Sam Francisco)*, Terence Stamp *(William Harcort)*, Kevin Major Howard *(Kipling)*, Leslie Bevis *(Cassandra)*, Peter Jason *(Fedorchuk)*, George Jenesky *(Quint)*, Jeff Kober, Roger Aaron Brown, Tony Simotes.

©20TH CENTURY FOX

ALIEN NATION is a terribly disappointing effort from producer Gale Ann Hurd, whose THE TERMINATOR and ALIENS set the standard for science fiction in the 1980s. Sporting a solid cast (James Caan, Mandy Patinkin, Terence Stamp), impressive makeup effects (Stan Winston), and excellent cinematography (Adam Greenberg of THE TERMINATOR and NEAR DARK), the film is, unfortunately, crippled by a thin script by first-time screenwriter Rockne S. O'Bannon and lackluster direction by Brit Graham Baker. Set in 1991, the movie presents us with an intriguing premise: How would America assimilate a race of outer-space aliens into its society? In the late 1980s, a giant spaceship full of genetically bred slaves takes a wrong turn and lands in the Mojave desert. Dubbed "Newcomers," the 100,000 aliens are given refuge by then-president Ronald Reagan and made citizens. By 1991, the Newcomers, called "Slags" by racist Americans, have been pushed into the slums of Los Angeles, where some overcome their economic disadvantage and rise to prominent positions and others turn to a life of crime. Looked down upon because they have reptilian heads, are stronger and smarter than humans, eat raw meat, get drunk on sour milk, and smell bad, the Newcomers find themselves the new despised minority (blacks, Hispanics, and Asians are suddenly acceptable). Caan, an alcoholic police detective, hates the aliens and resents the affirmative action programs that benefit them at "real" Americans' expense. When Caan's partner, a black man, is killed by criminal Newcomers during a hold-up, he gladly volunteers to be partnered with the first Newcomer cop promoted to the rank of detective, Patinkin. Although he hates Patinkin because of his race, Caan uses the alien to get an inside track on those who killed his partner. Of

course, now that he's met a Newcomer "up close and personal," Caan begins to like the guy and see him as an equal. As it turns out, their investigation uncovers a plot in which prominent Newcomer Stamp, a businessman whose political stock is rising, is conspiring to produce a drug once used to reward the Newcomer slaves and make them work harder. The sticky blue liquid is highly addictive for the Newcomers, and they will do anything to attain it. In addition, an overdose of the drug causes a metamorphosis in the Newcomers, changing them into rampaging, difficult to kill beasts. When Patinkin learns that Stamp is producing the drug, he becomes as mad for revenge as Caan, for he worries that if revealed, the Newcomer drug problem could destroy human-Newcomer relations. After much routine cops-and-robbers fare, Caan finally corners Stamp near an oil refinery. Gulping down a large glob of the drug, Stamp becomes a monster Newcomer and there is a fight to the death. Luckily, Caan is able to knock Stamp into the ocean, where salt water—which acts like hydrochloric acid on the aliens—eats the villain away. With the drug supply destroyed and its architect defeated, Caan agrees to keep his mouth shut about the whole thing in deference to his partner's wishes.

ALIEN NATION, which was titled "Outer Heat" until the release of DEAD HEAT and RED HEAT forced a change, could have been one of the best genre films of the year had Rockne O'Bannon's script been better. The first half-hour of the film plays well, with the backstory and premise set up in a fluid and interesting manner. Production design, special makeup, cinematography, and savvy acting mesh together perfectly to create a unique movie universe that successfully suspends our disbelief. After this promising buildup, however, the movie takes a steep nosedive into tired cop film cliches. The plot is nothing but warmed-over "Miami Vice" material, with blue glop substituted for cocaine and aliens taking the place of South Americans. Caan and Patinkin do their best to bring some spontaneity to their roles, but their relationship never moves beyond standard buddy film precepts, and the careful narrative development that marked the beginning is tossed aside for some woefully underwritten plotting that skids along haphazardly from one scene to the next. A sexy Newcomer stripper (Bevins) is introduced merely to provide a convenient escape for the two cops when they are cornered by the bad guys (she suddenly pulls a pistol and starts blasting away at the crooks when she learns that they killed her lover—a wholly unmotivated reaction that crashes down from the script like a thunderbolt). The last two-thirds of ALIEN NATION play more like a treatment for a movie than a film shot from a completed script. The whole thing seems rushed, as if there was no time to actually explore the nuance of a scene and ferret out a deeper subtext; instead, we are left with a collection of dramatic highlights that makes for a nice coming attractions trailer, but is ultimately unsatisfying. There never seems to be much at stake in the film; we have no feel for the extent of Stamp's plot or its implications. The climax—which is telegraphed long, long before it arrives—is so uninvolving and perfunctory that it totally fails, and the hokey, feel-good epilog is a blatant attempt to set up the inevitable sequel. As a producer, Gale Ann Hurd has shown an uncanny knack for assembling superior talent to work on her projects. Each one of her films *looks* great. But she should have concentrated on getting the script right before committing herself to a production as ambitious as ALIEN NATION. *(Violence, profanity, sexual situations, substance abuse.)*

p, Gale Anne Hurd, Richard Kobritz; d, Graham Baker; w, Rockne S. O'Bannon; ph, Adam Greenberg (DeLuxe color); ed, Kent Beyda; m, Curt Sobel; prod d, Jack T. Collis; art d, Joseph Nemec III; set d, Jim Duffy; cos, Erica Phillips; stunts, Conrad E. Palmisano; makeup, Zoltan, John Elliott.

Science Fiction   **Cas.**   **(PR:O MPAA:R)**

ALOHA SUMMER*½   (1988) 97m Hanauma Bay/Spectrafilm c

Chris Makepeace *(Mike Tognetti)*, Yuji Okumoto *(Kenzo Konishi)*, Don Michael Paul *(Chuck Granville)*, Tia Carrere *(Lani Kepoo)*, Sho Kosugi *(Yukinaga Konishi)*, Lorie Griffin *(Amanda Granville)*, Blaine Kia *(Jerry Kahani)*, Warren Fabro *(Kilarney)*, Andy Bumatai *(Kimo Kepoo)*, Ric Mancini *(Angelo Tognetti)*, Scott Nakagawa *(Scott Tanaka)*.

In 1959, Makepeace travels from the mainland to Hawaii with his parents for a vacation. In a series of vignettes, he meets five other teen boys: Japanese-American Nakagawa; his cousin, Okumoto, who has just arrived from Japan; Paul, the son of wealthy island parents; and two native brothers, Kia and Fabro. This is the year Hawaii gained statehood, and against that backdrop the six new friends set out to have some fun and learn about life in the process. The episodic film follows the youngsters as they learn about surfing, drinking, prostitutes, and prejudice. Middle-class Makepeace is attracted to Paul's sister (Griffin), a relationship strained by the vast difference in their social standings. Nakagawa's traditionalist Japanese father is outraged by the Western ways his son is adopting in speech and manner. American servicemen on the island make it obvious that they don't like children of Japanese ancestry. Fabro and Kia are ostracized by their fellow natives for befriending the outsiders. As the film rolls along to its climax—a surprisingly brutal confrontation between the friends and a group of drunken servicemen—the boys develop deep friendships, certain to remain vivid long after they've gone their separate ways.

As a "coming of age" picture, ALOHA SUMMER doesn't do much to enliven what has become a much overworked theme during the last few years. Nor is it particularly effective as social drama, since it is very heavy-handed in its characterizations and the delivery of its messages. Nevertheless, there is a nice rapport among the young actors, all of whom have enough appeal to make the movie fairly enjoyable. Chris Makepeace (MY BODYGUARD; MEATBALLS) is likable and moving as he futilely attempts to create relationships, first with an island girl and then with the wealthy Griffin, while Don Michael Paul, as the rich kid, is the strongest of the cast, displaying an easy charm. The island footage is pretty if nothing spectacular, and the shots of the surfers in action are quite impressive. While not a very good film, ALOHA SUMMER's heart is in the right place, and for that it should be commended. *(Violence, profanity.)*

p, Mike Greco; d, Tommy Lee Wallace; w, Mike Greco (based on a story by Mike), Bob Benedetto; ph, Steven Poster (CFI Color); ed, James Coblentz, Jack Hofstra, Jay Cassidy; m, Jesse Frederick, Bennett Salvay; art d, Donald Harris; set d, Airick Kredell; ch, Sho Kosugi; tech, Rabbit Kekai.

Comedy/Drama Cas. (PR:C MPAA:PG)

AMERICAN GOTHIC** (1988, Brit./Can.) 90m Manor Ground/Vidmark c

Rod Steiger *(Pa)*, Yvonne De Carlo *(Ma)*, Sarah Torgov *(Cynthia)*, Michael J. Pollard *(Woody)*, Fiona Hutchinson *(Lynn)*, William Hootkins *(Teddy)*, Janet Wright *(Fanny)*, Terry Kelly *(Psychiatrist)*, Mark Ericksen *(Jeff)*, Caroline Barclay *(Terri)*, Mark Lindsay Chapman *(Rob)*, Stephen Shelley *(Paul)*.

In AMERICAN GOTHIC, Torgov plays a young woman fresh out of the loony bin, to which she was committed after the death of her baby—who drowned in the tub when Torgov went to answer the phone and then got to cooking. With her husband (Ericksen), Torgov joins two other couples for a fly-in trip to a remote island in the Pacific Northwest. Not surprisingly, their small floatplane develops engine trouble, and they are forced to put in on an uncharted island. As the plane proves irreparable, Torgov begins to sense something foreboding. At first there is only the vague feeling that the group is being watched, of things moving in the brush. They discover a house at the other end of the island, all furnished straight out of the 1920s, complete with Victrola and photos of the Gish sisters in the nursery. Soon the occupants—Steiger and DeCarlo—arrive, and insist that everyone stay for supper and the night. Later that evening, the guests are introduced to the elderly couple's middle-aged daughter (Wright), who tells the young folks that her 11th birthday is imminent. Next morning, another child Pollard, shows up, and he and Wright knock off the first camper—enticing him into a clifftop swingset, then chopping the ropes. In short order everyone is dead but Torgov, who is practically gibbering by this point. Wright has made Torgov her special friend by now, though, and she joins the family in punishing a second son, loutish Hootkins, for raping one of her friends before murdering her. Soon Torgov is dressed up in a vintage party dress and whispering and giggling with Wright at her birthday party. The family shows Torgov their secret cellar, with all the interlopers they've killed over the years hanging around on the walls in various states of decay, including her companions. Later, when Wright tries to bathe her baby (a blackened, mummified infant, apparently the product of some incestuous activity with her brothers), something snaps afresh in Torgov (whose own baby-bath trauma you'll remember), and she goes through the family like a McCormick reaper, doing in DeCarlo with her own knitting needles. Steiger is the last to die; after delivering a monolog to God, Torgov dispatches him with a shotgun. The last scene shows Torgov, nutty as the cliched fruitcake, sitting alone.

Despite the rather obvious plotting, derivative of everything from PSYCHO and more recent spam-in-a-cabin epics to MOST DANGEROUS GAME, this Canadian-made effort (which made a cursory theatrical showing before blossoming on posters in video stores everywhere) does manage to incorporate some interesting facets that slightly distinguish it from the vast field of other horror videos. Without a doubt, what makes AMERICAN GOTHIC most worthy of attention are the performances of Steiger and Torgov. Steiger's Bible-spouting, moralizing patriarch is superb, given the weakness of the material in general. His final cry to heaven upon finding his family slaughtered is surprisingly heartfelt and effective. Torgov's part is better written and she makes the most of it, letting us see madness in her eyes better than anyone since the glory days of Barbara Steele. And Michael J. Pollard is always weird, even in normal films. *(Graphic violence, sexual situations, adult situations, profanity.)*

p, John Quested, Christopher Harrop; d, John Hough; w, Bert Wetanson, Michael Vines; ph, Harvey Harrison; ed, John Victor Smith; m, Alan Parker; prod d, David Hiscox; set d, Joe Gould; spec eff, Allen Benjamin; makeup, Gordon Kay.

Horror Cas. (PR:O MPAA:R)

AMERICAN WAY, THE (SEE: RIDERS OF THE STORM, 1988, Brit.)

AND GOD CREATED WOMAN zero (1988) 98m Crow/Vestron c

Rebecca De Mornay *(Robin Shay)*, Vincent Spano *(Billy Moran)*, Frank Langella *(James Tiernan)*, Donovan Leitch *(Peter Moran)*, Judith Chapman *(Alexandra Tiernan)*, Jaime McEnnan *(Timmy Moran)*, Benjamin Mouton *(Blue)*, David Shelley *(David)*, Einstein Brown *(Einstein)*, David Lopez *(Hawk)*, Thelma Houston *(Prison Singer)*, Gail Boggs *(Denise)*, Dorian Sanchez *(Alice)*, Maria Duval *(Maxine)*, Lee Ann Martin *(Shirley)*, Pat Lee *(Inmate)*, Connie Moore Kranz *(Warden)*, Elle Collier, Gilbert Anthony Silva, Danny S. Martin, Helen S. Pacheco, Nancy B. Kenney *(Guards)*, Tom Connor *(Chaplain)*, Gary Goetzman *(Al Lawrence)*, Lenny Vullo *(Lenny)*, Kenny Ortega *(Mike)*, Christopher Murray *(Harold)*, Gary Grubbs *(Rupert Willis)*, Allison Davies *(Tiernan's Secretary)*, J.D. Lincoln *(Governor Miller)*, Tommy Townsdend *(Owner, Las Quinellas Club)*, Rusty Dillen, Marlin K. Southerland *(Cowboys, Las Quinellas Club)*, Richard Kawecki, Barney Garcia *(Las Quinellas Sheriffs)*, Nelson Martinez *(Emcee)*, Mary McCorroll-Banner, Jim Terr *(Act at Las Quinellas Club)*, Erin Flynn *(Virginia)*, Doran Taylor *(Dale)*, Linda Bergman *(Emma)*, Kathryn J. Maitland *(Jenny)*, Anne O. Marshall *(News Broadcaster)*, Manfred Krause *(Political Aide)*, Samuel Leyba, David M. Vigil, David Dean, Jr., John Christopher Abeyta, David Borrego *(Mexican Band Members)*.

This worthless, pseudo-philosophical picture, an embarrassment from start to finish, stars De Mornay as a wrongly imprisoned young woman who aspires to be a rock'n-'roll star. Stir-crazy, she escapes from her women's reform facility (it looks too much like a college dorm to be called a prison) and scurries to a nearby Santa Fe freeway, where she is picked up by a limousine. In the back seat is Langella, a gubernatorial candidate whose stance on prison reform measures is expected to put him in the governor's mansion. Helping escapee De Mornay, however, could be a serious blot on his record, so he brings her back to prison, where her return is unnoticed by everyone except handyman Spano. As De Mornay changes back into prison garb, Spano watches. Naked except for socks and sneakers, De Mornay willingly "makes it" with Spano under the gymnasium stands. Later, she learns that she has little chance for parole, since she has no job or husband on the outside. Her easy solution is to ask Spano to marry her—as a business proposition. Upon her release, De Mornay is introduced to Spano's six-year-old son (McEnnan) and his synthesizer-playing brother (Donovan Leitch, son of the 1960s pop star). De Mornay is furious that she has gone from a real prison to the symbolic prison of a husband and family. Refusing to sleep with Spano, she devotes all her energies to forming a band. She reestablishes contact with Langella, seduces him on his pool table (he's married, but the wife's away for a few days), and manages to get a spot performing at an upcoming fund-raiser. Meanwhile, Langella has used De Mornay as a publicity tool to prove the success of his progressive ideas on reform. When a minor infraction threatens De Mornay's parole and some nude snapshots of her surface, Langella ends his involvement. However, De Mornay's band still manages to perform at the fund-raising event (which, curiously, is televised throughout the city) and everyone, including Langella, is thrilled. With the entire audience swaying, dancing, and clapping their hands, Langella thanks De Mornay and offers her freedom. Now officially free with a capital "F," she falls into place as Spano's wife—the two of them apparently in love.

In 1956, Roger Vadim directed AND GOD CREATED WOMAN (ET DIEU CREA LA FEMME), a low-budget, titillating, semi-intellectual French tale of love filmed in CinemaScope and color. It was not a particularly well-made film, but it was a great film in its effect. It not only made Brigitte Bardot an international star, it paved the way for a number of Vadim's counterparts (Francois Truffaut, Jean-Luc Godard, et al.) to get their films made. By bringing youth and sex to the screen, Vadim helped revolutionize and revitalize French cinema. In 1988, Vadim has directed AND GOD CREATED WOMAN, a Hollywood feature indistinguishable from much of the trash already littering the screen. Because this remake (in title and philosophy only) is directed by Vadim—a director with past ties to the New Wave, to Jean Cocteau, Andre Gide, and Colette, to the events of May 1968, and to the banned LES LIASONS DANGERUESES—its complete failure is even more resounding than if it were directed by a Hollywood lackey. Because Vadim, clearly an intelligent and capable director, has ignored his past and chosen to continue his career as a *cineaste a la mode*, his crime is unpardonable. The most important factor in the success of Vadim's original film was its assault on society—the (a)morality, freedom, and exhilaration it threw into the laps of otherwise complacent French moviegoers. Since, in 1988, it is quite difficult to shock audiences (sex in films no longer upsets the public unless it is coupled with religion, as in Godard's HAIL, MARY or Martin Scorsese's THE LAST TEMPTATION OF CHRIST), Vadim cannot be faulted for failing to create a sexual revolution with his remake. He can, however, be faulted for everything else wrong with the film. Rebecca De Mornay turns in the worst performance of her short career (She is infinitely better in RISKY BUSINESS; A TRIP TO BOUNTIFUL; and RUNAWAY TRAIN), while Vincent Spano and Frank Langella (who smartly underplays his cliched role) can offer little to save the film. If the acting, ludicrous dialog, and soft-core sex scenes (which have been steamed up for the video release) aren't bad enough, there's the rancid rock score, which is as safe as the original film's mamba score was threatening. Songs include De Mornay's big message tunes "Break Down the Walls" and "Newfound Freedom" (Greg Prestopino, Matthew Wilder), as well as "Happy Day (When I Found You)" (Prestopino, Wilder), "Any Fool," "We Touch" (Loz Netto, performed by Netto), "Too Far Gone" (David Shelley, Mike Piccirillo), "El Espejo" (Victor Ortiz, performed by Richie Ray, Bobby Cruz), "I Love You George" (Jim Terr, performed by Terr, Busy McCarroll), and "No Te Olvidare" (David H. Borrego, performed by Lumbre del Sol). A number of classical extracts are also included: "Dance of the Blessed Spirits" from "Orfeo ed Euridice" by Christoph Willibald von Gluck, "Brindisi (Libiamo)" from "La traviata" by Giuseppe Verdi, Serenade No. 13 in G Major for Strings, "Eine kleine Nachtmusik" by Wolfgang Amadeus Mozart, "The Wedding March" from Opus 61, No. 9 by Felix Mendelssohn. *(Nudity, sexual situations, profanity.)*

p, George G. Braunstein, Ron Hamady; d, Roger Vadim; w, R.J. Stewart; ph, Stephen M. Katz (DeLuxe Color); ed, Suzanne Pettit; m, Tom Chase, Steve Rucker, Christoph Willibald von Gluck, Giuseppe Verdi, Wolfgang Amadeus Mozart, Felix Mendelssohn; m/l, Loz Netto, David Shelley, Mike Piccirillo, Greg Prestopino, Matthew Wilder, Victor Ortiz, Jim Terr, David H. Borrego; prod d, Victor Kempster; set d, Robin Laughlin, Guido DeCurtis; cos, Sharman Forman-Hyde; makeup, Marianne Almasy.

Drama Cas. (PR:O MPAA:R)

ANGEL 3: THE FINAL CHAPTER* (1988) 99m NW c

Maud Adams *(Nadine)*, Mitzi Kapture *(Angel)*, Mark Blankfield *(Spanky)*, Kin Shriner *(Neal)*, Emile Beaucard *(Shahid)*, Richard Roundtree *(Lt. Doniger)*, Tawny Fere *(Michelle)*, Anna Navarro *(Gloria)*, Susan Moore *(Pam)*, Barbara Treutelaar *(Shirley)*, Floyd Levine *(Lt. Mallin)*, Kyle Heffner *(Tom Santangelo)*, Dick Miller *(Nick Pellegrini)*, Toni Basil *(Hillary)*, Steven Basil *(Porn Asst. Director)*, S.A. Griffin *(Roger)*, Cynthia Hoppenfeld *(Marie)*, Bob DeSimone *(Porn Director)*, Julie Kristen Smith *(Darlene)*, Kendall Carly Browne *(Gallery Woman)*, Ted Faye *(Companion)*, Paunita Nichols *(Black Hooker)*, Roxanne Kernohan *(White Hooker)*, Laura Albert *(Nude Dancer)*, Tyrone Granderson Jones *(L.A. Pimp)*, Kim McKamy, Barbara Hammond, Cheryl Starbuck *(Video Girls)*, Rick Paap *(Gallery Officer)*, Roxanna Hernandez *(Girl at Mansion)*, Michael Bandoni *(Mr. Fabazion)*, Hugh Karraker *(Croupier)*, Phillip Day *(Carlos)*, Bebop Bedlam *(Rap Group)*.

When we last left Molly, aka Angel, everyone's favorite "Honor Student by Day, Hollywood Hooker by Night," she was just finishing law school and planned to be a lawyer. Well, Molly must have flunked the bar exam, because in ANGEL 3 we find her in New York, working as a free-lance photographer. Although she had given up streetwalking at the end of part one, Molly—now played by Mitzi Kapture, the third actress to play the character (she was preceded by Donna Wilkes and Betsy Russell)-—is still concerned with the plight of street people, and is shooting photos for a book on the subject. As a means of making ends meet, she takes an outside assignment shooting a gallery opening and there she discovers her long-lost mother, Navarro, who abandoned her as a child. Kapture traces her mom back to Los Angeles, where she confronts her in an emotionally moving scene that takes place in Navarro's art gallery. "Can I help you?" asks Mom innocently. "You should have asked me that question 14 years ago!" spits the indignant Kapture. Charges and recriminations fly, but in the end mother and daughter make amends, after which Navarro informs Kapture that she has a half-sister (Fere) who is in danger. When Mom is blown up by a car bomb shortly thereafter, Kapture determines to find her half-sister and bring her mother's killer to justice by once again taking up her Angel identity and hitting the streets. While wandering Venice Beach she bumps into old pal Blankfield, a former male prostitute who now passes the hat as a street performer, and more great dialog follows. (Blankfield to Kapture: "My idea of an agreeable person is a person who agrees with me." Kapture: "Disraeli?" Blankfield: "You haven't forgotten!" Kapture: "God knows I've tried!") Blankfield lets Kapture stay at his place, lending her his "drag outfits" so that she can dress up like a hooker and work the strip. The streets are even meaner than last time and Kapture fails to get any information; however, through a filmmaker friend of Blankfield's (Shriner), she hooks up with a porno producer who hires her for his latest epic. Making friends with the other girls on the film, Kapture hears of Adams, the madam of an exclusive brothel that caters to foreign businessmen and the like. Kapture applies for a job with Adams and discovers Fere working there. She also learns that Adams is a white slaver in cahoots with swarthy Arab-ish Beaucard, who trades women for cocaine. After much derring-do, Kapture and her friends manage to save Fere, get the goods on Adams, and kill Beaucard, destroying his criminal empire.

Notwithstanding the implications of the concept "Honor Student by Day, Hollywood Hooker by Night," the first two ANGEL movies were surprisingly tame when it came to sex and nudity. Never was Angel shown plying her trade; instead, the films concentrated on the family atmosphere among Hollywood street people—how the homeless, runaways, and dispossessed were forced to do unsavory things to survive, but still cared for and watched out for one another. ANGEL 3, however, goes out of its way to exploit the gratuitous nudity and sexual titillation missing from the first two films. Director Tom DeSimone (REFORM SCHOOL GIRLS) wallows in the sleazier aspects of the material, without missing a chance to expose a breast or humiliate an actress willing to disrobe. The opening scene in ANGEL 3 has more nudity than the first two films put together, and DeSimone tosses naked women into nearly every subsequent scene. Employing the age-old exploitation trick of indulging a taste for social ills under the pretense of condemning them, DeSimone parades everything from streetwalking to porno filmmaking before the camera with drooling zeal. One almost unbearable scene, supposed to be comic, features a frenzied porno director urging his naked actress to put more passion into a scene, while she jiggles before DeSimone's leering camera for what seems like forever.

When not dollying in on naked body parts, DeSimone essays scenes of violent action, and the results aren't any better. The climactic shootout is poorly staged and, accordingly, pretty dull. Even worse is DeSimone's screenplay, which contains some of the most horrible dialog you're ever likely to hear. Some of the witty repartee has been quoted above, but DeSimone also tosses in such bon mots as "You're about as inconspicuous around here as a duck on the back of a horse." It is faint praise indeed to congratulate the fairly competent cast for being able to mouth such insipid stuff and keep a straight face. As Angel, Mitzi Kapture is the first actress to play the role who looks fairly convincing acting tough and street smart and wielding a large firearm (Wilkes and Russell were merely laughable). She also manages to be just about the only woman in the film who keeps her clothes on—continuing *that* fine ANGEL tradition. Although the title proudly exclaims that ANGEL 3 is "The Final Chapter," don't bet on it. Just about every series, from WALKING TALL to FRIDAY THE 13TH, has lied when similar promises were made. Songs include "Secrets" (Kim Darigan, Temmer Darigan, performed by Lou Rawls), "Cocteau's Dream" (Robert Fleischman, performed by Fleischman), "Five-O" (Deandre "Fish" Flemming, Joe Felix, performed by BeBop Bedlam), "She's Crying" (Sibling Rivalry, performed by Sibling Rivalry). *(Violence, nudity, sexual situations, profanity, substance abuse.)*

p, Arnold Orgolini; d, Tom DeSimone; w, Tom DeSimone (based on characters created by Joseph M. Cala, Robert Vincent O'Neill); ph, Howard Wexler (Getty Color); ed, Warren Chadwick; m, Berlin Game, Don Great, Alan Ett, Chris Spedding; m/l, Kim Darigan, Temmer Darigan, Robert Fleischman, Deandre "Fish" Flemming, Joe Felix, Sibling Rivalry; art d, Alexandra Kicenik; set d, Monette Goldman; stunts, John Branagan.

Action **Cas.** **(PR:O MPAA:R)**

ANGUISH*½** (1988, Sp.) 91m Pepon Cormina/Spectrafilm c

Zelda Rubinstein *(Mother)*, Michael Lerner *(John)*, Talia Paul *(Polly)*, Angel Jove *(Killer)*, Clara Pastor *(Linda)*, Isabel Garcia Lorca *(Caroline)*, Nat Baker *(Teaching Doctor (Cast of Old Movie))*, Edward Ledden *(Doctor)*, Gustavo Gili, Antonio Reguero, Joaquin Ribas *(Students)*, Janet Porter *(Laboratory Nurse)*, Patricia Manget, Merche Gascon *(Nurses at Clinic)*, Jose M. Chucarro *(Boyfriend)*, Antonella Murgia *(Ticket Girl)*, Josephine Borchaca *(Concession Girl)*, Georgie Pinkley *(Laura)*, Francesco Rabella *(Don)*, Diane Pinkley *(Popcorn Woman)*, Benito Pocino *(Popcorn Husband)*, Victor Guillen *(Sleepy)*, Evelyn Rosenka *(Bathroom Woman)*, Michael Chandler *(Projectionist)*, Vincente Gil *(Taxi Driver)*, Michael Heat *(Inspector)*, Pedro Vidal, Robert Long, Jalime Ros, Miguel Montfort, Jordi Estivill, Alberto Merelles, Javier Moya, John Garcia *(Policemen)*, Kit Kincannon *(Salesman)*, Tatiana Thaliven *(Ticket Girl)*, Joy Blackburn *(Concession Girl)*, Marc Maloney *(Elderly Man)*, Jasmine Parker *(Elderly Woman)*, Jean Paul Soto *(Manny)*, Javier Ducan *(Moe (Cast of New Movie))*, Marc Auba *(Jack)*, Randall Stewart *(First Murder)*, Eva Heald *(Granny)*, Rose Sherpac *(Granny's Friend)*, Emi Matias *(Hairy Woman)*, Elisa Crehvet *(Ann)*, Mingo Rafols *(Chicano)*, Maribel Martinez *(Hysterical Woman)*, Gustavo Guarino *(Hysterical Husband)*, Frank Craven *(Sleepy)*, Mario Fernandez *(Black Boy)*, May Vives *(Blond Girl)*, Craig Hill *(Doctor at Hospital)*, Anita Shemanski *(Nurse at Hospital)*, Fiacre O'Rafferty *(Projectionist)*, Maria Ricard *(Patty's Mother)*, John Shelly *(Patty's Father)*, Ricardo Azulay *(Police Captain)*, Joe Wolberg *(Swat Commander)*, Steven Brown, Fabia Matas, Mark Parker *(Swat Team)*, Philip Rodgers, Joan Lloveras, Jose Luis Amposta, Eric Pier, Claus Braun, Jorge Ferrer, Jorge Torcas, Pep Cukart, Tito Alvarez, John Heald, Dinky *(Policemen)*, Angelika Thiblant, Elvira Salles, Tatiana Gari, Margarita Borchaca, Julia Carrasco, Maria Guerin *(Nurses in Street)*.

A masterful example of audience manipulation, ANGUISH is a terrifically suspenseful horror film containing not one, but two classic gimmicks: a William Castle-style warning that the film may cause mental distress due to the hypnotic tricks on screen, and the film-within-a-film trick most recently seen in Lamberto Bava's DEMONS. While the first gimmick is silly, Spanish director Bigas Luna employs the second extremely well. The movie begins as loutish optometrist orderly Lerner louses up on the job and is dismissed. His mother, Rubinstein, is an odd little woman who totally dominates her docile son. Using a form of hypnosis, Rubinstein merges her mind with Lerner's and sends him out to get revenge on the patient who caused his dismissal (Lorca). Medical bag in hand, Lerner dutifully goes to the house of Lorca, killing her and her husband. He then produces a scalpel and methodically removes their eyes—which his mother collects. At this point, director Luna pulls back from the image to reveal that it is merely a horror film being watched by a small matinee crowd in a movie theater. While the lines, "This is disgusting" and "I can't take this," are heard from the audience, Luna's camera comes to rest on two teenage girls, Paul and Pastor. Pastor munches popcorn and stares at the screen, while Paul becomes queasy and wants to leave. Pastor has no intention of leaving and ignores her friend's insistence that the strange-looking man across the isle (Jove) is a lunatic. Quaking with fear, Paul staggers off to the bathroom, where, in her paranoia, she thinks the lunatic has followed her. She dashes back to her seat and begs Pastor to go see for herself. Pastor, who wants more popcorn anyway, goes to have a look. Meanwhile, on the screen, Lerner enters a movie theater (where the patrons watch the 1925 version of THE LOST WORLD) and begins silently killing the patrons one by one and removing their eyes. Back in the audience, Jove, who *is* a lunatic, gets up and goes into the lobby, where he produces a gun and kills the theater employees, dragging their bodies into the ladies' room—just like in the movie. Pastor witnesses the killings and hides in one of the stalls, terror stricken. Back in the theater, the action on the screen continues to parallel the action in the lobby, and Paul, her imagination running wild, sinks into her seat whimpering. Taking pity on the poor girl, a kindly patron goes to look for Pastor and is killed by Jove—as is his wife when she goes to find her husband. Shortly thereafter Jove locks everyone in the theater and holds Paul hostage while he continues to parallel what takes place onscreen. Pastor, in the meantime, has escaped and called the police. The theater is surrounded and snipers man the projection booth as Jove stands in front of the screen waiting for "Mother" in the movie to come and save him. Eventually he releases Paul and is shot by the police, but the girl whirls backward and looks at the screen just as a close-up shot of Lerner wielding a scalpel seems to stab her in the eye. Hysterical, Paul thinks she has actually been stabbed in the eye and she is taken to the hospital for psychiatric treatment. After the doctor bids the girl good night, an orderly enters and it is none other than Lerner—and he wants her eyes! As the credits roll, we see that the titles are on yet another screen and the "real" part of the story was just another movie-within-a-movie. As the credits proceed, we watch as the patrons in the movie theater slowly file out.

Although basically an empty-headed exercise in cinematic style, ANGUISH is a superbly crafted film and lots of fun to watch. Because mainstream audiences have no interest in experimental filmmaking techniques, commercial directors with an adventurous bent have found the horror genre an incredibly flexible venue in which to dabble with the unconventional. With an built-in audience whose only requirement is that the film be scary, directors have been able to get away with virtually plotless essays in style wherein they can indulge in any trick they care to as long as they deliver the occasional jolt. The NIGHTMARE ON ELM STREET series has been an exceptionally fertile testing ground for several clever new talents. ANGUISH, however, may be the best of the bunch. Director Bigas Luna spins an elaborate web of suspense, playing on audience expectations and perceptions. After 30 minutes he has the viewer in his grasp like a puppet on a string, skillfully manipulating his medium to produce the desired reactions. He also injects a sense of irony and humor into the proceedings, using the audience in the film to comment on the picture playing before them. Whereas some may find the grotesque obsession with eyes and the graphic removal thereof revolting, Luna is merely making literal what he does through cinema—he steals our eyes. Shot in 1986 on locations in Spain, New York, and Los Angeles, ANGUISH, for some unimaginable reason, didn't receive much of a release in the US and turned up on the home video heap. This is a great shame, for the effect of the film would have been heightened for audiences actually sitting in a movie theater while this movie-within-a-movie-within-a-movie—in which everyone is killed while watching a movie—flickered on a big screen. It would be impossible not to look over one's shoulder while watching ANGUISH at the local triplex. Unfortunately, home video is where most people will see this unique little film, and although it is still quite effective, it won't be as complete a cinematic experience. *(Violence, gore effects, profanity.)*

p, Pepon Coromina; d, Bigas Luna; w, Bigas Luna; ph, Jose Maria Civit (Eastmancolor, Agfa Color); ed, Tom Sabin; m, J.M. Pagan; prod d, Andreu Coromina; set d, Felipe de Paco; spec eff, Paco Teres; cos, Consol Tura; makeup, Matilde Fabregat.

Horror   Cas.   (PR:O MPAA:R)

ANOTHER WOMAN** (1988) 84m Jack Rollins-Charles H. Joffe/Orion c

Gena Rowlands (*Marion Post*), Mia Farrow (*Hope*), Ian Holm (*Ken Post*), Blythe Danner (*Lydia*), Gene Hackman (*Larry*), Betty Buckley (*Kathy*), Martha Plimpton (*Laura Post*), John Houseman (*Marion's Dad*), Sandy Dennis (*Claire*), David Ogden Stiers (*Young Marion's Dad*), Philip Bosco (*Sam*), Harris Yulin (*Paul*), Frances Conroy (*Lynn*), Kenneth Welsh, Bruce Jay Friedman, Michael Kirby.

Setting himself up for the usual round of critical lambasting, Woody Allen has again made a "serious" film (his second in a row, God forbid), and this time it's his most personal work to date. Comparable in some ways to Ingmar Bergman's WILD STRAWBERRIES, ANOTHER WOMAN stars Rowlands as an aging professor who comes to realize that she has led a harsh, unemotional life and must look back into the past in order to prepare herself for the future. The head of a university philosophy department, Rowlands leads the stereotypical life of an academic. She attends cocktail parties, discusses Brecht, reads Rilke, is on her second marriage, dabbles in political activism, and is, of course, writing a novel. She is a prime member of the subculture (or superculture) of intellectuals who recognize themselves as such. Rowlands is married to a physician (Holm), has a close relationship with her peppy stepdaughter (Plimpton), avoids her brother (Yulin), and fears the loss of her ailing father (Houseman). When distractions at home make concentrating impossible, Rowlands rents a studio apartment where she can work on her novel. There, as she sits down to her typewriter and stares at the blank pages before her, she hears voices coming from an air vent that connects to a psychiatrist's office. Although her initial reaction is to muffle the sound with pillows, she soon begins eavesdropping. One patient in particular attracts her attention. This character, named Hope (Farrow), is a pregnant woman who reminds Rowlands of her young self. Rowlands follows this "other woman" through the streets of New York—determined to find her, talk to her, get to know her. In the process, Rowlands is confronted with her own friends and family. Through a combination of heightened reality, flashbacks, and dream sequences (all of which are filmed realistically), Rowlands sees how she has isolated herself from everyone around her. She is thrilled at a chance meeting with a childhood friend (Dennis), only to learn that the friend, now a struggling actress, has for years hated Rowlands for luring away a former boy friend. Rowlands, who exists in her own little world, insists that she did nothing of the sort, at least not consciously. Through a flashback, it is also revealed that she was her father's favorite at her brother expense. For years her brother has held back his anger and, naturally, Rowlands knew nothing of his resentment. The only person to whom *she* has expressed her feelings is the openly emotional Hackman, a best friend of Holm's who professes his love for Rowlands and insists that she run away with him. By the end of this walk through her own life, Rowlands has discovered that there is "another woman" inside her, one she has been suppressing for some 50 years.

Without regard for audience or critical reaction, Woody Allen continues to take a brave creative stance in making only the type of films that he wants to make. His status in American cinema is unlike that of any other major American filmmaker: his already limited audience is getting smaller; he is an easy target of criticism from reviewers who habitually give him advice on how to bridge the gap between "serious" Woody and "funny" Woody; and he continues to receive the support of a major Hollywood studio (United Artists and, since 1982, Orion) and his two longtime producers, Jack Rollins and Charles H. Joffe. It is perhaps because Allen has already alienated most of his audience, and thereby negated audience expectations, that he is now able to make his greatest and most personal films. Unfortunately, the discourse on Allen's talent (or lack thereof) has grown repetitive and tiresome, and is inadequate to bringing us any closer to understanding this filmmaker. There are certain traits of his films (the debt to Bergman, the often embarrassing intellectual exchanges, the overbearing angst) that, by now, must be accepted as givens, as Allen's personality and nothing more. To expect Allen to refrain from references to Rilke, Freud, Brecht, Klimt, or Bach is to expect Allen to make dishonest, impersonal films that serve the status quo. One can hate intellectuals and still appreciate Allen's talent—just as one can hate the bourgeoisie and appreciate Claude Chabrol, or hate cowboys and appreciate John Ford. In all three cases (if one follows an auteurist line of criticism), one appreciates the filmmaker because of his ability to express his own personality in his work.

Aside from this expression of Allen's personality, ANOTHER WOMAN has, as has become expected with Allen's films, a superb ensemble cast. Gena Rowlands, in a complete turnabout from her films with John Cassavetes (FACES; A WOMAN UNDER THE INFLUENCE; LOVE STREAMS), is again a perfect mirror for her director. For Cassavetes, Rowlands turns in performances that expose emotions to an effect that proves as painful, uncomfortable, and honest as watching an autopsy. Under Allen's direction, everything that was once emotional in her acting becomes cerebral. She does what every great actor should do—interpret and reflect the personality of the author. The most brilliant scenes in the film are those between Rowlands and Ian Holm and between Rowlands and Gene Hackman, in which Rowlands must subtly adjust her performance to fit Holm's cold charm or Hackman's fiery passion. The acting is equally impressive all the way down the cast list (Mary Steenburgen had originally been cast in one small part that Allen reshot with Frances Conroy). Especially endearing is the final performance from a frail and obviously ailing John Houseman, who would die very shortly after the film's release. As expected, Sven Nykvist's photography is impeccable, as is Santo Loquasto's simple production design. (*Adult situations, profanity.*)

p, Robert Greenhut; d, Woody Allen; w, Woody Allen; ph, Sven Nykvist (Duart color); ed, Susan E. Morse; prod d, Santo Loquasto; art d, Speed Hopkins; set d, George DeTitta, Jr.; cos, Jeffrey Kurland.

Drama   Cas.   (PR:C MPAA:PG)

APPOINTMENT WITH DEATH* (1988) 102m Golan-Globus/Cannon c

Peter Ustinov (*Hercule Poirot*), Lauren Bacall (*Lady Westholme*), Carrie Fisher (*Nadine Boynton*), John Gielgud (*Col. Carbury*), Piper Laurie (*Mrs. Emily Boynton*), Hayley Mills (*Miss Quinton*), Jenny Seagrove (*Dr. Sarah King*), David Soul (*Jefferson Cope*), Nicholas Guest (*Lennox Boynton*), Valerie Richards (*Carol Boynton*), John Terlesky (*Raymond Boynton*), Amber Bezer (*Ginevra Boynton*), Douglas Sheldon (*Capt. Rogers*), Mike Sarne (*Healey*), Michael Craig (*Lord Peel*), Mohammed Hirzalla (*Hassan*), Ruggero Comploy (*Tourist Guide*), Danny Muggia (*Italian Policeman*), Lutuf Nuayser (*Boynton Driver*), Babi Neeman (*Arab Vendor*), Rupert Horrox (*British Official*), Hugh Brophy (*British Official at Ball*), Marcel Soloman (*Ship's Captain*).

In APPOINTMENT WITH DEATH, produced and directed by Michael Winner, Peter Ustinov returns as Hercule Poirot, Agatha Christie's fastidious Belgian detective whose presence bespeaks wit and cunning. As the film opens, in 1937, opportunistic attorney Soul is being blackmailed by the matriarch of the Boynton clan, Laurie, an intolerable stepmother who forces the lawyer to burn her late husband's will so she won't have to share the family estate with the children. An excursion to the continent soothes few feelings as the Boynton children discover they may have been cheated out of their inheritance. Guest, a broken spirit who lives masochistically under his mother's domination is able to give little solace to his spunky wife, Fisher, while siblings Richards and Terlesky plot their stepmother's demise. Even the youngest stepchild, Bezer, reads "Darling Detective," but to what purpose? In Trieste, the Boyntons board a ship bound for British-occupied Palestine and are joined by Seagrove, a doctor not above exercising her considerable will; Bacall, a member of Parliament; Mills, an archeologist; Soul, who is now Fisher's lover; and, of course, the indomitable Poirot (Ustinov). "There are six million Jews in Europe for whom the world is divided in two parts," says Ustinov. "Places in which they are not allowed to live and places in which they cannot enter." In the Holy Land, the pilgrims are greeted by Gielgud, a sympathetic colonel not above slinging a barb or two, and who proves himself to be immensely helpful when mystery flares en route to the party's destination, an archaeological dig near the Dead Sea. Soul and Mills vanish, then reappear. Is their return a portent of death for the wicked stepmother? In short order, Laurie *is* found dead, the victim of a fatal overdose of digitalis (a heart disease remedy). Ustinov promises to reveal the murderer within 48 hours, but before he can, an unknown assailant strikes again, murdering the mysterious Arab (Hirzalla) who might have held vital evidence of the crime. During the king's coronation ball, at the table of a family that has plotted murder, Ustinov reveals the culprit's identity. Fireworks, literal and figurative, burst, as the killer meets his fate.

Filmed on location in Israel, Italy, and England, APPOINTMENT WITH DEATH offers a tangled web to delight mystery lovers. Ustinov, a snappy Poirot, separates clues from red herrings with atypical finesse, Lauren Bacall creates a never-to-be-taken-for-granted character, and Carrie Fisher is the woman who might have provoked the dastardly deed. If the banal seems to creep into characters dominated by the venomous Piper Laurie, the viewer might look closer to discover how each is in essence confounded by reality. After all, as Ustinov confides to John Gielgud, "Everything is always fun for you English; the sun will never set on your games." One might wish for a bit more playfulness from Winner's film, but the chase is heady, lighthearted, and chancy. (*Violence, adult situations.*)

p, Michael Winner; d, Michael Winner; w, Anthony Shaffer, Peter Buckman, Michael Winner (based on the novel by Agatha Christie); ph, David Gurfinkel (Rank Color); ed, Arnold Crust; m, Pino Donaggio, Rafi Kadishzon, Frank Barber, DeWolfe; md, Natale Massara; prod d, John Blezard; art d, Avi Avivi; set d, Alan Cassie, Shlomo Tzafrir; cos, John Bloomfield; ch, Jakob Kalusky; makeup, Yvonne Coppard, Pat Hay.

Mystery   Cas.   (PR:A-C MPAA:PG)

APPRENTICE TO MURDER* (1988) 94m Hot Intl./NW c

Donald Sutherland (*John Reese*), Chad Lowe (*Billy Kelly*), Mia Sara (*Alice Spangler*), Knut Husebo (*Lars Hoeglin*), Rutanya Alda (*Elma Kelly*), Eddie Jones (*Tom Kelly*), Mark Burton (*Clay Meyers*), Adrian Sparks (*Irwin Myers*), Tiger Haynes (*Rufus*), Minnie Gentry, Blain Fairman, Mert Hatfield, Keith Edwards, Chris Langham, Lars Hiller, Ed Wiley, Agnette Haaland, Irina Eidsvold, Bembo Davis, Tor Hansen, Edel Eckblad.

Set in 1927 rural Pennsylvania, APPRENTICE TO MURDER is the saga of a teenage boy who falls under the influence of a Svengali-like faith healer (called a "powwow"), an association which eventually leads, as the title suggests, to a death. Teacher and apprentice meet when the boy (Lowe) seeks out the mysterious Sutherland for help in treating his acutely alcoholic father. Lowe is given a potion that, when sprinkled over Dad's breakfast, causes him to retch at the next gulp of Pennsylvania mountain moonshine and effectively solves his dependency problem. Thus convinced of the healer's validity, Lowe becomes Sutherland's sidekick-protege, accompanying him on a series of holistic healing house calls about the countryside. Trouble arises when Sutherland is arrested for practicing medicine without a license, after which he undergoes a kind of phantasmagoric persecution complex that comes to a head when he is nearly killed while exorcising a barn. He falls gravely ill and is spared death only by the incantations of another powwow, who informs Sutherland and

Lowe that the former is being cursed by Satan incarnate and they must find the man, "cut a lock of his hair and bury it eight feet deep." Satan, as it happens, turns out to be local hermit Husebo, whose appearance in the film up to this point has been limited to a few brief, low-angle doom shots heralded with loud mood music. The intrepid pair confront Husebo, who voices his objection to the haircut by spitting fire at them. There is a struggle and Husebo is killed, saving the community. Sutherland and Lowe are nevertheless sent up for Husebo's murder, though a tag line nullifies the unhappy ending by revealing that Lowe will, after a five-year stretch, move to New York and become a successful commercial artist.

Like so many post-MTV movies, APPRENTICE TO MURDER features often breathtaking (though occasionally trite) cinematography but is overwhelmed by a bewildering lack of narrative focus. Further confusing the peculiar logic of the main story is a vague coming-of-age subplot wherein Lowe's girl friend tugs at his soul, attempting to wrest him away from Sutherland and his pastoral community for the big city, where she aims to become a typist. This relationship and that between Lowe and his parents never quite crystalize, largely because the subsidiary characters are so blandly sketched that they become extraneous. What begins as a simple domestic morality tale degenerates under the weight of a plot structure seemingly born of panic. New and incongruous elements, gratuitous set pieces, and empty iconography thrown in helter-skelter cause the pace to lurch in fits and starts. Moreover, this film that purports to be a mystery/thriller is completely lacking in suspense or any real sense of menace due to its makers' failure to observe that most basic rule of cinema: show rather than tell. Expository dialog reduces any terrifying or potentially terrifying events to hearsay—making, for example, the Husebo-Satan character ludicrous (unless you happen to quake at the thought of tall, Nordic emigres). To compound the difficulty, Chad Lowe's is much too weak a central character, following instead of shaping events throughout, and Donald Sutherland's persona lacks the Elmer Gantry-Preacher Harry Powell forcefulness and charisma demanded by the plot. Suffering from these poor characterizations and sloppy story-telling, APPRENTICE TO MURDER resorts to feeble pyrotechnics in lieu of strong dramatic content. (*Adult situations.*)

p, Howard K. Grossman; d, R.L. Thomas; w, Alan Scott, Wesley Moore; ph, Kelvin Pike; ed, Patrick McMahon; m, Charles Gross; prod d, Gregory Bolton; cos, Elisabeth Ann Seley.

Mystery   **Cas.**   **(PR:C MPAA:PG-13)**

ARIA**   (1988, US/Brit.) 98m RVP-Virgin Vision/Miramax-WB c

Theresa Russell (*King Zog*), Stephanie Lane (*Baroness*), Roy Hyatt, George Ellis Jones (*Chauffeurs*), Sevilla Delofski (*Maid*), Ruth Halliday (*Companion*), Arthur Cox (*Major*), Dennis Holmes (*Colonel*), Paul Brightwell, Frank Baker, Chris Hunter (*Assassins*), Paul Collard (*Valet*), Danny Fitzgerald (*Mercedes Man*), Johnny Doyle (*Blind Balloon Man*), David Ross (*Doorman*), Lucy Oliver (*Woman in Background*), Gordon Winter (*Man in Background*), Derek Farmer (*Motorbike Man*), Michelle Read (*Nanny*), Maximillian Roeg (*Child*), Nicola Swain (*Marie*), Jackson Kyle (*Travis*), Marianne McLoughlin (*Kate*), Marion Peterson, Valerie Allain (*Les Jeunes Filles*), Jacques Neuville, Luke Corre, Christian Cauchon, Philippe Pellant, Patrice Linguet, Lionel Sorin, Jean Coffinet, Alexandre Des Granges, Gerrard Vives, Frederick Brosse, Pascal Bermont, Jean Luc Corre, Bernard Gaudray, Dominique Mano, Patrice Tridian (*Bodybuilders*), Buck Henry (*Preston*), Beverly D'Angelo (*Gilda*), Gary Kasper (*Jake*), Anita Morris (*Phoebe*), John Hostetter (*Elvis Impersonator*), Albie Selznick (*Bellboy*), Stan Mazin, Dominic Salinero, Jeff Calhoun (*Dancers*), Elizabeth Hurley (*Marietta*), Peter Birch (*Paul*), Bertrand Bonvoisin, Cris Campion, Anne Canovas, Sandrine Dumas, Jody Guelb, Julie Hagerty, Philipine Leroy-Beaulieu, Genevieve Page, Delphine Rich, Louis-Marie Taillefer, Bridget Fonda, James Mathers (*The Lovers*), Angie Tetamontie, Esther Buchanan, Lorraine Cote, Renee Korn (*Las Vegas Ladies*), Bertha Weiss (*Lady with Glove*), Diane Thorne, Howie Maurer (*Bride and Groom*), Derick Coleman, Quentin Brown (*Two Indian Boys*), Linzi Drew (*Girl*), Andreas Wisniewski, Kwabena Manso, Bella Enahoro, Bunty Mathias, Angela Walker, Amy Johnson (*Old Lady*), Tilda Swinton (*Young Girl*), Spencer Leigh (*Young Man*), Sophie Ward (*Young Girl*), Fernand Dumont, Voices of: Leontyne Price, Carlo Bergonzi, Robert Merrill, Shirley Verrett, Reri Grist, RCA Italiana Opera Chorus, Giorgio Tozzi, Ezio Flagello, Rachel Yakar, Zeger Vandersteene, Daniele Borst, Ensemble Vocale de la Chappelle Royale, Alfredo Kraus, Anna Moffo, Carol Neblett, Rene Kollo, Jennifer Smith, Anne-Marie Rodde, Philippe Langridge, Monteverde Choir, Jussi Bjoerling, Enrico Caruso.

A grand idea with bland results, ARIA is an omnibus film that combines the talents of ten directors and eight composers, but ends up with very little to show for it. It's more a showcase of brilliant packaging than of filmmaking, providing only a few segments of any real interest. The film opens with a portion of the connecting episode starring Hurt and directed by Bill Bryden. Hurt walks slowly through the deserted streets of Cremona, Italy, apparently in search of a lost love. This segment is returned to after every episode, as Hurt enters a church and, later, a theater dressing room, where he applies clown makeup for a performance of "Vesti la Giubba" from Ruggiero Leoncavallo's "I Pagliacci." Segment One, directed by Nicolas Roeg and set to extracts from Giuseppe Verdi's "Un Ballo in Maschera," is based on an actual historical incident, in which King Zog of Albania was the intended victim of an assassination plot. In Vienna, 1931, King Zog (played by a mustached Russell) attends a performance of Verdi's opera, but as he is leaving he is ambushed. The king, however, is prepared for the attack and shoots back at his assailants, gunning down all of them. While the segment is exquisitely staged and designed, with gentle framing scenes of a female Russell gazing out her window, the result is a rather empty and literal tale with all the depth of a student thesis project. Segment Two, directed by Charles Sturridge (of TV's "Brideshead Revisited") and set to the aria "La Vergine degli Angeli" from Verdi's "La Forza del Destino," is a surprisingly pleasant piece filmed in mono-

chromatic tones on the drizzly streets of London, but seems to be more of a moral than an operatic tale. Three dirty street kids, after gazing at a statue of the Virgin Mary, steal a Mercedes Benz. Cruising down slick streets at night, they are chased by police and eventually crash, dying in a ball of fire. Segment Three, directed by Jean-Luc Godard and set to "Enfin il est en ma puissance" and other excerpts from Jean Baptiste Lully's "Armide," is easily the most inventive episode, as Godard continues to experiment in modern sound construction and classical imagery. Without a conventional story line, the episode takes place in a gymnasium where a group of well-developed bodybuilders pump iron and a pair of barely dressed young women do cleaning chores. They dust the barbells and weights while the men press and jerk, and even try to polish the men's glistening, muscular bodies. They also try to seduce the men, twirling naked through the frame, but to no avail. One young woman then tries to plunge a butcher knife into a muscleman, but stops short of killing him. While the other directors of ARIA employ classical or overpowering architecture (grand ballrooms, castles, elegant bedrooms, weathered statues) to create an operatic set design, Godard surprises by presenting men and women who are built as if they themselves were architecture. (He had, in fact, intended to shoot his segment with two cleaning women in a gallery that had once been a studio of Rodin's.) As he has done in the past, Godard treats his music with an atypical reverence. In a move sure to send shivers through any opera purist, he freely chops up Lully's score by contrasting it with the clanging and banging of gymnasium sounds.

Segment Four, directed by Julien Temple (ABSOLUTE BEGINNERS) and set to "La Donna e Mobile" and other extracts from Verdi's "Rigoletto," is the most entertaining and comical of the bunch. Set in the gaudy Madonna Inn of San Luis Obispo, California, this overlong piece follows two couples as they spend a sexually charged evening together. Henry is married to Morris, but is having an affair with D'Angelo. He and D'Angelo hurry off to their Neanderthal Room at the inn, narrowly missing Morris and her muscular lover, Kasper, as they slip into the adjoining Heidi's Hideaway. The evening is a series of near misses for the adulterous husband and wife, as Temple's manic Steadicam camera twirls around the grounds, passing through walls and doors. Henry and Morris each videotape their respective dalliances, then the tapes get mixed up, and when they return home the truth is discovered. While his piece is a bit goofy, Temple does continue to show the visual flair he delivered in ABSOLUTE BEGINNERS. His episode also features one of the most memorable Elvis jabs in recent memory, showing the King, on stage and overweight in his white studded jumpsuit, as he belts out "La Donna e Mobile." Segment Five, directed by Bruce Beresford (TENDER MERCIES, CRIMES OF THE HEART) and set to "Gluck, das mir verblieb" from Erich Wolfgang Korngold's "Die Tote Stadt," is a boring, straightforward lip-synching of a Korngold duet between two lovers. In a massive bedroom in Bruges, Belgium, a man undresses a woman. Beresford intercuts some scenes of Bruges, then returns to the lovers as they sit naked on their massive bed. They then disappear, ending this short nothing of a segment that points sharply to Beresford's utter lack of inventiveness. Segment Six, directed by Robert Altman and set to "Lieux desoles," "Suite des Vents," and "Jouissons, Jouissons!" from Jean Philippe Rameau's "Les Boreades," shows a theoretically ambitious idea falling completely flat. Rather than filming the opera, Altman concentrates on the audience—a group of asylum inmates who jeer, hoot, cry, and flash one another during the 1734 premiere of "Les Boreades" at Paris' Ranelagh Theatre. "People used to go to the opera like it was Woodstock," Altman has explained. "They shouted, sang along with the performers, sold food in the aisles, moved around, like at a circus. There is no focus in my sequence, except that the people are insane." Unfortunately, Altman's execution of this admirable idea is thoroughly uninteresting. Segment Seven, directed by Franc Roddam (QUADROPHENIA, THE BRIDE), set to "Liebestod" from Richard Wagner's "Tristan und Isolde," parallels the passionate, perfect love of two innocent teenagers with the cheap, gunshot marriages of Las Vegas. Fonda (daughter of Peter Fonda) and Mathers, both in their film debuts, drive through the colorful, neon-lit strip, stopping in a bare-bones motel. The make love and seem to have reached a plateau of perfect, uncompromising union. Rather than return to the dishonesty and emptiness of real life, where their romance can only be diluted, the lovers kill themselves in the bathtub. Intertwined, they slit their wrists with a piece of broken glass and die together, in a truly tragic story that seems to best fit the themes of sex and death that run through so many operas. While some ARIA episodes are moral tales (Sturridge's) or historical statements (Roeg's or Altman's), Roddam has actually created a miniopera of perfect love that is strengthened by his choice of location—the loveless Las Vegas. Segment Eight, directed by Ken Russell and set to "Nessun dorma" from Giacomo Puccini's "Turandot," is a visual treat that is both repulsive and compelling. A young woman is seriously injured in an automobile accident. As she is being treated by doctors, she has visions that she is being decorated with marvelous jewels by some heavenly bodies. The contrast between the sparkling of diamonds and rubies and the oozing of the woman's bloody wounds is aesthetically confounding, making for the most purely visual segment of the film. Segment Nine, directed by Derek Jarman (CARAVAGGIO) and set to "Depuis le Jour" from Gustave Charpentier's "Louise," is a small piece featuring an aging woman who recalls a love affair from her youth. Jarman employs 8mm footage for the old woman's memories and has created a visual poem, but its connection with opera is a slim one. Segment Ten, directed by Bryden and set to "Vesti la Giubba" from "I Pagliacci," isn't actually a segment at all, but the climax of the numerous connecting episodes. Hurt, dressed in full clown attire, walks onto an empty stage and mimes Enrico Caruso as Ward watches from a private box. Hurt then collapses and dies. A 90-second coda montage by Chuck Braverman, tacked on for some unknown reason, includes out-takes and production stills from the various episodes.

Masterminded by producer Don Boyd (Jarman's THE TEMPEST, Temple's THE GREAT ROCK AND ROLL SWINDLE), ARIA is a noble attempt to bring together the talents of some of today's more notable directors. Unfortunately, however, some of today's more notable directors aren't up to much more here than third-rate trash that would be jeered at any film school screening. Since Boyd gave the directors the freedom to make the film they desired (providing they stay within a $75,000 budget, keep it to 7-12 minutes, and choose their music from the RCA library), one has to place the blame for ARIA's lack of creativity on the filmmakers. The film has been called MTV for opera fans, but that does a disservice to the infinitely more daring rock video directors. One would think that giving free rein to a director would encourage him to take a few chances. Instead, only Godard tries to make a connection between sound and image, addressing the very root of opera—music and visuals—and doing so in a popular setting. Roddam, though his approach is a bit saccharine, has at least given us a story that is operatic. (His visuals, photographed by Frederick Elmes of BLUE VELVET, are simply stunning, recalling Francis Coppola's ONE FROM THE HEART.) Temple also shows the visual and storytelling energy that one has come to expect from opera. The remaining directors, however, failed to meet their cinematic challenge (according to Boyd's original guidelines, to use the chosen aria as a source of inspiration); their segments lack either intelligent content or inventive visuals or (as in Beresford's and Bryden's work) both. What ARIA proves is that the top composers and stagers of opera today (Philip Glass and Robert Wilson, John Adams and Peter Sellars) are taking far greater steps in stretching the boundaries of their medium than this collection of supposedly top filmmakers are in stretching theirs. Instead of being a signal to other art forms that film, too, is an art, ARIA is a pitiful display of the lack of artistic imagination in filmmaking today. Perhaps if some of the other directors who were asked to participate (Federico Fellini, Jean-Jacques Beineix, David Byrne [who began shooting and reluctantly abandoned it after a dispute with RCA], Woody Allen, Peter Brook, and Werner Herzog) had actually contributed, then the film's creative power wouldn't have had to rest solely on Godard's shoulders and, just maybe, the film would have lived up to its original title: "Imaginaria." Screenings of ARIA were preceded in a number of venues by the Chuck Jones-directed Bugs Bunny-Elmer Fudd Warner Bros. cartoon "What's Opera, Doc?" *(Sexual situations, nudity, graphic gore effects.)*

p, Don Boyd; d, Nicolas Roeg, Charles Sturridge, Jean-Luc Godard, Julien Temple, Bruce Beresford, Robert Altman, Franc Roddam, Ken Russell, Derek Jarman, Bill Bryden; w, Nicolas Roeg, Charles Sturridge, Jean-Luc Godard, Julien Temple, Bruce Beresford, Robert Altman, Franc Roddam, Ken Russell, Derek Jarman, Bill Bryden, Don Boyd; ph, Harvey Harrison, Gale Tattersall, Carolyn Champetier, Oliver Stapleton, Dante Spinotti, Pierre Mignot, Frederick Elmes, Gabriel Beristain, Mike Southon, Christopher Hughes; ed, Marie Therese Boiche, Mike Cragg, Tony Lawson, Matthew Longfellow, Neil Abrahamson, Jennifer Auge, Rick Elgood, Michael Bradsell, Peter Cartwright, Angus Cook; m, Giuseppe Verdi, Jean Baptiste Lully, Erich Wolfgang Korngold, Jean-Philippe Rameau, Richard Wagner, Giacomo Puccini, Gustave Charpentier, Ruggiero Leoncavallo; md, Ralph Mace; prod d, Diana Johnstone, Andrew McAlpine, Stephen Altman, Piers Plowden, Scott Bushnell, John Hay, Matthew Jacobs, Paul Dufficey, Christopher Hobbs; set d, Arnaud De Moleron, Deborah Evans, Rossella Scanagatta; spec eff, Tom Harris; cos, Shuna Harwood, Leslie Gilda, John Hay, Elisabetta Rogiani, Jane Hamilton, Victoria Russell, Sandy Powell, Alison Chitty; ch, Terry Gilbert, Grover Dale; makeup, Jenny Shircore, Anni Buchanan, Vilborg Aradottir, Rick Casboro, Penny Delamar Shawyer, Dominique De Vorges, Philomene Sammartino, Angelo Dibiase, Morag Ross, Rick Casboro.

Opera Cas. (PR:O MPAA:R)

ARIZONA HEAT † (1988) 91m Arizona Heat/Spectrum c

Michael Parks *(Larry Kapinski)*, Denise Crosby *(Jill Andrews)*, Hugh Farrington *(Capt. Samuels)*, Ron Briskman *(Toad)*, Dennis O'Sullivan *(Paul Murphy)*, Renata Lee *(Lisa)*.

Shot on location in Phoenix and Scottsdale, this straight-to-video release was helmed by John Thomas, the director of last year's crash-and-burn epic BANZAI RUNNER. Michael Parks stars as a tough Arizona police detective with a bad reputation (similar to the Mel Gibson character in LETHAL WEAPON) who is hot on the trial of a serial cop killer. Assisting Parks is his new, unwanted, lesbian partner, Crosby, and the two engage in predictable buddy-film bickering while investigating the case. Songs include "The Pusher" (Hoyt Axton) and "Caught in the Heat" (Gary Stockdale).

p, John G. Thomas; d, John G. Thomas; w, Daniel M. Colmerauer; ph, Howard Wexler (United Color); ed, John G. Thomas; m, Gary Stockdale; art d, Brian Densmore; stunts, Spanky Spangler.

Action/Crime Cas. (PR:NR MPAA:R)

ARTHUR 2 ON THE ROCKS* (1988) 112m WB c

Dudley Moore *(Arthur Bach)*, Liza Minnelli *(Linda Marolla)*, Geraldine Fitzgerald *(Martha)*, Paul Benedict *(Fairchild)*, John Gielgud *(Hobson)*, Kathy Bates *(Mrs. Canby)*, Cynthia Sikes *(Susan Johnson)*, Stephen Elliott *(Burt Johnson)*, Barney Martin *(Ralph)*, Jack Gilford *(Super)*, Ted Ross *(Bitterman)*, Thomas Barbour, David O'Brien, Ron Canada.

Madcap dipsomaniac Arthur Bach (Moore) makes a less than triumphant return in ARTHUR 2 ON THE ROCKS, the sequel to the 1981 hit ARTHUR. When last seen in the original, Moore had just jilted his family-appointed fiancee for Minnelli, a hash-slinging would-be actress, and got to keep his $750 million inheritance to boot. ARTHUR 2 opens four years later: Moore and Minnelli are happily married (despite the fact that Moore's still a boozer), but Minnelli's just received the bad news that she can't have kids. A trip to the adoption agency follows, and the couple are told that finding them a kid should be a breeze. Ecstatic, Minnelli summons the decorators and plunks down a small fortune on toys for the tot. Enter Elliott, whose daughter, Sikes (Jill Eikenberry played the role in the first film), was dumped by Moore in the original. Intent on revenge, Elliott seizes control of Moore's family's business and delivers an ultimatum: Moore either ditches Minnelli and marries Sikes or he waves goodbye to the $750 million. Moore chooses Minnelli, and the now-impoverished couple are forced to cope with life in the slow lane—with Elliott thwarting them every step of the way. Meanwhile, Sikes tracks down Minnelli and imparts some not-so-friendly advice to her: If you love your husband, set him free. Guilt-ridden, Minnelli obliges. Alone, penniless, homeless, and drunk as a skunk, Moore roams the streets, at one point having a heart-to-heart talk with the ghost of his acid-tongued but tenderhearted butler (Gielgud, reprising his Oscar-winning role from ARTHUR), who tells him to stop whining and take control of his life. Revitalized—and sober—Moore digs up some dirt on Elliott and confronts him with it. Elliott goes berserk and pulls a gun. Sikes intervenes, persuading her father not only to let Moore go, but also to give him back his money. In one of the schmaltziest endings in movie history, Moore shows up at Minnelli's house rolling in dough, their baby arrives from the adoption agency, and Minnelli breaks the news that she's pregnant.

ARTHUR 2 is a romantic comedy with a fatal flaw: it's rarely funny. Dudley Moore is a gifted comedian—at times he's as maniacally brilliant as Robin Williams—but the writing isn't up to snuff. Too many jokes fall flat (one is lifted straight from ARTHUR), the characters lack depth, and most of the situational humor is either too predictable or too downright silly. The entire resolution depends on a single act—Sikes' intervention on Moore's behalf—that's unbelievable; it seems a mere contrivance to bring the story to a happy ending. Moreover, Moore's drunk act wears thin fast. In ARTHUR, Moore drinks because he's scared and lonely; his alcohol problem is a defense, and the viewer can forgive him for it. But in ARTHUR 2, Moore's boozing is just obnoxious.

The rest of the cast comprises a bevy of talented actors, but most of their talent is squandered. Liza Minnelli makes a sweet sweetheart, but her character, which was endearingly kooky in ARTHUR, is now bland. Moore's grandmother (Geraldine Fitzgerald), a lovable eccentric in the first film, is reduced to a cliche here. Cynthia Sikes is saddled with the film's least clearly defined character; Stephen Elliott, through no fault of his own, gives basically a one-note (rage) performance. Jack Gilford, who appears briefly as an apartment building super, performs adequately but isn't asked to do much. John Gielgud, however, is as distinguished and unflappable as ever, and provides a sorely needed touch of class. His appearance may not be one of the highlights of his career, but it's certainly a high point of this film. *(Profanity, adult situations, substance abuse.)*

p, Robert Shapiro; d, Bud Yorkin; w, Andy Breckman (based on characters created by Steve Gordon); ph, Stephen H. Burum (Technicolor); ed, Michael Kahn; m, Burt Bacharach; prod d, Gene Callahan; art d, Hub Braden; set d, P. Michael Johnstone; cos, Anna Hill Johnstone.

Romance/Comedy Cas. (PR:C MPAA:PG)

ASSAULT OF THE KILLER BIMBOS** (1988) 80m Titan/Empire c

Christina Whitaker *(Peaches)*, Elizabeth Kaitan *(LuLu)*, Tammara Souza *(Darlene)*, Nick Cassavetes *(Wayne-O)*, Griffin O'Neal *(Troy)*, Jamie Bozian *(Billy)*, Mike Muscat *(Vinnie)*, Patti Astor *(Poodles)*, David Marsh *(Shifty Joe)*.

This could have been truly wretched. The title doesn't promise much, except for the almost certain chance to ogle ample flesh. But ASSAULT OF THE KILLER BIMBOS manages to surprise, thanks to a certain loopy charm and the sensibility of director Anita Rosenberg, who keeps her characters "bimbos" without reducing them to objects. The film opens in a sleazy nightclub where Whitaker is the star dancer. ("Go-go is an art form," she proclaims. "It's interpretive dance with a rock'n'roll background.") She's a no-nonsense type, in contrast to Kaitan, a ding-a-ling waitress who admires Whitaker and hopes for her own big chance to take the stage. Kaitan's break finally comes when another dancer does a no-show. She begs Shifty Joe (Marsh), the manager, for a chance and he gives in, whereupon she totally bombs out. He calls both women "bimbos," infuriating Whitaker. A few moments later Marsh is murdered by a mob hit man (Muscat) just as Whitaker and Kaitan walk in demanding an apology. Muscat shoves the gun into Kaitan's hands and runs out, and when others arrive, they immediately assume that the dancers, who were seen arguing with the boss, are his murderers. The women light out for Mexico with the police on their tail. At a truck stop, they run into a trio of stoned surfers (Cassavetes, O'Neal, and Bozian) and a fed-up waitress (Souza). When a sheriff spots their car, the women escape by taking Souza hostage, but once on the road Souza decides to stick with them. After barely eluding the police several times, the trio finally arrives in Mexico, where they hole up in a cheap motel. The surfers also turn up there, as do Muscat and his moll, waiting for the heat to go down. The women realize that their only chance at clearing their names is to capture Muscat, and since Souza is the only one of them he doesn't know, she gets the job of luring him up to their room. There is a struggle that eventually leaves Muscat and his girl friend tied up. They are captured by the sheriff from the truck stop, who's arrived in an attempt to rescue Souza, even though he has no authority in Mexico. The film ends with the bimbos and the surfers on the beach and the vague and rather unlikely threat of a sequel.

The performances of the three principals are surprisingly good, with Christina Whitaker a standout as the leader of the trio. She's a brassy sort who can seem authoritative even while worrying about her hair. Elizabeth Kaitan (who, genre expectations notwithstanding, is the only actress who shows her breasts) is less effective, but she is likable, as is Tammara Souza. No one else manages to rise much above the level of a racy comic book, but that's really the point, isn't it? This is the second film to have this title. Another exploitation film was shot as ASSAULT OF THE KILLER BIM-

BOS and concerned a gang of girls who team up to clear out the scum in their town, but that film was eventually retitled HACK'EM HIGH and the ASSAULT moniker was given to this film—apparently so as not to waste such a great "high concept" title on something totally worthless. *(Nudity, substance abuse, comic violence.)*

p, David DeCoteau, John Schouweiler; d, Anita Rosenberg; w, Ted Nicolaou (based on a story by Anita Rosenberg, Patti Astor, Nicolaou); ph, Thomas Callaway; ed, Barry Zetlin; m, Fred Lapides, Marc Ellis; md, Jonathan Scott Bogner; prod d, Royce Mathew; cos, Susan Rosenberg; stunts, John Stewart; makeup, Ralph Rubalcava, Thomas Wayne Schwartz.

Comedy/Crime	Cas.	(PR:O MPAA:R)

ASTONISHED †   (1988) 103m Dream Bird c

Liliana Komorowski *(Sonia)*, Ken Ryan *(Det. Jonah Wylee)*, Rock Dutton, Theresa Merritt, Fred Neuman, Tommy Hollis.

In this film, Fyodor Dostoyevski's *Crime and Punishment* is reenacted on New York's Lower East Side, its main character becoming an impoverished young woman who kills her landlord after seeing him beat a prostitute. Set against a backdrop of nightclubs and pounding r & b rhythms, ASTONISHED was given a festival release in late 1988.

p, Sydney Kahn, Herman Kahn; d, Jeff Kahn, Travis Preston; w, Jeff Kahn; ph, Peter Fernberger, Rob Draper; ed, Peter Friedman, Bill Daughton; m, Michael Urbaniak; art d, Chris Barreca.

Drama		(PR:NR MPAA:NR)

AU REVOIR LES ENFANTS**½   (1988, Fr.) 104m Nouvelles Editions de
Films-MK2-Stella/Orion Classics c

Gaspard Manesse *(Julien Quentin)*, Raphael Fejto *(Jean Bonnet)*, Francine Racette *(Mme. Quentin)*, Stanislas Carre de Malberg *(Francois Quentin)*, Philippe Morier-Genoud *(Father Jean)*, Francois Berleand *(Father Michel)*, Francois Negret *(Joseph)*, Peter Fitz *(Muller)*, Pascal Rivet *(Boulanger)*, Benoit Henriet *(Ciron)*, Richard Leboeuf *(Sagard)*, Xavier Legrand *(Babinot)*, Arnaud Henriet *(Negus)*, Jean-Sebastien Chauvin *(Laviron)*, Luc Etienne *(Moreau)*, Daniel Edinger *(Tinchaut)*, Marcel Bellot *(Guibourg)*, Ami Flammer *(Florent)*, Irene Jacob *(Mlle. Davenne)*, Jean-Paul Dubarry *(Father Hippolyte)*, Jacqueline Staup *(Infirmary Nurse)*, Jacqueline Paris *(Mme. Perrin)*, Rene Bouloc, Alain Clement, Michael Rottstock, Detlef Gericke, Michael Becker, Thomas Friedl, Christian Sohn, Michel Ginot, Philippe Despaux.

©ORION

Like a scientific specimen viewed under a microscope, AU REVOIR LES ENFANTS is a well-developed world kept at a safe distance from the spectator. Photographing his memory of his Occupation-era childhood with a microscope, director Louis Malle has delivered a film of intelligence that, unfortunately, has been bled dry of any texture. As if Malle performed an autopsy on his own memory, AU REVOIR LES ENFANTS has exposed the very heart of the director's makeup—the lifeforce that "may well have determined [his] vocation as a filmmaker"—and in so doing has presented us with a film as lifeless as a cadaver. As filled with good intentions as it is with cliches, AU REVOIR LES ENFANTS is, not surprisingly, based on an incident from Malle's childhood. The bare-bones plot starts in 1944, as the 12-year-old Malle alter ego, Julien (Manesse), says goodbye to his bourgeois mother and, along with his brother, is sent off to a Catholic boarding school near Fontainbleau. Once there, he is asked by the headmaster, Morier-Genoud, to watch over one of the new pupils, Fejto, the only boy in the class as intelligent and curious as Manesse. The boys gradually become friends, despite the fact the mysterious Fejto is clearly hiding some truth from Manesse. What Manesse begins to suspect, and later confirms, is that Fejto is a Jew, hidden from the Gestapo by the school's anti-Fascist headmaster. All that Manesse knows about Jews is what he learns from his older brother: "They are smarter than us and they crucified Jesus." Manesse, however, has sense enough to know that the Romans did the crucifying, and that these labels are nothing but stereotypes. Meanwhile, the Gestapo has heard from an informant that there are three Jews at the

school. Fejto and two others are rounded up by the Gestapo and marched off along with their headmaster, while the rest of their classmates watch in frozen horror. A voice-over (Malle's) informs us that Fejto was killed at Auschwitz.

Roundly praised by a majority of critics and the recipient of numerous awards (seven Cesars, an Oscar nomination for Best Foreign-Language Film, top honors from the LA Film Critics and the Venice Film Festival), AU REVOIR LES ENFANTS, with its noble subject, is a picture perfectly calculated for success. It's not that the film is bad; it's not. But it is virtually nonsubstantive. There's nothing on the screen. Both main characters are cardboard cutouts that simply serve as Malle's mouthpieces for, simultaneously, the persecuted individual and the young boy coming of age. Nearly everything that happens to them has happened to every other child in French films over the last few decades, and undoubtedly also happened to Malle. Watching the film, one wonders where Malle's memory of real-life events merged with his memory of French cinematic history. This is not to say that there are not some profoundly moving moments in AU REVOIR LES ENFANTS. There is a memorable scene in which an elderly Jewish patron in a "No Jews" restaurant is pressured to leave, despite the fact that he has been dining there for years. There is also the film's sole burst of spontaneity, a scene in which Manesse and Fejto play a tune on the piano together. Also worthy of mention is an entertaining, albeit far too long, movie-viewing sequence in which Charlie Chaplin's THE IMMIGRANT is shown. This is worth watching, however, only because of Chaplin. Which leaves us with the film's finest scene—the brilliant and powerful ending in which the Gestapo leads its new prisoners out of the boarding school and towards their certain death. For a moment, as our young Jewish hero is led away, we hope that he will somehow survive the death camps. Malle's voice-over, however, drives home the bitter reality of it all when he tells us the boy died in Auschwitz. Sadly, this great ending is left desperately in search of an equally great beginning. (In French; English subtitles.) *(Adult situations.)*

p, Louis Malle; d, Louis Malle; w, Louis Malle; ph, Renato Berta (Eastmancolor); ed, Emmanuelle Castro; m, Franz Schubert, Camille Saint-Saens; art d, Willy Holt; cos, Corinne Jorry; makeup, Susan Robertson.

B

BABETTE'S FEAST*** (1988, Den.) 102m Panorama-Nordisk-Danish Film Institute/Orion Classics c

Ghita Norby *(Narrator)*, Stephane Audran *(Babette Hersant)*, Jean-Philippe Lafont *(Achille Papin)*, Gudmar Wivesson *(Lorenz Lowenhielm as a Young Man)*, Jarl Kulle *(Lorenz Lowenhielm as an Old Man)*, Bibi Andersson *(Swedish Court Lady-in-Waiting)*, Hanne Stensgaard *(Young Philippa)*, Bodil Kjer *(Old Philippa)*, Vibeke Hastrup *(Young Martina)*, Birgitte Federspiel *(Old Martina)*, Bendt Rothe *(Old Nielsen)*, Ebbe Rode *(Christopher)*, Lisbeth Movin *(The Widow)*, Prebe Lerdorff Rye *(The Captain)*, Pouel Kern *(The Vicar)*, Axel Strobye *(Driver)*, Ebba With *(Lorens' Aunt)*, Else Petersen *(Solveig)*, Therese Hojgaard Christensen *(Martha)*, Asta Esper Andersen *(Anna)*, Finn Nielsen *(Grocer)*, Erik Petersen *(Young Erik)*, Lars Lohmann *(Fisherman)*, Holger Perfort *(Karlsen)*, Tine Miehe-Renard *(Lorens' Wife)*, Thomas Antoni *(Swedish Lieutenant)*, Gert Bastian *(Poor Man)*, Viggo Bentzon *(Fisherman in Rowboat)*, Cay Kristiansen *(Poul)*, Michel Bouquet *(Voice of Narrator)*, Tina Kiberg *(Philippa's Singing Voice)*.

Named Best Foreign-Language Film of 1987 by the Academy of Motion Picture Arts and Sciences, BABETTE'S FEAST surprised many who had expected Louis Malle's autobiographical AU REVOIR LES ENFANTS to take the top honors. A small, quiet film from Denmark, it is an unlikely candidate for international success. There is no sex, violence, or nudity, just sermons and hymns, a dozen or so elderly Danes, and a *gastronomique* feast to end all feasts. The film is set up with the aid of voice-over narration and a half-hour expository flashback. It is in Denmark's Jutland peninsula, on the rugged North Sea, that the story takes place. A prophetic minister lives with his two daughters—Martina (Hastrup), who is named after Martin Luther, and Philippa (Stensgaard), named after Luther's closest friend and disciple, Philipp Melanchthon—and together they spread the word of the Lord to the people of their village. During their lives of devotion, each sister has a suitor but no romance ever blossoms. Hastrup's life changes when a brash army officer, Wivesson, comes to stay with his elderly aunt. He is immediately starry-eyed at the sight of Hastrup and works his way into her religious circle. Then, feeling insignificant in her presence, he decides to leave Jutland and devote himself to his military duties. When a Parisian opera star, Lafont, vacations in Jutland, he is enchanted by Stensgaard's angelic singing voice. He offers to give her lessons, but after they sing duets from *Don Giovanni* and exchange loving glances, Stensgaard abruptly cancels any further lessons. Heartbroken, Lafont returns to France. It is 30 minutes into the film before Audran, the Babette of the title, is properly introduced to the audience (she is seen briefly at the film's opening). The time shifts to 1871; Martina, now elderly, is played by Federspiel, and Philippa is played by Kjer. Their minister father has died and they must tend his flock by themselves, leading prayer meetings, singing hymns, and preparing the drab meals of cod and ale-bread. Enter Audran, a French woman who unexpectedly arrives at the sisters' door during a torrential downpour. Speaking only a smattering of Danish, she presents the spinsters with a letter from Lafont, the opera singer now long forgotten by his former admirers. Audran's husband and son have been killed by the Paris Communards, and Lafont has sent her to Jutland in the hope that the sisters, whom he fondly remembers, will provide for her. His note also points out that she "cooks a little." For 14 years, Audran works for the sisters, cleaning windows, cooking meals, and becoming a friend to the local merchants, who respect her savvy. Her only tie to France is a lottery ticket purchased each year by a friend. One day she receives a letter from France containing 10,000 Gold Francs, her winnings from the lottery. She announces that she would like to prepare the dinner for the upcoming celebration honoring the dead minister's 100th birthday—a French dinner. The sisters and their congregation assume that this is her farewell and agree to let her proceed. They have second thoughts, however, when the food arrives by boat from France: a gigantic turtle, a collection of quails, and, most sinful in their eyes, numerous bottles of wine. Fearing that Audran is planning a pagan celebration, the congregation agrees to attend her feast but to avoid tasting, or even speaking of, the food. When the evening of the feast arrives, Audran works diligently in the kitchen, with her nephew acting as server. Also in attendance is the now-aged officer (played by Kulle), who arrives at the sisters' home fearing that he will regret having devoted his life to the military instead of his beloved Martina. The meal is served and, to Kulle's surprise, it is some of the best food he has ever tasted, recalling a dinner at the Cafe Anglais in Paris, whose female *chef de cuisine* was the greatest in all of France. The rest of the guests, having vowed not to discuss the food, try to make small talk about the weather, but find that they cannot contain themselves. After sipping a bit too much wine, they begin to loosen up, settling all past differences, and when dinner has ended, they sing a hymn together under the stars. Kulle bids farewell to Federspiel and confesses that every night he will sit down at dinner thinking of her. After everyone has gone, Audran tells the sisters that she will not be returning to France because she has spent all her money on the dinner. The sisters are shocked that their feast cost 10,000 Gold Francs—the price of the same meal at the Cafe Anglais, where, Audran reveals, she was once the *chef de cuisine*. When the sisters tell Audran that she should not have prepared the feast for them, Audran says that she did so for herself. All that artists want, she explains, is "to have the opportunity to do the best we can do."

A gentle film that metaphorically examines the artist's relationship to her art, BABETTE'S FEAST is the sort of story that one cannot help but find uplifting. But while Gabriel Axel attempts to attain the purity, grace, and austerity of the works of Carl Theodor Dreyer or Andrei Tarkovsky, his direction is often too saccharine to be spiritually affecting. Much comedic mileage, for example, is gained by showing cute close-ups of elderly Danes discovering the inebriating power of liquor. Tipsy old ladies put down their water glasses and take another gulp of wine, and old men lick their lips after emptying a glass, all played for and receiving great guffaws from the audience. There is much in BABETTE'S FEAST that is beautiful—the sisters' devotion to the congregation, the officer's realization that he should have followed love instead of duty, the loneliness of the opera singer, the artistic contentment of Babette as she sips a glass of wine while preparing her feast—but there is also much that is simply predictably charming.

The performances are uniformly wonderful, and some of the actors will be familiar to art-house audiences: Stephane Audran, who frequently starred in ex-husband Claude Chabrol's films, and who appeared in another famous "dining" film, THE DISCREET CHARM OF THE BOURGEOISIE; Birgitte Federspiel of Dreyer's ORDET; Jean-Philippe Lafont of BIZET'S CARMEN; and Jarl Kulle and Bibi Andersson, who appeared in a number of Ingmar Bergman films. The story on which the film is based was penned by Karen Blixen (aka Isak Dinesen), the Danish writer portrayed by Meryl Streep in OUT OF AFRICA. It was written as a result of a bet between Blixen and a friend who wanted the author to crack the American market. "Write about food," the friend suggested. "The Americans have food on their minds constantly." The strategy worked for Blixen, as it did for Axel. (It also worked for Luis Bunuel, who won an Oscar for THE DISCREET CHARM OF THE BOURGEOISIE, and Louis Malle, whose MY DINNER WITH ANDRE was remarkably successful.) Turned down by *The Saturday Evening Post* and *Good Housekeeping*, "Babette's Feast" was finally published in 1950 by *The Ladies Home Journal*.

The success of BABETTE'S FEAST has led to a rather bourgeois movie tie-in scam wherein some of this country's more enterprising restaurants have been preparing "Babette's Feast" for their guests. One such evening in a Los Angeles restaurant will cost you $75 without wine, or $105 with. If you'd like to try your own "dinner with Babette," here's the menu: *Potage a la Tortue* (turtle soup), *Blinis Demidoff au Caviar Russe, Caille en Sarcophage avec Sauce Perigourdine* (quail stuffed with *foie gras* and baked in a pastry puff with truffles), *La Salade, Les Fromages Cantal, Fourme d'Ambert, Bleu D'Auvergne*, and *Baba au Rhum et Fruits Confits* (baba with rum and candied fruits). You can wash it all down (or kill the taste) with Amontillado Sherry, *Champagne Veuve Clicquot Brut, Louis Latour Clos Vougeot*, and *Tres Vielle Grande Champagne Cognac*. (In Danish; English subtitles.)

p, Just Betzer, Bo Christensen; d, Gabriel Axel; w, Gabriel Axel (based on the short story by Isak); ph, Henning Kristiansen (Eastmancolor); ed, Finn Henriksen; m, Per Norgard, Wolfgang Amadeus Mozart; art d, Sven Wichman; spec eff, Henning Bahs; cos, Annelise Hauberg, Pia Myrdal, Karl Lagerfeld; makeup, Lydia Pujol, Bente Moller, Elisabeth Bukkehave, Birthe Lyngsoe Sorensen, Sanna Dandanell, Grethe Hollenfer, Ase Tarp.

Drama **(PR:A MPAA:G)**

BAD DREAMS** (1988) 84m American Entertainment Partners II-No Frills/FOX c

Jennifer Rubin *(Cynthia)*, Bruce Abbott *(Dr. Alex Karmen)*, Richard Lynch *(Harris)*, Dean Cameron *(Ralph)*, Harris Yulin *(Dr. Berrisford)*, Susan Barnes *(Connie)*, John Scott Clough *(Victor)*, E.G. Daily *(Lana)*, Damita Jo Freeman *(Gilda)*, Louis Giambalvo *(Ed)*, Susan Ruttan *(Miriam)*, Sy Richardson *(Detective Wasserman)*, Missy Francis *(Young Cynthia)*, Sheila Scott Wilkinson *(Hettie)*, Ben Kronen *(Edgar)*, Charles Fleischer *(Ron the Pharmacist)*, Brian Katkin *(Physical Therapist)*, Stephen Anderson, Ellaraino, Alba Francesca, Maria Melendez, Chip Johnson, Diane Zolten Wiltse *(Reporters)*, Coleen Maloney *(Unity House Nurse)*, Annie Waterman *(Female Unity)*, Rex Lee Waddell, Jr., Tim Trella, Philip Granger *(Male Unities)*, Tony Cecere *(Fireman)*, James Purcell *(Paramedic)*, Don Sparks *(Policeman at Fire)*, Julianna McCarthy, Sarina Celeste Grant, Romy Rosemont *(Nurses)*, Thomas Oglesby *(Cynthia's Policeman)*, Charles Bouvier *(Ralph's Policeman)*.

This well-crafted and promising directorial debut from recent NYU film school graduate Andrew Fleming was the initial release of ambitious producer Gayle Ann Hurd's No Frills Film production company. Concentrating more on mood than on gore, BAD DREAMS begins in the early 1970s as the leader of a Jim Jonesish religious cult (Lynch) ceremoniously douses his followers with gasoline and then sets them and himself aflame. Twenty-seven men, women, and children die in the horrible fire, but there is one survivor, a 13-year-old girl who escapes the inferno but sinks into a coma. Fifteen years later, the girl, Rubin, awakens from her coma and is reluctantly placed in a group therapy session by the hospital's head psychiatrist, Yulin. The sessions, geared to the suicidal, are run by a handsome young psychiatrist, Abbott. Rubin doesn't get along with the rest of the group, for the narcissism of the 1980s is in direct contrast with her early 1970s' peace-and-love mentality. While she takes a spiritual approach, her fellow patients and the doctor look to science as the cure for mental illness. More troublesome are the terrible visions she has of Lynch returning to bring her back into the fold. He appears all over the hospital—sometimes looking normal, at other times horribly charred—beseeching Rubin to kill herself and make the cult's sacrifice complete. When Rubin refuses, Lynch begins to harass the other members of the therapy group and drives them to suicide one by one. Abbott is horrified by the deaths of his charges, and Yulin condemns his theories and methods, declaring him a failure. Although Rubin continues to believe it is the ghost of Lynch that is responsible for the deaths, Abbott turns up evidence that indicates it is Yulin who is inciting his patients to suicide. In a mad fit of professional jealousy, Yulin has tried to prove Abbott's theories wrong by giving the young doctor's patients mind-altering drugs and then driving them to suicide by suggestion. All of this is revealed in a rooftop climax that results in the crazed Yulin's death and Rubin's realization that she's not crazy after all.

Although much of this is very familiar territory, BAD DREAMS cowriter-director Fleming turns up some surprisingly effective moments. Producer Hurd (THE TERMINATOR; ALIENS) and Fleming use their low ($4.5 million) budget to their advantage, capitalizing on the claustrophobic nature of the production, which basically employs only two sets: the old house where the fire takes place and the hospital. While there are some concessions to the gorehounds, the bloody effects are few and fleeting. There are none of the lingering, clinical close-ups of effects-for-effects-sake that have threatened to destroy the entire genre over the last 10 years. Fleming sustains an air of dread and unease for most of the film, and one can never quite predict how or when the demonic-looking Lynch will next appear. The cult scenes are particularly memorable, benefitting from Fleming's clever use of the Chambers Brothers' classic rock tune "Time Has Come Today" as the segue between the 1973 and 1988 sections of the narrative. (Precious few films use pop music effectively; in most instances the songs are inserted by studios to promote rock stars who record for their subsidiaries and to sell soundtrack albums.)

Unfortunately, the moments of genuine spookiness are padded out with tiresome comic relief (mainly provided by Dean Cameron as a wisecracking manic-depressive), and played out within the standard "Ten Little Indians" plot line. In fact, the narrative gimmick—a therapy group bumped off by a nightmare bogeyman—bears a striking resemblance to last year's A NIGHTMARE ON ELM STREET PART III: DREAM WARRIORS (also featuring Jennifer Rubin as one of the Dream Warriors). Luckily, Fleming's imaginative and efficient direction propels the story at such a fast pace that viewers are given little opportunity to ponder the faults of the hackneyed screenplay. In interviews Hurd stated that she wanted to crank out a cheap and vigorous roller-coaster ride with little pretense of profundity that would herald a new era of competently made B pictures. In BAD DREAMS she and Fleming have succeeded admirably. Songs include: "Time Has Come Today" (Joseph Chambers, Willie Chambers, performed by The Chambers Brothers), "I Had Too Much to Dream (Last Night)" (Nancie Mantz, Annette Tucker, performed by Electric Prunes). *(Graphic violence, gore effects, profanity.)*

p, Gale Anne Hurd; d, Andrew Fleming; w, Andrew Fleming, Steven E. de Souza (based on a story by Andrew Fleming, Michael Dick, Yuri Zeltser, P.J. Pettiette); ph, Alexander Gruszynski (DeLuxe Color); ed, Jeff Freeman; m, Jay Ferguson; md, Bud Carr; prod d, Ivo Cristante; art d, A. Rosalind Crew; spec eff, Roger George, Lise Romanoff, Michele Burke, Richard Snell, Gill Mosko; stunts, Tony Cecere; makeup, Sheri Short.

Horror **Cas.** **(PR:O MPAA:R)**

BAGDAD CAFE*½** (1988, Ger.) 91m Pelemele-Project Filmproduktion-BR-HR/Island c

Marianne Sagebrecht *(Jasmin Munchgstettner)*, CCH Pounder *(Brenda)*, Jack Palance *(Rudi Cox)*, Christine Kaufmann *(Debbie)*, Monica Calhoun *(Phyllis)*, Darron Flagg *(Sal Junior)*, George Aquilar *(Cahuenga)*, G. Smokey Campbell *(Sal)*, Hans Stadlbauer *(Munchgstettner)*, Apesanahkwat *(Sheriff Arnie)*, Alan S. Craig *(Eric)*, Ronald Lee Jarvis *(Trucker Ron)*, Mark Daneri *(Trucker Mark)*, Ray Young *(Trucker Ray)*, Gary Lee Davis *(Trucker Gary)*, Baby Ashley.

Director Percy Adlon scored big on the art-house circuit with his 1985 West German film SUGARBABY, an eccentric love story starring the hefty Marianne Sagebrecht. For his follow-up, Adlon has again cast Sagebrecht and set his first English-language film in a run-down diner and motel in the middle of the Mojave Desert. Released in Europe at the end of 1987 as OUT OF ROSENHEIM, and winning the top prize at the Rio de Janeiro Film Festival and the Berlin Film Critics' Ernst Lubitsch Award as Best Comedy, the film has undergone a title change and been trimmed by 17 minutes for its American release.

As BAGDAD CAFE opens, Sagebrecht, dressed in a constricting Bavarian outfit and a decorative hat, is embroiled in an argument with her husband, Stadlbauer, as they drive through the sun-scorched desert. Stadlbauer tosses her out and drives away leaving the poor *hausfrau* in the middle of nowhere. By the time she gets *some*where—the dusty motel and a coffeeless diner that make up Bagdad, California—she is still essentially nowhere. The proprietor, a sharp-tongued black woman played by Pounder, has just thrown out her lazy husband (Campbell) and is in no mood to wrestle with Sagebrecht's name—Jasmin Munchgstettner. Sagebrecht takes a room and, in so doing, becomes just one more eccentric inhabitant of Bagdad. The other residents include Palance, a former Hollywood set painter; Flagg, Pounder's classical pianist son; Kaufmann, Pounder's sluttish but likable daughter; short-order cook Aquilar; tattoo artist Calhoun; boomerang-tossing backpacker Craig; and native American sheriff Aspesanahkwat. Initially, Pounder is suspicious of her German boarder, snooping through her things (a suitcase full of her husband's clothes, including his *lederhosen*) and calling the sheriff in to investigate. Meanwhile, Sagebrecht does all she can to prove that she means no harm. When she gives the motel's messy office a thorough cleaning, Pounder flies into a rage. Eventually, however, everyone grows to like and understand the strange Bavarian. It is Palance, though, who becomes most attracted to her. An animated, visionary painter, he leers at Sagebrecht and speaks to her in breathy rushes, as if his too-tight headband is forcing out his thoughts. As the film progresses, Palance paints a series of portraits of Sagebrecht in increasing stages of undress; in each she holds a sliced melon. Sagebrecht gains Kaufmann's trust when she exposes the teenager to her Bavarian background and lets her try on the *lederhosen*. When Flagg plays a Bach piece for Sagebrecht, they share a moment that transcends race, age, nationality, and culture. Sagebrecht takes up magic and begins practicing her trade in the diner, warming the heart of everyone, even Pounder. She agrees to let Sagebrecht help in the diner and, as word of the magic show spreads among truckers and travelers, the Bagdad Cafe becomes a hot spot. Soon, Pounder and Sagebrecht have turned the dusty little site into the Las Vegas of the Mojave. The plug is pulled, however, when the sheriff upholds the law and prevents Sagebrecht from working without a permit. With her tourist visa expired, Sagebrecht is forced to return to Rosenheim. Truckers enter the diner, inquire about the magic show, and promptly leave when they are told "the magic is gone." But there is still hope, and, after a long absence, Sagebrecht returns to Bagdad, bringing the magic back with her.

BAGDAD CAFE is a visually exhilarating and consciously modern film that is more concerned with projecting atmosphere and spirit than with telling a story. Presented as a fable about the magic that develops when two cultures meet, it is a film difficult, if not impossible, not to like. Sweet but not saccharine, this celebration of both friendship and filmmaking is an art film that is concerned with human *and* visual characteristics, not favoring one over the other and sacrificing neither to the usual demands of narrative form. Unlike so many films today, BAGDAD CAFE tells the viewer very little and instead makes us *feel*. In addition to using unorthodox camera angles and editing techniques, director Adlon and his cinematographer, Bernd Heinl, lend the film a warm golden hue (using a yellow filter throughout much of the film). While this effect may be initially disturbing or appear as a trite exercise in style, it soon has a psychological effect on the viewer. As a result, our impression of the film is one of warmth—the sun, the desert, and the characters' relations—and we walk away from it remembering not only the color of the image, but the "color" of the emotion and atmosphere.

A lasting impression is also made by the wonderfully warm Sagebrecht, who proves, as she did in SUGARBABY, that she is a very fine screen presence. CCH Pounder, whose character is too coarse at the film's start to elicit much sympathy, becomes increasingly likable as the friendship builds between the two women. The rest of the cast give commendable performances, but none even comes close to stealing Jack Palance's fire. In a full-blown, totally over-the-top, *tour-de-force* performance, Palance is unforgettable as the visionary romantic Rudy Cox—a throwback to Jeremy Prokosh, the warped, pontificating film director he played in Jean-Luc Godard's CONTEMPT. The series of short, wordless scenes between Palance at his easel and Sagebrecht as his model are pure magic, providing some of the film's best moments. Another plus is the billowy score by Bob Telson and the haunting theme song "Calling You" by gospel singer Jevetta Steele. (In English.) *(Brief nudity.)*

p, Percy Adlon, Eleonore Adlon; d, Percy Adlon; w, Percy Adlon, Eleonore Adlon, Christopher Doherty (based on a story by Percy Adlon); ph, Bernd Heinl (Eastman Color); ed, Norbert Herzner; m, Bob Telson, Johann Sebastian Bach; m/l, Bob Telson, Lee Breuer; art d, Bernt Amadeus Capra, Byrnadette di Santo; cos, Elizabeth Warner, Regine Batz; makeup, Lizbeth Williamson.

Comedy/Drama **Cas.** **(PR:C-O MPAA:PG)**

BANDITS** (1988, Fr.) 108m Films 13-TFI/AAA c

Jean Yanne *(Simon Verini)*, Marie-Sophie L. [Lelouch]*(Marie-Sophie)*, Patrick Bruel *(Mozart)*, Charles Gerard *(Tonton)*, Corinne Marchand *(Manouchka)*, Christine Barbelivien *(Mme. Verini)*, Helene Surgere, Herve Favre.

In 1976, a sophisticated outlaw (Jean Yanne) enjoys a moment of serenity on his family estate as he teaches his small daughter (Marie-Sophie L.) and a close family friend (Patrick Bruel) the refined art of fishing. When they return to Yanne's mansion, a television newscaster is bemoaning the loss of actor Jean Gabin, whose death, he feels, will bring about the decline of the gangster film. The subsequent announcement of a robbery at Cartier's famed jewelry store is seemingly ignored by the family in the wake of the great actor's demise. Bruel, the leader of the gang responsible for the theft at Cartier's, brings the stolen loot to Yanne so that he may exchange it for them at a premium price. Yanne's wife is then kidnaped and held for ransom by two of the gang members in an effort to get the jewels back. After the merchandise is returned, she is murdered by one of the fleeing bandits. Yanne's only visible reaction is to send his daughter to a Swiss boarding school to prevent her from learning of her mother's death. He is then framed for the theft, apprehended, and sentenced to ten years in prison. From his cell, he carries on a correspondence with his daughter, who is unaware of his whereabouts. She is regaled with an unending assortment of manufactured tales of her father's adventures around the world and her mother's mysterious activities in South America. In her own letters, she tells stories of her emotional and physical growth, much to the delight of her father. Eventually she learns her father is in a prison cell and her mother is dead. Moving forward to 1986, Marie-Sophie L., during her ten-year separation from her father, has created an image of her father based solely on his letters to her. After his release from prison occurs, he entertains her with his charmingly underhanded acts, and she concludes that they are extensions of his heroic character. She is invited to accompany her father to a festive dance where she happens upon Bruel, an outcast in the family since the death of her mother. While her father is busy uncovering the identities of the killers, she assesses Bruel and concludes that he did not murder her mother. Yanne suddenly packs up his daughter and her friend Bruel, and takes them to a small hotel where he guns down the pair of men who were responsible for the death of his wife. Marie-Sophie L. is appalled by her father's chilling act, and moves away with her new lover (Charles Gerard). Yanne, in the meantime, is transported back to prison when the body of his dead wife is excavated on his former estate. The moral dilemma quickly and effortlessly resolves itself for MarieSophie L., and she implores the shifty Bruel to help her father escape from jail. Through an utterly preposterous series of events, he does successfully obtain the older man's release. She reluctantly informs her present lover of the arrangement she has made—to marry Bruel if he successfully extricates her father from jail—and he accepts this as a fact of life. She broods about this new crisis at her father's hideout while she awaits the barge that will slip him out of the country. When she finds Bruel serenely fishing along the canal, she decides their relationship is one worth testing. The TV announcer commenting on the death of Jean Gabin asserts that, without Gabin, gangster films are sunk. Director Lelouch has wisely avoided an attempt at resurrecting the genre and uses Gabin's death as a springboard for his portrayal of the gangster as venerable and ultimately impotent rather than as iconographic and truly dynamic. But his real fascination lies with the presentation of the gangster's daughter (not surprising since Marie-Sophie L. is the real-life Mrs. Lelouch), her discovery and assessment of a questionable family background, and her attempts to forge a separate identity for herself. Moreover, the film continually engages the audience by promoting a fundamental but often forgotten principle of motion picture entertainment—to transform the presentation of a real state into the experience of an illusory one. In a noteworthy scene where Lelouch's sleight of hand is put to masterful use, Marie-Sophie L. watches from behind a closed automobile window as her father makes his entry from the enclosure of the prison walls into an expanse of open space. His movements toward the vehicle, viewed by the audience as a reflection in his daughter's section of the car window, enable father and daughter to magically occupy the same visual and emotional planes, but not the same material one. When he steps out of the reflection and into the vehicle to join her, he crosses the barrier that will transform the illusion of his resurgence into the recognition of his irrelevance. Unfortunately, the emphasis of Lelouch's story is placed on the plotting without much regard for narrative logic or character motivation. Characters are plunged into a series of critical situations, given a brief set of insipid lines of dialog to exchange, then bounced along to endure another series of excruciating events. By the conclusion of the film a lifetime of human crises have been exposed without the slightest insight into the experiences. *(Adult situations.)*

p, Claude Lelouch; d, Claude Lelouch; w, Claude Lelouch, Pierre Uytterhoeven; ph, Jean-Yves Le Mener (Fujicolor); ed, Hugues Darmois; m, Francis Lai.

Crime **(PR:C MPAA:NR)**

BAT 21* (1988) 105m Eagle/Tri-Star c

Gene Hackman *(Lt. Col. Iceal Hambleton)*, Danny Glover *(Capt. Bartholomew Clark)*, Jerry Reed *(Col. George Walker)*, David Marshall Grant *(Ross Carver)*, Clayton Rohner *(Sgt. Harley Rumbaugh)*, Erich Anderson *(Maj. Jake Scott)*, Joe Dorsey *(Col. Douglass)*, Rev. Michael Ng *(Vietnamese Man)*, Theodore Chan Woei-Shyong *(Boy on Bridge)*, Don Ruffin, Scott Howell, Michael Raden *(Helicopter Crew)*, Timothy Fitzgerald, Stuart Hagen *(EB-66 Officers)*, Jeff Baxter, Alan King *(Helicopter Gunners)*, Bonnie Yong, Willie Lai *(NVA/VC Officers)*, Martin Yong, Jim Aman, Freddie Chin, Dennis Chong, Liow Hui Chun, Fung Yun Khiong, Henry Lee, Michael Lee, Jeffrey Liew, Fredolin Leong, Benedict Lojingkau, Walter Lojingkau, Johnny Michael, Clarence Mojikon, Wilod Nuin, Harold Sinpang, Paul Yong, Conidon Wong *(NVA/VC Soldiers)*, Gary Douris, Muhandes HJ Mohamed *(Parachutists).*

A welcome change from the RAMBO-type Vietnam films, BAT 21 avoids excessive macho posturing and mindless shooting-gallery pyrotechnics, concentrating on the human dimension of the conflict by developing a few characters and putting a complicated face on the enemy. In this film based on a true story, Hackman plays Lt. Col. Iceal Hambleton, a 53-year-old military strategist who has spent his entire military career either in the air or on the ground behind a desk. When Intelligence reports that a major North Vietnamese offensive is mobilizing on a remote jungle road, Hackman decides to go up in a bomber and have a look before calling a massive air-strike on the entire area. As luck would have it, the bomber is hit by a missile over enemy territory and Hackman is the only man who manages to bail out. Alone in the middle of the jungle, with no infantry training and only a minimum of survival gear, Hackman must sit tight and wait for the military to pick him up. A spotter pilot, Glover, is dispatched to fly his small, fast Cessna low over the area and locate Hackman for a helicopter rescue. Codenamed "Birddog," Glover surveys the scene and reports any

nearby enemy activity to "Bat 21" (Hackman) over the radio so that he can act accordingly. Unfortunately, the entire area is too "hot" for Hackman to be picked up immediately, and he is forced to spend the night in the jungle. Frightened, tired, hungry, and alone, Hackman depends on Glover's pep talks to keep him going. As it turns out, the top brass does not want to delay the scheduled air strike, but Glover's commanding officer, Reed, pulls some strings and gets the bombing delayed by 24 hours. In the meantime, Hackman is getting a look at war from ground level for the first time in his life—and it horrifies him. Having spent his entire career giving orders and flying above the battles, Hackman has never really had to see the death and destruction his strategies bring. While raiding a peasant shack for some rice, Hackman is attacked by a farmer with a machete. Although Hackman tries to fend the man off, the farmer keeps coming and wounds him in the leg. Finally Hackman shoots the farmer dead, and then must face the man's family. Mumbling, "I'm sorry," Hackman hobbles off into the jungle and breaks down in tears—he has never killed before. Knowing that the enemy is listening to his and Glover's communications, Hackman, an avid golfer, devises a code based on golf terminology and creates a map based on nine holes from three different military golf courses to inform the Army of where he is heading. Glover, who knows nothing about golf, is given a golfer's handbook so that he can communicate with Hackman. With time running out, Hackman comes upon a clearing far away from the troop movements and big enough for helicopter landings. A rescue attempt is made, but Vietnamese soldiers in hiding open fire on the helicopters. Glover's friend, Grant, a gung-ho helicopter pilot, makes a foolhardy rescue effort against Reed's orders and he and his crew are killed. Because the air strike is so close and because so many men have already died trying to rescue Hackman, top brass order the rescue mission called off. If Hackman can make his way to a nearby river, a patrol boat will pick him up. Glover, who has become obsessed with rescuing Hackman, defies orders and steals Reed's own helicopter—which he barely knows how to fly—to make one last rescue attempt. Glover locates Hackman and manages to get him into the helicopter, but the whirlybird is shot down and the two soldiers have to race to the riverbank on foot. Hackman and Glover must avoid both the North Vietnamese and the American air strike on their way to freedom. Eventually they make it to the river and are picked up a patrol boat.

Competently directed by Peter Markle with an eye for military detail, BAT 21 manages to be compelling without lots of extended battle scenes. There are shootings, explosions, and bloodletting, but not on the scale of Sylvester Stallone/Chuck Norris Vietnam pictures. What also separates the violence in BAT 21 from the Stallone/Norris movies is that the human dimension remains. These are *people* getting killed, not faceless commie hordes. In having Hackman, a career military man, register disgust and horror at the violence he sees and commits, it reminds the viewer that war is not a playground for egotistical movie stars with overdeveloped muscles. While the film tends to become repetitive on this point and a little too melodramatic, it is preferable to the kind of jingoistic propaganda that presents armed conflicts as tests of true manhood and patriotism. Yes, there is plenty of male bonding here (after all, it's a variation on the black-white buddy genre), but it is balanced by the Hackman character's dawning awareness of the nature of the conflict and America's role in it. The Americans are shown knowingly killing civilians; the North Vietnamese are shown executing their own wounded and torturing prisoners of war. Hackman kills the patriarch of a civilian family, but is later saved by a young Vietnamese boy who shows him how to avoid a booby-trap he is about to walk into. Rather than making a pro-Vietnam or anti-Vietnam statement, BAT 21 refuses to take a stand on the war one way or the other and instead concentrates on the human beings involved and how the conflict affects their lives—an approach that will no doubt annoy those on both sides of the political fence.

With the larger geopolitical concerns removed, BAT 21 becomes a traditional male adventure story, and it works well on that level. Gene Hackman, as usual, turns in a solid performance as the career military man who has never really seen blood, and Danny Glover registers strongly as the dedicated pilot who develops a deep empathy for the officer's plight. One problem with the film—shared with this year's DIE HARD—is that the interaction between the two characters occurs almost entirely over the radio. While at times interesting, the device is extremely limiting when it comes to developing the relationship between the characters, and the impact of their meeting face to face isn't as powerful as it should be. Also notable in the cast are Jerry Reed (who was the executive producer), who does a fine job as the haggard commander, and young actor David Marshall Grant, as the hot-dog helicopter pilot—he nearly steals the film. Shot in the jungles of Malaysia because the political situation in the Philippines was deemed too unstable, the $10.5 million production received massive assistance from the Malaysian military and was on the vanguard of several productions that have discovered the region as a new location. For you aviation buffs (at least half the film takes place in the air), the Cessna 02 FAC flown by the Glover character was actually a Cessna Skymaster 337 converted to look like a military plane in Los Angeles, disassembled, shipped to Asia and then packed into a C130 military transports plane, and flown to the remote location where it was reassembled for the movie. While no ground-breaking treatise on the American involvement in Vietnam, BAT 21 is solid entertainment and worth a look. *(Violence, profanity.)*

p, David Fisher, Gary A. Neill, Michael Balson; d, Peter Markle; w, William C. Anderson, George Gordon (based on the novel by William C. Anderson); ph, Mark Irwin (DeLuxe color); ed, Stephen E. Rivkin; m, Christopher Young; prod d, Vincent Cresciman; art d, Art Riddle, Terry Weldon; set d, Karen Riddle; spec eff, Richard E. Johnson; cos, Audrey Bansmer; tech, Lt. Col. Iceal Hambleton; stunts, Everett Creach; makeup, Louis Lazzara.

War **Cas.** **(PR:O MPAA:R)**

BEACH BALLS † (1988) 77m New Classics/Concorde c

Phillip Paley *(Charlie Harrison)*, Heidi Helmer *(Wendy)*, Amanda Goodwin *(Toni)*, Steven Tash *(Scully)*, Tod Bryant *(Doug)*, Douglas R. Starr *(Keith)*, Leslie Danon *(Kathleen)*, Morgan Englund *(Dick)*, Charles Gilleran *(Babcock)*, Tami Smith

This throwback to the prehistoric Frankie-and-Annette beach party movies of the 1960s is spiced up with the usual contemporary T&A. Summertime beachfront antics include hapless hero Paley pursuing dreamgirl Helmer, while Paley's older sister, Danon, pines after Helmer's brother, lifeguard Bryant. Complete with a group of hoodlums patterned after the infamous Erich von Zipper and bad rock'n'roll provided by Douglas R. Starr, this independent effort was picked up by Roger Corman's Concorde Pictures for a fleeting theatrical run and then turned up on home video a few weeks later.

p, Matt Leipzig; d, Joe Ritter; w, David Rocklin; ph, Anthony Cobbs (Foto-Kem color); ed, Carol Oblath; m, Mark Governor; prod d, Stephen Greenberg.

Comedy **Cas.** **(PR:NR MPAA:R)**

BEACHES* (1988) 123m Touchstone-Silver Screen Partners IV-Bruckheimer South-All Girl

Bette Midler *(CC Bloom)*, Barbara Hershey *(Hillary Whitney Essex)*, John Heard *(John Pierce)*, Spalding Gray *(Dr. Richard Milstein)*, Lainie Kazan *(Leona Bloom)*, James Read *(Michael Essex)*, Grace Johnston *(Victoria Essex)*, Mayim Bialik *(CC, Age 11)*, Marcie Leeds *(Hillary, Age 11)*.

Near the end of BEACHES, as Barbara Hershey lies dying of viral cardiomyopathy, her best friend (Bette Midler) comes upon the scene and launches a diatribe accusing her of behaving as if she has already joined the dead. This exchange serves as a nice, albeit inadvertent, metaphor for the entire film, which is dead on arrival from its opening shot, wherein Ms. Midler performs a smarmy rendition of the Drifter's classic "Under the Boardwalk." At least Ms. Hershey has enough sense to lie down. This interminable melodrama purports to be a warm, humorous, and moving look at the relationship of two women over the course of 30 years. In reality, BEACHES is a pat, trite, maudlin, and terribly superficial effort of sub-made-for-TV quality, an insult to anyone who has ever befriended another human being. In BEACHES we are presented with the unlikely friendship of brassy, Jewish, Bronx-bred singer Midler, and icy, Waspy, San Francisco-based socialite Hershey from their meeting in Atlantic City until the day the latter is buried, having succumbed to the kind of disease that seems to only inflict characters in movies like this. An ego trip for star-executive producer Midler, the film tells its story mostly in flashback and entirely from Midler's point of view as the successful songstress drives a rented car from LAX to San Francisco to be with the dying Hershey. After meeting as 11-year-olds, the two correspond for years, chronicling the ups and downs of their very different existences (scenes of young Hershey dressed in a smart riding outfit astride a champion horse reading Midler's letters are intercut with young Midler sitting in a garish robe in her Bronx tenement reading Hershey's missives). By the time the 60s roll around, Midler is living in a seedy Greenwich Village flat trying to make a name for herself, while Hershey rebels against her bourgeois upbringing and comes to the Big Apple to be an ACLU lawyer. The old friends room together and everything is swell until ugly duckling Midler begins to resent that Off-Broadway theater producer Heard is more attracted to the pretty Hershey than to her. Hershey and Heard sleep together, much to Midler's dismay, but shortly thereafter Hershey returns to San Francisco to tend to her dying father. The old goat takes months to die and during Hershey's absence Midler and Heard fall in love and are married. Hershey, meanwhile, meets the son of another old-money family and marries him to please her father. Distance and lifestyle cause Midler and Hershey to grow apart. During this period Midler's career takes off, but instead of sticking to the kind of politically correct avant-garde theater to which Heard has dedicated his life, Midler winds up in bawdy Broadway productions designed to titillate the upper middle class. Hershey and her fuddy-duddy husband come to New York to see Midler and are horrified by the play she is in, though they cynically feign approval later. This, combined with the fact that Midler is now married to Heard, sends Hershey into a snippy jealous rage, and the two friends have a huge shouting match in a department store. Hershey returns to San Francisco and refuses to read Midler's letters, marking them "return to sender." In the coming years, Heard and Midler also grow apart and agree to an amicable divorce, while Hershey catches her husband cheating on her and dumps him. Hershey's situation is more complicated, however, as she finds herself pregnant and decides to have the baby alone. Meanwhile, Midler's career hits the skids and she winds up singing in a tacky San Francisco dance hall, where Hershey visits her and patches things up between them. Friends again, Midler vows to help Hershey through her pregnancy, but when given a chance to revive her career, she selfishly dashes back to New York. Hershey has a daughter and raises her on her own until she comes down with the aforementioned viral cardiomyopathy and is forced ask Midler—now a superstar—to put her career on hold and help care for her daughter. Midler agrees, the trio spends the summer at Hershey's beach house, and the singer represses her selfish instincts and does a wonderful job caring for both Hershey and her daughter. Eventually Hershey dies and leaves custody of her daughter to Midler, who is ready to accept the responsibility. BEACHES has to be one of the most superficial treatments of a 30-year relationship ever committed to film. Director Garry Marshall utterly fails to bring anything remotely resembling inspiration or spontaneity to screenwriter Mary Agnes Donoghue's terribly mundane disease-of-the-week script, leaving the viewer wondering why these two women would even speak to each other, let alone commit to an apparently deeply emotional relationship. The problems these characters face are wholly synthetic, dealt with in a flash, then forgotten until the next mini-crisis comes along. There is no sense of real joy, pain, or struggle here, merely a television version of them that is only tangentially related to actual human experience. Marshall's pacing is horrible, the scenes are abrupt, significant moments are rushed through, and the film is padded out with five unremarkable musical numbers performed by Midler. So desperate is Marshall to inject life into his film that he resorts to eccentric bit players and silly gags for occasional tedium-breaking laughs. The production values are shoddy as well. Notably, the period detail is nonexistent, failing so miserably to convey a sense of time passing that the film looks as if it takes place over the course of two weeks, not 30 years. In addition, all the New York City scenes were shot on a Hollywood backlot and look it, adding an incredibly artificial backdrop to the already artificial emotions. Perhaps worst of all are the performances of the two female stars. Hershey and Midler—both very different and, at times, very impressive actors—never connect on screen and their lack of rapport cripples the entire movie, making it a chore to watch. A few years ago Marshall showed promise as a competent director of commercial films with such efforts as THE FLAMINGO KID (1984) and NOTHING IN COMMON (1986), but judging from last year's Goldie Hawn vehicle OVERBOARD and now this, his talent seems to be on the wane, although, given the script, cast, and production problems of BEACHES, not even Douglas Sirk could have made it a viable project. *(Adult situations, profanity, sexual situations.)*

p, Bonnie Bruckheimer-Martell, Bette Midler, Margaret Jennings South; d, Garry Marshall; w, Mary Agnes Donoghue (based on the novel by Iris Rainer Dart); ph, Dante Spinotti (Metrocolor); ed, Richard Halsey; m, Georges Delerue; prod d, Albert Brenner; art d, Frank Richwood; set d, Harold L. Fuhrman; cos, Robert de Mora.

Drama **(PR:C MPAA:PG-13)**

BEAST, THE*½** (1988) 109m A&M/COL c

George Dzundza *(Daskal)*, Jason Patric *(Koverchenko)*, Steven Bauer *(Taj)*, Stephen Baldwin *(Golikov)*, Don Harvey *(Kaminski)*, Kabir Bedi *(Akbar)*, Erick Avari *(Samad)*, Shosh Marciano *(Moustafa)*, Haim Gerafi.

A perfect counterpoint to the absurdities of Sylvester Stallone's RAMBO III, THE BEAST is a fairly intelligent look at the Soviet-Afghan war from the point of view of its participants—as opposed to the jingoistic perspective of a musclebound American movie star who shows himself winning the war singlehandedly. Based on William Mastrosimone's stage play "Nanawatai" and stylishly directed by Kevin Reynolds, THE BEAST is set in 1981, during the second year of the Soviet occupation of Afghanistan. After viciously decimating a small Afghan village, a Soviet tank (nicknamed "The Beast" by the Afghans) takes a wrong turn and finds itself separated from its unit, trapped in a valley with no means of exit. Dzundza, the brutal and paranoid tank commander, blames his men for the mistake (although it was his own fault) and keeps them in line through fear and intimidation. He focuses his hatred on one man in particular, the tank navigator, an English-educated Afghan who supports the invasion. Determined to prove his worth to Dzundza, the navigator puts up with the abuse with stoic resignation. A bigger problem for Dzundza is his driver, Patric. A brave, intelligent, and compassionate soldier, Patric is the only crew member who dares to speak up to the commander, and there is great tension between them. This conflict is exacerbated as a tiny group of Afghan rebels, led by Bauer, decide to go after the lonely tank and avenge their village. Aided by an antitank device they managed to scrounge from the battlefield, the constantly bickering Afghans (two different factions have joined forces) launch a small-scale holy war against the Soviets. As the guerilla attacks become more successful, Dzundza becomes increasingly paranoid, until he actually executes the innocent navigator, whom he suspects of collaborating with the enemy. This outrages Patric, who had befriended the Afghan and learned about his culture. When Patric's attempt at a mutiny fails, Dzundza ties him to a rock and has a live grenade placed under his head. Left to die, Patric is found by a vengeance-seeking group of Afghan women who begin stoning him to death. Luckily, Bauer and his men come upon the scene, and when he speaks the Afghan word for asylum (an ancient social rule states that an Afghan must shelter even his sworn enemy if that man asks for asylum), Patric's life is spared. Eager to get revenge, he helps the rebels attack the tank. Eventually Dzundza realizes that the only way out of the valley is to go back the way they came, but the tank is running low on fuel and oil, and just as it gets to the pass, the Afghans launch a full-scale attack and cripple the tank. Although the Afghans want to kill the Soviets, Bauer accedes to Patric's wishes and lets them live (without his tank, Dzundza is nobody). Unbeknownst to Bauer, however, the angry Afghan women stone Dzundza to death. When a Soviet helicopter arrives on the scene, the Afghans scatter. Bauer urges Patric to join them, but, knowing he will never belong to their society, Patric signals for the chopper and willingly returns to his own people.

Dramatic and frequently moving, THE BEAST both delivers the genre goods and explores the nature of the Soviet-Afghan conflict and its combatants without resorting to polarizing rhetoric. Unlike the propagandistic RAMBO III, the movie is fairly even-handed in its portrayal of the two sides, and is more concerned with the human tragedy of war than its politics. Although the Soviets are the invaders, their perspective is presented right alongside that of the *mujahadeen*. RAMBO III ignored the Soviet perspective, and also glossed over the very real and potentially explosive internal disputes among various factions of the Afghan rebellion; THE BEAST makes it a point to show such dissention, hinting at the severe domestic problems Afghanistan will face after the Soviets leave. The extreme religious character of the rebellion is explored as well, another facet of the situation virtually ignored by Stallone. In fact, THE BEAST gives American audiences a better look at Afghanistan, its culture, and its people during its opening credits than can be found in the entire running time of RAMBO III.

Director Reynolds, shooting on location in Israel, makes good use of both the dry, expansive landscape and the cramped quarters of the tank. His imaginative camera placement, especially in the dark, claustrophobic tank, recalls the German submarine film DAS BOOT. Dale Dye, the military advisor on PLATOON, took the Soviet training manual and drilled the actors for 10 days, forcing them to behave according to rank in the oppressive desert heat. As in PLATOON, the end result is a team of actors who really work as a team. The performers, many of them veterans of the stage play, are excellent—especially Steven Bauer, who is very convincing as an Afghan rebel. One curious directorial choice that works against the film, however, is the decision to portray the Afghans as realistically as possible, but not the Soviets. Great pains were taken to make the Afghans appear authentic, including having the actors speak the native Pashtu dialect (their dialog is subtitled), but the Soviets characters all look and act like Americans, without even a hint of Russian accents. The effect is a bit disconcerting—its as if the *mujahadeen* are fighting a bunch of Southern Californians who took a wrong turn at Zuma Beach. That, however, may be the point: Reynolds may want the audience to see the parallels between the behavior of the Soviet Union in Afghanistan and American involvement in Vietnam. The two most powerful nations on earth may have more in common with each other than they do with the rest of the world, and there is much to learn from each other's example. Along similar lines, no one is purely good or purely evil in THE BEAST. Even Dzundza's unsympathetic character is shown to be a product of the horrors of WW II, rather than inherently evil. He represents the old guard leadership of the Soviet Union, while Patric embodies the changing face of the Soviet system and *glasnost*. THE BEAST ends on a strangely hopeful note, one that sees paranoid closed-mindedness ultimately destroyed because of its refusal to admit past mistakes and see the world as it is today—a much different place than it was in 1945. *(Violence, profanity.)*

p, John Fiedler; d, Kevin Reynolds; w, William Mastrosimone (based on his play *Nanawatai*); ph, Douglas Milsome (Rank color); ed, Peter Boyle; m, Mark Isham; prod d, Kuli Sander; art d, Richard James; cos, Ilene Starger; stunts, Paul Weston.

War **Cas.** **(PR:O MPAA:R)**

BEAT, THE*½ (1988) 98m Vestron c

John Savage *(Mr. Ellsworth, English Teacher)*, David Jacobson *(Rex Voorhaus Ormine)*, William McNamara *(Billy Kane)*, Kara Glover *(Kate Kane)*, Jeffrey Horowitz *(Dr. Waxman)*.

The only thing worse than a great stage play made into a lousy movie is a *bad* stage play made into a lousy movie. Originally conceived and presented as an Off-Broadway play by writer-director Mones, THE BEAT is a horribly pretentious and inept production that offers nothing but stock characters and sophomoric philosophy. Set in the ghettos of New York City, the film presents rival street gangs who must leave their hostilities outside when they enter the classroom of hip English teacher Savage. Young and dedicated, Savage runs his class in an informal manner in an attempt to get the kids to forget their posturing and open up. His efforts are relatively futile until a new kid, Jacobson, enters the classroom. Nerdy and sullen, Jacobson is at first looked upon as a "retard" by his fellow classmates. As the days go by, however, Jacobson reveals himself to be a strange bird who spouts torrents of bad beat-style poetry and seems to live in a world created in his imagination. McNamara and Glover, a brother and sister, warm to Jacobson and are willingly included in his imaginary world with the magic words "Lemme Lecke Solomon." He dubs Glover the Princess/Priestess and McNamara the Beggar, and the three of them wander his fictitious post-nuclear city ready to start a new civilization, all to the tune of their mantra, "The beat, the beat, dum, dum." Although at first their friends think they have all flipped out, Jacobson's imagination begins to fuel others and soon the rival gangs have patched up their differences and all are reciting beat poetry in class for the delighted Savage. Their enthusiasm leads them to take their act to the school talent show, calling themselves the Mutants of Sound. Just before the big day, the exasperated school psychiatrist decides that he's had enough of Jacobson's goofy antics and calls the men in the white coats. The kids help Jacobson escape and he hides in the park while the talent show goes up for grabs when a gang fight breaks out. To placate the mob, McNamara, Glover, and another friend perform their Mutants of Sound act without Jacobson. The combination of pretentious poetry and bongo drums wins the audience over and peace is restored. Hoping to share their triumph with Jacobson, they run to the park only to find that he has disappeared. They then rush to the shore of the river to find Jacobson gone, with only his jacket left as a memento. Muttering inane platitudes like "It's cool, he's free now" and the like, the kids turn and face the big, bad city skyline with renewed vigor and self-respect. THE BEAT plays like a botched collage of RIVER'S EDGE and an episode of "The Lone Ranger" (Who was that weird kid? Gosh, and we forgot to thank him!). Filmed in a deadeningly dull manner by writer/director Mones THE BEAT, which was shot in 24 days on a budget of $1 million, is about as uncinematic as they come. A standard TV visual style is employed here and the film is nothing but talk, talk, talk, with most of it in the form of bad poetry. Mones must be the only director in the history of film to have shot on location in NYC and then come away with an entire movie that looks as if it were filmed on a stage. The streets, the parks, the schoolyard, even the beach look stiff and artificial. Cinematographer DiCillo's lighting scheme is straight from Broadway and makes no allowances for subtlety or naturalism. Mones' dialog is even worse. Straining hard to capture the rhythms of the street, the lines are peppered with a ludicrous amount of slang and profanity. What is supposed to sound like realistic dialog merely becomes a playwright's self-conscious striving for it. Despite all the talk, there is precious little characterization in this film and none of the characters ring even remotely true. From the kids to the teachers, everyone is a stereotype and the young cast struggles mightily to wrest some meaning from it all (Glover and McNamara are fairly impressive). Although Mones has called his film "a fable for our times," it is nothing more than a dull, trite, banal, and deliriously selfimportant drama filmed in a flat, unimaginative manner. With the exception of some fresh young actors, there is nothing to recommend this movie. Shown at film festivals in 1987 and picked up by Vestron for distribution, THE BEAT received a brief theatrical release in 1988. *(Violence, substance abuse, excessive profanity.)*

p, Julia Phillips, Jon Klik, Nick Wechsler; d, Paul Mones; w, Paul Mones; ph, Tom DiCillo; ed, Elizabeth Kling; m, Carter Burwell; prod d, George Stoll.

Drama **(PR:C-O MPAA:NR)**

BEATRICE*** (1988, Fr./It.) 128m Clea-TF 1-Les Films de la Tour-AMLF-Scena-Little

Bernard-Pierre Donnadieu *(Francois de Cortemare)*, Julie Delpy *(Beatrice)*, Nils Tavernier *(Arnaud)*, Monique Chaumette *(Francois' Mother)*, Robert Dhery *(Raoul)*, Maxime Leroux *(Richard)*, Jean-Claude Adelin *(Bertrand Lemartin)*, Claude Duneton *(The Priest)*, Albane Guilhe *(Recluse)*, Michele Gleizer *(Helene)*, Jean-Luc Rivals *(Jehan)*.

BEATRICE, Bertrand Tavernier's follow-up to the internationally successful ROUND MIDNIGHT, is the director's most challenging film by far, and was unexpected by most critics and audiences. Here, as in his previous films LET JOY REIGN SUPREME; THE JUDGE AND THE ASSASSIN; and A SUNDAY IN THE COUNTRY, Tavernier's practice is to place a timeless story in a specific period, be it BEATRICE's medieval setting, 18th-century France, or (as in ROUND MIDNIGHT) 1959 Paris. Tavernier is also frequently concerned with relationships and conflicts between generations, chiefly between parent and child—the confused Descombes and his murderer son in THE CLOCKMAKER, the troubled Irene and her painter father in A SUNDAY IN THE COUNTRY, the devoted Francis and his weak idol, Dale Turner, in ROUND MIDNIGHT. In BEATRICE he combines both these tendencies with a severe intensity, setting his story in a heavily atmospheric age of feudal lords, castles, and witchcraft and concentrating on an incestuous, brutal relationship between a father and daughter. BEATRICE is an unexpected film only to those unfamiliar to the pre-ROUND MIDNIGHT Tavernier, whose work has encompassed a variety of subjects and tones. From the director of such idiosyncratic films as the brilliant COUP DE TORCHON (an adaptation of Jim Thompson's *Pop. 1280*) or the futuristic DEATH WATCH (in which death becomes a voyeuristic television program), nothing can be unexpected.

Set in the 14th century, BEATRICE opens as a 10-year-old boy sees his father off to war. The father gives the boy his dagger, telling him it is now his duty to protect his comely mother and the family's lands. The boy returns to his mother, finds her in bed with a lover, and coldly stabs the man. Finally, after spending months perched in a tower awaiting his father's return, the boy learns that his father has been killed in battle. Thirty years later that boy has grown into feudal lord Donnadieu. He and his son, Nils Tavernier (the director's real-life son), have been away from home for four years, having been taken prisoner by the English at the battle of Crecy during the One Hundred Years War. His estate is impoverished and his daughter, the angelic, blonde Delpy, has been forced to sell much of the family land and possessions to a neighboring lord, Adelin. Delpy wants nothing more than to see her father return, and fantasizes about his childhood while she wanders through the hills with her young confidante, Rivals, an idiot whose purity of soul attracts Delpy—herself a symbol of purity, virginity, and religious faith. When Donnadieu and Tavernier finally do come home, the peasants are thrilled at their lord's return, and a sumptuous feast awaits them, musicians poised to play. Although Tavernier is excited to see his sister and his grandmother, Chaumette, Donnadieu's reaction is frighteningly cold. He has barely dismounted his horse when he exclaims, "Already I want to flee," and he avoids any emotional contact with Delpy. When he sees Chaumette (whose honor so long ago was left in his charge), he grunts, "The very sight of you smites any remaining joy," for she represents a point of confusion for Donnadieu, as something he must protect and revere and, conversely, something he loathes. Donnadieu has returned from war a bitter, violent, sadistic beast who can no longer live the role of the feudal lord as one who is expected to respect life, land, and God. A diseased creature, he loathes everything around him, and focuses his hatred on the purest soul he knows, Delpy. He heaps indignities on all, but those he directs at his own flesh and blood are the most despicable. During a banquet in his honor, he admits with disgust that he wounded not one Englishman, instead trying to save his cowardly son, who had collapsed in his own excrement. Now, after verbally assaulting his effete son, he shoves the latter's face in a plate of food, barking, "When your father is done, you are done." Attracted by the challenge of corrupting his daughter's purity, and thereby spitting in the face of society and of God, Donnadieu rapes her and then announces his plan to wed her. The struggle between these two forces grows—Delpy resisting her father's evil, Donnadieu escalating his attacks—until, seeing no other way out, Delpy seeks help from a local witch, taking an effigy of her father. Donnadieu, however, defies death. To further break Delpy's spirit, Donnadieu offers to sell her to the neighboring Adelin (a handsome young man who showers Delpy with romantic words and vows to worship her above God), but then tells Adelin that Delpy has been deflowered and drives him away. When his brutality continues, Delpy finally takes her father's dagger and stabs him in the chest, having finally been turned by him against both God ("My Lord God, I hate you," she cries) and man—her father's corruption now inside her.

Difficult to watch, and more difficult to enjoy, BEATRICE alternates between audience-pleasing, beautiful pictures of the French countryside, with its rolling hills and misty mornings, and assaultive images of ugly violence. The film further destroys expectations by presenting an anti-Hollywood medieval world lacking pretty, buxom maidens, overflowing goblets, or picturesque troubadours. Tavernier's medieval era is more realistic than that, a time of raw emotion and intensity. Women are treated like dirt, referred to as "whores" or "wenches," beaten, raped, and humiliated. Children, if not crudely aborted by a kick in the stomach, are left to die (especially if female) or starve without milk. In such a world it is not surprising to meet a character like Donnadieu's lord. One expects bitterness and anger. What one does not expect is the character of Beatrice, a pure soul at odds with her surroundings, who refuses to submit to worldly brutality. But while BEATRICE is an accomplished film and Tavernier a director in command of his vision, the film never becomes as great and powerful as it attempts to be. It is a film about inner strength and purity of soul that, unfortunately, *tells* rather than *shows* us its meaning, and although one imagines one is supposed to feel something watching BEATRICE, in the end the film never quite draws out that emotion. Certain scenes have a greatness of both scale and affective power, but the film as a whole ebbs and flows between such scenes and a seemingly haphazard collection of medieval characters and vignettes. It is perhaps in the script (by Tavernier's ex-wife, Colo Tavernier O'Hagan) that the weakness lies, since the film's power derives more from Bruno de Keyzer's stunning photography and the rich performances by Bernard-Pierre Donnadieu and Julie Delpy, and in BEATRICE's 128 minutes it is difficult to recall even a single conversation between characters. In a film as emotionally complex in intent as this, however, clarification of a character's purposes and motivations would be better established through dialog than through a meaningful stare.

Donnadieu, best known to American audiences as the real Martin Guerre (opposite Gerard Depardieu) in THE RETURN OF MARTIN GUERRE, is frightening as the returning lord. Wrongly perceived by many as merely a hateful sadist, his character should be more sympathetically viewed as a broken, defeated man, whose earliest years were just like those of his own daughter, but who was more easily defeated than she. Delpy, who had brief roles in Jean-Luc Godard's DETECTIVE and KING LEAR and a more substantial part in Leos Carax's BAD BLOOD (MAUVAIS SANG), here receives her first starring role. At 18 years old, she proves herself a powerful actress with a pure and radiant face made for cinema, meant to be illuminated, photographed, and projected larger than life. As has been the case with all of Tavernier's films except ROUND MIDNIGHT, BEATRICE came and went in theaters (even a Best Foreign-Language Film Oscar nomination didn't do much for COUP DE TORCHON), receiving a less than courteous welcome from critics who felt the director should have continued producing pictures in the entertaining vein of ROUND MIDNIGHT. Jazz bassist Ron Carter, who had a cameo in ROUND MIDNIGHT as part of Dexter Gordon's New York combo, provides a medieval-cum-atonal jazz score that curiously tends to distance the viewer from the period Tavernier attempts to evoke. (In French; English subtitles.) *(Graphic violence, nudity, sexual situations, adult situations.)*

p, Adolphe Viezzi; d, Bertrand Tavernier; w, Colo Tavernier O'Hagan; ph, Bruno de Keyzer (Eastmancolor); ed, Armand Psenny; m, Ron Carter, Lili Boulanger; art d, Guy-Claude Francois; cos, Jacqueline Moreau; makeup, Paul Le Marinel.

Historical   Cas.   (PR:O MPAA:R)

BEETLEJUICE*½   (1988) 92m Geffen/WB c

Alec Baldwin (*Adam Maitland*), Geena Davis (*Barbara Maitland*), Michael Keaton (*Betelgeuse*), Catherine O'Hara (*Delia Deetz*), Glenn Shadix (*Otho*), Winona Ryder (*Lydia Deetz*), Jeffrey Jones (*Charles Deetz*), Sylvia Sidney (*Juno*), Patrice Martinez (*Receptionist*), Robert Goulet (*Maxie Dean*), Dick Cavett (*Bernard*), Annie McEnroe (*Jane Butterfield*), Simmy Bow (*Janitor*), Maurice Page (*Ernie*), Hugo Stanger (*Old Bill*), Rachel Mittelman (*Little Jane*), J. Jay Saunders, Mark Ettlinger (*Moving Men*), Cynthia Daly (*Three-fingered Typist*), Douglas Turner (*Char Man*), Carmen Filpi (*Messenger*), Susan Kellermann (*Grace*), Adelle Lutz (*Beryl*), Gary Jochimsen, Bob Pettersen, Duane Davis (*Dumb Football Players*), Marie Cheatham (*Sarah Dean*), Tony Cox (*Preacher*), Harold Goodman (*2nd Old Bill*), Jack Angel (*Voice of Preacher*).

The long-awaited second film from the promising 27-year-old director Tim Burton (PEE-WEE'S BIG ADVENTURE) is a wildly inventive and unique comedy that plays like a demented, surrealistic, cartoon remake of TOPPER (1937). The disjointed and often confusing narrative begins simply enough as we are introduced to a cute-but-childless yuppie couple (Baldwin and Davis) who have attained an idyllic existence in their *Better Homes and Gardens* New England farmhouse, decorated just so. One day, returning home from a short drive into town, Baldwin and Davis accidentally drive off a covered bridge and are killed. Much to their surprise, the couple makes it home, dripping wet, only to learn through a mysterious book sitting on their coffee table (titled *Handbook for the Recently Deceased*) that they have become ghosts. The pair adjusts easily to their spirit state, however, because at least they are still allowed to live in their perfect little home—unfortunately, whenever they try to leave the house they find themselves in another dimension, one which is populated by huge sandworms left over from DUNE (1984). Baldwin and Davis' ghostly existence is shattered when their house is sold and new tenants move in: a hopelessly pretentious family from Manhattan led by the distressingly hip would-be sculptor O'Hara. With her pompous SoHo interior designer, Shadix, in tow, O'Hara marches through the house with a can of purple spray-paint marking everything she wants changed, much to the chagrin of her hen-pecked husband, Jones, who merely wanted to escape to the country and likes the house the way it is. Indifferent to the entire affair is Jones' daughter by a previous wife, Ryder, a morose teenager with a funereal sense of fashion. As O'Hara and Shadix set about turning the country home into a icy palace for the terminally high-tech, the outraged Davis and Baldwin contact their spiritual caseworker, Sidney. Shocked at the log-jammed bureaucracy they find in limbo, the young couple is forced to sit in a waiting room populated by a variety of grotesque spirits who look exactly as they did when they died (a magician's assistant cut in half, the charred remains of a man who died smoking in bed, a big-game hunter with a normal body and a shrunken head, a skin diver with a shark still attached to his leg, etc.). To their horror, the couple learns from Sidney that they are stuck in the house for the next 125 years. Finding the situation intolerable, they decide to haunt the New Yorkers and scare them back to Manhattan. Regrettably, the basically decent pair's attempts at scaring the bejesus out of their unwelcome roommates prove merely quaint and ineffectual, inspiring Jones to market their new house as a sort of netherworld Disneyland. Although they cannot be seen by O'Hara and Jones unless they want to be, Ryder is able to see the ghostly couple at all times and soon becomes their friend. Frustrated by the lack of results, Davis and Baldwin contact a gruff, wild, and obnoxious ghost named Betlegeuse (a virtually unrecognizable Keaton)—though he'll answer to "Beetlejuice"—who sells his services as a "bio-exorcist." The miscreant spirit takes over the job of haunting the New Yorkers and does it in spades, employing a bag of wild tricks never before seen on the movie screen. Keaton, however, proves to have his own secret agenda (using his employers to reenter the "real" world) and it takes Davis, Baldwin, and Ryder to conquer the uncontrollable spook. In the end, after the banishment of Keaton, Davis and Baldwin strike a deal with O'Hara and Jones: the New Yorkers will live in the attic, and the ghost couple will live downstairs and raise the adoring Ryder themselves.

Any attempt to describe the action in BEETLEJUICE is an exercise in frustration, and, quite frankly, it's ultimately pointless. This is a film that must be seen to be understood, and even then understanding remains an iffy proposition. Director Burton gleefully charges through the expository twists of screenwriter-novelist Michael McDowell's script (coauthored by Warren Skaaren), taking little interest in clearly delineating just exactly what is happening and why. Instead, Burton serves up a strictly visual carnival of craziness, like a kid with his finger on the fast-forward button who says, "Let's get to the good stuff." This is not to maintain that Burton is derelict in his narrative duties—he is not—but by concentrating on the action and characters instead of the plot, he is able to free the structure of his film and let his imagination go wild without losing his audience. A former Disney animator, Burton brings an animator's sensibilities to his work and creates worlds in which surrealism and expressionism are the norms. Working closely with cinematographer Thomas Ackerman, the superb production designer Bo Welch, and a cadre of special effects wizards led by Robert Short and Chuck Gaspar, Burton presents a distinct and personal cinematic vision populated by eccentric characters, strange locations, and warped sets. And while in BEETLEJUICE Burton presents the truly macabre and grotesque, he presents it so lightheartedly that the entire film is silly and hilarious. One of his most inspired moments occurs with the dinner party held by the New Yorkers for their pretentious guests (Dick Cavett and Robert Goulet among them). In yet another attempt to spook the intruders, Davis and Baldwin possess O'Hara with the spirit of Harry Belafonte and she finds herself suddenly lip-syncing the "Banana Boat Song" while doing the limbo before her shocked guests. Then, in the scene's biggest surprise, the shrimps in the shrimp cocktails on the table become fingers of crustacean arms—all of which bolt out of their dishes to grab the guests by the face. Soon all are on their feet dancing around the table while O'Hara continues to belt out, "Work all night on a drink of rum! Daylight come and me wan' go home!" As stated previously, mere descriptions of this scene cannot properly convey the all-out wackiness of Burton's vision.

Although the entire cast is excellent, with Geena Davis, Winona Ryder, and Catherine O'Hara the standouts, BEETLEJUICE's insane energy is embodied by Michael Keaton as the foul-mouthed, rip-snorting maniac of the title. On-screen for less than half the film, Keaton makes up for lost time with a gruff, growling performance that grabs viewers by the throat and blows the moldy breath of the angry dead in their faces. His character would be perfectly at home in the equally wild and woolly netherregions of EVIL DEAD director Sam Raimi's demented imagination. Keaton is such a deranged presence in the film that he actually drives the previously light mood into darkly dangerous waters. Burton never allows his film to lose its sense of humor, however, and in the end good triumphs—and bad is forced to sit in the waiting room with a number in the millions while the "Now Serving" sign is still showing two digits. The only genuine heir to the inspired cinematic lunacy of Frank Tashlin, Tex Avery, and Bob Clampett, Tim Burton proves with BEETLEJUICE that PEE-WEE'S BIG ADVENTURE was no fluke. Songs include "Day-O" (Lord Burgess, William Attaway), "Man Smart, Woman Smarter" (Norman Span), "Sweetheart from Venezuela" (Fitzroy Alexander, Bob Gordon), "Jump in the Line (Shake, Shake Senora)" (Rafael Leon, Raymond Bell, performed by Harry Belafonte). *(Profanity, gore effects.)*

p, Richard Hashimoto, Larry Wilson, Michael Bender; d, Tim Burton; w, Michael McDowell, Warren Skaaren (based on a story by McDowell, Larry Wilson); ph, Thomas Ackerman (Technicolor); ed, Jane Kurson; m, Danny Elfman; m/l, Lord Burgess, William Attaway, Norman Span, Fitzroy Alexander, Bob Gordon, Rafael Leon, Raymond Bell; prod d, Bo Welch; art d, Tom Duffield; set d, John Warnke, Dick McKenzie; spec eff, Chuck Gaspar, Robert Short; cos, Aggie Guerard Rodgers; ch, Chrissy Bocchino; stunts, Fred Lerner; makeup, Ve Neill, Steve LaPorte.

Comedy/Horror   Cas.   (PR:C MPAA:PG)

BERSERKER zero   (1988) 85m American Video-Paradise Filmworks/Shapiro c

Joseph Alan Johnson, Valerie Sheldon, Greg Dawson, George Flower

BERSERKER is routine spam-in-a-cabin with a gimmick: this time it's actually the reincarnated spirit of a cannibalistic Viking warrior that's doing the mincing. Six interchangeable teenagers set out for a week of camping in a valley originally settled by Norwegians—or "descendants of the Vikings," as the smart kid portentously reads aloud from a book. He goes on to read of the legend of the "berserkers," fierce warriors who were so feared even by their own comrades that they were kept chained in the bows of their longboats until they hit the beaches and were unloosed upon the populace. They wore the skins of bears they killed in hand-to-hand combat (all this, incidentally, is true, and the word "berserker" comes from the Norse for 'bear shirt').

The brainy teen continues to read some mumbo-jumbo about the spirits of these warriors being doomed because they practiced cannibalism, never to find rest but to pass from generation to generation until the last of their descendants is killed. The other kids laugh it off. Arriving at the campground, they encounter a spooky caretaker (Flower) with a comic Norwegian accent, and, after getting on his bad side, they arrive at their campsite and proceed to carouse in such a way as to justify whatever reservations Flower may have had about letting them stay. That night the killings begin, with the first victim being the good girl, the one who wouldn't have sex or do drugs (in a switch from the usual morality found in these films, in which the nice girl is usually the one who survives). Some of the teens are attacked by a bear . . . or is it the berserker? No; a little later the berserker *does* come and kills one of them, then the bear and the berserker fight each other, with the bear coming out on top and the reincarnated Viking running off howling in pain (apparently he's not as tough as his ancestors). One kid goes for help, and comes back at dawn with the sheriff, who kills the beserker, who turns out to be—surprise!—the campground owner.

There's nothing here to attract even the most indiscriminate of horror fans, and the performances are all far below even the mediocre standard of the slice-and-dice genre. The kids are particularly idiotic, becoming hopelessly lost in the woods only steps away from their cabin and running around in circles over the same terrain without realizing they've been there just moments before. BESERKER is poorly plotted and lackadaisically directed, and it's little wonder that this one never graced a commercial screen and instead appeared straight on the video racks to lure the unwary into wasting $2, as well as valuable time that could be spent organizing sock drawers or studying atomic fission. *(Graphic violence, gore effects, nudity, sexual situations, substance abuse, profanity.)*

p, Jules Rivera; d, Jef Richard; w, Jef Richard; ph, Henning Shellerup; ed, Marcus Manton; m, Chuck Francour, Gary Griffin.

Horror	Cas.	(PR:O MPAA:R)

BETRAYED**½   (1988) 123m Irwin Winkler-UA/MGM-UA c

Debra Winger (*Katie Phillips/Cathy Weaver*), Tom Berenger (*Gary Simmons*), John Heard (*Michael Carnes*), Betsy Blair (*Gladys Simmons*), John Mahoney (*Shorty*), Ted Levine (*Wes*), Jeffrey DeMunn (*Flynn*), Albert Hall (*Al Sanders*), David Clennon (*Jack Carpenter*), Robert Swan (*Dean*), Richard Libertini (*Sam Kraus*), Maria Valdez (*Rachel Simmons*), Brian Bosak (*Joey Simmons*).

As anyone who has seen Z, or STATE OF SEIGE, or MISSING can tell you, Costa-Gavras is a political filmmaker concerned with liberal ideas and human rights. In 1969's Z, perhaps Costa-Gavras's greatest achievement, he exposed the political conspiracy behind the assassination of Greek leader Gregorios Lambrakis; his 1973 film, STATE OF SEIGE, drew on the assassination of a right-wing American anti-guerrilla expert by a group of Uruguayan revolutionaries; and his 1982 American film, MISSING, denounced the US government's role in supporting the Chilean dictatorship of Augusto Pinochet. Returning to the American film scene after a pair of unsuccessful pictures—HANNA K. and FAMILY BUSINESS (given only a festival release in the US)—Costa-Gavras has latched onto an explosive subject for BETRAYED, the frightening rise of white supremacist groups in America's heartland.

The film opens with the assassination of a controversial Chicago radio personality (an obvious rendering of murdered Denver on-air personality Alan Berg). Winger is an FBI agent sent to the Farm Belt to investigate the killing, specifically to check on Berenger, a widower who lives with his mother (Blair) and his two small children (Valdez and Bosak). Berenger, peeking out from under a cowboy hat, seems like a nice enough, albeit macho, guy who hangs out at the local saloon with his fellow farmers—the fatherly Mahoney and the crazed Levine. Winger adopts a fake name and pretends to be a traveling farmhand and combine operator. Soon she finds herself invited to a family dinner, making friends with Berenger's mother and kids. An early clue to Berenger's real nature is given when the little Valdez exclaims that her grandma makes some of the best food in the "whole white world." Winger, however, passes this off as standard rural prejudice. She reports back to FBI agent Heard that Berenger simply isn't their man and that she and the Feds are wasting their time. Heard has a gut instinct, however, and forces Winger, who also happens to be his former lover, to go back to Berenger. In the process, Berenger falls in love with Winger and, because he refuses to keep secrets from her, takes her hunting with him and the boys. The hunt, however, isn't for deer or pheasant, but for a defenseless young black man dragged into this nighttime trap by the local sheriff. The frightened man is sent into the wilderness, and the heavily armed good ol' boys chase him down for sport, corner him, and prepare to finish him off. Suspicious of Winger, Levine tells her to make her first kill. When she refuses, another of the farmers cold-bloodedly shoots the man in the back. Hysterical, Winger heads back to the safety of the FBI and reports her findings. It's not enough, however; they need proof of the radio personality's murder. They need a name. Winger goes back into the situation and, in order to gain Berenger's confidence, admits that she returned because she loves him. She is accepted by the others as a fellow white supremacist, but Levine continues to suspect her. She tags along on a family camping outing to a desolate forest preserve populated by KKK members, Nazis, survivalists, and other crazed "Americans" shouting White Power slogans. When she confesses to the soft-spoken Mahoney that she doesn't like killing—that she has a good heart—he understands her feelings and states, "The bank took my farm, and Vietnam took my son." He adds that he, too, has a "good heart," admitting to Winger, "I have to close my eyes every time I pull the trigger." He shares his friends' fear that "ZOG" (the Zionist Occupation Government) is destroying America because "the goddamn Jews are running our government with their nigger police." Later that night, Winger follows Berenger, Levine, and others as they run off to a secret rendezvous. Levine glimpses the spying Winger and tries to gun her down, though the others do not believe him. The situation heightens and Winger continues her charade, becoming more and more careless and growing more and more suspect. Moreover, she can no longer separate her feelings for Berenger from her job. When Berenger asks her to marry him, she agrees. Berenger also admits that his previous wife was murdered by Levine when she tried to run off and expose the group's activities. By now, these activities have grown to momentous proportions. Connected by computer with thousands of other white supremacists across the country, Berenger and his friends plan the assassination of a presidential candidate. It

is up to Winger to find out the name of the target and where and when the killing will take place. In the meantime, Berenger is given Winger's dossier, identifying her as an FBI agent. Berenger, the assigned hit man, takes Winger along to a presidential appearance by a right-wing senator supported by a friend of Berenger's—an intelligent and calculating white supremacist lunatic who fought with Berenger in Vietnam. As Berenger points his rifle at the senator, Winger reluctantly guns him down. However, an unseen second gunman kills the senator. Berenger's friend steps in and assumes the role as presidential candidate. Heard and his fellow FBI agents are thrilled that they've uncovered the network of white supremacists, but fail to accept Winger's claim that the assassination has now given the extreme Right a new hero and martyr.

Blessed with some fine acting—Tom Berenger and Debra Winger play nicely together and John Mahoney is excellent—BETRAYED is a standard Hollywood thriller with a lot to say about racism, the American heartland, and the US government. Unfortunately, the happenings become so absurd and insipid that what promises to be a powerful experience rapidly deteriorates into a series of thriller cliches. The subject matter alone is important enough to warrant seeing this film, but Costa-Gavras' unabashedly sensationalistic direction of Joe Eszterhas' familiar (see THE JAGGED EDGE) script threatens to overpower the essential ingredients. What begins as a believable series of events is soon sapped by so many digressions that the power of the subject matter loses its sting, and halfway through the film all concern shifts to the thriller aspects. Will the innocent Winger continue to love the murderous but charming Berenger? Will she be able to expose the darker side of his life and personality? (If Winger's character had seen THE JAGGED EDGE she might have learned from Glenn Close's mistake in loving Jeff Bridges.) Will Winger and the FBI be able to stop the extreme Right's plot to overthrow ZOG? By this point, the major thrust of Costa-Gavras' initially insightful and frightening premise—that the heartland of America is breeding racism and fascism in the name of patriotism—has long vanished from the screen. Instead of using the powerful medium of film as a forum for political discourse and awareness (as he has in the past), he has sacrificed its power in the name of entertainment.

The most interesting aspect of the film is the attempt by Costa-Gavras and Eszterhas to make Berenger and Mahoney likable villains. Much as THE GODFATHER paints mafiosos as honorable family men and compassionate human beings, BETRAYED shows us a man—Berenger—who loves his children and is deeply in love with Winger, but who sees his killing of blacks and Jews as a patriotic business necessary to the survival of American ideals. In his performance, Berenger never falters and, as an audience member, one is torn between hatred and sympathy. Less fortunate is Winger, whose profound performance far outweighs the intelligence of her character. One wonders how she ever was allowed in the FBI, though in comparison to John Heard's bone-headed character it is obvious that intelligence isn't a quality that is rewarded at the agency. One only wishes that Mahoney was on screen more. His performance is exceptional as a thoroughly likable man whose view of "good" is so warped that it is hard to hold him responsible for his actions. He is a man who believes that his mission is a moral one and that he is acting in the best interest of his countrymen. His character is the most powerful because, unfortunately, it is also the most real. If only Costa-Gavras and Eszterhas had realized that the reality of the situation was far more frightening than their fiction. . .*(Violence, adult situations, profanity, sexual situations.)*

p, Irwin Winkler; d, Constantin Costa-Gavras; w, Joe Eszterhas; ph, Patrick Blossier (Astro Color); ed, Joelle Van Effenterre; m, Bill Conti; prod d, Patrizia Von Brandenstein; art d, Stephen Geaghan; set d, Jim Erickson; cos, Joe I. Tompkins.

Political/Thriller	Cas.	(PR:O MPAA:R)

BIG***½   •   (1988) 104m FOX c

Tom Hanks (*Josh Baskin*), Elizabeth Perkins (*Susan Lawrence*), Robert Loggia ("*Mac*" *MacMillan*), John Heard (*Paul Davenport*), Jared Rushton (*Billy Kopeche*), David Moscow (*Young Josh*), Jon Lovitz (*Scotty Brennen*), Mercedes Ruehl (*Mrs. Baskin*), Josh Clark (*Mr. Baskin*), Kimberlee M. Davis (*Cynthia Benson*), Oliver Block (*Freddie Benson*), Erika Katz (*Cynthia's Friend*), Allan Wasserman (*Gym Teacher*), Mark Ballou (*Derek*), Gary Klar (*Ticket Taker*), Alec Von Sommer (*1st Brother*), Chris Dowden (*2nd Brother*), Rockets Redglare (*Motel Clerk*), Jaime Tirelli (*Spanish Voice*), Paul Herman (*Schizo*), Nancy Giles (*Administrative Woman*), Jordan Thaler (*Administrative Clerk*), Dana Kaminski (*Personnel Receptionist*), Harvey Miller (*Personnel Director*), Tracy Reiner (*Test Market Researcher*), James Eckhouse (*Supervisor*), Linda Gillen (*Woman in Red Dress*), Mildred R. Vandever (*Receptionist*), Bert Goldstein, Kevin Meaney, Peter McRobbie, Paul J.Q. Lee (*Executives*), Debra Jo Rupp (*Miss Patterson*), Keith W. Reddin (*Payroll Clerk*), Lela Ivey (*Bank Teller*), Dolores Messina (*Real Estate Agent*), Gordon Press (*Moving Man*), George J. Manos (*Limousine Driver*), Vinny Capone (*Photon Laser Gunfighter*), Susan Wilder (*Karen*), John Rothman (*Phil*), Judd Trichter (*Adam*), Pasquale Pugliese (*Tenor/Dough Man*), Vaughn Sandman (*Boy on Baseball Field*), Bruce Jarchow (*Photographer*), Samantha Larkin (*Girl Friend of Cynthia*), Edward Schick (*Piano Player*), Tom Coviello, Richard Devia, Teddy Holiavko, Augusto Mariani, Alfredo Monti, Sergio Mosetti, Armando Penso (*Singing Waiters*), F. Benjamin Stimler, Jonathan Isaac Landau (*Boys in Leaves*).

Without question the best of the recent spate of body-switching films, BIG features a brilliant and unforced performance by Tom Hanks as a New Jersey Little Leaguer who suddenly finds himself walking around in a 35-year-old body. Moscow (who plays the Hanks character before his transformation) is a shy, smallish 12-year-old with an unrequited crush on Davis, a taller classmate. At a carnival, Moscow drops a coin into Zoltar Speakes, a mechanized fortune-telling booth, and receives a card informing him his wish has been granted. The next morning it's Hanks, not Moscow, who jumps out of the top bunk with a tremendous thud—needing a shave, hilariously

©20TH CENTURY

overgrown for his Levi's, his voice changed. When Hanks approaches his mother, she refuses to believe he's her son, taking him for a kidnaper and chasing him from the house with a knife. He turns to his best friend, Rushton, for help, and his savvy-beyond-his-years buddy accompanies him to Manhattan, sets him up in fleabag hotel, and helps him land a job as a computer operator with a large toy company. Meanwhile, the "boys" have requested information from the city regarding carnival operations, hoping to catch up with Zoltar, but at least six weeks of red tape stands in their way. One Saturday, Hanks runs into the owner of the toy company, Loggia, in F.A.O. Schwartz, where Hanks has been having a wild time playing with the merchandise. Loggia recognizes his new employee and the two perform an extraordinary duet with their feet on an oversized piano keyboard whose keys not only sound but light up when someone steps on them. Bowled over by Hanks' discerning appreciation of playthings, Loggia promotes the transformed boy to vice president, a position that requires Hanks to play with and evaluate the company's toys. Heard, an ambitious junior executive, is incensed at Hanks' promotion and grows increasingly jealous as Hanks unwittingly charms not only Loggia but the other executive officers, including Perkins, Heard's girl friend. Soon after his 13th birthday, Hanks makes awkward but tender love with Perkins and she falls for him in a big way. Notwithstanding his professional success and his relationship with Perkins, Hanks aches to be back with his family. But he has become so caught up in the pressures and deadlines of his new life that he initially ignores Rushton when he presents Hanks with the location of Zoltar. Eventually, Hanks does go to the amusement park where the fantastic machine is located, followed by Perkins, and after telling her that she is the one thing he will miss after going back, he drops a coin in the slot and makes his wish. Perkins drives him home and as Hanks walks away he becomes Moscow again, dwarfed in Hanks' suit.

Released in June, BIG was the last of 1988's boy-in-a-man's-body films to be released, following the dismal 18 AGAIN and the entertaining VICE VERSA, both of which came in the wake of the unexceptional LIKE FATHER, LIKE SON (1987). Production began on BIG before any of these other films had hit the screen, but even after he became aware of the competition the film's producer, Academy Award-winning director James L. Brooks (TERMS OF ENDEARMENT; NETWORK), decided to continue working deliberately, rather than trying to beat these similarly themed productions into release. And despite its now-familiar premise, BIG is a winning, charming, and funny film, primarily because Tom Hanks—like Judge Reinhold in VICE VERSA—makes it work. Hanks and Reinhold are both extraordinarily convincing as adolescents who suddenly find themselves dealing with new, adult bodies, responsibilities, and romantic relationships while simultaneously trying to survive vicious corporate infighting. Both performances are first rate, but there is an important difference between them: the viewer frequently stops to marvel at the virtuosity of Reinhold's transformation, impressed by some small, childlike characteristic he has incorporated, whereas Hanks' amazing performance is seamless, taking the audience in immediately and allowing it to concentrate less on how well he conveys his situation than on the humor and pathos of the situation itself, and on the intricacies of his character. Hanks has always had an ingratiatingly boyish quality on-screen, but he has never used it to better effect than in BIG. He readied himself for his role by closely observing his own children and prepared for his scenes with Perkins by first watching her act them with Moscow, noting the young actor's reactions. Some of the credit for Hanks' success must go to the screenplay, which, unlike the other boys-will-be-men scenarios, concentrates on the changes that take place for *one* character, rather than becoming involved in body-and-mind switches *between* characters. As a result, Hanks' character is fully developed and the audience's sympathy completely engaged. BIG's screenplay was written by Gary Ross and Anne Spielberg, sister of Steven Spielberg—who, more than one critic speculated, may have been the inspiration for this story. Like Hanks' character, Steven Spielberg's disposition of childlike wonderment has made him millions. Coincidentally, at one time, Steven Spielberg was interested in directing the film, with Harrison Ford slated to appear in the Hanks role.

Hanks is surrounded by uniformly excellent performances. Elizabeth Perkins, who was so good as Demi Moore's roommate in ABOUT LAST NIGHT (1986), delivers a wonderfully restrained characterization here as the no-nonsense businesswoman whose habitual defensiveness is disarmed by Hanks' innocence. John Heard, playing her jilted lover, is handed a role calling for an essentially one-note performance, but he invests it with an inspired consternation and unremitting contempt for the rival he can ultimately cope with only by punching him in the nose. Robert Loggia is equally successful in his understated interpretation of the toy company's owner-director

whose love of toys and feeling for simplicity make him something of a man-child himself. Jared Rushton (OVERBOARD) contributes a fine portrayal of Hanks' best friend, balancing his cocky knowledge of the adult world with his adolescent pain at Hanks' seeming rejection of his friendship, and David Moscow is subtly shy and awkward as the pretransformation Little Leaguer, deftly paving the way for Hanks.

Much credit is due actress-director Penny Marshall—better known as Laverne from TV's "Laverne and Shirley" than as the director of the disappointing JUMPIN' JACK FLASH—for her handling of the actors and for her fine sense of comic pacing. Marshall serves up funny scene after funny scene, but also presents a not-overly-generous helping of emotion and sentiment, achieving a near-perfect balance. Hanks' touchingly tearful reaction to the gunshot he hears in his first night in the Manhattan hotel, for example, is countered by his nonchalance upon hearing more gunshots later, after he has begun to deal successfully with adult life in the Big City. Marshall has also created one of the most memorable song-and-dance numbers in recent years with the delightful scene in which Hanks and Loggia stomp out "Chopsticks" on the high-tech, oversized keyboard. That Marshall, in 1988, is able to incorporate such a magical scene so unobtrusively into her film is no small feat. She and cinematographer Barry Sonnenfeld (BLOOD SIMPLE; RAISING ARIZONA; THROW MAMA FROM THE TRAIN) often use the camera inventively, and seldom does the picture have the look of a TV sitcom transferred to the big screen. Sonnenfeld has also used his lighting effectively, giving Hanks' first return to his home a brown, memory-imbued tint, and when he returns for good the autumnal suburban streets are suffused in golden light, indicating that the story is coming to a happy end and that this has been a fairy tale all along, and a delightful one at that. (*Sexual situations, profanity.*)

p, James L. Brooks, Robert Greenhut; d, Penny Marshall; w, Gary Ross, Anne Spielberg; ph, Barry Sonnenfeld (DuArt Color); ed, Barry Malkin; m, Howard Shore; m/l, Alan Bergman, Marilyn Bergman, Marvin Hamlisch, Billy Idol, Steve Stevens, Bobby Gosh, Kimberly A. Bradstreet, Joel Frankel, Hoagy Carmichael, Frank Loesser, Mario Cipollina, Johnny Colla, Bill Gibson, Chris Hayes, Sean Hopper, Huey Lewis, Patrice Rushen, Freddie Washington, Glenn Miller, David Pomeranz; prod d, Santo Loquasto; art d, Thomas Warren, Speed Hopkins; set d, George DeTitta, Susan Bode; cos, Judianna Makovsky; ch, Patricia Birch; makeup, Mickey Scott.

Comedy	Cas.	(PR:A-C MPAA:PG)

BIG BLUE, THE*½   (1988, Fr.) 120m Gaumont-Weintraub/COL c

Rosanna Arquette (*Joanna Cross*), Jean-Marc Barr (*Jacques Mayol*), Jean Reno (*Enzo Molinari*), Paul Shenar (*Dr. Laurence*), Sergio Castellitto (*Novelli*), Jean Bouise (*Uncle Louis*), Griffin Dunne (*Duffy*), Andreas Voutsinas (*Priest*), Valentina Vargas (*Bonita*), Kimberley Beck (*Sally*), Patrick Fontana (*Alfredo*), Alessandra Vazzoler (*Mamma*), Geoffroy Carey (*Supervisor*), Bruce Guerre-Berthelot (*Young Jacques*), Gregory Forstner (*Young Enzo*), Claude Besson (*Jacques' Father*), Marika Gevaudan (*Angelica*), Jan Rouiller (*Noireuter*), Peter Semler (*Frank*), Jacques Levy (*Doctor*), Eric Do (*Japanese Diver*), Andre Germe (*Filipino Diver*), Ronald Teuhi (*Tahitian Diver*), Rosario Campese (*Waiter*), Franco Diogene (*Receptionist*), Tredessa Dalton (*Carol*), Constantin Alexandrov (*Dolphin Trainer*), Pierre-Alain De Garrigues (*Superintendent*), Claude Robin (*Taxi Driver*), Paul Herman (*Taxi Driver in US*), Nicolas Maltos (*Diving Coordinator on Platform*), Marc Planceon (*Paramedic*).

Frenchman Luc Besson has been heralded as a *wunderkind* since the then 24-year-old director's first film, LE DERNIER COMBAT, was released in 1983. He followed it with the vastly overrated SUBWAY, a Cesar award-winning exercise in style over content. Now, three years later, Besson's much-awaited new feature unspooled as the opening night gala premiere of the 1988 Cannes Film Festival. Costarring Rosanna Arquette, featuring a half-dozen exotic locales and much underwater photography, and bearing a hefty (for a French production) $12 million price tag, THE BIG BLUE is essentially a big-budget children's adventure about a boy and his dolphins (as was underscored by its re-rating from a PG-13 to a PG in order to assure that more children would see the film). It opens with a black-and-white segment, set in Greece, in which the two leads—played as adults by Barr and Reno—are seen as youngsters. Both are excellent free divers who can hold their breath underwater for phenomenal lengths of time. When the young Barr's father (played by Claude Besson), a coral fisherman, dies in an underwater accident, Barr explodes in a fit of despair. The story then picks up in 1988, with both boys grown into adults. Reno, looking something like Bluto of the Popeye cartoons, is the World Champion Free Diver, while Barr assists in scientific experiments involving studies of his lung capacity and his ability to slow his heart rate. Although Reno holds the world title, he knows that there is one man who can beat him—Barr. He has Barr located and invites him to compete in the World Championship at Taormina in Sicily. Enter Arquette, a mousy, bungling insurance investigator who meets Barr while checking an accident claim in a snowy mountain range in Peru. Arquette is immediately attracted to the quiet Barr and follows him to Sicily. While Barr and Reno renew their old friendship, Arquette falls in love with Barr—which seems a bit odd, as Barr rarely speaks and is more concerned with the welfare of a school of marineland dolphins than with anyone human. The World Championship gets under way, and Barr and Reno begin their battle. Competition is Reno's lifeblood; for Barr, however, it simply provides another chance for him to dive and experience the inspiration of the sea. While Reno becomes increasingly preoccupied with familial pressures, Barr, who has no family and no earthly attachments other than Arquette, is one in unity with the "Big Blue," effortlessly capturing a world depth record of 400 feet. But the competition is called unsafe (the water pressure could stop bloodflow and thus prevent oxygen from reaching the brain) by a scientific team under the charge of Shenar, and Barr appeals to Reno to call off his attempt to break Barr's record. Reno is compelled to continue, but cannot finish his dive. While Barr could not help his father many years before, he now can help his friend, who asks Barr before he dies to take him back to the depths so they may serve as his grave. Barr too is drawn to the sea and, after a remarkable dream sequence in which he and his bed are submerged in the sea's churning waters, leaves that bed in the middle of the night. Arquette follows and pledges her love, begging him to stay on land. Barr tells her that he loves her and then proceeds to the depths. After an encounter with a dolphin, he disappears into the oceanic darkness, having finally realized his lifelong dream.

As in Besson's previous picture, SUBWAY, THE BIG BLUE tells the story of a man who feels at home in a separate environment that exists below the "real" world. In SUBWAY it was Christopher Lambert who preferred to hide out in the labyrinthine tunnels of the Paris Metro, eventually falling in love with a woman (Isabelle Adjani) from above the surface. In THE BIG BLUE it is Jean-Marc Barr who retreats to another world, and Rosanna Arquette who tries to bring him back to the world she views as real. Like SUBWAY, however, THE BIG BLUE is desperately in need of depth—of character rather than of the sea. The film has no more insight into the human condition than a fairy tale; furthermore, it has none of the magic of a fairy tale. Barr is woefully lacking as the lead of a two-hour-plus film, and his chemistry with Arquette is nonexistent. Neither character has much to say to the other and their passionate romance is taken for granted or, worse yet, implied rather than shown. Of the leads, only Jean Reno emerges unscathed, in a comic book caricature of a macho Italian who shrivels in fear when confronted by his domineering mother. Perhaps the lack of an intelligent or insightful script could be excused had the much-publicized underwater footage been as remarkable as promised. Instead, the underwater camerawork (some actually shot by Besson) is neither suspenseful nor picturesque— surely no more impressive, and probably less so, than your average Jacques Cousteau special. Even the on-land photography, with its drastic low-angle shots and its even more drastic wide-angle lenses, which make the sea-sky horizon bend comically, wears thin after a while. Not much really happens in THE BIG BLUE; Besson tries to create suspense where there isn't any, and fails to put suspense where it should be. On all fronts—suspense, drama, acting, adventure—the film comes up with nothing more than cliches and yawns. The entire movie could be mapped out by any moderately knowledgeable audience member after just the first few minutes.

THE BIG BLUE's technical advisor was one Jacques Mayol, a World Champion free diver whose name became the character name for Barr. Beginning as a diver in the 1950s, Mayol became embroiled in an ongoing competition with the Sicilian Enzo Maiorca (a thinly veiled version of whom is Reno's Enzo Molinari). After the dives reached a depth of 249 feet, authorities put an end to the competitive aspect of the sport. By 1983, Mayol had reached a depth of 345 feet.

The film was rereleased in France at the beginning of 1989 with a longer, three-hour running time in order to satisfy "Blue Mania" in that country, where everything about THE BIG BLUE is a hit. (In fairness to the taste of the French, it should be noted that the film had a silly new ending and a wretched Bill Conti score tacked on for US release.) Although THE BIG BLUE does contain a party scene in which all three leads get quite soused, and a love scene between Barr and Arquette that is not graphic, it seems a perfect entertainment for youngsters. As indicated by the dedication of the film to his daughter, this seems to have been Besson's goal. (*Substance abuse, one sexual situation.*)

p, Patrice Ledoux; d, Luc Besson; w, Luc Besson, Robert Garland, Marilyn Goldin, Jacques Mayol, Marc Perrier (based on a story by Luc Besson); ph, Carlo Varini (CinemaScope); ed, Olivier Mauffroy; m, Eric Serra, Bill Conti; prod d, Dan Weil; set d, Patrick Barthelemy; spec eff, Alain Guille; cos, Magali Guidasci, Mimi Lempika, Martine Rapin, Patricia Saalburg, Malika Khelfa, Brigitte Nierhaus, Blandine Boyer; makeup, David Forrest.

Adventure   Cas.   (PR:A MPAA:PG)

BIG BUSINESS** (1988) 94m Touchstone-Silver Screen Partners III/BV c

Bette Midler (*Sadie Shelton/Sadie Ratliff*), Lily Tomlin (*Rose Shelton/Rose Ratliff*), Fred Ward (*Roone Dimmick*), Edward Herrmann (*Graham Sherbourne*), Michele Placido (*Fabio Alberici*), Daniel Gerroll (*Chuck*), Barry Primus (*Michael*), Michael Gross (*Dr. Jay Marshall*), Deborah Rush (*Binky Shelton*), Nicolas Coster (*Hunt Shelton*), Patricia Gaul (*Iona Ratliff*), J.C. Quinn (*Garth Ratliff*), Norma Macmillan (*Nanny Lewis*), Joe Grifasi (*Desk Clerk*), John Vickery (*Hotel Manager*), John Hancock (*Older Harlan*), Mary Gross (*Judy*), Seth Green (*Jason*), Leo Burmester (*Bum*), Lucy Webb (*Wenona*), Roy Brocksmith (*Dr. Parker*), Lewis Arquette (*Mr. Stokes*), Eddie Junior (*Young Harlan*), Ritch Brinkley (*Mayor Bill Finker*), Tony Mockus, Carmen Argenziano (*Board Members*), Maureen McVerry (*Hilda/Rose Photo Double*), Freddie Parnes (*Bellboy*), Dan Chambers (*Male Staffer*), Lois De Banzie (*Edwardian Room Hostess*), Al Mancini (*Waiter*), Nicholas Rutherford (*'Lil Levon*), Hunter Von Leer (*Petey*), Andrew Epper (*Zeke*), Andi Chapman (*Sadie's Secretary*), Chick Hearn (*Sports Announcer*), Troy Damien (*Hank Ratliff*), Ryan Francis (*Merle Ratliff*), Melanie Doctors (*Sadie Photo Double*), Louis Rukeyser (*Taxi Victim*), Kymberly Goldman (*Triplet No. 1*), Michelle Goldman (*Triplet No. 2*), Traci Goldman (*Triplet No. 3*), Crystal Field (*Bag Lady*), Everett Quinton (*Window Dresser*), Sandy Davis (*Saleslady in Dress Shop*), Natalie Dolishny, Nancy Lazarus (*Moramax Employees*), Shirley Mitchell, Charles J. Middleton, Irving Hellman (*Stockholders*), Judy Armstrong (*YMCA Desk Clerk*), Tom La Grua (*Cab Driver*), Matthew James Carlson (*Eufus*), Brianne Sommers (*Woman with Whippet*), Alice Gruenberg (*Attractive Woman with Yorkies*), Jane Butenoff (*Professional Hooker in Times Square*), Louise Yaffe (*Director's Mother in Lobby*), Bobby Bruce, Tommy Holden, Al Novis, Raymond Klein (*Swamp Mud Boys*), The Trinidad Serenaders Steel Band, North Hollywood High School Marching Band.

© BUENA VISTA

Two of America's funniest women, Bette Midler and Lily Tomlin, are paired in this mistaken identity farce directed by Jim Abrahams, the man in the middle of the Zucker-Abrahams-Zucker triumvirate that created AIRPLANE! and RUTHLESS PEOPLE. While traveling in West Virginia, a wealthy New York woman goes into labor and is rushed to the nearest hospital. Because the hospital caters only to employees of the Hollowmade Furniture factory, her millionaire husband buys the company on the spot and she is admitted, giving birth to twin daughters; however, in another room, a local woman also becomes the mother of twin girls, and a near-sighted nurse mixes up the babies. Years later, Midler and Tomlin are the two pairs of mismatched twins. Midler plays both Sadie Shelton, the tough-as-nails CEO of the Moramax Corporation, and Sadie Ratliff, a Hollowmade employee who dreams of a life of luxury far removed from her home in Jupiter Hollow. Tomlin portrays the wispy Rose Shelton, who worries more about saving whales than about Moramax's profit outlook, and Rose Ratliff, a headstrong Hollowmade foreman and union organizer who stomps off to New York City with her sister to fight Moramax's proposed sale of the furniture factory. Both sets of twins check into the Plaza Hotel, and confusion abounds as they are repeatedly mistaken for one another while never quite meeting. Placido, a suave Italian, attempts to buy Hollowmade (intending to convert the land to strip mining) and to put the make on Midler, but he receives mixed signals from Manhattan-bred Midler and the Jupiter Hollow version of the Divine Miss M., thinking they are the same person. Ward, down-home Tomlin's miniature golf-playing beau, has similar problems when he ventures to the Big Apple—while the big-city Tomlin's boy friend, Gross, and Manhattan Midler's ex-husband, Primus, are also ignorant of the mix-up. In fact, everyone is baffled (though occasionally charmed) by the erratic behavior of the twins, who finally meet in a ladies room, in a re-creation of the famous mirror scene from DUCK SOUP during which Midler comes face to face with herself ("My God, it's me with a bad haircut"). Both Tomlins team up with the Midler from the Mountain State to save Hollowmade en route a finale that delivers four happy couples.

This comedy of errors has more than a few laughs, but while it will satisfy Midler fans, it is not likely to win her many new converts; nor does it use Tomlin to her best advantage. The broad humor of BIG BUSINESS is well-suited to Midler's sassy, steamroller style, and she sashays through both of her roles with plenty of verve, employing the patented mincing and mugging that helped transform RUTHLESS PEOPLE and OUTRAGEOUS FORTUNE, her two previous Touchstone efforts, into Top 10 box-office hits. But while she creates two distinctive, and frequently funny, characters—linked by their instinctive love of luxury—she never brings much depth to either. Tomlin, on the other hand, appears to have tried too hard to bring depth to her two Roses, and the subtlety of her approach is lost in this broad farce. Unlike Midler, who spent her off-camera time reading or attending to her 18-month-old daughter, Tomlin consulted acting coach Susan Batson and worked meticulously on character details; however, her nuanced attempts to demonstrate that a Rose is a Rose too often leave even the viewer wondering which Rose is which. Both Midler and Tomlin began their film careers with Oscar-nominated dramatic roles (Midler for THE ROSE, Tomlin for NASHVILLE), but with the success of her recent work for Touchstone, Midler seems to have found her niche as a film comedienne, while Tomlin has yet to find a cinematic vehicle that offers her the opportunity to present the kind of insightful comedy that she demonstrates in her one-woman stage show, "The Search for Signs of Intelligent Life in the Universe."

Director Abrahams, working on his own for the first time, has some problems with pacing and with sustaining an essentially one-joke premise that never arrives at its big payoff and often misses the mark with smaller targets, but he does elicit some fine supporting performances that provide many of the best laughs in BIG BUSINESS. Fred Ward (THE ADVENTURES OF REMO WILLIAMS) gives his sincere downhome boy a nice edge, Edward Herrmann (OVERBOARD) and Daniel Gerroll are very funny as Sadie Shelton's corporate henchmen, Michele Placido is appropriately Eurosmooth, and Lucy Webb ("Not Necessarily the News"), who plays a Ratliff sister, brings charming backwoods naivete to her brief role. Perhaps the film's most important "performer," however, is the computerized camera technique that allowed two Midlers and two Tomlins to appear on the screen without the static quality of previous split-screen "twining." The VistaFlex computerized camera system, which was also used to shoot WHO FRAMED ROGER RABBIT?, made it possible to duplicate exactly camera movements for each character, whereas in the past the camera had to remain in one place to allow for as seamless as possible a vertical fusion of the split-screen image. Tomlin and Midler, acting against the void of a blue screen, still had to coordinate their actions with exact timing. Midler explained to the *San Fran-*

cisco Chronicle-Examiner that to perform her mirror scene she matched her movements to eight counts, then wore an earphone through which an assistant director monitoring a metronome counted.

Exteriors and some interior scenes were actually shot at the New York Plaza, but since most of the film takes place there it would have been impossible to interrupt business at the famous hotel for the amount of time required, so it was lavishly re-created at the Disney Studios, contributing to BIG BUSINESS' $18.5 million budget. Songs include "Higher Love" (Steve Winwood, Will Jennings, performed by Winwood), "On Broadway" (Jerry Leiber, Mike Stoller, Barry Mann, Cynthia Weil, performed by George Benson), "Little Ole Lady" (Richard Wilbur, Marc Shaiman), "Music Box Dancer" (Frank Mills, Shaiman, performed by The Trinidad Serenaders Steel Band), "Sing, Sing, Sing" (Louis Prima, performed by Benny Goodman), "Reilly Theme" (E. Shostakovich, Harry Rabinowitz), "Pennies from Heaven" (J. Burke, A. Johnson), "I'm in the Mood for Love" (Jimmy McHugh, Dorothy Fields). *(Adult situations, sexual situations.)*

p, Steve Tisch, Michael Peyser; d, Jim Abrahams; w, Dori Pierson, Marc Rubel; ph, Dean Cundey (Metrocolor); ed, Harry Keramidas; m, Lee Holdridge; m/l, Steve Winwood, Will Jennings, Jerry Leiber, Mike Stoller, Barry Mann, Cynthia Weil, Richard Wilbur, Marc Shaiman, Frank Mills, Louis Prima, E. Shostakovich, Harry Rabinowitz, J. Burke, A. Johnson, Jimmy McHugh, Dorothy Fields; prod d, William Sandell; art d, William Barclay; set d, James E. Tocci, Martha Johnston; cos, Michael Kaplan; stunts, Frank Ferrara, William Erickson; makeup, Michael Lorenz, Eugenia Weston.

Comedy	Cas.	(PR:C MPAA:PG)

BIG TOP PEE-WEE½   (1988) 86m PAR c

Pee-wee Herman *(Himself)*, Kris Kristofferson *(Mace Montana)*, Penelope Ann Miller *(Winnie)*, Valeria Golino *(Gina Piccolapupula)*, Susan Tyrrell *(Midge Montana)*, Albert Henderson *(Mr. Ryan)*, Jack Murdock *(Otis)*, Terrence Mann *(Snowball the Clown)*, Mihaly "Michu" Meszaros *(Andy)*, Franco Columbu *(Otto, the Strongman)*, Kevin Peter Hall *(Big John)*, Matthia Hues *(Oscar, the Lion Tamer)*, Lynne Stewart *(Bearded Lady)*, Joey Arias *(Shim)*, Benicio Del Toro *(Duke)*, Vance Colvig *(Clownie)*, John Sherrod *(Dell)*, Helen Siff *(Ruth, Siamese Twin)*, Carol Infield Siff *(Dot, Siamese Twin)*, Albert Henderson, Jack Murdock, David Byrd, Frances Bay, Mary Jackson, Leo Gordon, Anne Seymour, Kenneth Tobey, Jay Robinson, Eve Smith *(Townsfolk)*, Wayne White *(Voice of Vance the Pig)*.

© PARAMOUNT

This eagerly anticipated sequel to the incredibly popular PEE-WEE'S BIG ADVENTURE is a big disappointment. Lacking the delirious, magical, cartoonlike zaniness of the first film, BIG TOP PEE-WEE presents the audience with a slightly more adult Pee-wee, one who likes, indeed, *lusts after*, pretty girls (yuk!). The movie opens with a hilarious dream sequence wherein Pee-wee, decked out in a silver-spangled suit, croons a Frank Sinatra-style tune to an audience of screaming female admirers. Pee-wee's fantasy is interrupted, however, by the crowing of a rooster, and we see that he is the proud owner of a farm. With the help of his talking pet pig Vance, Pee-wee goes about the farm preparing breakfast for his animals—all of which sleep in their own beds. After the animals make their beds, they gather around picnic tables and are served pancakes made from fresh ingredients and chocolate milk from Pee-wee's brown cow. After breakfast, Pee-wee and Vance enter their private greenhouse to continue the top-secret botanical experiments they hope will change the face of agriculture. At noon, Pee-wee and Vance venture into the nearby town for lunch with beautiful young schoolmarm Miller. Despite the fact that she feeds him awful egg salad sandwiches every day, Pee-wee and Miller are engaged. Pee-wee can barely contain himself when he is around Miller, and is given to sudden amorous assaults on his betrothed. After lunch, a terrible storm blows into town and Pee-wee and Vance hightail back to the farm and gather the animals in the basement to wait out the tempest. After the storm, Pee-wee is amazed to find that a traveling circus run by Kristofferson has blown onto his property. Thrilled with the wild animals, clowns, midgets, strongmen, and jugglers in his midst, Pee-wee allows the circus to stay on his farm while its wagons are repaired. Better yet, Pee-wee is thunderstruck by beautiful young Italian trapeze artist Golino, and all thoughts of his fiancee fade as he falls

in love at first sight. Accompanied by a circus elephant, Pee-wee and Golino go on an idyllic walk and share a passionate first kiss beside a babbling brook while the strains of South Seas music Hollywood-style swell in the background (with a wailing vocal courtesy of Pee-wee). Unfortunately, the lovers are caught in the act by the horrified Miller and the engagement is off. Angry that Pee-wee didn't tell her he was engaged, Golino gives him a slap, and her red handprint remains plastered on his cheek for the rest of the night. While trying to figure a way out of this messy love triangle, Pee-wee attempts to find a place for himself in the circus. Although Kristofferson readily acknowledges that Pee-wee has "sawdust in his veins," the gentleman farmer has little talent for acrobatics, horseback riding, or even being shot from a cannon. Eventually Pee-wee's romantic difficulties are straightened out, with Miller falling for Golino's acrobat brothers and joining their act. Pee-wee makes a passionate apology to Golino and the couple is finally reconciled when she invites him into her trailer. This is immediately followed by stock footage of a train going into a tunnel, fireworks, molten lava, waves crashing into the shore, and writhing female mud wrestlers (Mom and Dad will know what all this means, kids won't get it). Inspired by Pee-wee's homestead, Kristofferson presents a new circus act based on scenes of the American farm. Having finally found his niche, Pee-wee becomes a tightrope walker and trains his animals—including a cow and a horse—to walk the high-wire with him. In the end, all is right with the world and Pee-wee and Golino clinch at the fade.

BIG TOP PEE-WEE is active proof of the *auteur* theory. Missing from most of this sequel is the inventive, manic goofiness that made the first film so much fun. The only movie released this year that comes close to the wacky vision of PEE-WEE'S BIG ADVENTURE is BEETLEJUICE, which just happens to have been directed by Tim Burton, the very same young man who directed Pee-wee's first film (surprise!). BIG TOP PEE-WEE, on the other hand, was directed by Randal Kleiser (GREASE; BLUE LAGOON; SUMMER LOVERS), a strong contender for the "Worst Hack Director Currently Working in Hollywood." His indifferent camera placement, and his ignorance of pacing, scene structure, and directing actors turns what should have been a dreamy, light-hearted comedic romp into a clunky, cheap-looking letdown. Only Paul Reubens (Pee-wee's alter ego) seems to understand what should be happening in front of the cameras and he tries hard to pull it off. Unfortunately, the rest of the actors don't seem to know how to handle him. Kris Kristofferson looks distinctly uncomfortable sharing the frame with Pee-wee; Susan Tyrrell (as Kristofferson's two-inch-tall wife) is grating as she overplays her part, and so is Penelope Ann Miller, who overdoes the bubbly but dim "small town girl" routine. Luckily for Valeria Golino, a newcomer to American audiences, all she has to do is act sexy and foreign.

Despite Kleiser's incompetence, much of the blame must be shared by Reubens. He coproduced and cowrote this mess, which began shooting in January 1988 and was released on July 22, 1988—a mere six-and-one-half months later, incredibly hasty for a major release. Why a director as colorless as Randal Kleiser was put at the helm is a mystery. Although Reubens claims that he had been planning the film for two-and-a-half years, one cannot help but wonder if this speedy production wasn't merely a cynical exercise designed to be hustled along so that it wouldn't interfere with Reubens' duties on "Pee-wee's Playhouse" while still capitalizing on the lucrative summer box office. To be sure, there are some delightful moments here—like when Pee-wee is cornered by a hungry circus lion that sees him as a huge steak—but they are too few and far between to recapture the magic of the first film. Cinema buffs, take note of the striking, albeit superficial, similarities between BIG TOP PEE-WEE and Wim Wenders' WINGS OF DESIRE. Most notably, the main character in both films falls in love with a foreign trapeze artist and loses his virginity to her. No doubt some student of film theory will write a doctoral dissertation comparing the two films. *(Mild sexual situations.)*

p, Paul Reubens, Debra Hill; d, Randal Kleiser; w, Paul Reubens, George McGrath; ph, Steven Poster; ed, Jeff Gourson; m, Danny Elfman; prod d, Stephen Marsh; art d, Beala B. Neel; set d, Stephen Homsy, William J. Newmon II, Richard W. Pitman, Carl Aldana; spec eff, Richard Edlund; cos, Robert Turturice.

Comedy	Cas.	(PR:A MPAA:PG)

BILOXI BLUES★★★½   (1988) 107m Rastar/UNIV c

Matthew Broderick *(Eugene Morris Jerome)*, Christopher Walken *(Sgt. Merwin J. Toomey)*, Matt Mulhern *(Joseph Wykowski)*, Corey Parker *(Arnold Epstein)*, Markus Flanagan *(Roy Selridge)*, Casey Siemaszko *(Donald Carney)*, Michael Dolan *(James J. Hennessey)*, Penelope Ann Miller *(Daisy Hannigan)*, Park Overall *(Rowena)*, Alan Pottinger *(Peek)*, Mark Evan Jacobs *(Pinelli)*, Dave Kienzle *(Corporal)*, Matthew Kimbrough *(Spitting Cook)*, Kirby Mitchell, Allen Turner, Tom Kagy *(Diggers)*, Jeff Bailey *(Mess-hall Corporal)*, Bill Russell *(Rifle Instructor)*, Natalie Canerday *(Girl at Dance)*, A. Collin Roddey *(Private Roddey)*, Christopher Ginnaven *(Corporal Ginnaven)*, Morris Mead *(Corporal Mead)*, David Whitman *(Tower Officer)*, Norman Rose *(Newsreel Announcer)*, Michael Haley *(Corporal Haley)*, Ben Hynum *(Private Lindstrom)*, Andy Wigington *(Corporal Wigington)*, Scott Sudbury *(Private Sudbury)*, Christopher Phelps *(Private Phelps)*.

Easily the best film based on a Neil Simon play since THE SUNSHINE BOYS (1975), BILOXI BLUES works better on the screen than it has any right to, thanks to the marvelously skillful direction of Mike Nichols and excellent performances from both Matthew Broderick and Christopher Walken. An adaptation of the second installment in Simon's autobiographical stage trilogy (preceded and followed, respectively, by "Brighton Beach Memoirs" and "Broadway Bound"), BILOXI BLUES follows Simon's alter ego, Eugene Morris Jerome (Broderick), as he is sent to Biloxi, Mississippi, for Army basic training during the waning days of WW II. An aspiring writer, New York born and bred, Broderick is bemused by the types he's thrown among (vulgar roughnecks Mulhern and Flanagan, hanger-on Siemaszko, nice farmboy Dolan), and takes notes that reveal his true feelings about them. "It was hard to believe they had mothers and fathers who worried about them," he comments. The only other Jew in his unit, Parker, a frail intellectual unafraid to voice his contempt for the Army and his fellow draftees, remains an enigma to Broderick. Adding to the shock of Broderick's new surroundings is the oppressive Biloxi heat, of which he moans, "I didn't know it would be so hot. Boy it's hot. This is *Africa hot*." Worse yet is the recruits' strange drill sergeant, Walken, who constantly reminds his charges that he has a steel plate in his head. Though he's surprisingly subdued for a DI, Walken's fundamental sadism works in quiet and mysterious ways, sowing dissension among his troops as he pits them against one another. The weeks of bad food, long marches, and humiliating conditions drag on, but are somewhat relieved by the weekend pass, during which Broderick loses his virginity to a prostitute, Overall, and falls in love with a Catholic girl, Miller. One night Broderick's buddies find his notebook and read his remarks about them. Most are insulted and hurt by his observations, but his speculations as to whether or not Parker is homosexual are especially damaging. Embarrassed and ashamed, Broderick discovers just how powerful the written word can be and learns to respect the responsibility that comes with it. This lesson is further enforced when, after two recruits are caught in the midst of a homosexual act, one of them escapes and is seen sneaking into Broderick's barracks by the MPs—who, however, can't see the suspect's face. The Army is now determined to ferret out and imprison the homosexual among the barracks-mates, and, because of what Broderick wrote in his journal, suspicion immediately centers on Parker. After several days of tension during which Walken acts particularly threatening toward Parker, the homosexual who was caught confesses that Dolan was the other man. As the well-liked Dolan is led off by MPs to certain imprisonment, all the recruits are given a sense of what persecution feels like. Soon afterwards, Walken gets drunk and finally flips out completely, cornering Broderick and holding a .45 to Broderick's head. In an incredibly tense scene, Broderick is able to talk Walken into giving up the gun, and, before turning himself in to military authorities, Walken insists that his platoon assign him a just punishment. With honors given to Parker, it is decided that Walken must do push-ups in the mud—just as he once made others do. By the time basic training ends, the war is over and Broderick returns home on the train that brought him to Biloxi.

With its breathtaking opening aerial shot, which follows the troop train across a massive steel trestle and eventually comes to rest on Broderick staring out the window, BILOXI BLUES immediately heralds itself as a very cinematic adaptation of Neil Simon's popular stage play. Mike Nichols, who directed the play on Broadway, understands the difference between stage and screen and makes the transition skillfully. He scales down the humor and avoids presenting the jokes in the hackneyed set-up-to-big-punchline formula so typical of Simon's style. The dialog flows naturally and the jokes come in a casual, almost offhand manner. This naturalistic approach helps make Simon's basically cliched military service comedy fresh and new, since the characters behave less like traditional "types" and more like real people. Matthew Broderick, who established the role on Broadway, re-creates that success on-screen by toning down his performance to suit the new medium. An actor in complete control of his craft, Broderick brings appealing nuance to a role he has essayed many, many times. The real surprise, however, is Christopher Walken as the drill sergeant. What could have been yet another entry in the long series of screaming, vein-popping DIs—of which FULL METAL JACKET's Lee Ermey was the ultimate incarnation—is instead turned into a quietly chilling, hauntingly ambiguous character in Walken's adroitly underplayed performance; once again, a new twist is added to old material.

Just as interesting is Nichols' and cinematographer Bill Butler's visualization of the play. The film was shot in a wide-screen format that really opens up the stage on which the action takes place. Not many directors have a good eye for wide-screen composition, and therefore waste its creative potential by merely settling for the obvious "panoramic" possibilities. Since most of the action in BILOXI BLUES takes place indoors or in a flat, dry, arid environment, there isn't much in the way of gorgeous vistas to exploit; instead, Nichols and Butler employ a complex visual style that advances the narrative's emotional movement through precise choreography of both actors and camera within the wider frame. This method takes scenes that are obviously of stage-bound origin and makes them very cinematic. For example, the scene in which Broderick and Miller dance at the USO is filmed with a dizzying circular camera movement that isolates the characters and conveys the delirious sensation of love at first sight. Such creative compositions occur throughout the film, and are not simply presented as a slick, self-conscious complement to Simon's set pieces; indeed, the entire film is intelligently directed and tightly constructed, without a single dull scene or wasted moment, as Nichols saves Simon's source material from becoming mired in sticky, wistful nostalgia by combining standard gags with hard realities. (In one scene, the director celebrates the service genre and simultaneously contrasts his film with its predecessors, as the GIs are shown watching a slapstick routine from Abbott and Costello's BUCK PRIVATES (1941).) While on the surface BILOXI BLUES may seem like just another Neil Simon film in which the playwright presents just another military service comedy, Nichols' direction of both camera and actors transforms what might have been routine material into entertaining art. Songs include "How High the Moon" (Nancy Hamilton, William Lewis, performed by Pat Suzuki), "Bourbon Street Parade" (Paul Barbarin, performed by Barbarin), "Fellow on a Furlough" (Bobby Worth, performed by Mark Warnow and His Orchestra), "Blue Moon" (Richard Rodgers, Lorenz Hart, performed by Jo Stafford and Her V-Disc Playboys), "Marie" (Irving Berlin, performed by Tommy Dorsey and His Orchestra), "Solitude" (Duke Ellington, Irving Mills, Eddie DeLange, performed by The Dorsey Brothers Orchestra), "Brass Boogie" (Phil Moore, performed by Bob Crosby and His Orchestra), "Goodbye Dear, I'll Be Back in a Year" (Mack Kay, performed by Dick Robertson and His Orchestra). *(Adult situations, sexual situations, profanity.)*

p, Ray Stark; d, Mike Nichols; w, Neil Simon (based on his play); ph, Bill Butler; ed, Sam O'Steen; m, Georges Delerue; m/l, Nancy Hamilton, William Lewis, Paul Barbarin, Bobby Worth, Richard Rodgers, Lorenz Hart, Irving Berlin, Duke Ellington, Irving Mills, Eddie DeLange, Phil Moore, Mack Kay; prod d, Paul Sylbert; set d, John Alan Hicks; cos, Ann Roth; makeup, Kevin R. Trahan.

Comedy/Drama **Cas.** **(PR:C-O MPAA:PG-13)**

BIRD**** (1988) 161m Malpaso/WB c

Forest Whitaker *(Charlie "Yardbird" Parker)*, Diane Venora *(Chan Richardson Parker)*, Michael Zelniker *(Red Rodney)*, Samuel E. Wright *(Dizzy Gillespie)*, Keith David *(Buster Franklin)*, Michael McGuire *(Brewster)*, James Handy *(Esteves)*, Damon Whitaker *(Young Bird)*, Morgan Nagler *(Kim)*, Arlen Dean Snyder *(Dr. Heath)*, Sam Robards *(Moscowitz)*, Penelope Windust *(Bellevue Nurse)*, Glenn T. Wright *(Alcoholic Patient)*, George Orrison *(Patient with Checkers)*, Bill Cobbs *(Dr. Caulfield)*, Hamilton Camp *(Mayor of 52nd Street)*, Chris Bosley, George T. Bruce *(Doormen)*, Joey Green *(Gene)*, John Witherspoon *(Sid)*, Tony Todd *(Frog)*, Jo de Winter *(Mildred Berg)*, Richard Zavaglia *(Ralph the Narc)*, Anna Levine *(Audrey)*, Al Pugliese *(Owner of Three Deuces)*, Hubert Kelly *(John Wilson)*, Billy Mitchell *(Billy Prince)*, Karl Vincent *(Stratton)*, Lou Cutell *(Bride's Father)*, Roger Etienne *(Parisian MC)*, Jason Bernard *(Benny Tate)*, Gretchen Oehler *(Southern Nurse)*, Richard McKenzie *(Southern Doctor)*, Tony Cox *(Pee Wee Marquette)*, Diane Salinger *(Baroness Nica)*, Johnny Adams *(Bartender)*, Natalia Silverwood *(Red's Girlfriend)*, Duane Matthews *(Engineer)*, Slim Jim Phantom *(Grainger)*, Matthew Faison *(Judge)*, Peter Crook *(Bird's Lawyer)*, Alec Paul Rubinstein *(Recording Producer)*, Patricia Herd *(Nun)*, Steve Zettler *(Owner of Oasis Club)*, Ann Weldon *(Violet Welles)*, Charley Lang *(DJ at the Paramount)*, Tim Russ *(Harris)*, Richard Jeni *(Chummy Morello)*, Don Starr *(Doctor at Nica's)*, Richard Mawe *(Medical Examiner)*.

It may seem incredible that superstar Clint Eastwood could have directed one of the finest films of 1988, but only to those who have not been paying attention to his impressive directorial output over the last 18 years. A magnificent tribute to the life and genius of jazz great Charlie Parker, BIRD (the title is Parker's nickname) opens with a powerful montage whose first image is a re-creation of a famous snapshot taken in Kansas City, Kansas, of Parker as a child astride a pony. The little boy blows on a toy instrument as another child leads the pony around the yard. We next see Parker as a teenager (played by Forest Whitaker's younger brother Damon), walking on the front porch and practicing the alto saxophone. The scene then dissolves, and the stunning sounds of Parker (Whitaker) playing "Lester Leaps In" fill the air as the camera prowls from behind the bandstand of a 52nd Street nightclub and moves around to face Parker as an adult—the Bird in glorious flight. After this exhilarating opening, we are brought back to earth with the crash of a cymbal thrown through the air. 1954: Parker comes home after a gig and almost immediately engages in an emotional fight with his common-law wife, Chan (Venora). Still in great pain over the death of their daughter, Pree, Parker goes into the bathroom and attempts suicide by drinking iodine. Although he survives, the heroin-addicted musician is taken to Bellevue hospital, where doctors recommend electroshock therapy. Chan refuses to give her permission for the (at the time) awful treatment and recollects the first time she saw Parker perform, at the Three Deuces on 52nd Street. Also in the audience was saxophone player Buster Franklin (David), who recognizes Parker as the youngster back in Kansas City in 1936 who fumbled during a cutting contest and was humiliated when the disgusted drummer tossed a cymbal at his feet. Although Franklin won that contest, he now realizes that Parker is a musical genius with whom he can never hope to compete. Walking home from the Three Deuces, Franklin admits defeat and tosses his saxophone into the river. Parker, meanwhile, attempts to seduce Chan, but instead is wrangled into a discussion of his reputation as a drug addict, boozer, and womanizer. When Parker declares that being with Chan somehow makes him feel peaceful, she takes offense at the notion and insists that she was born to "drive men crazy." The interracial couple have an off-and-on relationship over the years, and shortly after their meeting, Parker joins Dizzy Gillespie (Wright) on a trip to California to introduce their bebop style to the West Coast. The trip is a disaster. The music gets a cool reception, drugs are hard to find, and Parker subsequently drinks too much and ends up having to be hospitalized. Upon his return to New York, he learns that his behavior has caused him to be banned from the Three Deuces and he turns to Chan—who has showbiz connections—to help him get reinstated.

This act finally commits Parker to Chan firmly and they move in together. By 1949, Parker is famous within the jazz culture (but completely unknown outside it) and a club named Birdland in his honor opens. Parker takes his music to Europe, finding in Paris the mass adulation that has eluded him in the US. Although he loves Paris and craves the respect his music receives there, he returns to New York, where he finds it difficult to get work. Left with little choice, Parker forms a group and tours the Deep South, passing white trumpeter Red Rodney (Zelniker) off as a black albino so as not to violate segregation laws. In the South, Parker learns that Rodney has taken up the heroin habit and he angrily denounces the drug, begging Rodney give it up. The tour is a success and Parker makes a triumphant return to New York, only to learn that his daughter is ill. Seeking refuge in heroin, Parker goes into a steep decline. Because of his erratic behavior, his cabaret card is revoked and he is banned from playing at Birdland. Unable to take the pressure, Parker impulsively goes to California to play a gig with Gillespie, but the trip is a hazy mix of women, drugs, and alcohol. While in Los Angeles, Pree dies. The distraught Parker spends that night sending dozens of apologetic telegrams to Chan, with whom, back East, Parker subsequently moves to Chan's family home in Westchester. Offered an audition with a band, Parker drives to New York and stops off at 52nd Street. Shocked to find that the jazz scene there has vanished, he stumbles into a theater to find his old rival Franklin on stage, playing simplistic, honking rock'n'roll saxophone to a packed house of screaming teens. Thunderstruck that the crude music would attract such a crowd, Parker wanders backstage after the performance and "borrows" Franklin's saxophone. He walks down an alley playing one of his complex riffs, and is stopped by the angry Franklin, who demands to know what Parker is doing with the instrument. "I wanted to see if it would play more than one note at a time," replies Parker, handing the horn back to Franklin. Late to his audition, Parker loses the job and drifts over to the home of Baroness Nica de Koenigswarter, a rich European expatriate and jazz benefactor. While watching a variety show on television, Parker suffers a fatal heart attack and dies. When asked how old the musician was, the coroner estimates him to be 65 years old. Charlie Parker was thirty-four.

Breathtakingly ambitious, uncompromising, remarkably unsentimental, generally factual, complex, nonlinear, and valiantly uncommercial, BIRD should erase any doubts that Eastwood deserves to be ranked as a major American filmmaker. BIRD and Bertrand Tavernier's 'ROUND MIDNIGHT (a film Eastwood urged Warner Bros. to make) are easily the best films about jazz ever made. Although a shudder went through the jazz world when it was announced that Clint "Dirty Harry" Eastwood was slated to direct a movie about the great Charlie Parker, fears were quelled when it was learned that Eastwood was a lifelong jazz enthusiast who, as a teenager, saw Parker play and recalls it as one of the most vivid moments of his life. Eastwood directed from a script written by Joel Oliansky that had been kicking around Hollywood since 1981 and was at one time announced as a vehicle for Richard Pryor. Eastwood was excited by the script, which was owned by Columbia, and persuaded Warner Bros. to swap one of their projects for the BIRD script. Derived mostly from Chan Parker's unpublished memoir, *Life in E-Flat*, the story is told through a very intricate structure which jumps backward and forward in an ambitious attempt to create a narrative and visual equivalent of Parker's terribly complicated music. Eastwood's handling of this challenging material is often brilliant, full of breadth and meaning. Visually the film is pure *noir* —all dark, smoky jazz clubs and rainy urban nights. Production designer Edward C. Carfagno does a magnificent job of re-creating the bustling, postwar 52nd Street scene on a Hollywood backlot, and Eastwood lovingly highlights the details, giving, for example, prominent play to local character Pincus the doorman, who was known as the "Mayor of 52nd Street."

While Eastwood gets all the cosmetic details right, he also presents a compelling portrait of Parker the man. A lazy filmmaker would have taken a simplistic view of the material and proposed banal explanations of Parker's self-destruction, but Eastwood avoids such pitfalls and does not offer up pop-psychology or anti-drug preachiness. (Ironically, Parker himself was a vigorous opponent of heroin use and practically begged admiring musicians to give up the habit that they picked up in the misguided belief that the drug somehow fueled Parker's genius.) Also unemphasized for the most part are the racial pressures that hit Parker, a particularly sensitive man, very hard. Certainly Eastwood could have used Parker's story to examine American racism during the 1940s and 50s, but instead he chose to downplay it, perhaps because by now audiences are well aware of the problems faced by blacks in that era and the pressures are implicit. In any event, Eastwood allows the man's life its complexity and resists pointing to racism or drugs as the catalyst of Parker's downfall. Although the tragedy of his short, brilliant life is the driving force of the film, BIRD also captures Parker's intelligence, wit, eloquence, and passion. Most of the credit must go to young actor Forest Whitaker for his towering performance as the tortured musical genius. Avoiding cliches, Whitaker goes right to the soul of Bird and movingly conveys the terrible contradictions that drove the man to an early death. Equally impressive is Diane Venora as Chan. Tough, supportive, independent, courageous, and compassionate, Venora captures Chan's innate feistiness, and her scenes with Whitaker are marvelously nuanced. And, of course, there is the music. Aside from the script's occasional departure from fact, the film's treatment of the musical score has been its most controversial aspect among jazz buffs. Wisely opting to use Parker's actual solos on the soundtrack instead of having a modern musician re-create them, Eastwood and musical director Lennie Niehaus took several previously unreleased recordings of Parker and digitally stripped away his accompanists (mostly because of poor recording techniques that featured Bird at the expense of the others), replacing them with such modern musicians as Ron Carter, John Guerin, Ray Brown, Monty Alexander, Jon Faddis, and Charles McPherson. Red Rodney, who is still touring and recording, played the parts for his cinematic counterpart. While the trick works quite well for the purposes of the movie (and in the case of Parker's recordings with a string quartet *improves* on them), listening to the soundtrack album can be disconcerting for those who believe that removing Max Roach, Bud Powell, and Miles Davis from the mix is tantamount to sacrilege. Seen in the correct perspective, however, the high-tech manipulation of the music in BIRD is a fascinating experiment, and the fact that Leonard Feather, the dean of American jazz critics, endorsed the soundtrack album by writing the liner notes gives Niehaus' efforts some credibility.

What many critics and patrons have seen as a failing in BIRD, however, is Eastwood's inability to convey exactly *why* Charlie Parker was a musical genius who has been compared to Mozart and Stravinsky, an especially difficult problem when the artist in question received virtually no recognition from the wider world during his lifetime. The answer to Parker's genius is, quite frankly, that his music is impossible to describe. Thankfully, Eastwood recognizes this and doesn't bore viewers with a scene wherein a music critic pontificates on the nature of Parker's genius, thus "explaining" it to the audience. He merely presents the music and lets us hear for ourselves. Great music, especially jazz, either strikes a person or it doesn't, and no amount of exegesis is going to convert someone who simply can't dig it. Although he certainly didn't seek to alienate others, Eastwood made this film for jazz people and his vision is appropriately uncompromising. You can't be all things to all people, hence BIRD's failure at the US box office (it was a massive hit in France). While kudos must certainly go to Warner Bros. for putting up $10 million for a distinctly uncommercial film, one can easily conclude that—since Eastwood has raked in nearly one *billion* dollars for the studio over the years—they owed it to him. And to us. The music: "Maryland, My Maryland" (Lennie Niehaus), "Lester Leaps In" (Lester Young), "I Can't Believe That You're in Love with Me" (Clarence Gaskill, Jimmy McHugh), "All of Me" (Seymour Simon, Gerald Marks), "This Time the Dream's on Me" (Harold Arlen, Johnny Mercer), all performed by Charlie Parker, Monty Alexander, Ray Brown, and John Guerin; "Reno Jam Session" (Lennie Niehaus, performed by Niehaus, James Rivers, Red Rodney, Pete Jolly, Chuck Berghofer, John Guerin); "Young Bird" (Niehaus, performed by Rivers, Jolly, Berghofer, Guerin); "Why Do I Love You?" (Jerome Kern, Oscar Hammerstein II, performed by Rivers, Niehaus); "Moonlight Becomes You" (Johnny Burke, Jimmy Van Heusen, performed by Ronny Lang, Gary Foster, Bob Cooper, Pete Christlieb, Chuck Findley, Conte Candoli, Rick Baptist, Dick Nash, Bill Watrous, Barry Harris, Berghofer, Guerin); "Moose the Mooche" (Charlie Parker, performed by Charles McPherson, Jon Faddis, Walter Davis, Jr., Ron Carter, Guerin); "Ornithology" (Parker, Bennie Harris, peformed by Parker, Faddis, Mike Lang, Chuck Domanico, Guerin, Charlie Shoemake); "Lover Man" (Jimmy Davis, Roger 'Ram' Ramirez, Jimmy Sherman, performed by Parker, McPherson, Faddis, Davis, Jr., Carter, Guerin); "April in Paris" (Vernon Duke, E.Y. Harburg), "Laura" (Johnny Mercer, David Raksin), "Parker's Mood (with strings)" (Parker), all performed by Parker, Barry Harris, Berghofer, Guerin, plus strings; "Jewish Wedding" (Niehaus, performed by McPherson, Rodney, Davis, Jr., Guerin); "One for Red" (Niehaus, performed by Rodney, Lang, Domanico, Guerin); "Now's the Time" (Parker, performed by Parker, McPherson, Rodney, Davis, Jr., Carter, Guerin); "Albino Red Blues" (Niehaus, Joel Oliansky, performed by Rodney, Davis, Jr., Carter, Guerin); "Cool Blues," "Ko Ko" (Parker, performed by Parker, Davis, Jr., Carter, Guerin); "Be My Love" (Nicholas Brodszky, Sammy Cahn, peformed by Mario Lanza); "Parker's Mood" (Parker, performed by King Pleasure, John Lewis, Percy Heath, Kenny Clarke); "Buster's Last Stand" (Niehaus, performed by Ronny Lang); excerpt from the *Firebird Suite* (Igor Stravinsky, performed by the Vienna Symphony Orchestra, Wolfgang Sawallisch, conductor). *(Adult situations, profanity.)*

p, Clint Eastwood; d, Clint Eastwood; w, Joel Oliansky; ph, Jack N. Green (Technicolor); ed, Joel Cox; m, Lennie Niehaus; m/l, Lennie Niehaus, Lester Young, Clarence Gaskill, Jimmy McHugh, Seymour Simon, Gerald Marks, Harold Arlen, Johnny Mercer, Jerome Kern, Oscar Hammerstein II, Johnny Burke, Jimmy Van Heusen, Charlie Parker, Bennie Harris, Jimmy Davis, Roger "Ram" Ramirez, Jimmy Sherman, Vernon Duke, E.Y. Harburg, David Raskin, Joel Oliansky, Nicholas Brodszky, Sammy Cahn, Igor Stravinsky; prod d, Edward C. Carfagno; set d, Judy Cammer; spec eff, Joe Day; cos, Glenn Wright, Deborah Hopper; makeup, Michael Hancock.

Biography **(PR:C-O MPAA:R)**

BLACKOUT* (1988) 91m Ambient Light Entertainment c

Carol Lynley *(Mother)*, Gail O'Grady *(Caroline Boyle)*, Michael Keys Hall *(Uncle Alan)*, Joseph Gian *(Luke)*, Deena Freeman *(Angela)*, Joanna Miles *(Eleanor Carpenter)*.

This hopelessly wooden psycho-thriller written by Joseph Stefano, who adapted Robert Bloch's novel *Psycho* for Alfred Hitchcock and hasn't done anything of note since, has played around the country in festivals this year and seems a likely candidate for a quick conversion to video. Gail O'Grady stars as a troubled young woman who returns to the Northern California home she once ran away from after she receives a letter from her estranged father, whom she hasn't seen since she was seven years old. Her homecoming is a surprisingly cold one, for her mother (Lynley) doesn't want to see her or discuss anything having to do with her disappeared husband. Luckily, O'Grady is comforted by her kindly uncle, Hall, who co-owns the house and orange grove with his sister, and he allows O'Grady to stay. Once back home, O'Grady starts to experience flashes of a long-repressed memory regarding her father—something having to do with a bed, a screwdriver, and blood. Courted by Gian, a local lad who still holds a candle for her, the still-virginal O'Grady begins to have sexual rumblings. Unfortunately, these urges tend to manifest themselves violently, and when the hapless Gian tries to kiss her, O'Grady produces a screwdriver (there are more screwdrivers in this movie than there are at your local hardware store) and sinks it into the amorous guy several times. Gian survives the attack and, romantic fool that he is, demonstrates incredible sensitivity by forgiving the obviously deranged girl. When Lynley sees the blood on her daughter's white sweater, she demands to know what has happened. O'Grady tearfully relates the woeful tale. Lynley is horrified and mumbles something like "Oh my God, not again!" before reminding her daughter that her father was a child molester who attacked O'Grady when she was just seven. O'Grady herself stabbed dear old Dad to death with a screwdriver and faithful Mom buried the pervert in the orange grove. The trauma of the incident led to the block in O'Grady's memory. With the case solved, O'Grady decides to return to Chicago, but soon corpses begin piling up and she hears Mom making love to someone in the attic. When kindly uncle Hall tells O'Grady that it was not she, but her *mother* who stabbed Dad to death, O'Grady doesn't believe him and insists that Dad is still alive and hiding in the attic (which is conveniently furnished with a mattress, television, VCR, and impressive collection of hardcore porno videos). Hall goes upstairs to investigate and O'Grady hears the sounds of a struggle. Running up to the attic to see what's going on for herself, O'Grady finds that her kindly uncle was only foolin'—in fact, *he* is the killer! At this moment O'Grady finally gets her flashbacks straight and remembers that it was her uncle and her mother who were in bed together when Dad came home. Revolted by this incestuous scene, Dad began to throttle Mom. Just then buck-naked uncle Hall grabbed a screwdriver and stabbed Dad. Lynley lent a hand as well, and little seven-year-old O'Grady, who witnessed the whole thing, was the one who stopped them and ended up with the bloody screwdriver in her hands. Back in present time, horny uncle Hall begins chasing O'Grady around the house. O'Grady beats it out to the orange grove, screaming for help, and Lynley—who just happens to be several hundred feet above the ground, tending to a recalcitrant windmill—hesitates for a few seconds before shoving the entire unit on her brother's head. Not content to live life without her brother/lover, Lynley then takes a swan-dive off the platform to the ground below, landing right next to her dead sibling. She even clutches his hand as she goes, telling the understandably distraught O'Grady, "Don't waste your tears on me."

Well, O'Grady shouldn't waste her tears on Lynley and you certainly shouldn't waste your time with this movie. Stefano's screenplay is so poorly written that the vast majority of the plot is recited, not dramatized. The amount of expository dialog in this movie is mind-boggling, with scene after scene of characters explaining what is happening to one another. Thoughts, feelings, flashbacks, backstory, even shared pasts ("Remember when I . . .") are explained for the benefit of the camera. This, combined with the total ineptitude of the dialog itself, produces gems such as this exchange between O'Grady and her uncle: O'Grady: "I always hated flowers. I thought you knew that." Hall: "Why is that?" O'Grady: "Because they die and look putrid." Or this tidbit spoken by a bit player who is waiting to have her car repaired: "Excuse me, this is inexcusable!" First-time director Doug Adams (who also had a hand in the script) doesn't help matters much. Shot like a made-for-television movie, the film just doesn't move. Yes, there are a few mildly suspenseful moments, but most of them are stolen from Hitchcock, especially PSYCHO, including slow walks up creepy staircases, movement toward a chair from behind, and visits to an old musty bedroom full of dark antique wood furniture. One expects Mrs. Bates to show up at any moment. Visuals aren't the only elements lifted from PSYCHO, either; Don Davis' musical score plunders Bernard Hermann's as well. Stuck in the midst of all this are the actors. An incredibly weak lot as it is, these poor performers are also saddled with reams of unspeakable prose. O'Grady, while attractive, has great trouble speaking her lines with anything resembling conviction; Michael Keys Hall has "incestuous psycho-killer" written all over his kindly face; and poor Carol Lynley alternates between spitting venom at O'Grady and feigning ecstacy in an embarrassing sex scene in which, stark naked, she clutches the attic window frame and rocks back and forth while an unseen lover has at her from behind. The entire film, with its central themes of murder, child molestation, and incest, would feel even more sleazy if it weren't so damn boring. A low-budget independent, BLACKOUT seems unlikely ever to pick up a theatrical distributor and should die a quiet death at the video stores. *(Violence, nudity, sexual situations, profanity.)*

p, Doug Adams, Joseph Stefano; d, Doug Adams; w, Joseph Stefano (based on an original screenplay by Doug Adams, Laura Ferguson, Cynthia Williams); ph, Arledge Armenaki; ed, Zach Staenberg; m, Don Davis; prod d, Peter Kanter; set d, Effie Rosen; cos, Trudy Kapner.

Thriller **(PR:O MPAA:NR)**

BLOB, THE*** (1988) 92m Tri-Star c

Shawnee Smith *(Meg Penny)*, Donovan Leitch *(Paul Taylor)*, Ricky Paull Goldin *(Scott Jeskey)*, Kevin Dillon *(Brian Flagg)*, Billy Beck *(Can Man)*, Jeffrey DeMunn *(Sheriff Herb Geller)*, Candy Clark *(Fran Hewitt)*, Beau Billingslea *(Moss Woolsey)*, Art La Fleur *(Pharmacist/Mr. Penny)*, Del Close *(Rev. Meeker)*, Michael Kenworthy *(Kevin Penny)*, Douglas Emerson *(Eddie Beckner)*, Sharon Spelman *(Mrs. Penny)*, Margaret Smith *(Nurse)*, Jack Nance *(Doctor)*, Charlene Fox *(Woman in Doctor's Office)*, Paul McCrane *(Dep. Bill Briggs)*, Erika Eleniak *(Vicki De Soto)*, Teddy Vincent *(Sally Jeffers)*, Clayton Landey *(George Ruiz)*, Joe Seneca *(Dr. Meddows)*, Don Brunner *(White Suit #1*/Scientist), Jacquelyn Masche *(White Suit #2)*, Jack Rader *(Col. Hargis)*, Judy McCullough *(Susie)*, Daryl Marsh *(Lance)*, Wade Mayer *(Movie Patron)*, Jamison Newlander *(Anthony)*, Frank Collison *(Phil Hobbs Projectionist)*, Pons Maar *(Theater Manager)*, Judith Flanagan *(Eddie's Mother)*, Richard Crenna, Jr. *(Soldier Outside Town Hall)*, Charlie Spradling, Kristen Aldrich *(Co-Eds)*, Robert Axelrod *(Jennings)*, M. James Arnett *(Radio Man)*, Peter Crombie *(Soldier at Command Post)*, Rick Avery *(Soldier with Cracked Faceplate)*, David Weininger *(Soldier #1)*, Bill Moseley *(Soldier #2)*, Moss Porter *(Sergeant)*, Jennifer Lincoln *(Young Woman in Town Hall)*, Noble Craig *(Puddle Soldier)*, Portia Griffin *(Gospel Singer)*, Opelene Bartley *(Old Woman in Tent)*.

Most remakes of old movies, especially horror or science fiction movies, are pointless affairs that fail to either capture the spirit of the original or add anything new to the basic premise. Occasionally, a smart filmmaker will come along and actually improve upon the original, as was the case with David Cronenberg's remake of THE FLY (1986). Luckily, Chuck Russell's remake of the 1958 "classic" THE BLOB manages both to capture the giddy drive-in feel of the original *and* improve upon it. Savvy enough to quote from the highlights of the original film and clever enough to stand on its own, THE BLOB is set in the small town of Arborville, where high-school cheer-

© TRI-STAR

leader Smith finally lands a date with football star Leitch, while sheriff DeMunn is keeping an eye on leather-clad juvenile delinquent Dillon. Such routine goings-on are shattered, however, when a meteor from outer space crashes into the nearby woods. Beck, an elderly vagrant, finds the meteor and pokes at it with a stick. Immediately, a glutinous substance attaches itself to the stick and then crawls onto Beck's arm, dissolving it with some sort of corrosive. Dillon, Leitch, and Smith discover the old man and take him to the hospital, where the blob dissolves the vagrant completely and then eats Leitch. Since Dillon has left the scene and only Smith has actually seen the blob, the cops refuse to believe her outlandish story and suspect Dillon of Leitch's disappearance. Soon enough, however, the blob—which grows larger with each victim it consumes—is wreaking havoc on the entire town, absorbing short-order cooks, waitresses, teens necking in the moonlight, and even the Sheriff himself. Dillon and Smith, who at school despise each other, team up to defeat the monster. Just outside of town, however, they encounter a small army of spacesuit-clad government personnel led by scientist Seneca. The scientist informs the teens that the meteor has brought with it a deadly virus, and all surviving citizens must be quarantined in the town hall. Dillon doesn't buy the story, and, in fact, overhears that the meteor is actually an American satellite that contained a biological warfare experiment gone awry. Seneca and his men plan to seal off the town from the rest of the country and "neutralize" the problem (thus keeping it top secret) while trying to capture the blob alive for further use as the ultimate weapon. With the blob now having attained gigantic proportions after consuming patrons of the local movie theater, Dillon must help fend the beast off *and* convince the citizens who consider him a punk that the government is the true villain. Luckily, the blob comes along and kills Seneca, freeing the Army (who thought the scientist nuts) to attack the monster. Unfortunately, their superior firepower does nothing but destroy the town square and make the blob very angry. Smith, meanwhile, has discovered that cold repels the blob and she mobilizes townsfolk to fend off the monster with fire extinguishers. The heroic Dillon then shows up with an artificial snow-making machine and freezes the creature into submission. Although the horror is over for this small town, the crazed reverend Meeker—whose face was horribly scarred in the attack—has salvaged a few pieces of the frozen blob and has hit the tent revival circuit preaching the biblical prophecy of Armageddon—a prophecy he plans to fulfill when the thawed-out blob grows big enough.

Well directed by Chuck Russell (A NIGHTMARE ON ELM STREET PART III) this remake of THE BLOB is fast-paced, frightening, gross, and witty, delivering the goods that come with the genre while developing characters and themes at the same time. Although the state-of-the-art special effects are duly impressive and come at a breakneck pace, what works in this remake is not just the improvement in effects technology, but also a striking rethinking of the film's subtext. If one accepts the popular notion that the original BLOB was a reflection of American fears in the late 1950s, the new BLOB serves the same purpose for the post-Irangate/Pentagon scandal 1980s. The screenplay by director Russell and Frank Darabont is a Left-leaning reaction to the Reagan era. Whereas the original blob was seen as a representation of the creeping evil of communism, the remake sees the threat not as foreign, but as *domestic*, with a thoughtless, paranoid, and cynical American government whose obsession with communism leads to disastrous results for its own citizens. Although the Soviets are never mentioned by name, it is implicit that the biological weapons system that created the blob was designed to be used against them. In addition to its distrust of the government, the movie is fearful of fundamentalist religious zealots, represented by Close's Rev. Meeker, who are seen to endorse the use of American weapons technology to further their own obsessions with Armageddon and hasten its arrival. Quite a departure from the films of the 1950s—when, often, the power of prayer was shown to be a successful defense against alien attack (as in George Pal's THE WAR OF THE WORLDS).

Politics aside, THE BLOB is also delightfully self-reflexive in a cinematic sense. While the fond quotes from the original film are still effective and amusing (the old man poking the blob with a stick, the blob attacking the movie theater—a scene which in itself is wonderfully self-reflexive), Russell takes it one step further by making his good old-fashioned monster movie a statement against modern-day slasher pictures. In the film, Smith's little brother wants to go see a slasher film, but his mother won't let him and decries the fact that Hollywood makes the films in the first place. Later, after the little brother has defied his mother and is sitting in the theater watching the movie, we see a totally insipid clip from a fictitious slasher film that points out just how dumb these films are ("Say, this isn't hockey season," a dimwitted victim declares, just before being attacked by a hockey-masked, Jason-like killer with a chainsaw). In addition, a moronic patron sits behind the kid and easily predicts everything that will happen in the movie before it happens. Russell's final comment on slasher films is to have the blob destroy the film and the theater, thus heralding the triumphant return of the old-fashioned monster movie. This remake of THE BLOB is a fine, multilayered effort from a man who understands the genre and appreciates its traditions. Anyone who has been disheartened by the mindless, cynical, misogynistic, downright misanthropic direction science-fiction and horror films have taken lately should be delighted with the genuine thoughtfulness and fun behind THE BLOB. *(Violence, gore effects, profanity.)*

p, Jack H. Harris, Elliott Kastner; d, Chuck Russell; w, Chuck Russell, Frank Darabont; ph, Mark Irwin (Technicolor); ed, Terry Stokes, Tod Feuerman; m, Michael Hoenig; m/l, Keith Whitley, Mike Slamer, Alien, Janet Minto, Pam Barlow, Gary Cambra, Wayne Coster; prod d, Craig Stearns; art d, Jeff Ginn; set d, Anne Ahrens; spec eff, Hoyt Yeatman, Lyle Conway; cos, Joseph Porro; anim, Jeff Burks; stunts, Gary Hymes, Steve Holladay; makeup, Tony Gardner, Kathryn Miles Kelly.

Science Fiction	Cas.	(PR:O MPAA:R)

BLOOD ON THE MOON (SEE: COP, 1988)

BLOODSPELL † (1988) 88m Vista Street-Feifer/Miller c

Anthony Jenkins *(Daniel)*, Aaron Teich *(Charlie)*, Alexandra Kennedy *(Debbie)*, John Reno *(Luther)*, Edward Dloughy, Jacque J. Coon, Kimble Jemison, Heather Green, Christopher G. Venuti, Susan Buchanan, Douglas Vale, Tia Lachelle.

Yet another A NIGHTMARE ON ELM STREET 3 rip-off (check out this year's BAD DREAMS as well), BLOODSPELL features Jenkins as a telekinetic teen who has been sent to a psychiatric institution for his own protection. It seems that his father, Reno, is a dangerous man and has vowed to get his son. When the other patients begin dropping like flies, the hospital staff assumes that the deaths are accidental, but Jenkins knows better. Ultra low-budget horror, which went straight to home video.

p, Jessica Rains; d, Deryn Warren; w, Gerry Daly; ph, Ronn Schmidt; ed, Tony Miller; m, Randy Miller; prod d, Peter Kanter; makeup, Wade Daily.

Horror	Cas.	(PR:NR MPAA:R)

BLOODSPORT** (1988) 92m Cannon c

Jean Claude Van Damme *(Frank Dux)*, Donald Gibb *(Ray Jackson)*, Leah Ayres *(Janice)*, Norman Burton *(Helmer)*, Forest Whitaker *(Rawlins)*, Roy Chiao *(Senzo "Tiger" Tanaka)*, Philip Chan *(Capt. Chen)*, Pierre Rafini *(Young Frank)*, Bolo Yeung *(Chong Li)*, Kenneth Siu *(Victor)*, Kimo Lai Kwok Ki *(Hiro)*, Bernard Mariano *(Hossein)*, Bill Yuen Ping Kuen *(Oshima)*, Lily Leung *(Mrs. Tanaka)*, Joshua Schroeder *(Chuck)*, Keith Davey *(Eddie)*, Sean Ward *(Shingo)*, Johnny Lai *(Desk Clerk)*, Henry Ho, Henry Kot, Thomas Lam, Simon Lai *(Officials)*, A.P. George *(Referee/Judge)*, Charles Wang *(Chinese Doctor)*, John Foster *(Gustafson)*, John Cheung *(Toon)*, Dennis Chiu *(Chuan)*, Michelle Qissi *(Parades)*, Nathan Chkueke *(Parades' Opponent)*, Geoff Brown *(Parades' Friend)*, David Ho *(Pumola)*, Eric Neff *(Morra)*, Michael Chan *(Yasuda)*, Rick Erikson *(Cotard)*, John Law *(Luu)*, Samson Li *(Prang)*, Paulo Tocha *(Paco)*, Greg Richardson *(Aussie)*, Saheed Sahabuddin, Rocky Jasminder Singh *(Syrian Fighters)*, Wilson Lee *(Chong Li's Trainer)*, Mark Di Salle *(Boxer)*, Edward E. Ketterer *(Aide)*, Ken Boyle *(Col. Cooke)*, Joshua Schroeder, Keith Davey, Mark Wheelhouse, Wayne Morris, Darren Humphrey *(Older Boys)*, Tom Tam *(Young Tough)*, Claude Heme *(Mr. Dux)*, Susan Sheers *(Mrs. Dux)*, Mandy Chan *(Janitor)*, Wong Tak Ming *(Flagman)*, Tsui Siu Hung, Chung Shun Tak, Wan Kung Sung *(Policemen)*, Christopher Lay *(Butler)*, Andrew Rule *(Guard)*, Lois Gochnauer, Patricia McDonald, Mic Rieusset, Gloria Wu, Peggy Tam, Jacqueline Choy, Bernie Cilia, Rani Gill, Christine Redmen *(Special Ladies)*, Johnny Wong Tin Tok, Mak Shu Sun, Nip Kwok Chiu *(Big Spenders)*, David Tetter, Joao Gamez, Steve Daw, Henrik Wesslen, Wayne Archer, Mark Sharrock, Colin Bucknor, Hung Chi Shing, Chu Wah, Max Clsekedi, Benjamin Ling, Tse Kin Hung, Ng Yuk Shu, Paul Findley, Attilio Reale, Paul Treadwell, Roger Walker, Victor Wong, Eric Ng, Ronnie Li *(Fighters)*.

This film is based on true events in the life of Frank Dux, an American special forces commando and the first westerner to dominate the Kumite, a brutal martial arts competition, held clandestinely every five years in Hong Kong. Dux, played by Jean Claude Van Damme (a Belgian, with a disconcertingly thick accent), started his martial arts training as a boy in California. This is shown in flashback, and a good thing too, as it requires minimal acting—Van Damme has only to stare off into space and the camera dissolves to his mentor, Tanaka, a past Kumite champion, who has moved to the US from Japan after WW II to make a new life for himself. He engages the young Dux as a sparring partner for his son. When his son dies (this is never explained), Dux persuades Tanaka (Roy Chiao) to take him on as a student, and so begins an arduous apprenticeship culminating in the master's respect for his student's awesome ability and a strong emotional bond forged between the two. Now we follow Van Damme to Hong Kong. He is on leave from the Defence Intelligence Agency, determined to participate in the Kumite to bring honor to his ailing mentor. Unfortunately, his special forces unit feels he is too valuable to risk in such a dangerous contest and they send Forest Whitaker and Norman Burton to bring him back to the US. Whitaker, who plays Charlie Parker in 1988's BIRD, has little opportunity here to do anything with his cartoonish role as a bumbling operative. Dux divides his

time before the meet dodging the agents and anemically pursuing romantic interest Leah Ayres, a reporter willing to do almost anything to get the scoop on the Kumite. In an amusing twist, she is shown in bed with covers pulled to her chin ogling Van Damme as he flexes his muscles pulling on a pair of bikini underwear. These muscles get plenty of play in the competition scenes, which are bloody displays of martial arts technique, with Van Damme battling the sadistic incumbent, Chong Li, played with campy gusto by Bolo Yeung. Eventually of course, Van Damme is victorious, and so avenges a friend's cruel battering by Yeung, wins loving looks from Ayres, brings honor on Tanaka, and allows Whitaker and Burton to successfully conclude their mission by escorting him back home.

BLOODSPORT is strictly for martial arts buffs as there is little offered here in the way of plot, dialog, or acting, although the fight sequences are shot in a straightforward manner—generally not the case with this genre—affording the audience a chance to admire Van Damme's real skill as an athlete if not as an actor. Songs include "Fight to Survive" (Shandi, Paul Hertzog), "On My Own-Alone" (Shandi, Paul Hertzog), "Only a State of Mind" (Debbie Holland, Frankie "Blue" Sposato), "Keep On Dreaming" (Carl Sealove, Miriam Cutler, performed by Stan Bush). *(Extreme violence, sexual situations, profanity.)*

p, Mark DiSalle; d, Newt Arnold; w, Sheldon Lettich, Christopher Crosby, Mel Friedman (based on a story by Sheldon Lettich); ph, David Worth (TVC Color); ed, Carl Kress; m, Paul Hertzog; m/l, Shandi, Paul Hertzog, Debbie Holland, Frankie "Blue" Sposato, Carl Sealove, Miriam Cutler; prod d, David Searl; cos, Wei Sau Ling; stunts, Steve Lee Ka Ding; makeup, Chan Man Fai, Jennie Chui, Tommy Chan.

Action	Cas.	(PR:O MPAA:R)

BLOODY POM POMS † (1988) 88m Quinn/Prettyman-Prism-Daiei/Atlantic c

Betsy Russell *(Alison Wentworth)*, Leif Garrett *(Brent Hoover)*, Lucinda Dickey *(Cory Foster)*, Lorie Griffin *(Bonnie Reed)*, Buck Flower *(Pop)*, Travis McKenna *(Timmy Moser)*, Teri Weigel *(Pam Bently)*, Rebecca Ferratti *(Theresa Salazar)*, Vickie Benson *(Miss Tipton)*, Jeff Prettyman, Krista Pflanzer, Craig Piligian, William Johnson Sr., Kathryn Litton.

Released theatrically as BLOODY POM POMS, but available on home video as CHEERLEADER CAMP, this obscure low budget effort seeks to combine two classics of exploitation: the T&A cheerleader movie and the slice-and-dice splatter film. Betsy Russell (the second actress to play the "honor student by day, Hollywood hooker by night" in the popular ANGEL series), stars as a troubled cheerleader who suffers from horribly violent nightmares. Accompanied by six fellow cheerleaders and their mascot, Russell enrolls in a secluded rah-rah camp located in Sequoia National Forest. Russell's mental instability isn't helped any by her boy friend, Garrett, who gets wanderlust and pursues buxom rival cheerleader Pflanzer. When the horny pom pom wavers begin to die one by one, suspicion naturally falls on the obviously deranged Russell, but she, of course, is innocent and the real killer has yet to be discovered. It has been reported that while the gore effects remain intact in the home video release, the nudity has been trimmed and gratuitous profanity inserted in its place. Go figure.

p, Jeffrey Prettyman, John Quinn; d, John Quinn; w, David Lee Fein, R.L. O'Keefe; ph, Bryan England (Foto-Kem color); ed, Jeffrey Reiner; m, Murielle Hodler-Hamilton, Joel Hamilton; prod d, Keith Barrett; cos, Gini Kramer; ch, Lucinda Dickey; makeup, Ramona.

Horror	Cas.	(PR:NR MPAA:R)

BLUE IGUANA, THE* (1988) 90m Polygram-Propaganda/PAR c

Dylan McDermott *(Vince Holloway)*, Jessica Harper *(Cora)*, James Russo *(Reno)*, Pamela Gidley *(Dakota)*, Tovah Feldshuh *(Det. Vera Quinn)*, Dean Stockwell *(Det. Carl Strick)*, Katia Schkolnik *(Mona)*, Flea *(Floyd)*, Yano Anaya *(Yano)*, Michele Seipp *(Zoe, Bartender)*, Don Pedro Colley *(Boat Captain)*, John Durbin *(Louie Sparks)*, Eliett *(Veronica)*, Pedro Altamirano *(Rubberhead)*, Benny Corral *(Roy)*, Alejandro Bracho *(Hotel Clerk)*, Honorato Magaloni *(Smuggler)*, Enrique Garcia *(Drunken Man)*, Arturo R. Doring, Siro, Alberto Colin, Jorge Luis Corzo, Amelia Zapata *(Gangsters)*, Raul Araiza, Alvaro Carcano *(Teenagers)*, Jonathan Kano *(Solo)*, Carlos Romano *(Banker)*.

A hybrid parody of *film noir* and spaghetti westerns, THE BLUE IGUANA is nothing more than a showy film school nod to earlier movies. For what its worth, Dylan McDermott (HAMBURGER HILL) plays a bounty hunter who refers to himself grandly as a "recovery specialist." He's broke, living in a miserable apartment, and in trouble with the IRS. In order to square things with the government, he accepts (under pressure) an offer made by agents Stockwell and Feldshuh to travel south of the border to a place called El Diablo, where millions of dollars in drug money is being laundered. Since no one has paid any taxes on this money, it is McDermott's job to recover it. El Diablo is a tough place, however. People are murdered in the streets, wild types fire guns into ceilings, and coffin-making seems to be the only legitimate line of work. Harper, who runs the local bank, has so much power and provides such a necessary service to drug runners that she charges her *customers* interest. Gidley is a singer (a la Rita Hayworth's Gilda) at the Blue Iguana club who has an eye on McDermott. The film continues at an aren't-we-cool pace, with everyone double-crossing everyone else in an effort to get a hold of the millions in Harper's vault. At the end, everyone is dead except McDermott and his obnoxious teen cohort, Anaya, and things look great for the now-wealthy pair until tax agents Stockwell and Feldshuh appear and claim the cash.

The only reason to see THE BLUE IGUANA is Flea, whose pistol-packin' goon is killed off entirely too soon. His (and the film's) best moment comes in the scene in which he turns funkmaster and jams big time to James Brown's "Sex Machine." Songs include: "Blue Iguana" (Kurtis Blow, Michael Green, performed by Blow), "This Is Hardcore Is It Not" (T. Ray, T. Swain, T. Price, performed by White Boys), "Hell No" (D. Robinson, D. Wimbley, M. Morales, J. Glenn, G. Rottger, performed by the Fat Boys), "Get Up (I Feel Like Being A) Sex Machine" (James Brown, Bobby Byrd, Ronald Lenhoff, performed by Brown), "Nereidas" (Amador Perez, performed by Acerina y Su Danzonera), "Gee What a Guy" (Van McCoy, Dionne Warwick, performed by Pamela Gidley), "The Laziest Gal in Town" (Cole Porter, performed by Gidley, Ethan James, Glen Mont), "Teacher Don't Teach Me Nonsense" (Fela Anikulapo Kuti), "No Mercy" (T. Guns, M. Kripps, P. Lewis, N. Alexander, performed by L.A. Guns), "Song of the Chasqui" (Elizabeth Waldo), "Some Men" (Ethan James, Stephanie Shayne, performed by James), "Cruel and Unusual World" (James, Shayne, performed by James, Gidley), "You Cheated" (Don Burch, performed by the Del Vikings), "Born to Be Wild" (Mars Bonfire, performed by Zodiac Mindwarp), "Winner Take All" (Sid Wayne, Al Frisch, performed by the Platters), and "We Need Money" (Chuck Brown, J. Buchanan, D. Tillery, L. Fleming, C. Johnson, performed by Chuck Brown & the Soul Searchers). *(Sexual situations, profanity, substance abuse, violence.)*

p, Steven Golin, Sigurjon Sighvatsson; d, John Lafia; w, John Lafia; ph, Rodolfo Sanchez (CFI Color); ed, Scott Chestnut; m, Ethan James, Glen Mont, Freddie Ramos; prod d, Cynthia Sowder; art d, Jesus Buenrostro; set d, Sergio Nicolav, Heidy Gomez; ch, Felix Greco; stunts, John Escobar.

| Comedy/Crime | Cas. | (PR:O MPAA:R) |

BLUE JEAN COP   (SEE: SHAKEDOWN, 1988)

BLUE MOVIES †   (1988) 92m Blue Partners/Skouras c

Steve Levitt *(Buzz)*, Larry Poindexter *(Cliff)*, Lucinda Crosby *(Randy Moon)*, Darian Mathias *(Kathy)*, Christopher Stone *(Brad)*, Don Calfa *(Max)*, Larry Linville *(Dr. Gladding)*, Russell Johnson, Hardy Rawls, Seth Mitchell, Vickie Benson, Leland Crooke, Bert Rosario.

Aside from slasher films, sex comedies seem to be the most common straight-to-video releases. This one is even a bit self-reflexive. A nerd in debt (Levitt) and his buddy, an aspiring stand-up comedian (Poindexter), decide to make a quick buck by becoming hardcore porno movie producers. Gathering together a semiretired porno actress (Crosby), a washed-up screenwriter (Calfa), and a straight-out-of-film-school director (Crooke), the partners succeed in shooting their first adult film. Unfortunately, this gets them into hot water with the local mob, who feel that the boys are horning in on their turf, and trouble ensues.

p, Maria Snyder; d, Paul Koval, Ed Fitzgerald; w, Paul Koval, Ed Fitzgerald; ph, Vance Piper; ed, John Currin; m, Patrick Gleeson, Michael Shrieve; art d, John Wade; set d, Terese Mitchell.

| Comedy | Cas. | (PR:NR MPAA:R) |

BODY BEAT †   (1988) 96m RAI-1/Together/Vidmark c

Tony Dean Fields *(Moon)*, Galyn Gorg *(Jana)*, Scott Grossman *(Tommy)*, Eliska Krupka *(Patrizia)*, Steve La Chance *(Vince)*, Paula Nichols *(Paula)*, Julie Newmar *(Miss McKenzie)*, Serge Rodnunsky, Michelle Rudy, Read Scot, Virgil Frye, Leonora Leal, Patricia Zanetti, Timothy Brown.

This FAME-inspired dance film, previously titled DANCE ACADEMY, features Fields as a young student enrolled in Newmar's classical ballet academy who is determined to liven up the staid classical curriculum by injecting some jazz techniques into the mix. An Italian-US coproduction, filmed in both Los Angeles and Rome in 1986.

p, Jef Richard, Aldo U. Passalacqua; d, Ted Mather; w, Ted Mather (based on a story by Ted Mather, Guido De Angelis); ph, Dennis Peters (Alpha Cine color); ed, Rebecca Ross; m, Guido De Angelis, Maurizio De Angelis; m/l, Guide De Angelis, Maurizio De Angelis, Ted Mather, Chuck Francour; art d, Gene Abel, Francesco Cuppini; ch, Dennon Rawles, Sayhber Rawles; stunts, Greg Gault.

| Drama | Cas. | (PR:NR MPAA:PG) |

BODY COUNT †   (1988) 93m Poor Robert/Manson Intl. c

Bernie White *(Robert Knight)*, Marilyn Hassett *(Joanne Knight)*, Dick Sargent *(Charles Knight)*, Greg Mullavey *(Ralph Duris)*, Thomas Ryan *(Lt. Chernoff)*, Haunani Minn *(Kim)*, Steven Ford *(Tom Leary)*, Lauren Woodland *(Deborah)*, James Avery, Julia Campbell, Oceana Marr, Jennifer Rhodes, Richard Stanley.

A murderous psychopath (White) who was committed to a mental institution by his greedy uncle (Sargent) breaks out and heads back home, vowing revenge. Another straight-to-video bloodbath.

p, Paul Leder; d, Paul Leder; w, Paul Leder (based on a story by William W. Norton, Sr.); ph, Francis Grumman; ed, Paul Leder; m, Bob Summers; set d, Elpedio Vasquez.

| Horror | Cas. | (PR:NR MPAA:NR) |

BOOST, THE*½   (1988) 95m Becker-Blatt-Ponicsan/Hemdale c

James Woods *(Lenny Brown)*, Sean Young *(Linda Brown)*, John Kapelos *(Joel)*, Steven Hill *(Max)*, Kelle Kerr *(Rochelle)*, John Rothman *(Ned Lewis)*, Amanda Blake *(Barbara)*, Grace Zabriskie *(Sheryl)*, Scott McGinnis, Zina Bethune, Mark Poppel, Fred McCarren, Suzanne Kent.

Although it's a seemingly sincere attempt to chronicle the horrors of drug abuse, THE BOOST is so haphazardly scripted and directed that the film becomes an inadvertent self-parody. Salvaged only by an interesting, if not completely successful, performance from the great James Woods, THE BOOST chronicles the rise and fall of a head-over-heels in love couple, Woods and Young, who succumb to the lure of the fast lane. As the film opens, Woods is a two-bit New York City hustler trying to make ends meet as a salesman, while Young brings in the lion's share of their income as a paralegal. Self-conscious about his lack of higher education and harboring deep feelings of inadequacy—he constantly worries that he doesn't deserve his beautiful wife—Woods has a tendency to become overbearing, and occasionally explodes with resentment. His hyperkinetic, hard-sell style causes him to blow a job interview with some high-rolling investors, but one of the partners, Hill, is impressed by Woods' old-fashioned chutzpah and offers him a job selling real-estate tax shelters in Los Angeles. A relaxed, philosophical, self-made millionaire, Hill takes Woods under his wing and provides him with an impressive home in the Hollywood Hills, a Mercedes, and a huge office with a secretary. In awe of their new surroundings, Woods and Young begin to live the high life. Woods is incredibly successful in his first year and enthusiastically indulges in an orgy of conspicuous consumption, buying a small airplane and a Mexican nightclub, much to the always fretting Young's dismay. The couple also begin socializing with the smarmy, jaded, coke-snorting Hollywood jet set, especially car-wash king Kapelos and his bitchy blonde girl friend, Kerr. Staggering under a mountain of debt, Woods finds his bubble suddenly burst when Congress announces an end to tax shelters. His business dries up overnight and (while Hill takes things calmly and plans to regroup in six months) Woods goes into an emotional tailspin. Depressed and anxious, Woods finally accepts a snort of cocaine from Kapelos and, in the tradition of the drug-paranoia films of the 1930s, is instantly addicted to the "boost" the white powder gives him. Although hesitant, Young takes a snort as well and soon the two of them are hunched over with their faces in piles of white powder at every turn. Desperate for more cocaine, Woods embezzles $20,000 from Hill and is fired. From there the drop is steep, the drug-addled Woods and Young growing increasingly pale and gaunt while the repo men take everything they own (even their dog runs away). After a snort of some bad stuff sends him to the hospital, Woods vows to clean up his act. They move to the laid-back beachfront community of Santa Cruz, where Woods enrolls in an offscreen drug treatment program and gets a job managing a surfboard shop. Young, it turns out, is pregnant and she too gets off the drugs. Unfortunately, when Kapelos and Kerr come to visit and Woods is late getting home, Young succumbs to peer pressure and snorts some coke, subsequently falling down a flight of stairs and losing the baby. This sends the couple even further into the abyss. They head back to LA, this time moving into one of the most seedy sections of Hollywood. Now addicted to Quaaludes, Woods sleeps most of the day and dreams of making one good score that will put him back on top. He also takes to hitting Young on occasion, but she forgives him immediately. Surprisingly, Woods does cook up a solid money-making scheme and cons his way into a meeting with some big investors, but in his nervousness snorts too much coke and the meeting is a disaster. Back at home, Woods beats Young severely and, encouraged by her doctor, she finally leaves him. In the end, Woods is left a hopelessly pathetic wretch, snorting coke and raving about making a comeback. Considering the talent assembled, it's shocking that THE BOOST is a such a botch. One searches for Nancy Reagan's name during the credits, as Darryl Ponicsan's paint-by-numbers script and director Harold Becker's numbingly ham-handed direction are the stuff of government-sponsored educational films. Melodramatic in the extreme, the film is full of unintentionally funny moments that effectively remove the audience from any emotional involvement with the tragic characters. One such instance occurs in the scene wherein Woods drives home from the hospital following his bad trip. Blaming Los Angeles for their addiction, but still obsessed with scoring some coke, Woods suddenly veers violently off the road after the emaciated Young blurts out that she is pregnant. Instead of getting upset, the overjoyed Woods tearfully hugs his wife, with Stanley Myers' gushing musical score swelling in the background. Other risible moments feature Sean Young struggling with Ponicsan's awful dialog—mainly banal declarations of devotion like "As long as we've got each other," "I'd go to the end of the earth with you," and the breathy, desperate "Make love to me." Director Becker's idea of style is to make the lighting of each scene darker than the last as Woods and Young sink lower and lower. He also hits upon a laughable visual motif in chronicling the couple's rise and fall through the ebb and flow of their modes of transportation. Woods is first seen on foot, which turns into a leased Mercedes, then an owned Mercedes, and reaching his zenith in a private plane. Then the decline comes and the couple are seen driving a used Honda and finally a beat-up VW bug. The entire film operates on this excruciatingly simpleminded level. The plot is painfully predictable, most of the characters are stereotypes, and the central relationship between husband and wife is terribly sappy. Only James Woods succeeds in bringing any spontaneity or complexity to the mundane proceedings with his fairly compelling portrayal of an addictive personality, but, unfortunately, the deck is stacked against him, and even he fails to triumph over the misfired script and direction in several scenes.

None of this criticism is directed at the anti-drug subject matter. Most addiction films are pretty much the same and follow terribly predictable formulas; unfortunately, such films, if poorly done, tend to backfire and actually encourage an audience to mock the fate of the characters, thus allowing viewers to dismiss the anti-drug sentiment entirely. REEFER MADNESS and COCAINE FIENDS became big hits with the counter-culture in the 1960s and 1970s for exactly that reason. In the end, the films were used to promote drug use rather than condemn it. Ironically, in the case of THE BOOST, what drew most to the box office had nothing whatsoever to do with the film itself. Shortly after shooting was completed, Woods filed a $6 million lawsuit against costar Young, citing emotional suffering and harassment. Woods accused Young of tormenting him and his fiancee, Sarah Owens, by making abusive phone calls and leaving a mutilated doll on their doorstep. Young, who has had a history of stormy relationships with her costars (Kevin Costner in NO WAY OUT, Charlie Sheen in WALL STREET), denied the charges and filed a countersuit, making the rounds of television talk shows to defend herself. This good old-fashioned Hollywood scandal had more appeal at the box office than any Say-No-to-Drugs sentiment could possibly have. (Adult situations, violence, nudity, sexual situations, substance abuse, profanity.)

p, Daniel H. Blatt; d, Harold Becker; w, Darryl Ponicsan (based on the book *Ludes* by Benjamin Stein); ph, Howard Atherton; ed, Maury Winetrobe; m, Stanley Myers; prod d, Waldemar Kalinowski; art d, Ken Hardy; set d, Cindy Carr; cos, Susan Becker, Lisa Lovas.

Drama (PR:O MPAA:R)

BORN TO RACE † (1988) 98m Romax/MGM-UA c

Joseph Bottoms (*Al Pagura*), Marc Singer (*Kenny Landruff*), George Kennedy (*Vincent Duplain*), Marla Heasley (*Andrea Lombardo*), Antonio Sabato (*Enrico Lombardo*), Robert F. Logan (*Theo Jennings*), Dirk Blocker (*Bud*), Michael McGrady (*Walt*), La Gena Hart (*Jenny*).

Those hankerin' for the next Hal Needham effort will have to make do with this tepid race car movie, starring Heasley as a beautiful Italian auto designer who has invented a new engine that figures to revolutionize auto racing. Heasley decides to test her invention in the unlikely confines of North Carolina's Hickory Speedway, where she meets race car driver Bottoms and falls in love. When villains Kennedy (who makes $10,000 a day to appear in dreck like this) and Singer kidnap Heasley and her blueprints for the engine, Bottoms and his pit-stop buddies must race to the rescue. The distributors sensed they had a turkey on their hands and restricted its theatrical release to Detroit, Texas, and the Carolinas before turning it over to home video.

p, Andrew Bullians, Jean Bullians; d, James Fargo; w, Dennis McGee, Mary Janeway Bullians (based on a story by Mary Janeway Bullians); ph, Bernard Salzmann; ed, Tony Lombardo, Thomas Stanford; m, Ross Vannelli; prod d, Katherine G. Vallin.

Action **Cas.** (PR:NR MPAA:R)

BOYFRIENDS AND GIRLFRIENDS*** (1988, Fr.) 103m Films du Losange/AAA-Orion Classics c

Emmanuelle Chaulet (*Blanche*), Sophie Renoir (*Lea*), Eric Viellard (*Fabien*), Francois-Eric Gendron (*Alexandre*), Anne-Laure Meury (*Adrienne*).

It is often in their simplicity that Eric Rohmer's films are most complex, and in BOYFRIENDS AND GIRLFRIENDS Rohmer has made his simplest film yet. In order to get straight to the chaotic heart of youthful romantic entanglements, Rohmer has cleared away any obstacles that might pop up in his path. He has dismissed expressive camera angles or movements that might alter the viewer's psychological perception of a scene. He has almost completely ignored the use of music, relying instead on quiet background sounds. He has taken his characters away from the narrow streets and sidewalk cafes of Paris, and sets his story in the suburb of Cergy-Pontoise, a glass and concrete environment with man-made lakes—the perfect representation of orderly living. Finally, he has removed any extraneous characters or plotting that would divert attention from the romantic dilemmas of his main characters. In doing so, Rohmer, in this sixth and final installment of his "Comedies and Proverbs" series (begun in 1980), has created a perfectly crystal-clear, Rohmerian universe. The story is a simple comedy of manners made complex only when the characters, in their rage for chaos within the orderly Cergy-Pontoise, try to alter its form. Chaulet plays a 24-year-old, conservative-appearing, lower-level administrator of cultural affairs. She has no friends in Cergy-Pontoise until she meets Renoir, an exotic-looking, olive-skinned computer student who is a couple of years Chaulet's junior. Renoir lives a bohemian life with her live-in boy friend, Viellard. Despite the fact that she and Viellard have nothing in common—what she enjoys (dancing and partying) exhausts him, and what he enjoys (windsurfing) exhausts her—they remain together. Chaulet, on the other hand, *does* enjoy Viellard's lifestyle, though she has her eye on Gendron, a ladies' man in his early 30s who seems full of himself and his apparently impressive job at a national power company. Since this is Rohmer's world, no one really loves the person they are supposed to love. Renoir has no interest in Gendron; Gendron has no interest in Chaulet; and Chaulet has no interest in Viellard—or so they think. When Renoir makes a sudden decision to vacation at her grandparents' home (an excuse to meet a new lover), Chaulet and Viellard are pushed together. Although Viellard shows interest in Chaulet, she refuses to consummate the relationship for two reasons: Renoir is her best friend, and she still is infatuated with Gendron (she breaks down in tears after a perfectly wonderful afternoon with Viellard, because she wishes she could be as happy with Gendron). Chaulet has a problem, however, in her habit of getting tongue-tied whenever she gets the opportunity to speak to Gendron. Thinking, for a fleeting moment, that she and Viellard are meant for each other, Chaulet sleeps with him. When Renoir returns from her vacation and inquires about Chaulet's luck with Gendron, Chaulet is determined to keep her one-night rendezvous with Viellard a secret. Playing matchmaker, Renoir now intervenes in the seemingly hopeless Gendron-Chaulet courtship. In the process, *she* becomes attracted to

Gendron and sleeps with him. She too keeps her affair a secret from her best friend. At the film's end, Chaulet and Viellard are planning to vacation together, as are Renoir and Gendron. Both couples, unbeknownst to one another, plan lunches at a lakeside restaurant. Chaulet and Renoir are the first to arrive, without their respective men. Their initial discomfort leads a confession of secrets and, ultimately, to a misunderstanding (Chaulet is talking about Viellard, but Renoir thinks she is talking about Gendron) that is neatly cleared up. Gendron and Viellard both arrive at the table and the newly-formed pairs bond in even stronger friendship than before.

A fitting close to "Comedies and Proverbs"—its romantic optimism representing a new dawn for Rohmer—BOYFRIENDS AND GIRLFRIENDS is a culmination of all that has come before in the series, in which the characters themselves seem almost a combination of all the aspects of his previous characters. Sophie Renoir, for example, is some sort of amalgam of both the Arielle Dombasle and Beatrice Romand characters in LE BEAU MARIAGE. She initially appears similar to the independent and self-assured Dombasle, but gradually reveals herself to be more like the impulsive, romantically unpredictable Romand. (Curiously, she played Romand's little sister in LE BEAU MARIAGE.) Emmanuelle Chaulet's character also has elements of previous Rohmer heroines. At times she is reminiscent of Marie Riviere from SUMMER, a girl who is alone, but not necessarily lonely. At other times she is closer to Pascal Ogier's character in FULL MOON IN PARIS, caught in a problematic dichotomy—Ogier is split between two worlds (Paris and a suburb); Chaulet is split between her romantic idealization of Francois-Eric Gendron and her real love for Eric Viellard. While the previous "Comedies and Proverbs" films have ended essentially without achieving a romantic fulfillment, with the characters realizing that their quest is wrongly directed, BOYFRIENDS AND GIRLFRIENDS offers romantic bliss and a bond of friendship as a reward for the search. Here the lover's quest—no more mysterious or challenging than the quest for the Grail in Rohmer's PERCEVAL—ends in success, though the "Grail" (in this case, the perfect lover) can be found only in the place where one hasn't looked.

Not since the deceptively simple PERCEVAL (1978) has a Rohmer film been so perfectly realized and masterfully directed. Unlike some of his previous films, in which the cast was encouraged to improvise their dialog and conversations, BOYFRIENDS AND GIRLFRIENDS was written and planned entirely by Rohmer. This was not, however, done without input from his cast, especially in their youthful manner of speech. The 67-year-old Rohmer has made a working practice of spending many months getting to know his main actress—having tea, walking through the streets, visiting museums—recording their conversations as a basis for his films. The entire cast of BOYFRIENDS AND GIRLFRIENDS is superb as usual, but Chaulet is the latest Rohmer discovery to receive heaps of praise. Previously unseen in films, she is remarkable as she invisibly shifts from a conservative, cautious young woman to a woman as impulsive as her best friend, becoming more and more radiant as the film progresses and her passion emerges. Released last year in Paris and shown in late 1987 at the New York Film Festival before getting a theatrical release in the summer of 1988. (In French, English subtitles.) (Sexual situations.)

p, Margaret Menegoz; d, Eric Rohmer; w, Eric Rohmer; ph, Bernard Lutic; ed, Maria Luisa Garcia; m, Jean-Louis Valero.

Comedy/Drama (PR:A MPAA:PG)

BRADDOCK: MISSING IN ACTION III* (1988) 103m Golan-Globus/Cannon c

Chuck Norris (*Col. James Braddock*), Aki Aleong (*Gen. Quoc*), Roland Harrah III (*Van Tan Cang*), Miki Kim (*Lin Tan Cang*), Yehuda Efroni (*Rev. Polanski*), Ron Barker (*Mik*), Jack Rader (*Littlejohn*), Floyd Levine (*Gen. Duncan*), Melinda Betron (*Thuy*), Richard Pietro, Jan Schultz (*CIA Agents*), Keith David (*Embassy Gate Captain*), Robert Jocchiem (*Embassy Guard*), Thuy Lin Samora (*Embassy Secretary*), Pita Liboro (*Lin's Friend*), Jeff Habberstad, Howard Jackson (*U.S. Helicopter Pilots*).

Chuck Norris is back in Indochina for the third time, singlehandedly avenging the American defeat and rescuing a bunch of Amerasian children to boot. The film opens with a surprisingly effective re-creation of the fall of Saigon, as Marines hold off swarms of Vietnamese civilians from the US Embassy and helicopters evacuate

© CANNON

American personnel and Vietnamese employees and dependents. Norris arrives by helicopter and goes out into the strife-torn streets to find his Vietnamese wife, Kim, who is across town packing her bags. Just after she leaves, a bomb destroys the building, killing the friend to whom Kim has given a bracelet. Norris arrives a moment later, sees the charred body with the bracelet, and assumes Kim is dead. Meanwhile, Kim loses her passport when her bag is stolen en route to the embassy and is refused entrance. After returning to the US compound, Norris is wounded preventing some undeserving Vietnamese from climbing aboard a chopper and is put on the helicopter and evacuated. The story then picks up 13 years later with Norris drinking in a Washington, D.C., bar when a Polish priest tells him that he is a missionary in Vietnam who cares for Amerasian children and that Norris' wife is alive and has a son. At first Norris refuses to believe him, but when he is summoned to CIA headquarters and officially told not to believe the man, he knows it is all true. Sooner than you can say "One Man Army," Norris is flying into Vietnam, where the priest leads him to his wife and son (Harrah), who has long since given up ever seeing his father. Norris takes the pair to a boat he has hidden, but there they are confronted by soldiers under Aleong's command who shoot Kim on the spot and take Norris and Harrah to dungeons to be tortured. However, Norris manages to overpower his guards, and after he frees his son, the two head for the mission. Aleong anticipates this move and takes all of the mission children into captivity, including Harrah and the priest, while Norris watches from the jungle. The children are taken to another camp, and Norris stages a single-handed attack to free them, killing dozens of enemy soldiers. A long chase through the jungle then ensues, during which Aleong periodically cackles, "Now I've got you, Braddock." At the Thai border (notwithstanding the fact that Vietnam and Thailand share no border), another battle takes place, with American soldiers looking on, itching to take part. Aleong hovers overhead in a helicopter virtually screaming his "I've got you" line while Norris, badly wounded, has his gun lifted by Harrah. A burst kills the pilot, Aleong crashes to his death, and Norris leads the children over the bridge to freedom.

It is useless to try to relate BRADDOCK: MISSING IN ACTION III to any sort of reality except the disappointment some Americans still feel over the loss of the Vietnam War, so the only context in which to examine it is that of war films in general. As such it fails miserably. Norris is unquestionably the most wooden leading man to grace the screen since Victor Mature, and nothing is more boring than an invincible hero. Roland Harrah III is annoying in the way that only child actors can be, and the only three emotions he experiences—resentment, fear, and unbridled admiration—are exhibited in exactly that order, with no gradations between them. The only performance worth noting is that of Aki Aleong, who seems to have stepped right out of the most xenophobic, anti-Japanese WW II films. He appears to appreciate the irony of his role, however, and hams it up to the hilt, puncturing the incredible sense of self-importance that pervades the film, which concludes with a title stating that 15,000 children of American servicemen are still in Vietnam. This is a real issue, but BRADDOCK fails to address it, offering only invasion as a solution. Songs include "Freedom Again", "In Your Eyes" (Ron Bloom, performed by Bloom).

p, Menahem Golan, Yoram Globus; d, Aaron Norris; w, James Bruner, Chuck Norris (based on characters created by Arthur Silver, Larry Levinson, Steve Bing); ph, Joao Fernandes (Rank Color); ed, Michael J. Duthie, Ken Bornstein; m, Jay Chattaway; m/l, Ron Bloom; prod d, Ladislav Wilheim; art d, Rodell Cruz; set d, Pia Fernandez; spec eff, Danny Dominguez; cos, Tamy Mor; stunts, Dean Ferrandini, Renato Morado, Gil Arceo; makeup, Ilona Bobak, Tony Artieda.

Action **Cas.** **(PR:O MPAA:R)**

BRAIN DAMAGE½** (1988) 87m Henenlotter/Ievins/Palisades c

Rick Herbst *(Brian)*, Gordon MacDonald *(Mike)*, Jennifer Lowry *(Barbara)*, Theo Barnes *(Morris Ackerman)*, Lucille Saint-Peter *(Martha Ackerman)*, Vicki Darnell *(Blonde in Hell Club)*, Kevin Van Hentenryck *(Man with Basket)*, Joe Gonzales *(Guy in Shower)*, Bradlee Rhodes *(Night Watchman)*, Michael Bishop *(Toilet Victim)*, Beverly Downer *(Neighbor)*, Ari Roussimoff *(Biker)*, Michael Rubenstein *(Bum in Alley)*, Angel Figueroa *(Junkie)*, John Reichert *(Policeman)*, Don Henenlotter *(Policeman)*, Kenneth Packard, Artemis Pizzaro *(Subway Riders)*, Slam Wedgehouse *(Mohawked Punk)*.

Frank Henenlotter's first film since the cult favorite BASKET CASE (1982) is another grotesque "boy and his parasite" tale. Herbst is a nice young man who lives in a New York City apartment with his brother, MacDonald. His life is changed when a 1,000-year-old brain-eating parasite named Elmer slithers into his room. Elmer is the pet of Herbst's elderly next-door neighbors, Barnes and Saint-Peter, who keep the creature in their bathtub. More particularly, Elmer is an Alymer—a talking parasite that injects its hosts with a blue fluid that causes pleasant hallucinations. Because the hosts become addicted to the drug, Elmer is able to manipulate and use them to catch humans, whose brains the parasite eats. However, by feeding Elmer a steady diet of cattle brains, the old couple has managed to keep it weak and docile. Unfortunately, Elmer escapes and wriggles into Herbst's brain. As Herbst becomes addicted to Elmer's blue fluid, his brother and girl friend begin to notice radical shifts in his personality. Herbst goes on nocturnal jaunts with Elmer, during which the parasite attacks and sucks the brains out of assorted security guards, punk rockers, and flop-house tenants. Because he is experiencing drug-induced hallucinations, Herbst has no memory of the killings. Eventually, though, he realizes what is happening and tries to go cold turkey, but a confident Elmer sits in the sink and taunts him, knowing that Herbst will return to him because of the lure of the drug. What Elmer does not foresee, however, is that his former owners desperately want him back. This leads to a climactic confrontation between the old couple and Herbst. Unfortunately for Herbst, their attack occurs just as Elmer is giving the boy a dose of the drug. The couple's attempt to dislodge Elmer causes the parasite to inject a huge amount of the soup into Herbst's brain, and an ugly, pulsating tumor forms on his forehead. Meanwhile, Elmer sucks the brains of the old couple, but not before Barnes manages to squeeze the parasite to death. Suffering from a psychedelic overdose, Herbst stumbles off to his apartment, where he tries to kill himself by putting a gun to the tumor. When he pulls the trigger, a brilliant shaft of white light explodes out of Herbst's head—literally blowing his mind.

As in BASKET CASE, director Henenlotter combines some disturbing gore with an offbeat sense of humor that makes the entire disgusting exercise a bit more palatable. In fact, the little parasite Elmer is the most engaging character in the film. With his lines spoken by an uncredited actor, Elmer is an arrogant little slug whose soothing, measured tones prove very persuasive to anyone in his reach. Like a drug dealer snaring schoolchildren, Elmer seduces Herbst into accepting him. Giving the victim a taste of the drug for free and then moving in for the kill, Elmer makes a junkie out of Herbst. The most haunting scene in the entire film is a uneasy combination of horror and laughs as Herbst lies writhing on the floor trying to go cold turkey while Elmer sits in the sink and happily sings the Tommy Dorsey hit "Elmer's Tune." Henenlotter is a master at combining the horrid with the grimly humorous. One of Elmer's attacks is on a horny punk girl who has picked up Herbst in a nightclub. Eager for some quick sex, the girl ushers Herbst onto the roof, where she bends down and unzips his pants, only to have Elmer fly out and enter her brain through her open mouth. Although, in interviews, Henenlotter has vigorously denied a conscious "Say No to Sex and Drugs" subtext, it is evident throughout the film and impossible to ignore. In addition to the queasily funny scenes, there are also some out-and-out comedy bits, such as the scene in which Herbst and Elmer share a bath, and Henenlotter's hilarious *hommage* to himself, wherein Kevin Van Hentenryck, the star of BASKET CASE, with wicker basket in tow, takes a seat on the subway opposite the crazed Herbst and engages him in a wild-eyed stare-down.

Reportedly shot on a comparatively large budget ($2 million here, only $35,000 for BASKET CASE), BRAIN DAMAGE retains the cheap, seedy look of Henenlotter's previous effort. Although $2 million is paltry by Hollywood standards, for an independent filmmaker like Henenlotter it's a king's ransom. Unfortunately, the money really doesn't appear to be on screen. Elmer, for instance, is a rather crude-looking cable-controlled puppet. Luckily, Elmer's hokey design works in the film's favor and adds to the little monster's charm. As was the case with BASKET CASE, the cast is uniformly weak and the production values are nil. Compared with what John Waters did with 2 million dollars on HAIRSPRAY, one has to wonder where the money went on BRAIN DAMAGE. With his only two films sharing incredibly similar plots, one also wonders where Henenlotter—a filmmaker with a distinct and disturbing vision—will go next. *(Graphic violence, gore effects, adult situations, sexual situations, nudity, profanity.)*

p, Edgar Ievins; d, Frank Henenlotter; w, Frank Henenlotter; ph, Bruce Torbet (TVC Color); ed, James Y. Kwei, Frank Henenlotter; m, Gus Russo, Clutch Reiser; m/l, J. Calder, A. Buston, J.F. Garnett, B. Elsey, B.B. Burton, Elmer Albrecht, Sammy Gallop, Dick Jurgens; art d, Ivy Rosovsky; set d, Charles Bennett; spec eff, Al Magliochetti; makeup, Gabe Bartalos, Daniel Frye.

Horror **Cas.** **(PR:O MPAA:R)**

BRAVESTARR † (1988) 91m Filmation/Taurus c

Voices of: Charlie Adler, Susan Blu, Pat Fraley.

Filmmation, the animation studio that gave the syndicated television world "He Man and the Masters of the Universe," produced this new animated feature, which saw limited theatrical release before beating a hasty retreat to the home video shelves. Set in a science-fiction universe where high technology is combined with the icons of the Old West, the film features a cowboy named BraveStarr who must save planet New Texas from the villainous Stampede, a sci-fi cattle baron, and his enforcer, Tex Hex, who are determined to rule the universe. Together with his trusted companions Thirty-Thirty (a robot horse), J.B. (a lady judge), sidekick Deputy Fuzz, and mystic mentor Shaman, BraveStarr does battle with the forces of evil. Lackluster television-style animation and obvious borrowing from sources as diverse as "Gunsmoke" and STAR WARS conspired to make this a failure at the box office.

p, Lou Scheimer; d, Tom Tataranowicz; w, Bob Forward, Steve Hayes; ph, F.T. Ziegler (CFI color); ed, Ludmilla Saskova; m, Frank W. Becker; art d, John Grusd; anim, Brett Hisey.

Animation/Science Fiction **Cas.** **(PR:NR MPAA:PG)**

BRIGHT LIGHTS, BIG CITY½** (1988) 110m Mirage/MGM-UA c

Michael J.Fox *(Jamie Conway)*, Kiefer Sutherland *(Tad Allagash)*, Phoebe Cates *(Amanda)*, Swoosie Kurtz *(Megan)*, Frances Sternhagen *(Clara Tillinghast)*, Tracy Pollan *(Vicky)*, John Houseman *(Mr. Vogel)*, Charlie Schlatter *(Michael)*, Jason Robards, Jr. *(Alex Hardy)*, David Warrilow *(Rittenhouse)*, Dianne Wiest *(Mother)*, Alec Mapa *(Yasu Wade)*, William Hickey *(Ferret Man)*, Gina Belafonte *(Kathy)*, Sam Robards *(Rich Vanier)*, Zette *(Stevie)*, Marika Blossfeldt *(Bald Girl)*, Jessica Lundy *(Theresa)*, Kelly Lynch *(Elaine)*, Peter Boyden *(Maitre d')*, Annabelle Gurwitch *(Barbara)*, Russell Horton *(Walter Tyler)*, Peter Maloney *(Waiter)*, Maria Pitillo *(Pony-Tail Girl)*, Susan Traylor *(Leather Lady)*, Michael Fischetti *(Mannequin Craftsman)*, Mike Badalucco *(Policeman)*, David Hyde Pierce *(Bartender at Fashion Show)*, Jim Babchak *(Bartender at Disco)*, Peg Murray *(Receptionist)*, Barbara Rucker *(Elegant Lady)*, Pat Santino *(Security Guard)*, Mike Bacarella *(Bakery Man)*, Josie Bell, Anne Bezamat, Alva Chinn, Dianne DeWitt, Nathalie Gabrielli, Jennifer Houser, Lynn Howland, Sheila Johnson, Melanie Landestoy, Marisol Massey, Isabelle, Andrea Sande, Maud, Maria Von Hartz, Joko Zohrer (*Runway Models*).

Published in 1984, Jay McInerney's *Bright Lights, Big City* became the novel of choice for the hipeoisie; favorably compared with *The Catcher in the Rye* and *The Sun Also Rises*, it was hailed as the chronicle of a new lost generation. After a troubled production odyssey that took the property through two studios, three directors, and five screenwriters, this story of cocaine-fueled yuppie angst finally came to the screen burdened with the mantle of "THE GRADUATE of the 80s."

The novel's nameless protagonist is played here by Fox and given a name, Jamie. By day, would-be novelist Fox is a fact checker for *Gotham* magazine (*The New Yorker* cloaked in the thinnest of veils); by night, he prowls chic, pulsing Manhattan dance clubs, often in the company of preppy wastrel Sutherland, and almost always enlivened by healthy doses of "Bolivian Marching Powder" (Fox's euphemism for cocaine). Unable to pull his life out of the LOST WEEKEND-like tailspin it entered when his wife (Cates) left him to pursue her modeling career, Fox has incurred the wrath of Sternhagen, the schoolmarmish head of the fact checking department. Kurtz, a maternal coworker, does her best to watch over him, but when Fox is faced with an impossible deadline on a poorly researched story, there isn't much she or he can do to save his job. In an act of revenge, Fox and Sutherland take a ferret to Sternhagen's office at night, but the scheme backfires and Robards, the alcoholic fiction editor, becomes their victim. In the meantime, Cates has returned from Paris, accompanied by her new photographer boy friend, and Fox disrupts a fashion show in which she appears. Schlatter, Fox's younger brother, comes looking for him: It is nearly one year since the death of their mother (Wiest), periodically shown in flashback, and Fox still hasn't come to terms with his sense of loss. Throughout the film he follows the plight of an unborn child the tabloids have dubbed the "Coma Baby," the symbolic representation of his own arrested emotional existence. Eventually Fox meets Pollan, Sutherland's Princeton graduate student cousin, whom Fox is able to relate to even without the aid of a cocaine buzz. Later, Fox encounters Cates at a party, and though she hasn't spoken with him since she left him, she can only say, "How are you?" Sent into hysterics by the absurdity of it all, Fox suddenly has blood cascading from his coke-blown nostrils. After telephoning Pollan to tell her that his mother died, Fox leaves the party as day is breaking, trades his sunglasses for some fresh-baked bread, and prepares to take on the rest of his life.

BRIGHT LIGHTS, BIG CITY isn't THE GRADUATE of the 80s; however, it is an entertaining film that shouldn't disappoint fans of the book. In remaining faithful to the novel, director-coscreenwriter James Bridges has refused to allow his film to become the kind of sanitized "Say No to Drugs" spot that 1987's would-be GRADUATE, LESS THAN ZERO, became. Bridges realized that without his cocaine habit, McInerney's protagonist would be both considerably less complex and significantly less representative of the lifestyle the book captured. Deserted by his picture-perfect wife, fired from his status-lending job, McInerney's antihero is left without meaning in his life, and coke, instead of alleviating his problems, drags him down further until he sees that the only way out is out. Were it not for the winning quality that Michael J. Fox brings to Jamie, it would be difficult to empathize with a character who dwells so extravagantly in self-pity, but because Fox is so likable, his crash-dive seems undeserved. Fox conveys an appropriately wired quality as well, and his performance is assured and believable throughout the film. Kiefer Sutherland is also convincing as Tad Allagash—self-centered, dissipated, and snobbish, but still communicating genuine affection for Fox. Phoebe Cates, though given next to nothing to do, is nonetheless perfectly *cast* as Fox's mannequin of a wife. Swoozie Kurtz is suitably maternal and sympathetic as Fox's coworker and Frances Sternhagen is wonderfully prim, but the film's best performance is by Jason Robards, who, despite his limited screentime, delivers a full-blown portrayal of literary lion who has lost his teeth.

Bridges directs the film in a straightforward, craftsmanlike fashion that serves the narrative well, but that, unfortunately, doesn't lend the material a particularly cinematic quality. That the film is as polished and solid as it is, however, is no small accomplishment, given its tempestuous production history. After originating at Columbia, where Joel Schumacher was to direct from a McInerney screenplay with Tom Cruise as star, the project moved to United Artists, for whom Mark Rosenberg and Sidney Pollack agreed to produce, hiring Joyce Chopra (SMOOTH TALK) to direct. Chopra's agent also happened to represent Fox, and after he decided to become involved with the project, it was transformed from a low-budget effort to a major studio undertaking with a budget in excess of $15 million. Working from a script written by Chopra's husband, Tom Cole, the production began location shooting in New York, but 20 days into the shoot, studio executives began getting nervous. The Directors Guild of America's contract was to expire on June 30, with a strike threatened, and Fox had to be back in LA by mid-July to begin work on his last season of TV's "Family Ties." Chopra was fired, she claims because the studio didn't like the movie she was making. Publicly, United Artists contended that the situation demanded a veteran at the helm if the picture was to be completed by the end of June, but privately there were rumblings that Chopra was in over her head.

In either case, Bridges, who earned Oscar nominations for his screenplays for THE CHINA SYNDROME and THE PAPER CHASE, took over on the stipulation that he could scrap all of the film Chopra shot and start from scratch. After reading all of the existing scripts, Bridges holed up in a New York hotel room for seven days and completed a screenplay that was more faithful to the novel than even McInerney's first effort. Although Bridges kept much of the crew that had begun the project, he replaced cinematographer James Glennon with Gordon Willis (the "GODFATHER" films, MANHATTAN) and made some changes in the cast. (In the Chopra version, the Kurtz and Pollan roles were combined into one character, played by Megan Mully. Bridges also replaced Shirley Knight with Frances Sternhagen, and brought in John Houseman.) Working closely with McInerney, Bridges finished his shoot in a remarkable 36 days on June 29, adding no more than $300,000 to the budget. Ironically, the feared DGA strike never occurred. Bridges and McInerney both affixed their names to the screenplay, but the Writers Guild of America ruled that Bridges had not contributed enough to receive credit. He has, however, appealed their deci-

sion. Two endings were shot for the film. The one that didn't make it into the final version featured a flash forward to Fox sitting at his typewriter, where he has just finished writing a novel called *Bright Lights, Big City*. (*Substance abuse, profanity, sexual situations*.)

p, Marc Rosenberg, Sydney Pollack; d, James Bridges; w, Jay McInerney (based on his novel); ph, Gordon Willis (DuArt); ed, John Bloom; m, Donald Fagen, Robert Mounsey; m/l, Shannon Dawson, G. "Love" Jay, Martyn Young, Steve Young, New Order, Stephen Hague, Bryan Ferry, Prince, M.L. Gore, Oliver Leiber, Narada Michael Walden, Jeffrey Cohen, Jennifer Hall, Alan Tarney, Donald Fagen, Timothy Meher, Jimmy Reed; prod d, Santo Loquasto; art d, Thomas Warren; set d, George DeTitta; cos, Bernie Pollack; makeup, Bernadette Mazur.

Drama   Cas.   (PR:O MPAA:R)

BROKEN VICTORY †   (1988) 79m Carstens-Smith/Double Helix c

Jeannette Clift (*Sarah Taylor*), Ken Letner (*Matthew Taylor*), Jon Sharp (*Colonel*), Jonathan Turner Smith (*Joshua Taylor*), John Shepherd (*Kevin Taylor*), Bonnie Hawley (*Elizabeth*), Elias McCabe (*Nathanael*), Cheryl Slean (*Miriam*), Gerald Sharp (*Johnson*), Michael Conn (*Ben*), Jeff Kemnitz (*Gregory*), Gary Ballard (*Jeff*).

This futuristic cautionary tale, told from the Christian perspective, concerns a new world leader who declares that peace and prosperity can only exist if citizens will renounce their religious beliefs. While the vast majority capitulates, those who refuse are shoved into ghettos, where they are forced to wear gray uniforms and do hard labor. Despite the efforts of an evil colonel (Sharp) to force them to reject their faith, the Taylor family, led by Clift, steadfastly refuses and must suffer the consequences. No evidence of a theatrical release in 1988, the film will no doubt find life on home video.

p, David Carstens, Jonathan Smith; d, Gregory Strom; w, Jonathan Smith, Gregory Strom (based on a story by Jonathan Smith); ph, Brett Webster, David Carstens; ed, Pat Edmondson; m, Tom Howard; prod d, Heather Roseborough; art d, Paul Kinike; set d, Susan Strom; cos, Diana Creekmore.

Science Fiction   (PR:NR MPAA:NR)

BULL DURHAM*½   (1988) 108m Mount/Orion c

Kevin Costner (*Crash Davis*), Susan Sarandon (*Annie Savoy*), Tim Robbins (*Ebby Calvin* "*Nuke*" *LaLoosh*), Trey Wilson (*Joe* "*Skip*" *Riggins*), Robert Wuhl (*Larry Hockett*), Jenny Robertson (*Millie*), Max Patkin (*Himself*), William O'Leary (*Jimmy*), David Neidorf (*Bobby*), Danny Gans (*Deke*), Tom Silardi (*Tony*), Lloyd T. Williams (*Mickey*), Rick Marzan (*Jose*), George Buck (*Nuke's Father*), Carey "Garland" Bunting (*Teddy*), Greg Avelone (*Doc*), Robert Dickman (*Whitey*), Timothy Kirk (*Ed*), Don Davis (*Scared Batter*), Stephen Ware (*Abused Umpire*), Tobi Eshelman (*Bat Boy*), C.K. Bibby (*Mayor*), Henry G. Sanders (*Sandy*), Antoinette Forsyth (*Ballpark Announcer*), Shirley Anne Ritter (*Cocktail Waitress*), Pete Bock (*Minister*), Alan Mejia (*Chu Chu*), Sid Aikens, Craig Brown, Wes Currin, Butch Davis, Paul Devlin, Jeff Greene, Kelly Heath, Mo Johnson, Todd Kopeznski, John Lovingood, Eddie Matthews, Alan Paternoster, Bill Robinson, Dean Robinson, Tom Shultz, Sam Veraldi, El Chico Williams (*Baseball Players*).

©ORION

Featuring outstanding lead performances by Kevin Costner, Susan Sarandon, and Tim Robbins, a witty, literate script, and an insider's familiarity with life around minor league baseball, BULL DURHAM is both one of the best films ever made about the national pastime and a charming romantic comedy. Sarandon is the No. 1 fan of the Class A Durham Bulls of the Carolina League. No mere groupie, this part-time college English instructor approaches the game as a religion she practices every summer by choosing one of the most promising Bulls to be her student in the art of lovemaking, as well as in metaphysics and literature. This season she has narrowed the field to Robbins, a flamboyant bonus baby pitcher "with a million-dollar arm and a five-cent head," and Costner, a worldly catcher with 12 minor league seasons under his belt. Costner has been brought in by the organization to tame the wild Robbins, whose 90-mile-an-hour-plus fastball is as likely to hit the Bulls' mascot as it is to find the strike zone. Though clearly intrigued by Sarandon, Costner has no desire to compete with a *boy* for her affection. Sarandon, for her part, is attracted to the intellectually *sympatico* Costner, but, fearing commitment, she latches onto the callow hot shot instead. She introduces Robbins to Walt Whitman, bondage, and Mayan mysticism, points out a glitch in his pitching motion, and persuades him to wear a garter belt while on the mound, all in the interest of getting him to the big leagues. Costner works towards the same end, recognizing that Robbins has been blessed with the gift of a major-league arm. The catcher hasn't been so lucky, and though he has learned the game inside out, he has only been to "the show" (the majors) once, for 21 days that he still savors. He knows that Robbins has the physical ability to do what he can't, and sets about preparing Robbins mentally, teaching him not to think when he's pitching and not to worry about failing, providing him with a battery of sure-fire cliches to use with the press when he does make it. Robbins hits his stride, and before long is called up to the big club, but when he leaves Costner is given his release. Costner and Sarandon finally give in to their mutual attraction and make near nonstop love until Costner disappears suddenly, determined to finish out the season with another club so that he can break the record for career minor league home runs. After breaking the record, he returns to Sarandon, contemplating a future as a manager but determined just to exist and think about nothing for a while.

Working from his own screenplay, first-time director Ron Shelton—who wrote THE BEST OF TIMES and cowrote UNDER FIRE—has concocted a delightful romantic comedy that will charm even those who have no real interest in baseball. For baseball fans the pleasure is even greater, as Shelton, who spent five years toiling in the Baltimore Orioles farm system as a second baseman, suffuses his film with carefully realized details that brilliantly evoke the bush leagues. The uniforms and the stadiums are right; the players look and move like baseball players, not actors. Likewise, the emotions in Shelton's story have a ring of truth that echoes throughout the film, even if his characters are a trifle contrived and occasionally given to the kind of deft repartee that comes more easily in screwball comedies than in life. When Costner delivers his off-the-cuff speech detailing what he believes in ("that Lee Harvey Oswald acted alone, that the novels of Susan Sontag are self-indulgent, that there should be a constitutional amendment outlawing astroturf, and in deep, warm, wet kisses that last three days"), we know that this isn't the way people normally talk, but, like Sarandon, we are wowed just the same, caught up in a magical moment that promises that Costner's Crash Davis is no more your average ball player than Sarandon is your run-of-the-mill "Baseball Annie." Shelton has not stumbled into the wholly unbelievable universe of THE SLUGGER'S WIFE (1985), nor is he striving for the fairy tale quality that made THE NATURAL (1984) so winning. Instead, he uses his magical moments to illuminate the lives of his interesting and real characters. At its root, BULL DURHAM is about growing up, and by the film's end Sarandon and Costner have come to a self-awareness that is informed by their baseball experiences but that ultimately transcends it.

En route to its existential conclusion Shelton's film delivers laugh after rich laugh, due as much to his wonderful script (derived from his 1979 screenplay "A Player to Be Named Later") as to the extraordinary performances by the three leads. Sarandon sizzles as the woman who has built a shrine to baseball (with Thurman Munson's photograph as its centerpiece) and whose bed becomes a classroom. As familiar with William Blake as she is with Fernando Valenzuela and as smart as she is sexy, Sarandon's Annie may not be allowed actually to don a uniform, but she certainly leaves her mark on the game she knows as well as any of the men who play it. She and Costner make a terrific pairing, and BULL DURHAM is an extremely sexy movie that uses humor and sexual tension, bared souls rather than bared bodies, to turn up heat. Finally given a role that allows him to act rather than behave, Costner (THE UNTOUCHABLES; NO WAY OUT) delivers the best performance of his career. A one-time high school shortstop, he is not only obviously athletic but, swinging, running, and hitting with authority, he is also convincing as a professional baseball player. Costner (who turned down roles in two other sports films, EIGHT MEN OUT and EVERYBODY'S ALL-AMERICAN) wastes none of the wonderful smart-ass lines Shelton has given him; even the odd behind-the-plate laugh he comes up with is on the mark. Among the film's funniest moments are his mound conferences with Robbins after the pitcher has shaken off his signs and Costner has responded by telling the opposing batter what the next pitch will be, resulting in a home run ("Anything that flies that far should have a stewardess on it," quips Costner). Mixing bus-weary cynicism with undying romanticism, pie-eyed romping with a profound respect for the game, Costner is alternately hilarious and touching as the man who has spent his adulthood playing a boy's game and who, realizing his limitations, gives up his dream. Robbins (FIVE CORNERS) is also outstanding. More than just a necessary foil, he makes Nuke an equal partner in the love triangle (at least initially), investing his unsophisticated bonus baby with the right mixture of brashness, immaturity, randiness, and, eventually, humility on his way to the big leagues. Trey Wilson (RAISING ARIZONA) as the manager and Robert Wuhl (GOOD MORNING, VIETNAM) as the chatterbox coach also contribute fine performances, and Max Patkin, "the Clown Prince of Baseball," reprises some of antics he's used to delight baseball crowds for more than 40 years.

BULL DURHAM features plenty of on-field action, and Shelton uses the camera unobtrusively but skillfully to keep the ballplaying interesting—no mean trick. The diamond action was filmed at El Toro Field, the home of the real-life Durham Bulls (co-owned by the film's producer, Thom Mount), a Class A farm team for the Atlanta Braves. Though dealing with the summer game, BULL DURHAM was filmed much later in the year, so the performers are only *acting* as if they are warm. Few, however, will be left cold by BULL DURHAM. *(Sexual situations, profanity.)*

p, Thom Mount, Mark Burg; d, Ron Shelton; w, Ron Shelton; ph, Bobby Byrne (DeLuxe color); ed, Robert Leighton, Adam Weiss; m, Michael Convertino; m/l, John Fogerty, Jimmy DeKnight, Max Friedman, Harry Woods, Jimmy Campbell, Reg Connelly, William E. Ward, Rose Marks, Jeff "Skunk" Baxter, Pat DiNizio,

George Thorogood, Pat McLaughlin, Phil Everly, Gina Schock, Vance DeGeneres, Bennie Wallace, Ike Turner, Edith Piaf, Dave Alvin, Max Rebennack "Dr. John", C. Dumont, M. Vaucaire; prod d, Armin Ganz; art d, David Lubin; set d, Kris Boxell; cos, Louise Frogley; makeup, Cynthia Barr.

Comedy	Cas.	(PR:O MPAA:R)

BULLETPROOF zero   (1988) 94m Cinetel-Virgin c

Gary Busey (*Frank "Bulletproof" McBain*), Darlanne Fluegel (*Lt. Devon Shepard*), Henry Silva (*Col. Kartiff*), Juan Fernandez (*Pantoro*), Rene Enriquez (*Gen. Brogado*), Thalmus Rasulala (*Billy Dunbar*), L.Q. Jones (*Sgt. O'Rourke*), Mills Watson (*Colby*), James Andronica (*Agent Tarpley*), R.G. Armstrong (*Miles Blackburn*), William Smith (*Russian Major*), Luke Askew (*Gen. Gallo*), Lincoln Kilpatrick (*Capt. Briggs*), Lydie Denier (*Tracy*), Ramon Franco (*Camilo*), Jorge Cevera, Jr. (*Hermano*), Lucy Lee Flippen (*Sister Mary*), Redmond M. Glesson (*Father Riley*), Ken Medlock (*Jack Benson*), Don Pike (*Montoya*), Danny Trejo (*Sharkey*), Gray Fredrickson (*Border Guard*), Arnold Diaz (*lst Dude*), Drew Fischer (*2nd Dude*), Ron Shipp (*lst Paramedic*), Laura Crosson (*2nd Paramedic*), Christopher Doyle (*Duvail*), Bobbie Cummings, James Haley, Perry Blackburn (*Soldiers*), Frank Holtry (*Russian Lieutenant*), Gary Pike (*1st Guerilla*), Brad Orrison (*2nd Guerilla*).

© CINETEL

In BULLETPROOF, Busey plays individualistic LA cop Frank "Bulletproof" McBain, so called because he's pulled 37 bullets out of himself over the years. An ex-CIA agent who retired after his partner was shot, Busey now brings his expertise to the streets, where he shoots up would-be arms dealers. At a secret Pentagon briefing, it's revealed that a multinational terrorist group, The People's Liberation Army, has established a base just across the Mexican border. A raid is staged with a top secret assault vehicle, Thunderblast, headed by Busey's former girl friend, Fluegel. The raid goes awry, and Fluegel and others are taken prisoner by terrorists Silva and Enriquez. However, it turns out the whole thing is a setup to lure Busey out of retirement. He duly parachutes into Mexico, but is taken captive before he can live up to his eponymous nickname. Tied to a giant wooden spool, Busey is saved from execution when Fluegel throws a grenade and he conveniently rolls out of the scene. Busey then ambushes the convoy transporting Thunderblast, and he and Fluegel use the vehicle (whose huge insides don't match its small exterior) to destroy the terrorist camp and a few Russian helicopters. When Busey comes face to face with the Russian commander, Smith, he recognizes him as his partner's assassin and kills him. He and Fluegel then head back across the border.

Director Steve Carver, who was responsible for the Chuck Norris films AN EYE FOR AN EYE and LONE WOLF McQUADE, here shows little flair for action sequences, allowing the picture to flounder from scene to scene. Gary Busey is no better. He has shown that he can play volatile, daredevil characters (as in LETHAL WEAPON), but here all he can muster are sheepish, embarrassed looks toward the camera. Everyone concerned gets buried alive in a wash of shoddy sets, one-dimensional characters, and implausible plot twists. BULLETPROOF barely saw a theatrical run in 1987, going straight to the video market. *(Violence, sexual situations, profanity.)*

p, Paul Hertzberg, Neil C. Lundell; d, Steve Carver; w, Steve Carver, T.L. Lankford (based on a story by T.L. Lankford, Fred Olen Ray); ph, Francis Grumman (United color); ed, Jeff Freeman; m, Tom Chase, Steve Rucker; prod d, Adrian H. Gorton; art d, Monette Goldman, Gary Tolby; set d, Cosmas Demetriou; spec eff, Roger George; cos, Fred Long; stunts, Don Pike; makeup, Carla Fabrizi.

Action/Adventure	Cas.	(PR:O MPAA:R)

BUSTER**½   (1988, Brit.) 102m Hemdale-The Movie Group-NFH/Tri-Star c

Phil Collins (*Buster Edwards*), Julie Walters (*June Edwards*), Larry Lamb (*Bruce Reynolds*), Stephanie Lawrence (*Franny Reynolds*), Ellen Beaven (*Nicky Edwards*), Michael Attwell (*Harry*), Ralph Brown (*Ronnie*), Christopher Ellison (*George*), Sheila Hancock (*Mrs. Rothery*), Martin Jarvis (*Inspector Jack Mitchell*), Clive Wood

(*Sgt. Chalmers*), Anthony Quayle (*Sir James McDowell*), Michael Byrne (*Poyser*), Harold Innocent (*Justice Parry*), Rupert Vansittart (*Fairclough*), John Benfield (*Jimmy*), John Barrard (*Walter*), Carole Collins (*Linda*), Amy Shindler (*Susan*), David Shindler (*David*), Tony Collins (*Taxi Driver*), Jonathan McKenna, Vincenzo Nicoli, Timothy Davies, Roger McKern, David Arlen, Frank Ellis, Bill Rourke, Ian Lowe, Christopher Gray (*Gang Members*), Alan Cowan (*Fireman*), James Donnelly (*Rent Man*), Stewart Harwood (*Chip Shop Owner*), Graham Lines (*Vicar*), Pauline Little (*Sally*), Jean Ainslie (*Post Office Lady*), John Patrick (*Seaman*), Jessica Green (*Mandy*), Evangelina Sosa (*Maria*), Francisco Morales (*Mexican Doctor*), Martin Lasalle (*Mexican Waiter*), Rodolpho De Alexandra (*Market Stallholder*), Sergio Calderon (*Fruit Seller*), Yolanda Vazquez (*Hospital Receptionist*), Alvara Carcano (*Boat Captain*).

Small-time crook Buster Edwards refers to himself as "the lucky thief," because he's been plying his trade for years but has only spent two weeks in jail for his transgressions. As BUSTER opens in London, 1963, we watch the lucky Edwards (played by rock star Collins) pilfer clothing, toys for his baby daughter, and flowers for his wife, June (Walters). The couple are deeply in love and very happily married, although Walters, tired of hiding from the rent collector, wishes her husband would get a real job and bring some normalcy to their lives. Instead, Collins falls in with a group of big-thinking thieves and plays a role in Britain's Great Train Robbery, in which 15 hijackers made off with 2.6 million pounds ($7.3 million back then) stolen from the London to Glasgow Royal Mail Train. Collins and family go into hiding, but it isn't long before the police are identifying and arresting gang members. The thieves have been given almost folk hero status by the press, which government officials find inexcusable. To make an example of the convicted robbers, the prosecution asks for and gets stiff prison sentences of up to 30 years. It's getting hotter for Collins, and he departs for Mexico, where the gang's leader (Lamb) is already hiding out. Walters and daughter follow shortly thereafter, but the lifelong Londoners are soon overwhelmed by culture shock, finding Mexico a nightmare. Though they have plenty of money, Walters misses the food and weather of home, and hates the way the natives can't understand a word she says. When she is unable to get what she considers proper medical care for her daughter, Walters can't take it any longer and heads back to London with the child, and, although he knows it means certain capture, Collins misses his family so much that he too returns home. He is soon arrested, convicted, and sentenced to 15 years in prison. He is paroled after serving nine years of his sentence, and as the film ends, he's a London street vendor selling flowers.

Loosely based on the story of real-life Great Train Robber Edwards, BUSTER features strong performances from its two leads. Though Phil Collins hadn't acted for years until he was invited to play struggling con man "Phil the Shill" in an episode of "Miami Vice," BUSTER's director, David Green, saw the episode and decided Collins would be perfect in the title role. Collins is indeed funny and appealing as the working-class thief who views crime simply as a way to make a living and support his family. Costar Julie Walters (EDUCATING RITA; PERSONAL SERVICES) is subdued but quite convincing as June, who loves her husband but pines for a little more tranquility in her life. Collins and Walters are believable as a couple devoted to one another, but, while their relationship works, much of the rest of the movie doesn't. Switching gears from comedy to crime to romance to drama, BUSTER often stalls and sputters, never settling on a mood or pace. Still, it's worth seeing for the Collins-Walters pairing—as long as you're not the Prince or Princess of Wales, that is. The film's London premiere was to have been a major social event raising money for charity and featuring the royal couple in the audience; however, critics claimed the film glamorized crime and charged that Charles and Diana would be condoning criminal activities by attending the screening, and they subsequently declined the invitation. (Collins promised to send them a videotape of the film, however.) Though Collins has long been an enormously popular rock star, he was unable to attract his fans to this film. BUSTER got lost among the release of holiday pictures and quickly vanished from the theaters. Songs include "Two Hearts (One Mind)" (Lamont Dozier, Phil Collins), "Groovy Kind of Love" (T. Wine, C. Bayer-Sager, performed by Collins), "Goin Loco Down in Acapulco" (Dozier, Collins, performed by The Four Tops), "Big Noise" (Dozier, Collins), "Keep On Running" (J. Edwards, performed by The Spencer Davis Group), "Our Day Will Come" (Bob Hilliard, Mort Garson, performed by Ruby and the Romantics), "Atlantis" (Ferrie Lordan, performed by The Shadows), "Sweets for My Sweet" (Domus Shuman, performed by The Searchers), "Let It Be Me" (Gilbert Becaud, Delanoe & Curtis, performed by The Everly Brothers), "How Do You Do It" (Mitch Murray, performed by Gerry & The Pacemakers), "Just One Look" (Gregory Carroll, Doris Payne, performed by The Hollies), "I Just Don't Know What to Do with Myself" (Burt Bacharach, Hal David, performed by Dusty Springfield), "I Got You Babe" (Sonny Bono, performed by Sonny & Cher), "Nellie Dean" (Harry Armstrong), "Any Old Iron" (Charles Collins, F.A. Shepherd, Fred Terry). Also includes the theme from "Lawrence of Arabia" (Maurice Jarre). (*Profanity, violence, adult situations.*)

p, Norma Heyman; d, David Green; w, Colin Shindler; ph, Tony Imi; ed, Lesley Walker; m, Anne Dudley; m/l, Lamont Dozier, Phil Collins, T. Wine, Carole Bayer-Sager, J. Edwards, Bob Hilliard, Mort Garson, Ferrie Lordan, Domus Shuman, Gilbert Becaud, Delanoe & Curtis, Mitch Murray, Gregory Carroll, Doris Payne, Burt Bacharach, Hal David, Sonny Bono, Harry Armstrong, Charles Collins, F.A. Shepherd, Fred Terry, Maurice Jarre; prod d, Simon Holland; art d, Clinton Cavers; set d, Crispian Sallis; cos, Evangeline Harrison; stunts, Mark McBride; makeup, Norma Hill.

Romance/Crime/Comedy　　　Cas.　　　(PR:C-O MPAA:R)

CADDYSHACK II*   (1988) 103m WB c

Jackie Mason *(Jack Hartounian)*, Robert Stack *(Chandler Young)*, Dina Merrill *(Cynthia Young)*, Dyan Cannon *(Elizabeth Pearce)*, Jonathan Silverman *(Harry)*, Randy Quaid *(Peter Blunt)*, Brian McNamara *(Todd Young)*, Jessica Lundy *(Kate Hartounian)*, Chevy Chase *(Ty Webb)*, Dan Aykroyd *(Capt. Tom Everett)*, Chynna Phillips *(Miffy Young)*, Marsha Warfield, Paul Bartel.

It took eight years for them to get around to a sequel to the very successful CADDY-SHACK, but it was certainly not worth the wait. This time around, Jackie Mason, like Rodney Dangerfield in the original, plays a self-made millionaire who is loud, crass, and insulting. His social-climbing daughter (Lundy) talks him into becoming a member of a swanky country club, but the stuffy old-money club members have other ideas, especially Stack, who has filed a suit against contractor Mason to try to block his efforts to build low-income housing near the club. Stack, his wife (Merrill), and the rest of the snobs at the club find Mason to be thoroughly reprehensible and stop at nothing to crush his membership dreams. Mason does have one ally among the club set, though, Cannon, a widow who takes a liking to the brash builder. While her father fights his battles, Lundy has her cap set for Stack's son (McNamara), even as one of the club's young caddies (Silverman) is falling for her. As Mason's efforts to become a club member are thwarted, he becomes even more determined to get in, soliciting the help of his manic lawyer (Randy Quaid). Frustration mounts and he purchases most of the stock in the club, installing a garish amusement park and miniature golf business called "Jacky's Wacky Golf." He's still not satisfied, though, and his one chance to triumph over his adversaries comes in the form of a golf match in which he and Silverman are pitted against Stack and McNamara. As if Mason's ambitions haven't been complicated enough already, Stack retains a hired killer (Aykroyd) to eliminate him.

This production was in trouble before filming even started. Dangerfield was set to reprise his role from the original but he pulled out just before the cameras started rolling when the producers refused to meet his salary demands. Mason was hastily chosen to fill in and scripters Harold Ramis and Peter Torokvei had to do some quick rewriting so director Allan Arkush (GET CRAZY; ROCK 'N' ROLL HIGH SCHOOL) could begin shooting. The result is a disaster. Dangerfield's clearly defined comic persona enables him to milk laughs out of just about anything, much as he did in the original CADDYSHACK, which, though a big money maker, really didn't have much going for it in terms of its script. Mason, on the other hand, can be very funny if he's got the right material, and here he doesn't get it, so he flounders, as does the film. Further, his Jack Hartounian character is so obnoxious that he's not very likable. While the stuffed shirts he's battling are even less appealing, the film still doesn't generate much rooting interest. Chevy Chase gets a few laughs as he repeats his role as spacy golfer Ty Webb from the original, and Randy Quaid's overacting is well suited to the role of Mason's lawyer. Robert Stack and Dina Merrill are convincing snobs, while in his small role Dan Aykroyd once again demonstrates a remarkable lack of talent. If there's a bright spot in all this it's that CADDYSHACK II performed miserably at the box office, which means there's virtually no chance of another sequel. *(Profanity.)*

p, Neil Canton, Jon Peters, Peter Guber; d, Allan Arkush; w, Harold Ramis, Peter Torokvei; ph, Harry Stradling, Jr.; ed, Bernard Gribble; m, Ira Newborn; prod d, Bill Matthews; cos, May Routh.

Comedy   **Cas.**   **(PR:C MPAA:PG)**

CALL ME**   (1988) 96m Martel Media/Vestron c

Patricia Charbonneau *(Anna)*, Boyd Gaines *(Bill)*, Stephen McHattie *(Jellybean)*, Patti D'Arbanville *(Cori)*, Sam Freed *(Alex)*, Steve Buscemi *(Switch Blade)*, John Seitz *(Pressure)*, David Strathairn *(Sam)*, Ernest Abuba *(Boss)*, Olek Krupa *(Hannyk)*, Pi Douglas *(Nikki)*, George Gerdes *(Fred)*, Kevin Harris *(Dude)*, By Mirano *(Waitress)*.

A good cast is wasted in this monotonous would-be erotic thriller in which the *Penthouse* "Forum" fantasy of a beautiful woman getting off on obscene phone calls is exploited for all its worth. Set in Brooklyn and lower Manhattan, the film features Charbonneau as a street-smart journalist for a *Village Voice*-type alternative weekly who is stuck in an unfulfilling romantic relationship with self-centered yuppie magazine writer Freed. In her impossibly huge Brooklyn loft, Charbonneau receives an obscene phone call. Assuming it's Freed attempting to spice up their dull sex life, Charbonneau is turned on by the caller's demand that she wear something hot—without panties—and meet him at a local dive. She does so, but Freed doesn't show and she is hit on by the handsome-yet-seedy McHattie. Upset, Charbonneau tries to calm down in the ladies' room and accidentally happens upon a botched deal between drug dealers and a corrupt cop (Seitz). It seems McHattie works for a dealer and has left a payoff for Seitz in the paper towel dispenser. Before Charbonneau entered the restroom a transvestite found the money and passed it out the window to bug-eyed switchblade fetishist Buscemi, who just happens to be McHattie's enforcer. While Charbonneau hides in the far stall, Seitz enters and, failing to find the money, beats the drag queen to death. When the coast is clear, Charbonneau makes a beeline for the door, but

McHattie spots her leaving the ladies room and makes a vain attempt to stop her. Later, he gets roughed up by Seitz, who demands the money posthaste. McHattie assumes Charbonneau took the money, not knowing that his own partner has pocketed it, and is determined to find her. Meanwhile, her relationship with the bland Freed getting worse, Charbonneau begins to look forward to the erotic phone calls she now receives on a nightly basis, and has lengthy titillating gab-fests with the mysterious caller. She assumes the calls are from McHattie, and when she becomes aware that he is following her, she is sure that she is right. Eventually the phone calls build up to a mutual tele-masturbation in which oranges are used as an erotic prop. Of course the hapless Freed has the unfortunate luck to stumble in on the steamy scene. This is just about the last straw in his and Charbonneau's relationship and when Freed goes out of town to research a piece on fast food throughout the world, Charbonneau finds herself falling for harmless neighbor-friend Gaines. After some marathon love-making in his apartment, Charbonneau gets up and goes to his refrigerator for a drink, and, in addition to Perrier, she discovers . . . a dozen oranges! Livid at finding that Gaines is her obscene caller, Charbonneau dumps a humongous goldfish tank on the shocked phone-sex freak, who watches helplessly as she angrily stomps out of his place. Watching her out his window, Gaines notices that McHattie and Buscemi have followed Charbonneau into her building and he calls to warn her. She manages to escape and, joined by Gaines, beats it to a deserted warehouse where they hide on the catwalk. However (wouldn't you know it), Seitz also happens to turn up at the warehouse and beckons the couple. Thinking the cop has come to their rescue, Gaines and Charbonneau come out of hiding, only to have Seitz pull his gun on them and demand the money. But before he can pull the trigger the psychopathic Buscemi cuts the cop's throat to avenge the murder of his lover—the transvestite from scene two. Buscemi then goes after Gaines and Charbonneau, stabbing Gaines. McHattie, who finally realizes that it was Buscemi who stole the money, demands that he let Charbonneau go and threatens him with Seitz's (empty) gun. Buscemi will have none of it and is about to kill Charbonneau when the mortally wounded Gaines throws himself at Buscemi and they both go hurtling off the catwalk to their doom. Before he leaves, the dashing drug dealer writes his phone number on Charbonneau's hand and tells her to give him a call sometime. Charbonneau just stands there contemplating the offer as a nearby public phone begins to ring and the credits roll.

Although it features a strong cast and some decent direction, CALL ME goes bad in all the wrong places because of Karyn Kay's preposterous script. At the outset, Kay and director Sollace Mitchell do a credible job of capturing the pulse of life in Greenwich Village and introduce a believable cluster of streetwise characters with whom the audience can identify. Then, suddenly, most of these people come down with a case of terminal stupidity and begin doing things that a hayseed from Iowa would never do. For a savvy journalist, Charbonneau's character certainly goes goofy after witnessing a murder and opts to keep her mouth shut and go on with her life instead of investigating the case, as any reporter worth his or her salt would do. To make matters worse, she confides what she saw to an obscene phone caller she suspects to be one of the men involved in the murder. If this doesn't destroy your suspension of disbelief, there are the incredible coincidences Kay asks us to swallow in having McHattie, Buscemi, and corrupt cop Seitz happen to blunder across the much-sought-after Charbonneau, quite by accident, several times in a city of more than *seven million people*. The list goes on and on, and by the time the film is halfway over any faith the viewer may have had in CALL ME is irrevocably lost. On the plus side, director Mitchell does inject the suspense scenes with some flair, especially the murder in the ladies' room, and his handling of the ridiculous "erotic" phone sequences lends more credibility to the proceedings than they deserve. As for the actors, Patricia Charbonneau does her best to keep her character in the bounds of believability and nearly succeeds, Stephen McHattie makes for an off-beat and wonderfully ambiguous villain, and Steve Buscemi steals the show as the psychopathic switchblade artist. Also engaging is Patti D'Arbanville as Charbonneau's dippy, kitschy best friend. Unfortunately, the two most important males in Charbonneau's life, Sam Freed and Boyd Gaines, are two of the most bland guys you'd ever want to meet—and one of them is the obscene phone caller with the fruit fetish! What is most disturbing about the movie, however, is the apparent endorsement of the aforementioned *Penthouse* "Forum" mentality. The message here seems to be that if an obscene caller can dial the right number and hit on a beautiful, progressive, emotionally vulnerable, and sexually frustrated woman she will love every second of it and every sordid male fantasy will come true. This is nothing but a throwback to the "when they say no, they really mean yes" mentality and one wonders how any intelligent woman could have possibly penned such potentially damaging drivel. Songs include "Bar Polski," "Schlacker Polka," "You Stole More Than My Heart" (Michael Urbaniak, performed by The Michael Urbaniak Group), "To Tylko Slowa" (Urbaniak, Malgorzata Ostrowska, performed by The Michael Urbaniak Group and Ostrowska). *(Violence, adult situations, sexual situations, nudity, profanity.)*

p, John E. Quill, Kenneth F. Martel; d, Sollace Mitchell; w, Karyn Kay (based on a story by Karyn Kay, Sollace Mitchell); ph, Zoltan David (DuArt Color); ed, Paul Fried; m, David Frank; m/l, Michael Urbaniak, Malgorzata Ostrowska; prod d, Stephen McCabe.

Thriller   **Cas.**   **(PR:O MPAA:R)**

CANDY MOUNTAIN**** (1988, Switz./Can./Fr.) 91m Xanadu-Les Films du Plain Chant-Les Films Vision c

Kevin J. O'Connor (*Julius Book*), Harris Yulin (*Elmore Silk*), Tom Waits (*Al Silk*), Bulle Ogier (*Cornelia*), Roberts Blossom (*Archie*), Leon Redbone (*Huey*), Dr. John (*Henry*), Rita MacNeil (*Winnie*), Joe Strummer (*Mario*), Laurie Metcalf (*Alice*), Jayne Eastwood (*Lucille*), Kazuko Oshima (*Koko*), Eric Mitchell (*Gunther*), Mary Joy, Bob Joy (*Couple*), Arto Lindsay (*Alston*), Mary Margaret O'Hara (*Darlene*), David Johansen (*Keith*), David Margulies (*Lawyer*), Ralph Dillon, Tony "Machine" Krasinski (*Musicians*), Susan J. Kirschner (*Suzie*), Dee De Antonio (*Lou Sultan*), Jose Soto (*Musician's Son*), Bob Maroff (*Gas Station Attendant*), Rockets Redglare (*Van Driver*), Nancy Fish (*Maid*), Liz Porrazzo (*Lola*), Harry Fox (*Gas Station Owner*), Roy MacEachern (*Customs Officer*), Wayne Robson (*Buddy Burke*), Eric House (*Doctor*), Rosalee Larade, John Simon Beaton, Norman Rankin (*Kids*).

At the beginning of CANDY MOUNTAIN, failed rock'n'roll musician O'Connor overhears a conversation between rock star Johansen and his money men regarding Elmore Silk (Yulin), a legendary guitar maker who, 20 years before, dropped out of the scene at the height of his fame and hasn't been heard from since. His guitars are now worth $20,000 apiece, and Johansen would love to bring Yulin back into the fold and, of course, exploit him. Desperately looking for a way to carve out a career for himself in the music business, O'Connor, having never even heard of Yulin before that very moment, lies to Johansen and says that he knows the fabled guitar maker. The next day O'Connor is given a $2,000 advance to find Yulin and bring either him or his guitars back to New York City. Convinced that this is his big break and that the adventure will give his music an "edge," O'Connor, with his girl friend in tow, sets out for New Jersey to chat with Yulin's brother, Waits. Before he gets too far, however, his girl friend, tired of his grandiose dreams and freeloading, dumps him and takes her car with her. O'Connor then thumbs a ride to Waits' posh suburban home, where he learns that Yulin has moved in with his daughter near Niagara Falls. Waits gives O'Connor the address and sells him an old Thunderbird for $1,000. When O'Connor gets to the seedy trailer park Waits has sent him to, he finds himself in the midst of a routine domestic squabble between Yulin's daughter (Metcalf) and her husband, wheelchair-bound Dr. John. Yulin has recently moved out and a deal is struck by which, if O'Connor will trade the T-bird for their dilapidated VW van, Metcalf will tell him where Yulin went. O'Connor agrees, but on the road the van breaks down and he is forced to buy a broken-down pickup for several hundred dollars. It turns out Yulin is living in Canada, so O'Connor crosses the border and heads further north. Drunk, he accidentally veers off the main road and wanders onto private property where he hits a boat. He is captured by local sheriff Redbone and his ancient father, Blossom, the justice of the peace. The eccentric duo toss O'Connor into a home-made prison cell and leave him there for two days, releasing the American after he signs over his truck and gives them the money he has left. O'Connor now hitchhikes his way through Canada. When he finally arrives at the address Metcalf gave him, O'Connor finds only Yulin's former lover, Ogier, a French woman who has come to Canada to care for her dying mother. O'Connor and the lonely woman spend the night together and then O'Connor pushes on still farther north. Eventually, he catches up to Yulin in "the last town on the last street in North America." To O'Connor's dismay, Yulin is a self-absorbed, middle-aged man who is wholly unimpressed with his offer and couldn't care less about fame or fortune ("Sonny, you're not even on the board, not even on the tail end of my dance card," Yulin informs him). In fact, Yulin strikes a deal with a mysterious Japanese woman (Oshima) to sell her several of the guitars he has recently made and destroy the others, vowing never to make another (thus increasing the existing guitars' worth). With only vague plans, Yulin decides to begin wandering again. When Oshima sagely cites the Western tradition of the open road and freedom, Yulin shoots down such notions by declaring, "Freedom doesn't have much to do with the road one way or another." In the end, O'Connor is left alone, on the road, walking back to New York.

The product of a reportedly uneasy collaboration between photographer and filmmaker Robert Frank (PULL MY DAISY) and screenwriter Rudy Wurlitzer (TWO LANE BLACKTOP; WALKER), CANDY MOUNTAIN is an excellent road movie detailing the enlightenment of a callow young musician who mistakenly believes that simply pulling off a scam will somehow make him a successful artist. Filled with beautiful imagery, poetic dialog, sly humor, savvy cameos, and excellent music that runs the gamut from post-punk to regional folk, the film travels straight north from New York City instead of taking the usual east-west route shown in most American road movies. O'Connor's musician, named Julius Book, is a would-be rock star

whose romantic notions cloud the fact that he is an empty vessel with absolutely nothing to say. More interested in the trappings of stardom than in creating art, O'Connor babbles scenarios into a tape recorder as if he were a big-time star being interviewed by the rock press. O'Connor is also given to spouting hopelessly cliched notions, such as getting an "edge" for his music—as if he could simply purchase one at the store. As his adventure continues, his childish naivete is slowly destroyed by his encounters with a series of characters who have lived life and know the score. Frank and Wurlitzer chip away at O'Connor's romanticism by downgrading his mode of transportation at every step of his journey. Beginning in a new car, which is then taken from him, he goes from a slick old T-bird to a VW van, a dilapidated pickup, and eventually his thumb as he gets closer to his quarry. Ironically, O'Connor embarks on the trip with the hope that the adventure will someday bring him fame and fortune, but on the way he is forced to give up all his money and possessions before meeting the elusive Yulin—who voluntarily divested himself precisely of what O'Connor seeks. An American boy, O'Connor also believes that he can wheel and deal his way through life—and he can, until he hits the Canadian border, where such notions don't impress the father-and-son law enforcement team. There is no hustling these people; you commit a crime, you pay the price. By the time O'Connor gets to Yulin, he is profoundly shocked to discover that the "deal" he thought would bring him a career is dismissed outright. As Yulin destroys his guitars, O'Connor finally begins to understand that wisdom cannot be bought, but that it must come from within. As he is told early on in the film, "Life ain't no candy mountain." The last shot of the film, Julius walking alone down the road back to New York, is a hopeful image rather than a desperate one, for Julius has finally begun to attain the "edge" of experience he sought.

More Wurlitzer's film than Frank's, CANDY MOUNTAIN is an obvious relative of TWO LANE BLACKTOP; PAT GARRETT AND BILLY THE KID; WALKER; and Wurlitzer's fiction. Wurlitzer's characters are always hustling, always looking to score a good deal that will secure their future. Their belief in myth, their inability to see clearly, are their downfall. Luckily for O'Connor's character, his encounter with the guitar maker turns him around and puts him back on the right road. Typically, this quintessentially American film—one that embraces such outmoded notions as personal integrity, compassion, and honor during the selfish, superficial, and cynical Reagan era—was financed with money from Switzerland, Canada, and France because funding couldn't be found in the US. (*Sexual situations, profanity.*)

p, Ruth Waldburger; d, Robert Frank, Rudy Wurlitzer; w, Rudy Wurlitzer; ph, Pio Corradi; ed, Jennifer Auge; m, Max Rebennack "Dr. John", David Johansen, Leon Redbone, Rita MacNeil, Tom Waits; md, Hal Wilner; art d, Brad Ricker, Keith Currie; spec eff, Jacques Godbout; cos, Carol Wood.

Drama   Cas.   **(PR:C MPAA:R)**

CAPTIVE RAGE †   (1988) 92m The Movie Group-OKA c

Oliver Reed (*Gen. Belmondo*), Robert Vaughn (*Edward Delacorte*), Claudia Udy (*Chiga*), Lisa Rinna (*Lucy Delacorte*), Maureen Kedes, Sharon Schaffer, Diana Tilden-Davis, Deon Stewardson, Trish Downing, Frank Notaro.

The currently popular cycle of women-in-bondage films continues with this low-budget effort set in a mythical South American country called Parador. Reed stars as a renegade *generalissimo* whose son is arrested by the US Drug Enforcement Agency for trafficking in controlled substances. The incensed Reed vows revenge on DEA chief Vaughn and sends terrorists to hijack a plane full of college coeds, including Vaughn's daughter (Rinna). The flight is diverted to Parador, where the nubile young students will be tortured and otherwise abused unless the DEA releases Reed's son within 72 hours. The plucky Rinna and her pals manage to escape, however, and turn the tables on the psychopathic dictator. A better-than-usual cast for this sort of thing may make this direct-to-video feature worth a look for the undiscriminating.

p, Harry Alan Towers, Barry Wood, Keith Rosenbaum; d, Cedric Sundstrom; w, Rick Marx, Cedric Sundstrom (based on a story by Peter Welbeck [Harry Alan Towers]); ph, George Bartels; ed, Allan Morrison; m, Mark Mitchell, Mick Hope Bailie; prod d, George Canes; stunts, Ed Anders.

Action   Cas.   **(PR:NR MPAA:R)**

CARRIER, THE †   (1988) 99m Swan c

Gregory Fortescue (*Jake*), Steve Dixon (*Dr. Anthony King*), N. Paul Silverman (*The Reverend*), Paul Urbanski (*Joshua*), Patrick Butler (*Tim*), Stevie Lee (*Treva*).

An AIDS allegory and horror film, this feature concerns a small town that falls prey to the carrier of a fatal contagious disease that kills people on contact. Cut off from the outside world after a devastating rainstorm and flood, the community becomes enveloped in paranoia. A low-budget picture filmed in Michigan.

p, Jeffrey Dougherty; d, Nathan J. White; w, Nathan J. White; ph, Peter Deming; ed, Nathan J. White; m, Joseph Lo Duca.

Horror   Cas.   **(PR:NR MPAA:R)**

CASUAL SEX?½**   (1988) 87m Jascat/UNIV c

Lea Thomson (*Stacy*), Victoria Jackson (*Melissa*), Stephen Shellen (*Nick*), Jerry Levine (*Jamie*), Andrew Dice Clay (*Vinny*), Mary Gross (*Ilene*), Valeri Breiman (*Me-*

gan), Peter Dvorsky *(Matthew),* David Sargent *(Frankie),* Cynthia Phillips *(Ann),* Don Woodard *(Gary),* Danny Breen *(Dr. Goodman),* Bruce Abbott *(Keith),* Susan Ann Connor *(Dierdre),* Dan Woren *(Clerk),* Dale Midkiff *(Attractive Stranger),* John Edward Coburn *(55 Year Old Man),* Sheri Stoner *(New Wife),* Scott Thomson, Paul Lucas, John Boyle *(Men),* Niles Brewster *(Justice of the Peace),* Bradley Weissman *(Guy Who Dumped Stacy),* Tim McDaniel *(Kenny),* Ray Cochran *(Jim),* Matthew Walker *(Ronny),* Leslie Morris *(Gus),* Alan Berger *(Baylor Schneff),* Scott Utley *(Gunter),* Steve Oedekerk *(Joey),* Nicky Franklin *(Nicky),* Jarrett Lennon *(Jason).*

Written and directed by women, this intelligent little satire provides a funny, feminine slant on coupling in the AIDS era. Thompson, a would-be chef, and Jackson, a kindergarten teacher, are a pair of eligible bachelorettes in LaLaLand. In a blackout scene that reveals the film's theatrical origins, the two address the audience directly (as they do periodically throughout the film), explaining their sexual histories, which are shown in flashback. Thompson has been something of bed hopper; pleased with her promiscuity, she has been both a satisfied one-night stander and an easy mark for the artistic types she's attracted to, but the fear of sexually transmitted diseases has led to almost a year of celibacy for her. Jackson, on the other hand, has a considerably shorter lovemaking resume. The last virgin in her college dorm, she finally persuaded a bookish friend to help her gain some carnal knowledge, then became engaged to a dullard who urinated with the bathroom door open and was more involved with the NBA on CBS than with her. All of which has left Jackson, who has yet to experience an orgasm, convinced that there is simply no one out there for her. Thompson and Jackson leave LA behind for a vacation at an upmarket health spa, hoping to find plenty of *healthy* potential partners. Amidst the sunshine and swimming pools, exhausting aerobic workouts and foul-tasting spring water, they encounter a crowd of randy singles who are primarily interested in exercising their genitalia. Foremost among the male contingent is Clay, a hairy-chested, macho limo service owner from New Jersey whose "Hey, baby" come-ons have a preserved-in-Bryl Cream 50s quality. He has the "hot-hot-hots" for Thompson, but she couldn't be less interested in him; however, he ends up "doing it" with a drunken Jackson after she is rejected by Dvorsky, a psychologist who decides he isn't attracted enough to engage in any touching and feeling with her after she disrobes. Deep down, Jackson has fallen for Levine, a gentle staff member who is equally taken with her, and whom she wakes from a dream to find sitting beside her in the bus station when she remorsefully tries to go back to Los Angeles. Thompson, meanwhile, lusts after Shellen, a handsome exercise instructor and would-be singer-songwriter, and has her fantasy fulfilled when she sleeps with this hunk who is even prepared for safe sex. Shellen moves into Thompson's LA apartment, but it quickly becomes apparent that 1) Thompson has become involved with the same kind of guy that has proved disaster for her in the past, and 2) Shellen is a schmuck. Eventually, Thompson sends Shellen packing. Along the way, though, she again encounters Clay, who has continued to strike out even after trying to put into practice the lessons he has absorbed from the *Pretend You're Sensitive Handbook.* After returning to New Jersey, Clay writes Thompson, explaining the personality changes he is undergoing (including an interest in reading and a new wardrobe), and in the first of two epilogs, he appears with one of his limos outside the apartment of Levine and Jackson—now a happy couple—on New Year's Eve, just as Thompson is heading home. "I went for a drive and when I got to Chicago I realized I was coming to see you," he tells her before presenting her with a puppy as a present. The second epilog is set several years later at Christmastime, as Levine and Jackson visit Thompson and her husband . . . Clay, who plays perfect daddy to their young sons. "There's your boy friend," Jackson and Thompson say to each other, trotting out the inside joke they've shared throughout the film, usually applied to doddering old men or dogs, but this time used lovingly.

CASUAL SEX? first saw light as a three-song sketch performed by Wendy Goldman and Judy Toll for L.A.'s Groundlings. It was later fleshed out as a play, and upon the request of producer Ivan Reitman and his wife, director Genevieve Robert, Goldman and Toll collaborated on a screenplay, shifting the play's setting from a swanky singles hotspot to the health spa and adding a post-AIDS sensibility. A sketchlike structure remains and is put to good use by director Robert, who paces the film well and exercises a particularly deft hand in Jackson's and Thompson's funny dream sequences. This is hardly a film that is going to change anyone's life, but while profundity is not its aim, CASUAL SEX? has a ring of emotional truth as it cleverly pokes fun at the crisis-altered sexual mores of the 1980s. The characters here are all a bit over the top, but not so much so that it's impossible to recognize their real-life equivalents or to feel twinges of self-recognition. The film's sensibility is distinctly feminine, and, perhaps as a result, this is a sex comedy pleasantly lacking the kind of sophomoric lewdness that characterizes too many of its male-centered counterparts. That's not to say that we don't see sex or hear it discussed, but that it is handled more subtly or at least given a new spin, as in Mary Gross' particularly funny demonstration of the pelvic method she uses to gain maximum coital satisfaction.

The film benefits from fine lead performances by Lea Thompson (ALL THE RIGHT MOVES) and Victoria Jackson ("Saturday Night Live"), who conveys a lovable ditzy ingenuousness that makes Goldie Hawn look like Olivia de Havilland. The supporting performances are also solid, with Gross contributing some particularly nice work, but the real surprise here is Andrew Dice Clay, a stand-up comedian whose often-repulsive misogynist stage persona is modified here to produce the funny and ultimately very likable Vinny ("I'm the best in the East/I'm a beast/I'm the Vinman"). The film's happily-ever-after epilogs leave the viewer with a somewhat saccharine aftertaste, but in general, CASUAL SEX? asks a relevant question and provides some very funny answers. *(Nudity, profanity, sexual situations.)*

p, Ilona Herzberg, Sheldon Kahn; d, Genevieve Robert; w, Wendy Goldman, Judy Toll (based on the play by Wendy Goldman, Judy Toll); ph, Rolf Kestermann (CFI Color); ed, Sheldon Kahn, Donn Cambern; m, Van Dyke Parks; md, Peter Afterman; m/l, Alphonsus Cassell, August Darnell, Stoney Browder, Jr., Dan Hartman, Charlie Midnight, Reggie Calloway, Chaz Jankel, James Harris III, Terry Lewis, Stanley Dural Jr., David Eric Lowen, Dan Navarro, Arrow, Dave Grusin, Joe Beal, Jim Boothe; prod d, Randy Ser; set d, Julie Kaye Towery; cos, Grania Preston; ch, Susie Inouye; stunts, Eddie Paul; makeup, Ann Masterson.

Comedy Cas. (PR:O MPAA:R)

CELLAR DWELLER*½ (1988) 77m Dove/Empire c

Pamela Bellwood *(Amanda),* Deborah Mullowney *(Whitney Taylor),* Brian Robbins *(Philip),* Cheryl-Ann Wilson *(Lisa),* Vince Edwards *(Mr. Shelski),* Floyd Levine *(Taxi Driver),* Yvonne De Carlo *(Mrs. Briggs),* Michael S. Deak *(Cellar Dweller),* Jeffrey Combs *(Colin Childress).*

Filmed at Empire Studios in Rome, this modest horror film opens in 1951 with cartoonist Combs hard at work illustrating a horror comic book. His storyboard panels show a monster with a satanic symbol on its chest killing and eating a young woman. The inspiration for Combs' work is "The Curses of the Ancient Dead," and when he reads one of the curses, "Woe to you that gives the beast form," the drawing comes to life. Combs attempts to kill the enlivened creature by burning his drawings, but sets the house afire in the process, and dies himself. Twenty-five years later, Combs' mansion has become a rooming house for art students, where newcomer Mullowney attempts to create a comic book based on Combs' old "Cellar Dweller" series, setting up work in the basement and discovering the book of curses. The other residents of the house include the housekeeper, De Carlo; a painter, Robbins; a performance artist, Wilson; a mystery writer, Edwards; and video artist Bellwood, a bitter rival of Mullowney, her former art school classmate. Working from the same passage in the book that Combs used, Mullowney draws a number of panels depicting the monster killing Bellwood, and, in short order, the monster appears and rips Bellwood to shreds, then, after making its own drawings, kills Edwards. Mullowney and Robbins find these new panels, and as they watch in horror, further drawings appear showing the monster sucking off Wilson's face. They attempt to destroy the drawings, but the monster's claw reaches out from the paper, kills Robbins, and knocks Mullowney down. Using a bottle of whiteout, Mullowney drives the creature back, then makes sketches that bring her friends back to life. When she tries to burn the drawings of the monster, however, the creature causes the sketches of her friends to burn instead, killing them all over again. The monster then devours her, calling out, "Who's next?"

Enjoyable though not particularly distinguished effort, CELLAR DWELLER has a number of small worthwhile moments. The cast works well together and is given some offbeat material, such as the performance piece wherein Wilson hacks up a number of dolls and then exclaims, "Death is sad." Also to the film's credit, the integration of the drawings with the action is a nice touch and well handled. Director John Carl Buechler gets the most out of a somewhat limited script, pacing the action nicely, and the special effects are adequate, but like everything else in this film, small and limited in scale. Songs include: "Cellar Dweller Theme," "Mystery Baby" (Carlo Dante), "Nothing Changes" (David Young, Julius Robinson), "Master Dancer" (N. Ward, P. Penn). *(Gore effects, nudity, profanity.)*

p, Bob Wynn; d, John Carl Buechler; w, Kit DuBois; ph, Sergio Salvati (Technicolor); ed, Barry Zetlin; m, Carlo Dante; art d, Angelo Santucci, Roger McCoin; spec eff, John Carl Buechler, Gino Galliano; cos, Claire Joseph; makeup, Manilo Rocchetti.

Horror Cas. (PR:O MPAA:R)

CHAINSAW HOOKERS **(SEE: HOLLYWOOD CHAINSAW HOOKERS, 1988)**

CHEERLEADER CAMP **(SEE: BLOODY POM POMS, 1988)**

CHERRY 2000 † (1988) 93m ERP/Orion c

Melanie Griffith *(E. Johnson),* David Andrews *(Sam Treadwell),* Ben Johnson *(Six Finger Jake),* Tim Thomerson *(Lester),* Brion James *(Stacy),* Pamela Gidley *(Cherry 2000),* Harry Carey, Jr. *(Snappy Tom),* Cameron Milzer *(Ginger),* Michael C. Gwynne *(Slim),* Jennifer Mayo *(Randa),* Marshall Bell *(Bill),* Jeff Levine *(Marty),* Howard Swaim *(Skeet).*

Filmed way back in 1985, this troubled science fiction production, featuring the now-hot Melanie Griffith, finally saw a video release in 1988 after years of hemming and hawing by its studio, Orion. Set in the year 2017, the movie introduces an Earth that has squandered its natural resources, is rampant with disease paranoia, and has reverted to a MAD MAXish existence, a dystopia where "safe sex" means making love to robots. The tale begins as yuppie-type Andrews short-circuits his sex toy, a Cherry 2000 model (played by Gidley), by taking it into the bathtub. With spare parts available only from a remote desert location in a "lawless zone" that was once Las Vegas, Gidley is forced to hire Griffith, a tough female scavenger expert in scrounging up leftovers from America's high-tech age. Griffith takes the case, and a flesh-and-blood romance begins to develop between scavenger and client as they traverse the Nevada badlands trying to stay one step ahead of the region's sadistic overlord, Thomerson.

p, Edward R. Pressman, Caldecot Chubb; d, Steve de Jarnatt; w, Michael Almereyda (based on a story by Lloyd Fonvielle); ph, Jacques Haitkin (DeLuxe Color); ed, Edward Abroms, Duwayne Dunham; m, Basil Poledouris; prod d, John J. Moore; cos, Julie Wass.

Science Fiction Cas. (PR:NR MPAA:PG-13)

CHILD'S PLAY**½   (1988) 87m UA/MGM/UA c

Catherine Hicks *(Karen Barclay)*, Chris Sarandon *(Det. Mike Norris)*, Alex Vincent *(Andy Barclay)*, Brad Dourif *(Charles Lee Ray)*, Dinah Manoff *(Maggie Peterson)*, Tommy Swerdlow *(Jack Santos)*, Jack Colvin *(Dr. Ardmore)*, Edan Gross.

Is anyone ever going to make a really good toys-coming-to-life-to-kill-people movie? Although better than Stuart Gordon's disappointing DOLLS (1987), CHILD'S PLAY once again fails to milk the situation for all it's worth and delivers only half the chills it could have. Set in wintry Chicago, the movie opens with a thrilling nighttime chase scene in which police detective Sarandon has finally cornered crazed serial killer Dourif on Wabash Ave. Desperate to escape, Dourif breaks into a toy store and attempts to hide, but Sarandon shoots the killer and mortally wounds him. Dourif crashes into a display of "Good Guy" dolls—a large, expensive toy that responds to human voice commands and talks while moving its mouth and eyes. Dying, Dourif mutters a bizarre voodoo incantation and transfers his soul into one of the dolls. This is followed by a sudden storm of menacing clouds and a terrific bolt of lightning crashes into the store, blowing Sarandon across the room. The next morning, in another part of town, widowed mother Hicks and her six-year-old son, Vincent, celebrate the boy's birthday. A devotee of the Good Guy cartoon show—he wears Good Guy fashions, eats Good Guy breakfast cereal, and plays with Good Guy toys—Vincent receives several new Good Guy products, but is disappointed that he didn't get one of those new and very high-priced Good Guy dolls. Hicks is saddened by her son's despair, but that day at work she is able to buy the normally $100 doll from a back-alley peddler for only $30. Vincent is ecstatic over the doll, whose name is Chucky, but Hicks must work a double shift that night so her friend, Manoff, comes over to baby-sit. Well, wouldn't you know it, Chucky is indeed the doll possessed by the soul of serial killer Dourif and he stalks and kills Manoff, who falls out the apartment window and crashes into a parked vehicle on the street below. With all the evidence pointing to little Vincent as the killer, detective Sarandon is a bit suspicious of the kid. His suspicions seem confirmed the very next day when Chucky persuades the boy to ditch school and take the "El" to a bombed-out apartment building on the South Side. There Chucky/Dourif kills a former criminal associate who betrayed him by blowing up the building. The cops find Vincent and Chucky at the scene and bring the boy in for interrogation. When Vincent insists that his doll is responsible for the deaths, he is carted off to the loony bin, much to Hicks' dismay. Taking the Chucky doll home, Hicks decides to destroy the toy by throwing it into the fireplace. Suddenly Chucky comes to life and starts spewing vicious, hateful curses at Hicks. There is a struggle, Hicks is bitten in the arm by the doll, and Chucky escapes. Hicks gives chase and tries to convince Sarandon that the doll is alive. Sarandon thinks she's nuts, but when Chucky turns up in his car and tries to strangle him, he believes. In the fight, Sarandon manages to shoot Chucky in the arm. Shocked that he can feel pain, Chucky goes to Oliver, the black voodooist who taught him the chant. Oliver informs the evil Chucky that the longer his soul resides in the doll the more human it becomes. The only way Chucky can break the spell is to transfer his soul to the first person he revealed himself to—little Vincent. Chucky kills Oliver and then makes his way to the asylum where Vincent is being held. Now aware that Chucky is evil, Vincent is terrified when the doll shows up in his cell. The boy manages to escape and make his way home, but Chucky follows and there is a brutal showdown between Vincent, Hicks, Sarandon, and the evil Chucky. Although the doll is beaten, shot, and burned, it keeps coming back like the Terminator until Sarandon finally manages to shoot it through the heart, which destroys Chucky forever.

Buoyed by a good cast, strong direction, and excellent effects, CHILD'S PLAY almost works. Unfortunately, the screenplay by Don Mancini, John LaFia, and director Tom Holland (which Holland claims was mostly written by him) is full of plot holes, lapses of logic, and missed opportunities, and begins to run out of gas at the halfway point. While no one expects a horror film to be logical, it must stick to its own rules and have a sense of internal logic that makes its fantastical situations work in context. The voodoo aspect of the film is so perfunctory and underdeveloped that it calls undue attention to itself as a screenwriter's feeble plot device. How to bring a doll to life? Voodoo, of course! This is scriptwriting at its most fundamental and unimaginative, and it raises more questions than it answers. If Dourif had such impressive supernatural powers and could summon up devastating lightning storms, why didn't he use them earlier? Who is this voodoo witch doctor? How did he hook up with Dourif? Why did he teach him the darkest secrets of voodoo? None of this is dealt with. The script also has some amazing lapses of taste—even for a horror film. In one sequence, Hicks tries to track down the peddler she bought the doll from and there is a montage of homeless people, all of whom look sinister. When she does finally find the man, he immediately tries to rape her. This notion of the homeless as rapists is extremely distasteful and the entire sequence smacks of a suburban screenwriter's ignorant and paranoid view of an urban problem. There is also some unnecessary nastiness in the asylum scene. For starters, little six-year-old Vincent is kept locked in a barred cell with only a cot in the room, then there is a vicious murder in which Chucky straps an electroshock device on the head of a doctor and fries the guy to a crisp. Where is this place, Victorian England?

What *does* work in CHILD'S PLAY is some effective direction, some biting satire, and excellent special effects. As he proved in FRIGHT NIGHT, Holland can direct a movie. The first half-hour of CHILD'S PLAY delivers the chills in the old-fashioned way, by mood, atmosphere, and suggestion—not explicit gore. Unfortunately, as the film progresses it becomes more vicious, the characters more asinine, and the situations more repetitive. How many times do we have to see someone slowly pull up the dust-ruffle on a bed, couch, or whatever, and then ever-so-slowly stick his face near the floor and peer underneath, waiting for the knife-wielding Chucky to stick him in the eye? Holland's imagination seems to run out at the halfway point. Also strong in the first part of the film is the satiric look at modern toy marketing. The amount of Good Guy products on view is staggering, and, actually, not that greatly exaggerated. This, perhaps, is the most frightening aspect of the movie. Last but not least are the superb doll effects that bring Chucky to life. A combination of an articulated cos-

tume worn by a midget actor and several different puppets controlled by operators from beneath the soundstage, Chucky is downright scary and easily the most convincing "living doll" to grace the screen. The combined technical excellence of CHILD'S PLAY (acting, directing, and effects) ultimately makes the film all the more frustrating, for it *could have been* truly great had more care been taken with the script. *(Violence, gore effects, profanity.)*

p, David Kirschner; d, Tom Holland; w, Don Mancini, John Lafia, Tom Holland (based on a story by Don Mancini); ph, Bill Butler (Technicolor, Astro Color); ed, Edward Warschilka, Roy E. Peterson; m, Joe Renzetti; prod d, Daniel A. Lomino; set d, Cloudia; spec eff, Richard O. Helmer; cos, April Ferry.

Horror   Cas.   (PR:O MPAA:R)

CHILLERS †   (1988) 87m Big Pictures/Raedon c

Jesse Emery, Marjorie Fitzsimmons, Laurie Pennington, Jim Wolff, David Wohl, Gary Brown, Jesse Johnson, Thom Delventhal, Bradford Boll, Kimberly Harbour, David R. Hamm.

This low-budget horror picture from West Virginia is an anthology film set in a bus station where passengers waiting to ship out tell their tales of the macabre. One episode features a woman in love with a ghost, another concerns a lovelorn girl who falls in love with a news anchor man on her TV, and yet another involves an ancient Aztec demon. Strictly amateur in all departments, the film was shown briefly in West Virginia before hitting the video stores.

p, Daniel Boyd; d, Daniel Boyd; w, Daniel Boyd; ph, Bill Hogan; m, Michael Lipton.

Horror   (PR:NR MPAA:NR)

CHOCOLATE WAR, THE***   (1988) 100m Management Co. Entertainment c

John Glover *(Brother Leon)*, Ilan Mitchell-Smith *(Jerry)*, Wally Ward *(Archie)*, Doug Hutchison *(Obie)*, Adam Baldwin *(Carter)*, Brent Fraser *(Emille)*, Bud Cort *(Brother Jacques)*.

After 10 years of appearing in front of the camera, in such films as ALL THAT JAZZ (playing the young Roy Scheider), CHRISTINE (as a possessed dropout), and BACK TO SCHOOL (in which he played Rodney Dangerfield's son), 27-year-old Keith Gordon makes his directing debut with this dark, dazzling film in the tradition of IF and LORD OF THE FLIES. Working from his own adaptation of Robert Cormier's novel *The Chocolate War*, Gordon uses an inventive, nonstandard narrative and stylish visuals to tell this story of a teenager who takes a stand against an oppressive system but, in so doing, ends up playing the system's game.

Set at Trinity, a Catholic boys' high school, the film begins on the football field, where Mitchell-Smith, a 15-year-old "new kid," is trying out for the football team as a quarterback. Although he isn't able to get off a pass, Mitchell-Smith makes the team anyway; more important, he comes to the attention of Ward and Hutchison, two members of the Vigils, the school's secret society of bullies. Ward, the society's Assigner, singles out students to carry out cruel duties and Hutchison dutifully records their assignments. Even though Hutchison tells Ward that Mitchell-Smith's mother has died recently, Ward adds the new student's name to the list of assignees. In short order, we are introduced to Glover, a sadistic, pointer-wielding brother who moves from the classroom to the principal's office when the headmaster of the school takes ill. Glover is also in charge of the school's annual chocolate sale, and, raising the per student goal from 25 to 50 boxes and the total number of boxes to be sold from 10,000 to 20,000, he hopes to so impress the board of trustees that they will make his appointment as the head permanent. Determined to make the sale a success, he seeks the help of Ward, tacitly acknowledging both the power and the existence of the Vigils. Meanwhile, Mitchell-Smith is in the process of fulfilling his "assignment"—to refuse to sell any chocolates for 10 days, thus incurring the wrath of Glover, who is already on edge because the sale isn't going well. When the 10 days pass, however, Mitchell-Smith continues to refuse to sell any chocolates—not because the Vigils have told him to do so, or necessarily to anger them, but "for himself," to satisfy an inner need that he can't even describe. Mitchell-Smith's action is seen by some of the students as a challenge to the authority of the Vigils, who call him before them. When he still refuses to sell, Ward sees to it that life gets tough for Mitchell-Smith, trashing his locker, pestering him with menacing phone calls, and putting him at the mercy of a particularly brutal would-be Vigil who accuses Mitchell-Smith of being a "fairy" and then looses a pack young boys on him to beat him up. Still, Mitchell-Smith refuses to give in. Convinced that Mitchell-Smith's example is responsible for the sale's failure, Glover demands that Ward see to it that he comes around and that the Vigils put their full weight behind the sale. Baldwin, the imposing head of the secret society, also demands results from Ward, whose response is a devilish plan that calls for the Vigils to use their influence to make selling chocolates the "cool" thing to do. Soon, all of the chocolates are sold except for the 50 boxes that Hutchison has stolen from Mitchell-Smith's locker. Ward then offers Mitchell-Smith a chance for revenge in the boxing ring at a nighttime "students only" pep rally. Reluctantly, Mitchell-Smith accepts, and finds himself the object of a strange raffle: for the price of a ticket, the purchaser designates a punch and the combatant who is to throw it. Before the battle begins, however, Baldwin brings out a box containing five white balls and one black one. Tradition demands that the Assigner draw a ball from the box for each assignment he makes—white ball, the assignment stands; black ball, he must perform the task himself. Ward draws one ball for each of the boxers; the second is black, Ward takes the place of the student who was to have fought Mitchell-Smith and the contest begins. After being kneed in the groin, Mitchell-Smith lets fly with a barrage of punches that puts a bloody Ward to the canvas for good. Cheered by everyone, Mitchell-Smith slips in and out of a dream wherein he pictures his mother in the stands crying, prompting his realization that he has failed, that he has played the Vigils' game after all. As Hutchison and Ward slowly materialize in the corner of the frame and Mitchell-Smith dissolves, the action returns to the bleachers where the film began, with Hutchison now dictating assignments to Ward.

With much of his film's direction is dictated by dream logic, Gordon uses an arresting visual style to immerse the viewer in Mitchell-Smith's world. Despite his limited budget, the writer-director presents an array of memorable images, not only in the impressionistic, symbolic dream sequences that punctuate the narrative, but throughout the film. Gordon's choice of camera angles and movement is consistently surprising and informative, continually forcing us to view what is transpiring from a new perspective, slowly drawing us in, then gradually or suddenly distancing us from the proceedings. His hand-held camera (apparently the budget didn't allow for a steadycam) is particulary active and effective in the scene in which Mitchell-Smith is set upon by Ward's name-calling errand boy, circling tentatively, reversing its orbit around the boys in fits and starts, mirroring the situation's tension and threat, and literally showing us all sides of the confrontation. Director of photography Tom Richmond's use of lighting is equally expressive. THE CHOCOLATE WAR is not only a dark film in terms of tone and theme, but much of it is also performed in shadows or pools of light set against black backgrounds. Many of the film's crucial scenes are played by characters whose faces are half-cloaked in shadow; then, in an assembly in the chapel, the sunlight that pours through the window seems to bisect the students' faces not with shadow but light, as if this were somehow the negative image of most of the film's lighting.

Borrowing from the French New Wave, Gordon also uses abrupt flashes forward, showing part of an action, jumping back in time to reveal the circumstances that led up to it, then repeating the action. This technique is particularly effective in a sequence dealing with a prank played on a teacher hilariously limned by Bud Cort, wherein the students do a strange little dance every time he says the word *environment*. Another of Gordon's most inventive touches comes in one of Mitchell-Smith's dream sequences, when the voices of major players in the film come out of other characters' mouths. Most striking is that Gordon does not use his stylistic flourishes solely for style's sake, but to deepen our understanding of Mitchell-Smith's experience. If there is a major criticism of the film it is that Mitchell-Smith's character is not as well developed as we might want it to be, though much can be inferred from his dreams. Still, aided by strong performances—particularly by Adam Baldwin (MY BODYGUARD), Wally Ward, and John Glover as the on-the-edge, off-the-wall Brother Leon—Gordon has created a deeply involving film that has much to tell us, not just about the particular adolescent challenge faced by Mitchell-Smith, but also about the difficulty of nonconformity and how easily means and ends become confused. (*Profanity, violence.*)

p, Jonathan D. Krane, Simon R. Lewis; d, Keith Gordon; w, Keith Gordon (based on the book by Robert Cormier); ph, Tom Richmond; ed, Jeff Wishengrad; prod d, David Ensley; set d, Melissa Matthies; cos, Elizabeth Kaye.

Drama   **(PR:C MPAA:R)**

CITY OF BLOOD***   (1988, South Africa) 96m NW c

Joe Stewardson (*Joe Henderson*), Ian Yule (*Max Wharton*), Susan Coetzer (*Abigail*), Dudu Mkhize (*Elizabeth Mekana*), Gys De Villiers (*Stella*), Liz Dick (*Claire Henderson*), Sean Taylor (*Pimp*), Megan Kruskal (*Marina*), Norman Coombes (*College Professor*), Greg Latter (*Sgt. Phillips*), John Carson (*Prime Minister*), Ken Gampu (*Black Leader*).

Out of South Africa—where, surprisingly, the political content of feature films is little monitored by the government—comes this story of racial tension, murder, and mysticism. Stewardson is a medical examiner investigating a series of murders of prostitutes committed with a strange, spiked club. One day, signing a stack of death certificates but preoccupied with this mystery, he comes across a certificate with no name. His secretary knows nothing about it and he asks her to check it out. Shortly thereafter, two officials from the state security service turn up and tell him it would be best if he just signed the document. He refuses, but they continue to pressure him and his boss, eventually admitting that the nameless certificate is for a well-known black activist who was accidentally tortured to death by some overzealous interrogators while in detention. Since Stewardson is a known sympathizer with black causes, it is thought that his signing the certificate, listing cause of death as a heart attack, will keep the country from blowing up when the news gets out. Still he refuses. Meanwhile, he suffers from dreams in which masked warriors and streetwalkers pursue him. When Stewardson is shown a 2,000-year-old skull that bears the same wounds as did the murdered prostitutes, he heads to the rural site where the skull was found and encounters there an old man, who shows him a ceremonial club with five spikes and warns him to be careful. Back home, he is attacked by a number of the masked warriors of his dreams, who now turn out to be flesh and blood. Stewardson escapes and confronts a black leader, accusing him of ordering the murders to cause panic in the white community. You can't just kill people, Stewardson tells him, to which the man replies, "Why not? How many death certificates for children who have been shot have you signed?" With all his ideals made a mockery, Stewardson signs the death certificate, then blows his brains out.

Director Darrell Roodt is the first from the vigorous but hidden South African film industry to make an international name for himself, thanks to his 1986 A PLACE OF WEEPING. With the technically impressive CITY OF BLOOD, Roodt takes a compelling look at the dilemma of the white, liberal South African who loves his country but hates its repression, even as he benefits from it. Joe Stewardson is excellent in his portrayal of this conflicted, flawed character, a lonely man taken to picking up prostitutes when his wife and child leave the country. Packaged as a horror film, CITY OF

BLOOD will probably disappoint those expecting gore-caked scenes, and is unlikely to find the sophisticated audience it deserves. (*Violence, adult situations, sexual situations.*)

p, Anant Singh; d, Darrell Roodt; w, Mary Ann Lindenstadt, Darrell Roodt; ph, Paul Witte (Technicolor); ed, David Heitner; m, Lloyd Ross.

Thriller   **(PR:O MPAA:R)**

CLARA'S HEART*½   (1988) 108m MTM/WB c

Whoopi Goldberg (*Clara Mayfield*), Michael Ontkean (*Bill Hart*), Kathleen Quinlan (*Leona Hart*), Neil Patrick Harris (*David Hart*), Spalding Gray (*Dr. Peter Epstein*), Beverly Todd (*Dora*), Hattie Winston (*Blanche Loudon*), Fred Strother (*Bundy*), Dorthy Cunningham (*Buxom Woman*), Alaine Laughton (*Little Girl*), Randy Meeks (*Ching*), Kathryn Dowling (*Deena*), Tatum Adaire Gauthier (*Ashley Lafferty*), Joy Green (*Duty Nurse*), Tania Gauthier (*Jessica*), Forry Buckingham (*Coach Stillson*), Dan Griffith, Jason Schuyler, Kevin Colborn (*Swim Team Members*).

In CLARA'S HEART, Leona and Bill Hart (Quinlan and Ontkean) are a wealthy couple who live in a huge house in suburban Baltimore with their 15-year-old son (Harris) and infant daughter. When their baby daughter dies, the grief-stricken Quinlan feels she must get away and heads for Jamaica, where hotel maid Clara (Goldberg) senses the woman's grief and does all she can to help her through her pain. Quinlan is so taken with Goldberg that she invites her to the States to serve as Quinlan and family's maid, a proposition Goldberg accepts. As soon as she arrives, Goldberg is greeted with hostility by Harris, who makes it clear that he doesn't want her around. The relationship between his parents is rapidly deteriorating, however, and slowly he warms to Goldberg and starts to look to her for comfort, appreciating her ability to cut through nonsense and put things in perspective, especially as far as his selfish parents are concerned. For her part, Goldberg is very fond of Harris and often takes him to Baltimore's inner city to meet and party with her Jamaican friends. While Harris grows closer to Goldberg, his parents steadily grow farther apart. Quinlan learns of Ontkean's affair with an interior designer, spelling the end of their marriage as she in turn seeks comfort in the arms of an author of self-help books (a surprisingly restrained Spalding Gray). In the meantime, Harris and Goldberg continue their trips into Baltimore, where Dora (Todd), a Jamaican who doesn't like Goldberg, taunts Harris by telling him that Goldberg is hiding something from him. Eventually, Goldberg's deep secret is revealed: she was raped by her own son. Harris is at first appalled and withdraws from Goldberg, but the pair reconcile by the film's end.

After appearing in a series of action comedies (BURGLAR; FATAL BEAUTY; JUMPIN' JACK FLASH), Whoopi Goldberg here makes her first stab at drama since her film debut in THE COLOR PURPLE. She's well suited to the character of Clara, a woman full of humor, wisdom, and unshakable dignity. Compared to the characters who surround her in this film, however, it doesn't take much to seem to be wise, witty, and dignified. The Harts are already so insensitive, humorless, and demanding that it's overkill to add a character as strong as Clara to put them in their places. Goldberg's barbs directed at the wealthy couple are often funny, but they would have had greater impact if her targets weren't so easy. Still, the relationship between Neil Patrick Harris' and Goldberg's characters—though entirely predictable in its unfolding—is engaging, as Harris even begins to pick up Goldberg's Jamaican accent. More perfunctory is Clara's "secret," which is hinted at again and again throughout the film before it is finally revealed and seems designed simply to give Goldberg the chance to offer up a long dramatic monologue near the film's end. Based on a novel by Joseph Olshan, CLARA'S HEART was directed by Robert Mulligan (TO KILL A MOCKINGBIRD) and written by Mark Medoff (CHILDREN OF A LESSER GOD), who must share the blame for undermining Goldberg's chance to shine through this strong character. The film fared poorly at the box office; one hopes the experience won't cause Goldberg to wait another three years before again tackling a dramatic role. Songs include: "Jamming" (Bob Marley, performed by Bob Marley and the Wailers); "Extended Beat" (Eric B., Rakim, performed by Eric B. and Rakim); "The Determination Theme," "Shot a Lick Up" (Elon Wizzart, Michael Daly, Stephen Samuels, Michelle Cole, performed by The Determination Band); "Premature" (Toots Hibbert); "God Has Smiled on Me" (Isaiah Jones, Jr.) "See What the Lord Has Done" (Luther Barnes). (*Profanity*)

p, Martin Elfand; d, Robert Mulligan; w, Mark Medoff (based on the novel by Joseph Olshan); ph, Freddie Francis (Technicolor); ed, Sidney Levin; m, Dave Grusin; m/l, Bob Marley, Eric B., Rakim, Elon Wizzart, Michael Daly, Stephen Samuels, Michelle Cole, Toots Hibbert, Isaiah Jones, Jr., Luther Barnes; prod d, Jeffrey Howard; art d, Stephen Walker; set d, Anne H. Ahrens; cos, Bambi Breakstone; tech, Claire A. Nelson; makeup, Medusah.

Drama   **Cas.**   **(PR:C MPAA:PG-13)**

CLEAN AND SOBER***   (1988) 124m Image/WB c

Michael Keaton (*Daryl Poynter*), Kathy Baker (*Charlie Standers*), Morgan Freeman (*Craig*), M. Emmet Walsh (*Richard Dirks*), Brian Benben (*Martin Laux*), Luca Bercovici (*Lenny*), Tate Donovan (*Donald Towle*), Henry Judd Baker (*Xavier*), Claudia Christian (*Iris*), J. David Krassner (*Tiller*), Dakin Matthews (*Bob*), Mary Catherine Martin (*Cheryl Ann*), Pat Quinn (*June*), Ben Piazza (*Kramer*), Terri Hanauer (*Admissons Counsellor*), David A. Kimball (*Doctor*), Veronica Redd (*Head Nurse in Detox*), Sharie Doolittle (*Nurse*), Sharon Medearis (*Nurse*), Nick Savage (*Gary "Ike Turner"*), Sandra Foster (*Xavier's Girlfriend*), Pamela Dunlap (*Jane*), Leslie Neale

(Sheila), Anne Kerry Ford (Debbie Laux), Michael Francis Clark (Board Executive), Doug MacHugh (Board Executive), Claudia Robinson (Cleaning Lady), Harley Kozak (Ralston Receptionist), Serina Robinson (Karen Peluso), Al Pugliese (Detective), Stephanie Menuez (Ticket Agent), Michael Leopard (Steel Mill Foreman), Douglas Roberts (Mark), Jean Nash (Rita).

Playing against type, Michael Keaton stars as a repulsive cocaine- and alcohol-addicted real-estate hotshot forced to come to terms with himself in this poignant film directed by the creator of TV's critically acclaimed "Moonlighting," Glenn Gordon Caron. After "borrowing" $92,000 from his Philadelphia company's escrow account and losing it on the stock market, Keaton awakes one morning to find that his one-night-stand has OD'd in his bed. After hearing an advertisement on the radio, he checks into a 21-day chemical dependency program that promises anonymity, not because he thinks he has a drug problem, but because he wants to avoid the cops. Even as he undergoes detoxification, Keaton tries to score some coke over the phone, but Freeman, the recovering addict who oversees Keaton's group, is wise to every trick. As the treatment progresses, Keaton falls for Baker, a steel worker who is as addicted to her alternately abusive and whimpering boy friend (Bercovici) as she is to cocaine. Taken to an Alcoholics Anonymous meeting, Keaton tries to hook up with a gorgeous "sponsor," but ends up instead with the worldly-wise, patient Walsh, who helps him as he tries to readjust to the real world, where Keaton is fired from his job and finds his neighborhood blanketed with flyers declaring him a murderer. Desperately lonely, Keaton tries to maintain his relationship with Baker, pleading with her to move in with him, but she can't bring herself to leave Bercovici. It takes yet another tragedy before Keaton is finally able to see himself for what he is, and at the film's end, with a month of sobriety behind him, he has taken the first tentative steps towards bringing his life under control.

Reminiscent of THE DAYS OF WINE AND ROSES (1962), LOST WEEKEND (1945), and PANIC IN NEEDLE PARK (1971), this "problem" film doesn't offer many surprises. Here again the duplicity, self-deception, and pathetic dependency of the addict is meticulously and painfully etched. Keaton's recovery is predictable, the sympathetic presence of the seen-it-all counselor and kindly guardian angel is dramatically convenient, and the doomed love between the addicts is heart-wrenching but not unexpected; however, what makes CLEAN AND SOBER so moving are its outstanding performances, which make each moment in the story seem real and important. For most of the film, Michael Keaton is anything but likable; draining the good humor from his standard performance (MR. MOM; NIGHT SHIFT), he fashions his character from the edgy downside of his energetic presence. Convincingly glib and self-centered, he seems incapable of sincerity or sensitivity, yet, gradually, Keaton transforms his yuppie monster into a human being, and his testimony at the AA meeting that closes the film is both moving and enlightening. By the end of the picture we are unquestionably on his side. It isn't clear if he's going to make it, but we certainly are pulling for him.

CLEAN AND SOBER is definitely Keaton's film, but it also features some extremely strong supporting performances. Morgan Freeman, acting in his first film since his Oscar-nominated work in STREET SMART, infuses his selfless counselor with a streetwise, no-nonsense approach that makes him believable. Likewise, M. Emmet Walsh sells the altruism of his sponsor by underplaying his saintly qualities while still showing him to be a man who understands because he has clearly been there before. Kathy Baker, so wonderful in STREET SMART, is excellent again as the tough but tender female steelworker who shows that addiction doesn't only involve drugs and booze. Director Caron was so adamant about using the relatively unknown Baker that when Warner Bros. balked at her selection he had her do a marathon 14-hour screen test with Keaton to demonstrate the chemistry between them. After his success with "Moonlighting," Caron was given the opportunity to direct a number of comedy feature films, but he chose to make his debut with this serious film, based on a screenplay by former National Lampoon writer Tod Carroll. Given his fine direction of the actors and CLEAN AND SOBER's slow but effective pace, more involving films like this one may soon have his name on them. Includes the songs "Tighten Up" (Billy Buttier, Archie Bell, performed by Archie Bell and the Drells); "My Boyfriend's Back" (Robert Feldman, Gerald Goldstein, Richard Gottehrer, performed by The Angels); "If You Wanna Be Happy" (Frank Guida, Carmela Guida, Joseph Royster, performed by Jimmy Soul); "Since I Fell For You" (Buddy Johnson, performed by Lenny Welch); "Come Softly To Me" (Gary Troxel, Gretchen Christopher, Barbara Ellis, performed by The Fleetwoods); "Hello Stranger" (Barbara Lewis); and "Domino" (Van Morrison). (Substance abuse, brief nudity, sexual situations, adult situations, profanity.)

p, Tony Ganz, Deborah Blum, Jay Daniel; d, Glenn Gordon Caron; w, Tod Carroll; ph, Jan Kiesser (Technicolor); ed, Richard Chew; m, Gabriel Yared; m/l, Billy Buttier, Archie Bell, Robert Feldman, Gerald Goldstein, Richard Gottehrer, Frank Guida, Carmela Guida, Joseph Royster, Buddy Johnson, Gary Troxel, Gretchen Christopher, Barbara Ellis, Barbara Lewis, Van Morrison; prod d, Joel Schiller; art d, Eric W. Orbom; set d, Greg Papalia, Don Remacle; cos, Robert Turturice.

Drama   **Cas.**   **(PR:O MPAA:R)**

CLUB EARTH   **(SEE: GALACTIC GIGOLO, 1988)**

COCKTAIL*   (1988) 103m Interscope-Touchstone-Silver Screen Partners III/BV c

Tom Cruise (Brian Flanagan), Bryan Brown (Doug Coughlin), Elisabeth Shue (Jordan Mooney), Lisa Banes (Bonnie), Laurence Luckinbill (Mr. Mooney), Kelly Lynch (Kerry Coughlin), Gina Gershon (Coral), Ron Dean (Uncle Pat), Robert Donley (Eddie), Ellen Foley (Eleanor), Andrea Morse (Dulcy), Chris Owens, Justin Louis, John Graham, Richard Thorn (Soldiers), Robert Greenberg, Harvey Alperin, Sandra Will Carradine, Allan Wasserman, E. Hampton Beagle, Parker Whitman, Rick Liv-

ingston, Bill Bateman, Jean Pflieger, Rosalyn Marshall, Jeff Silverman, Rich Crater, Marykate Harris, Lew Saunders (Job Interviewers), Jack Newman (Economics Teacher), Paul Benedict (Finance Teacher), Diane Douglass (Mrs. Rivkin), George Sperdakos (English Teacher), David Chant (Chinese Porter), Dianne Heatherington, Arlene Mazerolle (Waitresses), Paul Abbott (Snotty Customer), Ellen Maguire, Joseph Zaccone (Bar Patrons), Larry Block (Bar Owner), Kelly Connell (Yuppie Poet), Gerry Bamman, James Eckhouse, Reathel Bean, Peter Boyden (Tourists), Luther Hansraj (Ambulance Attendant), Leroy Gibbons (Singer), Rupert "Ojiji" Harvey, Eric "Babyface" Walsh, Hal "Saint" Duggan, Walter "Crash" Morgan, Charles "Tower" Sinclair, Haile Yeates ("Messenjah" Band Members), Ken McGregor (Sculptor), Liisa Repo-Martell, Adam Furfaro (Young Couple in Deli), Kim Nelles (Female Artist), David L. Crowley (Doorman), James Mainprize (Butler), Gregg Baker (Bouncer), Dan MacDonald (Priest).

© BUENA VISTA

Tom Cruise stars as a flamboyant, upwardly mobile bartender in this glossy, cliched film from Roger Donaldson, the director of the 1987 box-office smash NO WAY OUT. Discharged from the Army, Cruise returns to his Queens home, but his sights are set on Manhattan, where he plans to make his fortune. When he fails to land a fast-track job, Cruise enrolls in some college business courses and begins tending bar at an upmarket watering hole, where veteran Aussie barkeep Brown makes him his protege, not only teaching him to mix drinks like a juggler and negotiate the bar like John Travolta, but also imparting his cynical philosophy of life, couched in "Coughlin's Laws." Eventually their behind-the-bar act becomes so spectacular that they are hired by a chic disco, where they twirl glasses, gyrate, toss off suggestive one-liners, and generally pour it on for bigger tips. Cruise loses faith in the practicality of his college classes but continues to devour secret-to-success books, hoping to come up with the money to have his own bar; Brown, on the other hand, is convinced that landing a "rich chick" is the ticket to the easy life. The two have a falling out over a woman and Cruise relocates behind a bar in Jamaica. A couple of years later Brown shows up on the island, newly married to wealthy and wanton Lynch, and Cruise sets out to prove that he, too, can land an upscale woman, becoming the lover of high-powered executive Banes, but blowing his deepening relationship with vacationing artist Shue. Back in New York Cruise tires of being a kept man and leaves Banes, but when he attempts to start things anew with Shue, she wants no part of him and neither does her super rich father! What's more, she's pregnant, and Brown is a miserable failure as a bar owner. Confused but determined, Cruise boldly does his best to set things right, but while he succeeds on one front, there is nothing he can do to avert catastrophe on another, and the film ends with a mix of triumph and tragedy.

After the success of NO WAY OUT, Kiwi director Donaldson (SMASH PALACE; THE BOUNTY) was deluged with screenplays, and why he chose the incredibly creaky one that became COCKTAIL is anyone's guess. Adapted by novelist and screenwriter Heywood Gould (THE BOYS FROM BRAZIL; FORT APACHE: THE BRONX) from his book based on his experiences as a Manhattan bartender, the film is loaded with cliches, particularly when its love story takes center stage. The athletic bartending that Cruise and Bryan Brown perform is certainly flashy and Donaldson and cinematographer Dean Semler (THE ROAD WARRIOR; THE COCA COLA KID) have given it the standard MTV treatment. In fact, featuring no less than 17 of Donaldson's favorite rock songs and lacking dramatic impetus, COCKTAIL would fare better as an extended-play music video. (Tellingly, the soundtrack album's supervisor receives a prominent credit.) Cruise and Brown learned their mixing magic from award-winning bartender J.B. Bandy and went behind the bars of several Manhattan beaneries to hone their skills, so presumably there are bartenders out there who perform such stunts, and there are certainly plenty of bars like those depicted in the film. Nonetheless, it's hard to imagine any bar where the patrons would continually stop what they are doing just to marvel at the "stars" on the other side of the counter.

Though given little to work with, Brown (BREAKER MORANT; F/X) and Elizabeth Shue (THE KARATE KID; ADVENTURES IN BABYSITTING) manage to make their characters believable if not especially compelling. As usual, Cruise is an appealing screen presence and in fleeting moments shows the fine acting that he has occasionally demonstrated in the past. Unfortunately, when Shue tells Cruise that his "sexy little smile isn't going to work this time," she says as much about his performance and the role he has been saddled with as she does about his Brian Flanagan's attempt to restart their relationship. Donaldson told Movieline that he was interested in exploring the ethics of characters who aren't necessarily admirable and he begins to scratch the surface of this idea with Cruise's character, but by the last reel he resorts to a "money isn't everything" moral, and Cruise is never able to bring much depth to his portrayal of Brian. Preview audiences found the film's original ending to be too upbeat, and a new, "darker" ending was shot on the days that Cruise was able to get away from the set of RAIN MAN. Donaldson serves up his COCKTAIL with plenty of glitzy showmanship, but he does the old short pour when it comes to the story, characterization, and reality. *(Nudity, excessive profanity, sexual situations, adult situations.)*

p, Ted Field, Robert W. Cort; d, Roger Donaldson; w, Heywood Gould (based on the book by Gould); ph, Dean Semler (Metrocolor); ed, Neil Travis; m, J. Peter Robinson; prod d, Mel Bourne; art d, Dan Davis; set d, Hilton Rosemarin; spec eff, Michael Cavanaugh; cos, Ellen Mirojnick; tech, John Bandy; stunts, Branko Racki; makeup, Rick Sharp, Linda Gill.

Drama **Cas.** **(PR:O MPAA:R)**

COCOON: THE RETURN½** (1988) 116m Zanuck-Brown/FOX c

Don Ameche *(Art Selwyn)*, Wilford Brimley *(Ben Luckett)*, Courteney Cox *(Sara)*, Hume Cronyn *(Joe Finley)*, Jack Gilford *(Bernie Lefkowitz)*, Steve Guttenberg *(Jack Bonner)*, Barret Oliver *(David)*, Maureen Stapleton *(Mary Luckett)*, Elaine Stritch *(Ruby)*, Jessica Tandy *(Alma Finley)*, Gwen Verdon *(Bess McCarthy)*, Tahnee Welch *(Kitty)*, Tyrone Power, Jr. *(Pillsbury)*, Mike Nomad *(Doc)*, Wendy Cooke *(Phil/Antareans)*, Herta Ware *(Rose)*, Brian C. Smith *(Dr. Baron)*, Fred Buch *(Alma's Doctor)*, Harold Bergman *(Dr. Erwin)*, Glenn Scherer *(Bess' Doctor)*, Tom Kouchalakos *(Doug)*, Alan R. Jordan, Fritz Dominique *(Orderlies)*, Iris Acker *(Mrs. Cashman)*, Will Marchetti *(Gen. Jefferds)*, Shelley Spurlock *(Rebecca)*, Ted Milford, Chris Fuxa *(Kids)*, Bill Wohrman *(Coach)*, Jay Smith *(Catcher)*, Tony Vila, Jr. *(Umpire)*, Brian Jay Andrews *(Visiting Catcher)*, David Easton, Matt Ford *(Players)*, Jack McDermott *(Spectator)*, Darcy Shean *(Woman in Restaurant)*, Barrie Mizerski *(Waiter)*, Madeline Lee *(Impatient Woman)*, Mal Jones *(Man at Kiosk)*, Patricia Rainier *(Man's Wife)*, Richard Jasen *(Little Boy)*, Patricia Winters *(Lamaze Teacher)*, Rachel Renick *(Janet)*, Ryan Szurgot, Anthony Finazzo *(Little Boys)*, Kelly Jasen, Stephanie Oldziej, Priscilla Ashley Behne *(Little Girls)*, Glenn L. Robbins *(Mr. Szydlo)*, Bruce McLaughlin *(Man on Glass Bottom Boat)*, Buddy Reynolds *(Airforce Policeman)*, Carlos Gonzalez *(Janitor)*, Kevin Corrigan *(Security Guard)*, Robert Gwaltney *(Clerk)*, Robert Short *(Technician)*.

This sequel to 1985's hugely successful COCOON picks up five years after the end of the original film. At the close of that movie, elderly couples Ben and Mary Luckett (Brimley and Stapleton), Joe and Alma Finley (Cronyn and Tandy), and Art Selwyn and girl friend Bess McCarthy (Ameche and Verdon) left Earth with the alien Antareans to go to a planet where no one ever gets sick or dies. Now the Antareans have returned (because the cocoons they left behind on the ocean floor have been disturbed by seismic activity), and the three couples have come along to check up on their family and friends. Back on Earth, the old folks have a chance to show their vigor, the men engaging in a physical game of basketball and the women heading off to try on the latest fashions and undergo makeovers at health spas. Subplots abound in this sequel and revolve around such points as the problems faced by Brimley and Stapleton's daughter and grandson, a day-care center job offered to Tandy, and Verdon's pregnancy. Gilford is also back from the original as the grumpy Bernie Lefkowitz, still mourning over the death of his wife. This time, however, he gets a love interest in the person of Ruby (Stritch), a lively woman who pulls Gilford out of the doldrums. Guttenberg returns (as the captain of a glass-bottom boat); so does Welch (as a beautiful Antarean), and they resume the relationship begun in the first film. There's one more subplot, dealing with the efforts of some nasty government agents who want to do horrible things to one of the cocoons, which is in the possession of a scientist played by Cox. Cox wants to protect the cocoon, but in the end it's the aliens and the old folks who must team up to save the day.

Probably this film's greatest achievement was to reassemble the large cast from the 1985 movie. The veteran actors are all once again in fine form and its good to see them on the screen. Unfortunately, the script isn't worthy of the cast. For the most part, the film focuses on a choice the leads have to make—should they stay on Earth with its joys and pains or return with the aliens to a life of immortality? Each character weighs the dilemma and each has at least one poignant soliloquy on the subject. Director Daniel Petrie (taking over for Ron Howard, one of the few people from the original not in on the sequel) seems competent enough, but a recurring plot device really bogs things down. Sad scenes always follow happy ones, to the point of predictability—the "boys" are exhilarated after beating some toughs in a basketball game, then Cronyn learns his leukemia isn't in remission; Tandy finds joy working in a day-care center, then gets hit by a car, etc. This unending sequence (and far too many trips to the hospital) make the film more and more tedious. COCOON: THE RETURN has some genuinely humorous moments, as when Ameche and Verdon begins attending a Lamaze class, but the humor stops about two thirds of the way through as all the leads begin to philosophize. While COCOON was fun and upbeat, the sequel goes for poignancy in attempting to deal with the weighty issues raised in the original. It's a commendable effort, but the result is a pretty dreary movie. Songs include "You Make Me Feel So Young" (Mack Gordon, Josef Myrow; performed by Frank Sinatra), "Sweet Georgia Brown" (Ben Bernie, Kenneth Casey, Maceo Pinkard). *(Profanity.)*

p, Richard D. Zanuck, David Brown, Lili Fini Zanuck; d, Daniel Petrie; w, Stephen McPherson (based on a story by Stephen McPherson, Elizabeth Bradley and characters created by David Saperstein); ph, Tak Fujimoto (DeLuxe color); ed, Mark Roy Warner; m, James Horner; md, Jim Henrikson; prod d, Lawrence G. Paull; set d, Frederick C. Weiler, Jim Poynter; spec eff, J.B. Jones, Greg Cannom, Robert Short; cos, Jay Hurley; tech, Roy Kieval; anim, Gordon Baker, Tim Berglund, Sean Turner.

Comedy/Science Fiction **Cas.** **(PR:A MPAA:PG)**

COLOR OF DESTINY, THE*½** (1988, Braz.) 104m Nativa/Embrafilme c

Guilherme Fontes *(Paulo)*, Norma Bengel *(Laura)*, Franklin Caicedo *(Victor)*, Julia Lemmertz *(Patricia)*, Andrea Beltrao *(Helena)*, Chico Diaz, Antonio Grassi, Anderson Schereiber, Antonio Ameijeiras, Marcos Palmeira, Paulinho Mosca, Anderson Muller, Duda Monteiro.

With THE COLOR OF DESTINY, Brazilian director Jorge Duran has created a sensitive portrayal of adolescent angst. Fontes is a teenager living in Rio de Janeiro with his parents, Bengel and Caicedo, the family having fled Chile for political reasons. Though faithful to his girl friend Beltrao, he is brokenhearted when he finally recognizes she has been engaged in an ongoing affair with their highschool art teacher. Fontes retreats to the privacy of his bedroom, where he creates experimental works of art. Fontes is burdened by the memory of an older brother who was tortured and killed for political activity in Chile. Fontes often confronts his late brother in dream sequences, while his parents worry that he will follow in their dead son's footsteps. Word comes from Santiago that Lemmertz, Fontes' cousin who was arrested by Chilean authorities during a demonstration, has been freed from prison. She is sent to her relatives in Brazil to recuperate from her experience, and is welcomed with open arms by her aunt and uncle. However, Fontes and Lemmertz develop a more antagonistic relationship. Still, Fontes can't help but admire his cousin for what she has undergone and slowly finds himself falling for her. Fontes finally realizes he must follow his brother's example by becoming involved in Chile's political turmoil. He asks his parents for permission to fly to Santiago, a request they repeatedly deny. Determined to take action, Fontes and Lemmertz plot an expression of their outrage toward the Pinochet government. Joined at the last minute by Beltrao, the teenagers go to Chile's Brazilian embassy under the pretense of obtaining information for a school assignment. Once inside, they make their way into an official's office and splash it with symbolic red paint. Fontes feels vindicated, and as an eight-year-old in a closing dream sequence, he finally is able to say goodbye to his older brother. What makes this film work so well are the naturalistic performances by its teenaged leads. We feel Fontes' pain and frustration as he undergoes enormous psychological changes. Fontes creates a complex character who experiences myriad emotional difficulties. Fontes' guilt over his brother's death constantly bubbles beneath the surface before finally surfacing after Lemmertz's arrival. Fontes allows his feelings to slowly seep through, a fine achievement for an actor of his age. Lemmertz is another find, and Duran's casting of her must have been based as much on her physical appearance as her talent. Thin and baby-faced, she looks more like a 12-year-old than an 18year-old, and when her features harden while Fontes questions her about the Chilean tortures, we know her innocent countenance hides a dark interior. That such a childlike woman should have suffered at the hands of her captors makes Lemmertz's ordeal all the more horrifying. Duran directs with great heart. He is sympathetic to these adolescents and never afraid to show his political leanings. The dream sequences are nicely integrated into the story, quietly revealing some of the terrible things plaguing Fontes. The last scene, in which Fontes finally is able to reconcile past and present, is a lovely moment that ties the film's themes together without forced sentiment. The parallel Duran creates between Fontes' emotional state and his artistic development is another good touch which speaks volumes in its simplistic presentation. This is Duran's debut feature as a director (following an apprenticeship as a screenwriter in the Brazilian film industry), and his ability to deal with multi-layered issues points towards a strong career behind the camera.

p, Jorge Duran; d, Jorge Duran; w, Nelson Natotti, Jorge Duran, Jose Joffily (based on a story by Jorge Duran); ph, Jose Tadeu Ribeiro (Eastmancolor); ed, Dominique Paris; m, David Tygel; set d, Clovis Bueno.

Drama **(PR:C-O MPAA:NR)**

COLORS*** (1988) 120m Orion c

Sean Penn *(Danny McGavin)*, Robert Duvall *(Bob Hodges)*, Maria Conchita Alonso *(Louisa Gomez)*, Randy Brooks *(Ron Delaney)*, Grand Bush *(Larry Sylvester)*, Don Cheadle *(Rocket)*, Gerardo Mejia *(Bird)*, Glenn Plummer *(Clarence Brown "High Top")*, Rudy Ramos *(Melindez)*, Sy Richardson *(Bailey)*, Trinidad Silva *(Frog)*, Charles Walker *(Reed)*, Damon Wayans *(T-Bone)*, Seymour Cassel *(Sullivan)*, Virgil Frye *(Sheriff Foster)*, Courtney Gains *(Whitey)*, Jack Nance *(Officer Samuels)*, Fred Asparagus *(Cook)*, Sherman Augustus *(Officer Porter)*, Bruce Beatty *(Spanky)*, Jo-Marie Payton-France, Paula Bellamy *(Women in Recreation Centre)*, Brandon Bluhm *(Tommie Hodges)*, Mark Booker, Eugene Collier, Gregg G. Dandridge *(Young Crips)*, Ron Boyd *(Cop at Sharon's)*, Verda Bridges *(C.R.A.S.H. Secretary)*, R.D. Call *(Rusty Baines)*, Steven Camarillo *(Gato)*, Carlos Cervantes *(Diaz)*, Lawrence Cook *(Officer Young)*, Nick Corello *(Phil)*, Troy Curvey, Jr. *(Preacher)*, Brian Davis *(Robert Craig)*, Romeo De Lan *(Felipe)*, Marianne Diaz-Parton *(Rita Gallegos)*, Howard Mungo, Nay K. Dorsey *(Men at Recreation Centre)*, Fabian Escobedo *(Flacco)*, Roy A. Nunez, Ted Markland, Dennis "Chicago" Fanning *(C.R.A.S.H. Officers)*, Tomas Goros *(Phillip)*, C.E. Grimes *(Oso)*, Trysh Jefferson *(Young Girl)*, Vaughn Tyree Jelks *(Boy)*, Annie-Joe *(Shouting Woman)*, Clark Johnson *(Lee)*, Kenia *(Maria)*, Leon Robinson *(Killer-Bee)*, Tina Lifford *(Mrs. Craig)*, Mario Lopez *(Felipe's Friend)*, Lawrence Low *(Cop at Car Wreck)*, Roberto Martin Marquez *(Grieving Husband)*, Shawn McLemore *(Willie Wright)*, Peggy Medina *(Angie)*, Micole Mercurio *(Joan Hodges)*, Nigel Miguel *(Snakedance)*, Karla Montana *(Locita)*, Allan Moore *(Shooter)*, Frances E. Nealy *(Neighbor Woman)*, Ray Oriel *(Homeboy)*, Roger Vernon Pamplin, Jr. *(Fighting Inmate)*, Kim Pawlik *(Female Officer)*, Anthony Pena *(Traffic Officer)*, Daniela Piquet *(Bird's Girlfriend)*, David Rayner *(J.C.)*, Tee Rodgers *(Dr. Feelgood)*, Richard Rust *(Hearing Officer)*, Sharon Schaffer *(Crip Girl)*, Geoffrey Thorne *(Lewis)*, Ara Thorpe *(Sharon Robbins)*, Tony Todd *(Vietnam Vet)*, Peter Mark Vasquez *(Veterano)*, Jeffrey Washington *(Dog-Man)*, Dion Williams *(Spooky)*, John Zenda *(Officer Rutley)*, Johnny Marr.

©ORION

Nothing mobilizes professional film critics faster than when artistic freedom is viciously attacked by politicians and special interest groups who, although they haven't even seen a controversial film, call for its censorship, suppression, or outright destruction. The only intelligent reaction to such an assault on the First Amendment is to rise to the defense of the film and its makers, extolling their constitutional right to make whatever film they see fit. While every citizen concerned with his right to freedom of expression should help defend the existence of the movie COLORS, it is regrettable that the film isn't better: if it were a masterpiece one could be much more passionate in its defense. Unfortunately, Dennis Hopper's reentry as a director into mainstream Hollywood is a distressingly routine effort that, while certainly not socially irresponsible, is not particularly distinguished by insight or artfulness either. What caused the entire controversy was Hopper's choice of subject matter—urban youth gangs. When the project was announced, those familiar with Hopper's work as a director (EASY RIDER; THE LAST MOVIE; OUT OF THE BLUE) looked forward to experiencing this unique and challenging filmmaker's perceptions of the subject. What was finally released amid all the hoopla was a bit of a disappointment.

Set in the barrios and slums of East Los Angeles, the film is basically an all-too-familiar tale of a confident veteran cop with one more year to go until his retirement (Duvall) and his relationship with his new partner (Penn), a young, cocky, hotheaded rookie who thinks he has all the answers. Their internal conflicts are played out amid shocking gang violence. The film begins at the start of a gang war between two black gangs, the Bloods (who wear red) and the Crips (who wear blue). When a member of the Bloods is murdered in a "drive-by" (wherein machine guns and shotguns are fired from a moving car) by members of the Crips, Duvall and Penn, members of the LAPD's elite anti-gang CRASH (Community Resources Against Street Hoodlums) unit, are called to the scene. There is little they can do in the aftermath of the violence other than try to find a witness who will testify. While investigating the murder, Duvall and Penn become sidetracked by a number of other crimes. On the street the wide difference between the two cops' methods is illustrated. Duvall, exuding a genuine toughness, attempts an uneasy dialog with gang members, treating them as human beings and giving them respectful, fatherly lectures. Penn, on the other hand, is sadistically brutal and foul-mouthed, treating gang members like wild animals. While this good cop/bad cop combination works on a superficial level, the clash of styles erodes Duvall's credibility with gang members. While cruising the barrios, Penn meets a young Hispanic woman (Alonso) who works at a taco stand and asks her out on a date. Meanwhile, the gang war between the Bloods and the Crips escalates. The Crips do a drive-by shooting of a church during the funeral of the Blood they previously murdered. Duvall, Penn, and a half-dozen other cops give chase, and the pursuit ends with the fiery crash of the Crips' car and Penn overturning his squad car. The next day Penn takes Alonso to a barbecue at Duvall's small home, and the young couple meets the older cop's loving wife and children. When Penn drives Alonso home, he demands to walk her to her door because its a dangerous neighborhood. "I'm a homegirl, remember? I'm safe here, you're the one in danger," she reminds him. Soon after, at a raid of a drug-smuggling operation at the docks, Penn earns the nickname Pacman from the gangs because of the new yellow undercover squad car he shares with Duvall. At the raid it is learned that a Blood pusher (Plummer), whom Duvall had previously turned loose over Penn's vehement objections, is the connection between South American drug dealers and the gangs. Duvall and Penn catch up with Plummer at Venice Beach and, after a violent fight, arrest him. During interrogation, Penn tricks Plummer into fingering the leader of the Crips (Cheadle) for the drive-by murder of the Blood. There is a raid on Cheadle's girl friend's home and a trigger-happy cop kills an unarmed black youth mistaken for Cheadle. Word on the street, however, is that Duvall pulled the trigger. Looking for information, Duvall turns to Silva, the leader of the relatively stable, multiracial 21st Street gang. Because he owes Duvall a favor, Silva informs him that the Crips have sentenced Penn to death. When the Crips get word that Silva talked to Duvall, they pull a drive-by on his gang during a house party. An innocent neighbor is killed in the attack, and when the police arrive at the scene, Penn is shocked to learn that Alonso is the lover of one of the gang members. The attack provokes the 21st Streeters to retaliate and there is a protracted shootout at the Crips' headquarters, in which many die—including Cheadle. As the surviving 21st Streeters regroup in the hills, the cops arrive unexpectedly to bust them. As the cuffs are slapped on the gang, Silva's brother—the youngest member—grabs a gun and shoots Duvall. The kid goes down in a hail of bullets, and as other cops call for an ambulance, Penn watches Duvall die (in one of the most uncomfortably realistic death scenes ever committed to celluloid), repeating: "Call my wife . . . call my wife . . . Just let me catch my breath . . . let me catch my breath . . ." At the close of the film we see a now-experienced Penn trying to break in a hotheaded rookie. No one should expect a Hollywood movie to address *and* cure complicated social ills, and in COLORS Hopper makes no attempt to provide solutions. He merely presents the disturbing reality of the situation as a backdrop for the narrative. In doing so he has not only made a bundle of money for Orion Pictures, but he has also brought about a firestorm of public debate on the problem of urban street gangs, a subject too often left off the social agenda. Cinematically, however, after all the controversy dies down and COLORS is just another rental in video stores, what will be left is an ordinary cop film that contains one great performance by a great actor (Duvall), one good performance by a sporadically great actor (Penn), and one long draw on the "Big Nipple" of Hollywood (to quote Bernardo Bertolucci) by a repentant bad boy (Hopper).

COLORS is the nadir of Hopper's recent Hollywood career resurgence. He spent decades alienating the establishment by adopting the stance of a notorious rebel who was hard to manage as an actor and, as a director, squandered good Hollywood money on the simultaneously underrated *and* overrated THE LAST MOVIE (1971), condemned as a self-indulgent, uncommercial disaster. In the last few years, however, Hopper's return to the screen has been a triumph, as he made the most of supporting roles in BLUE VELVET, HOOSIERS, and RIVER'S EDGE. His new visibility, combined with a strong "Say No to Drugs" stance, has suddenly made him the darling of Hollywood. Approached by Sean Penn to direct the already studio-approved COLORS, Hopper took the assignment. He had the reportedly awful screenplay (something about a black/white cop team battling a Chicago street gang pushing cough-syrup) rewritten into a merely bad one, and proved he could deliver an expensive studio-financed film on time and within budget. Unfortunately, these restrictions seem to have dampened the highly personal creative sensibilities that made OUT OF THE BLUE (1982) such a powerful and unforgettable experience.

COLORS is an unfocused and indifferent hodgepodge of documentary realism, expressionism, TV cop show, liberal message movie, and violent action film. Yet Hopper does none of these things particularly well. He has admitted in several interviews that if he had initiated the project himself he would have preferred that the film concentrate on the gangs and not the cops. Consequently, COLORS has a tentative, ambivalent feel to it, as if Hopper merely considered himself a hired-gun who should avoid imposing too personal a vision on the material. There are many slickly choreographed raids, shootouts, and car chases which vary in presentation from the brutally realistic to the patently absurd. However, for a film hailed by so many as the height of street realism, there are also a number of scenes of laughable mayhem that belong on the "A-Team" (the exploding car is unforgivable). Only occasionally does Hopper demonstrate his distinctive talent, especially at the beginning of the film, when the cops round up hundreds of Bloods and Crips. As the gangs are corralled into separate lockups, the frame becomes a turbulent sea of red and blue gang colors. But such moments are too infrequent to satisfy, for Hopper directs the rest of the film in an undeniably professional but wholly impersonal manner.

To be fair, Hopper is saddled with a cliched and terribly contrived screenplay that offers little more than familiar action-movie thrills. Attempting to combat this, he employs a herky-jerky narrative that mirrors actual police work. Like real cops—who are forced to solve a dozen cases at once—the heroes' pursuit is seldom effective and nothing is comfortably resolved. However, it is difficult to determine if this structure works to Hopper's advantage or merely disguises his own disinterest. Hopper also refuses to pass moral judgement on Duvall and Penn, preferring to remain neutral about what is right or wrong when it comes to dealing with gangs. Although Hopper's ambivalence infuriates those looking for easy answers to complex social problems, it is even more alarming to those looking for the intensely personal and passionate moments found in his other films. Passion and personality are missing in COLORS and no amount of big-budget pyrotechnics or polished acting can make up for their absence. Those curious enough to see Hopper's finest directorial work to date should rent OUT OF THE BLUE from your local video store—if they have it. Songs include "Colors", "Squeeze the Trigger" (Ice-T & Africa Islam, performed by Ice-T), "One Time One Night" (David Hidalgo, Louie Perez, performed by Los Lobos), "Raw" (Antonio Hardy, Marlon Williams, performed by Big Daddy Kane), "Go Girl" (Hardy, Williams, performed by Roxanne Shante), "Butcher Shop" (Nathaniel T. Wilson, Williams, performed by Kool G. Rap), "No Vuelvo Amar" (Alfonso Esparza Oteo, performed by Los Cadetes De Linares), "Angel Baby" (Rose Hamlin, performed by Rosie & The Originals), "Soon, and Very Soon" (Andrae Crouch, performed by Paula Bellamy, Marsha Bullock, Billy Griffin, Rick Howell), "Low Rider" (Jordan, Allen, Brown, Dickerson, Miller, Oskar, Scott, Goldstein, performed by War), "Sally Go 'Round the Roses" (Abner Spector, performed by Jaynetts), "Such a Night" (Mac Rebennack, performed by Dr. John), "Bloody Mary Morning" (Willie Nelson, performed by Nelson), "Land of 1000 Dances" (Kris Kenner, Fats Domino, performed by Cannibal & The Headhunters), "A Mind Is a Terrible Thing to Waste" (Shawn Moltke, Williams, performed by M.C. Shan), "Este Necio Corazon" (Cuco Escaler), "A Mi Pueblo" (Jose L. Martinez, performed by Maly y Su Playa Azul), "Makossa '87" (Manu Dibango), "Crumblin' Down" (John Cougar Mellencamp, performed by Mellencamp), "Rhythm Killer" (Robbie Shakespeare, Ally Dunbar, Bill Laswell, performed by Sly & Robbie), "Six Gun" (David Williams, Jeff Liles, performed by Decadent Dub Team), "Everywhere I Go (Colors)" (Rick James, performed by James), "Memories of El Monte" (Frank Zappa, Ray Collins, performed by The Penguins), "Mad Mad World" (Brent Bouldin, Sean Bouldin, Johnny Rivers, performed by 7A3), "Love Guarantee" (Kenia Hernandez, performed by Hernandez, Courtney Gains), "Oogum Boogum" (Alfred Smith, performed by Brenton Wood), "Let the Rhythm Run" (Fingerprints, performed by Salt-N-Pepa), "Paid in Full" (Eric B. & Rakim, performed by Eric B. & Rakim). *(Graphic violence, sexual situations, nudity, substance abuse, profanity.)*

p, Robert H. Solo; d, Dennis Hopper; w, Michael Schiffer (from a story by Schiffer, Richard DiLello); ph, Haskell Wexler (Metrocolor); ed, Robert Estrin; m, Herbie

Hancock; m/l, Ice-T & Afrika Islam, David Hidalgo, Louie Perez, Antonio Hardy, Marlon Williams, Nathaniel T. Wilson, Alfonso Esparza Oteo, Rose Hamlin, Andrae Crouch, Abner Spector, Max Rebennack "Dr. John", Willie Nelson, Kris Kenner, Fats Domino, Shawn Moltke, Cuco Escaler, Jose L. Martinez, Manu Dibango, John Cougar Mellencamp, Robbie Shakespeare, Ally Dunbar, Bill Laswell, David Williams, Jeff Liles, Rick James, Frank Zappa, Ray Collins, Brent Bouldin, Sean Bouldin, Johnny Rivers, Kenia Hernandez, Alfred Smith, Fingerprints, Eric B. & Rakim; prod d, Ron Foreman; art d, Charles Butcher; set d, Ernie Bishop; cos, Nick Scarano; ch, Patrick Alan; tech, Dennis "Chicago" Fanning, Gerald Ivory, Roy Nunez; stunts, Chuck Walters; makeup, Jim McCoy.

Crime	Cas.	(PR:O MPAA:R)

COMING TO AMERICA**½   (1988) 116m PAR c

Eddie Murphy *(Prince Akeem/Clarence the Barber/Saul the Old Jew)*, Arsenio Hall *(Semmi/Morris the Barber/ Extremely Ugly Girl/Rev. Brown)*, John Amos *(Cleo McDowell)*, James Earl Jones *(King Jaffe Joffer)*, Shari Headley *(Lisa McDowell)*, Madge Sinclair *(Queen Aoleon)*, Eriq LaSalle *(Darryl Jenks)*, Allison Dean *(Patrice McDowell)*, Paul Bates *(Oha)*, Louie Anderson *(Maurice)*, Clint Smith *(Sweets)*, Vanessa Bell *(Imani Izzi)*, Jake Steinfeld *(Cab Driver)*, Calvin Lockhart *(Col. Izzi)*, Don Ameche *(Mortimer Duke)*, Ralph Bellamy *(Randolph Duke)*, Garcelle Beauvais, Feather Simon, Stephanie Simon *(Rose Bearers)*, Victoria Dillard *(Bather/Dancer)*, Felicia Taylor, Michele Watley *(Bathers)*, Sheila Johnson *(Lady-in-waiting)*, Raymond D. Turner *(T-shirt Hawker)*, Billi Gordon *(Large Woman)*, Vanessa Bell *(Imani Izzi)*, Cuba Gooding, Jr. *(Boy Getting Haircut)*, Frankie Faison *(Landlord)*, Uncle Ray Murphy *(Stu)*, Ruben Hudson *(Street Hustler)*, Paulette Banoza *(Soul Glo Woman)*, Clyde R. Jones *(Soul Glo Man)*, Patricia Matthews *(Devil Woman)*, Mary Bond Davis *(Big Stank Woman)*, Kara Young *(Stuck-up Girl)*, Carla Earle *(Tough Girl)*, Karen Renee Owens, Sharon Renee Owens *(Ex-Siamese Twins/Dancers)*, Lisa Gumora *(Kinky Girl)*, June Boykins *(Strange Woman)*, Janette Colon *(Fresh Peaches)*, Vanessa Colon *(Sugar Cube)*, Monique Mannen *(Boring Girl/Dancer)*, Mindora Mimms, Cynthia Finkley *(Awareness Women)*, David Sosna *(Cartier Delivery Man)*, Vondie Curtis-Hall *(Basketball-game Vendor)*, Samuel L. Jackson *(Hold-up Man)*, Dottie *(Dottie Dog)*, Arthur Adams *(Mr. Jenks)*, Loni Kaye Harkless *(Mrs. Jenks)*, Montrose Hagins *(Grandma Jenks)*, Tonja Rivers *(Party Guest)*, Elaine Kagan *(Telegraph Lady)*, Michael Tadross *(Taxi Driver)*, Steve White *(Subway Guy)*, Helen Hanft *(Subway Lady)*, Birdie M. Hale *(Elderly Passenger)*, Jim Abrahams *(Face on Cutting-room Floor)*, Leah Aldridge, Aurorah Allain, Paula Brown, Dwayne Chattman, Stephanie Clark, Donna M. Perkins, Robin Dimension, Shaun Earl, Eric L. Ellis, Sharon Ferrol, Eric D. Henderson, Gigi Hunter, Debra L. Johnson, Tanya Lynne Lee, Jimmy Locust, Dionne Rockhold, Gina Consuela Rose, Randolph Scott, Robbin Tasha-Ford, Jerald Vincent, Eyan Williams *(Dancers)*.

© PARAMOUNT

This light romantic comedy is a refreshing change of pace from the phenomenally successful Eddie Murphy, who, in marked contrast to the irreverent, streetwise character expert in deflating staid white upper-crust society he portrayed in BEVERLY HILLS COP and BEVERLY HILLS COP II, here plays a polite, pampered, and fabulously wealthy African prince in search of true love. In Zamunda, the kingdom ruled by his father, Jones, Murphy's every need is catered to by a small army of beautiful female servants. On his 21st birthday he is to meet the bride his parents have selected for him. At the opulent engagement ball, Murphy is introduced to his betrothed, the beautiful Bell, a young woman who has been raised from birth to worship and serve the prince. Murphy is dismayed by the gorgeous-but-mindless girl and begs his father for the opportunity to go to America to find his own bride, a woman, as he says, who will "engage my intellect as well as my loins." Jones assumes that his son merely wishes to "sow his royal oats" before marriage, and agrees to finance a 40-day trip to the United States. Accompanied by his loyal and equally pampered friend Hall, Murphy decides that the best place in the United States for a king to find a queen is . . . Queens. Much to Hall's dismay, Murphy also decides to hide his true identity, in order to avoid attracting women who are merely interested in his money. To this end, once in Queens he checks them both into a skid row tenement apartment, where they

pose as African students, trading in their fabulous furs and jewels for New York City street clothes. After making friends in the local barber shop (both the barber and an old Jewish man are played by Murphy, and another barber is played by Hall), the Africans are invited to the neighborhood Black Awareness Rally. There Murphy sees his true love, Headley, the pretty daughter of Amos, who owns McDowell's, a fast-food hamburger chain that looks suspiciously like McDonald's. Wishing to be closer to Headley, Murphy and (under protest) Hall get jobs as janitors at McDowell's. In his polite, naive, and unassuming way, Murphy slowly starts to insinuate himself between Headley and her vapid boy friend, LaSalle, who is heir to the Soul Glo empire, a lucrative black hair-care products firm. When her social-climbing father announces her engagement to LaSalle without consulting her, Headley rebels and decides she likes Murphy better. Meanwhile, back in Zamunda, Jones has become worried that his son has fallen in love with a commoner and takes an entourage to New York to fetch him back. This leads to a confrontation between the king of Zamunda and the ambitious fast-food entrepreneur, who is suddenly delighted that his daughter is in love with a rich African prince. When Headley realizes that Murphy has been lying to her about his true identity, she breaks off their relationship and refuses to marry him, much to Amos' dismay and Jones' relief. Crushed, Murphy returns to Zamunda with his parents. Of course, by the film's end both Jones and Headley have a change of heart and she and Murphy are married in Zamunda.

Although the fairy tale script is as old as the motion picture industry itself, the wonderful cast of COMING TO AMERICA brings a charming freshness to the cliched material. Unfortunately, the incompetent direction of John Landis nearly ruins the film. Badly paced, indifferently shot, and sloppily edited, the movie lurches precariously from scene to scene, working against the best efforts of its performers. Stylistically, the film's only shining moment is its brilliant opening, when the camera dollies in on the Paramount logo, rises over the mountain, and descends into the mythical kingdom of Zamunda, all to the strains of "Mbube (Wimoweh)" as sung by Ladysmith Black Mambazo. It is a breathtaking and cinematically magical moment of a spirit that Landis fails to recapture for the rest of the film's lengthy running time. In fact, Landis' direction is so incompetent that by the end of the movie he is reduced to cutting to endless reaction shots of a white poodle for laughs during the excruciatingly long and unfunny climactic confrontation between the families of Murphy and Headley. The biggest laugh he does get, in the entire picture, is from an unexpected cameo by Ralph Bellamy and Don Ameche, reprising their roles from the Murphy/-Landis hit TRADING PLACES (1983).

Luckily, however, Eddie Murphy and his fellow actors somehow manage to override Landis' ineptitude. Murphy gives the sweetest, most touching, and most genuinely likable performance of his career as Akeem. Instead of showing contempt for society, Murphy embraces it here and proves to be compassionate. The scene in which he walks home from his first date with Headley, singing Jackie Wilson's "To Be Loved" in an African accent, is deliriously romantic in the way musicals from the golden age of Hollywood were. The most talked about aspect of Murphy's performance, however, is the cameo roles he plays under the remarkable makeup of Rick Baker. As Clarence, the old barber; Saul, the old Jewish man; and Randy Watson, the bloated, awful lead singer of the band Sexual Chocolate, Murphy's love of playing broad character types is showcased. Baker's makeup is truly amazing, especially for the Saul and Randy Watson roles, in which the actor is virtually unrecognizable. Arsenio Hall, in his first featured role, is also impressive. As Semmi, Akeem's loyal friend, he is relegated to merely reacting to Murphy, but he really shines in his cameos as Morris the barber, a transvestite, and—especially—a Baptist preacher known as Reverend Brown. Unfortunately, although the cameos provide the comedic highlights of the movie, Landis clumsily plops them into the film almost as an afterthought, calling attention to their gimmicky nature.

COMING TO AMERICA's supporting cast, like its leads, is also excellent. James Earl Jones, as the king of Zamunda, is masterful at skillfully turning a phrase to make it hilariously funny. His dignified and subtle comedic performance is reminiscent of that of John Gielgud in the original ARTHUR. Madge Sinclair, as the queen of Zamunda; Paul Bates, as the prime minister; John Amos; Eriq LaSalle; and stand-up comedian Louie Anderson (as a career fast-food worker) all contribute solid performances. Newcomer Shari Headley is sweet and pretty as Murphy's true love, and uses her acting inexperience to advantage in giving her character a somewhat naive, ingenuous quality. For a movie as loaded with charm as COMING TO AMERICA, it's a shame that Landis and/or Murphy chose to exploit some gratuitous female nudity and to indulge in a bit of scatological humor and excessive profanity. If Murphy had only had enough confidence not to fall back on raw humor, and enough sense to pick a better director than John Landis, COMING TO AMERICA could have been the best film of his career. Songs include "Coming to America" (Nile Rodgers, Nancy Huang, performed by The System), "Addicted to You" (Gerald Levert, Eddie Levert, Marc Gordon, performed by Levert), "All Dressed Up (Ready to Hit the Town)" (Jonathan Moffett, performed by Chico DeBarge), "Better Late Than Never" (Freddie Washington, Allan Scott, performed by The Cover Girls), "Come into My Life" (Paul Chiten, Pamela Phillips-Oland, performed by Laura Branigan, Joe Esposito), "Comin' Correct" (Dr. Dre, performed by J.J. Fad), "The Greatest Love of All" (Micheal Masser, Linda Creed, performed by Randy Watson [Eddie Murphy], Sexual Chocolate), "I Like It Like That" (Michael Rodgers, Lloyd Tolbert, performed by Rodgers), "I Got It" (Rodgers, Huang, performed by Eddie Murphy), "Mbube (Wimoweh)" (Solomon Linda, performed by Ladysmith Black Mambazo), "Livin' the Good Life" (Rodgers, Gardner Cole, performed by Sister Sledge), "Ooo Baby Baby" (William Robinson, Warren Moore, performed by Smokey Robinson and the Miracles), "Pride and Joy" (Norman Whitfield, Marvin Gaye, William Stevenson), "You're a Wonderful One" (Edward Holland, Lamont Dozier, Brian Holland, performed by Marvin Gaye), "That's the Way It Is" (Stock, Aitken, Waterman, performed by Mel & Kim), "To Be Loved" (Tyran Carlo, Berry Gordy, Jr., Gwendolyn Gordy, performed by Jackie Wilson), "Transparent" (Allee Willis, Danny Sembello, performed by Nona Hendryx). *(Nudity, profanity, adult situations).*

p, George Folsey, Jr., Robert D. Wachs; d, John Landis; w, David Sheffield, Barry

W. Blaustein (based on a story by Eddie Murphy); ph, Woody Omens (Technicolor); ed, Malcolm Campbell, George Folsey, Jr.; m, Nile Rodgers; m/l, Nile Rodgers, Nancy Huang, Gerald Levert, Eddie Levert, Marc Gordon, Jonathan Phillip Moffett, Freddie Washington, Allan Scott, Paul Chiten, Pamela Phillips-Oland, Dr. Dre, Michael Masser, Linda Creed, Michael Rodgers, Lloyd Tolbert, Solomon Linda, Gardner Cole, William Robinson, Warren Moore, Norman Whitfield, Marvin Gaye, William Stevenson, Edward Holland, Lamont Dozier, Brian Holland, Tyran Carlo, Berry Gordy, Jr., Gwendolyn Gordy, Allee Willis, Danny Sembello; prod d, Richard MacDonald; art d, Richard B. Lewis; set d, Greg Papalia, Ron Yates, Gil Clayton, Erin Cummins, Larry Hubbs; spec eff, Dan Cangemi, Syd Dutton, Bill Taylor; cos, Deborah Nadoolman; ch, Paula Abdul; stunts, John Sherrod; makeup, Bernadine Anderson, Rick Baker.

Comedy/Romance   Cas.   (PR:O MPAA:R)

COMPUTER BEACH PARTY †   (1988) 97m Vestron c

Hank Amigo (*Andy*), Andre Chimene (*Dennis*), Stacey Nemour (*Allison*), Rich Brakedale.

Having virtually nothing to do with computers, this amateurish beach party movie was filmed in Texas way back in 1985 and only now has managed to slink its way onto home video. Set in the Galveston area, the film features Amigo as a nerdy high school computer whiz who, along with his buddy Chimene, fight to keep the unspoiled beachfront from being turned into a tourist attraction by the ambitious mayor—who, coincidentally, believes that there is pirate treasure hidden nearby. Of course, Amigo's crusade threatens to destroy his relationship with the beautiful Nemour, the mayor's daughter. View at your own risk.

p, Gary Troy; d, Gary Troy; w, Gary Troy; ph, Robert E. Poimbeauf; ed, Gary Troy.

Comedy/Drama   Cas.   (PR:NR MPAA:NR)

CONSUMING PASSIONS   (1988, US/Brit.) 98m Goldwyn-Euston/Goldwyn c

Vanessa Redgrave (*Mrs. Garza*), Jonathan Pryce (*Mr. Farris*), Tyler Butterworth (*Ian Littleton*), Freddie Jones (*Graham Chumley*), Sammi Davis (*Felicity Stubbs*), Prunella Scales (*Ethel*), Thora Hird (*Mrs. Gordon*), William Rushton (*Big Teddy*), John Wells (*Dr. Forrester*), Timothy West (*Dr. Rees*), Mary Healey (*Mrs. Eggleton*), Andrew Sachs (*Jason*), Bryan Pringle (*Gateman*), Debbie Davies (*Mrs. Coot*), Patrick Newell (*Lester*), Preston Lockwood (*Josiah*), Angus Barnett (*Josiah's Son*), Adam Stoker (*Trevor*), Robert Bridges (*Wooster*), Leonard Trolley (*Mayor*), Linda Lusardi (*French Beauty*), Gerard Dimiglio (*Frenchman*), Archie Pool (*Rastafarian*), Marc Boyle, Paul Dalton (*Ambulancemen*), Helen Pearson (*Supermarket Assistant*), Geraldine Griffiths (*Thin Lady*), Jo Warne (*Fat Lady*), Julian Ronnie (*Piano Player*), David Neville (*Furniture Store Assistant*), Dick Brannick (*Butcher*), Donald Pelmear (*Porter*), Wincey Willis (*TV Presenter*), Susan Field, Vicky Ireland, Julie May (*Ladies on TV*), Paddy Ward (*Tramp*).

Based on a stage piece by Monty Python members Michael Palin and Terry Jones and performed by a strong cast of solid British actors, CONSUMING PASSIONS should have been a much better film. Unfortunately, the screenplay, cowritten by Paul D. Zimmerman (KING OF COMEDY) and Andrew Davies, is very weak, and the direction by first-timer Giles Foster is deadeningly dull. A black comedy attacking rampant capitalism, the film follows young "junior management trainee" Butterworth as he arrives for his first day on the job at Chumley's Chocolate Factory. It's a big day for Butterworth, who has absolutely no self-confidence and is totally inept at everything he tries to do. At the same time, Chumley's has been taken over by a giant corporate conglomerate called Anglo Foods and Haulage. Assigned to turn the unprofitable subsidiary around is Pryce, a long-haired British yuppie who ends every sentence with the word "Yah?" and then tosses his long locks with a twitch of his neck. As Pryce takes "... quality out of the product and put[s] it where it belongs. In the advertising!" Mr. Chumley (Jones), the third Chumley to run the company in its 100-year history, sits helplessly by and watches his beloved natural chocolates turned into synthetic mass-produced confectioneries. Meanwhile, the bumbling Butterworth wanders into the factory and accidentally knocks three workers into a huge vat of swirling chocolate. Before he can shut down the assembly line, the three men are processed into hundreds of bite-sized Passionelles, the Chumley company's new line of sweets. A test batch containing human flesh is shipped out to a small seaside town and becomes a new taste sensation, while all the batches *without* this special ingredient are horrible failures. Worried that word of the cannibalistic confectioneries will slip out, Pryce and Jones promote Butterworth and make him head of "Special Projects." His first assignment is to persuade the widows of the killed workers not to sue the company. Two out of three are no problem, but the third, Redgrave, an aging Maltese nymphomaniac (complete with gold tooth and tattoo), demands money and sex from Butterworth in exchange for her silence. Because the tainted chocolates have become a hit with the public, Pryce calls a meeting to discuss how to continue putting "meat" into the product. At first they try pork, but taste tests prove it to be a failure. Desperate, Pryce concocts a plan to murder Brits on the dole and use them in the chocolates, but Jones is horrified at the suggestion: "An accident is one thing, but grinding up the unemployed is quite another." Eventually, it is decided to buy up dead bodies from medical schools and mortuaries. This job, of course, is a "special project," and Butterworth now becomes a body snatcher. Sales skyrocket, causing Butterworth to be named Chocolate Man of the Year, but the young executive is dis-

gusted by his work and, with the support of his girl friend, Davis, decides to blow the whistle on the whole sordid operation. Pryce tries to intercept him, however, and there is a struggle above the chocolate vat in which they both plunge into the chocolate. Pryce is processed into Passionelles, while Davis rescues the chocolate-covered Butterworth. His mind finally snapped, Butterworth accepts chairmanship of the company and winds up becoming the youngest man ever knighted by the queen.

Inadvertent consumer cannibalism has figured in several plots ("Sweeney Todd" ; SOYLENT GREEN; MOTEL HELL; EATING RAOUL) to mostly comic effect, but never as ineptly as in CONSUMING PASSIONS. Basically a comic sketch (reminiscent of Monty Python's "Crunchy Frog" skit) stretched out to feature length, the film is ploddingly scripted and directed, with little in the way of comedic timing or satiric insight. Plot twists are telegraphed far in advance of occurrence and most of the humor is monotonously repetitive. Despite the superior cast, the performances are a dull collection of fussy facial tics, leers, and funny accents that are repeated ad nauseam. Pryce and Redgrave are both very funny in their first scenes, but then the script deserts them and they are forced to twitch and vamp over and over, until they have long worn out their welcome. The wonderful Sammi Davis (HOPE AND GLORY) is completely wasted as a dim bleached-blonde Liverpudlian, as is Prunella Scales ("Fawlty Towers") as an obnoxious secretary given to wearing outrageous/outdated mod fashions. Worst of all is Tyler Butterworth, as the nominal hero of the piece. This young actor has no screen presence and seems to think that to play a dullard one must give a dull performance. Most of the blame for CONSUMING PASSIONS' failure must certainly lie with Giles Foster, whose lifeless direction presents everything at the same ponderous pace. The material cries out for the manic lunacy of the Monty Python troupe and the wild direction of Terry Gilliam. Alas, what we are left with is a bad script envisioned by a bad director, both of which work to destroy the efforts of a good cast. (*Adult situations, sexual situations, profanity, comic violence.*)

p, William P. Cartlidge; d, Giles Foster; w, Paul D. Zimmerman, Andrew Davies (based on the play "Secrets" by Michael Palin, Terry Jones); ph, Roger Pratt (Eastmancolor); ed, John Grover; m, Richard Hartley; prod d, Peter Lamont; art d, Terry Ackland-Snow; set d, Michael Ford; spec eff, Ian Wingrove; cos, Barbara Kidd; stunts, Colin Skeaping, Paul Weston; makeup, Naomi Donne.

Comedy   Cas.   (PR:O MPAA:R)

COP*½**   (1988) 110m Atlantic c

James Woods (*Lloyd Hopkins*), Lesley Warren (*Kathleen McCarthy*), Charles Durning (*Dutch Pelz*), Charles Haid (*Whitey Haines*), Raymond J. Barry (*Fred Gaffney*), Randi Brooks (*Joanie Pratt*), Steven Lambert (*Bobby Franco*), Christopher Wynne (*Jack Gibbs*), Jan McGill (*Jen Hopkins*), Vicki Wauchope (*Penny Hopkins*), Melinda Lynch (*Sarah*), John Petievich (*Deputy*), Dennis Stewart (*Lawrence "Birdman" Henderson*), Randi Pelish (*Employee*), Annie McEnroe (*Amy Cranfield*), Rick Marotta (*Wilson*), Michael V. Allen (*Harry*), Helen Page Camp (*Estelle*), Scott Sandler (*Detective*), Christopher Blane, Matt Almond (*Punks*), Banks Harper (*Teddy Bailey*), Jim Wilkey (*Watchman*), Jimmy Woodward (*Robber's Voice*).

© ATLANTIC ENTERTAINMENT

Based on James Ellroy's novel *Blood on the Moon*, COP is an unrelentingly grim modern-day *film noir* starring James Woods as the most obsessive, vile, and amoral cop since Ralph Meeker played Mike Hammer in Robert Aldrich's KISS ME DEADLY (1955). Coproduced by Woods, and written and directed by his friend James B. Harris (who produced Stanley Kubrick's THE KILLING; PATHS OF GLORY; and LOLITA), COP combines brutal violence with a self-mocking sense of black humor and sets its action in a Los Angeles overwhelmed by hypocrisy, cynicism, and sleaze. Woods, an obsessive loner who is one of the LAPD's best detectives, finds himself investigating a murder that he believes is the work of a serial killer obsessed with innocent-looking women. Because the murders occur so infrequently, no one has made the connection that they are related. In fact, Woods' superior refuses to acknowledge this possibility because "the last thing LA needs is another serial killer." Undaunted, Woods continues his investigation under the protection of his mentor and only friend in the department, Durning. Clues lead Woods to the feminist bookstore run by a neurotic poet, Warren. Much to their surprise, the cop and the poet discover that they attended the same high school. Warren warms to Woods and reveals that, having felt ugly in high school, she formed a small clique of similarly withdrawn girls who vowed not to involve themselves with men. One horrible day, however, Warren was raped by a pair of jock types. When she told the clique of the ordeal, they ostracized her. Shortly thereafter, Warren began to receive poems and flowers from a secret male admirer who has continued to send gifts to this day. Warren delights in her romantic vision of her mysterious suitor, but doesn't care if she ever meets him. Ironically, Woods discovers that the dates on which Warren has received these gifts coincide with the dates of several murders. Through a series of complicated twists and turns Woods concludes that the killer is none other than Warren's mysterious admirer, who is determined to get revenge on the kind of innocent-looking, bookish women who shunned Warren after her rape. Despite the fact that he has been suspended by his superiors for his abrasive, immoral, and downright illegal methods, Woods persists in his "investigation" and baits the killer into the open, setting up a showdown at their old high school. In a taut cat-and-mouse game that climaxes in the school gymnasium, Woods finally gets the drop on the nerdy psycho. The killer just laughs, though, and declares that it's too bad Woods is a cop because ". . . now you've got to cuff me and take me in. I'll get off because I'm crazy." With his shotgun aimed right at the killer's head, Woods responds: "Well I got some good news and some bad news. The good news is that, yes, I am a cop and I do have to take you in. The bad news is, I just got suspended and I don't give a f______." With that Woods blows off the suspect's head. The screen goes black. The End.

Unrelentingly seedy and bleak, COP presents us with a world destroyed by the corruption of romantic notions. No one, except Woods, is what he seems to be. Durning, a well-respected superior, enjoys nocturnal, off-duty shootouts and lives vicariously through his protege, Woods. Their commanding officer, Barry, is a born-again Christian who is surprisingly pragmatic about the realities of the street. Warren runs a feminist bookstore, but is a hopeless romantic. County cop Haid, an alumni of Woods' high-school and one of Warren's rapists, lives in a sleazy little apartment and indulges in masochistic bondage games with young male street hustlers. Woods understands this warped milieu and is obsessed with the way society fills women's heads with fairy tale promises of security, decency, justice, and romance. "Innocence kills," he tells his shocked wife. "I see it every day." Woods is so determined that his own eight-year-old daughter will grow up with no such illusions that he tells her police-blotter bedtime stories complete with graphic language and department lingo. The girl delights in such tales, but Woods' wife is horrified and thinks her husband deeply disturbed—so disturbed, in fact, that she leaves him and takes their child with her.

While Woods understands the harsh realities of the street, he fails to realize that he continually crosses the razor-thin line between cop and criminal. He is not driven by an idealistic passion for "the Law" but by a perverted quest to prove to himself (or to his wife?) that his theories about the lethal implications of romantic innocence are correct. As the investigation proceeds he sinks deeper and deeper into a quagmire of filth, corrupting everything he touches, until he becomes as much of a social ill as the serial killer. In fact, the killer is eliminating the very women Woods loathes. The cop sleeps with hookers, informants, and Warren indiscriminantly, using sex either to gain information or as a reward. He breaks into both Warren's house and Haid's, obtaining evidence illegally. He tortures a confession from Haid, baits him into attempted murder, and then coolly shoots him dead. And in the end he finally snaps completely and kills a suspect—his mirror image.

Although directed and written with a sometimes unsure hand by Harris, COP is completely absorbing due to Woods' chillingly effective performance. Few actors can make an amoral, intelligent, sardonic, hyperactive, womanizing, violent, and downright warped character as disarmingly appealing as Woods can. As an actor, Woods juggles complex character contradictions with ease, showing an audience the various sides of his psyche with the skill of a magician. He takes us on a singularly unpleasant ride, but it is always an insightful and fascinating one. The supporting cast of COP is excellent as well. Although her character will no doubt rankle feminists, Lesley Ann Warren's Kathleen is a frank, realistic, and sensitive portrayal that has just as many shadings as Woods'. Durning is great as usual, and Haid essays a role that will put to rest memories of Andy Renko, his cop on "Hill Street Blues." Perhaps the weakest aspect of COP is the script, which asks the audience to swallow a lot of coincidences. Luckily, Harris' direction is on par with Woods' insolent character, constantly on the move and never pausing to reflect on past indiscretions. The film rushes headlong into an ending that is so inevitable, yet still so shocking, that it literally terminates the genre with an irrevocable bang. *(Graphic violence, sexual situations, nudity, excessive profanity.)*

p, James B. Harris, James Woods; d, James B. Harris; w, James B. Harris (based on the novel *Blood On The Moon* by James Ellroy); ph, Steve Dubin; ed, Anthony Spano; m, Michel Colombier; prod d, Gene Rudolf; set d, Kathy Curtis Cahill; spec eff, Larry Fioritto, Bill Myer; cos, Gale Parker Smith; tech, John Petievich; stunts, Steve Kelso; makeup, Deborah Figuly.

Mystery **Cas.** **(PR:O MPAA:R)**

COUCH TRIP, THE**½ (1988) 98m Orion c

Dan Aykroyd *(John Burns)*, Walter Matthau *(Donald Becker)*, Charles Grodin *(Dr. George Maitlin)*, Donna Dixon *(Dr. Laura Rollins)*, Richard Romanus *(Harvey Michaels)*, Mary Gross *(Vera Maitlin)*, David Clennon *(Lawrence Baird)*, Arye Gross *(Perry Kovin)*, Victoria Jackson *(Robin)*, Michael DeLorenzo *(Lopez)*, Mickey Jones *(Watkins)*, J.E. Freeman *(Unger)*, David Wohl *(Dr. Smet)*, Michael Ensign *(Hendricks)*, Carol Mansell *(Mrs. Blair)*, Robert Hirschfeld *(Night Watchman)*, Charles Levin *(TV Reporter)*, Kevin Rooney *(Cop at Hollywood Sign)*, Myrna White *(Policewoman)*, Scott Thomson *(Klevin)*, Tony Rolon *(Bellperson)*, Scott Weintraub *(Continental Agent)*, Donna Mitchell *(Stewardess)*, Linda Rae Favila *(Maitlin's Secretary)*, David Grant Hayward *(Waiter 'London')*, Jonathan Emerson *(Hendrick's Assistant)*, Beverly Archer *(Mrs. Guber)*, Gloria Dorson *(Ida V.O.)*, Jerry Belson *(Yuri V.O.)*, Charles Sweigart *(Cop)*, Susan Kellermann *(Woman on Bus)*, Don Stark *(Peterson)*, Benbow Ritchie, Jack Ritchie *(Men at Baseball Game)*, Jean Sterling *(Woman at Baseball Game)*, Susan Benn, Jan Cobler, Adrian Aron, Ralph Adano, Robert M. Dawson *(People at Party)*, June Claman *(Lady at Riviera)*, Michael Gregory *(Security at Riviera)*, John Sinclair, Kenneth Danziger *(Clerks in London)*, Corey Rand *(Airline Clerk)*, John Mahon *(Police Captain)*, John D. LeMay *(Dr. Smet's Resident)*, Neal Kaz *(Cop in Maitlin's Office)*, Tino Insana *(Jail Guard)*, Duane Tucker *(Guard in Squad Car)*, Rick Garcia *(Bellperson)*, Chevy Chase *(Condom Father)*.

Aykroyd stars in this film as John Burns, an antisocial con who got himself out of prison and into Illinois' Cicero County Mental Facility for Men by eating paint chips and licking the dust off radiators. At Cicero, Aykroyd has found his nemesis in the ineffectual Dr. Baird (Clennon), who is sure Aykroyd is not really crazy and decides to reward him for his disruptive antics by packing him off to a maximum security prison. Meanwhile, in Beverly Hills, Dr. George Maitlin (Grodin), psychiatrist to the very rich and radio call-in show personality, has had a nervous breakdown. He decides, following advice of his lawyer and best friend, Romanus, to hush it up. While he goes to London for six months to recover, under the guise of researching a book, a replacement will take over his million-dollar-a-year practice and radio show. Since the replacement has to be somewhat incompetent, Clennon, with his perfectly mediocre credentials, is selected. However, the call to Clennon is intercepted by Aykroyd, who escapes from the hospital and arrives in Los Angeles, impersonating Clennon. He is met by Romanus; the lawyer's young assistant, Arye Gross; and the beautiful Dr. Laura Rollins (Dixon), and insists on an advance of $200,000 cash upfront. Aykroyd makes an open reservation on a flight to Mexico, where he plans to go once he gets all the cash. He also strikes up a friendship with Matthau, a crusader for the rights of trees who accosted Aykroyd at the airport, and who sees right through his disguise. Within four days, "Dr. Baird" has taken LA by storm, shocking radio listeners with his graphic on-air descriptions of sexual neuroses; offering free counseling at Grodin's office; taking busloads of radio patients, categorized by neuroses, to a Dodgers game; and teaching one of Grodin's patients to bark and growl like a dog when she gets angry. In London, Grodin confesses to his wife (Mary Gross) that his depression is being caused by guilt over an affair with one of his patients, and she admits to him that she has been having a fling with Romanus. Grodin meets the real Dr. Baird at a conference, and they are both on the next flight to California, where Aykroyd is accepting an award for Grodin, and receiving his $200,000 advance, as they arrive. In the ensuing melee, Aykroyd escapes with the money, but has to stop Matthau from jumping off the Hollywood sign. Aided by Dixon, the two men are able to escape.

THE COUCH TRIP, while offering some funny moments, never reaches its potential. The script is full of incredible coincidences and heavy-handed plot devices, and has no sense of continuity. Dan Aykroyd is good in a tailor-made role, and Charles Grodin once again displays his impeccable comic timing. Mary Gross is also funny as Grodin's empty-headed, self-absorbed, shopaholic wife, and Richard Romanus and Arye Gross are suitably slimy as the lawyer and his ambitious assistant. Dixon delivers her lines with a Marilyn Monroe breathiness, but her character serves no point other than to act as a potential love interest for Aykroyd. She is supposedly a psychiatrist, but does nothing but hang around playing the straightman for Aykroyd's antics, and their relationship is so poorly developed that it is hard to believe she would help him escape, only to decide to stay behind. Walter Matthau, for his part, does more than his usual share of mugging—making the character, as well as himself, seem more pathetic than funny. The film's satirical touches, aimed at the psychiatric profession and Beverly Hills values, are recycled from a dozen better movies. THE COUCH TRIP has no particular personality of its own, and sometimes seems to be just going through the motions. While generally enjoyable to watch, it keeps reminding the audience of how funny it *could* have been. *(Adult situations, excessive profanity.)*

p, Lawrence Gordon; d, Michael Ritchie; w, Steven Kampmann, Will Porter, Sean Stein (based on a novel by Ken Kolb); ph, Donald Thorin (Deluxe Color); ed, Richard A. Harris; m, Michel Colombier; m/l, John Davenport, Eddie Cooley; prod d, Jimmie Bly; set d, Gary Fettis; spec eff, Cliff Wenger; cos, Eddie Marks; stunts, Chuck Walters; makeup, Ken Chase.

Comedy **Cas.** **(PR:O MPAA:R)**

CRIME ZONE † (1988) 93m Concorde-New Horizons/Concorde c

David Carradine *(Jason)*, Peter Nelson *(Bone)*, Sherilyn Fenn *(Helen)*, Michael Shaner *(Creon)*, Orlando Sacha *(Alexi)*, Don Manor *(J.D.)*, Alfredo Calder *(Cruz)*, Jorgo Bustamante *(Hector)*.

This futuristic crime tale from Roger Corman follows the exploits of a pair of lovers (Fenn and Nelson) as they embark on a crime spree at the behest of Carradine, who, it is later revealed, is a double-crossing government agent who recruits crooks to keep the police occupied.

p, Luis Llosa; d, Luis Llosa; w, Daryl Haney; ph, Cusi Barrio; ed, William Flicker; m, Rick Conrad; art d, Angel Valdez, Jose Troncojo, Susana Aragon, Adrian Arias; spec eff, Fernando Vasquez de Velasco; cos, Patricia Maguill.

Action/Crime/Science Fiction **(PR:NR MPAA:R)**

CRITTERS II: THE MAIN COURSE** (1988) 87m New Line-Sho/New Line c

Scott Grimes *(Brad Brown)*, Liane Curtis *(Megan Morgan)*, Don Opper *(Charlie McFadden)*, Barry Corbin *(Harv)*, Tom Hodges *(Wesley)*, Sam Anderson *(Mr. Morgan)*, Lindsay Parker *(Cindy Morgan)*, Herta Ware *(Nana)*, Lin Shaye *(Sal Roos)*, Terrence Mann *(Ug, Bounty Hunter)*, Roxanne Kernohan *(Lee, Bounty Hunter)*, Doug Rowe *(Quigley)*, Eddie Deezen.

©NEW LINE

When we last saw these Critters, they'd been annihilated by intergalactic bounty hunters and the normally peace-loving people of Grover's Bend, Kansas. Of course, even iron-jawed hair balls recognize that extinction is not a smart career move in this age of sequels, so they secreted dozens of their eggs away on the Brown family farm, which was laid to waste in Part One. Part Two picks up two years later, with Brad Brown (Grimes) returning to Grover's Bend to visit his grandmother (Ware). Many of the good townsfolk believe the Browns were somehow responsible for the appearance of the Critters, since they first popped up at the Brown farm. As a result, Grimes experiences some animosity when he first arrives, but, for the most part, finds that the locals prefer not to think about what happened two years earlier. That's the way Grimes feels about it, too, and besides, he's more interested in pursuing Curtis, daughter of the town's newspaper editor (Anderson), although he is curious to know what happened to his friend Opper, the town drunk, who has been missing since the night of the great Critter battle. Back at the Brown farm, the eggs have been discovered and are to be used in the town's annual Easter pageant. The warmth of that day is all the eggs need to hatch, and suddenly dozens of ravenous Critters burst forth and start eating everything in sight, including the sheriff. As they did in the original, Grimes and the Grover's Bend citizenry need help to combat the monstrous dustballs, and just as he did in the first film, space hunter Ug (Mann) shows up to help out. This time he's joined by Kernohan and Grimes' old friend Opper, who has been off with the aliens battling space criminals during the past two years. A scan of the Earth revealed Critters to still be living there, and Mann has returned to destroy them and collect the promised bounty. All this sets up a reprise of the action in first film as aliens and townspeople unite to complete the grisly job of eliminating the murderous creatures. At one point the Critters gather together in a huge ball that rolls through town eating everything in sight, but the aliens are equal to the threat, dispatch the Critters, and restore peace and order to the bedraggled residents of Grover's Bend.

As sequels go, CRITTERS II: THE MAIN COURSE is particularly bereft of imagination. Save for the opening 20 or 30 minutes, the film is pretty much a clone of the original. The form-changing aliens, the suspect Grimes (still "the boy who cried Critter" in the minds of the locals), the manic Critters—it was all done in Part One, and Part Two merely recycles the same plots and gags. It doesn't take itself very seriously, but then that's the case with so many movies these days that it's hardly significant. In reality, this is the third permutation of this premise, since CRITTERS is only a very thinly disguised appropriation of GREMLINS. If you've never seen any of these films, the Gremlins/Critters are so joyously evil that it's hard not to be entertained by them, and they maintain that level of unmitigated nastiness in this entry. If anything, the Critters, created by Chiodo Brothers, are a little more menacing this time out. CRITTERS was so successful for New Line that the company doubled the approximately $2-million budget for the sequel, and the Chiodos were able to upgrade the special effects accordingly. As for the actors, they're competent. Missing from the original is the always-interesting M. Emmet Walsh as the sheriff, but Barry Corbin does a nice job as the now-retired lawman who must return to duty after the Critters have his replacement for lunch. This picture did not perform nearly as well at the box office as CRITTERS, probably signaling the end of the series. Nevertheless, there are still places in Grover's Bend where an egg might be hidden. . . (Violence, profanity, gore effects.)

p, Barry Opper; d, Mick Garris; w, D.T. Twohy, Mick Garris; ph, Russell Carpenter (DeLuxe Color); ed, Charles Bornstein; m, Nicholas Pike; prod d, Philip Dean Foreman; set d, Donna Stamps Scherer; spec eff, Chiodo Brothers, Marty Bresin; cos, Lesley Lynn Nicholson; stunts, Dan Bradley.

Horror   Cas.   (PR:C MPAA:PG-13)

"CROCODILE" DUNDEE II   (1988) 110m PAR c

Paul Hogan (Mick "Crocodile" Dundee), Linda Kozlowski (Sue Charlton), Charles Dutton (LeRoy Brown), Hechter Ubarry (Rico), Juan Fernandez (Miguel), John Meillon (Walter Reilly), Ernie Dingo, Steve Rackman, Gerry Skilton, Gus Mercurio, Jim Holt, Alec Wilson, Maggie Blinco, Kenneth Welsh, Stephen Root, Dennis Boutsikaris, Marilyn Sokol, Bill Sandy, Carlos Carrasco, Luis Guzman.

This sequel to the phenomenally successful "CROCODILE" DUNDEE is a surpris-

ingly shoddy affair that abandons the unabashed romance of its predecessor for a rudimentary action-adventure plot involving guns and drugs. Directed at a stupefyingly sluggish pace, the film begins more or less where "CROC" I left off, with Australian Mick Dundee (Hogan) living in New York City with his reporter girl friend (Kozlowski). Feeling bored and useless, Hogan decides to find a job, although he hasn't a clue about what he would like to do. His job-hunting provides an excuse for the screenwriters (Hogan and his son Brett) to resurrect the same kind of fish-out-of-water jokes that worked so well in "CROC" I. This time Hogan goes fishing in New York harbor by tossing sticks of dynamite into the water; calmly walks out on the ledge of an office building to rescue a jumper (the punch line of this gag is distressingly homophobic); makes friends with a streetwise black man named LeRoy Brown (Dutton) who acts like a drug dealer to disguise the fact that he is actually a mild-mannered stationery salesman; mistakes a mechanical snake in a department store display for the real thing and snaps its neck; is mistaken for Clint Eastwood by Japanese tourists; and says, "G'day" and "No worries," to just about everyone he meets. Meanwhile, Kozlowski's ex-husband, a photojournalist, gets into trouble with a vicious Colombian drug kingpin (Ubarry) when he is caught taking pictures of his operation. He manages to send the film to Kozlowski before being murdered, but the drug runners trace the letter to New York and kidnap her. Hogan, however, has possession of the day's mail, and the kidnapers demand the film in exchange for Kozlowski's life. Instead of accepting the deal, Hogan and his friend, Dutton, enlist dozens of Manhattan punk rockers to create a diversion at Ubarry's Long Island compound while Hogan slips into the mansion to rescue Kozlowski. The trick works, and with the permission of the Drug Enforcement Agency, Hogan is allowed to take Kozlowski back to Australia with him so that he can protect her from the drug dealer on his own turf. Ubarry and his chief enforcer, Fernandez, follow and search the Australian outback for Hogan and Kozlowski with the help of some unscrupulous Aussie guides. The bumbling drug kingpin is no match for the clever Hogan, however, and during the course of the next interminable hour the charming Aussie toys with the Colombians, capturing them one at a time, aided by some bats, reptiles, water buffalo, and his loyal Aboriginie friends. In the end, only Ubarry and Fernandez die—one shot by the other, and the survivor plugged by the rifle-toting Kozlowski (Hogan does not indulge in lethal gunplay). An ecstatic Kozlowski embraces her rugged he-man and breathlessly declares that she would rather stay in the outback with him than go back to New York.

What was refreshingly charming in the first film is tired and boring here. Paul Hogan, a laid-back screen presence to begin with, is practically catatonic in CROC II, spouting the same quaint phrases and still reacting to every big-city situation like a naive child. The romance between him and Kozlowski—the basis of the first film's success—is given perfunctory treatment and left completely undeveloped. Moreover, Kozlowski's character has disintegrated into a clunky screenwriter's device used to introduce and motivate the absurd action-adventure plot line. But what is most alarming about a film with a premise as thin as this is that Hogan and director John Cornell (Hogan's partner, and the producer of CROC I) let this simpleminded material drone on for 110 minutes. The Long Island kidnaping sequence, in particular, is incredibly slow and dull, with scenes of Ubarry and Fernandez chatting away with a recalcitrant Kozlowski for what seems like days while Hogan rounds up the punkers and heads for the mansion. Likewise, the supposedly suspenseful rescue operation is a tedious set-piece wherein much screen time is devoted to little action, and the outback episode is simply an hour of watching people walk in circles.

Cornell is a dreadful director who seems to understand little more than the fundamentals of moviemaking (like keeping the image in focus). Unable to develop a romance and incapable of pacing an action scene, he allows the film to plod along like a dying water buffalo from its Manhattan beginning to its hokey freeze-frame ending. For some reason he chose to shoot the film in wide-screen, but, gorgeous Australian sunsets excepted, Cornell has done nothing of interest with the format, and most of his compositions are framed with a television cut-off ratio in mind. Hogan and son Brett's screenplay is also a lazy piece of work, and it is obvious that Hogan, who has said that this is the last CROCODILE DUNDEE film, is bored with Mick Dundee and would like to move on to something else. As well he should, because it is Hogan and Hogan alone who makes these films work, and if his heart isn't in it, the entire exercise is pointless. (Violence).

p, John Cornell, Jane Scott; d, John Cornell; w, Paul Hogan, Brett Hogan; ph, Russell Boyd (Duart Color); ed, David Stiven; m, Peter Best; prod d, Lawrence Eastwood; art d, Jeremy Conway; set d, Leslie Pope; cos, Norma Moriceau; tech, Dr. Grahame Webb, Harvey Cooper; stunts, Mal Graydon, Penny Graydon, Dennis Thompson, Henry Rainger, Graham Gow.

Adventure/Comedy   Cas.   (PR:C MPAA:PG)

CROSSING DELANCEY*   (1988) 97m WB c

Amy Irving (Isabelle "Izzy" Grossman), Reizl Bozyk (Bubbie Kantor), Peter Riegert (Sam Posner), Jeroen Krabbe (Anton Maes), Sylvia Miles (Hannah Mandelbaum), Suzzy Roche (Marilyn), Geroge Martin (Lionel), John Bedford Lloyd (Nick), Claudia Silver (Cecilia Monk), David Pierce (Mark), Rosemary Harris (Pauline Swift), Amy Wright (Ricki), Faye Grant (Candyce), Deborah Offner (Karen), Kathleen Wilhoite (Myla Bondy), Moishe Rosenfeld (Rabbi), Paula Laurence (Diva), Christine Campbell (Woman in Cab), Reg E. Cathey (Cab Driver), Susan Blommaert (Leslie), Delores Sutton (Aunt Miriam), Sam Corsi (Handball Champ), Vickilyn Reynolds (Woman in Sauna), Myra Taylor (Friend in Sauna), Young Ho Kim (Mr. Kim), Tudor Sherrard (Book Peddler), Jacob Harran (Guest at Bris), Bob Levine (Mr. Grossman), Mimi Bensinger (Mrs. Grossman), Arthur Rubin, Richard Frisch, Stan Page (Happy Birthday Singers), Michael Ornstein (Mickey), Susan Sandler (Molly), Tony Perez (Counter Boy), Arthur Tracey, Stan Rubin (Pickle Stand Customers), Debra Johanna Cole (Waitress), Brad O'Hare (Photographer), Freda Foh Shen (Self-Defense Teacher), Mina Bern (Would-be Victim), Ida Harnden, Ronnie Gilbert (Muggers), Kevin Rogers (Messenger), Miriam Phillips (Sarah Jacobs), De-

Gilbert *(Muggers)*, Kevin Rogers *(Messenger)*, Miriam Phillips *(Sarah Jacobs)*, Denis Belloco *(Maitre D')*, Pat Oleszko *(Pat Oleszko)*, Lee M. Linderman *(Waiter)*, Betty Rollin, Maria Antoinette Rogers *(Party Guests)*, Jayne Haynes *(Book Thief)*, Susan Braudy, Madge Cooper, Loring Eutemey, Vicki Goldberg, Hendrik Hertzberg, Stanley Leff, Quincy Long, Hugh Nissenson, Keith Reddin, Lore Segal, John Patrick Shanley, Scott Somer *(Celebrity Party Guests)*.

Set partly in New York's Lower East Side, where director Joan Micklin Silver's excellent tale of immigrant Jewish life in the 1890s, HESTER STREET (1975), also took place, this gentle romantic comedy is a fairy tale populated with real people. Irving, an attractive, intelligent Jewish woman in her early 30s, works in a classy Midtown bookstore frequented by well-known writers and editors. Like her parents, who live in Florida, she has opted not to live in the Old World neighborhood below Delancey Street, choosing instead an Upper West Side apartment more in keeping with the literary life she finds so fulfilling. Still, Irving dutifully treks Downtown for frequent visits with her *bubbe* (Bozyk), the grandmother who is so concerned about Irving's unwed status that she hires a marriage broker (Miles) to rectify the situation. Although Irving is already involved in a somewhat ambiguous relationship with a married friend and increasingly taken with Krabbe, the Dutch-born novelist who is one of the bookstore's star patrons, she consents to a meeting with the broker in the hope of putting an end to Bozyk's plotting. Miles' proposed match for Irving is Riegert, a soft-spoken man from the neighborhood who runs the pickle business started by his late father ("A joke and a pickle for only a nickel," reads a sign at his shop). Irving finds him nice enough, but tells him she has no interest in seeing him again. Not one to give up easily, however, Riegert continues trying to win Irving's heart, despite the mixed signals she gives him. Eventually, Irving begins to see that this pickle man has a poet's soul, but, unable to get around her disdain for his declasse occupation, she refuses to allow herself to get involved with him. She even tries a little matchmaking of her own, failing miserably when she attempts to arrange a "chance" meeting between Riegert and one of her friends, Roche (of the musical Roche sisters, who provide the film's sprightly soundtrack). Meanwhile, Krabbe, who has been slyly seducing Irving with some plum lines from Confucius, turns up the heat, inviting her to his apartment one night to be the first reader of a work in progress. Irving goes with him, despite the fact that it means standing up Riegert—who, she is beginning to realize, is not just a nice guy but a *wonderful* guy. Just as Irving starts to believe that Krabbe is in love with her, he asks her to become his assistant (read literary and literal whore). Disgusted, Irving rushes off to Bozyk's, where she was to meet Riegert hours earlier. Finding her grandmother drunk and passed out, she thinks she has ruined everything; then Riegert, dressed in a suit, the pickle smell washed from his hands with vanilla, appears. Love, needless to say, wins out.

CROSSING DELANCEY could easily have been just another saccharine, paint-by-numbers affair. On the contrary, guided by director Silver's gentle but sure hand and benefitting from strong performances by the leads, it is a sweet, funny movie, though not quite the magical film it might have been. Several critics have rightly called it a fairy tale, but what prevents the more or less cliched story line from dragging down the film are the nuanced performances of Peter Riegert and Amy Irving, who invest their characters with profound emotional verity. Riegert, in particular, creates a memorable character, despite the fact that he isn't given much to say. With subtlety of gesture and attitude, he provides his regular guy with an appropriately understated intelligence and sophistication, yet he doesn't take the nice-guy stance too far, giving his lovelorn romantic a pragmatic, slightly vindictive edge that makes him believable. Irving also prevents her "Izzy" from becoming a fairy tale princess, making her ambivalent feelings for Riegert's Sam convincing as she experiences self-satisfaction, confusion, disillusionment, and repentance en route to romance. Some may find fault with the presentation of a woman as intelligent and talented as Izzy who only seems to find happiness when the right man comes along, but Silver's film is less concerned with smashing sexual stereotypes than with musing on the possibility of love that can triumph despite class or lifestyle prejudices. The supporting performers are as strong as the leads, especially Reizel Bozyk, a 74-year-old veteran of Yiddish theater appearing not only in her first film but in her first English-language production, as the strong-willed *bubbe* who only wants the best for her granddaughter. Jeroen Krabbe also gives a solid portrayal of the self-involved expatriate novelist, but Sylvia Miles takes her marriage broker well over the top. Careful viewers will also note the presence of MOONSTRUCK screenwriter John Patrick Shanley at one of the literary soirees.

Like MOONSTRUCK, CROSSING DELANCEY uses its nicely etched ethnic milieu, not as a substitute for character, but to enhance the characters' emotional depth, giving the sense that they existed before the film began. Working from a screenplay by Susan Sandler, who also penned the semiautobiographical off-Broadway play on which the film is based, Silver has nicely captured Lower East Side Jewish life and the conflict between tradition and change while also offering resonant slice-of-life portraits of elsewhere in New York—from the self-defense class Bozyk attends to the up-market bistro where Irving introduces Riegert to Roche. With CROSSING DELANCEY, Silver again shows herself to be a gifted filmmaker, and though it's certainly not her best film, it is still a very satisfying one. Songs include: "Come Softly to Me" (Gretchen Christopher, Barbara Ellis, Gary Troxel, performed by The Roches); "Pounding" (Terre and Suzzy Roche, performed by The Roches); "Lieutenant Kije" (Serge Prokofieff, Paul Chihara); "It's Like That" (RUN DMC); "Some Enchanted Evening" (Richard Rodgers, Oscar Hammerstein II, performed by Paula Laurence); "Nocturne" (Margaret A. Roche, performed by The Roches); "Get Your Hands off Her" (Pat Oleszko, performed by Oleszko); "She's Going" (The English Beat, performed by The English Beat); "It Had to be You" (Isham Jones, Gus Kahn, performed by Benny Goodman) "Lucky" (Terre Roche, David Roche, performed by The Roches). *(Sexual situations, adult situations)*

p, Michael Nozik; d, Joan Micklin Silver; w, Susan Sandler (based on her play); ph, Theo Van de Sande (Duart color); ed, Rick Shaine; m, Paul Chihara; m/l, Gretchen Christopher, Barbara Ellis, Gary Troxel, Terre Roche, Suzzy Roche, David Roche, Serge Prokofieff, Margaret A. Roche, Pat Oleszko, Richard

Rodgers, Oscar Hammerstein II, Isham Jones, Gus Kahn; prod d, Dan Leigh; art d, Leslie E. Rollins; set d, Daniel Boxer; cos, Rita Ryack; stunts, Phil Neilson; makeup, David Forrest.

| Comedy/Romance | Cas. | (PR:C MPAA:PG) |

CRY IN THE DARK, A* ½**   (1988) 121m Cannon-Golan-Globus-Cinema Verity/WB c

Meryl Streep *(Lindy Chamberlain)*, Sam Neill *(Michael Chamberlain)*, Bruce Myles *(Barker)*, Charles Tingwell *(Justice Muirhead)*, Nick Tate *(Charlwood)*, Neil Fitzpatrick *(Phillips)*, Maurie Fields *(Barritt)*, Lewis Fitz-gerald *(Tipple)*.

A CRY IN THE DARK tells the true story of Michael and Lindy Chamberlain (Neill and Streep), the Seventh-Day Adventist minister and his wife whose infant disappeared from their tent during a family outing at Ayers Rock in the Australian province of Queensland in 1980. Streep suspects her baby was dragged off by a dingo she saw leaving the tent, and a search party of vacationers and aborigines is formed to plow through the heavy darkness, without success. A subsequent investigation into the child's disappearance absolves the parents of responsibility, but then a new investigator enters the case, and evidence points toward evil. Streep is indicted for the murder of her daughter and Neill is charged as an accessory to the crime. "Did she do it?" becomes a question publicly debated by the Australian populace, who are fed continuous reports by a press that won't let the story die. Streep adopts a hard exterior (one woman notes that "she's got a face to crack walnuts on"), while Neill struggles to maintain his faith in God. The marriage is strained. To exacerbate the couple's tragedy, the public is curiously unwilling to believe that a dingo was responsible. A rumor circulates that the infant's death was a ritual sacrifice. Hostility mounts, but Streep maintains her cool front, suggesting to Neill that he divorce her if she goes to prison. She becomes pregnant, but the timing of the trial is changed, and instead of delivering by its start as planned she has to appear in court pregnant. Streep is convicted, as is Neill, but, whereas Streep goes to prison, he is permitted to return home to take care of their boys. Streep gives birth in prison, but is not allowed to keep the baby. Years pass before new evidence appears in the form of a jacket worn by the missing infant, lending support to Streep's version, and she is released after five years' incarceration. Neill, her sons, and the daughter she has never seen welcome her home, although the battle to prove her innocence is not won until September 1988.

A CRY IN THE DARK is a poignant, if sometimes slow-moving, family-in-crisis drama. A long opening segment showing the Chamberlains at work and play establishes the couple's clean lifestyle and general ordinariness, but suffers from TV-movie weariness. Things gets more exciting with the baby's disappearance and again with the indictment, although too many shots of citizens debating Streep's innocence break the momentum. (Her delivery in prison of a baby she will not keep, on the other hand, is very moving.) On the whole, director-cowriter Fred Schepisi's film is lively enough, and is particularly aided by the music by Bruce Smeaton and spectacular performances from Meryl Streep and Sam Neill. Particularly affecting is Neill's depiction of Michael, struggling to keep his religious faith and to be supportive of his wife. Neill's job is made easier by virtue of Michael's being the more interesting character—weaker than Lindy, he nevertheless successfully resolves both his dilemmas, for by the movie's end he has returned to talking with confidence about God's providence, and, earlier, after a wrenching marital argument, he meaningfully takes Lindy's hand on the way up the courthouse steps, just before the verdict is read.

A CRY IN THE DARK is billed as "a true story of conscience, courage, and conviction" and it is indeed just that. Unfortunately, much of the dialog will be indecipherable to viewers unused to Australian accents. The film is based on a thriller-style book, *Evil Angels*, written in Lindy's favor by a Melbourne barrister who was critical of the prosecution's handling of forensic evidence and pointed out contradictions in old testimony. Movies like this reaffirm a role films sometimes play—to point out injustices, presumably with a view to correction and prevention. A CRY IN THE DARK, while falling short of greatness, succeeds in this, and as a work of art as well. *(Adult situations.)*

p, Verity Lambert; d, Fred Schepisi; w, Robert Caswell, Fred Schepisi (based on the book *Evil Angels* by John Bryson); ph, Ian Baker (Panavision); ed, Jill Bilcock; m, Bruce Smeaton; prod d, Wendy Dickson, George Liddle; art d, Dale Duguid, Brian Edmonds; cos, Bruce Finlayson; makeup, Noriko Spencer.

| Docu-drama | Cas. | (PR:C MPAA:PG-13) |

CRYSTALSTONE †   (1988) 103m TMS c

Kamlesh Gupta *(Pablo)*, Laura Jane Goodwin *(Maria)*, Frank Grimes *(Captain)*, Edward Kelsey *(Hook)*, Sydney Bromley *(Old Man)*, Terence Bayler *(Policeman)*, Patricia Conti, Helen Ryan, Ann Way, Brigit Forsyth, Ruth Kettlewell, Mario De Barros.

Despite winning the 1988 Award of Merit for Outstanding Achievement from the Academy of Family Films and the 1988 Award of Excellence from the Film Advisory Board, CRYSTALSTONE barely saw a theatrical release and will no doubt turn up on the home video shelves with little fanfare. A traditional children's tale of adventure set in Spain at the turn of the century, the film stars Gupta and Goodwin as a brother and sister (10 and six years old, respectively) who are left virtual orphans upon the death of their mother. Their drunken father (Grimes) having left long ago to live the life of a seaman, the children are dumped in the care of a cruel guardian who decides to separate them. Refusing to be split, the children run away and decide to search for the fabled Crystalstone, a much-coveted piece of quartz. Also looking for the quartz is a Captain Hook-type pirate (Kelsey), with whom the children have a few run-ins along the way.

p, John Williams, Britt Lomond; d, Antonio Pelaez; w, Antonio Pelaez; ph, John Stephens (Fotofilm); ed, Arnold Baker; m, Fernando Uribe; prod d, George Costello; art d, Maria Caso; cos, Julia Sanchez.

| Adventure/Children's | Cas. | (PR:NR MPAA:PG) |

D

DA*½** (1988) 102m FilmDallas c

Barnard Hughes (*Da*), Martin Sheen (*Charlie*), William Hickey (*Drumm*), Karl Hayden (*Young Charlie*), Doreen Hepburn (*Mother*), Hugh O'Conor (*Boy Charlie*), Ingrid Craigie (*Polly*), Joan O'Hara (*Mrs. Prynne*), Peter Hanly (*Young Oliver*), Jill Doyle, Maurice O'Donoghue, Amiee Clark, Frank McDonald, Marie Conmee, Ronan Wilmot, Kathy Greenblatt, Martin Dempsey, Marcus Colley.

Based on an autobiographical play by Hugh Leonard, which was in turn adapted from his book *Home Before Night*, DA is the heart-tugging story of a father-son reunion and reconciliation that takes place beyond the grave. Sheen, a middle-aged, Irish-American playwright with a play about to open on Broadway, learns that his 83-year-old father (Hughes) has died in Ireland and he returns to the coastal village of his youth to attend his da's funeral. As Sheen sits alone in his family's humble home and sorts through Da's belongings, he is visited by Hughes—more corporeal than ghostly, the invention of the grieving son's conscience. At first Sheen tries to ignore the apparition of this man, who spent 54 years tending the roses of a wealthy family only to be released with a miserable pension. Finally, he gives himself over to his imagination, exploring his love-hate relationship with his father, reminiscing with Da as he crosses a mental frontier and ventures into the past. There Sheen encounters Hughes and Hepburn, Sheen's mother; Hickey, the crotchety clerk who gave Sheen his first job and who remained an alternative father figure; and earlier incarnations of himself, most notably Hayden, who plays Sheen as a young man. In the process, he relives the most memorable—and most painful—moments of his life with his father, castigating Hughes along the way for his passivity, lies, stubbornness, and ignorance, but at the same time recognizing his essential decency and gentleness. With the wisdom of hindsight, Sheen hectors Hayden as he endures the anguish and embarrassment Sheen has been unable to put behind him, but the young man gets in his shots, too, at the man he will become. By the film's end Sheen's ambivalent feelings for his da have by no means been completely resolved, but he has come to understand both Hughes and himself better. At the fade, Hughes returns with Sheen to New York, a memory that he can live with, not run from.

Benefitting from wonderful performances by everyone involved, including Barnard Hughes' re-creation of his Tony Award-winning stage role, DA is an extremely moving film that is full of feeling but that does not resort to sentimentality. Instead, DA is a film that allows us to care. By evoking the youthful wounds and bitterness we all carry into adult life, as well more rose-colored memories, this first-time directorial effort by actor Matt Clark invites us to reexamine our own parent-child relationships. At the same time, Clark and screenwriter Hugh Leonard have opened up Leonard's play without giving the sense that they have done so purely out of necessity in converting a play into film. Instead, the transitions between past and present, between illusion and reality, that call attention to themselves on the stage are seamless in the film, adding to the immediacy of Sheen's imaginative experience. Clark and Leonard conjure up a "you are there" reality for Sheen in which the past doesn't appear as flashback, and in which Hughes' presence isn't quite supernatural. Shooting in Leonard's hometown, Dalkey, cinematographer Alar Kivilo uses the Irish landscape sparingly but effectively, and even when the action goes outdoors the camera setups maintain the intimacy of the stage.

For all its poignancy, DA is still a very funny movie, and the actors don't waste many opportunities. Barnard Hughes is charming, milking the humor, pathos, and humanity of his character, and only occasionally becoming *too* lovable. Martin Sheen, who was one of the film's executive producers and who labored for some years to bring the play to the screen, gives an insightful, sincere performance, believably balancing a sardonic sense of irony with less rational feelings. William Hickey (PRIZZI'S HONOR) contributes a terrific portrayal of the crotchety Mr. Drumm, whose 70 years of living have provided him with only one indisputable truth: ". . . in a public house lavatory incoming traffic has the right of way." Karl Hayden, as the young Sheen, and stage actress Doreen Hepburn, whose fine performance frequently shifts the focus of the film to Ma, also add much to this touching, funny film. (*Adult situations, profanity.*)

p, Julie Corman; d, Matt Clark; w, Hugh Leonard (based on his play "Da" and novel *Home Before Night*); ph, Alar Kivilo; ed, Nancy Nuttal Beyda; m, Elmer Bernstein; prod d, Frank Conway.

Fantasy **Cas.** **(PR:A-C MPAA:PG)**

DADDY'S BOYS** (1988) 85m Concorde c

Daryl Haney (*Jimmy*), Laura Burkett (*Christie*), Raymond J. Barry (*Daddy*), Dan Shor (*Hawk*), Christian Clemenson (*Otis*), Ellen Gerstein (*Mme. Wang*), Robert V. Barron (*Axelrod*), Paul Link (*Traveling Salesman*).

More interesting for the story *of* its filming than for the story actually filmed, DADDY'S BOYS is a vintage Roger Corman production. Realizing a brothel set he'd built for Angie Dickinson starrer BIG BAD MAMA II could be put to double duty, the King of the Bs had a cast, crew, and rough story put together in six days. AFTER HOURS screenwriter Joe Minion (who was probably already aware that Corman himself had been able to write THE TERROR in one night and then shoot it in three days) signed on with the promise of getting his directorial break. Writing as they went, and using a few vintage clothes, perhaps three cars, and a whole lot of gumption, Minion and crew shot DADDY'S BOYS from the hip in 22 days.

This Depression-era crime story features Barry as tough old Daddy, a psycho widower who leads his three morose or retarded sons on a midwestern bank-robbing spree while looking for a woman willing to play Mama to him and his clan. Haney (who gets screenwriting credit), the morose son, has had enough and strikes out on his own, much to Barry's consternation. Haney soon hooks up with kittenish whore Burkett (providing the requisite Corman topless scenes), and soon they're in love and finding out for themselves how liberating and sexy robbing banks can be. Barry catches up with them, however, and, after Barry murders an innocent family to give his own sick brood their home and threatens literally to crucify the ornery Haney like "God did his son," he and the boys wipe out some nasty real estate executives. They finally do get their Mama, in a not particularly happy ending.

A kind of male BIG BAD MAMA meets BONNIE AND CLYDE, DADDY'S BOYS is watchable, and sometimes even enjoyable, but mostly it's just dull. Too many scenes play like first-draft writing given first-take direction; as for action, because of budgetary limitations, almost no blood is shed onscreen until the wrap-up. The sets seem freshly painted, the lights porno-movie flat, and the cast can be called willing if not always able. Rising young character actor Christian Clemenson (BROADCAST NEWS) is superb and disturbing as dim brother Otis, but Laura Burkett's pouty hooker looks totally out of place and seems unable to get into the ironic swing of the proceedings. Raymond J. Barry has some chilly moments as Daddy, and the melon-shaped Daryl Haney throws a few curves into both his performance and his script. But, because its production schedule made it look so slipshod and sound so unthought-out, DADDY'S BOYS is easier to appreciate than to really like. Look for it on video shelves next to anything with Cameron Mitchell or Miles O'Keefe. (*Violence, nudity, profanity.*)

p, Roger Corman; d, Joe Minion; w, Daryl Haney; ph, David G. Stump (Foto-Kem Color); ed, Norman Hollyn; m, Sasha Matson; prod d, Gabrielle Petrissans; art d, Hernan G. Camacho; stunts, Mike Ryan.

Crime **Cas.** **(PR:O MPAA:R)**

DANCE OR DIE † (1988) 81m City Lights c

Ray Kieffer (*Jason Chandler*), Rebecca Barrington, Georgia Neu, Jerry Cleary, Jim Williams, Jerry Tiffe, Jack Zavorak, Rooney Tafeaga, Will Cavanaugh, Jake Jacobs, Joe Wheeler, Shane Devon, Jo Jo Bryan, Lauri Thompson.

DANCE OR DIE's lead character is a fellow named Jason Chandler, who, the film's press material tells us, "wants just two things in life: to stay off drugs, and to choreograph a dance show that rivals FLASHDANCE." The ambitious protagonist is helped with his chemical dependency by an older female friend, and his attempts to deliver a dance show in Las Vegas (complete with a creative use of fake blood) shows signs of becoming a hit, but he has another, as yet unconquered problem—his drug-dealing roommate is murdered and the woman with whom our hero has fallen in love is revealed to be a federal drug agent. Released straight to video.

p, Richard Pepin, Joseph Merhi; d, Richard Munchkin; w, Richard Munchkin; ph, Peter Jensen; ed, Paul Volk; m, John Gonzalez; spec eff, Judy Yonemoto, Kerby Brothers; ch, Minnie Madden; stunts, Perry Genovese; makeup, Judy Yonemoto, Kerby Brothers.

Crime/Dance **Cas.** **(PR:NR MPAA:NR)**

DANGEROUS CURVES † (1988) 93m Mark Borde/Lightning Pictures c

Tate Donovan (*Chuck*), Danielle Von Zerneck (*Michelle West*), Grant Heslov (*Wally Wilder*), Valeri Breiman (*Blake Courtland*), Karen Lee Scott (*Shawn Brooks*), Robert Klein ("*Bam Bam*"), Leslie Nielsen, Elizabeth Ashley, Robert Stack, Michael J. Rosenberg, Eva La Rue, Marie Cheatham, Armin Shimerman, Freeman King, Robert Romanus, Martha Quinn, Theresa Ring.

A couple of UCLA kids—one a party animal who wants nothing more out of life than a suntan, a beer, and a bikini-clad girl, the other a straight-laced teen with a bit more ambition—are hired by a wealthy industrialist (Stack) to drive a brand new Porsche to his daughter in Lake Tahoe. Along the way, the party animal persuades his friend to make a pit stop at the Miss Mission Beach Beauty Pageant. It should come as no surprise that DANGEROUS CURVES was released straight to video.

p, Mark Borde, Kenneth Raich; d, David Lewis; w, Michael Dugan, Michael Zand, Paul Brown; ph, David Lewis (DeLuxe color); ed, Bob Bring; m, John D'Andrea; prod d, Elliot Gilbert; stunts, Eddie Braun.

Comedy   Cas.   (PR:NR MPAA:PG)

DANGEROUS LIAISONS***½   (1988) 120m NFH-Lorimar/WB c

Glenn Close (Marquise de Merteuil), John Malkovich (Vicomte de Valmont), Michelle Pfeiffer (Madame de Tourvel), Swoosie Kurtz (Madame de Volanges), Keanu Reeves (Chevalier Danceny), Mildred Natwick (Madame de Rosemonde), Uma Thurman (Cecile de Volanges), Joe Sheridan, Peter Capaldi.

Choderlos de Laclos reportedly said of his epistolary, 1782 novel, Les Liaisons Dangereuses, "I resolved to write a book which would create some stir in the world and continue to do so after I had gone from it." That novel, on which British director Stephen Frears' first American feature film is based, has done much of what Laclos hoped. The first edition sold out in days and instantly became the succes de scandale of Paris. By late 1803, Laclos had "gone from" the world; in 1824, his novel was banned and labeled "dangerous." In 1959, Roger Vadim brought the novel's sexual depravity to the screen in a modernized version, set in a ski resort, which was banned in some parts of France. By 1987, Laclos' novel was still creating a stir, though not a scandal, when it was brought to the stage by the Royal Shakespeare Company in a play adaptation by Christopher Hampton that has had a successful and, as of this writing, ongoing 800-plus performance run. During 1988, two film productions of the novel were set into motion—the Milos Forman-directed, Jean-Claude Carriere-penned adaptation titled (for a 1989 release) VALMONT, and this Stephen Frears-directed, Hollywood-produced picture.

A costume drama set in pre-Revolution France, DANGEROUS LIAISONS' story is one of sexual power, depravity, cruelty, and deceit. Close and Malkovich are monsters of the aristocracy, former lovers who spend their days planning sexual seductions and vengeances. Malkovich is a professional rake notorious throughout France, an amoral game-player who views every seduction as a conquest in which the only variable is the degree of difficulty involved. Close makes Malkovich a proposition: if he deflowers the 16-year-old future wife (Thurman) of another of Close's former lovers, then she will gratefully invite Malkovich to her boudoir. Concerned for his reputation, Malkovich initially refuses such an easy conquest, intending instead to devote his attention to bedding Pfeiffer, a highly moral, married, and convent-bred young woman. Malkovich plies his trade with the greatest skill and precision, eventually breaking down Pfeiffer's resistance; in the meantime, to please his friend Close, he has also deflowered Thurman—who, since giving in to Malkovich, has become something of an insatiable teen, not only having a series of encounters with Malkovich but also writing increasingly suggestive letters to the young music teacher she really loves (Reeves). Malkovich's career as a rake takes a devastating turn, however, when he finds himself genuinely falling for Pfeiffer. Just as "good" girl Pfeiffer has become "bad," so, too, has Malkovich transformed from amoral to moral. When Malkovich tells the eager Close of his feelings for Pfeiffer (he admits he has never been so deeply under another's control), Close becomes furious. It becomes clear that her attraction for Malkovich, despite all her game-playing, is itself one of profound, albeit twisted, love. She demands that he break off the relationship, hinting that he use the excuse, "It is beyond my control." Fearing that his name as a seducer will be ruined and that he will become the laughingstock of the aristocracy, Malkovich heeds Close's wishes, and, after telling Pfeiffer of his decision, returns to Close with the expectation of bedding her. She refuses, however, and remains determined to keep Malkovich under her control. They then declare war upon one another—one that threatens to destroy everyone they have involved in their debauchery. As a result of their battle, Malkovich is killed by Reeves and Pfeiffer dies of a broken heart. Before breathing his final breath, however, Malkovich vows his eternal love to Pfeiffer and gives Close's private letters to Reeves, so that all her liaisons may be exposed.

Director Frears is best known in the US for his films about Britain's racially torn ghettoes and his left-wing, anti-Thatcher politics (MY BEAUTIFUL LAUNDRETTE; PRICK UP YOUR EARS; SAMMY AND ROSIE GET LAID), making it seem highly unlikely that he would film a costume drama based on an 18th-century French novel set among the upper class. Underneath the wigs and push-up corsets, however, there remains the one issue that concerns Frears most—the politics of power. DANGEROUS LIAISONS is less about debauchery and amorality than it is about the sexual and psychological domination of one person by another (the obvious theme of PRICK UP YOUR EARS, which detailed Joe Orton's subhuman treatment of Kenneth Halliwell), or, by political extension, of one class or country over another. (A sound argument could be made concerning American imperialism by examining the decision to cast all American actors and its implication in an adaptation of a British play about French aristocrats—the self-serving deceit and quest for power becoming even more apparent.) In many ways, however, DANGEROUS LIAISONS is closest to Frears' 1984 film THE HIT. Both are stories about an evil, callous professional (John Hurt's stone-faced hit man, Malkovich's amoral seducer) whose life is turned on its head when he finally begins to feel. Both these characters lose control, and are unable to function according to their predefined set of rules.

Much of DANGEROUS LIAISONS' success results from the performances of John Malkovich and Glenn Close. Instead of catering to expectation and adopting the stiff, ancient mannerisms one has come to associate with historical costume dramas, Malkovich and Close play their roles somewhere in between the archaic and the modern. As a result, the film can be more easily connected to present-day sexual morals, sexual politics, and thirst for power. The rest of the cast is also worthy of

commendation: Michelle Pfeiffer and Swoosie Kurtz do well in underwritten roles; 18-year-old Uma Thurman is wonderfully innocent and makes a delirious character switch upon losing her virginity; Keanu Reeves, the sloppy teen of RIVER'S EDGE and PERMANENT RECORD, is seen in a refreshing change of type; and the great Mildred Natwick delivers every line with pointed perfection.

The film's major fault is the decision to concentrate on the characters of Close and Malkovich—an evil pair who are seen as the chief designers of this architecture of depravity. In making this choice, Frears and screenwriter Hampton (who, at Frears' urging, at least restored the use of letters to the script—an aspect of the original that is unconsciously left out of the stage play) have destroyed the book's brilliant epistolary structure, a form by which all characters are shown as equally villain and victim. Still, despite the fact that it does not remain structurally true to Laclos (which, admittedly, would have been a difficult task), DANGEROUS LIAISONS is nonetheless an extremely well made, witty, and vulgar attack on the dangerously self-righteous morality of this country and of Frears' native land. (Nudity, sexual situations, adult situations.)

p, Norma Heyman, Hank Moonjean, Christopher Hampton; d, Stephen Frears; w, Christopher Hampton (based on his play and the novel Les Liaisons Dangereuses by Choderlos de Laclos); ph, Philippe Rousselot; ed, Mick Audsley; m, George Fenton; prod d, Stuart Craig; art d, Gerard Viard, Gavin Bocquet; set d, Gerard James; cos, James Acheson.

Historical   Cas.   (PR:O MPAA:R)

DANGEROUS LOVE †(1988) 94m Motion Picture Corp. of America/Concorde c

Lawrence Monoson (Gabe), Brenda Bakke (Chris), Peter Marc (Jay), Elliott Gould (Rick), Anthony Geary (Mickey), Sal Landi, Angelyne, Eloise Broady, Teri Austin, Robin Klein, Bernie Pock.

This low-budget thriller, which saw only a regional release, stars Gould as a gumshoe trying to stop a serial murderer who kills off girls in video-dating types while video-taping (a la Michael Powell's PEEPING TOM) their demise. The prime suspect is the dating service's new employee, a computer geek who clearly seems to be the culprit. Despite the strong case Gould builds against him, Gould's pretty partner manages to fall in love with the suspect and proclaim his innocence. Former soap opera star Anthony Geary has a supporting role, making this the second video dating movie he has appeared in this year—the other being YOU CAN'T HURRY LOVE.

p, Brad Krevoy, Steven Stabler; d, Marty Ollstein; w, Marty Ollstein; ph, Nicholas Von Sternberg; ed, Tony Lanza; prod d, Michael Clousen; art d, Greg Maher; set d, Chava Danielson; cos, Brian Cotton.

Thriller   Cas.   (PR:NR MPAA:R)

DARK AGE †   (1988, US/Aus.) 90m RKO-FGH c

John Jarratt (Steve), Nikki Coghill (Cathy), Max Phipps (John), Burnam Burnam (Oondabund), David Gulpilil (Adjaral), Ray Meagher (Rex), Jeff Ashby (Mac), Paul Bertram (Jackson).

In Australia, a 25-foot-long crocodile is washed downstream by heavy rains, terrorizing the local population. Hoping to prevent poachers from killing the creature, which is revered by the aboriginal people, a government ranger enlists the aid of two Aborigines and begins a quest to find the animal. The film, a US-Australian coproduction, saw a brief theatrical release before hitting the video shelves.

p, Basil Appleby; d, Arch Nicholson; w, Sonia Borg (based on the novel Numunwari by Grahame Webb); ph, Andrew Lesnie (Panavision, Eastmancolor); ed, Adrian Carr; m, Danny Beckerman; prod d, David Copping.

Adventure/Horror   Cas.   (PR:NR MPAA:R)

DARK BEFORE DAWN †(1988) 95m E.K. Gaylord-Lazy "E"-Kingpin/PSM c

Sonny Gibson (Jeff Parker), Doug McClure (James Kirkland), Reparata Mazzola (Jessica Stanton), Ben Johnson (Sheriff), Billy Drago (Cabalistas Leader), Rance Howard (Glen Logan), Morgan Woodward (J.B. Watson), Buck Henry (Charlie Stevens), Paul Newsom (Roger Crandall), Jeffrey Osterhage (Andy Peterson), Red Steagall (Hal Porter), John L. Martin (Sen. Henry Vance), Rex Linn (Don Haleys).

Conspiracy in the wheatfields is the subject of this farm thriller, which was released only in Kansas—where it was shot—and other small midwestern markets. When a reporter gets wind of the giant agribusiness conglomerate Farmco's plan to manipulate the wheat market to make them billions while skyrocketing the price of a loaf of bread to $6, he tips off Mazzola, a government investigator. The reporter subsequently turns up dead, and Mazzola goes to Kansas to investigate. With help from some independent farmers, local newspapermen, and a disgruntled ex-Farmco board member, Mazzola moves to stop the insidious corporation, but discovers that they are more than willing to kill again. This obviously heartfelt effort to highlight the plight of the American family farmer and alert the public to the rise of agribusiness was written by star Reparata Mazzola, who disowned the final cut. Seen by virtually no one during its theatrical release, DARK BEFORE DAWN is a likely candidate for rebirth on home video and cable television.

p, Ben Miller; d, Robert Totten; w, Reparata Mazzola; ph, Steve M. McWilliams (Panavision); ed, Ron Hanthaner, Tom Boutross; m, Ken Sutherland; art d,

Richard Carver.

Thriller (PR:NR MPAA:PG-13)

DEAD HEAT* (1988) 86m NW c

Treat Williams (*Roger Mortis*), Joe Piscopo (*Doug Bigelow*), Lindsay Frost (*Randi James*), Darren McGavin (*Dr. Ernest McNab*), Vincent Price (*Arthur P. Loudermilk*), Clare Kirkconnell (*Rebecca Smythers*), Keye Luke (*Mr. Thule*), Ben Mittleman (*Bob*), Peter Kent (*Smitty*), Robert Picardo (*Lt. Herzog*), Mel Stewart (*Capt. Mayberry*), Professor Toru Tanaka (*Butcher*), Martha Quinn (*Newscaster*), Cate Caplin (*Saleswoman*), Monica Lewis (*Mrs. Von Heiserberg*), Peggy O'Brien (*Jewelry Store Manager*), Chip Heller (*Wilcox*), Steven R. Bannister (*The Thing*), Lew Hopson (*Whitfield*), Tom Nolan (*Jonas*), Steve Itkin (*Freman*), Shane Black (*Patrolman*), Mike Saad, Monty Cox (*Guards*), Monty Ash (*Waiter*), H. Ray Huff (*Cop*), Pons Mar, Dawan Scott (*Pool Zombies*), Ivan E. Roth (*End Zombie*), Ron Taylor (*Shoot Out Zombie*), Yvonne Peattie (*Gertrude Bellman*), Clarence Brown (*Harry Latham*), Pamela Vansant, Beth Toussaint (*Lab Technicians*).

A disastrous comedy-horror film, DEAD HEAT could have been a decent time-waster had it not been for the inept direction of former editor Mark Goldblatt (THE TERMINATOR) and the crippling presence of the least funny comedian in the world, Joe "Muscles" Piscopo. Set in Los Angeles, the film begins as two police detectives, the uptight Williams and the wisecracking Piscopo, are called to assist officers who have cornered a pair of jewelry store robbers. The two thieves, armed with Uzis, trade machine-gun fire with a small army of cops, but, amazingly, the robbers refuse to die although they've been shot several dozen times. Finally, Williams runs one over with a squad car, while the other accidentally kills himself with a hand grenade. At the autopsy, coroner's assistant Kirkconnell realizes that she has already examined the corpses, and Williams and Piscopo, determined to get to the bottom of the mystery, trace a few clues to a high-tech drug lab where the company's public relations woman, Frost, gives them the grand tour. Piscopo goes nosing around on his own, however, and discovers a giant, ugly Hells Angel of a man on a slab beneath a machine that would make Dr. Frankenstein drool with envy. The monster comes to life and starts thrashing Piscopo, and in the melee that ensues Williams winds up getting killed, while Frost flees the scene. With Piscopo's help, Kirkconnell uses the mysterious machine to bring Williams back to life. Surprisingly, he feels just fine and is eager to crack the case and bring his murderer to justice. There is one catch, however: because his body is going to begin decomposing rapidly, he has only 12 hours to get the job done. Picking up Frost at her home, the two detectives begin piecing the conspiracy together. They learn that Luke, an inscrutable Chinese, invented the machine, but when the detectives go to his grocery to question him, he switches on his own version of the machine and brings a score of barbecued chickens and ducks to life. Piscopo has to fight a barbecued pig, Williams is attacked by a huge side of beef, and Luke escapes during the chaos. After the battle, Williams and Piscopo split up to cover more ground, with plans to meet back at Frost's house. When Frost and Williams arrive, however, they find Piscopo murdered. If that weren't enough, it's then revealed that Frost is herself one of the living dead as she rots before Williams' eyes. At this point the decomposing detective is not doing so well himself, and he hurries to solve the case before he falls apart completely. Eventually, Williams discovers that LA's top coroner, McGavin, is part of a conspiracy to reanimate the filthy rich in exchange for half their estates and that he and Luke have ironed out the bugs in the machine and made Price, who financed its development, their first immortal success. When McGavin and Luke make a presentation to Price's rich friends, using Piscopo's body for a demonstration, Williams breaks in on the scene and begins shooting up the joint. The reanimated Piscopo joins in and the bad guys are defeated, leaving the two zombie detectives to go off and rot together somewhere.

As written by Terry Black, the older brother of LETHAL WEAPON writer Shane Black, DEAD HEAT could have been a fairly amusing horror comedy, with its interesting premise. Unfortunately, Robert D. Yeoman's excellent cinematography, Steve Johnson's impressive special effects, and Treat Williams's engaging performance are compromised by Goldblatt's bumbling direction and Piscopo's ineptitude. With a horrible grimace plastered on his face and his pumped-up biceps gratuitously on display throughout the film, Piscopo sabotages the film's attempts at humor. Reportedly the former "Saturday Night Live" comedian was permitted to improvise at will, which may be why DEAD HEAT's laugh quotient is reduced to next to nothing. Further, there is absolutely no rapport between Piscopo and Williams, each doing his own thing without regard to the rhythms of the other. It's hard to blame Williams for this, however, Piscopo being so grating that one would hesitate to play off him for fear of ruining one's own performance. Obviously, director Goldblatt left the actors on their own, and while Williams and Darren McGavin contribute decent performances, the talents of Vincent Price are wasted. Simply put, Goldblatt's lack of direction destroys the film's comedy, and his action scenes don't fare much better. Since he has edited films for Joe Dante and James Cameron, one would assume that Goldblatt has learned that shot composition, camera movement, pace, and rhythm make or break a scene. He hasn't. With few exceptions, his directorial choices are misguided throughout the film, leaving the viewer wishing that this highly campy material had been helmed by the likes of Paul Bartel or Dante, who might have wrung the *proper* amounts of comedy and horror from it.

What keeps DEAD HEAT watchable (barely) are the inventive special effects of Johnson and his crew. Regrettably, some of his more graphic work was cut when the MPAA balked six different times and threatened the producers with an X rating if several gruesome items weren't removed. The trimming is obvious in the final version, and certainly doesn't help the action scenes any. Black's script, which is by no means

great, relies heavily on the 1950 *film noir* D.O.A. for inspiration (indeed, a clip from that film is seen on a television set) and even names Piscopo Bigelow after Edmond O'Brien's character in that film. What passes for humor are stupid character names—like Roger Mortis for Williams (get it?)—and the putrefying detective's constant reminders to others that he's dead. Luckily, Williams does bring some complexity to his role, acting more liberated and alive as the rotting increases. The rest of the script indulges in lengthy shootouts in which characters empty hundreds of rounds of ammunition into unaffected zombies for what, under Goldblatt's direction, seems like forever. Unless you're a special effects nut, avoid DEAD HEAT at all costs. (*Violence, gore effects, profanity.*)

p, Michael Meltzer, David Helpern; d, Mark Goldblatt; w, Terry Black; ph, Robert D. Yeoman (Technicolor); ed, Harvey Rosenstock; m, Ernest Troost; prod d, Craig Stearns; art d, Jon Gary Steele; set d, Greta Grigorian; spec eff, Patrick Read Johnson, Steve Johnson; cos, Lisa Jensen; stunts, Dan Bradley.

Comedy/Horror Cas. (PR:O MPAA:R)

DEAD MAN WALKING*½ (1988) 90m Metropolis-Hit c

Wings Hauser (*John Luger*), Brion James (*Decker*), Pamela Ludwig (*Lelia*), Sy Richardson (*Snake*), Leland Crooke (*Nomad Farmer*), Jeffrey Combs (*Chaz*), Joseph d'Angerio (*Gordon*), Tasia Vallenza (*Rika*), John Walter Davis (*The Body Counter*), Penelope Sudrow (*Pookie*), John Petlock (*Mr. Shahn*), Diz McNally (*Emcee*), Nancy Locke (*Mother*), Yvonne DePatis (*Customer*), Biff Yeager (*Security Man*), John Durbin (*Bartender*), Robert Factor (*Guard*), Darwin Swalve (*Skin Head*), Richard Epcar (*Driver*), Kent T. Smith, Forrest Witt, Nick Fragos, Robert Breeze (*Plague Victims*).

A direct-to-video feature, DEAD MAN WALKING marks the mainstream debut for filmmakers Gregory Brown and Walter Gernert, known previously for their documentary work and as the adult film and video team the Dark Bros. The action takes place in 2004, after a plague has wiped out half the earth's population. UNITUS, the ruling worldwide corporation has placed those infected with the disease into plague zones. Others infected with a fatal, but not contagious strain, the Zero Men, are allowed to live freely, but have a life expectancy of only one or two years. A trio of escaped prisoners, led by Zero Man James (essaying a role similar to the one he played in BLADE RUNNER), attacks the limo of a UNITUS industrialist who is working to create labor camps to quarantine contaminated people. After killing the fat cat and taking his daughter (Ludwig) hostage, James heads off into the plague zone. The police refuse to follow, so the industrialist's assistant, Combs (star of RE-ANIMATOR), looks for a Zero Man to help get her back, hiring Hauser, who hangs out at the Zero Club, passing the time before his death by defusing time bombs and playing Russian roulette with a chain saw. They track James and his pals into the zone's desert wasteland, but are over powered and left to die, buried to their necks in sand under the hot sun. After being rescued by a plague-stricken nomad and his sister, Hauser trades the strange pills that Combs is holding for ammo and gas, and the hunt continues. When his fellow escapees plot against him, James kills them, and he and Young end up at Cafe Death: a post-punk nightclub where the entertainment consists of burning audience members alive on stage. In the climax James electrocutes Hauser, nearly killing him, and stabs Combs, but Young, finally snapping out of her film-long trance, shoots James dead. After being stabbed, Combs reveals that the pills he has been carrying are actually an antidote for the plague kept secret by UNITUS. A newscast epilog reveals that police are searching for Hauser in connection with the theft of classified medical documents relating to the antidote.

A pastiche of everything from CAFE FLESH to THE ROAD WARRIOR, DEAD MAN WALKING, is ultimately too derivative and predictable to be effective. It's also surprisingly actionless, with the only good sequences coming at the end when it's too late to matter. The satirical TV news updates (a direct rip-off from ROBOCOP), with cheerily delivered items on LA gang wars over parking space, and baby-kissing presidential candidates spreading the plague, are amusing, but are poorly integrated into the script. Wings Hauser is well cast and Brion James gives a by-the-numbers psycho performance; however, everyone else is forgettable. Unfortunately, the nice touches concerning the human consequences of the AIDS-like disease, especially prominent in the death of the nomad's sister, are wasted by the film's overall lack of direction. (*Graphic violence, profanity, brief nudity.*)

p, Gregory Brown, Craig Thurman Suttle; d, Gregory Brown; w, John Weidner, Rick Marx; ph, Paul Desatoff (United Color); ed, Kert Vander Meulen; m, Claude (Coffee) Cave; prod d, Rick Wiggington; art d, Mike Villiers; spec eff, Dean C. Jones, William Jones, Thomas Powell; cos, Robyn Reichek, Claudia Cordk; stunts, Brian Smrz; makeup, Cynthia Farbman, Bright Hauser, Vicki Toler.

Action/Science Fiction Cas. (PR:O MPAA:R)

DEAD POOL, THE***   (1988) 91m Malpaso/WB c

Clint Eastwood (*Harry Callahan*), Patricia Clarkson (*Samantha Walker*), Evan C. Kim (*Al Quan*), Liam Neeson (*Peter Swan*), David Hunt (*Harlan Rook*), Michael Currie (*Capt. Donnelly*), Michael Goodwin (*Lt. Ackerman*), Darwin Gillett (*Patrick Snow*), Anthony Charnota (*Lou Janero*), James Carrey, Ronnie Clair Edwards, Christopher Beale, John Allen Vick, Louis Giambalvo.

THE DEAD POOL, the fifth entry in the "Dirty Harry" series, is a definite step backwards from the fascinating and ultimately disturbing progression of Clint Eastwood's Harry Callahan in SUDDEN IMPACT (1983), but a satisfying effort nonetheless. It is entirely likely that Eastwood made this film in a commercial trade-off with Warner Bros. to get the opportunity to direct the decidedly uncommercial BIRD, a biography of jazz saxophonist Charlie Parker. In this outing, Eastwood is the key witness in a trial that will put a powerful mafia boss away for good. He has, in the process, become a media hero and the exposure, especially from icy blonde TV reporter Clarkson, does not please him. His superiors want to take him off the street and make him a police force public relations liaison, but Eastwood refuses, snarling, "I'm no horse and pony show." Saddled, in the tradition of the series, with yet another partner, Asian-American Kim, Eastwood becomes embroiled in a string of murders involving a bettor's game called the "Dead Pool," a list of celebrities likely to die soon. Participants wager on who will die first. The game is being played on the set of a cheap horror film directed by infamous gore-monger Neeson, a filmmaker whose bloody work is taken seriously by colleges and film societies. Neeson is the instigator of the ghoulish game and, as the celebrities begin to die off, the most likely suspect in the murders. In-the-news Eastwood, of course, is himself on the list (because everyone knows that the mob is out to kill him before the trial) and he doesn't like it one bit. After the rock musician star of the horror film, a conservative TV talk show host, and a virulent critic of Neeson's movies are murdered in grisly fashion—virtual duplicates of scenes in Neeson's films—the police department becomes convinced that the horror director is the killer. Eastwood, however, isn't so sure. Eventually Eastwood discovers that it is not Neeson who is the killer, but a crazed fan of his films who has adopted the director's dress, speech patterns, and mannerisms. With reporter Clarkson as his hostage, the killer lures Eastwood to the waterfront for a showdown. Taking his fetish for big weapons to the most ludicrous extreme yet, Eastwood dispatches the psychotic horror film devotee with a giant harpoon gun.

While the weak screenplay by Steve Sharon would have trouble even filling out an episode of the "The Equalizer," the fascination of the film lies not in its thriller mechanics but in the character of Harry Callahan himself. Since everyone in the audience knows exactly what to expect from Dirty Harry in every situation, Eastwood has streamlined his portrayal to the point where all he has to do is *hint* at Harry's beloved sneer to get a reaction. His supremely controlled performance is a wonder to watch——some have called it bored and lazy, but it is really an engrossing experiment in minimalism. This description applies to the entire film: Harry's customary wisecracks are kept to a minimum, the gun fetish is held back until the big payoff, and violent episodes are quick and relatively understated. There is no "Make my day" scene in THE DEAD POOL. Eastwood has replaced all these time-worn elements with a sardonic sense of humor that pokes fun at the genre, his image, and his audience. Thus, the film's comedic highlight is a clever parody of the famous car chase in BULLITT (1968) in which Eastwood and Kim are pursued through the streets of San Francisco by a 12-inch, radio-controlled toy Corvette loaded with dynamite. Beneath the comedy, however, brews a grim and disturbing subtext. In apparently coming down hard on fans of violence and gore and on those who present it to us (the movies and news media), Eastwood chides his public for being a little *too* dedicated and the industry (including himself) a little too eager to pander to our baser instincts. Does Eastwood think his fans psychotic? Is he tired of the Dirty Harry image? Would he like to quit being Clint Eastwood the Star and become known as Clint Eastwood the Director of BIRD and other challenging, uncommercial projects? To put forth this agenda in a film full of horrific images and violence may seem hypocritical and contradictory, but it is Eastwood's seeming ambivalence regarding his career—the working out of his personal demons on film—that makes him such an absorbing figure. Although Eastwood didn't direct THE DEAD POOL, he continues to examine his persona on the screen, before his fans, and the results, while not always completely coherent, are fascinating to watch. (*Graphic violence, profanity.*)

p, David Valdes; d, Buddy Van Horn; w, Steve Sharon (based on a story by Sharon, Durk Pearson, Sandy Shaw from characters created by Harry Julian Fink, R.M. Fink); ph, Jack N. Green (Technicolor); ed, Ron Spang; m, Lalo Schifrin; prod d, Edward C. Carfagno; stunts, Richard Farnsworth.

Crime   **Cas.**   **(PR:O MPAA:R)**

DEAD RINGERS*******   (1988, Can.) 115m Mantle Clinic II/FOX c

Jeremy Irons (*Beverly and Elliot Mantle*), Genevieve Bujold (*Claire Niveau*), Heidi Von Palleske (*Cary*), Barbara Gordon (*Danuta*), Shirley Douglas (*Laura*), Stephen Lack (*Anders Wolleck*), Nick Nichols (*Leo*), Lynn Cormack (*Arlene*), Damir Andrei (*Birchall*), Miriam Newhouse (*Mrs. Bookman*), David Hughes (*Superintendent*), Richard Farrell (*Dean of Medicine*), Warren Davis (*Anatomy Class Supervisor*), Jonathan Haley (*Beverly, Age 9*), Nicholas Haley (*Elliot, Age 9*), Marsha Moreau (*Raffaella*), Denis Akiyama (*Pharmacist*), Dee McCafferty (*Surgeon*), Susan Markle

(*Operating Room Nurse*), Murray Chuchley (*Assisting Surgeon*), Jane Luk (*Lecture Hall Nurse*), Tita Trevisan (*Furniture Salesman*), Jacqueline Hennessy, Jillian Hennessy (*Escort Twins*), David Walden (*Director*), Liliane Stillwell (*Wardrobe Person*), Denise McLeod (*Art Gallery Lady*), Bob Bainborough (*Mr. Glaser*), Nicholas Rice (*M.C.*), Joe Matheson (*Sean*), Hadley Kay (*Delivery Boy*), Cynthia Eastman (*Sobbing Woman*), Nora Colpman (*Mrs. Randall*), Rena Polley, Madeleine Atkinson (*Soap Opera Characters*), John Bayliss (*Performance Double*), Graham Evans (*Picture Double*).

Having finally received long overdue mass critical and popular acclaim upon the release of THE FLY (1986), Canadian director David Cronenberg has resisted the pressures that come with commercial success and continued to explore his chief obsession, the conflict between mind and body, in DEAD RINGERS—a distinctly noncommercial effort that, surprisingly, does not contain the director's trademark visceralia. Instead, the film is a chilling character study, boasting a brilliant performance from Jeremy Irons and some of the most impressive (and unintrusive) special effects work yet to hit the screen. Cronenberg's latest was inspired by the real-life story of respected twin New York City gynecologists Steven and Cyril Marcus who, in 1975, were both found dead in their garbage-strewn Upper East Side apartment, a double suicide brought on by barbiturate addiction. Shortly after their deaths, it was revealed that both brothers had operated on patients while under the influence of drugs. The incident inspired a sensationalized (and fictional) account of the story in the novel *Twins* by Bari Wood and Jack Geasland.

Using the novel as a starting point to explore his own fascination with the subject, Cronenberg changes the setting from NYC to Toronto and introduces us to his twins, Elliot and Beverly Mantle, as eerily detached children, clinically intrigued by bodily functions—especially sexual reproduction. While medical students, the twins (played as adults by Irons) invent a surgical instrument that revolutionizes gynecology. Recognized as preeminent experts in the field, the uncommonly close siblings open a state-of-the-art fertility clinic together and share an opulent apartment. Although identical twins, they possess very different personalities. Elliot is something of a cad—suave, debonair, and self-confident to the point of arrogance. He is a supremely successful politician and fund-raiser for the clinic, while Beverly is shy, studious, and more sensitive. While this combination does wonders for their practice (Bev handles the patients while Elly charms the medical profession), it takes a toll on their personal lives, for the twins literally share everything. Ultimately, the relationship is suffocating, and individual identities become confused. The charming Elliot has always procured women for Beverly by seducing them first, then turning them over to his shy sibling when he was through—unbeknownst to the woman. The brothers discuss the details of their liaisons—more or less sharing notes on the women—and neither really feels he has experienced anything fully unless the other has done it as well. When a famous actress, Claire Niveau (Bujold), arrives at the clinic looking for answers to her infertility, trouble brews between the brothers. Upon examination, Elliot discovers that Claire has a trifurcated womb (a biological impossibility made real by Cronenberg), which prevents her from conceiving. Fascinated by the strong-willed, sexy actress, Elliot beds Claire and then passes her on to Beverly, who is likewise fascinated by her beauty, both external and *internal*. The brothers share the actress sexually, unbeknownst to Claire, who thinks she is seeing only Elliot. Bev, however, falls hopelessly in love with the fiercely independent actress and begins to separate himself psychologically from Elliot, wanting Claire for himself alone. This makes Elliot jealous, and when Claire finally learns that she has been sleeping with both brothers and publicly humiliates them in their favorite restaurant, Elliot is relieved. The distraught Beverly, however, continues to pursue Claire, and, attracted by Bev's sweetness, she begins seeing him again. Although the smart and hardened actress can regulate her indulgence in alcohol, barbiturates, and kinky sex, the totally naive and dependent Bev begins to sink into an anxious, guilt-ridden, drug-induced stupor, trying to keep up with Claire at the expense of his relationship with Elliot. When Claire leaves town for several weeks of filming, Bev becomes paranoid and imagines that she has cheated on him. Now a full-blown addict, he begins to go mad and takes his anger and frustration out on his shocked patients. He even commissions a local artist (played by SCANNERS star Stephen Lack) to make him a set of horrible-looking medical instruments to be used, as he puts it, for "examining mutant women." Seeing that Bev's erratic behavior threatens to destroy their practice, Elliot attempts to treat his brother's addiction but instead succumbs to it himself. The twins spend their last weeks wandering around their filthy clinic dressed in suit jackets and boxer shorts, shooting up and babbling incoherently. Finally, Beverly uses his grotesque new instruments on Elliot and then dies himself. The final shot resembles a religious painting, with Elliot sitting on the floor with his back against the wall and Beverly curled in a fetal position across his brother's lap—the two joined once again, in death.

A quietly devastating horror film, DEAD RINGERS is final evidence that David Cronenberg has matured into a truly great filmmaker. Continuing the detailed character study that blossomed in THE FLY and combining it with his trademark fixation on the metaphysical, Cronenberg has created yet another vividly realized film that is powerful, moving, and rich in ideas. Extremely unsettling, at times amusing, cold yet personal, DEAD RINGERS slowly creeps over the viewer, revealing its horrors at a deliberate pace, rather than shocking outright with such spectacular displays of gore as the exploding heads of SCANNERS, gaping stomach cavities of VIDEODROME, or vomiting Brundleflies of THE FLY. Because Cronenberg roots DEAD RINGERS in stark reality and refrains from the expected shocks, the few moments when he does indulge in bizarre or fantastical imagery—such as the crimson surgical gowns and the nightmare sequence wherein Claire chews apart the fleshy tie that binds Elliot and Beverly—are all the more effective. Cronenberg has always concerned himself with adult fears and obsessions, and DEAD RINGERS may be his most eloquent examination of the dichotomy between the mind and the flesh.

Much of the credit for this accomplishment must go to Jeremy Irons. One of the most skillful physical actors in movies today, Irons is able to convey which brother is which before ever uttering a line. The scenes in which he interacts with himself on screen are so subtle, relaxed, and natural yet precise, that some viewers unfamiliar with the actor actually believed that real-life twins played the parts. Of course, Irons' magnificent performance is enhanced by the superb optical work of the Film Effects crew. In the past, split-screen techniques required the camera to be locked down tight and the actor playing the dual role to restrict himself to one side of the frame per character. No matter how invisible the split in the screen, the effect still felt false, because the static camera setup restricted natural interaction and movement between characters. In DEAD RINGERS, however, the effects, supervised by Lee Wilson, freed Cronenberg and Irons from any such restrictions by combining a traveling split (so that Irons wouldn't have to be restricted to only one side of the frame), with a computer-controlled moving camera (the computer duplicated the camera move exactly so that both takes—Irons as Elliot and Irons as Beverly—would match perfectly). This allowed for some impressive, never-before-seen shots of Irons interacting with himself while the camera moved. The combined skills of Irons as actor and the technical crew are so effective that after the first half-hour the trickery becomes invisible; most viewers simply forget that Irons is playing a dual role. Also excellent is Genevieve Bujold, who breathes life into a part that could have been a mere plot device in different hands and plumbs the depths of a terribly complicated character. The other technical contributions in addition to the special effects are also superior, especially Peter Suschitzky's steely photography, Howard Shore's chilling score, Carol Spier's appropriately cold and clinical production design, and Denise Cronenberg's (sister of David) impeccable costuming.

Not your average horror roller-coaster ride, DEAD RINGERS asks some disturbing questions about the nature of individual identity, and within that net explores such outgrowths as eroticism, narcissism, and misogyny. While THE FLY was certainly a film that grappled with adult fears, the concept was suitably outlandish and the gruesome special effects sensational enough to attract a less discriminating audience looking for grotesque thrills. There is no such mainstream appeal in DEAD RINGERS. After a big opening weekend, business slacked off and the film left screens quickly—gynecological horror is not a big draw. But if the disappointing size of the audience is not surprising, it still remains a great pity. For 20 years, David Cronenberg has shared his deeply personal, provocative, and disturbing vision with cinemagoers. His early films were more interesting to talk about than to watch, since he had yet to fully appreciate the intricacies of the medium and articulate his ideas convincingly. In the last decade, however, he has matured into a filmmaker of remarkable scope, able to convey his obsessions with impeccable skill without sacrificing one iota of his own remarkable individuality. (*Adult situations, violence, sexual situations, profanity.*)

p, David Cronenberg, Marc Boyman; d, David Cronenberg; w, David Cronenberg, Norman Snider (based on the book *Twins* by Bari Wood, Jack Geasland); ph, Peter Suschitzky; ed, Ronald Sanders; m, Howard Shore; m/l, Fred Parris; prod d, Carol Spier; art d, James McAteer; set d, Elinor Rose Galbraith; spec eff, Gordon Smith; cos, Denise Cronenberg; makeup, Shonagh Jabour.

Horror   **(PR:O MPAA:R)**

DEADLY DREAMS*   (1988) 79m New Classics/Concorde c

Mitchell Anderson (*Alex*), Juliette Cummins (*Maggie*), Xander Berkeley (*Jack*), Thom Babbes (*Danny*), Timothy Austin (*Young Alex*), Beach Dickerson.

A surprising and refreshingly taut low-budget horror film, DEADLY DREAMS offers what most run-of-the-mill slasher films don't: a good story with a surprise ending. Anderson's parents were shot and killed 10 years earlier on Christmas Eve by a disgruntled business partner who then turned the gun on himself. Years later, Anderson is plagued with nightmares of a masked hunter and begins seeing him at every turn. Comforted by girl friend Cummins and best friend Babbes, Anderson begins a slow descent into madness. As the story unfolds, it reveals a conspiracy involving Anderson's brother, Berkeley, and *his* lover, Cummins, and an inheritance that is badly needed to save the family company. Slowly, Babbes catches on and is murdered. In a chilling finale, after Berkeley makes known his intentions to his younger brother, Anderson's throat is slashed as pseudo-girl friend Cummins watches, devoid of any emotion. The surprise ending has brother Berkeley haunted by dreams of the murdered Anderson, only to be killed by Cummins, who, it turns out, is the daughter of the original killer. The last scene has Cummins phoning her mother and saying, "It's all over, Mother. Dad can finally rest in peace."

Director Kristine Peterson (a former Roger Corman protege) handles the material with a sure hand and a keen eye. The numerous horror sequences are quite frightening—the viewer never sure of what is real and what is fantasy. Moreover, Peterson delivers the scares without overloading the blood, quite a change for the genre. All of the performances are convincing, especially that of Thom Babbes (author of the screenplay), who brings a freshness to the traditional role of the wise-guy buddy. Unfortunately, DEADLY DREAMS was not released theatrically, going straight to the home video market without much fanfare. It's a shame that this clever scare-show will not find the exposure that it rightly deserves. (*Graphic violence, nudity.*)

p, Matt Leipzig; d, Kristine Peterson; w, Thom Babbes; ph, Zoran Hochstatter (Foto-Kem color); ed, Bernard Caputo; m, Todd Boekelheide; prod d, Stephen Greenberg; spec eff, Deborah Zoeller.

Horror   **Cas.**   **(PR:O MPAA:R)**

DEADLY TWINS zero   (1988) 92m Prism c

Audrey Landers, Judy Landers, Harry Wolf, Joe Martinez, James McCartney, Wayne Allison, Gus Wood, Ellie Russell, Jan Fedder.

Audrey and Judy Landers are best known for their appearance as the first twin centerfold in *Playboy* history and for a series of undistinguished guest appearances on television, but in this wretched German-made feature, they get a chance to stretch and really show their talents. Moving from New York to Cologne when one sister (the two are virtually indistinguishable and the credits don't identify the characters) gets a job, the sisters supplement their income with a truly horrid singing act in a discotheque. After their show one night, they are raped and beaten by the thug son of the local mob chief and his pal. When one of them regains consciousness in the hospital, she learns that her sister has suffered a miscarriage. The miscarried child's father drives toward the hospital as fast as he can and ends up going over a cliff. The shock of the double loss is so devastating for his lover that she jumps out the hospital window, and although the fall doesn't kill her, she is confined to a wheelchair. Later, the twins manage to give a description of their attacker and his car to the police, but he is protected by his father's influence. Unable to get justice, the sisters follow in the well-trod B-movie footsteps of many a wronged woman and seek vengeance themselves. The ambulatory sister begins trailing the villain, photographing his shakedowns, robberies, and drug transactions. However, when these are shown to the kind policeman, he tells them there is still not enough evidence to make an arrest. The blonde duo then concocts another plan, going to the bad guy with the photos and threatening to turn them over to the cops unless he helps them with a payroll robbery. The guy is too dumb to recognize them, even together, but smart enough to scout the job himself. When he sees the payroll being delivered a day early, he moves in and takes the money before the police can set up their trap. What ensues is an interminable chase involving cars, motorcycles, helicopters, bulldozers, and a bunch of fistfights until he is finally caught. The epilog shows the sisters back in New York, the crippled one learning to walk again, with the nice policeman, who's narrating, saying he plans to quit the force and join them soon.

Shot on video with all the finesse of hardcore porn, DEADLY TWINS may be the absolute bottom of the barrel of 1988. The Landers sisters should stick to still photos, because while they are drop-dead gorgeous, as soon as they try to emote or even speak, their tremendous lack of talent is numbingly apparent. Tellingly, no writer is credited for DEADLY TWINS, indicating that either someone pulled his name off in disgust, or as seems more likely, everyone is just making it up as they go along. (*Violence, nudity, sexual situations, adult situations, profanity.*)

p, Joe Oaks; d, Joe Oaks; ph, Jim Banks; ed, Warren Banks; art d, Jeff Deena.

Crime   **Cas.**   **(PR:O MPAA:NR)**

DEATH CHASE †   (1988) 88m Action Intl. c

Paul Smith (*Steele*), Jack Starrett (*Lt. MacGrew*), William Zipp (*Steven Chase*), Bainbridge Scott (*Diana Lewis*), Reggie DeMorton (*Eddie*), Paul Bruno (*Sgt. Boone*), C.T. Collins (*Chairman*), Christine Crowell, Mike Hickam, Susanne Tegman, Francine Lapense, Brian O'Connor, Andria Savio.

The title says it all. This one is about a game of urban gunplay set in motion when a mysterious and malevolent corporate head organizes what is essentially a lethal game of tag. The action revolves around an innocent bystander (William Zipp) who gets drawn into the game when his sister is gunned down, and a pretty heroine (Bainbridge Scott) who becomes involved in the chase. Released straight to video.

p, Peter Yuval, Yakov Bentsvi; d, David A. Prior; w, James L. Hennessy, Jr., Craig L. Hyde, David A. Prior; ph, Keith Holland (United color); ed, Brian Evans; m, Tim James, Steve McClintick, Mark Mancina; art d, Leigh Nicolai; stunts, Fritz Matthews.

Action   **Cas.**   **(PR:NR MPAA:NR)**

DEATHSTALKER II †   (1988) 77m New Horizons/Concorde c

John Terlesky *(Deathstalker)*, Monique Gabrielle *(Evie)*, John La Zar *(Jarek)*, Toni Naples *(Sultana)*, Maria Socas *(Amazon Queen)*, Marcos Wolinsky *(One Eye)*, Deanna Booher *(Gargol)*.

For all of those diehard fans who were eagerly awaiting a follow-up to 1984's Richard Hill-Barbie Benton opus THE DEATHSTALKER, the wait is now over. Bearing almost no resemblance to its predecessor, the scant, 77-minute DEATHSTALKER II now stars John Terlesky as the sword-and-sorcery fantasy hero and Monique Gabrielle as a princess in exile. Topless women abound, as do muscular men, deformed and poorly made-up creatures, and fantasy mumbo-jumbo. Former *Penthouse* centerfold Monique Gabrielle gets to show off her acting abilities in dual roles—the exiled princess who wants to regain her throne *and* the clone who is placed on the throne by an evil, power-hungry sorcerer. As was THE DEATHSTALKER, this sequel was photographed in Argentina.

p, Frank Isaac, Jr.; d, Jim Wynorski; w, Neil Ruttenberg, R.J. Robertson (based on a story by Jim Wynorski); ph, Leonardo Solis (Film House Color); ed, Steve Barnett; m, Chuck Cirino, Christopher Young, Oscar Cardozo Ocampo; art d, Marta Albert.

Adventure/Fantasy   Cas.   (PR:NR MPAA:R)

DECEIVERS, THE**   (1988, Brit./India) 112m Merchant Ivory-Film Four/Cinecom c

Pierce Brosnan *(William Savage)*, Saeed Jaffrey *(Hussein)*, Shashi Kapoor *(Chandra Singh)*, Helena Michell *(Sarah Wilson)*, Keith Michell *(Col. Wilson)*, David Robb *(George Angelsmith)*, Tariq Yunus *(Feringea)*, Jalal Agha *(Nawab)*, Gary Cady *(Lt. Maunsell)*, Salim Ghouse *(Piroo)*, Neena Gupta *(Widow)*, Nayeem Hafizka *(Sepoy)*, Bijoya Jena *(Harlot)*, H.N. Kalla *(Nawab Servant)*, Kammo *(Official)*, Goga Kapoor *(Sher Dil)*, Manmohan Krishna *(Old Rajput)*, Harish Magon *(Sepoy)*, Manmaujee *(Ferryman)*, Giles Masters *(Captain Devril)*, Ramesh Ranga *(Rajput's Son)*, Dilip Singh Rathore *(Sowar)*, Hilla Sethna *(Chandra Singh's Maidservant)*, R.P. Sondhi *(Prisoner)*, Kanwaljit Singh *(Gopal)*, Shanmukha Srinivas *(Hira Lal)*, Dalip Tahil *(Daffadar Ganesha)*, Tim Van Rellim *(Reverend Matthias)*, Rajesh Vivek *(Priest)*, Amin, Akbar Bakshi, Ramesh Goyal, Kaushel, Haroon Khan, Nilesh Malhotra.

Producer Ismail Merchant's first collaboration with a director other than James Ivory is something of a departure from the genteel films with which Merchant and Ivory have made their considerable reputation—A ROOM WITH A VIEW; MAURICE; THE BOSTONIANS. Instead of E.M. Forster or Henry James, Merchant has turned to a 1952 novel by John Masters as the basis for this adventure, directed by Nicholas Meyer and set in colonial India in 1825. Masters' novel is based on the early 19th-century crusade by William Sleeman, an officer of the British East India Company, to rid the subcontinent of the deadly menace of the *Thugee*, a secret cult of murderers who took the lives of more than two million people. These "Deceivers," who claimed to serve Kali, the six-armed goddess of destruction, weaseled their way into the company of wealthy travelers and then strangulated them.

Pierce Brosnan (TV's "Remington Steele"), playing a character based on Sleeman, is a recently married officer of the East India Company. His wife (Helena Michell) is the daughter of his superior (Keith), and despite his frowned-upon proclivity for fair treatment of the Indians he administrates in his district, Brosnan seems well positioned to move up the company ladder. However, when a local woman prepares to undertake *suttee*—the self-immolation of a widow seeking to join her husband in the other world—Brosnan dons brownface and native dress in an attempt to impersonate her missing husband from afar, and thus put a halt to the ritual. In the process, he stumbles on a band of murderers as they brutally and efficiently strangle a group of travelers. Escaping their pursuit, he supervises an excavation the next day that unearths their victims, and, soon thereafter, he rounds up the murderers. One of them, Jaffrey, breaks down and tells Brosnan the secrets of his *Thugee* comrades, but his superior refuses to believe Brosnan's account and relieves him of his command. Determined to put an end to the killing, Brosnan masquerades as a *Thug* (right you are, that's where the word originates) and, accompanied by Jaffrey, whom he has convinced of the power of the Christian God, he infiltrates the deadly cult. In so doing, he not only perfects the *Thug* strangulation ritual but is forced to put it to use when his cover is threatened. More than this, Brosnan succumbs to the seductive goddess Kali, hallucinating under the influences of the *Thugee* drug of choice and indulging in post-massacre orgies. Jaffrey flees and informs Michell of her husband's dangerous predicament, but, rather than helping, Kapoor, a local native ruler and friend of Brosnan's, turns Jaffrey over to the Deceivers. Just as Brosnan's identity is about to be revealed, he escapes, though he is unable to save Jaffrey, who has been brought to be killed with the Englishman. A furious cross-country chases ensues, but just when it seems that Brosnan is a lost cause, the cavalry arrives, led to him by a loyal Indian servant. Brosnan is rescued and reunited with Michell, whose father sees the error of his ways, and the *Thugee* are about to become Indian history.

While THE DECEIVERS doesn't completely succeed as either a historical film or an adventure, it is never boring. When the adventure flags, the historical details maintain interest; when the finely etched setting becomes oppressive, the action generally picks up the slack. Director Meyer (TIME AFTER TIME; STAR TREK II: THE WRATH OF KHAN) deserves most of the credit for this, as his excellent pacing overcomes the lapses of dramatic impetus in Michael Hirst's screenplay, managing to maintain a level of tension that isn't inherent in the relatively pedestrian plot. Meyer also coaxes an effective, if uneven, performance from Brosnan, who is extremely convincing when he is in uniform, but less so when in the somewhat implausible process of deceiving the Deceivers. (One especially wonders how he continues to carry off his deception when disrobing for the orgies, or has he covered his whole body in brown makeup? And that must be pretty damn good makeup, eh? But, of course, the blame for this belongs with the screenplay, not with Brosnan.) The film is also helped along by excellent supporting performances from veteran Indian actors Saeed Jaffrey (MY BEAUTIFUL LAUNDRETTE) and Shashi Kapoor (SAMMY AND ROSIE GET LAID). With Merchant producing and working with his largest budget yet—$6.1 million—it comes as no surprise that the production design is exquisite and the Indian locations frequently stunning, yet, unlike the best-known Merchant-Ivory productions, the cinematography here is less spectacular. The slightly more prosaic look works in the film's favor, however.

Though THE DECEIVERS may not keep you on the edge of your seat, there was never a dull moment when it came to making the film. After having their scripts approved by the Indian government, the filmmakers began shooting on location in Rajasthan. Reportedly, a powerful local businessman was initially put on the payroll as a liaison, but when Merchant and company learned of his disreputable past, they gave him the sack. Using a number of front organizations, the vindictive businessman is then reputed to have begun a campaign to sabotage the production. A controversy was stirred up regarding THE DECEIVERS' portrayal of *suttee* : Alleging that the film glorified the outlawed practice—though it does anything but that—charges of "indecent portrayal of Indian culture" were brought against Merchant and coproducer Tim Van Rellim. In fact, more than 50 armed policemen were sent to arrest them. Although this court case (tried in the region due to the nature of India's judicial system) and Merchant and Van Rellim's countersuit didn't interfere with the production, other, more literal, sabotage did, as bolts were stolen from cranes and generators periodically dosed with water. In the final analysis, then, THE DECEIVERS isn't 1988's best adventure film—but when you stop to think about it, it probably wouldn't hurt for you to give it a chance, especially considering what the filmmakers went through to bring it to the screen. *(Violence, sexual situations, brief nudity.)*

p, Ismail Merchant, Tim Van Rellim; d, Nicholas Meyer; w, Michael Hirst (based on the novel by John Masters); ph, Walter Lassally; ed, Richard Trevor; m, John Scott; prod d, Ken Adam; art d, Gianfranco Fumagalli, Ram Yedekar; spec eff, Brian Smithies; cos, Jenny Beavan, John Bright; ch, Denny Martin Flinn; stunts, Gerry Crampton; makeup, Gordon Kay.

Adventure   Cas.   (PR:O MPAA:PG-13)

DEEP SPACE †   (1988) 90m Trans World c

Charles Napier *(Detective Macliamor)*, Ann Turkel *(Carla Sanborn)*, Bo Svenson *(Captain Robertson)*, Ron Glass *(Jerry)*, Julie Newmar *(Elaine Wentworth)*, James Booth *(Dr. Forsyth)*, Norman Burton *(Gen. Randolph)*, Anthony Eisley *(Dr. Rogers)*, Michael Forest *(Hawkins)*, Peter Palmer, Elisabeth Brooks, Jesse Dabson, Fox Harris, Dawn Wildsmith, Sandy Brooke, Susan Stokey.

This ALIEN-inspired horror thriller from Fred Olen Ray concerns a pair of LA detectives who are assigned to a case involving a space creature who crash-lands on Earth. Naturally, this alien life force is violent and begins killing off some hapless victims. What the detectives don't know, however, is that the alien's killing spree is the result of a problematic, top-secret government project. In a supporting role is Julie Newmar, once cast as "Cat Woman" on TV's BATMAN series. Released straight to video.

p, Alan Amiel; d, Fred Olen Ray; w, Fred Olen Ray, T.L. Lankford; ph, Gary Graver (Foto-Kem Color); ed, Natan Zahavi, Bruce Stubblefield; m, Robert O. Ragland, Alan Oldfield; art d, Corey Kaplan; spec eff, Steve Patino, Sho-Glass Effects, Steve Neill; stunts, John Stewart.

Horror/Thriller   Cas.   (PR:NR MPAA:R)

DEFENSE PLAY †   (1988) 93m Kodiak/Trans World c

David Oliver *(Scott Denton)*, Susan Ursitti *(Karen Vandemeer)*, Monte Markham *(Col. Mark Denton)*, Eric Gilliom *(Starkey)*, William Frankfather *(Gen. Philips)*, Jamie McMurray *(Norm Beltzer)*, Jack Esformes *(Eddie Dietz)*, Tom Rosqui *(Chief Gill)*, Milos Kirek *(Anton)*, Patch Mackenzie *(Ann Denton)*, Terrance Cooper *(Prof. James Vandemeer)*, Susan Krebs *(Margaret Fields)*, Jonathon Wise *(Nick)*, Dah Ve Choden *(Audrey Denton)*, Ron Recasner *(Mike Agee)*, J. Downing *(Joe Anderson)*, Glen Morshower *(Bartender)*, Rutanya Alda *(Victoria Vandemeer)*, Stacey Adams *(Kelly)*, Jim Beaver *(FBI Man)*, John Ingle *(Senator)*, Hal Johnson *(Ruxin)*, Alan Kolman *(Russian Officer)*.

Another WAR GAMES-inspired action thriller, DEFENSE PLAY pits precocious teens with computer knowledge against the superpowers. Oliver stars as a recent high school graduate who lands a summer job at a high-tech university, where he meets and falls for fellow teen Ursitti. Her father is an important scientist hired by the military to develop miniature remote-control helicopters that shoot deadly laser beams and it is Oliver's dad, an Army colonel (played by Monte Markham, who also directed), who is supervising the project. When Ursitti's father winds up dead in a mysterious accident and it looks like Markham's career may be doomed because of it, the teens decide to investigate and discover that Soviet agents, who are headquartered in a trawler just outside American territorial waters, are responsible. Their plan is to steal the advanced technology and sabotage the upcoming launch of Ronald Reagan's vaunted SDI project, and it is up to the teenagers to stop them. DEFENSE PLAY made the rounds at a few suburban theaters before hitting the home video market.

p, Wolf Schmidt; d, Monte Markham; w, Aubrey Solomon, Steven Greenberg (based on a story by Wolf Schmidt, Stan Krantman); ph, Tim Galfas (Foto-Kem color); ed, James Ruxin; m, Arthur B. Rubinstein; prod d, Petko Kadiev; art d, Michael Clausen; set d, Greg P. Oehla; spec eff, Pete Slagle; cos, Marjorie Bowers.

Thriller   **Cas.**   **(PR:NR MPAA:PG)**

DEMONWARP †   (1988) 91m Vidmark-Design Projects c

George Kennedy (*Bill Crafton*), David Michael O'Neill (*Jack*), Pamela Gilbert (*Carrie*), Billy Jacoby (*Tom*), Colleen McDermott (*Cindy*), Hank Stratton (*Fred*), Michelle Bauer (*Betsy*), Shannon Kennedy (*Tara*), John Durbin, Joe Praml, Jill Mern.

Kennedy is a tough guy with a shotgun who becomes the protector of a group of teenage campers who fall prey to an angry Bigfoot. It seems Kennedy has a personal vendetta against the creature, since, some time before, it killed his daughter. In fact, this Bigfoot is not some sort of missing evolutionary link but an alien spawn with a hunger for young, topless teenage girls in general. This straight-to-video release brings back memories of such other Camper's Nightmare classics as GRIZZLY and THE PROPHECY.

p, Richard L. Albert; d, Emmett Alston; w, Jim Bertges, Bruce Akiyama (based on a story by John Buechler); ph, R. Michael Stringer; ed, W. Peter Miller, John Travers; m, Dan Slider; spec eff, Bruce Barlow, Ed Yang, John Carl Buechler.

Horror/Science Fiction   **Cas.**   **(PR:NR MPAA:NR)**

DESTINY   **(SEE: TIME OF DESTINY, A, 1988)**

DESTROYER †   (1988) 94m Back East Money-Wind River/Moviestore c

Deborah Foreman (*Susan Malone*), Clayton Rohner (*David Harris*), Lyle Alzado (*Ivan Moser*), Anthony Perkins (*Director Edwards*), Tobias Andersen (*Russell*), Lannie Garrett (*Sharon Fox*), Jim Turner (*Rewire*), Pat Mahoney (*Warden*), David Kristin (*Fingers*).

When a film crew arrives at a recently-closed prison to film a women-in-prison picture entitled "Death House Dolls," they find themselves in a real-life horror situation. Closed 18 months before the film crew arrived, the prison is apparently haunted by a monstrous serial killer (former football star Alzado) who, despite having been juiced in the electric chair, still roams the various cell blocks. Perkins plays the film-within-the-film's director, Rohner its screenwriter, and Foreman the stuntwoman who comes face to face with the killer. Roddy McDowall was originally slated to star as the director, but was replaced by Perkins when illness forced him out of the picture.

p, Peter Garrity, Rex Hauck; d, Robert Kirk; w, Peter Garrity, Rex Hauck; ph, Chuy Elizondo (Foto-Kem color); ed, Mark Rosenbaum; m, Patrick O'Hearn; prod d, Paul Staheli; art d, Randy Holland; spec eff, Patrick Ryan Denver, Rex L. Whitney; stunts, Brian Veatch.

Horror/Prison   **Cas.**   **(PR:NR MPAA:R)**

DIE HARD***   (1988) 131m Gordon-Silver/FOX c

Bruce Willis (*John McClane*), Bonnie Bedelia (*Holly Gennaro McClane*), Reginald Veljohnson (*Sgt. Al Powell*), Paul Gleason (*Dwayne T. Robinson*), De'voreaux White (*Argyle*), William Atherton (*Thornburg*), Hart Bochner (*Ellis*), James Shigeta (*Takagi*), Alan Rickman (*Hans Gruber*), Alexander Godunov (*Karl*), Bruno Doyon (*Franco*), Andreas Wisniewski (*Tony*), Clarence Gilyard, Jr. (*Theo*), Joey Plewa (*Alexander*), Lorenzo Caccialanza (*Marco*), Gerard Bonn (*Kristoff*), Dennis Hayden (*Eddie*), Al Leong (*Uli*), Gary Roberts (*Heinrich*), Hans Buhringer (*Fritz*), Wilhelm von Homburg (*James*), Robert Davi (*Big Johnson*), Grand L. Bush (*Little Johnson*), Bill Marcus (*City Engineer*), Rick Ducommun (*City Worker*), Matt Landers (*Capt. Mitchell*), Carmine Zozzora (*Rivers*), Dustyn Taylor (*Ginny*), George Christy (*Hasseldorf*), Anthony Peck (*Young Cop*), Cheryl Baker (*Woman*), Richard Parker (*Man*), David Ursin (*Harvey Johnson*), Mary Ellen Trainor (*Gail Wallens*), Diana James (*Supervisor*), Shelley Pogoda (*Dispatcher*), Selma Archerd, Scot Bennett, Rebecca Broussard, Kate Finlayson, Shanna Higgins, Kym Malin (*Hostages*), Taylor Fry (*Lucy McClane*), Noah Land (*John Jr.*), Betty Carvalho (*Paulina*), Kip Waldo (*Convenience Store Clerk*), Mark Goldstein (*Station Manager*), Tracy Reiner (*Thornburg's Assistant*), Rick Cicetti, Fred Lerner (*Guards*), Bill Margolin (*Producer*), Bob Jennings, Bruce P. Schultz (*Cameramen*), David Katz (*Soundman*), Robert Lesser (*Businessman*), Stella Hall (*Stewardess*), Terri Lynn Doss (*Girl at Airport*), Jon E. Greene (*Boy at Airport*), Randall Bowers (*Kissing Man*).

The improbable Bruce Willis (who was reportedly paid $5 million for his work, despite the fact that his previous forays on the big screen have been relative flops) makes his bid for superhero status with this slickly directed actioner that, unfortunately, leaves a bad aftertaste. DIE HARD's script, by Jeb Stuart and Steven E. de Souza,

©20TH CENTURY FOX

panders to the blue-collar American's worst fears and resentments—foreigners are not to be trusted, feminism has destroyed the fabric of the American family, coke-sniffing yuppies have all the good jobs, bureaucrats are incompetent fools, the media is inherently evil—but all this knee-jerk reactionism is presented in such a sleek and entertaining format as to be positively insidious. On Christmas Eve, Willis arrives in Los Angeles to spend the holidays with his estranged wife, Bedelia, and his two young children. A New York cop, Willis has separated from his wife because the Japanese corporation she works for promoted her to a powerful position in their brand-new Los Angeles headquarters, an imposing state-of-the-art office building in Century City. Seeking a reconciliation, Willis struggles to accept his wife's independence, but he cannot get over his hatred of LA. He meets his wife at a Christmas party thrown on the 30th floor of the building. While washing up in his wife's executive bathroom, he grows resentful of the fact that she has begun using her maiden name again. Explaining that the Japanese don't hold much stock in married businesswomen, Bedelia says that she'll go further in the company if it appears she is single. Their quarrel is interrupted when Bedelia is asked to make a speech to the employees. Left alone in the bathroom, Willis is suddenly shocked to hear the sound of automatic gunfire. A group of German terrorists has seized the high-rise and are holding everyone at the party hostage. Barefoot and wearing only a T-shirt and jeans, Willis grabs his service revolver and high-tails it upstairs to camp out on the top, as yet uncompleted, floors of the building. From there he tries to figure out a way to rescue his wife and her coworkers. Meanwhile, the terrorists, led by the suave Rickman, escort Bedelia's boss, Shigeta, to his office, where they try to persuade him to reveal the secret computer codes that will open the massive company safe containing $670 million worth of negotiable bonds. Shigeta refuses and is killed instantly. Rickman dispatches one of his men, a computer whiz, to crack the code. Upstairs, however, Willis has run into and killed one of the terrorists, stealing his machine gun and walkie-talkie. Unfortunately, the victim happens to be terrorist Godunov's brother, and the psychotic Godunov wants revenge. Using the walkie-talkie, Willis gets on the roof of the building and calls for help. Thinking his cries a prank, the police send a desk sergeant (Veljohnson) already on his way home over to the building to have a look. Veljohnson sees no sign of trouble and begins to drive off, but a desperate Willis shoots out one of the windows and dumps the body of another terrorist he killed over the edge. The body lands on Veljohnson's squad car and he immediately calls for reinforcements and then aids Willis further by lending moral support. In a matter of minutes the LAPD SWAT team, led by the moronic Gleason, is on the scene and causing havoc, despite Veljohnson's common-sense warnings. Soon the equally incompetent FBI shows up and enacts a plan likely to kill 45 percent of the hostages ("I can live with that," one of the FBI agents says). At the same time, ambitious television news reporter Atherton is nosing around and, discovering that Willis is married to Bedelia, does a hit-and-run interview on their terrified children. When the interview is aired, the terrorists see it and realize that they have Willis' wife hostage. Many killings and explosions later, the terrorists break into the safe and pack up the bonds, Bedelia is being used to ferret out Willis, and the FBI plans to pretend to accede to the terrorists' demand for a helicopter and then open fire on them once they get on the roof. Rickman, however, knows the FBI playbook and plans to make his getaway by blowing up the roof (and the hostages) and then slipping out the back way. Willis discovers this and manages to get the hostages off the roof before it blows; unfortunately, the cretinous FBI agents are caught in the blast and killed. Eventually, Willis whittles down the terrorists to Rickman and one other, then tracks them both down and kills them, saving his wife. The ordeal over, Willis and Bedelia leave the building, met by Veljohnson. Grateful to Veljohnson, Willis gives the cop a hug. But wait! The movie's not over. The crazed Godunov, whom Willis had supposedly picked off earlier, comes back to life and shows up on the front steps firing his machine gun. Unarmed, Willis has no choice but to shield his wife. Luckily, Veljohnson, who had taken a desk job because he accidentally killed an unarmed child and never wanted to draw his weapon again, coolly blows away the terrorist. Grateful to Veljohnson once again, Willis and Bedelia make their way through the crowd, only to be confronted by reporter Atherton. Realizing that this is the man who invaded her home and put her kids on television—a move that further jeopardized her life and that of her husband—Bedelia punches the reporter in the jaw. Ever the professional, the stunned Atherton turns to his cameraman and asks, "Did you get that?" Having faced every conceivable obstacle and won, Willis and Bedelia finally climb into a limo and kiss.

Tautly directed by John McTiernan (PREDATOR), DIE HARD is skillfully shot and consistently thrilling throughout its lengthy running time. The high-rise location is cleverly employed to provide an array of unusual and breathtaking action scenes, lifting this film a cut above the dull line-em-up-and-mow-em-down pyrotechnics of RAMBO. Also unusual is the very vulnerable Willis, a man, in his bare feet, who does what he can to help without getting himself killed. In the first hour he is shown to be frightened and unsure of himself, but as the film progresses he becomes more confident and clever, killing all the terrorists single-handedly. Unfortunately, the more confident he gets, the less interesting his character becomes, and by the last half-hour Willis is running around bare-*chested* and mowing down terrorists as if he were suddenly transformed into Sylvester Stallone or Arnold Schwarzenegger. His "Moonlighting" -style wisecracks tend to grate as well, turning his likable character into a flippant jerk. Although Willis has certainly brought greater humanity to the persona of the American superhero killing machine, he succumbs to the genre's baser instincts and abandons emotional complexity in favor of ridiculous heroics. Naturally, the screenplay provides him with some pat monologs about how he loves his family and feels guilty for being an insensitive male chauvinist pig, but these feelings are hung on the character like a strange suit of clothes and he makes this emotional confession via walkie-talkie to *another man* (Veljohnson), not to his wife. As an actor, Willis has not gotten past the superficial television style of letting his character's emotions come tumbling out in one long, impassioned speech, thus getting all the sappy stuff out of the way quick so we can get back to the shooting. Compare this to Robert DeNiro's performance in MIDNIGHT RUN, in which his deep emotional scars are revealed slowly and reluctantly throughout the film—there is real pain and regret in DeNiro's character, as is not so with Willis. Reginald Veljohnson's character suffers the same fate, with a sketchy sitcom problem to overcome by the end of the movie. Given the inadequacies of the script, however, the performances are solid and engaging. Alan Rickman is especially memorable, creating one of the most quietly intimidating villains seen on the screen in some time.

DIE HARD is most disturbing in its wanton, cynical pandering to the audience's worst fears. The Japanese are seen to be building huge, vulgar monuments to themselves on American soil, and they have driven a wedge between a good American cop and his wife, who has been forced to conceal her marriage to get ahead in the invaders' game. The terrorists are almost all cynical foreigners who, rather than caring for some political cause, merely want money for their own gain. On the American side, the only hostage to get killed is a coke-snorting yuppie who is clearly shown to deserve what he gets. Commanding officers and the FBI are characterized as totally incompetent, egotistical imbeciles who pay no attention to the dedicated rank and file and send them to their doom with impunity. Where the media is concerned, it is suggested that all anchormen are pompous, ignorant jerks, and all street reporters are calculating, ambitious vampires who care nothing for the people about whom they report. While some of these perceptions may have a basis in incidental reality (as stereotypes often do), the worldview of DIE HARD is strictly black and white, with absolutely no room for modulation or ambiguity. The filmmakers seem to try to deflect the aforesaid criticisms by the racially "progressive" casting of several black actors in major roles both heroic and villainous, but this is merely a diversion, for the film comes down hard on the side of patriotic "average" Americans and makes a villain of everything they have come to resent in the 1980s. This kind of blind paranoia is just as backward and offensive as the mindlessness of the RAMBO films—and twice as insidious, because McTiernan is a good director and DIE HARD, despite its distasteful subtext, is a well-made, exciting film. *(Graphic violence, profanity, nudity, sexual situations, substance abuse.)*

p, Lawrence Gordon, Joel Silver; d, John McTiernan; w, Jeb Stuart, Steven E. de Souza (based on the novel by Roderick Thorp); ph, Jan De Bont (Panavision, DeLuxe Color); ed, Frank J. Urioste, John F. Link; m, Michael Kamen; prod d, Jackson DeGovia; art d, John R. Jensen; set d, E.C. Chen, Roland Hill; spec eff, Richard Edlund, Al Di Sarro; cos, Marilyn Vance-Straker; tech, Art Fransen, L. Gary Goldman; stunts, Charles Picerni; makeup, Scott H. Eddo.

Action   Cas.   (PR:O MPAA:R)

DIRTY ROTTEN SCOUNDRELS½   (1988) 110m Orion c

Steve Martin *(Freddy Benson)*, Michael Caine *(Lawrence Jamieson)*, Glenne Headly *(Janet Colgate)*, Anton Rodgers *(Inspector Andre)*, Barbara Harris *(Fanny Eubanks)*, Ian McDiarmid *(Arthur)*, Dana Ivey *(Mrs. Reed)*, Meagen Fay *(Lady from Oklahoma)*, Frances Conroy *(Lady from Palm Beach)*, Nicole Calfan *(Lady in Dining Car)*, Aina Walle *(Miss Krista Knudsen)*, Cheryl Pay *(Lady With Pearls)*, Nathalie Auffret *(Marion)*, Lolly Susi *(Lad in Rolls Royce)*, Rupert Holliday Evans, Hepburn Graham *(English Sailors)*, Xavier Maly *(Hotel Bellboy)*, Andre Penvern *(Waiter on the Train)*, Louis Zorich *(Greek Millionaire)*, Georges Gerrard Baffos *(Assistant Hotel Manager)*, Valerie Beaufils *(Pretty Beach Girl)*.

Set in the sun-drenched south of France, this well-crafted remake of BEDTIME STORY—a 1964 comedy that most critics found less than satisfying, due mostly to its odd-couple casting—stars Michael Caine in the role David Niven originated and Steve Martin in the Marlon Brando part. Caine is a suave, sophisticated con man who operates out of an elegant villa in the seaside town of Beaumont-sur-Mer. Masquerading as the exiled leader of a tiny nation whose patriotic freedom fighters are trying to liberate it from communist rule, he romances middle-aged American women and "accepts" their generous contributions to the cause. When Martin, a third-rate American hustler who poses as a tragic innocent with a sick grandmother, begins plying his trade on the Cote d'Azur, Caine first tries to get rid of him, then grudgingly takes him on as an apprentice. Although Caine instructs Martin in the nuances of continental refinement, when it comes to working the cons, the American is limited to playing the role of the exiled monarch's addled brother, Prince Ruprecht, whose slobbering presence discourages Caine's dowager victims from sticking around after they've forked over the cash. In time, Martin decides that he's ready to strike out on his own and

©ORION

anxious to use his newly polished skills in Caine's own backyard, much to his teacher's dismay. As a solution, they agree to a contest: the first one to get $50,000 from American "soap queen" Headly wins, with the loser to leave Beaumont-sur-Mer. Martin takes on the role of a US serviceman who is confined to a wheelchair, psychosomatically crippled after witnessing his dance-loving girl friend's infidelity. He explains to Headly that he needs $50,000 to be treated by a famous German physician, whereupon Caine quickly becomes the renowned healer, conveniently in town on vacation. Caine and Martin duel in character, trying to win Headly's trust and affections, hilariously reversing each other's gains with clever counteractions (in the film's funniest scene, Caine whips Martin's supposedly numb legs repeatedly to find out if he has any feeling in them while Martin, his eyes burning with pain, must pretend he feels nothing). Before long, though, they learn that Headly isn't a wealthy heiress at all, but a contest winner who is willing to sell everything she owns to come up with the money for Martin's operation. Or is she? As far as Caine is concerned all bets are off, but Martin is determined to prove a point. Ultimately, it is the con men who are conned, but in the end taker and taken join forces.

Notwithstanding popular opinion, BEDTIME STORY is arguably a more entertaining film than it is given credit as being. The teaming of Niven and Brando may seem strange at first and the idea of Brando doing comedy may seem equally foreign (despite his inspired performance as Sakini in THE TEAHOUSE OF THE AUGUST MOON), but at times the chemistry between the two is excellent, and Brando's Prince Ruprecht, wholly unlike anything else he's done on the screen, is wildly funny. Still, BEDTIME STORY is, at best, an uneven film, which cries out for reinterpretation. Originally, Mick Jagger and David Bowie indicated an interest in working on a project together, and screenwriter Dale Launer, whom Jagger hoped would pen a screenplay for them, suggested redoing the Niven-Brando film. A number of studios indicated an interest in remaking the film, but Universal refused to relinquish its rights to BEDTIME STORY. There was, however, one important bit of additional information: after 20 years the rights to the film reverted back to Stanley Shapiro, who cowrote the screenplay with Paul Henning. By the time this was discovered, Jagger and Bowie were no longer interested, but Eddie Murphy and director Michael Ritchie were—however, Paramount wasn't. Orion picked up the baton next, passing it to Jim Abrahams (BIG BUSINESS), who moved on to another project after three days; then Herbert Ross signed on, requesting five rewrites of the screenplay before he, too, decided not to make the film. Ultimately one-time Muppet manipulator-actor-director (LITTLE SHOP OF HORRORS) Frank Oz, who reportedly was interested all along, took over, provided that Steve Martin would be involved. Working from the screenplay Launer wrote with the help of Shapiro and Henning, Oz has fashioned an amusing comedy whose strengths and weaknesses both stem from his broad treatment of the material. In going for easy lowest-common-denominator laughs, Oz has lost much of the subtlety of the original, choosing also to veer from its occasionally dark humor; but, by the same token, moments that only brought smiles in BEDTIME STORY produce great guffaws here. Launer's screenplay, on the other hand, while sticking close to the original, throws in a number of new and interesting twists that make DIRTY ROTTEN SCOUNDRELS considerably more complex narratively than the original. Martin (who was initially considered for the Niven role) and Caine work well together, milking laugh after laugh from their symbiotic teacher-pupil relationship and their con game roles. Like Brando, Martin shines most as Ruprecht, his hair plastered down, sidesplittingly funny as he intimidates Caine's "contributors" with his outlandish behavior. Caine also does well in his part, bringing Niven-like refinement to his conscientious criminal. Perhaps the most surprising performance in the film, though, belongs to Glenne Headley (PAPERHOUSE; MAKING MR. RIGHT), who lends more than a little touch of Marilyn Monroe vulnerability to her smarter-than-she-looks-acts-or-sounds victim(izer). Director of photography Michael Ballhaus (THE COLOR OF MONEY) also makes the most of his Cote d'Azur locations, as the film was shot in Cap d'Antibes, Villefranche-sur-Mer, Cap Beaulieu, and St. Jean Cap Ferrat on a budget of $19 million. If it's subtlety you're after, look elsewhere, but if you're interested in having more than a few good laughs, DIRTY ROTTEN SCOUNDRELS is for you. *(Sexual situations, profanity.)*

p, Bernard Williams; d, Frank Oz; w, Dale Launer, Stanley Shapiro, Paul Henning; ph, Michael Ballhaus (DeLuxe Color); ed, Stephen A. Rotter, William Scharf; m, Miles Goodman; m/l, Irving Berlin, Dorothy Fields, Jerome Kern, Al Dubin, Harry Warren; prod d, Roy Walker; art d, Steve Spence, Damien Lanfranchi; set d, Rosalind Shingleton; cos, Marit Allen; makeup, Janet Flora, Pascal

Charbonnier.

Comedy/Crime **(PR:C MPAA:PG)**

DISTANT THUNDER** (1988, US/Can.) 114m PAR c

John Lithgow *(Mark Lambert)*, Ralph Macchio *(Jack Lambert)*, Kerrie Keane *(Char)*, Reb Brown *(Harvey Nitz)*, Janet Margolin *(Barbara Lambert)*, Dennis Arndt *(Larry)*, Jamey Sheridan *(Moss)*, Tom Bower *(Louis)*, John Kelly, Michael Currie, Hilary Strang, Robyn Stevan, David Longworth, Gordon Currie, Walter Marsh.

Mark Lambert (Lithgow) is a Vietnam veteran who withdrew from society after his 1970 discharge from the Army, deserting a wife and three-year-old son in Illinois. As DISTANT THUNDER opens, Lithgow is living in the woods of Washington state along with several other disaffected vets. He resides in a ramshackle hut and earns a meager income by gathering ferns and selling them to florists. When one of Lithgow's vet buddies (Bower) kills himself by walking in front of a train ("kissing a train," as the vets call it), Lithgow decides to head back to civilization, comes down from the mountains, and takes a job with a logging company. In the meantime, in a suburb of Chicago, Jack Lambert (Macchio), is delivering the valedictorian speech to his high-school graduating class. He hasn't seen his father since he was three, but Dad's presence is still felt, since Lithgow was a star football player at the same high school. Macchio, however, is no athlete, and his graduation speech deals with the need to work at relationships. A few weeks later, on his 18th birthday, he gets a letter from Lithgow saying he wants to get together. Macchio's mother (Margolin) objects, but Macchio immediately writes to say he'll come to Washington and begins planning his trip. Back in Washington, Lithgow has been befriended by Keane, who has taken him in and is working to help him adapt to society—it was she who encouraged him to write to his son. While the relationship is helpful to Lithgow, it infuriates Sheridan, Keane's boy friend. Lithgow gets Macchio's letter saying he's coming, which excites but also frightens him. He then has a violent fight with Sheridan in a bar, which sends him back to his hideaway in the mountains. Macchio arrives and he and Keane head into the woods to find Lithgow, followed by the still angry Sheridan. They find Lithgow, and he and Macchio try to work through their anger, pain, and resentment. Sheridan arrives on the scene and Brown, a seriously deranged member of the vet community, explodes in a violent rage, attempting to kill the interloper, whereupon Lithgow has to take on his friend, rekindling his painful memories of Vietnam. During the war, Lithgow was part of a Special Forces unit sent on a clandestine mission in North Vietnam. The unit was ambushed by Viet Cong and all were killed except Lithgow and a friend, who was seriously wounded. The wounded man howled in agony and Lithgow, afraid the noise would reveal his location to the enemy, was forced to kill the man. Back in the present, Sheridan has been seriously hurt in his fight with Brown, and Lithgow, Keane, and Macchio begin the arduous task of bringing him down from the mountains for treatment. During the journey, Macchio and Lithgow try to reconcile their differences, Macchio helping his father to deal with his wartime trauma and Lithgow trying to make his son understand his need to get away from society. It isn't easy, and Lithgow almost kisses a train himself, but by the fadeout the two have made peace and reached a better understanding of each other's needs.

To prepare for this role, the conscientious John Lithgow spent a week talking to Vietnam veterans who were receiving counseling for post-traumatic stress syndrome in Port Angeles, Washington. The film is dedicated to vets suffering from that syndrome, and scriptwriter Robert Stitzel obviously has done his homework on the subject. Yet all those noble intentions are undone by a film that succeeds only in trivializing the problems it pretends to explore. Yes, the film does make an effort to depict accurately the problems many vets still face in attempting to reenter society, but when the chips are down and the movie really needs some action to break things open, there's the old deranged, psychotic killer-vet on hand to explode on a rampage of violence. In addition, DISTANT THUNDER is slow moving and predictable. We know father and son will reconcile, and we know there will have to be some confrontations before hand, but the confrontations are so stagy and the dialog so cliched that we just want it to end. Lithgow, looking bedraggled and affecting a raspy voice, is solid as usual, and Denis Arndt and Reb Brown are effective as his buddies. Kerrie Keane is properly supportive, but poor Ralph Macchio is saddled with most of the worst dialog and is barely able to struggle through. British Columbia, standing in for Washington state, is dark and rainy, providing a suitable backdrop for the film. A Canadian-American coproduction, DISTANT THUNDER did little box-office business and quickly disappeared from theaters. *(Profanity, violence.)*

p, Robert Schaffel; d, Rick Rosenthal; w, Robert Stitzel (based on a story by Robert L. Stitzel, Deedee Wehle); ph, Ralf D. Bode (Technicolor); ed, Dennis Virkler; m, Maurice Jarre; cos, Tish Monaghan.

Drama **Cas.** **(PR:O MPAA:R)**

DISTORTIONS † (1988) 96m Cori c

Steve Railsback *(Scott)*, Olivia Hussey *(Amy)*, Piper Laurie *(Margot)*, June Chadwick *(Kelly)*, Rita Gam *(Mildred)*, Terence Knox *(Paul Elliot)*, Edward Albert *(Jason)*, Tom J. Castronova *(Detective Harry Cory)*, Leon Smith *(Detective Jackson)*, John Goff *(Coroner Tompkins)*, Don Clark *(Gary Walker)*, Kathleen Chin *(Receptionist Tielyn)*, Christopher Hayes *(Ralph)*.

Hussey plays a woman whose husband is killed in a car wreck, his face burnt beyond recognition. She moves into her aunt's mansion, where she becomes the victim of a plot to drive her insane and steal her insurance money. Shown in 1987 at the Cannes Film Festival market, DISTORTIONS was released on video in 1988. Produced by Jackelyn Giroux, former actress and wife of Hussey's costar Railsback.

p, Jackelyn Giroux; d, Armand Mastrioanni; w, John Goff; ph, John Dirlam; ed, Jack Tucker; m, David Morgan; md, Brian Leahy; art d, Michelle Sefman; set d, Lisa Schneider; spec eff, Don Clark; makeup, Noel De Souza, Lee Bryant.

Thriller **Cas.** **(PR:NR MPAA:NR)**

D.O.A.*½** (1988) 96m Touchstone-Bigelow-Silver Screen Partners III/BV c

Dennis Quaid *(Dexter Cornell)*, Meg Ryan *(Syndey Fuller)*, Charlotte Rampling *(Mrs. Fitzwaring)*, Daniel Stern *(Hal Petersham)*, Jane Kaczmarek *(Gail Cornell)*, Christopher Neame *(Bernard)*, Robin Johnson *(Cookie Fitzwaring)*, Rob Knepper *(Nicholas Lang)*, Jay Patterson *(Graham Corey)*, Brion James *(Detective Ulmer)*, Jack Kehoe *(Detective Brockton)*, Elizabeth Arlen *(Elaine Wells)*, Karen Radcliffe, William Forward, Lee Gideon, Bill Bolender, Hillary Hoffman, John Hawkes, Timbuk 3.

Remaking a classic Hollywood film always invites an onslaught of criticism from purists who hold the past close to their hearts, but occasionally improvements are made that justify a remake's existence. Such is the case with D.O.A., a remake (or, more exactly, a reworking) of the 1949 Rudolph Mate *film noir* that starred Edmond O'Brien and someone named Pamela Britton—a film that isn't really a "classic," but rather a mediocre film with a classic premise. Although it has some gritty location photography (seldom seen in the studio-bound films of the period), a gutsy performance by O'Brien, and a creepy villain in Neville Brand, the rest of the picture is fairly standard and, at times, downright silly (most notably, the whistling on the soundtrack that accompanies the appearance of a pretty woman). Taking the original's premise, husband-and-wife directing team Rocky Morton and Annabel Jankel and scriptwriter Charles Edward Pogue (PSYCHO III; THE FLY) have fashioned a murder mystery that is both modern and an homage to a genre of the past.

Quaid, who bears some resemblance to O'Brien, plays a once-brilliant author who has put down the pen after three increasingly unsuccessful follow-ups to a critically praised first novel. Retreating into the role of tenured college professor, he is jealous of one especially talented student, Knepper. For an assignment, Knepper has turned in a lengthy novel called *Out of Whack,* which Quaid has no desire to read despite Knepper's pleas and manic need for his approval. Quaid simply scribbles an "A" on the assignment and forgets about it . . . until Knepper's body crashes bloodily against his office window and onto the pavement below—an apparent suicide. Fortunately, Stern, a fellow faculty member and aspiring writer, helps Quaid through his initial shock at the incident, just as he has helped him cope with his pending divorce from Kaczmarek, who is no longer able to watch as Quaid wastes his life. Matters get even worse for Quaid, however, when he learns that Kaczmarek was having an affair with Knepper, who reminded her of her husband as a younger man. Turning to the bottle, Quaid heads for a college bar and tries to pick up Johnson, a grieving young woman who is whisked away by Nazi-like bodyguard Neame. Quaid then spots Ryan, a chipper, admiring student, and offers to buy her a drink. After a night of boozing, Quaid wakes up in her dorm room, having passed out after Ryan's unsuccessful advances. Suffering from more than a hangover, he stumbles into a hospital and learns that he has been given a dose of a radioactive poison that has no known antidote. Before long, he arrives at Kaczmarek's house to explain his predicament, but is moments too late—she has been bludgeoned by an unseen assailant. He then returns to Ryan's dorm, accuses her of poisoning him, and, in a variation of Alfred Hitchcock's THE 39 STEPS' handcuffing sequence, super-glues his hand to her forearm as they retrace their steps to find his "killer." While trying to avoid the police, who think he is guilty of both Kaczmarek's and Knepper's murders, Quaid and Ryan run through the city in search of clues. At Knepper's funeral service, he recognizes Johnson, the daughter of wealthy widow Rampling, who is about to give a eulogy. Rampling, as it turns out, paid for Knepper's schooling after his father, a professional thief, broke into her house and murdered her husband. Quaid approaches Johnson and learns that she, too, was having an affair with Knepper, but in the process he and bodyguard Neame exchange a few words, and Quaid is decked by the bruiser. Before he and Ryan can escape, they are attacked by an unseen assailant with a high-powered nail-gun. Eventually they do get away, but Ryan, no longer thrilled by the idea of risking her life—even for her favorite instructor—takes her leave of Quaid.

Quaid, however, is carried deeper into the skeleton closet of Rampling and her family. Thinking that Quaid knows too much about her life (though he really knows very little), Rampling orders Neame to drive him to a remote spot and kill him. Along the way, they are met by Johnson and, during an escape attempt by Quaid, Johnson is killed by Neame. Quaid returns to Rampling's to report that both Johnson and Neame (whom Quaid has killed) are dead. Rampling, having lost the will to fight, reveals the truth to Quaid: Knepper was her son (meaning that Johnson was unknowingly involved in an incestuous romance); Knepper's father, the supposed thief, was actually her first husband; and Rampling killed both her first and second husbands. Still unaware of what this has to do with his poisoning, Quaid leaves as Rampling turns a gun on herself. Returning to his office, Quaid remembers the foul taste of a drink Stern earlier offered him and realizes that it was his colleague who poisoned him. Shortly thereafter, Stern arrives and explains his mad motive. Gripped by "publish or perish" anxiety, Stern decided to murder Knepper after reading *Out of Whack,* which he considers to be a brilliant piece of writing. In order to carry out his plan, Stern has been forced to kill everyone who knew of student's novel, including Kaczmarek and, of course, Quaid. Stern then tries again to kill Quaid, but the dying professor shoots Stern, sending him and a manual typewriter flying out the window and onto the pavement below-on top of the chalk marks left by Knepper's body. Back in the police station where the film began in black and white, Quaid finishes relating his story, laughing about the number of murders that have occurred because of someone's "homework." He gets up, exits the office, and walks down a long hallway toward a door full of bright, blinding light, as the credits roll.

The first feature film from Morton and Jankel, creators of the British television episodes of "Max Headroom" (which gave rise to the Coca-Cola pitchman and the ABC-TV series), D.O.A. is a success on two levels—as a remake and on its own merits. While the 1949 mystery plot about international criminal gangs and secret bills of sale may have once been timely, it is not a truly "modern" scenario. Rather than be trapped by its dated contrivances, Morton and Jankel, working from Pogue's intricate script, have brought the film into the present. They have kept the original's basic structure—a man looking for his own killer—but they've dressed it up for the 80s. An idealistic student with a crush on a once-idealistic professor, a once-idealistic professor's wife involved with an idealistic young writer, and another man's desire to become a successful writer—these are characters with contemporary relevancy, especially in an era in which young writers like Jay MacInerney, Tama Janowitz, and Brett Easton Ellis have been hailed as superstars by the press. Beneath the murder mystery is a morality tale that hinges on Stern's obsession with "publishing or perishing." Of the three writers in D.O.A., the two most successful (Quaid and Knepper) are murdered by the least successful (Stern), who is then murdered himself (in a strange twist, Stern murders Quaid *and* Quaid murders Stern). An additional layer of meaning, wherein Quaid has considered himself "dead" ever since his lackluster second novel, is what separates the 1988 D.O.A. from the 1949 version, since the original only *suggests* the character's symbolic death (O'Brien is an accountant unable to reciprocate his fiancee's love).

D.O.A. has a visual style that, while not as intensely personal as that of Martin Scorsese (whose COLOR OF MONEY is more a Scorsese film than it is derivative of THE HUSTLER) or David Cronenberg (director of the Pogue-scripted update of THE FLY), does express an energetic technical flair. Photographed by Yuri Neyman (who also shot the visually aggressive LIQUID SKY), D.O.A. is a visual assault that refuses to take a back seat to the script or acting. After an abstract credit sequence, the film's black-and-white beginning pays homage to classic *film noir* visuals and then switches into color as Quaid scratches the word "color" onto his classroom chalkboard. This homage to *film noir* even extends to the character names: Nicholas Lang combines directors Nicholas Ray and Fritz Lang; Sydney Fuller refers to director Sam Fuller and perhaps more obliquely to Sylvia Sydney, star of two Lang films. Even Quaid's character name, Dexter Cornell, recalls pulp writer Cornell Woolrich. Perhaps the most interesting aspect of D.O.A. (original and remake alike) is that almost the entire mystery portion of the film is involved with a red herring. Having somehow taken a wrong turn, Quaid ends up tracking a series of clues that leads to the wrong mystery. It's as if he walked out of D.O.A. and into a Douglas Sirk melodrama starring Rampling as a widowed matriarch with a peculiar henchman, two dead husbands, and incestuous children. When Quaid arrives in *their* story everything goes haywire, and confused henchman Neame puts a bullet into the forehead of Rampling's daughter Johnson for no apparent reason, as if driven by some unseen force.

For the most part D.O.A. shows few concessions to Hollywood expectations, with the exception of the end. While the original has Edmond O'Brien die as "D.O.A." is stamped on the police report, Quaid exits the office looking healthier than when he arrived. His walk down the dark corridor towards a blinding white light, however, suggests that he, too, has died, without leaving the audience with too bleak an ending. Dennis Quaid, one of the busiest actors of 1987-88, is again superb, as is Meg Ryan (Quaid's real-life love and costar in INNERSPACE) in the rather thankless role of a starry-eyed college kid. Daniel Stern is effectively sleazy and the remainder of the cast adds able support, save for Charlotte Rampling, whose stone-faced character is given very little flesh and blood. The forgettable score is by forgotten dance musician Chaz Jankel, with a nightclub appearance by pop duo Timbuk 3. *(Brief nudity, violence, substance abuse, profanity.)*

p, Ian Sander, Laura Ziskin; d, Rocky Morton, Annabel Jankel; w, Charles Edward Pogue (based on a story by Pogue, Russell Rouse, Clarence Greene from an earlier screenplay by Rouse and Greene); ph, Yuri Neyman (CFI Color, Duart b&w); ed, Michael R. Miller; m, Chaz Jankel; prod d, Richard Amend; set d, Michael O'Sullivan.

Mystery **Cas.** **(PR:C-O MPAA:R)**

DR. HACKENSTEIN † (1988) 88m Feifer-Miller/Vista Street c

David Muir *(Dr. Elliot Hackenstein)*, Stacey Travis *(Melanie Victor)*, Catherine Davis Cox *(Leslie)*, Dyanne DiRosario *(Wendy)*, John Alexis *(Alex)*, Catherine Cahn *(Yolanda)*, William Schreiner, Sylvia Lee Baker, Jeff Rector, Anne Ramsey, Logan Ramsey, Phillis Diller, Michael Ensign.

This horror spoof set in 1909 concerns a mad doctor who tries to bring his dead wife back to life a la Dr. Frankenstein. He does so by borrowing body parts from an attractive threesome of young women, and employing a pair of gravediggers (one of them the late Anne Ramsey, of THROW MOMMA FROM THE TRAIN) to fetch additional parts.

p, Reza Mizbani, Megan Barnett; d, Richard Clark; w, Richard Clark; ph, Jens Sturup; ed, Tony Miller; m, Randy Miller; prod d, Leon King; art d, Craig Voigt.

Comedy/Horror **Cas.** **(PR:NR MPAA:R)**

DOMINICK AND EUGENE*** (1988) 111m Orion c

Ray Liotta *(Eugene* "Gino" Luciano), Tom Hulce *(Dominick* "Nicky" Luciano), Jamie Lee Curtis *(Jennifer Reston)*, Robert Levine *(Dr. Levinson)*, Todd Graff *(Larry Higgins)*, Bill Cobbs *(Jesse Johnson)*, Mimi Cecchini *(Mrs. Gianelli)*, Tommy Snelsire *(Mikey Chernak)*, Mary Joan Negro *(Theresa Chernak)*, Tom Signorelli *(Father T)*, John Romeri *(Choir Director)*, David Perry *(TV Announcer)*, Joe Maruzzo *(Guido)*, R. Scott Peck *(Joe)*, Charles Susan *(Leon)*, Jack Boslet, Matthew J. Ravenstahl, Shawn Ebbert *(Teens)*, Jaqueline Knapp *(Mrs. Vinson)*, David Strathairn *(Martin Chernak)*, Vincent Cinese *(Vince)*, Joe Marmo *(Tony)*, Daniel Krell *(Lew)*, Thomas Rocco *(Perry)*, Bingo O'Malley *(Abe)*, Amanda Picciafoco, Megan Picciafoco, Lindsay Harms, Lauren Harms *(Joey)*, John Naples Jr. *(Neighbor Boy)*, Mel Winkler *(Lt. Gage)*, Raymond Laine *(Reporter)*, O'Malley the Dog *(Fred)*, Victoria Dym *(Woman's Voice)*.

Tom Hulce, who received an Oscar nomination for his performance as Mozart in AMADEUS, and Ray Liotta, who made his stunning film debut as Ray Sinclair, the disturbing ex-con in SOMETHING WILD, are teamed in this often touching, unashamedly sentimental story of brotherly love. Hulce and Liotta play 26-year-old twins who live together over a poultry shop in a working-class neighborhood of Pittsburgh. Liotta (Eugene of the title, called Gino) is a hard-working medical student whom the good-natured but mildly retarded Hulce (Dominick, called Nicky) supports by working on a garbage truck owned by Cobbs. Because their parents are dead, the brothers share a special relationship and each looks after the other in his own way, Hulce acting as provider and Liotta as protector. The equilibrium of their relationship is threatened, however, when Liotta is given the opportunity to do his residency in a prestigious Stanford program, which would require a two-year separation from his brother. Liotta doesn't know how to break this news to Hulce and he frets that his simple-minded twin won't be able to care for himself in his absence. Liotta's fears are reinforced when he arrives home one day to find neighborhood punks harassing Hulce and later when he learns that Hulce has unknowingly been making deliveries for a local pusher. This last discovery sends the volatile Liotta into a rage that culminates with him punching out the dealer, sending his fist through a window on the way to his target's jaw. Meanwhile, Liotta has fallen in love with Curtis, another determined medical student, and Hulce, confused by the cynical predictions of coworker Graff, becomes jealous and fears abandonment. After Liotta is forced to cancel their birthday excursion to see professional wrestling, Hulce ends up at a drunken "party" with Graff and his lover, and, returning home, confronts Liotta, who explodes and then comforts him. A picnic that is meant to smooth things over only results in the death of Hulce's beloved dog, but the real trauma for him comes later, on the garbage route. Hulce sees Strathairn strike his young son, Snelsire (Hulce's pal and fellow comic-book lover), and the blow sends the boy down a flight of stairs. Witnessing this violent action calls up a long-buried memory from Hulce's childhood, and suddenly he knows that he is the way he is because a beating from his own father caused a fall that damaged his brain. Unable to tell anyone what he has seen, Hulce chases after the ambulance to the hospital, where he learns that Snelsire has died. That night, Hulce takes Cobbs' gun, goes to Strathairn's house, and steals off with the couple's baby, determined to protect it from harm. Roaming the darkened streets, trying to avoid police, Hulce is finally cornered in a warehouse, but before a SWAT team "takes him out," Liotta goes in to talk with him. High on a fire escape, with the baby in his arms, Hulce angrily asks Liotta why he never told him the truth about their father and his accident. With tears welling, Liotta explains that Hulce had protected him from their father when they were little and he confesses that he has always been afraid that he was like their father, scared that his violent temper would get the best of him, too. Filled with love for each other, Liotta and Hulce descend with the infant, and when Strathairn, in the presence of the police, pulls a gun on Hulce, the gentle garbageman finally fingers the abusive father. Later, after Curtis says her goodbyes, Liotta climbs into a car to drive to California to his residency, and Hulce, secure in the knowledge that he will reunited with his brother forever in two years, prepares to go on with his life. As the credits roll, we watch him do just that, following Hulce on the garbage route.

On paper, DOMINICK AND EUGENE has all the earmarks of a too-plaintive, three-hanky melodrama, and in its weakest and most obvious moments it is little more than that. Director Robert M. Young, who began his career as a documentary maker and whose feature films (NOTHING BUT A MAN, 1964; THE BALLAD OF GREGORIO CORTEZ, 1983) have been concerned with the triumph of human dignity, occasionally allows his film to become manipulative, though it is less a matter of strings showing than of sentimental overkill. The blame for this may be more properly laid on the script by Academy Award winner Alvin Sargent and Corey Blechman, although, in general, it steers clear of sentiment for sentiment's sake. Most of the time Young manages to push the right emotional and dramatic buttons unseen, and in these moments the film, buoyed by performances of considerable depth by Hulce and Liotta, is deeply affecting. Liotta's Ray Sinclair was darkly menacing —certainly one of the 1980s' most threatening film characters—and his Eugene is also capable of volcanic violence, but these outbursts represent the repressed side of a personality that is basically gentle and giving. Wrapping these two tendencies in a determined intensity, Liotta arrives at a complex, believable portrayal of a man torn between the immediate need to protect Hulce and the demand of doing what is best in the long run. Hulce's performance is riskier but no less successful than Liotta's. He obviously tosses aside any fears of looking foolish as he reaches for a monumental childlike simplicity, and though Hulce occasionally pushes his smiling, wide-eyed innocence over the top, he remains a deeply sympathetic character. Moreover, the interaction between Liotta and Hulce is excellent, the bond between them appears genuine, and, as the actors told the *Chicago Sun Times* Peter Keough, mirrors the closeness they felt working on the film. Jamie Lee Curtis is nicely understated as Liotta's love interest and David Strathairn (MATEWAN) lends a human touch to his creepy father, but the best supporting performance is turned in by Todd Graff as Hulce's opinionated, sleazy, but well-intentioned coworker—a far cry from his role as Jodie Foster's devoted but ineffectual boy friend in FIVE CORNERS.

Sargent and Blechman's screenplay is based on a story written by Danny Porfirio, a former Marine who sent his first literary undertaking to ex-Marine Mike Farrell after reading a magazine article about the former "M*A*S*H" star. Farrell encouraged Porfirio in his writing and some six months later the Pennsylvanian sent him the first draft of DOMINICK AND EUGENE, which became Farrell's first project as a motion picture producer. The entire film was shot in Pittsburgh, in the ethnic neighborhoods in which it is set. *(Violence, adult situations, profanity.)*

p, Marvin Minoff, Mike Farrell; d, Robert M. Young; w, Alvin Sargent, Corey Blechman (based on a story by Danny Porfirio); ph, Curtis Clark (Duart Color); ed, Arthur Coburn; m, Trevor Jones; md, Trevor Jones; m/l, Mike Piccirillo, Gary Goetzman, Andy Fairweather-Low, Peter Words, Glyn Johns, B. Maglia, J. Spousta, Jr., J. Stern, Bob Keane, D. Deen R. King, Jackie English, Fred Washington, Peter Allen, A. Anderson, Fred Campbell, Ben Peters, Winston Matthews, Lloyd McDonald; prod d, Doug Draner; set d, Derek R. Hill; cos, Hilary Rosenfeld; ch, Lenora Nemetz; makeup, Pamela S. Westmore.

Drama   Cas.   (PR:C MPAA:PG-13)

DON'T MESS WITH MY SISTER! †   (1988) 84m Vidamerica-Shotwed c

Joe Perce (*Steven*), Jeannine Lemay (*Wife*), Jack Gurci, Peter Sapienza (*Brothers-in-Law*), Laura Lanfranchi (*Annika*), Kit Bard, Roy Miller, Helen Perle, Janice Derosa, Pam La Testa.

This straight-to-video release follows the fortunes of an accounting student who works in a junkyard owned by his wife's brothers. When his wife throws him a surprise party complete with a belly dancer, the birthday boy falls for the exotic entertainer. The title line sums up the feelings of the two junkyard proprietors, who, with their Italian American blood boiling, set out to teach the unfaithful husband a lesson. Filmed in New York in 1983 under the less exciting moniker AMERICAN JUNKYARD.

p, Meir Zarchi; d, Meir Zarchi; w, Meir Zarchi; ph, Phil Gries; ed, Meir Zarchi; m, Todd Rice.

Drama   Cas.   (PR:NR MPAA:NR)

DOOM ASYLUM †   (1988) 78m Manhattan-Filmworld/Filmworld c

Patty Mullen (*Judy/Kiki*), Ruth Collins (*Tina*), Kristin Davis (*Jane*), William Hay (*Mike*), Kenny L. Price (*Dennis*), Harrison White (*Darnell*), Dawn Alvan, Farin, Michael Rogen (*The Coroner*).

This is one of those movies set in the sort of deserted asylum one never sees in real life. In this case, the aforementioned asylum is home to a blood-thirsty bogeyman who, 10 years earlier, sat up during his own autopsy and walked away. It seems that the monstrous killer is bent on vengeance and the members of an all-girl punk band (one of whom's mother was a victim in the same car wreck that claimed the villain) are getting in his way. This short, straight-to-video entry was filmed in New Jersey and, for some reason, includes clips from various British horror entries starring Tod Slaughter.

p, Steve Menkin; d, Richard Friedman; w, Rick Marx (based on a story by Friedman, Menkin, Marx); ph, Larry Revene (Precision Color); ed, Ray Shapiro; m, Jonathan Stuart, Dave Erlanger; prod d, Kosmo Vinyl; art d, Hank Liebeskind; spec eff, Vincent J. Guastini.

Horror   Cas.   (PR:NR MPAA:R)

DRACULA'S WIDOW*   (1988) 86m DEG c

Sylvia Kristel (*Vanessa*), Josef Sommer (*Lt. Lannon*), Lenny Von Dohlen (*Raymond Everett*), Marc Coppola (*Brad*), Rachel Jones (*Jenny*), Stefan Schnabel (*Von Helsing*), Traver Burns, Rick Warner, Candice Sims.

DRACULA'S WIDOW, the feature film debut of director Christopher Coppola (nephew of superstar director Francis Ford Coppola), is an ambitious but disappointing rehash of the Dracula myth. Kristel, the widow of the notorious count, is accidentally shipped from Castle Bran in Romania to a Hollywood wax museum. Using Von Dohlen, the museum's owner, as her pawn, Kristel plans to return to Romania to search for her long-lost husband; however, Von Dohlen informs her that Count Dracula is dead, killed by Dr. Von Helsing many years before. This news enrages the vamp, and she embarks on a killing spree, mutilating many helpless victims. Enter the police, who are confused and angered by the mysterious murders. Sommer, a detective who has seen it all, is assigned to the case and warned by his boss "to deliver or else". His investigation leads nowhere until Von Helsing's grandson conveniently pops up and explains everything to the disbelieving detective. After his partner and the grandson are brutally killed, Sommer finally accepts the vampire story and sets out to destroy Kristel. In the end, the vampire is killed (but not before turning into a hideous bat creature) by Von Dohlen, who thrusts a stake through her heart. To the amazement and relief of Sommer and Von Dohlen's girl friend (Jones), Kristel disintegrates and all is safe again in Hollywood.

Director Coppola sets up his film as a modern-day *film noir*, with Sommer's monotone voice introducing its mystery over a montage of flashing neon lights and rain-soaked streets. Giuseppe Macari's cinematography is appropriately moody, using color and shadows to convey the film's stylistic intent, and the vivid lighting, inspired by the E.C. horror comics of the 1950s, is occasionally effective, though mostly it is a distraction. (A similar technique was used with far better results in George Romero's CREEPSHOW.) From time to time, Coppola rises above his material by combining stylish camera movements with expressive editing techniques, but despite his technical bravado, the film fails on the crucial level of story content. Unfortunately, Coppola's characters are unengaging stereotypes, and the plot has been done better many times before. Vampire films are as old and worn as the fanged Count himself, and few filmmakers have succeeded in shedding new light on the tired sub-genre. Romero did so with MARTIN in 1977, as did Kathryn Bigelow with her fine 1987 entry, NEAR DARK. However, Christopher Coppola—quoted as saying, "You'll never see such an elegant horror film as DRACULA'S WIDOW" —has failed to provide the fresh blood that the vampire film desperately craves. *(Extreme violence, profanity.)*

p, Stephen Traxler; d, Christopher Coppola; w, Kathryn Ann Thomas, Christopher Coppola; ph, Giuseppe Macari (Technicolor); ed, Tom Siiter; m, James Campbell; prod d, Alexandra Kicenik; spec eff, Todd Masters, Dean Gates; cos, Ron Leamon.

Horror   Cas.   (PR:O MPAA:R)

DRAGON CHOW*½**   (1988, W. Ger./Switz.) 75m Novoskop-Probst-BernKuratorium Junger

Bhasker (*Shezad*), Ric Young (*Xiao*), Buddy Uzzaman (*Rashid*), Ulrich Wildgruber (*Cook*), Wolf-Dietrich Sprenger (*Herder*), Frank Oladeinde (*Dale*), Louis Blaise (*Louis*), Su Zeng Hua (*Wang*), Young Me Song (*Herder's Wife*).

A young Pakistani immigrant (Bhasker) who is seeking political asylum in Hamburg is tossed out of a Chinese restaurant by a waiter (Young) when he attempts to sell roses to the customers. Crestfallen, he trudges back through the dreary, wintry landscape to his room in a state-operated dormitory, where he learns that his friend and fellow countryman (Uzzaman) has been denied political asylum and is soon to be deported. Uzzaman instead opts for an illegal and complicated oceanic crossing that will eventually land him in the US. His friend gone, Bhasker finds illegal work in the kitchen of the Chinese restaurant from which he was evicted and is befriended by the Chinese waiter, Young. They decide to form a partnership in a restaurant and organize a contest for Bhasker's dormitory mates to decide whether Pakistani or Chinese food will be the featured cuisine. After Bhasker ingeniously manages to secure the necessary capital, construction begins on a Pakistani restaurant. A letter from the immigration authorities arrives for Bhasker, but he places it unopened inside a cabinet drawer. The restaurant opens to a full house and a receptive clientele, but the authorities arrive, forcibly remove Bhasker from the premises and, subsequently, from the country. An unknown immigrant later enters the establishment with a bundle of roses for sale, but leaves when he finds Young staring disconsolately at a photo of Bhasker. Jan Schutte's first feature film is a powerful and insightful look at the plight of Third World immigrants as they attempt to survive in the West. Presented in an understated manner, while using an approach that director Schutte describes as reductive, the film eliminates stylistic embellishments and narrative irrelevancies, providing, instead, the opportunity for the characters to tell their own stories. It is this directorial restraint that ultimately gives the film its remarkable strength, allowing the humanistic concern that Schutte feels for his characters to filter through without either elevating them to the status of victimized heroes or overtly attacking the society that seems to ignore them. Schutte developed this idea while filming an earlier documentary about an immigrant rose peddler. The main actor in the earlier film and several of his friends shared numerous stories about their immigrant experiences, inspiring Schutte to make DRAGON'S FOOD. A primary focal point of the film is the feeling of alienation the numerous immigrants feel when confronted by the dominant German culture, a feeling underscored as Schutte only translates one of the 12 languages (German) heard in the film. The German authorities continually take refuge in official decrees as their guidelines for handling the problems of the refugees. They are civil and sometimes even pleasant, but they are unable to provide any real help. Whenever faced with an emotional display, they react by reciting a statement of the designated policy that pertains to the individual case. Ultimately the struggles of the neglected immigrants bind them into a collective alien culture that gives them the will to survive. It is this resilience of human nature that DRAGON'S FOOD truly celebrates. *(Adult situations.)*

d, Jan Schutte; w, Jan Schutte, Thomas Strittmatter; ph, Lutz Konermann; ed, Renate Merck; m, Claus Bantzer.

Drama   (PR:C MPAA:NR)

DRIFTER, THE*   (1988) 90m New Horizons/Concorde c

Kim Delaney (*Julia*), Timothy Bottoms (*Arthur*), Al Shannon (*Kriger*), Miles O'-Keeffe (*Trey*), Anna Gray Garduno (*Matty*), Loren Haines (*Willie Munroe*), Larry Brand (*Morrison*), Thomas Wagner (*Capt. Edwards*), Ernest Alexander (*Eugene*), Joanne Willette (*Carrie*), Gil Christner (*Jambone*), Charles Zucker (*Joe*), Patrick McCord (*Biker*), Ken Stein (*Biker*), Myvanwy Jenn (*Milton*), Bruce Vilanch (*Cook*), Kerry Barden (*Hitchhiker*).

A low-budget ($400,000) Roger Corman production, THE DRIFTER casts Delaney (of TV's "All My Children") as a successful LA designer who, returning from a business trip, stops at a diner in a small desert town. While eating, she spies hitchhiker O'Keeffe. Another character present is the weird Shannon, who later turns out to be a private eye hired by Delaney's boy friend, Bottoms, to keep an eye on her. Soon after leaving the restaurant, Delaney gets a flat tire and gives O'Keeffe a lift in exchange for fixing it. Later that evening she invites him into her motel room, but, upon reaching LA, she informs him that it was just a one night stand. She does give him a keepsake, a 100-year-old pocketwatch given to Delaney by her grandfather and said to protect her as long as it keeps ticking. O'Keeffe, who is so detached he can barely run two sentences together, refuses to leave her alone, and is soon calling her to impart such information as "Sex is a forever thing" and "You'll always know where to find me." Bottoms, a lawyer who defends psycho mass murderers that Shannon digs up, is informed of Delaney and O'Keeffe's night together by the PI. Later, when Delaney's friend Garduno is murdered in her apartment, Bottoms and Delaney immediately suspect the phone calling hitchhiker. A police detective (writer-director Brand) is assigned to the case, but as he's never shown stepping out of his office it's not surprising that he fails to locate O'Keeffe. In the finale, Delaney discovers Bottoms with a bullet hole in his head, then is brutalized by the killer, Shannon. O'Keeffe shows up and is shot by Shannon but saved from death when the bullet strikes the keepsake pocket-watch—which he wears around his neck—allowing him to beat the killer up and save Delaney.

   The script has lots of holes, filled in at the end in a lumbering explanation from killer Shannon. The biggest plotting problem is that O'Keeffe's character is never built up to a point that would make him a convincing threat, while Shannon's dementia is introduced so late in the film that the ending is totally unbelievable. Despite the threadbare plot, however, THE DRIFTER does build up some genuine suspense and tension, mainly through the skills of Kim Delaney, an attractive and believable lead. Miles O'Keeffe does his best to add to the tension by striking laconic poses; Al Shannon is effective in the last scene that requires him to explain all, despite the ludicrous situation. The ultra-low budget is obvious throughout, with jump cuts and mike booms breaking up several scenes, and while director Larry Brand does a nice job of moving the film along, the very thin material undercuts his efforts. It's too bad, since with a somewhat better script this exploitation film could have added up to something more than the predictable product it is. THE DRIFTER had a brief theater run before heading off to home video. (*Violence, sexual situations, profanity.*)

p, Ken Stein; d, Larry Brand; w, Larry Brand; ph, David Sperling; ed, Stephen Mark; m, Rick Conrad; set d, Cara Haycak; cos, Daryl Binder; makeup, Deborah Zoller.

Thriller   Cas.   (PR:O MPAA:R)

DUDES½   (1988) 89m Vista/New Century-Vista c

Jon Cryer (*Grant*), Daniel Roebuck (*Biscuit*), Flea (*Milo*), Lee Ving (*Missoula, Thief Gang Leader*), Catherine Mary Stewart (*Jessie, Gas Station Owner*), Billy Ray Sharkey, Glenn Withrow, Michael Melvin, Axxel G. Reese, Marc Rude, Calvin Bartlett, Pete Willcox, Vance Colvig, Pamela Gidley.

First Alex Cox's STRAIGHT TO HELL and now this, the second punk western to hit the screen this year. DUDES begins as three New York City punkers, Cryer, Roebuck (sporting a massive bleach-blond mohawk), and Flea, decide that they are fed up with the Big Apple and are ready to give sunny Los Angeles a try. The trio set out in Cryer's old Volkswagen bug and somewhere in the Southwest they encounter Willcox, an Elvis impersonator/rodeo clown/stunt driver, etc. whose huge Airstream trailer (with "Daredelvis" painted on the side) is stuck in a ditch. The boys give Willcox a hand and earn his undying gratitude. One night while camping out among the bluffs and buttes in John Ford's beloved Monument Valley, the punkers are attacked by a band of vicious biker types led by Ving. After being robbed and tormented, the boys try to escape the marauders only to have Flea caught and brutally murdered by Ving. Cryer and Roebuck return with the unsympathetic sheriff who finds no evidence of murder (the body is gone) and tells the strange-looking youths to get out of town. Seething with anger and plagued by visions of a mythic cowboy on horseback, Cryer vows to take the law into his own hands and kill Ving, while Roebuck just wants to forget the whole thing and continue on to L.A. But Cryer picks up the Ving's trail and pursues his vendetta. On the road they meet Stewart, a tough, independent, and pretty female auto mechanic, and she teaches Cryer how to shoot and ride. Meanwhile, Roebuck, too, is visited by a vision where he sees himself as an Indian brave whose village is slaughtered by a cavalry unit led by Ving. Now both possessed with the spirit of the Old West, Cryer and Roebuck dress like a gunslinger and an Indian and prepare to do battle with Ving. With help from Elvis impersonator Willcox, they track Ving to a tiny town and corner him in a movie theater. As Henry

King's classic western JESSE JAMES reaches its climactic Northfield shoot-out sequence, Cryer and Roebuck open fire on Ving and one of his cronies. The shooting spills out into the street and develops into a chase in which Cryer kills one man and then corners Ving in an abandoned factory. After a brief struggle, Cryer manages to gun down Ving. His mission complete, Cryer watches as the ghostly cowboy and Indians, accompanied by the spirit of Flea, bid farewell and disappear in a cloud of dust. Penelope Spheeris *almost* pulls this off. Presented in a goofy what-the-hell manner, DUDES is a lot of fun at first and then bogs down in a screenplay that relies on too many outrageous coincidences to keep the limited amount of action flowing. Utah is a big state and these boys continually stumble across Ving, Willcox, and Stewart as if everyone in the film has been traveling in circles. Even with the massive suspension of disbelief required in this film, implausiblities abound and annoy. When Cryer, dressed like Jack Palance in SHANE, finally catches up to the killers and confronts them in a bar, neither of them recognizes him despite the fact that they had held a gun to his head just a few days before *and* that he had peppered their truck with bullets shortly thereafter. There are other problems as well. Spheeris pushes the spirit-of-the-West thing to the limit and wastes a lot of screen time on the phantom cowboys and Indians routine. Also the action scenes themselves are fairly uninspired. After it leaves the movie theater, the climactic shoot-out is a big disappointment and is padded with gratuitous after-the-fact optically-printed slow motion. The cast, however, does a pretty good job making this silliness palatable. Ving, former leader of the now-defunct L.A. punk band Fear (which was featured in Spheeris's first film, the documentary THE DECLINE OF WESTERN CIVILIZATION), makes a supremely evil villain. Stewart does what she can with a badly underdeveloped role, Flea is memorable as the doomed punker, Willcox is hilarious as the Elvis impersonator, and Roebuck (the hulking killer in RIVER'S EDGE) steals the film with all the best lines and lots of funny business. Cryer, unfortunately, isn't very convincing as the punker suddenly possessed by the "a man's gotta do what a man's gotta do" spirit and seems a bit lost.

p, Herb Jaffe, Miguel Tejada-Flores; d, Penelope Spheeris; w, J. Randal Johnson; ph, Robert Richardson; ed, Andy Horvitch; m, Charles Bernstein; prod d, Robert Ziembicki.

Western   Cas.   (PR:O MPAA:R)

EIGHT MEN OUT***   (1988) 119m Orion c

Jace Alexander (*Dickie Kerr*), John Cusack (*Buck Weaver*), Gordan Clapp (*Ray Schalk*), Don Harvey (*Swede Risberg*), Bill Irwin (*Eddie Collins*), Perry Lang (*Fred McMullin*), John Mahoney (*Kid Gleason*), James Read (*Lefty Williams*), Michael Rooker (*Chick Gandil*), Charlie Sheen (*Hap Felsch*), David Strathairn (*Eddie Cicotte*), D.B. Sweeney ("*Shoeless" Joe Jackson*), Jim Desmond (*Smitty*), John Sayles (*Ring Lardner*), Studs Terkel (*Hugh Fullerton*), Richard Edson (*Billy Maharg*), Michael Lerner (*Arnold Rothstein*), Robert Walsh (*Arnold Rothstein*), Christopher Lloyd (*Bill Burns*), Michael Mantell (*Abe Attell*), Kevin Tighe (*Sport Sullivan*), Eliot Asinof (*Heydler*), Clyde Bassett (*Ban Johnson*), Clifton James (*Charles Comiskey*), John D. Craig (*Rothstein's Lawyer*), Michael Laskin (*Austrian*), Randle Mell (*Ahearn*), Robert Motz (*D.A.*), Bill Raymond (*Ben Short*), Barbara Garrick (*Helen Weaver*), Wendy Makkena (*Kate Jackson*), Maggie Renzi (*Rose Cicotte*), Nancy Travis (*Lyria Williams*), Brad Garrett (*PeeWee*), Tay Strathairn (*Bucky*), Jesse Vincent (*Scooter*), Jack George, Tom Surber, Tom Ledcke, David Carpenter, Bert Hatch (*Fans*), Jerry Brent, Bruce Schumacher, Robert Walsh, Matthew Harrington, Richard Lynch, Garry Williams, Michael Harris (*Writers*), Ken Berry (*Heckler*), David Rice (*Enemy Fan*), Tom Marshall (*Browns Umpire*), Merrill Holtzman (*Grabiner*), Josh Thompson (*Winslow*), Leigh Harris (*Singer*), Julie Whitney, Dana Roi (*Women in Bar*), Philip Murphy (*Jimmy*), Stephen Mendillo (*Monk*), J. Dennis Newman (*Reds Player*), Charles Siebert II (*Reds Catcher*), Jim Martindale (*Cincinnati Umpire*), Bill Jennings (*Chicago Umpire*), David Hinman (*Announcer*), Danton Stone (*Hired Killer*), Patrick Grant (*Irish Tenor*), Tim Laughter (*Betting Man*), Brad Armacost (*Attendant*), Jim Stark, Brad Griffith, Steve Salge (*Reporters*), John Anderson (*Judge Kenesaw Mountain Landis*), Dick Cusack (*Judge Friend*), Eaton Randles (*Clerk*), Max Chiddester (*Nash*), Rich Komenich (*Jury Foreman*), Patrick Brown, John Greisemer, Charles Yankoglu, Michael Preston (*New Jersey Fans*).

©ORION

In 1919, major league baseball, America's most popular entertainment, was rocked by scandal when eight members of the Chicago White Sox, one of the sport's greatest teams, were accused of fixing the World Series. The "Black Sox" (so named because the team's tight-fisted owner, Charles Comiskey, refused to launder their uniforms after every game) lost to the Cincinnati Reds, five games to three, and later were tried on charges of conspiracy, tainting the national pastime so that it took a new, livelier ball and the heroics of the great Babe Ruth to save the game. Working from Eliot Asinof's assiduously researched *Eight Men Out*, writer-director John Sayles (RETURN OF THE SECAUCUS SEVEN; THE BROTHER FROM ANOTHER PLANET) has fashioned a gripping account of the scandal, underlain with the sort of unconventional (by Hollywood standards) workers vs. owners critique that has arguably made Sayles America's most important independent filmmaker.

The film begins with Comiskey (James) singing the praises of his players to the press as the Sox clinch the 1919 American League pennant, but when the team hits the clubhouse, they find that the bonus the notoriously cheap owner has promised them for taking the flag has turned out to be a case of flat champagne. Among the worst-paid players in the league, but locked into virtual servitude by the "reserve clause" that prohibits them from playing elsewhere, the Sox stew with resentment. At a bar that night, Boston gambler Sport Sullivan (Tighe) persuades first baseman Chick Gandil (Rooker) to set up a fix of the upcoming best-of-nine Series with the Reds. Shortly after Tighe makes this proposal, two other small-time gamblers (Edson and Lloyd) approach Rooker and make a similar deal. In quick fashion Rooker recruits shortstop Swede Risberg (Harvey), utility man Fred McMullin (Lang), and outfielder Hap Felsch (Sheen). Rooker has more trouble enlisting the team's aging, sore-armed pitching star, Eddie Cicotte (Strathairn), but he, too, joins the fold after James fails to deliver a bonus promised the knuckleballer if he won 30 games. (Strathairn has actually only won 29, but James has prevented him from taking his last five starts, allegedly resting him for the series.) With Strathairn aboard, Rooker has no

trouble involving the team's other star pitcher, Lefty Williams (Read), and the illiterate, hard-hitting "Shoeless" Joe Jackson (Sweeney) becomes party to the scheme almost without knowing it. Scrappy third baseman Buck Weaver (Cusack), who loves baseball as much as the kids who worship him do, refuses to take part but can't bring himself to tell manager Kid Gleason (Mahoney) what's going on. Meanwhile, Edson and Lloyd secure the backing of Abe Attell (Mantell), who claims to represent Big Apple big wheel Arnold Rothstein (Lerner)—who is, in fact, in league with Tighe. The Series begins and the heavily favored Sox throw the first game, arousing the suspicion of baseball writers Hugh Fullerton (famed Chicago journalist Studs Terkel) and Ring Lardner (Sayles). As the Series progresses, there are more double crosses than doubles and it quickly becomes apparent that the gamblers aren't going to make good on their promises. Cusack plays his heart out, Sweeney hits and runs as hard as ever, and the straight Sox (Alexander, Irwin, and Clapp), sensing what is going on, battle for two victories. After Strathairn decides to play for real, the Sox narrow the gap from four games to three, but when the gamblers threaten to kill Read's wife, he makes sure Cincinnati wins the next game and the Series. The rest of the film follows the intrigue leading up to and surrounding the conspiracy trial of the Sox, including an adorable kid uttering the memorable but manufactured line, "Say it ain't so, Joe." Although they are never allowed to testify in their own defense, the eight indicted Sox are acquitted when, as a result of crooked dealings by James and Lerner, their confessions are "lost." However, Judge Kenesaw Mountain Landis (Anderson), specially appointed by the baseball owners, prohibits the eight Black Sox from ever playing ball again. The film's final scene occurs six years later in a semi-pro ballpark, where Cusack watches as Sweeney, forced to play under an alias, works his magic. (The real Weaver spent the rest of his life protesting his innocence, with appeal after appeal for reinstatement turned down by subsequent commissioners; while Jackson, one of the game's greats, a lifetime .356 hitter, has been barred from the Hall of Fame.)

Sayles adheres closely to the events outlined in Asinof's book, and though many critics credit him with bringing a great deal of life to the lengthy game-by-game baseball sequences, several have faulted him for trying to do too much in too little time, with too many characters to keep straight in so complex a format. Others felt that Sayles dedicated too much of the film to the details of the scandal, at the expense of focusing on the motivations of individual players. However, a strong case can be made that Sayles has done just that—not necessarily with every player, but certainly with those portrayed so well by David Strathairn and John Cusack, who suffer the greatest moral anguish over their involvement. Strathairn, bitter at James and fearful that his sore arm may no longer be able to provide for his family, gives in to temptation; Cusack, whose baseball purism is well delineated, doesn't. Sayles might have looked at other individual motivations as well, but, interested in a broader, sociopolitical interpretation of the scandal, he has chosen instead to focus on class confrontation between an exploitative owner and his ill-used employees. However, like MATEWAN (1987), Sayles' film about the West Virginia coal wars of the 1920s, EIGHT MEN OUT is more than just a Marxist morality tale; it is also a study of corruption in an America that was fast losing its innocence in the wake of WW I. To that end, Sayles juxtaposes the mythic virtue associated with ball players in the popular mind (and reinforced in the press) with the cynical reality represented by the fix.

The film's biggest problem, a significant one, is the director's occasional heavy-handedness. Too often Sayles offers shots of gloves thrown in disgust, of angry glances exchanged between ball players, of meaningful looks by the gamblers. Otherwise he keeps the on-field action interesting (though some of the film's remainder might have been better paced), and elicits believable, if not always highly particularized, performances from an excellent ensemble cast—chosen from the intersection of the list of bankable names drawn up by Orion and the one containing actors Sayles hoped to work with. Many of the performers came to the film with some baseball or athletic background, and former White Sox outfielder Ken Berry was hired to give them the necessary polish to make the on-field action believable. D.B. Sweeney (GARDENS OF STONE), a promising ball player until he was injured in a motorcycle accident, even spent five months with the minor league Kenosha Twins, learning to bat left-handed to make a more convincing Shoeless Joe. In the interest of realism, Sayles employed continuous action takes as much as possible, and, determined to get one sequence right, he had an arm-weary Charlie Sheen make a throw from the outfield 10 times before he was satisfied.

Production designer Nora Chavooshian and costume designer Cynthia Flynt, who worked wonders on MATEWAN's low budget, have done the same here; Bush Stadium, home of the Indianapolis Indians, is masterfully transformed into both Comiskey Park and Redland Field; and Robert Richardson, the Oscar-nominated cinematographer for PLATOON, suffuses the film in blue-sky autumn crispness. The story of the Black Sox scandal might never have come to the screen had not David Susskind hired one-time Philadelphia Phillie farmhand Asinof to write a script about it, in 1959, for TV's "Dupont Show of the Month." Asinof had heard that Chicago writer James T. Farrell had already written a book about the scandal, but Farrell claimed that it was a "lousy" book and aided Asinof in his research, which included many especially enlightening barroom conversations with Abe Attell. Asinof's script never reached the tube, however, because then-baseball commissioner Ford Frick convinced the program's sponsor that the show was "not in the best interest of baseball." Asinof then published *Eight Men Out*, and Sayles, who was introduced to the scandal by a Nelson Algren short story, later read the book and, in 1977, wrote a script based on it to use as a screenwriter's calling card. When Sayles learned, in 1980, that producers Sarah Pillsbury and Midge Sanford (RIVER'S EDGE) had secured the rights to the book from Texan Wid Slick, he quickly joined them in trying to bring the project to the screen. Eight years and $6 million later, EIGHT MEN OUT arrived. (Profanity, adult situations.)

p, Sarah Pillsbury, Midge Sanford; d, John Sayles; w, John Sayles (based on the book by Eliot Asinof); ph, Robert Richardson (Duart Color); ed, John Tintori; m, Mason Daring; m/l, Jann Kenbrovin, John William Kelette, Henry Creamer, Turner Layton, John Sayles, Mason Daring; prod d, Nora Chavooshian; art d, Dan Bishop; set d, Lynn Wolverton; cos, Cynthia Flynt; makeup, Gigi Coker.

Sports	Cas.	(PR:C-O MPAA:PG)

18 AGAIN!*   (1988) 100m NW c

George Burns (Jack Watson), Charlie Schlatter (David Watson), Tony Roberts (Arnold), Anita Morris (Madelyn), Miriam Flynn (Betty), Jennifer Runyon (Robin), Red Buttons (Charlie), George DiCenzo (Coach), Bernard Fox (Horton), Kenneth Tigar (Professor Swivet), Anthony Starke (Russ), Pauly Shore (Barrett), Emory Bass (Art Teacher), Joshua Devane (J.P.), Benny Baker (Red), Hal Smith (Irv), Lance Slaughter (Mikey), Earl Boen (Robin's Dad), Toni Sawyer (Robin's Mom), Stephanie Baldwin (Robin's Sister), Nancy Fox (Waitress), Leeza Vinnichenko (Woman at Party), Kimberlin Brown (Receptionist), Kevin Haley, Mark Kamiyama, Karl Wiedergott (Team Members), Mark Kramer (Track Team Starter), Edwina Moore, Kate Benton (Nurses), Pat Crawford Brown (Old Lady), Nicholas Cascone, Darren Powell (Frat Members), Michael J. Shea, Freddie Dawson (Orderlies), Jim Jackman, Michael Rider (Asylum Orderlies), Parker Whitman (Doctor), Connie Gauthier (Artist's Model), Cathy Scott (Runner), Michael Fallon (Bewildered Art Student), The Dickies (Themselves).

© NEW WORLD

Although Hollywood's obsession with "high concept" films (those in which a supposedly marketable idea supercedes any notion of art or realism) appeared to be fading fast in 1988, you couldn't tell by 18 AGAIN, another in the recent cycle of body-and-mind-switching films that includes 1987's LIKE FATHER LIKE SON and 1988's VICE VERSA and the excellent BIG (sort of). In this version, Burns plays the well-to-do, young-at-heart owner of a successful company who is about to celebrate his 81st birthday. Schlatter is his 18-year-old grandson, a callow freshman fraternity pledge who is abused by his would-be brothers. His particular nemesis is Starke, the fraternity's president and boy friend of Runyon, on whom Schlatter has a massive crush. When Starke isn't humiliating Schlatter at the fraternity house, he's making the freshman's life miserable at track and field practice, where the older runner is a star. When Burns blows out the candles on his birthday cake (with his grandson's assistance), he wishes he could be 18 again. Go ahead, guess what happens! After the party the two are driving together and end up in an accident that lands Burns' bones in the hospital and his consciousness in Schlatter's body. Overcoming his initial confusion, Burns relishes the opportunity to strut his stuff on a pair of lively legs. Using 81 years' worth of wisdom and confidence, he goes about wooing and winning Runyon, setting a professor right about Harry Truman (who Burns knew), and putting Starke in his place, winning the adoration of most of the fraternity in the process. On the down side, Burns learns that Morris, his considerably younger, pneumatic, red-headed mistress, is much less interested in him than in his money. He also learns that his son (Roberts), Schlatter's father, whom he has long considered incompetent, is, in fact, full of creative ideas and doing a fine job running the company in his absence. In the meantime, however, Burns' hospitalized body (and presumably Schlatter's comatose mind) is about ready to expire. The frat pledge rushes to the hospital, where the decision has been made to take the body off of life support. While wheeling Burns' endangered body down the corridor, Schlatter's body loses control of the gurney and crashes through a window. Magically the right minds are back with the right bodies. The ailing Burns, who retains his memory of his experiences in his grandson's body, is revived, while Schlatter's mind returns to its own form without any idea of what has occurred. Returning to campus, Schlatter is surprised to discover that he has qualified for a big track meet in which Starke has promised to get even. Wearing his grandfather's ancient track shoes, Schlatter smokes his rival and wins Runyon's heart. Meanwhile, the recovered Burns tosses gold digger Morris out of his life.

Although the 92-year-old George Burns isn't onscreen much, he is heard in voice-over throughout the film, and brings his usual panache to the role. He is not, however, either particularly funny or affecting. Charlie Schlatter has a winning smile and delivers a fairly good interpretation of what Burns might be like with 18-year-old limbs, but his is essentially a two-note performance: bemused teenage-heartthrob cuteness substituting for character on the one hand, and increasingly irritating braggadocio on the other. Red Buttons is suitably sympathetic as Burns' longtime friend, but the other supporting actors don't do much with what little they have been given. 18 AGAIN's tired premise is a lot older than LIKE FATHER, LIKE SON or even Disney's 1977 FREAKY FRIDAY, in which Barbara Harris and daughter Jodie Foster exchanged places for a day. The transmigration of souls between characters is of more recent origin, but the idea of trading places has been around a long time, dating back at least to Shakespeare, and, more recently, Mark Twain's The Prince and the Pauper. In 1882, the year after Twain's classic was published, F. Anstey's similarly themed Vice Versa appeared, later becoming the basis for Peter Ustinov's 1948 film of the same name—which, in turn, lent its title to 1987's Judge Reinhold starrer VICE VERSA. One big problem with 18 AGAIN is that it doesn't bring anything new to either the oldster-youngster switch or to the trading places premise; another is that it simply isn't funny. In addition to these major flaws, the movie purports to be set in Ohio but is obviously filmed in southern California, and it presents its "big" track meet under the ridiculous banner of "The Midwest Regional Conference Track Meet." This Hollywood inanity might only barely call attention to itself in a better film, but with 18 AGAIN's paucity of laughs, it may just be the funniest thing about the picture. Songs include "I Wish I Was 18 Again" (Sonny Throckmorton), "By the Light of the Silvery Moon" (Gus Edwards, Edward Madden), "You Drive Me Ape (You Big Gorilla)" (Stan Lee, Chuck Wagon), "She's a Hunchback" (Leonard Phillips, Lee, performed by The Dickies). (Brief nudity.)

p, Walter Coblenz; d, Paul Flaherty; w, Josh Goldstein, Jonathan Prince; ph, Stephen M. Katz (DeLuxe Color); ed, Danford B. Greene; m, Billy Goldenberg; m/l, Sonny Throckmorton, Gus Edwards, Edward Madden, Stan Lee, Chuck Wagon, Leonard Phillips; prod d, Dena Roth; spec eff, Howard Jensen; cos, John Buehler; ch, Larry S. Blum; tech, Anna Biller, Chris Hutson; stunts, Charlie Croughwell; makeup, Gabor Kernyaiszky.

Comedy	Cas.	(PR:C MPAA:PG)

ELVIRA: MISTRESS OF THE DARK**   (1988) 96m NBC/NW c

Cassandra Peterson (Elvira), Edie McClurg (Chastity Pariah), Pat Crawford Brown (Mrs. Meeker), William Duell (Mr. Meeker), Susan Kellermann (Patty), Daniel Greene (Bob Redding), W.W. Morgan Sheppard (Uncle).

Cassandra Peterson, the actress-comedian-dancer who has found fame in the last seven years hosting the syndicated television "Movie Macabre" as Elvira, a well-endowed witch who lounges seductively on a couch and cracks bad jokes during the showing of rotten horror and science-fiction movies, brings her TV character to the big screen in this campy comedy (she also appeared as Elvira in BORN IN EAST L.A.). The film opens as Elvira concludes one of her shows (a screening of Roger Corman's 1956 classic IT CONQUERED THE WORLD). When she rejects the sexual overtures of the TV station's new owner, she is fired. Dejected, but hopeful that her upcoming stage act in Las Vegas will rejuvenate her career, Elvira is shocked to discover that the producers in Vegas want her to come up with $50,000 for the show. Luckily, at that very moment, she receives a telegram informing her that her aunt in Fallwell, Massachusetts, has died and left Elvira part of her estate. Hitting the street in the same slinky, low-cut dress she wears on television, Elvira drives from California to Massachusetts, shocking everyone she meets with her bizarre and voluptuous looks. Her arrival in staid, conservative Fallwell causes a major scandal and the sourpuss elderly population gives her the cold shoulder. Because of her bright personality and unconventional appearance, the bored teenagers are drawn to Elvira like pins to a magnet. Now that she's inherited her aunt's house, poodle, and cookbook, Elvira and her new friends set about renovating the rundown mansion in the hopes of selling it and using the money to finance her Las Vegas debut. Unfortunately, local parents and the school board conspire against Elvira and announce that any teen seen associating with her will be expelled from school. Things get complicated when it is learned that her aunt's cookbook is in reality an ancient book of witchcraft. Elvira's evil uncle, Sheppard, is a warlock and wants to get his hands on the tome and become all-powerful. Elvira discovers the secret when she uses the "cookbook" to fix a casserole for her new boy friend, Greene, the shy hunk who runs the local movie theater. She accidentally conjures up a monster and is forced to get rid of the creature by shoving it down the garbage disposal. After rummaging around in the attic, Elvira learns she is the daughter of a bona fide witch and has the power to conjure spells. Determined to get revenge on the stodgy folks of Fallwell, Elvira whips up another batch of stuff and plants it at the annual community picnic. Instead of producing a monster, however, the casserole makes those who eat it lose their inhibitions. Soon all the old folks in town are dancing, stripping off their clothes, and seeking carnal knowledge. Seeing his opportunity to get rid of Elvira and snatch the book, Sheppard persuades the embarrassed city fathers to use an ancient law and prosecute her as a witch. As Elvira is about to burned at the stake, Sheppard retrieves the book and begins the incantations that will turn him into the ultimate evil. But as the flames lick at her black pumps, Elvira suddenly uses her inherent powers to extinguish the flames and do battle with Sheppard, who is now rampaging through the town. Elvira wins the fight and Sheppard is destroyed. Now accepted by the townsfolk, Elvira learns that she has inherited her uncle's considerable estate as well, and can finance her show in Vegas.

Making full use of the freedom a PG-13 rating allows, this movie must set some kind of record for the number of sophomoric double entendres and amount of sexual innuendo spewed in a feature film. But despite its mildly raunchy tone and obsession with Elvira's considerable cleavage, the film is basically a decent, good-hearted comedy that never takes itself seriously. In fact, the screenplay by Peterson, John Paragon, and Sam Egan is an old-fashioned 60s-style slam against the establishment that takes a playful poke at Reagan-era morality. With the town named "Fallwell" (as in Jerry Falwell), there can be little doubt as to where the film's sentiments lie. Also amusing, in a hippie fantasy sort of way, is the notion that a dash of hallucinogenics in a conservative's system will suddenly turn them into lust-driven monsters whose repressed desires explode in wild and embarrassing fashion. Although frankly sexual and unafraid to strut her stuff, Elvira is shown to have a definite moral code and believe in truth, justice, and romantic love—while the self-righteous, hypocritical upholders of social order are seen to be the truly sick and sex-obsessed ones. In addition to the mild social subversion, the movie is a celebration of the low-budget school of genre filmmaking, full of references to classic B pictures and Roger Corman and even containing a film clip of the modern camp epic ATTACK OF THE KILLER TOMATOES (1978).

This is not to say that, under the direction of James Signorelli (EASY MONEY)-—or anyone else, for that matter—ELVIRA, MISTRESS OF THE DARK even comes close to mainstream notions of quality. It doesn't. What we have here is a silly, even stupid, way to waste some time with a rather engaging personality, Elvira. Even with her corny jokes and ultra self-conscious demeanor, there is something positively charming about Peterson's character and she is a minor delight to watch. Reminiscent of Mae West, Elvira makes the transition from one-liner TV host to feature film star with relative ease and she is able to hold the screen on her own whether or not her breasts are displayed prominently in the shot. With the return of sexual paranoia and Victorian values to the US, it's refreshing to root for a character who retains her sexual independence and isn't afraid to flaunt it when she's got it. *(Profanity, sexual situations, violence.)*

p, Eric Gardner, Mark Pierson; d, James Signorelli; w, Sam Egan, John Paragon, Cassandra Peterson; ph, Hanania Baer (CFI color); ed, Battle David; m, James Campbell; prod d, James De Cuir, Jr.; set d, Beverli Eagan; cos, Betsy Heimann.

Comedy/Horror **Cas.** **(PR:C MPAA:PG-13)**

END OF THE LINE*** (1988) 105m Guadalupe-Hudson-Sundance/Orion c

Wilford Brimley *(Will Haney)*, Levon Helm *(Leo Pickett)*, Mary Steenburgen *(Rose Pickett)*, Barbara Barrie *(Jean Haney)*, Henderson Forsythe *(Thomas Clinton)*, Bob Balaban *(Warren Gerber)*, Kevin Bacon *(Everett)*, Michael Beach *(Alvin)*, Holly Hunter *(Charlotte Haney)*, Trey Fancher *(Tommy)*, Robert Ginnaven, Steve Wilkerson *(State Troopers)*, Trey Wilson *(Sheriff Maxie Howell)*, Clint Howard *(Les Sullivan)*, Rita Jenrette *(Sharon)*, Lillian Grimes *(Lucy)*, Dan DeMott *(Travers)*, Howard Morris *(Hobo)*, Armando Garza *(Gonzalez)*, Velva Walthall *(Bartender)*, Clay Crosby *(Gas Station Attendant)*, Missy Platt *(Jeannie)*, Carroll Dee Bland *(Chester)*, Bruce McGill *(Billy Haney)*, Don Hood.

END OF THE LINE is a predictable, cliched, heartwarming, feel-good movie that says nothing new, but says it well. We've seen it all before—the good ol' folks of America's heartland are being bullied by the money-hungry city boys in their Brooks Brothers suits who value "progress" over tradition. Life in END OF THE LINE is sweet and whimsical even when its characters contemplate suicide. There's not a frame of cynicism anywhere to be seen, nor is there meant to be. The setting is Clifford, Arkansas, home of the Southland Railroad Yard and of local patriarch-railroad brakeman Brimley. Brimley, who has seen steam engines become diesel engines and now fears that technological progress will cost him his job, dreams of traveling across America in a trailer with his wife, Barrie. His bubble is burst when he arrives at work to find a crowd of his fellow workers locked out of the railroad yard, where a posted sign informs them that the rail line is closing in favor of the company's new air freight division. But Brimley has worked too long and too hard to let someone close the yard, so he tries to organize his fellow workers into traveling to Chicago to meet with Southland chairman Forsythe. The only one who agrees to make the trek is Helm, a hard-working, not-too-bright friend of Brimley's who assumes the role of the son Brimley has but doesn't really respect. (The real son is a rodeo rider in a body cast who refused to follow Dad's footsteps into the rail yard.) Brimley and Helm "borrow" a locomotive and head for the Windy City, along the way conversing about their lives, "fishin'," the railroad, and the Pledge of Allegiance (which Helm tries in vain to recite). When Arkansas authorities inform the Southland company that Brimley and Helm are on their way on the stolen train, Southland president Balaban and his assistant, Howard, cook up a public relations extravaganza to turn the pair from Arkansas into company spokesmen and American heroes. Brimley and Helm want no part of Balaban's cynical imagemaking, however, and insist that they and their friends get their *old* jobs back. Rather than deal with Balaban, they sneak into the office of chairman Forsythe, who is busy playing with an elaborate toy train setup. When Brimley fixes one of his miniature boxcars, Forsythe is impressed and invites the men to talk. They then inform Forsythe, who has relinquished all control of the company to Balaban (his son-in-law), that Southland is getting into the air freight business. Furious, Forsythe agrees to return, by rail, to Arkansas with Brimley and Helm. The three get along famously, with Brimley showing Forsythe how to engineer the train. They are met at the rail yard by Balaban and the local sheriff, but Brimley informs them that Forsythe has sold him the yard for $1, leaving the former workers in charge of the line.

Basically a Little Guys vs. Big Business fantasy, END OF THE LINE has very little basis in the real world. None of it makes much sense (if Forsythe no longer runs the company, how come he has the power to sell the yard for $1?), but that doesn't really matter. This film is no more about making sense than most of the whimsical populist films of the 1930s and 1940s were. It's about entertaining its audience, pure and simple. As a result, END OF THE LINE is both enjoyable (if one doesn't think too hard) and instantly forgettable. The film's biggest plus is its cast, since the script and direction by Arkansas-born, Columbia University-educated, and Sundance Institute-backed Jay Russell is nothing more than pedestrian. The standout, by far, is Levon Helm—the one-time drummer-vocalist for The Band and supporting player in COAL MINER'S DAUGHTER; THE RIGHT STUFF; SMOOTH TALK; and another Arkansas-based feature, MAN OUTSIDE—who never once appears to be acting or striking a good ol' boy pose. Wilford Brimley also does a fine job, which doesn't vary much from the usual Wilford Brimley performance. In supporting roles are such big names as Mary Steenburgen (who also exec produced), as Helm's hairdresser wife; Holly Hunter (pre-BROADCAST NEWS), as Brimley's tough and devoted daughter; and Kevin Bacon, as Hunter's ex-husband, soon to be her husband again. Despite this box-office thunder, END OF THE LINE came and went in the blink of an eye, only to find new life on the video shelf. A Ry Cooder-style score by ex-Police guitarist Andy Summers adds to the atmosphere of Americana. *(Profanity.)*

p, Lewis Allen, Peter Newman, Walker Stuart; d, Jay Russell; w, Jay Russell, John Wohlbruck; ph, George Tirl (Duart color); ed, Mercedes Danevic; m, Andy Summers; m/l, John Tiven, Sally Tiven, Jolyon Christopher Dantzig, Mitch Weissman, Allen Toussaint, E.E. Bagley, Paul Kennerly, John Wilf, Frank Quinn; prod d, Neil Spisak; art d, Vaughan Edwards; set d, Paul Kelly; cos, Vanbroughton Ramsey; makeup, Linda Castillo.

Drama **Cas.** **(PR:A-C MPAA:PG)**

ERNEST SAVES CHRISTMAS½** (1988) 90m Touchstone-Silver Screen Partners III/BV c

Jim Varney *(Ernest P. Worrell)*, Douglas Seale *(Santa)*, Oliver Clark *(Joe Carruthers)*, Noelle Parker *(Harmony)*, Robert Lesser *(Marty)*, Gailard Sartain *(Chuck)*, Billie Bird *(Mary Morrissey)*, Bill Byrge *(Bobby)*, Buddy Douglas *(Pyramus)*, Patty Maloney *(Thisbe)*.

In ERNEST SAVES CHRISTMAS, rubber-faced Ernest (Varney), the obnoxious and not-too-bright TV commercial pitchperson and star of 1987's ERNEST GOES TO CAMP, is a Florida cab driver who keeps a bumper sticker in his glove compartment that reads "Keep Christ in Christmas" (rather strangely, since this is the only reference to the holiday's religious origin) and sings Christmas carols while driving recklessly. He picks up a fare at the airport—Santa Claus, who seems to be cutting things rather close in traveling so far from home just when he should be going over last-minute details at the North Pole, since it's just a couple of days before Christmas. Well, in this version of the Santa story, Santa-ing is a career that has been taken and passed on by a series of Kris Kringles throughout history. This Santa (Seale) is ready to retire, and, having decided he should bequeath his magic to another, has come to talk a local children's TV show host (Clark) into taking the job. Varney and Seale are en route to Clark's when runaway teen Parker jumps in the cab and tags along for the rest of this adventure. Taking on the skeptical mantle of Natalie Wood in MIRACLE ON 34TH STREET, Parker doesn't believe in Santa, not even when she sees him face to face. In fact (but not surprisingly), no one believes that Seale is Santa; even Clark seems ready to turn his offer down. Clark's agent, preoccupied with "reality" and getting Clark a movie part, gets Seale arrested as a vagrant so he'll stop bothering his client, whereupon Seale spreads warmth and good cheer in the county pen and has the inmates harmonizing on "The 12 Days of Christmas" in no time. Varney, meanwhile, pretends to be a Jerry Lewis-style nerdish government employee to get Seale out of the slammer. In the meantime, a couple of goofs (a demented updating of Laurel and Hardy) who work in the airline baggage department seem to be stuck with some unclaimed crates . . . crates of reindeer, which are patiently grazing upside down on the ceiling. The precious minutes are ticking away, Christmas is getting closer and closer, and the misadventures keep on coming—involving Varney's delivery of a Christmas tree to a friend, the tracking down of Seale's missing sack, and Parker's resolution to leave town. It probably won't give away much of the story line to reveal that Varney proves the catalyst in Clark's realization that his next career move should be to the North Pole.

ERNEST SAVES CHRISTMAS is a combination of fresh twists, worn cliches, and frenetic camerawork. A little-used slant is the Yuletide Florida setting, which keeps production costs down and (thankfully) eliminates the need for fake-looking snow, while enabling Varney to wear his usual t-shirt and vest without having his lips turn blue. As the hero, Varney limits his acting to tirelessly mugging into a *very* wide angle lens that distorts his already unfortunate features to grotesque effect. A claustrophobic filming style, coupled with wildly spinning, shaking, and turning camera movement, provide the pacing, although sandwiched between spectacles of Ernest darting in and out of the wide-angle effects there are some quiet moments that serve primarily to advance the story line.

Adults may not relish the premise that even Santa gets old, tired, forgetful, and in need of replacement with fresh blood. No matter, since Ernest the moron-with-a-heart-of-gold aims to entertain the young set and generally hits his target in this film. Know-what-I-mean?

p, Stacy Williams, Doug Claybourne; d, John Cherry; w, B. Kline, Ed Turner (based on story by Turner); ph, Peter Stein (Continental color); ed, Sharyn L. Ross; m, Mark Snow; art d, Ian Thomas; set d, Chris August; spec eff, Tim McHugh; cos, Peter Mitchell.

Children's/Comedy/Fantasy **Cas.** **(PR:A MPAA:PG)**

ETERNAL EVIL † (1988, US/Can.) 85m Filmline Intl.-New Century/Seymour
Bourde c

Winston Rekert *(Paul Sharpe)*, Karen Black *(Janus)*, John Novak *(Det. Kaufman)*, Andrew Bednarsky *(Matthew)*, Patty Talbot *(Jennifer Sharpe)*, Lois Maxwell *(Monica)*, Vlasta Varna *(Scott)*, Walter Massey *(John Westmore)*, Bronwen Booth *(Iris)*, Joanne Cote *(Helen)*.

Shot in 1985 but making its US debut via home video in 1988, this Canadian horror film seeks to capitalize on the New Age hocus pocus called "channeling" —spirits from the past manifesting themselves in the bodies of modern day folk. Rekert stars as a director of television commercials who dabbles in astral projection. During one of his psychic trips he witnesses a murder and, much to his chagrin, winds up the chief suspect because of his detailed knowledge of the crime scene. Lucky for Rekert, the real culprits are the spirits of an ancient couple who have been channeling into the bodies of unsuspecting innocents.

p, Pieter Kroonenburg; d, George Mihalka; w, Robert Geoffrion; ph, Paul van der Linden (Sonolab color); ed, Yves Langlois, Nick Rotundo; m, Marvin Dolgay; art d, John Meighen.

Horror   Cas.   (PR:NR MPAA:R)

EVERYBODY'S ALL-AMERICAN**½   (1988) 122m New Visions/WB c

Dennis Quaid *(Gavin Grey)*, Jessica Lange *(Babs Rogers Grey)*, Timothy Hutton *(Donnie "Cake")*, John Goodman *(Ed Lawrence)*, Carl Lumbly *(Narvel Blue)*, Raymond Baker *(Bolling Kiely)*, Savannah Smith Boucher *(Darlene Kiely)*, Patricia Clarkson *(Leslie Stone)*.

Taylor Hackford (AN OFFICER AND A GENTLEMAN) directs this epic sports melodrama that focuses on the rise and fall of Gavin Grey (Quaid), a legendary fleet-footed halfback known as the "Grey Ghost." The film begins in 1956 as Quaid, on his way to being named a consensus All-American for the second straight year, leads the Louisiana University Tigers (why they aren't called LSU is a mystery) in pursuit of a national championship. Lange, his beautiful but seemingly vacuous fiancee, is crowned Magnolia Queen, but her hopes of becoming Miss America are dashed when she learns that married women are ineligible for the competition. She isn't about to delay her marriage to Quaid, however, particularly since they have (with great difficulty) abstained from sleeping together, adhering to 1950s nice girl standards. Quaid's best friends are Goodman, a gregarious behemoth of a lineman, and Hutton, Quaid's bookish cousin who sits with Lange—and falls in love with her—while she and 80,000 screaming Tiger fans worship at the temple of the Grey Ghost. The climax of the season comes in the Sugar Bowl. With just seconds remaining, Georgia appears to have locked up victory; however, Quaid, playing both ways, forces the Bulldog quarterback to fumble, and Goodman scoops it up and laterals to the Ghost, who races for the winning touchdown. Lange and Quaid are married, and he becomes a star for the Washington Redskins and opens a bar and grill that is managed by Goodman. Years pass, during which four children are born to Quaid and Lange, yet Hutton, a graduate student in history and eventually a professor, never stops loving Lange. Tragedy strikes when Goodman, an inveterate gambler, is murdered for his debts, and Lange learns that he has so mismanaged the restaurant that they are nearly bankrupt. Nonetheless, Quaid retires soon thereafter, determined to leave at the top of his game, and on the night that his teammates take him out on the town, Lange and Hutton make love. In retirement, Quaid continues to trade on his fame, acting as a spokesman for an artificial turf manufacturer and hanging out at the restaurant he now co-owns with Baker, a "jock sniffing" car dealer whom Quaid detests but must tolerate. Eventually Quaid can no longer stand rehashing stories of past greatness, and he comes out of retirement to play for the Denver Broncos. Football has changed, though, and, having lost more than a step, Quaid is a battered, bruised failure. Lange, who had also been working for Baker and became a shrewd businesswoman in the process, has remained behind with the kids and gotten a job with Lumbly, the black owner of a highly successful fast-food chain who might have been the equal of even the Grey Ghost were it not for segregation. The story then shifts to 1981: Lange, now a bigwig in Lumbly's operation, is supporting the family while a paunchy Quaid, the assistant pro at a golf club, dwells on past glory. The 1956 national champions are to be honored at a special banquet, and Hutton, who has brought his fiancee (Clarkson) south to meet Quaid and Lange, learns that the Ghost suspects his wife is having an affair. Hutton tries to ease his cousin's fears, but in the process Quaid figures out that Hutton has had an affair with Lange. At the banquet, after watching highlights of the Sugar Bowl victory, Quaid gives a speech, saying that maybe he should have been shot after that game, the high point in his life. He goes on to say, however, that he is glad that he wasn't, because Lange—who knows that Quaid knows about her and Hutton and stares tearfully at him across the room—has made him the happiest man alive.

Combining big emotions and the spectacle of college and professional football, EVERYBODY'S ALL-AMERICAN is a film about glory and its loss, and an occasionally touching three-cornered romance. Although Hackford, crew, and actors, employing excellent period detail, have done a commendable job of capturing the excitement of college football and the world surrounding it in 1950s Louisiana, as well as the more businesslike pro game, the film doesn't become compelling until after the glimmer has faded from Dennis Quaid's golden boy. His portrayal of the youthful football star is believable enough, but it is as the ghost of the Ghost, as a forgotten hero who has to search out people who will listen to his old stories, that Quaid brings complexity to his character. Much of the first three-quarters of the film moves slowly, playing out scenes that help to establish the passing of time and advance the plot but do little to develop the characters. But beginning with Quaid's comeback attempt with the Broncos—wherein fear and doubt first appear in his eyes as he looks

across the line—the film starts to take on real dramatic life. Despite a multicolor dye job that makes Rourke's hair in YEAR OF THE DRAGON look impeccable, Quaid manages to make his insecure old jock particularly touching and sympathetic. In his banquet speech, Quaid explains that he didn't play the game for glory but because he loved it. He is, as Hutton says when asked if anyone would still want to read the Ghost's memoirs, "the real thing," an old-fashioned athlete who believes that his legend brings with it responsibility. But even though Quaid knows very early on that the exhilaration of athletic accomplishment fades almost as soon as it occurs, it is only at the banquet, when he realizes that the real love of his life has been Lange and not football, that he finally comes to terms with his legend.

Jessica Lange also gives a strong performance as the faithful wife who helps protect the legend of the Ghost, the one-time Magnolia Queen whose brains prove far more important than her lasting beauty. Her metamorphosis from a coed majoring in being Quaid's wife into a woman who rises above sexist stereotyping to use her skills to the fullest is subtle and convincing. Less effective, however, is Timothy Hutton, whose performance hovers around a single note of earnest sensitivity. In the major supporting roles, John Goodman brings an appropriate thick-headed decency to his gargantuan good ol' boy, Ray Baker is suitably unctuous, and Carl Lumbly is proud without being stereotypically *noble*.

Hackford went to great lengths to get the action and the excitement of the football just right. After considering several southern universities, he decided to film much of EVERYBODY'S ALL-AMERICAN at Louisiana State University, which allowed him to shoot several key on-field action sequences before 80,000 spectators during halftime at some LSU games. Quaid also made a big commitment to the film's authenticity, putting on 30 pounds, bulking up by weight lifting, and practicing with some of the ex-pro players who performed in the film. (So real was the hitting in one scene that Quaid, who was to be popped hard enough lose his helmet, broke his collar bone and had to finish the film wearing a brace.) The screenplay by Tom Rickman is based on a novel by sportswriter and TV analyst Frank Deford, who appears in the film as the owner of the restaurant at which Lumbly stages a counter sit-in. Redeemed by the last reel, EVERYBODY'S ALL-AMERICAN is, in the final analysis, an entertaining melodrama that isn't going to change anyone's life, but that may bring tears to the eyes of those who are looking for a love story with a happy ending that is a little forced, a lot sincere, and not overly manipulative. *(Profanity, brief nudity, violence, adult situations, sexual situations.)*

p, Taylor Hackford, Laura Ziskin, Ian Sander; d, Taylor Hackford; w, Tom Rickman (based on the novel by Frank Deford); ph, Stephen Goldblatt (Technicolor); ed, Don Zimmerman; m, James Newton Howard; prod d, Joe Alves; art d, George Jenson; set d, Sig Tingloff; cos, Theadora Van Runkle; makeup, Dick Smith.

Sports   Cas.   (PR:C-O MPAA:R)

EVIL LAUGH †   (1988) 87m Wildfire/Cinevest c

Steven Baio *(Johnny)*, Kim McKamy *(Connie)*, Tony Griffin *(Sammy)*, Jody Gibson *(Tina)*, Johnny Venocur *(Freddy)*, Jerold Pearson *(Barney)*, Myles O'Brien, Susan Grant, Howard Weiss, Karyn O'Bryan, Gary Hays.

Medical students hired to refurbish an abandoned orphanage are slaughtered one at a time by a masked killer whose maniacal laugh provides the title for this no-budget slasher film that went the home video route after a brief regional release. Self-conscious comic relief is provided by a wisecracking character who notes the similarity between the events of the bloody weekend and scenes from HALLOWEEN and FRIDAY THE 13TH.

p, Dominick Brascia, Steven Baio; d, Dominick Brascia; w, Steven Baio, Dominick Brascia; ph, Stephen Sealy; ed, Brian McIntosh, Michael Scott; m, David Shapiro; art d, Jeffrey Diamond; spec eff, David Cohen.

Horror   Cas.   (PR:NR MPAA:R)

FAMILY VIEWING †   (1988, Can.) 86m Ego-Canada Council-Ontario Arts Council-Ontario Film c

David Hemblen *(Stan)*, Aidan Tierney *(Van)*, Gabrielle Rose *(Sandra)*, Arsinee Khanjian *(Aline)*, Selma Keklikian *(Armen)*, Jeanne Sabourin *(Aline's Mother)*, Rose Sarkisyan *(Van's Mother)*, Vasag Baghboudarian *(Young Van)*, David MacKay *(Man Behind Counter)*, Hrant Alianak *(Administrator)*, John Shafer *(Private Detective)*, Garfield Andrews *(Hotel Bellboy)*, Edwin Stephenson *(Video Salesman)*, Aino Pirskanen *(Mistaken Women)*, Souren Chekijian *(Priest at Funeral)*, Johnnie Eisen *(Aline's Client)*, John Pellat *(Television Voice-Overs)*.

One of the most highly praised new independent/experimental films of this year, Atom Egoyan's FAMILY VIEWING takes a look at a modern family. The teenage son is idealistic, his father is a VCR salesman, his father's girl friend is a sex fiend with eyes for the son, and the father's mother lives a quiet life vegetating in the local nursing home. What they all have in common is an obsession with television and video. The son is a coach potato. The father tapes over old home videos with sex scenes he records in his bedroom with his girl friend. Everyone communicates through electronic media—a thematic statement that relates, not only to our society in general, but to the art of filmmaking in specific. Photographed on video and transferred to 16mm film, FAMILY VIEWING was completed for $160,000. Screened at Montreal's International Festival of New Cinema, the film won support from Wim Wenders, who donated the prize money he had received to Egoyan—an action that says something about both directors.

p, Atom Egoyan; d, Atom Egoyan; w, Atom Egoyan; ph, Robert MacDonald; ed, Atom Egoyan, Bruce MacDonald; m, Mychael Danna; art d, Linda Del Rosario; cos, Nancy Duggan; makeup, Matti Sevink.

Drama   **(PR:NR MPAA:NR)**

FAR NORTH*½   (1988) 90m Alive-Nelson/Alive c

Jessica Lange *(Kate)*, Charles Durning *(Bertrum)*, Tess Harper *(Rita)*, Donald Moffat *(Uncle Dane)*, Ann Wedgeworth *(Amy)*, Patricia Arquette *(Jilly)*, Nina Draxten *(Gramma)*.

Pulitzer Prize-winning playwright Sam Shepard has already made his mark in motion pictures as a screenwriter (PARIS, TEXAS; FOOL FOR LOVE) and as an actor (DAYS OF HEAVEN; THE RIGHT STUFF, for which he received an Oscar nomination; and CRIMES OF THE HEART), now, with FAR NORTH, he goes behind the camera for the first time. Working from his own screenplay, Shepard directs his companion Jessica Lange in a story of family turmoil set in her native Minnesota North Country. Strangely ponderous and uncharacteristically lighthearted, this largely unfocused comedy is Shepard's SMILES OF A SUMMER NIGHT—as significant a departure from the intensity and psychological depth of his previous work as Ingmar Bergman's comedy was from his oeuvre.

Patriarch Durning is hospitalized after his horse runs out of control and overturns the wagon in which he is riding. Lange, his strong-willed eldest daughter, returns—pregnant and unmarried—to her rural Minnesota home from New York City to be with Durning. Bent on revenge, he makes her promise to shoot the horse, but back at the farm Lange's sister, Harper, who lives at home with her promiscuous teenage daughter (Arquette), does everything she can to prevent Lange from shooting the horse she grew up riding. Their prematurely senile mother (Wedgeworth) has her hands full trying to understand where all the men who used to crowd around her table have gone. She also has her own mother's (Draxten) 100th birthday party to prepare, and complicates rather than calms a situation that is rapidly, and surreally, spinning out of control. Harper hides the gun; accidentally brings about the escape of the horse, Mel; and sends Arquette to find him. By this time Lange has figured out that the execution she has been assigned is another in a long series of tests (shown in home-movie flashback) Durning has presented her with and decides she's through playing his game. On the way back from the hospital, where Durning has suffered a relapse after an evening of boozing with his alcoholic brother-in-law (Moffat), Lange nearly runs into Mel and leads him home. Lange and Harper then go in search of Arquette, finding her in the middle of the darkened woods, and, atop Mel, the three of them try to find their way back to the farm. Meanwhile, Durning and Moffat, still wearing their hospital gowns, journey through the night along the railroad tracks that lead home from town, with Moffat miraculously producing empty beer bottle after bottle to throw at Durning. When both parties have a frightful meeting, Durning collapses and, tossed over Mel's back, is transported home. As the film closes, Draxten celebrates her birthday, and the final shot follows Durning, gun in hand, and Mel as they disappear into the snow-covered landscape.

As with SMILES OF A SUMMER NIGHT (and its inspiration, Shakespeare's "A Midsummer Night's Dream"), the woods are the principal setting for FAR NORTH. Unfortunately, director Shepard is even more lost there than his characters and his attempt at melding offbeat comedy with family drama wanders the screen aimlessly, only occasionally providing a laugh and offering none of the insights into the human condition or arresting technique that have made Shepard the great playwright he is. Unlike fellow playwrights-turned-film directors David Mamet (HOUSE OF GAMES; THINGS CHANGE) and David Hare (WETHERBY), who made

smooth transitions from stage to screen, Shepard seems to be straining to convey a cinematic vision. And in the process of presenting a smattering of interesting images—juxtaposed in a style vaguely reminiscent of Alain Resnais—he allows his story to meander and his actors to stumble on, blithely unaware of their excessive performances.

The worst offender is Ann Wedgeworth. As the dotty mother, she is so "out there" that her peculiar locution and bearing seem more evidence of extraterrestrial citizenship than symptoms of a confused retreat to a happier, more ordered time. Tess Harper—who was nominated for a Best Supporting Actress Oscar for CRIMES OF THE HEART, which costarred Lange and Shepard, and which bears some resemblance to this film—substitutes whining and screaming for more modulated performance, as does Patricia Arquette. Jessica Lange doesn't indulge in this kind of excess, but she is guilty of what is essentially a lazy performance, presenting her character's dilemma as little more than a mildly perplexing enigma. The scene in which she contemplates her father's "tests" aloud in the car is particularly creaky. The men in the cast fare better, but though Charles Durning and Donald Moffat provide some of the film's best moments on their goofy trip home (Durning is especially funny when he confronts an onrushing car with an outstretched "finger" and announces, "This is for Korea"), they too are saddled with awkward dialog and struggle to fill the holes in Shepard's screenplay.

It's clear that Shepard hasn't attempted to fashion a standard Hollywood narrative, nor has he tried to move his film along at the pace one expects from more commercial movies; however, he hasn't succeeded making his characters or their plight particularly involving or amusing, either. There are some funny moments, snatches of good performances, and fleeting promises of character revelation, but for the most part, FAR NORTH is a disappointing directorial debut from one of America's most gifted writers. Made for $6.5 million, it was shot on location in a number of northern Minnesota communities. *(Profanity, adult situations.)*

p, Carolyn Pfeiffer, Malcolm Harding; d, Sam Shepard; w, Sam Shepard; ph, Robbie Greenberg; ed, Bill Yahraus; m, Red Clay Ramblers; prod d, Peter Jamison; cos, Rita Salazar.

Comedy/Drama   Cas.   **(PR:C MPAA:PG-13)**

FATAL PULSE † (1988) 86m Celebrity Home Entertainment/Great Entertainment c

Michelle McCormick, Ken Roberts, Joe Phelan, Alex Courtney, Kitty, Cindra Hodgdon, Maureen O'Hanlon, Steven Henry, Blair Karsch, Sky Nicholas, Roxane Kernohan, Christie Muccianti, Harvey Cowen [Herschel.

Only the appearance of Martin Sheen's little-known brother, Joe Phelan, makes this direct-to-video slasher movie worth noting. When dead bodies begin showing up at the fraternity house owned by Phelan, Roberts uses his unduly loyal girl friend McCormick to flush out the killer, while a dim-witted cop played by hardcore porno star Herschel Savage (billed as Harvey Cowen) tries to solve the case. Strictly for the undiscriminating flesh-and-blood crowd.

p, Anthony J. Christopher; d, Anthony J. Christopher; w, James Hundhausen; ph, David Lewis; m, Martin Mayo.

Horror   Cas.   **(PR:NR MPAA:NR)**

FEAR †   (1988) 95m Cinetel c

Cliff DeYoung *(Don Haden)*, Kay Lenz *(Sharon Haden)*, Robert Factor *(Jack Gracie)*, Scott Schwartz *(Brian Haden)*, Geri Betzler *(Jennifer Haden)*, Frank Stallone *(Robert Armitage)*, Charles Meshack *(Cy Canelle)*, Michael Watson *(Mitch Barnett)*, Eddit Banker *(Lenny)*.

Given a token release in Los Angeles the same month it appeared on home video, FEAR follows the fortunes of a troubled southern California family as they try to overcome their differences on a Winnebago trip to a remote mountain cabin. Screenwriters Rick Scarry and Kathryn Connell have just the remedy for what ails these campers, a quartet of escaped cons—one a crazed Vietnam vet (Factor)—ready to terrorize them into becoming a real family again. Guess what? Dad is a Vietnam vet, too! And with his family under seige, De Young is presented with the perfect opportunity to snap out of his post-warrior malaise by putting his old Army training to good use and setting a series of lethal booby-traps for the interlopers. Mom (Lenz), Sis (Betzler), and little brother (Schwartz) also help defeat the nasty convicts, proving that the family that slays together, stays together. Reportedly, first-time director Robert A. Ferretti performs miracles on a minuscule budget. You be the judge.

p, Lisa M. Hansen; d, Robert A. Ferretti; w, Rick Scarry, Kathryn Connell (based on a story by Ferretti); ph, Dana Christiaansen (Foto-Kem Color); ed, Michael Eliot; m, Alfi Kabiljo; art d, Fernando Altschul; set d, Trevor Norris; cos, Jan Rowton.

Action   Cas.   **(PR:NR MPAA:R)**

FEDS †   (1988) 83m WB c

Rebecca De Mornay (*Ellie DeWitt*), Mary Gross (*Janis Zuckerman*), Ken Marshall (*Brent Sheppard*), Fred Dalton Thompson (*Bill Belecki*), Larry Cedar (*Howard Butz*), James Luisi (*Sperry*), Raymond Singer (*Hupperman*).

Not screened for critics, dumped on the market shortly before the rash of Christmas films, and pulled from theaters one week later, FEDS was one of 1988's phantom releases. The script by coproducer Len Blum and first-time director Dan Goldberg (both part of the team that wrote MEATBALLS and STRIPES) combines the PO-LICE ACADEMY formula with the standard buddy movie format, then does a gender switch, making the green recruits females. DeMornay, a dim-but-athletic ex-Marine, and Gross, a meek, bookish type, are roommates at the FBI Academy, where they are subjected to the taunts of the sexist male recruits. Since both are on the verge of flunking out—DeMornay because she can't pass the written exams and Gross because she can't handle the physical requirements—the women team up to battle each other's weakness. In the film's climax, they take the academy's final test, a simulated crime exercise they must pass if they are to become FBI agents. The vast majority of critics who actually saw FEDS reported that it was a predictable, inoffensive, mildly amusing effort, with Rebecca DeMornay and Mary Gross struggling mightily to wring some spontaneity from the mundane material.

p, Ilona Herzberg, Len Blum; d, Dan Goldberg; w, Len Blum, Dan Goldberg; ph, Timothy Suhrstedt (CFI color); ed, Donn Cambern; m, Randy Edelman; prod d, Randy Ser; art d, Phil Dagort; set d, Sally Thornton; cos, Isabella B. Van Soest.

Comedy   Cas.   (PR:NR MPAA:PG-13)

FISH CALLED WANDA, A*½   (1988) 108m MGM/MGM-UA c

John Cleese (*Archie Leach*), Jamie Lee Curtis (*Wanda Gerschwitz*), Kevin Kline (*Otto*), Michael Palin (*Ken*), Maria Aitken (*Wendy Leach*), Tom Georgeson (*George*), Patricia Hayes (*Mrs. Coady*), Geoffrey Palmer (*Judge*), Cynthia Caylor (*Portia*), Mark Elwes (*Shop Customer*), Neville Phillips (*Shop Manager*), Peter Jonfield (*Inspector Marvin*), Ken Campbell (*Bartlett*), Al Ashton (*Warder*), Roger Hume (*Locksmith*), Roger Brierley (*Davidson*), Llewellyn Rees (*Sir John*), Michael Percival (*Percival*), Kate Lansbury (*Magistrate*), Robert Cavendish (*Copper*), Andrew MacLachlan (*Eebedee*), Roland MacLeod (*Vicar*), Jeremy Child (*Mr. Johnson*), Pamela Miles (*Mrs. Johnson*), Tom Piggot Smith, Katherine John, Sophie Johnstone (*Johnson Children*), Kim Barclay (*Nanny*), Sharon Twomey, Patrick Newman (*Defense Counsel*), David Simeon (*Court Clerk*), Imogen Bickford-Smith (*Stenographer*), Tia Lee (*Prosecution Counsel*), Robert Putt (*Police Officer*), Waydon Croft, John Dixon (*Prison Officers*), Anthony Pedley (*Irate Driver*), Robert McBain (*Hotel Clerk*), Clare McIntyre (*Airline Employee*), Charu Bala Chokshi (*Indian Cleaner*), Stephen Fry (*Hutchison*).

© MGM/UA

Combining the talents of Monty Python stalwart John Cleese and Ealing Studios veteran Charles Crichton, this hilariously offbeat post-caper comedy benefits from two of British film comedy's most accomplished traditions. Cleese, who wrote the screenplay, stars as an emotionally and sexually repressed English barrister whose life is thrown into upheaval by the appearance of Wanda—not the fish of the title, but a sexy American thief played by Curtis. She and her gang—Cockney tough guy Georgeson, stuttering animal rights advocate Palin, and ex-CIA assassin Kline—pull off a well-executed jewel heist, but in the thieves' subsequent rush to double-cross one another and grab all the loot, Georgeson ends up in jail and the booty remains hidden in safety deposit, the location of which is known only to him. Curtis has been dishing out sexual favors to her cohorts (save Palin, whose heart apparently belongs to the finned Wanda), but hides her lovemaking with fellow American Kline from Georgeson by claiming that he is her brother. Deciding that the best way to learn the whereabouts of the jewels is through Georgeson's barrister, Cleese, Curtis poses as an American law student studying the British system (and idolizing Cleese) and sweeps the uptight Englishman off his feet, liberating him from a stuffy suburban existence dominated by his nagging wife, Aitken, and his demanding, selfish daughter, Caylor (Cleese's real-life daughter). Their furtive affair is plagued by the insanely jealous, explosively violent Kline, who pops up and pops off at the most unexpected moments. Meanwhile, Georgeson has assigned the loyal Palin the task of eliminating Hayes, the

old woman who saw them fleeing from the scene of their crime. Palin's attempts to do her in become increasingly painful for him (both physically and psychically) as he accidentally brings about the destruction (in Wile E. Coyote fashion) of her three lapdogs before she keels over at last from the trauma of it all. The plot continues to thicken, and so to does Kline's head. Eventually, his terrorizing of Palin leads to a bizarre airport finale in which Curtis and Cleese's love wins out and Palin gets his revenge.

With British-American culture clash as its dominant theme, A FISH CALLED WANDA bristles with wit, enlivened by delightfully over-the-top ensemble acting. Cleese's screenplay, developed in association with director Crichton and actors Kevin Kline and Jamie Lee Curtis, uses a farcical framework to send up both British inhibition and formality and American intuitiveness and lack of sophistication. Although filled with clever twists and double-crosses, the film's where-are-the-diamonds-who's-got-the-key storyline is less important than the opportunities it provides for the actors to exploit their goofy characterizations. The love story between Cleese and Curtis is pleasant enough—with her American openness and vivacity freeing the same qualities that have been culturally repressed in Cleese—but what makes A FISH CALLED WANDA so wonderful are its hilarious performances.

Oddly, Cleese, playing the straightest role in the film, is the most subdued of the bunch. His Archie Leach (the real name of Cary Grant, who was born near Cleese's provincial hometown) is placed in several compromising situations and given his share of silly business, but he is, foremost, the film's romantic lead. Like Robin Williams in THE WORLD ACCORDING TO GARP, Cleese is given the chance to prove that he is a capable actor, and he makes the most of it. Fans of Cleese's Basil Fawlty won't be disappointed, though, as Cleese offers up one of his patented slow burns in a scene in which he tries to get some vital information from the stuttering Michael Palin. Fellow Pythoner Palin is t-t-terribly funny as the put-upon animal lover driven over the edge by the combination of his distasteful mission and unrelenting badgering of Kline. As the manipulative but likable Wanda, Curtis is unashamedly deceitful, salacious, and silly in just the right proportions. Kline, however, contributes the film's best performance, pulling out all the stops for his armpit-sniffing, common senseless, jealous, uproariously omnipresent Otto. Desperately insecure about his intelligence (with good reason), he compensates by ludicrously misreading Nietzsche, and whenever his brain fails him—as it almost always does—he explodes into uncontrollable violence.

Crichton's efficient direction is nearly invisible, save for the effectively flashy 180-degree camera tilt used in a scene in which Kline dangles Cleese out of a window. It had been more than 20 years since the 78-year-old Crichton, best-known as the director of THE LAVENDER HILL MOB, helmed a feature film. In the interim he directed for British TV, including "The Avengers." In 1969, Crichton and Cleese attempted to collaborate on a film, but never got the project off the ground; in 1983, after working together on management training films for Cleese's company, Video Arts, Crichton and Cleese began shaping the story for A FISH CALLED WANDA. On the set, Crichton oversaw the whole production, but Cleese worked with the actors, responding to their suggestions during the shooting as he had during the writing of the screenplay. After using approximately $100,000 of his own money for the project's start-up, Cleese approached MGM, who bankrolled the production, eventually delivered on time on a $7.3 million budget. Audiences at test screenings in New York and Los Angeles found the film's end a little too dark, and, at the request of MGM, a portion of a scene was reshot. The resulting film is still very much Cleese's, and it is very entertaining indeed. (*Violence, nudity, profanity, sexual situations.*)

p, Michael Shamberg; d, Charles Crichton; w, John Cleese (based on a story by John Cleese and Charles Crichton); ph, Alan Hume (Technicolor); ed, John Jympson; m, John Du Prez; prod d, Roger Murray-Leach; art d, John Wood; set d, Stephanie McMillan; spec eff, George Gibbs; cos, Hazel Pethig; stunts, Romo Gorrara; makeup, Paul Engelen.

Comedy/Crime/Romance   Cas.   (PR:C-O MPAA:R)

FIVE CORNERS½   (1988, US/Brit.) 92m Handmade/Cineplex Odeon c

Jodie Foster (*Linda*), Tim Robbins (*Harry Fitzgerald*), Todd Graff (*James*), John Turturro (*Heinz Sabantino*), Elizabeth Berridge (*Melanie*), Rose Gregorio (*Mrs. Sabantino*), Gregory Rozakis (*Mazola*), John Seitz (*Sullivan*), Kathleen Chalfant (*Mrs. Fitzgerald*), Rodney Harvey (*Castro*), Cathryn de Prume (*Brita*), Carl Capotorto (*Sal*), Daniel Jenkins (*Willie*), Michael R. Howard (*Murray*), Pierre Epstein (*George*), Jery Hewitt (*Mr. Glascow*), Jack McGee (*Desk Sergeant*), Jose Soto, Jr. (*Boy in Pet Store*), Mike Starr (*Bartender*), Kit Le Fever (*Esther*), Jerome Collamore (*Old Man in Bar*), Bill Cobbs (*Man in Coffee Shop*), Frances Foster (*Waitress*), Eriq LaSalle (*Samuel Kemp*), Ray Aranha (*Arthur*), David Brisbin (*Plainclothes Man*), Mary Small (*Woman in Deli*), Robert Lempert, Keith Reddin (*Neighborhood People*), Anthony Powers, Pepe Douglas, Dann Florek, Alex Kramarevsky, Thomas Kudlek, Mike Lisenco, Regis Mullavey, Frank Patton, James Ryan, Campbell Scott, Joel Segal, Victor Slezak, Richard Thomson (*Cops*).

Scripted by MOONSTRUCK's Academy Award-winning screenwriter, John Patrick Shanley, FIVE CORNERS is an arresting but flawed melange of comedy and melodrama, whimsy and violence. Set in the all-white working-class Bronx neighborhood of the title in 1964, the film traces several parallel stories to their ultimate convergence 36 hours later. One of the key players, Foster, a young woman who works in her family's pet store, becomes anxious when Turturro, the nut case who tried to rape her 18 months earlier, is freed from prison and returns to the old neighborhood. Her bartender boy friend, Graff, wants to protect her, but he has a permanent limp as a souvenir of his last unsuccessful attempt to do so, prompting Foster to seek help again from Robbins, who put Turturro out of commission before with a bottle to the head. Problem is, Robbins, the son of a slain policeman, has since become a pacifist crusader for social change; influenced by Martin Luther King, Jr., he has joined the

Student Non-Violent Coordinating Committee and is hoping to be allowed to travel to Mississippi to help register black voters. Meanwhile, in another part of the "hood," Capotorto, who has been cruising with his glue-sniffing fiancee (Berridge) and one of her friends (de Prume), grows bored with the giggling young women and pays Jenkins and Harvey $5 to take them off his hands. Looking for love in strange places, the foursome ends up riding atop a couple of elevators, off of which one of the girls nearly falls—in one of the film's most memorable scenes, buoyantly lyrical at first, then terribly frightening. Still elsewhere, a pair of cops (Rozakis and Seitz) investigate the bizarre murder of a high-school algebra teacher shot in the back by an arrow. Closer to the film's center, Foster (foolishly, with a capital "F") meets Turturro in a night-shrouded park, where he presents her with a stolen penguin and then beats it to a pulp when she doesn't respond as he'd hoped. Foster flees but Turturro catches and abducts her. Meantime, Robbins has gone to Rozakis and Seitz for help, but when the cops come upon Turturro, he makes off with one of their guns and Foster, driving wildly, crashing into a phone booth, and killing the cop who is staking out his mother's apartment. Gregorio, Turturro's equally loony mother, seems to have no idea how troubled her son is and pays for it by being tossed out the window by Turturro before he heads for the rooftop, cradling Foster, Fay Wray-like, in his simian arms. Robbins makes his way to the roof to challenge Turturro, putting his pacifist convictions to the test, but before the madman can hurt him, Turturro is shot in the back by an arrow.

Undeniably stamped with the signature of the "Bard of the Bronx," FIVE CORNERS, like MOONSTRUCK, is full of Shanley's rich dialog and careful observations about its specific milieu, but its radical tone shifts are what most distinguish the film. Moving frequently from moments of carefree, AMERICAN GRAFFITI-like levity to high tension, brooding melodrama, and brutal violence, Shanley's screenplay presents producer-director Tony Bill (MY BODYGUARD; SIX WEEKS) with a challenge that, unfortunately, he isn't up to. Certainly the emotional transitions required from the audience are abrupt, but these jarring mood swings wouldn't be so problematic if Bill had been able to synthesize them in the film's final reel, when the various narrative strands finally intertwine. Because he doesn't, FIVE CORNERS leaves the viewer feeling as if he or she has been lost in an emotional fun house, replete with both goofy mirrors and horrifying ghosts. Not surprisingly, FIVE CORNERS is more successful in its parts than as a whole: the gentle romance between Foster and Graff is touching, the thriller involving Turturro's abduction of Foster is frightening, the light-hearted romp of the good-time foursome is funny, and the examination of Robbins' involvement with the SNCC and the changing American political landscape is intriguing. Moreover, there are no weak performances in the film, and there are several particularly good ones, most notably Tim Robbins as the terribly serious MLK- and Bob Dylan-influenced would-be freedom rider–a performance that is even more impressive when contrasted with his flaky comic portrayal of the bonus baby pitcher in BULL DURHAM. Nearly as successful are John Turturro (THE SICILIAN), as the menacing, cartoonish, King Kong-like Heinz, and Jodie Foster, who returned to American screens in a big way this year after completing her studies at Yale, also appearing in THE ACCUSED; SIESTA; and STEALING HOME. Elizabeth Berridge (AMADEUS), Rose Gregorio, and Todd Graff also contribute fine work.

Interestingly, FIVE CORNERS came to the screen after Bill was impressed by a one-minute monolog an actor had used as an audition piece that turned out to be from a play by Shanley. When the producer-director sought out Shanley, he found that he had just completed the first (and last) draft of his first screenplay. Bill snatched up FIVE CORNERS and shot it in six weeks in Astoria, Queens, which looked more like the Bronx of 1964 than did the Bronx of 1987. Songs include: "In My Life" (John Lennon, Paul McCartney, performed by the Beatles), "The Times They Are a-Changing" (Bob Dylan, performed by Dylan), "Let the Little Girl Dance" (Glover Spencer, performed by Billy Brand), "Funky Soul" (Richard Thomas, performed by Thomas), "Uh, Uh, Uh," "Leave Me Alone" (Robbie Robertson, performed by the Canadian Squires). *(Violence, sexual situations, adult situations, profanity.)*

p, Forrest Murray, Tony Bill; d, Tony Bill; w, John Patrick Shanley; ph, Fred Murphy (Technicolor); ed, Andy Blumenthal; m, James Newton Howard; m/l, John Lennon, Paul McCartney, Bob Dylan, Glover, Spencer, Richard Thomas, Robbie Robertson; prod d, Adrianne Lobel; set d, Linda Ekstrand; spec eff, Bill Harrison; cos, Peggy Farrell; stunts, Jery Hewitt; makeup, Leslie Fuller.

Comedy/Drama **Cas.** **(PR:O MPAA:R)**

FOR KEEPS* (1988) 98m ML Delphi Premier/Tri-Star c

Molly Ringwald *(Darcy Elliot)*, Randall Batinkoff *(Stan Bobrucz)*, Kenneth Mars *(Mr. Bobrucz)*, Miriam Flynn *(Mrs. Elliot)*, Conchata Ferrell *(Mrs. Bobrucz)*, Sharon Brown *(Lila)*, Jack Ong *(Rev. Kim)*, Sean Frye *(Wee Willy)*, Allison Roth *(Ambrosia)*, Trevor Edmond *(Ace)*, Patricia Patts *(Desdemona)*, Brandon Douglas *(Trapper)*, Kimberly Bailey *(Baby Cakes)*, Darnell Rose *(Ron)*, J.W. Fails *(High Flyer)*, Monika Khoury *(Angel)*, Kelly McMahan *(Pediatric Nurse)*, Candy Peak *(Nurse)*, Robert Ruth *(Prom Photographer)*, Nancy Abramson, Sandra Jansen *(Nurses)*, Dr. Barry Herman *(Doctor)*, Michelle Downey *(Michaela Tuohy)*, Jeff Marshall *(Michaela's Boy Friend)*, Peggy Walton-Walker *(Bookkeeper)*, Bonnie Hellman *(Mrs. Sitwell)*, Larry Drake *(Night Clerk)*, Robin Morse *(Beth)*, Steve Eckholdt *(Ronald)*, Marty Zagon *(Manager of Quickie Nickie's)*, Annie Oringer *(Anastasia)*, Pamela Harris *(Beverly)*, Hailey Ellen Agnew *(Baby Thea)*, Rae Worland *(Student)*, David DeLange *(Uniformed Official)*, Roger Hampton *(Roofer)*, Tino Insana *(Capt. O'Connell)*, Steven Barr *(Sgt. Blaine)*, John Zarchen *(Chris)*, Pauly Shore *(Retro)*, Patricia Barry *(Adoption Official)*, Janet MacLachlan *(Miss Giles)*, Jaclyn Bernstein *(Mary Bobrucz)*, Matthew Licht *(Lou Bobrucz)*, Renee Estevez *(Marnie)*, Darcy DeMoss *(Elaine)*, Leslie Bega *(Carlita)*, Helen Siff *(Landlady)*, Anne Curry *(Push Nurse)*, John Di Santi *(Mr. Kolby)*, Robert Nadder *(Night School Teacher)*, Shane McCabe *(Amorous Porker)*.

© TRI-STAR

Continuing the on-screen transition into adulthood that she began in last year's THE PICK-UP ARTIST, Molly Ringwald stars here as a bright high-school student whose life takes an abrupt turn when she becomes pregnant by boy friend Batinkoff. Both have plans to attend college and make their way in the professional world—Ringwald wants to be a journalist, Batinkoff wants to study architecture at Cal Arts. Although they've been sweethearts for over two years, they've refrained from "going all the way." Finally, they give in to passion and make love in a torrential downpour. Ringwald has been on the pill for two years (because of a menstrual disorder), but she still becomes pregnant. At Thanksgiving dinner, she matter-of-factly breaks the news: "I'm pregnant, pass the turnips." Naturally, the parents are at odds. Ringwald's mother, a prissy Francophile who dreams of living in Paris with her daughter, sees an abortion as the only possible solution. Batinkoff's cartoonish parents believe it is morally right that she put the baby up for adoption. Only Ringwald and Batinkoff think they can make it work. They move into a run-down apartment, take lowly retail jobs, attend night school, and get married in a token ceremony. Worse yet, the ballooning Ringwald has to attend the prom and suffer the abuse of the least tactful girl in school, Downey, a smoking, drinking cheerleader who loves it when "smart kids do stupid things." In the meantime, Batinkoff turns down a full scholarship to Cal Arts, opting instead to stay with Ringwald. The birth of a baby daughter brings more complications than Ringwald and Batinkoff expected. Doctor's bills, utility bills, and rent payments pile high. Moreover, Ringwald's postpartum depression leaves her in a television-watching stupor, but Batinkoff takes care of the baby—changing diapers, washing, feeding, and cuddling. Soon, however, Batinkoff transforms into an uncaring ogre (explainable only through movie logic), hitting the bars at night with his friends. Eventually, the young couple is kicked out of the apartment and has to move in with Ringwald's mother. Ringwald then learns from a friend that Batinkoff was not turned down by Cal Arts (as he originally told her) but that he turned *them* down. She kicks him out of the house, requests an annulment, and refuses to even speak to him. Although it looks like they'll drift apart, their love is too strong and they decide to struggle through college and make it work.

FOR KEEPS opens with footage shot through a microscope (from "The Miracle of Birth") of the vaginal canal, an ejaculation, swimming sperm, and its union with the egg. Naturally, one gets the impression that this is going to be a relatively realistic teen coming-of-age film that will offer an intelligent look at teen pregnancy. No such luck. FOR KEEPS is a carelessly directed, paced, acted, and scripted film that, at best, offers a confused message to today's teenagers. Foremost among its endless problems is John Avildsen's pathetic direction. Under his uninspired guidance the actors appear to be performing in filmed rehearsals, guilty of glaring character inconsistencies from one scene to the next. Moreover, Avildsen's pacing (and it is truly *his* pacing since he also edited the film) is sporadic. Equally disturbing is his tendency to shoot nearly every scene with his camera on a Steadicam that floats and drifts as if it has a mind of its own.

Scripted by ABOUT LAST NIGHT writers Tim Kazurinsky and Denise DeClue (who disowned the film after Avildsen reportedly made massive changes), the cliche-ridden story throws in every possible obstacle to the young couple's happiness. The kids split with their Neanderthal parents, they live in a hovel without a bathroom, Ringwald is so pregnant she can't turn off the deep frier at the fast food restaurant where she works, she refuses to even hold the baby until an apparent burglar threatens its safety, and the once-caring Batinkoff inexplicably becomes a beer-chugging male chauvinist slob. Only birth defects are missing, but then maybe Avildsen thought a cleft palate would have been *too* realistic. As a result, Avildsen hasn't made a thoughtful, realistic film about his subject; he's made a sitcom in which the characters exist in a heightened, exaggerated sense of movie reality. There is certainly a need to address the subject of teenage pregnancy, and the casting of teen role model Ringwald (who, like her costar, struggles nobly to make this mess work) is a brilliant move. Unfortunately, FOR KEEPS simply perpetuates the ignorance that already exists. Buckling to the Hollywood convention of a happy ending, it also closes on an upbeat note, with Ringwald and Batinkoff last seen as a loving pair of parents who head off to college together—not an impossibility, but a fairy tale notion that works against the rest of the film.

Bill Conti's trumpet-blasting score sounds great next to the eviscerated version of the film's theme song, "Be My Baby," recorded by Ellie Greenwich. Oddly, Greenwich cowrote the song in 1963 with Jeff Barry and Phil Spector, but here it shows none of the spark heard in the Ronettes' version. Other songs include: "Sh-Boom" (performed by the Crew Cuts), "You Belong to Me" (performed by Jo Stafford), "Pow! You Got Me Where I Live" (performed by Lamont Dozier), "Smoke Gets in Your Eyes" (performed by Lawrence Welk). *(Adult situations, profanity.)*

p, Jerry Belson, Walter Coblenz; d, John G. Avildsen; w, Denise DeClue, Tim Kazurinsky; ph, James Crabe (Technicolor); ed, John G. Avildsen; m, Bill Conti; prod d, William J. Cassidy; set d, Bernard Cutler; spec eff, Jerry D. Williams, Bob Stoker, Jr.; cos, Colleen Atwood, Maritza L. Garcia; makeup, Robert Jiras.

Comedy/Drama	Cas.	(PR:A-C MPAA:PG-13)

FOR A NIGHT OF LOVE (SEE: MANIFESTO, 1988)

FRANKENSTEIN GENERAL HOSPITAL zero (1988) 92m New Star c b&w

Mark Blankfield (*Dr. Bob Frankenstein*), Lelsie Jordan (*Iggy*), Jonathan Farwell (*Dr. Frank Reutgar*), Kathy Shower (*Dr. Alice Singleton*), Irwin Keyes (*Monster*), Hamilton Mitchell (*Dr. Andrew Dixon*), Lou Cutell (*Dr. Saperstein*), Katie Caple (*Nurse Verna*), Dorothy Patterson (*Mildred Pennys*), Bobby " Boris"Pickett (*Man in Elevator*), Mark DeCarlo (*Dr. Skip*), Harry Murphy (*Dr. Biff*), Rebunkah Jones (*Elizabeth Rice*), Joleen Lutz (*Candy Stripper Patty*), Jessica Puscas (*Cindy Swanson*), Ben Stein (*Dr. Who*), John Young (*Dr. Alex Hoover*), Tom Fahn (*Zach*), Michael Franco (*Brad*), James Serrano, Ed Khmara (*Cops*), Chuck Kovacic (*Anesthesiologist*), Laura Bassett (*Cigarette Girl*), Kay E. Kuter (*Larry*), Ken Kallmayer (*Patient*).

©NEW STAR ENTERTAINMENT

Deep in the bowels of Los Angeles General Hospital lies the laboratory of the legendary Baron von Frankenstein's great-great grandson (Blankfield), a physician who has conveniently changed his name to Frankenheimer. Assisted by Jordan, a former short order cook who wears suspenders so tight they cause him to limp, Blankfield is secretly working on the creation of a perfect human being. He is also competing with Farwell, a doctor who is experimenting with a longevity serum, for funding from hospital director Mitchell. Jordan provides Blankfield with body parts for his experiment by killing off Cutell's patients, but in so doing arouses the suspicions of both Farwell and Cutell, who enlist psychiatrist Shower to find out what Blankfield is up to. Helped along by an occasional title card, the action limps from scene to scene with lots of dumb puns and running gags that simply don't work. After Jordan steals the head of a sex-crazed teen, instead of that of a genius, the monster (Keyes) is complete, and soon being fed baby food by Jordan, to the predictable accompaniment of belches and flatulence. In the film's climax, the monster gets loose, roams the hospital corridors in a stolen heavy metal outfit, and drinks Farwell's serum, which turns him into an articulate gentleman. At the fade, the monster strolls off hand-in-hand with Shower; Mitchell is dragged away babbling by the police; and Blankfield and Jordan begin putting together a new creature.

Wretched in nearly every respect, FRANKENSTEIN GENERAL HOSPITAL aspires to be a spoof of horror films somewhat along the lines of YOUNG FRANKENSTEIN; however, it fails to establish even the lowest level of credibility. Mark Blankfield, who appeared in another genre send-up flop, JEKYLL AND HYDE...TOGETHER AGAIN, tries hard, but is given such weak material that his efforts are wasted. The rest of the grossly overplayed performances are even worse. Director Deborah Roberts seems to have no idea how to pace the jokes or finish off a scene, and her idea of enlivening the proceeding appears to be having former Playmate Kathy Shower and Katie Caple take off their blouses. FRANKENSTEIN GENERAL HOSPITAL is so bad that it induces a certain strange fascination after a while, though it didn't captivate many in its brief regional theatrical release before being consigned to the home video market. About the only thing authentic in the picture is a brief appearance by Bobby Boris Pickett who recorded the "Monster Mash" with the Crypt Kickers in the late 1950s. *(Comic violence, sexual situations, profanity.)*

p, Dimitri Villard; d, Deborah Roberts; w, Michael Kelly, Robert Deel (based on the novel *Frankenstein* by Mary Wollstonecraft Shelley); ph, Tom Fraser; ed, Ed Cotter; m, John Ross; prod d, Don Day; art d, Thom Shepard; set d, Ginnie

Durden; cos, Virginia Krammer; stunts, Bud Graves; makeup, Kim Clouser, Doug White.

Comedy/Horror	Cas.	(PR:O MPAA:R)

FRANTIC**** (1988) 120m Mount/WB c

Harrison Ford (*Dr. Richard Walker*), Emmanuelle Seigner (*Michelle*), Betty Buckley (*Sondra Walker*), John Mahoney (*Williams*), Jimmy Ray Weeks (*Shaap*), Yorgo Voyagis (*The Kidnaper*), David Huddleston (*Peter*), Gerard Klein (*Gaillard*), Jacques Ciron (*Hotel Manager*), Dominique Pinon (*Wino*), Thomas M. Pollard (*Rastafarian*), Alexandra Stewart (*Edie*), Robert Barr (*Irwin*), Boll Boyer (*Dede Martin*), Djiby Soumare (*Taxi Driver*), Dominique Virton (*Desk Clerk*), Stephane D'Audeville, Roch Leibovici, Alan Ladd (*Bellboys*), Laurent Spielvogel, Alain Doutey (*Hall Porters*), Louise Vinceni (*Tourist*), Patrice Melennec (*Hotel Detective*), Ella Jaroszewicz (*Restroom Attendant*), Joelle Lagneau, Jean-Pierre Delage (*Florists*), Marc Dudicourt (*Cafe Owner*), Artus de Penguern (*Waiter*), Richard Dieux (*Desk Cop*), Yves Renier (*Inspector*), Robert Ground (*U.S. Security Officer*), Bruce Johnson (*Marine Guard*), Michael Morris, Claude Doineau (*U.S. Embassy Clerks*), Andre Quiqui ("Blue Parrot" Barman), Tina Sportolaro (*TWA Clerk*), Patrick Floersheim (*Man in Leather*), Marcel Bluwal (*Man in Tweed*), Isabelle Noah (*Houseboat Owner*), Fonky French Family (*Houseboat Band*), David Jalil (*Bodyguard*), Jean-Claude Houbard (*Dead Driver*), Rouf Ben Amor (*Dr. Metlaoui*).

The superbly crafted FRANTIC teams Harrison Ford with director Roman Polanski and is set against the romantic backdrop of Paris. Fashioned as a terse thriller, with a subplot about drug smuggling, the film works against expectations and ultimately concerns itself with one man's unfaltering and obsessive love for his wife of 20 years. with his wife, Buckley, to deliver a medical paper. Having been there only once before (on his honeymoon), Ford speaks no French and cannot even make a phone call without Buckley's help. The two arrive at the posh Le Grand Hotel physically exhausted, drained by jet lag. Dragging their leaden feet, Ford and Buckley try to unpack and shower, but even this proves a frustrating task when it turns out they've picked up the wrong suitcase from the airport. While Ford is taking his shower, Buckley receives a phone call; when he gets out of the shower, Buckley is gone. She has disappeared without an explanation, clue, or trace. Ford begins to search for her calmly, almost with annoyance; as the hours tick away, however, he becomes increasingly concerned. A street bum (Pinon) informs Ford that his wife was forced into a car by a couple of thugs, and a hotel worker tells Ford he saw a mustached Middle Eastern man with his arm around Buckley in the lobby. Ford's efforts to find his wife through American Embassy aides Weeks and Mahoney prove fruitless. Lacking any explanation for her abduction, Ford remembers the suitcase, but after busting open the lock he finds nothing inside but women's clothing, a toy streetcar from San Francisco, and a miniature Statue of Liberty. No hidden drug shipments. No microfilm. Nothing remotely suspicious. His only clue is the telephone number of a man named DeDe written on a pack of matches from the Blue Parrot nightclub. Ford puts out the word that he's looking for DeDe—who, he discovers, is a drug trafficker—and later discovers DeDe lying dead in his kitchen, his throat slit. An urgent message left on DeDe's answering machine gives Ford another lead, and he waits until the arrival of the caller, Seigner, a beautiful young Frenchwoman in black leather. Ford grabs her by the collar of her jacket and throws her down on the staircase, demanding to know his wife's whereabouts. Confused and frightened, Seigner convinces Ford that she knows nothing of his wife, she only traveled to San Francisco to pick up a shipment for DeDe. She knows the shipment was hidden inside the miniature Statue of Liberty, but she doesn't know the contents. Ford tells her the miniature is inside the suitcase he mistakenly picked up, and Seigner agrees to help Ford in his search only if he helps her deliver the shipment—since she has yet to be paid and is fearful of ending up like DeDe. Ford now must go deeper into the criminal underside of Paris, caught between two worlds: the civilized and orderly world in which he loves his wife, and the seedy, illegal world in which he is tempted by excitement, adventure, and Seigner's sensuality. Later, Ford is scaling the rooftop of Seigner's apartment with the suitcase in hand when he clumsily slips and falls, sending the contents down into the courtyard. Teetering on the roof's edge is the mini-Miss Liberty, which, as Seigner tries to recover it, smashes on the pavement below. Inside is not drugs but an electronic switch used to detonate nuclear weapons. Ford and Seigner now meet with Weeks and Mahoney of the Embassy, who fear that the switch will get into the hands of Arab terrorists, but they refuse to give the switch up (for Ford it represents Buckley's safety, for Seigner it means financial gain). Bloodshed follows when Ford and Seigner meet the terrorists in an underground parking garage, a plan foiled by the arrival of the Embassy's security men. Another meeting is arranged, this time at a bridge near the small-scale Statue of Liberty that stands on the banks of the Seine. Two terrorists arrive by boat with Buckley and set her free. Seigner approaches the terrorists but refuses to hand over the switch until she is paid. The terrorists, having no idea that DeDe never paid her, are dumbfounded and frantically search their pockets for the money. Another pair of agents, who also want the switch, arrives, and a gun battle follows that leaves both Arab terrorists dead. Seigner is also shot. She walks in a daze to Ford and Buckley, collapsing before them, and places the switch in Ford's pocket before she dies. Rather than give the switch to the agents, Ford throws it into the Seine and leaves Paris, his love for Buckley stronger than ever.

Bouncing back from his entertaining box-office bomb of 1986, PIRATES, Polanski has once more turned his talents to the psychology of suspense. Collaborating again with his longtime writing partner Gerard Brach (who coscripted 1987's JEAN DE FLORETTE and MANON DES SOURCES), Polanski has created a thriller with a realistic hero. Clearly the most commercially structured film of Polanski's career, FRANTIC is also blessed with the box-office draw of Ford, who is on-screen in almost every shot. Ford's costar, the 21-year-old, relatively unknown Emmanuelle Seigner (she played a character named Grace Kelly in Jean-Luc Godard's 1985 film DETECTIVE and has been Polanski's lover of three years) is superb, combining a tough punk quality with sensuality; and Betty Buckley, best known in America for her role in TV's "Eight Is Enough," is also perfect, though on the screen for only a few minutes. Ford is as good as he has ever been, brilliantly playing his role as a sort of missing link between the civilized common man and his famous Indiana Jones adventurer. His character is completely believable as he transforms from an exhausted, preoccupied medical lecturer into a man recklessly determined to save the life of the woman he loves. Like James Stewart's doctor in THE MAN WHO KNEW TOO MUCH, Dustin Hoffman's mathematician in STRAW DOGS, or Charles Bronson's architect in DEATH WISH, Ford's surgeon is a rational, cultured man who finds a different quality deep within himself that gives him the strength and character to confront death. The transformation does not take place instantaneously; rather, it appears as an evolutionary process as he walks, one step at a time, into the heart of the criminal world. This change is shown most concretely in the scene in which Ford creeps across the sloping rooftop of Seigner's apartment building. Six floors above ground, he struggles with the suitcase, slips, and nearly falls to his death in the courtyard. Realizing that he can get better traction in his bare feet, he removes his shoes. As he takes off his first shoe, he carefully balances it on the steep incline, neatly stuffing his sock inside it. Despite his careful efforts, however, the shoe slides off the edge. He becomes aware of the danger he faces and how powerless he now is—nothing he has learned in his life has prepared him for this. In order to survive and get his wife back, he must think and act differently, without fear or "sense." Taking his second shoe off, he flings it and his sock away.

Rather than simply making a thriller, Polanski has added his own personal brand of comedy to FRANTIC. As early as THE FAT AND THE LEAN and TWO MEN AND A WARDROBE (two short Polanski films made in 1959 and 1960, respectively), Polanski displayed the bizarre, almost slapstick sense of humor that cuts through this film and balances the tragic with the comic. Ford knocks things over, bumps into them, falls over them, but pays little attention to his pratfalls. They are merely symbolic obstacles, which Ford pushes his way past in order to get to Buckley. Ford's mind is focused completely on one thing in FRANTIC, the safe return of his wife. He disregards the security of America by refusing to cooperate with the American Embassy, and he cares little for his own safety because he knows he is completely lost without Buckley. Most interestingly and romantically (in light of the sexual mores of modern cinema), he ignores the sexuality of Seigner, persisting in his deep and undying love for his wife, which grows stronger every minute they are apart. Seigner's allure, in fact, presents the greatest obstacle for Ford. She is more of a danger to his reunification with Buckley than are all the world's terrorists, for she is the one who can extinguish Ford's love for his wife, and the one whose potential for harm is least easily identifiable. While the terrorists, with their weapons and swarthy mustaches, are clearly enemies, it is pretty Seigner who is available to comfort Ford in his most vulnerable moments and thereby ruin everything that exists between him and Buckley. It is this danger—the danger of falling in love with another—that Ford must defend himself from, and it is this danger that makes FRANTIC a purely Polanskian story of romance and devotion, which only masquerades as a thriller. Songs include "I'm Gonna Lose You" (Mick Hucknall, performed by Simply Red), "I've Seen That Face Before (Libertango)" (A. Piazzaola, B. Reynolds, D. Wilkey, N. Delon, performed by Grace Jones), "The More I See You" (Harry Warren, Mack Gordon, performed by Chris Montez), "Jah Rastafari" (Joseph Hill, performed by Culture), "I Love Paris" (Cole Porter), "San Francisco (Be Sure to Wear Some Flowers in Your Hair)" (John Phillips), "Chicago Song" (Marcus Miller, performed by David Sanborn), "The Song from Moulin Rouge (Where Is Your Heart)" (W. Engvick, G. Auric, performed by the 101 Strings Orchestra), "Something Tells Me" (Ish Ledesma, performed by Tiger Moon). *(Brief nudity, drug use, adult situations.)*

p, Thom Mount, Tim Hampton; d, Roman Polanski; w, Roman Polanski, Gerard Brach; ph, Witold Sobocinski; ed, Sam O'Steen; m, Ennio Morricone; m/l, Mick Hucknall, A. Piazzaola, B. Reynolds, D. Wilkey, N. Delon, Harry Warren, Mack Gordon, Joseph Hill, Cole Porter, John Phillips, Marcus Miller, William Engvick, Georges Auric, Ish Ledesma; prod d, Pierre Guffroy; cos, Anthony Powell; stunts, Daniel Breton, Remy Julienne, Vic Armstrong, Wendy Leech; makeup, Didier Lavergne.

Thriller **Cas.** **(PR:A-C MPAA:R)**

FREEWAY † (1988) 91m Gower Street/NW c

Darlanne Fluegel *(Sunny Harper)*, James Russo *(Frank Quinn)*, Billy Drago *(Edward Heller)*, Richard Belzer *(Dr. David Lazarus)*, Michael Callan *(Lt. Boyle)*, Joey Palese *(Gomez)*, Clint Howard *(Ronnie)*, Steve Franken, Brian Kaiser, Kenneth Tobey, Julianne Dallara, Laurie Foshay, Gloria Edwards.

FREEWAY, a thriller about random gunplay on Los Angeles roadways, exists somewhere between real-life news headlines, Peter Bogdanovich's classic TARGETS, Larry Cohen's GOD TOLD ME TO, and Oliver Stone's TALK RADIO. Drago is a psycho ex-priest who cruises LA freeways with a small arsenal and a cellular phone, chatting with a sarcastic radio talk show personality (stand-up comic Belzer) while offing unsuspecting drivers. When a doctor is blown away, his wife (Fluegel), angered by the LAPD's inability to solve the case, enacts her own investigation. Directed by rock-vid and television director Francis Delia (videos for the Ramones, episodes of "Crime Story" and "Max Headroom"), FREEWAY had remarkably good timing in being filmed and released during an actual spate of LA freeway shootings. After a brief theatrical release, it turned up on video (where one can watch it without fear of having to exit a parking lot with a bunch of potential copy-cat lunatics afterwards).

p, Peter S. Davis, William Panzer; d, Francis Delia; w, Darrell Fetty, Francis Delia (based on a novel by Deanne Barkley); ph, Frank Byers; ed, Philip J. Sgriccia; m, Joe Delia; prod d, Douglas Metrov; art d, Shane Nelson.

Thriller **(PR:NR MPAA:R)**

FRESH HORSES zero (1988) 105m Dick Berg-Weintraub Entertainment Grp./COL c

Molly Ringwald *(Jewel)*, Andrew McCarthy *(Matt Larkin)*, Patti D'Arbanville *(Jean McBaine)*, Ben Stiller *(Tipton)*, Leon Russom *(Larkin's Dad)*, Molly Hagan *(Ellen)*, Viggo Mortensen *(Green)*, Doug Hutchison *(Sproles)*, Chiara Peacock *(Alice)*, Marita Geraghty *(Maureen)*, Rachel Jones *(Bobo)*, Welker White *(Christy)*, Christy Budig *(Laurel)*, Larry Ketron *(Roy)*, Ken Strunk *(Dr. Lippincott)*, William Youmans *(Gary)*, Richard Woods *(Buddy)*, Kent Poole *(Stephen)*, Dan Davis *(Fletcher)*, Barry Williams *(Fairgate)*, Carol Schneider *(Jane)*, Joan Macintosh *(Larkin's Mother)*, Sheri Norton-Stearn *(Mrs. Price)*, K.C. Jones *(Dr. Price)*, Jacqueline Verdeyen *(Jewel's Mother)*, Ann Johnson *(Girl No. 1)*, Jessica Browne *(Woman at Engagement Party)*, Jennifer P. Born *(Waitress)*, Peter Duchin *(Piano Player)*.

FRESH HORSES is a completely worthless rehashing of PRETTY IN PINK in which Molly Ringwald and Andrew McCarthy essay mirror images of their former John Hughes-penned selves. In 1986's PRETTY IN PINK, Ringwald was an outcast high school punklet from the wrong side of the tracks who fell in love with McCarthy, a fairly likable rich kid with equally rich friends. Because of their social differences, the high schoolers had to conduct their romance in secrecy, for fear of what friends and family would say. Turn the calendar ahead to 1988: Ringwald is now a 16-year-old, barely literate piece of po' white trash whose stepfather molested her until she married a gun-totin' good ol' boy (Mortensen) with whom she has supposedly never had sex. Along comes McCarthy, a fairly likable rich kid with equally rich friends (hmm, sound familiar?) who is preoccupied with college and his upcoming marriage to a whiny, prissy debutante (Peacock). But lo and behold, when McCarthy meets Ringwald it's love at first sight. Before long, McCarthy has given the big blow-off to his fiancee, forgotten about that degree in engineering, ignored the advice of best pal Tipton (Stiller, son of Jerry Stiller and Anne Meara), and mapped out a romantic future with his loving, pouty cavegirl. At first, their romance is nothing but heavenly bliss, but McCarthy soon starts hearing rumors about Ringwald (about her real age—she told him she was 20—and her marriage, which she never mentioned) from a campus acquaintance (Hutchison) who seems to have the inside line on everyone in town. Now McCarthy wants the truth, goshdarnit, and by golly he's gonna get it. When Ringwald 'fesses up, however, he can't take it, and, rather than sacrifice his whole future, decides to give up on her. He and Tipton get themselves some eager young ladies and some booze and sneak off to a little hideaway. McCarthy and Ringwald just can't stay away from each other, however, and try to make another go of it. The film ends at some point in the future, as McCarthy bumps into Ringwald, arm-in-arm with a new guy, at an outdoor skating rink. McCarthy's gone back to school, and guess what? Ringwald is even taking a couple of classes! They say goodbye and just chalk up their relationship to one of those crazy teen things.

Just in case there weren't already enough mindless, predictable, fill-in-the-blanks films on America's movie screens, this dull piece of drivel has come along to waste everybody's precious holiday hours. Appropriately released on time for Thanksgiving turkey, FRESH HORSES adapts a fairly well-respected New York play and misses on all counts. Surprisingly, the film comes from David Anspaugh, who directed the insightful and intelligent HOOSIERS, and was scripted by Larry Ketron, who penned the original stageplay and the commendable teen suicide film PERMANENT RECORD. It's rather tough to pinpoint just how and when FRESH HORSES starts to misfire—it all seems to fall apart at once. Contributing elements certainly include the hilariously contrived dialog, which forces the actors to say things no right-minded individual would dare mumble in public; the total lack of chemistry between the Ringwald and McCarthy—they didn't have much in PRETTY IN PINK, either—as if they've done this whole routine before (they have); Ringwald's supposed portrayal of a sultry bumpkin, in which she tends to lose her accent when emotions run high; and the fact that one never believes for a moment that McCarthy even *likes* Ringwald, much less that he is willing to throw away his entire existence because of his uncontrollable obsession. The film is ostensibly about such passion, but passion is the one thing FRESH HORSES lacks the most. Perhaps part of this can be blamed on the fact that although this was being touted as Ringwald's first "adult" role (read: sex scenes and nudity), there is in fact very little in her so-called "cagey, sensual, sexy" (as Ketron has described her) demeanor to suggest that she enjoys so much as holding hands.

Although FRESH HORSES isn't jampacked with rock tunes like most teenage pictures, there is one rock video segment that is worse than anyone can possibly imagine—a incredibly awful pool party in which McCarthy, Stiller, and three bikini-clad young women splash about, do Tom Cruise's COCKTAIL tumbler routines behind the poolside bar, dance in a drunken chorus line, and exchange lustful looks, all to the tune of Aretha Franklin's "Think" (Franklin, Ted White)—but thinking is one thing the filmmakers obviously never bothered to do. *(Sexual situations, adult situations, profanity, substance abuse.)*

p, Dick Berg; d, David Anspaugh; w, Larry Ketron (based on his play); ph, Fred Murphy (CFI color); ed, David Rosenbloom; m, David Foster, Patrick Williams; md, Tim Sexton; prod d, Paul Sylbert; spec eff, Sam Barkan; cos, Colleen Atwood; makeup, Robert Jiras.

Drama/Romance **Cas.** **(PR:C MPAA:PG-13)**

FRIDAY THE 13TH PART VII—THE NEW BLOOD zero (1988) 90m PAR c

Jennifer Banko *(Young Tina)*, John Otrin *(Mr. Shepard)*, Susan Blu *(Mrs. Shepard)*, Lar Park Lincoln *(Tina Shepard)*, Terry Kiser *(Dr. Crews)*, Kevin Blair *(Nick)*, Jennifer Sullivan *(Melissa)*, Heidi Kozak *(Sandra)*, Kane Hodder *(Jason Voorhees)*, William Clarke Butler *(Michael)*, Staci Greason *(Jane)*, Larry Cox *(Russell)*, Jeff Bennett *(Eddie)*, Diana Barrows *(Maddy)*, Elizabeth Kaitan *(Robin)*, Jon Renfield *(David)*, Craig Thomas *(Ben)*, Diane Almeida *(Kate)*, Michael Schroeder, Debora Kessler.

©PARAMOUNT

Jason kills a bunch of teenagers and a couple of adults using a variety of sharp instruments. A girl with CARRIE-like psychokenetic powers appears to defeat him once and for all. Sure she did. Paramount Pictures has no shame. (*Graphic violence, gore effects, substance abuse, sexual situations, nudity, profanity.*)

p, Iain Paterson; d, John Carl Buechler; w, Daryl Haney, Manuel Fidello; ph, Paul Elliott (Technicolor); ed, Barry Zetlin, Maureen O'Connell, Martin Jay Sadoff; m, Harry Manfredini, Fred Mollin; prod d, Richard Lawrence; spec eff, Lou Carlucci; cos, Jacqueline Johnson; stunts, Kane Hodder; makeup, John Carl Buechler.

| Horror | Cas. | (PR:O MPAA:R) |

FRIENDSHIP'S DEATH*   (1988, Brit.) 78m British Film Institute c

Bill Paterson (*Sullivan*), Tilda Swinton (*Friendship*), Patrick Bauchau (*Kubler*), Ruby Baker (*Catherine*), Joumana Gill (*Palestinian*).

Peter Wollen's first solo directorial outing (he previously codirected with Laura Mulvey) is a unique, deceptively simple science-fiction film that revolves around the Palestinian situation in the 1970s. Although structured like a standard narrative (Wollen has written that Val Lewton's B pictures at RKO were his inspiration), FRIENDSHIP'S DEATH is more closely related to that neglected genre, the "film essay." The film opens with documentary footage from 1970's "Black September" in Amman, Jordan. Gunfire is exchanged in the streets, and the city is reduced to rubble. An airport runway is enveloped in a mushroom cloud of thick, black smoke as PLO terrorists explode a jetliner. Against this backdrop, a woman, Swinton, is detained because she has arrived in the city without a passport. A PLO-leaning journalist, Paterson, pretends to know her, secures her release, and invites her back to his hotel room. Suspecting that she may be a secret agent, Paterson begins questioning Swinton, and learns that she is an alien from the galaxy Procryon. (Her planet had been ruled by creatures resembling tree shrews, but computers have since taken over.) Moreover, she explains that she is not a woman, as she appears, but a prototype computer, code-named "Friendship," sent to Earth on a peacekeeping mission. She was meant to land at MIT and later address the United Nations; instead, she crash-landed in Jordan in the midst of a civil war. Naturally, Paterson is reluctant to believe her—until she downs two glasses of whiskey with no noticeable effect. Swinton doesn't really drink, though; she simulates the act of drinking. Having carefully studied the outward signs of human behavior, she is able to perfectly mimic them, without always comprehending their meaning. Initially she is dependent on Paterson to provide her with identification so she can proceed to MIT, but the more time Swinton spends in his hotel, the more she empathizes with the Palestinians, who, like her, have been stranded in this land without a home. Life grows more and more dangerous in their region. Mortar fire rocks nearby buildings. The sound of gunfire echoes throughout the hotel, then a bullet is shot into their room. Some of Paterson's contacts warn him of the danger, and he prepares to leave, but Swinton has chosen to stay. Donning khakis, a Palestinian headdress, and a machine gun, she joins the PLO. Years later, Paterson has returned home. Still working as a journalist, he no longer hammers on the keys of his manual typewriter, but now writes at a computer keyboard. His adolescent daughter, a computer whiz, examines one of her father's mementos—a colored plastic communication device that Swinton gave Paterson in Jordan. After having the device analyzed and transferred to videotape, Paterson and his daughter put the tape into their video player. As they watch, multicolored computer-generated forms and shapes fill the screen. Bits and pieces of conversation between Paterson and Swinton are heard, a soccer match that Swinton watched on television is replayed, body-scan images and microscopic blood cells appear. However, all Paterson can do is watch these symbols, unable to decode them and apply any sort of meaning.

An impressive film with a number of layers to examine, FRIENDSHIP'S DEATH is perhaps more exciting to think about than it is to watch, a description that is not necessarily a negative one. Photographed on a single studio set with essentially only two characters, the film is unrelentingly talky—its science fiction-political-dramatic treatises overshadowing the visuals. While the frame is obviously composed with

painstaking care (note the interplay between sunlight and shadow) and the soundtrack densely populated, the film never really explodes with the energy that one might expect.

It is in its ideas, though, that the film is most interesting. Adapted from a short story Wollen wrote in the mid-1970s for Emma Tenant's science-fiction journal *Bananas*, the film explores a compendium of compelling ideas: the relationship between man and machine (one of friendship but not romance, as symbolized by the journalist and the alien), the gap between modern machinery and archaic machinery (the alien has a fondness for the journalist's typewriter, viewing it as a "distant cousin"), the relationship of signs to meanings (for Friendship the actions of humans can be duplicated but not truly understood; for the journalist, Friendship's message exists as a series of symbols without any code to decipher them), and parallels between Friendship and the cinema (the alien is not an actual woman but an icon; in the cinema, an image is not the actual object but a projected representation). All of these layers make for a fiendishly clever and conceptually sound picture, which, perversely, can be seen as an adaptation of Wollen's own theoretical writing in *Signs and Meanings in the Cinema*. More concretely, FRIENDSHIP'S DEATH emerges, as Wollen has already pointed out, as a sequel to Michelangelo Antonioni's 1975 film, THE PASSENGER, which starred Jack Nicholson as a Third World journalist and was coscripted by Wollen. (This year's HIGH SEASON, scripted by THE PASSENGER'S other cowriter, Mark Peploe, also has elements of being a sequel to the Antonioni film.) As Wollen told British writer Simon Field: "THE PASSENGER is a road movie, whereas this one is about being trapped, not being able to get out rather than constantly moving on."

p, Rebecca O'Brien; d, Peter Wollen; w, Peter Wollen (based on his short story); ph, Witold Stok (Technicolor); ed, Robert Hargreaves; m, Barrington Pheloung; prod d, Gemma Jackson; set d, Denise Rubens; cos, Cathy Cook; makeup, Morag Ross.

| Political/Science Fiction | | (PR:A MPAA:NR) |

FULL MOON IN BLUE WATER*½   (1988) 94m Turman-Foster/Trans World c

Gene Hackman (*Floyd*), Teri Garr (*Louise*), Burgess Meredith (*The General*), Elias Koteas (*Jimmy*), Kevin Cooney (*Charlie*), David Doty (*Virgil*), Gil Glasgow (*Baytch*), Becky Gelke (*Dorothy*), Marietta Marich (*Lois*), Lexie Masterson (*Annie*), William Larsen (*Jack Hill*), Mitchell Gossett (*Marone*), Mark Walters (*Johnny Gorman*), Ed Geldart (*Man # 1*), Lawrence Elkins (*Roy*), Tiny Skaggs, Bill Johnson (*Strangers*), Sharon Bunn (*Announcer*), Brandon Smith (*Talk Show Guest*), Sandra Zimmer (*Guest's Wife*), Ben Jones (*Digby*), Billy Donahue (*Vocalist*).

©TRANS WORLD

Skillfully directed by Peter Masterson, who called the shots on 1985's exceptional THE TRIP TO BOUNTIFUL, this "small" comedy-drama takes place mostly in the Blue Water Grill, a near-patronless small-town bar on Texas' Gulf Coast. Oblivious to the bar's failure, it's owner, Hackman, passes his days watching home movies of his wife (Gelke), who disappeared during a boating accident a year ago and has been given up for dead by everyone but him. The other resident of the Blue Water Grill is the "General" (Meredith), Hackman's wheelchair-bound father-in-law, a cantankerous stroke victim who is cared for by the slow-thinking Koteas. The one-time mental patient plays chess all day with Meredith, and also indulges him in his favorite activity, "walking the plank" —racing the old man down a walkway and coming to an abrupt halt at the water's edge. This routine is interrupted by Cooney, who offers to buy the Grill for $45,000 and warns Hackman that he could lose the place if he doesn't pay his back taxes. In short order, Cooney's partner, a local government official, confronts Hackman with an ultimatum—either pay the taxes or else. Against this backdrop, Garr, a pretty bus driver who sleeps with Hackman despite his "devotions," makes her play to become a more permanent part of his life. Hackman, however, refuses to acknowledge his feelings for Garr, wallowing in self-pity instead and holding onto his love for his wife even after her remains are finally discovered. This rejection becomes too much for Garr, and to make Hackman jealous, she goes out with the ineffectual Doty. While on their date, Garr learns that the long-rumored bridge that will connect the little town of Blue Water with the rest of civilization is actually going to be built. Knowing that this news is behind real estate man Cooney's offer, Garr punctures the tires on his car so that he will be late for his meeting with Hackman, who at that moment is preparing a suicide cocktail of beer and lye. In the meantime, Koteas has taken off with Meredith, not very convincingly threatening never to return his charge if Hackman doesn't pay him the $200 in back wages he needs to buy a car. Koteas and Meredith walk the plank again, but this time the old man accidentally falls into the shallow water and passes out. Koteas panics, fearing that he will be institutionalized again; returns to the Grill; and uses a gun to hold Doty, Garr, and Hackman hostage. Back at the walkway, the thick-headed sheriff (Glasgow) discovers Meredith, revives him, and brings him to the bar, where Koteas holds his gun to Garr. After Glasgow leaves, Hackman overpowers Koteas and puts him to work cleaning up the mess he's made. Next Hackman sends a humiliated Doty on his way, and when Cooney finally arrives, certain he has pulled off his deal, Hackman punches him in the nose. As the film ends Garr has become Hackman's partner, in business and life, and the credits roll over a best-of-all-possible-worlds party wherein everyone in town is dancing joyously at the Blue Water Grill.

With A TRIP TO BOUNTIFUL, director Masterson proved he could make an entertaining, moving film about *people*. This may not seem like a particularly distinctive accomplishment, but given Hollywood's predilection for "high concept," action-packed, effects-laden product, small films about people dealing realistically with their problems and each other still stand out. FULL MOON IN BLUE WATER is another such film. Structurally, it has much in common with a stage play, not surprising given that Masterson came to film by way of the theater (after writing and directing "The Best Little Whorehouse in Texas") and that the film was scripted by playwright Bill Bozzone ("Rose Cottages"). Not only does most of the story take place in one spot, but conflict builds incrementally as in a stage play, growing more intense as the principal players enter the enclosed environment of the Grill. This is not to say, however, that the film feels stage-bound or that the tension of the final reel is forced. Rather, the story moves along a leisurely pace that is perfectly suited to the Texas characters it delineates so carefully, allowing conflict to develop organically as a believable product of the personalities and situations presented.

Masterson, who is himself an actor, has a reputation as an actor's director, and—as with his first film—he is blessed with a fine cast, whom he rehearsed for two weeks before the cameras started rolling. Instead of being the human props that so many big-budget films require, the actors are given plenty of wonderful dialog and the screen time to fully develop their characters. Not surprisingly, the performances are all first-rate. Gene Hackman is masterfully restrained as the man who refuses to accept his wife's death, but who has himself given up on life in the process. The fundamental decency that defines Hackman's screen persona is never far from the surface here, even as he cruelly snubs Garr's affections. FULL MOON IN BLUE WATER is an often serious film, but a playful tone underlies the whole proceedings, and Hackman, like the other actors, does a wonderful job of finding the humor in the story's darkest moments. The film does in fact have many very funny moments, but the laughs are never cheap, springing naturally from character development, often informed by irony.

Much of the humor in the film comes from Burgess Meredith's excellent portrayal of the crotchety but life-loving "General" and from his relationship with his minder, Elias Koteas, a film newcomer who brilliantly essays the well-intentioned dimwit. Giving a performance that's extraordinarily reminiscent of Robert De Niro's Rupert Pupkin in THE KING OF COMEDY, Koteas wields a gun menacingly, but the viewer questions whether he really intends to use it. The threat is there, so tension exists, but the aura of mild danger conveyed by Koteas' presence is perfect for the film's tone. Equally appropriate for her role is Teri Garr, who uses her usual manic energy to create a convincing portrait of the independent woman of action whose love is strong enough to overcome the ghostly presence of Hackman's wife but who maintains her self-esteem in the process. Fine supporting work is also contributed Kevin Cooney, David Doty, and Gil Glasgow.

With its carefully observed characters, strong sense of locale, and adept mix of drama and comedy, FULL MOON IN BLUE WATER might have come from the pen of Lanford Wilson. Surprisingly, it is the first screenplay attempted by Bozzone, whose play "Rose Cottages" brought him to the attention of producer Lawrence Turman. Still, for all its theatrical origins, FULL MOON makes extremely effective use of its coastal Texas setting, due in no small part to the beautiful photography of Fred Murphy, who was responsible for A TRIP TO BOUNTIFUL's painterly cinematography, and whose credits include HOOSIERS; THE DEAD; and FIVE CORNERS. The film was shot with a predominantly Texan crew in Laporte, Seabrook, Clear Lake, and Kemah, Texas, where production designer Neil Spisak (another BOUNTIFUL collaborator) converted the Castaway Tavern into the Blue Water Grill. Songs include: "Don't Get Around Much Anymore" (Duke Ellington, Bob Russell, performed by Willie Nelson); "I Know I Belong to You," "Not a Tooth in Her Head (But Man Could She Beat a Drum)" (John Dumke, performed by the Bayou City Beats); "Survivor of Love" (Phil Marshall, performed by the Mersh Brothers Band). (*Profanity, adult situations, sexual situations.*)

p, Lawrence Turman, David Foster, John Turman; d, Peter Masterson; w, Bill Bozzone; ph, Fred Murphy (Technicolor); ed, Jill Savitt; m, Phil Marshall; m/l, Duke Ellington, Bob Russell, John Dumke, Phil Marshall; set d, Jeannette Scott; cos, Rondi Davis; stunts, Spiro Razatos; makeup, Ronnie Spector.

Comedy/Drama   **(PR:O MPAA:R)**

FUNNY FARM*½   (1988) 101m Cornelius-Pan Arts/WB c

Chevy Chase (*Andy Farmer*), Madolyn Smith (*Elizabeth Farmer*), Joseph Maher (*Michael Sinclair*), Jack Gilpin (*Bud Culbertson*), Brad Sullivan (*Brock*), MacIntyre Dixon (*Mayor Barclay*), Caris Corfman (*Betsy Culbertson*), William Severs (*Newspaper Editor*), Mike Starr (*Crocker*), Kevin O'Morrison (*Sheriff Ledbetter*), Dakin Matthews (*Marion Corey, Jr.*), Alice Drummond (*Mrs. Dinges*), William Newman (*Gus Lotterhand*), Nicholas Wyman (*Dirk Criterion*), Bill Fagerbakke (*Lon Criterion*), William Duell (*Old Character*), Glenn Plummer (*Mickey*), William Severs

(*Newspaper Editor*), Helen Lloyd Breed (*Old Operator*), Kit LeFevre (*Young Operator*), Nesbitt Blaisdell (*Hank*), George Buck (*Peterbrook*), Audrie J. Neenan (*Ivy*), Raynor Scheine (*Oates*), Peter Boyden, Reg E. Cathey, Dan Desmond, Don Plumley (*Reporters*), Brett Miller, Jamie Meyer (*Teenagers*), David Woodberry (*Ike*), Kevin Murphy (*Ewell*), Dennis Barr (*First Base Coach*), Barbara Baker (*Woman in Stands*), David Williams (*Marcus*), Steve Jonas (*Driving Instructor*), Russell Bletzer (*Councilman*), Evelyn McLean, Steven John, Robert Conner, Judson Duncan, Alison Hannas, Robert Ingram, Mary Johnson, Kristin Kellom, Paul Link (*Carolers*).

If you've happened to see any "fish-out-of-water" motion picture in, say, the last 75 years, or by chance caught any television sitcom (preferably of the "Newhart" variety) over the last few decades, then the chances are excellent that you've seen every single one of the gags that fill FUNNY FARM. Despite its title, FUNNY FARM is not funny and doesn't take place on a farm, though it is about a couple named the Farmers—by all rights, the film should probably have been called UNFUNNY FARMERS. Directed by the usually underrated George Roy Hill (BUTCH CASSIDY AND THE SUNDANCE KID; THE STING; A LITTLE ROMANCE), this tale of a city couple who retreat to the great life of the country stars a relatively laid-back Chevy Chase as Andy Farmer, a sportscar-driving Yuppie sportswriter who lives in a posh Manhattan apartment. After receiving a $10,000 advance to write one of those Great American Novels, Chase hops into his little roadster with his wife, Smith, and heads for paradise. This modern-day Mr. and Mrs. Blandings have bought their dream house in the middle of a heavenly plot of land. There are even ducks in their pond ("honey, we're duck owners!" Chase exclaims in all sincerity) and a delicate little sparrow in a birdhouse outside the bedroom window. Everything seems just perfect as the camera swirls deliriously around the thrilled Yuppie pair; however, little do they realize that they have descended into . . . Yuppie Hell. After a number of initial mishaps—the furniture arrives a day late, the happy couple does a pratfall over a Dutch door, they cannot make a phone call without depositing 20 cents into a nonexistent coin slot, they find a snake in the pond and a corpse in the garden, and the local mailman (who is only one of a collection of local eccentrics) nearly kills Chase as he speeds by in his old pickup—Chase and Smith wonder if they've made a mistake. The plot (when it surfaces from beneath the nonstop series of familiar gags) concerns Chase's inability to write his novel, while, unbeknownst to him, Smith is penning a charming children's tale herself. When Chase presents his wife with the first few chapters of his "The Big Heist," she breaks down in tears because she can't bear to tell him how bad it is. He, of course, tells her she knows nothing about writing. Then, just a couple of days after she mails out her own unsolicited, untyped manuscript, Smith receives a $5,000 advance and great praise as a writer of children's books. Smith's success and the subject of her book—a city squirrel named Andy and his mishaps in the country—hit a sensitive nerve with Chase. Eventually, divorce papers are filed and they plan, in the true style of this Me generation, to sell the house to the *next* dumb Yuppie couple that wanders along. Country life is no longer like it was in Norman Rockwell's magazine covers. Knowing that no one will buy the house if they discover how strange the locals are, Chase offers the town a hefty reward if they will help him sell the house by acting and dressing like Rockwell characters, and, upon the arrival of two prospective buyers—Gilpin and Cofman, a couple with the same idyllic vision of country life Chase and Smith once had—the town shifts into high Rockwell gear. As a result, everything seems perfect to Gilpin and Cofman and they can hardly contain themselves. This is their dream come true—the house is gorgeous, the neighbors are warm and hospitable—and they are determined to buy the house, offering even *more* than Chase and Smith's asking price. In the ultimate display of consumerism and materialism, Gilpin and Cofman want to buy it all: the house, the dishes, the furniture, even Chase's dog. But, at the last minute, Chase and Smith have a change of heart. They call off their divorce and take the house off the market, determined to live out their dream in the country.

Since judging comedy is a subjective matter, one cannot definitively say that a film is not funny. FUNNY FARM managed to thrill an inordinate number of film reviewers who praised Chase's comic genius and subdued performance, Hill's exceptional handling of sight gags and slapstick comedy, and the script's characterizations and biting satire. But as the less-than-spectacular box office tallies rolled in and FUNNY FARM rapidly disappeared from movie theaters, it became clear that most of the American public didn't find much to laugh at. Although there are some nice jabs at the Yuppie ideal of buying one's dreams, the film's main thrust lies in stringing together a number of familiar gags that are as predictable as night and day. As for characterization and emotional complexity, there have been more insightful entries by the Three Stooges. If you can imagine the slapstick style of Moe, Larry, and Curly reworked for popular consumption in the 1980s race for box office results, you'll have some idea of FUNNY FARM. Even the tone of the comedy is dark and brutal—one scene, for example, shows Chase hooking a fellow fisherman in the throat with a fishing lure, then trying to knock the struggling victim unconscious in order to pull out the hook. Unfortunately, this perverse, black sense of humor is not maintained throughout, as it was in Hill's similar THE WORLD ACCORDING TO GARP, adapted from the John Irving novel, or in Tony Richardson's adaptation of Irving's HOTEL NEW HAMPSHIRE. Nor does FUNNY FARM tackle the city mouse/country mouse theme as deftly as the previous Yuppie dream-come-true tale BABY BOOM. While it aspires to subversive social satire, FUNNY FARM is instead little more than a dumb comedy that seems more determined to make people laugh than to make them think. (*Comic violence, profanity.*)

p, Robert L. Crawford; d, George Roy Hill; w, Jeffrey Boam (based on the book by Jay Cronley); ph, Miroslav Ondricek (Technicolor); ed, Alan Heim; m, Elmer Bernstein; prod d, Henry Bumstead; set d, Judy Cammer; cos, Ann Roth.

Comedy   **Cas.**   **(PR:C MPAA:PG)**

FURTHER ADVENTURES OF TENNESSEE BUCK, THE****   (1988) 90m
Trans World Entertainment c

David Keith (*Buck Malone*), Kathy Shower (*Barbara Manchester*), Brant Van Hoffman (*Ken Manchester*), Sillaiyoor Selvarajan (*Sinaga*), Tiziana Stella (*Che*), Patrizia Zanetti (*Monique*), Sumith Mudanayaka (*Chief*), Pearl Vesudeva (*Chief's Mother*), Somi Ratanayaka (*Witch Doctor*), Solomon Hapte-Selassie (*Tui*), Steve Davis (*Argo*), Sydney Lassick (*Wolfgang Meyer*), Piyadasa Wijekodn (*Panang Chief*), Lilani Perera (*Panang Chief's Wife*), Augustus Pietrangali (*Chief Manoot*), Kapila Sigara, Reglus Perera, Presanna Fonseka, Sampath Fernandd (*Policemen*).

A knockoff of the "Indiana Jones" movies—with the addition of four-letter words and lots of jiggling breasts—THE FURTHER ADVENTURES OF TENNESSEE BUCK stars Keith as the drunken big-game hunter hero who is bailed out of jail by Van Hoffman. A nerd with too much money and a beauty queen wife (Shower), Van Hoffman wants Keith to take him and Shower to a jungle island where he can bag a white tiger, even though Keith tells him the isle is cannibal country. Van Hoffman is insistent, however, and when he names the right figure Keith agrees. Arriving on the island in Keith's seaplane, they are treated to a feast of monkey by the friendly coastal natives before setting out for the interior on foot. Keith gives Van Hoffman and Shower details on the cannibals, explaining that he used to live among them. It isn't long before they gain first-hand experience of the man-eaters, however, as they are captured and taken back to the cannibal camp. The chief takes a liking to Shower and has her taken to his hut, where she is oiled up in preparation for his enjoyment. Van Hoffman is cut loose and allowed to run away, then is hunted down and killed, his head tossed at Shower's feet before she is raped. Luckily, the chief's mother recognizes an amulet around Keith's neck and realizes that he is the one who had lived among them. She turns him loose during the night and he frees Shower before heading to the coast, with the chief and his warriors in pursuit. Keith kills several, and several more abandon the chase, but the chief is relentless, wanting the woman and the amulet, not to mention Keith's head. Meanwhile, the skimpily clad Shower shows a remarkable recovery from the rape and her husband's death, falling in love with Keith. They finally reach the coast and their plane, leaving the chief hopping up and down on the beach.

   David Keith is a good actor who made a memorable impression in AN OFFICER AND A GENTLEMAN. Lately he has turned director, debuting in this capacity with THE CURSE, and as a director he does show some slight ability. He is also a relaxed, likable hero and gives the film whatever charm it has with his leading portrayal. On the other hand, to say former Playmate of the Year Shower's thespian talents are limited would be the kindest place to leave the matter. This whole picture is little more than a live-action cartoon, but, accepted on that level, it can be entertaining. Not as mean-spirited as many of the "Indiana Jones" ripoffs, TENNESSEE BUCK is not for kids but adults could do worse . (*Violence, nudity, sexual situations, adult situations, substance abuse, excessive profanity.*)

p, Gideon Amir, Peter Shepard; d, David Keith; w, Barry Jacobs, Stuart Jacobs (based on a story by Paul Mason); ph, Avraham Karpick; ed, Anthony Redman; m, John Debney; m/l, Steve Gray, Alan Hankshaw, Clive Hicks, R. Gilks, Andy Clarke, John Devereaux, Richard Myhill; prod d, Erroll Kelly; spec eff, Adams Calvert; cos, Audrey Bansmer; stunts, Gregg Brazzel; makeup, Camille Calvet.

Adventure   **Cas.**   **(PR:O MPAA:R)**

GALACTIC GIGOLO zero   (1988) 82m Titan-Generic/Urban Classics c

Carmine Capobianco *(Eoj)*, Debi Thibeault *(Hildy Johnson)*, Ruth Collins *(Dr. Ruth Pepper)*, Angela Nicholas *(Peggy Sue Peggy)*, Frank Stewart *(Waldo Crabbo)*, Michael Citriniti *(Sonny Corleone)*, Tony Kruk *(Carmine)*, David Coughlin *(Tony)*, Donna Davidge *(Kay)*, Will Rokos *(Pie Vendor)*, Todd Grant Kimsey *(Big Peter Dick)*, Barry Finkel *(Billy Joe Bob)*, Bill L. Gillogy *(Tommy Jerry Joe)*, J.L. Gitter *(Sammy Harry Bill)*, Lee Anne Baker *(Lucy)*, Toni Whyne *(Kelly)*, Lisa Schmidt *(Joanne)*, Jenny Bassett *(Alison)*, Don Sirasky *(Pa Goldberg)*, Cassandra Cole *(Mike)*, Michele Gabrill *(Lori)*, Courtenay James *(Lisa)*, Judy Coppola *(Riva)*, Danny Noyes, Ed Powers, Mike Brady, Gary Rakow *(Reporters)*, Karen Neilsen *(Kathy)*, Lisa Patruno *(Sandy)*, Taylor Neary *(Veronica)*, Herb Klinger *(William)*, Frank Christopher, Rich Thibeault *(Indians)*, Elizabeth Rose *(Lemonade Vendor)*, Shaun Cashman *(New Spaceman)*.

GALACTIC GIGOLO opens on Crowak, a planet populated by vegetables. There, Eoj (Joe spelled backwards, and of no significance to the plot), played by writer-associate producer Carmine Capobianco, has just won a two week trip to Earth on the game show "You Bet Your Fertilizer." Capobianco, being a broccoli (a Groucho Marx carrot), chooses as his disguise on Earth the appearance of the "Lovable Sleazeball." He's sent to Prospect, Connecticut, the horniest spot in the world according to the Crowakians, and lands in a cheap silver Elvis outfit complete with goggles and cape. (This all makes sense when it's later revealed that Elvis himself was a Crowakian who chose not to return when his two-week trip was up, but has since been taken forcibly home.) On a mission to make love to every woman in Prospect, Capobianco immediately sets to work using pick up lines like "Hi, I'm Eoj from the planet Crowak, and I'm here to partake in sexual relations with Earth women." This works because he has the hypnotic power to make any woman have the instant hots for him, and soon he's in numerous hot *tubs* sipping champagne. At a televised press conference, Capobianco explains his purpose in coming to Earth (arousing the interest of countless numbers of females), and shows off his protean capabilities by becoming a kitten. The show is seen by a bunch of buffoonish Italian mobsters (led by Citriniti) who want to use him to help pull bank robberies, and by a family of backwoods—Jewish—rednecks who want to kill him for being a Commie. A journalist, Thibeault, persuades the alien to let her and her nerdy photographer (Stewart) tag along with him, so she can bring his exploits to the world. After an endless number of idiotic jokes, (such wordplay as "extra-testicle" for "extra-terrestrial"), stupid sound effects, and dismal bits of slapstick, Capobianco defeats the mob and hillbilly clan with the aid of bananas, household appliances, and a few cream pies. He then heads for home, saying, "You know it's time to go when your jokes get predictable," just as a new Crowakian winner appears, again in the guise of Elvis.

An awful mix of puns, bargain-basement production values, and muddled plot lines, GALACTIC GIGOLO is truly wretched. Tasteless, stupid jokes abound and the main thought behind the editing seems to be: when in doubt, cut to a shot of breasts. The production barely reaches home movie quality, with the amateurish camerawork particularly annoying, and it all ends up as painful to watch despite the short running time. Even the occasional funny line gets butchered by the flat, uninspired readings. Perhaps the cast was tired out from having to perform many of the production chores as well. Producer Gorman Bechard claims this mess was meant to be a nonanimated adult cartoon and was ruined in the color timing and the editing, but with a premise as wrong as this one it's hard to see how that could have made a difference. *(Comic violence, sexual situations, excessive profanity.)*

p, Gorman Bechard, Kris Covello; d, Gorman Bechard; w, Carmine Capobianco, Gorman Bechard; ph, Gorman Bechard (Foto-Kem color); ed, Joe Keiser; m, Bob Esty, Michael Bernard; set d, Shaun Cashman, George Bernota; cos, Debi Thibeault; makeup, Frank Stewart.

Science Fiction/Comedy   Cas.   **(PR:O MPAA:R)**

GANDAHAR   (SEE: LIGHT YEARS, 1988, Fr.)

GHOST TOWN**   (1988) 85m Empire/Trans World c

Franc Luz *(Langley)*, Catherine Hickland *(Kate)*, Jimmie F. Skaggs *(Devilin)*, Penelope Windust *(Grace)*, Bruce Glover *(Dealer)*, Zitto Kazann *(Blacksmith)*, Blake Conway *(Harper)*, Laura Schaefer *(Etta)*, Michael Aldredge *(Bubba)*, Ken Kolb *(Ned)*, Will Hannah *(Billy)*.

Produced by Charles Band's recently defunct Empire Pictures, GHOST TOWN combines elements of the horror and western genres, resulting in a mixed bag of pretty pictures and stale story-telling. Present-day deputy sheriff Luz stumbles upon a ghost town while searching for missing socialite Hickland, who, at the film's opening, was snatched up by a man in black appearing out of a dust cloud on horseback. Luz, quite to his amazement, discovers that the town is full of the undead, the townsfolk bound in an old curse that keeps them ageless. Skaggs (the lead bad guy, suggestively named Devilin) oversees the town with an iron hand, intimidating the populace with the threat of throwing them into nothingness. Luz, upon being deputized by the crumbling yet verbal remains of the ex-sheriff, stands up to Skaggs and, after the nec-

essary allotment of shootouts and saloon scenes, kills the beast by throwing his badge into Skaggs' forehead. With the rescued Hickland at his side, Luz subsequently watches with amazement as the town disappears before his eyes.

GHOST TOWN has a lot going for it. Director Richard Governor brings a sense of poignancy to the material, a quality that is, to say the least, absent from most horror films. The movie is beautifully photographed by Mac Ahlberg and the performances (especially those of Franc Luz and Jimmie F. Skaggs) are convincing. What starts out as an interesting premise, however, soon turns into a run-of-the-mill, Saturday afternoon bad-guy western, the only difference being that here the villains are zombies. It should have been fun, but, instead of exploiting the concept's potential, the film falls prey to tired western cliches and lacks the strong narrative drive that could have kept it one hoof ahead of the rest. Because of its own laziness, GHOST TOWN falls from the saddle and quickly strays from the path. *(Violence, sexual situations.)*

p, Timothy D. Tennant; d, Richard Governor; w, Duke Sandefur (based on a story by David Schmoeller); ph, Mac Ahlberg (Foto-Kem Color); ed, Peter Teschner, King Wilder; m, Harvey R. Cohen; prod d, Don De Fina; art d, Rick Brown; spec eff, MMI, John Carl Buechler, Eddie Surkin; stunts, Kane Hodder.

Horror/Western   Cas.   **(PR:C-O MPAA:R)**

GHOULIES II*   (1988) 90m Charles Band/Empire c

Damon Martin *(Larry)*, Royal Dano *(Uncle Ned)*, Phil Fondacaro *(Sir Nigel)*, J. Downing *(P. Hardin)*, Kerry Remsen *(Nicole)*, Dale Wyatt *(Dixie)*, Jon Maynard Pennell *(Bobby)*, Sasha Jensen *(Teddy)*, Starr Andreeff *(Alice)*, William Butler *(Merle)*, Donnie Jeffcoat *(Eddie)*, Christopher Burton *(Leo)*, Mickey Knox *(Ray)*, Romano Puppo *(Zampano)*, Ames Morton *(Patty)*, Michael Deak *(Bozo)*, Anthony Dawson *(Priest)*, Don Hodson *(Barker)*, Carrie Janisse *(Carol)*, Steve Pelot *(Security Guard)*, Larry Dolgin, Mark Peter D'Auria *(Policemen)*, Fidel Bauna *(Hot Dog Vendor)*, Lucilla Potasso *(Bearded Lady)*, Ettore Martini *(Shooting Gallery Owner)*, Maurizio Gaudio *(Operator)*, Fiorella Ceneetti *(Fat Lady)*, Luea Mazzaeurati *(Half & Half)*, Livia Bonelli *(Gene)*, Robert Spafford *(Supervisor Boxer Booth)*, G. Lorenzo Bernini *(Big Guy)*, Ignazio Blonde *(Little Guy)*, Filli Campagna *(Blonde Girl)*, R. Colombaioni *(Fire Eater)*, Patrizia Fazi, Barbara Grazzi, Nadia Canelias, Laura Battistini *(Dancers)*, Hal Rayle *(Ghoulies' Voices)*.

A typically lame production from the now defunct Empire Pictures, this straight-to-home-video release is a sequel to the moderately successful GREMLINS rip-off of 1985, GHOULIES. This time out, the badly articulated ghoulie puppets—denizens of hell—are kidnapped from a group of satanists by a priest. Although the priest tries to destroy the little demons, he fails and they wind up hiding out in a haunted house called Satan's Den. Part of a traveling carnival, Satan's Den is run by the alcoholic Dano and his nephew Martin. Down on their luck and running their exhibit at a loss because kids today are used to graphic gore and not the more genteel scares offered by a simple haunted house, Dano and Martin find their livelihood threatened by Downing, a yuppie accountant who represents the conglomerate that owns the carnival. If the show doesn't make a profit soon, Satan's Den will be replaced by female mud wrestlers. Things look grim for Dano and Martin until the ghoulies begin showing themselves to patrons. Mistaking the vile little creatures for spectacular special effects, patrons soon come flocking to Satan's Den for a chance to see them. Unfortunately, the ghoulies begin killing off their public, and soon all hell breaks loose at the carnival. Realizing that the demons can only be dispatched by magic, Martin, his girl friend (Remsen), and their dwarf buddy, Fondacaro, recite an incantation from a book of spells and summon up a huge ghoulie. The giant ghoulie stomps around the carny eating all the little ones up, but when it is finished, it mistakes Fondacaro for a ghoulie and gives chase. The quick-thinking Martin grabs a demon suit Fondacaro wore in his haunted house act and sticks a molotov cocktail inside it and the big ghoulie mistakes the costume for a demon and gobbles it down. After experiencing some bad gastronomical pains, the giant ghoulie explodes. With the carny saved, Martin and Remsen decide to head out on their own, leaving Fondacaro to run the haunted house.

Certainly no improvement over the original, GHOULIES II instead offers the same dull chills, bad special effects, and juvenile humor that made its predecessor so boring. Since the plot is a merely an excuse to put the ghoulies in a series of scary-yet-funny situations, one would expect that John Buechler's low-budget special effects team would have improved their designs from last time. Perhaps they could have made the ghoulies a little more mobile, a bit more expressive. Alas, this is not the case and, just like last time, the little critters simply aren't up to carrying an entire movie by themselves. The ghoulies are still quite obviously hand-puppets intermingled with some very brief scenes of stop-motion animation done by David Allen Productions. Despite their limited technical ability, the ghoulies do have a sort of shabby charm that might endear them to small children. Unfortunately, the vicious bloodletting and crude sexual innuendo here should preclude viewing of this movie by kids. If scenes of teenagers taunting a dwarf, heavy-metal kids making out in a haunted house, and a ghoulie chewing off the private parts of a yuppie accountant while he sits on a toilet is your idea of a good time, by all means rent GHOULIES II. *(Violence, gore effects, sexual situations, profanity, substance abuse.)*

p, Albert Band; d, Albert Band; w, Dennis Paoli (based on a story by Charlie Dolan); ph, Sergio Salvati (Technicolor); ed, Barry Zetlin; m, Fuzzbee Morse; m/l, Paul Sabu, Charles Esposito, Neil Citron, George Fenton, John Leach; prod d, Giovanni Natalucci; spec eff, John Carl Buechler.

Horror   Cas.   (PR:C-O MPAA:PG-13)

GLITCH †   (1988) 90m Omega c

Will Egan (Todd), Steve Donmyer (Bo), Julia Nickson (Michelle), Dick Gautier (Julius Lazar), Ted Lange (DuBois), Teri Weigel (Lydia), Dan Speaker (Brucie), Dallas Cole, Ji-Tu Cumbuka, Fernando Carzon, John Kreng, Lindsay Carr, Susan Youngbluth, Bunty Bailey, Joy Rinaldi, Lisa Erickson, Caroldean Ross, Penny Wiggins, Christina Cardan, Kahlena Marie, Laura Albert, Debra Lamb, Bridget Boland.

Low-budget action master Nico Mastorakis, who last year turned out the impressive thriller THE WIND, changes gears with this comedy about filmmaking. Gautier plays a Hollywood filmmaker whose new film, "Sex and Violence" is about to start production. Because a large number of scantily-clad young women are auditioning, two enthusiastic young girl-chasers pretend to be the film's producer and director in the hope of bedding a few of them. Released straight to video.

p, Nico Mastorakis; d, Nico Mastorakis; w, Nico Mastorakis; ph, Peter Jensen (CFI color); ed, Nico Mastorakis; ed, George Rosenberg; m, Tom Marolda; prod d, Gary New.

Comedy   Cas.   (PR:NR MPAA:R)

GOOD MOTHER, THE★★   (1988) 103m Touchstone-Silver Screen Partners IV-Arnold Glimcher/BV c

Diane Keaton (Anna Dunlap), Liam Neeson (Leo Cutter), Jason Robards (Muth), Ralph Bellamy (Grandfather), Teresa Wright (Grandmother), James Naughton (Brian Dunlap), Joe Morton (Frank Williams), Katey Sagal (Ursula), Tracy Griffith (Babe).

During an extended opening sequence, a little girl is shown to be very much taken with her bold, lively young aunt (Griffith), whose life falls apart when she becomes pregnant. After giving up the child for adoption, Griffith eventually drowns, most likely a suicide. The film then jumps forward to the present where the little girl has grown into Keaton, the divorced mother of a six-year-old who lives in Boston, supporting herself by working as a lab technician and teaching piano, while her lawyer ex-husband (Naughton) is remarried and lives in Washington. Keaton is devoted to her daughter and seems reasonably content with her simple existence, declining the financial assistance offered by her grandparents (Bellamy and Wright). One day in a laundromat she meets Neeson, an Irish-born sculptor. Though she is normally cautious around men, she is immediately attracted to the handsome and thoroughly charming Neeson. Soon they are having a passionate affair that serves to liberate the repressed Keaton. Little Vieira also takes to Neeson and before long he is spending most of his nights with Keaton. One evening, Vieira, frightened by a nightmare, climbs in bed with her mother as Keaton and Neeson are making love. As Vieira sleeps, the couple continues making love. Time passes and then an irate Naughton shows up one day, claims that Vieira has told him that Neeson molested her, and vows that he will never return the child to Keaton. A custody battle ensues in which it is revealed that Neeson and Keaton were sometimes nude in the presence of Vieira, and that the "molestation" in question occurred one day while Keaton was away and Neeson was emerging from the shower. Vieira was in the bathroom and asked if she could touch his penis, which Neeson allowed, believing that the liberated Keaton would find nothing wrong in giving in to a child's normal curiosity. It becomes apparent that the liberal atmosphere created by Keaton and Neeson is not one the court finds well suited to child rearing. In response, Keaton's attorney (Robards) tells her she has only one chance to maintain custody of her daughter: she must renounce Neeson for his actions and say that she will never see him again. Keaton, however, finds this option reprehensible, and the court finally awards permanent custody of the little girl to Naughton.

Based on Sue Miller's 1986 bestseller, THE GOOD MOTHER, as directed by Leonard Nimoy (THREE MEN AND A BABY; STAR TREK IV: THE VOYAGE HOME); refuses to provide simple answers. But in distancing itself from the material, the film becomes rather lifeless and uninvolving. We feel for Diane Keaton and the wrenching conflict in which she is trapped, but the script never lets the emotion out with any force. Keaton, who was last seen with an unwanted baby in BABY BOOM, here is convincing as the devoted mother and repressed woman, although less so following her liberation. Exhibiting the potential to be a major star in his own right, Liam Neeson (SUSPECT) is very appealing. However, in this case, he is perhaps a little too appealing, since, in order to make Keaton's dilemma all the more poignant, he isn't just a passionate sexual partner but also a warm and caring person who is gentle and kind with his lover's daughter. Jason Robards is effective as the lawyer forced to propose the unthinkable to Keaton, as are Ralph Bellamy and Teresa Wright as the conservative grandparents who are appalled by the direction their granddaughter's life has taken. Overall, THE GOOD MOTHER is a competent meditation on a complex subject, but one wishes it had been injected with a little of the passion that Neeson is supposed to have awakened in Keaton. (Profanity, adult situations, sexual situations, substance abuse.)

p, Arnold Glimcher; d, Leonard Nimoy; w, Michael Bortman (based on the novel by Sue Miller); ph, David Watkin (Metrocolor); ed, Peter E. Berger; m, Elmer Bernstein; prod d, Stan Jolley; art d, Richard Harrison, Hilton Rosemarin; set d,

Anthony Greco; cos, Susan Becker.

Drama   Cas.   (PR:O MPAA:R)

GOODBYE, CHILDREN   (SEE: AU REVOIR LES ENFANTS, 1988, Fr.)

GORILLAS IN THE MIST★★★   (1988) 129m Guber-Peters-Arnold Glimcher/UNIV c

Sigourney Weaver (Dian Fossey), Bryan Brown (Bob Campbell), Julie Harris (Roz Carr), John Omirah Miluwi (Sembagare), Iain Cuthbertson (Dr. Louis Leakey), Constantin Alexandrov (Van Vecten), Waigwa Wachira (Mukara), Iain Glenn (Brendan), David Lansbury (Larry), Maggie O'Neill (Kim), Konga Mbandu (Rushemba), Michael J. Reynolds (Howard Dowd), Gordon Masten (Photographer), Peter Nduati (Batwa Chief), Helen Fraser (Mme. Van Vecten).

©MCA (UNIVERSAL)

During the 1970s, Dian Fossey journeyed to Africa, where years of dedication and patience enabled her to closely study the mountain gorilla. A National Geographic television special recounted her exploits, as did her own book, Gorillas in the Mist, and, most recently, Farley Mowat's Woman in the Mists. In this film biography, Sigourney Weaver portrays the late, controversial Fossey, beginning with her 1963 meeting in Louisville, Kentucky, with anthropologist Louis Leakey (Cuthbertson). She persuades him that her skills as a physical therapist would be of use to him in his studies of the African mountain gorilla, and he allows her to accompany him to the Belgian Congo. Once there, Cuthbertson sets out by himself, leaving Weaver and her guide (Miluwi) to search for the gorillas on their own. They sight a group of gorillas, but before they can make any meaningful contact, war breaks out and Weaver is forced to leave the Congo. She takes refuge with Roz Carr (Harris), who talks her into setting up a new camp on the Rwanda side of the Congo border. Once camp is established, Weaver and Miluwi begin patiently to follow and study the gorillas. Eventually, she is able to overcome their natural fear of humans and achieves a remarkable closeness with the animals. But while Weaver is passive and playful with the gorillas, she feels nothing but hostility toward the local Batwa pygmy poachers and the government bureaucrats who want to exploit "her" gorillas (an endangered species) as a tourist attraction. Meanwhile, romance enters Weaver's life in the form of National Geographic photographer Bob Campbell (Brown). His photos tell her story to the world and they fall in love. Brown is married, but offers to divorce his wife so that he and Weaver can wed; however, the romance comes to a quick end when he suggests that Weaver give up her work and follow him around on his assignments. He departs, but the magazine articles have created a lot of interest in Weaver and her work and lead to the filming of the special to be aired in the US on public television. Unfortunately, during the filming, Weaver's famous, favorite gorilla companion Digit is slaughtered by poachers, who remove the animal's hands and head. Thereafter, Weaver continues her studies, but becomes more and more obsessed with protecting the animals from humans. She engages in black magic rituals to terrify the natives, stages mock hangings, burns huts, and organizes her own militia to patrol the mountain. She becomes alienated from all other humans, and one night, alone, surrounded by pictures of gorillas, she dozes off and is slain while sleeping by an unidentified assassin. She is buried (as was Fossey) near the gorillas she spent 18 years studying.

There was interest in bringing Dian Fossey's story to the screen long before this film went into production. Fossey had sold the rights to her book and was to meet with producer Arnold Glimcher on Dec. 27, 1985, to discuss the project. She was murdered the night before, and several studios then battled to tell her story. In 1986, Universal and Warner Bros. reached a rare agreement to collaborate on the picture, and production began on the $24 million film. The complex Fossey presented a problem for writer Anna Hamilton Phelan and director Michael Apted (COAL MINER'S DAUGHTER; GORKY PARK). Hollywood does not often produce films centered on "unlikable" characters, and Fossey, though her work unquestionably advanced scientific knowledge in her field, could be irrational, compulsive, and perhaps more than a little mad. Weaver is stunning as Fossey, a woman driven by a cause that eventually put her at odds with nearly everyone she knew. The film teeters ambivalently, however, in its depiction of Fossey's enemies the Batwa pygmies, sometimes showing them as mere villains, at other times taking into account the failing Rwanda economy and their very real need to hunt in the area.

Upon its release, GORILLAS IN THE MIST generated much publicity concerning the manner in which the cast and crew filmed many of the same gorillas Fossey studied. Little was said, however, about the work of Rick Baker, who created the gorilla costumes donned by human stunt players for many of the scenes. In fact, Baker's work is so well done that it is impossible to tell the real gorillas from the guys in the suits.

GORILLAS IN THE MIST fails to offer any insights into Fossey's courage and obsessions. Weaver's performance and a glimpse of the endangered and magnificent mountain gorillas, however, make the film worth viewing. (Profanity, adult situations, violence.)

p, Arnold Glimcher, Terence Clegg, Robert Nixon, Judy Kessler; d, Michael Apted; w, Anna Hamilton Phelan (based on the story by Harold T.P. Hayes); ph, John Seale, Alan Root (Technicolor); ed, Stuart Baird; m, Maurice Jarre; prod d, John Graysmark; art d, Ken Court; set d, Simon Wakefield; spec eff, David Harris; cos, Catherine Leterrier; makeup, Christine Beveridge, Rick Baker.

Drama   Cas.   (PR:C MPAA:PG-13)

GRAND HIGHWAY, THE**½   (1988, Fr.) 107m Flach-Selena Audiovisuel-TF 1/Miramax c

Anemone (Marcelle), Richard Bohringer (Pello), Antoine Hubert (Louis), Vanessa Guedj (Martine), Christine Pascal (Claire), Raoul Billerey (Priest), Pascale Roberts (Yvonne), Marie Matheron (Solange), Daniel Rialet (Simon), Jean-Francois Derec.

Praised to the high heavens in France, where it was the number one French-produced film of the year and the recipient of six Cesar nominations, THE GRAND HIGHWAY has in its US release been compared to Jean Renoir and Marcel Pagnol for its portrayal of provincial life and to Francois Truffaut for its handling of childhood. Unfortunately, THE GRAND HIGHWAY is an uninventive, calculated look at the charm, innocence, and simplicity of country life and childhood that falls flat in all but a few scenes. Closer to Rene Clement's traditional and superficial FORBIDDEN GAMES than to the above-mentioned prototypes, THE GRAND HIGHWAY focuses on Hubert, a high-strung Parisian nine-year-old who is taken to the country for a few weeks while his mother (Pascal) has her baby. Hubert's father is long gone—as Hubert knows, although his mother continues to try to deceive him in the matter. Hubert is taken to a peaceful little village and an idyllic life of relaxation for most adults—but a hell of boredom for a child. When Hubert learns there isn't even a place to swim, he becomes more disenchanted. He stays with his mother's close friend, Anemone, a 30ish peasant woman who is thoroughly content plucking chickens and skinning rabbits for dinner. When Hubert first meets his temporary guardian, she has just scooped out a hanging rabbit's eye and is in the process of skinning the creature. "Do you want to see how Mr. Rabbit's pajamas come off?" she asks the horrified youngster. Even more frightening to Hubert than the gory rabbit is Anemone's gruff husband, Bohringer. A carpenter who constructs all the village's coffins, Bohringer is a hard drinker who treats Anemone with contempt and has an aura of violence and anger that sends Hubert running for comfort. Anemone is thrilled that she now has a little boy to take care of, watching over him with a stifling possessiveness and devoting more time to him than to Bohringer. Hubert's only escape is his new-found friend, Guedj, a 10-year-old country girl who wanders around in her bare feet and freely shows her underwear to her new pal. She takes Hubert to all her favorite spots, including a treetop hideout where they can spy on her older sister as she undresses. A loud, precocious youngster, Guedj is a walking encyclopedia of taboos and tells Hubert about menstruation, gonorrhea, toilet habits, and funerals, all the while teasing the young boy with the sight of her underwear. Not surprisingly, Hubert is a bit frightened by Guedj, but he is also fascinated as she forces him to confront things he would never have been exposed to in the safety of his Parisian home. Her antics often become too much for Hubert, like when she tosses a handful of baby eels into his pants; later, she berates him into climbing atop the town cathedral and peeing into a gutter gargoyle so an unsuspecting nun below gets wet. As Hubert is fascinated by Guedj, so too is he fascinated by Bohringer. Hoping to anger his wife, Bohringer begins competing with Anemone for Hubert's affections. He presents the boy with a miniature wooden ox cart that he made and forbids anyone to touch. When Anemone sees Hubert playing with this cart (using it to feed beans to his rabbit friends), she takes it away from him. Despite her interference, Hubert and Bohringer grow closer, and one day on the way home Hubert puts his small hand in Bohringer's bearish paw and the two walk together. Anemone soon comes along and drags the boy away for dinner. Bohringer even takes Hubert fishing one Sunday morning instead of allowing Anemone to take him along to church. Again Bohringer and Hubert have a pleasant father-and-son time. It is then that Hubert confronts Bohringer with something he has learned—that Bohringer and Anemone had a child who died at birth nine years earlier. Since then Bohringer and Anemone have been unable to love each other. Anemone refuses to forget the past, even making a shrine of the baby's room that she prepared nine years ago—a room filled with furniture built by Bohringer, who, though once he could build cribs and rocking horses, can now only fashion coffins. Fearing that his own mother will die in childbirth, Hubert runs away, taking refuge on the roof of the cathedral. Taking a dangerous stroll at the roof's pinnacle, Hubert vows to join his mother, not knowing that she has just given birth to a healthy child. Bohringer tries to climb to the boy's aid while everyone watches from below. The boy slips, slides down the roof, and is saved when he becomes lodged in the gutter. His mother later arrives to take him home, and teary goodbyes follow—the most powerful being Bohringer's farewell. He scoops the boy into his arms, hugging him as if he were the son that he never had. As Hubert and his mother take the bus back to Paris, Bohringer and Anemone are liberated from their past, embracing each other as they haven't done in years.

This is the third film from writer-director Jean-Loup Hubert and the first to be an unqualified success. His first picture was a well-received but inconsequential romantic comedy, L'ANNEE PROCHAINE SI TOUT VA BIEN (1981), which starred Isabelle Adjani and Thierry Lhermitte as a yuppie couple nearly torn apart when they cannot agree on having a family. The unsuccessful LA SMALA (1984) is also concerned with a family, this time a tribe of five. With THE GRAND HIGHWAY, Hubert takes a different turn, focusing on a couple who wanted to have a family, but who were not destined to have their wish fulfilled. When a surrogate child comes temporarily into their lives, their lives are finally renewed. In light of Hubert's other films, it's easy to see where THE GRAND HIGHWAY goes wrong. The most interesting characters in this film are the couple—Bohringer and Anemone—who have been in a state of suspended animation since the death of their child. Unfortunately, however, Hubert, bent on making a semiautobiographical story (this seems to be the era for it, judging from AU REVOIR LES ENFANTS, MY LIFE AS A DOG, and HOPE AND GLORY), concentrates most of his efforts on the children in the film—Antoine Hubert (the director's son) and Vanessa Guedj. He has tried for realism in the children's performances, but instead their parts seem self-conscious and heavily screenwritten. It's as if director Hubert, not confident that his child actors were convincing enough, filled their mouths with charming and precocious lines of dialog to compensate. Only occasionally does the film come alive and break out of the static, conventional boundaries Hubert seems to have set up for himself, most notably in the finale. Its ending is a masterful one during which, no matter how indifferent one is to the characters, one cannot help but be moved by the rediscovery of life experienced by Bohringer and Anemone. Rarely is an actor as great as Richard Bohringer is in THE GRAND HIGHWAY. On the surface, his character is a frightening, callous, hated man who sinks so low as to torment children and rape his wife, but underneath he is a sensitive, confused, and hurting man who carries the burden of his loss without ever displaying it. Nominated for six Cesars, THE GRAND HIGHWAY was awarded two—for the performances of Bohringer and Anemone. (In French, English subtitles.) (Nudity, sexual situations, adult situations, graphic violence, profanity.)

p, Pascal Hommais, Jean-Francois Lepetit; d, Jean-Loup Hubert; w, Jean-Loup Hubert; ph, Claude Lecomte (Eastmancolor); ed, Raymonde Guyot; m, Georges Granier; art d, Thierry Flamand.

Drama   Cas.   (PR:O MPAA:NR)

GREAT OUTDOORS, THE*   (1988) 92m UNIV c

Dan Aykroyd (Roman Craig), John Candy (Chet Ripley), Stephanie Faracy (Connie Ripley), Annette Bening (Kate Craig), Chris Young (Buck Ripley), Ian Giatti (Ben Ripley), Hilary Gordon (Cara Craig), Rebecca Gordon (Mara Craig), Robert Prosky (Wally, Lodge Manager), Zoaunne LeRoy (Juanita), Lucy Deakins (Cammie), Nancy Lenehan (Waitress), John Bloom (Jimbo), Lewis Arquette (Herm), Britt Leach (Reg), Cliff Bemis (Boat Yard Owner), Paul Hansen (Hot Dog Vendor), Debra Lee Ortega (Dancing Biker Girl), Sierra Somerville (Girl in Arcade), Christine Spiotta (Woman in Crowd), Chris Bass (Lodge Patron), Shirley Harris (Lodge Customer), Christopher Kinsman (Irate Customer), Andy Prosky (Grill Chef), Raleigh Bond (Grandpa), Barry Thompson (Kitchen Help), Brian Healy (Man in Crowd).

©MCA (UNIVERSAL)

Scripted by the extraordinarily prolific John Hughes, directed by Howard Deutch (Hughes' collaborator on PRETTY IN PINK and SOME KIND OF WONDERFUL), and starring John Candy and Dan Aykroyd, this disappointing comedy should have been much funnier given the talent of those involved. Candy stars as a genial Chicago auto parts salesman who takes his family—wife Faracy, sons Young and Giatti—to Peck's Pine Log Resort in Wisconsin so that he, like his father before him, can introduce his boys to the wonders of nature. But Candy's best-laid plans are upset by the uninvited appearance Faracy's sister, Bening; her husband, Aykroyd, a blustering, boastful investment consultant; and their quiet red-haired twin daughters. A nouveau riche materialist who views the great outdoors as one big investment opportunity, Aykroyd has a very different vacation in mind from the one Candy has planned. Instead of a quiet pontoon boat, Aykroyd insists on taking out a speedboat emblazoned with "Suck My Wake," and before long Candy is unwillingly water-skiing behind it, holding on for dear life as he negotiates a slapstick obstacle course. Mis-hap follows misadventure as Aykroyd and nature—bears, leeches, scavenging raccoons, and a bat—combine to make a nervous wreck of Candy. In the meantime, Candy's teenage son, Young, strikes up a relationship with Deakins, a pretty local girl leery of tourists who win her heart and then disappear. Eventually, tensions between Candy and Aykroyd, and their families, become so great that Aykroyd and his brood decide to leave, though not before Aykroyd bamboozles Candy into sinking his savings into a phony investment scheme. Plagued with guilt, Aykroyd returns to confess, and in the finale everybody is pulled together by a crisis that involves a storm, the twins, and another bear.

Sadly, THE GREAT OUTDOORS is neither very funny nor insightful. The situations, gags, and characters are all vaguely familiar, and with good reason. Candy played a similarly unlucky vacationer in SUMMER RENTAL (1985), Aykroyd's obnoxious con man is a not-so-distant cousin of his Vic in NEIGHBORS (1980), and Hughes' screenplay for NATIONAL LAMPOON'S VACATION (1982) took Chevy Chase and family on holiday. However, THE GREAT OUTDOORS most nearly resembles the Hughes-scripted-and-directed PLANES, TRAINS, AND AUTOMOBILES (1987). In many ways, Candy, who menaced Steve Martin in that film, has simply taken over the Martin role, with Aykroyd doing Candy's part. Vacation mishaps have replaced transportation snafus and Candy plays a somewhat nicer guy here than Martin's self-interested businessman, but essentially this is still the story of one man who won't get out of another man's hair. PLANES, TRAINS, AND AUTOMOBILES was more affecting, however, in the reality of its characters and the humanity at the core of Martin and Candy's relationship. In THE GREAT OUTDOORS, Hughes and Deutch have tried to re-create the pathos and dignity of the earlier film's scene in which Candy defends himself against Martin's big put-down, but Aykroyd's confession of failure and deceit lacks the depth of its predecessor. This is due mostly to Hughes' failure to develop his characters, and though Candy and Akroyd create amusing antagonists, they never become more than the victims of funny (sometimes) occurrences. Hughes and Deutch are more successful in their handling of the teen romance (a thematic specialty of both Hughes and his protege), but despite their honesty, the scenes between Young and Deakins feel tacked on, as if they belong in another film. Deutch's direction, overall, is competent, though the pacing is a little uneven. The real problem with THE GREAT OUTDOORS is Hughes' screenplay. With TRAINS, PLANES, AND AUTOMOBILES, the master of the teen comedy-drama (SIXTEEN CANDLES; THE BREAKFAST CLUB) proved that he is capable of making interesting films about adults, but, judging from THE GREAT OUTDOORS and this year's SHE'S HAVING MY BABY, he still has a lot to learn. (*Profanity, sexual situations.*)

p, Arne L. Schmidt; d, Howard Deutch; w, John Hughes; ph, Ric Waite (CFI color); ed, Tom Rolf, William Gordean, Seth Flaum; m, Thomas Newman; prod d, John W. Corso; set d, Sharon Busse; spec eff, John Frazier; cos, Marilyn Vance-Straker; ch, Ken Ortega; stunts, Walter Scott; makeup, Ben Nye, Jr., Alan Friedman.

Comedy   Cas.   (PR:A-C MPAA:PG)

GROTESQUE †   (1988) 79m United Filmmakers/Concorde c

Linda Blair (*Lisa*), Tab Hunter (*Rod*), Donna Wilkes (*Kathy*), Brad Wilson (*Scratch*), Nels Van Patten (*Gibbs*), Guy Stockwell (*Orville Kruger*), Sharon Hughes, Michelle Bensoussan, Charles Dierkop, Chuck Morrell, Lincoln Tate, Luana Patten, Robert Zdar, Billy Frank, Bunki Z, John Goff, Mikel Angel, Stacy Alden, Mike Lane.

Hunter and Blair costar in this special effects exercise about a gang of punk rockers who invade the home of a special effects makeup man and begin killing off his family. Escaping the mayhem is Blair, whose uncle (Hunter), a plastic surgeon, devotes himself to tracking down the punk killers and methodically deforming their faces. Linda Blair and supporting player Lincoln Tate are billed as the film's associate producers.

p, Mike Lane, Chris Morrell; d, Joe Tornatore; w, Mikel Angel (based on characters and concept by Tornatore); ph, Bill Dickson (Foto-Kem Color); m, Bill Loose, Jack Cookerly; art d, Richard McGuire; spec eff, John Naulin; stunts, Eddie Donno.

Horror   Cas.   (PR:NR MPAA:R)

GUILIA E GUILIA   (SEE: JULIA AND JULIA, 1988, It.)

H

HAIRSPRAY*½ (1988) 90m New Line c

Sonny Bono *(Franklin Von Tussle)*, Ruth Brown *(Motormouth Maybell)*, Divine *(Edna Turnblad/Arvin Hodgepile)*, Colleen Fitzpatrick *(Amber Von Tussle)*, Michael St. Gerard *(Link Larkin)*, Debbie Harry *(Velma Von Tussle)*, Ricki Lake *(Tracy Turnblad)*, Leslie Ann Powers *(Penny Pingleton)*, Clayton Prince *(Seaweed)*, Jerry Stiller *(Wilbur Turnblad)*, Mink Stole *(Tammy)*, Shawn Thompson *(Corny Collins)*, Ric Ocasek *(Beatnik Cat)*, Pia Zadora *(Beatnik Girl)*.

©NEW LINE

What began as a celebration of the terrifically entertaining, downright wholesome mainstream breakthrough of the infamous gross-out team of John Waters and Divine suddenly became a rueful farewell when Divine was found dead from an apparent heart attack in his Los Angeles hotel room on March 7, 1988. The tragedy occurred a mere two weeks after HAIRSPRAY opened to glowing notices—most of which singled out Divine as an honest-to-gosh star. In HAIRSPRAY writer-director Waters has finally hit his stride. Instead of selling out to the Hollywood establishment by abandoning his more perverse obsessions, Waters has parlayed his keen social observation and great compassion for society's outsiders into an "all-talking, all-dancing, sort-of-big-budget civil rights comedy dealing with glamour-starved teenage celebrities, their blue-collar mothers, and their quest for mental health." Waters has graduated from the somewhat inarticulate rage that fueled his first 10 films and matured as a writer and, especially, as a director. His personal obsessions are still very much in evidence—suburban mores, warped families, local Baltimore eccentrics, dance music, bouffant hairdos, polyester clothes, tacky furnishings, and all-around garishness—but this time he has left the shock tactics behind. After all, he has already explored every avenue of shock, and as he himself put it, making HAIRSPRAY a PG-rated movie was ". . . intentional. It was the only shock left."

Set in Waters' beloved Baltimore circa 1962, HAIRSPRAY details the last days of 1950s American naivete as the country moves from postwar complacency to massive social upheaval. As Divine's character, Edna Turnblad, states, "The times they are a'-changin'. I feel it blowin' in the wind." Caught up in all this is the "Corny Collins Show," a wildly popular Baltimore television dance program featuring local teenagers twisting to all the latest pop records. Queen of the show is the spoiled and snobbish Amber Von Tussle (Fitzpatrick), whose father (Bono) is the owner of an amusement park called "Tilted Acres." Fitzpatrick's domineering mother (Harry) drills the exhausted teen on all the latest dance steps in a supreme effort to keep her darling daughter before the cameras. Meanwhile, in the working-class section of town, obese teenager Tracy Turnblad (Lake) and her skinny girl friend, Penny Pingleton (Powers), rush home every day to watch the Corny Collins Show, much to the chagrin of Lake's overworked mother (Divine), who complains, "I've got hampers of laundry to do and my diet pill is wearing off!" Although Lake's father, Wilbur (Stiller), the owner of a novelty shop, thinks the teen's obsession with rock music is harmless, Divine worries that her daughter will become a hopeless "hair-hopper." When the show's producers announce a round of tryouts for new dancers, Lake and Powers sneak off to the station for an audition. Although she's overweight, Lake's sensational dancing earns her a spot on the show and the admiration of Fitzpatrick's boy friend, Link Larkin (St. Gerard). At the same time, trouble is brewing in Baltimore. Despite the fact that the white teens routinely dance to black R & B tunes, black kids are only allowed on the show once a month for the segregated "Negro Day" hosted by local black singer Motormouth Maybell (Brown). Although Corny Collins (Thompson) disagrees with the unfair policy, repugnant station owner Arvin Hodgepile (also played by Divine) insists on segregation. Lake is outraged by the state of affairs and openly associates with blacks in her own neighborhood and at school. The shy Powers, meanwhile, has fallen in love with a handsome black teen named Seaweed (Prince), and her horrified parents hire quack psychiatrist Waters to "cure" her. While the racial storm brews, Lake finds herself rapidly becoming the most popular teen in Baltimore and threatens to depose the distraught Fitzpatrick as "Miss Auto

Show of 1963." Lake's newfound fame even wins over her parents, bringing the family closer together when mother and daughter don snappy new clothes purchased at the "Hefty Hideaway" and indulge in some outrageously large hairdos. During this period Lake's social consciousness is also raised, and after a run-in with beatniks Zadora and Ocasek, Lake abandons her bouffant and embraces social change. Outspoken and unafraid, she also uses her popularity to help advance desegregation, offering herself as a martyr for the cause by forcing the repressive powers-that-be to persecute her for her views. Uniting with her black friends, Lake leads a triumphant march on the Corny Collins live broadcast from the "whites only" Tilted Acres and forces Baltimore to accept integrated dancing.

Easily director John Waters' finest film to date, HAIRSPRAY is a milestone of sorts, in that it is a very rare example of a fiercely independent and eccentric director entering the Hollywood mainstream while still managing to advance his unique and intensely personal vision. A relatively large $2 million budget and all the restrictions that accompany it have enabled the outrageous Waters to hone his craft and allowed him to produce the most coherent and satisfying film of his career, without any apparent concession to mainstream sensibilities. Obviously a labor of love, HAIRSPRAY feels like a film that Waters has wanted to make for some time. Working from an article he wrote about The Buddy Deane Show, the real-life counterpart of "The Corny Collins Show," Waters re-creates the Baltimore of his youth with his usual distinct eye for broad characters and kitsch detail. This a vibrant film full of bright colors, great music, and skillful, lovingly re-created dances, including the Madison, the Bug, the Mashed Potato, the Dog, the Roach, and the Limbo Rock (both Divine and Waters tutored the 1980s teens in the dance steps that they had learned watching The Buddy Deane Show in the early 1960s). Cinematographer Dave Insley's fine camerawork is a real surprise, especially after his not-so-fine work on Waters' POLYESTER (probably attributable to that film's $200,000 budget). What HAIRSPRAY's large budget (though still minuscule by Hollywood standards) has allowed Waters to do is elevate himself from talented amateur to promising professional. His cast, half unknowns and half guest stars, is perfect. Nineteen-year-old Riki Lake is a wonderfully energetic actress who exudes youthful enthusiasm and hopefulness—a true champion of Waters' favorite kind of people: society's "others." What makes even Waters' most revolting work so compelling and, in a strange way, *moving*, is his total devotion to characters who are scoffed at and scorned by "normal" people. The fat, the ugly, the disenfranchised, the alienated, and those whose sexuality deviates from the accepted norm are heroes in Waters' universe, and he is their tireless advocate, pointing out that it is the so-called normal people who live hypocritical, pathetic lives.

One of Waters greatest strengths as an artist is his dizzyingly hilarious grasp of character and dialog ("Your hairdo is a hair-don't!" says the principal to Tracy), and no one delivered his lines better than Waters' longtime friend and associate Divine. Cast in a comparatively small dual role, Divine manages to steal the film from its vivacious young star. Divine is superb as the put-upon working-class housewife Edna Turnblad, a strong woman who literally blossoms under the spotlight of her daughter's newfound fame, much to the delight of her supportive husband. As the repugnant racist Arvin Hodgepile, Divine embodies the ugliness and stupidity of racism. His performance here, and his marvelous appearance as a gangster in Alan Rudolph's excellent TROUBLE IN MIND (1985), had finally begun to bring him the recognition he so long deserved. Divine seemed to be on the verge of superstardom, convincing the mainstream that he was an *actor* and not merely a sideshow freak, and it is a pity he was not around long enough to enjoy the fame due him. One naturally must wonder what Divine's death will do to the career of John Waters. Waters made only one film without him (DESPERATE LIVING, 1977) and it will be difficult, if not impossible, to find another actor so in tune with his own obsessions. While waiting to see what the future holds, however, we can don our cha-cha heels and practice our dance steps to make Corny Collins proud.

Songs include: "Hairspray" (Rachel Sweet, Anthony Battaglia, Willa Bassen, performed by Sweet), "The Madison Time" (Eddie Morrison, Ray Bryant, performed by The Ray Bryant Combo), "I'm Blue (The Gong-Gong Song)" (Ike Turner, performed by The Ikettes), "Mamma Don't Lie" (Curtis Mayfield, performed by Jan Bradley), "Town Without Pity" (Ned Washington, Dimitri Tiomkin, performed by Gene Pitney), "The Roach (Dance)" (Alonzo B. Willis, Kathie Venetoulis, performed by Gene and Wendell), "Foot Stompin'" (Aaron Collins, performed by The Flares), "Shake a Tail Feather" (Verlie Rice, Otis Hayes, Andre Williams, performed by The Five Du-Tones), "The Bug" (Jerry Dallman, Milton Grant, performed by Jerry Dallman and The Knightcaps), "You'll Lose a Good Thing" (Barbara Lynn Ozen, performed by Barbara Lynn), "I Wish I Were a Princess" (George David Weiss, Hugo and Luigi, performed by Little Peggy March), "Nothing Takes the Place of You" (Toussaint McCall, performed by McCall).

p, Rachel Talalay, Stanley F. Buchthal, John Waters; d, John Waters; w, John Waters; ph, David Insley; ed, Janice Hampton; md, Bonnie Greenberg; m/l, Rachel Sweet, Anthkony Battaglia, Willa Bassen, Eddie Morrison, Ray Bryant, Ike Turner, Curtis Mayfield, Ned Washington, Dimitri Tiomkin, Alonzo B. Willis, Kathie Venetoulis, Aaron Collins, Verlie Rice, Otis Hayes, Andre Williams, Jerry Dallman, Milton Grant, Barbary Lynn Ozen, George David Weiss, Hugo and Luigi, Toussaint McCall; art d, Vincent Peranio; cos, Van Smith; ch, Edward Love; makeup, Van Smith.

Comedy   Cas.   (PR:A-C MPAA:PG)

HALLOWEEN IV: THE RETURN OF MICHAEL MYERS*** (1988) 88m Galaxy c

Donald Pleasence (*Dr. Loomis*), Ellie Cornell (*Rachel Carruthers*), Danielle Harris (*Jamie Lloyd*), George P. Wilbur (*Michael Myers*), Michael Pataki (*Dr. Hoffman*), Beau Starr (*Sheriff Meeker*), Kathleen Kinmont (*Kelly*), Sasha Jenson (*Brady*), Gene Ross (*Earl*), Carmen Filpi (*Jack Sayer*).

The best of the sequels to John Carpenter's seminal slasher movie HALLOWEEN, this one hit the screen just in time to celebrate the 10th anniversary of the original. Picking up 10 years after HALLOWEEN II left off (part three had nothing whatsoever to do with the other two), we learn that the infamous "Shape," Michael Myers, has survived the fiery blast that appeared to have killed both him and his perennial pursuer, the slightly mad Dr. Loomis (Pleasance). Having been in a coma all these years, Myers finally comes to, slaughters his handlers, and escapes while being transferred from one federal mental hospital to another. When Pleasence—who also survived the blast, with only some facial scars and a limp to show for it—hears the news, he immediately heads for Haddonfield, Illinois, the site of Myers' rampage a decade ago. Knowing that Myers has a grade-school-aged niece (Harris) in Haddonfield, Pleasence assumes that the psychotic killer will go home to finish her off. Meanwhile, we see that little Harris (the daughter of the original's Jamie Lee Curtis character) has been orphaned and is now living with a local family. Adjusting to a new family is difficult for Harris, who feels left out and resented by her teenage step-sister, Cornell—who learns that she must forgo a hot date with boy friend Jenson to baby-sit Harris on Halloween night. By nightfall, Pleasence has blown into town and urges local sheriff Starr to close all the businesses and get the citizens off the streets until Myers can be found. Some local good ol' boys get wind of this and form a vigilante group to hunt down Myers themselves. While trick-or-treating with Harris (who wears a clown costume just like the one the six-year-old Michael Myers wore at the beginning of the original film), Cornell is shocked to discover her boy friend making out with the buxom Kinmont—who just happens to be the sheriff's daughter. Shortly thereafter, the cops clear the streets and Cornell finds herself and Harris being barricaded in the sheriff's house with both her boy friend and his new gal until Myers can be found. Unbeknownst to everyone, however, Myers—who by now has cut off all the power to the town and ransacked the police station—is in the house with them. While Pleasence is out looking for Myers and the sheriff is off trying to stop the rednecks from accidentally killing half the population, Myers makes hamburger out of a deputy, Kinmont, and Jenson. The terrified Harris and Cornell are chased to the roof by the killer and Cornell falls. Harris makes it down to safety and is discovered by Pleasance. They go to the grade school for shelter, but Myers turns up there and throws Pleasence through a window. Harris and Cornell (who survived the fall) are rescued by the vigilante group and taken out of town, but Myers hides in their pickup truck and kills the girls' protectors. Thrown to the side of the road when the pickup crashes, Myers is finally killed by a hail of police bullets that send him tumbling into an old well. Back at home, Harris' step-mom runs some hot water so that the bloodied and shell-shocked child can take a bath while the her step-dad, the sheriff, Pleasence, and Cornell wait downstairs. Suddenly the camera goes to a Halloween-mask point-of-view shot and we see a hand pick up a pair of scissors from the bathroom sink and stab the step-mother to death. Pleasence, et al., run to the staircase after hearing the screams and are horrified to see little Harris in her Halloween costume clutching the bloody scissors. Realizing that the girl has just committed the same crime that the six-year-old Michael Myers had so many years ago, Pleasence flips out and starts screaming, "No, no, no." Michael Myers has transfered his evil soul to a little girl.

Although Carpenter has disowned the HALLOWEEN series and had nothing whatsoever to do with this sequel, HALLOWEEN 4: THE RETURN OF MICHAEL MYERS is easily the best entry since Carpenter's original. Directed with flair by Dwight H. Little (KGB—THE SECRET WAR), who does not blatantly ape Carpenter's style, the movie delivers a number of effective chills without relying too heavily on the kinds of tired tricks and bloody gore that have made this genre a boring cliche. The solid script by Alan B. McElroy takes time to develop its characters, exploits each situation to the fullest, has a fairly complicated structure with several simultaneously running subplots, and taps into childhood fears in the way that made the first film so memorable. Aided by a terrific performance from child actress Danielle Harris, the filmmakers do an excellent job of conveying the loneliness and alienation experienced by the orphaned youngster and her efforts to assimilate into both her new family and at school (in an in-joke, her character is named Jamie, after actress Jamie Lee Curtis). Harris is also able to show pure childhood terror and reacts to Myers with total fear—this is not one of those smart-mouthed, precocious kids who are braver than any adult found in many slasher movies. The Harris character is a normal, sensitive kid, and her conversion at the shocking conclusion therefore seems perfectly logical, not to mention horrifying. Also excellent, again, is Donald Pleasence as the crazed Dr. Loomis. With his scarred face and painful limp, he has begun to take on the mantle of a modern day Captain Ahab madly pursuing his white whale. Pleasence turns in a wonderfully hammy performance, despite the fact that he was surreptitiously conned into taking the part by the producers, who told him that John Carpenter had approved the script and called it "the best of the HALLOWEEN series." Reportedly, Carpenter, who didn't want to participate in any more HALLOWEEN films and was forced to divest his financial interest in the series after being threatened with a lawsuit by his partners Moustapha Akkad, Irwin Yablans, and Debra Hill, never even saw the script—something Pleasence didn't discover until after the filming was completed. In fact, Carpenter didn't even want his name on the film, forgoing the credit, "Based on characters created by John Carpenter and Debra Hill." The producers were determined to place Carpenter's name prominently in the credits anyhow, and his name appears by itself on-screen when the HALLOWEEN theme music is credited to him. Despite Carpenter's misgivings, HALLOWEEN 4 is a worthy successor to his original and nothing to be ashamed of. Given the twist ending, a Part Five, for once, may actually be worth viewing. (*Violence, gore effects, sexual situations, nudity, profanity.*)

p, Paul Freeman; d, Dwight H. Little; w, Alan B. McElroy (based on a story by Dhani Lipsius, Larry Rattner, Benjamin Ruffner and Alan B. McElroy); ph, Peter Lyons Collister; ed, Curtiss Clayton; m, Alan Howarth; art d, Roger S. Crandall; set d, Nickle Lauritzen; spec eff, Larry Fioritto; stunts, Fred Lerner.

Horror   Cas.   (PR:O MPAA:R)

HANDFUL OF DUST, A**½ (1988, Brit.) 118m LWT-Stagescreen Prods./New Line c

James Wilby (*Tony Last*), Kristin Scott Thomas (*Brenda Last*), Richard Beale (*Ben*), Jackson Kyle (*John Andrew Last*), Norman Lumsden (*Ambrose*), Jeanne Watts (*Nanny*), Kate Percival (*Miss Ripon*), Richard Leech (*Doctor*), Roger Milner (*Vicar*), Tristram Jellinek (*Richard Last*), Anjelica Huston (*Mrs. Rattery*), Rupert Graves (*John Beaver*), Judi Dench (*Mrs. Beaver*), Pip Torrens (*Jock Grant-Menzies*), Beatie Edney (*Marjorie*), Stephen Fry (*Reggie*), Graham Crowden (*Mr. Graceful*), John Quentin (*Brenda's Solicitor*), Timothy Bateson (*MacDougal*), Moyra Fraser (*Mrs. Northcote*), Marsha Fitzalan (*Polly Cockpurse*), Annabel Brooks (*Daisy*), Tamsin Olivier (*Veronica*), Mareueen Bennett (*Marjorie's Maid*), Hugh Simon (*Travel Agent*), Alan Hay (*Club Porter*), Matthew Ryan (*Club Page*), Cathryn Harrison (*Milly*), Alice Dawnay (*Winnie*), John Junkin (*Blenkinsop*), Peggy Aitchison (*Waitress*), Alec Guinness (*Mr. Todd*), Christopher Godwin (*Mr. Messinger*), Jeannette Baillie (*Rosa*), Julian Infante (*Indian Spokesman*), William Gonzalez (*Indian Singer*), Duke of Norfolk (*Gardener*).

This film version of what many consider to be Evelyn Waugh's finest novel is the handiwork of Derek Granger and Charles Sturridge, the producer-director team responsible "Brideshead Revisited," the popular TV adaptation of another Waugh novel. Reteaming James Wilby and Rupert Graves, the homosexual lovers in 1987's MAURICE, the film is mounted in the lavish Merchant-Ivory fashion and re-creates the well-appointed London drawing rooms, sumptuous manor houses, and arid gentility of the British upper class circa 1932. Wilby is the lord of Hetton Abbey, a gothic monstrosity in southern England whose upkeep devours most of the family's resources. He loves the ancestral residence, however, and the world of tradition, honor, and breeding it represents. It and his family—young son Kyle and beautiful wife Scott Thomas—are his reasons for living. Scott Thomas, on the other hand, is bored by this staid lifestyle and begins an affair with Graves, a handsome but dim social climber with little wealth of his own. Scott Thomas cavorts with Graves in London, where she eventually takes a flat, and though all of London seems to know about the affair, Wilby remains in the dark. When Kyle is killed in a fox hunting accident, Scott Thomas' initial reaction to the awful news is relief that it is her son and not her lover who has died. Not long after Kyle's death, Scott Thomas leaves Wilby and requests a divorce. At first, Wilby is compliant, honorably venturing to Brighton with *another woman* so that Scott Thomas might have grounds, but when she requests so much alimony that Wilby would have to give up Hetton, he decides that enough is enough. Wilby accompanies an explorer on an ill-fated search for a lost city in South America, Graves begins to lose interest in Scott Thomas when she is left without resources, and the ironic ending finds both Wilby and Scott Thomas isolated.

Many of those who have read A Handful of Dust have been disappointed by Sturridge's film, finding that it fails to capture Waugh's biting satire. This is not to say, however, that Sturridge has watered down the emotional impact of the story, or that A HANDFUL OF DUST is an unsatisfying film. It remains a tale of horrible selfishness and cruelty, but while retaining much of Waugh's dialog and keeping as much of the story intact as is possible in two hours of film, Sturridge has, nevertheless, altered the tone of the proceedings. While there are still a number of funny moments in the film, Sturridge for the most part approaches his subject straight on, revealing the selfishness that lurks beneath the veneer of gentility that passes for decency. Rather than satirizing Scott Thomas and Graves, he stacks his moral deck against them. He does so without preaching: Sturridge's point of view is more detached than didactic or ironic, and, as a result, the fall of nice guy Wilby appears less as the predictable fate of a fool who believes in a nonexistent honorable world than as the wronging of an innocent.

The performances are all first rate. Radiating self-satisfaction and complacency in his time-honored position in the world, Wilby is particularly sympathetic as the trusting cuckold. He goes almost, but not quite, too far in his portrayal of the nice-guy, making his assertive self-defense in the last reel all the more effective.   Kristin Scott Thomas (UNDER THE CHERRY MOON) is convincing as she thoughtlessly drifts into adultery, and Graves is appropriately limpid and spineless as the fop she pursues. Judi Dench delivers a nicely understated, quickly etched portrayal of Graves' money-minded mother, Alec Guinness gives an oddly appealing performance as the half-Englishman who forces Wilby to read Dickens to him in the jungle, and Anjelica Huston strides across the screen with a brazenness befitting her strong-willed American flyer. The period production design is excellent and the photography is, not surprisingly, beautiful—both in its misty English country scenes and in its lush South American jungle settings.

Waugh's novel, which takes its title from T.S. Eliot's "The Waste Land" ("I will show you fear in a handful of dust"), was published in 1934, not long after the failure of his first marriage and his own real-life excursion to South America. Ismail Merchant and James Ivory also showed interest in filming the novel, but Waugh's literary executor, his son Auberon, was so pleased with Sturridge and Granger's adaptation of *Brideshead Revisited* that he gave them the rights to *A Handful of Dust* for nothing. Sturridge has not betrayed his faith. Something may be lost in the transition from novel to movie, but A HANDFUL OF DUST is still an involving, if unspectacular, film. *(Adult situations.)*

p, Derek Granger; d, Charles Sturridge; w, Tim Sullivan, Derek Granger, Charles Sturridge (based on the novel by Evelyn Waugh); ph, Peter Hannan (Technicolor); ed, Peter Coulson; m, George Fenton; md, George Fenton; prod d, Eileen Diss, Chris Townsend; set d, Stephanie McMillan; cos, Jane Robinson; makeup, Sally Sutton.

Drama   **Cas.**   **(PR:C MPAA:PG)**

HANNA'S WAR**½   (1988) 148m Golan-Globus/Cannon c

Ellen Burstyn *(Katalin Senesh)*, Maruschka Detmers *(Hanna Senesh)*, Anthony Andrews *(Squadron Leader McCormack)*, Donald Pleasence *(Rosza Gabor)*, David Warner *(Capt. Julian Simon)*, Vincenzo Ricotta *(Yoel Palgi)*, Christopher Fairbank *(Ruven Dafne)*, Rob Jacks *(Peretz Goldstein)*, Serge El-Baz *(Tony)*, Eli Gorenstein *(Aba Berdichev)*, Josef El-Dror *(Yonah Rosen)*, Rade Serbedaij *(Capt. Ivan)*, Miodrag Krivokapic *(Col. Illya)*, Dorota Stalinska *(Maritza)*, George Dillon *(Milenko)*, Teri Tordai *(Baroness Hatvany)*, Yehuda Efroni *(Sandor)*, Agi Margitai *(Professor Ravas)*, John Stride *(Dr. Komoly)*, Patrick Monckton *(Kalosh)*, Jeff Gerner *(Lt. Colonel Simmonds)*, Shimon Finkel *(Ben Gurion)*, Ingrid Pitt *(Margit)*, Jon Rumney *(Uncle Egon)*, Magda Faluhelyi *(Aunt Ella)*, Emma Lewis *(Cousin Evi)*, Russell Porter *(George)*, Nigel Hastings *(Jancsi)*, Patsy Byrne *(Rosie)*, Istvan Hunyadkurthy *(Smuggler)*, Barry Langford *(Air Commodore Hadley)*, Rami Baruch *(Enzo Sireni)*, Avi Koren *(Eliyahu Golomb)*, Mordechai Tenenbaum *(Avigur)*, Peter Czajkowski *(Andy)*, Tamas Philippovich *(Andras)*, Jozsef Lakky *(Ticket Clerk)*, Terez Varhegyi *(Marietta)*, Gabor Varadi *(Young Sergeant)*, Jozsef Imcze *(Hungarian Policeman)*, Gyorgy Gonda *(German Officer)*, Miklos Nagy, Istvan Lakatos *(Detectives)*, Tamas Farkas *(Hotel Clerk)*, Zsuzsa Palos, Laura Bokonyi, Magda Darvas *(Female Prisoners)*, Jon Varady *(Guard)*, Balazs Blasko *(Male Secretary)*, Arpad Ladanyi *(Jewish Refugee)*, Csaba Pethes *(Porter)*, Imre Szalai *(Sergeant)*.

One of Israel's great martyrs is Hanna Senesh, a Hungarian-born poet and daughter of a prominent playwright who emigrated to Palestine in 1938. Recruited into the British secret service in 1944, she was parachuted into Yugoslavia with instructions to make her way into Hungary, where she was to help establish escape routes for downed Allied fliers. Promptly captured, she was taken to Budapest, tortured, tried, and finally executed even as Soviet tanks were entering the city, and today she lies in the martyr's cemetery on Mt. Herzl. That this fascinating story, the stuff of true heroes, deserves wider renown is almost certainly what prompted Israeli producers Menahem Golan and Yoram Globus to make HANNA'S WAR. Unfortunately, the Golan-Globus touch that has graced such sensitive examinations of current affairs as DEATH WISH 4; DELTA FORCE; and INVASION U.S.A. similarly doom this film. Maruschka Detmers (of Godard's PRENOM: CARMEN, but best known for her role in THE DEVIL IN THE FLESH and its notorious oral sex scene) plays Senesh, who flees to Palestine after Hungarian fascists prevent her from becoming president of the literary society at school because she is Jewish. In Palestine she studies agriculture, then mysteriously becomes a fisherwoman, living in a tent on the beach and writing poems by candlelight. Recruited by the British along with an international collection of Jewish refugees, she guts out the training and is soon parachuting into Yugoslavia, but is captured crossing into Hungary, coming up against tag-team villains Warner and Pleasence. Both want to know the usual—codes, contacts, and the like—but Detmers refuses even to give her name. Eventually, though, the daily round of torture and degradation proves too much and she admits her identity. Immediately they track down her mother, Burstyn, who has been living more or less in hiding, and arrest her. With the Russians closing in on Budapest, Detmers suddenly finds herself receiving much kinder treatment and at one point even believes she will be freed, until it is suddenly announced that all prisoners are to be taken to Germany. Warner, however, infuriated at the way she has refused to cooperate, has Detmers taken off the trucks and turned over to him for trial. In court she is found guilty of treason, then gives a stirring speech that makes everyone in the court ashamed of their collaboration with the Germans. In fact, the presiding judges are so shaken by her remarks that they disappear before the sentencing, and Warner takes it on himself to sign the death warrant and have the execution carried out.

This could have been a fine film in different hands, but under Golan's direction it all becomes utterly trivialized. The absolute nadir occurs as the Jewish fighters join with the Yugoslavian guerrillas to attack a German train they believe to be carrying weapons. To a thumping, Eurodisco, pseudo-CHARIOTS OF FIRE score, they charge, taking heavy casualties and killing lots of Nazis before they capture the train, which turns out to hold half-dead Jews bound for the camps—in a scene with the potential

for real power, but which ends up flat and banal, simply because of its music. The gorgeous Detmers' commitment to the part is obvious, but, with the exception of the torture scenes, she seems just too glamorous and single-mindedly devoted to her mission to ring true; Ellen Burstyn, despite top billing, is in only a few scenes and leaves little lasting impression. On the plus side, however, are the performances of David Warner and Donald Pleasence, two of the best bad guys in the business. Released in Israel on the 40th anniversary of independence, this is clearly Golan's heartfelt attempt to make a patriotic classic. Just as clearly, he has fallen short of the mark. *(Violence, adult situations.)*

p, Menahem Golan, Yoram Globus; d, Menahem Golan; w, Menahem Golan (based on the books *The Diaries of Hanna Senesh* by Hanna Senesh and *A Great Wind Cometh* by Yoel Palgi); ph, Elemer Ragalyi; ed, Alain Jakubowicz; m, Dov Seltzer; prod d, Kuli Sander; art d, Tividar Bertalan, Tibor Nell, Michal Japhet; set d, Fred Carter; spec eff, Fereni Habetler, Gabor Budahazy, Nany Rosenstein, Alon Meir, Moshe Klugman; cos, John Mollo; stunts, Pinter Tamas; makeup, Vered Hochman Shubert, Christine Allsopp.

War   **(PR:C-O MPAA:NR)**

HEARTBREAK HOTEL*   (1988) 93m Touchstone-Silver Partners III/BV c

David Keith *(Elvis Presley)*, Tuesday Weld *(Marie Wolfe)*, Charlie Schlatter *(Johnny Wolfe)*, Angela Goethals *(Pam Wolfe)*, Jacque Lynn Colton *(Rosie Pantangellio)*, Chris Mulkey *(Steve Ayres)*, Karen Landry *(Irene)*, Tudor Sherrard *(Paul Quinine)*, Paul Harkins *(Brian Gasternick)*, Noel Derecki *(Tony Vandelo)*, Dana Barron *(Beth Devereux)*, T. Graham Brown *(Jerry Schilling)*, Dennis Letts *(Alan Fortas)*, Stephen Lee Davis *(George Klein)*, Blue Deckert *(Jones)*, Michael Costello *(Dr. Charles Devereux)*, John L. Martin *(Sheriff Abrams)*, John Hawkes *(Talent Show M. C.)*, Jerry Haynes *(Mr. Hansen)*, Clark Devereux *(Teacher)*, Miles Mutchler *(Furniture Salesman)*, Ruth Sadlier *(Aunt Anne)*, Cheryl Beckham *(Nurse)*, Al Dvorin *(Himself)*, Monica Devereux *(Monica)*, Hal Ketchum *(Steve's Friend)*, Urban Kneupper *(Accordian Player)*, Debra Luijtjes *(Cheryl)*, Christine M. Poole *(Judy)*, Diane Robin *(Donna)*.

© BUENA VISTA

Easily one of the worst releases from a major studio this year, HEARTBREAK HOTEL is a torturously inept effort that asks, What would happen if Elvis Presley came into your life? Sanctioned and sanitized by the all-powerful Graceland representatives who protect *His* image, the film presents an idealized Elvis, one untouched by the weight, drug, and mental problems that began to destroy him circa 1972, the year in which this movie is set. The story takes place in a small town in Ohio, where teenage rock 'n' roller Schlatter is once again prevented from participating in the high-school talent show because the conservative selection committee won't abide by the anti-Vietnam War lyrics of his song. Depressed, Schlatter would like to turn to his mother, Weld, for comfort, but she is too busy getting drunk with her redneck boy friend, Mulkey. Divorced, lonely, and a devoted Elvis fan, Weld has neglected her teenage son, young daughter (Goethals), and her business—a run-down hotel named "Flaming Star" (the title of a 1960 Elvis film). After a bitter confrontation, Weld tries to make up with her children by taking them to an Elvis Presley double-feature at the drive-in. During the show Schlatter bemoans the terminal "un-coolness" of Elvis since he has rejected rock 'n' roll, gone Las Vegas, donned ridiculous Liberace-like jumpsuits, and ended his shows by singing "The Battle Hymn of the Republic." Weld counters with her memories of the rebellious and dangerous Elvis that first burst onto the scene in the mid-1950s. This rejuvenated family situation does not last long, however, as Weld goes off with Mulkey once again, is physically abused by him, gets in an auto accident, and is hospitalized. Determined to improve the quality of his mom's life, Schlatter decides to bring Elvis to see her (he just happens to be playing in Cleveland that very week). Knowing that it would be impossible to get close to Elvis, Schlatter baits the King with a local waitress (Colton) dressed up to look like Elvis' beloved mother, Gladys, and then kidnaps the singer after the concert. When Elvis (Keith) comes to (the teens have chloroformed him), he angrily rejects Schlatter's pleas for help. He is stopped in his tracks, however, when the boy attacks him for selling out to the establishment and becoming a glorified lounge lizard, saying, "You used to be cool, you used to be a rebel. . . a badass." This hits the King right where he lives (before the concert he had expressed a desire to get back in touch with "the kids" of America) and he agrees to help Schlatter. With his bushy sideburns shaved to their 1950s length and dressed up in his Schlatter's father's vintage clothing, Elvis once again looks like the man who sang "Blue Suede Shoes." When Weld comes back from the hospital, she is shocked and thrilled to have Elvis in her home, and soon the King is entertaining the neighbors, cutting the lawn, helping renovate the hotel, coaxing little Goethals to sleep with the lights off, bedding Weld, and lecturing Schlatter about patriotism. Unfortunately, Elvis also turns the hotel into a mini Graceland and tension builds between him and Schlatter. Sensing it is time for him to go, Elvis patches things up with Schlatter by invading the high-school talent show and performing a rousing duet of "Heartbreak Hotel" with the teen that melts the cold hearts of the selection committee. Meeting the "Memphis Mafia" at a small airport outside of town, Elvis bids good-bye to his new family and thanks Schlatter for reminding him what it felt like to be a "badass."

Poorly written and clumsily directed by 29-year-old Steven Spielberg protege Chris Columbus, HEARTBREAK HOTEL would be pure torture if it were not so unintentionally funny. The film is so ineptly executed that one actually starts to wonder if it is intended as camp or parody. Under the control of a director with some grasp of the magnitude of Presley's influence on popular culture, this film could have been a powerful examination of the effect Elvis had on us and the forces that ultimately destroyed him. Instead, we are left with an inane "high concept" Hollywood product that will please no one—especially the blindly devoted Elvis fans who *adored* his Vegas persona. Director Columbus' idea of a visual style is to impose cartoonish blue and red gels on the lighting scheme and toss in an occasional sweeping camera move that makes no logical sense and lends a false sense of drama to the shot. His attention to period detail is nonexistent. Though set in 1972, HEARTBREAK HOTEL looks and feels like a contemporary made-for-television movie. The haircuts are wrong, the clothes are wrong, the attitudes are wrong, the original music is wrong, and the dialog is wrong. No effort was made to capture the feel of the early 1970s, save for a few tie-dyed shirts and a scene where Elvis and young Goethals play the old board game "Mystery Date."

Columbus' direction of the actors is even worse. Charlie Schlatter (18 AGAIN) must be the most unappealing young actor working in films today, and his performance here is self-conscious, smug, arrogant, condescending, and thoroughly perfunctory. As for the adults, they are allowed to simply flounder. The usually wonderful Tuesday Weld, who actually appeared in an Elvis movie (WILD IN THE COUNTRY, 1961), is reduced to staring lovingly at her idol while he sets about straightening out her life. Given the unenviable task of playing Elvis Presley, David Keith, who bears no resemblance to him, resorts to copying the well-known body movements and voice of the King. While the choreography is correct, the essence is missing and Keith never succeeds in persuading the viewer that he is Elvis. On the other hand, Jacque Lynn Colton, as the waitress who masquerades as Gladys Presley, is wonderfully funny and seems to be the only actor in the entire film who understands how the material should be played.

The ultimate blame for the film's failure must be laid on the shoulders of Columbus, however. His wretched screenplay is so artless that one becomes numbed by the onslaught of insipid and treacly cliches. The opening titles inform us that the film is a fantasy, and it is, but not for the reasons stated. Made in conjunction with the watchdogs from Graceland, the true fantasy here is not what would happen if Elvis entered your life, but that Elvis, by 1972, was still a salvageable talent. It is both absurd and amusing to think that the Elvis of 1972 *even for a fleeting moment* thought that he had abandoned his musical roots or fretted about losing touch with the youth of America. The Elvis of 1972 was a totally self-indulgent, lazy entertainer who was content to live excessively while squandering his considerable talent on mundane material intended to pander to the lowest common denominator. He had become the symbol of everything that was wrong with the music business and it is this image that the punks rebelled against. Yes, the film does make a token effort to address the dismaying direction that Elvis' career had taken after his stint in the Army, but the Elvis presented here is the fantasy that the fans would prefer to believe in and not the pathetic self-parody he had become. Columbus' screenplay is so incoherent that it seems to be criticizing the conservative Elvis persona that Colonel Parker had created while, at the same time, embracing blindly patriotic values (there is much flag-waving and an implicit criticism of the anti-war movement here). What makes this notion even more insidious is that Elvis is shown to uphold traditional, wholesome American values, while there is no hint of the pill-popping, gun-wielding, cruel, paranoid, and abusive Elvis that had taken hold by 1972. At the end of this film there is no indication that Elvis would become horribly obese and die due to severe drug abuse a mere five years later. Like visiting Graceland, which is bereft of any reference to Elvis Presley's horrifying decline, HEARTBREAK HOTEL is indeed a fantasy and just as dishonest. (*Profanity, sexual situations.*)

p, Lynda Obst, Debra Hill; d, Chris Columbus; w, Chris Columbus; ph, Stephen Dobson (Metrocolor); ed, Raja Gosnell; m, Georges Delerue; md, Robert Kraft; prod d, John Muto; art d, Dan Webster; set d, Anne Kuljian; spec eff, Randy E. Moore; cos, Nord Haggerty; ch, Monica Devereux; makeup, Gigi Coker.

Fantasy   Cas.   (PR:C MPAA:PG-13)

HEAT AND SUNLIGHT**   (1988) 98m Snowball-New Front Alliance bw

Rob Nilsson (*Mel Hurley*), Consuelo Faust (*Carmen*), Don Bajema (*Mitch*), Ernie Fosselius (*Bobby*), Bill Bailey (*Barney*), Bill Ackridge, Lester Cohen, Bob Elross, Burns Ellison, Dan Leegant, Herb Mills, Richard A. Rohleder (*Salesmen*), Russell Murphy (*Adam*), Lynn "Chrystie" Ana (*Raven De La Croix*).

Powerful, disturbing, excruciatingly honest, and occasionally hilarious, HEAT AND SUNLIGHT is the extraordinary fourth film from Rob Nilsson, a San Franciscan who has become one of America's most important independent filmmakers. After cowriting, codirecting, and coproducing NORTHERN LIGHTS, which won the

award for Best First Film at the 1979 Cannes Film Festival, Nilsson went on to write and direct two films on his own: ON THE EDGE (1985), starring Bruce Dern as an aging distance runner in a story that one critic called "ROCKY for Social Democrats," and SIGNAL 7, which follows two San Francisco cab drivers through one eventful night. Dedicated to John Cassavetes, whose style Nilsson's most closely resembles, SIGNAL 7 introduced the essence of the filmmaking technique that Nilsson calls "direct action cinema," whereby he films his improvising actors on videotape and transfers the edited results to 35mm film. In HEAT AND SUNLIGHT, which focuses on the final 16 hours of a collapsing love affair, Nilsson polishes that approach, and also steps from behind the camera to give a deeply emotional performance as the film's star.

On the day before his 40th birthday, photojournalist Nilsson returns to San Francisco after an assignment in the Nevada desert, expecting to be met by his dancer-choreographer girl friend, Faust. When she doesn't appear, he believes it confirms his suspicions that Faust is having an affair with her dance partner (Murphy), and, consumed by jealousy, Nilsson begins to withdraw into himself, periodically flashing back 17 years to his impassioned attempts to use his camera to bring attention to the misery and starvation that devastated Biafra during the final days of its unsuccessful struggle for national liberation. His best friend, pilot Bajema, was with him then, and now he tries to persuade Nilsson to confront Faust with his fears rather than "getting Norwegian" about them—avoiding Faust and sinking into anguished, self-destructive isolation. Nilsson listens to Bajema but doesn't hear him, and when another friend, Fosselius, comes to his apartment to try out his new stand-up comedy routine, Nilsson is impatient, his obsession and insecurity mushrooming, his rage boiling over. Alone, he plasters his walls—still covered by photos of Biafran children with distended stomachs—with erotic photos of Faust, imagines her with Murphy, and winds tighter and tighter until he appears ready to snap. Finally, he goes with Bajema to a bar, where they listen to a group of aging conventioneers talk about relationships, and, inspired by them, Nilsson phones Faust, only to discover that Murphy is at her apartment. After racing there, he orders the bigger Murphy to leave. When he won't, Nilsson absurdly tries to force him to take a banana, as if this action will drive Murphy away. Then Nilsson begins stuffing the banana and other pieces of fruit inside his own shirt, and when this, too, fails, he desperately tackles Murphy, who easily subdues him and then leaves. Nilsson and Faust have a rapprochement, but when he notices that she has taken his picture from her wall, he flies into rage, punches a mirror, and throws something at Faust before she slaps him. Almost immediately, however, their violence becomes violent lovemaking—one of the most kinetic and erotic love scenes in recent memory. Afterwards, in repose, Nilsson demands that Faust choose between him and Murphy. She does. They are finished. Although devastated, Nilsson goes with Bajema to the strip club where Fosselius is performing his punchlineless jokes. ("It was really hot today. How hot was it? It was pretty darn hot.") After performing, Fosselius disappears into the streets of the down-and-out Tenderloin district, and Murphy and Nilsson go searching for him. At the end of a darkened alley, Fosselius, some bums, strippers, and the conventioneers are waiting to begin a surprise birthday party for Nilsson. Later he returns to his apartment and takes both the photos of Faust and Biafra from his walls. This passionate lover of both humanity and a woman who has chosen another takes the first steps to letting go of a painful past. From beginning to end, HEAT AND SUNLIGHT vibrates with stunningly real emotions, its characters so believable and its sense of poignant intimacy so all-encompassing that one even hesitates to talk about *performances*. At the film's center, Nilsson is magnificent, an electric bundle of exposed nerve endings as he delivers an astonishingly honest and passionate portrayal of man driven by jealousy and insecurity to the breaking point. He is by turns morose, contemplative, volcanic, violent, tender, irrational, and absurdly funny, but there is never any question of the genuineness of his emotions, and at times his pain is so real that it becomes difficult to watch. Likewise, there is a tremendous immediacy and sincerity in the performances of the other actors, particularly that of Don Bajema, the faithful buddy who, having experienced a similarly painful end to a relationship and gone through his own period of isolation and self-destruction, stands by Nilsson, demonstrating the redemptive power of friendship that is one of HEAT AND SUNLIGHT's main themes.

Means and ends are so closely related in HEAT AND SUNLIGHT that it is impossible to evaluate the film without considering it in terms of Nilsson's "direct action cinema" technique. As with SIGNAL 7, most of the dialog and many of the situations here are improvised, using Nilsson's 30-page script as an outline. He and the other actors rehearsed for several months and delved deeply into their characters' backgrounds before going before the cameras. Nilsson's freewheeling visual approach to filmmaking is as indebted to video technology as it is to the documentary style of his *cinema verite* predecessors. With HEAT AND SUNLIGHT he has again recorded the action on videotape, but this time, instead of working in color, Nilsson shot his film in black and white, using the Betacam format, three-tube color cameras, and a recorder that was set to receive only the signal from the green tube, which provided the best flesh tones and shades of gray. This technique allowed for a sharper (though still grainy) film-to-video transfer and avoided some of the "smearing" of images that plagued SIGNAL 7. By choosing to work on videotape, Nilsson was able to do considerably longer takes than film generally affords, and by employing 360-degree lighting and two hand-held cameras for every scene, he allowed the actors to act, react, and range over the sets and locations without ever having to consider their relation to a camera setup, providing the best possible environment for his cast's inspired, naturalistic improvisations. Although Tomas Tucker, the director of photography for SIGNAL 7, served in that capacity again for HEAT AND SUNLIGHT, no less than nine cameramen shot the movie and were given a free hand by Nilsson to do their own framing, keeping in mind his desire to "see tension in the frame." Sixty hours of tape were then skillfully edited down to 98 minutes of film, and the results are nothing less than fascinating.

Occasionally, the film's pace lags a little, but this is less the result of pedestrian editing or the dramatic lulls that have plagued so many improvised projects than of the film's adherence to the way events unfold in real life. The narrative flow is also punctuated with expressionistic visualizations of Nilsson's thoughts, fantasies, and memories—including repeated footage of Biafra and romantic interludes with Faust. Often HEAT AND SUNLIGHT has the look of the kind of still photography that adorns Nilsson's walls (those photos were actually taken by the film's producers, photographers Steve and Hildy Burns), and the tempestuous love scene between Nilsson and Faust is reminiscent of painter Robert Longo's anguished, societally tossed subjects. Moreover, the film's arresting visuals are evocatively reenforced by a score taken from David Byrne and Brian Eno's inventive fusion of African music and Western bric-a-brac speech, "My Life in the Bush of Ghosts." The cost for shooting all of this was $68,000, and the budget for the entire production was under $500,000, with everyone who worked on the project deferring their salaries. The result is an amazingly moving, wholly believable, visually dazzling study of romance, passion, rage, jealously, compassion, and friendship that may not be for everyone, but that will be unforgettable for many. *(Nudity, sexual situations, adult situations, profanity.)*

p, Steve Burns, Hildy Burns; d, Rob Nilsson; w, Rob Nilsson; ph, Tomas Tucker; ed, Henk Van Eeghen; m/l, David Byrne, Brian Eno, Mark Adler, David Schickele, Michael Small; prod d, Hildy Burns, Steve Burns; ch, Consuelo Faust.

Drama **(PR:O MPAA:NR)**

HELL COMES TO FROGTOWN** (1988) 86m NW c

Rowdy Roddy Piper *(Sam Hell)*, Brian Frank *(Comdr. Toty)*, Sandahl Bergman, William Smith.

Another of those futuristic, post-Apocalypse science-fiction dramas, HELL COMES TO FROGTOWN features a retired professional wrestler, a couple of good-looking babes, some familiar faces, and a bunch of giant frogs. Piper is Sam Hell, one of the last fertile males in the world and a notorious outlaw. As the film opens, he has been captured and is being beaten by Smith, whose daughter Piper raped (she drops the charges when she learns she is pregnant). Piper is rescued by "Medtech," an agency charged with repopulating the world, who fit him with an electronic codpiece so that they can control his procreative urges and assure that he doesn't waste his precious fluids consorting with infertile women. He is then forced to go on a dangerous mission into mutant territory to rescue a bevy of fertile women who have been captured by Commander Toty (Frank), the frog ruler of Frogtown. Piper is accompanied on the mission by Bergman and Verrell, who keep him in a perpetual state of arousal for the job at hand. Arriving in Frogtown, their plan quickly goes awry when Bergman and Piper are captured, and the former is forced to do the Dance of the Three Snakes while Piper is tortured. He manages to escape, however, with the help of a disenchanted frog exotic dancer and his old desert rat buddy Calhoun. With a cry of "Eat lead, Froggies!" Piper rescues Bergman and the fertile girls and flees into the desert, the big amphibians in hot pursuit, until the escapees' vehicle is damaged and Piper is forced into combat with the mysterious figure who has been selling arms to the frogs. He turns out to be Smith, who rants something about it having been a "man's world" before and whose alias, Commander Sodom, fills in the rest of that particular puzzle. Piper dispatches him, then wrestles with Frank until he throws him off a cliff. Now Piper and Bergman express their love for each other, even though it is clear he still has to impregnate all those gals he rescued earlier.

A case study in how to botch a film, HELL COMES TO FROGTOWN was originally planned as a $150,000 project intended to go straight to video. Then it was decided to cast Bergman, who was under contract to New World for another film. This meant that the whole thing now had to be cast with Screen Actors Guild actors, instantly boosting the budget to $500,000. This was too much for New World's video unit to put up, so it went to the feature division. There the producer decided that the film had more stunts and effects than could be done on $500,000, so the budget soared to $1 million. Next it was determined that Donald G. Jackson, who had originated the project, was not to be trusted with that much money, so R.J. Kizer was brought in as codirector, despite a lack of interest in the project. The two fought constantly, with Jackson coming in at night to age down the spiffy sets Kizer had constructed for Frogtown. Eventually, Jackson was ordered to talk with Kizer only in the trailer and not on the set. When the film was finished, the feature division took one look and decided they didn't want it; apart from one brief booking in Texas, it went straight to video. Jackson, apparently undeterred, is now planning a sequel. *(Nudity, violence, profanity.)*

p, Donald G. Jackson; d, Donald G. Jackson, R.J. Kizer; w, Randall Frakes; spec eff, Steve Wang.

Science Fiction **Cas.** **(PR:O MPAA:R)**

HELLBOUND: HELLRAISER II** (1988) 96m Film Futures/NW c

Ashley Laurence *(Kirsty Cotton)*, Claire Higgins *(Julia)*, Ken Cranham *(Dr. Channard)*, Imogen Boorman *(Tiffany)*, William Hope *(Kyle Macrae)*, Oliver Smith *(Browning)*, Sean Chapman *(Uncle Frank)*, Doug Bradley *(Skinhead Cenobite)*, Simon Bamford *(Butterball Cenobite)*, Barbie Wilde *(Female Cenobite)*.

This much-anticipated sequel to Clive Barker's successful directorial debut, HELLRAISER, is, unfortunately, a chaotic affair that assaults the viewer with a jumble of horrific images but fails to leave a lasting impression. Although publishing commitments kept Barker's participation to a minimum here (he's listed as executive producer), he did write the treatment and assigned the screenplay to fellow Liverpudlian Peter Atkins, whom Barker had known since their days together at the Dog Company theater ensemble. First-timer Tony Randel, a New World veteran who has worked at everything from the mail room to special effects to marketing to editing, was chosen to direct.

Picking up a mere two hours after HELLRAISER left off, the sequel finds young Laurence in a mental hospital in the aftermath of the horrific events she witnessed at the first film's climax. Her case comes to the attention of the urbane Dr. Channard (Cranham), who takes a special interest in Laurence and persuades the police to take the bloody mattress upon which Laurence's stepmother, Higgins, was flayed (check HELLRAISER for the details) to his home for further research. A young intern, Hope, befriends Laurence and introduces her to another patient, Boorman, a mute, autistic girl expert at solving puzzles. Unbeknownst to anyone is the fact that Cranham has a collection of Chinese puzzle boxes that caused all the trouble in HELLRAISER, and that he is obsessed with opening the gate to hell—the land of the Cenobites. Laurence, whose outlandish stories are scoffed at by Hope, sees the skinless form of her father in her room one day and watches in horror as he writes a message in his own blood that begs for her help. It seems he is trapped in hell, and wants his daughter to rescue him. Meanwhile, Cranham brings home a deeply disturbed patient (he thinks his body is covered with bugs) and sets him down on the bloody mattress. After handing the madman a straight razor, Cranham watches in horror as his patient slashes himself to death. The blood seeps into the mattress and reanimates Higgins, who emerges from the fabric skinless. Hope, who has become suspicious of his superior and broken into his office to look for information, witnesses the disgusting spectacle and is terrified. Although she has no skin, Higgins succeeds in seducing Cranham into providing her victims so that she can suck the life from them and grow her epidermis back. In return, Higgins agrees to show the perverse Cranham the gates of hell, where the line between pain and pleasure is blurred for eternity. Hope escapes undetected and, now believing Laurence's outlandish tales, checks her out of the hospital. The pair returns to the house to find Higgins, who now has skin. She seduces Hope, sucking the life out of him, knocks out Laurence, and then lives up to her end of the bargain by taking Cranham hellbound. While Cranham marvels at the myriad of sensual tortures there, Laurence takes Boorman from the hospital and has her solve one of the puzzle boxes, thereby allowing her to enter the Dark Side and rescue her father. Avoiding the bizarre Cenobites at every turn, Laurence and Boorman search for the former's father, while Cranham himself is turned into the most powerful Cenobite of all. To Laurence's horror, she discovers that it was her evil Uncle Frank (Chapman) who summoned her into hell, not her father. In a flurry of betrayals, high weirdness, and special effects, Higgins, Chapman, and the original Cenobites (who learn they were once human), are killed and it looks as if Cranham will rule hell. Just as he is about to kill Boorman, however, a once-again revitalized Higgins appears and rescues the girl. As it turns out, the hero is really Laurence in Higgins' skin, and together the two young women escape hell and reenter the living world.

When one considers the distinct lack of any new or impressive talent in horror films of late, it's not surprising to find genre aficionados flocking to Clive Barker as if he were the messiah. Unfortunately, Barker's output does not appear to match his promise. Fans of his early fiction have recently expressed dismay at a perceived decline in his writing, and it seems that with his newfound popularity—which spans several mediums—he may be spreading his talents a bit too thin. What made HELLRAISER both so interesting and so frustrating was that it introduced of a fresh, intelligent, obsessive, and highly personal vision to the screen, then disarmed it with a haphazard cinematic style that concentrated on the peaks at the expense of the valleys—in fact, there are damn few valleys at all. Instead, the film is a constant barrage of grotesqueness that barely slows down to develop into anything intelligible. This style may work in a wild roller-coaster ride like THE EVIL DEAD, but Barker has intellectual pretensions that are ill-served by the slam-bang treatment. Certainly there are some unforgettable images in both HELLRAISER and HELLBOUND, but the glue that binds these moments together is missing, and both films tend to fall apart. While the obsessive lust that drives the Higgins character to horrific extremes in HELLRAISER was almost enough to carry that film, there is no such straw to cling to in HELLBOUND. A token effort is made to explain the origins of the intriguing Cenobites, but there is little else in the way of character or thematic development, and the film collapses into a bloody mess of bravura set-pieces that never add up to a satisfying whole. Barker, Atkins, and director Randel may succeed when it comes to the gut-churning elements, but they fail to present Barker's peculiar psychosexual obsessions in an even remotely coherent or affecting manner, nightmare logic notwithstanding. Barker devotees will dismiss such charges by claiming the extensive cuts required by the MPAA effectively watered down the more challenging portions of the film (the film went before the MPAA seven times before the initial "X" rating was changed to an "R"), but this again applies to the visceral rather than the intellectual, and Barker purports to be concerned with both.

The $4 million film is also haphazard on the purely technical level. Although Robin Vidgeon's cinematography is slick and effective, the set design and optical work in the hellbound sequences leave much to be desired. The endless series of hallways and tunnels that make up hell have a cut-rate haunted house look to them, and in several spots supposedly stone walls bend inward when actors lean against them. The glass painting and matte work look rather cheap as well, and one must assume that most of the effects budget went to the duly impressive Cenobite makeup and costumes. As was the case in HELLRAISER, the acting in HELLBOUND is terribly variable. Clare Higgins, whose character is easily the most interesting in both films, reprises her role but is given little to do—having become more an icon than a character. Ken Cranham is the best addition to the cast and does a fine job as the suave, creepy, and obsessive psychiatrist who just happens to be depraved, too. The Cenobites, again led by Doug Bradley as "Pinhead," are a treat as always. Unfortunately, Ashley Laurence has not developed much as an actress since HELLRAISER and again is not particularly adept at anything besides running and screaming. William Hope, as the heroic intern, is killed off just as his limited range becomes glaringly apparent; newcomer Imogen Boorman barely opens her mouth and makes no impression at all. Gorehounds desperate for a movie they can feel good about will no doubt heap all kinds of undue praise on HELLBOUND, extolling it as an example of intelligently presented graphic bloodletting. In fact, Barker has yet to make a movie on par with the work of George Romero or David Cronenberg, though some have praised him as their equal. One shouldn't close the book on Barker yet; still, he had better fulfill his promise soon, or he may wear out his welcome. *(Extreme violence, gore effects, sexual situations, profanity.)*

p, Christopher Figg; d, Tony Randel; w, Peter Atkins (based on a story by Clive Barker); ph, Robin Vidgeon; m, Christopher Young; prod d, Mike Buchanan.

Horror Cas. (PR:O MPAA:R)

HERO AND THE TERROR** (1988) 96m Golan-Globus/Cannon c

Chuck Norris *(Herrara* "Hero" O'Brien), Brynn Thayer *(Kay Griffith)*, Steve James *(Bill Robinson)*, Jack O'Halloran *(Simon Moon)*, Jeffrey Kramer *(Dwight Hopkins)*, Ron O'Neal *(Mayor)*, Murphy Dunne *(Theater Manager)*, Heather Blodgett *(Betsy)*, Tony DiBenedetto *(Doheny)*, Billy Drago *(Dr. Highwater)*.

Oh, what a sensitive "Man of the 80s" is Chuck Norris! After being beaten to a pulp by a hulking psycho (O'Halloran) who snaps the necks of women and then collects their corpses in a deserted seaside restaurant, police detective Norris is saved when his assailant steps on a rotting ladder rung and falls, knocking himself out. The press assumes Norris beat O'Halloran into submission and declares him a hero. Norris, however, knows the truth and lives in fear that the killer will return to pick up where he left off. Plagued by sweat-drenched nightmares of O'Halloran, Norris goes to see a pretty psychiatrist, Thayer, and falls in love with her. Three years later, she is pregnant with his child, but, being a stubborn modern woman, she refuses to marry him. Norris accepts this, persuades her to move in, and is a doting boy friend catering to her every need during the emotional roller coaster of the last few weeks of her pregnancy. Meanwhile (in a scene that is patently absurd), the clever but mute O'Halloran breaks out of his cell at the mental institution by cutting through the iron bars with dental floss dipped in pumice. Lumbering across the grounds, O'Halloran steals a van and proceeds to drive it off a cliff and into the ocean. Although his body is never found, the authorities assume he is dead. We, and Norris, know better, however, and when women begin disappearing from the ladies' room at a newly refurbished movie theater (the Wiltern, a 2,400-seat palace built in 1931), the press begins clamoring that the "Terror" is alive and up to his old tricks. After talking with O'Halloran's psychiatrist (the oddly cast Drago), Norris comes to believe that O'Halloran, who behaves like an animal, has made a den for himself somewhere inside the bowels of the movie theater. Norris' partner, Kramer, is stationed at the theater to listen for any disturbances after closing. Predictably, O'Halloran makes quick work of Kramer and dumps the body in the alley. This scene is intercut with Thayer finally giving birth to Norris' daughter (death, birth, the cycle of life, get it?). An initial sweep of the theater fails to flush out the killer, but after Norris finally thinks to check the building's floor plan, he discovers an old prop room that had been bricked over and decides that must be where the Terror is hiding. Determined to face his fears alone, Norris delays the back-up team so he can fight O'Halloran *mano a mano*. After much grunting, kicking, and punching, the Hero and the Terror stagger onto the rooftop of the theater, where Norris manages to heft the huge O'Halloran onto his shoulders and dump him through a skylight. The weighty villain crashes through the glass, scaffolding, a heavy wooden drop ceiling, and finally comes to rest with a resounding thud on the back of seats J, K, L, and M, aisle 47, in the main theater. Sporting a few cuts and bruises, Norris returns to the hospital. Upon entering the building, he spots a priest and in the next shot he flings open the room to Thayer's door. With blood coagulating on his mighty brow, Norris smiles and puts his arm around the priest. Thayer smiles back and gushes an immediate "I do." Cut back to Norris grinning and the priest looking a bit uncomfortable. Freeze frame. Roll credits.

Norris' attempt to broaden his screen persona by portraying a vulnerable human being instead of a macho killing machine is both admirable and desirable. Unfortunately, the silly script by Dennis Shryack and Michael Blodgett (from his novel) and the routine direction by William Tannen aren't up to Norris' enthusiasm. Norris is an engaging performer and under the right supervision, as in the Andrew Davis-directed CODE OF SILENCE (1985), he demonstrates the same sort of appeal that his mentor, Steve McQueen, had. HERO AND THE TERROR, however, is too disorganized a film to balance genre thrills with the charming scenes of intimacy between a man and a woman. In fact, the scenes between Norris and Brynn Thayer are the best in the film and there is a nice, natural rapport between the actors. It is gratifying to see a more progressive Norris somewhat stumble over his lines in an effort to be understanding and patient with the woman he loves. He does not particularly like her unwillingness to marry, but he seems to respect her position. Only when the script starts to pander to audience expectations do the scenes take on a rather sappy feel, and the ending—where motherhood suddenly compels Thayer to reject her independence—is insulting to women.

Despite their flaws, these scenes work better than the thriller aspect of the film. Although the opening is suspenseful and exciting, the action goes downhill from there. Moreover, from the first shot to the last, Jack O'Halloran's villain is not given an iota of characterization. He is merely a plodding, hulking id that, considering his massive size, does an amazingly good job of hiding itself in small places. The explanation of what drives the Terror is laughable, and because an actor as villainous-looking as Billy Drago is cast as the killer's psychiatrist, one wonders if the doctor and his patient have been in collusion. Without a particularly compelling villain, the action scenes are downright boring. The only thing that makes the rather lethargic investigation interesting is the guided tour of the architecturally wonderful Wiltern Theater. Although crippled by problems, HERO AND THE TERROR is definitely a step in the right direction for Norris, and maybe he will soon prove that CODE OF SILENCE wasn't just a fluke. *(Violence, profanity.)*

p, Raymond Wagner; d, William Tannen; w, Dennis Shryack, Michael Blodgett (based on the novel by Blodgett); ph, Eric van Haren Noman (TVC Color); ed, Christian Adam Wagner; m, David Frank; prod d, Holger Gross; art d, Douglas Dick, Mark Haskins.

Crime Cas. (PR:O MPAA:R)

HIDE AND GO SHRIEK † (1988) 90m New Star/New Star c

Brittain Frye, Donna Baltron, George Thomas, Annette Sinclair, Scott Fults, Ria Pavia, Sean Kanan, Rebunkah Jones, Jeff Levine, Scott Kubay.

Given a brief regional release at the end of 1987, HIDE AND GO SHRIEK is now gaining general release on home video, in an unrated version that promises more graphic gore than an R-rating allows. The standard slasher plot sends four teenage couples sneaking late at night into a department store to celebrate their high school graduation. While playing a game of hide and seek, the kids are killed off one at a time by an unseen maniac.

p, Dimitri Villard; d, Skip Schoolnik; w, Michael Kelly; ph, Eugene Shlugleit; m, John Ross.

Horror Cas. (PR:NR MPAA:R)

HIGH SEASON*½** (1988, Brit.) 104m British Screen-Hemdale-Film Four-Curzon/Hemdale c

Jacqueline Bisset *(Katherine)*, James Fox *(Patrick)*, Irene Papas *(Penelope)*, Sebastian Shaw *(Basil* "Sharpie" Sharp), Kenneth Branagh *(Rick Lamb)*, Lesley Manville *(Carol Lamb)*, Robert Stephens *(Konstantinis)*, Geoffrey Rose *(Thompson)*, Paris Tselois *(Yanni)*, Ruby Baker *(Chloe)*, Mark Williams *(Benny)*, Shelly Laurenti *(June)*, George Diakoyorgio *(Mayor)*, Father Bassili *(Pappas)*, Captain Stelios *(Fisherman)*.

It's tourist season in the small Greek village of Lindos, off the coast of Rhodes, and the once-traditional town is becoming diseased with the commercialism. An enterprising young man, Tselios, is in the process of closing the shop that bears his dead father's name and reopening it as a tourist trap called "Lord Byron," much to the consternation of his mother, Papas. Besides selling t-shirts imprinted with Lord Byron's face, he manufactures and sells modern, silver-studded single-breasted bikinis. He has also commissioned a modern artist, Fox, to create a sculpture for the village square dedicated to the "Unknown Tourist." Fox's estranged wife, Bisset, a celebrated photographer, also lives in the village with their teenage daughter; however, she is in dire financial straits due to the failure of her latest book, *The Light of Greece*, and fears she will have to sell her home. Shaw, a British art expert and a true antique of a man who makes an annual visit to Lindos to see his dear friends Bisset (for whom he openly declares his love) and Baker, suggests Bisset marry him, so that he can support her with his pension. She, however, still loves Fox and plans to sell an ancient Grecian urn given to her by Shaw. When an art dealer offers her $300,000, her financial woes appear to be over. Meanwhile, a daft young British couple—Branagh and Manville—arrive in the village. Branagh is a bottom-rung special agent on assignment for British intelligence who keeps his work a secret from his wife. He is instantly infatuated with Bisset, and Manville and Tselios are drawn to each other because Manville's name (Carol Lamb) is nearly the same as that of Byron's great love, Lady Caroline Lamb. Soon, Manville discovers that Bisset and Shaw are selling the urn, which requires that they smuggle it out of the country, as it is a national treasure. During an evening of excessive drinking and partying in which both locals and tourists partake, the drunken Manville accidentally breaks the urn. Branagh shoves the pieces under the furniture and rushes home. His guilt is discovered, though, by Shaw, who has known all along that the urn was a fake. While Fox and Bisset try to reunite, settling both personal and artistic differences, Shaw informs Bisset that he is about to be arrested for his espionage work in WW II. Back in the town square, Tselios has unveiled the "Unknown Tourist," a grotesque, blockheaded caricature with camera in hand. Driven into a Rambo-like rage, Papas rides into the square on a donkey and, sporting a gunbelt, rifle, and pistol, shoots the statue's head off. Shaw is then greeted by a British intelligence official who, instead of arresting him, assigns him a new identity and home in the Soviet Union. Saddened by Shaw's departure, Bisset and Baker accompany him to his boat and wish him well, shouting *opisthea*—a Greek term which means "the future is behind you." As the boat speeds off, Shaw waves to the friends who stand on the shore behind him.

A witty satire that takes a jab at tourism and commerce, HIGH SEASON, while constructed in a rather sprawling manner, manages to be both comic and serious, not unlike the classic films of Preston Sturges. This is the first feature for Clare Peploe (who won an Oscar for her 1981 short COUPLES AND ROBBERS) and she directs in a loose style perfectly suited for her "on holiday" subject matter. As Diane Kurys did in her underrated 1987 film, A MAN IN LOVE, Peploe shows a promising talent for juggling a number of story lines and characters—a talent that seemed to have disappeared from currency with the death of Jean Renoir. The strong point of HIGH SEASON is its casual structure, which may or may not have been wholly intentional. Characters seem to drift effortlessly from scene to scene, place to place, encounter to encounter. Everything interconnects in this small village and characters continuously run into one another, creating a familial atmosphere. In addition to the main characters, there is a group of a half-dozen pneumatic vacationers who bounce in and out of a number of scenes, dressed in their single-breasted bikinis. There is also a loud, obnoxious fellow who makes a habit of wandering into frame. Like the villagers, the movie audience knows nothing about these peripheral characters other than the fact that they are typical, obnoxious tourists.

Peploe is concerned with more than loud tourists, however. Of deeper interest is the part that native Greeks play in the tourist trade, foregoing their own heritage to make money. It is this strained relationship between the commerce of tourism and the value of classicism that forms the conflict between Bisset's and Fox's characters. While Fox represents all that is modern in art (receiving commissions for sculptures of gigantic cigarettes in equally gigantic ashtrays), Bisset represents the beauty of the past as she tries to recapture the power of the sunlight that hits the Aegean coast (though it is worth remembering that she attempts to peddle a piece of Greek history, her fake urn, in exchange for cash). While Bisset accuses Fox of creating modern monstrosities, he attacks the falseness of her work: "That's not the 'Light of Greece,' that's the Light of Kodak."

HIGH SEASON is a prime example of the sort of work that James Fox and Jacqueline Bisset can do when given rich material. Bisset, in her first theatrical film since 1984's UNDER THE VOLCANO (her appearance in TV's "Napoleon and Josephine" is best forgotten), turns in one of her most praiseworthy performances, while Fox continues a recent string of quality work (ABSOLUTE BEGINNERS; THE WHISTLE BLOWER). The rest of the cast also does a fine job, including Irene Papas in the self-parodying role of the mourning Greek widow; Kenneth Branagh and Lesley Manville as the flighty couple; and veteran stage actor Sebastian Shaw, performing magnificently as the film's most sympathetic and complex character. It is Shaw who professes the philosophy that is at the heart of the film—*opisthea*, the respect one must have for history, for it is from the past that the future hails.

Although this is Peploe's first feature, she is a film veteran, having coscripted Michelangelo Antonioni's ZABRISKIE POINT and husband Bernardo Bertolucci's LUNA. Here she collaborated with brother Mark Peploe (cowriter of THE PASSENGER and THE LAST EMPEROR) and enlisted the service of brilliant cinematographer Chris Menges (THE MISSION; SHY PEOPLE). Also lending a hand was investor Jack Nicholson, a friend of the Peploes' since his appearance in Antonioni's THE PASSENGER. The Nicholson-Mark Peploe connection in HIGH SEASON is pointed to in an in-joke when Shaw is given his new identity—David Locke, Nicholson's character name in THE PASSENGER. *(Nudity, sexual situations.)*

p, Clare Downs; d, Clare Peploe; w, Mark Peploe, Clare Peploe; ph, Chris Menges; ed, Gabriella Cristiani, Peter Dansie; m, Jason Osborn; md, Jason Osborn; m/l, Gioacchino Antonio Rossini, Miklos Theodorakis, Stavros Xarchakos, Vasili Tsitsanis, Youssou Ndour; prod d, Andrew McAlpine; art d, Caroline Hanania, Petros Kapouralis; spec eff, Yannis Samiotis; cos, Louise Stjernsward; makeup, Nicholas Forder.

Comedy/Drama	Cas.	(PR:C-O MPAA:R)

HIGH SPIRITS**   (1988) 96m Vision PDG-Palace/Tri Star c

Peter O'Toole *(Peter Plunkett)*, Steve Guttenberg *(Jack)*, Beverly D'Angelo *(Sharon)*, Daryl Hannah *(Mary Plunkett)*, Liam Neeson *(Martin Brogan)*, Peter Gallagher *(Brother Tony)*, Jennifer Tilly *(Miranda)*, Ray McAnally *(Plunkett Senior)*, Martin Ferrero *(Malcolm)*, Connie Booth *(Marge)*, Aimee Delamain *(Great Granny Plunkett)*, Krista Hornish *(Wendy)*, Donal McCann *(Eamon)*, Mary Coughlan *(Katie)*, Liz Smith *(Mrs. Plunkett)*, Tom Hickey *(Sampson)*, Tony Rohr *(Christy)*, Matthew Wright *(Woody)*, Paul O'Sullivan *(Graham)*, Ruby Buchanan *(Great Aunt Nan)*, Preston Lockwood *(Great Uncle Peter)*, Hilary Reynolds *(Patricia)*, Isolde Cazelet *(Julia)*, Little John Gateman.

© TRI-STAR

This is a surprisingly disjointed movie from one of the most promising directors in the UK, Neil Jordan, whose previous efforts DANNY BOY, THE COMPANY OF WOLVES, and MONA LISA have shown him to be a filmmaker of vision, with an impressive grasp of the medium, who refuses to be pegged. With HIGH SPIRITS, Jordan has again shifted gears and attempted an old-fashioned haunted house comedy-romance along the lines of BLITHE SPIRIT (1945), THE GHOST AND MRS. MUIR (1942), and THE CANTERVILLE GHOST (1944). While the attempt is admirable, the execution is incredibly sloppy—perhaps in part due to some last-minute tampering by the studio. Set in Ireland, the film presents O'Toole as the heir to the ancient Castle Plunkett, a huge, spooky, drafty, leaky castle that has fallen into severe financial straits. Unable to pay the mortgage, O'Toole faces foreclosure by his American lender, who threatens to take ownership and dismantle the castle, ship it to Malibu, and turn it into a theme park called "Irish World." This absurd notion provides O'Toole with the inspiration to make one last ditch-attempt to save his home.

Since the castle is rumored to be haunted by his ancestors, O'Toole and his staff prepare a low-budget version of Disneyland's haunted mansion, taking out ads to lure gullible American tourists as guests. O'Toole's elderly mother (Smith), however, insists that the castle really *is* haunted and that she is regularly visited by the ghost of O'Toole's father (McAnally). Before long the first busload of Americans arrives, and it is an odd lot of characters indeed, including unhappily married couple Guttenberg and D'Angelo; parapsychologist Ferrero, his wife Booth, and their three obnoxious children; dim-witted bombshell Tilly; and quiet priest-to-be Gallagher, who is on a little vacation before taking his final vows. As the bus approaches the castle, O'Toole urges his hapless staff to take their places and begin the phony haunting. The ensuing melee is a disaster, though the plucky castle help do their best to scare the wits out of the Americans. Unfortunately, nobody's buying it, and the evening turns out to be such a failure that all the guests declare their intent to leave the following morning. All except one, that is. Guttenberg learns that his wife's father holds the mortgage on the castle and that Daddy sent D'Angelo on the trip, which she cynically billed as a second honeymoon, to investigate. Guttenberg actually likes the castle and its staff and, after getting blotto with O'Toole, vows that he will do his best to save the place. That night, the drunken Guttenberg stumbles into the wrong room and is witness to a nightly apparition that has been occurring regularly for more than 300 years. The ghostly Hannah, on her wedding night, is chased by her brutish ghost husband Neeson and stabbed. As legend has it, Hannah did not love Neeson and, when she refused to consummate their marriage, he assumed she was in love with another and killed her in a jealous rage. Taken with the beautiful ghost, Guttenberg steps between Hannah and Neeson just as Neeson is about to stab Hannah. Having interceded on her behalf, Guttenberg can now free Hannah from her ghastly fate by declaring his love for her, but this is a bit too much for the American to handle, and, although he is attracted to the spirit, he needs time to think about it. Meanwhile, McAnally—who has revealed himself to O'Toole—leads all the other family ghosts in a haunting designed to convince the Americans that the place is indeed bespooked. After much slapstick comedy, the Yanks are convinced and Guttenberg falls in love with Hannah. At the same time, D'Angelo falls for the ghostly Neeson. In an amiable switch, Hannah and D'Angelo change places, the ghost becoming human and the human dying and becoming a spirit. Hannah is now betrothed to Guttenberg and Neeson spends eternity with D'Angelo, and all's well that ends well as the happy couples dance together in the great hall of Castle Plunkett.

While enough of HIGH SPIRITS succeeds to keep the film watchable, its jerky construction, haphazard comedy, and overwhelming sense of opportunities missed work against it from the very first scene. Despite the considerable amount of production support that went into the filming (it was shot on location in Ireland and on a massive interior castle set at England's famed Shepperton studios), this is easily the weakest effort in director-screenwriter Jordan's solid career. Some of the film's problems may be due to cuts made by the studio. While as of this writing there have been no reports of any such cutting, there are several indications that it may indeed have occurred. In the closing credits, for example, Lynzee Klingman is listed as an "editorial consultant"—the sort of credit that often appears on films with a troubled production history and often is an indication that studio chiefs sent some of their own people in to tinker with the film after the director delivered his final cut. And while the editorial consultant listing is a solid clue to studio tampering, the real test is the film itself. The first third of HIGH SPIRITS is very disjointed, with a rushed feel to it, as if scenes are being cut away from before they have been played out. This truncates the pace and characterizations, robbing the viewer of a chance to get into the film's rhythm and to get to know the characters. All that seems to be left is the slam-bang comic highlights—which often aren't very funny. Another clue potentially supporting the missing footage theory is that scenes mentioned in on-the-set interviews with Jordan and others do not appear in the final cut, although this is not all that uncommon and directors often willingly remove scenes they have shot. Still, there is enough evidence to suggest some final-hour studio interference, and this helps to explain why the film is such a sloppy product from a heretofore controlled director.

Jordan cannot be absolved of blame entirely, however. Regardless of any studio tampering that may have occurred, there are still crippling problems with what did make it onto the screen. In HIGH SPIRITS, Jordan does a much better job at making interesting characters out of the Irish than he does with the Americans. The Irish are warmer, more detailed, and less stereotyped than the Americans, who are a uniformly dim and boorish bunch and behave in cartoonish fashion. Jordan doesn't seem to understand Americans and their behavior is boiled down to a caricature of self-importance, tactlessness, repression, greediness, and superficiality. Some of the actors in the American roles, like the wonderful Connie Booth (who created "Fawlty Towers" with her then-husband John Cleese), are barely given anything to do or say, while others spend the entire film bleating out such "Americanisms" as "Awesome!" With the exception of the puppy-like Guttenberg, Jordan presents us with a fairly unsympathetic and unpleasant bunch, which, combined with its broadly slapstick sense of humor, makes much of HIGH SPIRITS predictable and tedious. Only when Daryl Hannah and Liam Neeson appear on the scene does the film really begin to kick in and take hold in the manner of the 1940s ghostly romances Jordan emulates. Hannah—an actress who can be either wonderful (ROXANNE) or awful (WALL STREET) depending on the director—is a delight here and makes a charming ghost despite her imperfect Irish accent. Her scenes with the miscast Guttenberg (who, for some reason, is Jordan's vision of a typical American) have a persuasive romance and sparkle that almost make one forget the miscues preceding them. Neeson is excellent as well, delivering an exuberant performance that takes the hysterical edge off Beverly D'Angelo's one-note contribution. For his part, Peter O'Toole is allowed to ham it up in a manner reminiscent of late John Barrymore—spending much of the film spouting drolleries while clutching a drink. With these wonderful performances to hang on to, one can almost forgive the ham-handed humor, over-reliance on cheap special effects, and stumbling pace of what could have been a thoroughly entertaining movie. *(Sexual situations.)*

p, Stephen Woolley, David Saunders; d, Neil Jordan; w, Neil Jordan; ph, Alex

Thomson (Rank Color); ed, Michael Bradsell; m, George Fenton; prod d, Anton Furst; art d, Nigel Phelps; set d, Barbara Drake; spec eff, Derek Meddings; cos, Emma Porteous; ch, Micha Bergese; anim, Peter Chiang; stunts, Martin Grace; makeup, Peter Robb-King.

Comedy/Romance   Cas.   (PR:C MPAA:PG-13)

HOLLYWOOD CHAINSAW HOOKERS † (1988) 74m Savage Cinema/Camp Motion Pictures-American Independent

Gunnar Hansen (Cult Leader), Linnea Quigley (Samantha Kelso), Jay Richardson (Jack Chandler), Michelle Bauer (Mercedes), Dawn Wildsmith (Laurie), Dennis Mooney, Jerry Fox, Esther Alyse, Tricia Burns, Michael D. Sonye, Jimmy Williams.

This is another grade-Z horror film from the prolific Fred Olen Ray, a low-budget *auteur* who cranks out several movies a year. A combination of comedy, horror, and *film noir*, the picture begins as private detective Richardson is hired to track down teenage runaway Quigley. The trail leads to a strip club, where Richardson finds the girl doing the bump-and-grind for the slobbering crowd. Before Richardson can haul her in, however, she slips him a mickey, leaving him to come to in the middle of a bizarre blood cult ritual presided over by Gunnar Hansen—"Leatherface" from the original TEXAS CHAIN SAW MASSACRE. Much to his dismay, Richardson discovers that these cultists do not worship Satan, but chainsaws! With lots of blood, female flesh, and campy humor, HOLLYWOOD CHAINSAW HOOKERS went the direct-to-video route.

p, Fred Olen Ray; d, Fred Olen Ray; w, Fred Olen Ray, T.L. Lankford; ph, Scott Ressler (United Color); ed, William Shaffer; m, Michael Perilstein; prod d, Corey Kaplan; cos, Jill Conner.

Comedy/Horror   Cas.   (PR:NR MPAA:NR)

HOLLYWOOD COP †   (1988) 100m Peacock c

Jim Mitchum (Feliciano), Cameron Mitchell (Capt. Bonano), David Goss (Turkey), Julie Schoenhofer (Rebecca), Lincoln Kilpatrick (Jaguar), Troy Donahue (Lt. Maxwell), Aldo Ray (Fong), Larry Lawrence (Joe Fresno).

An all-star cast of low-budget exploitation actors—Cameron Mitchell, Jim Mitchum, Aldo Ray, and Troy Donahue—helps carry this action picture about a husband and wife who are trying to get back their kidnaped son from mobsters determined to collect on the husband's $6-million debt.

p, Moshe Bibiyan, Simon Bibiyan; d, Amir Shervan; w, Amir Shervan; ph, Peter Palian; ed, Ruben Zadurian, Bob Ernst; m, Elton Farokh Ahi; spec eff, Bill Kulzer.

Action   Cas.   (PR:NR MPAA:R)

HOME REMEDY †   (1988) 100m Xero/Kino c

Seth Barrish (Richie Rosenbaum), Maxine Albert (Nancy Smith), Richard Kidney (P.J. Smith), David Feinman (Moshe), John Tsakonas (Donnie), Alexa (Mary), Cynde Kahn (Bambi).

An independent feature from New Jersey that had short theatrical runs in both New York and LA, HOME REMEDY is a film about boredom and how to overcome it. As one character states early on, "Life is boring, then you die." Barrish is Richie Rosenbaum, a 30-year-old bachelor whose home is his fortress. Refusing to leave it or to attempt to battle boredom, he sits around, watches paint dry, plays his harmonica, pays for phone sex, and videotapes the world that passes by his window. Enter Albert, a 40ish neighbor who sets up camp outside Barrish's window and manages to become his friend.

p, Kathis Hersch; d, Maggie Greenwald; w, Maggie Greenwald; ph, Thomas H. Jewett; ed, Pamela Scott Arnold; m, Steve Katz; prod d, Robert P. Kracik.

Comedy   (PR:NR MPAA:NR)

HOT TO TROT*   (1988) 83m WB c

Bob Goldthwait (Fred P. Chaney), Dabney Coleman (Walter Sawyer), John Candy (Voice of Don), Virginia Madsen (Allison Rowe), Jim Metzler (Boyd Osborne), Cindy Pickett (Victoria Peyton), Tim Kazurinsky (Leonard), Santos Morales (Carlos), Barbara Whinnery (Denise), Garry Kluger (Pomeroy), Mary Gross (Ms. French), Liz Torres (Bea), Jocko Marcellino (Marvin), Deanna Oliver (Lorraine), Harry Caesar (Gideon Cole), Allen Williams (Ted Braithwaite), Lonny Price (Frank), Chino "Fats" Williams (Messenger), Angel Salazar (Snake), Henry "Hank" Levy (Marv), John Lisbon Wood (Mike), Jack Whitaker (Himself), Tom Wolski (Michael Murphy), Kevin Furlong (Dennis Riday), Edmund Stoiber (Head Steward), Frank Morriss (Track Announcer), Gilbert Gottfried (Dentist), Dennis Tufano, Alison Moir (Party People), Virginia Eubanks (Sawyer's Secretary), Don (Himself).

The long-awaited teaming of comedian Bob Goldthwait and a talking horse finally materializes in HOT TO TROT, with John Candy providing the voice for the chatty equine. Goldthwait's mother has passed away, leaving half of the family's successful brokerage business to her son and the other half to his skirt-chasing stepfather (Coleman, wearing a ridiculous set of buck teeth). Mom knew how much Coleman hated

her son, and this is her way of getting even for his infidelity. She has also left her son a horse named Don that not only is able to speak but also seems to be more intelligent than a lot of humans, including the simple-minded Goldthwait. While Goldthwait isn't much of a stockbroker, Don helps him out by feeding him stock tips he's overheard at the stable. Soon, Goldthwait's made a fortune and moved into a posh apartment, with Don, who trashes the place when he invites over some "party animals" (birds, goats, etc.). At the office, a beautiful blonde (Madsen) has taken a liking to Goldthwait, while Coleman is plotting to ruin his stepson. Coleman's scheming is not in vain, as Goldthwait soon finds himself bankrupt, with only one chance to redeem himself: he has to ride Don to victory in a horse race in which he will be pitted against a steed owned by Coleman. Put all your money on Don to win.

Yes, it's all very silly, but unfortunately it isn't very funny. HOT TO TROT tries to update the old talking-animal routine by giving Don a talking family (a TV-addicted brother and a philosophical father who dies and is reincarnated as a horse fly) and by giving him a lot of four-letter words to throw around (something Francis the Talking Mule never would have tolerated). John Candy's upbeat delivery works well as the voice of Don, despite the horse's lack of worthwhile dialog, but Dabney Coleman, who has shown a wonderful ability to create memorable characters in the past (DRAGNET), seems hamstrung here by those buck teeth. The manic Goldthwait is a little less manic than in his appearances in the "Police Academy" series (wherein he is billed as "Bobcat"), but his voice is still filled with desperation and it wears thin over the course of the film. On the distaff side, Virginia Madsen (SLAMDANCE) is gorgeous, and only in a movie like this would such a woman be attracted to the likes of Goldthwait. HOT TO TROT had only a brief theatrical run, indicating that the movie-going public just isn't ready for a rebirth of the talking animal movie. Songs include: "Tutti Frutti" (Richard Penniman, Dorothy La Bostrie, Joe Lubin, performed by Little Richard); "Fight for Your Right" (Adam Yauch, Adam Horowitz, Rick Rubin, performed by Beastie Boy); "Shooting Dirty Pool" (Paul Westerberg, Thomas Stinson, Christopher Mars, performed by The Replacements); "Heartbreak Hotel" (Mae Boren Axton, Tommy Durden, Elvis Presley); "Off to See the Wizard" (Harold Arlen, E.Y. Harburg); "Merry-Go-Round Broke Down" (Cliff Friend, Dave Franklin); "We're in the Money" (Harry Warren, Al Dubin). (*Profanity*)

p, Steve Tisch, Wendy Finerman; d, Michael Dinner; w, Stephen Neigher, Hugh Gilbert, Charlie Peters (based on a story by Stephen Neigher, Hugh Gilbert); ph, Victor J. Kemper (Technicolor); ed, Frank Morriss; m, Danny Elfman; m/l, Richard Penniman, Dorothy La Bostrie, Joe Lubin, Adam Yauch, Adam Horowitz, Rick Rubin, Paul Westerberg, Thomas Stinson, Christopher Mars, Mae Boren Axton, Tommy Durden, Elvis Presley, Harold Arlen, E.Y. Harburg, Cliff Friend, Davd Franklin, Harry Warren, Al Dubin; prod d, William Matthews; set d, Judy Cammer; spec eff, Peter Albiez; stunts, Mike McGaughy; makeup, Michael Hancock.

Comedy   Cas.   (PR:C MPAA:PG)

HOUSE ON CARROLL STREET, THE*   (1988) 101m Orion c

Kelly McGillis (Emily Crane), Jeff Daniels (Cochran), Mandy Patinkin (Ray Salwen), Jessica Tandy (Miss Venable), Jonathan Hogan (Alan), Remak Ramsay (Senator Byington), Ken Welsh (Hackett), Christopher Rhode (Stefan), Charles McCaughan, Randle Mell (Salwen Aides), Michael Flanagan (Senator), Paul Sparer (Randolph Slote), Brian Davies (Warren), Mary Diveny (Maid), Bill Moor (Dr. Teperson), Patricia Falkenhain (Woman in the House), Frederick Rolf (FBI Director), Anna Berger (Funeral Woman), Cliff Cudney (McKay), Alexis Yulin (Sackadorf), Trey Wilson (Lt. Sloan), William Duff-Griffin (FBI Librarian), George Ede (Conductor), John Carpenter (Gateman), Jamey Sheridan (Porter), P.J. Barry (Barber), Boris Leskin (Hurwitz), Marat Yusim (Bistrong), James Rebhorn (The Official), Howard Sherman (Boria), John Randolph Jones (Agent Simpson), David Hart (Stage Manager), Maeve McGuire (Mrs. Byington), Suzanne Slade (Senator Byington's Daughter), Todd De Freitas (Senator Byington's Son), Gregory Jbara (Office Boy), James Tew (Sam), Polly O'Malley, Maureen Moore (Manicurists), Alice Drummond (Woman at Hearing), Tony Carreiro (Xanthias), Robert Stanton (Dionysus), Daniel Mills (Bartender), Jim Babchak (Salwen Aide in Senate Hearing), Melba La Rose (Receptionist), Stephen Gleason (Man at Theater Bar), Christopher Cusack, Elizabeth A. Reilly (Theater-goers), Skip Rose (Sloan's Partner), Frank Patton (Sergeant), Gaylord C. Mason (Theater Manager), Rabbi Morris S. Friedman (Rabbi), John-Kenneth Hoffman (Waiter).

Of the three Hollywood thrillers released in early 1988 (the others were FRANTIC and MASQUERADE), THE HOUSE ON CARROLL STREET is easily the most traditional. Hearkening back to the romantic thrillers of the 1950s, THE HOUSE ON CARROLL STREET takes innocent, trustworthy characters and places them in mysterious and dangerous situations. Set in 1951, the film and its characters express the era's mood of uncorrupted patriotism and a blind trust in America's government. McGillis, the film's central character, is a concerned citizen who has faith in both elected officials and the American people. A symbol of the average American of the day, McGillis becomes increasingly distrustful of the government as it indulges in Communist witch-hunts, rabid McCarthyism, and the trampling of First Amendment rights. The picture opens as the Left-leaning McGillis, a *Life* magazine employee, is under fire from Patinkin, a Roy Cohn-type senator with slick hair plastered away from his stern face, for refusing to "name names." Patinkin comes down hard on McGillis, spearheading an FBI smear campaign that results in her being fired from *Life*. Desperate for work, she takes a job reading to Tandy, a wealthy matron with failing eyesight. Coincidentally, there is a mysterious house across from Tandy's backyard in which German refugees are being hidden by none other than Patinkin. Peering inside the house a la an Alfred Hitchcock heroine, McGillis becomes a witness to a mysterious plot involving government importation of Nazi scientists. She comes in contact with a frightened young German who requests her help. Before she can save him, however, he is stabbed to death by an unseen assailant. Meanwhile, the FBI continues to pester her, putting Daniels on her trail. During a routine inspection of her apartment, Daniels gets "personal" with her—an FBI term meaning he has treated her like a person instead of an object—and together they proceed to unearth a series of clues pointing to Patinkin as the mastermind behind a plot to sneak Nazis into the country as Jewish refugees. Not surprisingly, this all leads to the bedroom for McGillis and Daniels, though both are aware that they are "like oil and water"—he being a right-wing patriot and she a patriot of the Left. When FBI officials learn of Daniels' emotional involvement, they remove him from the case; in the meantime, Patinkin, tiring of McGillis' interference, has her stove rigged with a bomb. Clues lead McGillis and Daniels to New York's Grand Central Station, where Patinkin has arranged for the Nazis to travel by train to Chicago. When McGillis is spotted, Patinkin and his men try to apprehend her, but she escapes into the maze of underground train tunnels. The chase leads upward, to the glass-domed roof of the terminal, with McGillis edging her way 150 feet above the crowded station. On a catwalk above the roof, Patinkin appears out of nowhere and confronts the seemingly helpless McGillis, asking, "Where is your patriotism? Our country is in danger." As McGillis tries to escape his grasp, she kicks him off the catwalk and onto a surface of plaster and wire mesh. The plaster crumbles underneath the weight of his body and leaves him dangling in a trap of wire, perilously high above the crowd that scurries from the falling plaster. As the mesh wire slowly rips apart, Patinkin has a few seconds to contemplate his end (this scene has a tension not unlike Norman Lloyd's fall from the Statue of Liberty in Hitchcock's SABOTEUR as his coat sleeve tears apart a thread at a time), then falls to his spectacular death. McGillis and Daniels rush to the Chicago-bound train and, covered in dust and dirt, approach the very dignified "Jewish refugees" and place them under arrest. Later, after the excitement is over, Daniels meets McGillis outside her apartment. He expresses his hope that they have a future together, but both know it can't work. She responds to him as if he is just another nosy FBI agent: "I have nothing to say." Then, in one of recent Hollywood's most realistic endings, the one-night lovers part ways.

Directed by Peter Yates (BULLITT; BREAKING AWAY; and most recently SUSPECT, 1987), THE HOUSE ON CARROLL STREET is a wonderful example of craftsmanship. Clearly influenced by Hitchcockian thriller devices and iconographic characters, Yates has delivered a film that, on a technical level, is a pure joy to watch. Its thrills have more in common with those of 1950s films than of the present—and this is the film's strong point. There is none of the cluttered plot "sophistication" of today's movies; none of the witty, tongue-in-cheek characters; none of the high-tech, action-packed chases and gun battles. THE HOUSE ON CARROLL STREET succeeds best in its subtlety and understatement. As in Roman Polanski's FRANTIC, the characters' heroics are limited by the bounds of realism. McGillis and Daniels (like Harrison Ford and Emmanuelle Seigner in FRANTIC) are ordinary people placed in extraordinary situations. Paradoxically, however, while McGillis' character is basically a regular girl her actions are dictated, not by real-life logic, but by the definitions of the thriller heroine. Her character, while essentially an innocent, is motivated by the thriller dictum that characters must snoop and put themselves in ridiculously dangerous situations. Like Grace Kelly in REAR WINDOW, Kelly McGillis is compulsively driven to spy, probe, investigate, search, and ultimately make herself a sitting duck for her antagonist, be it Mandy Patinkin or Raymond Burr. Not surprisingly, then, Jeff Daniels' character is the equivalent of James Stewart's—a likable, tender, soft-spoken, and not easily excited type. But one crucial difference between the Yates-McGillis-Daniels world and the Hitchcock-Kelly-Stewart world lies in the respective levels of obsession. THE HOUSE ON CARROLL STREET's chief drawback is not its Hitchcockian construction (Yates' work is technically the equal, rather than derivative, of Hitchcock's), nor the convenience (rather than implausibility) of its plot twists. It is the near-total absence in Yates' film of three-dimensional characters who exhibit a dark side, an obsession, or a perversity that compels them to plunge themselves into danger. For all its intelligence, refusal to pander to the audience, political overtones (the script is from the once-blacklisted Walter Bernstein of THE FRONT), and subtle romance, THE HOUSE ON CARROLL STREET remains frightfully devoid of any real substance. It is a shell of a film that boasts fine acting, meticulous production design and concern for period detail (on a relatively low budget of $11.5 million), a pleasant score by the increasingly formulaic Georges Delerue, exceptional camerawork by cinematographer extraordinaire Michael Ballhaus, and the spectacular finale in Grand Central Station, with its marvelously staged fall in which Patinkin (doubled by stuntman Ken Bates) crashes through the roof and plummets down onto the marble floor below. Covered with a three-camera setup by Ballhaus (thereby enabling the editor to cover the shot with a variety of angles), the "decelerated fall" has Bates, connected to the ceiling by a body harness and an undetectable wire, free-falling 118 feet, at which point his fall is broken—just a few feet from the floor.

Although production wrapped in late 1986, the film kicked around for some time, first set for release in October 1987. One of the delays concerned the film's title. Originally called THE HOUSE ON SULLIVAN STREET, the film ran into some problems when the title was already taken by another project. A name change followed, one reason viewers will find no references to either Carroll or Sullivan streets in the film. The executive producers were Arlene Donovan and Robert (PLACES IN THE HEART; NADINE) Benton, of whom the latter was originally slated to direct. Includes the song "Because of You" (A. Hammerstein, D. Wilkinson, performed by Dan Kroll and the Ambassadors). (Brief nudity.)

p, Peter Yates, Robert F. Colesberry; d, Peter Yates; w, Walter Bernstein; ph, Michael Ballhaus (DeLuxe Color); ed, Ray Lovejoy; m, Georges Delerue; m/l, A. Hammerstein, D. Wilkinson; prod d, Stuart Wurtzel; art d, W. Steven Graham; set d, David Weinman; cos, Rita Ryack; stunts, Ken Bates; makeup, Richard Dean.

Thriller   Cas.   (PR:C MPAA:PG)

HOWLING IV: THE ORIGINAL NIGHTMARE   (1988, Brit.) 92m John Hough/Allied c

Romy Windsor (Marie), Michael T. Weiss (Richard), Antony Hamilton (Tom), Suzanne Severeid (Janice), Lamya Derval (Eleanor), Norman Anstey (Sheriff), Kate Edwards (Mrs. Orstead), Clive Turner (Tow Truck Driver).

It seems that any successful horror film spawns at least a few sequels. Unfortunately, as the roman numerals climb, the commitment to good filmmaking seems to deteriorate. This installment of the "Howling" series does little to reverse that trend, and even less to whet viewer appetites for a possible fifth installment. Romy Windsor plays Marie, an attractive, best-selling author plagued by unsettling visions of a young nun and a demonic wolf-like creature. Convinced that the visions are the result of stress and exhaustion, Windsor and her husband, Michael T. Weiss, retreat to a quaint cottage near the small town of Drago. There she is visited by Janice (Susanne Severeid), a former nun and a fan of Marie's books who is investigating the traumatization of a friend found wandering near Drago. She produces a photograph of the trauma victim and, voila, the identity of the nun in Windsor's visions is revealed. Further visions reveal that the mysterious nun witnessed a gruesome killing by an unknown attacker in Windsor's cottage. It takes longer than it should, but Windsor slowly begins to suspect that her visions are not stress-related hallucinations at all but in fact warnings of danger and evil from beyond the grave. Meanwhile, a number of mysterious events are being downplayed or covered up by the authorities and inhabitants of Drago. It would seem that the combination of the strange howling sounds Windsor hears every night and the local canine folklore would be enough to convince any sane person that a werewolf is on the loose, but Windsor is again slow to pick up on the rather obvious clues. By the time she puts the pieces together and tries to warn Weiss, he has fallen into the clutches (and bed) of a seductive local shopkeeper who is also a werewolf. Soon afterwards, the wolves come out to devour Windsor and indoctrinate her husband into wolfdom. In the film's most ambitious effects sequence, Weiss is then reduced to a gurgling puddle of protoplasm, from which he is resurrected as a werewolf. As Windsor races here and there, vainly searching for help, she discovers that everyone in Drago is a werewolf. In the film's climax, Severeid sacrifices herself by luring the wolves to a belltower, which Windsor torches with an enormous, automotive molotov cocktail.

It would be unfair to judge the players in this film too harshly. The material is so thin, and the characters so inconsistent and poorly drawn, that it's hard to imagine any actor doing a credible job with the script. Marie's inability to recognize even the most obvious warnings of danger are hard to swallow in light of the fact that she is supposed to be not only a wildly successful novelist but a former medical student as well; worse yet, clues to unraveling the werewolf mystery are telegraphed so unmistakably by the screenwriter that five or 10 minutes later, when the characters are finally figuring them out, the audience is way ahead of the game.

The film's special effects are cheesy at best, though this is well concealed by some quick editing cuts. The big meltdown scene with Marie's husband has a few good moments, but there are several in which it is obvious that the effects team is cutting back and forth between a mannequin and the actor. In the end, the scene simply goes on for too long for it to have any lasting impact. The film's only truly striking aspects occur during Marie's visions: director Hough is adroit in creating the sense that the world itself has stopped whenever the mysterious nun or unfortunate former tenants of Marie's cottage appear. But a few good moments do not a movie make, and HOWLING IV eventually succumbs to its own poor script and story. Songs include "Something Evil, Something Dangerous" (Justin Howard, Barrie Guard, performed by Howard), "Winter Rain" (Lauren Danielle, performed by Danielle). Also includes "Spring" from "The Four Seasons" (Antonio Vivaldi, performed by The Orchestra Da Camera Di Miland). (Nudity, sexual situations.)

p, Harry Alan Towers; d, John Hough; w, Clive Turner, Freddie Rowe (based on a story by Turner from novels by Gary Brandner); ph, Godfrey Godar; ed, Claudia Finkle, Malcolm Burns-Errington; m, David George, Barrie Guard; m/l, Justin Howard, Barrie Guard, Lauren Danielle, Antonio Vivaldi; spec eff, Steve Johnson; stunts, Reo Ruiters.

Horror   Cas.   (PR:O MPAA:R)

IJK

I MARRIED A VAMPIRE †   (1988) 93m Full Moon/Troma c

Rachel Golden (*Viola*), Brendan Hickey (*Robespierre*), Ted Zalewski (*Gluttonshire*), Deborah Carroll (*Olivia*), Temple Aaron (*Portia*), David Dunton, Kathryn Karnes, Marcus Chase, Steve Monahan, Ken Skeer, Rit Friedman.

This low-budget entry from 1983, after a very brief 1986 theatrical showing, was picked up by Troma and subsequently released on video this year. The story concerns a young woman's attempt to move out of her parents' home and start life on her own. She rents an apartment that turns out to be rat-infested and without hot water. Her neighbor steals her money. Her lawyer also rips her off. Finally, she is introduced to a 100-year-old vampire—whose thirst for blood is no worse than any of the other parasites she's dealt with lately. Vampire and ingenue fall in love and take revenge on everyone who has taken advantage of the young woman.

p, Vicky Prodromidov, Jay Raskin; d, Jay Raskin; w, Jay Raskin; ph, Oren Rudavsky (Duart Color); ed, Jay Raskin; m, Steve Monahan; art d, Vicky Prodromidov.

Comedy/Horror   **Cas.**   **(PR:NR MPAA:NR)**

ICED †   (1988) 85m Mikon Releasing Corp. c

Debra DeLiso (*Tina*), Doug Stevenson (*Cory*), Ron Kologie (*Carl*), Elizabeth Gorcey (*Diane*), John C. Cooke (*John*), Joseph Alan Johnson (*Alex*), Dan Smith (*Jeff*), Michael Picardi (*Eddie*), Lisa Loring (*Jeanette*), Sharon Bingham (*Suzanne*).

A homicidal manic who has been driven over the edge after a fatal skiing accident invites those he holds responsible to his winter resort several years later, then picks off the unsuspecting skiers one by one. Released straight to video.

p, Robert Seibert; d, Jeff Kwitny; w, Joseph Alan Johnson; ph, Eugene Shlugleit; ed, Carol Oblath; m, Dan Milner; prod d, Tim Boxell; makeup, Mike Klint.

Horror   **Cas.**   **(PR:NR MPAA:NR)**

ILLEGALLY YOURS★★½   (1988) 102m Crescent Moon-DEG-UA/MGM-UA c

Rob Lowe (*Richard Dice*), Colleen Camp (*Molly Gilbert*), Kenneth Mars (*Hal B. Keeler*), Harry Carey, Jr. (*Wally Finnegan*), Kim Myers (*Suzanne Keeler*), Marshall Colt (*Donald Cleary*), Linda MacEwen (*Ruth Harrison*), Rick Jason (*Freddie Boneflecker*), Jessica James (*Mrs. Evelyn Dice*), Ira Heiden (*Andrew Dice*), George Morfogen (*Judge Norman Meckel*), Tony Longo (*Konrat*), Howard Hirdler (*Harry Crumrine*), L.B. Straten (*Sharon Woolrich*), David Reeves (*Arnie, the Blackmailer*), Jay Glick (*Mailman*), Cynthia Costas (*Sonja*), Jim McDonald (*Sonja's Boyfriend*), Donald Wassler (*Gas Station Attendant*), Jim Shipp (*Old Guard*), C.T. Wakefield (*Jury Selection Man*), Lee Ralls (*Mrs. Sobel*), Laura Sullivan (*Defense Counsel*), Leon Rippy (*Prosecutor*), Tom Nowicki (*Court Clerk*), Nell Schaap (*Mrs. Kockenbakker*), Delight McCoy, Philadelphia Springfield, Thomas Henchy, Jan DiNicola, Patricia Jackson, Alan J. Mandell, Andy Fitzpatrick, Lori Robinson, William Reed, Herbert Huff (*Jurors*), Ruth Reddinger (*Alternate Juror*), Theresa Hassett, Richard Lavery, Robert J. Wedyck (*Reporters*), Steve Foley (*Taxi Driver*), Jason Klassi (*Keeler's Workman*), Eric Small (*Jerome*), Steve Zurk (*Security Guard*), Thomas Fallon (*Wall Hanger*), Anna Thea (*Ms. Temple*), Richard DeSpain (*Record Store Manager*), Earl Poole Ball (*Party Singer/Pianist*), Anthony Pellicano (*Mr. Norris*), Hilroy Distin, Antonia Bogdanovich (*Reggae Singers*), Victor Helou (*Lamar*), Irma Plummer (*TV Announcer*), Dominick "Nick" Nicklo (*Radio Policeman*), Doreen Chalmers (*Mrs. Walker*), Wendy Catherine Hummel (*Girl with Dart Rifle*), Bobby Mencner (*Kid with Helmet*), J. Michael Tiedeberg (*Kid's Father*), Kathy "Kat" Estocin, F.R. Haire, Jr. ("Fountain of Youth" Tourists), Phyllis Alexion (*Tour Bus Woman*), Ernest Goldsmith (*Tour Bus Man*), Tim Y.T. Chin (*Ambassador Ting*), Dan Foley (*TV Technician*).

It doesn't take long to figure out that ILLEGALLY YOURS' director Peter Bogdanovich is again in this film trying to fashion a screwball comedy of the sort that Cary Grant helped make memorable in films like TOPPER, THE AWFUL TRUTH, BRINGING UP BABY, and HOLIDAY. Under the expert direction of a Howard Hawks or Leo McCarey, Grant, with his sophisticated style of comedy, was an unbeatable funnyman: the situations his character became involved in were riotously absurd, the dialog rapid-fire, and the romantic angle always present. Forty years later, the screwball style is a lost art that only Bogdanovich seems intent on keeping alive. Unfortunately, ILLEGALLY YOURS does little to breathe life into the old genre.

Opening with a lengthy, confusing, and dull voice-over, the picture begins as nearly all its major characters converge on one house. It seems that one member of the group has been blackmailing a number of the others, and has now been caught in a nearby assassin's gunsights. He is murdered, the audiotape he has been secretly recording is hidden in a pile of other cassettes, and two of the blackmail victims (Colt and MacEwen) wrap the corpse in a carpet and toss it into a car trunk. Meanwhile, Camp, who was previously unrelated to the blackmailing scheme, arrives at the house

to collect some personal belongings from her previous boy friend, Colt, and picks up the blackmailer's audiocassette in the process. Caught in a crossfire of events, Camp tries to gun down MacEwen and inadvertently shoots a mailman in the leg. All of this is witnessed by two more of the blackmailer's victims, a pair of teenage girls (Myers and Straten), one of whom (Myers) was trying to keep a drug rap secret from her millionaire father. As it all happens, Camp is pegged as the fall guy and charged with the blackmailer's murder. Into these madcap events (and the Grant role) steps Lowe, a bespectacled dork who has just returned from a failed semester at college. Jobless and loveless (having been jilted), Lowe nonetheless optimistically expects to turn his life around. So far he has encountered only one obstacle—jury duty—and arrives at the courthouse in the hope of getting excused. When he learns that the jury selection is for Camp's trial, however, he stays on—for, as coincidences go, Lowe, while a first-grader, wandered into the girl's bathroom by mistake and was met by Camp, then a sixth grader. She accused him of being a pervert, and for Lowe it's been love ever since. Camp, however, doesn't remember him, and when Lowe is asked if he knows the defendant, he perjures himself. Convinced that she must be innocent, Lowe tries to find proof. At every turn he is met by the ubiquitous Myers and Straten, who not only witnessed the murder, but, like everyone else, are also trying to find the missing audiocassette. After countless comic twists and turns, Lowe gets the tape, but still needs to find the corpse—entailing much sleuthing and even more coincidences, after which Lowe learns that the blackmailer's body has been hidden in the base of a statue about to be shipped to Cairo. Lowe rescues Camp from the courtroom, where she has just been convicted of the murder (Lowe had to file a guilty vote in order to get out of court on time to stop the statue's shipment), and, together with Myers and Straten, they manage to save the day.

Although all the necessary elements are here, ILLEGALLY YOURS never gels and never quite kicks into gear as a screwball comedy. Most disconcerting about this failure is that it's difficult to pinpoint where things went wrong. The film isn't funny, but it's hard to figure out why. The script is filled with humorous ideas and situations; the Hawksian direction is fast, intelligent, and witty; the plot turns and character eccentricities are sufficiently "screwball"; the romantic angle has an emotional and psychological basis that lends credibility; and the supporting characters (including Harry Carey, Jr., as a likeable tow-truck operator, Colleen Camp as the energetic fall guy, former "Combat" star Rick Jason as a maniacal cop, and Kim Myers and L.B. Straten as the ubiquitous teens) are enjoyable. Even the questionable casting of Rob Lowe in a comic turn is successful. While no one can replace Cary Grant, Lowe, who like Grant has proven himself as a dramatic actor (SQUARE DANCE) and a heartthrob (everything else he's been in), displays a comic flair in a number of the scenes. His casting here is not unlike that of John Ritter, who was brilliant in his very similar role in Bogdanovich's superior THEY ALL LAUGHED, or of Ryan O'Neal, whose work in WHAT'S UP DOC? was the best he's done for Bogdanovich.

Perhaps the film's failing derives from the irreversible truth that the Hollywood style of filmmaking made famous by the likes of Hawks, John Ford, McCarey, Raoul Walsh, and Allan Dwan is a lost art. Bogdanovich, who has done the bulk of his critical writing on these filmmaking masters, understands as well as anyone what makes old Hollywood films tick. Displaying more of Dwan's craftsmanship than Hawks' and Ford's genius, Bogdanovich is a spotty director who can make great or mediocre films, but never truly bad ones—since even his worst pictures are of some interest. ILLEGALLY YOURS falls into the mediocre category. Like a paint-by-numbers replica of an Old Master's canvas, the film follows the guidelines of great filmmaking but lacks the inventive spark to bring it to explosive life. As much as it tries, ILLEGALLY YOURS just lays there.

Something more than a box-office bomb, the film played one week in the San Francisco area before hitting the video shelves. Despite the top billing of teen-dream Lowe (whose name carried the much worse MASQUERADE), ILLEGALLY YOURS was one of a couple of Dino De Laurentiis-produced pictures (another was William Friedkin's unreleased RAMPAGE) that were victims of DEG's financial woes. One interesting footnote is the appearance, in her first film role, of L.B. Straten (sic), the 20-year-old sister of Dorothy Stratten, the former *Playboy* centerfold and lover of Bogdanovich whose gruesome, much-publicized murder was the basis of Bob Fosse's STAR 80. About six months after ILLEGALLY YOURS' theatrical release, Bogdanovich and the ingenue Straten wed. Includes three songs copenned by Bogdanovich and performed by Johnny Cash; "Love Is a Gambler," "The Lady of Love," and "One Wish" (Bogdanovich, Earl Poole Ball). The soundtrack also includes "Yesterday Only" (Ramon Farran, Robert Graves, performed by Tamara Champlin), "Who Wins" (Champlin, Bruce Gaitsch, performed by Champlin), "Thinking About It" (Steve Wood, Champlin, performed by Wood, Champlin), "When Love Breaks" (Steve McClintock, Tim James, Tim Heintz, performed by McClintock), and "The Black and White Bus" (Hilroy Distin, performed by Distin, Antonia Bogdanovich).

p, Peter Bogdanovich; d, Peter Bogdanovich; w, M.A. Stewart, Max Dickens; ph, Dante Spinotti (Technicolor); ed, Richard Fields, Ronald Krehel; m, Phil Marshall; m/l, Robert Graves, Ramon Farran, Peter Bogdanovich, Earl Poole Ball, Hilroy Distin, Tamara Champlin, Bruce Gaitsch, Steve McClintock, Tim James, Tim Heintz, Steve Wood; prod d, Jane Musky; art d, Harold Thrasher; set d, Robert Kracik; cos, Nancy Fox; stunts, Greg Walker; makeup, Cindy Cruz.

Comedy/Romance   **Cas.**   **(PR:A MPAA:PG)**

ILLUSORY THOUGHTS †   (1988) 72m Patrick Chu Prod. c

Patrick Chu.

This short, independent, episodic film concerns a Chinese choreographer's wanderings through the city and his "illusory" voice-over thoughts on life, love, religion, and art. Directed by Hong Kong-born American Patrick Chu, and shown in New York as part of the Asian American International Film Festival.

p, Patrick Chu; d, Patrick Chu; w, Patrick Chu; ph, Paul Gibson, Mark Trottenberg; ed, Tom Agnello, Philip Rucci; m, Janet Lund; prod d, Dale Chan; ch, Patrick Chu.

Dance/Drama   **(PR:NR MPAA:NR)**

I'M GONNA GIT YOU SUCKA***   (1988) 88m Ivory Way-UA/MGM-UA c

Keenen Ivory Wayans *(Jack Spade)*, Bernie Casey *(John Slade)*, Antonio Fargas *(Flyguy)*, Steve James *(Kung Fu Joe)*, Isaac Hayes *(Hammer)*, Jim Brown *(Slammer)*, Ja'net DuBois *(Ma Bell)*, Dawn Lewis *(Cheryl)*, John Vernon *(Mr. Big)*, Clu Gulager *(Lt. Baker)*, Clarence Williams III, Eve Plumb, Anne-Marie Johnson, Chris Rock.

Keenan Ivory Wayans, one of the most promising members of the so-called "Black Pack" that boasts Robert Townsend and Eddie Murphy as members, wrote and directed this very funny parody of the black-oriented exploitation films of the 1970s. Dubbed "blaxploitation" by the trade journal *Variety*, these low-budget films featured such stars as Richard Roundtree (SHAFT, 1971), Ron O'Neal (SUPERFLY, 1972), Fred Williamson (BLACK CAESAR, 1973), Jim Brown (SLAUGHTER, 1972), Isaac Hayes (TRUCK TURNER, 1974), and Bernie Casey (HIT MAN, 1972). Blaxploitation had women heroes too, like the beautiful Pam Grier (COFFY, 1972) and Tamara Dobson (CLEOPATRA JONES, 1973). Obscure (to whites) comedians soon joined the fray, such as the rhymin' and rappin' Rudy Ray Moore (DOLEMITE, 1975), and the success of blaxploitation even spawned a bizarre subgenre of horror epics like BLACULA (1972), BLACKENSTEIN (1973), and DR. BLACK AND MR. HYDE (1975). The popularity of blaxploitation spilled over into kung-fu films as well, and soon black martial arts experts like Jim Kelly were fighting alongside Bruce Lee in ENTER THE DRAGON (1973). Sociologists and some film historians tend to view the incredible popularity of these films, which invariably pitted the black heroes against corrupt whites, as a response to the frustration felt by urban blacks whose lot in life was rapidly worsening, despite the civil rights movement. Whatever the reason, blaxploitation films boomed at the box office for several years before slowly dying off and eventually being replaced by the phenomenal cross-over success of black stars like Murphy, who was able to have big-budget Hollywood at his beck and call. Murphy, Townsend, and other new black stars who grew up watching the blaxploitation movies of the early 1970s are intimately familiar with all the conventions of the genre and often refer to the archetypes in their films and comedy routines to get laughs. Now Keenan Ivory Wayans has finally turned a series of amusing gags and observations into a comedy that pokes fun at black popular culture, both past and present, while retaining affection for the source.

Set in "Any Ghetto, U.S.A.," I'M GONNA GIT YOU SUCKA begins as the police find the body of yet another black youth who has "O.G.'d," in other words, died from wearing too many gold chains. When the sheet covering the body is pulled back we see a man covered from head to toe in gold chains and pendants (including a gold hubcap), the weight of which has finally dragged him down and suffocated him. The victim's upstanding younger brother, Wayans, returns home from the Army to attend the funeral and vows vengeance on the ruthless gold-chain pusher known as Mr. Big (Vernon). Since his experience in the armed forces is mostly bureaucratic, Wayans seeks the help of his childhood hero, John Slade (Casey), a SHAFT-like character who has since gone into retirement and now sponsors inner-city youth athletic events like street-gang foot races (where gang members must run the 100-yard dash while carrying a large TV set and being chased by dobermans) and car-stripping contests. Casey wants nothing to do with the obviously inexperienced Wayans, but when he finds out the young man is the son of his old flame, he agrees to assemble a small army of former black action heroes to help collapse Vernon's operation. Casey's first stop is to see Hammer (Hayes) and Slammer (Brown), a pair of old heroes who were driven out of the business by black-image pressure groups and who now run a struggling barbecue joint. In addition to Hayes and Brown, Casey gets help from James, a more modern black hero who is expert in the martial arts. To glean information, Casey visits black pimp Flyguy (Fargas) in prison. Scoring an unbelievable amount of weapons from a local arms dealer, the gang of old black heroes is now ready to go. Casey dons his all-black-leather costume and assembles a roving band of musicians to follow him so that he can have his "theme music" wherever he goes (appropriately enough it is the theme from SHAFT, which was composed by Hayes). The attack on Vernon's headquarters, of course, is an almost total botch, because the old heroes just don't have it anymore. Hayes, who has about 30 handguns strapped to his body, slips on a bullet lying on the floor and falls, setting off all the guns. Brown, who has sore feet, aggravates a bunion on his toe that inflates and threatens to explode. Casey, who plans to swing on a rope from the rooftop and burst through the window carrying a stick of dynamite a la SHAFT, mistimes his descent and the dynamite explodes *before* he crashes through the window. This leaves Wayans to battle Vernon's dim-witted minions alone, and he adopts a RAMBO-like style that includes cauterizing a tiny sliver with a hot needle (a direct slam at the absurd scene in RAMBO III in which Sylvester Stallone cauterizes a gaping wound in his side with some gunpowder and a burning stick). Luckily, Wayans' mother, DuBois, who is really the toughest character in the movie, arrives on the scene to save the day.

Although the above synopsis conveys the basic plot of the movie, most of what makes I'M GONNA GIT YOU SUCKA so enjoyable is the torrent of gags that crowd the margins. Owing as much to AIRPLANE! as he does to THE HOLLYWOOD SHUFFLE, Wayans keeps the jokes coming fast and thick, never giving the audience time to stop laughing. Much of the humor is based on blaxploitation film conventions or modern-day black social standards; those unfamiliar with either may find themselves wondering what is so funny. In featuring many of the stars of the old blaxploitation movies, the film gains added weight and authenticity, and it is a joy to see the likes of Casey, Brown, Hayes, and Antonio Fargas having a good time poking fun at themselves. Although Wayans offers up a rich, savvy, and affectionate parody of the old movies, he also turns a satiric eye on black culture in general by gently mocking black fashion, speech, music, dances, sexual mores, family life, businesses, machismo, and even political movements, as represented by former "Mod Squad" star Clarence Williams III in a side-splitting cameo as a 60s-style radical still living in the past. What keeps I'M GONNA GIT YOU SUCKA from straying into offensiveness is its light-hearted approach—the gags are never vicious or insulting. Wayans also does a better job of deflating black stereotypes than Townsend did in THE HOLLYWOOD SHUFFLE: whereas Townsend took an indignant stance toward stereotypes, then got most of his laughs by using them, Wayans takes a more successful approach by presenting the image, getting a laugh, then deflating the image and getting an even bigger laugh. The perfect example of Wayans' style occurs when pimp Fargas finally gets out of prison after nearly 20 years and then hits the street in his finest pimp regalia, circa 1972—huge hat, yellow suit, bell-bottoms, and a pair of gargantuan platform shoes with goldfish tanks as heels. Wayans gets laughs from the stereotype, and then the heels of the shoes break and modern-day blacks mock Fargas as he sadly limps off. The collapse of the stereotype gets an even bigger laugh than the image itself. To be sure, in films of this type not all the gags work, and Wayans is still an inexperienced director who hasn't yet quite mastered his craft (the pacing sometimes lags; some jokes don't pay off as well as they should), but I'M GONNA GIT YOU SUCKA is on target often enough to make Wayans a talent worth watching. *(Comic violence, sexual situations, profanity, brief nudity.)*

p, Peter McCarthy, Carl Craig; d, Keenen Ivory Wayans; w, Keenen Ivory Wayans; ph, Tom Richmond (DeLuxe Color); ed, Michael R. Miller; m, David M. Frank; prod d, Melba Farquhar, Catherine Hardwicke.

Comedy   **(PR:O MPAA:R)**

IN A SHALLOW GRAVE †   (1988) 92m American Playhouse-Skouras-Lorimar-Film Trustees/Skouras c

Michael Biehn *(Garnet Montrose)*, Maureen Mueller *(Georgina Rance)*, Michael Beach *(Quintas Pearch)*, Patrick Dempsey *(Potter Daventry)*, Thomas Boyd Mason *(Edgar Doust)*, Mike Pettinger *(Milkman)*, Prentiss Rowe *(Postman)*, Ron Rosenthal, Muriel Moore.

An American Playhouse film that barely received a release from Skouras Pictures, this Southern Gothic adaptation of James Purdy's novel begins in 1943 when a young man, Biehn, is hit in an explosion at Guadalcanal. He returns to his Virginia farm with hideous facial scars and, less obvious to those around him, equally disfiguring emotional scars. He becomes a recluse, unable even to meet with his former love, Mueller. A likeable drifter, Dempsey, happens along and becomes friendly with Biehn, agreeing also to deliver Biehn's letters to Mueller. Following the course of such events, it is only natural that Biehn comes to suspect an affair between Dempsey and Mueller. A chance to see Michael Biehn (TERMINATOR; ALIENS) in an all-together different role, though much of Purdy's deeper thematic shading (the religious imagery, the homoeroticism) is reportedly absent from the film.

p, Kenneth Bowser, Barry Jossen; d, Kenneth Bowser; w, Kenneth Bowser (based on the novel by James Purdy); ph, Jerzy Zielinski (Foto-Kem Color); ed, Nicholas C. Smith; m, Jonathan Sheffer; prod d, David Wasco; art d, Sharon Seymour; set d, Sandy Reynolds Wasco; cos, Molly Maginnis; makeup, Michele Burke.

Drama   **Cas.**   **(PR:NR MPAA:R)**

INVASION EARTH: THE ALIENS ARE HERE †   (1988) 83m NW-Rearguard/NW c

Janice Fabian *(Joanie)*, Christian Lee *(Billy)*, Larry Bagby, III *(Tim)*, Dana Young *(Mike)*, Mel Welles *(Mr. Davar)*, Corey Burton, Tony Pope *(Voices)*.

A small-town movie theater is the sight of an alien invasion: space creatures are taking over the bodies of audience members after turning them into catatonic pods by subjecting them to an endless screening of horror/sci-fi films and trailers. Four youths team up to try to stop the invasion. Mel Welles, as the theater manager, and a collection of vintage 1950s film clips, are an added plus. Released straight to video.

p, Max J. Rosenberg; d, George Maitland; w, Miller Drake; ph, Austin McKinney (Foto-Kem color); ed, Miller Drake, William B. Black; m, Anthony R. Jones; prod d, Michael Novotny; spec eff, Dennis Skotak, Michael McCracken.

Horror   **Cas.**   **(PR:NR MPAA:NR)**

INVISIBLE KID, THE zero   (1988) 95m Elysian/Taurus c

Jay Underwood *(Grover Dunn)*, Karen Black *(Mom)*, Wally Ward *(Milton McClane)*, Chynna Phillips *(Cindy Moore)*, Brother Theodore *(Dr. Theodore)*, Mike Genovese *(Officer Chuck Malone)*, Jan King *(Singer)*, Nicolas de Toth *(Donny Zanders)*, John Madden Towen *(Principal Baxter)*, Thomas Cross *(Officer Terell)*.

THE INVISIBLE KID, a rehash of such mid-80s pictures as MY SCIENCE PROJ-ECT and TEEN WOLF, does nothing but recycle the cliches of earlier films. Under-wood plays a high school brain working on a project to complete the notes of his late father, a science teacher, while his befuddled mother, Black, camps out in front of the TV set, watching an advice show hosted by Brother Theodore. Searching for a miss-ing secret ingredient, Underwood creates an explosion of green slime that, after some pigeon guano falls into it, converts to a pile of glittery powder that, when ingested, makes one invisible for 30 minutes thereafter. Underwood has no idea that the drop-pings complete his father's formula (originally meant to be a toilet bowl cleaner), but wants to take the powder to a scientific convention. Ward, Underwood's friend, wants to put it to another use: to spy on the girl's locker room and catch a glimpse of leading lady Phillip's chest. While invisible, Ward and Underwood discover a plot by school principal Towen and some local mobsters to throw the high school basketball championship. With the help of police officer Genovese—who uses the powder to turn invisible, climb a basketball backboard and kick balls away from the hoop—Underwood, Phillips, and star player deToth foil the attempt to rig the game and catch the crooks.

The second film written and directed by Avery Crounse, (his first was the uneven but interesting 18th-century ghost story EYES OF FIRE), INVISIBLE KID seems to be an attempt to make as commercial a film as possible, with predictably lame re-sults. The humor is forced and miserable, the slapstick poorly played and dull. Crounse's direction is barely noticeable, with individual scenes completely lacking in flow or pacing. The finale is an endless inane mess with neither a set-up or a conclu-sion to the flaccid slapstick routines. Choppy editing and nearly invisible production values characterize the technical aspects of the film; the special effects consist of using a first-person Steadicam to simulate characters' invisibility. Karen Black has a point-less role as the mom, Brother Theodore is thoroughly wasted, and the rest of the per-formances are forgettable. The film played in theaters but should have gone straight to video. (*Comic violence, brief nudity, profanity.*)

p, Philip J. Spinelli; d, Avery Crounse; w, Avery Crounse; ph, Michael Barnard (United Color); ed, Gabrielle Gilbert; m, Steve Hunter, Jan King; art d, Charles Tomlinson; spec eff, Tassilo Baur, Ernie Farino; stunts, John Stewart; makeup, Annie Maniscalco.

Comedy/Science Fiction   Cas.   (PR:C MPAA:PG-13)

IRON EAGLE II*   (1988) 105m Alliance-Harkot/Tri-Star c

Louis Gossett, Jr. (*Chappy*), Mark Humphrey (*Cooper*), Stuart Margolin (*Still-more*), Alan Scarfe (*Vardovsky*), Sharon H. Brandon (*Valeri Zuyeniko*), Maury Chaykin (*Downs*), Colm Feore (*Yuri*), Clark Johnson (*Graves*), Jason Blicker (*Hick-man*), Jesse Collins (*Bush*), Mark Ivanir (*Balyonev*), Uri Gavriel (*Koshkin*), Neil Munro (*Strappman*), Douglas Sheldon (*Dmitriev*), Azaria Ropoport (*Stepanov*), Nicolas Colicos (*M.P. Connors*), Gary Reineke (*Bowers*), Michael J. Reynolds (*Sec-retary*), Jerry Hyman (*Commanding Officer*), Janine Manatis (*Reporter*).

© TRI-STAR

At the conclusion of TOP GUN, the American pilots blow a squadron of Russians out of the sky and World War III doesn't begin because both sides decide to keep it a secret. Apparently this sort of thing goes on all the time, because here it is again at the beginning of IRON EAGLE II, as an aerial game of tag over the Bering Straits be-tween two Americans and two Russkies gets out of hand and one of the Americans gets shot down. Once again, nothing of this is ever made public. Right. At any rate, it just so happens that the pilot who went down is the young hero of IRON EAGLE, a film in which that character teamed with Gossett to free the former's pilot father from some unnamed Arab hellhole where he was a prisoner. Next thing we know, Gossett is being pulled out of retirement for IRON EAGLE II and charged with a top secret mission. He is given a team of misfits, including Humphrey, the surviving pilot of the Arctic showdown, and told to team up with a similar squad of Russian misfits at a base in Israel, where they will train for a combined air and land mission to destroy a nuclear missile site in yet another of those unnamed Arab countries. Naturally, there are tensions between the two teams, leading eventually to a big fight after which ev-eryone respects everyone else. One of the Russians is a beautiful woman (Brandon)

and, of course, she and Humphrey fall in love once she has proved she is a good pilot. Gossett, however, learns that his superior, Margolin, has been out to sabotage the mission so that he can ruin detente and use his own missile to blow up the site. Gos-sett rouses the troops with this information and the mission finally is launched. The combined forces manage to penetrate the Arab defenses, and, after some fancy can-yon flying (lifted from the attack on the Deathstar in STAR WARS), they blow up the missile base.

With so much idiotic flag-waving with the nice Russians on our side and swarms of faceless Arabs as the victims, it's not surprising that this film is an Israeli coproduc-tion. The plot of misfits coming together for a suicide mission is one of the most hoary in the war genre, best done in THE DIRTY DOZEN. But while that film had an ex-cellent cast and an action director in Robert Aldrich, IRON EAGLE II has only Gossett and a bunch of unknowns and director Sidney J. Furie, whose successes (THE IPCRESS FILE; THE BOYS IN COMPANY C; LADY SINGS THE BLUES) are no great shakes and outweighed by his failures, including GABLE AND LOMBARD and SUPERMAN IV: THE QUEST FOR PEACE. The only things to recommend here are the aerial sequences, which utilized a modified Lear Jet, and even these pale in comparison to TOP GUN. None of this, however, made any difference at the box office, where IRON EAGLE II was one of the top grossing movies for sev-eral weeks—we may as well resign ourselves to IRON EAGLE III. (*Violence, adult situations, profanity.*)

p, Jacob Kotzky, Sharon Harel, John Kemeny; d, Sidney J. Furie; w, Kevin Elders, Sidney J. Furie; ph, Alain Dostie (Bellevue Pathe color); ed, Rit Wallis; m, Amin Bhatia; md, Sam Feldman, Bruce Allen, Steve Love; art d, Ariel Roshko; set d, Giora Porter; spec eff, George Erschbamer; cos, Sylvie Krasker; stunts, Terry Leonard; makeup, Louise Mignault.

Action   Cas.   (PR:C MPAA:PG)

IT COULDN'T HAPPEN HERE*   (1988, Brit.) 90m Liberty-Picture Music
                                                          International c

Neil Tennant, Chris Lowe, Joss Ackland, Dominique Barnes, Neil Dickson, Carmen Du Sautoy, Gareth Hunt, Barbara Windsor, Nicholas Haley, Jonathan Haley, Wyn McLeod, The Beach Bikers, The X Posse, Audrey Kirby, Kevin Duffield, James Downie, Lillian Coyle, Christopher Coyle, Christopher Gabriel, Chris Chering, Ga-vin Watson, Paul Sexton, Simon Lawes, Mitzi Mueller, Klondyke Kate, Terry Fisher, S.J. Versey, Tabby, Clair Becker, Stephanie Buttle, Lyndsey Cole, Hugh Craig, Christopher Hall, Emma Hendry, Hevon Grant, Lisa Hendry, Lisa Jones, Mi-chelle Nelson, Natalie Roles, Chris Tudor, Tom Searle, Voyd and H.S.H. Penge Latin Team at the Regal Uxbridge, Michale Bayliss, Peter Salem.

Not exactly A HARD DAY'S NIGHT, IT COULDN'T HAPPEN HERE brings British pop duo The Pet Shop Boys (Chris Lowe and Neil Tennant) and their music to the big screen in a surreal travelog. The narrative is nearly nonexistent: Tennant visits an English seaside resort where he chooses some postcards, which conjure an assortment of strange memories as he and Lowe embark on a cross-country journey. Along the way they encounter some naughty nuns, a blind priest (Ackland) who reappears as a murderous hitchhiker, a businessman who is oblivious to the flames raging on his body, a ventriloquist (Hunt) and his loquacious dummy, and a de-ranged pilot (Dickson). Tennant and Lowe, who say next to nothing, are as unaf-fected by the metaphysical ramblings of the other characters as they are by the ab-surd, often catastrophic, occurrences they witness. Not surprisingly, the soundtrack is full of Pet Shop Boys' tunes, including "West End Girls" and "Always on My Mind." Occasionally the Boys lip synch along; at other times the lyrics are recited without musical accompaniment.

Director Jack Bond has aspired to make IT COULDN'T HAPPEN HERE into more than a feature-length music video, and he arrives at more than a few arresting images, especially the stunningly photographed seaside scenes (some of which were filmed without the aid of wind machines; Bond kept his cameras running when a hur-ricane struck the UK during the shoot). Bond makes no attempt to illustrate the Boys' songs literally; instead, he creates an alternative reality that has more to do with dreams than the waking world. Yet, despite its often captivating cinematogra-phy and the room (lots of room) that it leaves for subjective interpretation, IT COULDN'T HAPPEN HERE is painfully slow-moving and frequently just plain dull. The performances—and it would be stretching it to say that these include Ten-nant and Lowe's sleepwalking—are less than inspiring, even including the quirky turn by the usually excellent Joss Ackland. Some may be able to find metaphors for Thatcher's England in the bizarre, ravaged landscape, others may see the picture as another illustration of the Pet Shop Boys' keen understanding of the process of pop consumption, and some critics have likened the film favorably to the work of Jean-Luc Godard and Ken Russell. But for many, IT COULDN'T HAPPEN HERE will simply seem like MTV from hell. Songs include "It Couldn't Happen Here", "Subur-bia", "It's a Sin", "West End Girls", "Rent", "Two Divided by Zero", "King's Cross", "One More Chance", "Wake Up" (Neil Tennant, Chris Lowe), "Always on My Mind" (Thompson, James, Christopher, performed by Pet Shop Boys), "What Have I Done to Deserve This?" (Tennant, Lowe, Willis, performed by Pet Shop Boys, Dusty Springfield). (*Nudity, adult situations, sexual situations.*)

p, Jack Bond; d, Jack Bond; w, Jack Bond (based on a story by Bond, James Dillon); ph, Simon Archer (Fujicolor); ed, Rodney Holland; m/l, Neil Tennant, Chris Lowe; art d, James Dillon; cos, Leah Archer; ch, Arlene Phillips; stunts, Paul Weston; makeup, Marella Shearer.

Musical   (PR:C-O MPAA:NR)

IT TAKES TWO †   (1988) 81m UA/MGM-UA c

George Newbern (*Travis Rogers*), Leslie Hope (*Stephi Lawrence*), Kimberly Foster (*Jonni Tigersmith*), Barry Corbin (*George Lawrence*), Anthony Geary (*Wheel*), Frances Lee McCain (*Joyce Rogers*), Patrika Darbo (*Dee Dee*), Marco Perella (*Dave Chapman*), Bill Bolender (*Judd Rogers*).

From David Beaird, the director of MY CHAUFFEUR and PASS THE AMMO, two flawed but relatively interesting pictures, comes this latest opus—a teen comedy about a 20-year-old Texan who is just 10 days away from tying the knot with his childhood sweetheart. Eager to live a wild and reckless final week-and-a-half, the young man heads to the bright lights of Dallas with $5,000 in his pocket, buys a Lamborghini replica, and rolls down the highway with the sultry car saleswoman at his side. After all this free living, however, he must make that climactic choice. Once again former soap opera star Anthony Geary, who seems determined to become a cult character actor, is cast in a spaced-out, Zen-practicing type role.

p, Robert Lawrence; d, David Beaird; w, Richard Christian Matheson, Thomas Szollosi; ph, Peter Deming; ed, David Garfield; m, Carter Burwell; md, Peter Afterman; prod d, Richard Hoover; art d, Mark Hillerman, Gregory Bolton, Michael Okowita; set d, Suzette Sheets; spec eff, Greg Hull, William Purcell; cos, Reve Richards.

Comedy   Cas.   (PR:NR MPAA:R)

IT'S ALIVE III: ISLAND OF THE ALIVE**½   (1988) 91m Larco/WB c

Michael Moriarty (*Steve Jarvis*), Karen Black (*Ellen Jarvis*), Laurene Landon (*Sally*), James Dixon (*Dr. Perkins*), Neal Israel (*Dr. Brewster*), Art Lund (*Swenson*), Ann Dane (*Miss Morrell*), Macdonald Carey (*Judge Watson*), Gerrit Graham (*Ralston*), William Watson (*Cabot*), C.L. Sussex (*Hunter*), Patch Mackenzie (*Robbins*), Rick Garia (*Tony*), Carlos Palomino, Tony Abatemarco (*Cubans*), Gladys Portugese, Joann Lara (*Waitresses*), Bobby Ramsen (*T.V. Host*), Jill Gatsby (*Girl in Cab*), Kevin O'Conner (*Cab Driver*), John Woehrle, Richard Duggan (*Cops*), Lauri Riley (*Medic*), Marilyn Staley (*Miss Garson*), Mitchell Edmonds (*Stewart*), Elizabeth Sanders (*Autograph Seeker*), Steven Alan Green (*Comic*), Kathleen Kickya (*Girl on Beach*), Lynda Clark (*2nd Woman*), Dan Rycerz (*Court Officer*).

When we last left the mutant killer babies of IT'S ALIVE (1974) and IT LIVES AGAIN (1978), a panicked American government was in the midst of forcing abortions on pregnant mothers suspected of carrying mutants, and executing those monster kids already born. At the opening of this, the third installment of the series, most of the babies have been destroyed. A few, however, have survived and the father of one of them, Moriarty, has taken the government to court in order to stop his child's destruction. Horrified by what she has given birth to, the baby's mother (Black) has fled the family, leaving Moriarty to deal with their child's fate. An actor in commercials, Moriarty finds that he cannot get work because sponsors don't want their products associated with the man who fathered a mutant baby. After successfully proving to the court that the monster child has emotions and recognizes its father, Moriarty wins a reprieve for his baby. Instead of being executed, the child will be taken to a remote island, where it will be allowed to live out its days. Several other surviving mutant babies are dumped on the island, and, five years after the trial, Moriarty is asked to participate in a scientific expedition to the island in order to study their development. Moriarty is shocked to discover that his child has grown into adulthood and become the leader of the other mutants on the island. Even more amazing is that the mutants have begun to procreate and Moriarty has become a grandfather. Unfortunately for the scientists, there is a rebellion among the mutants and all are killed, save Moriarty, who is forced to pilot the boat containing the escaping mutants. The mutants (three males, one female, and the infant) head for Florida, but when it appears that some of the escapees want to kill Moriarty, his mutant son persuades them to let Moriarty be set adrift in the ocean. Washing up in Cuba, Moriarty finds officials sympathetic to his plight and they take him to Cape Vale, Florida, where the mutants have already gotten into trouble. Although one of the mutants is killed by police, Moriarty's son merely wants to track down his mother to see if she can cure their illness—a simple case of measles. As the police close in on the mutants, a tearful family reunion is played out on the roof of Black's apartment building. Moriarty finally succeeds in getting his wife to accept their child—and grandchild—but it is too late for the adult mutants, for they are dying from the measles. Before he succumbs to the disease, the son turns his child over to Black and Moriarty, knowing that they will care for it. The mutant and his mate die together, holding hands. Now desperate to save the baby, the grandparents manage to hide the child from the authorities and escape to parts unknown—the reunited nuclear family.

Larry Cohen's latest installment in the "It's Alive" series, one of the most thematically rich horror series ever produced, once again tackles American political and social attitudes in a genre context, but this time in an even more mocking manner. Here Cohen takes a swipe at abortion, the "Baby M" case, the court system, fear of AIDS (people avoid Moriarty because he is the father of a monster child, and a prostitute becomes hysterical with fear after learning of Moriarty's identity just before having sex with him—"Oh God, he touched me!"), media stardom, merchandizing (Moriarty becomes a celebrity after writing a book called *A Parent's Story*), and a host of other issues debated in the 1980s. Much of the success of the film once again lies in the incredibly strange performance of Cohen veteran Michael Moriarty. At first a rather normal, straight-laced kind of guy, Moriarty slowly becomes harsh and cynical toward the society that wanted to destroy his child and made him a pariah. In addition to the rich thematics and Moriarty's strong performance, IT'S ALIVE III is also one of the most visually interesting films of Cohen's career. The opening courtroom scene is a marvel of camera movement and lighting, lending an expressionistic air to the bizarre proceedings. Cohen also quotes from classic horror films, including wry visual

references to KING KONG and NOSFERATU. Another of his projects designed specifically for home video, IT'S ALIVE III was shot in only four weeks on locations in Hawaii and Los Angeles. Steve Neill's special makeup for the adult mutant babies is based on the original design by Rick Baker and is quite effective, given the limited amount of money he had to work with, as is the brief stop-motion animation by William Hedge. Also notable is Laurie Johnson's haunting score, which builds upon the main theme originally composed by Bernard Herrmann. A trivia note: footage from the precredits sequence to IT'S ALIVE III (a mutant baby born in a taxi cab) turned up as an example of fictitious horror director Peter Swan's work in a scene from the latest Dirty Harry movie, THE DEAD POOL. (*Violence, gore effects, adult situations, sexual situations, profanity.*)

p, Paul Stader; d, Larry Cohen; w, Larry Cohen; ph, Daniel Pearl (Technicolor); ed, David Kern; m, Laurie Johnson, Bernard Herrmann; m/l, David Shapiro, Lauri Riley; art d, George Stoll; spec eff, Steve Neill, Rick Baker, William Hedge.

Horror   Cas.   (PR:O MPAA:R)

JACK'S BACK***   (1988) 97m Palisades c

James Spader (*John/Rick Wesford*), Cynthia Gibb (*Christine Moscari*), Rod Loomis (*Dr. Sidney Tannerson*), Rex Ryon (*Jack Pendler*), Robert Picardo (*Dr. Carlos Battera*), Jim Haynie (*Sgt. Gabriel*), Wendell Wright (*Capt. Walter Prentis*), Chris Mulkey (*Scott Morofsky*), Danitza Kingsley (*Denise Johnson*), John Wesley, Bobby Hosea, Kevin Glover.

In Hollywood, everyone has a script in his or her back pocket and most harbor a desire to direct someday. This is especially true among members of film crews, many of whom have taken entry-level jobs in hopes of getting their big break. On occasion the breaks come and promising new talent is given a chance to shine. Such is the case with the unjustly ignored JACK'S BACK, a surprisingly effective low-budget mystery written and directed by ex-gaffer Rowdy Herrington and coproduced by ex-key grip Tim Moore. Boasting a strong dual-role performance by James Spader (LESS THAN ZERO), the film is set in Los Angeles as the city is menaced by a serial killer who patterns himself after the infamous Jack the Ripper. Exactly 100 years after the original murders, this new Jack kills prostitutes in the same manner as his forbearer and duplicates the surgical mutilations performed on the victims. As the film begins, it is the anniversary of the last Ripper murder, and police are sure the new killer will seek out a pregnant prostitute (the historical Ripper's final victim). At a free clinic in Echo Park, we meet Spader, a young medical student dedicated to progressive social causes. Although his tireless crusades irritate his boss (Loomis), Spader earns the respect and admiration of his patients and fellow doctors, especially pert young intern Gibb. Spader is shocked to discover, however that his high-school sweetheart has become a hooker, when she arrives at the clinic pleading for an abortion despite the fact that she is well into her seventh month. Morally indignant, Loomis kicks the woman out of the clinic. That evening, Spader goes to visit her and finds that she has been hacked to pieces. Standing over the body is Spader's colleague Ryon, who protests his innocence, but admits that he had come to give the woman an illegal abortion. In a panic, Ryon flees and Spader gives chase. The young doctors end up back at the clinic and the desperate Ryon strangles Spader and then hangs him to make his death look like suicide. The film then cuts to Spader sitting bolt upright in bed, having suffered a nightmare. He walks to the balcony of the apartment for a breath of fresh air, and it is then that we notice he sports an earring and a scar above his right eye. Young doctor Spader is indeed dead; this man is his identical twin brother—the black sheep of the family. When Spader learns of his brother's death, he tells the police about his dream. They, however, have made the dead doctor a scapegoat for the Ripper murders (assuming he killed the girl and then himself) and don't want to hear about it. But once they discover that the twin has a lengthy rap sheet, they begin to suspect that he is both the and his brother's murderer. Meanwhile, Spader launches his own investigation, and, with the help of the wary Gibb, he begins to track down Ryon. As plot takes many clever twists and turns, we realize that, although Ryon did kill Spader, he is not responsible for the serial murders. While the police waste their time trying to connect Spader to the killings, the real Ripper is still at large. Eventually, Spader catches Ryon and avenges his brother's murder. The cops assume Ryon was the Ripper and close the case, but Spader continues to have nightmares, and with the help of criminal psychologist Picardo, who hypnotizes him, Spader realizes who the Ripper actually is. Spader then races to Gibb's home, just in time to save her from the crazed killer.

Despite a few clunky plot devices designed to get the story going, JACK'S BACK is a gripping, edge-of-your-seat thriller that will keep even the most ardent mystery fans guessing. Cleverly scripted and well directed by Herrington, the movie feels like a project that he thought about for a long time, and, when given the opportunity, filmed exactly as planned. There isn't a wasted moment here, and Herrington knows how to sustain suspense while he skillfully negotiates the complicated shifts and reversals of his plot. Although the picture does have its share of red herrings, Herrington is never dishonest with the audience and keeps everything ambiguous until the closing moments. A sense of dread and unease permeates the film as the characters, and the audience, can't decide whom to trust, including Spader in *both* his incarnations. Herrington not only combines an absorbing plot line with interesting characters, but he tells his story in a wonderfully visual manner (although the smoky look favored by cinematographers lately is overused here and becoming tiresome in general). This sort of approach used to be quite common, but nowadays movies are either high-concept narratives, plotless character studies, or hollow visual exercises. Rarely does Hollywood successfully, and unpretentiously, integrate all three elements into an artistically satisfying and entertaining whole. Luckily, JACK'S BACK succeeds on all levels.

Herrington is also good with actors, and Spader is superb in a dual role that finally breaks the string of sleazy yuppie types he has played from PRETTY IN PINK to WALL STREET. The "nice" brother is a genuinely dedicated, progressive, and charming guy, while the "bad" brother is a dour, brooding young man who is basically decent at heart. Spader shows the contradictory shades of gray that make up the brothers' personalities, and Herrington exploits this ambiguity to keep the audience ill at ease with both characters. Cynthia Gibb makes a wonderfully spunky heroine, and Rod Loomis, Rex Ryon, and Robert Picardo exude menace in every scene in which they appear. Also strong in a small role is Chris Mulkey (THE HIDDEN; PATTI ROCKS) as a police detective given to an occasional wisecrack. Receiving spotty distribution and little critical support, JACK'S BACK failed to find a wide audience during its theatrical release; however, it will most likely become a popular video rental. (*Violence, brief gore effects, adult situations, excessive profanity.*)

p, Tim Moore, Cassian Elwes; d, Rowdy Herrington; w, Rowdy Herrington; ph, Shelly Johnson; ed, Harry B. Miller III; m, Danny Di Paolo; prod d, Piers Plowden; set d, Deborah Evans; spec eff, John Naulin.

Mystery	Cas.	(PR:O MPAA:R)

JAILBIRD ROCK**   (1988) 92m Transworld/Continental c

Robin Antin (*Jessie Harris*), Valchie Gene Richards (*Peggy*), Robin Cleaver (*Echo*), Rhonda Aldrich (*Max*), Jacquelyn Houston (*Samantha*), Debra Laws (*Lisa*), Erica Jordan (*Judy*), Perry Lange (*Denny*), Ron Lacey (*Warden Baumann*), Victoria Lustig (*Dr. Lunde*), Maria Noel (*Mary*), Sebastian Larreta (*Lamont*), Perla Cristal (*Jesse's Mother*), Ted McNabney (*Stepfather*), Maria Carmen (*Woman in Street*), Yolanda Pedroza (*Denny's Friend*), Arthur Brown (*Guard*), Mariana Cedon, Marina Magali, Jessica Schultz, Georgina Campiglio, Andrea Cribben (*Jailbait*), George Baza (*Congressman Knowles*), Frank Cano (*Governor*).

After a hiatus in the late 1970s and early 80s, the women-in-prison film has made an impressive comeback in the last few years, most visibly in the high camp but hollow REFORM SCHOOL GIRLS, but primarily in the large number of films that have little or no theatrical release before going to the video racks. JAILBIRD ROCK is a better than average contribution to the genre, less exploitative than the general run.

Antin is a talented dancer and high school student who comes home one day to find her stepfather beating her mother, apparently a regular occurrence. Antin tries to make him stop and, when he doesn't, shoots him. Sent to the big house for a two-year stretch on a manslaughter rap, she immediately falls afoul of Aldrich, the top-dog inmate inevitably present in these movies. Aldrich derives her power from the fact that Noel, a female guard, is hopelessly in love with her, providing Aldrich with drugs (which she resells) and keeping her from being punished for her offenses. When Aldrich starts a fight and tries to kill Antin, all the women involved go to solitary (except Aldrich, of course). There Antin is persuaded by the other prisoners, talking through the walls, into helping them put together a variety show. The warden sees an opportunity to pick up some easy publicity through the project, so he allows the show to go on, booking a hall outside the walls. At first, Aldrich sets out to sabotage the production, but after Noel catches her in bed with her cellmate she knows the free ride is over and makes plans to escape. She pretends to make up with Antin in order to join the show, planning to take off during the big finale. The production is a success, with the governor, congressmen, and Antin's boy friend among those in the enthusiastic audience. Aldrich makes her break, but is gunned down by Noel, who is fatally shot in return. Titles at the end tell us that Antin and her boy friend married after her release and she works as a choreographer.

With a premise that's sort of like throwing Mickey and Judy into the joint, JAILBIRD ROCK rises above the usual run with good performances, catchy songs, and some decent dancing. The women-in-prison plot is usually an excuse for endless topless scenes, but this film eschews them, shifting the emphasis of the inevitable lesbianism away from sexuality and towards the affectionate, even loving relationships among the female inmates (even Aldrich tells her cellmate she loves her before making her break). For a genre in which the basic elements haven't changed much in decades, this may be progress. Songs include: "Can't Shake the Beat" (Tommy Dunbar, Charles Judge, performed by George Black), "Over and Out" (Black, Howard Huntsberry, performed by Huntsberry), "Wind on My Wings" (Black, Rick Nowels, performed by Black), "Heart of Me" (Nowels, Terry Abrahamson, performed by Debra Laws), "Just Lust" (Nowels, Abrahamson, performed by Lucy Sustar), "Gotta Move" (Nowels, Judge, Black, performed by Laws). (*Violence, brief nudity, sexual situations, adult situations, substance abuse, excessive profanity.*)

p, J.C. Crespo; d, Phillip Schuman; w, Carole Stanley, Edward Kovach (based on a story by Eduard Sarlui); ph, Leonardo Solis (Technicolor); ed, Peter Teschner, Raja Gosnell; m, Rick Nowecs; prod d, Gustavo Acosta; art d, George Marchegiani; cos, Gloria Van Hartenstein; ch, Dennon Rawles; makeup, Alice Adamson.

Prison/Musical	Cas.	(PR:O MPAA:R)

JOHNNY BE GOOD zero   (1988) 98m Orion c

Anthony Michael Hall (*Johnny Walker*), Robert Downey, Jr. (*Leo Wiggins*), Paul Gleason (*Wayne Hisler*), Uma Thurman (*Georgia Elkans*), Steve James (*Coach Sanders*), Seymour Cassel (*Wallace Gibson*), Michael Greene (*Tex Wade*), Marshall Bell (*Chief Elkans*), Deborah May (*Mrs. Walker*), Michael Alldredge (*Vinny Kroll*), Jennifer Tilly (*Connie Hisler*), Jon Stafford (*Bad Breath*), Pete Koch (*Pete Andropolous*), Howard Cosell (*Himself*), Jim McMahon (*Himself*), George Hall (*Grandpa Walker*), Lucianne Buchanan (*Lawanda Wade*), Tony Frank (*Joe Bob*), Tim Ros-

sovich (*Gas Attendant*), Robert Downey, Sr. (*NCAA Investigator*), David Denny (*Benny Figg*), Chris Dunn (*Flick Weaver*), John DeLuna (*Jose Popupu*), Larry Wolf (*Recruiter Larry*), Michael Colyar (*Recruiter Mike*), Lee Ritchey (*Recruiter Lee*), Linwood Phillip Walker (*Recruiter Linwood*), Ted Dawson (*TV Reporter*), Adam Faraizl (*Randy Walker*), Megan Morris (*Raylene Walker*), Jack Gould (*Priest*), Dennis Letts (*Army General*), Craig Tonelson (*Pete Provolone*), John F. Cunningham (*Substitute*), Denise Thorson (*Eunice Elkans*), Hayley Ladner (*Joanie Dorfman*), Holly Harrington, Philisha Sanders (*Cheerleaders*), Jamie Goss, Donna Willson, Ann Matush (*Strippers*), Traci Ann Dutton, Karen Cecka, Barbara Cecka (*Girls at Motel*), Deanna Maddox, Coquina Dunn (*Sorority Girls*), John Hawkes, Scott Bate (*Pizza Boys*), Michael Petty, Van Dykes (*Hari Krishnas*), Gary Hartwell (*Male Stripper*), Thethia Hanson, Clara Paul (*Tupperware Ladies*), Harlan Jordan (*Exterminator*), Doris V. Hargrave (*Woman at Piermont*), Gary G. GeLaune (*Local TV Reporter*), Catherine Alexander (*Waitress at BBQ*), Thomas Anthony Patti (*Chauffeur*).

Anthony Michael Hall, the likable teen star of the John Hughes comedy SIXTEEN CANDLES, has been trying desperately to change his nerdy, virginal image over the last couple of years. After a brief stint on TV's "Saturday Night Live," Hall appeared in the unwatchable OUT OF BOUNDS (1986) as a macho action hero. Missing from the big screen for all of 1987, he returned in JOHNNY BE GOOD with a new image as a squeaky clean All-American quarterback, a gridiron Bruce Springsteen.

The first infraction (worth five yards) in this penalty-laden film is the unabashed misuse of Chuck Berry's song title. Infraction No. 2 (costing another five yards) is the heavy-metal Judas Priest version of the song. And the next three infractions are Anthony Michael Hall, in that order (adding up to 15 more penalty yards). A horribly ungifted actor (his talent has mysteriously vanished between SIXTEEN CANDLES and JOHNNY BE GOOD), Hall tries unceasingly to be a "dude" in this film, but comes off as nothing more than a phony, pesty geek. Yet, we, the moviegoing audience, are supposed to believe that he is the hottest high-school quarterback in the entire nation. Now, if, perhaps this film were set in Costa Rica, or Liechtenstein, or Burkina Faso, then maybe, just maybe, Anthony Michael Hall would be a contender. But as far as American football goes, he's no contender. Infraction No. 6 (worth 10 yards and putting JOHNNY BE GOOD out of field goal range) is a script that has possibilities as a biting satire but instead plays on male fantasies, sexual double entendres, toilet humor, and an unhealthy portrait of women and minorities. Hall is being courted by all the top college football programs, but some are more persuasive than others. "Ol' Tex" (a thinly veiled SMU) promises cars, girls, and money if Hall will sign with that institution. UCC, a competing California school, promises the same. Hall, however, has a steady girl friend (Thurman) with whom he has promised to attend the generic State University. State has a very good football program but expects its students to . . . (gasp!) attend class, pass exams, and play for the love of the game instead of recruitment promises. While Hall is being courted by the recruiters, Thurman has just about written him off, and his family is embarrassed beyond words. By the end, Hall has seen the light, denounces the corrupt recruitment programs, and signs with State.

Infraction No. 7 (another 15 yards, pushing the film deep into its own territory) is the colorless, anemic direction of Bud Smith, the coeditor of THE EXORCIST and FLASHDANCE (both of which earned him an Oscar nomination); SORCERER; FALLING IN LOVE AGAIN; PERSONAL BEST; CAT PEOPLE; THE KARATE KID; and TO LIVE AND DIE IN L.A. He has also cut films for underground director Robert Downey (PUTNEY SWOPE; POUND; and GREASER'S PALACE), which explains why Downey appears in a cameo as an NCAA investigator, and why his son, Robert Downey, Jr., is cast as Hall's best buddy. Despite Smith's past association with generally respectable films, JOHNNY BE GOOD is a sub-PORKY'S pandering to the T & A aspects of today's marketplace. Infraction No. 8 is the film's overall lack of morality. Although it preaches family values (what family would name their child after a brand of Scotch?), the importance of education, and standing up to corrupt institutions, it only does so out of one side of its mouth. Out of the other side comes shameful and reprehensible exploitation—the usual parade of women in bikinis, women exposing their breasts, women in their underwear, women bending over in various states of undress, extreme close-ups of gyrating strippers, phallic jokes, excrement jokes, anti-Oriental jokes, and anti-Texan jokes. Infraction No. 9 (roughing the quarterback) is the commercial that appears halfway through the film in which Chicago Bears star Jim McMahon is visited on the set as he is shooting a promotional spot. The implication is that someday, Hall will be as successful as McMahon. In the process, the viewer is subjected to a 30-second spot that is the same as the one McMahon does for the product on television. The 10th and final infraction is Orion Pictures' decision to release on videotape an R-rated version of the film with "new, sexually explicit footage." By adding more sex scenes and nudity, they've provided a more saleable film than the theatrically released PG-13 version.

There is simply no reason to see JOHNNY BE GOOD, unless you are related to Downey, Jr., who appears to be trying his darnedest to make his character lively. As is the norm with this sort of drivel, a soundtrack album swiftly appeared in the bins. Songs include: "Johnny B. Goode" (Chuck Berry, performed by Berry), "Johnny B. Goode" (Berry, performed by Judas Priest), "Been There, Done That" (John Astley), "If There's Any Justice" (Steve Diamond, Sam Lorber, performed by Fiona), "Caviar" (Myles Goodwin), "Skintight" (Ted Nugent), "Perfect Stranger" (Jimmy Erichson, Michael Sadler, John Bettis, performed by Saga), "Ring Around Rosie" (Donie Purnell, Taylor Rhodes, performed by Kix), "No Place Like Home" (Bettie Shanahan), "Rock Still Rolls Me" (Arnold Lanni, performed by Frozen Ghosts and Friends), "It's Not the Way You Rock" (Dirty Looks), "Heaven Knows" (Michael Woody, performed by Prisoner), "Loneliness Doesn't Live Here Anymore" (Gary Prukop, Jon Milligan, performed by Prisoner), "Mack the Knife" (Bertolt Brecht, Kurt Weill, Marc Blitzstein, performed by Bobby Darin), "When Johnny Comes Marching Home" (arranged by Robert Clark), "La Negra," "Jarabe Tapatio" (arranged by Louis Garcia), and "Ol' Tex Fight Song" (David Obst). (*Profanity, nudity, sexual situations, substance abuse.*)

p, Adam Fields; d, Bud Smith; w, Steve Zacharias, Jeff Buhai, David Obst; ph, Robert D. Yeoman (Foto-Kem Color); ed, Scott Smith; m, Dick Rudolph; md, Dick Rudolph; m/l, Michael Woody, Gary Prukop, Jon Mulligan, B. Nazarian, R. Matlock, D. Bradley, Kurt Weill, Bertolt Brecht, Marc Blitzstein, Robert Palmer, Tommy Dunbar, Charles Judge, David Obst; prod d, Gregg Fonseca; art d, Sharon Seymour; set d, Dorree Cooper; spec eff, Jon G. Belyeu; cos, Susie DeSanto; stunts, Russell Towery; makeup, Devorah Fischa, Michelle Vittone.

Comedy/Sports   Cas.   (PR:O MPAA:PG-13)

JOURNEY TO SPIRIT ISLAND½   (1988) 93m Pal-Seven Wonders c

Bettina (Maria), Marie Antoinette Rodgers (Jimmy Jim), Brandon Douglas (Michael), Gabriel Damon (Willie), Tarek McCarthy (Klim), Tony Acierto (Hawk), Nick Ramus (Tom), Atilla Gombacsi (Phil).

Beautifully photographed by premier cinematographer Vilmos Zsigmond, JOURNEY TO SPIRIT ISLAND is good-hearted family fare that, unfortunately, is marred by a hopelessly naive conclusion that rewrites history and tends to invalidate whatever message the film was aiming for. Set on the Olympic Peninsula and San Juan Islands of the Pacific Northwest, the film concerns a tribe of native Americans who are faced with a dilemma. Acierto, a college-educated member of the tribe, has returned to his hometown with a white college friend who is involved in real estate development. The two propose a plan to turn a sacred island burial ground into a multimillion-dollar resort. Although the older members of the tribe are against violating the sacred burial ground of their ancestors, younger members only see a lucrative windfall in the offing and vote in favor of the resort. Meanwhile, Bettina, the teenage granddaughter of one of the tribe's most respected elders, begins having strange dreams about her great-great-grandfather, who, as legend has it, sent his only son to persuade the white man to leave the sacred island alone. When the boy never returned, the ancient shaman went to the island himself and disappeared. The Indians believe that there has been a curse on the island ever since. Bettina doesn't know what to make of the dreams and they frighten her. When the children of her father's white college chum come to visit from Chicago, Bettina is put in charge of a three-day kayak expedition to the various islands. The two Chicago boys, Douglas and Damon, have preconceived notions of what Indians are like and undergo an education through interaction with Bettina and her younger brother, McCarthy. While kayaking, the teens find their boat mysteriously drawn toward the sacred island, which no one has visited in generations. On the island they discover the remains of the son of Bettina's great-great-grandfather and give them a proper burial. At the same time, Acierto has arrived on the island to destroy the nests of the rare bald eagles that inhabit the area (federal law prohibits man-made disruption of bald eagle nesting sites). The kids try to stop the ambitious Acierto, but he seals them in a cave and leaves them to die. Guided by the spirit of her great-great-grandfather, Bettina finds an escape route and the kids hurry back to the mainland to blow the whistle on the evil Acierto before the city council signs the real estate contracts. Unfortunately, they are too late, arriving just after the contracts are signed. After the kids excitedly tell the council of their brush with death, Acierto scoffs at their story and coldly announces that there's no proof of their allegations and, besides, the contracts have already been signed. Much to his dismay, however, the white real estate speculator stands up and tears the contract in half, announcing that "good business depends on trust" and that he does not make deals with men who respond to allegations of wrongdoing with a casual "You can't prove anything." Defeated, Acierto slams his briefcase shut and storms out of the room, leaving the joyous Indians to celebrate.

Ostensibly a lesson in environmental protection, respect for native American culture, and the terrible exploitation of that culture by the white man, JOURNEY TO SPIRIT ISLAND negates whatever impact it might have had by making an Indian the villain and a white businessman the noble hero who turns his back on a multimillion-dollar deal because of some notion of fairness. Given the atrocious history of European settlers' brutal dealings with native Americans—total contempt for their culture, treaty after treaty broken, and virtual genocide—asking modern audiences to swallow the heartwarming conclusion of this film is absurd. Since when does white American business give a hoot about the feelings of those they seek to displace—especially people of color? If one can get past this ludicrous notion and the distasteful transfer of guilt to an educated, ambitious Indian who sells out his own people (which really smacks of blame-the-victim logic), one may be able to relax and enjoy the absolutely gorgeous Pacific Northwest scenery captured by Zsigmond's camera. As a Disneyesque sort of adventure, with well-scrubbed, plucky teenagers as the protagonists, the film works fairly well and should appeal to youngsters. The interaction of the Indian and Caucasian teens is undeniably charming, with the bemused Indians poking fun at the ignorant whites for believing what they see in the movies. Several universal truths about teenagers in general—white or Indian—are suggested, and this portion of the film is presented as a rather wholesome coming-of-age tale. It is when director Laszlo Pal and screenwriter Crane Webster veer into larger issues that the film falls flat. Luckily, cinematographer Zsigmond found all the truth and poetry he needs in the scenery and the wonderful faces of the native Americans, and perhaps that alone is enough to get the real message across—in spite of the script. (Violence, profanity.)

p, Bruce Clark; d, Laszlo Pal; w, Crane Webster; ph, Vilmos Zsigmond (Alpha Cine color); ed, Bonnie Koehler; m, Fred Myrow; prod d, Bruce Jackman.

Drama   (PR:AA MPAA:NR)

JUDGMENT IN BERLIN½   (1988) 92m Bibo TV-January/New Line c

Martin Sheen (Herbert J. Stern), Sam Wanamaker (Bernard Hellring), Max Gail (Judah Best), Jurgen Heinrich (Uri Andreyev), Heinz Hoenig (Helmut Thiele), Harris Yulin (Bruno Ristau), Sean Penn (Gunther X), Carl Lumbly (Edwin Palmer), Max Volkert Martens (Hans Schuster), Cristine Rose (Marsha Stern).

©NEW LINE

Essentially a courtroom drama, JUDGEMENT IN BERLIN is the true story of the 1978 hijacking of a Polish airliner and the controversial trial of two East Germans who sought to escape to the West. Martens is a West German contractor who works on both sides of the Iron Curtain and has fallen in love with East Berliner Speidel. He plans an escape for Speidel, her young daughter, and Hoenig, a friend whose children live in West Germany. The scheme calls for the East Berliners to meet Martens in Gdansk, Poland, where he will give them false documents they can use to make their way to the West; however, Martens is picked up by the police and Speidel and Hoenig are forced to come up with an alternative plan. They sneak a toy gun onto their flight to East Berlin, and Hoenig uses it to hijack the plane to West Berlin's Tempelhof Airport, where they, as well as several other passengers, are seemingly given political asylum. But it's not that simple. International accords have recently been signed to prevent sky piracy and the American and West German governments have come under pressure from the Soviets to take action. The Bonn government washes its hands of the matter and leaves it to the occupying Americans to prosecute, with an American judge presiding. The Justice Department, determined to obtain a conviction to assuage the Soviets, wants a tough judge who'll come in and get the trial overwith as quickly as possible. Sheen seems to fit the bill, but the fair-minded former prosecutor proves to be more than they bargained for, demanding that the defendants, who are being tried under US law, be given every right guaranteed by the Constitution, including the right to trial by jury. Despite the objections of the prosecutors (Sinclair, Lumbly), who are, in essence, State Department mouthpieces, Sheen seats a jury of Berliners. Early in the proceedings, the case against Speidel is dropped when her silver-tongued lawyer, Wanamaker, proves that she was coerced into signing a confession. Wanamaker then joins Gail in the defense of Hoenig, and demonstrates through cross-examination that the crew of the Polish airliner, intimidated by Polish officials, have committed perjury. Finally, Penn, one of the passengers who defected after the hijacking, comes forward and testifies. He was outside the cockpit when the hijacking occurred and he explains that the crew realized immediately that Hoenig's gun was a toy, but landed in West Berlin anyway out of sympathy for him. The German jury finds Hoenig innocent on all counts except one, but Sheen decides not to sentence him.

JUDGEMENT IN BERLIN is based on a book by Herbert J. Stern, the presiding judge, and Martin Sheen, who was the film's executive producer, is very much center stage as Stern, delivering a portrayal that oozes integrity and determination. Unfortunately, a weak script and choppy, pedestrian direction by Leo Penn (Sean's father) prevent Sheen's performance and the film from becoming gripping, despite the inherently compelling nature of the real-life events. To its credit, the script succeeds in ironically juxtaposing Eastern repressiveness with its American equivalent in the prosecutors' unwillingness to accord the victims due process and in Sheen's brave refusal to allow the State Department to turn the proceedings into a kangaroo court, but on the whole, the trial and Sheen's internal struggle for justice are presented with little imagination. Most of the performances are adequate but unexceptional, although Wanamaker does an assured turn as the speechifying defense lawyer who likens the trial to the one proposed by the cat to the mouse in Alice Through the Looking Glass. The film's most noteworthy performance, however, is Sean Penn's. Carrying himself as if he has been physically repressed by his years behind the Iron Curtain and delivering his lines in halting English with a finely nuanced German accent, Penn presents a minutely detailed but too studied portrayal of Gunther X, so that his acting detracts from the depth of emotion he also brings to his character's heartfelt testimony. Penn, who had been sentenced to a 60-day jail term for punching an extra on the set of COLORS—a flagrant violation of the probationary sentence he received for an earlier battery charge—was permitted to delay the start of his incarceration to go to Berlin and complete his work in this low-budget production.

p, Joshua Sinclair, Ingrid Windisch; d, Leo Penn; w, Joshua Sinclair, Leo Penn (based on the book by Herbert J. Stern); ph, Gabor Pogany (Eastmancolor); ed, Teddy Darvas; m, Peter Goldfoot; art d, Jan Schlubach, Peter Alteneder; cos, Ingrid Zore.

Drama   Cas.   (PR:A MPAA:PG)

JULIA AND JULIA*½ (1988, It.) 97m RAI-TV/Cinecom c

Kathleen Turner *(Julia)*, Sting *(Daniel Osler)*, Gabriel Byrne *(Paolo)*, Gabriele Ferzetti *(Paolo's Father)*, Angela Goodwin *(Paolo's Mother)*, Lidia Broccolino *(Carla)*, Alexander Van Wyk *(Marco)*, Renato Scarpa *(Commissioner)*, Norman Mozzato, Yorgo Voyagis, Mirella Falco, Francesca Muzio, John Steiner.

© CINECOM

JULIA AND JULIA is the first English-language picture for American-born Italian director Peter Del Monte, but, perhaps more important, it is also the first feature-length film shot in HDVS, a high-definition video system that is then transferred to 35mm film for distribution. Boasting a more detailed image than standard video systems (1125 lines instead of the usual 625), High Definition Video has been hailed but some as the wave of the future. But while the technology may be revolutionary and the subject of much discussion, this film is far less noteworthy.

Turner stars as the title Julias. As the film gets underway, we realize that we are witnessing Turner's wedding day. As she and her new husband, Byrne, are driving along they are run off the road by a truck. Byrne is killed, while Turner, who was thrown from the moving car, is left screaming in her wedding dress. Time passes and Turner is still having difficulty getting over her loss. She lives in Trieste, Italy, but is urged by Byrne's mother (Goodwin) to return home to America—if only for the sake of her sanity. Turner, however, attempts to make the best of life, living in a lovely apartment and working at a travel agency. Then one evening, after driving through a mysterious fog, she comes home and cannot unlock her apartment door. A crabby woman answers the door and claims she has lived there for years. Turner is baffled. So is the audience. And Maurice Jarre's already irritating electronic score kicks into high gear. Turner is then reunited with Byrne and, much to her surprise, a son she doesn't remember bearing. Suddenly, she seems to be living a happy family life, but when she goes to work, no one recognizes her. In her pocket she finds a the key to Room 12 at the Hotel Savoy; later, she receives a phone call from her lover, Sting, but doesn't recognize his voice or name. Deciding to play Nancy Drew, Turner calls the Hotel Savoy, Room 12, and, hearing Sting's voice, she hangs up. She goes to his room, where she finds slides that picture her naked in Sting's bed. Jarre's music reminds us things are not what they seem, and we keep waiting for Rod Serling to walk into frame and say, "Trieste, Italy, Planet Earth . . ." Instead, Sting appears and is delighted to see his lover. Turner is considerably less thrilled and runs away. Later, at the travel agency, Turner (recognized again by her fellow employees) is at her desk when Sting walks in to purchase a plane ticket. Guess what? He doesn't remember her. Turner, however, recognizes him. After he leaves, she follows him to his room, but though he doesn't seem to know her, he is eager to become intimate. Turner noses around but can't find the slides she saw earlier. She tries to run off, but Sting's animal magnetism keeps her in his grasp. They make love and, come morning, Turner returns home, where Byrne is waiting for her. Knowing that she has been unfaithful, he leaves. Wait a minute, isn't he supposed to be dead? Is Turner really cheating on Byrne, or just on her memory of Byrne? We don't know, and Turner doesn't seem to either, as she runs back to Sting, convinced that she shouldn't see him anymore because she still loves her husband. Byrne, however, has departed, so Sting grabs Turner and, in no time, rapes her in a piazza. Later, Sting returns home to again find Turner there. They embrace and Turner plunges a scissors into Sting's back, dumps his body, and attempts to resume a normal life again. Turner now seems content, baking in her kitchen while Byrne gives their son a bath. She runs to the store, but along the way is picked up by a police car and hauled in for questioning on the disappearance of Sting. When Turner provides her alibi—that she was with Byrne—the inspector looks as if his been dealt a swift right hook and reminds Turner that her husband has been dead for six years. Turner is sent to jail and, during a visit by Byrne's mother, admits that she is now finally happy.

There are certain debates in the history of civilization that just aren't worth pondering for long, like "If a tree falls in the forest and no one hears it, does it make a sound?" or "What are Razzles—a candy or a gum?" With the release of JULIA AND JULIA, we can now add "What is JULIA AND JULIA about, really?" In his last film, PICCOLI FUOCHI (Little Flames), Del Monte played head games with his audience by presenting a child whose playmates may be fantasies or alien creatures. The result is an interesting perversion of a childhood fairy tale that is tedious, pretentious, and ultimately pointless. Before that, in 1982, Del Monte made INVITATION AU VOYAGE, a French-Italian coproduction that was given a limited US release. Not even remotely interesting, that film is just tedious, pretentious, and pointless. With JULIA AND JULIA, Del Monte has again made a film with those same qualities from a script better suited to "Twilight Zone" or "Tales from the Darkside." Although there are some interesting ideas in the script (most notably, that Turner's attachment to her dead husband is so strong that she not only imagines that he is still alive, but invents the life of the child they never had), they are so flatly executed that it's difficult to care. As for the acting, Kathleen Turner seems to try with her material but gives basically a one-note performance conveying perplexity and little else. Sting and Gabriel Byrne are in the film, but there's little more one can say about their performances—they're just pawns in Del Monte's mind game. This leaves nothing left to consider but the quality of the High Definition Video. Untrained eyes probably won't notice anything different, as JULIA AND JULIA looks pretty much like an expensive soap opera, but people who love the quality of film and appreciate the importance of light in a projected image will be a bit distressed. *(Adult situations, sexual situations, nudity, violence.)*

d, Peter Del Monte; w, Silvia Napolitano, Peter Del Monte, Sandro Petraglia (based on a story by Peter Del Monte, Silvia Napolitano); ph, Giuseppe Rotunno (Technicolor); ed, Michael Chandler; m, Maurice Jarre; art d, Mario Garbuglia; cos, Danda Ortona.

Drama **Cas.** **(PR:C MPAA:NR)**

KANDYLAND* (1988) 93m NW c

Kim Evenson *(Joni Sekorsy)*, Charles Laulette *(Frank)*, Sandahl Bergman *(Harlow Divine)*, Cole Stevens *(Roy)*, Bruce Baum *(Mad Dog)*, Alan Toy *(Eppy)*, Irwin Keyes *(Biff)*, Steve Kravitz *(Bruce Belnap)*, Catlyn Day *(Diva)*, Ja-Net Hintzen *(Vampira)*, Chrissy Ratay *(Scarlet)*, Brenda Winston *(Betty)*, Israel Juarbe *(Lumpy)*, Beth Peters *(Mrs. Pruitt)*, Ken Olfson *(Cleaner Customer)*, Richard Neil *(Vinnie)*, Natalie Sumara-Janiec *(Lucille)*, Deanne Jacobs *(Debbie)*, Shelby Gregory *(Contest Emcee)*, Ray Saniger *(Rowdy)*, Jim Mapp *(Leon)*, Hugh McPhillips *(Minister)*, Alan Popper, Robert Kash *(Hecklers)*, Don Barber *(Pedestrian)*, Kahlena Marie *(China Doll)*, Anet Anatelle, Margie Barron, Elise Bernbach, Demona Kirk, Diana London, Charmaine Spears *(Waitresses)*.

Taking itself far too seriously, KANDYLAND is not so much a movie as an excuse to show off a number of nightclub strippers performing their dance routines. Former *Playboy* centerfold Evenson stars as a pretty young Californian who is struggling to make it financially with her mechanic boy friend, Laulette. When Evenson meets Bergman, a stripper whose career as a ballerina never materialized, she decides to try stripping at Kandyland, a trendy, neon-lit, yuppie strip joint. Although Laulette is initially against the idea, he gives in to her wishes, thinking them just a passing whim. Bergman offers to teach the eager Evenson the ropes, insisting that stripping "isn't something you just stand up and you do . . . it's an art." Soon Evenson is perfecting her striptease before Bergman. They become the best of friends and, after a titillating audition, Evenson is hired (and performs under the name "Lotta Love"). Laulette breaks off his relationship with Evenson, but still finds himself thinking about her. Meanwhile, Evenson has moved in with Bergman and the pair make big plans to leave town and try their luck in either Las Vegas or Atlantic City. Laulette has a change of heart and gives Evenson his blessing. A heartbroken Bergman, believing that her friend has abandoned her and given up on their plans to travel together, gets mixed up with Kandyland's sleazy, ultra-macho bartender, Stevens, who gives her a dangerous dose of drugs just before she is about to go onstage. While trying to perform her Jean Harlow routine, Bergman stumbles around embarrassingly as the audience jeers. The drugged Bergman flees to the rooftop and, despite Evenson's efforts, falls to her death on the street below. Stevens, in an effort to silence Evenson, beats and attempts to rape her before she is rescued by Laulette and the police. Everything is patched up between Evenson and Laulette and the pair make plans to marry.

With half of the film's running time devoted to topless dancing girls, there isn't a lot of room left for a plot. Still, although the film starts out painfully slow, by the second half there is some actual character development and complexity—a real rarity in this sort of film. The relationship between Evenson and Laulette begins typically, but is eventually revealed to have an innocent quality in which both characters truly seem to love each other. More curious, however, is the friendship between Evenson and Bergman, which has more than its share of lesbian undercurrents. Kim Evenson, while no great actress, has an ingratiating ingenuousness that takes over when her acting fails. Despite his character's introduction as a macho stud, Charles Laulette creates a likeable character who actually shows his true feelings to Evenson. Sandahl Bergman's performance is serviceable in a part that stretches her acting ability to the breaking point. The rest of the film is peppered with some eccentric characters that manage to pump some life into the picture, namely Bruce Baum, as the club comic; Irwin Keyes, as the dumb bouncer; and Alan Toy, as the crippled club owner. The film contains much technical flash in its production design, lighting, and editing, but is still little more than an excuse to titillate. The sex club atmosphere and the life of strippers received a much more interesting treatment in Abel Ferrara's 1984 thriller FEAR CITY. Besides a snippet of Tchaikovsky's "Swan Lake" (arranged by George Michalski), the soundtrack includes "Let's Fly Away," "Ask Me To Dance" (Michalski, Freddy Herrick, performed by Naomi Delgado); "John and Diane" (Robert Berry, performed by Berry); "My Car, His Car" (IC3, performed by IC3); "Stolen Kisses" (Alex Bendhan, performed by Alex Guinness and the World Records); "You Make Me Come Alive (Scarlet's Dance)" (Jimmy Lifton, performed by Siri Lini); "Butterfly Cocoon (Harlow's Dance #1)," "Harlow's Dance #2" (Alan Howarth, performed by Howarth); "Trying Very Hard" (Gene Tambor, Holly Tambor, Ed Subitzky, performed by Wheels); "As I Move (Joni's Dance)" (Marc Decker, performed by Doctor Daddio and the L.A. Mints); "Eyes on Me (Vampira's Dance)" (Patrick Henderson, Ollie Brown, performed by Brenda Price); "This Heart" (Hiroshi Upshur, Kathleen Ann Parker, performed by Bobby Van Rooy), "Do the Dance" (Ben Merlene, P.J. Wilde, performed by Trance Dance); "When I Get to Heaven Will

There Still Be Rock n' Roll" (Johnny Flynn, performed by Flynn). *(Nudity, profanity, violence, sexual situations, substance abuse.)*

p, Rich Blumenthal; d, Robert Schnitzer; w, Robert Schnitzer, Toni Serritello; ph, Robert Brinkman (Technicolor); ed, Jeffrey Reiner; m, George Michalski; m/l, George Michalski, Freddy Herrick, Robert Berry, IC3, Alex Bendhan, Jimmy Lifton, Alan Howarth, Gene Tambor, Holly Tambor, Ed Subitzky, Marc Decker, Patrick Henderson, Ollie Brown, Peter Tchaikovsky, Hiroshi Upshur, Kathleen Ann Parker, Ben Marlene, P.J. Wilde, Johnny Flynn; prod d, Paul Sussman; art d, Archie D'Amico, Billie Greenbaum; set d, Marina Kieser; cos, Vicki Graef; makeup, Bridget Bergman.

Drama	Cas.	(PR:O MPAA:R)

KANSAS*   (1988) 106m Trans World c

Matt Dillon *(Doyle Kennedy)*, Andrew McCarthy *(Wade Corey)*, Leslie Hope *(Lori Bayles)*, Alan Toy *(Nordquist)*, Andy Romano *(Fleener)*, Brent Jennings *(Buckshot)*, Brynn Thayer *(Connie)*, Kyra Sedgwick *(Prostitute Drifter)*, Harry Northup *(Governor)*, Clint Allen *(Ted)*, Arlen Dean Snyder *(George Bayles)*, James Lovelett *(Governor's Driver)*, Louis Giambalvo *(Army Sergeant)*, Craig Benton *(Patrolman Casson)*, James Lea Raupp *(Man With Shirt)*, John Lansing *(Governor's Aide)*, Gale Mayron *(Bank Teller)*, T. Max Graham *(Mr. Kennedy)*, Annie Kellogg *(Governor's Daughter)*, Mimi Wickliff *(Mrs. Bayles)*, Linda Dawson *(Governor's Wife)*, George Mason Kuhn *(Bank Guard)*, Ken Boehr *(Ferson)*, Robert J. Peters ("Fair" Farmer), Patricia Ann Grit *(Farm Girl)*, Tracy Martin Smith *(Farm Boy)*, Gary Cosey *(Shoeshine)*, Bobby Enriquez *(Bartender)*, Joseph R. Scrivo *(Rodriguez)*, Bart Petty *(Rookie Cop)*, Greg Gilstrap *(Reporter)*, Art Dilks *(Pharmacist)*, Brett Pearson *(Alvin)*, Gail Dicus *(Female Reporter)*, Brent Wright, Holmes Osborne *(Deputies)*, Roger Richman *(Officer Ellwood)*, Rusty Howard *(Officer Swift)*, Lori Gooch *(Lady With Child)*, Robert Hagerman *(Farmer)*, Hank Rector *(Businessman)*, Jacquie Litto *(Friend of Mrs. Bayles)*.

© TRANS WORLD

This predictable melodrama is the tale of two young drifters—one mostly good, the other mostly bad—brought together by fate on a boxcar rumbling through the windblown wheat fields of the American heartland. Dillon, a gregarious ex-con, persuades McCarthy, who had been driving east for the wedding of a friend when his car caught fire, to return with him to his small Kansas hometown, where a big Fourth of July festival is taking place. Before he knows what's happening, McCarthy is drawn into Dillon's robbery of the local bank, and, pursued by police, the two flee and then split up. While hiding under a bridge, McCarthy watches as a car in which the governor's daughter is a passenger slides into the river. Even though the police are nearby, McCarthy rescues the little girl, returning her to the riverbank. A handicapped journalist (Toy) takes a photo of this heroic act before McCarthy disappears. Leaving the stolen loot hidden under the bridge, McCarthy makes his way to Snyder's farm and is hired to work the wheat harvest. Fate is still on the job, though, as Snyder's daughter, Hope, just happens to be the attractive lass who mesmerized McCarthy at the holiday parade. She already has a law school-bound boy friend, however, and, assuming that she knows all about McCarthy's kind, she turns up her nose at his attentions. He works hard and watches from the sidelines as Hope plays tennis and acts the privileged brat with her boy friend, but, of course, McCarthy isn't about to give up. Meanwhile, Dillon has been laying low as a ride operator with a carnival. On the stormy night that he and McCarthy are to meet to split the money, McCarthy finally gets his chance for a roll in the hay (literally) with Hope. Still, she refuses to see any future in their relationship. What's more, a furious Dillon shows up, and, to ensure McCarthy's presence at their next meeting, sets fire to the barn. When reporter Toy arrives to cover the fire, he recognizes McCarthy as the hero from his photograph (but not as a bank robber, because the police have been looking for only one man, Dillon) and overnight McCarthy becomes a celebrity, honored by the governor and a huge party. Hope decides that McCarthy is all right after all, but he still has to deal with Dillon, who has told Toy that McCarthy was in on the robbery. The two outlaws battle on the bridge at night, and though Dillon walks away with the money, he also ends up in the hands of the law, and McCarthy, whom Toy decides not to finger, ends up with Hope.

There aren't many surprises in KANSAS—not in its plot, its performances, or its look. Very early on, we suspect that McCarthy will eventually get the girl and that Dillon will get his comeuppance, but these inevitabilities would more palatable if screenwriter Spencer Eastman and Australian director David Stevens led us to them by a less-traveled route. Instead, their film is not only predictable but overly dependent on coincidence. Presumably, the filmmakers' intent was to explore two personalities that are more alike than we might at first think—to show the decent side of Dillon's violent criminal and the dark, duplicitous side of McCarthy, and that heroism and villainy can coexist in the same person. However, because the screenplay is more concerned with its formula plot than with character development, neither McCarthy nor Dillon are able offer any real insights into this theme.

Matt Dillon is convincing as the sometimes good-natured but ultimately menacing bad boy; however, McCarthy, displaying too many of his increasingly familiar acting ticks, is less successful and his character never comes into focus. Andrew McCarthy being Andrew McCarthy, his drifter is also unremittingly middle class, which flies in the face of the suggestion that his relationship with Hope is impeded by class barriers. Obviously, McCarthy, as both a hero and bank robber, isn't what he appears to be, but if Eastman and Stevens intended his backstory to also work against Hope's perception of him, they have failed to offer enough of a sense his background to give his relationship with Hope any real resonance. As it is, his romance with Hope—whose performance, like those of the supporting players, is unmemorable—is overheated without generating any real passion or insight.

The film's cinematography, by David Eggby (MAD MAX), is polished but predictable, his wheat field sunsets pretty but familiar. KANSAS was shot on location in the eastern part of the Jayhawk State, but because the production didn't get under way until after the Kansas wheat harvest, those scenes were shot in North Dakota. Interestingly, screenwriter Eastman had never been to Kansas when he undertook the film's screenplay, but rather than make a quick get-acquainted tour, he subscribed to five small-town Kansas newspapers and got to know the state and its people that way. Reportedly, Eastman's story was also inspired by newspaper accounts he had read of "spontaneous heroism." Unfortunately, the characters in KANSAS have a second-hand feel to them—not so much as if they have come from newspaper stories but rather as if they have come from other movies. *(Violence, profanity, adult situations, sexual situations.)*

p, George Litto; d, David Stevens; w, Spencer Eastman; ph, David Eggby (DeLuxe color); ed, Robert Barrere; m, Pino Donaggio; md, Natale Massara; prod d, Matthew Jacobs; set d, Stewart K. McGuire; cos, Nancy G. Fox; stunts, Wally Crowder; makeup, Gigi Williams.

Crime/Romance	Cas.	(PR:C-O MPAA:R)

KILLER KLOWNS FROM OUTER SPACE*½   (1988) 88m Trans World c

Grant Cramer *(Mike)*, Suzanne Snyder *(Debbie)*, John Allen Nelson *(Officer Dave Hanson)*, Royal Dano *(Farmer Green)*, John Vernon *(Officer Mooney)*, Michael Siegel *(Rich)*, Peter Licassi *(Paul)*.

In KILLER KLOWNS FROM OUTER SPACE a potentially interesting concept is turned into a merely dull and repetitive one by the men who created the critters in CRITTERS, Stephen, Charles, and Edward Chiodo, known collectively as the Chiodo brothers. Set in a small town, the movie begins on the lover's lane where most of the local college students are drinking and necking. Suddenly, a shooting star cuts across the sky and appears to crash nearby. Cramer and Snyder decide to postpone their necking and go search for the astral object. While combing the area where the "star" fell, the couple discover a giant circus tent with many colorful passageways inside it. They stumble upon a huge storage room full of giant pink cotton candy cocoons. Wrapped up in the cocoons are dead bodies. To their horror, Cramer and Snyder learn that they have encountered killer klowns from outer space, an alien race of beings that resemble maniacal circus clowns. The klowns discover the human intruders and chase after them, firing their candy-striped guns loaded with popcorn "bullets" that fly through the air and stick to the victims' clothing. Cramer and Snyder manage to escape and rush to the police station to tell young deputy Nelson of the invasion. Although incredulous, Nelson makes an effort to hear the youths out. Dour cop Vernon, however, believes that the college students are mocking the police department by pulling an elaborate prank. Nelson, who once dated Snyder and still carries a torch, asks Cramer to show him the site where they discovered the circus tent. But first, Nelson insists on taking Snyder home. Meanwhile, the killer klowns have left their tent spaceship and have invaded the town, zapping its citizens with their colorful weapons, which entomb the humans in the cotton candy cocoons. After witnessing a killer klown at work, Nelson finally believes Cramer's story. Unfortunately, by this time nearly the entire town has been swathed in cotton candy and Snyder has been captured and is being held inside a giant beach ball. Nelson and Cramer are determined to rescue the girl and, aided by a pair of ice cream men, take on the killer klowns. It is discovered that the klowns can be killed by a shot to their big red noses, so the heroes follow the klowns into their circus-tent spaceship for a showdown. After dispatching several klowns, the guys manage to rescue Snyder and attempt to leave, but they are cornered by a giant killer klown. Nelson creates a diversion so that his comrades can escape, but later finds himself trapped on the spaceship as it begins to take off. In a heroic effort, Nelson punctures the nose of the giant klown and the spaceship explodes in midair, destroying all the klowns. The young deputy survives, however, because he took shelter in a klown car that shielded him from the blast.

Certainly one of the most colorful films of the year, KILLER KLOWNS FROM OUTER SPACE has its moments, but suffers from a lack of development beyond the concept stage. Obviously the Chiodo brothers enjoyed creating the incorrigible klowns, but, with a simple-minded script that borrows heavily from THE BLOB (1958), the movie simply becomes dull and repetitive, and isn't half as funny as it should be. The acting, save that of veteran character actor John Vernon, is uniformly weak and Suzanne Snyder is particularly atrocious. Not that one expects superior thesping in a low-budget science fiction film, but this actress is downright annoying. Stephen Chiodo is not much of a director, either. The film is haphazardly shot and poorly paced, making its brief running time seem longer than it actually is.

What does work are the sets and the klowns. Klown-makers Charlie Chiodo, Derrick De Voe, and Dwight Roberts, art director Philip Dean Foreman, and especially prop-maker Gene Rizzardi create a truly unique and clever alien universe in which brightly colored circus costumes and candy-striped toys become menacing items of death and destruction. The klowns' heads are fully articulated foam rubber masks that are worn by the actors and manipulated mechanically by technicians. These are capable of many different expressions, including an evil smile that shows off rows of sharp teeth. Four basic klown heads were created and then made to look different with a variety of wigs, makeup, and costumes. The many optical effects—most of which are excellent—were handled by the Fantasy II company. Unfortunately, all this superior low-budget effects technology is devoted to only a few gags, which are repeated with little variation throughout the movie. KILLER KLOWNS could have been an interesting and enjoyable addition to a tired genre, but the Chiodos bobbled the ball and presented a film full of unfulfilled promise. *(Cartoon violence, profanity.)*

p, Edward Chiodo, Stephen Chiodo, Charles Chiodo; d, Stephen Chiodo; w, Charles Chiodo, Stephen Chiodo; ph, Alfred Taylor; ed, Chris Roth; m, John Massari; prod d, Charles Chiodo; art d, Philip Dean Foreman; spec eff, Fantasy II Film Effects, Charles Chiodo; cos, Darcee Olson.

Horror/Science Fiction Cas. (PR:C-O MPAA:PG-13)

KILLING AFFAIR, A † (1988) 100m Tomorrow Ent./Hemdale c

Peter Weller *(Baston Morris)*, Kathy Baker *(Maggie Gresham)*, Bill Smitrovich *(Pink Gresham)*, John Glover.

Filmed in 1985, screened at the American Film Institute Festival early in 1988, but yet to receive a wide release, A KILLING AFFAIR is a WW II-era southern Gothic adapted from the novel *Monday, Tuesday, Wednesday* by Robert Houston. Set in the backwoods of West Virginia, the film centers on a farm woman, Baker, whose vile, two-timing husband turns up murdered in the outhouse. Enter a mysterious stranger, Weller, who freely admits to the killing, claiming that it was an act of vengeance. It seems that the deceased had tried to run off with Weller's wife and children. Now Weller holds Baker hostage in her isolated cabin for three days, and a complicated psycho-drama of compassion, complicity, hatred, lust, and violence plays out between the two before the sheriff arrives. Writer-director David Saperstein, who wrote the novel *Cocoon*, makes his feature debut here, assembling an impressive cast that includes John Glover as Kathy Baker's Bible-thumping brother. Given the talent involved (three of the fine lead actors appeared in this film before their respective breakthrough movies: Peter Weller in ROBOCOP, Baker in STREET SMART, and Glover in 52 PICKUP), A KILLING AFFAIR may get a wider release in 1989 and will most certainly turn up on videocassette.

p, Michael Rauch, Peter R. McIntosh; d, David Saperstein; w, David Saperstein (based on the novel *Monday, Tuesday, Wednesday* by Robert Houston); ph, Dominique Chapuis (Technicolor); ed, Patrick McMahon; m, John Barry; prod d, John J. Moore; set d, Lynn Wolverton; cos, Elisabeth Ann Seley.

Drama (PR:NR MPAA:R)

KILLING GAME, THE † (1988) 83m City Lights Home Video c

Chard Hayward, Cynthia Killion, Geoffrey Sadwith, Robert Zdar, Bette Rae, Julie Noble, Monique Monet, Brigitte Burdine, Janet Jimmi Parker, Ron Gillchrist, Leia Luahiwa.

Another made-for-videocassette release from City Lights Home Video (see L.A. CRACKDOWN parts I and II), THE KILLING GAME stars Chard Hayward as a hit man-gambler who finds himself a blackmail victim after he ices a man and his mistress. The prime suspect is Zdar (also seen this year in the title role in MANIAC COP), a Las Vegas crime lord who wants Hayward to work as his triggerman *and* peddle dope.

p, Richard Pepin, Joseph Merhi; d, Joseph Merhi; w, Joseph Merhi; ph, Richard Pepin; m, John Gonzalez.

Crime Cas. (PR:NR MPAA:NR)

KING LEAR**** (1988, US/Fr.) 90m Cannon/Cannon c

Burgess Meredith *(Don Learo)*, Peter Sellars *(William Shakespeare, Jr. the Fifth)*, Molly Ringwald *(Cordelia)*, Jean-Luc Godard *(Professor)*, Woody Allen *(Mr. Alien)*, Norman Mailer *(Himself)*, Kate Mailer *(Herself)*, Leos Carax *(Edgar)*.

In 1606, William Shakespeare's "King Lear" first appeared on the stage. Three hundred and seventy-nine years later, Jean-Luc Godard was pelted in the face with a meringue pie at a Cannes Film Festival press conference for his film DETECTIVE. The following day, Godard sat at a hotel table with Cannon Films production head Menahem Golan and signed, on a napkin, the most publicized picture deal in recent years—an adaption of "King Lear" from a script by Norman Mailer. According to Golan, the deal "gives us the most modern and controversial director in the world dealing with Shakespeare's far-sighted view of the generation gap." After some talk that Marlon Brando or Rod Steiger would be cast as Lear, and that Ellen Burstyn and members of the Actors Studio would participate, Godard's much-anticipated KING LEAR surfaced as a work-in-progress at the 1987 Cannes festival and later appeared at a handful of other festivals. It was not until 1988, however, that KING LEAR received its theatrical release.

With no credits (contractually, everyone's names have been left off and none can be used to promote the film, not even on its poster), KING LEAR opens over black with a conversation between Menahem Golan and Godard in which they discuss the progress of the film and its pending release. Already the film's peculiar tone is set, since this conversation is moot—not only has the film been released, we're watching it. The opening segment (Godard's structure cannot be divided into "scenes") takes place in a hotel room as Mailer, "the Great Writer" (a parallel to Shakespeare, the Great Writer of his era), discusses his script with daughter Kate. His script, titled "Don Learo," is set against a Mafia background, much to Kate's consternation. The Mailers (Godard's filmic parallel to Lear and daughter Cordelia) walk onto their balcony, which overlooks the coast of Nyon, Switzerland. The squawking of the seagulls reaches a deafening level. The scene repeats, with only slight variance. The narrating Godard, in a Boris Karloff voice, tells us that only one day into the production the Mailers returned to America. (Writer and director parted ways because, according to Godard, Mailer had a "ceremony of star behavior." This claim is disputed by associate producer Tom Luddy, who stated that the Mailers would gladly have continued had they not been playing themselves, since there is an incestuous subtext to Godard's direction.) The scene shifts to a hotel dining room, which always seems to be empty except for the film's main characters. Avant-garde theater whiz kid Sellars stars as William Shakespeare Jr., V, a vice-president of the Cannon Cultural Affairs division. The time is apocalyptic post-Chernobyl, during a period when "movies and art no longer exist and must be reinvented." Sellars is, therefore, seeking out his ancestor's once-great writings. He ponders a phrase of Shakespeare's. "As you . . . wish," he quotes. That doesn't sound correct. He tries again. "As you . . . witch." "As you . . . watch." Meanwhile, at a nearby table, the powerful Don Learo (Meredith) talks with his virtuous daughter Cordelia (Ringwald). "As you . . . like it!" Sellars blurts out, fully aware that he has hit upon the title of the great play. He approaches Ringwald, but is verbally attacked by Meredith, who barks, "Are you trying to make a play for my daughter?" Well, actually, Sellars *is* —and that play is "King Lear." This nonstop, zig-zagging, multilayered confusion persists throughout. Sellars continues his search for Shakespeare's writings. Meredith and Ringwald try to work out their tragic relationship—she unable to show her love in a way he understands. While her two less-devoted sisters make false displays of their love, Ringwald refuses such insincerity. Meredith sees only that Ringwald gives him nothing. Ringwald, however, is giving him "no thing." Godard repeatedly resorts to title cards "No Thing," "Fear and Loathing," "Power and Virtue," "Three Journeys into King Lear," "KING LEAR—a Film Shot in the Back," and "King LEAR—A Film in the cLEARing" a technique he has long used to make the verbal visual. Sellars meets Carax, a young man trying to reinvent fire, who is keeping company with a girl friend who is not around. This girl friend, Delpy, spends much of her time ironing (an electric form of fire put to a practical use) and is, perhaps, a descendent of Virginia Woolf. (Virginia Woolf Jr., V, maybe?) In any case, a copy of Woolf's *The Waves* can be spotted by the seaside, where Sellars gets pounded by fierce waves as he struggles to write Shakespearean quotes in his journal. Through Carax, Sellars meets Godard, playing Professor Pluggy, a former filmmaker turned Rastafarian wizard with a noisy hairdo of electric patch cords, dog tags, hotel keys, and pop tops. He smokes a cigar, talks out of the side of his mouth, pontificates about America being "Las Vegasized," and is violently flatulent. He talks about images and carries with him a miniature shoebox projection room, which he illuminates with a sparkler. Pictures of great paintings are intercut—lit by the flame of a lighter. Plastic toy dinosaurs are illuminated by a swinging lightbulb sun. Eventually the cast comes together for a screening of a film. A New York film critic interviews the evasive Pluggy. Back in the editing room Allen, as Mr. Alien (the Fool of the original), wears a black T-shirt with white letters that read "Picasso." Very seriously, he quotes from Shakespeare and splices together two pieces of motion picture film . . . using a safety pin, needle, and thread.

It should come as no surprise that Godard shows very little concern for plot, though the plot of KING LEAR is the most coherent of the films in his third period (1980-present). As with every addition to the Godard canon, KING LEAR further stretches his previous ideas, preoccupations, and experiments. His first "adaptation" in 20 years, KING LEAR does for Shakespeare what LE MEPRIS (CONTEMPT) did for Homer and Alberto Moravia, what MASCULIN-FEMININ (MASCULINE-FEMININE) did for Guy de Maupassant, what PRENOM: CARMEN (FIRST NAME: CARMEN) did for Georges Bizet, and what JE VOUS SALUE, MARIE (HAIL MARY) did for the Bible—nothing, and everything. It does nothing (no thing) for Shakespeare because what little Shakespeare manages to sneak through is relegated to the wings while Godard takes center stage. In a different sense, however, it does more with the original than any number of faithful, literary adaptations—it allows the material to transcend its medium and find new power in a modern time. Godard's KING LEAR rejuvenates Shakespeare's play—no longer a literary relic, but a piece of work placed at the very edge of artistic advancement. KING LEAR also represents Godard's greatest achievements in sound. (Special credit must go to sound recordist Francois Musy.) For the first time in his career, the sound has become more important than the visuals. It is his wish that "movies and art . . . be reinvented," and by creating a separate aural world in KING LEAR he comes closer than ever to this goal. Unfortunately, his Dolby experiments go unheard in most of the venues in which KING LEAR appears. Not only has Godard advanced further than his contemporaries in the art of filmmaking, he has now moved beyond the technicians in creating a soundtrack that cannot be accommodated by standard means of projection.

In KING LEAR, Godard has moved further towards an international cinema (it is fitting that he lives and works in neutral Switzerland). The film is in English, was produced by a major American company, and features a big-name cast. Although previous Godard films have featured "stars" (such as Yves Montand and Jane Fonda in 1972's TOUT VA BIEN and, most recently, Hanna Schygulla and Isabelle Huppert in PASSION), none have been so filled with box-office names as KING LEAR. Although the casting of Burgess Meredith, Norman Mailer, Peter Sellars, and Woody Allen is highly unorthodox, the shocker is Molly Ringwald, star of SIXTEEN CANDLES; PRETTY IN PINK; and this year's wretched FOR KEEPS. A superstar who is the very embodiment of that species known as Teenager, Ringwald is just about the last person you could imagine in a Godard film. Interestingly, however, she is able to fit into what was surely an alien situation for the actress. Godard manages to use her in much the same way as he has Isabelle Huppert—as a virtuous, fresh-faced innocent who seems uneasy with the world around her. Stepping into the Jean-Pierre Leaud role of such films as LE GAI SAVOIR; WIND FROM THE EAST; or WEEKEND is Sellars, who wanders around, book in hand, in his bemusing quest for culture. Godard, who connects his film with cinema's past (photos are shown of Jean Cocteau, Orson Welles, Fritz Lang, and others), also connects with its future by casting Leos Carax, the young French director whose BAD BLOOD (France, 1986, though released only at festivals in the US) had numerous critics calling him the "new Godard." Julie Delpy, featured in BAD BLOOD and Godard's DETECTIVE, also appears, making the link between the two directors on another level. KING LEAR is not for everyone. Unlike Akira Kurosawa in his "King Lear" adaptation RAN, Godard is not adapting but inventing. This is Jean-Luc Godard's KING LEAR, not Shakespeare's. Shakespeare's is about power and virtue; Godard's is about the invention and continued reinvention of the ways we create and perceive cinema. (In English.) (*Profanity.*)

p, Menahem Golan, Yoram Globus; d, Jean-Luc Godard; w, Jean-Luc Godard (based on the play by William Shakespeare); ph, Sophie Maintigneux.

Drama   **(PR:A-C MPAA:NR)**

KISS, THE †   (1988) 101m Tri-Star-Astral-Trilogy/Tri-Star c

Pamela Collyer (*Hilary Halloran*), Peter Dvorsky (*Father Joe*), Joanna Pacula (*Felice*), Meredith Salenger (*Amy Halloran*), Mimi Kuzyk (*Brenda Carson*), Nicholas Kilbertus (*Jack Halloran*), Sabrina Boudot (*Heather*), Shawn Levy (*Terry*), Jan Rubes (*Tobin*), Celine Lomez (*Aunt Irene*), Dorian Joe Clark (*T.C.*), Richard Dumont (*Abe*), Priscilla Mouzakiotis (*Young Felice*), Talya Rubin (*Young Hilary*), Philip Pretten (*Father*), Johanne Herelle (*Old African Woman*), Tyrone Benskin (*Train Station Conductor*), Shannon McDonough (*Eileen*), Vlasta Vrana (*Bishop*), Marty Finkelstein (*Boy in Classroom*), Claire Rodger (*Nurse*), Norris Domingue (*Security Guard*), Robin Bronfman (*Stewardess*), Nevin Densham (*Boy in Pool*), Andrew Johnson (*Gunshop Owner*).

© TRI-STAR

Tri-Star apparently realized they had quite a stinker on their hands in THE KISS, delaying its distribution twice and finally, quietly, giving it a swift regional release late in the year, before dumping it on the home video market. Sounding like a combination of THE OMEN and THE HIDDEN, this supernatural horror tale features Pacula as a mysterious fashion model who, as a child living in the Belgian Congo, was possessed by an evil spirit as the result of a kiss administered by a voodoo priestess. Twenty-five years later, Pacula shows up for the confirmation of her niece (Salenger), and soon the blood begins to flow. With her mother killed by an out-of-control pickup truck, her best friend mutilated by an escalator, her boy friend slain in yet another "accident," and her ineffectual father seduced by Pacula, Salenger begins to suspect that her aunt is up to no good. As it turns out, Pacula wants to pass along the family curse to her young niece, but to do so she has to get close enough to lay a long, wet kiss on the distinctly *lesbophobic* child. This reportedly laughable horror film was the directorial debut of Pen Densham, who never cared much for horror films before accepting the job and took a crash course in the genre by screening financially successful horror films and reading 25 books on the subject before production began. (Sounds real promising, eh?) Special effects designer Chris Walas (who has since directed the sequel to THE FLY) handled the whiz-bang stuff.

p, Pen Densham, John Watson; d, Pen Densham; w, Stephen Volk, Tom Ropelewski (based on a story by Stephen Volk); ph, Francois Protat (Bellevue Pathe color); ed, Stan Cole; m, J. Peter Robinson; m/l, J. Peter Robinson, Tom Canning, Pen Densham, Richard B. Lewis, Larry Williams; prod d, Roy Forge Smith; art d, Suzanna Smith; set d, Gilles Aird; spec eff, Louis Craig; cos, Renee April; stunts, Steve Davison; makeup, Louise Mignault.

Horror   **Cas.**   **(PR:NR MPAA:R)**

L

L.A. CRACKDOWN †   (1988) 84m City Lights c

Pamela Dixon *(Karen Shore)*, Tricia Parks, Kita Harrison, Jeffrey Olsen, Robert D'Lorrio, Michael Coon, Tyron Van Haynes, Achmed Rubell, Pete Shaner, Tom Dewier, John Gonzalez.

City Lights Home Video is a company that specializes in producing movies exclusively for the home video market, and this seems to be their most popular release. Dixon stars as an idealistic police psychologist who is determined to rid Los Angeles of its gang and drug problem. Not content merely to play cop, Dixon goes so far as to take in two troubled teenage girls, a black prostitute (Harrison), and a member of a crack-dealing gang (Parks) who wants out. Despite Dixon's efforts to rehabilitate the girls, Harrison and Parks become victims of the street and Dixon vows revenge on the social parasites who killed them. The national obsessions with crack dealers and pornographers are exploited for all they're worth here and the video spawned a sequel that was also released in 1989.

p, Joseph Merhi, Richard Pepin; d, Joseph Merhi; w, Joseph Merhi; ph, Richard Pepin; ed, Richard Pepin; m, John Gonzalez.

Crime   Cas.   (PR:NR MPAA:NR)

L.A. CRACKDOWN II †   (1988) 87m City Lights c

Pamela Dixon, Anthony Gates, Joe Vance, Cynthia Miguel, Lisa Anderson, Cheri Readon, Donna Erickson, Bo Sabato.

The sequel to the made-for-video feature once again stars Dixon as a dedicated female cop determined to clean up the mean streets of Los Angeles. This time out Dixon is after a vile serial killer who has been brutally mutilating taxi dancers. Ever enthusiastic, Dixon poses as one of the girls to ferret the killer out and, together with her new female partner, Anderson, makes sure that justice triumphs.

p, Joseph Merhi, Richard Pepin; d, Joseph Merhi; w, Joseph Merhi; ph, Richard Pepin; ed, Paul Volk; m, John Gonzalez; spec eff, Judy Yonemoto; stunts, Red Horton.

Crime   Cas.   (PR:NR MPAA:NR)

LA PASSION BEATRICE   (SEE: BEATRICE, 1988, Fr./It.)

LADY IN WHITE* 1/2**   (1988) 112m New Century-Vista c

Lukas Haas *(Frankie Scarlatti)*, Len Cariou *(Phil)*, Alex Rocco *(Angelo Scarlatti)*, Katherine Helmond *(Amanda)*, Jason Presson *(Geno Scarlatti)*, Renata Vanni *(Mama Assunta)*, Angelo Bertolini *(Papa Charlie)*, Jared Rushton *(Donald)*, Gregory Levinson *(Louie)*, Joelle Jacob *(Melissa)*, Tom Bower, Lucy Lee Flippen, Sydney Lassick, Rita Zohar, Hal Bokar.

Independent filmmaker Frank (FEAR NO EVIL) LaLoggia's long-awaited second feature is an impressive, if overly ambitious, semiautobiographical ghost story that rejects gore in favor of genuine gothic chills. Surprisingly rich in character, period, and place, LADY IN WHITE begins as a successful Stephen King-type writer (played by LaLoggia himself) returns to the small upstate New York town of his youth. He visits the graves of a young girl and her mother, and in a flashback he recalls Halloween 1962, when he first met their ghosts. The youngest son of widower Rocco, Haas lives with his loving dad, his older brother (Presson), and his old-country Italian grandparents (Vanni and Bertolini). Decked out in a Dracula cape and Bela Lugosi mask, young Haas pedals his bicycle to school, where, during the class Halloween party, he is asked to read a story he has written titled "The Monster That Ate New York." After school, two of Haas' prankster buddies (Rushton and Levinson) lock him in the cloakroom and leave him there for the night. Resigned to his fate, Haas climbs up on the top shelf and tries to get some sleep. Suddenly he is awakened by the ghost of a little girl (Jacob) about his age who was murdered in the cloakroom many years before. To his horror, Haas watches as the murder of the child is reenacted before his eyes. During her struggle with the unseen killer, the girl's barrette falls into the air vent on the floor. Her body is then carried out of the cloakroom. Shortly thereafter the locked door of the cloakroom is jimmied open and a flesh-and-blood man enters. Although young Haas isn't sure at first if this is another vision, he decides the man is real and sits silently on the shelf, attempting to be inconspicuous. The man, whose face is obscured, is the killer, and he has returned to the scene of the crime to retrieve the barrette, having learned that the school plans to install a new heater the very next day. Unfortunately for Haas, the intruder notices the masked boy and tries to strangle him. As Haas blacks out, he has an out-of-body experience that takes him flying over his town and into the clouds. When he awakes, he finds his father and several paramedics on the scene attempting to revive him. The police arrest a drunken black janitor who was asleep in the basement and charge him with the attempted murder of Haas and suspect him of being the child killer who has plagued the town for several years. While recuperating in his bedroom, Haas is again visited by the ghost of the little girl, who asks him to help find her mother. Meanwhile, the

janitor goes on trial and is obviously a scapegoat. When the jury acquits the innocent man—a husband and father himself—the distraught mother of one of the child murderer's victims shoots and kills him in front of the courthouse. During the trial, Haas has begun to investigate the ghostly girl's background and learned that her mother had killed herself after discovering the girl's lifeless body on the rocks below their cliffside house. Her ghost, known as the "Lady in White," now haunts the rocky seaside cliffs. Haas has also opened the air vent in the cloakroom and found both the girl's barrette and a high-school ring left behind by the killer. In a complicated series of plots and subplots, Haas and his brother begin to piece the whole thing together and eventually realize that close family friend Cariou is the real killer. When Cariou discovers that Haas knows the truth, he tries to kill the boy at the very same cliffs where he dumped the little girl's body. Luckily, the angry Lady in White rescues Haas, and Cariou falls to his doom. As Rocco, Presson, and the police arrive on the scene, young Haas watches happily as the ghost of the little girl and her mother are reunited.

An intensely personal film, LADY IN WHITE is an incredibly ambitious low-budget effort, which attempts to combine a good ghost story with a childhood reminiscence about growing up during the early 1960s. Fortunately, writer-director-composer LaLoggia pulls off this unlikely combination, although his narrative is a bit too diffuse at times and he runs the risk of being accused of indulging in some of the most cloying Steven Spielbergisms by those who don't understand the difference between reflection and sentimentality. However, LaLoggia, for starters, isn't as saccharine as Spielberg, and there is an authentic edge to this work that is mostly alien to the latter's movie universe. Instead of using Haas' encounter with ghosts to escape the mundane realities of everyday life, LaLoggia's film is firmly rooted in the real world. Child murders, racism, and cruelty share the spotlight here and are contrasted with the warm, loving, and secure family of which Haas is proud to be a part—he doesn't want to escape. What does trouble young Haas, however, is the death of his mother. The boy's subconscious longing for her is at the root of his quest, and he fulfills his desire to be with her again by helping the ghostly little girl become reunited with her mother.

LaLoggia shares his unique vision with the viewer using an imaginative and innovative visual style that flows skillfully from traditional naturalism into surreal dreamlike fantasies and back again without ever seeming gratuitous or clumsy (Russell Carpenter's cinematography is excellent, although due to budget restrictions the quality of the special visual effects is only fair to middling). Instead of turning his narrative into a launching pad for a series of special-effect set pieces, LaLoggia creates a vivid "real" world of love, ethnic heritage, and good humor to which both Frankie and the viewer are happy to return after a dose of the supernatural. LaLoggia has a mature sensibility that does not seek to recapture the lost innocence of childhood, but rather reflect upon it with new understanding. Whereas Spielberg is always blatant, LaLoggia is subtle and ambiguous, leaving the viewer to wonder if Frankie actually has seen these ghosts or if the entire supernatural experience is merely the product of a healthy imagination struggling to cope with an actual loss.

For a director with such a strong visual sense, LaLoggia proves himself quite capable with actors as well. Lukas Haas (WITNESS, 1985; THE WIZARD OF LONELINESS, 1988) continues to be an impressive young actor who knows how to skillfully underplay a role instead of employing the kind of flashy histrionics considered by some to be mature acting. The supporting cast is equally remarkable, with Alex Rocco, Jason Presson, Len Cariou, and Gregory Levinson (BIG), lending solid, naturalistic support. Katherine Helmond is remarkably effective as a creepy old lady who lives in the neighborhood spook house, and the elderly Renata Vanni and Angelo Bertolini are on hand for some amusing comedy relief. With LADY IN WHITE, LaLoggia has confirmed that the promise shown in his very Catholic horror film of 1981, FEAR NO EVIL, was no fluke. With bigger budgets and better resources he may well get the attention he deserves from the public and critics alike. *(Violence, profanity.)*

p, Andrew G. La Marca, Frank LaLoggia; d, Frank LaLoggia; w, Frank LaLoggia; ph, Russell Carpenter (DeLuxe Color); ed, Steve Mann; m, Frank LaLoggia; prod d, Richard K. Hummel; art d, Howard Kling; set d, Sarah Burdick; spec eff, Image Engineering, Fantasy II Film Effects; cos, Jacqueline Saint Anne.

Thriller   Cas.   (PR:C MPAA:PG-13)

LAIR OF THE WHITE WORM, THE ** 1/2**   (1988, Brit.) 94m White Lair/Vestron c

Amanda Donohoe *(Lady Sylvia Marsh)*, Hugh Grant *(Lord James D'Ampton)*, Catherine Oxenberg *(Eve Trent)*, Sammi Davis *(Mary Trent)*, Peter Capaldi *(Angus Flint)*, Stratford Johns *(Peters, the Butler)*, Paul Brooke *(P.C. Erny)*, Imogen Claire *(Dorothy Trent)*, Chris Pitt *(Kevin)*, Gina McKee *(Nurse Gladwell)*, Christopher Gable *(Joe Grant)*, Lloyd Peters *(Jesus Christ)*, Miranda Coe, Linzi Drew, Caron Anne Kelly, Fiona O'Conner, Caroline Pope, Elisha Scott, Tina Shaw *(Maids/-Nuns)*, Paul Easom, James Hicks, David Kiernan, Matthew King, Ross King, Andy Norman, Bob Smith *(Soldiers/Witchdoctors)*, Jackie Russell *(Snakewoman)*.

After having a bash at Mary Wollstonecraft Shelley in last year's disastrous

GOTHIC, director Ken Russell has turned his feverish imagination loose on Bram Stoker in this very campy adaptation of Stoker's last novel, *The Lair of the White Worm* (known in the US as *The Garden of Evil*). Updated and set in the Derbyshire region of modern-day England, the film begins as a young Scottish archaeologist, Capaldi, uncovers an unidentifiable skull while digging up the garden of the inn where he is staying. Run by sisters Davis and Oxenberg, whose parents have recently disappeared, the house just happens to sit on a site that, centuries ago, was a convent during the Roman occupation. Urged by the sisters to attend a party thrown at the nearby mansion of Lord Grant, Capaldi reluctantly abandons his digging for a little relaxation. At the party he learns of local legends regarding a giant white worm/snake creature that terrorized the area in ancient times. One of Grant's ancestors is credited with having slain the evil worm and each year there is a party celebrating the event. Strangely, the skull that Capaldi has just discovered bears a distinct resemblance to paintings of the fabled worm. Meanwhile, the mysterious and sultry Lady Donohoe returns to her giant mansion, which is left empty for most of the year. When she learns of the discovery of the skull, she slips into the inn and steals it—revealing herself to be a vampire-like creature with huge fangs. Donohoe worships the giant white worm, which still exists, living in deep tunnels beneath the earth. Her bite, when not fatal, transforms her victims into vampire followers (a fate suffered by Oxenberg and Davis' parents). To feed the hungry beast, Donohoe seduces hapless strangers and then gives them to the giant white worm, which slithers up into Donohoe's mansion—a veritable worm temple—through a hole in the basement floor. Looking to restore the beast to its former glory, Donohoe searches for a beautiful female virgin to sacrifice to the worm. At the same time, Oxenberg begins having hallucinations in which she sees herself as a nun at the Roman governor of the region's crucifixion, as the governor's body is squeezed by the great white worm and the nuns at the convent are brutally raped and murdered by the Romans. Oxenberg, a virgin, is kidnaped by Donohoe and is about to be sacrificed to the ancient beast when, through the combined efforts of Davis, Grant, and Capaldi, she is saved, while Donohoe and the hideous worm are destroyed.

Given a distinctly playful treatment by director Russell, who fills each frame with all manner of phallic snake/worm imagery, THE LAIR OF THE WHITE WORM is a relatively entertaining and offbeat horror film, which, of course, delights in breaking every social taboo known to man. In addition to the visual puns, Russell (who scripted as well) has fun with the ludicrous situation and stretches it to its satiric limits. One example comes near the climax when, to entice the reptilian Donohoe from her mansion, Grant digs through his explorer father's record collection and comes up with a platter devoted to snake charmer's music. Blasted from huge loudspeakers placed on the mansion roof, the airs succeed in seducing Donohoe, who heads for the door with a slithering walk, like Theda Bara in a silent movie (eventually she puts in earplugs, defeating Grant's plan). In addition to all the silliness, Russell indulges in his usual stylistic fetishes, such as pagan ritual, sexual repression, and Grand Guignol gore. The hallucinations look like a combination of ALTERED STATES and THE DEVILS, and contain more sacrilegious imagery in 30 seconds than the entire three hours of THE LAST TEMPTATION OF CHRIST. (Perhaps due to the skimpy $2 million budget, the hallucination sequences look as if they were shot on videotape and then transferred to film, giving them an odd, grainy quality.) In fact, Russell seems to be stirring up memories of many of his previous pictures. He even parodies himself by echoing the famous nude male wrestling scene in WOMEN IN LOVE (1970) with a dream sequence featuring Donohoe and Oxenberg dressed like stewardesses and wrestling in the aisle of an airplane while passenger Grant stares at their legs—clad in pumps, thigh-high stockings and garter belts. The climax, in which Oxenberg hangs from a rope in her white underwear and Donohoe runs around wearing nothing but garish body paint, looks like an outtake from GOTHIC. The performances are all tongue-in-cheek as well, with the villains acting especially villainous and the heroes acting especially virtuous. Amanda Donohoe, as the snake-like Lady Sylvia Marsh, is the real standout as she slinks through the movie in a variety of kinky outfits (black lingerie, thigh-high black leather boots, wild sunglasses, reptilian jumpsuits, body paint, etc.), striking the perfect balance between sensuality and danger. She also manages to be extremely funny without ever becoming totally ridiculous. Hardcore horror fans may be put off by Russell's mocking humor and may view it as a put-down of the genre, but the director really seems to be poking fun at himself and the film should be taken in that spirit. Includes the song "The D'Ampton Worm" (*Stephan Powys Emilio Perez Machado*). *(Violence, nudity, sexual situations, profanity.)*

p, Ken Russell; d, Ken Russell; w, Ken Russell (based on the novel by Bram Stoker); ph, Dick Bush (Technicolor); ed, Peter Davies; m, Stanislas Syrewicz; m/l, Emilio Perez Machado, Stephan Powys; set d, Anne Tilby; spec eff, Geoff Portass; cos, Michael Jeffrey; ch, Imogen Claire; stunts, Stuart St. Paul; makeup, Pam Meager.

Horror **Cas.** **(PR:O MPAA:R)**

LAND BEFORE TIME, THE*½** (1988) 70m Sullivan Bluth-Amblin Ent./UNIV c

Voices of: Pat Hingle *(Narrator/Rooter)*, Helen Shaver *(Littlefoot's Mother)*, Gabriel Damon *(Littlefoot)*, Candice Houston *(Cera)*, Burker Barnes *(Daddy Topps)*, Judith Barsi *(Ducky)*, Will Ryan *(Petrie)*.

Released to compete head-to-head with the Disney studios' new animated feature OLIVER & COMPANY, Don Bluth's THE LAND BEFORE TIME is, ironically, much more reminiscent of the classic Disney style than the Disney film. In fact, Bluth once worked in Disney's animation department and led a much-publicized walkout of animators from Disney in 1979, citing the drastic decline of artistic values at the studio. Subsequently, Bluth set up his own animation studio, first located in Studio City and now in Ireland, where he has continued the high-quality Disney tradition in such films as THE SECRET OF NIMH (1982) and AN AMERICAN TALE

©MCA (UNIVERSAL)

(1986), making the latter under the auspices of Steven Spielberg, a lifelong animation enthusiast. In his latest work, done this time under the tutelage of George Lucas and Spielberg, Bluth capitalizes on the amazing recent resurgence of interest in dinosaurs among children, setting his tale millions of years ago and creating what has been called a sort of prehistoric BAMBI. The movie opens as dozens of baby dinosaurs are born to happy dino parents. One such baby, a brontosaurus named Littlefoot (Damon), is fatherless and must rely on his mother (Shaver) and elderly grandparents for support. Because of climate changes and terrain upheavals, the once-lush landscape has gone barren and the plant-eating dinosaurs begin an exodus to the fabled Great Valley, which is lush and green, but very far away. While on the trail, Littlefoot attempts to befriend a feisty baby triceratops named Cera (Houston), but there has long been segregation among dinosaur species and they do not associate with one another. Soon after, tragedy befalls Littlefoot when his mother must fight off the dangerous, carnivorous "sharp-tooth," a vicious tyrannosaurus rex. It is a brutal battle, and, although Littlefoot's mother succeeds in waylaying the sharp-tooth, she is mortally wounded. At the same time a violent earthquake hits the area and separates many baby dinosaurs from their parents. Littlefoot, who is separated from his grandparents because of the quake, becomes determined to find the Great Valley on his own, because his mother once told him the way. Distraught and lonely after the loss of his mother, Littlefoot imagines he sees her walking along a rock formation, but realizes after running toward it that all he saw was his enlarged shadow. Littlefoot also sees his mom's shape in cloud formations, and the sight comforts and reassures the little dinosaur that she will never leave him. As Littlefoot continues on the long journey he spots Cera and asks her to join him. The independent and proud Cera at first refuses Littlefoot's help, but after she has a close run-in with the sharp-tooth she grudgingly comes along. As their journey progresses, several other baby dinosaurs of different species are found stranded and join the group. Among them are a restless, chatty anatosaurus named Ducky (Barsi), a pterodactyl who's afraid to fly named Petrie (Ryan), and a mute, dull-witted stegosaurus named Spike. Putting aside the species distrust taught them by their parents, the baby dinosaurs band together and learn to use each others' strengths for the good of the group. With the nasty sharp-tooth threatening at every step of the way, Littlefoot is able to guide his friends through volcanoes and tar-pits until they finally come upon the beautiful Great Valley, lushly verdant as his mother said it was. The valley is full of hungry dinosaurs who have come from all points to feast and there Littlefoot's friends are reunited with their parents and Littlefoot with his grandparents.

A gorgeous production from beginning to end, THE LAND BEFORE TIME contains all the essential elements missing from the Disney OLIVER & COMPANY. When Bluth left the studio he took the Disney magic with him, for he is committed to the high quality animation and adroit story-telling that produces classics—not merely product. While AN AMERICAN TALE was crippled by the tell-tale Spielberg influence—breakneck pace, avoidance of realistic struggle or suffering, and cloying sentimentality—THE LAND BEFORE TIME seems relatively free of his sometimes overbearing hand. Bluth understands that the greatest Disney films took us on an emotional journey that presented horror, tragedy, loss, sadness, friendship, humor, renewal, and love as elements in a cycle that everyone must face in the course of life. These films didn't hide from reality, but presented sadness, hardship, and setbacks as natural occurrences, tempered them with optimism, and helped prepare children for the future. The best Disney features put us in a dreamlike state in which all our hopes and fears are played out in a vivid fantasy world where anything can happen.

Whereas the short-sighted OLIVER & COMPANY corrupts the Dickens source material, confronts children with adult problems (gangsters, juice loans, stealing), and skids into some thoughtless racism, THE LAND BEFORE TIME is a much more positive film that balances its portrayal of common childhood tragedy (loss of loved ones) with its depiction of companionship, determination, and good humor and an antiracist message. Bluth does stumble in some of his narrative (details are rushed through or glossed over), but does not shy away from the Disney formula; in fact, for much of the film he presents us with a surprisingly bleak environment. The tiny dinosaurs must fight their way through a dry, harsh, and barren terrain, avoiding life-threatening volcanoes, earthquakes, and tar-pits—not to mention the sharp-tooth. It is a vivid and uncompromising landscape, but one that, in its own way, is quite beautiful to behold; Bluth's crew of animators put much more thought, time, effort, and care into rendering their setting than the Disney studio did on the sketchy New York City background of OLIVER & COMPANY. Better yet is Bluth's character animation, which is truly in the classic Disney mode. From the giant sharp-tooth to the tiny

Ducky, Bluth infuses his characters with vibrant, fluid movement. Each character's signature is its movement and the Bluth crew does a magnificent job with them all. It is wonderful to watch the baby Littlefoot, achingly cute, awkward and unsure of himself in the early reels, become more mature, confident and determined as the film progresses. While the voice talents assembled add to the overall effect, the voices are merely part of the recipe and call much less attention to themselves than the cast of recognizable stars do in OLIVER & COMPANY. Movement and color are what animation is all about and that is Bluth's primary concern. There are dozens of breathtakingly beautiful moments in THE LAND BEFORE TIME, scenes that will affect adults as well as children, and it is all done through the magic of paint on acetate, a movie camera, and a great deal of imagination and hard work from Don Bluth and his skillful crew. Song: "If We Hold On Together" (James Horner, Will Jennings, performed by Diana Ross). *(Violence.)*

p, Don Bluth, Gary Goldman, John Pomeroy; d, Don Bluth; w, Stu Krieger (based on a story by Judy Freudberg, Tony Geiss); ed, Dan Molina, John K. Carr; m, James Horner; m/l, James Horner, Will Jennings; prod d, Don Bluth; spec eff, Dorse A. Lanpher; anim, John Pomeroy, Linda Miller, Ralph Zondag, Dan Kuenster, Lorna Pomeroy, Dick Zondag.

Animation/Children's Cas. (PR:AA MPAA:G)

LANDLORD BLUES † (1988) 96m Double Helix Films c

Mark Boone, Jr. *(George)*, Raye Douell *(Viv)*, Richard Litt *(Albert Streck)*, Bill Rice *(Roth)*, Rosemary Moore *(Mrs. Streck)*, Susan Lydia Williams *(Rose)*, George Schneeman *(Walter)*, Mary Schultz *(Drug Queen)*, Gigi Williams *(Liz)*, Dino Leon *(Billy)*, Bill Rose *(Myron Stramsky)*, Nona Hendryx *(Sally Viscuso)*, Gerard Little.

Shown at the Berlin Film Festival but yet to get a commercial release, LANDLORD BLUES should have the tag line, "Direct from the Pages of the *Village Voice!*" in its advertising, for its plot is a cry against yuppie gentrification of low-income neighborhoods in New York. Boone is the proud owner of a bike shop located on Manhattan's Lower East Side. Unfortunately, his greedy yuppie landlord (Litt)—who sells cocaine on the side to support his wife's BMW-and-fur habit—is trying to terminate his lease on a technicality so that he can rent the shop space to an art galley at inflated prices. Litt has his own problems, however. Hoping to restrict his drug-selling to the safe suburban addicts, the landlord finds himself involved with some tough characters who play for keeps. Meanwhile, the legal battle wages between Boone and Litt over the shop, while angry tenants attempt to blackmail Litt with photos and tape recordings of his illegal activities. The situation boils over and murder is the result. The second feature from independent filmmaker Jacob Burckhardt (IT DON'T PAY TO BE AN HONEST CITIZEN, 1984), LANDLORD BLUES seems likely to get a release —at least in Manhattan art houses—sometime in 1989.

p, Jacob Burckhardt; d, Jacob Burckhardt; w, Jacob Burckhardt, William Gordy (based on a story by George); ph, Carl Teitelbaum (Kodak Color); ed, Jacob Burckhardt, William Gordy; m, Roy Nathanson, Marc Ribot; m/l, Nona Hendryx, Oliver Lake; prod d, Wendy Walker; cos, Linda Mancini; makeup, Gigi Williams, Gayle Tufts.

Drama (PR:NR MPAA:NR)

LASER MAN, THE** (1988) 92m Peter Wang-Hong Kong Film Workshop c

Marc Hayashi *(Arthur Weiss)*, Maryann Urbano *(Jane Cosby)*, Tony Ka-Fei Leung *(Joey Chung)*, Peter Wang *(Lt. Lu)*, Joan Copeland *(Ruth Weiss)*, George Bartenieff *(Hanson)*, David Chang *(Jimmy Weiss)*, Sally Yeh *(Susu)*, Neva Small *(Martha Weiss Chung)*.

Another low budget independent film from Peter Wang, the director of A GREAT WALL (1986), THE LASER MAN pokes fun at everything from cultural identity to the military-industrial complex in highly quirky fashion. Disjointed and rambling, the essentially plotless movie is set in the near future (political posters saying "Reelect Ollie for President" can be seen) and focuses on Hayashi, a somewhat nerdy, apolitical young New York City laser researcher, half-Chinese, half-Jewish, who accidentally kills his assistant during an experiment. Blackballed from the laser industry because of the accident, the divorced Hayashi spends his time trying to find other work, eating his Jewish mother's horrible Chinese meals, hanging out with his small-time hood brother-in-law (Leung), taking his son to the park, and falling in love with Urbano, a Caucasian woman obsessed with things oriental. Director Wang himself plays an NYC police detective and Hayashi family friend who narrates the film and keeps tabs on the young laser scientist and his crooked brother-in-law. Hayashi finally does land a job in laser research, but he is hired by a very mysterious corporation that wants the laser scientist to build them a powerful weapon. As it turns out, the men are working for the government and Hayashi is unknowingly helping to develop the Strategic Defense Initiative (SDI), aka Star Wars. His invention, a small, light, and very lethal laser gun, is to be tested on the noggin of his crooked brother-in-law, who has sold Hayashi's employers some bad merchandise and made them angry. After years of blithely doing weapons research without even considering the practical implications, Hayashi suddenly realizes the horrible nature of his work and decides to fight back. By now, however, it's too late and Leung apparently is killed by the laser. In a decidedly goofy climax, Hayashi finally takes some personal responsibility and fights back. With the help of his family, girl friend, brother-in-law (who isn't dead after all), and detective Wang, Hayashi is able to double-cross his employers and frustrate their plans for Star Wars.

A character comedy with political and societal overtones, THE LASER MAN is almost too idiosyncratic for its own good. For every telling and relevant moment, there are half a dozen comic or dramatic bits that fall very flat. Director Wang's satiric eye is everywhere, commenting on race relations, family life, dating, sex, marriage, politics, religion, New York City, crime, defense, New Age, the generation gap, modern technology, etc., etc. While Wang's fervent approach is indeed spirited, the film is too scattershot to be truly engaging. Wang seems to have much on his mind, but he fails to present it in a persuasive, coherent way. Part of the problem is his comedic approach, which borders on the sophomoric. One must wonder if the flip, and sometimes even crude, humor is tongue-in-cheek and supposed to be viewed ironically, or if Wang does indeed have a very indifferent attitude toward his subject matter. Although the movie seems to be a plea for the populace to wake up and become politically and socially committed, its humor is far from biting and Wang fails to persuade the viewer that anything important is at stake.

While he bobbles the bigger issues, Wang does succeed in creating some vivid characters. Although Hayashi himself remains a bit vague by the end of the film, the supporting cast is wonderful. Joan Copeland, as the quintessential Jewish mother who has "a Chinese soul," is hilarious, as is Maryann Urbano as the white woman searching for fulfillment through Eastern culture. Director Wang is also memorable as the eccentric police detective. When one considers that the film was shot by Spike Lee's cinematographer, Ernest Dickerson (whose work is better here than in Lee's SCHOOL DAZE), it would seem to indicate that once again a small group of socially and politically committed independent filmmakers is on the rise in New York City. Although they have shown promise, their cinematic skills have yet to attain a truly strong and graceful authority. Perhaps their best work is yet to come. THE LASER MAN premiered at film festivals in the US in 1988, but may not get a general release until 1989. *(Adult situations, sexual situations, violence, nudity, profanity.)*

p, Peter Wang; d, Peter Wang; w, Peter Wang; ph, Ernest Dickerson; ed, Grahame Weinbren; m, Mason Daring; prod d, Lester Cohen; art d, Daniel Talpes; cos, Barbara Weis.

Comedy (PR:O MPAA:NR)

LAST RITES* (1988) 103m MGM/MGM-UA c

Tom Berenger *(Father Michael Pace)*, Daphne Zuniga *(Angela)*, Chick Vennera *(Nuzo)*, Anne Twomey *(Zena Pace)*, Dane Clark *(Carlo Pace)*, Paul Dooley *(Father Freddie)*, Vassili Lambrinos *(Tio)*, Adrian Paul *(Tony)*, Deborah Pratt *(Robin Dwyer)*, Tony Di Benedetto *(Lt. Jericho)*.

Catholic priests have had a rough time of it in movies lately. From the inanities of THE UNHOLY to the deadly silver sphere that skewers a man of the cloth and drills his brains out in PHANTASM II, priests have been fodder for the grotesque imaginations of Hollywood filmmakers in 1988. To make matters worse, along comes LAST RITES, a terribly inept thriller that ranks among the worst films of the year. The *auteur* of LAST RITES is writer-director Donald P. Bellisario, the man who brought you such macho television action heroes as "Magnum P.I.," here trying to parlay that success onto the big screen for the first time. Notwithstanding his TV track record, Bellisario's incompetent script and bumbling direction conspire to make LAST RITES the unintentional laff-riot of the year. Pity poor Tom Berenger, as Bellisario's ruggedly handsome New York City priest, Father Michael. Not inclined to go out in public wearing the tell-tale collar, Berenger must continually fend off the lustful advances of beautiful blondes, who are profoundly shocked to learn of his vow of celibacy. His buddy from the old neighborhood, police detective Vennera, feels compelled to chide these hussies for even tempting the good father. As the film opens, a classily dressed woman (Twomey) enters a swank hotel room and shoots a man in the crotch and head while he makes gymnastic love to the much younger Zuniga. Buck-naked, Zuniga manages to survive the attack by hiding out in the bathroom. As it turns out, both Berenger and Vennera know the victim, and the dedicated priest administers last rites as the cops draw the chalk line around the corpse. That night, the killer shows up in Berenger's confessional at St. Patrick's Cathedral and begs divine forgiveness. Shortly thereafter, Zuniga, a Mexican immigrant, also turns up to confess and asks to meet the father later to discuss the details of her case. Berenger meets the girl at a seedy loft, where it is revealed that the murder victim was Berenger's brother-in-law, that his sister did the shooting, and that he and his sister are the children of powerful mafia boss Clark. Zuniga is horrified by the knowledge at first, but when Berenger declares that he has renounced his organized crime heritage she decides to trust him. This scene is interrupted when Twomey and some mob goons show up to finish Zuniga off. Berenger helps the girl escape and takes her to his priestly bachelor pad in the rectory. When the stuttering ex-Vietnam chaplain Father Freddie (Dooley) walks in on Zuniga as she is taking a shower, hasty explanations are made. Zuniga spends the night sleeping naked in Berenger's bed, as the handsome priest sits in his chair and fantasizes a torrid sex scene with the nubile Mexican girl. At this point the nearly indecipherable plot goes into overdrive. First, there is a suggestion of incest between Berenger and his sister. Then it is revealed that Clark is about to go to prison and Twomey is to take over the mob. After that, Berenger's buddy Vennera is gunned down during a drug bust gone bad and the priest must again administer last rites. Having fallen in love with Zuniga, Berenger spirits the girl back to Mexico for safekeeping and then makes love to her for real, breaking his vow of celibacy. Of course, shortly thereafter it is learned that Zuniga was actually being paid by the mob to set up Twomey's husband for the hit and she's just using Berenger for protection against the mob (or something). Berenger discovers this and, feeling betrayed, sets up Zuniga to be killed by his sister. Finally accepting his lot in life, the confused priest rejects his divine calling and rejoins his mafia family.

LAST RITES is about as dumb as they come. Bellisario's writing and directing are just plain incoherent and it is extremely difficult to decipher just what the hell is going on in this film. The plot is foggy, the characterizations are nothing but a variety of cliches (Berenger is handsome, Dooley is a stutterer, Twomey is icy, Clark is paternal, Zuniga is naked), and the bold "theme" —the struggle between the spirit and the flesh—is really just an excuse to titillate the audience with Roman Catholic taboos. With years of television experience under his belt, one would think that Bellisario might understand the fundamentals of dramatic filmmaking; indeed, most American television is nothing *but* rudimentary situations told in the clearest and most direct manner possible. Bellisario, however, is so incompetent that he fails to make this highly exploitable material even remotely engaging. As a writer, he doesn't seem to have an inkling of how to develop his narrative in a consistent, logical manner. Significant character details and potentially shocking plot twists come tumbling out of the script willy-nilly and fail to have any impact on the audience—other than eliciting unintended laughter. Bellisario's handling of his narrative is so inexpert that the viewer begins to wonder if potentially significant character details, such as the incest subplot, have actually been introduced, or if one has merely misinterpreted the director-screenwriter's intentions.

As confusing as the narrative is, Bellisario's dialog is even worse. His script contains such gems as the profound "Nuthin' is what it seems anymore" and the dramatic "What do you want from me? An act of contrition?" When the lines aren't inadvertently hilarious, they are stupifyingly banal. Bellisario isn't an actors' director either. Poor Berenger looks absolutely lost through the entire film, and seems extremely uncomfortable performing weddings, mass, and the inevitable last rites. He even seems to find playing basketball with a group of inner-city kids a chore. Still, Berenger looks like Olivier when compared to the hapless Daphne Zuniga. Utterly unconvincing as a Mexican, Zuniga's attempt at an ethnic accent sounds more like a speech impediment than Spanish. In an apparent attempt to convey Latin volatility and demonstrativeness, Zuniga moves spastically around the room, most of the time completely nude, making sweeping, melodramatic gestures. Watching an illicit and unholy romance develop between Berenger and Zuniga is a distinctly unpleasant experience. Well then, perhaps Bellisario is really a visual stylist who is more interested in the purely cinematic aspects of the medium and has used his script as a mere springboard to that end? Not hardly. The rather mundane visual style seems to have been left up to cinematographer David Watkin, and there isn't a scene in the film that could be considered even remotely dazzling. A total failure, LAST RITES was justifiably dumped by the studio and only given a scant release in the East and Midwest before quietly vanishing and then rematerializing on home video. As for Bellisario? It's back to the boob-tube for him, with a series—tentatively titled "Quantum Leap" —in which the protagonist is a time traveler who winds up in a different era each week. If one could only travel back in time to the day the deal was made for LAST RITES . . . *(Violence, adult situations, sexual situations, nudity, profanity.)*

p, Donald P. Bellisario, Patrick McCormick; d, Donald P. Bellisario; w, Donald P. Bellisario; ph, David Watkin (DeLuxe Color); ed, Pembroke J. Herring; m, Bruce Broughton; prod d, Peter Larkin; art d, Victor Kempster, Fernando Ramirez; set d, Steven Jordan; cos, Joseph G. Aulisi.

Thriller **Cas.** **(PR:O MPAA:R)**

LAST TEMPTATION OF CHRIST, THE**** (1988) 164m UNIV-Cineplex Odeon/UNIV c

Willem Dafoe *(Jesus Christ)*, Harvey Keitel *(Judas Iscariot)*, Barbara Hershey *(Mary Magdalene)*, Harry Dean Stanton *(Saul/Paul)*, David Bowie *(Pontius Pilate)*, Verna Bloom *(Mary, Mother of Jesus)*, Andre Gregory *(John the Baptist)*, Juliette Caton *(Girl Angel)*, Roberts Blossom *(Aged Master)*, Irvin Kershner *(Zebedee)*, Gary Basaraba *(Andrew, Apostle)*, Victor Argo *(Peter, Apostle)*, Michael Been *(John, Apostle)*, Paul Herman *(Phillip, Apostle)*, John Lurie *(James, Apostle)*, Leo Burmester *(Nathaniel, Apostle)*, Alan Rosenberg *(Thomas, Apostle)*, Tomas Arana *(Lazarus)*, Nehemiah Persoff *(Rabbi)*, Barry Miller *(Jeroboam)*, Paul Greco *(Zealot)*, Steven Shill *(Centurion)*, Russell Case, Mary Seller, Donna Marie *(People at Sermon)*, Mohamed Mabsout, Ahmed Nacir, Mokhtar Salouf, Mahamed Ait Fdil Ahmed *(Other Apostles)*, Peggy Gormley *(Martha, Sister of Lazarus)*, Randy Danson *(Mary, Sister of Lazarus)*, Robert Spafford *(Man at Wedding)*, Doris von Thury *(Woman with Mary, Mother of Jesus)*, Del Russel *(Money Changer)*, Donald Hodson *(Saducee)*, Peter Berling *(Beggar)*, Penny Brown, Gabi Ford, Dale Wyatt, Domenico Fiore, Tomas Arana, Ted Rusoff, Leo Damian, Robert Laconi, Jonathon Zhivago, Illeana Douglas, David Sharp *(People in Crowd)*, Khalid Benghrib, Redouane Farhane, Fabienne Panciatili, Naima Skikes, Souad Rahal, Otmane Chbani Idrissi, Jamal Belkhayat *(Dancers)*, Leo Marks *(Voice of the Devil)*.

In some respects it is heartening to know that in this day and age a work of art can still engender so much controversy. Reviled by fundamentalist Christians who hadn't seen it but denounced it as blasphemy nonetheless, Martin Scorsese's adaptation of Nikos Kazantzakis' controversial novel *The Last Temptation of Christ* is one of the most heartfelt and passionately committed American films in recent memory. While certainly not wantonly blasphemous, Scorsese consciously took a different approach to the New Testament material, seeking to emphasize the human aspects of Jesus Christ, a figure described in the Bible as both fully God and fully man. Acknowledged from the very opening as a work of fiction not meant to be taken as a literal adaptation of the Gospels, the film opens with Jesus of Nazareth (Dafoe), a carpenter, making crosses upon which the Romans crucify rebellious Jews. Judas (Keitel), a Zealot, angrily accuses Jesus of collaborating with the Romans, but Jesus insists that it is all part of His destiny—which He does not yet understand. Wracked by confusion and doubt about His calling—is it from God or the Devil?—Jesus is subject to painful headaches and fainting spells. Jesus goes to a brothel to visit His childhood friend Mary Magdalene (Hershey), now a prostitute, and waits while she services her customers. Although He feels great love for Magdalene—and she for Him—Jesus has always resisted the temptation of her flesh and begs for her forgiveness (it is suggested that his refusal to marry Magdalene has driven her to prostitution). She angrily de-

© MCA (UNIVERSAL)

nounces Him as a coward and sends Him away. While Jesus travels the desert seeking guidance, Judas has been ordered by the Zealots to kill the carpenter. Once in His presence, however, Judas decides that Jesus may be the Messiah and chooses to follow Him until he understands Christ's nature. When Jesus and Judas happen upon the group that is about to stone Magdalene, Jesus stops the killing and gives the Sermon on the Mount. Shortly thereafter, Jesus gathers together a group of disciples and they travel the country spreading a message of love. On Judas' suggestion, Jesus visits John the Baptist (Gregory) in Judaea. John, who espouses violent revolution, rejects Jesus' message of love and sends Him into the desert to ask God's guidance. Jesus survives 40 days and nights of challenges before John appears in the desert and believes that He is indeed the Messiah. While wandering alone in the desert spreading the word of God, Jesus meets Martha and Mary, learning that John the Baptist has been beheaded by Herod. Jesus returns to His disciples an angrier God and He begins to perform His miracles, making the blind see, turning water into wine, and, most importantly, raising Lazarus from the dead. Jesus then leads His disciples to the temple and violently throws out the money-changers. Concerned that Jesus' following is becoming too large and powerful, Saul the Zealot (Stanton) murders Lazarus, thus destroying proof of Jesus' greatest miracle. Meanwhile, Jesus rides into Jerusalem on a donkey and is hailed by the Jews. A mass assault on the temple begins, and Jesus asks God for a sign as to what He should do next. Bleeding stigmata appear on His hands, and Judas helps Jesus escape the Romans. Alone, Jesus begs Judas to betray Him to the Romans so that He will be crucified and return as a martyr. Judas is reluctant to betray his friend, but Jesus tells him that this is God's plan and He must fulfill His destiny. That evening, Jesus says farewell to his disciples at the Last Supper and goes to the Garden of Gethsemane, where He is captured by the Romans. Brought before Pontius Pilate (Bowie), He is condemned to death and crucified at Golgotha. As Jesus suffers on the cross, He is faced with a last temptation, a visit from a guardian angel. The beautiful, blonde, female child tells Him that God has decided He has suffered enough and can now live a normal life. The angel removes the nails from Jesus' feet and hands and helps Him off the cross, then, taking Him by the hand and leading Him to a lush, green valley, the angel presents Jesus to Magdalene and they are married. Jesus and his wife make love and Magdalene is impregnated. Tragically, she dies before giving birth, and the distraught Jesus turns to the angel for comfort. In the years that follow, the angel leads Jesus to Mary and Martha, and he lives with them in a polygamist marriage, raising several children. One day, Jesus encounters Saul, who is preaching the story of the Messiah's crucifixion and resurrection to a group of onlookers. Jesus is outraged by Saul's false story and condemns him. Saul is unswayed, however, and tells Jesus that the truth isn't important—it's the myth that gives people hope in their desperate lives. Later, as Jerusalem burns and the elderly Jesus lies dying, Judas appears and blames the destruction of Jerusalem on Jesus' cowardice, condemning Him for not dying on the cross. Jesus tells Judas that God sent Him the guardian angel, but Judas reveals that the angel was really the Devil in disguise. Horrified, Jesus rejects this last temptation, and begs God's forgiveness, then suddenly finds Himself back on the cross—only a fleeting moment has passed. Jesus accepts His destiny with a triumphant, "It is accomplished," and dies on the cross. A myriad of colorful lights representing the resurrection plays across the screen and the film ends.

Martin Scorsese, who once seriously considered entering the priesthood, had been obsessed with telling Christ's story on-screen for 30 years, and, after a false start in 1983, he was finally able to realize his vision. Like so many other films that have boiled in a filmmaker's brain for many years, THE LAST TEMPTATION OF CHRIST is not the masterpiece one would have hoped it to be. Powerful, haunting, and at times very moving, the film shows Scorsese's seriousness, passion, and commitment in every frame. Unfortunately, however, one senses that, despite his determination to offer a different vision of the life of Christ, Scorsese held back, was somehow still intimidated by the material and didn't go far enough. Throughout his career, Scorsese has been making remarkable films that tread the same thematic ground—the struggle between the spirit and the flesh—but placed them in gritty urban settings where his unique and complex vision could have free reign. Now faced with making a film based on the actual figure that gave rise to his concerns as an artist, Jesus Christ, he seems to have reined in some of the creative energy that marked him as one of the most important American directors of the last 20 years. The first and last sections of THE LAST TEMPTATION OF CHRIST are the most powerful, affecting, and controversial portions of the film. The middle portion, however, is a more or less straightforward retelling of events familiar to most moviegoers (the assembly of the disciples, the miracles, etc.) with nothing that really separates it from more traditional dramatizations of the story (although there is some charming humor, and a joyous moment when Jesus actually dances at Canaan's wedding).

This is not to say that THE LAST TEMPTATION OF CHRIST is a weak film—it is merely a bit disappointing. It should have been Scorsese's masterpiece; it is not. It is, however, one of the most vivid interpretations of the life of Christ in cinema history. Whatever the theological and dramatic pitfalls of Paul Schrader's script (the contemporary American street lingo in place of familiar Biblical dialog—for the sake of freshness—is a questionable call, and the women characters, especially the Virgin Mary, get remarkably short shrift), Scorsese triumphs over them with his magnificent visuals. Striving for historical accuracy, Scorsese's Jerusalem is a flat, arid, harsh land suffering under the oppressive thumb of Roman rule. Cinematographer Michael Ballhaus and production designer John Beard create an evocative vision of the Holy Land that, combined with Peter Gabriel's excellent musical score derived mostly from traditional and contemporary Arabic rhythms, vividly conveys what Christ's world must have really been like—and it is not the lush, picturesque, sanitized Hollywood version. The opening crucifixion; the first sight of John the Baptist conducting a fiery, rhythmic baptism; the 40 days and nights in the desert; the Last Supper; the arrest in the garden; the meeting with Pilate; all are unforgettably presented by Scorsese and his talented cast and crew. Most effective of all, however, is the painful walk to Golgotha, as Jesus carries the crossbeam to which His hands will soon be nailed through the narrow streets of Jerusalem, a jeering crowd surrounding Him. The viewer feels Jesus' pain with each step as, filmed in slow motion, He maneuvers the crossbeam between buildings, bumping and scraping the walls as He stumbles down the narrow path (the shot was inspired by Bosch's *Bearing of the Cross* and is one of the most unforgettable images in the film). This leads to the crucifixion scene, which was carefully researched and based on recent archaeological discoveries and classic religious paintings. While Jesus is hung on the cross, the thieves are crucified on barren, gnarled trees. Scorsese brilliantly creates an image that is both unbearably cruel and starkly beautiful. At this point the film goes into the lengthy and extremely moving "last temptation" sequence, which details exactly what it was that Jesus had sacrificed to fulfill His destiny as the savior of mankind. When the temptation is resisted and Jesus accepts His role as savior, dying on the cross, it is the most poignant and effective presentation of that moment ever committed to film.

The acting is generally excellent, with Willem Dafoe contributing what is perhaps the most skillful *physical* interpretation of Jesus Christ. Where most actors playing Christ stand ramrod straight with arms outstretched, using their hypnotic eyes like some sort of biblical Svengali, Dafoe uses body language to convey the inner struggle of Jesus. (His Anglo-Saxon looks are Scorsese's only concession to the latter-day European and Hollywood representations of Christ; the rest of the cast is suitably Middle Eastern in appearance.) Also strong is Harvey Keitel, virtually unrecognizable in a curly red wig and nose makeup. His Judas—the characterization prompting one of the most strident fundamentalist objections to the film—is strong, dedicated, and heroic, Jesus' closest friend and most loyal disciple. The scenes of discussion between Jesus and Judas are among the best in the film, and the shot in which they fall asleep in each other's arms beneath a tree is quite touching. Harry Dean Stanton as Saul, another character designed to raise the wrath of the self-righteous, is also remarkably effective. Somewhat disappointing, however, is Barbara Hershey as Mary Magdalene. Considering that she was the actress who first introduced Scorsese to the Kazantzakis novel (during the shooting of BOXCAR BERTHA [1972]) and had waited to play the role all these years, her performance seems somewhat vague and hesitant, and she fails to register strongly.

Made on a remarkably low budget of $6.5 million and shot very quickly, the film marvelously attests to Scorsese's skills in looking as good as it does. Although LAST TEMPTATION is flawed and not quite up to the very high standards of his best work, Scorsese must be commended for having the commitment and passion to stick with the project for so long and to do it the way he saw fit. It is ironic that the one American filmmaker whose main concern as an artist is to explore the spiritual nature of man has been reviled by those seeking to protect Jesus' image—as if it needed protecting.

What of the protests, then? What should concern most Americans regarding the controversy over THE LAST TEMPTATION OF CHRIST are not the accusations of blasphemy or that Hollywood engaged in wanton "Christian-bashing," but that during the last decade the level of intellectual discourse in this country has fallen so low that a group of self-appointed spokesmen for the Bible and media-savvy organizations pursuing their own agenda (political influence, censorship, anti-Semitism, anti-intellectualism, fund-raising) can secure a sort of credibility from the media in their attempts to censor a work of art that the vast majority of the protestors had not even seen. While most of the people on the picket lines were no doubt sincere in their distress, it also seems likely that the focus on the film's "blasphemy" (especially the "events" of the last temptation) was intensified by fundamentalists' need to recapture media credibility and popular support lost in the Jim Bakker-Jimmy Swaggart scandals. The disturbing undercurrent of anti-Semitism (most notably, as directed toward MCA head Lew Wasserman) and intolerance of opposing viewpoints that ran through the protests suggested more about the overall agenda of those protesting than did their overwrought claims of "Christian-bashing" (an organization calling itself "Mastermedia," for example, has already begun selling a book that details the Holy Struggle to censor LAST TEMPTATION to their subscribers). Not content merely to voice their concern that Scorsese's film would be taken as gospel, the most vocal conservative Christian protestors really wanted to prevent *anyone* from seeing the film and deciding for him- or herself, calling for boycotts and pressuring venues not to show the picture. All of which begs the question: What were these people afraid of? To those who supported Scorsese's right to make and screen his film unmolested and according to his own theological light, the answer was, finally, freedom of thought and expression, as legitimate concerns were lost in the stridency with which LAST TEMPTATION's opponents condemned—and insisted that others condemn—the film.

Although far too many theater chains and local municipalities were intimidated by the protestors, an impressive number of Americans defied the pressure tactics and went to see THE LAST TEMPTATION OF CHRIST at theaters brave enough to book the film. Ironically, this decidedly uncommercial film would have done much worse at the box office had the picketers, et al., stayed home and kept their mouths shut. A low-budget production by Hollywood standards, THE LAST TEMPTATION OF CHRIST is well on its way to making a tidy profit, despite the claims of victory from the religious Right, and Universal Studios should be applauded for defending artistic freedoms and not knuckling under to the pressure of those who would censor it. *(Violence, adult situations, sexual situations, brief nudity.)*

p, Barbara De Fina; d, Martin Scorsese; w, Paul Schrader (based on the novel by Nikos Kazantzakis); ph, Michael Ballhaus (Technicolor); ed, Thelma Schoonmaker; m, Peter Gabriel; prod d, John Beard; art d, Andrew Sanders; set d, Giorgio Desideri; spec eff, Gino Galliano, Iginio Fiorentini; cos, Jean-Pierre Delifer; ch, Lahcen Zinoune; stunts, Franco Salamon; makeup, Manilo Rocchetti.

Religious   Cas.   (PR:O MPAA:R)

LATE SUMMER BLUES***   (1988, Israel) 101m Blues Ltd./Nachshon c

Dor Zweigenbom *(Arale)*, Yoav Zafir *(Mossi)*, Noa Goldberg *(Naomi)*, Vered Cohen *(Shosh)*, Sahar Segal *(Margo)*, Sharon Bar-Ziv *(Kobi)*, Ada Ben Nahum, Edna Fliedel, Miki Kam, Moshe Havatzeleth, Amith Gazith.

Four members of a graduating Tel Aviv high school class enjoy their final weeks of freedom prior to their induction into the Israeli army and subsequent service at the front during the Suez War in 1970. Each is exposed to the realities of the war. The opening segment focuses on Vered Cohen, who is drafted just ten days after his final class. He will miss his graduation ceremonies which are postponed because a graduate from the previous year's class has died at the front. During his last night before induction, he attends a farewell party, and he notes in his diary that he is proud, as the first draftee, to have a song written about him. He laments, however, that he will be a soldier before he has had the opportunity to either get a driver's license or go to bed with a girl. His classmates, in an effort to maintain the ephemeral closeness, try to ignore the war, which, as they realize, will soon control their lives. One member of the group, Sahar Segal, a budding filmmaker who likens himself to Fellini, roams through the crowd with his camera constantly poised to capture the moments of this last evening with his friends. The second part begins during the graduation ceremonies and concentrates on Dor Zweigenbom, the most radical of the graduating class. As the principal is to take the stage, she receives a phone message in her office that Cohen has been killed during his army training program, a conversation overheard by Zweigenbom and his group of friends. Zweigenbom confronts her during the ceremonies when she refuses to announce Cohen's death to the student body, and she breaks down. When Cohen's coffin is returned from the front, Segal records his funeral on film, and combines it with the earlier footage of his departure as a salute to his departed friend. Soon Zweigenbom, whose anti-war activities are incomprehensible to the majority of his classmates, is accused of cowardice because of his pacifist sentiments. Zweigenbom retreats into solitude in an effort to come to terms with the accusations. The third part features Yoav Zafir, a musician who is advised by an army officer to lower his draft rating to escape enlistment so that he may serve in the military band. During the graduation ceremonies, Zweigenbom quickly becomes suspicious that the songfest, arranged and conducted by Zafir, is being orchestrated to promote his musical talents and to enable him to escape army induction. Zafir, while asserting that he did what he thought was right, nevertheless joins the inductees when they depart for training camp. During the fourth part, the epilog, even Zweigenbom has enlisted due, as he says, to a moment of weakness. Only Segal, whose bout with diabetes has prevented him from serving in the army, remains in Tel Aviv. Segal moves to Paris and embarks upon a filmmaking career. Renen Schorr's feature-film debut is a strong indictment of the compulsory draft that forces Israeli adolescents to surrender three prime years to the army. The fact that Israelis have been reluctant to criticize the army because it is such a protective force in their lives makes the production of this film noteworthy. Even more noteworthy is the fact that the film was partially subsidized by the government. Schorr's choice of the more distant events of 1970 perhaps has made the film seem less threatening. While the film is critical of the prevailing attitudes, it presents a restrained and thoughtful look at its subject. Perhaps the strength of Schorr's film is in its recreation of the world of 1970. The use of the film within the film structure serves to enhance this sense of objectivity. Ultimately we watch as the four main characters, all of whom protest, with varying degrees of intensity, against the draft, give in to stronger forces and climb aboard the recruitment bus. Schorr's most intriguing character is the amateur filmmaker, a member of the group, but one who cannot experience the intensity of the emotional issues because he does not truly partake of them. In fact, he uses his camera to completely escape the emotional experiences. *(Adult situations.)*

p, Ilan De-Vries, Renen Schorr, Doron Nesher; d, Renen Schorr; w, Doron Nesher; ph, Eitan Harris; ed, Shlomo Hazan; m, Rafi Kadishzon.

Drama   Cas.   (PR:C MPAA:NR)

LE GRAND BLEU   (SEE: BIG BLUE, THE, 1988, Fr.)

LE GRAND CHEMIN   (SEE: GRAND HIGHWAY, THE, 1988, Fr.)

LETHAL OBSESSION** (1988, Ger.) 88m Lisa-CTV 72-K.S. Film/Vidmark c

Peter Maffay *(Don Bogdan)*, Tahnee Welch *(Daniela Santini)*, Bernhard Freyd *(Mario Santini)*, Massimo Ghini *(Toni Black)*, Elke Krings *(Henry Black)*, Elliott Gould *(Serge Gart)*, Joachim D. Mues *(Salt)*, Marquard Bohm *(Pepper)*, Andras Goczol *(Kouba)*, Werner Pochath *(Resch)*, Monika Bleibtreu *(Cilly)*, Uwe Hacker *(Giant)*, Klaus Bueb *(Paul)*, Didi Mossmer *(Thug)*, Armin Mueller-Stahl *(Axel Baumgartner)*, Michael York *(Dr. Proper)*.

A violent, German-made cop movie notable chiefly for its cast, including Elliott Gould, Michael York, and Tahnee Welch (Raquel's daughter), LETHAL OBSESSION features Maffay and Freyd as partners on the police force of a German city (Hamburg, perhaps). They are investigating the murder of a trio of drug smugglers by a professional killer, known as Dr. Proper (York), who is so correct that he calls the police himself after his killings and who works for Gould, the local mob kingpin who operates a menswear wholesaler as his cover. Maffay's girl friend, Welch, the daughter of an Italian restaurant owner, is having an affair with Freyd, something not unsuspected by Maffay. When Welch's father tries to stand up to some mobsters muscling in on his business, he winds up dead and his restaurant is blown up while Maffay is inside, leaving the policeman paralyzed. Embittered and forced out of his job, Maffay has a special wheelchair constructed and sets out to avenge his tragedy. Finding the underworld much more willing to talk now that he is no longer a cop, he manages to contact York, who, for reasons of his own, puts Maffay on the track of the men responsible for the blast. Maffay kills one of them with an attack dog, but in retaliation the mobsters murder Freyd. This does nothing to slow up Maffay, though, and he receives more help from York, who is upset that Gould has broken the "rules" in killing a policeman. With his investigation getting closer to Gould, Maffay begins to realize that Gould is being tipped off, and barely escapes several attempts on his life; meanwhile, it becomes clear that his paralysis is only psychological. Eventually, Welch is kidnaped by some of Gould's goons in order to lure Maffay into a trap. He arms himself to the teeth and goes into the bomb-damaged restaurant to confront them. Naturally, a shootout ensues, with Maffay forced to take to his legs to finish off the last bad guy. He then sets out to confront Gould, who offers him a partnership even as another of Gould's henchmen sneaks up behind Maffay, who kills them both. In an epilog, Maffay is running the restaurant and meets with York, who has taken over Gould's position. York tells Maffay that his old boss, Mueller-Stahl, was Gould's contact on the force. Maffay meets Mueller-Stahl and tells him what he knows, then goes out with Welch to watch some fireworks by a carousel. He is shot in the back and dies in Welch's arms.

This downbeat, unexplained ending is the final bummer in a pointless exercise in the detective genre. Like a Teutonic Chuck Norris, Peter Maffay wears the same grim expression throughout the film, while Gould seems to be in it only for the European vacation. York's character is rather interesting, but skimpily utilized. Technically proficient though it is, LETHAL OBSESSION can't overcome the inherent weakness of its material. (Nudity, violence, adult situations, profanity.)

d, Peter Patzak; w, Jonathan Carroll, Peter Patzak (based on a story by Mortimer Ellis); ph, Igor Luther, Dietrich Lohmann; ed, Michou Hutter; m, Toney Carey, Carl Carlton, Frank Diez, Peter Maffay; set d, Claus Kottman; cos, Heidi Melinc.

Crime Cas. (PR:O MPAA:NR)

LICENSE TO DRIVE* (1988) 88m Davis-Licht-Mueller/FOX c

Corey Haim *(Les)*, Corey Feldman *(Dean)*, Carol Kane *(Les' Mom)*, Richard Masur *(Les' Dad)*, Heather Graham *(Mercedes)*, Michael Manasseri *(Charles)*, Harvey Miller *(Professor)*, M.A. Nickles *(Paolo)*, Helen Hanft *(Miss Heilberg)*, James Avery *(DMV Examiner)*, Nina Siemaszko, Grant Goodeve, Grant Heslov, Michael Ensign, Parley Baer.

Two of 1988's hottest young actors, Corey Haim and Corey Feldman, made up quite a draw for the high-school set in the destructive LICENSE TO DRIVE—in which, strangely, even though they're billed together, only one (Haim) has what could be considered a starring role, Feldman being relegated to a much less visible supporting position. In its most detailed form, the entire plot of LICENSE TO DRIVE is contained in the fact that a lad (Haim) suffers the ultimate humiliation of failing his first driving examination. Undaunted, he deceives his dad and pregnant mom (Masur and Kane) and takes his grandfather's precious classic car without permission when an opportunity too good to refuse (read: "hot date") presents itself. For maximum realism, the film sets this high schooler off on an evening with the kind of 16-year-old girl (Graham) who lives in a house all by herself, dresses to the nines, visits all-night discos, and drinks to her heart's content. Never without a smirk or wink, the filmmakers always present this unlikely and undesirable influence as nothing less than the ultimate reward for being male. What the poor guy does and goes through to please this great catch goes beyond any behavior perceived as acceptable.

To appreciate everything that a picture like LICENSE TO DRIVE *isn't*, one need only look as far as such a minor examination of teenage life as John Hughes' earlier FERRIS BUELLER'S DAY OFF. In that film, adolescents are given brains and maturity as well as hormones; in LICENSE TO DRIVE all that's provided is the hormones. The teenage natural target audience for LICENSE TO DRIVE should (if they're as smart as they think they are) notice how short they've been sold. Unfortunately, with teen idols like these, audiences shouldn't have been too hard to drum up, since, in light of its story line, it could be said that the film aims to please anyone who has ever been embarrassed when his or her parents picked them up at school and can therefore identify with the young hero's predicament. What could be better fodder for teenagers to relate to and parents to learn from? But while the premise of getting or not getting a first driver's license is a solid enough base for 90 minutes of teenage comedy, LICENSE TO DRIVE misses the point on all counts.

Insidious double standards undermine any heartfelt attempts to entertain even on a high-school level. There is, for example, the typical parental reaction when the son is punished for lying and gets bawled out after his evening ends in the destruction of his grandfather's car. What about his twin sister? She's the "good" kid, of course, and there's no mention of *her* date the same evening, which entailed a riot, staying out until dawn, and never even returning the car *she* borrowed. In the parents' eyes, she remains a model child. But, by the same token, in applauding reckless teenage behavior like no other film of its ilk, LICENSE TO DRIVE provides exactly the worst disciplinary standards possible. Moreover, not only is its message potentially dangerous, its PG-13 rating makes it easily accessible as well.

For the record, neither of the two Coreys—who also appeared together in 1987's rock'n'roll vampire thriller THE LOST BOYS—has developed much in acting ability since their earlier days, which included sensitive portrayals in LUCAS (Haim) and STAND BY ME (Feldman). Creative and technical credits are perfunctory, with first-timer Greg Beeman directing Neil Tolkin's screenplay. *(Profanity, substance abuse.)*

p, Jeffery A. Mueller, Andrew Licht; d, Greg Beeman; w, Neil Tolkin; ph, Bruce Surtees (DeLuxe Color); ed, Wendy Greene Bricmont; m, Jay Ferguson; prod d, Lawrence G. Paull; set d, Greg Papalia; stunts, Joe Dunne.

Comedy Cas. (PR:O MPAA:PG-13)

LIGHT YEARS** (1988, Fr.) 83m Colimason-Films AZ-Revcom TV/Miramax c

Voices of: Glenn Close, Jennifer Grey, Christopher Plummer, John Shea, Penn Jilletta, David Johansen, Terrance Mann, Charles Busch, Bridget Fonda, Sheila McCarthy, Paul Shaffer, Teller, Earl Hyman, Earl Hammond, Alexander Marshall.

French director Rene Laloux began developing this animated feature in 1974, a year after the release of his FANTASTIC PLANET (his second film, 1982's TIME MASTERS, remains unreleased in the United States). What has emerged more than a decade later is a fascinating, but ultimately pretentious, arty jumble. The story takes place on the planet Gandahar, a perfect world of bountiful crops, tranquil landscapes, and contented people. One day a village is attacked by an unseen enemy, whose weapons turn the fleeing citizens into stone. As the countryside is laid waste, Queen Ambisextra (Close) calls a meeting of the ruling female council. In order to determine the source of the attacks, it is decided to send out a male soldier, Sylvain (Shea), the queen's young son. He goes forth and encounters the Deformed, a race of genetic mutants created through bungled Gandaharian experiments. A tribesman, Shaol (Johansen), sends Shea on to meet the Metal Men, the unseen army of mindless killing machines, armed with this strange prophecy: "In a thousand years Gandahar will be destroyed, and all its inhabitants massacred. A thousand years ago Gandahar will be saved, and what cannot be avoided will be." The Metal Men turn out to be created by Metamorphis, an omnipotent living mass that is the result of yet another Gandaharian experiment gone awry. In a confusing climax, Shea destroys Metamorphis and saves Gandahar.

The murky narrative, with its past-present-future story line, is just one of the film's problems. The simplistic symbolism of the story—with its Nazi-like Metal Men and the warrior who saves a planet from evil technology—is not much above Saturday morning television fare. Likewise for the bland characterizations and readings by the American cast and the poorly animated backgrounds (credited to a South Korean crew). What redeems the film are some of the surreal images that Phillipe Caza, who also handled the animation for FANTASTIC PLANET, has created. The various slithering animals, the freakish looking Mutants, and Queen Ambisextra's city of Jaspar, which is in the shape of a woman's head, are all memorable and stylish. Isaac Asimov turns in a workmanlike job adapting the French script into English, but the film has little to do with his oeuvre; it is much closer in spirit to European comics (Laloux has worked with illustrators Roland Topor and Moebius) or the visual flair seen in *Heavy Metal* magazine. All things considered, LIGHT YEARS is an interesting piece of work, which should appeal to fans of animation. *(Violence, sexual situations.)*

p, Bob Weinstein, Henri Rollin, Jean-Claude Delnyre; d, Rene Laloux, Harvey Weinstein; w, Isaac Asimov (original screenplay (Fr.) by Raphael Cluzel adapted by Rene Laloux from the novel *Robots Against Gandahar* by Jean-Pierre Andrevan); ed, Christine Pansu; m, Gabriel Yared, Bob Jewett, Jack Maeby; anim, Philippe Caza.

Animation/Science Fiction Cas. (PR:C MPAA:NR)

LIGHTHORSEMEN, THE½** (1988, Aus.) 115m Picture Show/Cinecom c

Jon Blake *(Scotty)*, Peter Phelps *(Dave Mitchell)*, Tony Bonner *(Lt. Col. (Swagman Bill) Bourchier)*, Bill Kerr *(Lt. Gen. Sir Harry Chauvel)*, John Walton *(Tas)*, Gary Sweet *(Frank)*, Tim McKenzie *(Chiller)*, Sigrid Thornton *(Anne)*, Anthony Andrews *(Maj. Meinertzhagen)*, Anthony Hawkins *(Gen. Sir Edmund Allenby)*, Gerard Kennedy *(Ismet Bey)*, Shane Briant *(Reichert)*, Serge Lazareff *(Rankin)*, Ralph Cotterill *(Von Kressenstein)*, John Heywood *(Mr. Mitchell)*, Di O'Connor *(Mrs. Mitchell)*, Grant Piro *(Charlie)*, Patrick Frost *(Sgt. Ted Seager)*, Adrian Wright *(Lawson)*, Anne Scott-Pendlebury *(Nursing Sister)*, Brenton Whittle *(Padre)*, Jon Sidney *(Grant)*, Graham Dow *(Hodgson)*, James Wright *(Fitzgerald)*, Gary Stalker *(Nobby)*, Scott Bradley *(Lt. Burton)*, Peter Merrill *(Young German Officer)*, Peter Browne *(Arch)*.

During WW I most major armies of the world came to the conclusion that cavalry had no place on the modern battlefield—early engagements showing the expensive, lightly armed mounted troops to be little more than machine-gun fodder. Today cavalry has come to mean tanks or, in its newest incarnation, helicopters. There was, however, one successful use of mounted troops in WW I: the charge of the Australian Light Horse at Beersheba, a desert town in Palestine held by Turkish troops with German advisors. Guarding the only water for miles, it was the region's strategic key and a crucial objective in the advance on Jerusalem. THE LIGHTHORSEMEN is the second film the Australians have made about the battle (the first, released in 1940, was directed by Charles Chauvel, a pioneer Australian filmmaker and the son of the commander of the actual charge). The film itself is almost two hours long, most of it one long string of war movie cliches that leads up to the famed charge, but the wait is worth it. The plot concerns a quartet of Lighthorsemen (Blake, Walton, McKenzie, and Sweet) who survive the Gallipoli invasion and are sent to Palestine, where their unit is consistently misused by its British superiors. One of the men is wounded and replaced by Phelps, a green trooper who has the usual problems being accepted by the veterans. When he can't bring himself to shoot the enemy, Phelps is transferred to the Ambulance Corps, where he has a romance with a nurse. The day of the big attack eventually arrives, and the troop is finally to be allowed to charge all the way, instead of dismounting and fighting on foot as they have been commanded to do in the past. Calculating that they will be susceptible to Turkish artillery fire for approximately two miles—until they are too close for the big guns to be effective—they begin the attack. Magnificently, the 800 horsemen advance at a trot, then a gallop, and finally a full-tilt charge, overwhelming the Turkish positions and securing the all-important wells.

The care that went into THE LIGHTHORSEMEN is obvious, and its $10-million budget shows. The charge itself is unlike anything that's been done in Hollywood in decades, and the only cinematic cavalry action that compares is the climactic attack in THE CHARGE OF THE LIGHT BRIGADE. Apart from that, the film is such a rehash of stock scenes that the audience will have a hard time staying interested until the finale. The performances are nothing special, though all are competent; but the photography is superb, and the production design, including the creation of Beersheba in the Australian desert, is nothing short of superb. The charge, though, is the reason this film exists, and in an age of reappraisal of the conventional war film, we may not see the likes of it again. *(Violence, brief nudity, adult situations, mild profanity.)*

p, Ian Jones, Simon Wincer; d, Simon Wincer; w, Ian Jones; ph, Dean Semler (Panavision, Eastmancolor); ed, Adrian Carr; m, Mario Millo; prod d, Bernard Hides; spec eff, Steve Courtley; cos, David Rowe; stunts, Grant Page.

War **(PR:A-C MPAA:PG)**

LITTLE DORRIT**** (1988, Brit.) 360m Sands-Cannon Screen Ent. c

Alec Guinness *(William Dorrit)*, Derek Jacobi *(Arthur Clennam)*, Cyril Cusack *(Frederick Dorrit)*, Sarah Pickering *(Little Dorrit)*, Joan Greenwood *(Mrs. Clennam)*, Max Wall *(Flintwinch)*, Amelda Brown *(Fanny Dorrit)*, Daniel Chatto *(Tip Dorrit)*, Miriam Margolyes *(Flora Finching)*, Bill Fraser *(Mr. Casby)*, Roshan Seth *(Mr. Pancks)*, Roger Hammond *(Mr. Meagles)*, Sophie Ward *(Minnie Meagles)*, John Savident *(Tite Barnacle)*, Edward Burnham *(Daniel Doyce)*, Eleanor Bron *(Mrs. Merdle)*, Michael Elphick *(Mr. Merdle)*, Robert Morley *(Lord Decimus Barnacle)*, Alan Bennett *(The Bishop)*, Patricia Hayes *(Affery)*, Luke Duckett *(Young Arthur)*, Molly Maureen *(Mr. F's Aunt)*, Diana Malin *(Mr. Casby's Maid)*, Janice Cramer *(Young Flora)*, Kathy Staff *(Mrs. Tickit)*, Amanda Bellamy, Tracey Wilkinson *(Housemaids)*, Julia Lang *(Henry Gowan's Mother)*, Pip Torrens *(Henry Gowan)*, Graham Seed *(William Barnacle)*, Beth Ellis *(Mrs. William Barnacle)*, Ian Gelder *(Rev. Samuel Barnacle)*, Lee Fox *(Richard Barnacle)*, Robert Mill *(Hugh Stilstalking)*, Morwenna Banks *(Georgina)*, Nadia Chambers *(Agnes)*, Dawn Charatan *(Mrs. Ismay)*, Patricia Napier *(Dolly)*, Sophie Brew *(Lydia)*, Brian Pettifer *(Clarence Barnacle)*, John Harding *(Ferdinand Barnacle)*, Alec Wallis *(Discreet Clerk)*, Michael Mears *(Clerk with the Quill)*, Ken Morley *(Mr. Wobbler)*, John Quarmby *(Circumlocution Office Porter)*, Stuart Burge *(Head)*, Donald Pelmear *(Mr. Clive)*, Arthur Nightingale *(Shabby Footman)*, David Stoll *(Hesitant Weighty Gentleman)*, Donald Bisset *(Enthusiastic Weighty Gentleman)*, Christopher Birch *(Cautious Weighty Gentleman)*, Harold Innocent *(Mr. Rugg, Legal Adviser)*, David Pugh *(Mr. Parker, a Creditor)*, Terence Conoley *(Mr. Fogg, a Creditor)*, Richard Henry *(Smiles, Foreman)*, Steve Ismay, Johnny Irving *(Workers)*, David Doyle *(Pepper, Apprentice)*, Christopher Whittingham *(Mr. Plornish)*, Ruth Mitchell *(Mrs. Plornish)*, Eric Francis *(Old Nandy, Mrs. P's Father)*, Anna Whittingham, Eve Whittingham, Harry Whittingham, Nicholas Whittingham *(Plornish Children)*, Kate Williams *(Mrs. Greasby)*, Ronnie Brody *(Broke Tenant)*, Joan Dainty *(Broke Tenant's Wife)*, Susan Field *(Mrs. Tiffin)*, Robert Demeger *(Mr. Braddle)*, Cordelia Ditton *(Mrs. Braddle)*, David Thewlis *(George Braddle)*, Gerald Campion *(Mr. Tetterby)*, Rita Triesman *(Mrs. Tetterby)*, Betty Turner *(Mrs. Kidgerbury)*, Johnny Clayton *(Fiddler)*, Moya Brady *(Fiddler's Daughter)*, John Fahey *(Second-Hand Furniture Seller)*, Joanna Maude *(Second-Hand Furniture Seller's Wife)*, Iris Sadler *(Shirtmaker)*, Joanna Brookes *(Shirtmaker's Daughter)*, Nat Pearn *(Mr. Strong)*, Cyril Epstein *(Mr. Strong's Friend)*, Alan Bungay *(Principal Messenger)*, Mark Arnold *(Boy)*, Howard Goorney *(Bob, the Turnkey)*, Liz Smith *(Mrs. Bangham, Midwife)*, Gwenda Hughes *(Mrs. Dorrit)*, Celia Bannerman *(Milliner)*, Murray Melvin *(Dancing Master)*, Darlene Johnson *(Mrs. Robinson)*, Bernard Padden *(Newcomer)*, Dermot Crowley *(Mr. Simpson)*, Richard Cubison *(Mr. Simpson's Friend)*, Arthur Blake *(Herbert Smangle)*, John Scott Martin *(Faded Involvent)*, David Trevena *(Tidily Buttoned Man)*, David Bale *(Lucky Skittle Player)*, Anthony Benson *(Unlucky Skittle Player)*, Ian Lindsay *(Capt. Martin)*, Doug Roe *(Capt. Martin's Friend)*, Tom McCabe *(Rough Fellow)*, Ramon Martino *(Gruff Fellow)*, Joan Stafford *(Rough Lady)*, Terry Day *(Mrs. Hurt)*, Cate Fowler, Carol Street *(Women at Dance)*, Siobhan Nicholas *(Mrs. Fray)*, Katherine Best *(Lady Visitor)*, Yvonee D'Alpra *(Motherly Lady)*, Robin Meredith *(Ruined Speculator)*, Marcel Steiner *(Whistler)*, Charles Reynolds *(Mr. Timms)*, Tony Jay *(Doctor)*, Lizzie McKenzie *(Drunken Woman)*, Harry Cross, Sarrina Caruthers, Susan Tanner *(Little Dorrit as a Child)*, Sandra O'Rourke, Joanna Hurley *(Fanny as a child)*, Ricky Cave *(Tip at Age 12)*, Zephyr Steer, Sam Steer *(John Chivery at Ages 4 and 8)*, Robert Putt *(Mr. Chivery, the New Turnkey)*, Richard Stirling *(John Chivery)*, Pauline Quirke *(Maggy, Little Dorrit's Protegee)*, Heathcote Williams *(Dr. Haggage)*, Charlie Bartle *(Mr. Battens)*, David Foxxe *(Mr. Mivvins)*, James Coyle *(Horace Kinch)*, Maurice Elliot *(Snuggery Gambler)*, Jack Gittings *(Old Gambler)*, John McEnery *(Capt. Hopkins)*, Marilyn Milgrom *(Mrs. Hopkins)*, Stewart Permutt, John Levitt *(Quarrelling Debtors)*, Marjorie Somerville *(Lady by Snuggery)*, Seymour Green *(Tailor)*, John Warner *(Bootmaker)*, Peter Miles *(Mr. Dubbin)*, Laura Cox *(Orange Juggler)*, John Halstead *(Mr. Mortimer)*, Charles Hunter *(Mr. Mortimer's Friend)*, Richard Graden *(Slingo)*, Richard Clifford *(Jerry)*, Doris Littlewood *(Old Wife)*, Irene Frederick *(Mrs. Pitt)*, Harry Webster *(Pickton)*, Leonard Maguire *(Knowledgeable Debtor)*, Judy Laister *(Anxious Wife)*, Alfred Hoffman, Lelia Hoffman *(Old Couple)*, Mike Carnel *(Lonely Debtor)*, Tommy Shand *(Mr. Cain)*, Imogen Millais Scott *(Mrs. Bee)*, Olivier Pierre *(Hotel Manager)*, Tim Wright *(Hotel Porter)*, Rosemary Smith, Lin Sagovsky *(Hotel Maids)*, Odette Bennett *(Fanny's Maid)*, Michael Mears *(William's Valet)*, Tusse Silberg, Elizabeth Archer, Nadine Large *(Ladies at Concert)*, Simon Dormandy *(Sparkler Merdle)*, Ian Hogg *(Butler)*, Brenda Bruce *(Duchess)*, Edward Jewesbury *(Magnate from the Lords)*, Jonathan Cecil *(Magnate from the Bench)*, Brian Poyser *(Treasury)*, Malcolm Tierney *(Bar)*, Trevor Ray *(Magnate from the City)*, Rosalie Crutchley *(Magnate from the Bench's Wife)*, Betty Marsden *(Mrs. Phoebe Barnacle)*, Paul Rhys *(Bright Young Gentleman)*, Malcolm Mudie *(Officer)*, Barbara Peak *(Countess)*, Ronald Russell *(Elderly Gentleman)*, Arthur Hewlett *(Physician)*, Giles Oldershaw *(Imposing Gentleman)*, John Atkinson *(Baron)*, Sally Ashby, Anthea Holloway, Ruth Sheen *(Society Ladies)*, John Tordoff *(Waiter in the Coffee House)*, Christopher Hancock *(Customer in the Coffee House)*, Jo Warne *(Mrs. Chivery, Tobacconist)*, Fred Beauman *(Flower Seller)*, Alan Foss *(Mr. Bead)*, Michael Eaves *(Narrow Faced man)*, Alison Dowling *(Pretty Milliner)*, Chris Darwin, Leon Davis *(Fraudulent Grooms)*, Sidney Johnson *(Print Seller)*, Mark Knox *(Print Seller's Clerk)*, Frank Shelley *(Disagreeable Man)*, Jenny Galloway *(Polly)*, John Dalby *(Mr. Jobling)*, Danny Schiller, Arthur Kelly *(Revellers in the Slap Bang)*, David Cardy *(3 Thimble Man)*, Eric Richard *(Sir George Wills)*, Guy Nicholls *(Mr. Wabe)*, David Whitworth *(James Simms)*, Eli Woods *(Greedy-Eyed Old Man)*, Charles Simon *(Sharp Speculator)*, Stanley Lloyd *(Mr. Wrosley)*, Peter Waddington *(Boy at Theatre)*, Arthur Cox *(Stage Carpenter)*, Billy Gray *(Stage Doorman)*, Jackie Ekers, Rebecca Ham, Fiona MacAlpine, Amanda Maxwell, Shona Morris, Diana Paris, Cazz Scattergood *(Dancers at Theatre)*.

Little Dorrit is one of Charles Dickens' greatest and least-read novels. Written in the same period that produced *Bleak House* and *Hard Times*, it shares the dark tone and satiric social vision of these more popular novels, with a minimum of the exaggerated caricatures and cheery sentimentality that dominate his earlier work in particular. As far as these aspects of Dickens' universe can be separated, it is Dickens the beloved hearthside caricaturist that has been most favored in film adaptations of his work. With her massive, six-hour LITTLE DORRIT, however, director-screenwriter Christine Edzard has created a work that is at once faithful to Dickens' depiction of a corrupt Victorian society and one of the finest of all Dickens screen adaptations.

The film plays in two three-hour parts. Part I, "Nobody's Fault" (Dickens' original title) is told from the point of view of Jacobi, a middle-aged bachelor returning home to London after 20 years in China, where he helped his recently deceased father run the family business. Jacobi tells his grimly Protestant mother (Greenwood) that he has decided to give up the business, news she receives coldly. He further provokes her wrath—and gets no reply—when he asks her if his father had some unrighted wrong on his conscience when he died. While staying in Greenwood's gloomy house, Jacobi notices a slight, quiet seamstress known as "Little Dorrit" (Pickering), whom Greenwood seems inexplicably to favor. Intrigued by Pickering's sweet manner and his own suspicions, Jacobi begins investigating her case. He traces her to the Marshalsea debtors' prison, where her debilitated, pseudo-genteel father, Guinness—known as "The Father of the Marshalsea" —is interred, and begins making inquiries to improve the family's lot. One route leads him to the Kafkaesque Circumlocution Office (the government's ultimate example of "How NOT to Do It"), and an inevitable dead end. Jacobi's attempts to find more work for Pickering meet with more success, as he finds her a situation with Margolyes, the former love of his life grown hugely fat and garrulous, but still kind-hearted. At Margolyes' home he meets Seth, who collects rents for Margolyes' father at Bleeding Heart Yard, site of the engineering business of Burnham, with whom Jacobi goes into partnership. Seth, too, takes an interest in the Dorrits' case, and eventually unearths information that leads to Guinness' reclaiming a lost inheritance and release from prison. As the *nouveau riche* Dorrits go off on a continental Grand Tour, Burnham dies. Jacobi invests all the company's resources in the schemes of financier Merdle (Elphick), the universally hailed Lord of English Capitalism. Elphick proves a fraud, however, and kills himself, taking half the country with him—including Jacobi, who winds up in the Marshalsea, in the very room Guinness inhabited. Part I ends as, to his self-lacerating regret, Jacobi learns from a Marshalsea "turnkey" that the shy Pickering was in love with him.

Part II, told from Pickering's point of view, begins with her birth in the Marshalsea and follows her as, early on, she becomes the "mother" of her selfish, pretentious, and irresponsible family. She tries to find work for her shiftless brother (Chatto), launches her sister (Brown) on a career as a dancer in her uncle's (Cusack) theater, and cares for her pathetic father, who encourages his children's snobbery and plays patriarch to the other Marshalsea inmates while cadging "testimonials" from outgoing prisoners and exploiting the devoted Pickering. She finds work with Greenwood, and learns that Jacobi is not really Greenwood's son, a fact of which he is ignorant. When Jacobi arrives in England, she falls in love with him—he is one of the few truly unselfish people she has met, and genuinely interested in her case—although she knows he loves another (unrequitedly). After the discovery of Guinness' fortune, the family is shown traveling through Europe. The other Dorrits constantly criticize Pickering for retaining her old ways, committing the grave offense of remembering old acquaintances fondly, and shunning "society." Society takes the form of Mrs. Merdle (Bron), whose son has fallen in love with Brown. Guinness and Brown, moved by a repressed sense of inferiority, seize this chance to ally with the Merdle name, and Brown lovelessly weds his idiotic son. Everyone returns to London for the wedding, where, upset by a visit from a Marshalsea turnkey, Guinness breaks down and makes a speech before the wedding guests in his old guise as the Father of the Marshalsea, scandalizing all. He dies soon after, and his children lose their fortune in the same downfall of Elphick that landed Jacobi, now gravely ill, in the Marshalsea. Pickering goes to nurse him there, and confronts Greenwood, demanding her help in paying off his creditors. Greenwood now confesses that she swindled Jacobi's real mother (a dancer in Cusack's theater) when his father sent her money for the woman's care, a fortune she kept for herself as an act of revenge. Although her servant (Wall) tries to secure the money for himself, a fortunate accident foils him, removing all obstacles to a happy ending as Jacobi and Pickering depart the Marshalsea and marry.

LITTLE DORRIT is one film in two feature-length parts, not, as some have called it, two films. Part II is necessarily the stronger, developing themes and filling out the plot, but the two halves are interdependent. Part I, told from Jacobi's viewpoint, is visually and emotionally darker. Interiors are dimly lit; it rains, even on a country home; Greenwood's house and Jacobi's Covent Garden lodgings are shown at their gloomiest. Dickens' famous prison imagery is suggested by the enclosed quality of each shot: a garden is trellised and hedged in such a way as to admit no view of sky, while heavens and horizons are similarly excluded in city scenes, where buildings entirely fill the background. Edzard has been faulted by some historians for failing to show the true squalor of Dickens' London; still, Part I very effectively presents the city as a claustrophobic, dark, damp, haphazard maze. The goodness and passivity in Jacobi's character, and a general sense of helplessness, is suggested in the repeated phrase "it's nobody's fault"; while the unmastered energy of the Industrial Revolution is given in Edzard's fascinated shots of Burnham's whirring machinery. Pickering is only a glimpsed presence in Jacobi's dreamy view, a mere woman-child.

In Part II, "Little Dorrit's Story," Edzard rectifies Jacobi's oversight and makes her most significant departure from the novel. Dickens' Little Dorrit—though not quite Little Nell—belongs in the sentimental company of colorless, selfless, naively intuitive heroines so essential to the Victorian moral imagination and so intolerable today. In Edzard's version, the character takes on a much more forceful consciousness; she becomes, in a sense, the Dickensian conscience of the novel's narration. Of the original characters eliminated from the film, the most notable absence is that of the killer Rigaud, who in Dickens' version proves the key that unlocks the Greenwood character's guilty secrets. Here, it is Pickering who learns of Greenwood's duplicity and confronts her at the end, rescuing Jacobi's character herself where the Rigaud deus ex machina rescues him in the novel. (Dickens' parallels between Jacobi's and Guinness' natures are strengthened in this emergence of Pickering as a stronger circumstantial agent.) Moreover, it is within the discrete context of "Little Dorrit's Story" that Dickens' important comparisons between Marshalsea society and the elder Dorrit's self-excusing self-pity with society at large and bureaucratic irresponsibility are established (and brilliantly dramatized by Edzard in placing Guinness' breakdown at the London wedding before assembled lords of English capitalism, rather than at the novel's dinner in Rome). Edzard's Pickering emphatically informs Jacobi that his plight is "everybody's fault"—a conviction she does not, and could not, express in the novel. She is also shown cleaning windows and raising curtains, as her vision literally sheds light on Jacobi's Part I despair. Interiors grow lighter and more spacious, the sky now spreads above the buildings. "Replayed" scenes reveal new nuances, seen from the prescient Pickering's eye, and Pickering herself emerges from the shadows she dwelt in in Part I.

Boasting a 211-member cast, LITTLE DORRIT is packed with fine performances. Joan Greenwood, Sarah Pickering (in her film debut), Derek Jacobi, Eleanor Bron, and Roshan Seth are standouts; Miriam Margolyes and Max Wall do strong work with their more limiting Dickensian caricatures. Best of all is veteran Dickensian Alec Guinness (GREAT EXPECTATIONS, 1946; OLIVER TWIST, 1948; SCROOGE, 1970) as William Dorrit. In one of Edzard's rare closeups, as Guinness learns of his inheritance, his face is a revelation, registering panic, shock, and a dim idea of life as a free man; his breakdown at the wedding dinner is at once terrifying and clearly foreshadowed. (A nice touch is the shared tic of Guinness and Jacobi, a childish way of putting their fingers to their mouths that stresses their common weaknesses.)

After two years' preparation, LITTLE DORRIT was shot on a low budget by Sands Films, the studio of Edzard and her husband, coproducer (with John Brabourne) Richard Goodwin. Goodwin and Brabourne previously produced MURDER ON THE ORIENT EXPRESS and A PASSAGE TO INDIA; Edzard, a former opera designer, most recently directed BIDDY. Sets and details were scrupulously researched and re-created (all costumes were designed and hand-sewn from original patterns and fabrics), and all scenes were filmed in the Sands studios in London—to extremely handsome effect. Cinematographer Bruno de Keyzer (of Bertrand Tavernier's A SUNDAY IN THE COUNTRY and ROUND MIDNIGHT) achieves beautiful effects, from the darkness of Part I, reminiscent of Rembrandt, to the light-suffused interiors and cityscapes of Part II, recalling Vermeer; Edzard's direction augments the force of her script's dialectical structure in its simplicity. Further proof of Edzard's talents is that the six-hour LITTLE DORRIT rarely drags, and has played to enthusiastic audiences in London. This feat deserves repetition in the US, where Edzard's labor of love will please novices and diehard Dickensians alike.

p, John Brabourne, Richard Goodwin; d, Christine Edzard; w, Christine Edzard (based on the novel by Charles Dickens); ph, Bruno de Keyzer (Technicolor); ed, Olivier Stockman, Fraser Maclean; m, Giuseppe Verdi; md, Michael Sanvoisin; art d, John McMillan; set d, Neale Brown, John Tyson, Ronnie Barlow, Bill Reid, Richard Feroze, Malcolm May, Paul Colombo, Scott Loom, Terry Thompson, John Whybrow, Charles McMillan, Peter Feroze, Mary McGowan, Peter Seatter, Hugh Doherty; cos, Barbara Sonnex, Judith Loom, Joyce Carter, Jackie Smith,

Sally Neale, Claudie Gastine, Danielle Garderes.

Comedy/Drama   (PR:A MPAA:G)

LITTLE NIKITA**½   (1988) 98m COL c

Sidney Poitier (Roy Parmenter), River Phoenix (Jeff Grant), Richard Jenkins (Richard Grant), Caroline Kava (Elizabeth Grant), Richard Bradford (Konstantin Karpov), Richard Lynch (Scuba), Loretta Devine (Verna McLaughlin), Lucy Deakins (Barbara Kerry), Jerry Hardin (Brewer), Albert Fortell (Bunin), Ronald Guttman (Spassky), Jacob Vargas (Miguel), Roberto Jimenez (Joaquin), Robb Madrid (Sgt. Leathers), Chez Lister (Tom), Bill Stevenson (Tony), Tom Zak (Brett), Newell Alexander (Drill Sergeant), Ingrid Rhoades (Corp. Hogan), Lisa McCullough (Water Skier), Richard Holden (Young Russian Diplomat), Vojo Goric (Joe), Kim Strange (DMV Clerk), Lou Hancock (Nursery Customer), David M. Paynter (Spike), Biff Wiff (Bucky), Tasha Stewart (Dolphin Trainer), John Spafford (Trainer #2), Brooke Theiss (Dilys), Jonathan McMurtry (Tour Boat Guide), Charles T. Salter, Jr. (Trolley Conductor), Rick L. Nahera (Trolley Passenger), Jim Parrott (U.S. Border Patrolman), Martine Van Hamel (Princess Aurora, in Ballet), Robert Hill (Prince Desire, in Ballet Scene), Michael Owen (The Fairy Carabosse, in Ballet), Christine Dunham (The Lilac Fairy, in Ballet Scene), Arlin L. Miller (TV Announcer), Julio Medina (Soccer Announcer).

A timely espionage thriller with plot holes that you can fly a Stealth bomber through, LITTLE NIKITA stars Phoenix as (no, not young Khrushchev) a seemingly average teenager in sunny Fountain Grove, California. He's so average, in fact, that he's a straight-A student who lies about his grades in order to fit in better with his friends. He's also a good American with plans to enlist in the Air Force. To top it off, he seems quite well bred. Mom and Dad (Kava and Jenkins) have a nice house, run a prosperous neighborhood nursery, and belong to the PTA and the United Way. Mom and Dad also have a secret: their son's real name is Nikita, not Jeffrey, as they've led him to believe. That's because they're not really honest-to-goodness Americans, but Soviet "sleeper" agents who 20 years ago were given new identities and homes in the US. Their mission is to just sit back patiently, fit into their surroundings, raise a family, and wait until they're called upon to serve their country. Unfortunately, however, director Richard Benjamin turns them into pawns in his game of international intrigue. Benjamin sets up the premise deftly enough: FBI agent Poitier, while doing a routine background check on Phoenix for the Air Force Academy, notices that the applicant's parents are listed as having been born in the mid-19th century, leading Poitier to suspect that Phoenix and family may be foreign agents who have used false names and documents to enter the US. Meanwhile, a powerful KGB agent (Bradford) has received an assignment from the Soviet Embassy in Mexico. He must locate and apprehend a Soviet agent named Scuba (Lynch), a "loose cannon" who is blackmailing the embassy and killing off a number of sleeper agents. While Bradford—with his conspicuous accent, hair, hat, coat, cigarettes, and overall demeanor—has traced Lynch to Fountain Grove, Poitier has moved in across the street from Phoenix's family and become the friendly neighbor. Spotted as an FBI man by Kava and Jenkins, Poitier states his true identity to Phoenix, and keeps the teenager in suspense for some time before finally dropping the bomb and telling Phoenix that his parents are Soviet spies. Unknown to Phoenix, Bradford has arranged to meet Kava and Jenkins at a symbolic ballet performance of "Sleeping Beauty" (awakening agents, awakening beauty, get it?) and given them the assignment of paying Lynch his blackmail money. Naturally, the family ties that bind Kava, Jenkins, and Phoenix prove stronger than any brand of patriotism. Phoenix does not want to cooperate with Poitier because he fears his parents will be sent away (they have not yet committed any crimes, Poitier assures him), while Kava and Jenkins have learned to love the stability of their family and, presumably, these United States. (Mom and Dad even suggest running away with Phoenix and hiding out, but dismiss this choice as being unfair to their son—not to mention too similar to the plot of another Phoenix film, RUNNING ON EMPTY.) Now the plot devices spin out of control, as Bradford takes Phoenix hostage; Kava and Jenkins meet Lynch with the cash; Poitier follows and wounds Lynch; Lynch drops the money and tries to flee; and by screenwriting happenstance all six characters, after a standard TV-style car chase, end up together on a trolley car heading for the US-Mexican border. Bradford, with a gun to Phoenix's head, tries to force the boy across the Mexican border and recruit him as an agent; Poitier, with a gun to Lynch's head, wants to make a prisoner exchange. The parents look on in horror. A big emotional subtext here is Poitier's past—his partner was brutally murdered by Lynch and the FBI man has been hunting him down for the last 20 years. Now he finally has him, but, in order to assure Phoenix's safety, must hand him over. By the film's end, Lynch is killed (presumably from two gunshots—one by Poitier, one by Bradford), Poitier has atoned, and the family of Americanized Soviet agents remains united.

The premise of LITTLE NIKITA is a great one—worthy of Alfred Hitchcock, the master of espionage thrillers—but the execution here by director Benjamin is as rickety as can be. If a film is well directed, plot holes will generally be overlooked; viewers will become so engrossed with the goings-on that discrepancies will not distract them. About two-thirds into LITTLE NIKITA, however, the film deteriorates so rapidly that the characters cannot help but fall through the holes. The film desperately needs some character, some honesty, and some emotion; Benjamin inserts in their place plot mechanisms and genre expectations, which just don't leave the audience satisfied. The best guide to a film of this type is its running time. LITTLE NIKITA's 98 minutes feels about one half-hour too short—as if, after carefully setting up the plot and relationships, Benjamin decided to hurriedly cram all the loose ends into the last few scenes. The actions of the characters do not evolve as part of a natural progression, but out of a necessity to end the film.

Adding to the frustration of watching this otherwise promising movie fall apart at the end are its superb performances. Sidney Poitier, who also played a G-man in this year's SHOOT TO KILL, proves that his return to the screen was worth the wait; and River Phoenix (the only contemporary teen idol who deserves his lionization) again manages to play his troubled youngster role with enough variation from film to film to make his performance exciting. Caroline Kava and Richard Jenkins do well as the parents (although one never believes that they have a hidden past), but Benjamin's characterization of the Soviets, especially the stereotypical Bradford, seem more influenced by Hollywood films of the 1950s than by the real world. Desperately in need of some daring and more adroit direction, LITTLE NIKITA is no more than a diverting entertainment that becomes more and more disappointing the more one thinks about it. The unsuspenseful Marvin Hamlish score is supported with some additional music by Joe Curiale and the following songs: "Shattered" (Mike Slamer), "Fountainbleu" (Grace Lane), "Along the Way" (David Kurtz, Jack Allocco), "Paradise" (Charlie Mitchel, Kaylee Adams; performed by Adams), "You'll Know Love (When You Feel It)" (Mark Mangold, Al Fritsch; performed by Sandra St. Victor), "'Til the Next Time" (Mitchel; performed by Mitchel). *(Profanity.)*

p, Harry Gittes; d, Richard Benjamin; w, John Hill, Bo Goldman (based on a story by Tom Musca, Terry Schwartz); ph, Laszlo Kovacs (DeLuxe Color); ed, Jacqueline Cambas; m, Marvin Hamlisch, Joe Curiale; m/l, Mike Slamer, Grace Lane, David Kurtz, Jack Allocco, Charlie Mitchel, Kaylee Adams, Mark Mangold, Al Fritsch; prod d, Gene Callahan; art d, Hub Braden; set d, Ann Harris; spec eff, Michael E. Edmonson; cos, Patricia Norris; ch, Sir Kenneth MacMillan; stunts, Conrad E. Palmisano.

Spy/Thriller   **Cas.**   **(PR:A-C MPAA:PG)**

LONE RUNNER, THE †   (1988) 85m Trans World c

Miles O'Keeffe *(Garrett, the Lone Runner)*, Savina Gersak *(Analisa Summerking)*, Michael J. Aronin *(Emerik)*, John Steiner *(Skorm)*, Hal Yamanouchi *(Nimbus)*, Donald Hodson *(Mr. Summerking)*, Ronald Lacey *(Misha)*.

Earning a quick release before hitting the home video circuit, LONE RUNNER is a mildly violent action film featuring O'Keeffe as the familiar rugged-loner-with-three-days-of-beard-stubble who rides a horse through the Moroccan desert and carries a crossbow armed with explosive arrows. When beautiful European heiress Gersak is kidnaped by a gang of desert thieves and ransomed for a sackful of priceless diamonds owned by her father, O'Keeffe gets the call to come to the rescue. Filmed in 1986 by a mostly Italian crew.

p, Maurizio Maggi; d, Ruggero Deodato; w, Chris Trainor, Steven Luotto; ph, Roberto Forges Davanzati (Technicolor); ed, Eugenio Alabiso; m, Carlo Maria Cordio; art d, Bob Glaser; spec eff, Burt Spiegel.

Action   **(PR:NR MPAA:PG)**

LONELY PASSION OF JUDITH HEARNE, THE*   (1988, Brit.) 110m
                                                            Handmade/Island c

Maggie Smith *(Judith Hearne)*, Bob Hoskins *(James Madden)*, Wendy Hiller *(Aunt D'Arcy)*, Marie Kean *(Mrs. Rice)*, Ian McNeice *(Bernard Rice)*, Alan Devlin *(Father Quigley)*, Rudi Davies *(Mary)*, Prunella Scales *(Moira O'Neill)*, Aine Ni Mhuiri *(Edie Marinan)*, Sheila Reid *(Miss Friel)*, Niall Buggy *(Mr. Lenehan)*, Kate Binchy *(Sister Ignatius)*, Martina Stanley *(Sister Mary Paul)*, Veronica Quilligan *(Mrs. Mullen)*, Frank Egerton *(The Major)*, Leonard McGuire *(Dr. Bowe)*, Kevin Flood *(Owen O'Neill)*, Catherine Cusack *(Una O'Neill)*, Peter Gilmore *(Kevin O'Neill)*, James Holland *(Shaun O'Neill)*, Aiden Murphy *(Youth at Liquor Store)*, Emma Jane Lavin *(Young Judith)*, Dick Sullivan *(Priest)*, Alan Radcliffe *(Young Priest)*, Seamus Newham, Paul Boyle *(Taxi Drivers)*, Isolde Cazelet, Marjorie Hogan *(Old Women)*, Gerard O'Hagan *(Waiter)*, Anna Murphy, Gemma Murphy *(Girl Gigglers)*, Paddy Joyce *(Drunk in Pub)*, Richard Taylor *(Tin Whistle Player)*, Sue Hampson *(Cellist at Aunt D'Arcy's)*, Mike Rennie *(Violinist at Aunt D'Arcy's)*.

The vicious cycle of isolation and despair is a hard one to break. So learns Judith Hearne in this moving film based on the novel by Brian Moore. Smith plays the lonely Miss Hearne—an aging Irish spinster whose occasional bouts with the bottle lead her from boardinghouse to boardinghouse. Her days are empty save for the piano lessons she sporadically gives and frequent chats with the photograph of her late Aunt D'Arcy, whom she tended during the last months of the cantankerous old woman's life. At the movie's beginning, Smith has just moved into a boardinghouse run by Mrs. Rice (Kean) and her overweight, lazy, and—in Smith's naive eyes—worldly and sophisticated son, Bernard (McNeice). As boardinghouses go, this one is quite ordinary, with the exception of one guest who fills Smith's world with dreams and hope. Kean's brother, James Madden (Hoskins), has recently returned to Ireland from New York City. He is middle-aged, single, and—in Smith's naive eyes—worldly and sophisticated. With the innocence of a schoolgirl, Smith pursues Hoskins to the best of her ladylike ability, and they strike up an amiable relationship with two very different motives. Smith, of course, is looking for a husband, a partner to ease the emptiness of her solitary existence. Hoskins, however, mistakes Smith for a wealthy spinster and perceives her as nothing but a potential business partner. His taste in women runs more toward innocent young things like the housgirl, Mary (Davies), whom he rapes in a scene that reveals just what a swine he really is. When Smith realizes how gravely she has misjudged the philandering Hoskins, the impact is devastating. She gets drunk and sings away the night in her little room, provoking a scandal that forces her out of yet another home. A devout woman her entire life, Smith questions her beliefs, unable to comprehend why she has been left so alone. Religion gives way to alcoholism and an unsettling hospital stay during which she is visited, and once again humiliated, by the opportunistic Hoskins. The movie ends on a disturbingly unsatisfying note, as Smith moves on once again and the cycle of loneliness and despair continues.

Bleak and disquieting, THE LONELY PASSION OF JUDITH HEARNE is nevertheless a finely acted, gripping film. Maggie Smith, the epitome of British propriety, is just about perfect as the abandoned woman who manages to maintain an innate dignity despite the staggering emptiness of her life. Smith portrays the intimidated Miss Hearne with as much finesse as she brought to the title character in THE PRIME OF MISS JEAN BRODIE, and Bob Hoskins is just as effective as the sleazy, alienated loser James Madden as he was playing a frantic investigator in WHO FRAMED ROGER RABBIT. The striking contrast between these two characters thrown together gives life to an essentially slow-paced story, making for a movie that is both disturbing and thought provoking. *(Substance abuse, brief nudity, sexual situations.)*

p, Peter Nelson, Richard Johnson; d, Jack Clayton; w, Peter Nelson (based on the novel by Brian Moore); ph, Peter Hannan (Fuji Color); ed, Terry Rawlings; m, Georges Delerue; m/l, Mark Fisher, Joe Goodwin, Larry Shay; prod d, Michael Pickwoad; art d, Henry Harris; set d, Josie MacAvin; cos, Elizabeth Waller; makeup, Kevin Lintott.

Romance/Drama   **Cas.**   **(PR:O MPAA:R)**

LURKERS †   (1988) 90m Reeltime/Crown c

Christine Moore *(Cathy)*, Gary Warner *(Bob)*, Marina Taylor *(Monica)*, Carissa Channing *(Sally)*, Tom Billett *(Leo "The Hammer")*, Dana Nardelli *(Cathy as a Girl)*, Roy MacArthur, Peter Oliver-Norman, Nancy Groff.

Once again, low-budget splatter *auteur* Roberta Findlay (BLOODSISTERS) serves up a bloody supernatural tale full of nightmares, possessions, visions, ghosts, and, of course, sex and violence. Saddled with an unwieldy flashback structure, the film tells the story of pretty professional cellist Moore, who is plagued by the "lurkers" of her past. It seems that, as a child, Moore was tormented by her mother and some of the neighbor folk—all of whom happened to be satanists. Suffering from horrible nightmares, Moore turns to faithful boy friend Warner for comfort, but he too is a representative of Satan and is determined to capture her soul. Given a quick regional release before going the home video route, LURKERS promises to be an amateurish production all the way, given Findlay's previous output and the bargain-basement quality of special effects man Ed French's work.

p, Walter E. Sear; d, Roberta Findlay; w, Ed Kelleher, Harriette Vidal; ph, Roberta Findlay (Studio Film Labs Color); ed, Walter E. Sear, Roberta Findlay; m, Walter E. Sear; art d, Ivy Rosovsky, Jeffrey Wallach; spec eff, Ed French; cos, Ivy Rosovsky, Jeffrey Wallach.

Horror   **Cas.**   **(PR:NR MPAA:R)**

M

MAC AND ME † (1988) 91m Orion c

Christine Ebersole (*Janet Cruise*), Jonathan Ward (*Michael Cruise*), Katrina Caspary (*Courtney*), Lauren Stanley (*Debbie*), Jade Calegory (*Eric Cruise*), Vinnie Torrente (*Mitford*), Martin West (*Wickett*), Ivan Jorge Rado (*Zimmerman*), Danny Cooksey (*Jack, Jr.*), Laura Waterbury (*Linda*), Jack Eiseman (*Splatter Car Driver*), Barbara Allyne Bennet (*Scientist*), Richard Bravo, J. D. Hall (*Movers*), Joseph Chapman, Gary Brockette (*Doctors*), Sherri Stone Butler (*Checkout Girl*), Sheila Chambers, Alyce Coleman (*Girls in Car*), John Curtin (*Control Room Chief*), Andrew Divoff, Ray Forchion (*Policemen*), James C. Duke (*Sears Store Manager*), Bud Ekins (*Gardner*), Buck Flower (*Security Guard*), Tom Fuccello (*Mr. Ryan*), Ernie Fuentes (*Store Manager*), Michael Geary, Jack Ong (*Technicians*), Heather Green (*Mars Sister*), Roger Hampton (*Water & Power Man*), Dixon Harding (*Kid*), Christopher Law (*Air Force Major*), Mayah McCoy (*Dancing Double for Mac*), Elena Moure (*Mars Mother*), Buckley Norris (*Highway Man*), J. Jay Saunders (*Judge*), Lowell Sexton (*Counter Man*), Sean Simmons (*Sheriff's Deputy*), Sterling Swanson (*Police Captain*), Jack David Walker (*Mars Father*), Richard Wright (*Elrod*), Ronald McDonald (*Himself*).

Unabashed consumerism abounds in this full-scale rip-off of Spielberg's E.T., which, like that 1980 classic, tells the story of a young boy from a fatherless family who lives a happy life in the sterility of the Valley. The only difference here is that the young boy is confined to a wheelchair. He gets the usual ribbing from schoolmates because he is different from the rest. What is extraordinary about his life, however, is the arrival of MAC—Mysterious Alien Creature—an ugly little MacE.T. that has been separated from its family. If you haven't already guessed, our young hero helps MAC find his family. In the process, the boy dies and is magically revived, a la E.T. The film is filled with references to Coca-Cola, Big Macs, and Skittles candy, and includes a visit to a MacDonalds restaurant and a "special guest appearance" by Ronald Mac-Donald. MAC AND ME deserves to be soundly criticized for this unconscionable mix of marketing aimed at easily impressionable children. To attempt to sell fast food and soft drinks as some sort of food of redemption is more than suspect. On the other hand, the film provides a fine model in its young hero, played by Jade Calegory, an 12-year-old actor and sufferer of spina bifida, and the spokesman for an Easter Seals Campaign called "Friends Who Care." Orion Pictures must also be commended for donating a portion of the film's profits (which, at the box office, were pretty scant) to Ronald MacDonald's Children's Charity. Includes the songs: "Down to Earth" (Allee Willis, Danny Sembello, performed by Ashford & Simpson), "Send out a Signal" (Larry Hart), "Wait and Break My Heart Tomorrow" (Greg Allen, performed by the Flint River Band), "You Knew What You Were Doing (Every Inch of the Way)" (Jeff Barry, Marcy Levy, performed by Levy), "Waves" (Marti Sharron, Glen Ballard, performed by Debbie Lytton), "Take Me/I'll Follow You" (Alan Silvestri, Bobby Caldwell, performed by Caldwell), "You're Not a Stranger Anymore" (Alan Silvestri, Bob Gaudio, Judy Parker, Mike Curb, performed by Jara Lane).

p, R.J. Louis; d, Stewart Raffill; w, Stewart Raffill, Steve Feke; ph, Nick McLean (CFI color); ed, Tom Walls; m, Alan Silvestri; prod d, W. Stewart Campbell; set d, John Anderson; spec eff, Dennis Dion, Chris Burton; cos, Richard Bruno, Arlene Encell; ch, Marla Blakey; stunts, Fernando Celis; makeup, John Elliott, Margaret Elliott.

Comedy/Drama/Fantasy Cas. (PR:NR MPAA:PG)

MADAME SOUSATZKA* (1988, Brit.) 122m Sousatzka-Cineplex Odeon/UNIV c

Shirley MacLaine (*Mme. Irina Sousatzka*), Navin Chowdhry (*Manek Sen*), Peggy Ashcroft (*Lady Emily*), Twiggy (*Jenny*), Shabana Azmi (*Sushila Sen*), Leigh Lawson (*Ronnie Blum*), Geoffrey Bayldon (*Mr. Cordle*), Lee Montague (*Vincent Pick*), Robert Rietty (*Leo Milev*), Jeremy Sinden (*Woodford*), Roger Hammond (*Lefranc*), Christopher Adey (*Conductor*), Barry Douglas (*Pianist at Portman Hall*), Sam Howard (*Edward*).

It's been five years since Shirley MacLaine's Oscar-winning performance in TERMS OF ENDEARMENT and she returns with a vengeance in MADAME SOUSATZKA, directed by Oscar-winning director John Schlesinger (MIDNIGHT COWBOY), scripted by Oscar-winning writer Ruth Prawer Jhabvala (A ROOM WITH A VIEW), and costarring Oscar-winning actress Dame Peggy Ashcroft (A PASSAGE TO INDIA). Not surprisingly, MADAME SOUSATZKA seems to be making a headfirst dive into Oscar contention. "I teach not only how to play the piano, but how to live," is the truest phrase that explodes from MacLaine's title character, a jittery, loud, fiery fascist of a piano teacher. Born of a Russian father and an American mother, this highly respected teacher has spent the last 30 years living in a London boarding house. Although the neighborhood is falling victim to regentrification—other houses on the block are being swallowed up by real estate developers—MacLaine stands tall and has no intention of letting progress knock her over. Also living in the building is a sweet old landlady, Ashcroft; a kindly old osteopath and closest homosexual, Bayldon; and a pretty pop singer and former model, Twiggy. Into this eccentric microcosm steps Chowdhry, a gifted 15-year-old Indian pianist whose talent and charisma attract MacLaine. She believes she can turn him

into a brilliant musician, but that means starting from scratch and molding him into a new whole. She yells at him, forces him to sit straight, tears down his showy playing, buys him a suit and tie, makes him promise to throw away his roller skates for fear that he will hurt himself, implores him to become cultured and read the classics, then rewards him with a motherly smile and a fresh-baked cookie. MacLaine's overbearing ways come to the attention of Chowdhry's mother, Azmi. An attractive woman who earns a meager income from the Indian food she supplies to ritzy merchants, Azmi has devoted her entire life to her dream of seeing her son become a concert pianist. She is eager to see him perform, and Chowdhry is just as eager to begin supporting his mother. MacLaine, however, in accordance with her perfected Sousatzka System, is infuriated at the very thought of selling one's talent. She feels her pupils must wait, and wait, until they are ready to reach the stage. This last step, she believes, should not be dictated by a desire for money. As a result, MacLaine has, over the years, lost all her best pupils—instead of remaining under her iron fist, they move on to performance halls and MacLaine's rival teacher, Rietty. Pulling Chowdhry away from MacLaine's guidance is talent scout Lawson, who, while passing MacLaine's flat on the way to girl friend Twiggy's (his real-life partner), has heard the teenager's exceptional playing. He offers him a chance to play in a prestigious festival—an offer that grossly insults MacLaine. She is even more insulted when Chowdhry accepts. It is MacLaine's fear that he will fail, as she did when she was 18 and her pushy and demanding mother forced her into a recital. Unable to handle the pressure, the young MacLaine fumbled at the keyboard and ran off the stage—a traumatic incident from which she never recovered. MacLaine reluctantly attends Chowdhry's first performance. With orchestral accompaniment, Chowdhry attacks the piano and earns the respect of his entire audience. Even MacLaine is impressed. Near the end, however, he fumbles and loses eight bars. The conductor is able to adjust and Chowdhry, instead of running from the stage as the young MacLaine did, recovers and finishes the piece. The audience is thrilled, hardly noticing his mistake. Later, Chowdhry must decide if he should return to MacLaine's instruction. Before he confronts her, however, he visits Twiggy. Infatuated with her and preying on her vulnerability (she has broken off with Lawson, packed up and prepared to move, and now questions her own talent), Chowdhry convinces her to let him spend the night. The following morning, he presents MacLaine with the news that he will be studying with Rietty. Instead of slamming the door in his face, she accepts his decision and gives him her blessing. But although the neighborhood is being torn down around her, this piano teacher's presence will still be felt. Coming down the street towards her flat is a new student, fearful of what this legendary teacher may have in store.

MADAME SOUSATZKA features a cast so good they cannot be sunk, not even by the film's script and direction, both of which are tired and pedestrian. Surprisingly, there is very little plot in this two-hour film, giving the characters freedom to live and breathe. Shirley MacLaine, who shared the Best Actress prize at the Venice Film Festival with Isabelle Huppert, has been widely praised in the past for her acting talent, and offers another tour-de-force performance here. Curiously, however, Mac Laine's acting style is not a realistic one. One never really believes that Madame Irena Sousatzka exists; rather, one sits back and watches MacLaine tackle her role. MacLaine doesn't so much play a part in this film as move her face, twinkle her eyes, flail her arms, and bark her lines. Her entire body gives the performance, as if Shirley MacLaine is sitting inside this shell of Madame Sousatzka and piloting this acting machine through the frame, or guiding her body as a puppet master does a marionette. Hers is a style rarely seen today in films—one which harkens back to Bette Davis and to the acting of the silent cinema. In light of MacLaine's performance, one has to say that her costar, young newcomer Navin Chowdhry, is doing his acting duty above and beyond the call. Bursting with charisma, this bright and energetic young actor (in contrast to MacLaine) makes viewers believe they are watching a piano prodigy on the verge of a major breakthrough. The scene of his festival recital is the film's greatest moment, in large part due to Chowdhry. A lengthy scene that incorporates all the characters and shows Schlesinger at his best, it contains more suspense than a handful of FATAL ATTRACTIONs, taking the viewer on a musical rollercoaster ride. The supporting cast also deserves a hearty round of applause, especially Twiggy, whose character is an endearing woman, if a rather thick-headed one. MADAME SOUSATZKA's chief fault is its insistence on social relevancy. Its trite and heavy-handed underlying theme of change vs. tradition, commerce vs. art, and the general destruction of history and values is clear from the situations and dialog. Schlesinger, however, has to continuously fill his frame with "For Sale" signs, renovation crews, moving trucks, and wrecking balls. Although these hyperreal stylizations and anti-Thatcher stances have worked well for British director Stephen Frears (in SAMMY AND ROSIE GET LAID, for example), Schlesinger's success in the film comes in small moments and the nurturing of emotional responses. MADAME SOUSATZKA is not the great or important film that it tries to be; rather, it is a warm and touching human drama, made so by its exceptional performances. (*Profanity, adult situations, substance abuse.*)

p, Robin Dalton; d, John Schlesinger; w, Ruth Prawer Jhabvala, John Schlesinger (based on a novel by Bernice Rubens); ph, Nat Crosby (Rank color); ed, Peter Honess; m, Gerald Gouriet; md, Yonty Solomon; prod d, Luciana Arrighi; art d, Ian Whittaker, Stephen Scott; cos, Amy Roberts.

Drama Cas. (PR:A-C MPAA:PG-13)

MADE IN U.S.A. † (1988) 87m Hemdale/DEG c

Adrian Pasdar *(Dar)*, Christopher Penn *(Tuck)*, Lori Singer *(Annie)*, Jackie Murphy *(Cora)*, Judy Baldwin *(Dorie)*, Dean Paul Martin *(Cowboy)*.

A satirical, independent road movie, MADE IN U.S.A. follows three characters who travel across America from Centralia, Pennsylvania, to Los Angeles. Penn (younger brother of Sean) and Pasdar play buddies who leave the urban wasteland of the industrial belt behind them, traveling in stolen cars.

p, Charles Roven; d, Ken Friedman; w, Ken Friedman (based on a story by Friedman, Nick Wexler); ph, Curtis Clark (CFI Color); ed, Curtiss Clayton; m, Sonic Youth; prod d, James Newport; art d, Tom Southwind; set d, Cynthia Redman.

Drama **(PR:NR MPAA:R)**

MAJORETTES, THE † (1988) 92m Major Films c

Kevin Kindlin *(Jeff)*, Terrie Godfrey *(Vicky)*, Mark V. Jevicky *(Sheriff Braden)*, Sueanne Seamens *(Judy)*, Denise Huot *(Helga)*, Carl Hetrick *(Roland)*, Mary Jo Limpert, Harold K. Keller, Tom E. Desrocher, Jacqueline Bowman, Colin Martin, Russ Streiner, John Russo, Bill Hinzman.

This straight-to-video release features a hooded murderer who is offing high-school football cheerleaders. The serial murders become a cover for a ruthless nurse who wants her granddaughter to become a victim, leaving a half-million dollar inheritance. Produced and written by John Russo, the screenwriter of George Romero's NIGHT OF THE LIVING DEAD. Two actors in the Romero horror classic are also involved—this film's director, Bill Hinzman, had a bit part in the Romero film; and Russell Streiner (the smart-aleck brother who is killed off at the start of Romero's movie) here has a supporting role.

p, John Russo; d, Bill Hinzman; w, John Russo (based on his novel); ph, Paul McCollough (WRS color); ed, Bill Hinzman, Paul McCollough; m, Paul McCollough; spec eff, Gerald Gergely; makeup, Gerald Gergely.

Horror **Cas.** **(PR:NR MPAA:R)**

MAN OUTSIDE* (1988) 109m Stouffer/Virgin Vision c

Robert Logan *(Jack Avery)*, Kathleen Quinlan *(Grace Freemont)*, Bradford Dillman *(Frank Simmons)*, Levon Helm *(Sheriff Leland Laughlin)*, Andrew Barach *(Leo Greenfield)*, Alex Liggett *(Toby Riggs)*, Rick Danko *(Jim Riggs)*, Patricia Ralph *(Velma Riggs)*, Mary Ingalls *(Momma)*, Patricia Brandkamp *(Evelyn)*, Roger Gross *(Detective)*, Tom Earnhart, Philip Steele *(Plainclothesmen)*, Garth Hudson *(Cheney)*, Cecily Stormdelk *(Rita)*, Sarge West *(Deputy in Office)*, Jerry Rushing *(Deputy in Library)*, David Huie, John Gallagher, Stratton Leopold, Kent Brown *(Buddies)*, Becky Hernreich *(Sexy Woman)*, Dash Goff *(Theo)*, Elizabeth Reha *(Maggie)*, Pashal Porta *(Newsman on TV)*, Richard Manuel, Robert Illjes *(Vigilantes)*, Jamie Gallagher *(Radio Dispatcher)*, Earl Bond *(Jail Guard)*, Shobie Partos, Sloan Wilson *(Coeds)*, Nancy Johnson, Cassandra Currie, Melanie McLain, Eric Boyd *(Students)*, Floyd Bohannan, Bill Ramsey *(Firemen)*, Jason Coates *(Billy Avery)*, Harry Shadden *(Bartender)*, Bill Dickson *(Baggage Handler)*, Kelly Householder *(Woman in Flames)*, Chessie the Diving Dog *(Roger)*.

MAN OUTSIDE features Logan as a lawyer who, one day, runs his Porsche into the Arkansas backwoods and stays there, living off the land and reverting to a hermit's existence. Anthropology student Barach takes photos of Logan as part of a class project; professor Quinlan, upon seeing Barach's presentation, tells her students that such solitary isolation is a form of self-punishment, then becomes intrigued as to why Logan has exiled himself out there. She heads off to investigate, but has little luck at coaxing information out of him—although they do begin a touch-and-go romance that sputters on through the rest of the film. Logan decides to take Quinlan up on her offer to tell his story for cash so that he can pay off some back land taxes. Even as he begins to crawl out from under his rock, however, other forces are out to get him. A little boy is kidnaped by psycho land surveyor Dillman, and the evidence—a shoe picked up by Logan's dog—points to the mountainman as the pervert. Picked up by a vigilante group led by the boy's father, Logan is beaten up and tortured with a blow torch, but rescued by sheriff Helms and thrown in jail. From behind bars, Logan finally tells Quinlan about the past he's running from: He feels responsible for his wife's death in a fire. With Quinlan's assistance, Logan escapes from jail and the pair flee into the countryside, where they are given shelter by a backwoods couple. Barach then helps Logan get to Dillman's house, discovering his evil mother upstairs and the boy in the cellar. With his romance with Quinlan firmly established, Logan sets off to visit his own son, whom he hasn't seen since the fire.

MAN OUTSIDE marks the feature directorial debut of nature documentarist Mark Stouffer, so it should come as no surprise that there are lots of scenic shots of the Arkansas countryside. Indeed, the good technical work on such a modest budget (3.5 million) is one of the better aspects of this picture. The story, however, sticks to tried-and-true formulas and is far too drawn out, with the same territory being covered time and again, so that the film never gathers any momentum. The story line of child molester Dillman is quite superfluous; the filmmakers shy away from actually confronting the issue of sexual molestation, and the subject is just a complicated means through which Logan confronts his past (although, given the film's middle American values, it's perhaps not surprising that the problem gets treated this way). Robert Logan and Kathleen Quinlan work well together, with nice support from Levon Helm (COAL MINER'S DAUGHTER; END OF THE LINE), ex-drummer from the Band (other members of which [Richard Manuel, Rick Danko, and Garth Hudson] are also in the cast). Bradford Dillman's performance, on the other hand, is absurd and annoying, as is much of the backing score. Songs include: "Lowlands" (Gary Scrugg; performed by Vince Gill), "Reunion Theme" (Dennis Burnside), "Ashcroft" (Ted Pillzecker). *(Violence, brief nudity, adult situations.)*

p, Mark Stouffer, Robert E. Yoss; d, Mark Stouffer; w, Mark Stouffer, Ira Steven Levine, Pat Duncan (based on a story by Stouffer); ph, William Wages; ed, Tony Lombardo; m, John McEuen; m/l, Gary Scrugg, Dennis Burnside, Ted Pillzecker; prod d, Deborah Stouffer; set d, Michael Taylor; cos, Elisabeth Scott; makeup, Lynn Barber Rosenthal.

Drama **Cas.** **(PR:C MPAA:PG-13)**

MANIAC COP*½ (1988) 85m Shapiro Glickenhaus c

Tom Atkins *(Lt. McCrae)*, Bruce Campbell *(Jack Forrest)*, Laurene Landon *(Theresa Mallory)*, Richard Roundtree *(Commissioner Pike)*, William Smith *(Capt. Ripley)*, Sheree North *(Sally Noland)*, Robert Z'ar *(Matt Cordell)*.

MANIAC COP comes as something of a disappointment from the prolific pen of Larry Cohen, the one-man movie machine who has written, produced, and directed such modern genre classics as the IT'S ALIVE trilogy, GOD TOLD ME TO, and Q. Serving only as producer and writer here, Cohen turned over the directing chores to Bill Lustig, whose MANIAC (1980) is one of the most repulsive splatter movies ever made. Written with tongue firmly in cheek, the film begins as New York City is terrorized by a homicidal killer in a police uniform whom the press dubs "Maniac Cop." Although the police department officially denies that the killer is from their ranks, homicide detective Atkins isn't so sure. As the murders continue, it becomes apparent that the killer is getting his information from inside the department and Atkins begins digging for clues among his brothers. Meanwhile, a young married police officer, Campbell, is clandestinely carrying on an affair with female officer Landon. At the same time, his wife receives anonymous phone calls telling her that her husband is the maniac cop. Suspicious, she follows Campbell to a seedy motel and bursts in on him and Landon in bed. Relieved that Campbell is not the killer, but upset at his infidelity, the wife runs from the motel, only to be snatched by the real maniac cop. The next morning her body is found in the very motel room that was used by her husband. Campbell is arrested for the murder and made a convenient scapegoat for the killings. Atkins, however, doubts that Campbell is the maniac, and teams up with Landon to solve the crimes. As their investigation proceeds, Atkins and Landon come to believe that the maniac cop is a police officer (Z'ar) thought to be long dead. It seems that Z'ar was a notoriously gung-ho cop who cared little for civil rights or due process of law. Although his arrest record was impressive, his storm-trooper tactics made him a political liability for the NYC major and for police commissioner Roundtree. To relieve themselves of this troublesome peace officer, the powers-that-be framed Z'ar on a trumped-up murder charge and he was sentenced to a maximum security prison. Soon after his arrival, Z'ar was attacked in the showers by knife-wielding inmates and cut to ribbons. Although brain-dead, Z'ar continued to live. A sympathetic prison coroner declared him dead and allowed the officer's cop girl friend, North, to obtain custody of the body. Now the zombified Z'ar is back out on the street, seeking vengeance on those who sent him to prison. Before he can inform the commissioner and mayor of this discovery, however, Atkins runs afoul of Z'ar and is killed. Landon breaks Campbell out of jail and together they try to defeat the maniac cop while avoiding a statewide manhunt for Campbell (who police believe murdered Atkins and several others during his escape). Ignoring warnings from Landon, commissioner Roundtree goes to attend the annual St. Patrick's Day parade, only to be murdered by Z'ar before getting into the elevator. A chase ensues, with Campbell and Z'ar battling in a paddy wagon as the vehicle careens onto a rotting NYC wharf. Moving at high speed, Z'ar is impaled by a pole and drives the paddy wagon into the river as Campbell jumps to safety. When the wagon is dredged out of the river, however, Z'ar's body is not to be found. Beneath the dock, unseen, a hand emerges from the water.

Larry Cohen has made some surprisingly complex and interesting low-budget genre films that are rich in characterization and thematics. MANIAC COP, however, is basically a one-idea concept enlivened ever so slightly by fleeting moments of Cohen's patented sociopolitical subtext and goofy black humor. Cohen's script takes potshots at the news media, police department, city hall politicians, and citizens of New York City. The various murders, although graphically presented, have elements of macabre humor about them. In one instance, a young man whose throat is cut is flung onto the hood of his car. With blood spurting all over the windshield, the victim's terrified girl friend instinctively turns on the windshield wipers, in order to see where she's going as she drives off to escape the killer. In another scene, the maniac cop smothers a man in a freshly poured concrete sidewalk. The next morning it takes jackhammers to remove the cemented victim. Okay, so the humor is repulsive, but at least Cohen and director Bill Lustig aren't taking the obligatory generic elements very seriously. The title, in fact, is Cohen's most inspired contribution, one that will forever be remembered alongside such howlers as THREE ON A MEATHOOK (1973) and NAIL GUN MASSACRE (1987) for its lay-all-the-cards-on-the-table frankness. Unfortunately, there is not enough freshness in Lustig's direction to elevate MANIAC COP from the dregs of the merely competent. As was the case with last year's mainstream thriller BEST SELLER, one is left with the feeling that only Larry Cohen can properly direct a script written by Larry Cohen. A low-budget *auteur* if ever there was one, Cohen employs quirky direction to bring bizarre legitimacy to his outlandish ideas and makes them work cinematically. Other directors, no matter how talented, fail to tap into Cohen's wholly unique sensibility. Lustig does borrow a few of Cohen's tricks, however, and shoots in the streets of NYC off-the-cuff, incorporating real events like the St. Patrick Day parade into the narrative (Cohen did the same thing in GOD TOLD ME TO). Another Cohenesque element is the casting. Cohen always assembles a fairly remarkable array of new and old talent, and this film is no exception to the rule. Relative newcomer Bruce Campbell, whose only other films have been Sam Raimi's EVIL DEAD and EVIL DEAD II, fits right in here, while Richard Roundtree (a Cohen veteran from Q), Tom Atkins, Sheree North, and William Smith—all veteran genre film actors with familiar faces—lend weighty credibility to the absurd proceedings. Laurene Landon, however, is a weak and unremarkable actress, and Robert Z'ar is merely a hulking shape that could have been played by any bodybuilder. Also appearing in brief cameos are Jake "Raging Bull" LaMotta, as a detective, and EVIL DEAD director Raimi as a reporter at the parade. Cohen's contributions make MANIAC COP more interesting than most mad-slasher films, but not by much. (*Graphic violence, gore effects, sexual situations, profanity.*)

p, Larry Cohen; d, William Lustig; w, Larry Cohen; ph, Vincent J. Rabe (Foto-Kem Color); ed, David Kern; m, Jay Chattaway; art d, Jonathon Hodges.

Horror   Cas.   (PR:O MPAA:R)

MANIFESTO***   (1988) 96m Golan-Globus/Cannon c

Camilla Soeberg (*Svetlana Vargas*), Alfred Molina (*Avanti*), Simon Callow (*Police Chief Hunt*), Eric Stoltz (*Christopher*), Lindsay Duncan (*Lily Sacher*), Rade Serbedzija (*Emile*), Svetozar Cvetkovic (*Rudi Kugelhopf*), Chris Haywood (*Wango*), Patrick Godfrey (*Dr. Lombrosow*), Linda Marlowe (*Stella Vargas*), Gabrielle Anwar (*Tina*), Enver Petrovci (*The King*), Ronald Lacey (*Conductor*), Tanja Boskovic (*Olympia*), Zeljko Duvnjak (*Martin*), Danko Ljustina (*Baker*), Rahela Ferari (*Grandmother*), Djani Segina (*Old Mailman*), Tom Gotovac, Mirko Boman (*Agents*), Matko Raguz (*Engineer*), Branko Blace (*Stoker*), Ivo Kristof, Marijan Habazin (*Orderlies*), Drew Kunin (*Singer*), Alan Anticevic (*Boy*), Svjetlana Grzelja (*Girl*), Sinisa Cmrk (*Man in the Water*).

Having returned to Yugoslavia after 17 years in exile, Dusan Makavejev has also returned to the type of political satire he departed from in 1985's THE COCA-COLA KID. Unfortunately, while this return marks a step in the right direction, MANIFESTO disappoints when compared to Makavejev's earlier, more confrontational works—WR: MYSTERIES OF THE ORGANISM or SWEET MOVIE. The film takes place in 1920, in a fictional Eastern European town called Waldheim, "where nothing is what it seems." (The actual town is Skofja Loka in the Yugoslavian republic of Slovenia.) Traveling by train into Waldheim are Soeberg, a beautiful young woman who hasn't been back to her hometown in many years and who is now involved in a plot to assassinate a visiting king (she hides her revolver in her lacy underthings), and Molina, an outwardly prim-and-proper secret policeman driven by ways of the flesh. Soeberg has barely stepped into town when she witnesses the seemingly unwarranted arrest of Cvetkovic, an energetic schoolteacher who is really a revolutionary. Meanwhile, Molina is preparing for the king's arrival, working at the side of Callow, the nincompoop local police chief. Others in town are obviously revolutionaries—baker Ljustina, photographer Haywood, postmaster Stoltz—but their roles in the day-to-day activities of the town are too integral for the authorities to have them sent away. Although everyone in town has duties that pertain to the king's arrival—whether these be protecting his majesty or assassinating him—they all seem more interested in getting into one another's knickers. Soeberg, who reveals some fleshy part of her body throughout much of the film, spends much energy fighting off and submitting to the advances of her widowed mother's servant, Serbedzija, a brutal animal of a man. Although Molina tries to keep his identity and mission secret, it is clear to everybody that he is an undercover agent. Instead of performing his duties, however, he wanders off for a secluded rendezvous with Anwar, an orphaned nymphet who earns a living as an ice cream merchant. While Molina is busy seducing Anwar, Soeberg is trying to get her revolver to chosen assassin Cvetkovic, who has been hauled of to Bergman's Sanatorium, a secluded asylum with radical methods of torturing and treating political prisoners. The apparently mad Cvetkovic's treatment consist of imprisoning him in a large exercise wheel (the sort one would find in a hamster cage). Because this revolutionary believes so strongly in "The Movement," the doctors give him what he wants—movement. Disguised as a nun, Soeberg manages to get the revolver, which has been hidden in a loaf of bread by the baker, to Cvetkovic. Meanwhile, the king has arrived in town, but Molina is unable to give him a royal greeting. Discovered in a compromising position with Anwar by Duncan, the town's highly moral schoolteacher, he has been beaten and bound. Naturally, this radical action gets Duncan sent to the sanatorium for a treatment. Acting as a silent observer to much of the goings-on is Stoltz, the postmaster who has long loved Soeberg from afar. He pledges his allegiance to her, is rewarded with a night in her bed, and eventually learns that wrapped in a carpet at the foot of Soeberg's bed is Serbedzija's fresh corpse. After more than one unsuccessful attempt on the king's life, Soeberg's mission has completely failed, ending with her accidentally killing a servant rather than a king. Stoltz helps her dump the corpse, but he too is killed in the process. By the film's end, Soeberg and Molina leave town as lovers, while, outside their train compartment window, they see the once-reserved schoolteacher Duncan. Now a devoted, wild-eyed, gun-waving revolutionary, she has taken up the cause all the others have forsaken for the flesh.

Described by Makavejev as an "irresponsible comedy" because, as opposed to a traditional comedy, it is the "good guys who suffer" in the film, MANIFESTO can be praised as the director's return to a cinema of subversion. It is a film that takes subjects not usually viewed as comic—political revolution and eroticism—and treats them as such, and bears similarities even to such previous madcap political satires as KING OF HEARTS or THE MOUSE THAT ROARED. What is curious about Makavejev's last three films (MONTENEGRO [1981], THE COCA-COLA KID [1985], and MANIFESTO) is that they appear (in varying degrees) to be "normal" in a westernized, Americanized, Hollywoodized way. But while beautifully shot, starring reasonably well-known actors, and retaining a relatively straightforward narrative line, these recent films do not deal with "normal" situations or subjects—as in the

fictional town of Waldheim, "nothing is what it seems." MANIFESTO is less daring structurally and theoretically than either WR or SWEET MOVIE, but is even more subversive because of its presentation, its accessibility. Instead of making an "art film" that will preach only to the converted few, Makavejev has created an entertainment that may just twist the minds of the masses. He has, indeed, achieved his stated goal of merging a "subversive spirit with a formal strategy." Despite the fact that the Cannon Film Group of Menahem Golum and Yoram Globus have long been pegged as the bottom of the filmmaking barrel, they must be given credit for supporting such respected but unbankable directors as Makavejev, Ivan Passer (HAUNTED SUMMER), Jean-Luc Godard (KING LEAR), Norman Mailer (TOUGH GUYS DON'T DANCE), Andrei Konchalovsky (SHY PEOPLE), Lina Wertmuller (CAMORRA), and John Cassavetes (LOVE STREAMS). Songs include "Why Stars Come Out at Night" (Ray Noble, performed by Camilla Soeberg), "I'd Give a Million Tomorrows" (Jerry Livingston, Milton Berle, performed by Nick Curtis). (*Nudity, profanity, sexual situations, adult situations.*)

p, Menahem Golan, Yoram Globus; d, Dusan Makavejev; w, Dusan Makavejev (based on a story by Emile Zola); ph, Tomislav Pinter (Rank Color); ed, Tony Lawson; m, Nicola Piovani; m/l, Ray Noble, Jerry Livingston, Milton Berle; prod d, Veljko Despotovic; cos, Marit Allen; stunts, Ivo Kristof; makeup, Mary Hillman.

Comedy/Political   (PR:O MPAA:R)

MARRIED TO THE MOB***   (1988) 103m Mysterious Arts/Orion c

Michelle Pfeiffer (*Angela Demarco*), Matthew Modine (*Mike Downey*), Dean Stockwell (*Tony "The Tiger" Russo*), Mercedes Ruehl (*Connie Russo*), Oliver Platt (*Ed Benitez*), Alec Baldwin (*Frank "The Cucumber" DeMarco*), Anthony J. Nici (*Joey DeMarco*), Sister Carol East (*Rita Harcourt*), Paul Lazar (*Tommy Boyle*), Trey Wilson (*Franklin, FBI Field Director*), Joan Cusack (*Rose Boyle*), Ellen Roley (*Theresa*), O-Lan Jones (*Phyllis*), Charles Napier (*Ray, Hairdresser*), Nancy Travis (*Karen Lutnick*), David Johansen (*Priest*), Maria Karnilova (*Frank's Mom*), Chris Isaak (*Arrowhead "The Clown"*), Joe Spinell (*Leonard "Tiptoes" Mazzilli*), Tracey Walter (*Chicken' Lickin' Mgr*), Warren Miller (*Johnny King*), Frank Gio (*Nick "The Snake"*), Gary Klar (*Al "The Worm"*), Steve Vignari (*Stevarino*), Captain Haggerty (*The Fat Man*), Marlene Willoughby (*Mrs. Fat Man*), Frank Acquilino (*Conductor*), Jason Allen (*Tony Russo, Jr.*), Diana Puccerella, Suzanne Puccerella (*Three-card Monte Victims*), Tara Duckworth (*Tara*), Frank Ferrara (*Vinnie the Slug*), Gary Goetzman (*Guy at the Piano*), Carlos Giovanni (*Carlo Whispers*), James Reno Pelliccio (*Butch*), Daniel Dassin (*Maitre d'*), Colin Quinn (*Homicide Detective*), Dodie Demme (*Pigs Knuckles Shopper*), Gene Borkan (*Goodwill Executive*), Wilma Dore (*Uptown Saleslady*), Joseph L. "Mr. Spoons" Jones (*Mr. Spoons*), Lezli Jae (*Chicken Lickin' Server*), Alison Gordy (*Chicken Lickin' Feminist*), Pe De Boi (*Samba Band*), Buzz Kilman (*Ruthless Sniper*), Kenneth Utt (*Sourpuss F.B.I. Man*), Tony Fitzpatrick (*Sourpuss Immigration Man*), Al Lewis (*Uncle Joe Russo*), Tim O'Connell (*Abused Ticket Agent*), D. Stanton Miranda (*Gal at the Piano*), Luis Garcia (*Honeymoon Suite Bellboy*), Janet Howard (*Abused Stewardess*), Ralph Corsel (*Jimmy "Fisheggs" Roe*), Bill Carter (*The Ambassador*), Obba Babatunde (*The Face of Justice*), George "Red" Schwartz (*Shotgun Marshal*), Ellie Cornell (*Pushy Reporter*), Roy Blount, Jr. (*Humane Reporter*), Todd Solondz (*Zany Reporter*), Roma Maffia (*Angie's First Customer*), Patrick Phipps (*Goodwill Hunk*), Carlos Anthony Ocasio (*Joey's New Pal*).

Disappointed with the indifferent public response to his excellent SOMETHING WILD (1986), director Jonathan Demme has here produced a less ambitious comedy, which does not possess the disturbing edge of his previous work—it's "Something Mild," one might say. But though it's not as challenging as SOMETHING WILD, MARRIED TO THE MOB has the idiosyncratic Demme touch and there is plenty here to amuse and delight, including fine performances from Michelle Pfeiffer, Matthew Modine, and Dean Stockwell. A gangster film with a twist, the movie begins on Long Island, the suburban hotbed of the modern-day Mafia, where the homes are full of gilded Mediterranean furniture, the men dress in pin-striped suits, and the women don garish outfits complemented by junk jewelry while spending most of their time getting their hair teased at the local beauty salon. Pfeiffer is the dissatisfied wife of up-and-coming hit man Baldwin. She is tired of the criminal mentality that passes as normal among their friends and family and moans that everything that they own, eat, and wear somehow "fell off a truck." She tearfully tells Baldwin that she wants a divorce, but the notion strikes the gangster as so ludicrous he merely laughs it off. That night, Baldwin makes a bad career move in getting caught by his boss, Mafia don Tony "the Tiger" Russo (Stockwell), in a love nest with the boss' mistress. Stockwell personally "ices" Baldwin and the chippie, unwittingly freeing Pfeiffer from the family. The amorous Stockwell, however, has the hots for Pfeiffer—much to the dismay of his insanely jealous wife, Ruehl. Meanwhile, FBI agent Modine and his partner, Platt, have been running surveillance on Stockwell and his "family." Overeager to establish a motive for Baldwin's killing, Modine—who enjoys donning disguises to ferret out information—assumes that Pfeiffer and Stockwell are lovers and that the Mafia don removed her husband so that they can be together. When Pfeiffer, who is actually desperate to break away from the mob, gives away everything she owns, packs her son (Nici) into the station wagon, and moves into a seedy apartment on Manhattan's lower East Side, the Feds follow. Her attempts to find a job prove futile until East, the kindly Jamaican owner of the "Hello Gorgeous" beauty salon across the street, gives her work. Following her heels at every step, Modine—dressed as a plumber—eventually bumps into Pfeiffer just after placing a bug in her apartment. He lies and says he lives in the building and she asks him for a date. The two become close, and soon Modine learns that Pfeiffer is not Stockwell's lover and is trying to escape him. Worried that Modine's relationship with Pfeiffer will ruin their case, the Feds bring her in and blackmail her into helping to ensnare Stockwell during his meeting with the heads of other Mafia families in Miami. Reluctantly, she returns to Long Island and pretends to be in love with Stockwell. By the time they get to Miami, however, he is suspicious of Pfeiffer, and his wife thinks he's run off with her. In a screwball conclusion that includes the livid Ruehl shooting at her husband and Modine taking on the mob goons single-handedly, Stockwell is captured by an army of FBI agents and carted off to prison. At the fade, Pfeiffer forgives Modine for his duplicity and decides to give their relationship another chance.

One of the most distinctly populist American directors working today, Jonathan Demme continues his obsession with the hodgepodge of ethnicity, class, and crass consumerism that makes the United States such a vibrant, strange, and contradictory nation. Demme delights in all his eccentric characters, from the somber FBI chief to a Mr. Spoons who stands on a New York City street corner. Where some filmmakers would exploit such characters and present them in a condescending manner, Demme has respect and understanding for all the people that populate his movies—even Mr. Chicken Lickin' (Walter), who subjects Pfeiffer to her first bout of on-the-job sexual harassment, is allowed some dignity. And that is what the crux of this film—and most of Demme's work—is about: not being judgmental and giving yourself and others a second chance in life. Demme's America is a wonderful place that allows people to be who they want to be; no one is stuck living an unhappy or mundane existence unless they choose to do so. In many of his films, Demme shows us people who finally take control of their lives and enact their repressed desires by entirely reinventing themselves (like Jeff Daniels in SOMETHING WILD and Michelle Pfeiffer in MARRIED TO THE MOB). Change is not easy in Demme's films; his protagonists must pass through the crucible before attaining true freedom, but in the end they are reborn better people. His movies are so vibrant, so full of humor, music, and dancing, that his themes of personal liberation and freedom virtually leap off the screen. But, although a hopeless romantic, this director is not blind to the darker side of the American Dream. In his best work (MELVIN AND HOWARD; SOMETHING WILD) the joy is tempered by a sometimes violent force that jealously reacts to the liberation of others. Those who would impose strict order are seen to be afraid of change. Demme does not condemn these forces, but instead presents them with understanding and compassion. Unfortunately, this sort of richness is mostly missing from MARRIED TO THE MOB. The Mafia does represent a perverse element of American society, but the gang is played strictly for laughs and they never seem as frightening, dangerous, or truly threatening as Ray Liotta's character was in SOMETHING WILD. Also, the screenplay by Barry Strugatz and Mark R. Burns is a haphazard affair that drops some characters (Pfeiffer's son virtually disappears from the movie), never bothers to introduce others, and sets up a climactic conclusion that just doesn't work. What MARRIED TO THE MOB does have to offer, however, is a whole lot of silly fun. The wonderfully tacky production design by Kristi Zea, the bizarre costumes by Colleen Atwood, the clash of musical styles from David Byrne, and the eccentric performances of the entire cast combine to create a dizzying array of forces swirling around Pfeiffer—who plays her part fairly straight, thus making everyone else seem that much more bizarre. Unfettered by "seriousness," Demme lets his fondness for American *populuxe* run rampant and the result is an incredibly kitschy visual feast that yields a hearty giggle in every frame. MARRIED TO THE MOB may not be top-flight Jonathan Demme, but it is certainly more interesting than just about anything else released by the majors this year. Songs include "Mambo Italiano" (Robert Merrill, performed by Rosemary Clooney), "Bizarre Love Triangle" (New Order, performed by New Order), "Queen of Voudou" (William Berg, Stuart Arbright, Steve Breck, performed by The Voodooist Corporation), "Ghost In A Bikini" (David Bean, performed by The Judy's), "The Same Melody", "Burger World Town", "Tony The Tiger", "Uncle Ron's Country Cars" (Gary Goetzman), "Jump In The River" (Sinead O'Connor, Marco Pirroni, performed by O'Connor), "Suspicion of Love" (Chris Isaak, performed by Isaak), "She's Got Everything" (Bean, performed by Bean, Dickie Malone), "Welcome To The Real World" (Jane Child, performed by Child), "Happy Birthday To You" (Mildred J. Hill, Patty S. Hill), "Traveling Stranger" (A. Gourdine, E. Wright, performed by True Image), "Work It" (Willie Lemon, Shelly Lemon, Reggie Stewart, Geraldine Berry, performed by Lemon Lime), "Isla De Encanta" (Black Francis, performed by The Pixies), "Gummy Duppy" (Nina Ramsey, performed by Ramsey), "Time Bums" (Ziggy Marley, performed by Marley and The Melody Makers), "Devil Does Your Dog Bite?" (Chris Frantz, performed by Tom Tom Club), "Too Far Gone" (Glenn Mercer, Bill Million, performed by The Feelies), "Zazueira" (Jorge Ben, performed by Pe De Boi), "Goodbye Horses" (William Garvey, performed by Q. Lazzarus), "You Don't

Miss Your Water" (William Bell, performed by Brian Eno), "Liar, Liar" (James Donna, performed by Debbie Harry), "Chemin Victoire" (Jean Jacques, Clark Parent, performed by Les Freres Parent), "Veye-Yo" (Jacques, Parent, performed by Les Freres Parent), "Kramtorn Avenges The Puttbundles" (Lawrence Grennan, performed by Wazmo). (Violence, sexual situations, nudity, profanity.)

p, Kenneth Utt, Edward Saxon; d, Jonathan Demme; w, Barry Strugatz, Mark R. Burns; ph, Tak Fujimoto (Duart Color); ed, Craig McKay; m, David Byrne; m/l, Robert Merrill, New Order, William Berg, Stuart Arbright, Steve Breck, David Bean, Gary Goetzman, Sinead O'Connor, Marco Pirroni, Chris Isaak, Jane Child, Mildred J. Hill, Patty S. Hill, A. Gourdine, E. Wright, Willie Lemon, Shelly Lemon, Reggie Stewart, Geraldine Berry, Black Francis, Nina Ramsey, Ziggy Marley, Chris Frantz, Glenn Mercer, Bill Million, Jorge Ben, William Garvey, William Bell, James Donna, Jean Jacques, Clark Parent, Lawrence Grennan; prod d, Kristi Zea; art d, Maher Ahmad; set d, Nina Ramsey; spec eff, Efex Specialists, Inc.; cos, Colleen Atwood; stunts, Frank Ferrara, John Robotham; makeup, Bernadette Mazur.

Comedy/Crime	Cas.	(PR:O MPAA:R)
MASQUERADE*½		(1988) 91m MGM/MGM-UA c

Rob Lowe (Tim Whalan), Meg Tilly (Olivia Lawrence), Kim Cattrall (Brooke Morrison), Doug Savant (Mike McGill), John Glover (Tony Gateworth), Dana Delany (Anne Briscoe), Erik Holland (Chief of Police), Brian Davies (Granger Morrison), Barton Heyman (Tommy McGill), Bernie McInerney (Harland Fitzgerald), Bill Lopatto (Weyburn), Pirie MacDonald (Cantrell), Maeve McGuire (Aunt Eleanor), Ira Wheeler (Uncle Charles), Timothy Landfield (Sam), Cristen Kauffman (Holly), Karen McLaughlin (Jillian), Nada Rowand (Mrs. Chase), Carl Tye Evans, Maryann Urbano (Cousins), Edwin Bordo (Mortician), Bruce Tuthill (Lt. Wacker), James Caulfield, John Henry Cox (Cops), Paddy Croft (Bridget), Henry Ravelo (Alberto), Peter Carew (Tailor), Lois Diane Hicks (Judge), Dorothy Lancaster (Nun), Marilyn Raphael (Maid), Mary McTigue (Morrison Maid), Dick Wolf (Sedgewick), Evan O'Neill (Debutante), James Raitt (Store Manager), Robert D. Wilson, Sr. (Dock Man), Michael Tadross (Kid on Dock), Benjamin Lee Swaim, Christopher Thomas Swaim (French Boys), Bob Swaim (Man in Diner).

© MGM/UA

The delicate balance that exists between the lawbreaker and the law enforcer often makes it impossible to tell good from bad. If one looks hard enough, the criminal can be seen as virtuous or victimized, the policeman perceived as abusive and insensitive. This idea of the masquerade (the cop as a false symbol of social justice, the crook as a false symbol of moral decay) is seen in all four of the films of Bob Swaim, an American expatriate residing in France. Swaim is best known as the director of the 1982 Cesar-winning LA BALANCE, a hard-edged *policier* in which a prostitute and her low-level mobster boy friend (Nathalie Baye and Philippe Leotard) are portrayed in a sympathetic light, while a Parisian cop (Richard Berry) destroys their life together by pressuring them into becoming informers. Similarly, Swaim's first feature, 1977's LA NUIT DES ST. GERMAINE-DES-PRES, concerns a cop who protects a murderer who happens to be the cop's son. And in 1986's unredeemable HALF MOON STREET, Sigourney Weaver is a high-class whore who also happens to be an expert on world affairs, and whose world is bursting with people who are not what they seem—sheiks who are drug-running murderers, diplomats who are perverts, etc. In his first film shot in America, Swaim rises from the gutter of the criminal underworld and sets MASQUERADE (an all-revealing title that refers simultaneously to a character's yacht, the theme of this film, and the thread that runs through Swaim's previous films) in the fresh ocean air of the Hamptons along the southern fork of Long Island.

The film opens with a yacht race in which Lowe tries unsuccessfully to skipper his boat to victory. He's the new kid at the harbor and has impressed just about everyone he's met, including Cattrall, the whorish "rich bitch" wife of Lowe's millionaire boss. Lowe's purely physical affair with Cattrall is brought to a halt, however, when he meets the shy and mousy Tilly, an orphaned heiress who inherited a $300-million fortune when her parents died. Soon Tilly falls in love with Lowe, despite the objections of her despicable stepfather (Glover), an alcoholic playboy who lives off her inheritance, and local police officer Savant, a childhood friend whom she once girlishly promised to marry. Early on, it is revealed that Lowe is in league with Glover. Their plan is to have Lowe marry Tilly, kill the newlywed bride, and split the inheritance. Lowe, however, is becoming attached to Tilly, and suggests that she is more valuable alive than dead. The psychopathic Glover will hear nothing of this, and threatens to reveal Lowe's unsavory past if he makes waves. Later that evening, as planned, Glover barges into Tilly's bedroom as she and Lowe are making love, drunkenly brandishes a handgun, and stages a brawl with Lowe as Tilly looks on in fright. Improvising, Lowe kills Glover, making it appear accidental. Fearing that the police will try to pin a murder charge on Lowe, Tilly convinces her lover to leave. When she reports to the police that Glover tried to rape her and was killed in self-defense, Savant investigates. While searching through her bedroom, he finds a pair of wine glasses and puts two and two together. Rather than reporting the evidence to his superior, Savant suppresses it and confronts Tilly, who sticks to her original story. In a bizarre and thoroughly unbelievable twist, nice cop Savant is now revealed to be a frothing lunatic—like Glover—who is in on the plan to kill Tilly (he's upset because she reneged on that childhood promise of marriage, and now wants his cut from her millions). Lowe has by now wed Tilly and is about to become the father of her child, but Savant still has the wine glasses that could pin the murder on Lowe. After a couple of aborted attempts by Lowe to shake off Savant, the riled cop rigs the couple's yacht by cutting their propane line so that Tilly will accidentally blow herself to bits. Savant even tosses a rat on board to make it appear that the rodent chewed through the line. Just minutes before Tilly is to arrive, however, Lowe uncovers the plot and races to the harbor. He rushes onto the yacht ahead of Tilly and fixes the severed line. But wait! Lowe gets bit by the squealing rat, jumps back in fright, and bumps into a switch that blows the yacht into a ball of fire. When Savant realizes that Tilly wasn't on board, he goes into a mad frenzy and tries to kill her. Tilly fights back and pushes him from a window, where he and a shower of glass shards fall to a slow-motion death. Later, at Lowe's funeral, Tilly (who has since been informed of Lowe's involvement in the original scheme) learns that Lowe has had himself completely removed from her will—thereby proving that he indeed married her for love and not money.

While emulating the psychological undercurrents of the *film noir* of the 1940s, Bob Swaim has added the contemporary "look" of the 1980s thriller to his film. In its favor, there are no dark corners in which terror lurks, no low-key lighting through venetian blinds or glistening rainy night scenes. MASQUERADE is, in fact, the visual antithesis to *film noir*. It has a beachfront house, yacht racing, seagulls, sunlit bedrooms—none of which feels even remotely threatening. This, it may seem, would make for an interesting twist on the genre. Instead of becoming an update of the *film noir*, however, MASQUERADE is a shockingly dumb thriller crippled by its implausibility. Swaim heaps one outlandish character and situation on top of the next, until the film's back breaks under the weight. Tilly, the heroine around whom this absurd world swirls, is sometimes a sheeplike young woman, at other times exhibits a savvy business sense. Then, just when you think you've got her figured out, she does something stupid for the sake of advancing the story. Even more unbelievable is Savant, the local cop. Originally, he's painted as a clean-cut, All-American type keen on courting Tilly. Instead of being a cop, however, this kid should become an actor, because underneath it all he's a lunatic who has masterminded a plot to kill an heiress, killed a local woman to lay suspicion at Lowe's feet, abused his position as a policeman, and tried to smash Tilly's skull with a wrench. Swaim isn't just trying to make a thriller in MASQUERADE, he's trying to come up with as many ways as possible to make the audience look like fools. "Ha ha," he seems to say, when you realize you've stupidly been duped into thinking Lowe was an okay guy. Ditto when you discover that Savant is a madman. The whole situation becomes so absurd that it *is* laughable; one wonders why Swaim doesn't just give Tilly the hackneyed evil twin and pin the whole silly mess on *her*. , Everything in MASQUERADE is exaggerated and overblown (using a killer rat to set off the climactic explosion is the film's high/low point). Instead of assuming that the audience has at least a modicum of intelligence, Swaim panders to them and tries to slip elephantine absurdities past the viewer's eye. With all its faults, however, MASQUERADE does manage to toss in a couple of moral messages—a woman *can* get pregnant even if she is on the pill (an admonition that supports an identical claim made by Molly Ringwald in this year's FOR KEEPS) and, by wearing a seat belt, a driver *can* live through a high-speed crash into a telephone pole. For what it's worth, the acting in MASQUERADE is fine. Rob Lowe does an admirable job as an unscrupulous sleaze transformed by love. Meg Tilly, who was so good in PSYCHO II and AGNES OF GOD, unfortunately isn't given much to do besides be victimized. The rest of the cast, when not busy with exaggerated characteristics (the ultra-bitchy Cattrall, the ultra-odious Glover), turns in some okay support. Like the characters in Swaim's previous films, MASQUERADE is a film that has tipped the balance, ending up as a laughable product instead of a quality film. *(Nudity, sexual situations, profanity, violence.)*

p, Michael I. Levy; d, Bob Swaim; w, Dick Wolf; ph, David Watkin (Duart color); ed, Scott Conrad; m, John Barry; prod d, John Kasarda; art d, Dan Davis; set d, Steve Jordan; spec eff, Connie Brink; cos, John Boxer; stunts, Peter Hock; makeup, Irv Buchman.

Thriller **Cas.** **(PR:O MPAA:R)**

MASS IS ENDED, THE*½** (1988, It.) 96m Faso/Titanus c

Nanni Moretti *(Don Giulio)*, Margarita Losanno *(Mother)*, Ferrucio De Ceresa *(Father)*, Enrica Maria Modugno *(Valentina)*.

An insightful, moving, and often hilarious comedy-drama directed by and starring Moretti as a young priest struggling to maintain his faith. Having been a radical college student in the 1960s, Moretti has now rejected his long hair and liberal ideals in favor of the church and its simple approach toright and wrong. He has himself transferred to his home parish, only to discover the church empty and the town indifferent. The parish's previous priest has rejected the church in favor of the love of a woman and a family (the woman became pregnant while the man was still the parish priest). Moretti is at first shocked by this, but comes to see the couple as happy and productive until he becomes fed up with the former priest's obnoxious and mindless doting on his family (Moretti is jealous). Meanwhile, Moretti's friends from his radical days begin popping up. One has cloistered himself in his apartment and refuses to talk to anyone because his wife has left him (his phone answering machine message says, "I'm home right now, but I don't want to talk. Don't leave a message."). Another old friend, a bookstore owner, disposes of his store's stock of Marxist literature and turns out to be a closet homosexual who tries to pick up young boys in movie house bathrooms. Yet another of his friends, a jazz pianist, has decided to become a Catholic and enrolls in Moretti's catechism class (the grown man sits among the children and tries to answer all the questions but when he tells Moretti he has decided to become a priest, the impatient Moretti kicks him out of the class). Perhaps the most shocking is the one friend who has not turned his back on his radical ideals and is now standing trial for his acts of terrorism. All this craziness serves to confuse and frustrate Moretti even further and he seeks solace with his beloved family. Unfortunately, his family is in chaos. His father leaves his mother to live with a woman barely into her 20s, and his sister is pregnant by a boy friend who has left her to live in the mountains and watch birds. The sister, Modugno, wants an abortion and the outraged Moretti ventures into the mountains in an attempt to bring the father of the baby back. His attempt fails, as does his effort to bring his parents back together. Tragically, his mother commits suicide, but her death changes nothing. All of this proves too much for Moretti and he has himself transferred to a faraway parish in the mountains where he thinks he can escape.

THE MASS IS ENDED is a wonderful film which examines one man's struggle to escape the difficult realities of everyday life—by becoming a priest. He is shocked when the traditional respect he should be getting from the community is nonexistent, and this attitude manifests itself violently when he is almost drowned in a public fountain by thugs who have stolen his parking space. His growing disillusionment with the order is marked by his increasing unwillingness to listen to the problems of others, his impatience with human quirks and foibles, and, eventually, his total self-absorbtion with his own problems. Moretti is confused and frustrated because the strict moral codes and religious approach to life are no longer valid. He clings to his beliefs because he wants his life to be simple, but as his friends and family prove, there aren't any easy, comforting answers to life's problems. Moretti the director presents all his characters in loving detail. None of the family members, friends, or villagers are cardboard caricatures, they are all shown as living, breathing, real people who each have individual and distinct personalities. He does not condescend to their craziness and instead embraces them as symphetic people trapped in an insane world. The character Moretti is hardest on is the one he plays himself, and his performance, along with the rest of the cast, is superb. While the viewer maintains sympathy for the priest, Moretti shows that his selfish reasons for joining the order can only lead to dissatisfaction and frustration. The priest is the architect of his own unhappiness and at the end flees to the mountains (just like his sister's boy friend) because he can no longer deal with the fact that no one lives up to his expectations. Most of his friends are hiding as well. The bookstore owner hides his sexuality, his divorced friend hides in his apartment, his father tries to hide his aging by living with a younger woman, and the jazz pianist floats from life choice to life choice in search of something he can't define. The only two characters in the film who seem to know exactly what they want, his sister and the terrorist, intimidate and frighten him because of their self-confidence. THE MASS IS ENDED is a loving tribute to the human spirit and proves to the world that mindless slasher-movie king Dario Argento isn't the only person making films in Italy these days. THE MASS IS ENDED won the Special Jury Prize at the Berlin Film Festival in 1986, receiving a limited theatrical release in 1988.

p, Achille Manzotti; d, Nanni Moretti; w, Nanni Moretti, Sandro Petraglia; ph, Franco Di Giacomo; ed, Mirco Garrone; m, Nicola Piovani.

Comedy/Drama **(PR:C MPAA:NR)**

MELO***** (1988, Fr.) 110m MK2-Films A2-CNC/MK2-European Classics c

Sabine Azema *(Romaine Belcroix)*, Pierre Arditi *(Pierre Belcroix)*, Andre Dussollier *(Marcel Blanc)*, Fanny Ardant *(Christiane Levesque)*, Jacques Dacqmine *(Dr. Remy)*, Hubert Gignoux *(Priest)*, Catherine Arditi *(Yvonne)*.

Since appearing on the international film scene in 1959 with his brilliant HIROSHIMA, MON AMOUR, Alain Resnais has become recognized as a great innovator whose experiments with nonlinear structure and the relationship between the past and one's memory of the past have placed him among the ranks of the greatest directors working today. From the bewildering narrative puzzles of LAST YEAR AT MARIENBAD to the intricate narrative complexities of MON ONCLE D'AMERIQUE, Resnais has consistently surprised audiences and critics alike with his predictably unpredictable deconstruction of film form. It is because of his previous accomplishments that MELO is such a shock. MELO is a traditionally constructed linear narrative adapted from a 1929 Parisian melodrama written for the stage by Henry Bernstein, a forgotten and once-popular playwright. Deceptively simple in appearance, MELO is the story of two musicians—Dussollier and Arditi—whose friendship dates back to their days at the conservatory. Dussollier has gone on to international fame as a soloist while Arditi has settled down in a Parisian suburb to lead a simple life with his wife Azema. After a quiet evening of drink and reminiscence, Dussollier is fascinated by Azema and she with him. The following day she visits him at his apartment in Paris and the two begin a passionate affair. Rather than confess the affair to the unsuspecting and good-natured Arditi, Azema plots to gradually poison her husband. When a doctor nearly discovers her plot, Azema jumps to her death in the Seine. Her suicide note for Arditi makes no mention of Dussollier, instead declaring her love for her husband. Three years later, Arditi (now a father and married to Azema's cousin Ardant) calls on Dussollier, whom he has not seen since Azema's funeral, and accuses him of having had an affair with Azema. Rather than lose Arditi's friendship and destroy the image Arditi has created of Azema, Dussollier insists that no secret romance ever existed. The film ends as Dussollier agrees to accompany Arditi in playing Brahms' Sonata for Violin and Piano—a piece of music both men had previously played in duet with Azema. Masterfully directed, MELO contains all of Resnais' usual themes and places them not in a complex structure but in a popular form of entertainment—the melodrama. The result is a pure work of art which can be enjoyed on one level as an entertaining romantic melodrama and on a second, more complex, level as an extension of Resnais' ideas about memory and imagination, reality and fiction. As he did in HIROSHIMA MON AMOUR, Resnais gives us characters who are haunted by their memories—so haunted that their past continues to live on into the present, thereby blurring the line between the two. From the opening scene of MELO the characters become lost in reminiscence. While visiting with Arditi and Azema, Dussollier recounts the story of a love affair that has since ended. In one long, unbroken shot Dussollier describes "Helene" and how she became attracted to another man during one of Dussollier's concerts. He is not, however, merely *telling* Arditi and Azema a story, but *reliving* it. Although the camera shows only a close-up of his face, it is as if the entire scene is played out before our eyes. Like Dussollier, Arditi is given to reminiscing—recalling days when both men were music students at the conservatory. However, Azema, the spontaneous and unpredictable woman of the present, can take no part in their reminiscing. It is this superb and lengthy (lasting some 20 minutes) opening that sets the stage for the rest of MELO. By the end of the film both Dussollier and Arditi are filled with the memory of Azema. Arditi refuses to let his dead wife's memory fade away and asks Dussollier to accompany him as they play Brahms—the piece of music which Arditi and Azema would always play together and the same piece that Dussollier played with Azema. It is during the finale, when Azema's two lovers play Brahms together, that Azema ceases to be a thing of the past. One of the most interesting aspects of MELO is Resnais' paradoxical interplay between theatricality and reality. The film begins with its opening credits printed on the turning pages of a playbill. A stage curtain then dissolves into the patio scene—an obvious set which comes complete with a painted moon and stars. (With the exception of Azema's suicide, the entire film is shot on sets.) Resnais' use of long takes, however, adds a contrasting dimension. Long argued by French film theorist Andre Bazin as a technique of realism, the long take in MELO simultaneously gives a sense of reality and of theatricality. This paradox is achieved through Resnais' ability to combine theatrical techniques with realism. Although the theatricality of the melodrama is evident in every frame, the viewer never forgets he is watching a film. As always in a Resnais film, one can sense that the director is in perfect control of the frame—the camera movement, the production design, the sound, and the actors themselves. In MELO, unlike other Resnais films, the concentration is purely on the actors instead of on film technique. Like his 1984 picture, L'AMOUR A MORT (unreleased in the US), MELO stars Ardant, Arditi, Azema, and Dussollier—all of whom perform beautifully in roles which combine melodramatic and silent film acting techniques with modern mannerisms and emotions. Only rarely is a film this simple *and* this complex. Such filmmakers as Carl Dreyer, Ernst Lubitsch, Jean Renoir, and Charles Chaplin have consistently reached such a level and now, with MELO, so, too, has Resnais. MELO was showered with Cesar nominations, winning two awards—Azema for Best Actress and Arditi for Best Supporting Actor. Other nominations were for Best Picture/Best Director, Best Actor (Dussollier), Best Cinematography, Best Production Design, and Best Costumes. Bernstein's play was filmed previously on five occasions—in 1932, in French, as MELO starring Gaby Morlay and Pierre Blanchar; the same year, in German, as DER TRAUMENDE MUND and starring Elisabeth Bergner; in 1937, in English, as DREAMING LIPS and again starring Bergner; in 1938, in French, as MELO; and then in 1953 as DER TRAUMENDE MUND (released in the US in 1958 as DREAMING LIPS) starring Maria Schell. The first version was to star Charles Boyer in his first talkie. He had appeared in the stage version with Morlay and Blanchar and was a protege of Bernstein, but he was instead lured to Hollywood. The play opened in Paris at the Gymnase on March 11, 1929, and had a successful run of over a year. Bernstein, largely forgotten today, has an ardent admirer in Resnais, who has, as a result of MELO, renewed interest in the playwright. Bernstein, who died in 1953, wrote nearly 30 plays in his career, 14 of which were produced on Broadway. Throughout the 1920s, one could always find a Henry Bernstein play being staged somewhere in Paris; and at one point, 80 performances of his plays were being staged throughout Europe. (In French; English subtitles.)

p, Marin Karmitz; d, Alain Resnais; w, Alain Resnais (based on the play "Melo" by Henry Bernstein); ph, Charlie Van Damme (Agfa-Gevaert Color); ed, Albert Jurgenson; m, Johannes Brahms, Johann Sebastian Bach, Philippe Gerard; prod d, Jacques Saulnier; cos, Catherine Leterrier; makeup, Dominique De Vorges.

Drama/Romance **(PR:A MPAA:NR)**

MEMORIES OF ME** (1988) 105m MGM-Odyssey/MGM-UA c

Billy Crystal *(Dr. Abbie Polin)*, Alan King *(Abe Polin)*, JoBeth Williams *(Lisa McConnell)*, Sean Connery *(Himself)*, Janet Carroll *(Dorothy Davis)*, David Ackroyd *(First Assistant Director)*, Phil Fondacaro, Robert Pastorelli, Mark L. Taylor, Peter Elbling, Larry Cedar, Sheryl Bernstein, Joe Shea, Jay (Flash) Riley, Billy Beck, Margarito Mendoza, Noni White, Zachary Benjamin.

Written by star Billy Crystal and directed by the former "Fonz," Henry Winkler (in his dubious feature debut), MEMORIES OF ME is a hopelessly maudlin father-and-son drama brimming with insipid dialog, cardboard characters, misty sentimentality, and pat resolutions to hackneyed problems. Crystal is a wise-cracking Jewish New York City doctor who suffers a mild heart attack. This brush with death leads Crystal to sit at home with his WASPy girlfriend, Williams, and look at old black-and-white home movies of his childhood. Attributing the physically fit Crystal's heart attack to the inner turmoil he feels regarding his estranged father (or some such nonsense), Williams urges the young doctor to fly to Los Angeles and see the old man. Upon landing at LAX, Crystal is dismayed and embarrassed to find that his dad, King, hasn't changed a bit. Having left the family to become a movie actor, King has spent the last 40 years playing bit parts as a nonspeaking extra. Despite his obvious failure, King comforts himself with the notion that he is looked upon as the "King of the Extras" by his peers. A boisterous, friendly, outgoing man among his friends, King seems incapable of an intimate relationship with his own flesh and blood. Crystal and King's first day together does not go well and ends with the two of them about to have a fist-fight in the middle of a tunnel. Realizing how stupid the whole scene is (as does the audience), Crystal gives up before the first punch is thrown. Since the two men have reached an emotional impasse, it's a lucky thing that Williams shows up in LA unannounced, so that she can serve as the buffer between them. With Williams in place, the film becomes a series of scenes in which Crystal and King bicker with each other, while confiding to Williams how they *really* feel. Of course, things improve between father and son, and it looks like everything is going to be fine when it is suddenly revealed that King has a brain aneurism and could die at any moment (we are given hints of this throughout the film, because Dad occasionally launches into theatrical monologues at inappropriate moments). Determined to make King's final days productive, Crystal decides to finally get his father a speaking part in a movie. Pretending to be an agent, Crystal bluffs his way into a casting call and King's natural charm melts the heart of a tough female casting agent. Given the part of a maitre d with 10 lines, King is elated. But he is more concerned with whether or not he will die on a weekend. "If I die on a weekday, no one will come to my funeral because everybody is working," says King. Crystal dismisses the concern as nonsense, but, wouldn't you know it, the old man croaks on the eve of his talkie debut. As Crystal and Williams stand by the coffin, it looks as if King's prediction has to come pass. But wait! Suddenly hundreds of extras—still in costume—come wandering into the cemetery and gather around King's grave to give the "King of the Extras" an especially sappy sendoff.

Although MEMORIES OF ME was no doubt a sincere and heartfelt effort from all concerned, it is executed in such an inept and cloying manner as to be positively mawkish. The screenplay by Crystal and Eric Roth hits the audience over the head with sledgehammer symbolism and dialog, such as Williams telling Crystal, "You know, you're great in bed, but then don't know how to hold my hand!" and this exchange between King and Crystal: "What do you want from me?" says King. "How about love?" snaps Crystal. Subtlety is obviously not Crystal and Roth's forte. Not only do the characters spout dialog that sounds like it was cribbed from a self-help best seller, but screenwriters Crystal and Roth also infect *both* their main characters with life-threatening maladies. This film, combined with the vastly superior NOTHING IN COMMON (1986), leads one to believe that fathers and sons can't relate to each other unless they're visiting hospitals. Why is Hollywood incapable of telling a heartwarming reconciliation story without putting somebody's life in jeopardy? Reportedly, Crystal wrote the script seven years ago in order to purge the demons created by his relationship with his own father, who died when he was 15. During production, Alan King and Winkler added anecdotes from their personal lives to the script, creating a panoply of patriarchal estrangement unparalleled in Hollywood history. Simply ticking off all the thoughtless things that fathers and sons do to each other does not an insightful movie make. There is no nuance, no resonance, no effort to move beyond the obvious and sappy. Director Winkler does nothing to elevate this melodramatic material. His idea of a cinematic visual style is strictly television sitcom, and he seems to have let the actors modulate their own performances. Crystal, who can be very effective in the right vehicle, is unconvincing as a dramatic actor. He rushes through his lines as if he's uncomfortable speaking them and has two expressions on his face throughout, namely exasperation and pouting. King, luckily, makes the film bearable—mainly because he has all the best lines. His robust characterization, while cliched, shoots some life and humor into this otherwise flaccid film. JoBeth Williams wrestles with yet another vapid second-banana role beneath her talents, relegated to massaging the egos of her co-stars. Her part is so underdeveloped that she serves merely as a clumsy screenwriter's device—materializing and vanishing when it suits the needs of the narrative. We are never given any sense of this woman or why she willingly submits to Crystal's sniveling self-pity. For those who find the average television movie of the week satisfying entertainment, MEMORIES OF ME will suffice. Those looking for a bit more substance, however, will be disappointed. *(Sexual situations, profanity.)*

p, Alan King, Billy Crystal, Michael Hertzberg; d, Henry Winkler; w, Eric Roth, Billy Crystal; ph, Andrew Dintenfass; ed, Peter E. Berger; m, Georges Delerue; prod d, William J. Cassidy.

Comedy/Drama **Cas.** **(PR:C MPAA:PG-13)**

MESSENGER OF DEATH † (1988) 90m Golan-Globus/Cannon c

Charles Bronson *(Garret Smith)*, Trish Van Devere *(Jastra Watson)*, Laurence Luckinbill *(Homer Foxx)*, Daniel Benzali *(Chief Barney Doyle)*, Marilyn Hassett *(Josephine Fabrizio)*, Jeff Corey *(Willis Beecham)*, John Ireland *(Zenas Beecham)*, Penny Peyser *(Trudy Pike)*, Gene Davis *(Junior Assassin)*, John Solari *(Senior Assasin)*, Jon Cedar *(Saul)*, Tom Everett *(Wiley)*, Duncan Gamble *(Lt. Scully)*, Charles Dierkop *(Orville Beecham)*, Don Kennedy *(Cyrus Pike)*.

Bronson—who doesn't even carry a gun in this picture—stars as a reporter for the *Denver Tribune* who takes a story involving the murder of the three wives and six children of an expelled Mormon farmer. It seems the farmer, and now Bronson, are caught in the crossfire of a religious war involving two extremist factions of the Mormon religion. (There has been enough real-life violence in recent years linked to the Mormon church to make this all credible.) Instead of becoming a DEATH WISH-style vigilante, Bronson serves as a peaceful go-between who, nonetheless, gets involved in some car chases, explosions, and fist-fights. Directed by the 74-year-old veteran J. Lee Thompson (helmer of such Bronson films as ST. IVES; 10 TO MIDNIGHT; THE EVIL THAT MEN DO; MURPHY'S LAW; DEATH WISH 4: THE CRACKDOWN; and dozens of other well-crafted entertainments), MESSENGER OF DEATH suffered at the box office from typically poor Cannon distribution.

p, Pancho Kohner; d, J. Lee Thompson; w, Paul Jarrico (based on the novel *The Avenging Angel* by Rex Burns); ph, Gideon Porath (TVC color); ed, Peter Lee Thompson; m, Robert O. Ragland; art d, W. Brooke Wheeler; set d, Susan Carsello-Smith; cos, Shelley Komarov.

Action/Mystery	Cas.	(PR:NR MPAA:R)

MIDNIGHT CROSSING**   (1988) 96m Team Effort-Limelight/Vestron c

Faye Dunaway (*Helen Barton*), Daniel J. Travanti (*Morely Barton*), Kim Cattrall (*Alexa Schubb*), John Laughlin (*Jeffrey Schubb*), Ned Beatty (*Ellis*), Pedro De Pool (*Captain Mendoza*), Doug Weiser (*Miller*), Vincent Fall (*Officer on Launch*), Michael Thompson (*Shore Patrol Officer*), Chick Bernhardt (*Young Morley*), Janet Constable, Mara Goodman (*Coast Guard Women*), Armando Gonzales, Pat Selts (*Paramedics*), Rhonda Johnson (*Waitress in Bar*), Lynn Syvante, Dana Mark, Lori Bivins, Tonda Weeder, Kami Grigsby (*People on Dock*), Debra Schuster (*Waitress*).

This complicated mystery opens with a background scene from 1959, as, under cover of darkness, US Navy personnel unload cases from a small motorboat onto an island 35 miles off Cuba. One sailor removes money from a case and stashes it in a seabag in a deserted building. He kills a naval officer who comes to investigate and then argues with his CO, the only one who knows how to find the hiding place again. The story then shifts to present-day Miami, where Laughlin is married to the unhappy Cattrall and is struggling to make a living by chartering the yacht his father left him. Cattrall's boss (Travanti) charters the boat to celebrate his and Dunaway's 20th wedding anniversary, proposing that Laughlin and Cattrall sail with them to the Bahamas. In a bar one evening, Travanti tells them about the cache of money he hid in 1959 and offers to split it 50-50 with Laughlin, who, as the son of Travanti's CO, now has the coordinates to find the island. The truth, however, is that Travanti and Cattrall plan to run off together after they get the money. On the trip, Dunaway, who is blind as a result of glaucoma, grows close to Laughlin. She warns Laughlin about Travanti and Cattrall and tells him that Travanti murdered Laughlin's father, whom Dunaway loved. Double-crossing the double-crossers, Laughlin moves the money and Travanti can't find it. They fight, and in the confusion Cattrall hits Laughlin with a board, apparently killing him. While Travanti searches for the money on the yacht, another boat shows up with armed men on board, including Beatty, who overheard Travanti's story in the bar. Travanti blows up their boat, after which Laughlin miraculously shows up alive and wounds Travanti. Dunaway unties the boom in an effort to kill Travanti, but it knocks Cattrall overboard and Travanti jumps in after her, followed by Laughlin. Now Dunaway is alone—but no, Travanti is back on board, taunting her to shoot him. Magically, her eyes clear and she does shoot him, smiling in satisfaction. The next day the Coast Guard finds her huddled on the boat, babbling about men with machine guns. They tow the yacht to Miami, where they find Laughlin alive, tied to the stern. He laughs hysterically at Dunaway, hanging onto the seabag. The money isn't there. In the final scene, Laughlin and Dunaway sail off together.

With so much background to fill in and such confusing interrelationships, much of MIDNIGHT CROSSING drags, while several scenes meant to plant clues seem off base. (One steamy sex scene, for instance, shows Laughlin uncharacteristically pulling a knife to cut Cattrall's bikini string, foreshadowing violence. Travanti watches them make love, but the scene suggests voyeurism rather than jealousy.) The cast, unfortunately, doesn't add much interest. Daniel J. Travanti was highly praised as Capt. Furillo on TV's "Hill Street Blues," but he is weak as the villain here; Faye Dunaway begins admirably in her role as a woman trying to cope with blindness, but turns melodramatic toward the end, probably as a result of embarrassment over the script. As for John Laughlin, no wonder his character is hysterical in Miami. Fatally injured, he has not only survived most of the night in the sea, but also the 90-mile tow to shore. Too many scenes in MIDNIGHT CROSSING stretch credence to impossible lengths. Moreover, there is no sense of place here, although the setting could have been an effective and enjoyable part of the film. Instead, in the only use of scenery, Dunaway, still blind, stands alone on the yacht gazing at a gorgeous sunset. Good mysteries make for fun challenges, but this one is too slow and confusing to be worth figuring out. Songs include "Love Thing" (Steve Tyrell, Ashley Hall, Stephanie Tyrell, performed by Garry Glenn), "After Midnight" (Mark Rogers, performed by Hollywood Beyond), "Erika" (Bob Mann, performed by Mann, Phil Krawzak), "Alone" (Peter Brown, Rodney Saulsberg, performed by Saulsberg), "EAO, EAO, AHH" (Ashley Hall, Paul Buckmaster, performed by Hall), "Barbados" (Barry Coffing, Phil Settle, performed by The Coffing-Settle Band), "Lost in You" (Coffing, Larry Sotoodeh, Robert Ginsburg, performed by Coffing). (*Violence, profanity, adult situations, sexual situations.*)

p, Mathew Hayden, Doug Weiser; d, Roger Holzberg; w, Roger Holzberg, Doug Weiser (based on a story by Roger Holzberg); ph, Henry Vargas (Technicolor); ed, Earl Watson; m, Paul Buckmaster, Al Gorgoni; m/l, Steve Tyrell, Ashley Hall, Stephanie Tyrell, Mark Rogers, Bob Mann, Phil Krawzak, Peter Brown, Rodney Saulsberg, Paul Buckmaster, Barry Coffing, Phil Settle, Larry Sotoodeh, Robert Ginsburg; prod d, Jose Duarte; art d, Carter Lee Cullen; spec eff, J.B. Jones; cos, Beverly Safier; stunts, Artie Melesci; makeup, Ken Diaz.

Mystery	Cas.	(PR:O MPAA:R)

MIDNIGHT RUN***½   (1988) 122m City Lights/UNIV c

Robert De Niro (*Jack Walsh*), Charles Grodin (*Jonathan Mardukas*), Yaphet Kotto (*Alonzo Mosely*), John Ashton (*Marvin Dorfler*), Dennis Farina (*Jimmy Serrano*), Joe Pantoliano (*Eddie Moscone*), Richard Foronjy (*Tony Darvo*), Robert Miranda (*Joey*), Jack Kehoe (*Jerry Geisler*), Wendy Phillips (*Gail*), Danielle DuClos (*Denise*), Philip Baker Hall (*Sidney*), Thom McCleister (*Red Wood*), Mary Gillis (*Bus Ticket Clerk*), John Toles-Bey (*Monroe Bouchet*), Thomas J. Hageboeck (*Sgt. Gooch*), Stanley White (*Stanley*), Scott McAfee (*Boy on Plane*), Linda Margules (*Car Rental Clerk*), Lois Smith (*Mrs. Nelson*), Fran Brill (*Dana Mardukas*), Michael D. Gainsborough, John Hammil (*FBI Agents*), Lou Felder (*Airline Pilot*), Cameron Milzer, Sonia M. Roberts (*Stewardesses*), Sam Sanders (*Train Porter*), Frank Pesce (*Carmine*), Paul Joseph McKenna (*Ohio Policeman*), Matt Jennings (*Jason*), Rosemarie Murphy (*Coffee Shop Waitress*), Jack N. Young (*Amarillo Desk Sergeant*), Robert Coleman, William Robbins, Wilfred Netsosie, Sherman L. Robbins, Dale Beard, Jr., Thomas Nez (*Native Americans*), Richard Gonzalez (*Bar Cashier*), Bill Fritz (*Bar Customer*), Pete Jensen (*Flagstaff Police Captain*), Andy Charnoki (*Flagstaff Sheriff*), Tracey Walter (*Diner Counter Man*), Robert Vento, Joe "Tippy" Zeoli, Jim Portese, Armando Muniz (*Serrano Bodyguards*), Dan York, Rowdy Burdick (*Las Vegas FBI Agents*), Varnoy Lee (*Airport Porter*), Bob Maroff (*L.A. Taxi Driver*), Tom Irwin (*FBI Agent Perry*), Jimmy Ray Weeks (*FBI Agent Tuttle*).

©MCA (UNIVERSAL)

Easily the most engaging action film of the year, MIDNIGHT RUN boasts a superb cast that transforms its rather mundane story line into something memorable, funny, and moving. The film opens in Los Angeles as tough, foul-mouthed bounty hunter De Niro is hired by seedy bail bondsman Pantoliano to bring back Mafia accountant Grodin, who has embezzled $15 million from the mob and given the money to charity. Grodin was caught and arraigned, but, fearing he would be killed by the mob in prison, skipped bail. Pantoliano stands to lose $500,000 if Grodin isn't returned in 72 hours, and he agrees to pay De Niro $100,000 upon delivery. De Niro, who is sick and tired of bounty hunting, takes the job with hopes of retiring and opening up a coffee shop. Immediately after leaving Pantoliano, however, De Niro is accosted by FBI agent Kotto and told to lay off lest he ruin the Feds' case against Grodin's former employer, Mafia kingpin Farina. De Niro, of course, ignores the warning and steals Kotto's FBI badge to boot (using it throughout the movie, infuriating Kotto). Tracing Grodin to New York City, De Niro easily captures the fugitive accountant and takes him to the airport. Pantoliano is ecstatic that De Niro has found Grodin so quickly and awaits his return to LA. Unbeknown to the bail bondsman, though, his assistant, Kehoe, is an informant for Farina, and he notifies the mobster of De Niro's impending arrival. Farina, based in Las Vegas, sends his goons to LAX to kill Grodin before he can be turned over to the Feds. Before the plane takes off in New York, however, the persnickety Grodin throws a fit, claiming he is claustrophobic and can't fly. The pilot kicks them off the plane, and the exasperated De Niro is forced to book passage on a train. This turn of events frustrates the FBI, Pantoliano, and the Mafia. Kotto and his men give chase; Farina sends moronic hit men Foronjy and Miranda to kill Grodin and De Niro; and Pantoliano, fearing a double-cross, hires Ashton, another bounty hunter and De Niro's professional nemesis, to bring in Grodin. In the extended cross-country chase that ensues, De Niro, flat broke, drags Grodin on board nearly every modern mode of transportation in an effort to avoid their pursuers and get back to LA on time so he can collect his money. During their adventure the dour bounty hunter and nerdy accountant get to know each other. Prompted by Grodin's constant insistence that he get in touch with his feelings, the taciturn De Niro slowly reveals his past. Once an honest Chicago cop, he was entrapped by mobster Farina and given the choice of going on the Mafia payroll, quitting the force, or going to jail on a framed heroin rap. Fed up with the corruption he found in the police department, De Niro quit and became a bounty hunter so that he could catch criminals and not have to depend on anyone else to be honest. De Niro sees himself as a lonely crusader for law, order, and justice. Grodin also views himself as an idealist. Thinking that he had joined a legitimate firm, the accountant was horrified to discover that he was working for the mob, and, to get revenge, he embezzled as much as he could and gave most of the proceeds to charity. In fact, if De Niro lets him go, Grodin can lead the ex-cop to information that will destroy Farina's entire empire. As the plot takes a series of complicated twists and turns, the two men begin to actually like and respect each other, and in the end De Niro helps the FBI nail Farina and then lets Grodin go. Moved by De Niro's sacrifice (no Grodin, no money), the accountant reaches under his shirt and removes the money belt containing $300,000 he has secretly carried throughout the entire adventure and gives it to De Niro. Suddenly wealthy beyond his wildest dreams, De Niro still must walk home because he can't get change for a $1,000 bill.

Back in the golden age of Hollywood, when there was a steady supply of strong directors and good actors who understood that it wasn't the plot so much as the characters that made people flock to the theater, movies like MIDNIGHT RUN were fairly common. Directors like Howard Hawks would take familiar story lines and turn them into pure gold by casting solid, reliable performers in all the roles, from the hero to the smallest bit player, and then allowing them to explore the depths of their characters before an unobtrusive camera. Those movies were brimming with action, laughs, drama, pathos, intelligence, and insight—they were also marvelously entertaining. Modern Hollywood, however, has fed the public a steady stream of stoic, muscular, automaton heroes whose only function is to kill faceless villains in a fancy display of state-of-the-art pyrotechnics. Formula and "high concept" have overpowered character development and poignancy to such an extent that in RAMBO one man simply slaughters hundreds of extras without saying a word.

MIDNIGHT RUN, thankfully, is a welcome return to proper form. BEVERLY HILLS COP director Martin Brest takes a tired "odd couple" concept and transforms it into something much greater by allowing his amazing cast to create vivid human beings on-screen, not mindless killing machines. Although the story has been told a hundred times before, the delight of MIDNIGHT RUN is watching two superior actors, De Niro and Grodin, put a new spin on overly familiar situations. Director Brest has allowed the actors to improvise, and the result is an interaction between them that is more realistic, funny, and surprising than any buddy film released in the last several years. What further separates MIDNIGHT RUN from the current action-film pack is that these characters, especially De Niro, have weight and convey a sense of having lived full lives that have brought them to this place at this time. De Niro, physically and mentally, carries his character's past into this film and it is there, on his haggard face, for the audience to see. Compare this to DIE HARD, where in empty soliloquies whispered over walkie-talkies pass for characterization and backstory (relating sitcom problems that must be resolved before the end credits roll). The characters in MIDNIGHT RUN feel real—not only as if they existed before we met them, but also as if they will continue on after the movie ends. There is emotional human drama in MIDNIGHT RUN. More is at stake than getting the accountant to the bail bondsman on time. De Niro's humanity hangs in the balance and his relationship with Grodin helps him to regain it—a rare enough occurrence in a straight dramatic film, now almost unheard of in an action picture.

However, for everything that Brest does right in MIDNIGHT RUN, he also capitulates to the current cartoonish genre expectations. The "action" scenes here are decidedly excessive (100 police cars when 10 would do, exploding helicopters, thousands of bullets, endless panes of glass shattering, etc.), not particularly well-directed, and tend to bog down the narrative, making the film longer than it need be. This, luckily, is a minor annoyance that just makes the audience that much more eager for the next dialog scene between DeNiro and Grodin, which is where the magic in MIDNIGHT RUN really happens. (Violence, excessive profanity.)

p, Martin Brest; d, Martin Brest; w, George Gallo; ph, Donald Thorin (Astro Color, Metrocolor); ed, Billy Weber, Chris Lebenzon, Michael Tronick; m, Danny Elfman; prod d, Angelo Graham; art d, James J. Murakami; set d, Peter J. Kelly; spec eff, Roy Arbogast; cos, Gloria Gresham; stunts, Glenn H. Randall, Jr.; makeup, Dan Striepeke, Frank Griffin.

Comedy/Crime   Cas.   (PR:O MPAA:R)

MILAGRO BEANFIELD WAR, THE**½   (1988) 118m UNIV c

Ruben Blades (*Sheriff Bernabe Montoya*), Richard Bradford (*Ladd Devine*), Sonia Braga (*Ruby Archuleta*), Julie Carmen (*Nancy Mondragon*), James Gammon (*Horsethief Shorty*), Melanie Griffith (*Flossie Devine*), John Heard (*Charlie Bloom*), Carlos Riquelme (*Amarante Cordova*), Daniel Stern (*Herbie Platt*), Chick Vennera (*Joe Mondragon*), Christopher Walken (*Kyril Montana*), Freddy Fender (*Mayor Sammy Cantu*), Tony Genaro (*Nick Rael*), Jerry Hardin (*Emerson Capps*), Ronald G. Joseph (*Jerry G*), Mario Arrambide (*Carl*), Roberto Carricart (*Coyote Angel*), Alberto Morin, Frederico Roberto, Natividad Vacio, Pablo Trujillo, Eloy Vigil (*The Senile Brigade*), Consuelo Luz, Olga Merediz, Eva Cantu, Donald Salazar, Alfredo Romero, Cipriano Vigil, Trinidad Silva, Mike Gomez, Leandro Cordova, Astrea Romero, Reynaldo Cantu, Arnold Burns, Rudy Fernandez, Frederick Lopez, Marcos L. Martinez, Eddie G. Baros, Douglas Yanez, Bonnie Apodaca, Adelita Sandoval, Roberto Mondragon, Victoria Plata, Cletus Tafoya, Waldo Cantu, Ishmael A. Avila, Jimmy Martinez, Ruby Marchant, Marco A. Oviedo (*Townspeople of Milagro*), Eric Treisman, Juanita Nichols, Patricio Chavez, Nat Shipman, Margo Cutler, China Bell (*Devine's Friends*), Basil Hoffman, Gene Ornales, Sam Vlahos, Phil Mead, Ron Frazier, Lynda Witz (*Governor's Office Staff*), M. Emmet Walsh (*The Governor*).

Eight years after winning an Oscar for his first film behind the camera, ORDINARY PEOPLE, Robert Redford returned to directing with this charming movie based on novelist John Nichols' cult favorite *The Milagro Beanfield War*. As the film opens, Carricart, a "coyote angel," dances through the predawn landscape of Milagro (Spanish for miracle), an impoverished, predominantly Chicano town in northern New Mexico. That day, Vennera, a feisty local handyman, fails to get work on a construction crew involved in a huge recreation development overseen by Bradford, the local Anglo land baron. Returning to the arid land that was once worked by his father but that has remained disused since a decades-old water rights act prohibited the area's subsistence farmers from irrigating their property, Vennera accidentally kicks open a sluice gate and sends water rushing down to his field. Almost before Vennera decides

to plant beans on the land as an act of rebellion against the forces of "progress," the rest of the people in the tiny community are aware of what he has done and begin taking sides. Braga, the strong-willed owner of the town's auto repair shop and plumbing service, persuades Heard—a 60s refugee from the East—to help organize the citizens of Milagro against the recreation area, which threatens their way of life. Bradford, meanwhile, looks to governor Walsh for help, and Walken, a tough-as-nails special agent, is assigned to the case. Caught between the warring factions is Blades, the bumbling but fair-minded sheriff, and into the middle of all this local color comes Stern, an NYU graduate student befriended by Riquelme, Vennera's ancient neighbor who spends much of his time chasing down his itinerant pet pig. The action heats up, some surprising alliances are formed, and, before long, events take a violent turn. But by the film's uplifting end, Vennera's beanfield has become a symbol of The People's victory.

The Milagro Beanfield War, the first novel in Nichols' New Mexico trilogy, is a sprawling, funny, often mystical story many have likened to the "magical realism" of Gabriel Garcia Marquez. At 630 pages, with more than 200 characters, the novel presented a tremendous challenge for screen adaptation. Devotees of the book may be somewhat disappointed by the elimination or alteration of some characters and events in the film, but taken on its own merits, THE MILAGRO BEANFIELD WAR is quite delightful. Director Redford has kept much of Nichols' story and structure intact and, more important, he has retained the novel's whimsical, buoyant spirit. The most striking difference between book and film is that in the film Vennera accidentally kicks open the sluice gate, whereas in the novel Joe's opening salvo is voluntary—though impulsive. This change alters the story's tone, making Joe a less revolutionary hero, but while Redford has toned down the class conflict of the story, his film remains pointedly political, focusing on a traditional culture threatened by profit-motivated development.

THE MILAGRO BEANFIELD WAR is hardly a political tract, however; instead of haranguing, it pokes gently at the funny bone and is sympathetic without becoming overly sentimental. A danger in having an Anglo direct a film that is predominantly Chicano in temperament is that the film might be patronizing, but though many of the characters are ah-inspiringly endearing, they seldom become too quaint. In this respect, the film benefits from several outstanding performances. Ruben Blades (CROSSOVER DREAMS) brilliantly essays the sheriff who holds the lid on the war through his judicious inaction. Carlos Riquelme, a 74-year-old veteran Mexican actor appearing in his first US production, is equally affecting as the lovable old Amarante. Chick Vennera, best known for his work on the New York stage, captures Joe's feisty but fearful iconoclasm, subtly interpreting a role that at one time appeared destined to be played by Cheech Marin. Daniel Stern nicely underplays a part that could have been unbearably cloying, and Julie Carmen is convincing as Vennera's caustically supportive wife. Less successful are Sonia Braga (KISS OF THE SPIDER WOMAN), the Brazilian bombshell who sheds her image as a siren to portray the earthy, strident Ruby, and John Heard, who is unable to bring his usual depth to a role that lost much in its screen adaptation. Christopher Walken, badly miscast as the undercover agent, plays the character as a one-dimensional heavy (the role cries out to be played by Redford himself, slightly against type).

The Milagro Beanfield War's journey from printed page to the screen took more than 13 difficult years. While the project was under development for Tomorrow Entertainment, Paramount, and then Lorimar, screenplays were written by Tracy Keenan Wynn and Leonard Gardner (FAT CITY). In 1979 Moctesuma Esparza—activist, documentary maker, and producer of THE BALLAD OF GREGORIO CORTEZ—secured the rights to the novel, determined to make a small production for PBS consumption. Eventually, however, he agreed to coproduce with Redford. Nichols undertook several rewrites of the script and was then asked to collaborate with Frank Pierce (DOG DAY AFTERNOON), the Writers Guild president who had denied Nichols credit for his rewrite of the Oscar-winning screenplay for MISSING. Eventually David Ward (THE STING) arrived at a structure with which the story could finally be filmed.

With Redford's name behind the project, it was picked up by Universal and budgeted at $8-10 million. Shooting was to have begun in June 1986 in Chimayo, New Mexico, but in a development that paralleled the story itself, a small group of townspeople adamantly opposed having the film shot there out of concern that an 18th plaza would be despoiled. The production then moved to Truchas; however, it was August when shooting began, and Truchas, located at a high elevation, became the victim of the earliest winter in the region's history. When November brought snow, everything was put on hold, and shooting was unable to resume until the following year. Meanwhile, a lawsuit had been filed by the producers of "King Tiger," a film project based on the life of land-grant activist Reies Tijerina that had been in development at Columbia and then dropped, apparently because of its similarity to THE MILAGRO BEANFIELD WAR. The suit alleged that MILAGRO's screenplay was based on Tijerina's life, but approximately a month after the suit was filed, Tijerina dropped his name from the suit and little has been heard of it since. In August 1987, Redford and company returned to northern New Mexico for a week, and shooting was completed.

The location, legal, and weather problems, combined with Redford's meticulousness and chronic tardiness, pushed the production schedule back months and ballooned the budget to $18-22 million. For Robbie Greenberg's cinematography alone, the wait was nearly worth it. It's hard to go wrong when the American West is used as a canvas, and Greenberg has captured northern New Mexico in all its sky blue and purple mountain splendor. As with the production, there are problems with the finished product, but in the final analysis this is a film that it is difficult not to be entertained by, or to leave without having been touched.

p, Robert Redford, Moctesuma Esparza; d, Robert Redford; w, David Ward, John Nichols (based on the novel by John Nichols); ph, Robbie Greenberg (MGM color); ed, Dede Allen, Jim Miller; m, Dave Grusin; art d, Joe Aubel; set d, Thomas L. Roysden; spec eff, Tom Ward; cos, Bernie Pollack; makeup, Gary Liddiard, Tom Hoerber.

Comedy/Drama   **Cas.**   **(PR:C MPAA:R)**

MILES FROM HOME*   (1988) 112m J&M Entertainment/Cinecom c

Brian Dennehy (*Frank Roberts Sr.*), Jason Campbell (*Young Frank*), Austin Bamgarner (*Young Terry*), Larry Poling (*Nikita Khrushchev*), Richard Gere (*Frank Roberts, Jr.*), Kevin Anderson (*Terry Roberts*), Terry Kinney (*Mark*), Laurie Metcalf (*Ellen*), Penelope Ann Miller (*Sally*), Helen Hunt (*Jennifer*), Moira Harris (*Frank's Girl*), John Malkovich (*Barry Maxwell*), Francis Guinan (*Mr. Root*), Judith Ivey (*Frances*), Laura San Giacoma (*Sandy*), Randy Arney (*Farmer*), Jo Anderson (*Farmer's Wife*), Daniel Roebuck (*Young Trooper*).

This debut feature from Gary Sinise, co-founder of Chicago's Steppenwolf Theatre company, addresses the plight of America's farmers but is really concerned with the relationship between two brothers. The film begins with a nostalgic, black-and-white silent sequence, as Soviet leader Nikita Khrushchev (Poling) visits America's "Farm of the Year," owned by Dennehy. As the Soviet entourage approaches Dennehy's front porch, the proud farmer stands with his two young sons. Flash bulbs burst as photographers seize photo opportunities with the Soviet and Dennehy. Years later, the farm has changed—the price of a combine has increased from $6,500, to over $100,000, while the price of corn has increased only 20 cents. Dennehy's sons (Gere and Anderson) have done their best with the farm but cannot continue the legacy of their late father. Trying to fend off creditors, Gere, Anderson, and farm worker Kinney organize a sale of their belongings. One potential buyer is Miller, who is entertaining her visiting city cousin (Hunt), and Anderson and Miller are instantly attracted to each other. Rather than surrender the farm to a childhood friend who is now a banker, Gere decides to burn it to a cinder. Anderson, the younger and more idealistic brother, goes along with Gere, out of devotion rather than shared purpose. After setting the farm ablaze—house, barn, silo, and crops—they escape in their battered pickup truck, only to learn that the police have organized a manhunt for them, charging the brothers with the destruction of government property. Unwittingly, Gere and Anderson become outlaw heroes. After meeting a friendly stripper (Metcalf) in a rundown bar, they are introduced to a reporter (Malkovich) who pays them a handsome sum for their story and even hires a photographer to take some slick, high-fashion pictures of the outlaw pair. Their heroic status is elevated to media stardom when they appear on the cover of *Rolling Stone*. This folk heroism soon goes to Gere's head, as he realizes that people love him just as they loved his father. The gross irony is that Gere, like his father, owned the "Farm of the Year" (this was also the film's initial title)—but while Dennehy's farm was celebrated for its success, under Gere's charge it is celebrated for its failure. Gere and Anderson's position on the "Most Wanted" list grows more prominent as Gere steps up his crimes, assaulting a police officer, stealing cars, and attempting to rob a bank. Meanwhile, Anderson has become more attracted to Miller and the domestic stability she represents. With Gere drawn toward rebellion and Anderson pulled the opposite way, the strain on the brothers' relationship grows to a breaking point. By the finale, Gere is heading for a friend's farm in Canada to find work, while Anderson stands at Miller's side and turns himself in to the police.

Far from your typical "farm" film, MILES FROM HOME is not about saving the farm—not about the struggles of farming, making ends meet, or pulling together to overcome the threat of foreclosure. (Just a short while into MILES FROM HOME, the brothers have already *lost* their farm.) The film is far more concerned with surviving tragedy than with preventing it. Even the folk hero status of Gere and Anderson is downplayed, left in the background for other characters to react to. Gere and Anderson do not create their heroic image, the media do. The brothers are merely affected by it. The film, then, is not PLACES IN THE HEART or COUNTRY, nor is it BONNIE AND CLYDE or BADLANDS; it places its emphasis on the relationship between the brothers and their individual reactions to a tragedy that affects both of them. Richard Gere, as the older brother forced to assume responsibility for the farm's failure, turns in a superb performance—masterfully essaying an insecure, sensitive man who has no choice but to act tough and dangerous. For years, Gere's character has been forced to prove himself to his fellow farmers and to the legacy of his father. Now that the farm's "days of heaven" are gone, he must continue to prove himself to those who view him as a folk hero. He is not a hero, but he must act like one. Equaling Gere's performance is that of Kevin Anderson, a former Steppenwolf ensemble actor, in his fourth film (though only his second major release). Having pre-

viously stunned audiences in the barely seen ORPHANS, Anderson again proves himself with his soft-spoken yet powerful delivery. His scenes with Penelope Ann Miller (also seen this year in BIG TOP PEE-WEE and BILOXI BLUES) are some of the best in the film, providing a quiet, romantic break from the tension of the sibling relationship. Acting is the definite strong point of MILES FROM HOME, and director Gary Sinise has surrounded himself with familiar Steppenwolf actors—John Malkovich, Terry Kinney, Laurie Metcalf, Randy Arney, Francis Guinan and Moira Harris (Sinise's real-life wife). Of the non-Steppenwolfers (of which there aren't many), Helen Hunt, as usual, delivers a shining, fresh performance. While Sinise may not yet be a great American director, MILES FROM HOME shows that the man who brought so much recognition to a small Chicago theater company may someday attract as much attention to himself as a filmmaker. (*Violence, profanity, substance abuse.*)

p, Frederick Zollo, Paul Kurta; d, Gary Sinise; w, Chris Gerolmo; ph, Elliot Davis; ed, Jane Schwartz Jaffe; m, Robert Folk; prod d, David Gropman; art d, Nicholas Romanac; set d, Karen Schulz; cos, Shay Cunliffe.

Drama   **Cas.**   **(PR:C MPAA:R)**

MISFIT BRIGADE, THE*   (1988) 101m Panorama-Manley/Trans World c

Bruce Davison (*Porta*), David Patrick Kelly (*The Legionnaire*), Don W. Moffett (*Capt. von Barring*), Jay O. Sanders (*Tiny*), Keith Szarabajka ("*Old Man*"), Oliver Reed (*The General*), David Carradine (*Col. Von Weisshagen*), Slavko Stimac (*Sven*), Andrija Maricic (*Stege*), Boris Komnenic (*Bauer*), Bane Vidakovic (*Muller*), Irena Prosen (*The Madam*), Svetlana, Gordana Les, Lidija Pletl, Annie Korzen.

In 1943 Germany, the Nazis were so desperate for able-bodied fighting men that they began raiding prisons for recruits, and THE MISFIT BRIGADE episodically recounts the exploits of a brigade made up of prison inmates attached to a Panzer division. Jailbirds though they may be, their crimes aren't exactly heinous, ranging from bigamy to desertion to preaching Marxism. None is much enamored with Nazism, but they find being warriors preferable to being prisoners. Under the leadership of Kelly, they booze, brawl, cheat at cards, and generally raise hell until a colonel (Carradine) has the brigade sent to the Russian front. The misfits may not be Hitler devotees, but they prove their mettle in battle and are chosen by Carradine for the dangerous job of blowing up a train in the Russian village of Dankau. To Davison's objection that this is really a suicide mission, Carradine replies that, if the men are successful, they will be permanently transferred from the Russian front and given long leaves. With that incentive, the brigade takes off for Dankau, raiding a Russian munitions warehouse along the way to capture explosives and change into Russian uniforms. Before they reach Dankau, however, they come across an idyllic setting in which a half-dozen Russian and German soldiers are sitting out the war with their girl friends. The brigade members skinny dip, drink, and play cards with their new friends and are tempted to remain with them, but Kelly believes that if he doesn't try to accomplish the mission his wife and child will be killed, and the others join him when he presses on. They are able to make it to Dankau and succeed in blowing up the targeted train. Upon returning to Germany, the brigade is to be decorated for its bravery and Carradine is to be honored for hatching the plan. A general (Reed) arrives to present the honors, but when Carradine tells the men they are going to be sent back to the Russian front despite his earlier promise, the men break ranks and make clear their disgust. This infuriates Reed, who screams that they will be sent to the front for the rest of their lives. His tirade is interrupted as Allied fighters strafe the base, and he and Carradine head for a plane that will take them to safety. But their pilot is nowhere to be found, and the two men find themselves surrounded by members of the misfit brigade, who raise their weapons and are poised to execute the officers at the fadeout.

This film's greatest asset is its cast. David Patrick Kelly, Bruce Davison, the huge Jay O. Sanders, and the other members of the brigade are all properly cynical and world-weary, while David Carradine does a terrific job as the arrogant colonel. The film also has its amusing moments, one of the best occurring when the brigade is in a bunker on the night after a major battle. They hear music and, knowing what's coming next, rush outside. A movie screen rises across the battlefield and a voluptuous Russian woman appears on it, encouraging the Germans to surrender so that they can be sent to Russian prisons, which are really "luxury resorts where you can enjoy suckling pig, red cabbage, and caviar, and wash it all down with champagne." For the most part, however, the script is decidedly weak, especially when it departs from the humorous for the dramatic. Though the brigade's assignment to blow up the train is supposed to be a suicide mission, there is no sense of tension or danger and it's all accomplished pretty easily. Director Gordon Hessler previously specialized in martial arts pictures (PRAY FOR DEATH; RAGE OF HONOR). (*Profanity, violence, brief nudity, sexual situations.*)

p, Just Betzer, Benni Korzen; d, Gordon Hessler; w, Nelson Gidding (based on the novel *Wheels of Terror* by Sven Hassel); ph, George Nikolic (Eastmancolor); ed, Bob Gordon; m, Ole Hoyer; prod d, Vladislav Lasic.

War   **Cas.**   **(PR:O MPAA:R)**

MISSISSIPPI BURNING*   (1988) 128m Frederick Zollo/Orion c

Gene Hackman (*Rupert Anderson*), Willem Dafoe (*Alan Ward*), Frances McDormand (*Mrs. Pell*), Brad Dourif (*Deputy Pell*), R. Lee Ermey (*Mayor Tilman*), Gailard Sartain (*Sheriff Stuckey*), Stephen Tobolowsky (*Townley*), Michael Rooker (*Frank Bailey*), Pruitt Taylor Vince (*Lester Cowens*), Badja Djola (*Agent Monk*), Kevin Dunn (*Agent Bird*), Frankie Faison (*Eulogist*), Tom Mason (*Judge*), Geoffrey Nauffts (*Goatee*), Rick Zieff (*Passenger*), Gladys Greer (*Hattie*), Jake Gipson

©ORION

(Mose), Dianne Lancaster *(Waitress)*, Stanley W. Collins *(Hollis)*, Daniel Winford *(Fennis)*, Marc Clement *(Floyd Swilley)*, Larry Shuler *(Earl Cooke)*, Stephen Wesley Bridgewater *(Wesley Cooke)*, Bob Penny *(Curtis Foy)*, James F. Moore *(Barber)*, Park Overall *(Connie)*, Georgia F. Wise, Lois Allen *(Beauty Parlor Women)*, Barry Davis Jim, Sr. *(Choctaw Man)*, John P. Fertitta, Dan Desmond *(TV Commentators)*, Darius McCrary *(Aaron Williams)*, Lou Walker *(Vertis Williams)*, Billie Jean Young *(Mrs. Williams)*, Alisa R. Patrick, Barbara Gibson *(Church Soloists)*, Pat Funderburk *(Pell Maid)*, Dawn Boyd, Dwight Boyd, Linda Fuller, George Isbell, Ethel L. Mayes, James Arnold Mayes *(Interviewees)*, George Mason *(Farmer)*, Charles Franzen *(Interviewer & Reporter)*, Harry Franklin *(SNCC Inteviewer)*, Virginia Bennett, James Lloyd *(SNCC Interviewees)*, Jesse Merle Speaks *(Pecan Vendor)*, Simeon Teague *(Obie Walker)*, Tonea Stewart *(Mrs. Walker)*, Rev. Harry Quick *(Doctor)*, Cullen Gilliland, Zeke Davidson *(Lawyers)*, Robert F. Colesberry *(Cameraman)*, Frederick Zollo *(Reporter)*, Judy Sasser *(Neighbor Woman)*, Ralnardo Davis *(Willie)*, Mark Jeffrey Miller, Ed Geldart, Mert Hatfield, James Eric *(Fire Bombers)*, Paul Savelis *(Trooper)*, Ron De Roxtra, Doug Jackson, Gary Moody, Robert Erickson, John Brook *(Reporters)*, Tobin Bell *(Agent Stokes)*, Daniel Chapman *(Agent Macmillan)*, Rick Washburn *(Agent Brodsky)*, Bob Glaudini *(Agent Nash)*, Kenneth Magee *(Agent Reilly)*, E.A. Thrall *(Agent Tubbs)*, Bernice Poindexter *(Grieving Mother)*, Brenda Dunlap *(Mrs. Cowens)*, Lannie Spann McBride *(Gospel Singer)*.

During the last eight years there has been an alarming increase in racial tension, resentment, and violence in the United States. The Howard Beach incident, the Tawana Brawley case, and the reaction of some whites to the Jesse Jackson campaign have reopened the old wounds of American racism. This development, combined with the general apathy toward, attacks on, and outright subversion of key civil rights statutes by the Reagan administration, has brought about a renewed tolerance and tacit approval of bigotry, to the extent that a presidential candidate could openly provoke the racist instincts of frightened whites to get votes while the mainstream media turned a blind eye (the Bush's campaign's use of the Willie Horton issue). Given this alarming trend, a major motion picture designed to remind viewers of the horrors perpetrated against people of color just 25 years ago should have been one of the most important films of the year. Instead, Briton Alan Parker (ANGEL HEART) has presented the wholly superficial MISSISSIPPI BURNING.

Using the shocking murders of three civil rights workers (James Chaney, a Mississippi black, and Andrew Goodman and Michael Schwerner, two Jews from New York) by the Ku Klux Klan in Mississippi on June 21, 1964, as its inspiration, MISSISSIPPI BURNING presents a fictionalized version of the events and turns it into another cop-buddy movie. DaFoe and Hackman are two very different FBI agents sent to Mississippi to investigate the disappearance of the young men (their car was sunk in a swamp and their bodies buried in an earthen dam). DaFoe is the man in charge, one of Bobby Kennedy's young hotshots from the Justice Department, a by-the-book type who is morally outraged by the racism he finds in the South and is determined to do something about it. The older Hackman, a former sheriff of a small southern town, does not see the assignment as a crusade, but is determined to do his job to the best of his ability, using his understanding of the region and its people to crack the case. This means taking off his tell-tale dark jacket and wandering the streets like a good ol' boy, chatting with the townsfolk to ferret out clues. DaFoe, on the other hand, invades the small town with hundreds of FBI agents and attempts to bully the locals, both black and white, into talking. This only incites more violence against blacks and the situation begins to spin out of control. While DaFoe uses approved high-tech (for the time) FBI methods, Hackman meets McDormand, a sympathetic member of the community who is willing to talk. Apparently the only liberal in all of Mississippi, she is disgusted by recent events. Bored and frustrated with her marriage to weasel-like deputy Dourif ("Down here girls marry the first boy in high school who makes them laugh"), McDormand is vulnerable to the charming Hackman's questions and she eventually reveals that her husband is a member of the Klan and tells the FBI agent where the bodies are buried. Word of McDormand's betrayal spreads through the community like wildfire, and an incensed Dourif gives his wife a severe beating while fellow Klan members look on approvingly. Although the bodies have been found, the FBI still does not have the murderers. As Hackman notes, "Rattlesnakes don't commit suicide," by which he means that the feds will have a tough time identifying the conspirators. When Hackman learns of McDormand's beating, he goes over the edge and demands that DaFoe allow him to finish the investigation his way—that is, by any method necessary. To uncover the conspirators, Hackman imports a mysterious black man who kidnaps the town's mayor (Ermey), then threatens to cut off his testicles with a hot razor blade (a torture used by the Klan on blacks) unless he reveals the identity of the murderers. Although he isn't a Klan member, Ermey knows the information and spills it. Hackman and the feds, using a variety of illegal means—including harassment, intimidation, detainment, and unauthorized wiretaps—pit the conspirators against each other until they finally crack and begin betraying each other. Because a murder charge would be a state matter and local judges would be disinclined to hand out harsh sentences, the feds decide to prosecute the Klan members on civil rights charges, which are under federal jurisdiction. Most of the conspirators get five to ten year sentences. The case over, Hackman goes to visit McDormand, who has finally come home from the hospital. Although her home has been vandalized by the Klan or Klan sympathizers and Hackman suggests she leave town with him, McDormand plans to stay and rebuild her life. Hackman understands and bids her adieu.

As is to be expected from any Alan Parker film, MISSISSIPPI BURNING *looks* great. From the sets, costumes, props, and Mississippi locations to the gorgeous cinematography of Peter Biziou, Parker and his crew created a film that is unquestionably watchable. But despite all the attention to the visual, something essential is missing here, and it can be found in the faces of the local Mississippians cast as extras—genuine human experience. Parker is at his best with surface details, but he fails to dig deeper into the twisted psyche of racism to reveal anything that is moving or significant. Part of the problem is attributable to a recent filmmaking trend, the well-meaning, and mainly British, proclivity for taking on "socially significant" material that attempts to awaken the white bourgeoisie to their indifference to brutal oppression of the "other" (THE MISSION and CRY FREEDOM being other noteworthy examples). Unfortunately, these filmmakers tend to depict the "other" as nebulous mass of childlike innocents with the words "helpless," "long-suffering," "spiritual," and most importantly "victim," practically tattooed on their saintly foreheads. Little or no individuality is given to these characters and, therefore, no insight is attained. (Chris Menges' powerful A WORLD APART, which personalizes the struggles of all its South African characters, black and white, proves that a more nuanced approach is infinitely more effective.) For a political movement that was mainly engineered by blacks for blacks, the notion that a few white knights willing to bend the law could set things straight is demeaning.

Why does Hollywood insist that these types of stories be told from the white perspective? This approach smacks more of a "white man's burden" mentality than anything truly progressive. Moreover, the oppressors are given a one-dimensional treatment as well. With the exception of the McDormand character—who serves mainly as a plot device—every white southerner is portrayed as a slobbering racist animal. In Parker's universe, pure good is pitted against total evil, and there are no shades of gray. The screenplay by Chris Gerolmo (MILES FROM HOME), which was subjected to extensive rewrites by the dictatorial Parker without the writer's approval, contains one clue to what the film could have been in a speech made by Hackman to DaFoe. In it Hackman speaks of his childhood and his father, a poor white farmer who became insanely jealous when a black sharecropper neighbor was able to buy a mule and improve his lot in life. One day the mule turned up poisoned and Hackman knew his father had done it. "Where does that leave you?" asks DaFoe. "With an old man so full of hate he didn't know that being poor was what was killing him," replies Hackman. The point here is that the rich have long used notions of white supremacy to divide economically oppressed blacks and whites. As Parker says in his notes on the production, "The black underclass had always been there as pathetic comforter to the poor whites—there was always someone worse off than they were. The threat of black political equality (and possible economic equality) is obviously not the only explanation for the bigotry, but an important one." If it is so important (and it is), why dismiss it in a three-minute monolog and then cut back to the chase (ending the scene with gunshots exploding the motel room window). It would be more valuable to witness the seeds of racism being planted—to understand why such irrational hate exists—than to merely be told about it in a brief speech that is really just a breather between action scenes. Parker's insistence on pandering to the lowest common denominator by delivering genre thrills is the ruination of what could have been a significant film. In MISSISSIPPI BURNING, the very core of the subject is relegated to the role of filler between the seemingly dozens of burnings, bombings, beatings, shootings, and lynchings that make up most of the running time. The biggest insult to the memory of the Civil Rights movement is that the film seems to *endorse violence* as a catalyst for change instead of depicting what was one of the most successful *non-violent* movements in history. True, in the real-life incident on which the film is based the FBI was rumored to have used illegal means to crack the case, but showing other methods to be ineffectual is dishonest and reactionary.

Since MISSISSIPPI BURNING utterly fails as an artistic statement, what little the viewer does have to cling to—mainly another terrific performance from Gene Hackman—is all the more precious. Volumes have been written on his wonderfully naturalistic acting style, his consummate skill at playing "ordinary" men, so suffice to say that he adds another honorable notch to his belt and is a joy to watch. Also excellent is Frances McDormand, who turns a nothing role into a moving and substantial character in her honest, open, and tender scenes with Hackman. Lee Ermey, the psychopathic drill sergeant from FULL METAL JACKET, proves here he is capable of playing more than one role. Less fortunate is Willem DaFoe, who struggles mightily to portray a human being, despite the endless series of speeches he is forced to give. MISSISSIPPI BURNING was sold as an important film about an important subject, but that film has yet to be made. *(Violence, profanity)*.

p, Frederick Zollo, Robert F. Colesberry; d, Alan Parker; w, Chris Gerolmo; ph, Peter Biziou (Duart color); ed, Gerry Hambling; m, Trevor Jones; m/l, Thomas A. Dorsey, Jimmy Work, Roberta Martin, Emily D. Wilson, Eliza E. Hewitt, James Cleveland; prod d, Geoffrey Kirkland, Philip Harrison; art d, John Willett; set d, Jim Erickson; spec eff, Stan Parks; cos, Aude Bronson Howard; stunts, John Robotham; makeup, David Forrest.

Drama **Cas.** **(PR:O MPAA:R)**

MR. NORTH** (1988) 92m Heritage/Goldwyn c

Anthony Edwards *(Theophilus North)*, Robert Mitchum *(James McHenry Bosworth)*, Lauren Bacall *(Mrs. Amelia Cranston)*, Harry Dean Stanton *(Henry Simmons)*, Anjelica Huston *(Persis Bosworth-Tennyson)*, Mary Stuart Masterson *(Elspeth Skeel)*, Virginia Madsen *(Sally Boffin)*, Tammy Grimes *(Sarah Baily-Lewis)*, David Warner *(Dr. Angus McPherson)*, Hunter Carson *(Galloper Skeel)*, Christopher Durang *(YMCA Clerk)*, Mark Metcalf *(George Harkness Skeel)*, Katharine Houghton *(Mary Skeel)*, Judge Thomas H. Needham *(Judge)*, Richard Woods *(Willie)*, Harriet Rogers *(T. Liselotte)*, Layla Sommers *(Natalie Denby)*, Lucas Hall *(Joseph Denby)*, Thomas-Lawrence Hand *(Luther Denby)*, Linda Peterson *(Mrs. Denby)*, Cleveland Amory *(Mr. Danforth)*, Christopher Lawford *(Michael Patrick Ennis III)*, Albert H. Conti *(Arresting Officer)*, Katherine Wiatt *(Eloise)*, Jason Adams *(Johnny)*, Arthur Bowen *(Claybourne Turhommounde)*, Marieta Tree *(Amanda Venable)*, Richard Kneeland *(Butler Venable)*, Allegra Huston *(Miss Wetmore)*, Barbara Blossom, Mara Clark, Belle McDonald, Bill L. McDonald, John Heeney McKay *(YMCA Visitors)*, William Lynch *(Bartender)*.

An unrelentingly tedious directorial debut from the late John Huston's 26-year-old son, Danny, MR. NORTH strives for the sparkle of old-fashioned Hollywood magic but does not even rise to the level of mundane PBS fare. Based on the semiautobiographical novel *Theophilus North* by Thorton Wilder, the film begins as young Yale graduate Edwards pedals his bicycle into the snobby high-society world of Newport, Rhode Island, circa 1926. With a charming smile, a good education, fluency in several languages, and a mysterious ability to generate excess amounts of static electricity in his body that manifests itself in mild shocks coming from his hands, Edwards soon ingratiates himself with most of the community. His greatest champion is the elderly and wealthy Mitchum, who has hired Edwards to read him the Bible. Housebound for the last eight years due to a weak bladder, Mitchum has spent his time pursuing philosophical knowledge. Unbeknownst to Mitchum, however, his greedy daughter (Grimes) and his quack doctor (Warner) have conspired to make him feel like an invalid in the hope of spurring his early demise. Edwards identifies the problem and cures Mitchum by prescribing placebos (peppermints) and giving him rubber underwear. Liberated, Mitchum goes out for long drives again and plans to spend the rest of his fortune building a college in Newport dedicated to the pursuit of philosophy. At the same time, Edwards has "cured" a shy debutante (Masterson) of her migraine headaches, and encouraged a pretty maid (Madsen) to pursue her abandoned romance with the scion of a wealthy family. Predictably, word of Edwards' healing powers spreads and soon the entire town is coming to him to cure their ills. This causes Warner to have Edwards arrested for practicing medicine without a license and he is put on trial. In the courtroom the townsfolk come to Edwards' defense. Under questioning from the judge, Edwards reveals that his only power is that of optimism and positive thinking—he took the time to befriend those who were suffering and their maladies vanished. The case is dismissed and Edwards becomes the toast of Newport.

Although MR. NORTH tries earnestly to be charming, the end result is nothing but an overqualified bore. The amazing cast assembled by Danny Huston—Edwards, Madsen, Masterson, Stanton, Bacall, Mitchum, Warner, and Angelica Huston, good actors all—is given little more than underdeveloped cameo roles that frustrate rather than enlighten the material. The adaptation by John Huston, Janet Roach, and James Costigan is terribly literate, and the subsequently stilted dialog appears to be nearly unspeakable for the actors, especially Robert Mitchum, miscast in an upper-crust comedy of manners. It is, however, unfair to single out Mitchum, for he did the role as a favor on short notice when John Huston, who was originally cast in the part, fell ill during shooting and was hospitalized (he died several weeks later). Unfortunately, the role seems tailor-made for John Huston. The notion of a once-powerful man turned decrepit for fear of wetting his pants in public is perfect for Huston's craggy face and frail frame, and his eager pursuit of knowledge suits the sly twinkle in Huston's eye and the brimming enthusiasm of the late director's speech. The part is perfect for an old ham, and John Huston, as an actor, was certainly that. Mitchum, however, does not convince. His tired eyes and lazy voice do not convey a hunger for knowledge, and his massive frame and strong appearance makes ludicrous the notion that he would not go outside for fear of wetting himself. (This is, after all, *Robert Mitchum* we're talking about.) It's not that he gives a bad performance, it's just that he is totally wrong for the role. Others, especially the younger actors, fare well. Mary Stuart Masterson, in the scant screen time she is given, transcends the banality of her role and contributes a moving portrayal of a shy teenager coming to grips with adulthood. Virginia Madsen, with a surprisingly good Irish accent, is the liveliest character in the film. Also charming is Harry Dean Stanton, having fun with his obviously fake Cockney accent. Angelica Huston, looking absolutely stunning in a variety of gorgeous gowns, is totally wasted as Mitchum's granddaughter and the object of Anthony Edwards' desire, and Edwards himself struggles mightily to appear eager and spontaneous while spouting mouthfuls of unutterable prose. The rest of the actors, Lauren Bacall included, either sputter, bluster, or slur their way through their performances, overacting unashamedly (Mark Metcalf, the infamous ROTC student Neidermeyer in NATIONAL LAMPOON'S ANIMAL HOUSE, is simply embarrassing as Masterson's father). Worst of all, however, is young Danny Huston's direction. Uninspired, unimaginative, and wholly awkward, the movie plods along from badly paced scene to badly paced scene, with no sense of lightness, spontaneity, or timing. Huston has delivered a film dead on arrival—and, as an adaptation of a literary work set in a wealthy community some 60 years ago, it is a commercial disaster. Only Danny's father, John, could make unfilmable books cinematic, and even his batting average was spotty at best. Fine actors, lush settings, and gorgeous costumes are simply not enough; there must be a strong, fiery, thoughtful presence with clear vision at the helm, and in MR. NORTH there isn't. It's like watching a newborn pony struggling to stand up for the first time. Perhaps, in a few years, if he ever gets another chance, Danny Huston will gain the confidence and strength to direct again. Until then he should study his father's work and try to unearth the sparkle that made so many of his films shine.

p, Steven Haft, Skip Steloff; d, Danny Huston; w, Janet Roach, John Huston, James Costigan (based on the novel *Theophilus North* by Thornton Wilder); ph, Robin Vidgeon (Metrocolor); ed, Roberto Silvi; m, David McHugh; md, Seth Kaplan; prod d, Eugene Lee; set d, Sandra Nathanson; makeup, Robert Arrollo.

Comedy/Drama Cas. (PR:A MPAA:PG-13)

MODERNS, THE****** (1988) 126m Alive c

Keith Carradine *(Nick Hart)*, Linda Fiorentino *(Rachel Stone)*, Genevieve Bujold *(Libby Valentin)*, Geraldine Chaplin *(Nathalie de Ville)*, Wallace Shawn *(Oiseau)*, John Lone *(Bertram Stone)*, Kevin J. O'Connor *(Ernest Hemingway)*, Elsa Raven *(Gertrude Stein)*, Ali Giron *(Alice B. Toklas)*, CharlElie Couture *(Charley)*, Ranee Lee *(Black Chanteuse)*, Michael Rudder *(Buffy)*, Gailard Sartain *(New York Critic)*, David Stein *(Critic # 1)*, Marthe Turgeon *(Proprietress)*, Didier Hoffman *(Priest)*, Michael Wilson *(Surrealist Poet)*.

Arguably the only visionary working in the arena of commercial American filmmaking, Alan Rudolph has delivered his second film in one year's time with THE MODERNS. After elevating the pedestrian Hollywood fantasy MADE IN HEAVEN (1987) to a level of Cocteauesque poetry (within the limitations of the Hollywood studio system), Rudolph has realized this long-standing project about the spirit of Paris in the 1920s—this century's most aesthetically explosive period in Western art. It was in this time and place that (according to myth) one could walk into a Left Bank cafe and spot Ernest Hemingway scribbling notes for *A Moveable Feast*, or listen to Erik Satie kerplunking away on a piano in the corner, or spy Georges Braque doodling a cubist sketch on a tabletop. It was an era of playfulness, irresponsibility, and creativity during which anything could happen . . . and usually did. From this atmosphere emerged some of the world's most influential and important artistic works and philosophies, and not only was it a time of modern art, it was a time of modern love. Expatriate Americans—Hemingway, F. Scott Fitzgerald, Gertrude Stein, and Alice B. Toklas being the most celebrated—flocked to the center of this world. It wasn't the architecture or the food that attracted them. The Paris of the 1920s was, and still is, a state of mind—a *modern* state of mind, which has come to represent all that is *modern* in this world.

Carradine plays Nick Hart (pronounced "art" with the silent French "h"), an American who earns a living as an illustrator, though his heart lies in painting. He frequents his favorite cafe, the Selavy (as in "C'est la Vie," or as in Marcel Duchamp's alter-ego Rose Selavy), along with his friends: Shawn, a gossip columnist known as "l'Oiseau" ("the bird") who wants nothing more than to quit his job and run off to the "city of the future" —Hollywood—and O'Connor, in a tour-de-force performance as the introspective, slightly drunken Ernest Hemingway. Into Carradine's cafe walks Lone, a proud American businessman who has amassed a fortune in the prophylactic business and who now wants to buy himself the best collection of modern art in Paris. On Lone's arm is his lovely wife, Fiorentino, a seemingly shallow young woman whose comments are emptily pedantic and whose mannerisms are out of place, like those of a little girl playacting in a grown-up's world. From across the room, Carradine spots Fiorentino and, despite warnings that Lone is powerful and perhaps a murderer, demands that Shawn introduce her to him. Only later do we learn that this woman, Lone's bride, had a few years earlier married (and never divorced) Carradine when they lived in Chicago. Since Lone is trying to buy himself a collection, Carradine's friend, art dealer and former nun Bujold (as Libby Valentin—another romantic name), suggests that he show Lone his work. A sale would be especially nice for Carradine, who has nothing but contempt for the business end of art, having sold only one painting in six years. Through Bujold, Carradine meets patroness of the arts Nathalie de Ville (or "devil," if you Anglicize your accent), played to perfection as a grotesque caricature by Chaplin. She is planning to leave her husband and secretly ship her three favorite paintings in his ownership—a Modigliani, a Matisse, and a Cezanne—to New York for display in the newly opened Museum of Modern Art (MOMA). In order to make her plan work, she wants Carradine to make copies of the paintings that she can leave behind for her duped husband. Carradine, whose late father was once a renowned art forger, initially resists, preferring to make his own art. Although he finally agrees, his work goes in vain when Chaplin's husband unexpectedly dies, rendering his services unnecessary. Refusing to pay Carradine for his work, she steals "her" paintings from his studio. Carradine, however, has hidden away the originals and, without realizing her error, Chaplin ships the completed *forgeries* off to MOMA. While struggling with his art, Carradine is also struggling with his heart, as Fiorentino continually wanders in and out of his life. Carradine wants her to leave Lone, but she has become too complacent in her lifestyle—that of an alcoholic, bon-bon eating concubine—with the wealthy Lone. Carradine's intense feelings for her erupt one evening at Gertrude Stein's apartment. When Lone insults Carradine's art and his suit, calling them both "cheap," Carradine responds by slapping the laughing Fiorentino across the face. In a modern form of the duel, the men agree to settle the dispute, not with pistols, but with three rounds in the boxing ring—a fight that Carradine "loses" to his kicking, kidney-punching adversary. Still stuck with the widowed Chaplin's three original paintings, Bujold and Carradine decide to sell them to Lone, along with a work of Carradine's. While Bujold and Lone go through the rituals of dealmaking, Carradine, under the premise that he is returning to his studio, is upstairs making love to Fiorentino. Lone later invites the Parisian art world to an exhibit of his collection, and Chaplin attends and makes a fool of the collector by (mistakenly) identifying his new paintings as forgeries. Dilettante art critics agree—one claims that Matisse would never paint such awful nipples on a nude. What follows is a battle of art and commerce in the confrontation between Lone and his aesthete guests. He argues that a masterpiece is a masterpiece only because a collector pays a high price for it—his most-loved paintings being those that are the most expensive. The critics argue that a painting is a masterpiece because they say it is a masterpiece and, therefore, Lone's Matisse is a fake because they say it is a fake. Lone then tosses the Matisse painting in the fireplace, cuts the breast out off one canvas, and burns the canvas of the third—the critics growing more apprehensive with each action, doubting their own previous declarations that the works were forgeries. In revenge for this debacle, Lone has his thugs destroy all the paintings, including Carradine's, in Bujold's gallery. Having nothing left, Bujold decides to leave town. Carradine and Fiorentino finally come to terms and plan to return to America. Lone, however, begs Fiorentino to stay, pulling a gun on her and Carradine. Another fight ensues between the men, during which Fiorentino, fed up with both of them, runs off. As Carradine chases after her, Lone jumps to his death in the Seine. The following morning, Carradine waits at the train station for Fiorentino to arrive. When she doesn't show, he and Shawn depart for New York, en route to Shawn's golden city of Hollywood. Their arrival in the US takes them to MOMA, where Carradine's three forgeries are on display and are being praised by an art critic who pontificates wildly about the genius of the work and how such brilliance cannot be duplicated. Carradine looks on, as do Shawn and Fiorentino, who has somehow managed to find them. As they exit, Hemingway walks in—the modern moveable feast having re-opened in New York.

Alan Rudolph's finest film to date, THE MODERNS is a culmination of all the things that have made Rudolph's past films so exciting. Displaying a vision of the world uniquely his own, Rudolph has succeeded in making a very modern period film that can be viewed as a documentary—not of an actual time or place, but of a feeling. Better than any piece of newsreel footage or recorded documents, THE MODERNS re-creates the spirit of Paris in the 1920s, and it is this *spirit* that is the most important aspect of that era and the essence of all art of that period. It is the spirit that Picasso and Braque uncovered in their Cubist creations, it is the spirit that Hemingway pinpointed in *A Moveable Feast*, it is the spirit that was most important to the Dadaists. Because of Rudolph's "heart" and "art," it is that spirit that also exists in THE MODERNS. Unlike TROUBLE IN MIND or MADE IN HEAVEN, in THE MODERNS Rudolph has not *created* another world, but has conjured one up from the past. But THE MODERNS is not just about Paris in the 1920s, or even Paris as a state of mind. (As a point of reference, last year's BEYOND THERAPY by Rudolph's mentor, Robert Altman, was also about Paris, the state of mind; while Roman Polanski's CHINATOWN similarly dealt with an abstract mental state as embodied in a concrete place.) It is also about ways of seeing art. While it is common for foreign filmmakers to question the nature of art, or the relationship between art and commerce, rarely do American directors address such issues. Rudolph, however, confronts these questions straight on. THE MODERNS is an essay on forgery—real art and fake art, real love and fake love. THE MODERNS tells us that the importance of art is in the perception of that art, not in the piece of art itself. To Nick Hart, the most significant aspect of a painting is the emotion it elicits in the viewer. In that respect, his copy of Cezanne is as brilliant as the original—a statement to which the art critic (Rudolph regular Gailard Sartain) in the Museum of Modern Art testifies. What makes the character's arguments all the more potent is Rudolph's own place in film. The director is a renegade who, like Nick Hart, has been victimized by the Bertram Stones of this world. When patroness Nathalie de Ville says to Hart, "I've followed your career with interest and concern . . . I always believed you would be more successful by now," the remark has added meaning in its applicability to Rudolph, who has received measured critical success but has reaped no financial profits from any of his last six pictures.

A longtime project of Rudolph's, THE MODERNS dates back to 1975, when he and producer Carolyn Pfeiffer began what amounted to 12 years of preproduction. Rejected by every studio, the script (penned by Rudolph and Jon Bradshaw) kicked around Hollywood for some time before the cameras were ready to roll. Twice Rudolph and Pfeiffer came close to shooting—and both times watched the plug get pulled. One cast included Mick Jagger (as Bertram Stone) and Charles Aznavour, but lack of a major distribution deal led to a shutdown. Another cast included Meg Tilly (as Rachel Stone), Sam Shepard (as Bertram), and Isabella Rossellini (as Nathalie de Ville). This time scheduling conflicts interfered. What could have been a final setback occurred in November 1986, when coscripter (and husband of producer Pfeiffer) Bradshaw, to whom the film is dedicated, died of a heart attack. Determined to make the project live, Rudolph, Pfeiffer, and coproducer David Blocker recast and went ahead with shooting. They also switched locations—from Paris to Montreal, which not only shaved about $1.5 million off the budget, but also, according to Rudolph, looked more like Paris of the 1920s. The production design is exceptional—with backgrounds that are paintings, rooms that look as if they belong in a Matisse—"forging" the real settings of the period. The cast, as always in a Rudolph film, is as important to the atmosphere as the film's design. While everyone is superb, there are standouts: Lone, fresh from his role as the Emperor Pu-Yi in Bernardo Bertolucci's THE LAST EMPEROR, shines as Bertram Stone; Wallace Shawn adds a sharp, fresh sense of comedy that cuts through the smokiness of the Selavy cafe and the overcast Parisian skies; and Kevin J. O'Connor—whose billing might as well read "and Ernest Hemingway as himself." The film is, not surprisingly, filled with paintings, including one by Carradine (itself something of a forgery) that is used as the poster art. Painting the "originals" of the Matisse, Cezanne, and Modigliani, as well as the copies, was David Stein, a Frenchman (his real name is Henri Haddad) who served time in prison in the early 1970s for passing off forgeries of paintings by Picasso and Chagall. Stein now sells his copies legally, signing the name of the original artist *and* his own. *(Nudity, sexual situations.)*

p, Carolyn Pfeiffer, David Blocker; d, Alan Rudolph; w, Alan Rudolph, Jon Bradshaw; ph, Toyomichi Kurita (CFI color); ed, Debra T. Smith, Scott Brock; m, Mark Isham; prod d, Steven Legler; set d, Jean-Baptiste Tard; cos, Renee April.

Drama **Cas.** **(PR:O MPAA:R)**

MONKEY SHINES: AN EXPERIMENT IN FEAR**** (1988) 113m Orion c

Jason Beghe *(Allan Mann)*, John Pankow *(Geoffrey Fisher)*, Kate McNeil *(Melanie Parker)*, Joyce Van Patten *(Dorothy Mann)*, Christine Forrest *(Maryanne Hodges)*, Stephen Root *(Dean Burbage)*, Stanley Tucci *(Dr. John Wiseman)*, Janine Turner *(Linda Aikman)*, William Newman *(Doc Williams)*, Tudi Wiggins *(Esther Fry)*, Tom Quinn *(Charlie Cunningham)*, Chuck Baker *(Ambulance Driver)*, Patricia Tallman *(Party Guest)*, David Early *(Anesthetist)*, Michael Naft *(Young Allan)*, Tina Romero, Michael Baseman, Lia Savini *(Children Playing)*, Tim Dileo, Melanie Verlin *(Vandals)*, Dan Fallon *(Allan's Friend)*, Alice Shure, Leslie Dane Shapiro, Christina Galesi *(Nurses)*, Boo the Monkey *(Ella)*.

©ORION

George Romero, who will always be remembered for NIGHT OF THE LIVING DEAD (1968), continues to bolster his reputation as America's preeminent horror film writer-director. His entire output marks him as a fiercely independent and uncommonly intelligent filmmaker whose thematic concerns are unapologetically liberal, humanistic, and gleefully subversive. While his technique may at times be crude, his films are undeniably effective, and he has cultivated a legion of dedicated supporters. His latest film, the outstanding MONKEY SHINES: AN EXPERIMENT IN FEAR, is a terrifying psychological horror film, which, unfortunately, is marred by a cliche, crowd-pleasing coda and a terribly sappy musical score by David Shire, both imposed on Romero by the film's producer. Filmed mostly in Romero's beloved Pittsburgh, the film begins as handsome young track star-law student Beghe is hit by a truck while jogging and is paralyzed from the neck down. After weeks in the hospital, the wheelchair-bound Beghe is returned to his home to find that his overbearing mother (Van Patten) has taken over his life and hired a disagreeable nurse (Forrest, Romero's wife) to care for him. To make matters even worse, Beghe's girl friend (Turner) has abandoned him and taken up with the smarmy, ambitious surgeon (Tucci) who saved his life. Meanwhile, Beghe's best friend (Pankow), an idealistic medical student who shoots drugs to stay awake for several days at a time, has been trying to increase the intelligence of capuchin monkeys by injecting them with a serum made from human brain tissue. Pankow is under tremendous pressure from his loathsome advisor, Root, who is anxious for results and determined to steal Pankow's serum. Looking for a way to keep Root from his most successful case—an incredibly intelligent female monkey named Ella—Pankow takes the monkey to animal behavior expert McNeil, who trains capuchins to assist the handicapped. Pankow gives Ella to Beghe and the monkey proves to be a great boon. Through McNeil's training, Ella is soon combing Beghe's hair, feeding him, dialing the phone, turning the pages of his textbooks, and even raising her hand for him in class. A strange, almost unnatural bond develops between Beghe and Ella, and the monkey even shuts off the lights and plays Peggy Lee tapes so that she can nuzzle romantically with her human charge. This serves to further alienate the resentful Forrest, who despises Ella and constantly threatens to harm her. Ella's arrival also brings an unexpected bonus as the beautiful and outgoing McNeil takes a liking to the wheelchair-bound law student and the two begin seeing each other frequently. The monkey begins to have another unforeseen effect, however: somehow, Ella brings out Beghe's repressed anger and resentment over his condition. In dreams, he has visions seen from Ella's point of view as she gets out at night and scurries throughout the neighborhood. The monkey seems to sense Beghe's anger and acts upon the hate he feels. One night Ella kills Forrest's beloved parakeet (which Beghe hates), an incident that finally causes Forrest to quit. This brings back Beghe's mother, who has impulsively sold her house and business to move in with her son and care for him as if he were a baby again. Beghe begins to detest his mother's presence, especially her obvious jealousy over his relationship with McNeil. Shortly thereafter, Beghe learns from a new doctor that Tucci—the one who stole away Turner—misdiagnosed Beghe's spinal problem and could have fixed it. Soon after that, both Tucci and Turner are killed in a fire that Beghe believes was caused by Ella. Although his friends think he is overreacting, Beghe demands that Ella be removed from the house. Pankow returns Ella to the lab, but she escapes and goes back to the house, and, although he doesn't see her, Beghe feels Ella's presence because he is suddenly very angry and abusive toward his mother. Upset, Van Patten tries to relax in the bath, but Ella appears and tosses a blow dryer into the water, electrocuting her. Meanwhile, Pankow has armed himself with several hypodermic needles filled with a fatal dose of tranquilizer, and goes to Beghe's house to do battle with Ella. In a nerve-wracking cat-and-mouse game, Pankow and Beghe try to capture Ella, but the monkey is too clever and she manages to inject Pankow with his own hypodermic needle, killing him. In the meantime, McNeil suspects trouble and comes to the house to help, where she too is waylaid by Ella and knocked unconscious. As Ella contemplates plunging the hypodermic needle into McNeil's eye, Beghe makes a superhuman effort and manages to move his hand to the tape deck and play Ella's favorite song. Although suspicious at first, Ella drops the needle and climbs up to Beghe's neck to cuddle. Beghe speaks to Ella in soothing tones and the monkey lets down her guard, giving Beghe the opportunity to sink his teeth into Ella's neck and viciously shake her from side to side, as if he were an animal at the kill. With Ella dead and McNeil saved, Beghe goes back into surgery to see if his spine can be corrected. As the doctor makes the incision, a bloody Ella leaps out of the wound. Of course the shocking image is just a dream, and the operation is a success.

In MONKEY SHINES, as in most of his best films, George Romero again poses the question: What does it mean to be human? This notion has been the overriding concern of the "Living Dead" trilogy. In the unjustly ignored third film of the series, DAY OF THE DEAD (1985), the catalyst for Romero's inquiry was an incredibly intelligent zombie named Bub, and the parallels between Bub in DAY OF THE DEAD and Ella in MONKEY SHINES are strong. Both are nonhuman, and posited by Romero as the missing link between pure animal instinct and civilized human behavior. Both creatures are fed human brain tissue (Ella through injections and Bub through feedings), which subsequently causes them to become more human-like, without relinquishing their violent instinctive behavior. Both Bub and Ella are catalysts for conflict between supposedly civilized characters, as the line between human and animal begins to blur. And while both films have scenes of talky scientific mumbo-jumbo that verbalize Romero's ruminations on humanity, they are much more effective when Romero articulates his theories visually.

Claustrophobic, gripping, and incredibly intense throughout, MONKEY SHINES is an extremely complicated emotional drama that taps into the dark side of family ties, friendship, dependency, nurturing, and love. At times, MONKEY SHINES is like a Douglas Sirk film taken to fantastic extremes. Beghe's character, who is the opposite of Romero's zombies (they are brainless mobility, while he is immobile intellect), is surrounded by four very different females (his mother, the nurse, his new girl friend, and especially Ella) who all want to care for him, but view one another as threats to their monopolization of his gratitude and love. Ella, the most complex character in the piece, is the wild card, for she will act upon the animal instincts the other characters repress; to his horror, Beghe discovers that Ella is all too willing to fulfill his own violent instincts, for she is unable to understand that to stifle one's darker impulses is to be human. (Because women are the focus of Beghe's rage some have accused Romero of misogyny, but nothing could be further from the truth. Romero takes great pains to paint his characters in full detail. Although the mother may be overbearing and the nurse ill-tempered, the women remain sympathetic because, in the end, they really just want to help and to be appreciated. Their extreme reaction to Beghe's sometimes brutal rejection of their efforts is perfectly understandable.) The characters in MONKEY SHINES are operating under trying circumstances, and emotions are at a heightened pitch throughout. In addition, although the film gets off to a rough start due to some unwieldy dialog and weak performances from Janine Turner and Stanley Tucci; Romero has progressed as a director of actors, with strong performances from Jason Beghe, John Pankow, and, amazingly, a capuchian monkey named Boo as Ella. Luckily, while improving his work with actors, he has not surrendered his uncanny ability to grip an audience viscerally. While he is easily the most interesting and intelligent director working in the horror genre today, mass commercial success has eluded George Romero. He tried for years to finance MONKEY SHINES independently, but failed and was forced to go to executive producer Charles Evans for the money. This also, unfortunately, led to a lack of control over the project, and Evans imposed the tired, CARRIE-like shock of the operation scene and the sappy happy ending after test audiences were dissatisfied with Romero's conclusion (when has a Romero film *ever* ended with two people grinning at each other like lovesick idiots?), which contained his trademark ironic dark humor. In Romero's cut the scientist played by Root, who has stolen Pankow's serum, arrives at his lab to be accosted by a militant group of anti-vivisectionists. Hit on the head by a rock, Root angrily turns to the protestors and tells them, "You deserve whatever you get!" He then enters the lab and we see hundreds of highly intelligent killer monkeys like Ella, waiting to be unleashed on mankind—a sort of miniversion of Romero's original plans for DAY OF THE DEAD (also frustrated), which called for an army of intelligent zombies controlled by humans. Unfortunately, Romero's cut was not restored for the videocassette release. The new ending didn't make a damn bit of difference, for the film was ineptly marketed by Orion and was yet another box-office flop for Romero. Despite the slight damage done by its producers, MONKEY SHINES, along with David Cronenberg's DEAD RINGERS, stand as shining examples of what the horror genre can be when a director with vision is at the helm. *(Violence, sexual situations, nudity, profanity.)*

p, Charles Evans; d, George Romero; w, George Romero (based on the novel by Michael Stewart); ph, James A. Contner (DeLuxe Color); ed, Pasquale Buba; m, David Shire; md, Brenda Hoffert, Paul Hoffert; m/l, Peggy Lee, Hubie Wheeler, Richard Whiting, Raymond B. Egan, Gus Kahn, Alan Brandt, Bob Haymes, Billy Hill; prod d, Cletus Anderson; art d, J. Mark Harrington, Jim Feng; set d, Diana Stoughton; spec eff, Tom Savini, Steve Kirshoff; cos, Barbara Anderson; makeup, Jeanee Josefczyk.

Horror **Cas.** **(PR:O MPAA:R)**

MOON OVER PARADOR** (1988) 105m UNIV c

Richard Dreyfuss *(Jack Noah)*, Raul Julia *(Roberto Strausmann)*, Sonia Braga *(Madonna)*, Jonathan Winters *(Ralph)*, Fernando Rey *(Alejandro)*, Sammy Davis, Jr. *(Himself)*, Michael Greene *(Clint)*, Polly Holliday *(Midge)*, Milton Goncalves *(Carlo)*, Charo *(Madame Loop)*, Marianne Sagebrecht *(Magda)*, Richard Russell Ramos *(Dieter Lopez)*, Jose Lewgoy *(Archbishop)*, Dann Florek *(Toby)*, Roger Aaron Brown *(Desmond)*, Dana Delany *(Jenny)*, Dick Cavett *(Himself)*, Ike Pappas *(Himself)*, Edward Asner *(Himself)*, Carlotta Gerson *(Momma)*, Lorin Dreyfuss *(1st Dictator)*, Nika Bonfim *(Carmen)*, John C. Broderick *(Director)*, David Cale *(Edgar Low)*, Reuven Bar-Yotam *(Menachem Fein)*, Rod McCary *(Gordon Boyd)*, Lora

©MCA (UNIVERSAL)

Milligan *(Alice)*, Jill Mazursky *(Assistant Director)*, Nina Fineman *(Casting Secretary)*, Regina Case *(Clara)*, Bianca Rossini *(Tilde)*, Ariel Coelho *(Paulo)*, Guilherme Karan *(Forte)*, Vera Buono *(Nightclub Singer)*, Ursula Cantu *(Showgirl)*, Guara *(Bearded Man)*, Giovanna Gold *(Carnival Girl)*, Carlos Augusto Strasser *(Drunk on Street)*, Betsy Mazursky *(Woman at Buffet)*, Rui Resende *(Man on the Beach)*, Flavio R. Tambellini *(Dante Guzman)*, Nelson Xavier *(Gen. Sinaldo)*, Mario Guimaraes *(Umberto Solar)*, Nildo Parente *(Gray Man)*, Jorge Cherques, Neville de Almeida, Renato Coutinho, Catalano, Helio Souto, Patricio Guzman *(Family Members)*, Lutero Luiz *(Samuel)*.

Throughout his career, writer-producer-director Paul Mazursky has used old movies as sources for his own films, remaking them in his distinctive comedic style. Not surprisingly, he has followed his most commercially successful film, DOWN AND OUT IN BEVERLY HILLS (a remake of Jean Renoir's BONDU SAVED FROM DROWNING), with another movie-inspired movie. This time a 1939 film, THE MAGNIFICENT FRAUD, which starred Akim Tamiroff as a French actor who is coerced into playing the role of an assassinated South American dictator, provided the basis for Mazursky's uneven comedy MOON OVER PARADOR.

Dreyfuss plays a second-rate American actor shooting a film on location in the fictional Caribbean-Latin American nation of Parador. Parador is ruled by a dictator who is not so much inhumane as ineffectual and inebriated. When the dictator, a dead ringer for Dreyfuss, keels over from a heart attack caused by drinking too many *Poonas* (the national specialty), Julia, the chief of police who is the country's unseen, de facto ruler, coerces Dreyfuss into playing the late dictator, thereby insuring a smooth transition of power that will protect the government from the threat of revolution. Although the actor has earlier demonstrated a better than average impersonation of the ruler, he is hesitant to take the role. Julia makes the decision easy for him, however, by appealing first to Dreyfuss' actor's vanity and then, more directly, by threatening to kill him if he doesn't take the part. The prime fringe benefit of the gig is the dictator's vivacious mistress (Braga), who spots Dreyfuss as a phony immediately but, attracted by his neurotic charm, falls in love with him anyway. Dreyfuss doesn't fool the dictator's maid and valet (Charo and Rey) either, but his speeches to his countrymen who pack the palace plaza to listen are big hits as he improvises on Julia's script, incorporating lyrics from "The Man of La Mancha." As time passes, the American grows more confident in his masquerade, leading his subjects in a campaign for better health that includes Dreyfuss-led aerobicizing; however, he grows increasingly bored with his role and longs for other parts being cast in New York. Moreover, influenced by Braga, Dreyfuss has come to see that injustice is rampant in Parador, although Julia is not about to let him upset the apple cart of privilege and oppression. Just when it looks as if there is no way out for Dreyfuss and no hope for the people, the special effects expert of the film that originally brought Dreyfuss to Parador returns to the country for the annual festival—the same festival from which Julia had Dreyfuss kidnaped a year earlier. With the special effects man's help, Dreyfuss stages a fake assassination and flees the country, which, thrown into turmoil, comes out all for the better with Braga as the leader of a new, democratic government. The action then shifts back to New York's Public Theatre, where the film began, as Dreyfuss finishes wistfully recounting the story of his adventures in Parador.

Striving to mix social consciousness with comedy, Mazursky has come up short on both counts. MOON OVER PARADOR's one-joke premise needed a tour-de-force performance from Richard Dreyfuss to succeed, and though Dreyfuss has his moments, he relies too heavily on the self-absorbed persona that hasn't always worked for him in the past and ultimately fails him here. Mazursky and cowriter Leon Capetanos' screenplay is sadly underdeveloped, so that once the viewer begins to lose interest in the nuances of Dreyfuss' charade there is nothing left to hold one's interest. Along the way there are a few laughs—generated mostly by the humorous cultural details supplied by Mazursky and production designer Pato Guzman to give Parador a goofy tangibility—but in the end MOON OVER PARADOR is not a funny movie. Nor is it politically insightful. Using comedy to make a political statement is not an easy trick, and Mazursky has treated the themes of authoritarian oppression and US covert meddling in the affairs of its southern neighbors so lightly that they seem inconsequential. He comes closer to the mark in drawing a parallel between Dreyfuss' literally acting the role of the dictator and the Reagan presidency—when Dreyfuss cups his ear while boarding a helicopter, indicating to reporters that he won't answer their questions because he can't hear, the distance between the White House and Parador vanishes—but fails to explore the deeper implications of having an actor as head of state. Instead, Mazursky is content merely to show Dreyfuss as a puppet,

Julia as the power behind the throne, and the US (in the person of CIA operative Jonathan Winters) as a shadowy evil presence. Once these relationships have been introduced, the viewer is left waiting for the development of the story, which never comes.

The film does benefit from the capable performances surrounding Dreyfuss' game but problematic one. Sonia Braga is both sultry and sincere as the dictator's paramour who becomes a sort of Paradoran Eva Peron, and Raul Julia, his hair dyed blond, captures a certain depraved stoic charm as the descendent of escaped Nazis. Sadly, Jonathan Winters' brief appearance as the CIA agent and Marianne Sagebrecht's (BAGHDAD CAFE) even briefer role leave the viewer wanting more. There are a number of other celebrity cameos in the film, including Sammy Davis, Jr.—who delivers a wonderful over-the-top self-parody during the festival—and Dick Cavett, who appears as himself. The scene in which Dreyfuss the actor meets Dreyfuss the dictator was accomplished by the use of an extra Dreyfuss, Richard's brother Lorin; and when Judith Malina (who was to have played Dreyfuss' mother) was unavailable, Mazursky, who began his career as an actor, donned drag and did the role himself.

Having viewed THE MAGNIFICENT FRAUD at a friend's suggestion and decided that it was a good premise but a bad movie, Mazursky and Capetanos traveled to Guatemala, El Salvador, Mexico, Trinidad, Jamaica, and other Caribbean nations in search of dictators to inspire their story. They then watched plenty of news footage and undertook their screenplay, shopping it to Universal, who held the rights to the original and weren't going to relinquish them. The hunt for the perfect location led to Brazil, where the colonial town of Ouro Preto in the mountains of Minas Gerais provided beautifully preserved 18th-century buildings and a plaza that Mazursky would fill with some 6,000 extras for one of Dreyfuss' speeches. (During the filming of that scene, the non-English-speaking extras simply moved their lips when they were supposed to be singing Parador's national anthem, and visitors on one of Universal Studios' tours later provided the actual vocals.) Made on a budget of $19 million, the biggest yet for Mazursky, MOON OVER PARADOR also benefited from the cooperation of the Brazilian army, which provided equipment and 700 soldiers for the dictator's army. Other locations used for the production were the 400-year-old coastal city of Salvador De Bahia and Rio de Janeiro, whose neo-classical Teatro Municipal became the dictator's palace.

Before the film could be made its script had to be approved by the Brazilian national film agency, *Concine*, and three army officers read it scrupulously for references that might reflect badly on the Brazilian military's rule. Apparently they didn't find anything offensive. This is not surprising, since there isn't much that could be called politically sensitive in the film—which is also exactly the problem with MOON OVER PARADOR. *(Sexual situations, adult situations, profanity.)*

p, Paul Mazursky, Pato Guzman, Geoffrey Taylor; d, Paul Mazursky; w, Leon Capetanos, Paul Mazursky (based on a story by Charles G. Booth); ph, Donald McAlpine (DeLuxe Color); ed, Stuart Pappe; m, Maurice Jarre; prod d, Pato Guzman; art d, Markos Flaksman; set d, Alexandre Meyer; spec eff, Pat Domenico; cos, Albert Wolsky; ch, Bianca Rossini; stunts, Bill Catching; makeup, Gary Liddiard.

Comedy **Cas.** **(PR:C MPAA:PG-13)**

MORGAN'S CAKE † (1988) 87m Rick Schmidt c

Morgan Schmidt-Feng *(Morgan)*, Willie Boy Walker *(Morgan's Dad)*.

Independent American filmmaker Rick Schmidt delivers his fourth feature (A MAN, A WOMAN, AND A KILLER; 1988—THE REMAKE; and EMERALD CITIES preceded), a low-low-budget 16mm tale of a teenager who is named Morgan after the Karel Reisz black comedy of 1966. This young man wishes that life were a bit more like that movie—"unserious and funny." As was the case here, each of Schmidt's previous features have been made for under the phenomenally small sum of $10,000.

d, Rick Schmidt; w, Rick Schmidt; ed, Rick Schmidt.

Comedy/Drama **Cas.** **(PR:NR MPAA:NR)**

MOVING* (1988) 89m WB c

Richard Pryor *(Arlo Pear)*, Beverly Todd *(Monica Pear)*, Dave Thomas *(Gary Marcus)*, Dana Carvey *(Brad Williams)*, Randy Quaid *(Frank/Cornell Crawford)*, Stacey Dash *(Casey Pear)*, Raphael Harris *(Marshall Pear)*, Ishmael Harris *(Randy Pear)*, Robert LaSardo *(Perry)*, Ji-Tu Cumbuka *(Edwards)*, King Kong Bundy *(Gorgo)*, Morris Day *(Rudy)*, Rodney Dangerfield *(Banker)*, Tony Rolan *(Parking Attendant)*, Claire Malis *(Helen Fredericks)*, John Wesley *(Roy Henderson)*, Jason Marin *(Paperboy)*, Traci Lin *(Natalie)*, Will Gill, Jr. *(Security Guard)*, Don Franklin *(Kevin)*, Gordon Jump *(Simon Eberhart)*, Julius Carry III *(Coach Wilcox)*, Stephan Michael Cole *(Young Husband)*, Diedre Madsen *(Young Wife)*, Anne Gee Byrd *(Realtor)*, Paul Willson *(Mr. Seeger)*, Lynne Stewart *(Mrs. Seeger)*, Dorothy Meyer *(Grandma)*, Al Fann *(Grandpa)*, Don Draper *(Homeowner)*, Alan Oppenheimer *(Mr. Cadell)*, Brooke Alderson *(Mrs. Cadell)*, Dave Johnson *(Race Track Announcer)*, Darrah Meeley *(Mrs. Davenport)*, Bill Wiley *(Arnold Butterworth)*, Bibi Osterwald *(Crystal Butterworth)*, Molly McClure *(Puzzle Lady)*, Patrick Cranshaw *(Packer)*, Anne Bellamy *(Woman at Yard Sale)*, Joseph Feinstein, Audree Chapman, Bif Hutton, Michael Briggs *(Reporters)*, David L. King *(Kitchen Couple Man)*, Bever-Leigh Banfield *(Kitchen Couple Woman)*, Gene Ross *(Bike Buyer)*, Lori Doran *(Waitress)*, Shirley Brown *(Mrs. Messina)*, Jacque Lynn Colton *(Mrs. Griffin)*, Shirley Jo Finney *(Junior High Secretary)*, Joe Praml *(Ted Barnett)*, Roger Reid *(Bob Delaney)*, Lisa Moncure *(Nina Franklin)*, J.J. Barry *(Bartender)*, Dian Kobayashi *(Anchorman)*, Rae Allen *(Dr. Phyllis Ames)*, Newell Alexander *(Announcer)*, Leslie Jordan *(Customer At Bar)*, Michael Casey *(Hank)*, Denise Kendall *(Girl In Limbo)*.

After the rather hapless and bland comedies THE TOY (1986) and CRITICAL CONDITION (1987), Richard Pryor has at least surrounded himself with some high quality talent in this, his most recent film. MOVING was scripted by Andy Breckman of TV's "Saturday Night Live" and "The David Letterman Show," and directed by Alan Metter (BACK TO SCHOOL), but, unfortunately, it ends up in the same depressingly lame quagmire as its Pryor priors. Pryor plays Arlo Pear, an upper middle-class New Jersey mass transit engineer who loses his job in a merger. The only new position he can find requires a move to Boise, Idaho. His wife and twin sons initially rebel against the prospective relocation, but Pryor's daughter, Dash, is especially upset, since she is in her last year of high school and has a new boy friend. She does her best to sabotage the move, even going so far as attempting to marry a pick-up "fiance," played by former Prince cohort Day. The constant harassment from next-door neighbor Quaid, who loves to buzz Pryor with a remote control helicopter and guzzle beer, also complicates the move. Further horrors ensue: demented moving men, multiple-personality auto delivery drivers, a company scandal that gets Pryor fired on his first day at work, and a new Boise neighbor who turns out to be Quaid's brother. After drowning his sorrows in drink, Pryor paints his face, dons a Rambo outfit and kicks some people around till there's a happy ending.

The film has its moments, mainly from the fine group of supporting actors. Beverly Todd is fine as Pryor's wife; Dana Carvey (the "Saturday Night Live" Church Lady) is funny as the schizo driver grappling with his eight personalities; and wrestler King Kong Bundy is one of the road warrior movers. Thomas, as Pryor's new boss, and Dangerfield, as a bank loan officer, put in brief appearances in supporting roles. Ultimately, however, none of this matters. Pryor barely moves through some of the scenes, displaying none of his old manic energy, and the film follows suit, proceeding with murderous deliberation. At one point, Pryor laments his lost New Jersey home, mumbling, "If you're happy, don't change." And, despite his starring in this film in which action revolves around change, it's clear that Pryor has no desire to move on, either. He appears to be quite happy using his talent for nothing more than light, diverting entertainment. Songs include: "Moving" (Ollie F. Brown, performed by Brown), "Salty Dog" (performed by The George Lewis Band of New Orleans). *(Violence, excessive profanity.)*

p, Stuart Cornfeld, Kim Kurumada; d, Alan Metter; w, Andy Breckman; ph, Donald McAlpine (Technicolor); ed, Alan Balsam; m, Howard Shore; m/l, Ollie Brown; prod d, David L. Snyder; art d, Joe Wood; set d, Linda DeScenna; spec eff, Clay Pinney, Michael Lantieri; cos, Deborah L. Scott; stunts, David Ellis, Mickey Gilbert; makeup, Gary Liddiard.

Comedy **Cas.** **(PR:O MPAA:R)**

MURDER ONE*** (1988, Can.) 95m SC/Miramax c

Henry Thomas *(Billy Isaacs)*, James Wilder *(Carl Isaacs)*, Stephen Shellen *(Wayne Coleman)*, Errol Slue *(George Dungee)*.

Based on a true crime spree that began in Maryland and ended in Georgia in 1973, MURDER ONE is an unrelentingly bleak look at the carload of killers who murdered six members of the Alday family. Seen through the eyes of 15-year-old Billy Isaacs (Thomas), the film begins in an economically depressed area of Baltimore. Working at a gas station and living with his older brother's former girl friend, Thomas is surprised to learn that his brother Carl (Wilder), 19; his half-brother, Wayne (Shellen), 26; and Wayne's cellmate, George (Slue), a 36-year-old black man with a 64 IQ, have escaped the minimum security prison where they had been incarcerated for a variety of petty crimes. Later that night the escapees show up at Thomas' apartment asking for some money and a change of clothes. When his brothers inform Thomas that they intend to visit their mother before pushing on, the teenager decides to go with them. The family reunion, however, is a disaster. While their stepfather gets drunk watching television, Mom, a prostitute, is parked out in front of the house with a young sailor. Rebuked by their mother, the fugitives prepare to flee, and, thinking he'll just go for a joy ride, Thomas goes with them. After destroying a hated uncle's home and stealing a few shotguns, the brothers head south. When the car breaks down in a remote area, they decide to steal a station wagon parked by a nearby house. Before Wilder can hot-wire it, however, a college-age neighbor happens upon the scene and demands that they leave. The college boy's condescending attitude and his vain attempt to grab a pistol enrage Shellen, and while Thomas watches, his brother shoots the young man in the back of the head. The convicts then steal the victim's car and continue their journey. Eventually they end up in rural Georgia with no money or gas and decide to rob a house. While the gang is ransacking the place, the family members begin to return home, singly and in pairs. Their adrenalin flowing, Wilder and Shellen kill the family one at a time, piling the bodies in the bedroom and living room. After murdering the five male members of the household, Wilder rapes the sole woman and then brings her with them. Stripped naked, she is taken to a remote area and Wilder pressures the childlike Slue into killing her. Shortly thereafter, they are caught in a police roadblock. After a brief gun battle the fugitives manage to run off into the woods, but they are easily captured by a small army of law officers. As they are being handcuffed, Thomas remarks in voice-over narration: "I felt like I was watching my brothers in a movie and now it was over. . . It seemed like all those people they killed should get up and take a bow. But they couldn't. They would never get up again."

Reminiscent of IN COLD BLOOD (1967) and BADLANDS (1974) in its portrayal of senseless rural crime, and AT CLOSE RANGE (1986) in its look at the dark side of the American family, MURDER ONE is a methodical and detailed account of the Isaac brothers' 13-day crime spree presented in a chilling, matter-of-fact manner by director Graeme Campbell. Although MURDER ONE will prove to be either infuriating or nauseating for many viewers, Campbell and screenwriter Tex Fuller (who previously directed an award-winning documentary about the killers) do not seek to judge or moralize about these remorseless killers. They merely present the facts in numbingly casual fashion. The only obvious cinematic liberty the filmmakers take is the insertion of hauntingly flat narration by Thomas, who expresses what was going through his head while the horrifying events unfolded (perhaps this is a nod to Terrence Malick, who uses the device brilliantly in both BADLANDS and DAYS OF HEAVEN). Otherwise it is up to the viewer to make sense of this tragic and senseless crime, and the clues to its cause are everywhere.

There is a palpable sense of claustrophobia and doom in the opening scenes. Poverty, hopelessness, despair, and apathy hang like a dark cloud in every frame. The superbly dingy set design captures the kind of depressed, resigned environment that produces killers like the Isaacs. Denied participation in the mythic American Dream, these warped, angry young men make their mark on society the only way they know how—through shocking acts of violence. Wayne is shown to be incapable of having a good time without destroying something, Carl seems to be consciously carving out a heinous name for himself, while Billy—who never participates in the killing and wants to go home—is trapped at first by his sense of family obligation and then by simple fear of his siblings. Perhaps the most tragic is George, a likable, childlike man who was sent to prison for nonpayment of a $7 child support check and was only three weeks from gaining release when he joined the Isaacs in escape. A seemingly gentle man who was obviously incapable of logical judgment, he appears to have simply gone along for the ride with his only friends and gotten caught up in events over which he had little control.

The performances are uniformly excellent, with James Wilder making an unforgettable mark as the most profoundly disturbed member of the family and Errol Slue equally memorable in his complex and dignified portrayal of George. Henry Thomas, who will forever be remembered as young Elliott in E.T. (1982), makes a strong case for serious consideration as an adult actor with his subtle, haunting performance. With its passionless surface and its almost pathological fetish for unblinking detail, MURDER ONE will no doubt deeply disturb anyone who sees it expecting answers. What Campbell and Fuller do is pose questions, questions that may not have answers. Carl Isaacs, Wayne Coleman, and George Dungee were all sentenced to be executed by the state and are still sitting on death row. Billy Isaacs is currently serving a life sentence. (*Violence, nudity, excessive profanity, substance abuse.*)

p, Nicolas Stiliadis; d, Graeme Campbell; w, Tex Fuller; ph, Ludek Bogner; ed, Michael McMahon; m, Mychael Danna; prod d, John Dondertman, Bora Bulajic.

Crime   Cas.   (PR:O MPAA:R)

MURDER RAP †(1988) 107m Image Films/Resolution Films/United Home Video c

John Hawkes, S. Kathleen Feighny, Coquina Dunn, Tim Mateer, Sara Roucloux, Kerry Awn, David Frizzell, James Michael Costello, Julius Tennon.

Filmed in Austin, Texas, this straight-to-video title is about a young man who gets caught in a web of murder, violence, and deception when he becomes friendly with a sensual but manipulative young lady who involves him in a killing. In order to beat her at her own game, he fakes his own death and outmaneuvers her. The title has a double meaning, referring also to a rap record the hero makes.

p, Kliff Kuehl, Joe M. South; d, Kliff Kuehl; w, Kliff Kuehl; ph, Michael Delahoussaye; m, Robert Renfrow.

Thriller   Cas.   (PR:NR MPAA:NR)

MY BEST FRIEND IS A VAMPIRE †   (1988) 90m Kings Road c

Robert Sean Leonard (*Jeremy Capello*), Evan Mirand (*Ralph*), Cheryl Pollak (*Darla Blake*), Rene Auberjonois (*Modoo*), Cecilia Peck (*Nora*), Fannie Flagg (*Mrs. Capello*), Kenneth Kimmins (*Mr. Capello*), David Warner (*Prof. McCarthy*), Paul Wilson (*Grimsdyke*).

When a teenage delivery clerk drops off some groceries at a creepy gothic mansion, he is seduced by the sexy vampiress that lives there. He leaves with fang marks in his neck and a new thirst for blood. It should come as no surprise that his friends and family are a bit distressed at his curious new habits. To add to the fun, there's even a subplot about a pair of vampire hunters (Warner and Willson) who are trying to track down our blood-sucking young hero. The film received a brief regional release.

p, Dennis Murphy; d, Jimmy Huston; w, Tab Murphy; ph, James Bartle (Technicolor); ed, Janice Hampton; ed, Gail Yasunaga; m, Steve Dorff; prod d, Michael Molly; set d, Richard Huston; cos, Rona Lamont; makeup, Christy Belt.

Comedy/Horror   Cas.   (PR:NR MPAA:PG)

MY STEPMOTHER IS AN ALIEN* (1988) 108m Weintraub-Franklin R. Levy-Ronald Parker-Catalina/COL c

Dan Aykroyd (*Dr. Steve Mills*), Kim Basinger (*Celeste*), Jon Lovitz (*Ron Mills*), Alyson Hannigan (*Jessie Mills*), Joseph Maher (*Dr. Lucas Budlong*), Seth Green (*Fred Glass*), Wesley Mann (*Grady*), Adrian Sparks (*Dr. Morosini*), Juliette Lewis (*Lexie*), Tanya Fenmore (*Ellen*), Karen Haber (*Kristy*), Amy Kirkpatrick (*Kimberly*), Suzie Plakson (*Tenley*), Robyn Mundell (*Kat*), Jim Doughan, Jay McCaslin, Jim Jackman (*Party Guests*), Kevin McDermott (*Olaf*), Robert Benedetti (*Drill Sergeant*), Maxine (*Porn Actress*), James Edwards (*Porn Actor*), Tony Jay (*Council Chief*), Peter Bromilow (*Second in Command*), Earl Boen (*Reverend*), Barbara Sharma (*Mrs. Glass*), Michele Rogers (*Skippy Budlong*), Nina Henderson (*Cashier*),

© WEINTRAUB ENTERTAINMENT

Chere Rae (*Station Wagon Driver*), Lisa Croisette (*Comdr. Winnek Wolfet*), Sophia Bowen, Shea Bowen, Gabi, Gina Raymond, Susan Carlsberg (*12th Navigational Command*), Dave the Dog (*Peanut*), Ann Prentiss (*Voice of Bag*), Harry Shearer (*Voice of Carl Sagan*).

In MY STEPMOTHER IS AN ALIEN, an extraterrestrial is sent to Earth to find information that will save her planet, but instead learns about life and love. Aykroyd, a widowed astronomer bent on proving the existence of life on other planets, accidentally transmits a radar signal "92 light years and two solar systems away," losing his job when the powerful signal shakes the research facility where he works to its foundations. Later, Aykroyd and his 13-year-old daughter (Hannigan) go to a party at the home of his brother (Lovitz). There the lonely astronomer finds himself attracted to the outlandishly dressed Basinger, an alien with a talking handbag who has been sent to the Earth to learn "the composition of [the]radar beam" so it can be reproduced to return her planet to its normal state. A romance develops between Aykroyd and Basinger as she presses him for information, even agreeing to marry him, in the belief that he will concentrate more on his work if he thinks she won't leave. (By this time, her handbag has imitated Carl Sagan's voice to convince Aykroyd's boss to rehire him.) Alone with Basinger while her father is at work, Hannigan sees her talking to a serpentlike creature in the handbag and summons Aykroyd home. Although the creature continues to torment Hannigan, it disappears when her father arrives, and, unable to make him believe her story, Hannigan rides off on her bike into the path of an oncoming car, only to be miraculously saved by Basinger, who reveals her alien origins in the process. Although upset, Aykroyd asks Basinger to stay anyway. While they are talking, a lightning storm begins, and Basinger gets an electric shock from the metal snaps on Aykroyd's shirt, prompting his realization that a similar conductor is necessary to duplicate the signal. They rush off to the lab, where they are joined by Lovitz, bearing the handbag, which has faked Basinger's voice to convince him to transport it there. The transmission is made, the bag is electrocuted before it makes good on its threat to destroy the earth, Basinger convinces the leaders on her planet to allow her to stay, and Lovitz volunteers to leave Earth in her stead to teach the aliens about being human.

A standard formula comedy, MY STEPMOTHER IS AN ALIEN tries to emulate popular alien-on-earth films like STARMAN. Had it actually been told from the perspective of the scientist's daughter, as the title suggests, it might have been more appealing, but instead a predictable, amateurish script shifts the focus elsewhere. Granted, Hannigan is the one who first witnesses Basinger's unusual behavior (like eating batteries), but the viewer automatically identifies with Basinger as she awkwardly adjusts to human life, and what could have been an interesting approach is lost. The script also contains a number of logical inconsistencies and suffers from too many stock characters: the innocently inquisitive alien, the befuddled scientist, his lecherous brother, and his self-serving boss, none of whom develops during the course of the story. Moreover, scattered throughout the script are several misplaced critiques of human society—"Earth is a backward culture," "We're where you'll be in 55 centuries, if you make it," and "Enjoy your humanity, while it lasts." More important, the film is sorely lacking as a comedy, as too much time is spent on the tired jokes surrounding Basinger's introduction to kissing, sex, and marriage. For instance, when she summons a council of elders from her planet to ask them to define marriage, she is told, in effect, you cook, you clean, and you bring him martinis. Ultimately, MY STEPMOTHER IS AN ALIEN is predictable, dull, and not particularly funny. (*Profanity, sexual situations.*)

p, Ronald Parker, Franklin R. Levy; d, Richard Benjamin; w, Jerico Weingrod, Herschel Weingrod, Timothy Harris, Jonathan Reynolds; ph, Richard H. Kline (DeLuxe Color); ed, Jacqueline Cambas; m, Alan Silvestri; prod d, Charles Rosen; set d, Harold L. Fuhrman; spec eff, John Dykstra, Philip C. Cory; cos, Aggie Guerard Rodgers; ch, Don Correia; stunts, Richard Ziker; makeup, Dan Striepeke, Brad Wilder.

Comedy/Science Fiction   Cas.   (PR:C MPAA:PG-13)

MYSTIC PIZZA**½   (1988) 104m Goldwyn c

Julia Roberts (*Daisy Araujo*), Annabeth Gish (*Kat Araujo*), Lili Taylor (*Jojo Barboza*), Vincent Phillip D'Onofrio (*Bill Montijo*), William R. Moses (*Tim Travers*), Adam Storke (*Charles Gordon Winsor*), Conchata Ferrell (*Leona Valsouano*), Porscha Radcliffe *(Phoebe Travers)*, Joanna Merlin *(Margaret)*, Arthur Walsh *(Manny)*, John Fiore *(Jake)*, Gene Amoroso *(Ed Barboza)*, Janet Zarish *(Nicole)*, Ray Zuppa *(Mitch)*, Louis Turenne *(Everyday Gourmet)*, Wiley Moore *(Newscaster)*, Ann Flood *(Polly)*, Suzanne Sheperd *(Aunt Tweedy)*, Jody Raymond *(Teresa)*, Matt Damon *(Steamer)*, Marrisa Carey *(Flower Girl)*.

Taking its title from a pizza parlor in the seaside tourist town of Mystic, Connecticut, this romantic comedy follows the fortunes of three Portuguese-American friends (Taylor, Roberts, and Gish) who waitress together at the title restaurant, where Ferrell concocts "traditional" pizzas from her father's secret recipe and longs for the recognition of the "Everyday Gourmet," a pompous TV restaurant critic. At the film's opening, the tourist season is winding down with the approach of fall. Taylor faints during her wedding ceremony, unable to go through with her marriage to D'Onofrio, the lumbering fisherman she loves but to whom she can't yet commit herself. Her friends, sisters Roberts and Gish, give her support but become involved in their own romantic entanglements as the autumn progresses. Roberts, the older, more overtly sexy of the two, has no real plans for the future except to get the hell out of Mystic. Bookish and sexually inexperienced Gish, their hard-working mother's "perfect daughter," is bound for Yale on a partial scholarship. In addition to her waitressing duties, would-be astronomer Gish works at the local planetarium and begins babysitting for the young daughter of Moses, a handsome, 30-year-old architect (Yale, class of 1979) whose wife has gone abroad for an extended visit. As time passes, 18-year-old Gish falls for Moses, and, captivated by the attentions of this pretty and intelligent young woman, he plays along with her. Roberts becomes involved with Storke, the preppie, Porsche-driving son of a prominent lawyer, who has been thrown out of law school for cheating. As these events unfold, Taylor and D'Onofrio continue their stereotype-reversing romance: she continually anxious to go to bed, he determined to marry first, to make a life-long commitment. Before long her refusal to set another date becomes too much for D'Onofrio, and he breaks off their relationship. Roberts' affair is also threatened. Her dinner visit to meet Storke's parents is a disaster, ending in a tumultuous father-son confrontation that leaves Roberts convinced that Storke has simply exploited her commonness to get back at his father. Gish, on the other hand, appears to be luckier. Moses seems to be falling for her, but on the night that their candle-lit dinners finally give way to sexual intimacy, his wife returns, and their affair comes to an abrupt halt that shatters Gish. At season's end, it looks as if the three waitresses have painfully come of age—a little older, a little wiser, but without much else to show for their romantic autumn. Not so. Storke returns to prove that his feelings for Roberts go much deeper than she had imagined, Taylor and D'Onofrio are married (though he has promised to respect her independence), Ferrell presents Gish with a big "loan" for her schooling, and Mystic Pizza's house specialty is given four stars by the Everyday Gourmet.

Part WHERE THE BOYS ARE, part LOVE STORY, and grounded in ethnicity a la MOONSTRUCK, MYSTIC PIZZA is a feel-good movie with a gentle melancholic undercurrent. It is also both annoyingly predictable *and* refreshingly surprising. Of the three love stories, the cross-class relationship between Julia Roberts (sister of actor Eric Roberts) and Adam Storke (making his film debut) is the most familiar, and despite their competent performances the film is least interesting when their romance is front and center. However, Vincent D'Onofrio's on-again, off-again courtship of Lili Taylor provides an interesting twist to the usual movie mating rituals. An imposing figure—though a far cry from the bloblike psychotic time bomb he portrayed so well in FULL METAL JACKET, and given too little to do here—D'Onofrio is strong and just silent enough to sell his character's you-only-want-me-for-my-body insistence on marriage and his confusion at Taylor's randy unreadiness to tie the knot. For the most part, Taylor also does a good job of conveying not only her conflicting lust for D'Onofrio and desire for independence, but also a simplicity that has nothing to do with being stupid. The chemistry between Taylor and D'Onofrio isn't as strong as it should be, however, so scenes like that in which Taylor's parents discover the fisherman in their living room with his pants around his ankles aren't as funny as they could have been.

More poignant and believable, primarily because of the excellent performance by Annabeth Gish (so wonderful in DESERT BLOOM), is the painful relationship between Gish and William R. Moses, who delivers a portrayal that appropriately alternates between warm, fuzzy nice-guyness and chilly "but I love my wife" desertion. Their affair is also predictable, but its development successfully teases the viewer. We suspect that they will eventually sleep together, but are kept wondering when, and what will happen after that. It doesn't seem likely that their relationship will be anything more than a fling, but the filmmakers keep us guessing, and, because Gish is so charming, we are nearly as surprised and affected (even though we know better) as she is when Moses drops her cold.

MYSTIC PIZZA is hardly a seamless film. Some of the plot development is forced—as is some of the humor, conflict, and pathos—but, for the most part, first-time director Donald Petrie (the son of director Daniel Petrie [FORT APACHE, THE BRONX]and brother of screenwriter Daniel Petrie, Jr. [THE BIG EASY]) has created an entertaining and poignant film about friendship, love, and growing up. Amy Jones—who scripted SLUMBER PARTY MASSACRE and directed MAID TO ORDER—wrote the original screenplay, but Randy and Perry Howze and playwright Alfred Uhry ("Driving Miss Daisy") also put their pens to MYSTIC PIZZA's script before it was completed. Most of the shooting was actually done on location in Mystic, Connecticut. *(Excessive profanity, sexual situations.)*

p, Mark Levinson, Scott Rosenfelt; d, Donald Petrie; w, Amy Jones, Perry Howze, Randy Howze, Alfred Uhry (based on a story by Amy Jones); ph, Timothy Suhrstedt (Duart color); ed, Marion Rothman, Don Brochu; m, David McHugh; m/l, Franke Previte, Brad Fiedel; prod d, David Chapman; art d, Mark Haack; set d, Mark Haack; spec eff, Ken Levin; cos, Jennifer Von Mayrhauser; makeup, Vera Yurtchuk, Steven Frank, Nan Piascik.

Comedy/Romance   Cas.   (PR:O MPAA:R)

N

NAKED GUN, THE½   (1988) 85m PAR c

Leslie Nielsen (*Lt. Frank Drebin*), George Kennedy (*Capt. Ed Hocken*), Priscilla Presley (*Jane Spencer*), Ricardo Montalban (*Vincent Ludwig*), O.J. Simpson (*Nordberg*), Nancy Marchand (*Mayor*), John Houseman (*Driving Instructor*), Reggie Jackson (*Right Fielder*), Jeannette Charles (*Queen Elizabeth II*), Curt Gowdy, Weird Al Yankovic, Dr. Joyce Brothers, Ken Minyard, Bob Arthur.

©PARAMOUNT

One of the most overrated movies of the year, THE NAKED GUN, while quite funny in spots, is certainly not one of Zucker, Abrahams, and Zucker's best efforts. The ZAZ team, which made a huge splash after AIRPLANE! (1980), based their latest comedy on their short-lived television show, "Police Squad," which was deemed too daring for that medium and lasted only four episodes. While "Police Squad" was a delightful slam at hackneyed television conventions that managed to stay hilarious for most of its half-hour running time, expanding the concept to feature length posed problems for ZAZ that they failed to overcome. Leslie Nielsen reprises his role as the bumbling police lieutenant Frank Drebin, who opens the film by beating up Khomeini, Khadafi, Gorbachev, and Idi Amin (?) look-alikes while on vacation in Beirut. Upon his return to Los Angeles, Drebin becomes embroiled in a case involving suave heroin smuggler Montalban, who uses his shipping business as a front. During his investigation the hapless Nielsen meets and falls for Montalban's assistant, Presley, who is just as dim and clumsy as he is. Meanwhile, Nielsen's boss, Kennedy, learns that there will be an assassination attempt on Queen Elizabeth (played by look-alike Jeannette Charles) during her visit to Los Angeles. For reasons never made clear, Montalban is behind the nefarious plan and has programmed an unnamed assassin, a la THE MANCHURIAN CANDIDATE, to kill the queen while she attends a California Angels home game. Nielsen surmises that the assassin must be a ball player, so he poses as an umpire and frisks the batters as they step to the plate. Chaos ensues (to the tune, inexplicably, of Randy Newman's hit song "I Love L.A."), and during the confusion outfielder Reggie Jackson is revealed to be the assassin. Jackson walks like a robot over to second base, where he has hidden a handgun. Just as he is about to shoot the queen, Nielsen saves the day, Montalban is exposed and killed, and all's well that ends well.

   Merely recounting the plot of any ZAZ comedy utterly fails to convey the lunacy of the production and, therefore, its charm. From the credits sequence, which has the camera mounted on top of a police car that drives through the city streets, into a house, and finally into a girl's locker room and shower; to the villainous Montalban falling off a tier at the ball park and being crushed by a bus, a steamroller, and then a marching band, THE NAKED GUN throws the gags at the viewer fast and furious. Unfortunately, for every gag that works there are 10 that don't. At their worst, ZAZ have a penchant for vulgarity that would embarrass a 10-year-old, and they tend to fall back on it whenever they discover a dead spot in the narrative (the "beaver" joke comes to mind). For all its attempts at unpredictability, the film is terribly calculated—even to the extent of staging a dull shoot-out in a grungy meat-packing plant merely to set up a rather unfunny gag in which Montalban, three scenes later, bites into a hot dog and finds a human finger. Wouldn't this rather feeble gross-out have been just as effective without the elaborate setup? In addition, some of the physical humor is repeated ad infinitum—Nielsen crashes into things every time he parks his car—until it just isn't funny anymore. Also misguided is the flag-waving opening, wherein Nielsen beats up international terrorists. Given the absurdities of the Sylvester Stallone and Chuck Norris machismo fantasy films, one would assume that ZAZ would zero in on them as a target for satire, but instead ZAZ seems to *endorse* the fantasy rather than mock it (Keenan Ivory Wayans does a better job of parodying RAMBO in the climactic shootout of I'M GONNA GIT YOU SUCKA). The slapstick in THE NAKED GUN isn't as successful as it has been in past ZAZ films, and their true forte, the snappy, stupid, and incredibly funny dialog that peppers AIRPLANE!, is used only sparingly here.

When bits do work, however, they are very funny, especially the "falling in love" montage between Nielsen and Presley that turns out to be a rock video, and the inspired lunacy of spicing up standard baseball "bloopers" footage with such scenes as a runner sliding into second base, then being mauled by a tiger, and an outfielder slamming against a wall to catch a fly ball only to have his head come off and fall into the stands. In the end, critical judgements about comedies like THE NAKED GUN are fairly useless. The jokes either make you laugh or they don't, and your reaction, of course, is purely subjective. (*Adult situations, comic violence, sexual situations, brief nudity, profanity.*)

p, Robert K. Weiss; d, David Zucker; w, Jerry Zucker, Jim Abrahams, David Zucker, Pat Proft; ph, Robert Stevens (Technicolor); ed, Michael Jablow; m, Ira Newborn; prod d, John J. Lloyd; art d, Donald B. Woodruff; set d, Rick T. Gentz; cos, Mary E. Vogt.

Comedy   Cas.   (PR:C-O MPAA:PG-13)

NEST, THE †   (1988) 88m Concorde c

Robert Lansing (*Mayor Elias Johnson*), Lisa Langlois (*Elizabeth Johnson*), Franc Luz (*Sheriff Richard Tarbell*), Terri Treas (*Dr. Morgan Hubbard*), Stephen Davies (*Homer*), Diana Bellamy (*Mrs. Pennington*), Jack Collins (*Shakey Jake*), Nancy Morgan (*Lillian*), Jeff Winkless (*Church*), Steve Tannen (*Mr. Perkins*), Heidi Helmer (*Jenny*), Karen Smyth (*Diner*).

THE NEST is the proud winner of *The Motion Picture Annual* award for "Best Exploitation-Film Ad of 1988" for its unforgettable newspaper advertisement that showed a man recoiling in horror from his open refrigerator and exclaiming, "Why is the cheese moving?!" Unfortunately, the film's distributor, Roger Corman's Concorde Pictures, unceremoniously dumped THE NEST onto the drive-in circuit and it went the home video route before the masses had a chance to savor its subtle ad campaign. Trouble brews in the sleepy little community of North Port, California, after the ambitious mayor strikes a deal with a powerful corporation known as INTEC, allowing it to do some top-secret experimenting in the town. As it turns out, INTEC has created a vicious breed of meat-eating super roaches that have gone on the rampage eating cattle, house pets, and an occasional tourist. Poisons do not stop the killer roaches, and to make matters worse, the vile bugs literally become what they eat, mutating into hideous half-roach, half-whatevers. Can repentant INTEC scientists devise a poison capable of killing the nasty beasts? Will the entire populace be devoured by the creatures? Will beachfront property values go down? Isn't it true that a filmmaker *cannot fail* to give an audience the willies merely by showing thousands of cockroaches? The answer to these and other questions can be found by renting THE NEST.

p, Julie Corman; d, Terence H. Winkless; w, Robert King (based on a novel by Eli Cantor [Gregory A. Douglas]); ph, Ricardo Jacques Gale; ed, James A. Stewart, Stephen Mark; m, Rick Conrad; art d, Carol Bosselman; set d, Craig Sulli; spec eff, Cary Howe.

Horror   Cas.   (PR:NR MPAA:R)

NEW ADVENTURES OF PIPPI LONGSTOCKING, THE   (1988) 100m COL c

Tami Erin (*Pippi*), David Seaman, Jr. (*Tommy*), Cory Crow (*Annika*), Eileen Brennan (*Miss Bannister*), Dennis Dugan (*Mr. Settigren*), Dianne Hull (*Mrs. Settigren*), George Di Cenzo (*Mr. Blackhart*), J.D. Dickinson (*Rype*), Chub Bailly (*Rancid*), Dick Van Patten (*Glue Man*), John Schuck (*Capt. Efraim*), Branscombe Richmond (*Fridolf*), Evan Adam (*Freckled Face Boy*), Fay Masterson (*Head Girl*), Romy Mehlman (*Lisa*), Geoffrey Seaman (*Billy*), Bridget Ann Brno (*Chrissy*), Christopher Broughton (*Manuel*), Carole Kean (*Miss Messerschmidt*), Leila Hee Olsen (*Miss Ward*), Clark Neiderjohn (*Jake*), Louis Seeger Crume (*Fire Chief*), Joe Gilbride (*Horseman*), Jim Grimshaw (*Police Chief*), Joseph John Kurtzo, Jr. (*Janitor*), Russ Wheeler (*Ice Cream Vendor*), Gail Klicman (*Townswoman*).

This is the third film based on Astrid Lindgren's precocious and unorthodox little heroine, following PIPPI IN THE SOUTH SEAS (1974) and PIPPI ON THE RUN (1977). This time Tami Erin plays the little girl with the wired pigtails and immovable smile, with the film opening on board a pirate vessel that is captained by her father. A violent storm sends Erin into the sea with her horse and monkey, and she winds up on land in a dilapidated old house. The two children who live next door (Seaman and Crow) quickly take a liking to Erin and her philosophy about life, which is that it is to be lived in the most irresponsible way possible. Erin encourages her young friends to spill their food, skate in the house, and shake feathers out of pillows—activities the kids relish. Then the social worker at the local orphanage (Brennan) arrives on the scene. She's understandably appalled by Erin's behavior and sets out to see to it that the new girl starts attending school. Erin continues her errant ways—at one point buying ice cream for all the local children, then throwing it at them—but Brennan

© COLUMBIA

persists, and Erin finally ends up in school. When her teacher asks her questions, however, Erin responds by saying that if she doesn't know the answer she has no business being a teacher. So much for education. Soon thereafter, Erin's father shows up, and she is all set to sail away with him, but just as they are about to leave, Erin notices her friend is crying. Saying that no one should leave a crying friend, Erin elects to stay behind as her father sails off to a Pacific island where the natives have made him a king.

Without question, this film can't be accused of moralizing in the manner common to most children's films. In fact, it stops just short of promoting anarchy. Erin is given a chance to be heroic when she saves a couple of kids from a fiery grave, but that seems merely a plot device to advance the relationship between the little girl and Eileen Brennan. For her part, Brennan is strangely subdued in a role that required histrionics. It's all pretty sloppy, as some scenes end suddenly, while others just drag on. Ken Annakin, directing from his own script, seems bored, though he does make sure that every child in the cast has at least one appallingly bad acting habit. The kids will like it, though parents may not be fond of the questionable behavior this film seems to endorse.

p, Gary Mehlman, Walter Moshay, Ken Annakin; d, Ken Annakin; w, Ken Annakin (based on the books by Astrid Lindgren); ph, Roland "Ozzie" Smith (DeLuxe Color); ed, Ken Zemke; m, Misha Segal; m/l, Harriet Schock, Misha Segal; prod d, Jack Senter; art d, Stephen B. Merger; set d, Chris Senter; spec eff, Richard Parker, Richard Huggins; cos, Jacqueline Saint Anne; ch, Nancy Gregory; stunts, Joe Gilbride; makeup, Sherry Caudle.

Children's   Cas.   (PR:A MPAA:G)

NEW LIFE, A**   (1988) 104m PAR c

Alan Alda (Steve Giardino), Ann-Margret (Jackie Giardino), Hal Linden (Mel Arons), Veronica Hamel (Dr. Kay Hutton), John Shea (Doc), Mary Kay Place (Donna), Beatrice Alda (Judy), David Eisner (Billy), Victoria Snow (Audrey), Paul Hecht, Celia Weston, Bill Irwin, John Kozak, Alan Jordan.

In the late 1940s and 50s, Joseph L. Mankiewicz made his reputation with a series of films that explored relations between intelligent, mature, professional men and women (A LETTER TO THREE WIVES; ALL ABOUT EVE; PEOPLE WILL TALK). In the 1980s, Alan Alda covers much the same territory and one-ups Mankiewicz by acting in his own creations (as well as writing and directing them). Unfortunately, Alda lacks the biting incisiveness and wit as a director that his predecessor used to such advantage. A NEW LIFE is a too glib, emotionally arid delineation of male menopause with characters who have all the depth of cartoons.

Steve Giardino (Alda) is a New York stock trader whose wife, Jackie (Ann-Margret), has left him, citing general neglect. Alda is nonplussed, but his coworker and friend, Mel (Hal Linden), a confirmed bachelor of the "women are only good for one thing" school, urges him to dye his hair, smarten up sartorially, and hit the singles scene. His experiences there are less than wonderful, running the gamut from coke addicts to nefarious transvestites (a hoary device twice employed here for low laughs). Meanwhile, Ann-Margret, abetted by her girl friend, Donna (Place), after equally negative encounters with the opposite sex, takes up with a young sculptor, Doc (John Shea), and discovers what it's like to be attended to day and night. At the gym one day, Alda suffers a mild heart attack and ends up meeting a physician (Hamel) with whom he promptly falls in love. Hamel is a paragon of modern, gorgeous professionalism, and in no time the two are married. Things begin to sour, however, for Ann-Margret who realizes that 24-hour puppylike devotion was not what she had in mind for her new life. She breaks with Shea and throws herself happily into her new career as a teacher. After much argument, Alda gives in to Hamel's wish for a baby, but must then unwillingly deal with the challenge of contemporary conception (Lamaze classes, being present at the birth). At the eleventh hour, he rises to the joyous occasion and becomes a proud, fully cooperative Daddy.

The film is as cozily pat as its synopsis, and a viewer's eyes can begin to glaze over when confronted with the unceasing surge of cliches Alda doles out. Whatever real tensions or conflicts exist between him and his wives or forgotten daughter (Beatrice Alda) are either avoided entirely or resolved so facilely that even Neil Simon would blanch. Whatever his failings as a writer-director (including his characters' uniform Disneyesque blandness), Alda remains a likably intelligent performer. In a few scenes

with Hal Linden, he shows a rude abrasiveness that is a refreshing antidote to his Teddy-bear image, and he has a nice moment, hugging Hamel close, where he radiates the joyful wonder of newfound love. His character starts from a ridiculous premise, however. What kind of man could take any woman played by Ann-Margret for granted? From her debut as the musically precocious sex-kitten of BYE BYE BIRDIE and VIVA LAS VEGAS to her lovely maturation as a performer of wit and empathy in CARNAL KNOWLEDGE; TOMMY; and A TIGER'S TALE, she has evinced real growth. With a sketchily devised role that has her breaking out into nervous hives at the hint of any crisis, she nonetheless continues to exhibit that effulgent womanliness and quiet humor that make her the closest American equivalent of a Moreau or a Signoret (would that she had the roles!). Linden enlivens things no end with his scabrous, unashamedly macho Mel. His are the only lines in the film that approach satire and he hits those consonants like Dempsey. Hamel is attractive and competent as Kay, although it's a shame the script has her turning overnight from dream girl to petulant shrew. Mary Kay Place is wasted in yet another heroine's best buddy role, and John Shea struggles manfully with Doc, a character for whom Alda seems to have saved all of his bile. It's not enough that he has Doc turning Jackie off by being more protective than any five Jewish mothers; this young threat is unrelentingly callow as well, with his hideous sculptures and habit of rattling off I Ching/Tarot card insipidities at crucial moments in the plot.

Kelvin Pike's photography is glossily appropriate—a grittier approach would have exposed the Hollywood-ized view of adult behavior for the sham that it is. Adding to the general air of well-heeled unreality are the sets: Doc, supposedly a waiter struggling to support his art, enjoys a capacious Manhattan loft, while Kay reaps the benefits of a large rooftop garden overlooking Washington Square. Moreover, the score shrewdly uses classical music (Bach, Haydn) to propel the scenes along—the effect of all that violin-induced brio is at least minimally counteractive to boredom. A NEW LIFE is the type of movie one inevitably runs into aboard airplanes. (Profanity, adult situations.)

p, Martin Bregman; d, Alan Alda; w, Alan Alda; ph, Kelvin Pike (Medallion Color); ed, William Reynolds; m, Joseph Turrin; prod d, Barbara Dunphy; art d, Lucinda Zak; set d, Anthony Greco, Alan Hicks; cos, Mary McLeod.

Comedy/Romance   Cas.   (PR:C MPAA:PG-13)

NEW YORK'S FINEST zero   (1988) 86m Platinum c

Jennifer Delora (Loretta Michaels), Ruth Collins (Joy Sugarman), Heidi Paine (Carley Pointer), Scott Baker (Dougie), Jane Hamilton (Bunny), Alan Naggar (Fillmore), John Altamura (Brian Morrison), Alan Fisler (Tennison Alderman), Josey Duval (Papillion), Daniel Chapman (Wire), T. Boomer Tibbs (Boss), Harvey Siegel (Max), Russ Batt (Axel Witherspoon), Loretta Palma (Mrs. Flanagan), Rick Savage (Mr. Smith), Andy Anderson (Mr. Fullright), Murray Pilch (Mr. Walker), Miriam Zucker (Mrs. Rush), Frank Cole, Craig Derrick, Preston Cody (Cops), Gary Warner, Kurt Schwoebel (Detectives), Judy Wiener (Waitress), Rocky Dilorenzo, Houston B. Franklin (Hunks), Ken Marchinko (Host/Salesman), Karen Nielsen, Denise Torek, Catherine Shelter (Hookers), Mollie O'Mara (Salesgirl), James McCaffrey (Maitre d'), Christine Nicholson, April Hampton (Rabbits), Joey Mennonna, Richard Guide, Ryan Grayson, Adam Fried, John Pierce, Joseph Z. Pritchard (Band), Fabien Torek, Kim Gittens, Ute Hanna, Tasha Voux, Jill Amber, Karen Scabrini, Nicky Nite, Suzy London, Wendi Blot (Girls in Loft).

The tag line for this sex comedy reads, ". . . so funny it should be illegal," and after the first few minutes one wishes it actually were against the law, so that some sort of legal retribution awaited filmmaker Chuck Vincent. This one is so bad it makes ASSAULT OF THE KILLER BIMBOS look like THE WHALES OF AUGUST. Three no-class Queens hookers—Delora, Collins, and Paine—are tired of being harassed by the vice squad, so they enlist the aid of good friend Baker, a transvestite who gives them "lady lessons." After strenuous training that includes balancing books on their heads, reading from a dictionary, learning the names of California wines, and doing push-ups while topless, the trio shed their label as "hookers" and become "ladies." In their quest for millionaire husbands, they also rent a luxury apartment on the Upper East Side of Manhattan, are chauffeured around town in a limousine, purchase new wardrobes, and even adopt high-class names: Muffy, Tittles, and Poodle. However, when a former madame locates the threesome, they are forced to lead double lives, both turning tricks with sleazy johns and going out on the town with the elite. Things aren't what they seem among the upper class, though. One of the wealthy suitors is a sadomasochist with a torture chamber, another is just a doorman masquerading as a playboy, and the third has a domineering mother who won't agree to a wedding. To raise the money they need to pay off the blackmailing madame (porn star Veronica Hart, here billed as Jane Hamilton), they organize a high society fund-raising event to help fallen opera singers, calling it "Save the Divas." A police raid breaks up the festivities, and the real identities of Muffy, Tittles, and Poodle are revealed. Despite their pasts, however, the "ladies" still find three guys who want to marry them. Believe it or not, by the time this mess ends, a sense of morality creeps into the proceedings, although this is far from Bible Belt propaganda. There are a few redeeming moments here (Scott Baker's Carmen Miranda impersonation being the highlight), but to get to them one has to suffer through some of the most abrasive performances to ever reach the screen. (Nudity, profanity, sexual situations.)

p, Chuck Vincent; d, Chuck Vincent; w, Craig Horrall; ph, Larry Revene; ed, James Davalos, Marc Ubell; m, Joey Mennonna; art d, Mark Hammond; set d, Faizool Husain.

Comedy   Cas.   (PR:O MPAA:R)

NEWLYDEADS, THE † (1988) 77m City Lights c

Jim Williams, Jean Levine, Jay Richardson, Roxanna Michaels, Scott Kaske, Rebecca Barrington, Michael Springer, Michelle Smith, Doug Jones, Rene Way, Ron Preston.

One suspects that the title is the high point of this straight-to-video slasher movie centering on a cursed honeymoon hotel. It seems that 15 years previously the hotel's owner, Williams, unknowingly picked up a transvestite and took him back to his room for some fun and games. When Williams discovered that *she* was really a *he*, he flipped out and killed his companion, dumping the body in the lake. Now Williams plans to be married and the rotting corpse of the vengeful transvestite returns to wreak havoc on the wedding party.

p, Richard Pepin, Joseph Merhi; d, Joseph Merhi; w, Sean Dash, Joseph Merhi; ph, Richard Pepin; m, John Gonzalez; spec eff, Judy Yonemoto.

Horror **(PR:NR MPAA:NR)**

NIGHT BEFORE, THE † (1988) 85m Kings Road c

Keanu Reeves *(Winston Connelly)*, Lori Loughlin *(Tara Mitchell)*, Theresa Saldana *(Rhonda)*, Trinidad Silva *(Tito)*, Suzanne Snyder *(Lisa)*, Morgan Lofting *(Mom)*, Gwil Richards *(Dad)*, Chris Hebert *(Brother)*, Michael Greene *(Capt. Mitchell)*, Pamela Gordon *(Burly Waitress)*, David Sherrill *(Danny Boy)*, P-Funk All Stars *(Rat's Nest Band)*.

Although director Thom Eberhardt's WITHOUT A CLUE, featuring Michael Caine and Ben Kingsley, got all the attention in 1988, this low-budget effort he filmed back in 1986 also opened this year—albeit in only one theater in Minneapolis. A teenage sex comedy, THE NIGHT BEFORE features Keanu Reeves as a hapless young man who awakens with a powerful hangover and tries to piece together the previous night's events. In flashback, we see that he was to have taken Loughlin, the beautiful daughter of a police captain, to the school prom, but on the way, they get lost and wind up in the wrong part of town. Things only get worse, however, as Reeves accidentally sells Loughlin to an infamous pimp for $1,500, loses his virginity to a prostitute, and has to rescue his date and get her home before midnight, or face the service revolver of her father. Although Loughlin was forced into the date after losing a bet, her trying experience brings her closer to Reeves, with whom she falls in love. Obviously a likely candidate for home video.

p, Martin Hornstein; d, Thom Eberhardt; w, Gregory Scherick, Thom Eberhardt (based on a story by Scherick); ph, Ron Garcia; prod d, Michel Levesque.

Comedy **(PR:NR MPAA:PG)**

NIGHT IN THE LIFE OF JIMMY REARDON, A*** (1988) 92m Island/FOX c

River Phoenix *(Jimmy Reardon)*, Ann Magnuson *(Joyce Fickett)*, Meredith Salenger *(Lisa Bentwright)*, Ione Skye *(Denise Hunter)*, Louanne *(Suzie Middleberg)*, Matthew L. Perry *(Fred Roberts)*, Paul Koslo *(Al Reardon)*, Jane Hallaren *(Faye Reardon)*, Jason Court *(Mathew Hollander)*, James Deuter *(Linus Spaulding)*, Marji Banks *(Emma Spaulding)*, Margaret Moore *(Mrs. Bentwright)*, Anastasia Fielding *(Elaine)*, Kamie Harper *(Rosie Reardon)*, Johnny Galecki *(Toby Reardon)*, Melva Williams *(Maid)*, Regan Andreas *(Sailor Cap)*, E.J. Murray *(Alice)*, Mark Winsten *(Red Blazer)*, Jack McLaughlin-Gray *(Carnation)*, Craig Wright Huston *(Waiter)*, Kristin Weithas, Lisa Stodder *(Coffee House Girls)*, Kurt Bjorling, Alan Goldsher *(Musicians)*.

Unjustly ignored by the vast majority of the critics and public, who dismissed it as just another teenage sex comedy, A NIGHT IN THE LIFE OF JIMMY REARDON is yet another interesting film from writer-director William Richert (WINTER KILLS; THE AMERICAN SUCCESS CO.) whose sparse but brilliant output has doomed him to relative obscurity. Based on an autobiographical novel Richert wrote at age 19, the film is set circa 1962 in Evanston, a wealthy suburb north of Chicago, and follows 17-year-old Jimmy Reardon (Phoenix), a disarmingly shifty lad who fancies himself a romantic and beat poet, as he desperately tries to make some sense of life in his last summer before college. Under great pressure to attend his stern, working-class father's (Koslo) alma mater, a local all-boys business school, Phoenix has his own ideas and tries to scam a way to visit Hawaii with beautiful young socialite Salenger. Phoenix is obsessed with the girl and considers her his one true love, mainly because he hasn't gotten past second base with her. To raise money, the teenage lothario taps all the women he knows, including his sister; the eccentric, elderly mother of his boss; and his mother. Having scraped together the necessary funds, Phoenix types out a farewell note to his parents, but is interrupted as his mother introduces her friend Magnuson, an attractive divorcee whom his father despises. Told to drive Magnuson home in his father's beloved car, Phoenix winds up being seduced by the older woman. This escapade causes him to be late for a country club dance to which he was supposed to take Salenger, and he finds that she has gone without him, accompanied by Court, an upper-class BMOC of whom her parents approve. Phoenix crashes the swank party and spirits Salenger away from her date. She confesses that she has finally decided to lose her virginity to Phoenix, but he is unable to comply (because he just made love to Magnuson) and she storms back to the dance without him. Hooking up with another female friend, the incredibly wealthy and sardonic Middleberg, Phoenix learns that Court, who also fancies himself a poet, has deflowered most of the girls in their graduating class. Making a last-ditch attempt to steal Salenger back, Phoenix returns to the party and follows Court's reading of pretentious doggerel with a deliberately scandalous poem that angrily mocks the ruling-class crowd. Humiliated, Salenger leaves the party with Court, Phoenix gives chase, and, in a confrontation, the much larger Court beats Phoenix to a pulp and leaves him lying in the road. The depressed and frustrated Phoenix then drives his father's car into downtown Chicago and accidentally crashes it into an El platform. With no one to turn to, Phoenix phones Magnuson for help and realizes that his father is also having an affair with her. He then phones his dad and lets it be known that he is aware of the tryst. This little secret successfully placates his father, who comes downtown to pick Phoenix up. When father and son come face to face, a new understanding between them develops and they ride back home on the elevated together in silence, with Phoenix vowing to himself to try and please his father more often—maybe. A NIGHT IN THE LIFE OF JIMMY REARDON is a film with much more on its mind than the juvenile pranks and drooling titillation found in the youth-oriented epics with which it has been compared. Basing his film on his novel *Aren't You Ever Gonna Kiss Me Goodbye?* writer-director Richert seems to have resisted the temptation to impose a more adult perspective on material he wrote when still a teen. Richert does a fine job capturing the alienation, confusion, and desperation that can follow high school, as well as the very real class distinctions that begin to define students' future—with some bound for Harvard, others for community college—upon their graduation from a public school where the children of the wealthy and the working class intermingle. Richert also continues to explore adversarial father-son relationships, a theme which has marked his other work, and, since the material is autobiographical, it may be assumed that this film indicates how the seeds of his obsession were sown.

Set in a diverse community where the very rich reside alongside the lower middle class and poor, JIMMY REARDON vividly conveys the class struggle between status seekers like Phoenix's character's father and the old-money rich, who really have nothing but contempt for his type. Phoenix realizes that no matter how hard his father works, he will never be accepted by the social elite (Middleberg even remarks to Phoenix's rich friend Perry that the former's family will never be accepted because they haven't lived in Evanston for three generations), but Phoenix himself attempts to insinuate himself into their world by seducing the daughters of wealth. Unfortunately, he doesn't see until the end of the film that the girls treat him like the kitchen help, and will use him to satiate desires unfulfilled by their spineless men (such as Perry) but never really accept him as an equal. This realization finally dawns on Phoenix when he is given the chance to capture his obsession—Salenger's virginity—and can't perform. He always thought that he was using the women, when, in reality, the opposite was true. This dawning of self-awareness is reenforced when Phoenix learns of his father's affair and finally begins to understand that his father hides his vulnerabilities behind a jumble of resentment, frustration, and rage. In the end both father and son seem to realize how similar they are—not because they have slept with the same woman, but because they, as Richert puts it in his notes on the film, "are subject to the same limitations and desires." Through the disastrous events of 36 hours, both Phoenix and his father realize that they are not alone, not outsiders, for they are cut from the same mold, are blood, and have each other. Although Phoenix's character winds up with nothing at the end, Richert doesn't show this as a defeat. On the contrary, he seems to endorse the fight, not for acceptance by the rich, but for carving out your own niche. By finally accepting who he is and moving forward with that knowledge, Phoenix can heed the words he reads on a billboard: "Nothing is beyond you."

As in THE AMERICAN SUCCESS CO. and WINTER KILLS, Richert is able to combine his superior narrative sense with solid visuals and good direction of actors. River Phoenix is quite good as Jimmy Reardon, although some have complained that the character is self-centered and unlikable. When one considers that the film is highly personal, told from a teenager's perspective, and concerns a search for identity, however, it must be conceded that the character cannot appear to be anything but self-absorbed. It is to young Phoenix's credit that he nonetheless makes Jimmy sufficiently compelling and sympathetic, rather than succumbing to the self-satisfied smugness of Matthew Broderick in FERRIS BUELLER'S DAY OFF. Paul Koslo, as Jimmy's father, is marvelous, a barely suppressed bundle of frustration trying to claw his way to the top while hiding his deepest feelings from his family. The climactic scene between father and son—almost entirely without dialog—is skillfully played and wonderfully nuanced. Also excellent is Ann Magnuson as the woman who undergoes a quiet moral dilemma before deciding to sleep with the much younger Phoenix, while Louanne, as Jimmy's sardonic rich friend Suzie Middleberg, almost steals the film. There is one weak link in the cast, however, namely Meredith Salenger as Lisa. A competent actress, Salenger just doesn't quite ring true as the confused socialite torn between her physical attraction to Phoenix and the realities of her upbringing. Her line readings seem somewhat vague and are not quite convincing.

All of Richert's films have been concerned about American wealth, status, and power, and A NIGHT IN THE LIFE OF JIMMY REARDON is no exception. As with most successful semiautobiographical works, it also provides a fascinating glimpse into what created the artist's perspective, and—as is the case with all of Richert's films—it deserves to find an audience. The use of period music on the soundtrack is pleasingly restrained, and includes the songs "Shop Around" (William Robinson, Berry Gordy, performed by Smokey Robinson and the Miracles), "I Know" (Barbara George, performed by George), "Just One Look" (Doris Payne, Gregory Carroll, performed by Doris Troy), "Goodnight, It's Time to Go" (James "Pookie" Hudson, Calvin Carter, performed by The Spaniels), "Theme from 'A Summer Place'" (Max Steiner, performed by Percy Faith and his Orchestra), "You're the One (That I Adore)" (Deadric Malone, performed by Bobby Bland), "He's So Fine" (Ronald Mack, performed by The Chiffons), "The Adventures of Robin Hood" (Erich Wolfgang Korngold, performed by the Utah Symphony Orchestra), "Chances Are" (Al Stillman, Robert Allen, performed by Johnny Mathis), "Wiggle Wobble" (Les Cooper, performed by Cooper), "Saved" (Jerry Lieber, Mike Stoller, performed by LaVern Baker), "I'm Not Afraid to Say Goodbye" (Elmer Bernstein, Don Black, performed by Johnny Mathis), "I'm a Man" (Bo Diddley, performed by Diddley), "Green Onions" (Steve Cropper, Louis Steinberg, Al Jackson, Jr., Booker T. Jones, performed by Booker T. and the MGs), "Boom Boom" (John Lee Hooker, performed by Hooker). *(Adult situations, sexual situations, violence, profanity.)*

p, Russell Schwartz; d, William Richert; w, William Richert (based on his novel *Are't You Even Gonna Kiss Me Goodbye?*); ph, John Connor (Metrocolor); ed, Suzanne Fenn; m, Bill Conti; m/l, Erich Wolfgang Korngold, Elmer Bernstein, Don Black, Doris Payne, Gregory Carroll, Bo Diddley, Deadric Malone, Steve Cropper, Louis Steinberg, Al Jackson, Jr., Booker T. Jones, Les Cooper, John Lee Hooker; prod d, Norman Newberry; art d, John R. Jensen; set d, Hilton Rosemarin; spec eff, Curtiss Smith; cos, Robert de Mora; ch, Bobby Wells; stunts, Rick Lefevour; makeup, Rodger Jacobs.

| Comedy | Cas. | (PR:O MPAA:R) |

NIGHT OF THE DEMONS †   (1988) 89m Meridian-Paragon Arts/Intl. Film Marketing c

Lance Fenton *(Jay)*, Cathy Podewell *(Judy)*, Alvin Alexis *(Roger)*, Hal Havins *(Stooge)*, Mimi Kinkade *(Angela)*, Linnea Quigley *(Suzanne)*, Phillip Tanzini *(Max)*, Jill Terashita *(Fran)*, Allison Barron *(Helen)*, William Gallo *(Sal)*, Donnie Jeffcoat *(Billy)*.

NIGHT OF THE DEMONS is more low-budget horror from the gang that created the better-than-average-for-this-sort-of-thing WITCHBOARD (1987), this time taking place at an abandoned funeral home said to be haunted. A group of teens gather at the site on Halloween night for fun and games, but get more than they bargain for after two of the girls, Kinkade and Quigley, hold a seance that sends them into the pit of hell. Possessed by a vicious demon, the two girls return to the party and wreak havoc on their friends. NIGHT OF THE DEMONS received a scant city-by-city release late in 1988—beating Tri-Star's THE KISS at the box office in Los Angeles——and will probably do well on home video and cable.

p, Joe Augustyn; d, Kevin S. Tenney; w, Joe Augustyn; ph, David Lewis; ed, Daniel Duncan; m, Dennis Michael Tenney; art d, Ken Aichele; set d, Sally Nicolav; cos, Donna Reynolds; stunts, John Stuart; makeup, Steve Johnson.

| Horror | | (PR:NR MPAA:R) |

NIGHT VISION †   (1988) 100m Prism-Flash c

Stacy Carson, Shirley Ross, Tony Carpenter, Ellie Martins, Stacy Shane, Tom Henry, Glenn Reed.

This direct-to-video horror entry offers Stacy Carson as a would-be writer from Kansas who ventures to Denver to ply his trade. Since writing jobs are scarce, he takes a job in a video store and falls in love with coworker Ross. Their romance is interrupted, however, when a stolen VCR containing a tape made by a satanic cult somehow takes possession of Carson, turning him into a crazed killer.

p, Sarah Liles-Olson, Douglas Olson; d, Michael Krueger; w, Nancy Gallanis, Leigh Pomeroy, Michael Krueger; ph, Jim Kelley; ed, Jonathan Moser; m, Bob Drake, Ron Miles, Eric Jacobson.

| Horror | Cas. | (PR:NR MPAA:NR) |

NIGHT ZOO**   (1988, Can.) 115m Cinema Plus-Les Productions Oz c

Roger Le Bel *(Albert)*, Gilles Maheu *(Marcel)*, Lynne Adams *(Julie)*, Lorne Brass *(Georges)*, Germain Houde *(Charlie)*, Jerry Snell.

A much-heralded Canadian picture from first-time director Lauzon which sets a father-son relationship against a glossy backdrop of Quebec's criminal underworld. Maheu, a former drug dealer for a corrupt cop Houde, emerges from prison after a two-year stint. The night before his release, however, a homosexual prisoner rapes Maheu on orders from Houde. The rape is a warning to Maheu, who, before beginning his term, skimmed $200,000 and a cache of cocaine from Houde. The money is safely hidden away in Maheu's uncle's restaurant, but when Maheu goes to retrieve it, he finds it missing. The money is later returned to Maheu by his father, Le Bel, an old man with a heart condition who has kept the loot out of Houde's reach. Le Bel, whose wife has just left him, wants nothing more than to be reunited with his son. He dreams of going fishing and hunting like a father and his son should. Houde, who is now partnered with the sadistic homosexual Brass, keeps a close watch on Maheu, threatening to harm his father and his former girl friend, Adams, if the missing cash doesn't surface. Maheu then pays a visit to Adams, a leather-clad punk, whom he violently makes love to on a rooftop before riding off into the night on his motorcycle. In an effort to renew his relationship with his father, Maheu takes him on a fishing trip. Drifting on a placid, fog-shrouded lake, father and son strengthen their bond—fishing, making moose calls, and sharing laughs. For Le Bel's birthday, Maheu buys a hunting rifle and promises to take his father moose hunting. In the meantime, Maheu has been pressured by Houde and Brass into paying back the money after the pair nearly kill Adams in the peep show booth where she works. Maheu, however, outsmarts the cops and guns down both of them in a seedy sex motel. In the meantime, Le Bel has a heart attack and is hospitalized. Rather than forget about the hunting trip, Maheu arrives at his father's bedside with a movie projector. He blows some cocaine up his father's nose and together they watch a super-8 wilderness film of a moose. If that isn't enough excitement for one night, Maheu puts his father in a wheelchair, arms him with his hunting rifle, and takes him to the nearest zoo. Since this zoo doesn't have a

moose, the ecologically minded father and son decide to bag an elephant. Later, Le Bel's condition worsens, leaving Maheu to care for him. Le Bel then dies happily, having regained the devotion of his son. Carried by its highly polished visual style, NIGHT ZOO is a brutal, misanthropic, sleazy crime film which is only made worthwhile by the heartfelt and somewhat sappy father-son relationship that offsets the violence. NIGHT ZOO attempts to show the contradictions of a nasty character who survives in a dangerous world, yet has very human and gentle feelings towards his father. Unfortunately, the film doesn't reach the level of complexity that one hopes it would, failing to capture the more profound ambiguity of Coppola's GODFATHER films. The seedy underbelly of Quebec that is exposed is no different from that captured in countless other flashy crime films of late, from DIVA to SUBWAY to 1987's dazzling Canadian entry BLIND TRUST (POUVOIR INTIME)—sadistic, perverse, and essentially one-dimensional. In NIGHT ZOO's criminal universe all the men are super macho, wearing tight blue jeans and leather jackets, flashing their big guns and riding down the street on their even bigger motorcycles. Along with all this macho posing comes a built-in misogyny that is directed at Adams, the only woman in the film. Apparently her only purpose in life is to be physically, verbally, sexually, and emotionally abused by every man she meets. What separates NIGHT ZOO from other films in this league is the parallel father-son story. Although director Lauzon seems content to fill his criminal world with cliches, he treats the father-son relationship with some heart. Le Bel's character is a truly sympathetic one who will do anything to impress his son. He is a beaten man who has been deserted by his wife, ignored by his relatives, and victimized by his ailing heart. However, just when Lauzon gains audience sympathy (in the hospital scene), he resorts to the pathetic (but supposedly funny) scene in which Maheu blows cocaine into his father's nose, nearly choking the already weak-hearted man. The two then become thoroughly reprehensible when they proceed to the zoo and kill an elephant. While these scenes could have meant something had they explored the pathetic qualities of the two characters, they instead are played for laughs. Along with I'VE HEARD THE MERMAIDS SINGING, NIGHT ZOO has attracted a great deal of attention, continuing to arouse an interest in Canadian cinema which reached a high point in 1987 with Denys Arcand's THE DECLINE OF THE AMERICAN EMPIRE, Anne Wheeler's LOYALTIES, and Leon Marr's DANCING IN THE DARK. (In French and English; English subtitles). *(Violence, sexual situations, substance abuse.)*

p, Roger Frappier, Pierre Gendron; d, Jean-Claude Lauzon; w, Jean-Claude Lauzon; ph, Guy Dufaux; ed, Michel Arcand; m, Jean Corriveau; set d, Michele Forest; cos, Andree Morin.

| Crime | Cas. | (PR:O MPAA:NR) |

NIGHTFALL †   (1988) 80m Concorde c

David Birney *(Aton)*, Sarah Douglas *(Roa)*, Alexis Kanner *(Sar)*, Andra Millian *(Ana)*, Starr Andreeff *(Bet)*.

Concorde Pictures gave this adaptation of an Issac Asimov short story the ultralow-budget treatment and a scant regional release before consigning it to home video. Set on a faraway planet in a three-sun solar system, NIGHTFALL introduces us to a culture on which the sun literally never sets. A blind seer (Kanner), however, forecasts that night *will* soon fall on the planet, and his prediction is confirmed by astronomer Birney. Fearing that a period of massive death and destruction will commence with the coming of night, the populace divides into two camps—the ritualistic and irrational, led by Kanner, and the Birney-led survivalists, who plan to live underground until daylight returns. When Birney's wife (Douglas) joins the rival faction, he becomes smitten with a mysterious and sexy young woman (Millian) who has appeared from out of the desert. As a result his leadership ability wavers and the future of the planet is jeopardized. Adapted and directed by Paul Mayersberg, who wrote Nicolas Roeg's THE MAN WHO FELL TO EARTH and directed the strange British film CAPTIVE.

p, Julie Corman; d, Paul Mayersberg; w, Paul Mayersberg (based on a story by Isaac Asimov); ph, Darlusz Wolski; ed, Brent Schoenfeld; m, Frank Serafine; art d, Carol Bosselman.

| Science Fiction | Cas. | (PR:NR MPAA:PG-13) |

NIGHTMARE ON ELM STREET 4: THE DREAM MASTER, A**½   (1988) 93m New Line-Heron-Smart Egg/New Line c

Robert Englund *(Freddy Krueger)*, Rodney Eastman *(Joey)*, Danny Hassel *(Danny)*, Andras Jones *(Rick)*, Tuesday Knight *(Kristen)*, Toy Newkirk *(Sheila)*, Ken Sagoes *(Kincaid)*, Brooke Theiss *(Debbie)*, Lisa Wilcox *(Alice)*, Brooke Bundy *(Kristen's Mother)*, Jeff Levine *(Paramedic)*, Nicolas Mele *(Johnson)*, Hope Marie Carlton *(Waterbed Bunny)*.

Although this latest installment in the series broke the box office record set by the previous NIGHTMARE entry ($12,833,403 for the first three days—the most successful opening weekend of any independently released film), it seems that with part four, Freddy Krueger has just about run out of gas. Getting further and further away from creator Wes Craven's original concept, the series has declined into a plotless series of special effects set pieces featuring Freddy slicing and dicing a variety of teenagers in their dreams. Luckily, New Line Cinema's CEO, Robert Shayne, has avoided some of the pitfalls of this approach by drafting strong young directors who have superb visual sense. What the films lack in narrative they make up for with pure cinematic panache. The latest installment is no exception; Finnish director Renny Harlin (PRISON) contributes what may be the best-directed NIGHTMARE film since Craven's. Picking up where part three left off, we see the teenage Dream Warriors (Eastman, Sagoes, and Knight—the last replacing Patricia Arquette, who played the role in the previous film) suddenly being plagued in their dreams by the supposedly dead and buried Krueger (Englund). In a rather unconvincing resurrection scene, Englund rises from the grave and makes quick work of the three surviving Dream Warriors. Having finally dispatched all the children of the parents who murdered him years before (check out the original film for all the details), Englund moves on to new territory by invading the dreams of mousy teen Wilcox. Englund is able to snare fresh teens when Wilcox unwittingly includes her brother and friends in her nightmares. What the child-killer doesn't anticipate, however, is that after he kills them, Wilcox begins taking on the strongest characteristics of her friends and soon becomes a complete Dream Warrior blessed with the impressive athletic prowess of her brother (Jones), the strength of her bodybuilder friend Theiss, and the intelligence of straight-A pal Newkirk. She eventually comes face to face with Englund in her dreams, and the two fight to the death in a deserted old church. Just as it looks as if she will be added to the list of Englund's victims, Wilcox remembers a nursery rhyme that states that evil cannot face itself. Quickly, she grabs a piece of stained glass and holds it before Englund. Catching a glimpse of himself in the reflection, Englund writhes in horror and reels backward. Suddenly the arms, legs, and heads of all the teenage souls he had consumed come bursting forth out of his body, tearing him to shreds. As the spirits of the teens vaporize and soar toward the heavens, all that is left of Englund are his tattered clothes, slouch hat, and taloned glove.

In the original A NIGHTMARE ON ELM STREET, Freddy Krueger was the embodiment of pure evil. Since then his appearance and behavior have been softened by New Line to make him more of a cartoon figure—still very lethal, but less threatening, more playful. What was once the ultimate, unforgiving horror has now become the real hero of the series. The guy teens love to hate. The edge is gone from Freddy and what we are left with is a wisecracking psycho who appears to be a cross between the Terminator and Bruce Willis—and who is now seen in the daytime almost as often as at night. This shift in the series has not been lost on actor Robert Englund, who has played Freddy in every film. Although the character has catapulted him to stardom, he has expressed dismay at the disintegration of Wes Craven's concept and has hinted about taking a break from the series, knowing full well that New Line probably wouldn't hesitate to replace him. Which brings us to the basic problem of the NIGHTMARE series: it has become an extremely lucrative, money-making industry—the glue that holds New Line Cinema together. Therefore, it must become more middle-of-the-road, tamer, more able to reach across genre barriers and attract people who don't necessarily like horror films. And that is why, with each entry, the films become more removed from their source. Freddy just isn't scary anymore. We are left then, to marvel at the handiwork of a talented crew of special effects people under the guidance of a director who may some day prove himself to be a major talent. With his impressive, creative, and offbeat camera moves and his flawless sense of space, composition, and rhythm, Harlin is certainly an interesting director. There are several unforgettable sequences in NIGHTMARE 4, including scenes of a kid who is drowned in the depths of his waterbed, the life literally being sucked out of a girl, a pizza covered with the tiny faces of previous victims, and a girl being turned into a cockroach. One of the most remarkable also happens to be an *hommage* to Buster Keaton's classic SHERLOCK, JR. (1924), as Wilcox is pulled from a movie theater audience and into the screen, where she is seamlessly integrated into the black and white movie being shown. Harlin's grasp of the medium is tight, but the script (which went through a small army of writers) throws narrative development and logic to the wind, using the passages between nightmares as mere breathers, rather than developing the concept or characters any further. With PART 4 it is obvious that the series has run its course. This does not mean that the series will end, however—just look at how long the FRIDAY THE 13TH films have droned on. Luckily, the Freddy films have always been more interesting than the Jason movies, but if the series continues on this path, Freddy will soon become as big a joke as the guy in the hockey mask. It's a shame that Wes Craven lost control of the series. *(Graphic violence, gore effects, nudity, substance abuse, profanity.)*

p, Robert Shaye, Rachel Talalay; d, Renny Harlin; w, Scott Pierce, Brian Helgeland (based on a story by William Kotzwinkle, Brian Helgeland); ph, Steven Fierberg; ed, Michael N. Knue, Chuck Weiss; m, Craig Safan; md, Kevin Benson; prod d, Mick Strawn, C.J. Strawn; art d, Thomas A. O'Conor; spec eff, Jim Doyle; cos, Audrey Bansmer; makeup, Kevin Yeager, Steve Johnson, Magical Media Industries, Screaming Mad George, R. Christopher Biggs.

Horror   Cas.   (PR:O MPAA:R)

NIGHTWARS †   (1988) 88m Action Intl. c

Brian O'Connor *(Trent Matthews)*, Dan Haggerty, Cameron Smith, Steve Horton, Chet Hood, Jill Foor, Mike Hickam, David Ott, Kimberley Casey.

Apparently a combination of A NIGHTMARE ON ELM STREET 3 and PLATOON, this low-budget feature played the Times Square circuit before turning up on home video. O'Connor and Smith are Vietnam veterans suffering from nightmares that propel them back into the jungle. Racked with guilt for having left a buddy behind, the duo relive that horror every night, then awake to find the wounds suffered in their nightmares have appeared on their bodies. When they turn to vet-turned-psychiatrist Haggerty for help, O'Connor and Smith are scoffed at and sedated. This time nightmare machine-gun fire kills O'Connor's wife, and Haggerty finally takes notice. Determined to end the terror, O'Connor and Smith don their uniforms and arm themselves to do battle with their demons in dreamland.

p, Fritz Matthews; d, David A. Prior; w, David A. Prior; ph, Stephen Ashley Blake; ed, Reinhard Schreiner; m, Tim James, Steve McClintick, Mark Mancina.

Horror/War   Cas.   (PR:NR MPAA:R)

1969**   (1988) 90m Atlantic c

Robert Downey Jr. *(Ralph)*, Kiefer Sutherland *(Scott)*, Bruce Dern *(Cliff)*, Mariette Hartley *(Jessie)*, Winona Ryder *(Beth)*, Joanna Cassidy *(Ev)*, Christopher Wynne *(Alden)*, Keller Kuhn *(Marsha)*, Steve Foster.

Telling a story of teenagers opposed to the Vietnam War and their parents during that pivotal year in recent American history, 1969 captures only the anguish of a nation in conflict and little of the passion or hope that set off a social revolution. As the movie opens, college sophomores Downey and Sutherland hitchhike home in time to see Wynne, Sutherland's Marine brother, shipped off to Vietnam. Later, their mothers (Hartley and Cassidy) and Downey's sister (Ryder) visit them at school, where they watch as student protestors take over a campus building in what turns into a violent confrontation with police. When one bloodied demonstrator falls on Ryder, her consciousness is raised. She protests the war in the valedictory speech at her high school graduation, but is upstaged by the acid-tripping Downey, who runs amok through the auditorium in his underwear. Ryder replaces her brother as Sutherland's traveling partner after Downey is imprisoned for breaking into the draft office. They head for the Canadian border, then decide to return home and continue the fight instead of running away. Upon returning, their first deed is to lead a march to the local jail to demand Downey's release.

Apparently operating on the premise that a movie about the Vietnam era is bound to be profound, writer-director Ernest Thompson neglects to give much depth to the characters or action of 1969. The result is a downbeat tale of rebellion and the generation gap—a surprising failure for Thompson, who was responsible for the poignant family drama ON GOLDEN POND. It's tough to take issue with a film "dedicated to peace," as the narrator says 1969 is, but it's also tough to care a lot about the characters without knowing more about them. The audience is expected to do so merely on the basis of the youngsters' noble ideals, since their development is weak and muddled. Downey, defined only by his near-obsessive fear of being drafted, is so confused he can't decide whether to hit the road or run back to Mom. Wild and irreverent, he chooses the most peculiar times to submit to authority, virtually turning himself in to the police. The parents have nothing but superficial personalities that demand no more of the actors than scowling (Dern) and giggling (Cassidy). Hartley, the most glum of all, is apparently disturbed by her older son's departure for Vietnam, but, puzzlingly, goes for a jog instead of accompanying him to the bus station and can muster only the advice, "Don't die," for a farewell.

Incidents that might otherwise stir emotion, such as the love story between Sutherland and Ryder, are overly predictable. In the first conversation in the movie, Sutherland laments his virginity—so that as soon as you see Ryder's smiling face, you know they're destined for that romantic night beneath the stars. Sutherland and Ryder do make an appealing couple, but a romantic comedy would take more advantage of their charm. One of the few laughs in 1969 is provided in a seaside nudist colony visited by Downey and Sutherland. Questioning Downey's desire to go home, Sutherland reminds him, "We have naked people giving us free food!"

1969 does capture the look and sound of the era well. The costumes and art design lend authenticity, while the soundtrack offers up vintage Jimi Hendrix, Creedence Clearwater Revival, and Moody Blues, among others. Unfortunately, the movie's gloominess outweighs its nostalgia or commentary. *(Profanity, nudity, substance abuse.)*

p, Daniel Grodnik; p, Bill Badalato; d, Ernest Thompson; w, Ernest Thompson; ph, Jules Brenner; ed, William Anderson; m, Michael Small; md, Jolene Cherry; prod d, Marcia Hinds; art d, Bo Johnson; set d, Jan K. Bergstrom; cos, Julie Weiss.

Drama   (PR:C MPAA:R)

NOCE IN GALILEE   (SEE: WEDDING IN GALILEE, 1988, Bel./Fr.)

NOT OF THIS EARTH*   (1988) 80m Concorde c

Traci Lords *(Nadine Story)*, Arthur Roberts *(The Alien)*, Lenny Juliano *(Jeremy)*, Ace Mask *(Dr. Rochelle)*, Roger Lodge *(Harry)*, Michael Delano *(Vacuum Cleaner Salesman)*, Rebecca Perle *(Alien Woman)*, Cynthia Thompson, Becky LeBeau.

As a pair of lovers start to get passionate in a parked car at the beginning of NOT OF THIS EARTH, a man (Roberts) dressed in a suit, wearing sunglasses, and carrying a metal suitcase appears. He kills the male, then removes his glasses to reveal two fluorescent eyeballs, the sight of which immediately kills the woman. The killer then attaches a device to her neck and begins removing her blood. Next, we see Roberts entering a doctor's office and demanding that the nurse, Lords, give him a blood transfusion. Lords says he'll have to be tested first, and ushers him in to see the doctor (Mask). Mask reiterates Lords' admonition, but Roberts uses telepathic powers to force the doctor to provide the transfusion, then gets Mask to agree to allow Lords to move into Roberts' house and regularly provide him with transfusions. Though her police officer boy friend (Lodge) doesn't much like the arrangement, Lords takes up residence in Roberts' house, where she meets his man-servant, Juliano. Roberts, locked in his room, takes a camera-like device from his bureau and points it at the wall. A bearded man in front of a long neon tunnel appears, and, as he and Roberts talk, it is revealed that Roberts is from a distant planet where years of nuclear war have led to rampant radioactivity, which is killing off inhabitants by destroying their blood cells. Roberts has come to Earth to see if the blood of Earthlings is compatible with that of his people, hence the need for transfusions. He is also sending samples of blood back to his planet for study, and, in order to obtain more study samples, has to find some more humans to kill and drain. Among his victims are a trio of prostitutes and a persistent vacuum cleaner salesman, all done in by the alien's withering stare. In the meantime, Lords finds Roberts' strange behavior suspicious and she and

Juliano start snooping around, looking for incriminating evidence. One night Roberts has another visitor from the neon tunnel, this time a blonde female, who tells him she left their planet because the situation had become even more desperate. She is also in need of blood and Roberts takes her to Mask's office, where he mistakenly give her a transfusion of blood contaminated with rabies. The female alien then goes on a murder spree, brutally killing some punkers and a woman out for a walk before dying herself. Lords somehow connects the death to Roberts and she and Juliano begin searching the house in earnest for clues to Roberts' identity. They are interrupted by Roberts, who kills Juliano with "the look," then chases Lords, threatening to send her back to his planet as a specimen for study. Lodge shows up and begins pursuing Roberts, turning on the siren on his police motorcycle. The piercing wail of the siren is something Roberts can't stand and, as he tries to cover his ears, his car crashes and he is killed. In the final scene another man appears, wearing a suit and sunglasses and carrying a metal suitcase in the cemetery where Roberts is buried, as "The End?" appears on screen.

NOT OF THIS EARTH was billed as a science-fiction satire—which, in this case, apparently meant the filmmakers didn't have the imagination to make a true science-fiction film or the wit to make a comedy. The science-fiction component of the amalgam is pretty lame (SF plots don't come any less original than aliens visiting Earth because their own planet has become inhospitable), and the special effects are limited to Roberts' fluorescent eyeballs when he turns on the look that kills. For comedy, the filmmakers rely on tired references to Elvis and Jim and Tammy Bakker and on a strip-o-gram bimbo who disrobes at the wrong house because she misreads the address. Traci Lords is on hand primarily to display her body, while Arthur Roberts has little to do but hide behind sunglasses and speak with that clipped dialog aliens always seem to favor. Lenny Juliano is the film's one bright spot, displaying timing and delivery that deserve a chance to shine in a more ambitious project. Overall, NOT OF THIS EARTH is a rather abysmal offering, and one hopes the question mark appended at the end of the film doesn't indicate a planned sequel. *(Nudity, profanity, sexual situations, gore effects.)*

p, Jim Wynorski, Murray Miller; d, Jim Wynorski; w, R.J. Robertson, Jim Wynorski (based on the original script by Charles B. Griffith, Mark Hanna); ph, Zoran Hochstatter (Foto-Kem Color); ed, Kevin Tent; art d, Hayden Yates; cos, Libby Jacobs.

Science Fiction/Comedy　　　　　**Cas.**　　　　　**(PR:O MPAA:R)**

NOT SINCE CASANOVA**　　　　(1988) 80m Owen-Thompson Prod. c

Charles Solomon *(Prepski Morris)*, Diana Frank *(Gina)*, Tomi Griffin *(Tommi)*, Leslie Mitts *(Laurie)*, Lucy Winn *(Denise Harrington)*, Karen Smith *(Serina Skelly)*, Kare N. Marcus *(Hilary)*, Robyn Reichek *(Lorna Doom)*, Erol Landis *(Jeff)*, Doug Self *(Teen Prepski)*, Dr. Klaus Hoppe *(Prepski's Analyst)*, Burt Auerbach, M.D. *(Prepski's Doctor)*, Trevor LaPresle *(Young Prepski)*, Gavin Hamilton *(Prepski's Father)*, Andrea Summerstein *(Prepski's Mother)*, Shannon Lloyd *(Champagne Customer)*, James Hole, Diana Becronis *(Schoolmates)*, Linda Cervon *(Guidance Counselor)*, Leota Thomas *(Dreamland Artist)*, Marc Davis *(Roy Francis)*, Bodie Plecas *(Mike)*, Kevin LaPresle *(Kevin)*, Jeff Zabludoff *(Dave)*, Anne Cheetham *(Jeff's Wife)*, Marciella Cervon, Lorraine Graham, Judith Harding *(Fantasy Lovers)*, Susanne Gilmore *(ULTRA Leader)*, Tessa Gaynor *(Mrs. Harrington)*, Benjamin Snedeker, Ashley Snedeker, Kiersten Phipps, Molly Phipps, Tyler Phipps *(Hilary's Children)*, Marvin Ramos *(Marvin)*, Harry Sabin *(Dreamland Narrator)*, Claudia Cordic, Maria Passantino *(Prepski's Father's Floozies)*, Mary Mitchell *(Voice of Ophelia Grimm)*, Ian Mitchell *(Voice of TV Station Manager)*.

NOT SINCE CASANOVA is the tale of Prepski Morris, a young man who refuses to accept adult responsibilities, especially romantic commitment. Young Prepski grows up "when Eden was in suburbia," the product of a broken marriage between a champagne salesman and a June Cleaver-style mom who dresses him in a Peter Pan outfit and promises he'll never have to grow up. His two great passions are rocket ships and a local amusement park called "Dreamland" (read Disneyland) created by master animator Davis. The teenage Prepski (Self) discovers a third interest—girls—in the person of Smith, a sweet Annette Funicello-look-alike who sits enthralled as Self narrates the wonders of rocket mechanics. (Their first kiss takes place before the phallic image of the Mercury lift-off on a TV screen, as John F. Kennedy's voice proclaims, "We choose to go to the moon!") Smith loses Self when he goes to work for his idol, Davis, at Dreamland; in voice-over, she tells us she never saw him again. When the *audience* next sees Prepski, he's 30ish, and played by Solomon. At a party, he meets Griffin, a sexy aerobics instructor; Winn, a rich Total Woman who spearheads a "Ladies Against Women" crusade; and Reichek, an overly made-up "spinster" at 30, desperate to catch a husband. Solomon dates all three (lured by the prospects of "physically fit" sex, wealth and power, and Mom-style homemaking, respectively), but although they all fall for him, he finds each lacking (he's worried about catching AIDS from Griffin; intimidated by Winn's iron will and oversexed mother; and turned off by Reichek, who serves him tater tots and Green Giant succotash for dinner in her hideously kitschy home). He much prefers to sit in his apartment glutted with 60s memorabilia and commune with his ideal girl (Frank), a blonde fantasy who adores him unreservedly and, being a creature of his imagination, makes no demands. Solomon swears off women in favor of meditation in the forest, but as soon as he arrives in the woods he meets Mitts and then Marcus, an ex-hippie earth mother with whom he builds a yurt. Soon Solomon is juggling *five* women (not counting Frank), feeling alternately enticed and threatened by them while refusing to admit to himself that he is falling in love with Mitts. As his analyst informs him, Solomon is suffering from the "Peter Pan Syndrome" (also known as the "Casanova Complex"), born of a sense of inadequacy, in which the over-idealized *Self* seeks out the over-idealized *Other* in a narcissistic search for perfect, no-catches fulfillment. Indeed, Solomon is so insecure about his feelings that he can't express his love for Mitts to her face, although he gets it down on tape so she can hear it later through headphones. After a final dream sequence in which Griffin, Marcus, Reichek, Smith, and Winn offer Solomon a Faustian contract (he gets to keep them all, plus the grand prize of Frank made flesh, if he gives up Mitts), culminating in a partially animated vision of the menage, Solomon finally does the mature thing and marries Mitts—though not without a note of wistfulness. The film ends as it began: with the image of Solomon and all his women traipsing hand in hand through a meadow, silhouetted against a purple sunset.

In his first feature film, Brett Thompson, NOT SINCE CASANOVA's director-screenwriter-coeditor, presents Prepski Morris' predicament with an assured pace and a flair for employing pop-culture images to tell this pop-culture child's story. Mixing documentary techniques (one of a number of superficial resemblances the film bears to Spike Lee's far superior SHE'S GOTTA HAVE IT), cinematic references and cliches, and visual pastiche (the fantasy final temptation combines elements of 60s TV animation and commercials, "The Wonderful World of Disney," Vargas pinups, and "Lifestyles of the Rich and Famous"), Thompson draws viewers fully into Solomon's Peter Pan mentality. Unfortunately, Thompson—a California kid who hung around the Disney studios as a teen, received a Disney fellowship to study film at Cal Arts, and lists Steven Spielberg and Robert Wise as his cinematic heroes—is entirely *too* sympathetic to his would-be eternal youth's point of view. NOT SINCE CASANOVA exemplifies as much as it portrays Solomon's immaturity, and ultimately allows its shallow protagonist to have his cake and eat it too. Solomon's sexist, reductive views of women are hardly challenged—of his "seven beauties," only locker-room pal Griffin even approaches realistic characterization, while Reichek's Lorna Doom is a particularly cruel caricature, right down to her sophomoric character name. True, Mitts chides Solomon's photos of his girl friends as "sexist" and sarcastically likens his apartment to the Smithsonian. But it's not long before she too has succumbed to Solomon's charm and sits happily listening to him talk while she wears his coonskin cap, in a scene that reprises the Smith-Self puppy love as adult *true* love. Mitts herself is merely an updated fantasy—the image of late 80s cool with a not inconsistent dash of feminism, she might appear in any number of TV ads or music videos—and it's difficult to marry Solomon's decision to marry her as an indication of maturity. He's simply traded one fantasy girl (Frank) for a hipper model (Mitts).

While the film's tendency to revel in pop imagery undeniably contributes to its enjoyment, it also tends to override characterization and to belie any substantive examination of the role mass media may have played in creating Solomon's narcissism. Instead, the images are presented as enthralling absolutes—Dreamland *is* the ideal. Also taken for granted is Solomon's devastating attractiveness. It's suggested that he's great in bed, but he shows little in the way of intelligence, sensitivity, or charisma—as character, script, and actor (the acting is cartoonish throughout) all bank on the endless appeal of boyish charm to win us over. Only in a subplot, involving the breakup of Solomon's friends' "ideal" marriage as a result of the husband's philandering, is the psychological syndrome in question taken out of the context of fantasy and caricature, and lent emotional resonance. Ultimately, NOT SINCE CASANOVA's assessment of its protagonist's refusal to grow up amounts to little more the a knowing wink, and 80 minutes is a long time to keep one eye shut. On its own, Thompson's vision is well-suited to today's TV-limited attention spans; feature-length story-telling, however, requires more thematic depth. *(Nudity, sexual situations, adult situations, substance abuse.)*

p, Bradford Owen, Brett Thompson; d, Brett Thompson; w, Brett Thompson; ph, Andreas Kossak; ed, Arthur Farkus, Brett Thompson; m, John Debney; prod d, Robyn Reichek; art d, Doug Miller; cos, Robyn Reichek; anim, David Cutler.

Comedy/Drama　　　　　　　　　　　　　　　**(PR:O MPAA:NR)**

O

OFF LIMITS** (1988) 102m FOX c

Willem Dafoe *(Buck McGriff)*, Gregory Hines *(Albaby Perkins)*, Fred Ward *(Sgt. Benjamin Dix)*, Amanda Pays *(Nicole)*, Kay Tong Lim *(Lime Green)*, Scott Glenn *(Col. Dexter Armstrong)*, David Alan Grier *(Rogers)*, Keith David *(Maurice)*, Raymond O'Connor *(Staff Sgt. Flowers)*, Richard Brooks *(Preacher)*, Thuy Ann Luu *(Lanh)*, Richard Lee Reed *(Col. Sparks)*, Woody Brown *(Co-Pilot)*, Ken Siu *(Ploughboy)*, Viladda Vanadurongwan *(Sister Agnes)*, Arun Sunantalod, Suksanti Cherpat, Chumpon Sunetara *(Sappers)*, Nguyen Kim Hoa *(Sapper's Mother)*, Norah Elizabeth Cazaux *(Mother Superior)*, Look Nam, Rungsima Kasikranund *(Whores)*, Coconut *(Dead Whore's Baby)*, Mayura Srisittidecharak *(Bar Girl)*, Boonchai Jakraworawut *(ARVN Interpreter)*, Pradit Prasartthong, Terd Porn Manophaiboon, Pravit Piyasirikul, Tawan Mahathavorn *(V.C. Prisoners)*, Piathip Kumwong *(Dragonlady)*, Wasun Uttamayodhin *(Rogersan)*, Kovit Vatanakul, Pipot Nalinat *(V.C.s)*, Peter MacKenzie, Clive Gray, Tom Schroeder, Robert Langlois, Greg Knight *(M.P.s)*, Tongaow Taveprungsenukul *(Aborigine)*, Prae Petchompoo *(Francine)*, Jim Kinnon *(Top)*, Louis Roth *(Captain)*, Kanya Wongsawasdi *(Nguyen Tri Quan)*, Kamsine Spinog *(Gen. Vin)*, "Arm" Suvinit Pornvalai *(V.C. Taxi Driver)*, Elizabeth LeCompte *(Nurse)*, Father Buncha *(Bishop)*, Greg Elam *(Batman)*, Teerapat Tanapum, Praput Puuyatip, Trachi Chaivan, Thommas Pestony *(Bar Band)*, Jean Phuturoj, Somboun Phuturoj, Elizabeth Nguyen Thi, Hoang Nga *(Vietnamese Interpreters)*.

Combining a traditional whodunit with the elements of the currently popular cycle of Vietnam films could have yielded an interesting reflection on the larger issues raised by the American presence in Southeast Asia. Unfortunately, OFF LIMITS disintegrates into an annoyingly obvious murder mystery full of cliche characters, ludicrous plot devices, and frequently laughable dialog, effectively burying any complex socio-political subtext that the filmmakers may have hoped to explore. Set in Saigon in 1968, the film stars Willem Dafoe and Gregory Hines as two plainclothes investigators of the Criminal Investigations Department of the Military Police (CID). The pair rabidly embraces the mantle of "Ugly American," caring little or nothing for Vietnam or the millions of "slopes" that inhabit it. When it is discovered that a number of Vietnamese prostitutes with Amerasian children have been murdered, Dafoe and Hines take the case. After some preliminary sleuthing, the investigators come to suspect that a high-ranking American military officer may be the culprit. Supported by their immediate superior, Ward, the investigators continue their search, determined to ferret out the murderer no matter what his rank. Unfortunately, their investigation only serves to rankle in their already poor relationship with Vietnamese police chief Kay Tong Lim, especially when their digging leaves behind the predictable trail of bodies—both American and Vietnamese. The investigators are assisted by a beautiful French novice nun, Pays, who has worked closely with the prostitutes and their children. Dafoe is quite taken with Pays, and the specter of "forbidden love" hangs heavy through much of the film. Eventually, the investigators single out a prominent colonel (Glenn) as the most likely suspect. Dafoe and Hines follow the colonel on his nocturnal wanderings through Saigon and discover that he enjoys tying up young Vietnamese girls and spanking them with a riding crop. Dafoe and Hines are caught, however, by Glenn's fanatically loyal men and taken out into the bush for a confrontation with the colonel. Tossed into a helicopter along with a trio of Viet Cong soldiers under interrogation, the investigators question Glenn while he tries to get information out of his Vietnamese prisoners. When the first prisoner refuses to talk, Glenn nonchalantly tosses the man out of the helicopter to his death. He does the same with the remaining two, and after admitting that Dafoe and Hines' discovery of his carnal predilections will cause a career-ending scandal, Glenn jumps out of the helicopter himself. Back in Saigon, the investigators are pleased to report that the mystery is solved; Glenn was indeed the culprit. Ward congratulates them and hands over orders directing them to leave Vietnam several weeks early. As the investigators head for the airport, they suddenly discover yet another murder—one that has taken place after Glenn's suicide. Realizing they had the wrong man, Dafoe and Hines go AWOL and continue their investigation illegally. Eventually, the trail leads to Ward himself, and in a hopelessly corny climax, the investigators trace the crazed CID master sergeant to Pays' church and burst in just as he is about to kill the nun. Ward, of course, is shot several times and his body goes crashing though a stained-glass window, falling several stories and landing in a bloody heap in the courtyard. Although mightily tempted by the physical charms of Dafoe, Pays goes through with her spiritual commitment and becomes a full-fledged nun.

Directed in a terribly slick and artificial manner by television veteran Christopher Crowe, this poorly scripted effort wastes the skills of its talented cast and the considerable financial resources provided for its production. Shot in Bangkok, Thailand, much of OFF LIMITS takes place at night, and Crowe, along with Australian cinematographer David Gribble, presents a Saigon infested with literally dozens of three-foot-long fluorescent light bulbs that hang in every doorway, alley, and porch in the film. These lights emit an eerie blue haze and even turn up at a MASH unit, placed arbitrarily in the midst of the action. This visual scheme, while quite in vogue on television, only serves to betray Crowe's creative roots. His daytime scenes aren't much better, although he does milk a tension-filled standoff between Dafoe and Hines and hundreds of angry Vietnamese citizens for all it's worth. Unfortunately, cowriters Crowe and Jack Thibeau boxed themselves into a corner and were forced to introduce one of the more blatant examples of deus ex machina seen on the screen in quite some time when a US Army helicopter suddenly (and quite noiselessly) appears in the middle of downtown Saigon to rescue the investigators from certain death. OFF LIMITS is full of credibility problems such as this. In another ridiculous scene that was filmed at great expense, Dafoe and Hines are allowed to travel to the bloody battlefield of Khe Sanh during the height of the Tet offensive to question *one soldier* about the murder case. With shells exploding all around them, the investigators run through what seems like miles of trenches only to find that the man they seek refuses to talk. So Dafoe and Hines hightail it back to the C-130 transport plane, which lands amidst a hail of shells exploding in picturesque patterns along the runway, only to have the soldier they questioned experience a change of heart and chase after the C-130 with an all-important envelope containing clues. This entire "spectacular" action is so contrived as to be laughable.

Luckily, some cast members rise above the material to contribute a few very watchable performances. Hines, who has once again been saddled with the role of second banana (he deserves to be the lead of any movie in which he appears), plays a character wrapped so tight he seems ready to explode at any moment. His furious gum-chewing throughout the film is a marvelous tension builder and demonstrates just how much excess energy his character has pent up inside him. At any given moment, he is just as likely to whip out a pair of pistols as he is to say hello. With limited dialog and little to do other than stand next to Dafoe looking intense, Hines is able to convey an incredibly complex individual. Fred Ward is also fine, lending rock-solid support throughout and underplaying his role just enough to make one actually wonder whether he is indeed the killer. At the other end of the thesping spectrum is Scott Glenn, who transforms a tiny red-herring role into a memorable one by making Robert Duvall's performance in APOCALYPSE NOW look restrained. Not as effective are Amanda Pays as the nun and Dafoe as the lead. A beautiful and promising young actress, Pays fails more because of the cliched and gratuitous nature of her character than because of her own inability. Dafoe, however, appears if he'd like to get the hell out of Southeast Asia, after working on PLATOON and now this. Looking distracted and bored, he scowls his way through the film and conveys what appears to be a bad case of puppy-love rather than lustful infatuation in his scenes with Pays. Moreover, there is little rapport between him and Hines, which is actually somewhat refreshing after scads of buddy films that border on the homoerotic. Although OFF LIMITS does manage to be one of the only Vietnam films to portray the American presence in that country as entirely corrupt, diseased, racist, and irredeemable, this message is lost amid the twists and turns of an illogical and unsatisfying plot. Songs include "Pretty Ballerina" (Michael Brown, performed by The Left Bank), "Funky Broadway" (Lester Christian, performed by Wilson Pickett), "Down on Me" (Janis Joplin, performed by Joplin), "Yummy, Yummy, Yummy" (Arthur Resnick, Joe Levine, performed by The Ohio Express), "Tighten Up" (Archie Bell, Billy H. Buttier, performed by Bell and the Drells), "Dang Me" (Roger Miller), "Foxy Lady" (Jimi Hendrix, performed by Hendrix), "It's a Man's Man's World" (James Brown, Betty Jean Newsome, performed by Brown), "Stand" (Sylvester Stewart, performed by Sly and the Family Stone). *(Graphic violence, extreme profanity, sexual situations, nudity.)*

p, Alan Barnette; d, Christopher Crowe; w, Christopher Crowe, Jack Thibeau; ph, David Gribble (DeLuxe Color); ed, Douglas Ibold; m, James Newton Howard; m/l, Michael Brown, Lester Christian, Janis Joplin, Arthur Resnick, Joe Levine, Archie Bell, Billy Buttier, Roger Miller, Jimi Hendrix, James Brown, Betty Jean Newsome, Sylvester Stewart; prod d, Dennis Washington; art d, Scott Ritenour; set d, Crispian Sallis; spec eff, Joe Digaetano; cos, Peter V. Saldutti; stunts, Buddy Van Horn, Richard Ziker, Tawan Mahathavorn; makeup, Felicity Bowring, Joan Petch.

Mystery/War Cas. (PR:O MPAA:R)

OLIVER & COMPANY**½ (1988) 72m Walt Disney-Silver Screen Partners III/BV c

Voices of: Joey Lawrence *(Oliver)*, Billy Joel *(Dodger)*, Richard "Cheech" Marin *(Tito)*, Bette Midler *(Georgette)*, Dom DeLuise *(Fagin)*, Roscoe Lee Browne *(Francis)*, Richard Mulligan *(Einstein)*, Sheryl Lee Ralph *(Rita)*, Natalie Gregory *(Jenny)*, Robert Loggia *(Sykes)*, Taurean Blacque *(Roscoe)*, Carl Weintraub *(Desoto)*, William Glover *(Winston)*.

OLIVER & COMPANY is another disappointing animated feature from Walt Disney productions, the faults of which seem even more glaring when compared to Don Bluth's excellent THE LAND BEFORE TIME, which opened nationwide on the very same weekend. Ostensibly based on Dickens' *Oliver Twist*, OLIVER & COMPANY is set in the mean streets of modern-day New York City and follows the adventures of a wide-eyed kitten, Oliver (Lawrence), as he tries to survive on his own. Little Oliver hooks up with a scrappy dog, Dodger (Joel), who brings him into a doggy gang of thieves whose headquarters are on the wharf. Dodger and the other canine gang members—the sultry Rita (Ralph), hambone actor Francis (Browne), dull-witted Einstein (Mulligan), and the hyperkinetic Chihuahua Tito (Marin)—are owned by human being Fagin (DeLuise), a kindly down-and-out sort who owes money to evil loan shark Sykes (Loggia). Fagin has only a few days to raise the money to pay off Sykes, otherwise there will be hell to pay. Accepted by the gang, Oliver hits the streets with them the next day to learn the ins and outs of stealing. While pulling a con with Tito, Oliver winds up in the limousine of lonely little rich girl Jenny (Gregory), whose parents are in Europe on business. Cared for by her rotund butler, Winston (Glover), Jenny adopts little Oliver and takes him home to her palatial Fifth Avenue brownstone. Oliver is overjoyed to be owned by someone who loves him, but he runs into trouble with the prissy family poodle, Georgette (Midler). Georgette, who is used to having free reign of the house, resents Oliver's presence and schemes to rid herself of the bothersome little kitten. Meanwhile, the doggy gang misunderstands what has happened to Oliver and assume that he's been kidnaped. They track Oliver down and invade the house, rescuing him against his will. Although happy to see his friends again, Oliver really wants to go back. Dodger resents this and treats the kitten with disdain. Fagin, however, concocts a scheme to get the money he needs by pretending to hold Oliver hostage, so that Jenny's rich parents will pay him ransom. When little Jenny shows up on the wharf with only Georgette and a piggy bank, the soft-hearted Fagin can't go through with it and gives Oliver back to the girl. Sykes, however, witnesses the whole thing and kidnaps Jenny himself in the hopes of attaining a big ransom. Through the heroic efforts of Oliver, Fagin, Dodger, and the others, Jenny is rescued and Sykes killed when his car runs into a train. In the end, Oliver and Jenny are reunited and retire to Fifth Avenue, while Dodger and his gang prefer the rhythm of the streets.

Although OLIVER & COMPANY is fairly entertaining and better looking than the average Saturday morning cartoon show, it certainly isn't up to classic Disney standards. Aided by computers, the animation is relatively stiff and inexpressive. With the exception of the peppy Tito, none of the characters possess the trademark Disney movement that makes or breaks an animated character. By imbuing an animated character with a distinct, detailed, and fluid pattern of movement, a vivid screen personality is created out of acetate and paint; OLIVER & COMPANY's characters seem more like sketches. In fact, the filmmakers rely much more heavily on the voice talents of the cast than on the animation to convey the characters' personalities. Another distressing aspect of the animation design are the rather cheap-looking background paintings, which lack the kind of lush detail one expects from Disney. Granted, top-notch animation is almost prohibitively expensive nowadays, but compared with the twin artistic successes of this year's WHO FRAMED ROGER RABBIT and THE LAND BEFORE TIME, OLIVER & COMPANY looks shoddy. The movie also stumbles when it comes to the script. Only tangentially related to the Dickens novel, the film is short on character development and lacks a plot that will either engage or move a child, let alone an adult. Yes, there are enough songs and action scenes to maintain interest, but the film lacks the deep emotional pull found in classic Disney efforts. Aside from the opening, which shows poor little Oliver as the only kitten unsold from an entire litter, the film stays away from childhood concerns of abandonment and loneliness, instead preferring to concentrate on its standard television adventure plot.

Much more disturbing, however, is the mob-related violence shown as Fagin begs Sykes for more time to repay his loan. At one point, Sykes uses his electric car window to crush Fagin, whose head is in the car, into submission. Do dangerous gangsters, juice loan debts, strong-arm tactics, and stealing to pay off said debts really belong in a film aimed at children? Why is the script more willing to depict unpleasant *adult* situations than the universal fears experienced by children? Also a bit dismaying are the subtle hints of racism that pop up during the course of the film. Sykes' two mean, very dangerous Doberman pincers have voices that sound unmistakably street-black, while the Chihuahua Tito, although Cheech Marin's vocal performance is marvelous, is an Hispanic stereotype right down the line and merely re.inforces the notion that Hispanics are fast-talking, boastful, hyper, and sexually aggressive. Again, why do the Disney people run the risk of engendering such criticism in a film aimed at small children? Because of the amazing financial success of the company over the last several years (which now seems to be slipping—at least at the box office), Disney management seems to think that anything they release will be met with mass approval—including truncated rereleases of their classic library. (*Violence.*)

d, George Scribner; w, Jim Cox, Timothy J. Disney, James Mangold (based on a story by Vance Gerry, Mike Gabriel, Roger Allers, Joe Ranft, Gary Trousdale, Jim Mitchell, Kevin Lima, Chris Bailey, Michael Cedeno, Kirk Wise, Pete Young, Dave Michener, Leon Joosen, Gerrit Graham, Samuel Graham, Chris Hubbell, Steve Hulet, Danny Mann and the novel *Oliver Twist* by Charles Dickens); ed, Jim Melton, Mark Hester; m, J.A.C. Redford; m/l, Barry Mann, Howard Ashman, Tom Snow, Dean Pitchford, Ron Rocha, Robert Minkoff, Dan Hartman, Charlie Midnight, Barry Manilow, Jack Feldman, Bruce Sussman, Rocky Pedilla, Michael Eckhart, Jon St. James, Ruben Blades; art d, Dan Hansen; anim, Mike Gabriel, Hendel Butoy, Glen Keane, Mark Henn, Ruben A. Aquino, Doug Krohn.

Animation/Children's   (PR:AA MPAA:G)

ONE MINUTE TO MIDNIGHT †   (1988) 103m Curtin c

Lawrence Curtin *(David Lawrence)*, Diane Coyne *(Bo)*, Rob Fuller *(Brock)*, Nelson Brungart *(Mike)*, Sydney Messett *(First Wife)*.

This bizarre vanity production written, executive produced, and starring Lawrence Curtin (brother of Jane), chronicles Curtin's own psychological trials and tribulations, albeit in fictionalized fashion. Having suffered a nasty divorce from his first wife, who seems to have taken all his money and continues to harass him for finances, Curtin undertakes a secret Drug Enforcement Agency mission to Colombia, but winds up with a job selling billboard advertising. He then meets another woman, Coyne, whom he marries, only to be divorced again when she catches him cheating on her. This sends him into a spiral and a three-day trip to the mental hospital—against his will—follows. On the verge of suicide, Curtin stops himself from pulling the trigger after having some sort of spiritual revelation. Curtin reportedly was able to finish

the film with money he raised by threatening the mental hospital that held him with a lawsuit. Ultra low-budget and available on videocassette through Curtin's own company, Curtin International, this highly personal film was directed by Robert Michael Ingria, whose previous effort was a wrestling film titled HAMMERHEAD JONES.

p, Dara Murphy; d, Robert Michael Ingria; w, Lawrence Curtin; ph, Robert Michael Ingria (Continental color); ed, Lawrence Curtin, Dara Murphy.

Drama   Cas.   (PR:NR MPAA:NR)

ORDER OF THE BLACK EAGLE †(1988) 93m Polo Players/International Film Marketing c

Ian Hunter *(Duncan Jax)*, Charles K. Bibby *(Star)*, William Hicks *(Baron von Tepish)*, Anna Rapagna *(Maxie Ryder)*, Jill Donnellan *(Tiffany Youngblood)*, Flo Hyman *(Spike)*, Shan Tai Tuan *(Sato)*, Stephan Krayk *(Dr. Brinkman)*, Gene Scherer, Wolfgang Linkman, Typhoon the Baboon.

The sequel to another straight-to-video title, UNMASKING THE IDOL, this action-adventure epic with international locations was filmed mostly at Earl Owensby's studios in South Carolina. Hunter stars as a secret agent, with a tuxedo-wearing baboon for a sidekick, who must stop the evil villain Hicks from taking over the world using stolen laser technology. To make matters worse, Hicks has the body of Adolf Hitler on ice and plans to revive *der Fuehrer* so he can pick up where he left off in 1945. Filmed back in 1985, this silly-sounding espionage picture borrows much of its business from the James Bond pictures, including lots of big-chested women. Olympic volleyball star Flo Hyman, who died suddenly shortly after the film was completed, is featured as a mercenary named "Spike" (get the volleyball reference?). The producers dedicated the film to Hyman, a dubious honor at best.

p, Betty J. Stephens, Robert P. Eaton; d, Worth Keeter; w, Phil Behrens; ph, Irl Dixon (Technicolor); ed, Matthew Mallinson; m, Dee Barton; art d, Mack Pittman.

Action/Adventure   Cas.   (PR:NR MPAA:R)

OUT †   (1988) 88m Cinema Group Home Video c

Peter Coyote, O-Lan, Jim Haynie, Grandfather Semu Haute, Scott Beach, Danny Glover, Michael Grodenchik, Gail Dartez.

This low-budget independent film bypassed theatrical distribution entirely and went directly to home video. Although based on a novel by coscreenwriter Ronald Sukenick, it seems that Jack Kerouac was the main inspiration for this road picture, which features Peter Coyote as a Greenwich Village denizen who leaves NYC and heads out west on a cross-country trip that ends in Venice, California. During his journey, Coyote runs into the same few people, who keep popping up in different towns with different identities. The film is structured like a novel, with episodes in the narrative separated by chapters shown as numerical title cards appearing in descending order (10, 9, 8, etc.).

p, Eli Hollander; d, Eli Hollander; w, Eli Hollander, Ronald Sukenick (based on a novel by Sukenick); ph, Robert Ball; ed, Eli Hollander; m, David Cope.

Drama   Cas.   (PR:NR MPAA:NR)

OUT OF ROSENHEIM   (SEE: BAGDAD CAFE, 1988, Ger.)

OUTLAW FORCE †   (1988) 95m Outlaw Film/Trans World-TBJ c

David Heavener *(Billy Ray Dalton)*, Paul Smith *(Inspector Wainwright)*, Frank Stallone *(Grady)*, Robert Bjorklund *(Washington)*, Devin Dunsworth *(Jesse)*, Stephanie Cicero *(Holly Dalton)*, Warren Berlinger *(Capt. Morgan)*, Cecilea Xavier *(Billy's Wife)*, Mickey Morton, John Reistetter, Steve Keeley, Mark Richardson, Arvid Homberg, Jeff D. Patterson, Francesca Wilde.

Quite the Renaissance man is singer David Heavener, who wrote, directed, co-produced, acts, and yes, sings his own songs in this, his low-budget feature film debut. What Heavener was not able to do, however, was get his movie into theaters, for it went directly to home video. Derivative of everything from DEATH WISH to Sergio Leone's westerns, OUTLAW FORCE sees kind and decent family man Heavener pay dearly for helping a black gas station attendant who was attacked by a gang of vicious rednecks. In retaliation, the rednecks track down Heavener's wife, whom they rape and kill, and kidnap his young daughter with plans to sell her to a kiddie porn producer. Being a reasonable citizen, Heavener turns to the LAPD (represented by, of all people, Stallone and the burly Smith) for help, but there is nothing they can do. Well, a man's gotta do what a man's gotta do, so Heavener arms himself heavily and sets out to kill the scum-sucking redneck peckerwoods who ruined his life.

p, David Heavener, Ronnie Hadar; d, David Heavener; w, David Heavener; ph, David Huey, James Mathers (Foto-Kem Color); ed, Peter Miller; m, Donald Hulette; m/l, David Heavener; art d, Phil Schmidt, Naomi Shohan; spec eff, Fritz Matthews.

Action   Cas.   (PR:NR MPAA:R)

PQ

PARAMEDICS †   (1988) 91m Ruddy-Morgan/Vestron c

George Newbern (*Uptown*), Christopher McDonald (*Mad Mike*), Javier Grajeda (*Bennie*), Lawrence-Hilton Jacobs (*Blade Runner*), Elaine Wilkes (*Savannah*), Lydie Denier (*Lisette*), John P. Ryan (*Capt. Prescott*), James Noble (*Chief Wilkens*), Karen Witter (*Danger Girl*), John Pleshette (*Dr. Lido*), Ray Walston (*1st Patient*).

A pair of goofy paramedics are sent on a mission to bust up a ring of villains who traffick in internal organs. Along the way, the paramedics get involved in a number of embarrassing sexual adventures and other zany encounters. Includes songs by Jim Messina (Loggins' former sidekick), who acts as the film's music supervisor.

p, Leslie Greif; d, Stuart Margolin; w, Barry Bardo, Richard Kriegsman; ph, Michael Watkins; ed, Allan A. Moore; m, Murray MacLeod; md, Jim Messina; prod d, Jack Marty; stunts, Randy Fife.

Comedy   Cas.   (PR:NR MPAA:PG-13)

PARTY LINE †   (1988) 91m Westwood/SVS c

Richard Hatch (*Lt. Dan Bridges*), Shawn Weatherly (*Stacy Sloane, Asst. D.A.*), Leif Garrett (*Seth*), Greta Blackburn (*Angelina*), Richard Roundtree (*Capt. Barnes*), James O'Sullivan (*Henry*), Terrence McGovern (*Simmons*), Shelli Place (*Mrs. Simmons*), Tara Hutchins (*Alice*), Marty Dudek (*Butch*).

This timely thriller capitalizes on the recent spate of 976 party line numbers—the ones on which groups of hormonally active teens chatter on with *sympatico* peers and run their parents' phone bill into the thousands. It seems that these party lines are the perfect place for a brother-sister murdering tandem to find victims. Sis lures the victim into her bedroom, while her razor-wielding brother (played by former teen idol Garrett) slits his throat. On the trail of these killers is a guy-girl investigating team who stumble upon every cliche in the book on the trail of the killers. Released regionally in late 1988.

p, Tom Byrnes, Kurt Anderson, William Webb, Monica Webb; d, William Webb; w, Richard Brandes (based on a story by Tom Byrnes); ph, John Huneck; ed, Paul Koval; m, Sam Winans; art d, Mark Simon; stunts, Jeff Smoleck.

Thriller   (PR:NR MPAA:R)

PASCALI'S ISLAND*½   (1988, Brit.) 104m Avenue-Initial-Film Four Intl.-Dearfilm/Avenue c

Ben Kingsley (*Basil Pascali*), Charles Dance (*Anthony Bowles*), Helen Mirren (*Lydia Neuman*), George Murcell (*Herr Gesing*), Sheila Allen (*Mrs. Marchant*), Nadim Sawalha (*Pasha*), Stefan Gryff (*Izzet Effendi*), Vernon Dobtcheff (*Pariente*), T.P. McKenna (*Dr. Hogan*), Danielle Allan (*Mrs. Hogan*), Nick Burnell (*Chaudan*), Josh Losey (*Turkish Soldier*), Kevork Malikyan (*Mardosian*), George Ekonomou (*Greek Rebel*), Alistair Campbell (*Captain*), Ali Abatsis (*Boy in Bath*), Brook Williams (*Turkish Officer*).

Just as FATAL ATTRACTION was beginning to appear on American screens, well before it became a huge box-office smash, James Dearden, who received an Oscar nomination for its screenplay, was already involved in another project in making his first feature film as a director, PASCALI'S ISLAND. Working from Barry Unsworth's 1979 epistolary novel of intrigue, Dearden ventured to Greece to re-create the twilight of the Ottoman Empire on one of its more remote outposts, the island of Nisi. For the 20 years leading up to 1908, Basil Pascali (Kingsley), half-Turkish and half-European, has called this sun-drenched island home, spying on its visitors and its potentially rebellious Greek inhabitants and sending off long missives to the sultan in Constantinople detailing any suspicious comings and goings. Although he is regularly sent small compensation for his loyal efforts, he has never received so much as a note confirming that his elegantly written letters have even been read. A number of expatriates reside on the island, including Mirren, an Austrian painter who is Kingsley's only real friend. When Dance, a handsome but mysterious British archaeologist, appears, claiming to be in search of the island's past treasures, Kingsley does some investigating that later proves Dance to be a con man. In the meantime, Kingsley acts as Dance's interpreter in his dealings with the Turkish pasha who rules the island and from whom Dance leases some land for exploration. Kingsley begins to grow close to Dance and uncovers the Englishman's scheme to swindle the pasha, eventually becoming his confederate. All the while, an American yacht maintains a mysterious presence offshore (waiting to supply the Greek rebels on the island with arms), and Dance and Mirren have an affair. When pseudo-archaeologist Dance stumbles upon a genuine treasure—a perfectly preserved, centuries-old statue—Kingsley helps him unearth it. Later, Kingsley becomes convinced that both Dance and Mirren are going to take the statue and desert him, a known informer on an island where the Turks maintain only tenuous control. Feeling betrayed, he informs the local Turkish authorities of the pair's activities, bringing about the story's violent climax and ironic denouement.

PASCALI'S ISLAND is a beautifully shot tale of political and psychological intrigue undone by its choppy editing, ham-fisted symbolism, and absence of passion. Writer-director Dearden draws the viewer slowly and skillfully into his complex story, only to lose him with flurries of logical inconsistencies, oblique plot complications, and symbolic overkill, and then hooks him again with the story's narrative thrust—repeating this frustrating pattern until the film's conclusion. Ben Kingsley plays a man torn between cultures and between his sense of self-preservation and his loyalty to a distant, uncaring imperial government that he doesn't want to admit has already seen its greatest days. His Basil Pascali has come to wonder if his life has been in vain. When the two people he cares most about, Mirren and Dance (there is a suggestion of homoeroticism), appear to have forsaken him, Kingsley, ever the observer, makes a disastrously wrong choice when he finally does take action. With his eyes speaking volumes—whether in his patented unfocused glare or in narrowed scrutiny—Kingsley brings his usual intensity to the film's central role. His intelligent, measured performance is nicely complimented by Charles Dance, who captures the essence of British rectitude while making his sun-tanned "archaeologist" both devious and heroic. Seemingly interested in promoting only his own cause, he ultimately proves to be fair, a true student of antiquity, and a champion of Greek independence. Helen Mirren is equally convincing as the free-thinking Austrian artist who is both the object of Kingsley's unspoken love and his rival for Dance's regard. Yet, despite the fact that these principal characters are all romantics in their own way, the performances are surprisingly dispassionate. Dearden has said that the actors gave him just what he wanted, but had he allowed them and his film to enter more into the realm of emotion PASCALI'S ISLAND would be less disappointing.

Shot in seven weeks on a budget of $3.8 million, PASCALI'S ISLAND was filmed on the islands of Rhodes and Simi. Because tensions still run high in the Aegean Sea, the Greek government prohibited the filmmakers from so much as flying a Turkish flag, fearing that it would support the legitimacy of Turkish territorial claims in the region. Although this is the first feature film for Dearden (son of British director Basil Dearden), he had previously made several shorts, a 45-minute film called "Diversion" that was the basis for FATAL ATTRACTION, and "The Cold Room" for HBO. (*Violence, nudity, sexual situations.*)

p, Eric Fellner; d, James Dearden; w, James Dearden (based on the novel by Barry Unsworth); ph, Roger Deakins (Metrocolor); ed, Edward Marnier; m, Loek Dikker, Franz Schubert; prod d, Andrew Mollo; art d, Philip Elton, Petros Kapouralis; set d, Jennifer Williams; spec eff, Special Effects Universal Ltd.; cos, Pam Tait; stunts, Paul Weston; makeup, Peter Frampton.

Drama   Cas.   (PR:C-O MPAA:PG-13)

PASS THE AMMO**½   (1988) 97m Vista/New Century-Vista c

Bill Paxton (*Jesse*), Linda Kozlowski (*Claire*), Tim Curry (*Rev. Ray Porter*), Annie Potts (*Darla Porter*), Dennis Burkley (*Big Joe Becker*), Glenn Withrow (*Arnold Limpet*), Anthony Geary (*Stonewall*), Brian Thompson (*Kenny Hamilton*), Logan Ramsey (*Jim Bob Collins*), Jim Holmes (*Governor*), Leland Crooke (*Sheriff Rascal Lebeaux*), Richard Paul (*G.W. Wraith*), John Cody (*Billy*), Paul Cody (*Dean*), Elizabeth Ward (*Christie Lynn*), Debra Sue Maffett (*Miss Dallas*), Brad Kepnick (*Rickey Marcell*), Paul Ben-Victor (*Eddie DePaul*), Daniel Hirsch (*Lee*), James C. Mullins (*Tiny*), Robert A. Ginnaven (*Mean*), Gerald F. Leray (*Chew*), Karren Dille (*Lorette*), Vance Colvig (*Fritz*), Randy Bame (*Major*), Georgia A. Adams (*Tubby*), Jill Augustine (*Marie*), Jorden Baker (*Diane*), Cindy Brooks (*Debbie*), Lynn Rose (*Operator*), Jordana Capra (*Mary Trenton*), Tommy Sanders (*Reporter*), Susan Carlsberg (*July*), Caleb Edwards (*Guard*), Gene Gephardt (*Choir Boy*), Megan Blake (*Cherry*), Austin Goss (*Dick*), Terry Haskell (*Tank Pilot*), Scott Linden (*Dispatcher*), Robert Peters (*Cameraman*), Phil Phillips (*Local Newscaster*), Frank

©NEW CENTURY/VISTA

Thomas Roberts III *(Network Newscaster)*, Jackie Stewart *(Sergeant)*, Gregg Michael Vogt *(Deputy)*, Chris F. Thompson *(Cop)*, Barry Mines *(Rescue Worker)*, Eddie Maples *(Lester Odin)*, Julie Uribe *(Anna Becky)*, Dorotha Yager *(Davine)*, Shirley Jean Young *(Juletta)*, Jean Tharp *(Wife in Grocery Store)*, Craig O'Neal *(Bull)*, H.T. Lester *(Socket)*, Terry Lee Sneed *(Bottle)*, Tracy Pearce *(Jonsey)*, Judy Dockrey Young *(Big Alice)*, Bud Cook *(Moose)*, Mark W. Johnson *(Knuckle)*, Lyle E. Armstrong *(Armstrong)*, Dick Canady *(Zachery)*, Burke Hully *(Josh)*, Dawn Duncan, Debra Johnson, Kelley Radusch, Margo Harris, Mia Togo, Joyce Allison, Beverly Boatright, Dana Tanner, Joanna Simmons *(Dancers)*, Sherry Dodson, Kelly Householder, Chris Martin, Patty Pasternostro, Sherry Williams, Pam Lawrence *(Angels)*, Lucious Spiller, David Kendrick, Darrell Claypool, Eric Ware, Derrick Spiller *(Band)*, Dennis Glascock, Jerr Kimes, Dan Carter *(Backup Singers)*, Melaine McClain, Melissa Fant, Babette Crowder, Tamara Wooten, Crystal Smith, Krista Belote, Rose Bunch, Kathy Trumbo *(Telephone Girls)*.

Filmed just before the Jim and Tammy Bakker scandal broke and released just as Jimmy Swaggart was blubbering, "I have sinned," on the airwaves, this anti-televangelist comedy couldn't have asked for better free publicity. Unfortunately, the film's distributor, New Century/Vista, went out of business on the very day the movie hit the screens, and the film was taken out of circulation posthaste. While certainly no masterpiece, PASS THE AMMO has a certain charm and is a promising development in the directing career of David Beaird, whose previous effort, the essentially sweet-hearted MY CHAUFFEUR (1986), was marred by some vulgar scenes of gratuitous nudity inserted by the producer. Set in rural Arkansas, PASS THE AMMO takes aim at a lucrative teleministry run by the greedy husband-and-wife preaching team of Curry and Potts. Oozing false sincerity, the preachers regale their audience with ridiculously overblown Las Vegas-style production numbers that supposedly recreate scenes in the Bible, then launch into game show-like ministry fund-raisers that con viewers into contributing more than they can afford. Enter likable young redneck Paxton and his girl friend, Kozlowski. Angry that Curry has conned $50,000, her life savings, out of Kozlowski's dying grandmother, Paxton recruits two of Kozlowski's ex-con cousins, Burkley and Withrow, to help him steal the money back from the minister. With help from a man on the inside, Paxton, Kozlowski, Burkley, and Withrow arm themselves, invade Curry's fortress-like "Tower of Bethlehem," and rob the vault of hundreds of thousands of dollars. Unfortunately, a silent alarm goes off and the ministry is surrounded by dozens of police cars. Seeing that there is no escape, Paxton leads his band of outlaws into the television station and takes control of the show while it is on the air. Not really wanting anyone hurt, Paxton lets sympathetic Cajun sheriff Crooke talk him into letting the studio audience go. During the standoff, the robbers begin blowing holes in Curry's hypocritical persona on live TV, telling his audience about his Rolls Royces, ritzy summer homes, and other sundries paid for with money earmarked for starving children. Curry's technical director, Geary, a hippie who has feigned born-again status to keep his job, is delighted by the revelations and does everything he can to keep the show on the air. Meanwhile, the Arkansan political powers that be—every one corrupt to the gills and beholden to the fundamentalists for their jobs—conspire to stop this disaster by any means possible. Paul, a Jerry Falwell lookalike, orders the spineless governor to send in the National Guard and blast the intruders off the air. At the same time, it is revealed that Curry has been having an affair with one of the chorus girls and, in a desperate attempt at damage control, he goes before the cameras, weeping, "I have sinned!" (a remarkable coincidence, considering the film was in the can long before Swaggart's confession). With a gang of angry redneck vigilantes at the back door and a National Guard tank at the front, all hell breaks loose in the studio and a volley of shots are fired. Although it appears that Paxton and Kozlowski have been killed in the exchange, they had anticipated just such a move and collaborated with Geary to fake their deaths on television. In an implausible ending, the ministry building is totally destroyed, Curry's reputation is ruined, and the outlaws are able to escape with the $50,000 for which they came.

A fairly vicious satire with more than its share of hearty laughs, PASS THE AMMO also suffers from a haphazard script that gets the outlaws on the air, but then doesn't know what to do with them or how to resolve their dilemma in an even remotely satisfying way. The first half of the film is wickedly funny, especially during the hilarious production number scenes, complete with funny songs like "Lay Your Money down for Jesus," sung by a twin-brother team who look and dress like Robert Goulet. Tim Curry is excellent as the cynical preacher who simply places his hand on a stack of letters from deaf people and mumbles a prayer meant to cure them. Also very funny is Annie Potts, whose character is a direct parody of Tammy Faye Bakker, a woman who claims that God likes to see her all dolled up and festooned with expensive baubles. The sexually repressed preacher's wife lives out her carnal fantasies through the elaborate religious production numbers, in which she wears slinky dresses and gets to bump and grind for Jesus. Once director Beaird runs through the litany of accusations leveled against television preachers, however, the film grinds to a halt and begins to disintegrate into an explosive show of pyrotechnics. In addition, the central performances of Bill Paxton (ALIENS, NEAR DARK) and Linda Kozlowski (of "Crocodile Dundee" fame) are very weak and fail to drum up much interest or sympathy for their characters. Luckily, the supporting work is fine, especially from thieves Dennis Burkley and Glenn Withrow, who deliver some of the movie's best laughs. The hulking Burkley contributes a priceless bit when he sings an ode to the police force he wrote in prison—a ditty that brings tears to the eyes of the cops trying to arrest him—and Withrow is a genial idiot who spends half the movie dressed up in a silly devil costume. Some funny lines ("The crack of dawn ain't safe around that man!") in reference to Curry's infidelity also pop up now and then to make the last 30 minutes of the film watchable. Surprisingly sympathetic to all its characters, including the preachers, the film isn't as didactic as it could have been—but then it isn't as rich or deft as the average Jonathan Demme movie either. What PASS THE AMMO will be remembered for is its sense of timing, both good and bad. Good in that it was handed a priceless advertising campaign by the Bakkers and Swaggart, bad because it was released on the day its distributor folded—disappearing from theaters before it could capitalize on all the free publicity. Songs: "You're in Paradise Now," "Samson and Delilah" (David Newman, Nan O'Byrne), "You're a Policeman" (Jim Cushinery), "Lay Your Money down for Jesus" (John Cody, Paul Cody). *(Violence, adult situations, profanity.)*

p, Herb Jaffe, Mort Engelberg; d, David Beaird; w, Neil Cohen, Joel Cohen; ph, Mark Irwin (DeLuxe Color); ed, Bill Yahraus; m, Carter Burwell; m/l, David Newman, Nan O'Byrne, Jim Cushinery, John Cody, Paul Cody; prod d, Dean Tschetter; art d, Mayling Cheng; set d, Michele Starbuck; spec eff, Rick Josephson; cos, Reve Richards.

Comedy **Cas.** **(PR:O MPAA:R)**

PASSAGE, THE † (1988) 105m Spectrum-Carrera/Manson Intl. c

Alexandra Paul *(Annie May Bonner)*, Ned Beatty *(Matthew Bonner)*, Barbara Barrie *(Rachel Bonner)*, Brian Keith *(Byron Monroe)*, Dee Law *(Jesse Monroe)*.

Set during the Depression, this melodrama tells the story of a tough Southern landowner (Beatty) who disowns his college-educated daughter when she become pregnant by the son of one of his employees. Years pass, Beatty's wife dies, the young lovers wed and have other children, and the old codger finally warms to his daughter, son-in-law, and four grandchildren.

p, Raul Carrera; d, Harry Thompson; ph, Peter Stein (Eastmancolor); ed, Peter Appleton; m, Paul Loomis.

Drama **(PR:NR MPAA:NR)**

PATTI ROCKS*** (1988) 87m FilmDallas c

Chris Mulkey *(Billy Regis)*, John Jenkins *(Eddie Jenks)*, Karen Landry *(Patti Rocks)*, Buffy Sedlachek, Joy Langer, Grian Lambert, Joe Minjares, David L. Turk, Stephen Yoakam, Sally Tronnes, Ken Tronnes, Ralph Estlie, May Mayhew.

In 1975, independent filmmaker David Burton Morris made LOOSE ENDS, a movie about a recently divorced Minneapolis mechanic (Mulkey) who persuades one of his coworkers (Jenkins) to desert his wife and children and start a new life in Denver. They only get as far as Iowa before returning to their old lives in the Twin Cities, but 12 years later, after the men have more or less reversed roles—Mulkey is married with two daughters and Jenkins divorced—Morris brings them together again in PATTI ROCKS. Mulkey now works on a barge that travels between the Twin Cities and LaCrosse, Wisconsin, where he has been carrying on an affair with a woman who has recently informed him that she is pregnant, but who refuses to consider abortion. Experiencing some of the first remorseful feelings of his life, Mulkey meets Jenkins, who is now the manager of an auto repair shop, in a bar and persuades him to accompany him on a drive through the winter night to LaCrosse. Equipped with a six-pack and a Neanderthal's view of women, Mulkey launches into a nonstop, profanity-laden discourse on sex that is only occasionally punctuated by the more thoughtful Jenkins' amused questions and comments. For half the film, Mulkey turns his car into a locker-room forum, frequently employing his telling euphemism for copulation, "chopping beef." As Mulkey blabbers on—baffled by homosexuals who have sex changes only to become lesbians, fantasizing about a "Star Trek" -like transporter that could return him to his favorite watering hole immediately after orgasm during a one-night stand—Jenkins bonds with him only reluctantly, becoming increasingly put off by his friend's crotch-driven view of relationships and growing more sullen as he reflects on his own failed marriage and loneliness. En route, Mulkey is sprayed by a skunk that is hit by the car, and, tossing out his own stinking clothes, he demands that Jenkins allow him to wear his underwear. Dressed only in his coat, boots, watch cap, and Jenkins' boxer shorts, Mulkey is later propositioned on the roadside by a dolled-up older woman who wants to have a romp with him in the back seat of her car, and whose approach is a distaff parody of Mulkey's own crudity. In the middle of the night, the men arrive at the LaCrosse apartment of Patti Rocks (Landry, of TV's "St. Elsewhere"), and the tone of the film shifts dramatically with the appearance of this strong-willed, independent woman who refuses to consider abortion and who, in direct opposition to Mulkey's predictions, doesn't really give a damn if she ever sees him again. Mulkey is slow to pick up on Landry's rejection of him and is still afraid to tell her that he is married. Eventually, Jenkins disappears into the bedroom with Landry and half-heartedly pleads Mulkey's case, but, finding her to be sympathetic, the lonely romantic mostly shares his own disappointment. Feeling pity or a momentary connection, or just because she enjoys sex, Landry seduces him. Before the men leave to return to Minneapolis, Landry makes clear to Mulkey that she neither expects nor wants anything from him and takes a snapshot of him, to provide the only connection she feels her child will ever need with this father.

The key word to characterize the mixed reviews PATTI ROCKS received is "verisimilitude." Some critics found Chris Mulkey (THE HIDDEN) and John Jenkins' funny blue-collar MY DINNER WITH ANDRE conversation to be extraordinarily frank and true, more like the way people talk than the dialog in most films; others found their remarks to be either stagy or needlessly profane. Certainly, when Jenkins gets around to verbalizing his worldview, he does so with the kind of eloquence one doesn't always expect in off-the-cuff conversation, but, tempering his intelligence with plenty of regular-guyisms and sincerity, Jenkins is convincing in his profundity. His excellent performance is matched by Mulkey and Karen Landry (who are, surprisingly, husband and wife in real life). Mulkey's Billy is unquestionably a swine, and the actor plays him with a mix of jocklike swagger and thick-headedness, while at the same time making him human in his occasionally charming simplicity and in his devotion to his family. Landry's *strong* performance was another point of contention with the critics: several of them found her fiercely independent Patti to be a feminist cliche, but others felt that the film doesn't become real until she enters the scene. Without Landry's determined independence to serve as a counterpoint to Mulkey's boneheaded outlook on women and Jenkins' less overt sexism, PATTI ROCKS might still make its point. The duo's cross-country conversation is damning enough in its male solipsism, but when it is contrasted with Landry's complete refutation of the characteristics they have assigned women the director's point is driven home, if perhaps a little too heavy-handedly. But even if Landry is independent almost to a fault, she is still believable; it is, after all, not the least bit surprising that she would rather raise a child alone than allow Mulkey to do any behavior modifying.

All three actors and director Morris are given script credit, and much of the dialog is the result of improvisation, though there isn't really much that happens in the film. Two friends who have grown apart over the years get together, go for a long ride, talk a lot, and arrive at their destination, with one of them discovering (maybe) that he has something to learn about women as people, and the other momentarily escaping a self-imposed exile from romanticism. Morris' subtle use of the camera is simple but evocative in reinforcing the story's development. Throughout the film the camera is essentially static, mirroring the film's emotional inertia, but when one of the characters does reveal some deeper feeling, the camera's slight movement has the impact of a 360-degree pan, heightening the viewer's connection with these moments.

Mulkey and Jenkins' profanity was the cause of some controversy. The Classification and Rating Administration of the Motion Picture Association of America gave the film an "X", not for its single love scene (which is sensitively shot, as if the camera had stumbled onto an extraordinarily intimate moment), but for its language. Upon appeal, however, the rating was reduced to an "R", a much fairer assessment of this funny and poignant film that uses rough language not to shock, but in the interest of realism. PATTI ROCKS was shot in Minnesota in 18 days, on a budget of $350,000. *(Extreme profanity, sexual situations, nudity.)*

p, Gwen Field, Gregory M. Cummins; d, David Burton Morris; w, David Burton Morris, Chris Mulkey, John Jenkins, Karen Landry (based on characters created by Victoria Wozniak for the film LOOSE ENDS); ph, Gregory M. Cummins (Foto-Kem Color); ed, Gregory M. Cummins; m, Doug Maynard; art d, Charlotte Whitaker; cos, Charlotte Whitaker.

Comedy   **Cas.**   **(PR:O MPAA:R)**

PATTY HEARST**½   (1988) 108m Atlantic-Zenith c

Natasha Richardson *(Patricia Hearst)*, William Forsythe *(Teko)*, Ving Rhames *(Cinque)*, Frances Fisher *(Yolanda)*, Jodi Long *(Wendy Yoshimura)*, Olivia Barash *(Fahizah)*, Dana Delany *(Celina)*, Marek Johnson *(Zoya)*, Kitty Swink *(Gabi)*, Pete Kowanko *(Cujo)*, Tom O'Rourke *(Jim Browning)*, Scott Kraft *(Steven Weed)*, Ermal Williamson *(Randolph A. Hearst)*.

Paul Schrader's film recounts events beginning in 1974, when Patty Hearst (Richardson), a pleasant, less-than-brilliant, spoiled rich girl (an heir to the Hearst fortune), is kidnaped by members of the Symbionese Liberation Army, a group of urban revolutionaries. The SLA members whisk Richardson away to their hideout, blindfold her, and toss her into a dark closet. For the next 57 days, they bombard her with their confused political rhetoric and worldview. The male members of the group attempt to seduce and then rape her; the women try to instill the belief that it's her duty to be sexually receptive to everyone in the organization. Thinking that they've succeeded in winning Richardson over to their cause, they release her from her closet jail and offer her the chance to either leave or join them as a member. Completely brainwashed and broken, she chooses the latter and is given the SLA name "Tanya." During Richardson's initial days of SLA membership, it becomes apparent that the "army" is nothing but a haven for half-witted, uncertain egomaniacs who see themselves as brilliant American radicals. Their leader, Rhames, has tremendous charisma and a gift for oratory, but lacks a true vision for the future and is, at times, laughably pathetic, as are his dedicated followers Forsythe and Fisher. Despite their faults (which are apparent to the audience, not Richardson), Rhames and his SLA cohorts *are* dangerous and the threat of violence and death hangs over Richardson like an ugly cloud. As the SLA begins a series of armed robberies—with Richardson along as a willing accomplice—its members vie for Richardson's attention. It's as if her approval will somehow validate their actions. Although the group isn't supposed to succumb to bourgeois feelings of jealousy, Fisher becomes angry over husband Forsythe's fascination with Richardson and continually tries to convince the group that Richardson isn't truly loyal. As the media begins to paint a picture of Richardson as a traitor, the FBI cracks down on the SLA and destroys their Los Angeles hideout. Richardson, Forsythe, and Fisher manage to escape, flee across the country to hide out in Long's secluded home, and are eventually captured by the FBI. Succumbing to public pressure, the authorities rush Richardson into a trial and, despite clear evidence of brainwashing, she is convicted and sentenced to prison. Clearly fed up with all forms of bureaucracy and any type of organization, a cynical Richardson expresses her utter contempt for American society and marches off to jail.

For the first third of PATTY HEARST, director Schrader forces the audience to share Richardson's ordeal during her 57-day period of captivity with the SLA. He and talented cinematographer Bojan Bazelli film the entire episode from Richardson's point of view. *We* see shadowy figures, *we* hear angry voices shouting, and *we're* shoved into a dark, black closet. This is a very effective, Kafkaesque sequence that, on its own, would be the stuff of a study into subjective cinematic technique. However, once this section is completed, Schrader pulls away from his protagonist and observes her and her activities with the SLA from a cold distance. Although we've seen things through Richardson's eyes, we really don't *know* her, and are never given that chance. Schrader's Patty Hearst is supposed to be seen as a classic victim, whose personal trials and tribulations are not taken into consideration by a hostile public, but

this theme (present in almost every Schrader film), is never fully developed, resulting in an emotionally unsatisfying viewing experience. Schrader is an intellectually challenging director, but he never seems to be able to (or willing) to present fully the passionate, emotional sides of his characters.

Devotees of real-life crime dramas will be disappointed by PATTY HEARST as well, since it's too much the product of a quirky personal vision to appeal to fans of such thrillers as IN COLD BLOOD or THE ONION FIELD. What's truly remarkable about the film are the performances. William Forsythe and Frances Fisher are compelling as the frightening yet pathetic Bill and Emily Harris, Ving Rhames is wonderful as SLA leader Cinque, and Dana Delaney (now a star of TV's "China Beach") turns in a notable brief appearance as a "soldier" duped by SLA rhetoric. Most captivating, however, is Natasha Richardson. Her performance as the title character is stunning and, like all great performances, does not call attention to itself. Richardson, the daughter of Vanessa Redgrave and director Tony Richardson, effortlessly slips into the personality of Patty Hearst and makes an unremarkable woman seem, well, remarkable. In what is an extremely rare occurrence in film, Natasha Richardson manages to transcend the mishandled material and create a character that's much more real and stimulating than anyone could have imagined. *(Profanity, sexual situations, violence.)*

p, Marvin Worth; d, Paul Schrader; w, Nicholas Kazan (based on the autobiography *Every Secret Thing* by Patricia Campbell Hearst with Alvin Moscow); ph, Bojan Bazelli (DeLuxe Color); ed, Michael R. Miller; m, Scott Johnson; prod d, Jane Musky; art d, Harold Thrasher; set d, Jerie Kaelter; cos, Richard Hornung.

Biography   **(PR:O MPAA:R)**

PENITENT, THE**½   (1988) 94m Ithaca-Cinevest/New Century-Vista c

Raul Julia *(Ramon Guerola)*, Armand Assante *(Juan Marco)*, Rona Freed *(Celia Guerola)*, Julie Carmen *(Corina)*, Lucy Reina *(Margarita)*, Eduardo Lopez Rojas *(Major)*, Jose Gonzales Rodriguez *(Rezador)*, Paco Mauri *(Pitero)*, Justo Martinez *(Enfermero)*, Enrique Novi *(Jose)*, Valentina Hernandez *(Dolo)*, Martin Lasalle *(Miguel)*, Jose Antonio Estrada *(Tomas)*, Juana Molinero *(Ramon's Mother)*, Jose Chavez Trowe *(Old Man)*, Daniel Stewart *(Pepito)*, Tina Romero *(Susana)*, Demian Bichir *(Roberto)*, Alejandra Benitez Vargas *(Little Girl)*, Roberto Munoz, Fernando Elizando, Ignacio Gomez Gil *(Penitentes)*.

Bolstered by some fine photography and strong performances from Raul Julia and Armand Assante, THE PENITENT nearly overcomes its plodding pace and predictable melodramatics. The wild card here is its examination of the little-known Penitente religious cult, a mainly Spanish-speaking splinter group of the Catholic church that believes in self-flagellation and literal reenactment of Christ's crucifixion as atonement. Set in an unspecified location somewhere in Mexico or the American Southwest, the film begins as Assante—fresh from a five-year prison sentence for manslaughter—travels to the small village where his old friend Julia has married and become a simple farmer. Having adopted the ways of the Penitente, the dour Julia has become very devout and, in fact, seems to be using his religion as a refuge from his frustrations with his young wife, Freed, who is afraid to consummate their marriage. Although on his way to accept a job, Assante lets Julia talk him into hanging around for a few weeks. Predictably, the rugged and charming Assante has no trouble seducing his friend's wife. Julia knows of this, but says nothing in the hope that once Assante leaves, Freed will no longer be frigid. Assante, much to his own surprise, falls in love with Freed and wants to run off with her. Meanwhile, the end of Lent approaches and the Penitentes select the one among them who will play the role of El Christo and hang on the cross for one full day. The man chosen, however, falls ill on the day of the crucifixion, and Julia, his *compadre*, must take his place. Learning of this, a guilt-ridden Freed dons the robes of a widow and runs off to be with her husband as he drags a 300-pound cross up a steep hill to where he is to be crucified. Informed that if the Christo dies, his wife must remain celibate for the rest of his life, Assante tries to persuade Julia to let him take his place. Stronger and more used to suffering (because of his prison experience) than Julia, Assante knows he will not die, and after confessing his love for Freed, he talks Julia into allowing him to be his substitute so that they can fight for her when the ceremony is concluded. Soon, Assante is strapped onto the cross while a life-size wood carving of the crucified Christ is placed opposite him. As the hours drag on, Assante suffers more than he bargained for and cannot help but stare into the lifelike eyes of the Christ statue. Assante survives the ordeal, however, and returns to Julia's farm to claim Freed, but the woman will have nothing to do with him, protesting, "You are the Christo. You hung on the cross." Realizing that his suffering has paid for their sins and saved his friend's marriage, Assante wanders off into the mountains, alone.

Slow moving and very predictable until the last 20 minutes, THE PENITENTE, given its bizarre religious subtext, screams to be directed by the likes of Luis Bunuel. The Spanish master would have taken this simple tale and transformed it into a truly gripping and artful examination of love, lust, and religion. Instead, what we have is a competently directed and only marginally interesting romantic triangle that exploits a religious sect. Writer-director Cliff Osmond, a former character actor and sometime scriptwriter, presents his tale in an unrelentingly somber manner wherein all is played out with a tired air of inevitability. As a result, Osmond fails to convey the romantic and religious passion necessary to fully explore his characters' motivations. Compare the films of Martin Scorsese, including the controversial LAST TEMPTATION OF CHRIST, which always draw audiences into the fevered passions of his characters, and in which, through draining catharsis, viewers attain a state of grace. His films are powerful because the viewer is run through the wringer *with* Charlie, Travis Bickle, Jake Lamotta, and Jesus Christ. Osmond, however, distances his audience from his characters and forces us to watch them like bugs under the microscope. Thus, his film is not terribly engaging, and one is left to admire the game performances of the two male leads and ponder the beautiful scenery until the crucifixion scene, with which the film actually begins to come to life. Unfortunately, it is too little too late, and most will have lost interest by then. The film's distributors must have felt likewise, for THE PENITENT received an extremely limited release and made a quick transition to home video. Note: Surprisingly, the Penitente sect has been presented on film at least once before, in an extremely obscure movie from 1936 titled THE PENITENTE MURDER CASE, which contained actual footage of a Penitente ritual filmed clandestinely. *(Nudity, sexual situations, adult situations.)*

p, Michael Fitzgerald; d, Cliff Osmond; w, Cliff Osmond; ph, Robin Vidgeon (Technicolor); ed, Peter Taylor; m, Alex North; makeup, Lucrecia Munoz.

Drama   **Cas.**   **(PR:C-O MPAA:PG-13)**

PERFECT VICTIM †   (1988) 100m Vertigo c

Deborah Shelton *(Liz Winters)*, Lyman Ward *(Steven Hack)*, Tom Dugan *(Brandon Poole)*, Clarence Williams III *(Lt. Kevin White)*, Nikolette Scorsese *(Melissa Cody)*, Jackie Swanson *(Carrie Marks)*, Phil Roberson, Geoffrey Rivas, John Agar.

An AIDS-infected killer is on the loose, has raped a pair of fashion models, and has top-flight agency head Shelton in his sights as his next victim. On his trail is a tough cop (Clarence Williams III, formerly Link of TV's "The Mod Squad") who must stop this lunatic before he can kill or infect anyone else. Lead Deborah Shelton, of TV's "Dallas" and the drilled heroine of Brian De Palma's BODY DOUBLE, also doubled as executive producer; her husband, Shuki Levy, served as director and co-screenwriter.

p, Jonathon Braun; d, Shuki Levy; w, Shuki Levy, Joe Hailey, Bob Barron; ph, Frank Byers, Michael Mathews (CFI color); ed, Jonathon Braun; m, Shuki Levy; art d, Shane Nelson; set d, Ann Banks; stunts, Eric Cord.

Thriller   **Cas.**   **(PR:NR MPAA:R)**

PERMANENT RECORD★★½   (1988) 92m PAR c

Alan Boyce *(David Sinclair)*, Keanu Reeves *(Chris Townsend)*, Michelle Meyrink *(M.G.)*, Jennifer Rubin *(Lauren)*, Pamela Gidley *(Kim)*, Michael Elgart *(Jake)*, Richard Bradford *(Leo Verdell, Principal)*, Dakin Matthews *(Mr. McBain, Drama Teacher)*, Barry Corbin *(Jim Sinclair)*, Kathy Baker *(Martha Sinclair)*, Joshua Taylor *(Lee Sinclair)*, Sam Vlahos *(Mr. Townsend)*, David Selberg *(Dr. Moss, School Superintendent)*, Ron Jaxon *(Woody)*, Kevin Brown *(Tiny)*, Paul Ganus *(Randy)*, Phil Diskin, Lou Reed, Garrett Lambert, Carolyn Tomei.

©PARAMOUNT

Marisa Silver's first feature, 1984's OLD ENOUGH, dealt with an 11-year-old girl's struggle to become an adolescent. In PERMANENT RECORD, Silver's second feature, teenage characters struggle to *live* as adolescents—without succumbing to teen pressures and committing suicide. With a rising national teenage suicide rate and a barrage of media reports heightening public awareness, PERMANENT RECORD is both timely and socially relevant. Unfortunately, the power of its subject far outweighs the power of the film. For the first half-hour, we are shown a typical group of high-school friends: Boyce, the intelligent, well-liked musician who everyone predicts will find fame and fortune; Reeves, his best friend, a guitarist whose skills improve with Boyce's tutoring; Meyrink, the loner who hopes to be a writer; Rubin, the aspiring singer; Gidley, the cool blonde who has no-questions-asked sex with Boyce; and their tough but respected principal, Bradford, who is responsive to their needs. These teens do what many do—listen to rock'n'roll, play in a band, hang out and drink beer, have sex, and throw parties. They're not delinquents, however. All are intelligent and involved (with varying degrees of enthusiasm) in a school production of Gilbert and Sullivan's "H.M.S. Pinafore." Boyce has the most responsibility, arranging the music charts for the production. He is also working towards a college music scholarship and writing a song for his band's big recording date (where real-life rocker Lou Reed makes a cameo). He's good-looking, personable, and respected by friends and teachers alike until, during the biggest party of the year, he jumps to his death from a nearby cliff. For a few days, everyone assumes the death is accidental. His friends plan a memorial service and lament the unfairness of his being taken away. Then Reeves receives a parcel containing Boyce's completed charts for the school production—and a suicide note. Opinions of Boyce change, the memorial service is cancelled by Bradford's superior, and Reeves bears the weight of not having been able to prevent his friend's death. When the memorial is cancelled, Reeves rebels, insults Bradford's refusal to stand up to his superior, heaves a brick through the principal's office window, and is consequently expelled. As punishment, his unfeeling father leaves on a business trip and takes the boy's guitar with him. Without his best friend or his guitar, Reeves turns to Boyce's parents, Corbin and Baker. Longing to fill a personal void, they become surrogates. Corbin lets him have an old guitar of his—a prized Fender Stratocaster—and even Boyce's little brother, who is growing emotionally distant, looks up to Reeves. Boyce's death now brings more responsibility to Reeves, who experiences the same pressures that Boyce did as people rely on him to take over Boyce's role. His band members breathe hot down his neck, demanding that he write a song for their rapidly approaching recording date. Drunk, he gets into his car and heads for Boyce's parents' home. When he swerves, crashes, and nearly runs over Boyce's little brother, Baker rushes to protect her only living son, while Corbin tries to shake some sense into the drunken teenager. Reeves completely breaks down, clinging to the father and crying, "I should have stopped him." Unlike Boyce, however, Reeves can handle the pressure. He comes through in the clutch—his band loves his song (composed of his lyrics and Boyce's music), and he feel some self-worth. The production of "H.M.S. Pinafore" also goes smoothly, though Rubin interrupts the proceedings with a forbidden tribute to Boyce as she delivers a song that Reeves wrote in his friend's honor *a cappella.* The audience—students, parents, and faculty—burst out in applause. At the film's end, the same group of students are gathered at their "spot" near the edge of the cliff—a fence now separating them from the rocky shore below. Meyrink speaks for all her friends when she tells Reeves she has found her own voice in her writing, discovering a self-worth and realizing that her life is important.

PERMANENT RECORD is a clumsy film that, in spite of itself, at times manages to be quite powerful. Its opening half-hour is an attempt at naturalism—showing these kids in their everyday lives—that becomes ho-hum tedium on a par with an "Afterschool Special." Despite everyone's attempt to make this high school "scene" appear real, it comes off as forced, and, until the suicide, the entire audience sits in anticipation, simply waiting for *something* to happen. In effect, the movie doesn't really start until Boyce commits suicide. Before that it is just a standard canvas upon which Silver paints her standard characters. Once Boyce finally kills himself, the clumsiness of the script and direction persist; in addition, except for those who saw the film before critics and friends revealed the premise, everyone in the audience knows Boyce will commit suicide, which diminishes some of the film's impact. It is in Keanu Reeves' character that one finds the film's remaining power. An exceptionally gifted actor (he was wonderful as the voice of conscience in last year's similar, but far superior, RIVER'S EDGE), Reeves carries this film on his shoulders. Its two finest scenes—which show Reeves receiving the suicide note and his breakdown in Corbin's arms—both revolve around Reeves. The rest of PERMANENT RECORD simply falls flat, with Richard Bradford proving the only other major character (Boyce's family is unfortunately relegated to the background) able to rise above its treacly surroundings. For some reason, Silver injects the film with countless scenes of the production of "H.M.S. Pinafore"—we get auditions, rehearsals, more rehearsals, backstage drama, and the show itself, until we just can't stand the thought of ever hearing the names of Gilbert and/or Sullivan again.

Because of its subject matter, the casting of Reeves, and the photography of Frederick Elmes, one can't help but recall RIVER'S EDGE when viewing Silver's film. Reeves' Matt from RIVER'S EDGE and his Chris from PERMANENT RECORD are similar types in similar situations (although while Matt and his friends are trying to cope with the *murder* of a friend, Chris and his friends are confronted with a *suicide*). In both films, Reeves' characters are the moral centers. In both films, it is not the death of the friend that is important, but the survivors' ability to cope. PERMANENT RECORD, despite its premise, never really addresses the act of suicide, or suicide as a disturbing phenomenon of 1980s teen culture. Only once in this film that dramatizes teenage suicide is the matter even discussed—one brief exchange of dialog between Reeves and Meyrink, that's it. While RIVER'S EDGE is a film about modern culture's twisted outlook on passion and murder, PERMANENT RECORD isn't really about anything; it even makes its suicide a clean, bloodless one that never even produces a corpse and, thereby, won't repel anyone in the audience. PERMANENT RECORD is a film filled with good intentions that should be seen and discussed by teens and even preteens (despite some foul language and excessive beer drinking) and, perhaps more importantly, parents. It performs a service for which Marisa Silver, producer Frank Mancuso, Jr. (who, interestingly, has also produced the FRIDAY THE 13TH films), and Paramount Pictures should all be congratulated. One just wishes the filmmakers had had enough guts and insight to do more than scratch the surface. *(Profanity, substance abuse, adult situations.)*

p, Frank Mancuso, Jr.; d, Marisa Silver; w, Jarre Fees, Alice Liddle, Larry Ketron; ph, Frederick Elmes; ed, Robert Brown; m, Joe Strummer; md, Neil Portnow, Becky Mancuso; prod d, Michel Levesque; art d, Steven Karatza; cos, Tracy Tynan.

Drama	Cas.	(PR:A-C MPAA:PG-13)

PHANTASM II**   (1988) 93m UNIV c

James Le Gros *(Mike Pearson)*, Reggie Bannister *(Reggie)*, Angus Scrimm *(The Tall Man)*, Paula Irvine *(Liz)*, Samantha Phillips *(Alchemy)*, Kenneth Tigar *(Father Meyers)*, Ruth C. Engel *(Grandma)*, Mark Anthony Major *(Mortician)*, Rubin Kushner *(Grandpa)*, Stacey Travis *(Jeri)*, J. Patrick McNamara *(Psychologist)*.

©MCA (UNIVERSAL)

Content with recycling the highlights of Don Coscarelli's 1979 cult favorite PHANTASM without ever establishing its own identity, this shockingly dull sequel only approaches the wild imagination and surrealistic horrors of the original when it steals from it. More a remake than a sequel, the film begins promisingly enough with a well-crafted transition between footage from 1979 and new material. The story picks up exactly where it left off, with young Mike being captured by the "Tall Man" (Scrimm), a supernatural mortician with yellow embalming fluid in his veins. Ice cream vendor Bannister hears the commotion and comes to the teenager's rescue. After fighting off a hoard of Scrimm's little helpers (which resemble the Jawas in STAR WARS), Bannister manages to wrest the boy from certain death. Years later, we see that Mike has grown into an adult (played by Le Gros) and has been in a mental hospital since the incident. He is finally released after he declares that all the events were hallucinations. Bannister picks up Le Gros at the hospital and is dismayed to discover that he continues to believe everything that happened was real. In addition, Le Gros has begun receiving psychic messages from a young woman (Irvine) who shares his visions of Scrimm. Le Gros senses that Scrimm is still after them, and he's proved correct when Bannister's house explodes, killing his entire family. Convinced that Le Gros is right, Bannister vows to help the young man track down and destroy Scrimm, who, apparently, is traveling across the country creating ghost towns by invading cemeteries, snatching the corpses, and turning them into slaves (the Jawa-like creatures) who toil for him in another dimension. To prepare for battle, Le Gros and Bannister break into a hardware store and arm themselves with all manner of weapons, including a quadruple sawed-off shotgun and a chain saw. Rigging harnesses that resemble those worn by the soldiers in ALIENS, the two become a very lethal mobile force. In time, Le Gros and Bannister hook up with Irvine, and the three of them do battle with Scrimm. Of course, Scrimm's deadly flying silver spheres, dubbed the "Flying Cuisinarts" by some critics, are back for the sequel and they whiz about drilling people's brains out. After a furious climax that contains all manner of nightmarish imagery, Scrimm is finally dispatched when Bannister mixes acid into the embalming fluid that is the Tall Man's life force. With Scrimm destroyed, the warriors jump into a nearby hearse and drive off, only to discover that the horror is not yet over. Bannister is killed, leaving Le Gros and Irvine to chant, "It's only a dream. It's only a dream." But just when the audience thinks that may be the case, Scrimm appears in the back window of the hearse and declares, "No it isn't." End of movie.

The beauty of the first PHANTASM was the fever-dream quality that paved the way for A NIGHTMARE ON ELM STREET. Coscarelli was in his early 20s when he made PHANTASM, and the film seemed the product of the warped imagination of a teenager, full of creative and original scares rooted in basic fears of abandonment, loneliness, sex, and death. Although viewers left the theater buzzing about the flying silver sphere, it was only one element in a film filled with unique, personal, witty, and, at the same time, terrifying imagery rarely seen in low-budget horror films. The sequel, however, lacks that delirious youthful imagination. While its last 20 minutes are exciting, they are wholly derivative of the first film, and Coscarelli takes a long, long time getting there. Structured like a traditional road movie with its protagonists involved in a quest, PHANTASM II drags along from ghost town to ghost town with

the heroes peering into empty graves. There are some memorable moments along the way—fleeting images scattered throughout the film that have a cumulative effect——but when the shocks do come, they are mostly retreads of the highlights from the first film, including a virtually identical sequence wherein the guys get momentarily sucked into the other dimension for a look at the poor slaves trudging along an arid, other-worldly desert.

This is not to say that Coscarelli was obligated to explain the intriguing ambiguities regarding the Tall Man and his origins left over from the first film, but there is little new story development here, leading one to wonder why, after so many years, he felt the need to create a sequel to the film for which he will be remembered the rest of his life, when it is obvious he has run out of ideas? The unfortunate answer must surely be that, after a series of setbacks that had stalled his career, he sought to recapture the success that brought him attention in the first place. Too bad the audience, especially those who thrilled to the first film, found his uninspired sequel a bore and told their friends to stay away. PHANTASM II did poorly at the box office and it appears Coscarelli has made yet another bad career move. That is unfortunate, for, despite this rather mundane effort, Coscarelli continues to exhibit a glimmer of unique, personal cinematic vision, a rare commodity these days. *(Graphic violence, gore effects, nudity, sexual situations, profanity.)*

p, Roberto A. Quezada; d, Don Coscarelli; w, Don Coscarelli; ph, Daryn Okada (Foto-Kem Color); ed, Peter Teschner; m, Fred Myrow, Christopher L. Stone; prod d, Philip Duffin; art d, Byrnadette di Santo; set d, Dominic Wymark; spec eff, Mark Shostrom, Wayne Beauchamp; cos, Carla Gibbons; makeup, Melnie A. Kay.

Horror	Cas.	(PR:O MPAA:R)

PLAIN CLOTHES †   (1988) 98m Sierra Alta/PAR c

Arliss Howard *(Nick Dunbar/"Nick Springsteen")*, Suzy Amis *(Robin Torrence)*, George Wendt *(Chet Butler)*, Diane Ladd *(Jane Melway)*, Seymour Cassel *(Ed Malmburg)*, Larry Pine *(Dave Hechtor)*, Jackie Gayle *(Coach Zeffer)*, Abe Vigoda *(Mr. Wiseman)*, Robert Stack *(Mr. Gardner, Principal)*, Alexandra Powers *(Daun-Marie Zeffer)*, Loren Dean *(Matt Dunbar)*, Harry Shearer *(Simon Feck)*, Peter Dobson *(Kyle Kerns)*, Reginald Veljohnson, Max Perlich.

In 1983, Martha Coolidge directed VALLEY GIRL, a teen comedy that was a big hit and pointed to Coolidge as one of the top women directors in Hollywood. Then came THE JOY OF SEX, an embarrassingly unfunny picture. REAL GENIUS followed in 1985 and, while not a complete failure, was surely disappointing. This year PLAIN CLOTHES, another nothing picture from Coolidge, receiving a token release in just a few cities across the country, came and went with little ado. Howard stars as a young cop who goes undercover as a high school student to solve a teacher's murder. Since the chief suspect is Howard's younger brother, the undercover cop has a vested interest in finding the real killer. Along the way, he falls for the gym teacher's daughter and becomes the object of his home room teacher's desires.

p, Richard Wechsler, Michael Manheim; d, Martha Coolidge; w, A. Scott Frank (based on a story by Frank, Dan Vining); ph, Daniel Hainey (CFI Color); ed, Patrick Kennedy, Edward Abroms; m, Scott Wilk; prod d, Michel Levesque; art d, William Apperson; set d, Marya Delia Javier; spec eff, Robert Riggs; cos, Tracy Tynan.

Mystery	Cas.	(PR:NR MPAA:PG)

PLATOON LEADER**   (1988) 100m Breton/Cannon c

Michael Dudikoff *(Lt. Jeff Knight)*, Robert F. Lyons *(Sgt. Michael McNamara)*, Michael De Lorenzo *(Pvt. Raymond Bacera)*, Rich Fitts *(Robert Hayes)*, Jesse Dabson *(Joshua Parker)*, Brian Libby *(Roach)*, William Smith, Tony Pierce.

It usually doesn't take as long for an American war to make its way to the big screen as the war in Vietnam did, but in the last couple of years the floodgates have opened. While some of the recent Vietnam films, like PLATOON, are superb depictions of the deep ambivalence and dislocation American troops felt there, some have more modest intentions, namely just to be entertaining. PLATOON LEADER is in the latter class, pale in comparison to PLATOON or APOCALYPSE NOW or GO TELL THE SPARTANS, but—when considered in the context of the war film as an entire genre—not bad, either. Dudikoff is the title character, a young lieutenant fresh from the States. He is stationed at a small firebase, from which the last commander has already taken off. At first, Dudikoff's inexperience makes him the butt of jokes from his battle-hardened troops, but under the tutelage of sergeant Lyons, he soon learns the ropes and leads daily patrols into the bush. In one particularly effective scene, the dawn light finds a small group directly in the path of a large number of Viet Cong. Lying low in the grass, they watch as hundreds of the enemy run in slow motion over and all around them. In another scene, a soldier overdoses on heroin while on patrol, whereupon Lyons pulls the needle out of his arm and machine guns the body to give the appearance that the man died in action. When intelligence reveals that the Viet Cong are preparing a major attack on the base and the village it protects, Dudikoff gets permission to lead a preemptive strike against enemy troop concentrations. There is a breakdown of communications, however, and the attack fails. Lyons is wounded and Dudikoff waits to put him on a helicopter before heading for the village, which is now getting the brunt of the VC attack. By the time they arrive, the Viet Cong have left, leaving the village in flames, its inhabitants dead or scattered, and the firebase without a purpose.

Despite its pandering title (changed from NAM to capitalize on the success of PLATOON) and no-name cast, PLATOON LEADER is not that bad. Aaron

Norris' direction shows some improvement over his debut in brother Chuck's BRADDOCK: MISSING IN ACTION 3, and he may yet make a serviceable action director, at least as skilled as, say, Michael Winner. Michael Dudikoff has just the right square-jawed sincerity to portray the young officer trying in vain to make his training jibe with the reality in which he finds himself. Best, though, is Robert F. Lyons, whose performance as the combat-wise sergeant is in the finest tradition of this rather cliched character. The rest of the cast is less memorable, but do well just the same. While not the penetrating look at America's Vietnam experience that APOCALYPSE NOW was, PLATOON LEADER sure beats MISSING IN ACTION. (Violence, excessive profanity, substance abuse.)

p, Harry Alan Towers; d, Aaron Norris; w, Rick Marx, Andrew Deutsch, David Walker, Peter Welbeck [Harry Alan Towers] (based on the book by James R. McDonough); ph, Arthur Wooster (Rank color); ed, Michael J. Duthie; m, George S. Clinton; art d, John Rosewarne; set d, Emilia Roux; cos, Kady Dover; stunts, Jannie Weinand.

War   Cas.   (PR:O MPAA:R)

POKAYANIYE   (SEE: REPENTANCE, 1988, USSR)

POLICE ACADEMY 5: ASSIGNMENT MIAMI BEACH*   (1988) 90m WB c

Matt McCoy (Nick), Janet Jones (Kate Stratton), George Gaynes (Commandant Lassard), G.W. Bailey (Capt. Harris), Rene Auberjonois (Tony Stark), Bubba Smith (Moses Hightower), David Graf (Eugene Tackleberry), Michael Winslow (Larvelle Jones), Leslie Easterbrook (Debbie Callahan), Marion Ramsey (Lawrence Hooks), Lance Kinsey (Proctor), George R. Robertson (Hurst), Tab Thacker (House), Archie Hahn (Mouse), James Hampton (Mayor of Miami), Jerry Lazarus (Sugar), Dan Burrows (Bob the Janitor), Dana Mare (Graduating Policewoman), Richard Jansen (Kid with Toy Plane), Ruth Farley (Airport Information), Kathryn Grey, Via Van Ness (Stewardesses), A.L. Meet (Cigar Smoker), Don Fitzgerald (Commissioner Murdock), Arthur Edwards (Thief in Drag), Jeff Gillen (Thief's Victim), Susan Hatfield (Mayor's Wife), Ed Koynes (Dempsey), Tom Kouchalakos (Manny), Rubin Rabasa (Julian), Angelo Reno (Pete), Scott Weinger (Shark-attack Kid), Pam Bogart (Harris' Pick-up), Tony Crabtree (Activities Announcer), Nelson Orames (Crowd-control Cop), Julio Oscar Mechoso (Shooting-range Cop), Joni Siani (TV Interviewer), Jeff Breslauer (News Photographer).

Like a cartoon villain reappearing time and again after a series of dramatic setbacks, the "Police Academy" movies, seemingly impervious to the consensus of negative critical response, keep on coming, reinforcing the Hollywood dictum that nothing succeeds like box-office success. The film opens as the scheming Capt. Harris (Bailey) and his bumbling assistant break into the police commissioner's office and rifle through his files. Bailey searches for and ultimately finds evidence supporting his suspicion that the endearingly disoriented Police Academy Cmdt. Lassard (Gaynes) is past mandatory retirement age. After four movies' worth of frustrating near misses, he's convinced that his long-awaited opportunity to succeed Gaynes is at hand. Once made aware of Gaynes' age, the commissioner arranges to have him anointed police chief of the decade and have his impending retirement feted at a convention in Miami, where the commandant will be joined by a loyal core of Academy graduates (Smith, Graf, Winslow, and Easterbrook). Initially, Bailey savors the chance to remain at the Academy in Gaynes' absence, but he subsequently opts to attend, availing himself of a chance to distinguish himself in the eyes of the assembled police hierarchy. Running parallel to scenes on the plane en route to Miami and at the airport terminal is a jewel heist pulled off by a trio of inept professional thieves. As Gaynes arrives at the terminal with his charges, he characteristically triggers a chain reaction of Rube Goldberg mishaps. In a slapstick encounter, Gaynes runs into the thieves and mistakenly picks up their gem-laden luggage (his bag and their's look identical). While the zany Police Academy veterans party at the convention site and take part in a host of staged demonstrations (crowd control techniques, etc.), the bungling robbers try to recover the jewels, with Gaynes unwittingly thwarting them at every turn. When they finally panic and take him hostage, Gaynes is convinced the kidnaping is merely another in the series of demos and genially complies. Bailey seizes his opportunity to play the hero and rescue Gaynes, but is undermined by his incompetent aide. It's up to the Academy regulars, who are mobilized and, in a high-speed chase across the Everglades, overtake the "perpetrators." In a final flourish, Gaynes throws his kidnaper off the hydroplane and assures the safe return of the jewels. Gaynes' accidental heroism is rewarded: he is asked to stay on as commandant, in the crowning indignity to be heaped upon the thoroughly defeated Bailey.

The first "Police Academy" film was a disarming combination of light satire and sophomoric spoof. POLICE ACADEMY 5, however, is more a product of inertia than originality—it neither adds fresh comedy to its antecedents (there is a limit to the humor to be derived from recycled references to breasts and flatulence), furthers the story, nor deepens the relationships. In addition, the script repeatedly announces what is taking place on the screen, indicating an offensive lack of confidence in its audience (thus, Bailey thumbs through the commissioner's files and broadcasts his actions as if an explanatory caption were needed). Aside from merely rehearsing its by now standard formula (the only real "twist" is in transplanting the action to Miami), POLICE ACADEMY 5 present a patchwork of ideas borrowed from a score of wittier and better-done comedies (the bag mix-up is a shopworn convention of 30s screwball comedy and boulevard farce; an in-flight scene is a weak diversion of AIRPLANE; the relationship between Gaynes and Bailey is a brazenly obvious appropriation from the "Pink Panther" movies, etc.). As for the acting and direction, it's hard to determine whether they are hobbled by a hackneyed script or whether the entire dismal enterprise is a true ensemble effort. POLICE ACADEMY 5 is a cops-and-robbers film that places everyone under suspicion. (Violence.)

p, Paul Maslansky, Donald West; d, Alan Myerson; w, Stephen J. Curwick (based on characters created by Neal Israel, Pat Proft); ph, James Pergola (Technicolor); ed, Hubert C. de La Bouillerie; m, Robert Folk; prod d, Trevor Williams; set d, Don Ivey; spec eff, Roy Downey, Wayne Beauchamp, Robert Cooper; cos, Robert Musco; stunts, Gary Hymes; makeup, Marie Del Russo.

Comedy   Cas.   (PR:C MPAA:PG)

POLTERGEIST III*½   (1988) 97m MGM/MGM-UA c

Tom Skerritt (Bruce Gardner), Nancy Allen (Patricia Gardner), Heather O'Rourke (Carol Anne Freeling), Zelda Rubinstein (Tangina Barrons), Lara Flynn Boyle (Donna Gardner), Kip Wentz (Scott), Richard Fire (Dr. Seaton), Nathan Davis (Kane), Rober May (Burt), Paul Graham (Martin), Meg Weldon (Sandy), Stacy Gilchrist (Melissa), Joey Garfield (Jeff), Chris Murphy (Dusty), Roy Hytower (Nathan), Meg Thalken (Deborah), Dean Tokuno (Takamitsu), Catherine Gatz (Marcie), Paty Lombard (Helen), E.J. Murray (Mary), Sherry Narens (Mrs. Seaton), Phil Locker (Bill), Maureen Steindler (Old Woman), Alan Wilder, Brent Shaphren, Mindy Bell (Observers), Conrad Allan (Young Boy), Maureen Mueller (Gallery Woman), John Rusk (Gallery Man), Sam Sanders (Security Guard), Laurie V. Logan (Elevator Woman), Jerry Birn (Elevator Man), Jane Alderman (Scott's Mother), Mary Hogan, Laura Koppel, Chris Montana, Harold Taulbee, Lynn Koppel, Mark Zweigler, Wendy Wolfman, Christy Davis.

© MGM/UA

This second sequel to the hit 1982 haunted house extravaganza is an erratic affair containing some promising ideas and clever effects, which are, unfortunately, haphazardly presented in a narrative so perfunctory as to be almost nonexistent. The brainchild of writer-director Gary Sherman (who had the project dumped in his lap by the studio), POLTERGEIST III shifts the focus of the series from the suburbs to the city, setting the action in Chicago, in a newly constructed, state-of-the-art high-rise complex full of shops, offices, and apartments. Little blonde-haired Carol Anne (O'Rourke) lives with her Aunt Trish (Allen), her Uncle Bruce (Skerritt), and her teenage cousin (Boyle). Allen resents having to take care of her sister's child so soon after her own marriage to Skerritt has begun. After already making the adjustment to the presence of her husband's daughter from another marriage, she finds O'Rourke yet another unwanted distraction in her busy life. Skerritt is the general manager of the brand-new high rise, Allen is in the process of opening a swank art gallery on the retail level, and O'Rourke is enrolled in a school for highly intelligent but emotionally disturbed youngsters. Her therapist, the pithy Dr. Seaton (Fire), attributes the poltergeists that have haunted O'Rourke's past to mass hypnosis caused by her suggestions and ignores her protests that the ghost of the evil Rev. Kane (Davis) has found her in Chicago. Davis has indeed found O'Rourke in the Windy City, and he appears in mirrors and reflections beckoning her "into the light." The little girl is frightened, but because she knows no one will listen to her, she keeps her mouth shut and tries to ignore the malicious ghost. On the opening night of Allen's art gallery, however, Davis decides to strike. He lures O'Rourke out of the apartment to the parking garage, where he snatches her into another dimension through a puddle on the floor. Boyle and her boy friend, Wentz, try to save the girl, but they, too, are pulled into the netherworld. Meanwhile, the diminutive psychic Tangina (Rubinstein) senses that O'Rourke is in trouble and flies across the country to come to her aide. Soon Skerritt and Allen are dragged into the supernatural conflict, and they team up with Rubinstein to fight the poltergeist. Sadly, Allen's lack of love for O'Rourke is a weak link that the spirits exploit, and it looks like the girl may be lost forever. During the tumultuous battle even Rubinstein is sucked into the void, but Allen eventually feels guilty and declares her love for the child. The spirits then release all those they possess, and the family is reunited. Rubinstein, however, chooses to stay in the spirit world to help guide Davis to a more peaceful afterlife.

This movie works perfectly well as an excuse to parade a number of cleverly conceived and executed in-camera (live) special effects before the public, but when the handful of truly remarkable tricks have passed, what is left behind is an incoherent mess filled with bad dialog, weak performances, unintentional humor, and some surprisingly dull scenes of poltergeist mayhem. Writer-director Sherman's idea to set the action in a modern skyscraper is a good one, and, shooting in Chicago's John Hancock Center and the Water Tower Place complex, he uses the enclosed, claustrophobic feel of such places to his advantage. Regrettably, however, his screenplay is short on inspiration, and the film soon disintegrates into a repetitive, underdeveloped, and uninvolving chase scene.

Sherman's lack of interest in the narrative infects his direction of the actors as well. Veteran character actor Tom Skerritt looks distinctly bored throughout the proceedings, Nancy Allen's performance is appallingly apathetic, and, as the disbelieving therapist, Chicago actor-playwright Richard Fire ("Bleacher Bums") draws gales of unintentional laughter with his mannered, over-the-top characterization. Nathan Davis (father of ABOVE THE LAW director Andrew Davis) is given little to do other than leer from under pounds of heavy facial makeup designed to make him look more like the late Julian Beck, who played Kane in POLTERGEIST II. Likewise, the only two actors brought back from the first two POLTERGEIST films, Zelda Rubinstein and Heather O'Rourke, are underutilized by Sherman and treated more like icons of past success than vital characters.

Twelve-year-old O'Rourke, who died from a bowel obstruction six months after filming was completed, looks ill in the film, her cheeks large and puffy from the cortisone doctors had given her to combat what they thought was Crohn's disease (chronic inflammation of the bowel). The illness, however, had been misdiagnosed, and the film is dedicated to the young starlet, who died on January 31, 1988. At this point there seems to be nowhere else to go with the POLTERGEIST concept and one would hope that part three will be the last, but when studios are asked to choose between a proven money-maker and common sense, the latter usually loses. *(Violence, gore effects, profanity.)*

p, Barry Bernardi; d, Gary Sherman; w, Gary Sherman, Brian Taggert; ph, Alex Nepomniaschy (Astro Color); ed, Ross Albert; m, Joe Renzetti; prod d, Paul Eads; spec eff, Cal Acord; cos, Tom McKinley; ch, T. Daniel; stunts, Ben R. Scott; makeup, John Caglione, Jr., Jerry Turnage.

Horror   **Cas.**   **(PR:C-O MPAA:PG-13)**

POUND PUPPIES AND THE LEGEND OF BIG PAW***   (1988) 76m
Atlantic-Kushner-Locke-Maltese/Tri-Star c

Voices of: George Rose *(McNasty)*, B.J. Ward *(Whopper)*, Ruth Buzzi *(Nose Marie)*, Brennan Howard *(Cooler)*, Cathy Cadavini *(Collette)*, Nancy Cartwright *(Bright Eyes)*, Greg Berg, Ryan Davis, Joe Deido, Ashley Hall, Janice Kawaye, Alwyn Kusher, Mark Vieha, Jasper Kushner, Robbie Lee, Tony Longo, Hal Rayle, Wayne Scherzer, Susan Silo, James Swodek, Frank Welker.

This animated kids' film opens with a gang of crooks breaking into a museum, attempting to steal the "Bone of Scone." According to legend, the bone is responsible for "Puppy Power," which makes it possible for youngsters and dogs to communicate with each other. A villain named McNasty wants the bone, believing it will give him magical powers and enable him to rule the world. While making off with the bone, the thieves break it in half, thereby creating a world in which dogs and children cannot communicate. Enter the quadruped Cooler, who takes it upon himself to retrieve the sacred object and restore communication between canines and kids. McNasty and his gang are formidable opponents, however, and Cooler is going to need help if he is to get the bone back. He and his dog pack find Whopper, the Big Paw of the title, a huge pooch who's had a rough life and is hiding in the swamp. It takes some doing, but Cooler and the gang are able to make friends with Whopper and then enlist his aid in regaining the bone. Naturally, they are able to defeat McNasty, take possession of the bone, and put children and dogs back on speaking terms.

Only the very young are likely to be entertained by this pallid feature-length cartoon, and even they may find it all very confusing. To tell the story, the script shifts from the present to the 1950s, to ancient times and back again, and little ones may find all this time travel mind-boggling. The animation is basic low-budget dull, and the voices don't add much to the characterizations. There are some nice songs, done in 1950s doo-wop rock style, but overall the film is limp and forgettable. Produced in conjunction with the Tonka toy company, the film seems likely to have been conceived as a vehicle for promoting stuffed replicas of the animated canines that appear in the film. Since POUND PUPPIES received only very limited release, however, it's unlikely the filmmakers reaped any substantial benefits from promotional tie-ins.

p, Donald Kushner, Peter Locke; d, Pierre DeCelles; w, Jim Carlson, Terrence McDonnell; ed, John Blizek; m, Richard Kosinski, Sam Winans, Bill Reichenbach; md, Steve Tyrell; m/l, Ashley Hall, Stephanie Tyrell, Steve Tyrell; art d, Pierre DeCelles.

Children's/Animation   **Cas.**   **(PR:AA MPAA:G)**

POWWOW HIGHWAY †   (1988, US/Brit.) 91m Handmade c

A. Martinez *(Buddy Red Bow)*, Gary Farmer *(Philbert Bono)*, Amanda Wyss *(Rabbit Layton)*, Joanelle Nadine Romero *(Bonnie Red Bow)*, Sam Vlahos *(Chief Joseph)*, Wayne Waterman *(Wolf Tooth)*, Margo Kane *(Imogene)*, Geoff Rivas *(Sandy Youngblood)*, Roscoe Born *(Agent Jack Novall)*.

Screened at the Montreal World Film Festival but yet to get a major release, this British-US coproduction from George Harrison's Handmade Films concerns two American Indians from the Northern Cheyenne Reservation (Farmer and Martinez) who fight against greedy mining companies who want to despoil their sacred lands. Playing dirty, the mining company teams up with unscrupulous federal agents and stages a phony drug bust on A Martinez's sister, who lives in Santa Fe. Outraged, A Martinez and Farmer head out to Santa Fe to rescue her. On the road, the two native Americans are exposed to life on many different reservations, the insensitive and racist attitudes of uncomprehending whites, and the fact that the once-bountiful lands of

the American West are on the verge of vanishing. The film features songs by former Band guitarist Robbie Robertson.

p, Jan Wieringa; d, Jonathan Wacks; w, Janet Heany, Jean Stawarz (based on the novel by David Seals); ph, Toyomichi Kurita; ed, James A. Stewart; m, Barry Goldberg; prod d, Cynthia Sowder; cos, Isis Mussenden.

Drama   **(PR:NR MPAA:R)**

PRESIDIO, THE*½   (1988) 97m PAR c

Sean Connery *(Lt. Col. Alan Caldwell)*, Mark Harmon *(Jay Austin)*, Meg Ryan *(Donna Caldwell)*, Jack Warden *(St. Maj. Ross "Top" Maclure)*, Mark Blum *(Arthur Peale)*, Dana Gladstone *(Lt. Col. Paul Lawrence)*, Jenette Goldstein *(Patti Jean Lynch)*, Marvin J. McIntyre, Don Calfa, Susan Saiger, Robert Lesser, Rick Zumwalt, Tracy Tanen, James Hooks Reynolds.

©PARAMOUNT

This cut-and-dried picture features far more talk than action and is saved only by the unwavering professionalism of Sean Connery, appearing in his first role since his Oscar-winning performance in THE UNTOUCHABLES. Directed and photographed by Peter Hyams (RUNNING SCARED; 2010; and Connery starrer OUTLAND), THE PRESIDIO is set in San Francisco and pairs an aging Army lieutenant colonel (Connery) with a slick young cop (Harmon) in the investigation of the murder of a military policewoman. The killing took place during a break-in at the officer's club on the Presidio (a military compound within the city's borders), leaving Connery and Harmon bickering over which of them has jurisdiction in the case. As it just so happens, Harmon had been an MP under Connery's command until, under threat of court-martial, he quit the military after arresting and punching out a drunken colonel (Gladstone). Harmon still holds a grudge because he feels Connery should have supported him and his partner, who, coincidentally, was the murdered MP. Complicating matters is Connery's frisky daughter, Ryan, who has recently returned from college with burning loins. Naturally, she and Harmon have a wicked passion for each other. The next hour or so is devoted to an excess of pointless exposition: Ryan can't forgive Connery for her mother's suicide some 20 years previously; Ryan has trouble committing to Harmon because of her relationship with her domineering father; and Connery has been hardened by a rough time in Vietnam, where he was saved by the heroic Warden, a sergeant who runs a military museum and acts as Ryan's surrogate father and confidante. In the last 20 minutes, director Hyams remembers that, about an hour earlier, he began a film about a murder in the officer's club, and in a last-ditch effort to tie the film together, Connery and Harmon dig up some answers. A powerful businessman with CIA connections turns out to be masterminding a plot to smuggle diamonds from the Philippines to the US via bottled water. This sets up the shoot-'em-up finale in a water-bottling warehouse, giving Hyams and friends the chance to splash about in the liquid. It turns out that Warden, who is brutally gunned down in another heroic effort to save Connery, was a reluctant party to the smuggling scheme. After a teary graveside eulogy, Connery, Ryan, and Harmon all wander off into the sunset arm in arm.

A thoroughly uninvolving picture, THE PRESIDIO is chiefly the victim of a horrendous screenplay by Larry Ferguson (BEVERLY HILLS COP II and the 1985 Connery vehicle HIGHLANDER—both of which suffer from wretched writing). When it isn't providing mundane dialog, Ferguson's script assaults the viewer with senseless exposition continuously dredged up from the characters' pasts. This is one of the few pictures you'll see in which the characters spend more time complaining about the past than doing anything in the present. Structurally, the film is even worse off, stressing the big, steamy romance between Ryan and Harmon and painting the lovers as fleshy magnets. Unfortunately, however, all of this takes place off-screen and is *told* rather than *shown*. Reportedly a number of scenes between Ryan and Harmon ended up on the editing room floor, which would explain why even though they are supposedly deeply involved with each other they hardly appear together on-screen.

There are, however, a couple of noteworthy moments in the film. The opening chase (a rehash of BULLITT, filmed at night) is a real roller-coaster ride, but since the drivers are unidentified, there's zero audience identification. Another fun scene is a saloon confrontation between Connery and a drunken thug, in which Connery uses only his right thumb, poking and jabbing at the bruiser and finally debilitating him by attacking a pressure point his throat. Connery is the film's saving grace, but one can't help but feel a bit embarrassed for him as he puts up with such listless filmmaking. Mark Harmon's "St. Elsewhere" TV image follows him onto the screen, and his performance is fairly likable, albeit unmemorable. The lovely Meg Ryan, who spiced up D.O.A. with her presence, isn't given much to do here. Having nothing to do with the murder plot, she basically serves as a token character to bridge the gap from one Harmon-Connery scene to the next. Her big pseudo-sexual, game-playing line—"cut to the chase" —sparks an apparently metaphoric, but ultimately pointless, car chase between her and Harmon, an okay idea that is poorly executed. Last seen in Woody Allen's SEPTEMBER, Jack Warden, like Connery, is a consummate professional who refuses to allow his performance to be dragged down by Ferguson's waterlogged script and Hyams' uninspired direction. Just a month before shooting commenced, Paramount was reportedly attempting to persuade Marlon Brando to take the Warden role, and THE PRESIDIO was originally to be directed by Tony Scott (TOP GUN; BEVERLY HILLS COP II). *(Profanity, sexual situation.)*

p, D. Constantine Conte; d, Peter Hyams; w, Larry Ferguson; ph, Peter Hyams (Panavision, Technicolor); ed, James Mitchell; m, Bruce Broughton; m/l, Johnny Mercer; prod d, Albert Brenner; art d, Kandy Stern; set d, Roland E. Hill, Jr., Harold L. Fuhrman, Bernard Cutler; spec eff, Philip C. Cory; tech, Major Mary Rupert, Lt. Col. Alex Zwirner; stunts, Glenn Wilder.

Action/Thriller **Cas.** **(PR:C-O MPAA:R)**

PRIMAL SCREAM* (1988) 92m Anything Under-Hellfire/Unistar c

Kenneth J. McGregor *(Corby McHale)*, Sharon Mason *(Samantha Keller)*, Julie Miller *(Caitlin Foster)*, Jon Maurice *(Capt. Frank Gitto)*, Joseph White *(Nicky Fingeas)*, Mickey Shaughnessy *(Charlie Waxman)*, Stephan Caldwell *(Olan Robert Foster)*, Edward Fallon *(Dr. Charles Kesselman)*, Vivian Nothaft *(Dirty Mary)*, Michael Laird *(O.E. Karp)*, Stephen Emhe *(Barman)*, Ryn Hodes *(Lisa)*, Morton Hodge *(Anton Kirar)*, Jenny Albert *(Vice-President Clarke)*, Steve Langone *(Boyle)*, Susan Farrell *(Santhany)*, Lon Hoffman *(Truck Driver)*, Herb James, Peter Harp *(Traffic Controllers)*, Gary Hollrah *(Bartender)*, Anne Horne Foulkrod *(Paramedic)*, Leonard Reino *(Pilot)*, Vincent Langone *(Officer)*, Sven Widecrantz *(Hot Room Foreman)*, Kevin Morrisey *(Thug)*, Sadistic Exploits *(Sand Box Band)*.

Set at the start of the 21st century, this utterly incomprehensible mishmash of science fiction/detective thriller opens with the successful test of Hellfire, an energy catalyst developed by the Thesaurus Corporation. Cut to a space station that is being attacked by rebels in protest over the existence of Hellfire—spaceships crashing, explosions thundering, men dying screaming. Back on earth, the pair in charge of the rebels are murdered. Suddenly, the film shifts gears and follows two-bit private eye McGregor, hired by Miller, the sister of Thesaurus' chairman, who claims her brother is spying on her and ruining her life. She wants it stopped. What follows is a befuddling series of nasty murders (Hellfire turns its victims into smoking embers) as McGregor wanders around confused, getting beaten up, arrested, and occasionally laid. When his girl friend is kidnaped by Fallon—Hellfire's creator and apparently the perpetrator of some of the murders—McGregor rescues her. Miller then turns out to be responsible for the rest of the deaths, and she and McGregor fight aboard his hovercraft until it is shot down by police, killing Miller.

This is one of those films that may have made more sense on paper than it does on the screen, but director-writer William Murray most certainly fails in one of his roles, probably behind the camera. None of the actors shows much interest in the proceedings, though Joseph White is okay as Kenneth McGregor's low-life sidekick. Not much of interest here for anybody. *(Violence, gore effects, sexual situations, excessive profanity.)*

p, Howard Foulkrod; d, William Murray; w, William Murray; ph, Dennis Peters (TVC Color); ed, Keith L. Reamer; m, Mark Knox; m/l, Mark Knox, Gerald Veasey, Bryan Lathrop, The Mob; art d, Robert Zeier; set d, Janet Coward, Carol Melman; spec eff, David Di Pietro; cos, Francesca Chay.

Science Fiction **Cas.** **(PR:O MPAA:NR)**

PRINCE OF PENNSYLVANIA, THE † (1988) 87m New Line c

Keanu Reeves *(Rupert Marshetta)*, Amy Madigan *(Carla Headlee)*, Bonnie Bedelia *(Pam Marshetta)*, Fred Ward *(Gary Marshetta)*, Joseph De Lisi *(Roger Marshetta)*, Jeff Hayenga *(Jack Sike)*, Tracy Ellis *(Lois Sike)*, Jay O. Sanders *(Trooper Joe)*.

Set in the rural coal mining town of Mars, Pennsylvania, Keanu Reeves stars as an alienated teenager who is driven to distraction by his dad, Ward, a Vietnam-vet right-wing conservative nut, and his mother, Bedelia, who is having an affair with her husband's best friend, Hayenga. Frustrated and troubled, Reeves rejects his unstable homelife and falls into the arms of Madigan, an ex-hippie who runs the Twin Twister Ice Cream Drive-In. Using Reeves for her own gain, Madigan encourages the teen to get back at his family by kidnaping his father and holding him for ransom. This offbeat black comedy was the directorial debut of screenwriter Ron Nyswaner (MRS. SOFFEL, SMITHEREENS), but it was given a scant theatrical release where it failed to ignite critical favor and died a swift death at the box office.

p, Joan Fishman, Kerry Orent; d, Ron Nyswaner; w, Ron Nyswaner; ph, Frank Prinzi; ed, Bill Sharf; prod d, Toby Corbett; set d, Marlene Marta; cos, Carol Wood.

Comedy **(PR:NR MPAA:NR)**

PRISON½** (1988) 102m Empire c

Viggo Mortensen *(Connie Burke)*, Chelsea Field *(Katherine Walker)*, Lane Smith *(Ethan Sharpe)*, Lincoln Kilpatrick *(Cresus)*, Tom Everett *(Rabbitt)*, Ivan Kane *(Lasagna)*, Andre De Shields *(Sandor)*, Tom "Tiny" Lister, Jr. *(Tiny)*, Steven E. Little *(Rhino)*, Mickey Yablans *(Brian Young)*, Larry Flash Jenkins *(Hershey)*, Arlen Dean Snyder *(Horton)*, Hal Landon, Jr. *(Wallace)*, Matt Kanen *(Johnson)*, Rod Lockman *(Kramer)*, Jeff L. Deist *(Gate Guard)*, Kane Hodder *(Charlie Forsythe/Gas-mask Guard)*, George D. Wallace *(Joe Reese)*, Luciana Capozzoli *(Claxton)*, Duke Spencer *(Scully)*, Pat Noonan *(Collins)*, Lyle D. Kelsey *(Guard)*, Rob Brox *(Pervis)*, Larry Moore *(Reptile Guard)*, John Hoke *(Old Warden)*.

Easily the best non-Stewart Gordon film to be released under the auspices of Empire Pictures, PRISON is an effective and unique chiller that successfully combines two genres: the prison film and horror. Conceived and produced by HALLOWEEN executive producer Irwin Yablans, the film begins at Creedmore prison in 1964 as an innocent man is being executed for the murder of an inmate who was really killed by brutal prison guard Smith. During the next 20 years Creedmore, which was built at the turn of the century, is closed down and Smith moves up the penal system ladder —although he is plagued by nightmares. In 1984, because the system has become overcrowded, the state decides to reopen Creedmore and make Smith its warden. Hundreds of prisoners are bused in and Smith immediately launches into a series of harsh actions designed to strike terror into the hearts of the inmates. Meanwhile, a detachment of prisoners is sent down into the bowels of the prison to knock through a wall and reopen the bricked-up execution chamber. When they do so, a bright blue light shines forth, and the vengeful ghost of the executed prisoner is loose. After the macabre and unexplainable deaths of several prisoners and guards, Smith begins to realize that the ghost is after him. As terror mounts, the frightened prisoners rebel and a full-scale riot ensues. After much bloodletting, Smith tries to make his escape, but is stopped in his tracks when the spirit of the prisoner—still in the electric chair—erupts out of the ground and claims the evil warden.

An intriguing genre hybrid boasting a stronger-than-usual cast and excellent, atmospheric direction from Finnish newcomer Renny Harlin, PRISON is an impressive piece of low-budget genre work. With the film played as a straight prison drama for close to half of its running time, the filmmakers take the time to develop the characters and set the mood before pouring on the gore. Filming in the abandoned Wyoming State Prison, director Harlin used the inherently creepy location for all it's worth. Cold stone walls, cramped cells, low-key lighting, and flooded floors all contribute to the dank, dark, claustrophobic feel of PRISON. The gore effects, while graphic, are handled with dispatch and are not lingered over any longer than need be. The entire film plays almost like a good old-fashioned horror excursion in which mood is more important than gut-churning carnage. Among the actors, Lane Smith (who, ironically, was recently featured as an inmate in WEEDS) is the real standout. His performance as the psychotic guard-turned-warden is intense without becoming ridiculously overblown. The supporting cast is good as well, with Viggo Mortensen, as a morose James Dean-ish inmate; Lincoln Kilpatrick, as the old black prisoner who shares Smith's secret; Andre De Shields, as a devout voodooist; Tom "Tiny" Lister, Jr., as the most physically intimidating inmate; and Arlen Dean Snyder, as a sympathetic guard, all contributing greatly to the scary goings-on. Actress Chelsea Field, the only woman in the picture, is fine in what is essentially an unnecessary and incongruous role. Harlin, who would go on to direct A NIGHTMARE ON ELM STREET IV later in the year, writer C. Courtney Joyner (who wrote the interesting THE OFFSPRING in 1987), and Yablans, who also produced FADE TO BLACK (1980), all understand what makes the horror genre work and have collaborated to produce one of the more effective and original low-budget genre works seen in quite some time. *(Violence, gore effects, profanity.)*

p, Irwin Yablans; d, Renny Harlin; w, C. Courtney Joyner (based on a story by Irwin Yablans); ph, Mac Ahlberg; ed, Andy Horvitch; m, Richard Band, Christopher L. Stone; md, Richard Band; m/l, Margaret Connell, Melissa Connell, Ron Jankowski, Sunny Hilder; prod d, Philip Duffin; set d, Jim Shumaker; spec eff, John Beuchler; cos, Stephen Chudej; stunts, Kane Hodder; makeup, Suzanne Sanders.

Horror/Prison **Cas.** **(PR:O MPAA:R)**

PROMISED LAND*** (1988) 102m Wildwood/Vestron c

Jason Gedrick *(Davey Hancock)*, Tracy Pollan *(Mary Daley)*, Kiefer Sutherland *(Danny Rivers)*, Meg Ryan *(Bev)*, Googy Gress *(Baines)*, Deborah Richter *(Pammie)*, Oscar Rowland *(Mr. Rivers)*, Sandra Seacat *(Mrs. Rivers)*, Jay Underwood *(Circle K Clerk)*, Herta Ware *(Mrs. Higgins)*, Walt Logan Field *(High School Coach)*, Kelly Ausland *(Schroeder)*, Todd Anderson *(Pat Rivers)*, Dave Valenza *(Glenn)*, Theron Read *(Harting)*, Richard Matthews *(Mel)*, Cindy Clark *(Vera)*, Charles Black *(Preacher)*, Tony Kruletz *(Charlie)*, James Cash *(Park Employee)*, Matthew Karas *(Park Employee Dultz)*, Dave Jensen *(College Coach)*, Michael Rudd *(Cowboy in Casino)*, Victoria Holloway *(Cleo)*, Herb McGarvey *(Riley Riddle)*, Don Steffey *(Rudy Riddle)*, Spence Ashby, Fenton Quinn, Jr. *(Flagmen)*, L.L. West *(Toy Store Clerk)*, John Garrison *(Mr. Daley)*, Deborah Green *(Kate)*, Dorothy Conrad *(Mary's Grandmother)*, Gae Cowley *(Mrs. Daley)*, Lisa Macfarlane *(Jenny)*, Joseph Yeates *(Kate's Husband)*, Gene Pack *(Mayor of Ashville)*, Grant Gottschall *(Bassford)*, Kelly Ausland, Adam Christensen, Shane Perry, Greg Weichers *(Ashville Basketball Players)*, Bob Bedore, Troy Bench, Tom Thornquest, Zeke Totland, Jeff Lindsay *(Falcons Basketball Players)*.

Following the fortunes of four young adults, this third picture from the producer-director team of Rick Stevenson and Michael Hoffman seeks to examine the unfulfilled promises of the American Dream. The film opens in 1984, with a high-school basketball district championship game that is won by the last-minute heroics of Gedrick (IRON EAGLE) and witnessed by his cheerleader girl friend Pollan and by Sutherland, nicknamed "Senator" because of his father's oft-stated belief that with enough hard work any American can be one. Gedrick is bound for college on a basketball scholarship, and Pollan wonders if things will change between them. Sutherland, who sees himself as a loser, drops out of school and leaves the little town of Ashville, Utah. Two years later, Christmas draws near. Gedrick is now an Ashville policeman, having failed to make the grade in college ball. Pollan is home from college for the holidays. Gedrick tries desperately to keep their romance going, but, with her horizons broadened and a boy friend back at school, Pollan wants out. Meanwhile, in Nevada, Sutherland marries Ryan, an impetuous hellraiser with pink hair, whom he has known for only three days. The film then cuts back and forth between Gedrick's attempts to hold on to Pollan and Sutherland and Ryan's journey through the mountainous expanse of Nevada and Utah to meet his parents. En route it becomes clear that Ryan's outrageous behavior—running a road block, shoplifting, excessive drinking—is more than just a wild streak. Drugs and a tough-luck background have made her frenetic and fearless, yet she is touched by the attention paid her by the mildmannered, sensitive Sutherland and anxious to make a good impression on his family. Back in Ashville, Pollan is confused by the feelings she still has for Gedrick, but realizes they inhabit different worlds now. Sutherland and Ryan arrive but things don't go well. Sutherland tries to talk with his sickly father Rowland, but nothing of consequence is said. Sutherland explains to Ryan that if he and his father really talked, Rowland would have to admit that Sutherland wasn't the son he hoped for, and Sutherland would have to tell him that he wasn't the father he wanted. Sutherland wants to leave town, but they are out of money. He and Ryan go to a convenience store, and, to his shock, she pulls a gun. Gedrick and Pollan, who have been arguing, pull up in a car. In the confused moments that follow, Gedrick, acting the policeman, shoots and kills Sutherland. The next day, Gedrick goes to console Rowland, and later turns in his badge.

PROMISED LAND is a well-intentioned film, but despite strong performances, an engaging plot, and some arresting photography, its ambitious reach exceeds its grasp. In attempting to show that the American Dream is a pipe dream for many, writer-director Hoffman has taken a stance that flies in the face of Reagan-era optimism. Rather than making his characters poor people, Hoffman has chosen to place the action in a small town and, with the significant exception of Pollan (whose background gives her choices unavailable to the others), to focus on the lives of working-class Americans. The locale is important, particularly in Sutherland and Ryan's pilgrimage (the car is a Plymouth, its prominent hood ornament an angel) through wide open spaces and majestic mountains of Utah and Nevada. Long the symbol of unbounded opportunity, the West has provided little for either Sutherland or Ryan. Reno's neon-lit casinos are also a poignant symbolic reminder of the gamble and promise of the big pot at the heart of capitalism. What is disappointing about PROMISED LAND is that these symbolic elements seem to exist on a different plane. Instead of being shown as the stuff of which American Dreams are made, the film's symbolism has a grafted-on quality. The presidential portrait that hangs in Rowland's shabby living room makes Hoffman's point too heavy handedly. Similarly, Rowland himself is a caricature of lumpen enervation.

That said, Hoffman still delivers an intriguing, well-paced story that draws the viewer in as it builds to its tragic climax. His characters come across as real people both because they have been well-written and because of the convincing performances of the four leads. All-American pretty, Pollan (formerly of TV's "Family Ties") makes the inner struggle of the young woman with a future believable. Gedrick's portrayal of the frustrated one-time basketball star is affecting because he knows exactly why Pollan is drifting away from him. The best performances, though, are by Sutherland and Ryan, playing emotional polar opposites. Sutherland underplays his quiet, sensitive loner (a departure from his recent tough-guy roles in STAND BY ME and THE LOST BOYS) without allowing him to disappear or become too pathetic. Drugged, drunken, and psychotic, Ryan (TOP GUN, INNERSPACE) is a jittery ball of unfocused energy, a bad-news comet that catches Sutherland in her tail and hurtles him towards disaster.

The photography of the mountains, plains, and huge Western skies is gorgeous and Hoffman's use of the camera is occasionally dazzling. There are many memorable images in PROMISED LAND, but the most unforgettable is the Plymouth and the distant mountains reflected on the shimmering salt flats. Hoffman is himself from a small town in Idaho where a shooting similar to the one in the film occurred. He knew both of the former high-school friends who were involved and has dedicated his film to them. Developed at the Sundance Institute, PROMISED LAND was shot on location in Utah and Reno, Nevada. Robert Redford served as an executive producer and all the actors worked for scale. This is the third collaboration (following PRIVILEGED and RESTLESS NATIVES) for Hoffman and producer Stevenson, Americans who met while studying at Oxford and who will bear watching in the future. *(Profanity, nudity, sexual situations, violence.)*

p, Rick Stevenson; d, Michael Hoffman; w, Michael Hoffman; ph, Ueli Steiger, Alexander Gruszynski; ed, David Spiers; m, James Newton Howard; m/l, Giovanni Pierluigi da Palestrina, Reba McEntire, Janey Street; prod d, Eugenio Zanetti; art d, Jim Dultz; set d, Clif A. Davis; spec eff, Bob Rigga; cos, Victoria Holloway; stunts, David Boushey, Bob Miles; makeup, Thomas Nellen, Sheri Short.

Drama Cas. (PR:O MPAA:R)

PULSE*** (1988) 91m Aspen Film Society/COL c

Cliff De Young *(Bill)*, Roxanne Hart *(Ellen)*, Joey Lawrence *(David)*, Matthew Lawrence *(Stevie)*, Charles Tyner *(Old Man)*, Dennis Redfield *(Pete)*, Robert Romanus *(Paul)*, Myron D. Healey *(Howard)*.

PULSE (the title refers to the flow of electricity into one's household) is an original, intense thriller that becomes horrific as it weaves its tale of everyday household items run amok. One evening, DeYoung and his wife, Hart, are awakened by a neighbor who is destroying his house, having presumably gone mad. The next day, DeYoung's son (Joey Lawrence) arrives from Colorado to visit his father and step-mother. He's not happy to be there, and after talking to a neighborhood youngster (Matthew Lawrence), he's downright anxious to leave. Son Lawrence's small friend tells him how the crazy neighbor's wife was killed just before the man himself lost control. It seems that the woman died when a piece of metal was spewed from her garbage disposal, piercing her eye. Lawrence becomes afraid, and lies awake at night listening to the strange sounds the house makes. Slowly, the electrical world around Lawrence begins to change, and to damage—the TV burns out, the furnace shoots flames. Lawrence, eager to discover the truth of these ruptures, breaks into the house across the street, where he meets an elderly electrician who tells of voices in the wires and hints about "them." "I've seen dozens of houses just like this one," he says eerily. Lawrence's father is reluctant to heed the warnings, until he is almost killed by poisonous gasses while trapped in the garage and Hart is nearly burned to death while taking a shower. At the film's climax, De Young and Lawrence are trapped in the house, battling fire, water, and electricity. They escape, and as the neighbors watch and the police arrive—all convinced that he is insane—De Young cuts down the electrical pole outside his house and watches happily as its fall demolishes his home.

Writer-director Paul Golding succeeds here where many horror directors fail: in making the incredible believable. The idea of electricity having a mind of its own is silly, of course, but with Golding's guidance the notion becomes frighteningly possible as he generates fear from the recognition that most of us don't consider exactly how an electrical device works, just take for granted that it will. Especially effective is Golding's refusal to provide an exact reason as to why the chaos is happening (a device used successfully by Hitchcock in THE BIRDS, for example). Some talk by electrician Tyner hints that aliens from outer space might be communicating to the machines for an unknown purpose, and several moments showing John Carpenter's STARMAN as it plays throughout the film on the family's VCR seem to back this notion up. Still, no one steps forth to say exactly what is going on. The filmmakers leave it to our imagination, and because we are put in the same position as the characters themselves, we can identify with their fear.

Golding builds his tension well. The movie is played through the point of view of young Lawrence, who, mostly because of his age, accepts what is happening without question—only the adults are doubtful, until it's too late. Golding's visual technique is also excellent. His camera is almost always in motion, a dizzying effect that succeeds in conveying the family's growing paranoia. All of the performances are engaging and convincing, especially those of Joey Lawrence and Roxanne Hart. The terror in Lawrence's eyes as he watches his world turn into a giant mosquito lamp is believable and moving; Hart, as the step-mom with a heart, provides the exact amount of sympathy required and realistically underplays the horror. Cliff DeYoung has the more thankless task of playing the doubting father, and he delivers throughout. The technical credits also shine: P.L. Collister's footage is sharp and clean, and the music by Jay Ferguson enhances the terror perfectly. Columbia Pictures opened PULSE for a limited time in March 1988, whereupon it slipped away with little notice. *(Violence.)*

p, Patricia A. Stallone; d, Paul Golding; w, Paul Golding; ph, Peter Lyons Collister (DeLuxe Color); ed, Gib Jaffe; m, Jay Ferguson; prod d, Holger Gross; art d, Maxine Shepard; set d, Greta Grigorian; stunts, Mike Cassidy.

Thriller Cas. (PR:C MPAA:PG-13)

PUMPKINHEAD** (1988) 86m UA-Lion/MGM-UA c

Lance Henriksen *(Ed Harley)*, Matthew Hurley *(Billy Harley)*, Jeff East *(Chris)*, John DiAquino *(Joel)*, Kimberly Ross *(Kim)*, Joel Hoffman *(Steve)*, Cynthia Bain *(Tracy)*, Kerry Remsen *(Maggie)*, Madeleine Taylor Holmes *(Witch-woman)*, Tom Woodruff, Jr. *(Pumpkinhead)*, Florence Schauffler.

The fairly promising directorial debut of Oscar-winning special effects man Stan Winston (TERMINATOR; ALIENS; PREDATOR), PUMPKINHEAD had its release set for Halloween of 1987, but was held up due to severe financial problems at De Laurentiis Entertainment, the film's original studio. Now DEG has been bought out by MGM/UA and the film was finally released, ironically, just in time for Halloween 1988. Old-fashioned and atmospheric, PUMPKINHEAD is a surprisingly moralistic tale and presents a horror steeped in rural folklore and legend. Set in an unnamed area of impoverished rural America, the film stars Henriksen as a kindly farmer who runs a ramshackle general store with his 10-year-old son. A widower, Henriksen is a dutiful and caring father who loves his boy more than anything in the world. Tragedy strikes, however, when six city kids arrive in town for a wild weekend of dirt biking. Henriksen's son is accidentally hit by one of the bikers, DiAquino, who fears he will be sent to jail and leaves the boy to die. One of the youths, East, stays behind with the boy while the others go for help, but the panicked DiAquino prevents them from calling an ambulance. When Henriksen finds his dying son, he says nothing to East, but gives him a look that could kill. East returns to his friends while the little boy dies in his father's arms. Blinded by hatred and the desire for vengeance, Henriksen goes to the remote cabin of an ancient witch (Schauffler) and begs her to bring his boy back to life. That she cannot do, but Henriksen also knows of Pumpkinhead, a vicious demon that can be summoned to avenge wrongful death. Although it's thought to be a legend by most, Henriksen actually saw the beast when he was a child and knows that it actually exists. Despite Schauffler's warnings that Pumpkinhead is an unforgiving beast, Henriksen demands that she conjure it up. Sent by Schauffler to a surreal-looking pumpkin patch, Henriksen digs up a small rotting corpse and brings it to the witch. Revived with a combination of the blood of Henriksen and his son, the beast awakens and begins to grow until it is a huge eight-foot ALIENesque creature capable of ripping off a human head with a single twist. The beast then proceeds to track down the boy's killers and dispatch them one at a time. A particularly sadistic demon, Pumpkinhead toys with its victims before finally killing them and then makes sure that the victim's loved ones get a good look at the corpse. Unfortunately for Henriksen, each time Pumpkinhead kills he experiences a seizure and sees the killings from the demon's point of view. Each time Pumpkinhead kills, it starts to look more and more like Henriksen. Wracked with guilt over what he has wrought and unable to call the beast off, Henriksen decides to destroy Pumpkinhead before it kills again. Finding that bullets and flames are of no use, Henriksen accidentally discovers that when he feels pain, Pumpkinhead feels pain. Left with no choice, Henriksen commits suicide and Pumpkinhead dies with him. The film ends as the witch buries a small shriveled corpse that looks like Henriksen in the pumpkin patch.

Having worked closely with director James Cameron on THE TERMINATOR and done some second-unit directing on Cameron's ALIENS, special-effects whiz Winston felt that he could direct a feature himself—and he was right. Combining a strong visual sense with a surprisingly good feel for character development, PUMPKINHEAD is actually stronger in the first hour than in its climactic last half. Taking his time to develop a vivid sense of place and some memorable characters, Winston allows the audience a level of emotional involvement not found in many contemporary horror films. The relationship between Henriksen and his son is especially effective; the viewer actually feels a deep sense of loss and outrage when the boy dies. Winston encourages the audience to feel just as vindictive as the Henriksen character when he demands that Pumpkinhead be summoned, and then turns the tables on them by showing Henriksen calm down, have second thoughts, and then try to stop the terror he created. The message: Revenge is wrong. Not a common theme in modern horror. With the director's good feel for atmosphere and character, the first part of PUMPKINHEAD is quite engaging and scary, but Winston begins to lose control when the monster is on the rampage. By now the "Ten Little Indians" method of killing characters one at a time has gotten so old, boring, and stale from the innumerable FRIDAY THE 13TH films that no matter how well shot or how impressive the monster is, the resulting sequence is inevitably tedious and predictable. The dull script by Mark Patrick Carducci and Gary Gerani gives Winston nowhere to go once the killing begins, and, to his credit, Winston keeps this section moving at a breakneck pace in an attempt to bulldoze over the screenplay's deficiencies. Unfortunately, it doesn't really work and the climax is a letdown—not even Lance Henriksen's solid performance can fill in the script's blanks.

Created by Winston's talented special effects team (Shane Mahan, Alec Gillis, John Rosengrant, Tom Woodruff, Jr., and Richard Landon), but without his supervision, the Pumpkinhead monster is fairly impressive, considering the film's low $3.5 million budget. Eight feet tall and capable of a remarkable array of facial expressions, Pumpkinhead is a suitably frightening creature and looks the stuff of folklore. Also excellent is the aging makeup used on Florence Schauffler to make her look like an ancient witch. There is very little outright gore in PUMPKINHEAD, with Winston preferring the time-honored method of mood and suggestion to carry off most of the chills. This is not to say that the film is for kiddies—it is still very violent—but there is none of the kind of gratuitous sexual titillation and gore-for-gore's-sake indulgence that has marred horror films in the past decade. *(Violence, profanity.)*

p, Richard C. Weinman, Howard Smith; d, Stan Winston; w, Mark Patrick Carducci, Gary Gerani (based on a story by Mark Patrick Carducci, Stan Winston, Richard C. Weinman); ph, Bojan Bazelli (Technicolor); ed, Marcus Manton; m, Richard Stone; spec eff, Alec Gillis.

Horror **Cas.** **(PR:O MPAA:R)**

PUNCHLINE*½** (1988) 128m COL c

Sally Field *(Lilah Krytsick)*, Tom Hanks *(Steven Gold)*, John Goodman *(John Krytsick)*, Mark Rydell *(Romeo, Comedy Club Owner)*, Kim Greist *(Madeline Urie)*, Paul Mazursky *(Arnold)*, Pam Matteson *(Utica Blake)*, George Michael McGrath *(Singing Nun)*, Taylor Negron *(Albert Emperato)*, Barry Neikrug *(Krug)*, Angel Salazar *(Rico)*, Damon Wayans *(Percy)*, Joycee Katz *(Joycee)*, Mac Robbins *(Billy Lane)*, Max Alexander *(Mister Ball)*, Paul Kozlowski *(Jerry Petroviak)*, Barry Sobel *(Robyn Green)*, Marty Pollio *(Juggling Comic)*, Katie Rich *(Eve)*, Charles David Richards *(Maitre d')*, Casey Sander *(Ernie the Bartender)*, Michael Pollock *(Piano Player)*, Wanda Balay, Christiane Eden, Susan Michael, Consuela Nance, Darunee Doa Hale, Tiffany Terry, Renna Bogdanowicz, Kimberly Ryusaki, Barbara Collier, Andrea Adams, Marcy Del Campos *(Gas Station Waitresses)*, Candace Cameron, Laura Jacoby, Bianca Rose *(Lilah's Children)*, Ron Ulstad, Howard Weller, Richard Parker *(Talent Scouts)*, George Wallace *(Man with Arm in Cast)*, Andrew Parker *(Boy on Gurney)*, Randy Fechter *(Young Doctor)*, Sam H. Ginsburg *(Sam, the Laughing Patient)*, Angela Bennett *(Nurse)*, Cameron Thor, George Novogroder, Susan Avants, Carin Badger, Eva Dunlap, Mark Helm, C. James Lewis, Suzanne Rains, Scott Williams, Sharon Lyn Borne, Bob Zmuda *(Audience Participants & Hecklers)*, John Kirby *(Marketing Man)*, Robina Suwol *(Buffy)*, Robert Britton *(Murray)*, Mark Goldstein *(Mark)*, Melissa Tufeld *(Mark's Wife)*, Dottie Archibald *(Mrs. Ball)*, Susie Essman *(Lilah's Hairdresser)*, Joey Vega *(Waiter in Coffee Shop)*, Ben Hartigan *(Older Clergyman)*, Jimmy Brogan *(Younger Clergyman)*, George D. Wallace *(Dr. Wishniak)*, Crane Jackson *(Second Faculty Examiner)*, Rich Ramirez *(Taxi Driver)*, Michael Starr *(Man with Bullhorn)*.

© COLUMBIA

There is always something frightening about those little comedy clubs where humor-starved patrons sit at their tables and squirm as the funnyperson on stage does everything possible to coax a laugh out of an unimpressed audience. Everyone just sort of looks at one another with a sense of embarrassment—they don't want to be there anymore, they feel bad for the fool onstage. They just want that person up there to disappear and be replaced by someone who'll make them laugh. PUNCHLINE, the first major release to hit on this subculture of comedy clubs and struggling comedians, is both funny and sad. Tom Hanks, coming off his excellent performance in BIG (though PUNCHLINE was actually filmed first), plays a callous, down-and-out comedian who spends more time delivering routines than studying for medical exams. As a result, he gets booted out of med school and must face the wrath of his surgeon father. In contrast to Hanks is Field, a New Jersey housewife with a husband, three kids, and a roast in the oven, who tells dirty Polish jokes about her husband (the only thing "long and hard" about him is his last name) and even resorts to buying jokes on the black market. Her husband, Goodman, is an insurance salesman who just wants a wife that will be by his side, and has lost his patience with her frequent evenings in Manhattan. Field, like everyone else at The Gas Station, a typical comedy club, knows that Hanks is the funniest guy around. Even the professionals are starting to pick up on him: talent scout Greist loves his act and promises that someone (she won't say who) will come down to the club (she won't say when) to watch his routine and make an offer (she won't say what). Hanks, however, is tired of being strung along. After 18 months in stand-up, he is broke, has been kicked out of his apartment and dropped from med school, and seems not to have any friends; nonetheless, Field decides to turn to him for advice. He's less than courteous—insulting her, ignoring her, telling her she's funny when she's obviously not. Hanks has seen her kind before—someone who wants to make it, but doesn't want to give up everything in a headlong effort. She'd rather make excuses about her duties as a wife and mother. When Field finally agrees to go with Hanks as he performs for a group of hospital patients, however, he realizes that she *is* serious about her comedy. Eventually she begins to come out of her shell. Her act loosens up and she becomes funny, managing to make even Hanks laugh. While Hanks is a success onstage, he's an emotional mess otherwise, and when his distinguished-looking father appears in the audience the comic completely crumbles during his act. Gradually, he finds himself becoming attracted to Field, who is some 10 years his senior, not to mention her being a married mother. "I love my husband," Field reminds him. "If we're going to get married you'll have to get over that," he quips. After another meeting with Greist, Hanks learns that she is planning a TV comedy contest, the winner of which will receive a guest shot with Johnny Carson. Everyone at the club realizes this is their big chance—the man (Paul Mazursky) who dresses in a nun's habit and sings "The Name Game" with Jesus' name; a chubby high-school history teacher who can make his students laugh, but not his audience; a hip young Chicano with a gigantic boom box; and a half-dozen others. (One regular, an old-timer whose style is better suited to the Catskills, gets cut from the program before it starts. Stunned and depressed, he consoles himself with the fact that he once appeared on the "Ed Sullivan Show.") Field has told her family she would consider giving up comedy, but still enters the contest. Goodman decides to support his wife and asks if he might watch her perform—he has not done so before. Both Field and Hanks knock 'em dead, but when the winner is announced, it's Field. She, however, is content with earning the love and respect of her husband, and drops out of the contest. A recount is taken and Hanks comes out on top.

A surprisingly dark film, PUNCHLINE manages to catch that peculiar breed of the human animal—the stand-up comic. While the American public sees the comedy success stories—the Jay Lenos, Arsenio Halls or Richard Lewises—most know nothing of those everyday people who think they're funny enough to become stars, too: the teachers or housewives who stand before the microphone and break out into a sweat, mumble, or read jokes from index cards. With the recent rise in comedy clubs and cable TV shows featuring stand-up, it's not surprising that a film should venture into the hitherto uncharted land of the comedy circuit. PUNCHLINE is a success because it doesn't try to glorify its surroundings, and presents instead a world in which far more get laughed *at* than get laughs. In a sense, the film does for aspiring comedians what JAWS did for swimmers: it warns them away from the maneaters.

Taking the plunge, however, are Sally Field and Tom Hanks. Performing stand-up comedy is tough enough, but it's even tougher for an actor who's untrained in stand-up to do a routine convincingly and humorously. If moviegoers sit stonefaced while the onscreen characters are laughing themselves senseless, the film will have failed completely. Fortunately, Hanks and Field rarely fall flat. Hanks took stand-up lessons from the film's "comedy consultant," Barry Sobel, and it shows, especially in his excellent routine before the hospital patients—a scene which has an almost documentary feel. Field, in what is perhaps a more difficult role, also does a fine job. She initially must come off as a mousy, unfunny housewife, then emerge from her shell to make us laugh, even though we are predisposed against her.

Along with strong performances (John Goodman, best remembered from RAISING ARIZONA and TV's "Roseanne," is simply amazingly as Field's husband), PUNCHLINE is brimming with "moments." Writer-director David Seltzer, who previously directed LUCAS, is not afraid to stop his narrative and let a scene linger in order to add subtext. The role of the old Catskills comic is a perfect example—a character so sympathetic and complex he could provide the basis for an entire film, though Seltzer makes him live in just a few shots. Early on, after the inconsiderate Hanks has finished his routine at the hospital, he stops for a minute to talk to a sick child—the comedian's feeling for medicine and pediatrics momentarily emerging. Perhaps the film's most moving scene comes at Field's home just after she has gotten a new hairstyle and stands at the door with tears streaming down her face, complaining how ugly her hair is. For the first time, we see Goodman and the children support Field: Goodman tells her in all honesty that she is beautiful, and one of the kids insists she looks like Miss America. Although PUNCHLINE occasionally falters—in its contrived contest ending (similar to the Rocky-isms of LUCAS), insistence on a happy outcome for both Hanks and Field, and saccharine tendencies—it is still an endearing and honest achievement. In theme it even recalls the 1951 Luchino Visconti masterwork BELLISSIMA, the Italian neo-realist film of a woman (Anna Magnani) who is a pushy stage mother to her beautiful daughter and, like Field's character, nearly destroys her family to achieve a measure of success. *(Profanity.)*

p, Daniel Melnick, Michael Rachmil; d, David Seltzer; w, David Seltzer; ph, Reynaldo Villalobos (DeLuxe Color); ed, Bruce Green; m, Charles Gross; md, Daniel Allan Carlin; m/l, Michael Pollock; prod d, Jackson DeGovia; art d, John R. Jensen; set d, Joe Hubbard, Pete Smith; cos, Dan Moore, Aggie Lyon; makeup, Lee Harmon.

Comedy/Drama   **Cas.**   **(PR:C MPAA:R)**

PURPLE PEOPLE EATER, THE †(1988) 92m Motion Picture Corp/Concorde c

Ned Beatty *(Grandpa)*, Neil Patrick Harris *(Billy Johnson)*, Shelley Winters *(Rita)*, Peggy Lipton *(Mom)*, James Houghton *(Dad)*, Thora Birch *(Molly Johnson)*, John Brumfield *(Mr. Noodle)*, Little Richard *(Mayor)*, Chubby Checker *(Singer)*.

One of the strangest films to hit the theaters in some time, this low-budget release is based on Sheb Wooley's popular novelty song of 1958. When a preteen boy meets the one-eyed, one-horned Flying Purple People Eater of the title, he and some of his pals from the neighborhood form a pop band with the musically inclined creature. Following a plot line most recently seen in *BATTERIES NOT INCLUDED, the heroes and their alien cohort then help prevent eviction of Beatty and Winters. Also helping save the day are Little Richard and Chubby Checker.

p, Brad Krevoy, Steven Stabler; d, Linda Shayne; w, Linda Shayne (based on the song by Sheb Wooley); ph, Peter Deming (Foto-Kem color); ed, Cari Coughlin; prod d, Stephen Greenberg; cos, Terry Dresbach; ch, Ted Lin.

Children's/Fantasy/Musical   **(PR:NR MPAA:PG)**

R

RAIN MAN***½   (1988) 128m Guber-Peters-UA/MGM-UA c

Dustin Hoffman *(Raymond Babbitt)*, Tom Cruise *(Charlie Babbitt)*, Valeria Golino *(Susanna)*, Jerry Molen *(Dr. Bruner)*, Jack Murdock *(John Mooney)*, Michael D. Roberts *(Vern)*, Ralph Seymour *(Lenny)*, Lucinda Jenney *(Iris)*, Bonnie Hunt *(Sally Dibbs)*, Kim Robillard, Beth Grant.

Given the tumultuous production history of this picture, which saw four different directors over the course of two years, it is truly remarkable that RAIN MAN is as good as it is. Cruise costars as a self-centered Los Angeles hustler who illegally imports expensive sports cars for a living. Arrogant, ruthless, and venal, Cruise is used to getting things his way and leaves a lackey to unload four Lamberghinis while he takes a quick trip to Palm Springs with his secretary-girlfriend Golino, an Italian import herself. En route, Cruise gets a call on his car phone informing him that his father has died and that the funeral is in Cincinnati. An only child, Cruise left home on bad terms while still a teenager and never patched things up with his widowed father. Cancelling his trip, Cruise attends the funeral merely to collect a $3 million inheritance. Much to his dismay, however, he learns that he has inherited only his father's 1949 Buick Roadmaster and beloved rose bushes—items Cruise despises. The bulk of the estate is turned over to a trustee, who will administer it to a person unnamed in the will. Determined to get his inheritance, Cruise does some snooping and discovers that the trustee, Molen, is the head of a respected home for the mentally disabled. Although Molen refuses to divulge the name of the person who will get the inheritance, Cruise stumbles upon Hoffman, an older patient who recognizes the Roadmaster and claims to have driven it. To Cruise's amazement, he learns that Hoffman is his elder brother, an autistic savant institutionalized when Cruise was an infant. Although quite brilliant at processing numbers and memorization, Hoffman is shut off from the rest of the world and cannot look anyone in the eye; he also does not want to touch or be touched. Both out of anger that he never knew he had a brother and out of determination to get half his father's estate, Cruise more or less kidnaps Hoffman from the home and holds him hostage until Molen agrees to turn over $1.5 million. Disgusted by his behavior, Golino leaves Cruise and flies back to Los Angeles. The situation proves difficult, however, because while in the home Hoffman has become used to a strict daily routine; therefore, he must eat meals that coincide with the institutional schedule (pepperoni pizza with tapioca pudding on Monday, etc.), must arrange motel rooms to a facsimile of his room at the home, refuses to go out in the rain, and *must* watch "The People's Court" every day, otherwise he will become extremely agitated and upset. To make things as easy as possible, Cruise attempts to fly Hoffman back to Los Angeles, but Hoffman—who can cite airline crash statistics in astounding detail—refuses to fly, forcing the pair to drive from Cincinnati to LA in their father's car. As they make their way across the country ever so slowly, stopping to watch "The People's Court" and find motel rooms before 11 p.m. (Hoffman's lights-out time) Cruise begins to warm up to his brother, despite the extreme frustration of trying to connect with him emotionally, and marvels at his amazing abilities. At one stop, Cruise discovers that Hoffman, whose name is Raymond, is the Rain Man, Cruise's childhood imaginary friend who used to sing to him when he was scared. Cruise always assumed that the Rain Man was imaginary, because he didn't remember having a sibling. As it turns out, their father institutionalized Hoffman after he accidentally burned the infant Cruise with scalding bath water. This revelation causes Cruise's feelings toward Hoffman to deepen and now the money doesn't seem as important as retaining custody of his brother. As they approach California, Cruise learns that the Lamberghini deal has fallen through and he must pay back $80,000 in down payments, which he doesn't have, to his customers. Given Hoffman's incredible memory for numbers, Cruise takes him to Las Vegas, where Hoffman counts cards while his brother plays poker. With Hoffman's help, Cruise wins $86,000 and triumphantly returns to Los Angeles determined to fight a custody battle for Hoffman. Molen arrives in LA from Cincinnati to meet with Cruise, Hoffman, and another doctor, Levinson, who will assess the case and recommend to the court whom Hoffman would be better off with. Cruise is very forthright and admits the initially mercenary nature of his plans, but is quite sincere when he states that he would prefer Hoffman live with him. After a few tests, however, it is obvious Hoffman couldn't really care less where he lives and would be better cared for by a staff of professionals. Wanting what is best for Hoffman, Cruise concedes custody to Molen and plans to visit his brother at the home in two weeks' time.

Well written, smartly directed, and sensitively performed, RAIN MAN rises above the banality of its concept, which in essence is yet another buddy movie crossbred with a road picture, to become a genuinely moving and intelligent look at what it means to be human. What separates RAIN MAN from the pack is its refusal to deal in stereotypes and easy sentimentality, instead concentrating on the brutal realities of life, as well as its joys, with an autistic person. As much as the audience would like to see the Hoffman character change and improve during his journey—endorsing the notion that removal from a regimented environment is somehow liberating for autistic people—the filmmakers refuse to indulge in that fantasy, and Hoffman remains the same at the end as he was at the beginning. But if there is no emotional breakthrough for Hoffman, he is the catalyst for Cruise's transformation from a completely self-absorbed character seemingly incapable of true intimacy (shades of his brother) into a caring and sympathetic human being.

Although Dustin Hoffman's magnificent performance will no doubt overshadow Tom Cruise's contributions, the young superstar has begun to actually reach beyond the charming smile and sexy swagger that has enabled him to sleepwalk through such drivel as TOP GUN and COCKTAIL and dig deeper into himself and his craft. This was no doubt encouraged by Hoffman, whose performance literally forces Cruise to struggle in order to make an honest emotional connection. For his part, Hoffman will probably be unjustly criticized for being an acting machine whose total self-absorbtion and obsession with detail prevents him from connecting with the other actors. While that may be true of some of Hoffman's other work, in RAIN MAN it is entirely appropriate, since his character is *incapable* of traditional notions of meaningful interaction—he is in his own world. To prepare for the role, Hoffman (and sometimes Cruise) spent a year meeting with people who were autistic, some of whom were retarded and others of whom were savants. One man in particular, who lives on the east coast and, ironically, is cared for by his brother, became the focus for Hoffman, who patterned his performance on the man. This prototype's brother was extremely helpful to both Hoffman and Cruise, providing insight into the situation that no script could hope to duplicate.

© MGM/UA

While the work of the two leads is exemplary, Barry Levinson again assembles an impressive group of supporting players, including many people found on location. The real standout among the supporting players, however, is Valeria Golino, last seen in BIG TOP PEE WEE. Using the fact that she is Italian, Golino keeps her performance spontaneous by putting an odd spin on her exchanges with Cruise. Not bound by American modes of behavior, she unhesitatingly questions and chides the arrogant Cruise, blowing holes in his slick demeanor. Her spontaneity makes a wonderful counterpoint to the internal studiousness of Hoffman and it gives the film an extra spark.

Levinson, who came to the project after Martin Brest, Steven Spielberg, and Sydney Pollack (all of whom had varying degrees of commitment) had tried their hand, does a fine job here, using his much-praised staging of dialog scenes to good advantage, underplaying the more sentimental aspects of the piece, and exploiting the American landscape in new and unexpected ways. Tackling a project with many potential pitfalls in RAIN MAN, Levinson, Hoffman, and Cruise have avoided the banal and created something special. *(Adult situations, profanity.)*

p, Mark Johnson; d, Barry Levinson; w, Ronald Bass, Barry Morrow (based on a story by Morrow); ph, John Seale (DeLuxe Color); ed, Stu Linder; m, Hans Zimmer; prod d, Ida Random; art d, William A. Elliott; set d, Linda DeScenna; cos, Bernie Pollack.

Drama   Cas.   (PR:C-O MPAA:R)

RAMBO III*½   (1988) 101m Carolco/Tri-Star c

Sylvester Stallone *(John Rambo)*, Richard Crenna *(Colonel Trautman)*, Marc de Jonge *(Colonel Zaysen)*, Kurtwood Smith *(Griggs)*, Spiros Focas *(Masoud)*, Sasson Gabai *(Mousa)*, Doudi Shoua *(Hamid)*, Randy Raney *(Gen. Kourov)*, Marcus Gilbert *(Tomask)*, Alon Abutbul *(Nissem)*, Mahmoud Assadollahi *(Rahim)*, Yosef Shiloah *(Khalid)*, Harold Diamond *(Stick Fighter)*, Seri Mati, Hany Said El Deen *(Gun Dealers)*, Shaby Ben-Aroya *(Uri)*, Marciano Shoshi *(Afghan Girl)*, Sadiq Tawfiq, Julian Patrice, Tal Kastoriano, Benny Bruchim, Tikva Aziz, Milo Rafi *(Helicopter People)*.

After trivializing the experiences of Vietnam veterans in RAMBO: FIRST BLOOD PART II, Sylvester Stallone turns his ego loose on the tragic war in Afghanistan and makes a mockery of that conflict as well in RAMBO III. Reportedly the most expensive film ever made ($63 million, but that figure does not include Stallone's $20 million salary), RAMBO III begins in Thailand, where the taciturn Stallone has fled the pressures of being the world's greatest warrior and is hiding out in a Buddhist monastery. It is here that Stallone's only friend, Green Beret colonel Crenna, tracks him down. Crenna, accompanied by an American government official (Smith), informs Stallone that he is about to embark on a covert mission in Afghanistan to deliver Stinger missiles to the *mujahedeen* (anti-Soviet Afghan rebels). Crenna asks if Stallone would like to come along. Mumbling that his "... war is over," Stallone declines. Disappointed, Crenna gently berates Stallone for not coming "full circle" and accepting the fact that he is an ancient warrior and other such nonsense. But Stallone still refuses to participate and bids adieu to Crenna. Minutes later Crenna and several *mujahedeen* are captured by the Soviets immediately after crossing the border. Smith returns to the monastery in Thailand and tells Stallone of Crenna's capture. Although indifferent to geopolitics, Stallone won't let the capture of his only friend slide by unanswered, so he launches a one-man invasion of Afghanistan to rescue Crenna from the sadistic clutches of the Evil Empire. Stallone hooks up with the *mujahedeen*, and while the rebels brief him on the particulars of the Soviet fortress where Crenna is being held, a Soviet helicopter arrives and strafes the area. Many are killed and the remaining rebels decide to hightail it back across the Pakistan border to wait for reinforcements. Stallone continues on his mission, joined by his loyal Afghan guide, Gabai, and an 11-year-old *mujahedeen* fighter (Shouda). From this point on the entire film is one long series of huge explosions in which Stallone takes on brutal Soviet commander de Jonge and his minions. Using his trusty knife, bow-with-exploding-arrows, and whatever weapons he picks up along the way, Stallone manages to wipe out scores of Russians and rescue Crenna. Just as it looks as if they have made it to the border, however, a helicopter, a dozen tanks, and hundreds of Soviet troops intercept them. Being the true-blue Americans that they are, Stallone and Crenna refuse to surrender and face this army by themselves. Luckily, hundreds of *mujahedeen* troops on horseback arrive in the nick of time to help out. In the last massive battle, Stallone singlehandedly kills the crew of a Soviet tank and then drives the deadly contraption right into the helicopter carrying the evil de Jonge. The chopper is destroyed, de Jonge is killed, Stallone survives, and the battle is over. Although the *mujahedeen* beg him stay and continue the fight against the Soviets, Stallone gracefully declines and drives off with Crenna as the song, "He Ain't Heavy, He's My Brother," swells up under the closing credits.

Released the same month that Soviet troops began to pull out of Afghanistan and Ronald Reagan went to Moscow to embrace Soviet Secretary General Mikhail Gorbachev, RAMBO III became an instant anachronism in the era of *glasnost*. Better US-Soviet relations notwithstanding, the film is destined to make a ton of money at the box office from easy-to-please action fans who are impressed by expensive pyrotechnics but care nothing about drama or character development. Following the much more realistic war films PLATOON, FULL METAL JACKET, and HAMBURGER HILL, the absurd adventures of Stallone and Chuck Norris (the latter in MISSING IN ACTION parts I, II, and III) seem more cartoonish than ever.

The filming of RAMBO III was unusually troubled. First off, Stallone and Carolco Pictures executive producers Mario Kassar and Andrew Vajna couldn't decide on a proper place to shoot the film. Arizona, Nevada, Utah, Mexico, Morocco, Australia, and Italy were all considered and sets were even built in Mexico, only to be torn down and rebuilt in the country finally decided upon, Israel. Fearing terrorist attacks on Stallone and the crew, the producers hired scads of security personnel for protection from real bombs and bullets. Stallone was equipped with 10 bodyguards, a bulletproof car, and a supply of his own blood in case he was injured. No actual violence occurred during the production, but the RAMBO III press kit claims that on November 8, 1987, while Stallone and the editors were working on a rough cut of the film in an Israeli hotel, gunfire broke out just 150 yards away. Urged by security personnel to evacuate the hotel, Stallone at first refused, stating, "Yeah, but we've got to edit this." Eventually the star was persuaded to leave and on his way to the shelter claimed that he "could see that there was machine-gun fire and at least one direct hit." The official Israeli Army version of the story claims that there was never any gunfire, and that Israeli soldiers shot off several flares in an attempt to scare a French tourist who was trying to climb a fence on the Israeli-Jordanian border to pick some fresh dates. Considering the self-serving aspects of Stallone's anecdote and the questionable veracity of Israeli Army official explanations, the truth of this matter must fall somewhere in between.

What the RAMBO III press kit does not mention, however, is that nearly everyone on the crew, from the director to the still photographer, was fired. First, cinematographer Ric Waite (48 HRS., FOOTLOOSE) was sacked and replaced by Israeli David Gurfinkel, who shot Stallone starrer OVER THE TOP. Fired along with Waite were first assistant director Andy Stone and the entire camera department. The official reason for Waite's dismissal was that he had "creative differences" with director Russell Mulcahy that had caused the production to fall three days behind schedule. Waite contends, however, that he was fired in a cost-cutting maneuver that allowed producers to hire an Israeli crew for one tenth of what Waite and his crew was being paid. Two days later, Australian director Russell Mulcahy (RAZORBACK, HIGHLANDER), the man Stallone had originally picked to helm the film, was let go. Once again, producers blamed costly delays—this time caused by Mulcahy—for the firing and claimed that the director was overwhelmed by the scope of the project. Ironically, he was replaced by second unit director Peter MacDonald—a man who had never directed a feature film. Subsequently, property master Sam Moore and his entire crew quit, but they returned several weeks later. The next major loss was replacement cinematographer Gurfinkel, who quit, citing "creative differences" with Stallone. Replacement director MacDonald took over the cinematographer chores until producers were able to get British cinematographer John Stainer to replace Gurfinkel. Next to be fired was second unit director Andy Armstrong (who had replaced MacDonald) and his crew. In addition to these major firings, there were cameramen, costume people, and publicists who either were fired, quit, or quit and returned during the course of the turbulent shoot. Many of them cited the egotistical Stallone as the main source of tension.

The end result of all these hirings and firings? An unbelievably expensive action film so rudimentary in concept and presentation that it actually manages to be boring and predictable during its lengthy scenes of mass mayhem. The political rhetoric aside, the only reason for this film to exist are the action scenes; unfortunately, they are not particularly memorable. The battle scenes, by and large, are shot with the creation of epic scope in mind and rarely does the audience feel a sense of personal danger. Director MacDonald directs like a second unit director and much of the action is filmed in panoramic long shots so that viewers can see the huge explosions, impressive masses of extras, props, horses, helicopters, tanks, and other vehicles assembled. To simpletons, this is proof that "every dollar spent is on the screen." To people who know the difference between a well-shot action film and a poorly shot action film, this is known as "lazy direction." Because there is little in the way of good coverage, there is little in the way of good editing. MacDonald alternates his wide-angle long-shots with head-banging close-ups of Stallone's big brown eyes. For a film with expansive terrain, hundreds of extras, props, horses, hardware, explosions, etc., an inordinate amount of footage is wasted on Stallone's totally inexpressive face and bulging muscles. These tributes to Stallone's narcissism may be what the fired crew members meant by citing "creative differences" with the star.

Good action films should establish characters the audience cares about, convey a real sense of danger, create a vivid milieu for scenes of mayhem, and follow rudimentary rules of spatial relationships (i.e., where are the good guys, where are the bad guys, who is getting killed, etc.). RAMBO III is amazingly spotty on most of these counts. Stallone is such a superhero that one never worries for a moment that he might not win. Watching the RAMBO films is like watching a hunter shoot fish in a barrel. There is no sense of danger, no sense of time or place, no characterization, and nothing but total chaos on screen. Among the handful of effective moments there is, however, one fairly memorable sequence in which Stallone and Crenna battle some Soviet soldiers in a cave. Scaled down, the violent action actually becomes somewhat gripping in this scene, and there is some clever lighting, camerawork, and editing (with no less than four cinematographers and two directors over the course of the shoot, there is no way to guess who shot the scene). In the characterization department, Stallone has finally allowed Rambo a slight sense of humor. Some progress.

Although not as slapdash or outright offensive as RAMBO: FIRST BLOOD PART II, RAMBO III is just as distressingly simpleminded as its predecessor and continues to trivialize complex political situations while exploiting them to make big money. While the film does call attention to the war in Afghanistan and makes mention of the heinous tactics used by the desperate Soviet army, it ignores the reasons for the Soviet invasion, the violent dissension among rebel factions, the religious nature of the resistance, the incredibly volatile situation that will remain there once the Soviets leave, and other substantive aspects of the struggle. It turns a tragic real-life war into an ego trip for its star and a cheap thrills joyride for its jingoistic audience. Make no mistake, RAMBO III is not an impassioned plea of support for the Afghan people, it is Hollywood exploitation at its most base and cynical. *(Graphic violence, profanity).*

p, Buzz Feitshans; d, Peter MacDonald; w, Sylvester Stallone, Sheldon Lettich (based on characters created by David Morrell); ph, John Stanier (Technicolor); ed, James Symons, Andrew London, O. Nicholas Brown, Edward Warschilka; m, Jerry Goldsmith; prod d, Bill Kenney; art d, Pier Luigi Basile, Benjamin Fernandez, Adrian Gorton; set d, Giorgio Postiglione; spec eff, Thomas Fisher; cos, Richard La Motte; stunts, Vic Armstrong; makeup, Giannetto De Rossi.

Action **Cas.** **(PR:O MPAA:R)**

RED HEAT*** (1988) 103m Carolco-Lone Wolf-Oak/Tri-Star c

Arnold Schwarzenegger *(Capt. Ivan Danko)*, James Belushi *(Det. Sgt. Art Ridzik)*, Peter Boyle *(Police Comdr. Lou Donnelly)*, Ed O'Ross *(Viktor Rostavili)*, Larry Fishburne *(Lt. Stobbs)*, Gina Gershon *(Cat Manzetti)*, Richard Bright *(Sgt. Gallagher)*, J.W. Smith *(Salim)*, Brent Jennings *(Abdul Elijah)*, Gretchen Palmer *(Hooker)*, Pruitt Taylor Vince *(Night Clerk)*, Michael Hagerty *(Pat Nunn)*, Brion James *(Streak)*, Gloria Delaney *(Intern)*, Peter Jason *(TV Announcer)*, Oleg Vidov *(Yuri Ogarkov)*, Savely Kramarov *(Gregor Moussorsky)*, Gene Scherer *(Consul Stepanovich)*, Tengiz Borisoff *(Josep Baroda)*, Roger Callard *(Pytor Tatomovich)*, Gabor Koncz *(Vagran Rostavili)*, Geza Balkay *(Col Kulikov)*, Zsolt Kortvelyessy *(Lt. Redetsky)*, Janos Ban *(Officer)*, Masanori Toguchi *(Mongol Hippy)*, Sven-Ole Thorsen *(Nikolai)*, Norbert Novenyi *(Sacha)*, Istvan Etlenyi *(Yegor)*, George Gati *(Piano Player)*, Peter Marikovsky *(Waiter)*, Gabor Nemeth, Istvan Vajas, Peter Kis, Atilla Fasi *(Gangsters)*, Eric Mansker *(Ali)*, Lew Hopson *(Jamal)*, Jason Ronard *(Nelligan)*, Gigi Vorgan *(Audrey)*, Allan Graf *(Prison Guard)*, Kurt Fuller, Bruno Acalinas *(Detectives)*, Christopher Mankiewicz *(Cop in Hospital)*, Bob O'Donnell *(Newsie)*, Marjorie Bransfield *(Waitress)*, Luis Contreras *(Lupo)*, Christopher Anthony Young *(Hooligan)*, William McConnell, Ed Defusco *(Police Photographers)*, Joey D. Vieira *(Man at Phone Booth)*, Mike Adams *(Railroad Engineer)*.

Just as the much touted RAMBO III began to take a nosedive at the box office, RED HEAT arrived on the scene to prove once again that veteran director Walter Hill is the preeminent talent in the action film genre. Filled with interesting characters, a hearty sense of humor, an insightful social subtext, and some breathtaking scenes of mayhem, RED HEAT is head and shoulders above the mindless RAMBO films both in terms of filmmaking technique and pure entertainment value. The film opens in Moscow (where, for the first time, an American production was allowed to film in Red Square) as dedicated policeman Schwarzenegger goes undercover at a bizarre coed steam bath in search of information on a Georgian drug dealer. After pummelling the information out of a recalcitrant stoolie, Schwarzenegger traces the drug kingpin (O'Ross) to a bar, but before he can make an arrest a vicious shootout ensues. Although his partner loses his life, Schwarzenegger kills O'Ross's brother; however, the drug dealer escapes and flees to the US, where he arranges a major cocaine deal with a black Chicago street gang. When O'Ross is thrown in jail on a fluke for driving without a license, the Soviets send Schwarzenegger to Chicago to get him. In the Windy City, two grubby Chicago detectives, Bright and Belushi, are assigned to work with Schwarzenegger. The Soviet is single-minded about his mission and has no interest in the US or motor-mouthed Belushi's wisecracks. As O'Ross is being led out of the lockup and to the airport by Schwarzenegger and Bright, the gang with which O'Ross is doing business shows up; dressed as armored car guards, they help O'Ross escape. Bright is killed in the shootout and now Belushi has a personal vendetta against O'Ross. Although they dislike each other, the Chicago cop and the Soviet policeman team up to find the vicious drug dealer. Schwarzenegger decides to continue his pursuit in plain clothes and dons a hideous green suit, prompting Belushi to call the him "Gumby." The two cops begin ferreting out information from a variety of sources, including powerful drug kingpin Jennings (in a superb performance), who runs his operation from his cell at Stateville Penitentiary, and Gershon, a young dance instructor who married O'Ross for $10,000, allowing him to remain in the US. After several violent run-ins with both O'Ross and his American drug partners, Schwarzenegger and Belushi finally catch up to the Soviet criminal at a bus terminal. O'Ross escapes by stealing a bus, and Schwarzenegger gives chase in another one. The two giant vehicles reach top speeds as they career through downtown Chicago destroying everything in their path. Finally both buses crash in a train yard, and Schwarzenegger and O'Ross finally face each other man-to-man. Belushi bows out of the gunfight, claiming that the whole vendetta is "too Russian" for him, and watches as Schwarzenegger blows away O'Ross. The case completed, Schwarzenegger and Belushi sit at the airport watching a baseball game. Schwarzenegger finally lightens up enough to tell Belushi that he considers him a friend. Before the flight back to Moscow leaves, the two cops exchange their wrist watches as a remembrance, and Schwarzenegger returns to the Soviet Union, his mission accomplished.

Although the plot conceit is virtually identical to that of his own 1982 hit 48 HRS., Hill is such a confident filmmaker that he can take the same formula and deliver a completely different movie. Schwarzenegger's Ivan Danko is an ultraserious, dedicated Soviet policeman who will stop at nothing to accomplish his mission. While a lesser director would have had Schwarzenegger become so captivated by American capitalism that he would defect at the film's end, Hill remains true to his character's nature and has Schwarzenegger return to the Soviet Union eagerly—after all, he is a proud Russian, and Hill allows him his patriotism with no apologies to American audiences. In fact, Schwarzenegger has nothing but disdain for the West and American culture. He finds capitalism corrupting and venal and worries that its disease will affect the Soviet Union.

While Hill understands Schwarzenegger's perspective, he also offers an alternative view embodied by Belushi's Art Ridzik. Belushi initially is leery of Schwarzenegger because he is a "commie," but after the rival cops begin to develop a rapport, Belushi doesn't hesitate to remind Schwarzenegger of the shortcomings of the Soviet system. In RED HEAT, Hill establishes a casual and useful dialog between the superpowers that is telling, evenhanded, ironic, amusing, and remarkably topical given the advances of *glasnost* since the film was shot.

Hill also includes a chilling third perspective, however, and it cuts even closer to the bone than the capitalism vs. communism argument. In the Stateville sequence, Schwarzenegger has a chat with drug lord Jennings wherein the black Islamic gang leader informs the Soviet cop that the world was built on the backs of the black slaves. Jennings plans to avenge this injustice and free his people from the oppression of the decadent white race by selling whites as many drugs as they can blithely consume. Eventually, according to Jennings, the whites will destroy themselves and he and his followers will be left to rebuild a new society. Jennings has nothing but contempt for both the US and the USSR, claiming that *he* is the ". . .only real Marxist in the room." It is a disturbing and powerful scene, made doubly so by actor Brent Jenning's memorable performance, and points out that repressed minorities in both the US (blacks) and the Soviet Union (Georgians) have been forced by circumstance into running drugs to survive.

The many layers of subtext and shadings of character found in RED HEAT are practically nonexistent in most action films produced today. What inferior directors (and stars) fail to understand about the genre is that violence defines the existence of these characters and illuminates different aspects of their personalities. Action that is not consistent with character is gratuitous and pointless. One of RED HEAT's weaknesses is that Hill has allowed the action scenes to become absurd and cartoonish, a capitulation to audiences who have come to expect the unchecked lunacy of Stallone's films. On the other hand, Hill has made the best use of Arnold Schwarzenegger since THE TERMINATOR. With his thick Austrian accent and unreal musculature, Schwarzenegger is an odd movie star, but the former body builder understands his limitations and has done a decent job sticking to his strengths. His most inspired defense is the sly, self-deprecating sense of humor that has crept into his screen persona. Unfortunately, a little bit of that goes a long way, and when allowed to perform unchecked, as in last year's THE RUNNING MAN, Schwarzenegger can come off as crass, insensitive, and insulting.

While most directors concentrate on Schwarzenegger's muscles, Hill understands that the actor's greatest asset is his remarkable face. As a director, Hill has always cast on the basis of facial features, and a glance at his usual stable of supporting performers reveals a rogues gallery of eccentric mugs. By forcing Schwarzenegger to rely on his ironlike face and imposing size instead of having him perform feats of strength like a sideshow freak, Hill has gone a long way toward humanizing Schwarzenegger's screen persona and has gotten him to give the best performance of his career. In pairing the stoic Schwarzenegger with the sloblike, motor-mouthed Belushi, Hill has created a memorable buddy team composed of total physical and temperamental opposites.

Although he is likely to be overlooked because of Schwarzenegger's impressive showing, Belushi turns in a well-rounded performance as well. He is thoroughly convincing as an action hero, and his wisecracks have a relaxed, improvisational feel that flows naturally from his character. As is typical of Hill's films, the supporting players are solid and memorable, especially Larry Fishburne as an uptight police lieutenant, Peter Boyle as Belushi's pragmatic captain, and Ed O'Ross as the particularly menacing Georgian drug dealer. Although the project may not be as visionary or personal as Walter Hill's best work (HARD TIMES, THE DRIVER, THE WARRIORS, SOUTHERN COMFORT), RED HEAT is a fine action film and a welcome break

from the shallow shoot-'em-ups that have become the standard in the 1980s. *(Graphic violence, excessive profanity).*

p, Walter Hill, Gordon Carroll; d, Walter Hill; w, Harry Kleiner, Walter Hill, Troy Kennedy Martin (based on a story by Walter Hill); ph, Matthew F. Leonetti (Technicolor); ed, Freeman Davies, Carmel Davies, Donn Aron; m, James Horner; m/l, Mickey Oliver, Cheese Mixin' Music, Acker Bilk, Robert Mellin; prod d, John Vallone; art d, Michael Corenblith; set d, Nick Navarro; spec eff, Bruce Steinheimer; ch, Ginger Farley, Mark Gomez; stunts, Bennie Dobbins; makeup, Michael Germain, Jeff Dawn.

Action   Cas.   (PR:O MPAA:R)

RED HEAT zero   (1988, US/Ger.) 104m TAT-Aida United-Intl Screen/Vestron c

Linda Blair *(Chris Carlson)*, Sylvia Kristel *(Sofia)*, Sue Kiel *(Hedda)*, William Ostrander *(Michael)*, Elisabeth Volkmann *(Einbeck)*, Albert Fortell *(Ernst)*, Herb Andress *(Werner)*, Barbara Spitz *(Meg)*, Kati Marothy *(Barbara)*, Dagmar Michal-Schwarz *(Lillian)*, Sissy Weiner *(Uta)*, Norbert Blecha *(Kurt)*, Sonja Martin *(Evelyn)*, Evelyn Engleder *(Eva)*, John Brett *(Roger)*, Michael Troy *(Howard)*, Helmuth Janatsch *(Lecture)*, Elvira Neustadtl *(Limmer)*, Fritz von Friedel *(BND Agent)*.

© TRI-STAR

RED HEAT is a thoroughly stupid and illogical women-in-prison film, just one of about 30 or 40 in Linda Blair's filmography. She plays a dizzy college student from Pennsylvania who travels to Germany to meet her fiance, Ostrander, an enlisted man who has one month of duty left before he can return home. One night, Blair takes a walk and witnesses as an East German woman who has just defected is abducted and tossed into a van. The abductors also grab Blair. The next morning, Ostrander wakes up to an empty bed. He turns to the hotel staff, army intelligence, and the US Embassy for help, but to no avail. He'll just have to find her on his own. In the meantime, Blair is tried and convicted of acts of espionage and tossed into a women's prison. It's the sort of jail that exists only in women-in-prison films—everything is strictly *verboten*, lesbianism runs rampant, and the toughest gal in prison, Kristel, is feared by everyone. Naturally, no one knows Blair is incarcerated there—she can't send out any information, and the US Embassy has made no attempt to find her. She might as well be in Oz—a place that is far more realistic than this Iron Curtain jail. Blair is next used as a pawn for the prison authorities who want her to pry information from the jailed defector and, of course, she has no choice but to comply. She's not easily pushed around, however, and soon becomes a rebel leader for her cellmates, who finally stand up to their sadistic oppressors. Ostrander, meanwhile, has hooked up with a gang of mercenaries who have organized a prison break—the prison being conveniently located directly above the city's sewer system. Needless to say, it's a success, and the lovers safely make their way across the border, but after some ho-hum gunplay.

If you like women-in-prison films, you'll probably enjoy RED HEAT, despite the fact that it's utterly worthless. The film is nicely photographed and boasts a score by Tangerine Dream, but it's nothing more than an excuse to heap indignities on a number of unsightly German actresses. It does, however, contain one immortal line of dialog, spoken by the vengeful Kristel in an awful German accent to Blair: "I killed three people . . . at least. The first one was my stepfather . . . he ate my pet snake." Unfortunately, Kristel never tells us what pets the other two victims swallowed up. Photographed with a largely German crew in 1984, RED HEAT didn't see a US release until its 1988 video release. *(Nudity, graphic violence, sexual situations, excessive profanity.)*

p, Ernst R. Theumer; d, Robert Collector; w, Robert Collector, Gary Drucker; ph, Wolfgang Dickmann; ed, Anthony Redman; m, Tangerine Dream; art d, Livia Kovats, Ernst Wurzer; cos, Erika Navas, Monika Hinz, Margit Ogris Thiel; makeup, Britta Kraft, Ingrid Thier.

Action   Cas.   (PR:O MPAA:NR)

RED NIGHTS † (1988) 89m Trans World c

Christopher Parker *(Randy)*, Brian Matthews *(David)*, Tom Badal *(Bruce)*, Patti Bauer *(Betty)*, Jack Carter *(Uncle Solly)*, James Mayberry *(Jeff)*, William Smith *(Phillip)*, Ivan E. Roth *(Peter)*, Tawny Capriccio *(Helen)*, Anna Louise *(Stripper)*.

A straight-to-video drama with some bizarre casting, RED NIGHTS follows young would-be actor Parker as he leaves his New Hampshire hometown—where he had a bit part in a movie shot on location there—to seek fame and fortune in Hollywood. Obviously somewhat naive, Parker hopes to star in westerns, a genre that has been dormant for the last 10 years. To pay the rent, he takes a job in a novelty shop owned by the oddly cast Smith (veteran of innumerable biker movies). While trying to get a break, Parker falls in love with the beautiful Bauer, but is shocked to learn that she stars in porno films produced by—get ready for this—comedian Jack Carter. Meanwhile, Parker's best pal, Matthews, has gotten himself tangled up with some tough drug dealers and is murdered. Vowing vengeance, Parker puts his acting career on hold long enough to go after Matthews' killer. The synthesizer musical score is by Tangerine Dream, a band that seemingly will work for just about anyone these days.

p, Ron Wolotzky; d, Izhak Hanooka; w, Izhak Hanooka; ph, Jacob Eleasari; ed, David Lloyd; m, Tangerine Dream; prod d, Rina Binyamini; set d, Myron Emery.

Drama **Cas.** **(PR:NR MPAA:R)**

REJUVENATOR, THE † (1988) 86m Jewel/SVS c

Vivian Lanko *(Elizabeth Warren/Monster)*, John MacKay *(Dr. Gregory Ashton)*, James Hogue *(Wilhelm)*, Katell Pleven *(Dr. Stella Stone)*, Marcus Powell *(Dr. Germaine)*, Jessica Dublin *(Ruth Warren)*, Roy MacArthur *(Hunter)*, Louis F. Homyak *(Tony)*, Poison Dollys *(Themselves)*.

In a plot that sounds like it was borrowed from an old Roger Corman movie, aging former movie queen Dublin uses what's left of her fortune to fund mad-scientist MacKay's research into age reversal. Discovering a portion of the brain that controls aging, MacKay develops a serum—derived from human gray matter—that is capable of turning back the clock. MacKay tests the serum on the eager Dublin, and is amazed to find that she reverts back to her younger self (now played by Lanko). Unfortunately, as a nasty side effect (there are *always* nasty side effects in these movies), she becomes a raging monster and requires even bigger doses of the serum to become normal again. When MacKay can't procure enough cadavers to keep up with Lanko's demand for serum, the monster-woman turns murderer and feasts on her victims' brains.

p, Steven Mackler; d, Brian Thomas Jones; w, Simon Nuchtern, Brian Thomas Jones; ph, James McCalmont (Technicolor); ed, Brian O'Hara; m, Larry Juris; prod d, Susan Bolles; art d, Lynn Nigro; spec eff, Ed French.

Horror **Cas.** **(PR:NR MPAA:R)**

REMOTE CONTROL* (1988) 88m Vista Organization c

Kevin Dillon *(Cosmo)*, Deborah Goodrich *(Belinda)*, Christopher Wynne *(Georgie)*, Frank Beddor *(Victor)*, Jennifer Tilly *(Allegra)*, Kaaren Lee *(Patricia)*, Bert Remson *(Bill Denver)*.

With REMOTE CONTROL, director Jeff Lieberman attempts to capture the flavor of the 1950s science-fiction film and combine it with the subject of today's video revolution. Dillon works at a video store that receives an elaborate display for a film titled "Remote Control." Along with the display, the store is given several promotional copies of the film, which quickly becomes a hot rental. Unknown to the public, the film hypnotizes its viewers and makes them commit acts of extreme violence. Dillon catches on to the scheme and, with the help of girl friend Goodrich and best friend Wynne, sets out to locate the plant that manufactures the videotape. Upon arriving at the plant, the three are captured and told of a plan to overtake Earth by a bunch of land-greedy outer space aliens. Naturally, this doesn't sit well with Dillon, and the trio attempts to destroy the plant and all of the remaining tapes. In the climax, Dillon, under the spell of one of the tapes, almost kills Goodrich, only to break free of his trance and destroy the videocassette thought to be the last. Of course, Dillon's tape *isn't* the last—a forgotten cassette left in the heroes' car is, and at the end a factory worker grabs it, laughing hysterically, and holds it above his head as an offering to the remote gods above.

REMOTE CONTROL doesn't know whether it wants to be a spoof or a thriller, and because of its indecision fails on both levels. Attempting to capture the mood of the 50s' goofy sci-fi films, Lieberman overplays his hand in trying to make the present day look otherworldly. Characters walk around in metallic clothing, sport bizarre haircuts, and live in homes that look like something out of LOST IN SPACE. The end product is a film that rings false on all levels—we are never quite sure if we are supposed to be laughing or gasping—until finally the film falls flat on its face, tripped up by its own ridiculousness. The performances are all similarly flat, except that of Kevin Dillon, who is convincing in a sharp and energetic portrayal of a man-who-knows-it-all-but-whom-no-one-will-believe. It's a shame he didn't have a better script to work with. Lieberman is obviously a fan of this film's spacy prototypes, but needs to take a closer look to see what makes them fly, since, if REMOTE CONTROL's heart is in the right place, its head is from a different world. *(Violence, profanity.)*

p, Scott Rosenfelt, Mark Levinson; d, Jeff Lieberman; w, Jeff Lieberman; ph, Timothy Suhrstedt (DeLuxe Color); ed, Scott Wallace; m, Peter Bernstein; prod d, Curtis Schnell; set d, Douglas Mowat; cos, Daniel Paredes; stunts, William Lane.

Science Fiction **Cas.** **(PR:C MPAA:R)**

RENT-A-COP** (1988) 95m Kings Road c

Burt Reynolds *(Tony Church)*, Liza Minnelli *(Della Roberts)*, James Remar *(Dancer)*, Richard Masur *(Roger)*, Dionne Warwick *(Beth)*, Bernie Casey *(Lemar)*, Robby Benson *(Pitts)*, John Stanton *(Alexander)*, John P. Ryan *(Chief of Police)*, Larry Dolgin *(Capt. James)*, Roslyn Alexander *(Miss Barley)*, Michael Rooker.

RENT-A-COP stars Burt Reynolds as a Chicago police officer who, after being the only surviving member of a botched drug bust, is dumped from the force and becomes resigned to hiring himself out as a security guard to anyone who will have him, to the extent of dressing as Santa Claus and prowling department stores looking for shoplifters. Minnelli plays a bouncy hooker who unwittingly witnessed the raid in which all of the cops (minus Reynolds) were killed. The killer, Remar, is armed with an arsenal of futuristic weapons, including a light-bomb that can temporarily blind its victims. Reynolds saves Minnelli from near death, but not before the killer has a good look at her. Flash forward two months: Reynolds, now a veteran rent-a-cop, is approached by former cop Masur, a flashy dresser who obviously isn't hurting for a paycheck. Masur tries to convince Reynolds to work for his people, but, when Reynolds wants to know just what type of work he does, Masur clams up, realizing he shouldn't divulge such information freely. It's about this time that Remar makes another attempt on the life of Minnelli, the only person who can identify him as the cop killer. She survives the attack, and hunts down Reynolds, who is still working in the department store. After a few refusals, Reynolds agrees to be her bodyguard. The quarrelsome couple return to the hotel where the murders occurred, and, after retracing her steps, Minnelli recalls the killer's face. She remembers that the man had devil eyes and smelled like a dancer, whatever that means. Reynolds now begins an extensive investigation, at the same time falling for Minnelli. After Minnelli's madam, Warwick, is savagely executed by Remar, they begin finding some answers. It seems that Minnelli recalls meeting the flashy Masur, as well as many other ex-cops, at a lavish party thrown by Chicago drug lord Stanton—and a computer check reveals that Remar had been on the force but was fired for using excessive violence. He now works for Stanton. Bingo! Minnelli recognizes Remar's evil eyes and identifies him as the killer, while the amazing computer also manages to identify the nightclub where he dances. Masur admits that he, too, works for Stanton, but maintains that he had no part in the cop slayings. Reynolds buys his story, and, shortly thereafter, Masur becomes Remar's latest target. Minnelli locates the killer at his favorite disco, where he kidnaps her, setting up the final showdown between Good and Evil. Reynolds calls in his former partner, Casey, along with Benson, for backup, and the ensuing battle leaves a beautiful mansion destroyed and a good portion of Chicago's bad guys dead. Reynolds and Minnelli are left to walk away into the sunset.

RENT-A-COP subscribes to the basic cop-movie ingredients, but rarely rises above mediocrity. Reynolds' has been in some very good films, but this isn't one of them, and his charm simply isn't enough to mask the weak script. Director Jerry London makes room for virtually every stereotype in this film, including the sleazy police chief, the squinty-eyed psychopathic killer, and the omnipotent drug czar. London does manage to move things along at a brisk pace, but speed cannot make up for the lack of meaty content. The ever-reliable Richard Masur rises above the material, but Liza Minnelli is simply miscast as Della the hooker, and her performance is overblown in all but a few scenes. Her character's lines are often absurd, as in this classic: "Hookers and baseball players, when their legs give it's time to get out." The audience can't expect much sincerity in such dialog. Bernie Casey, as Reynolds' former partner, does a nice turn, while Robby Benson looks as if he'd rather be somewhere else. The film never settles on one style, going from road-picture dialog between the lead characters to cold-blooded killings, and the result is a film with little to say and nothing new to offer. *(Violence, profanity.)*

p, Raymond Wagner; d, Jerry London; w, Dennis Shryack, Michael Blodgett; ph, Giuseppe Rotunno (Technicolor); ed, Robert Lawrence; m, Jerry Goldsmith; prod d, Tony Masters; art d, Aurelio Crugnola; set d, Franco Fumagalli; cos, Moss Mabry.

Action/Drama/Comedy **Cas.** **(PR:C MPAA:R)**

RENTED LIPS zero (1988) 80m Vista/Cineworld c

Martin Mull *(Archie Powell)*, Dick Shawn *(Charlie Slater)*, Jennifer Tilly *(Mona Lisa)*, Edy Williams *(Heather Darling)*, Robert Downey, Jr. *(Wolf Dangler)*, June Lockhart *(Archie's Mother)*, Kenneth Mars *(Rev. Farrell)*, Shelley Berman *(Bill Slotnik)*, Mel Welles *(Milo)*, Jack Riley *(Herb the Auditor)*, Pat McCormick *(Winky)*, Eileen Brennan *(Hotel Desk Clerk)*, Michael Horse *(Bobby Leaping Mouse)*, Tony Cox *(Tyrell)*, Eric Bruskotter, Karl Bruskotter *(Farrell's Goons)*.

Archie Powell (Martin Mull) and Charlie Slater (Dick Shawn, in his last screen appearance) are struggling filmmakers who specialize in documentaries. During a screening of their latest effort, an ode to aluminum, they are approached by the manager of the local public television station (Berman), who offers the pair the chance to finish "Rented Lips," an "art film" he's financing. It seems the original director died during shooting and Berman has to have the film completed in 12 days. Mull complains that he and Shawn are about to begin shooting a documentary on Indian farming techniques, but Berman tells him they can use the cast and crew from "Rented Lips" to shoot that film as well. Mull and Shawn thereupon agree to take over the project, though Mull is appalled to find that he is shooting a porno epic about sexual practices in Nazi Germany. Meanwhile, Mull's mother (Lockhart), unhappy about her son's dull life, arranges for him to meet young singer Mona Lisa (Tilly), and Mull immediately falls in love with her. Since she's a singer, he decides to make both of his productions musicals and to cast Tilly in the leads. He also sets about to raise the artistic level of "Rented Lips," retitling it "Halloween at the Bunker" and dispensing with the sex, much to the chagrin of the film's male star, Wolf

Dangler (Downey, Jr.). Mull moves the production to a ranch outside of town and works feverishly to complete both his projects. His work attracts the attention of Rev. Farrell (Mars), a TV evangelist who is also a porno filmmaker and the father of Tilly. Mars doesn't want Mull to complete his film, and does all he can to block the production, including having his black dwarf henchman, Cox, set fire to the barn in which Mull is shooting. Still Mull perseveres, and completes his film on Indian farming techniques, which includes an elaborate musical production number in which Berman plays a giant ear of corn. As the movie plays on a theater screen, the audience breaks into raucous cheers. Cut to Mull dozing at his typewriter. He awakens, says, "Guess I better finish this," and begins typing. The film then cuts back to the theater and a joyous Mull and Tilly accepting congratulations from all corners.

RENTED LIPS is a pretty excruciating experience. It's not funny, not by a long shot, and to see people who have been involved with successful comic efforts in the past (Mull, Shawn, Kenneth Mars, Shelley Berman, director Robert Downey) caught in this sorry mess is quite painful. Of course, Mull, who also served as producer and writer, has to take a lion's share of the blame for this failure. More distressing than the film's inability to amuse is the fact that it borrows so blatantly from Mel Brooks' THE PRODUCERS. Seeing singing and dancing Nazis in a production called "Halloween at the Bunker" can't help but conjure images of the singing and dancing Nazis in "Springtime for Hitler" in the Brooks film. But, while Brooks' effort was captivating in its unbridled offensiveness, Mull's is hollow. Mull started his career as a writer and performer of satirical songs, and one keeps waiting for a hint of that wit in the musical numbers in RENTED LIPS, but instead he offers lyrics like "Shuck your fears and shuck your ears and sit with us for a while / We're gonna show you how we party Indian-style." In the acting category, the disheveled Mull adequately portrays the nerd devoted to the craft of filmmaking, while Mars overacts mightily. Only Robert Downey, Jr. (son of the director, with appearances in PICK-UP ARTIST and LESS THAN ZERO to his credit), brings any life to the production. His porno veteran Wolf Dangler is manic, insecure, demanding, and altogether quite amusing. Then there's Shawn. Sporting sunglasses and a floppy hat throughout the picture, he is so subdued that his place could have been filled by Peter Fonda. The saddest thing about this dismal film is that it will have to stand forever as Shawn's final film appearance. *(Nudity, profanity.)*

p, Mort Engelberg; d, Robert Downey; w, Martin Mull; ph, Robert D. Yeoman (DeLuxe Color); ed, Christopher Greenbury, Brian Berdan, Jay Ignaszcwski; m, Van Dyke Parks; m/l, Van Dyke Parks, Martin Mull; prod d, George Costello; cos, Lisa Jensen.

Comedy **Cas.** **(PR:O MPAA:R)**

REPENTANCE**** (1988, USSR) 150m Gruziafilm/Cannon c

Avtandil Makharadze *(Varlam Aravidze/Abel Aravidze)*, Iya Ninidze *(Guliko, Varlam's Daughter-in-Law)*, Merab Ninidze *(Tornike, Varlam's Grandson)*, Zeinab Botsvadze *(Katevan Barateli, Sandro's Daughter)*, Ketevan Abuladze *(Nino Baratelli, Sandro's Wife)*, Edisher Giorgobiani *(Sandro Baratelli, Painter)*, Kakhi Kavsadze *(Mikhail Korisheli)*, Nino Zakariadze *(Elena Korisheli)*, Nato Otijigava *(Ketevan as a Child)*, Dato Kemkhadze *(Abel as a Child)*, Veriko Anjaparidze, Boris Tsipuria, Akaki Khidasheli, Leo Antadze, Rezo Esadze, Amiran Amiranashvili, Amiran Buadze, Dato Papuashvili, Srota Skhirtladze, Beso Khidasheli, M. Makhviladze, T. Tsitsishvili, M. Kakhiani, R. Kiknadze, Kh. Khobua, L. Kapanadze, K. Makhazadze, Z. Kavtaradze, D. Dvalishvili, N. Djavakhishvili, M. Djojua, T. Koshkadze, P. Nozadze, T. Tavariani, M. Shembeli, I. Vasadze, R. Baramidze, G. Gogoberidze, T. Saralidze, S. Gozichaishvili, G. Otarashvili.

As the 1980s draw to a close, it seems likely that Tengiz Abuladze's REPENTANCE will emerge as the decade's most significant Soviet film, a historically important document of the springtime of Gorbachev's *glasnost* policy. Written in 1981 and okayed under the Brezhnev administration by Eduard Shevardnadze, REPENTANCE was filmed in Soviet Georgia, the homeland of Stalin, as a television project. It was shelved in 1984, remaining thus until 1987, when, under Gorbachev, the Union of Cinematographers headed by filmmaker Elem Klimov reviewed the film and liberated it from state censorship. Before the year came to a close, REPENTANCE won the Special Jury Prize at the Cannes Film Festival, received a Gold Hugo (for best picture) and a Silver Hugo (for best actor) from the Chicago International Film Festival, and was named as the Soviet Union's official entry in the Academy Awards' Foreign-Language Film category. In 1988, the Cannon Film Group gave the film a US theatrical release. These facts would be relatively insignificant did they not illustrate the very theme of REPENTANCE: that the post-Stalin generation's sin of silence in refusing to admit to the brutality of Stalin's reign is as contemptible and severe in its consequences as Stalin's purges were. While the suppression of REPENTANCE only adds fuel to the fire of Abuladze's thesis, its theatrical release is a marked sign of hope—a sign recognized by the reported 60 million-plus Soviet citizens who saw the film, making it the most widely seen Soviet picture of all time.

The film's plot is relatively simple, though structured in a brilliantly complex manner. REPENTANCE begins and ends with a framing scene of a middle-aged woman, Botsvadze, a cake decorator who makes confections in the shape of churches. While at work, she learns of the death of the aged Varlam Aravidze (brilliantly played by Avtandil Makharadze, who also plays the deceased man's son), a highly revered Georgian mayor whose physical appearance and personality is a composite of fascist leaders—a Georgian like Stalin, he has a similar haircut; like Mussolini, he cloaks his intimidating physique in a black shirt; like Hitler, he sports a small mustache; like Lavrenti Beria, Stalin's chief of secret police, he wears *pince-nez* and is an opera buff; and like Charlie Chaplin's "Hynkel," he is a comic buffoon. Botsvadze tells a visitor that she once knew the mayor. The scene then shifts to the mayor's burial, attended by the mayor's son, Abel (Makharadze again); the son's wife (Iya Ninidze); and the mayor's grandson (Merab Ninidze). Later that evening, at the home of the mayor's son, the freshly buried corpse appears in the garden. Again it is buried. Again it appears in the garden. Police arrive, arrest the corpse, and bury it again. Again the stiffened corpse appears. Again it is buried. Exasperated by the events, the authorities post sentries in the cemetery to catch the person responsible. When the grave robber appears, the dead man's grandson fires his rifle and attacks this desecrator of his ancestor's tomb. It is the cake decorator Botsvadze, who is wrestled to the ground, bleeding from a bullet wound to the arm. She stands trial and admits to digging up the corpse, declaring, "As long as I live, Varlam Aravidze will not be in a grave." She shocks her jurors and the courtroom spectators by telling them a story of what their dear mayor was really like, as the scene shifts to an earlier era, when Botsvadze was just a girl of eight, the daughter of a creative and highly expressive painter, Giorgobiani. The painter, upset that a local 6th-century church is being used as a test sight for scientific experiments and is crumbling as a result, visits his mayor along with two concerned town elders. Later the elders are arrested and detained for 24 hours, while the painter voices his strong protest to his mentor, Kavsadze, an intellectual and advisor to the mayor. When the mayor hears of the painter's protests, he pays a visit to the painter's home and studio. The mayor entertains the painter's family, singing arias with his two aides and reciting a sonnet by Shakespeare. The mayor and the painter discuss the purpose and importance of art in society. The following day, the painter's mentor receives an anonymous letter accusing the painter of antinationalism. The painter is arrested and "exiled" (read: executed), nor is he the only one to suffer this fate, as the mayor and his aides vow to ferret out the enemy. In a public speech, the mayor proclaims that "Four out of every three persons are enemies. Numerically, one foe is greater than one friend . . . Our Motherland is in danger!" As his fear grows greater, so too do his crimes, and many other intellectuals and artists are accused of being spies and arrested. A whole truckful of people whose only crime is to share the same last name are exiled. People wait in hope that an "exiled" husband or father isn't a dead one. Some gather at a lumber mill, hoping to find a loved one's name carved into the tree trunks. Meanwhile, those accused try to devise a plan to stop the purges. When the painter is allowed to meet face to face with his accuser (as a blind-folded figure of Justice looks on), the latter explains that if everyone, even the innocent, is accused of taking part in illegal activities then the government will take heed, since they will be unable to arrest the entire population. (History, however, proved this theory wrong as some 20 million Soviets disappeared during Stalin's rule.) Later, the painter's wife (Katevan Abuladze) is also arrested, never to be seen again, leaving her child an orphan. The film returns to Botsvadze's trial, where, their consciousness raised, the jury is unable to convict her. Instead, they declare her insane and make plans to admit her to an asylum. Disgusted by his father's silence, the mayor's grandson, Merab Ninidze, speaks out against his father and the whole of his father's generation. He accuses his father of ignoring the facts, and of naming the innocent as guilty and the sane as insane—all in an effort to protect his own reputation and status. Rather than be part of such hypocrisy, Ninidze kills himself with the rifle he received as a gift from his grandfather. The father, who has already lost his own father and the history he represents, now loses his son and the future he represents—all because of his own silence. As his act of repentance, he digs up the mayor's corpse and tosses the body from a precipice. The film shifts back (or ahead?) to the opening scene of the cake decorator, as Botsvadze continues her work and her discussion of the dead mayor she once knew. From outside her window an old passerby asks the way to the church, becoming indignant when she learns that the road on which she is traveling—Varlam Street—doesn't lead to a church. She believes that if a road doesn't lead to such a destination then there is no point in having a road at all.

A powerful, intelligent, and visually poetic picture, REPENTANCE condemns not only Stalinism but those who try to bury it away. The film's greatest villain, arguably, is not the fascist mayor (who is painted as an indecisive clown), but the mayor's son. The film's greatest hero is the character initially viewed as a madwoman—the grave-robbing cake decorator. She is the one who defies and defiles in the name of her people's freedom, even though it means a life in a lunatic asylum. Like the characters in two previous Abuladze films (1968's MOLBA [Supplication] and 1977's THE WISHING TREE—the first and second parts of a trilogy that ends with REPENTANCE), the mayor's son and the cake decorator display what Abuladze has called "the guilt of the innocent".

While its anti-Stalinist line is obvious, what has, curiously, been most overlooked in the numerous reviews and articles to appear this year surrounding the film's release is Abuladze's plea for religious freedom. More Georgian than Soviet, the deeply moral and spiritual REPENTANCE is filled with religious iconography—crucifixes, churches, the Christ-like painter, the satanic mayor—as well as a plea for a spiritual leader, rather than an artistic or political one. It is thus, however, that REPENTANCE tends to sink under the weight of its own visual symbolism. While many of the film's dreamy images are unforgettable (such as that of the painter and his wife buried, except for the faces, under a pile of rocks while the mayor sings an aria, or the chillingly sad scene at the lumber mill), Abuladze's use of them sometimes becomes too generous. Nonetheless, REPENTANCE can stand, not only as one of the finest films to be released as a result of *glasnost*, but as a great example of Georgian filmmaking. (In Georgian; English subtitles.) *(Violence, nudity, adult situations).*

d, Tengiz Abuladze; w, Nana Djanelidze, Tengiz Abuladze, Rezo Kveselava; ph, Mikhail Agranovich (Orwo Color); ed, Guliko Omadze; m, Nana Djanelidze; prod d, Georgi Mikeladze; set d, Navruz Abdul-ogli; makeup, Guram Barnabishvili.

Drama/Fantasy/Political **Cas.** **(PR:C MPAA:PG)**

RESCUE, THE* (1988) 98m Touchstone-Silver Screen Partners III/BV c

Kevin Dillon *(J.J. Merrill)*, Christina Harnos *(Adrian Phillips)*, Marc Price *(Max Rothman)*, Ned Vaughn *(Shawn Howard)*, Ian Giatti *(Bobby Howard)*, Charles Haid *(Cmdr. Howard)*, Edward Albert *(Cmdr. Merrill)*, Timothy Carhart *(Lt. Phil-*

lips), Michael Gates Phenicie *(Wicks)*, Mel Wong *(Kim Song)*, James Cromwell *(Adm. Rothman)*, Ellen Barber *(Virginia Phillips)*, Anne E. Curry *(Sybil Howard)*, Joyce Reehling *(Vella Rothman)*, Lorry Goldman *(Sec. Gates)*, Leon Russom *(Capt. Miller)*, Shim Sung Sool *(Tae Kwon Do Instructor)*, Cmdr. Tom Nelson *(Capt. Stillman)*, Herbert Wong *(Riverman)*, Rocky Wing Cheung Ho *(Cell Guard/Fighter)*, Ock Youn Chang *(Commandant)*, Stephen Ng, Trevor Sai Loue, Pak Kun Tang, No Tran *(Kim Song Men)*, Seong Hee Lee *(Border Gun)*, Tony Lee *(Patrol Boat Officer)*, Norman Palacio *(Base Gate Guard)*, Wendy Jill Gordon *(Newscaster)*, Squadron Leader Radar O'Reilly *(C130 Pilot)*, Steve Moore, John Benfel *(A-4 Pilots)*.

© BUENA VISTA

"Incredible, incredible!" exclaims a Korean freedom fighter toward the climax of THE RESCUE, a RAMBOesque action film which attains new heights in macho absurdity. Incredible indeed. This anachronistic release takes all the paranoid, jingoistic, patriotic propaganda spewed by the likes of superheroes Sylvester Stallone and Chuck Norris and installs it in the mouths of babes. Opening titles tell us of the extreme tension still felt along the DMZ between North and South Korea. We are then brought into an American army base in Seoul, where it is learned that one of our nuclear submarines has gone down and is beginning to drift into North Korean waters. Base commander Cromwell dispatches his top Navy SEALS unit (Haid, Albert, Carhart, and Phenicie) on a secret mission to rescue the submarine's captain and destroy the sub so that our advanced American military technology won't fall into the hands of the evil communists. Well, not surprisingly, the SEALS are captured by the North Koreans—despite the fact that they were in international waters—and tossed into a dank POW camp where they are routinely beaten by the cruel and unreasonable reds. Although the president of the United States has declared the men hostages and the military has drafted a detailed plan, dubbed Operation Phoenix, to rescue them, the powers that be in Washington decide it would be politically injudicious to launch the mission. This outrages the children of the prisoners (teenagers Dillon, Harnos, and Vaughn, and 10-year-old Giatti), who have eavesdropped on the top secret meeting via a bugging device invented by base commander Cromwell's precocious son, Price. Determined not to sit by and let their fathers be tortured, the kids steal the plans to Operation Phoenix and launch it themselves. After much ridiculous derring-do, the kids manage to break their fathers out of the North Korean prison camp and, with the help of some friendly Korean freedom fighters, are able to blast their way to a nearby airstrip, where they steal a cargo plane to fly back to South Korea. There is a final tense moment, however, when two American fighter jets are scrambled to shoot down the unidentified plane. With no radio, the heroes cannot identify themselves as Americans, so the quick thinking kids send young Giatti up the hatch at the top of the plane where he reveals a red, white, and blue Bruce Springsteen concert t-shirt to the fighter pilots. With its crew finally identified as true-blue Americans, the cargo plane is allowed to land at the Air Force base where the kids and their fathers are reunited with their anxious mothers.

It is difficult to describe just how mind-numbingly stupid this movie is. From the somber opening crawl to the ridiculous ending, THE RESCUE is one unintentional howl after another. British television director Ferdinand Fairfax is fairly adept at scenes of mayhem, but his direction of actors (mostly from TV themselves) is downright embarrassing, as is the horrible script by Jim and John Thomas. Haid, Albert, and the other SEALS spend the entire movie striking macho poses and exchanging meaningful glances. This, one must assume, is supposed to convey the impression that these men are a no-nonsense, tightly-knit unit that can read each other's minds. On-screen, however, they look like a bunch of inarticulate dunderheads. Even worse are the perfunctory scenes of family life designed to introduce the children and drum up sympathy for the prisoners' plight. Whereas Haid's family is all warmth and discipline, Albert and his rebellious son Dillon have a shouting match, with dad calling his son "mister" and son calling dad "sir" at the end of each sentence. This, perhaps, is really the most touching relationship, for Dillon is able to swallow his pride, ignore the fact that his dad is a sullen jerk, and rescue him from the clutches of the yellow peril anyway. As for tomboy Harnos and her father, Carhart, there seems to be an unnatural attraction between the two. What makes THE RESCUE so unintentionally funny is the utter seriousness imposed on the absurd proceedings. The dialog by the Thomas brothers is laughably bad, full of grim declarations of machismo, insipid attempts at humor ("What a beautiful daughter you have!" "Oh yeah—you should see her room!"), and self-aggrandizing exclamations designed to remind the audience just how amazing the whole movie is ("It's crazy, isn't it?" "Incredible!"). The only

actor in the entire film who plays his role the way it should be played—with tongue firmly in cheek—is Marc Price (Skippy from TV's "Family Ties"). Making wisecracks and overplaying at just the right moments, Price does a fine job of letting the audience know that he recognizes just how ludicrous this whole thing is while the other actors work overtime to appear convincing. Visually, too much of the running time is handed over to dull second-unit work, mainly panoramic views of the beautiful terrain (ironically, the film was shot in New Zealand) and fetishistic close-ups of huge military hardware. There is a cheap, made-for-television feel to the entire lamebrained affair. It would seem even Touchstone realized what a dog they had on their hands, because coming-attractions trailers for THE RESCUE were shown in theaters almost a year before the film finally crawled onto screens in the midst of the summer glut. This would indicate that the studio was waiting for a time to sneak it into release when few would notice so it would die a quick death and then be reborn on home video—where it belongs. *(Violence, profanity.)*

p, Laura Ziskin; d, Ferdinand Fairfax; w, Jim Thomas, John Thomas; ph, Russell Boyd; ed, David Holden, Carroll Timothy O'Meara; m, Bruce Broughton; prod d, Maurice Cain; art d, Robin Tarsnane, Dan Hennah; set d, Thomas L. Roysden; spec eff, Nick Allder; cos, Mary Malin; tech, Comdr. Tom Nelson; stunts, William Erickson; makeup, Rosalina Da Silva.

Action/Adventure   **Cas.**   **(PR:A-C MPAA:PG)**

RETRIBUTION*   (1988) 107m Renegade/United c

Dennis Lipscomb *(George Miller, Artist)*, Leslie Wing *(Dr. Jennifer Curtis, Psychiatrist)*, Suzanne Snyder *(Angel)*, Jeff Pomerantz *(Dr. Alan Falconer)*, George Murdock *(Dr. John Talbot)*, Pamela Dunlap *(Sally Benson)*, Susan Peretz *(Mrs. Stoller)*, Clare Peck *(Carla Minelli)*, Chris Caputo *(Dylan)*, Hoyt Axton *(Lt. Ashley)*, Ralph Manza *(Amos)*, Mario Roccuzzo *(Johnny Blake)*, Harry Caesar *(Charlie)*, Jeffrey Josephson *(Joe Martinez)*, Danny D. Daniels *(Rasta Doctor)*, Mike Muscat *(Vito Minelli, Sr.)*, Pearl Adell *(Waitress)*, Ed Berke *(Mickey)*, George Caldwell *(Paramedic)*, Brian Christian *(Bus Driver)*, Tony Cox *(Hotel Resident)*, David Dunard *(Lt. Lupo)*, Trish Fillmore *(Desiree)*, Kenneth Gray *(Rev. Dr. Baxley)*, Richard Jamison *(4th Killer)*, Joan-Carol Kent *(Paramedic)*, Steve Lerman *(Bus Passenger)*, Guy Magar *(Taxi Driver)*, Muriel Minot *(Gallery Attendant)*, Matthew Newmark *(Vito Minelli, Jr.)*, Diane Robin *(Crash Victim)*, Michelle Roth *(Newscaster)*, Miss Holly the Dog *(Hotel Dog)*.

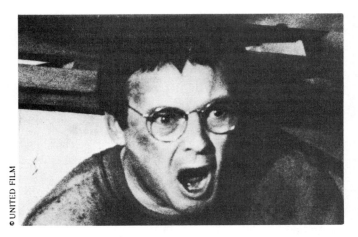

© UNITED FILM

RETRIBUTION is an incredibly tedious, low-budget ($1.5 millon) horror film that tries to make up for its lack of narrative inspiration with hyperactive camerawork. Set in Los Angeles, the film opens on Halloween night as a destitute, wimpy artist, Lipscomb, stands on the roof of his flophouse, about to make a suicide leap. As masked revelers look on, Lipscomb does a swan dive splat onto the pavement below. The camera simulates an out-of-body experience, green laser lights cut through clouds of smoke, and a horribly scarred face comes zooming out of the darkness toward the camera. Amazingly, Lipscomb survives the fall, but his soul is possessed by the green light show and he suffers from terrible nightmares. Through therapy with patient psychiatrist Wing, Lipscomb recovers his sanity, and after three months in the sanitarium he is allowed to go home. There he is welcomed back by the extended family of hookers, bums, thugs, junkies, and drunks who live in the hotel. Everything is looking up for Lipscomb—until he falls asleep, when he has nasty dreams in which he goes places he's never been, meets people he's never seen, and murders them in a variety of horrible ways. When he wakes up, news of the murders are splashed across the front page. Convinced that he is somehow the killer, Lipscomb is plagued by guilt and begs Wing to cure him. She thinks he is suffering from delusions and decides not to call the cops until she can sort things out. Her boy friend, however, does call the police, and detective Axton shows up with a subpoena demanding Lipscomb's psychiatric records from Wing. Meanwhile, Lipscomb has finally been able to piece together the source of his troubles and concludes that he has been possessed by the angry soul of a small-time hood named Vito who was brutally tortured and murdered by other unsavory types on Halloween night. Apparently Vito's soul was zooming around the ozone at the time Lipscomb tried to kill himself and, seeing that the wimpy artist was about to die, entered his body (or some such nonsense). Since then, the possessed Lipscomb has been stalking and killing those who murdered Vito.

There is one victim left, but Lipscomb is determined to prevent another killing. While Axton and his partner stake out the flophouse, Lipscomb—who has split into two bodies, one his own, one Vito's—is in his room struggling for possession of his eternal soul. Wing shows up to help, but only manages to get throttled by Vito until Lipscomb tackles him and they both crash out the window. Lipscomb's body goes splat on the pavement once again, causing a woman driver to swerve into a garbage hopper. As Wing clutches Lipscomb's dead form, Axton and his partner fish the driver out of her car, only to find that the ever-angry and persistent Vito has now possessed her.

RETRIBUTION is the feature debut of director Guy Magar, who racked up 25 hours of television helming ("Lady Blue," "Hunter," "The A-Team") before trying his hand at the big screen, but it sure seems like he didn't learn much in TV. The film is dull, repetitive, and much, much too long. In interviews, Magar has expressed dissatisfaction with the tight restrictions of the TV medium, and longed for the creative freedom theatrical films provide. Unfortunately, set length seems to be one of the things that annoyed him about television, because every scene in RETRIBUTION is pointlessly drawn out, with loads of unnecessary camera movement. The opening sequence alone runs at a painfully extended eight minutes for no apparent reason. The film has no drama, no suspense, and no surprises—it's just plain slow and terribly pretentious. Scene after scene simply pads out the narrative until the next killing; one sequence, a trip to a Jamaican witch doctor, feels like it's from another movie. When the death scenes finally manage to chug their way onto the screen, they too are sadistically lingered over and gory (the film had to be cut to avoid an "X" rating). Worse yet are the scenes of "characterization." Lipscomb, a good character actor, tries hard to make his whiny milquetoast character likable, but the script by Magar and Lee Wasserman doesn't give him a chance. Banal, trite, extremely expository dialog abounds, with characters explaining, explaining, and explaining what the audience has already seen again, again, and again. The kooky cast of street folks who inhabit Lipscomb's flophouse look like there were bought wholesale from the series of ANGEL ("Honor Student by Day, Hollywood Hooker by Night") movies, and the psychiatric staff of the sanitarium is strictly from the Snideley Whiplash school of villainy. As the police detective, Hoyt Axton looks as bored as the audience and makes his appearance so late in the movie that his character is really superfluous. The whole premise of the film is woefully underdeveloped and doesn't make much sense—not even for a supernatural horror film. Granted, Magar does manage to put together a relatively impressive-looking film on a low budget, but RETRIBUTION hardly seems worth the effort. (*Violence, gore effects, sexual situations, nudity, adult situations, substance abuse, profanity.*)

p, Guy Magar; d, Guy Magar; w, Guy Magar, Lee Wasserman; ph, Gary Thieltges (Fujicolor); ed, Guy Magar, Alan Shefland; m, Alan Howarth; m/l, Tavabonn, Michael G. Ashley; prod d, Robb Wilson King; set d, Marcie Dale; spec eff, John Eggett, Kevin Yagher; stunts, Bob Yerkes; makeup, Nina Kent.

Horror   **Cas.**   **(PR:O MPAA:R)**

RETURN OF THE KILLER TOMATOES †   (1988) 98m Four Square/NW c

Anthony Starke (*Chad*), George Clooney (*Matt*), Karen Mistal (*Tara*), Steve Lundquist (*Igor*), John Astin (*Prof. Gangrene*), Charlie Jones, Rock Peace, Frank Davis, C.J. Dillon, Teri Weigel.

This seemingly unnecessary sequel to the 1977 cult item ATTACK OF THE KILLER TOMATOES picks up where the latter left off, as, over footage from the first film, we are told that the human race has survived the onslaught of the giant killer fruit, yet some are still traumatized even at the sight of a normal-sized tomato. The story centers on Starke, a delivery boy for a pizzeria that uses only non-tomato sauces in their pies. He falls in love with Mistal, the beautiful assistant of evil scientist Astin. The romance has tragic consequences for Starke, however, for he learns that Mistal is really a killer tomato genetically altered into human form by the crazed Astin. RETURN OF THE KILLER TOMATOES ran briefly as a midnight show before being released on home video.

p, J. Stephen Peace, Lowell D. Blank; d, John DeBello; w, John DeBello, Stephen F. Andrich, Constantine Dillon; ed, John DeBello, Stephen F. Andrich; m, Rick Patterson, Neal Fox; prod d, Constantine Dillon; art d, Roger Ambrose.

Comedy/Science Fiction   **Cas.**   **(PR:NR MPAA:PG)**

RETURN OF THE LIVING DEAD PART II**   (1988) 89m Greenfox/Lorimar c

Michael Kenworthy (*Jesse Wilson*), Thor Van Lingen (*Billy*), Jason Hogan (*Johnny*), James Karen (*Ed*), Thom Mathews (*Joey*), Suzanne Snyder (*Brenda*), Marsha Dietlein (*Lucy Wilson*), Suzan Stadner (*Aerobics Instructor*), Jonathon Terry (*Colonel*), Dana Ashbrook (*Tom Essex*), Sally Smythe (*Billy's Mom*), Allan Trautman (*Tarman*), Don Maxwell (*Billy's Dad*), Reynold Cindrich (*Soldier*), Philip Bruns (*Doc Mandel*), Mitch Pileggi (*Sarge*), Arturo Bonilla (*Les*), Terrence Riggings (*Frank*), James McIntire (*Officer*), Larry Nicholas (*Jesse's Double*), Forrest J. Ackerman, Douglas Benson, David Eby, Nicholas Hernandez, Annie Marshall, Richard Moore, Steve Neuvenheim, Brian Peck, Derek Loughran (*Special Zombies*).

Burdened with one of the most unwieldy sequel titles in recent memory (why not simply "Return of the Return of the Living Dead"?), this movie is not so much a continuation of the surprise horror hit of 1985 as it is a remake. Considering that the original movie ended with the nuclear annihilation of the entire cast, one would imagine that it would be a bit difficult to continue that particular plot line. Maintaining the goofy black humor that made the first film tolerable, the sequel begins as a military

© LORIMAR

transport loaded with those nasty canisters containing rotting corpses steeped in experimental nerve gas that reanimates the dead hits a bump, causing a single canister to fall from the truck. The canister rolls down an embankment and into a creek, on which it floats to a Spielbergian subdivision. The canister is then discovered by a trio of boys. One of the kids, Kenworthy, is a bit apprehensive about the contents and goes home, leaving the other two—both local bullies—to open it. When the seal is broken a strange green gas is emitted. Meanwhile, in a nearby cemetery, two hapless grave robbers (Karen and Mathews, the only original cast members to return) are raiding a crypt for valuable human skulls. The mist from the canister seeps into the cemetery, contaminating the humans who breathe it and reanimating the buried corpses. In a comic dead-rising-from-their-graves sequence, dozens of corpses interred during a variety of historical periods come stumbling out of their coffins with a sudden craving for brains (a zombie resurrection that is most reminiscent of Alan Ormsby's 1972 cult item CHILDREN SHOULDN'T PLAY WITH DEAD THINGS). From here the film becomes an extended chase wherein Kenworthy, his older sister Dietlein, intrepid young cable installer Ashbrook, and Mathews' obnoxious girl friend Snyder try to escape the horde of marauding zombies, with the ailing Karen and Mathews in tow. They happen upon befuddled local doctor Bruns and whisk him to the hospital, where he examines the grave robbers. Much to his surprise, he finds no heartbeat, brain-waves, or other signs of life—despite the fact that they can still move and talk. Eventually, his patients, too, become brain-hungry zombies. The remaining humans try to leave town, but discover that the military has earlier evacuated the other citizens and blocked all roads leading out. Meanwhile, the zombified Mathews eats his girl friend's brains, Karen feasts on a unfortunate soldier, and young Kenworthy's nemesis—the local bully—is now a zombie and out looking for him. Ultimately, the humans decide to electrocute the bothersome flesh-eaters, luring them to a nearby power station by leaving a trail of cattle brains. Once the zombies have been rounded up, the heroes set up live wires around the muddy premises and turn on the juice, frying the living dead en masse.

Fans of this sort of thing will appreciate the special gore effects, which are superior to the ones employed in RETURN OF THE LIVING DEAD. Perhaps the highlight of the sequel is a sequence that takes place in the hallway of the hospital in which a zombie has its legs separated from its torso. Played for laughs, but also quite frightening and technically impressive, the sequence features the zombie's legs continuing to walk around—bumping into walls and changing direction like a wind-up toy—while the upper half of the creature walks on his hands, attempting to retrieve his legs. These and other striking special effects were done by Kenny Myers, an effects technician who had replaced effects coordinator Bill Munns late in the shooting of the first RETURN film. One effect, a decapitated zombie head that is still able to talk, so delighted the producers that they insisted it be used as a running character throughout the movie. The head, apparently that of a southern woman, continues to turn up in a variety of unlikely places making sassy wisecracks. The humor here, as in the first film, is strictly sophomoric and mostly slapstick. Director Wiederhorn is a competent, if unremarkable, talent and he handles the action scenes in a professional manner. His writing talent, however, is not equal to that of the first film's writer-director, Dan O'Bannon. Missing from the sequel is the snappy, biting dialog and O'Bannon's satiric slant, which lampooned everything from the military to punk rockers. Wiederhorn, on the other hand, gives us lines like "No, duh." Although not nearly as successful financially as the first film, RETURN OF THE LIVING DEAD PART II made enough to turn a profit and will no doubt spawn yet another sequel. (*Graphic violence, gore effects, profanity.*)

p, Tom Fox; d, Ken Wiederhorn; w, Ken Wiederhorn; ph, Robert Elswit (Foto-Kem Color); ed, Charles Bornstein; m, J. Peter Robinson; md, David Chackler; m/l, Joe Lamont, Brian Cadd, Julian Cope, Geoffrey Gayer, Carey Howe, Michael Olivieri, Dean Roberts, Paul Carmen, John Moon Martin, Robert Palmer, Mantronik, M.C. Tee, Joseph Belladonna, Dan Spitz, Scott Ian, Frank Bello, Charles Benante, John Rooney, Zodiac Mindwarp, The Love Reaction, Bobby Pickett, Leonard Capizzi, art d, Dale Allan Pelton; set d, Suzette Sheets; spec eff, Terry Frazee, Geno Crum, Gene Grigg; stunts, Gary Davis; makeup, Kenny Myers, Del Armstrong.

Comedy/Horror   **Cas.**   **(PR:O MPAA:R)**

RETURN TO SALEM'S LOT, A**½   (1988) 95m Larco/WB c

Michael Moriarty (*Joe Weber*), Ricky Addison Reed (*Jeremy*), Samuel Fuller (*Van Meer*), Andrew Duggan (*Judge Axel*), Evelyn Keyes (*Mrs. Axel*), Jill Gatsby (*Sherry*), June Havoc (*Aunt Clara*), Ronee Blakley (*Sally*), James Dixon (*Rains*), David Holbrook (*Deputy*), Katja Crosby (*Cathy*), Tara Reid (*Amanda*), Brad Rijn (*Clarence*), Georgia Janelle Webb (*Sarah*), Robert Burr (*Dr. Fenton*), Jacqueline Britton (*Mrs. Fenton*), Gordon Ramsey (*Allen*), David Ardao (*Car Salesman*), Kathleen Kichta (*Vampire Woman*), Edward Shils, Richard Duggan (*Farmer Vampires*), Stewart G. Day (*Jeremiah*), Lynda A. Clark, Ron Milkie (*Townspeople*), Nancy Duggan (*Farm Girl*), Ted Noose, Jim Gillis (*Hobos*), Rick Garcia (*Cameraman*), Bobby Ramsen (*Jungle Guide*), Peter Hock (*Farmer Drone*).

Another one of those bizarre, personal, and very quirky genre films from the fevered brain of low-budget *auteur* Larry Cohen—this one produced directly for home video. A sequel in name only to the made-for-TV movie based on Stephen King's novel *Salem's Lot* (although King is credited as creative consultant), Cohen's film stars Moriarty as an ambitious anthropologist who travels to Salem's Lot, Maine, with his estranged teenage son, Reed, to renovate a house left to him by his aunt. To their surprise, the small New England town is populated by vampires who breed semi-humans they call "drones" to protect them during the day. Led by the grandfatherly Duggan (a Cohen favorite who died in May of 1988; see Obits), the vampire community is 300 years old, having crossed the Atlantic at the same time as the *Mayflower*. Ostracized by normal settlers, the vampires landed in New England and created their own community. Having grown rich from real estate values alone, they have become wealthy old Republicans, the literal embodiment of "old money" in America. Although they drink human blood from time to time, they have primarily turned to cattle blood for sustenance because, as Duggan explains, human blood has become unsafe what with alcohol, drugs, hepatitis, and "that AIDS virus." Because he is a famed anthropologist, the vampires want Moriarty to write their history—to dispel the myths about their race and set the facts down once and for all. Intrigued, Moriarty agrees, but he begins to have second thoughts when he realizes that his son is slowly being seduced into the vampire lifestyle. Parental responsibility soon overwhelms greed, and Moriarty decides to abandon the project and leave town with his son. Unfortunately, the drones will not allow them to do so. Luckily, a tough old stranger (Fuller) wanders into town. As it turns out, Fuller is a Nazi hunter looking for an escaped Gestapo officer. Good with a gun and unafraid, Fuller decides to help Moriarty get rid of the vampires. During the day the pair goes from Victorian house to Victorian house finding coffins and driving stakes through sleeping vampires. Because there are too many vampires to kill in just one day, Fuller and Moriarty creep around that evening and set all the empty coffins on fire. Eventually, there is a nighttime showdown between the vampire killers and an extremely angry Duggan—who shows his true face, that of an ugly monster. Just when it looks like Moriarty is doomed, young Reed grabs an American flag and stabs Duggan through the heart. With Fuller at the wheel of a bus, Moriarty and Reed leave Salem's Lot forever. "I wonder if one hundred years from now anybody would believe that there were vampires?," Moriarty muses. To which Fuller gruffly responds, "One hundred years from now people won't even believe there were Nazis!"

A RETURN TO SALEM'S LOT is not your typical vampire movie. Presenting very little in the way of traditional chills, Cohen takes a somewhat satiric poke at the genre. Although much is played for laughs, Cohen never condescends and it is apparent that he respects that with which he is having fun. Character is everything in Cohen's films and once again he does not disappoint. Michael Moriarty contributes yet another extremely eccentric performance (he has appeared in Cohen's Q; THE STUFF; IT'S ALIVE III: ISLAND OF THE ALIVE) as the brutally honest anthropologist who is struggling to become a decent father to the son he has ignored for 13 years. Richard Addison Reed is excellent as the smart-mouthed son who covers his loneliness with a mask of tough bravado. The complicated relationship between Moriarty and Reed is well played, funny, and telling—and is also one of the most refreshing father-son relationships seen on the screen in some time. But the movie is stolen by a pair of older performers: namely Andrew Duggan, in one of his last roles, and director Samuel Fuller as the crotchety vampire hunter. As the leader of the vampires, Duggan combines a folksy, Judge Hardy-type persona with a subtle sense of menace that hints at the "true face" that lies underneath his amiable facade. Given Cohen's left-wing political proclivities, one cannot help but see Ronald Reagan in Duggan's performance.

Better yet is Fuller, the director of such grungy classics as THE STEEL HELMET (1950); PICKUP ON SOUTH STREET (1953); RUN OF THE ARROW (1957); and THE BIG RED ONE (1979), and a personal friend of Cohen's. Having appeared as an actor in films as diverse as Jean Luc Godard's PIERROT LE FOU (1965), Dennis Hopper's infamous THE LAST MOVIE (1971), and Wim Wenders' THE AMERICAN FRIEND (1977), Fuller gets his biggest role yet as Cohen's cigar-chomping Van Meer. Grumbling and running around Salem's Lot like a man half his age (which is 77), Fuller is wonderfully funny and dominates the last half of the film. A cigar is in his mouth in every scene, except when he is asleep, and even then it is pinched between his fingers, ready to be popped into his mouth at any moment. According to Cohen, the cigar, as well as Fuller's inability to remember his lines, created headaches in the continuity department, and his scenes had to be methodically reconstructed in the editing room so that the cigar didn't appear to be leaping from his hand to his mouth, or from side to side in his mouth, between shots.

Thematically Cohen continues his use of the fantasy genres to explore modern-day political and social ills, and visually the film is an eclectic collection of clever set-ups designed for maximum impact on a low-budget, five-week shoot. Those expecting a reverent sequel to the Stephen King tale will no doubt be disappointed. However, those with a taste for the offbeat and unusual should make a point of viewing this latest entry from the strange and fertile mind of Larry Cohen. (*Violence, gore effects, nudity, sexual situations, profanity.*)

p, Paul Kurta; d, Larry Cohen; w, Larry Cohen, James Dixon; ph, Daniel Pearl; ed, Armond Leibowitz; m, Michael Minard; art d, Richard Frisch; spec eff, Steve

Neill; cos, Catherine Zuber; stunts, Jery Hewitt, Danny Aiello III; makeup, Gigi Williams.

Horror	Cas.	(PR:O MPAA:R)

RETURN TO SNOWY RIVER: PART II***   (1988, Aus.) 100m Burrowes Film Group-Hoyts-Silver Screen Parteners III/BV c

Tom Burlinson (*Jim Craig*), Sigrid Thornton (*Jessica Harrison*), Brian Dennehy (*Harrison*), Nicholas Eadie (*Alistair Patton*), Mark Hembrow (*Seb*), Bryan Marshall (*Hawker*), Rhys McConnochie (*Patton, Sr.*), Peter Cummins (*Jake*), Cornelia Frances (*Mrs. Darcy*), Tony Barry (*Jacko*), Wynn Roberts (*Priest*), Alec Wilson (*Patton's Crony*), Peter Browne (*Reilly*), Alan Hopgood (*Simmons*), Mark Pennell (*Collins*), Charlie Lovick (*Charlie*), Wayne Lovick (*Jack's Son*), Greg Stroud (*Jockey*), Nick Waters (*Announcer at Harrison's*), Cae Rees (*Barmaid*), John Raaen (*Lout in Bar*), Bruce Clarkson (*Bystander at Harrison's*), Peter Tulloch (*Bystander outside Church*), Christopher Stevenson (*Harrison's Waiter*), Geoff Beamish (*Frank*), Gerald Egan (*Jamie McKay*), Charlie Lovick, Ken Connley, Clive Hodges, Jim Campbell, John Harper, Noel Elliott, Greg Purcell, Dick Forrest, Kevin Nicholson, Max Scanlon, Wayne Anderson, Barry Stephen, Wayne Pinder, Gary Neil, Julien Welsh, John Bird, Derek Scott, Graeme Stoney, Rusty Connley, Kevin Higgins, Graeme Fry, Lloyd Parks, Tony Lovick, Robert Purcell, John Coombs, Paul Purcell, Bruce McCormack, Basil Egan, Robert Gough, Curly McCormack, Graig Edwards, Dennis Vickery, Tony Larkins, Steve Harrison (*Crack Riders*), John Lovick, Col Reynolds, Brendan Purcell, John Klingsporn, Mark Arbuthnot, Graydon Marks, Chris Stoney, Peter Purcell, Max Jeffries, Martin Myors (*Patton's Roughriders*), Peter McElroy, Brendan Egan, John Johnston, Steve Arbuthnot (*Patton's Friends*).

© BUENA VISTA

Five years after their characters were introduced in THE MAN FROM SNOWY RIVER, Tom Burlinson and Sigrid Thornton complete this romance about horse-lovers. The time is the 1880s and the setting is dusty horse country, but this is not the usual Western film because it takes place in the high country of Australia. Burlinson is returning to his beloved rustic cabin in the mountains after travelling thousands of miles rounding up a herd of wild horses. He plans to tame and sell the animals to provide him with the stake he needs to continue his courtship of the beautiful tom-boy daughter (Thornton) of flatlands rancher, Brian Dennehy. However, during the boy's long absence the cattle breeder has come up with a breeding program for his daughter. To assure approval of the application he's made for a loan to keep his place growing, Dennehy has tried to get his daughter to accept the attentions of the banker's son (Eadie.) But with her true love back in town the willful girl will have nothing more to do with the sullen kid born with a silver spoon in his mouth. After a nasty confrontation with her father she runs off to live with her mountain boy in his aerie in the hills. The rejected suitor quickly strikes back, stealing the couple's herd of horses and starting a drive to the district border with them. Coming to Burlinson's aid at just the right moment is a wild old stallion, notorious in the region for leading a pack of rampaging horses. The black beauty allows himself to be tamed in minutes and ridden in hell-bent pursuit of the rustlers. With the horses recovered, father and daughter reconciled, and the mountain people's sudden and unexplainable acceptance of the rich girl, the lovers are now free to return to their hilltop home to run their horse business together.

The plot is a simplistic love triangle, with some tired old story cliches thrown in; such as a father with a mysteriously absent wife who suddenly stings his daughter with the taunt, "You're just like your mother," and then later only has to say "I'm sorry" to mend the deep wound. But Dennehy can bring to life sparse and unconvincing dialog with a well-aimed glance, and the golden-skinned Burlinson, and winsome Thornton win over the most cynical in the audience. Repeated helicopter pull-away shots of mountain grandeur make experiencing the film seem like a vacation in the wilderness. And never have horses been so lovingly captured on film; this will surely become a cult film for all horse lovers. The credits show almost a hundred riders, wranglers, and handlers were involved in the filming, and the exciting scenes of thundering hooves across the mountains make full use of the talent. The story stands alone, but it's helpful to have seen the precursor for background information it provides, confusing though it may be at first to adjust to Brian Dennehy playing the role originated by Kirk Douglas in THE MAN FROM SNOWY RIVER. Comparison of the two films is inevitable, for they have strong elements in common. Either one is as good a travelog for the Australian countryside as "CROCODILE" DUNDEE. The first had a more complex story to hold attention. But when producer Geoff Burrowes assumed directing chores for the sequel, he was able to compensate for slim story values by outdoing even the original film in dramatic use of scenic splendor, quivering horse flesh, and winning performances.

p, Geoff Burrowes; d, Geoff Burrowes; w, John Dixon, Geoff Burrowes; ph, Keith Wagstaff (Panavision, Eastmancolor); ed, Gary Woodyard; m, Bruce Rowland; prod d, Leslie Binns; art d, Robert Leo; set d, Viv Wilson, Rick Bell; spec eff, Brian Pearce; cos, Jenny Arnott; stunts, Chris Anderson; makeup, Di Biggs.

Adventure/Romance/Western	Cas.	(PR:A MPAA:PG)

RICKY 1 †   (1988) 90m Tapeworm c

Michael Michaud (*Ricky Wanero*), Maggie Hughes (*Angela*), James Herbert, Lane Montano, Peter Zellers, Jon Chaney, Brent Beckett.

This low-budget spoof takes a comic look at a Rocky-ish boxer who gives up the game for his girl friend, but still hopes to get a chance to fight the champion, known as the Silver Shadow. While training for the big fight, the hero pays his dues working in a fish market, a far cry from the meat market that employed Sylvester Stallone's Rocky. Filmed in 1983, RICKY 1 never saw a theatrical release and ended up on video this year.

p, Bill Naud; d, Bill Naud; w, Bill Naud; ph, David Golia; ed, Bill Naud; m, Joel Goldsmith.

Comedy	Cas.	(PR:NR MPAA:NR)

RIDERS OF THE STORM**   (1988, Brit.) 92m Miramax c

Dennis Hopper (*Captain*), Michael J. Pollard (*Doc*), Eugene Lipinski (*Ace*), James Aubrey (*Claude*), Al Matthews (*Ben*), William Armstrong (*Jerry*), Nigel Pegram (*Sen. Willa Westinghouse*), Michael Ho (*Minh*), Derek Hosby (*Sam*), Mark Caven (*Don*), Craig Pinder (*Irving*), Jeff Harding (*Doug*), Linda Lou Allen (*Mary*), Norman Chancer (*Dr. King*), Gwen Humble (*Linda*), Manning Redwood (*Martinez*), Bill Bailey (*Gen. Motors*), Bruce Boa (*Col. Parker*), John Alderson (*Col. Sanders*), Jim Carter (*Castro*), Julian Littman (*Raoul*), Catherine Chevalier (*Rosita*), Ted Maynard (*Leonardo*), Don Fellows (*Capt. War Hero*), Beryll Nesbitt (*Mrs. War Hero*), Lou Hirsch, Sam Douglas, Tony Sibbald, Anthony Porrest (*Vets*), George Harris, Michael Feast (*Vet Cameramen*), Tara Ward (*Donna*), Bill Hutchinson (*Baker Gaspard*), Barbara Rosenblat (*Betsy Blanket*), William Roberts (*Calley*), Ian Tyler (*Carson*), Josie Lawrence (*Guerillette*), Tony Spiradakis (*Vet Announcer*), Britt Walker (*Panther*), Michael Fitzpatrick (*Ecorilla*), Colin Bruce (*X'an*), Michael John Paliotti (*Zavaroni*), Danny Brainin (*Radar Operator*), Chuck Julian (*TV Presenter*), Keith Edwards (*WTV Director*), Gay Baynes (*WTV Vision Mixer*), R.J. Bell (*Big Drummer*), Francis Drake (*Farmer*), Jennifer Sternberg (*Farmer's Wife*), Johnny Myers (*Scientist*), Suzie Savoy (*Brunette*), Scott Prescott, Scott Riley, Tony Cisneros (*Urban Animals*), Pete Sayers and His Band (*Tony Manyana & His Tomcats*), Ozzy Osbourne, Dave Cash.

A throwback to some of the more bizarre political satires of the 1960s, RIDERS OF THE STORM is a chaotic affair lampooning the right-wing American values of the 1980s. The feature film debut of British rock video director Maurice Phillips, RIDERS follows the wild exploits of a group of wacked-out Vietnam veterans, led by Hopper, who, for the last 15 years, have been flying across the US in a B-29 jamming network airwaves with pirate telecasts of their station, S&M TV. Pledged to prevent the government from conning the public into another Vietnam, Hopper and crew monitor the mainstream media for lies and then periodically invade the airways to tell the people the truth. Their latest crusade is against Mrs. Willa Westinghouse, a conservative candidate running for president who advocates rabid anti-communism, a strong military, and a host of other Reagan/Thatcher-type platforms. The candidate is shown to be a cynical and shrewd politician, willing to suddenly become a born-

again Christian just to garner more votes. Hopper, with the help of his electronics engineer, Pollard, and the rest of his loyal crew, launch an attack against the politician in an effort to reveal her true militaristic goals. Courting the military brass, the candidate promises generous defense budgets if they will "accidentally" shoot down Hopper's plane. The video pirates get wind of the plan and are able to defend themselves, but the candidate is not about to give up. Using the greedy resources of evangelical television, the candidate begins pandering to the Christian masses in an effort to clinch the election. Hopper counterattacks by getting the goods on the candidate when he is able to confirm a rumor that *she* is really a *he*. Dispatching his guerilla cameramen, Hopper obtains footage of the male candidate donning his female disguise. Before he can get the footage on the air, however, one of Hopper's crew flips out and drops an unarmed bomb on the country music fair at which the candidate is appearing. Before a huge audience of horrified onlookers—not to mention the folks at home watching on television—the candidate's clothes are torn off during the crash of the bomb and her true identity is revealed. His job done, Hopper decides to dismantle his S&M network and take a stab at running for president himself.

Trying too hard to tap into the same absurdist intensity that fueled DR. STRANGELOVE and CATCH 22, RIDERS OF THE STORM is a curious collection of hip images, video art, improvisation, surrealism, and sophomoric comedy. While enough of it works to maintain interest, none of it really gels. Director Phillips simply throws everything he can think of at the viewer in the hopes that some of it may stick. His targets are the standard right-wing fare that has entrenched itself in American society during the 1980s, but Phillips and screenwriter Scott Roberts are unable to say anything new or fresh about them. Conservative Christians and politicians are seen as conniving evildoers who easily manipulate the moronic military while zombielike farmers and suburbanites stare at the television and dutifully write out checks to any hustler who asks for money. The limited cleverness extends to the character names, with a network news anchor called "Betsy Blanket" and military men named General Motors, Colonel Parker (Elvis' agent), and Colonel Sanders. This narrow, stereotyped representation may work in a three-minute "Saturday Night Live" sketch, but stretched out to feature length it becomes childish and off-putting. What *is* refreshing about the film is its wholehearted 1960s sensibility. The film plays like a crazy underground comic book from the hippie era, and there is an earnestness to the whole thing that is endearing. Phillips resurrects the establishment-as-enemy attitude and seems to really want his viewers to think about the possibility that government propaganda comes across the airwaves as news. Also interesting is the endorsement of alternative forms of broadcast communication, an idealistic vision that has its roots in the 60s and has begun to become a reality in the 80s—what with affordable, sophisticated electronic equipment allowing amateur operators to jam network and cable airwaves. Hopper's broadcasts are a hip, eye-catching mix of news footage, old movies, rock concerts, and left-wing propaganda, usually hosted by himself in a variety of outlandish outfits. The nonstop rock'n'roll soundtrack boasts classic tunes like "Layla," "Purple Haze," and "Won't Get Fooled Again." Filmed several years ago, Dennis Hopper's performance is uneven and seems improvised. The rest of the cast is merely bland, with the exception of Brit Nigel Pegram, who plays the drag-queen presidential candidate as a combination of Ronald Reagan, Margaret Thatcher, and Jeanne Kirkpatrick. The film, which was originally titled THE AMERICAN WAY until the distributors removed the more biting title in favor of the perplexing RIDERS OF THE STORM, was awarded the "Best Science Fiction Film of the Year" prize at the Avoriaz Film Festival. (*Excessive profanity, sexual situations, substance abuse*).

p, Laurie Keller, Paul Cowan; d, Maurice Phillips; w, Scott Roberts; ph, John Metcalfe; ed, Tony Lawson; m, Brian Bennett; prod d, Evan Hercules.

Comedy/Science Fiction	Cas.	(PR:O MPAA:R)

RIKKY AND PETE½   (1988, Aus.) 101m Cascade/MGM-UA c

Stephen Kearney (*Pete*), Nina Landis (*Rikky*), Tetchie Agbayani (*Flossie*), Bill Hunter (*Whitstead*), Bruno Lawrence (*Sonny*), Bruce Spence (*Ben*), Dorothy Alison (*Mrs. Menzies*), Don Reid (*Mr. Menzies*), Lewis Fitz-gerald (*Adam*), Peter Cummins (*Delahunty*), Peter Hehir (*Police Officer*), Ralph Cotterill (*George*).

Rikky (Landis) and Pete (Kearney) are the children of a wealthy Melbourne couple. Their father is cold and distant; their mother is confined to a wheelchair after having been hit by a police car driven by Sgt. Whitstead (Hunter). Because of the accident, Kearney hates police officers in general and Hunter in particular, and spends a lot of time plotting revenge against the cop. An amateur inventor, Kearney is always tinkering with machines, including a vehicle he uses on his paper route that folds newspapers into giant paper airplanes and then attempts to sail them onto customers' porches, and a "work of art" called the "eggs terminator," by which eggs are crushed by hammer. When Kearney unveils his work at a local gallery, it performs well enough to splatter gallery patrons with eggs, much to the artist's delight. His sister is more serious minded. She has a job as a geologist, and also spends her evenings singing in nightclubs. She's concerned about her brother, though, and fears that his arguments with their father and ongoing battles with Hunter and other members of the police department will lead to grave trouble. When Dad decides to quit giving money to his children, and the police are near arresting Kearney for his numerous pranks, Landis takes a job with a mining company in the Outback and persuades Kearney to join her on the journey to her new job. The siblings take their mother's Bentley and head across the vast Australian expanses to the mining town of Mount Lena. Once there, Kearney gets a job in the mine, but it isn't long before he is once again playing the inventor. Feeling that the traditional mining methods are outdated, he builds a machine that "does the work of three." Landis then finds a place where ore is more accessible than at the old mine, and she and her brother go into business for themselves. Romance also enters the picture as Kearney falls for Agbayani, a beauty from the South Seas, while Landis eyes a miner played by Bruno Lawrence (SMASH PALACE). At the film's end, Landis and Kearney have sold the mine for a small fortune and seem all set for a life of happiness.

RIKKY AND PETE tries to be a charming film about nonconformists beating the system, but doesn't quite pull it off. Leads Nina Landis and Stephen Kearney are engaging enough, but they're let down by a thoroughly predictable script in which the quirkiness of the characters, particularly Kearney with his madcap inventions, is simply too calculated to be enjoyable. Further, the film lacks continuity; subplots are picked up and dropped randomly throughout the film. Husband-and-wife filmmaking team David Parker and Nadia Tass chose this project as a follow-up to their mildly successful MALCOLM (1986). In picking this film up for release in the US, MGM/UA was no doubt betting that the success of CROCODILE DUNDEE and the growing interest in Australia would mean solid box office for RIKKY AND PETE. They were wrong: the film disappeared from theaters after a brief release and quickly ended up on the video shelves. (Profanity, nudity.)

p, Nadia Tass, David Parker; d, Nadia Tass; w, David Parker (based on a story by Parker); ph, David Parker (Eastmancolor); ed, Ken Sallows; m, Phil Judd, Eddie Raynor; prod d, Josephine Ford; art d, Graeme Duesbury; spec eff, Visual Effects; cos, Phil Eagles; stunts, Glenn Ruehland; makeup, Rosalina Da Silva.

Comedy/Drama	Cas.	(PR:O MPAA:R)

ROCKET GIBRALTAR †   (1988) 100m Ulick Mayo Weiss/COL c

Burt Lancaster (*Levi Rockwell*), Suzy Amis (*Aggie Rockwell*), Patricia Clarkson (*Rose Black*), Frances Conroy (*Ruby Hanson*), Sinead Cusack (*Amanda "Billi" Rockwell*), John Glover (*Rolo Rockwell*), Bill Pullman (*Crow Black*), Kevin Spacey (*Dwayne Hanson*), John Bell (*Orson Rockwell*), Nicky Bronson (*Max Hanson*), Dan Corkill (*Kane Rockwell*), Macaulay Culkin (*Cy Blue Black*), Angela Goethals (*Dawn Black*), Sara Goethals (*Flora Rockwell*), Emily Poe (*Emily Rockwell*), Sara Rue (*Jessica Hanson*), George Martin (*Dr. Bonacker*).

A much-awaited Hollywood release, ROCKET GIBRALTAR stars Lancaster as a 77-year-old patriarch whose children and grandchildren come to visit him on his birthday at his coastal Long Island estate. A once-blacklisted writer, Lancaster spends his days thinking back on his youth and the events of his life. Arriving for the visit is his single daughter (Amis), a promiscuous young woman who sleeps with whomever she finds; his Hollywood filmmaker son (Glover), who is never seen without his portable phone; his eldest daughter and her washed-up major league pitcher husband (Clarkson and Pullman); another daughter and her unfunny comedian husband (Conroy and Spacey); and a collection of small-fries. Lancaster captures the children's attention when he tells them of an ancient Viking belief that immortality is achieved by setting a seafaring ship afire. Later, the children overhear a doctor telling Lancaster that he is terminally ill. Hoping that their grandfather might live forever, the children ready his old boat—the Rocket Gibraltar—for a Viking journey. When the old man finally dies, the children, apparently taking the Viking myth too literally, drag his corpse towards the shoreline. A hold-over at Columbia Pictures from the days of David Puttnam's reign, ROCKET GIBRALTAR received only a token theatrical release, which, judging from the negative reviews it received, was probably a good thing. The film was written by the urban-minded Amos Poe, the former New York underground director who made a name for himself by making Super8 and 16mm shorts before graduating to such feature films as SUBWAY RIDERS and ALPHABET CITY, for whom ROCKET GIBRALTAR seemed an odd directorial turn. Columbia apparently agreed, and, two weeks into the production, put craftsman Daniel Petrie in the driver's seat.

p, Jeff Weiss, Marcus Viscidi; d, Daniel Petrie; w, Amos Poe; ph, Jost Vacano (Duart color); ed, Melody London; m, Andrew Powell; prod d, Bill Groom; set d, Betsy Klompus; cos, Nord Haggerty.

Drama	Cas.	(PR:NR MPAA:PG)

ROLLING VENGEANCE †   (1988) 90m Apollo/Apollo c

Don Michael Paul (*Joey Rosso*), Lawrence Dane (*Big Joe*), Ned Beatty (*Tiny Doyle*), Susan Hogan (*Big Joe's Wife*), Lisa Howard (*Misty*), Barclay Hope (*Steve*), Todd Duckworth (*Vic Doyle*), Michael J. Reynolds (*Lt. Sly*), Michael Kirby, Michael Dyson, Hugo Dann, Lawrence King Phillips.

Receiving a brief theatrical release in 1987, this low-budget action entry found its way onto video shelves in early 1988. This film, as the ads say, is "the ultimate monster truck" movie, though fans of Steven Spielberg's television film DUEL may want to counter. When the tough young hero's family is killed and girl friend raped, he builds a humungous 8-ton killing machine that destroys any and every thing in its path. Its destination is a strip joint owned by the villainous Beatty and his nasty redneck family. If you've seen any of those monster truck competitions on cable TV, you know what to expect in ROLLING VENGEANCE.

p, Steven H. Stern; d, Steven H. Stern; w, Michael Montgomery; ph, Laszlo George; ed, Ron Wisman; m, Phil Marshall; art d, Harold Thrasher.

Action	Cas.	(PR:NR MPAA:R)

R.O.T.O.R. zero   (1988) 90m Imperial c

Richard Gesswein, Margaret Trigg, Jayne Smith, James Cole, Clark Moore, Carroll Brandon Baker.

A cheapjack knockoff of THE TERMINATOR (which it even mentions) and

ROBOCOP, R.O.T.O.R. (the acronym stands for Robot Officer Tactical Operation Research, if anyone cares) is a sophisticated robot being developed by Gesswein for the Dallas police. Conceived as the ultimate law enforcement machine and intended for use decades in the future on streets beyond redemption, R.O.T.O.R. is being pushed into service too soon because of political pressures. Gesswein is fired when he protests this move, and his doltish assistant is put in charge. When a janitor's switchblade comb somehow activates the robot, it makes itself a (male) face and hits the street looking for criminals on whom to exercise his prime directive: "Judge and Execute." Trigg and her fiance drive by and R.O.T.O.R. determines that they are speeding. Pulling them over, he shoots the man, and Trigg drives away with the android in hot pursuit. Gesswein, who is quickly called back to duty, manages to contact Trigg long enough to tell her to keep moving, setting a rendezvous for the next morning. He also calls a scientist colleague (Smith), who's also a female bodybuilder and an even more impressive specimen than Gesswein—not exactly small-boned himself. Together they track down R.O.T.O.R., who by this time has trashed a truck stop and left a wake of dead bodies in his pursuit of Trigg. Smith is electrocuted when she goes at the rogue robot *mano a mano*, leaving Gesswein to blow his creation up with some primer cord he has with him. Back at the office, he threatens to expose his boss's negligence in rushing the project, whereupon his superior shotguns him in the parking lot.

Thoroughly derivative and thoroughly boring, R.O.T.O.R. is easily one of the lamest pictures of the year. The performances by Richard Gesswein and Jayne Smith bring new meaning to the term "wooden," though Margaret Trigg (whose character never seems to figure out that honking her horn incapacitates the robot) is somewhat better. Perhaps the most jarring thing here, though, are the odd moments of tossed-in philosophy, reaching some kind of berserk peak as the rugged Gesswein and the massive Smith begin quoting *Paradise Lost*. If you were stranded on a desert island with a VCR, a TV, and this tape, it would be hard to stop yourself from swimming just to get away.

p, Cullen Blaine, Budd Lewis, Richard Gesswein; d, Cullen Blaine; w, Budd Lewis; ph, Glenn Roland; ed, Douglas Bryan; m, David Adam Newman.

Horror	Cas.	(PR:O MPAA:NR)

RUNNING ON EMPTY***   (1988) 116m Lorimar-Double Play/WB c

Christine Lahti (*Annie Pope*), River Phoenix (*Danny Pope*), Judd Hirsch (*Arthur Pope*), Martha Plimpton (*Lorna Phillips*), Jonas Arby (*Harry Pope*), Ed Crowley (*Mr. Phillips*), L.M. Kit Carson (*Gus Winant*), Steven Hill (*Mr. Patterson*), Augusta Dabney (*Mrs. Patterson*), David Margulies (*Dr. Jonah Reiff*), Lynne Thigpen (*Contact at Eldridge St.*), Marcia Jean Kurtz (*School Clerk*), Sloane Shelton (*Mrs. Phillips*), Justine Johnston (*Librarian*), Herb Lovelle (*Hospital Clerk*), Bobo Lewis (*Home Ec Teacher*), Ronnie Gilbert (*Mrs. Taylor*), Leila Danette (*Maid*), Michael Boatman (*Spaulding*), Jenny Lumet (*Music Girl*), William Foeller (*Man at Meeting*), Carol Cavallo (*Woman at Meeting*), Alice Drummond (*Mrs. Powell*), Joey Thrower (*Catcher*), Donna Hanover (*Reporter*), Thomas Fraioli (*Violinist*), Burke Pearson (*Julliard Man*), Elzbieta Czyzewska (*Julliard Woman*), Angela Pietropinto (*English Teacher*), Daniel Dassin (*Waiter*).

© WARNER BROS.

Sidney Lumet, one of America's most consistently political filmmakers, fuses the personal with the political in this film that is part teenage romance, part family drama, and nearly always compelling. In 1971, antiwar activists Hirsch and Lahti planted explosives in a Massachusetts university lab that was being used for the manufacture of napalm. What they didn't know was that a janitor was still in the building, and their blast blinded and paralyzed him, putting Hirsch and Lahti on the FBI's Ten Most Wanted list. Fifteen years later, Hirsch and Lahti are still on the run, and as the film opens Phoenix, their 17-year-old son, is returning home from baseball practice when he notices the telltale signs of the encroaching FBI. Even before his parents return from a Greenpeace meeting, Phoenix begins the familiar, well-planned escape procedures that protect his parents and his 10-year-old brother (Abry) from capture. Leaving this small Florida town behind, the family travels north to New Jersey, where, after cutting and dying their hair, they establish new identities. For 15 years, the process has been the same: find a middling-sized town; adopt new names and pasts; take innocuous jobs (preferably ones that pay in cash); enroll the kids in school, claiming that their records have been lost; but, above all else, remain a family. This time something different is happening. Phoenix is ready to graduate from high school, and Crowley, a music teacher, upon discovering that the boy is an extremely gifted piano player, encourages him to apply to Juilliard, frustrating and confusing Phoenix, who knows he can never produce the transcripts necessary for admission. What's more, Phoenix and Plimpton, Crowley's rebellious, smart-alec daughter, become each other's first real love. Without warning, Carson, another radical gone underground, who now sees violence as the only alternative, appears and tries unsuccessfully to recruit Lahti (his one-time lover) and Hirsch for a bank robbery. Meanwhile, Phoenix performs a stellar audition for the Juilliard examiners, and Crowley tries to persuade Lahti to allow him to attend the school, emphasizing the importance of getting hold of his transcript. Hirsch is dead set against Phoenix's matriculation, knowing that he will never be able to see his son again if the boy leaves the underground. Lahti, torn between losing her son and wanting him to live his own life, arranges a meeting with her industrialist father (Hill), whom she hasn't seen in 15 years. In the film's most emotional scene, she pleads with Hill to take in Phoenix so that he can attend Juilliard, and Hill explains to his daughter how painful it has been to be separated from her for so long, knowing that she has squandered her life. Eventually, Phoenix reveals the family's secret to Plimpton, who is dazzled by her boy friend's "cool" parents at Lahti's birthday party, the high point of which is some joyous dancing to James Taylor's seemingly undanceable but deeply nostalgic "Fire and Rain." Before long the hour of decision is at hand, and with the FBI breathing down their necks, Hirsch instructs his son to stay behind, to go to Juilliard, to "go out and make a difference."

Neither a BIG CHILL-style attempt to revel in 1960s nostalgia nor an effort to make a definitive statement about the impact or fate of the flower generation, RUNNING ON EMPTY is a melodrama about an age-old dilemma: the difficulties that arise when the time comes for children to leave the nest. The film is, however, informed from start to finish by the 60s values Lahti and Hirsch have passed on to their sons. Ironically, in attempting to hold together what is in fact a traditional family unit—albeit with an alternative sociopolitical worldview—Lahti and Hirsch have, for appearances' sake, adopted the very staid, middle-class lifestyle they so adamantly rejected in their youth. Moreover, in teaching their sons to question authority, they have left themselves vulnerable to charges of hypocrisy when Hirsch, concerned with protecting the family's anonymity, strictly prohibits Phoenix from, first, performing at a recital, then from going to Juilliard. Lahti, who gave up her own future as a promising musician, is more immediately sympathetic to her son's needs and prepares for his departure, even though she knows how painful her forced separation from her own parents has been. In the emotional final scene, Hirsch plays both the universal role of the father who is finally able to let go of his son and that of the 60s idealogue who remains true to his belief in freedom and autonomy, convinced that his very decent son has learned his lessons well and will indeed go off into the world and make a difference.

Lumet develops his story at a leisurely but effective pace, allowing the dynamics of a family in conflict and not the sudden appearance of the FBI or an action-paced chase to give the film its tension. The threat of capture is constantly present, giving this particular family conflict its edge, and the appearance of the gun wielding Kit Carson (who scripted TEXAS CHAINSAW MASSACRE and the remake of BREATHLESS) shows just how high the stakes are, but Lumet never forgets that his film is about a family in transition. Among the family players, though Judd Hirsch and Christine Lahti are center stage very nearly as much as River Phoenix, RUNNING ON EMPTY is Phoenix's story, seen from his perspective. The fine young actor delivers a sincere, serious performance, as convincing in his tentative romantic scenes with the excellent Martha Plimpton (with whom he set off fewer sparks in THE MOSQUITO COAST) as he is in his moments of high drama with his parents. Though all of the actors, save for the miscast Hirsch, give strong performances, Lahti is the film's other standout. While Hirsch's portrayal is too broad; Lahti, as she has done so many times before (most especially in HOUSEKEEPING), underplays to perfection. With this in mind, Lumet, an actor's director who believes less is more, cast Lahti before anyone else, and her days as an activist at the University of Michigan during the late 1960s also provided her with a wealth of firsthand experience to draw on for her character. Similarly, Phoenix, as the son of quintessential 60s parents who moved their family 40 times in 17 years, including stints in communes and in South America, was well prepared for his role.

Screenwriter Naomi Foner (VIOLETS ARE BLUE)—an activist at Barnard College, veteran of the civil rights movement, and campaign worker for Eugene McCarthy in 1968—also had the right sort of background to draw on for the script. After their success with AFTER HOURS (1985), producers Griffin Dunne (who also starred in that Martin Scorsese-directed film) and Amy Robinson wanted to make a film with a 60s theme and began collecting newspaper articles. When they came across an article about a family of radicals who were arrested in upstate New York, they knew they had the beginnings of their film and they went to Foner, with whom they had worked on an earlier project. Using as a basis her own experience and that of Eleanor Stein, a friend who had been a Weatherman and gone underground, Foner arrived at a story that also recalled events that took place at a lab at the University of Wisconsin in 1970, in which a young researcher was killed when the building, thought to be empty, was bombed.

Most of the location shooting for RUNNING ON EMPTY, made on a budget of $7 million, was done in Tenafly and Englewood, New Jersey, and the interior shooting was done at Empire Studios in Long Island City, New York. (Profanity, adult situations.)

p, Amy Robinson, Griffin Dunne; d, Sidney Lumet; w, Naomi Foner; ph, Gerry Fisher (Technicolor); ed, Andrew Mondshein; m, Tony Mottola; prod d, Philip Rosenberg; art d, Robert Guerra; set d, Philip Smith; cos, Anna Hill Johnstone; makeup, Toy Russell.

Drama   Cas.   (PR:C MPAA:PG-13)

S

SAIGON COMMANDOS † (1988) 83m Concorde c

Richard Young (*Sgt. Mark Stryker*), P. J. Soles (*Jean Lassiter*), John Allen Nelson (*Tim Bryant*), Jimi B., Jr. (*Will Thomas*), Spanky Manikan (*Jon Toi*), Joonee Gamboa (*Nguyen Huu Tri*), Fred Bailey (*Capt. Daniels*).

When an MP stationed in Saigon in 1970 gets caught up in a series of drug-related killings, his methods clash with those of the South Vietnamese authorities. Helping uncover the facts is a careless AP reporter (P.J. Soles, the bopping teenage punk in cult favorite ROCK AND ROLL HIGH SCHOOL), who finds a link between the murders and a group of corrupt politicians. Photographed in the Philippines in 1987, SAIGON COMMANDOS was released straight to video this year.

p, John Schouweiler, Isabel Sumayao; d, Clark Henderson; w, Thomas McKelvey Cleaver (based on the novel *Saigon Commandos—Mad Minute* by Jonathan Cain); ph, Juanito Pereira, Conrado Baltazar (Motion Picture Color); ed, Pacifico Sanchez; m, Samuel Asuncion, Noli Aurillo; prod d, Mariles Gonzales.

Crime   *Cas.*   **(PR:NR MPAA:R)**

SALAAM BOMBAY*** (1988, India) 113m Mirabai/Jane Balfour c

Shafig Syed (*Krishna/Chaipau*), Sarfuddin Qurrassi (*Koyla*), Raju Barnad (*Keera*), Raghubir Yadav (*Chillum*), Nana Patekar (*Baba*), Aneeta Kanwar (*Rekha*), Hansa Vithal (*Manju*), Mohanraj Babu (*Salim*), Chandrashekhar Naidu (*Chungal*), Shaukat Azmi, Dinshaw Daji, Alfred Anthony, Ramesh Deshavani, Anjan Srivastava, Chanda Sharma.

Photographed in the slums of Bombay, this first fiction feature from documentarian Mira Nair is a well crafted and moving story of an 11-year-old orphan, Syed (a non-professional, as are the rest of the film's child actors) who is abandoned by his family when he burns his brother's scooter. Unable to read or write, unsure even of the name of his native village, Syed arrives in the Bombay slums. He hopes to raise enough money to return to his family, but life on the streets is not easy. He makes a few rupees a day delivering an opium-like tea, and in the process comes into contact with a variety of seedy characters, including a nasty pimp (Patekar), his prostitute wife (Kanwar), a drug addicted pusher (Yadav) who works for and is dependent on the pimp, the pimp's vulnerable but streetwise daughter (Vithal), and a peasant girl called "Sweet Sixteen" (Sharma), a prostitute-to-be whose virginity is being auctioned off to the highest bidder. The streets are clearly not a desirable place in which to grow up, but the young orphan Syed hasn't a choice and must make the best of his surroundings, and, despite the poverty and violence, there are times of joy, such as a visit to the local cinema in which all the children mimic a ridiculous matinee idol. As time wears on, however, the youngster's surrogate family collapses around him. He falls in love with the virginal Sharma, but their love is stifled. The pimp's drug runner (Yadav) dies of an overdose and receives a chilling street funeral. Syed and the even younger Vithal are eventually arrested and sent to a reform camp—a government-run children's prison that is no better or worse than street life.

While the structure, themes, and characters of SALAAM BOMBAY may remind viewers of other films photographed in the city streets that follow the lives of lost children—such as Roberto Rossellini's GERMANY YEAR ZERO, Luis Bunuel's LOS OLVIDADOS, and Hector Babenco's PIXOTE—the story behind its filming is uniquely compelling. Nair, a 31-year-old India-born, Harvard-educated director now living in a Manhattan loft, had previously directed a few documentaries relating to Indian subjects (SO FAR FROM INDIA; INDIA CABARET; CHILDREN OF A DESIRED SEX) when she decided to take to the streets of Bombay with a script that former Harvard classmate Sooni Taraporevala had written from Nair's original story. For months, Nair and Taraporevala immersed themselves in the lives of the city's street urchins, deciding to recruit some 125 children to take part in an acting workshop. Under the direction of Nair and British theater director Barry John, the children, paid about $2 a day, were taught, not how to act, but how to appear naturally in front of the cameras. After initially mimicking the style of India's box-office stars, the children's acting became more realized, and eventually 17 of them were chosen for the film, with payment of a lump sum in advance and additional money placed into a trust fund. From these 17 youngsters, Shafiq Syed emerged as the lead actor. After the production ended, Nair and her coworkers offered assistance to the children. Some chose to work (one teaches sculpture to blind children, another runs a gambling den), others—including Syed, after a stint of schooling—chose to return to the streets. (One hopes that Syed will fare better than the young star of PIXOTE, Fernando Ramos da Silva, whose shooting death in the streets of Sao Paulo was reported to Nair and her crew on the day they began filming.)

Coming from a country where some 800 films a year are released, most of them "entertainments" far removed from real life (and very few of them bearing any resemblance to those of its internationally most respected director, Satyajit Ray), a film like SALAAM BOMBAY is a promising sign that, as in the Neorealist movement of Italy and the Nouvelle Vague of France, filmmakers in India may also begin taking to the streets. In addition, the fact that SALAAM BOMBAY (which was funded by Indian, French, and British sources) received the Cannes Film Festival Camera D'Or as best first feature and was named the most popular film by the festival's paying public proves there is potentially a strong interest in Indian cinema; in light of the interna-

tional reception given to Mali's BRIGHTNESS, it may also suggest that US and European audiences are ready for "Third World cinema" in general. (In Hindi; English subtitles.) (*Adult situations, sexual situations, violence, substance abuse.*)

p, Mira Nair; d, Mira Nair; w, Sooni Taraporevala (based on a story by Mira Nair and Sooni Taraporevala); ph, Sandi Sissel; ed, Barry Alexander Brown; m, L. Subramaniam; prod d, Mitch Epstein.

Drama   **(PR:O MPAA:NR)**

SALOME'S LAST DANCE*½ (1988) 89m Vestron c

Glenda Jackson (*Herodias/Lady Alice*), Stratford Johns (*Herod/Alfred Taylor*), Nickolas Grace (*Oscar Wilde*), Douglas Hodge (*John the Baptist/Lord Alfred "Bosie" Douglas*), Imogen Millais-Scott (*Salome/Rose*), Denis Ull (*Tigellenus/Chilvers*), Russell Lee Nash (*Pageboy*), Alfred Russell (*Cappadodem*), Ken Russell (*Kenneth*), David Doyle (*A. Nabda*), Warren Saire (*Young Syrian*), Kenny Ireland, Michael Van Wuk (*Soldiers*), Paul Clayton, Imogen Claire (*Nazarenes*), Tim Potter (*Pharlose*), Matthew Taylor (*Saddocean*), Linzi Drew, Tina Shaw, Caron Anne Kelly (*Slaves*), Doug Howes (*Phony Salome*), Mike Edmonds, Willie Coppen, Anthony Georghiou (*Jews*), Leon Herbert (*Nauman*), Lionel Taylor (*Police Sergeant*), Colin Hunt, David Addison (*Police Constables*), Robert Goodey (*Black Maria Driver*), Danny Godfrey (*Hansom Cab Driver*), Alison Cella, Frank Cella, Simon Gilbey, James Harte, Martino Lazzeri, Sinead Lightly, Sheree Murphy, Charles Richards (*Children*).

Ken Russell's most impressive offering in years features a faithful rendering of Oscar Wilde's "The Tragedy of Salome" (translated from the French by the director's wife, Vivian Russell), which serves as a play-within-a-film attended by Wilde himself and a Kris Kringle-type still photographer played by Russell. Set entirely on a single set, the film takes place in London on the rainy evening of November 5, 1892. Wilde (Grace) and his lover, Lord Alfred Douglas (Hodge), visit a local bordello, where a clandestine performance of his banned play "The Tragedy of Salome" is to be staged just for the author. Playing Herod, the gluttonous king, is Johns, who is also the bordello's proprietor. Other bordello employees fill out the remaining roles, including Cockney servant girl Millais-Scott in the pivotal role of Salome, step-daughter of Herod, and Hodge as the prophet John the Baptist. With Grace reclining on a cushioned sofa and sipping champagne, the play begins. Hodge, confined to a small cage, is exposed to the temptations of three large-chested, topless vixens, but refuses to succumb to their lewd gyrations. He is then removed to his smoky dungeon (actually the bordello's dumb-waiter) where his prophecies echo from the depths. Inside the palace sits the king's bored step-daughter, Millais-Scott. Rather than partake in the festivities of the evening, she wanders outside, where the palace guards watch over their prisoner. Under the painted full moon, stars, and clouds, Millais-Scott convinces the guards to let her see this prophet that her mother hates and her father fears. When Hodge is pulled up from below, Millais-Scott is overjoyed, wriggling and giggling at the possibilities of what she can do with him. Chained, spread-eagle, at the ankles and wrists, Hodge stands before Millais-Scott. Determined to have this man of God for herself, she taunts him, lustfully breathing, "I am in love with your body." When he resists and calls her the "cursed daughter of an incestuous mother," she gleefully has him lashed. Again she tries: "I am in love with your hair." Again, Hodge counterattacks with words. Finally, Millais-Scott, now seething with a dangerous determination, declares, "I am in love with your mouth. Let me kiss your mouth." She moistens her own lips, licking them longingly for Hodge. He responds by spitting in her face. Ecstatic, she continues to lick her lips and emphatically states, "I *will* kiss your mouth, John the Baptist." After Hodge is lowered back into his dungeon, the king (Johns) and his wife (Jackson, in Lady Macbeth garb) leave their feast to locate Millais-Scott. Johns, who ceaselessly ogles the virgin flesh of his step-daughter, refuses to go back inside until she dances for him. She teases him, coyly eating a banana and stretching her naked legs in front of his face, until he can barely control himself. Meanwhile, the voice of the prophet thunders from below, promising that the true King of Man will rule. Although Jackson dismisses Hodge as a blubbering drunk, Johns respects him and believes his prophecies. Unable to resist his step-daughter's wriggling any longer, Johns begs her to dance for him, promising her anything, even half his kingdom, in return. Millais-Scott agrees to perform the "Dance of the Seven Veils" for him. Shrouded in sheer veils, the dancer moves wildly around the room, leaping, stretching, twirling—whipping the drunken king into a mad sexual frenzy as each veil is tossed aside. When the final veil is thrown off, however, the king has a shock: male genitalia are revealed. There are two dancers standing before him—a nude male transvestite and the nude Millais-Scott. Having been marvelously entertained, Johns asks Millais-Scott what she desires. "Bring me, on a silver platter . . . the head of John the Baptist." Hodge tries desperately to change her mind, offering instead rare white peacocks, gold jewelry, sacred treasures, and half his kingdom. But she is determined to have the prophet's head. Hodge gives in and sends his executioner down in the dumb-waiter. Up comes the platter upon which is served the severed head. Overjoyed at her victory, Millais-Scott takes her prize and mocks the prophet. She then kisses the mouth, as she had earlier vowed to do. (Meanwhile, the author watches his play, a tear rolling down his cheek.) Disgusted by his step-daughter's trickery, the king orders that she be killed. The play ends and Grace thanks everyone involved. They are interrupted by a group of London bobbies at the door, who inform the group that they are under arrest, charging the author with "gross sexual indecency and the corruption of minors."

As usual with Ken Russell, he has taken a biographical subject and literary source in SALOME'S LAST DANCE and breathed his own brand of life into it. Russell's films transform his source materials into his own personal vision, or perhaps the vision they were intended to present before censors and societal morality reshaped them. In this film, however, unlike his previous misfire GOTHIC, Russell has taken the events of a single evening and placed them on the overlapping border of theater and real life. SALOME'S LAST DANCE is not an adaptation of Wilde's play, but a dramatization of a performance of Wilde's play. As in Francois Truffaut's THE LAST METRO or even Ernst Lubitsch's TO BE OR NOT TO BE (not that Russell has much in common with these directors), the events that take place off the stage are as important as, or perhaps even more important than, those which occur on the proscenium. Further obfuscating the separation between stage and reality is the fact that "The Tragedy of Salome" is being performed not by professionals in a professional arena, but by servants, common whores, and male prostitutes. What we (the cinema audience) and they (the bordello audience) are watching is the synthesis of real-life decadence, historical decadence, and that particular decadence which flowed from Wilde's pen. In an effort to stretch these boundaries even further, Russell casts himself as the photographer, who captures and frames the images, and as the stagehand who creates the sound effects—the aural counterpart to the imagemaker. Within Russell's structure, the performances of Jackson, Johns, Millais-Scott, et al., must be judged on a more complex level than usual, not as standard portrayals ("Is Millais-Scott convincing as Salome?") but as portrayals of commoners performing onstage ("Is Millais-Scott convincing as an uneducated Cockney servant who is performing the part of Salome for the benefit of the author?").

Russell is clearly not for all tastes and the Salome presented here is hardly as innocent as that of Rita Hayworth, who, in 1953's SALOME, danced in order to *save* John the Baptist's head. (Other Salomes have included Sarah Bernhardt, for whom Wilde's text was penned, Theda Bara, Russian actress Alla Nazimova, and Yvonne DeCarlo.) The world Russell presents here is one of decadence and vulgarity, but also one of passion, energy, and deep devotion. When Wilde cries at the finale of his own play it is because he is seeing not a weak Herod or a disgusting Salome, but the beauty of two characters mad with the fruits of life. In seeing how touched the playwright is by the show, one can also see how moved Russell, its director, must be. Despite what are called Russell's "excesses," SALOME'S LAST DANCE is not the work of a madman but a film of genuine warmth. In its battle of character Herod and Salome are the central players, so that Stratford Johns and Imogen Millais-Scott must carry the film. Johns, as Herod, is remarkable as a man who is too honest with himself to turn back on his own word, too weak to ignore the pleasures of his step-daughter's flesh, and too blind to see what a fool he has become. Millais-Scott, in her film debut, is stunning. Part pixie, part vixen, she is portrayed as neither female or male, but the very embodiment of sexual power. Made on a tiny (especially for someone of Russell's status) budget of $1.3 million, SALOME'S LAST DANCE looks as if it cost much more, for which much credit must go to the art direction of Michael Buchanan and the set design of Christopher Hobbs. Since the estate of Richard Strauss reportedly blocked the use of the composer's music (a feud erupted in 1970 when Russell's BBC film THE DANCE OF SEVEN VEILS: A COMIC STRIP IN SEVEN EPISODES ON THE LIFE OF RICHARD STRAUSS exposed the composer's involvement with the Nazis), the score is a compilation of classic pieces, including works by Erik Satie, Claude Debussy, and Frederick Delius. *(Excessive profanity, nudity, violence, adult situations, sexual situations).*

p, Penny Corke, Robert Littman; d, Ken Russell; w, Ken Russell (based on the play *Salome* by Oscar Wilde); ph, Harvey Harrison (Technicolor); ed, Timothy Gee; md, Richard Cooke, Ray Beckett; art d, Michael Buchanan; set d, Christopher Hobbs; cos, Michael Arrals; ch, Arlene Phillips; makeup, Pat Hay.

Comedy/Religious **Cas.** **(PR:O MPAA:R)**

SALSA*** (1988) 97m Golan-Globus/Cannon c

Robby Rosa *(Rico)*, Rodney Harvey *(Ken)*, Magali Alvarado *(Rita)*, Miranda Garrison *(Luna)*, Moon Orona *(Lola)*, Angela Alvarado *(Vicki)*, Loyda Ramos *(Mother)*, Valente Rodriguez *(Chuey)*, Daniel Rojo *(Orlando)*, Humberto Ortiz *(Beto)*, Roxan Flores *(Nena)*, Robert Gould *(Boss)*, Deborah Chesher *(Sister)*, Debra Ortega, Renee Victor *(Aunts)*, Joanne Garcia *(Waitress)*, Leroy Anderson, Chain Reaction, Celia Cruz, The Edwin Hawkins Singers, Grupo Latino, Mongo Santamaria, Tito Puente, Bobby Caldwell, Willie Colon, Mavis Vegas Davis, Marisela Esqueda, La Dimencion, Kenny Ortega, Michael Sembello, H. Wilkins *(Themselves)*, Patrick Alan, Marty Alvarez, Robert Alvarez, Eryn Bartman, Marylynn Benitez, Tony Burrer, Joanne Caballero, Juan Cabral, Tina Cardinale, Joyce Carlsen, Greg Carrillo, Bernard Ceballos, Carlos Eduardo Correa, Baruch Kozlo Darling, Charlie De Cali, Marco De La Cruz, Jose De Leon, Gregory De Silva, Toledo Diamond, Melissa Fahn, Daisy Flood, Jesus Fuentes, Joanne Garcia, Rafael Garcia, Marcial Gonzalez, Christiane Calil Hanson, Naomi Hernandez, Ruth Hernandez, Christina Hinestrosa, Monica Hinestrosa, Veronique Hinestrosa, Dr. Memo Huang, Liz Imperio, Louise Kawabata, Daniel Klein, Constance Marie Lopez, Tiger Martina, Steve Messina, David Norwood, Lisa Nunziella, Debra Ortega, Michael Parker, Marla Rebert, D.A. Pawley, Kamar Reyes, Jaqueline Rios, Kirk Rivera, Robert Rossi, Ana Marie Sanchez, Paul Guzman Sanchez, Thomas Guzman Sanchez, Pallas Sluyter, Linda Talcott, Nancy Todescheni, Paula Venise Vasquez, Eddie Vega, Renee Victor, Allen Walls, Adria Wilson, Mari Winsor, James Woodbury *(Featured Dancers)*.

SALSA is a second-rate reworking of everything that clicked in SATURDAY NIGHT FEVER and DIRTY DANCING, albeit with a Latin background. The thin plot, merely an excuse to justify the almost wall-to-wall dancing that is SALSA's sole saving grace, follows Rosa as he hoofs his and girl friend Angela Alvarado's feet off in an attempt to be crowned the "King of Salsa." So single-minded is his effort that even his bedroom is strung with revolving mirrored balls. When Rosa's best "bro," Harvey, an Anglo, falls in love with his high-school-aged sister, Magali Alvarado, we know trouble lurks around the bandstand. The aging "Queen of Salsa," Garrison, a sexy, scheming club owner, is bent on making a comeback by replacing Angela as Rosa's partner. She does so with ease and immediately unleashes her queenly temperament. "You're the frame," she snaps at him. "I'm the picture!" When Rosa discovers his buddy necking with Magali, he beats him to a pulp. Magali drives off in a huff, has a car accident, and (yes, you guessed it) everyone is reconciled around her bedside. Harvey and Magali get together to neck again, Rosa and Angela team up once more and go for the prize, and everybody dances the bejeepers out of the salsa as the credit crawl rolls.

Strictly a Golan-Globus exploitation effort, SALSA has the look of an under-budgeted TV special. The direction by Boaz Davidson, who co-wrote the flimsy scenario with three (count 'em, three) other writers, is perfunctory, as is David Gurfinkel's photography. The lighting is sometimes downright awful, and the sound levels are noticeably uneven. Further, the film slips from realism, to unrealism, to fantasy without reason. It even includes an embarrassing and less than half-baked imitation of Astaire and Rogers' "Face the Music" routine, with the dancers working in front of a billboard with a Puerto Rican beach rather than a movie screen. In another scene, the entire crew of an auto repair shop unbelievably breaks into a lengthy salsa "ballet" with barely a peep from the boss. The film's sole first-class effort comes from choreographer Kenny Ortega, whose moves are stunning, sensual, and deftly worked out in the group numbers. SALSA's highlight is the appearance by the Tito Puente group, but Davidson makes the mistake of letting him go home too early, perhaps because of budget limitations. With the delicate sensual looks of Prince, but without his cloying vanity, Robby Rosa is a decent actor who can dance up a storm. The rest of this mostly young cast is upbeat, energetic, and comport themselves quite respectably. Unfortunately, the script and direction in this throwaway production provide them with little stuff to strut. Songs include "The Magic of Your Love" (David Friedman, Amanda George, performed Laura Branigan), "Every Teardrop" (Joyce Carlsen, Donald Cromwell, performed by Carlsen, Bobby Caldwell), "Which Way?" (Gabor Presser, Larry Kahn, performed by Nick Cortez), "Son Matamoros" (Tata Guerra, performed by Celia Cruz, Willie Colon), "Chicos y Chicas" (Michelle Aller, Bob Esty), "My Blood Is Hot" (Michael Bishop, John Bigham, Wayne Linsey, performed by Mavis Vegas Davis), "Maybe Baby" (Norman Petty, Charles Hardin, performed by Buddy Holly and the Crickets), "Take It Easy" (Jean-Claude Naimro, Georges Decimus, Alex Masters, performed by Kassav), "Spanish Harlem" (Jerry Leiber, Phil Spector, performed by Ben E. King), "Loco" (Marco Antonio Cossio, Arturo Cabrera, performed by Grupo Latino), "Lime Juice (Canto Limon)" (Javier Rivera, Reina Rivera, Oswald Bernard, performed by La Dimencion), "I Know" (Barbara George, performed by Marisela with The Edwin Hawkins Singers), "Cali Pachanguero" (Jairo Vorela, Georges Sigara, performed by Grupo Niche), "Good Lovin'" (Arthur Resnik, Rudy Clark, performed by Kenny Ortega with Chain Reaction and The Edwin Hawkins Singers), "Oye Como Va", "Mambo Guzon" (Tito Puente, performed by Puente), "Blue Suede Shoes" (Carl Perkins), "Under My Skin" (Michael Sembello, Randy Waldman, Cliff Magness, performed by Robby Rosa), "Apple Salsa" (Pat Kelly, Bill Boydstun, performed by Salt and Pepe), "Salsa Heat" (Sembello, Rick Bell, performed by Sembello), "Puerto Rico" (Sembello, Bobby Caldwell, Waldman, H. Wilkins, performed by Sembello, Charlie Palmieri, Mongo Santamaria, Marisela, H. Wilkins, Caldwell), "Margarita" (Sembello, Waldman, Wilkins, performed by Wilkins), "Mucho Money" (L. Dermar, J. Galdo, R. Vigil, performed by Gloria Estefan and the Miami Sound Machine). *(Some violence, profanity, sexual situations.)*

p, Menahem Golan, Yoram Globus; d, Boaz Davidson; w, Boaz Davidson, Tomas Benitez, Shepard Goldman (based on a story by Boaz Davidson and Eli Tabor); ph, David Gurfinkel (TVC color); ed, Alain Jakubowicz; m/l, David Friedman, Amanda George, Joyce Carlsen, Donald Cromwell, Gabor Presser, Larry Kahn, Tata Guerra, Michelle Aller, Bob Esty, Michael Bishop, John Bigham, Wayne Linsey, Norman Petty, Charles Hardin, Jean-Claude Naimro, Georges Decimus, Alex Masters, Jerry Leiber, Phil Spector, Marco Antonio Cossio, Arturo Cabrera, Javier Rivera, Reina Rivera, Oswald Bernard, Barbara George, Jairo Vorela, Georges Sigara, Arthur Resnick, Rudy Clark, Tito Puente, Carl Perkins, Michael Sembello, Randy Waldman, Cliff Magness, Pat Kelly, Bill Boydstun, Rick Bell, Bobby Caldwell, R. Vigil, H. Wilkins; prod d, Mark Haskins; set d, Kate Sullavan; spec eff, Joe Knotts; cos, Carin Hooper; ch, Kenny Ortega; stunts, Al Jones; makeup, Lesa Nielsen.

Musical/Romance **Cas.** **(PR:C MPAA:PG)**

SATISFACTION* (1988) 92m FOX c

Justine Bateman *(Jennie Lee)*, Liam Neeson *(Martin Falcon)*, Trini Alvarado *(May "Mooch" Stark)*, Scott Coffey *(Nickie Longo)*, Britta Phillips *(Billy Swan)*, Julia Roberts *(Daryle Shane)*, Debbie Harry *(Tina)*, Chris Nash *(Frankie Malloy)*, Michael De Lorenzo *(Bunny Slotz)*, Tom O'Brien *(Hubba Lee)*, Kevin Haley *(Josh)*, Peter Craig *(Mig Lee)*, Steve Cropper *(Sal)*, Alan Greisman *(Bob Elden)*, Sheryl Ann Martin *(Sylvia)*, Lia Romaine *(Lexie)*, Wyatt Pringle *(Man in Wild Pants at Party)*, Greg Roszyk *(Guy at Party)*, "The Killer Whales" *(The Blow Fish)*.

In SATISFACTION, Bateman stars as Jennie Lee, an orphan and high-school honor student who dreams of a career in rock'n'roll. Bateman's older brother (O'Brien) insists that his sister get the college education he never got, but when Bateman wants to spend her first summer after graduation playing rock music at a seaside resort, big brother grants his permission. So Bateman packs up the van and heads for the sea with her band: Phillips, the pill popper; Alvarado, the tough girl drummer; Roberts, who's leaving her lover, Nash, behind; and Coffey, the classically trained pianist who was recruited for the band at the last minute when the regular keyboardist found Jesus and abandoned rock'n'roll. The group auditions to be the summer house band at a club owned by Martin Falcon (Neeson), a Grammy-winning songwriter of the 1960s who hit the skids after his wife died. Bateman and band get the job and begin a summer of fun and games at the beach. Adventures include the development of a relationship between Alvarado and Coffey, Roberts' brief infatuation with a snobbish law student, Phillips' conquest of her substance addiction, and Bateman and Neeson's falling for each other. The last proves therapeutic for Neeson, who stops drinking and begins writing songs again, but he finally tells Bateman the affair can't go on. She is at first furious, but then realizes that Neeson is merely being realistic. All the while, Neeson has been telling the group members that he's got a friend who books American bands in Europe and who's in the market for a new group. The agent finally shows up at the club, hears the band, and offers a booking. However—major surprise here—he doesn't want the whole band, only Bateman. Bateman turns down the offer, and, at the fadeout, the older, wiser, and happier band members head for home, with Bateman determined to get that college degree.

SATISFACTION is directed by Joan Freeman (STREETWALKIN'), who spends a lot of time showing that Bateman and her friends are an alienated and hostile lot. Strangely, once that's been established, SATISFACTION is then transformed into an 80s version of the 60s' "Beach Party" movies. Certainly the action in the later film is no less absurd than that found in the Frankie and Annette pictures. Of all the inane subplots, one is particularly noteworthy for its lunacy: Over the course of the film, Phillips' substance abuse becomes more and more frequent, until she finally overdoses. While she is passed out, Bateman goes through her luggage, finds her drug stash and throws it out. When Phillips awakens, she's distraught over the loss of her pills and confronts Bateman, who forcefully replies, "Hey, this isn't funny anymore. You've got to shape up." With that—in what is most certainly a major breakthrough in drug therapy—Phillips is immediately cured of her addiction.

Bad though the story may be, the cast is for the most part equal to it. Irish-born Liam Neeson, who has been impressive in SUSPECT and THE GOOD MOTHER, among others, doesn't belong here—the shadings of his portrayal of the struggling Falcon are wasted in this shallow effort. In contrast, playing the intelligent, talented, fiery Jennie Lee proves to be too much of a stretch for Justine Bateman, whose previous acting has been confined to playing the airhead daughter on TV's "Family Ties." Her very limited vocal abilities are showcased in far too many musical numbers, most of which were produced by Steve Cropper, the legendary rock guitarist who broke into the business in the 1950s with Booker T and the MGs. For some reason, the film pays a lot of homage to early rock. Most of the songs Bateman and her band sing are 20 or 30 years old and, at one point, Neeson plunks out "Dedicated to the One I Love" on the piano, noting that the song predates even *him*. Bateman replies, "Yeah, but that's when all the best rock came from." That may be so, but you couldn't prove it by the uninspired renditions offered here. Songs include: "(I Can't Get No) Satisfaction" (Mick Jagger, Keith Richards), "Knock on Wood" (Steve Cropper, Eddie Floyd), "Iko, Iko" (Joan Johnson, Joe Jones, Marilyn Jones, Sharon Jones, Jes Thomas, Barbara Hawkins, Rosa Hawkins), "C'mon Everybody" (Eddie Cochran, Jerry Capeheart), "Talk to Me" (Cropper), "Mr. Big Stuff" (Joe Broussard, Carol Washington, Ralph Williams), "Lies (Are Breaking My Heart)" (Beau Charles, Buddy Randell), all performed by Jennie Lee and the Mystery [Trini Alvarado, Justine Bateman, Scott Coffey, Britta Phillips, Julia Roberts]; "Dedicated to the One I Love" (Ralph Bass, Lowman Pauling; performed by Bateman); "Loving You Is Like a Suicide Mission" (David Bethany, performed by The Killer Whales); "Rock & Roll Rebel" (John Kay, Michael Wilk, Rocket Ritchotte, performed by John Kay and Steppenwolf); "Stimulation" (Paul Gray, performed by Wa Wa Nee); "I've Been Down Before" (Antonina Armato, Kerry Knight, performed by Knight); "Maybe" (Richard Barret, performed by the Chantels); "Just Jump into My Life" (Mona Lisa Young, performed by Paul Gurvitz); "God Bless the Child" (Billie Holiday, Arthur Herzon, Jr.); Prelude No. 7, Op. 28 (Frederic Chopin). *(Profanity, sexual situations, substance abuse.)*

p, Aaron Spelling, Alan Greisman; d, Joan Freeman; w, Charles Purpura; ph, Thomas Del Ruth (DeLuxe Color); ed, Joel Goodman; m, Michel Colombier; md, Peter Afterman; m/l, Mick Jagger, Keith Richard, Steve Cropper, Eddie Floyd, Robert Schumann, Joan Johnson, Joe Jones, Marilyn Jones, Sharon Jones, Jess Thomas, Barbara Hawkins, Rosa Hawkins, Frederic Chopin, David Bethany, Eddie Cochran, Jerry Capehart, John Kay, Michael Wilk, Rocket Ritchotte, Billie Holiday, Arthur Herzog, Jr., Ralph Bass, Lowman Pauling, Joe Broussard, Carol Washington, Ralph Williams, Paul Gray, Antonina Armato, Jerry Knight, Paul Gurvitz, Richard Barrett, Beau Charles, Buddy Randell; prod d, Lynda Paradise; set d, Ernie Bishop; spec eff, John Gray; cos, Eugenie Bafaloukas; makeup, Arlette Greenfield, Cheri Minns.

Musical **Cas.** **(PR:C-O MPAA:PG-13)**

SATURDAY NIGHT AT THE PALACE** (1988, South Africa) 88m Davnic c

Bill Flynn *(Forcie)*, John Kani *(September, Head Waiter)*, Paul Slabolepszy *(Vince)*, Joanna Weinberg.

Based on a play by Paul Slabolepszy, who also wrote the screenplay and stars here, this film presents a look at the turmoil in South Africa. Slabolepszy plays an unemployed racist lout, whose obnoxious behavior and failure to pay his share of the rent cause his housemates to decide to toss him out. The task of telling Slabolepszy falls on his best friend, Flynn, a milquetoast who idolizes Clint Eastwood. In another part of Johannesburg, Kani, a black man, prepares for his last shift at Rocco's Burger Palace before traveling to his Zulu homeland to see his family, whom he has been away from for two years. The film cuts back and forth between these characters as Kani carries out his duties as the drive-in's crew chief and the white men go to a party, where Flynn makes shy conversation with a woman only to have her disappear into the back seat of a car for a romp with the drunken Slabolepszy. Later, with Slabolepszy as a passenger, Flynn heads home on his motorcycle, but stops at the nearly deserted Rocco's, claiming engine trouble. The truth is he doesn't want to tell his friend that he has been kicked out and tries to get him to phone one of the other housemates to receive the news. Meanwhile, Kani, the last person left at Rocco's, is trying to close up. When the pay phone doesn't work and Kani refuses to serve him (insisting that the drive-in is closed), Slabolepszy turns hostile and directs his pent-up wrath toward the black man. Slabolepszy manages to get a hold of Kani's keys and begins tearing up Rocco's. Flynn sympathizes with Kani, but other than making a few discouraging comments, he does nothing to stop Slabolepszy. After being thoroughly humiliated, Kani attacks Slabolepszy, but doesn't slit his throat when the opportunity arises. Later, while staging an arm-wrestling contest for the keys, Slabolepszy, who now knows that he has lost his home, claps Kani into the handcuffs Flynn uses as a lock for his motorcycle. The vicious racist continues to taunt Kani, and when Flynn's protests grow more vehement, Slabolepszy tells him that he's had his way with the woman that Flynn was so fond of at the party. In a rage, Flynn grabs Kani's knife and stabs and kills Slabolepszy. As the realization of what he has done hits him, the panicked Flynn decides to pin the murder on Kani. "It's not my fault. I didn't do anything," Flynn cries before running off. The political message of SATURDAY NIGHT AT THE PALACE is obvious. With the main characters functioning as representatives of the three factions of South African society, the tragedy of apartheid is played out in microcosm at Rocco's Burger Palace. The symbolism is transparent. Slabolepszy is the heinous proponent of apartheid, Kani is his and its victim, and Flynn represents those South Africans who may be opposed to the institutionalized class system but whose passive acceptance of it allows it to continue. Flynn's final words are an indictment of this latter group. It *is* their fault precisely because they haven't done anything. The problem with the film is not its intent or its political analysis; it is that the characters are such obvious symbols. There is little depth to any of them and as a result the conflicts between them and are not as compelling or tension-filled as they should be. While it is difficult to argue with Slabolepszy's portrayal of Vince as an unredeemable monster, a more complex depiction might have been more enlightening. Kani, on the other hand, is too decent, too perfect. Black South Africans in the plays of Athol Fugard ("Master Harold and the Boys," "A Lesson From the Aloes") are real people with both good and bad characteristics and because of this their trampled dignity and their struggles to overcome the inhumanity perpetrated upon them affect us much more profoundly. Though Flynn is somewhat complex, he is still more a *study* in contradictions than a man with contradictory feelings. Though director Davies has taken great pains to avoid merely filming a stage play—particularly in the cinematic elements he introduces in the opening section before the conflict at the drive-in—SATURDAY NIGHT AT THE PALACE is occasionally caught with its theatrical roots showing. Too often the dialog has the well-formed quality that works on stage but that calls too much attention to itself in film. Slabolepszy's play was produced in London's West End and a number of European cities as well as in South Africa. The film was shown at US festivals in 1987. *(Profanity, violence.)*

p, Robert Davies; d, Robert Davies; w, Paul Slabolepszy, Bill Flynn (based on the play by Paul Slabolepszy); ph, Robert Davies (Irene color); ed, Lena Farugia, Carla Sandrock; m, Johnny Cleff.

Drama **(PR:C MPAA:NR)**

SCARECROWS** (1988) 88m Effigy/Forum c

Ted Vernon *(Corbin)*, Michael Simms *(Curry)*, Richard Vidan *(Jack)*, Kristina Sanborn *(Roxanne)*, Victoria Christian *(Kellie)*, David Campbell *(Al)*, B.J. Turner *(Bert)*, Dax Vernon *(Dax (The Dog))*, Tony Santory *(Jacob Fowler)*, Phil Zenderland *(Norman Fowler)*, Mike Balog *(Benjamin Fowler)*.

After an apparently spectacular (but nevertheless off-screen) heist of a Marine base payroll, a gang of paramilitary types led by Vernon hijacks a DC-3 with its pilot and his daughter (Christian). As they head for their escape, the thieves are double-crossed by one gang member, who jumps out with the money after gassing the others, tossing a grenade as he leaves. The rest of the gang manages to get the grenade out of the plane, then come back looking for blood, landing in a wild, remote area with only one house (abandoned, naturally) around. There they are confronted with dozens of scarecrows hanging in groups throughout the dark woods. After much chasing around in the forest, the hijackers begin to fall victims to the scarecrows, who, it turns out, do in their victims with scythes, then gut them and stuff them with straw. The victims then come back to life themselves, proving very difficult for their former comrades to rekill. The survivors are trapped in the house, from which they are occasionally lured by the possibility of escape or by the stolen money, which litters the lawn (one victim ends up stuffed with cash). Eventually, Christian and Vernon make their way back to the plane, where Christian's father has already fallen victim to the scarecrows. As Christian lifts the plane off the ground, her reanimated dad attacks, but Vernon manages to throw him off the plane and blow him up at the cost of his own life.

SCARECROWS is impressively relentless in its refusal to explain just what the heck is going on. The combination of a photograph of three men on the wall of the house, three active scarecrows, and three credited but otherwise unexplainable characters leads the viewer to an obvious conclusion, but the people in the film never put things together or even speculate thereupon. They just accept the notion that their former compatriot is somehow running around stuffed with money. This makes the already creepy scarecrows doubly frightening. Shot in Florida, the action takes place in virtually real time during a few hours in the dead of the night. The sense of foreboding is surprisingly high, though the performances are two dimensional at best. Without any kind of serious theatrical release, SCARECROWS seems promised a long life on the video shelf. (Gore effects, excessive profanity.)

p, Cami Winikoff, William Wesley; d, William Wesley; w, Richard Jefferies, William Wesley (based on a story by Wesley); ph, Peter Deming; ed, William Wesley; m, Terry Plumeri; set d, Tony Bondanella; spec eff, J.B. Jones, Norman Cabrera; cos, Juliet Provo; makeup, Laura Krewatch.

Horror	Cas.	(PR:O MPAA:NR)

SCAVENGERS*   (1988) 94m Anglo Pacific/Triax c

Kenneth David Gilman (Tom Reed), Brenda Bakke (Kimberly Blake), Crispin De-Nys (Col. Chenko), Cocky "Two-Bull" Tihothalemaj (February), Norman Anstey (Boris), Somizi Mhlongo (Jeffry), Patrick Mynhart (Pavloski), Graham Clarke (Lt. Provmilc), Peter Elliot (McKenzie), Jon Maytham (Turner), Ron Smerczak (Capt. Barlow), Joe Stewardson (Air Controller), Ken Gampu (Dr. Nomus), Michael Richard (Priest), Robin Smith (Patrick), Shalom Kenan (Yudalman), Koos Straus (Stanov), Phillip Van Der Bijl (Povin), Stanley Tabama (Napolan), Thapejo Mofekeng (Scab), Billy Mashigo (Customs Offical), Hugh Rouse, Arthur Hall (Archeologists), Simon Sabela (Terrorist Leader), John Lesley (Prof. Stanton), Ruth Cela (Sister), Merle Malon (Nurse), Jonathan Piernaan (Punk), Llia Mpanga (Receptionist), Percy Molefe (Hotel Waiter), Martin LeMaitre (Russian Simpleton), Fats Bookhalane (Witchdoctor).

SCAVENGERS casts Gilman as an American ornithologist who's passion is for vultures, while reporter Bakke is his former girl friend and next-door neighbor. A priest pursued by a KGB agent stuffs into Gilman's mailbox a Bible that contains microfilm linking the CIA and the KGB in dope smuggling. Gilman is mistaken for an agent, the "Vulture Man," and soon he and Bakke are in Africa, chased by Russian agents and African drug runners. After this initial setup the film settles down for one long chase sequence, with Gilman and Bakke escaping time and time again in predictable fashion. The pair fight off agents while in a cargo plane with no door, steal a Russian armored truck, and even elude a troop of CIA bikers who parachute into the African bush, motorcycles and all, to get in on the pursuit. With the aid of a local pilot played by one Cocky (Two-Bull) Tihothalemaj, the drug smuggling ring is smashed and Gilman and Bakke are given up for dead by all concerned when their Land Rover blows up in a fiery crash. Bakke the journalist, of course, writes her story, and the two happily head off to study vultures.

Filmed in Zimbabwe, SCAVENGERS' plot is unbelievable and played mainly for laughs between Brenda Bakke and Kenneth David Gilman. Writer-director Duncan McLachlan seems to give up on the action sequences midway through the picture, but manages to get some nice moments out of the two leads. Like many recent B pictures, the aptly named SCAVENGERS is little more than a messy, inept, low-budget copy of Hollywood's financially successful big-budget films. With no personality of its own, the little credibility created in the film by Bakke and Gilman is quickly forgotten. (Violence, profanity.)

p, Chris Davies, David Barrett; d, Duncan McLachlan; w, Duncan McLachlan; ph, Johan Van Der Veer (J.T. Avanti color); ed, C.J. Appel; m, Nic Picknard, Ferdi Brendgen; prod d, Roy Rudolphe; art d, Jay Avery; set d, Chelsea; spec eff, Janne Wienard, Max Poolman; cos, Cynthia Schumacher; makeup, Betty Church.

Adventure	Cas.	(PR:C MPAA:PG-13)

SCENES FROM THE GOLDMINE †   (1988) 105m Hemdale c

Catherine Mary Stewart (Debi DiAngelo), Cameron Dye (Niles Dresden), Steve Railsback (Harry), Joe Pantoliano (Manny), John Ford Coley (Kenny Bond), Timothy B. Schmit (Dennis), Jewel Shepard (Dana), Lee Ving (Ian Weymouth), Alex Rocco (Nathan DiAngelo), Pamela Springsteen (Stephanie), Mark Michaels (Kerry DiAngelo), Lotus Weinstock, Lisa Blake Richards, Nick Gilder, Lesley-Anne Down, Bobby Woods.

This behind-the-scenes look at back-stabbing in the glamorous world of rock 'n' roll follows the rise of a promising female keyboardist/songwriter (Stewart) who hooks up with a band that is just about to hit it big. Stewart and the band's leader (Dye) begin an affair, only to have him, at the urging of his unscrupulous manager, take credit for songs she has written. Included in the supporting cast are a couple of actors with strong connections to the music world: Lee Ving, ex of the LA punk band Fear, and Pamela Springsteen, sister of Bruce. Songs include: "Lonely Dancer" (Melissa Etheridge), "Every Good Girl Falls" (Bobby Woods), and "Play to Win" (Bryan Adams, Jim Vallance). After a brief regional theatrical release, this Hemdale film quickly hit the video shelves.

p, Danny Eisenberg, Marc Rocco, Pierre David; d, Marc Rocco; w, Marc Rocco, John Norvet, Danny Eisenberg; ph, Cliff Ralke (Foto-Kem color); ed, Russell Livingstone; m, Steve Delacy, Marc Rocco, Danny Eisenberg; m/l, Bobby Woods, Bryan Adams, Jim Vallance, Melissa Etheridge, Timothy B. Schmit, James House; prod d, Matthew Jacobs; art d, Pola Schreiber; set d, Scott Mulvaney.

Drama	Cas.	(PR:NR MPAA:R)

SCHOOL DAZE*½   (1988) 120m Forty Acres and a Mule/COL c

Larry Fishburne (Vaughn "Dap" Dunlap), Giancarlo Esposito (Julian "Big Brother Almighty" Eaves), Tisha Campbell (Jane Toussaint), Kyme (Rachel Meadows), Joe Seneca (President McPherson), Ellen Holly (Odrie McPherson), Art Evans (Cedar Cloud), Ossie Davis (Coach Odom), Bill Nunn (Grady), James Bond III (Monroe), Branford Marsalis (Jordan), Kadeem Hardison (Edge), Eric A. Payne (Booker T.), Spike Lee (Half-Pint), Anthony Thompkins (Doo-Doo Breath), Guy Killum (Double Rubber), Dominic Hoffman (Mustafa), Roger Smith (Yoda), Kirk Taylor (Sir Nose), Kevin Rock (Mussolini), Eric Dellums (Slim Daddy), Darryl M. Bell (Big Brother X-Ray Vision), Rusty Cundieff (Big Brother Chucky), Cylk Cozart (Big Brother Dr. Feelgood), Tim Hutchinson (Big Brother Lance), Joie Lee (Lizzie Life), Alva Rogers (Doris Witherspoon), Delphine T. Mantz (Delphine), Terri Lynette Whitlow (Terri), Tanya Lynne Lee (Tanya), Jacquelyn Bird (Jacquelyn), Traci Tracey (Traci), Sharon Ferrol (Sharon), Laurnea Wilkerson (Laurnea), Stephanie Clark (Stephanie), Eartha Robinson (Eartha), Angela Ali (Velda), Jhoe Breedlove (Kim), Paula Brown (Miriam), Tyra Ferrell (Tasha), Jasmine Guy (Dina), Karen Owens (Deidre), Michelle Whitney Morrison (Vivian), Greta Martin (Greta), Sharon Owens (Sharon), Frances Morgan (Frances), Monique Mannen (Monique "Mo-Freak"), Gregg Burge (Virgil Cloyd), Cinque Lee (Buckwheat), Kasi Lemmons (Perry), Toni Ann Johnson (Muriel), Paula Birth (Carla), Tracy Robinson (Roz), A.J. Johnson (Cecilia), Cassandra Davis (Paula), Michelle Bailey (Tina), Samuel L. Jackson (Leeds), Edward G. Bridges (Moses), Dennis Abrams (Eric), Albert Cooper (Spoon), Tracey Lewis (Counter Girl), Kelly Woolfolk (Vicky), Florante P. Galvez (Student in Bathroom), Leslie Sykes (Miss Mission), Dawn Jackson, Angela Lewis (Attendants), Phyllis Hyman, Bill Lee, Consuela Lee Morehead, Harold Vick, Joe Chambers (Phyllis Hyman Quartet), Valentino "Tino" Jackson, "Go-Go" Mike Taylor, Gregory "Sugar Bear" Elliot, Jenario "Foxy Brown" Foxx, Kent Wood, Edward "Junie" Henderson, William "Ju Ju" House, Ivan Goff, Darryl "Tidy" Hayes (EU Band), Keith John (Singer at Coronation), Reginald Tabor, Robert L. Cole, Jr., Lester McCorn, William N. Ross, Keith Wright, Derrek W. Jones, Harold L. Boyd III, Rod Hodge (Alpha Phi Alpha).

© COLUMBIA

After the release of his first feature, SHE'S GOTTA HAVE IT, director Spike Lee was hailed as one of the freshest new talents in film. With the release of his second film, however, Lee has fallen victim to that nasty "sophomore jinx," delivering a film far below expectations, one that casts doubt in the minds of those who championed his previous effort. SCHOOL DAZE is, as the ads describe it, "a comedy with music" set during homecoming week at Mission College, a fictional all-black school in Atlanta. As the film begins, the militant Fishburne is trying to rally his fellow students to protest against Mission's refusal to divest from South Africa. Opposing Fishburne's revolutionary tactics is Esposito, the head of the campus fraternity, Gamma Phi Gamma. These two characters represent the two factions at Mission College: Fishburne's "Jigaboos"—the darker-skinned, lower-class kids with natural hairstyles who are concerned with the plight of their race—and Esposito's "Wannabees" (as in "wanna be white"), the light-skinned, straight-haired blacks who want BMWs and Brooks Brothers suits. Wedged in between these stereotypes is "Half-Pint," played by director Lee, who is Fishburne's cousin but who wants desperately to become a member of Esposito's Gamma Phi Gamma. While the tension grows between Fishburne and Esposito, it grows even greater between Fishburne and school president Seneca, who promises to expel the rebellious student if he continues to speak out against the administration. Meanwhile, Lee and his fellow pledges are continually humiliated by Esposito (who must be addressed in reverence as "Big Brother Al-might-EEE"). The pledges have their heads shaved and the letter "G" stenciled on their foreheads, are chained together, are forced to get on all fours and bark, and must even eat Alpo from a dog bowl. Although the Mission College football team loses its Homecoming Game—as it always does—the students continue their activities with the greatest of enthusiasm. By the finale, everyone has settled their differences and men and women, students and faculty, Wannabees and Jigaboos come together as Fishburne and Esposito deliver their plea to "Wake Up."

Except for the brief spell in the 1970s when directors Gordon Parks and Melvin van Peebles were particularly active, there has not been a black filmmaking movement since the 1930s, when Oscar Michaeux was the reigning figure. After the 1986 release of SHE'S GOTTA HAVE IT and the 1987 appearance of Robert Townsend's HOLLYWOOD SHUFFLE, the film establishment again began to take notice of black filmmakers. When Island Pictures announced that Lee would be directing, with a black cast and crew, a musical comedy about class divisions within the black community, expectations and anticipation quickly rose. Lee became not only a spokesperson for his race, but for the independent filmmaking community as well. (The publication of his book *Spike Lee's Gotta Have It: Inside Guerrilla Filmmaking* contributed to his status, as did his next book, *Uplift the Race: The Construction of School Daze*.) Not one to back away from controversy, Lee attracted attention even before cameras began to roll when he and Island parted ways. When Lee's budget swelled to $6 million, Island (a relatively small company that distributed SHE'S GOTTA HAVE IT) was forced to back out. Island expressed a lack of confidence in Lee and his crew, while Lee claimed he "outgrew" Island. Two days later, Lee struck a deal with the Columbia Pictures of David Puttnam's reign and secured himself a budget of $6.1 million. Three weeks into shooting, Lee's alma mater, Atlanta's Moorhouse College, refused to let him and his crew continue, forcing them to move the production to Atlanta University.

Just as he upset some viewers with his hard-hitting and rough-edged portrayal of sexuality among blacks in SHE'S GOTTA HAVE IT, Lee again stirred up controversy here by bringing to the screen black-on-black racism—a subject that most non-black audiences never even knew existed. A strongly negative reaction began to emerge even before the film's release: The United Negro College Fund cancelled plans for a premiere benefit, fashion enterprise WilliWear cancelled a screening party, and many critics took exception to Lee's negative portrayal of fraternity life, citing Martin Luther King, Jr., and Jesse Jackson as fraternity men. As a result, not surprisingly, the film's subject (even before its release) had already overshadowed the film itself.

While SCHOOL DAZE must be commended for its subject matter, little else can be said in its favor. Certainly, SCHOOL DAZE raises a number of relevant and compelling questions about the conservatism of black institutions and their financial dependence on white dollars, the issue of South African divestment, treatment of black women by black men, degradation of fraternity pledges, and the division between the so-called "Wannabees" and "Jigaboos." Instead of addressing any of these conflicts, however, Lee merely tosses them up on the screen, then jumps ahead to a musical number or instance of fraternity hazing in which the viewer completely forgets about the previous scene. Rather than making a strongly defined statement, Lee falls back on sweeping generalities about characters based on their skin color and hairstyle.

Suffering from an attempt to say *too* much, SCHOOL DAZE splits apart into three films—an ANIMAL HOUSE-style attack on fraternities pledging that gets its laughs by offering up a variety of degradations that have been seen far too often; a haphazard collection of a half-dozen musical numbers; and an unfocused drama about four characters, none of whom are terribly sympathetic. The result is a rambling mess that crumbles under its total lack of a structure. In SHE'S GOTTA HAVE IT, which is a free-form, non-narrative film, Lee was liberated from the standard conventions of filmmaking and storytelling. SCHOOL DAZE, however, is far more dependent on a narrative, dramatic drive, for which Lee shows very little directing aptitude. The imagination and invention of SHE'S GOTTA HAVE IT rarely surface. Most disappointing are the self-described "Busby Berkeley dance numbers." The only standout is "Straight 'n' Nappy," which occurs in a hair salon and centers on a conflict between the prissy Wannabees, with their dyed and straightened coiffures, and the tough Jigaboos, with their more traditional hairstyles. Only moderately interesting (any MGM musical has more energy and flair, as does NEW YORK, NEW YORK or ONE FROM THE HEART), "Straight 'n' Nappy" is miles above the other numbers, which are little more than onstage performances. Supposedly set over a weekend, the film carelessly jumps from scene to scene, giving one the impression that the scenes could be reshuffled in a different order with little negative impact. It all leads to a Sunday morning finale in which everyone gathers to make the film's plea to the audience to unite. Unfortunately, this ending resolves none of the conflicts or questions raised throughout the film, especially the steadily inflating tension between Lee and cousin Fishburne.

Besides its confused script (written by Lee before SHE'S GOTTA HAVE IT as "Homecoming") and aimless direction, SCHOOL DAZE suffers on a technical level as well. Some musical numbers are inexplicably out of sync and the camerawork and lighting, in many instances, is unforgivably amateurish. The photography by Ernest Dickerson, who shot SHE'S GOTTA HAVE IT and did the fine color cinematography of John Sayles' BROTHER FROM ANOTHER PLANET, has some unnerving faults. Many scenes are heavily diffused and bathed in amber (a sorority meeting in the girl's dorm), while others are atrociously lit (Ossie Davis' brilliantly acted locker room speech). Since his faults can no longer be explained by miniscule budgets, Lee is a strange case in filmmaking—a probing, exciting, and powerful voice whose talent for heightening awareness overshadows all else. Enhanced by some exceptional acting, especially that of Larry Fishburne and Giancarlo Esposito, SCHOOL DAZE, while failing as a film, succeeds at raising questions that are important not just to blacks but to an entire nation. Songs include "I'm Building Me a Home" (Uzee Brown, performed by The Morehouse College Glee Club), "Straight and Nappy" (Bill Lee, performed by Jigaboos & Wannabees Chorus), "Be Alone Tonight" (Raymond Jones, performed by The Rays), "I Can Only Be Me" (Stevie Wonder, performed by Keith John), "Perfect Match" (Lenny White, Tina Harris, performed by Tech and the Effx), "Kick It Out Tigers" (Consuela Lee Morehead, performed by the Morehouse, Clark and Morris Brown College Marching Bands), "Da Butt" (Marcus Miller, Mark Stevens, performed by E.U.), "Be One" (Bill Lee, performed by Phyllis Hyman), "We've Already Said Goodbye (Before We Said Hello)" (Raymond Jones, performed by Pieces of a Dream), "Wake Up Suite" (Bill Lee, performed by The Natural Spiritual Orchestra).

p, Spike Lee, Monty Ross, Loretha C. Jones; d, Spike Lee; w, Spike Lee; ph, Ernest Dickerson (DuArt Color); ed, Barry Alexander Brown; m, Bill Lee; m/l, Bill Lee, Raymond Jones, Stevie Wonder, Lenny White, Tina Harris, Consuela Lee Morehead, Marcus Miller, Mark Stevens, Uzee Brown; prod d, Wynn Thomas; art d, Allan Trumpler; set d, Lynn Wolverton; cos, Ruthe Carter; ch, Otis Sallid;

makeup, Teddy Jenkins.

Comedy/Musical	Cas.	(PR:O MPAA:R)
SCROOGED*½		(1988) 101m Art Linson-Mirage/PAR c

Bill Murray *(Frank Cross)*, Karen Allen *(Claire Phillips)*, John Forsythe *(Lew Hayward)*, John Glover *(Brice Cummings)*, Bobcat Goldthwait *(Eliot Loudermilk)*, David Johansen *(Ghost of Christmas Past)*, Carol Kane *(Ghost of Christmas Present)*, Robert Mitchum *(Preston Rhinelander)*, Nicholas Phillips *(Calvin Cooley)*, Michael J. Pollard *(Herman)*, Alfre Woodard *(Grace Cooley)*, Mabel King *(Gramma)*, John Murray *(James Cross)*, Jamie Farr *(Jacob Marley)*, Robert Goulet *(Himself)*, Buddy Hackett *(Scrooge)*, John Houseman *(Himself)*, Lee Majors *(Himself)*, Pat McCormick *(Ghost of Christmas Present (TV))*, Brian Doyle Murray *(Earl Cross)*, Mary Lou Retton *(Herself)*.

©PARAMOUNT

Bill Murray's first film in four years (excluding his cameo in LITTLE SHOP OF HORRORS), this only partly successful comedy updates Charles Dickens' *A Christmas Carol*. Murray takes on the Scrooge role as Frank Cross, the youngest network executive in television history, a mean-spirited, wise-cracking creep whose sole interest is attracting viewers . . . no matter what it takes. As Christmas draws near, he personally supervises "Scrooge," a $40 million production of the Dickens' classic featuring Buddy Hackett, Jamie Farr, John Houseman, the Solid Gold Dancers, and Mary Lou Retton as Tiny Tim. To scare viewers into watching, Murray has commissioned hideous, violent commercials for the extravaganza, and when Goldthwait, one of his sycophants, dares to take issue with Murray's approach, he is fired—on Christmas Eve. Meanwhile, Murray does his best to please his boss, Mitchum, who is convinced that programming should be directed to the millions of feline and canine viewers that research has indicated are out there watching. Worried that Murray doesn't have "Scrooge" under control, Mitchum has summoned slick LA director Glover to help the production along, much to the dismay of Murray, who begins to worry about job security. Alone that night, Murray is visited by the grizzly specter of his former boss, Forsythe, and told to expect visits from three more ghosts. The first, Johansen (aka Buster Poindexter), the cab-driving Ghost of Christmas Past, takes Murray for a reckless ride back to his loveless, TV-soothed childhood (Murray's brother Brian Doyle plays his father). Then Johansen transports Murray back to 1968, when he worked in the network's mail room; and finally back to his stint as the dog-suited host of a kids' show, where his career ambitions and selfishness forced Allen, his patient social worker girl friend, out of this life. Deposited back in the present, Murray returns to the production of "Scrooge," but not before leaving a phone message for Allen, whom he dismisses when she comes to visit him and later pursues to a shelter for the homeless. His next visitor, Kane, the Ghost of Christmas Present as sugarplum fairy, floats into Murray's life like THE WIZARD OF OZ's Good Witch of the North. However, though spouting lovely words, she proceeds to pummel, kick, and gouge Murray in the process of showing him what is transpiring in the home of his secretary, Woodard, whose six-year-old son was struck mute by his father's death. Kane then "escorts" Murray to the home of his brother (Murray's brother John), where he and his wife and friends (one of whom is yet another real-life brother, Joel) are celebrating, disappointed that Murray has spurned their invitation but delighted with the VCR he has sent as a gift—though he actually intended to give only his standard present, a towel. Finally, Murray is confronted by the terrifying high-tech Ghost of Christmas Future, and the cumulative effect of these eye-opening visits transforms him, prompting him to interrupt the live broadcast of "Scrooge," take over the microphone, and begin an impassioned NETWORK-like diatribe on the true meaning of Christmas and a plea to Allen and his brother. As hearts are warmed, Woodard's young son speaks his first words, and everyone joins Murray in a joyous rendition of Jackie DeShannon's "Put a Little Love in Your Heart."

Scripted by veteran "Saturday Night Live" writers Mitch Glazer and Michael O'Donoghue, SCROOGED plays like a series of extended sketches from that program. Occasionally, in its salad days, "Saturday Night" presented "serious" interludes that gave the Not Ready for Prime Time Players a chance to show their range; but in the wake of the cool reception to Murray's biggest stretch as the dramatic lead in THE RAZOR'S EDGE (1984), he and director Richard Donner (LETHAL WEAPON; SUPERMAN; THE LOST BOYS) seem unsure of how to approach SCROOGED. Some of the time it h   the feel of one of those "serious" sketches, at other moments it is more like standard "Saturday Night" satirical fare, but the two approaches never really come together. Given O'Donoghue's participation in the screenplay, it isn't surprising that a dark undercurrent runs through the proceedings. Nonetheless most of the film's malevolent feeling comes directly from Murray's performance, which, depending on whether you accept his metamorphosis in the final scene, either gives the film its oomph or sinks it. Murray is one nasty Scrooge, and for some it may be hard to believe that even the presence of the angelic Allen, the happiness in the face of tragedy of Woodard and her family, or the threatening future posited by the third ghost would be enough to change this creep. Murray is front and center throughout, and though a number of talented actors appear, only a few are able to make much of a mark given their limited screentime. Most notably, John Glover, Carol Kane, David Johansen (the one-time New York Doll who made such an impression in this year's CANDY MOUNTAIN), and Bob Goldthwait more or less hold their own in their scenes with Murray. This is not to say that Murray's performance doesn't work, only that it is a strange, often venomously sarcastic one that doesn't immediately ingratiate him with the viewer—which, on the other hand, would seem to be pretty appropriate for Scrooge. You'll have to be the judge.

It's important to note that neither SCROOGED nor Murray (who reportedly did a great deal of improvising) are particularly funny. Those who enjoyed O'Donoghue's warped Mr. Mike tales are bound to appreciate Murray's most sardonic putdowns and more cruel inclinations (like his request that antlers be stapled onto mice to transform them into tiny reindeer for "Scrooge"), and his sly, self-mocking expressions after his first ghostly encounters are vintage Murray, but much of his humor falls flat. In fact, Murray doesn't participate in the film's funniest moments, the teasers for upcoming Christmas specials shown at the beginning of the film. In "The Day the Reindeer Died," Lee Majors leads the defense of the North Pole against a commando raid, and "Bob Goulet's Old-Fashioned Cajun Christmas" features the crooner poling through a bayou swamp. Ultimately, SCROOGED, like Disney's disappointing animated adaptation of *Oliver Twist*, OLIVER & COMPANY, is far less satisfying than the year's other filmed Dickens' classic, the wonderful LITTLE DORRIT. *(Profanity, adult situations, comic violence.)*

p, Richard Donner, Art Linson, Ray Hartwick; d, Richard Donner; w, Mitch Glazer, Michael O'Donoghue; ph, Michael Chapman (Technicolor); ed, Fredric Steinkamp, William Steinkamp; m, Danny Elfman; prod d, J. Michael Riva; art d, Virginia Randolph, Thomas Warren; set d, William J. Teegarden, Nancy Patton, Dianne Wager; spec eff, Thomas R. Burman, Bari Breiband-Burman; cos, Wayne Finkelman.

Comedy **(PR:C MPAA:PG-13)**

SENIOR WEEK † (1988) 98m Upfront-Stuart Goldman-Matt Ferro/Skouras c

Michael St. Gerard *(Everett)*, Gary Kerr *(Jody)*, George Klek *(Jamie)*, Jennifer Gorey *(Tracy)*, Leesa Bryte *(Stacy)*, Alan Naggar *(Kevin)*, Barbara Gruen *(Miss Bagley)*, Devon Skye, Jaynie Poteet, Gordon MacDonald.

It's Senior Week, just seven days until graduation, and three New Jersey lads are determined to get away to Daytona Beach for the usual teen merriment. However, one of them still hasn't finished his last term paper, so the boys kidnap the "class brain" and force him to write it, permitting them to soak up some rays, down an excess of beer, and fantasize about topless beachgoers. Filled with surprises, no doubt.

p, Ken Schwenker, Matt Ferro; d, Stuart Goldman; w, Jan Kubicki, Stuart Goldman, Stacey Lynn Fravel; ph, John A. Corso (Technicolor); ed, Richard Dama; m, Ken Mazur, Russ Landau; prod d, John Lawless.

Comedy **Cas.** **(PR:NR MPAA:R)**

SERPENT AND THE RAINBOW, THE*** (1988) 98m UNIV c

Bill Pullman *(Dennis Alan)*, Cathy Tyson *(Marielle)*, Zakes Mokae *(Dargent Peytraud)*, Paul Winfield *(Lucien Celine)*, Brent Jennings *(Mozart)*, Conrad Roberts *(Christophe)*, Badja Djola *(Gaston)*, Theresa Merritt *(Simone)*, Michael Gough *(Schoonbacher)*, Paul Guilfoyle *(Andrew Cassedy)*, Dey Young *(Mrs. Cassedy)*, Aleta Mitchell *(Celestine)*.

The moviegoing public has been fascinated with voodoo and zombies since the release of the Halperin brothers' WHITE ZOMBIE in 1932. The incredible success of the Halperin film spawned a rash of inferior imitations, and by 1941 wound up as fodder for comedy with KING OF THE ZOMBIES starring Mantan Moreland. Then producer Val Lewton and director Jacques Tourneur resuscitated the genre with the lyrical and haunting masterpiece, I WALKED WITH A ZOMBIE (1943). Ever since, cinematic zombies have been detached from their religious roots (voodoo) and been made the marauding, cannibalistic hordes popularized by the "Living Dead" films of George Romero. With THE SERPENT AND THE RAINBOW, director Wes Craven (A NIGHTMARE ON ELM STREET) returns the zombie to the Caribbean, exploring the culture from which it sprang in this ambitious tale of Haitian voodoo. Loosely based on Harvard ethnobotanist Wade Davis' best-selling nonfiction account of his adventures in Haiti, the film stars Pullman as a young scientist hired by a major American pharmaceutical company to go to Haiti and uncover the secrets of zombification. Recent studies had proven the existence of actual zombies and scientists suspect a drug or potion—the discovery of which could mean a fortune to drug manufacturers looking for a new anesthetic—is involved in the process. Pullman's trip, however, happens to coincide with the collapse of the Duvalier government, and he finds himself tossed into the resulting violent social upheaval. In Haiti Pullman is teamed up with beautiful local psychiatrist Tyson, who introduces him to the mysterious world of voodoo. In her clinic is a catatonic woman said to be a real-life zombie, but Pullman wants to meet Roberts, a lucid man who can recall having been contaminated with the zombie powder, being declared dead by a doctor, his subsequent burial, and then the resurrection that condemned him to wander the countryside a passive slave. After speaking with Roberts in a graveyard, Pullman discovers that deep religious beliefs, combined with a strong anesthetic powder, are the cause of zombification. The subjects never die, but are instead given an incredibly potent drug that paralyzes them so that no vital signs are evident. The victim is then buried and later unearthed just as the potion wears off. Because of their deep religious faith, the victims simply *believe* that they are dead and society treats them as such. Pullman hires Jennings, a *houngan* (voodoo priest), to make the powder for him. It is derived from a variety of symbolic ingredients (including human bones); the only truly active ingredient is the deadly poison of a puffer fish. Unfortunately, Pullman's expedition is noticed by sadistic *Ton Ton Macout* (Haitian secret police) chief Mokae, who also happens to be the most powerful and feared *bokor* (sorcerer) in all of Haiti. Mokae at first tries brutal physical violence to dissuade Pullman from continuing his quest, but when the American persists the *bokor* uses voodoo to invade Pullman's dreams and make him experience what it is like to become a zombie. Pullman fights back, however, and in a whirlwind climax featuring exploding fireballs and flying bodies, Pullman defeats the evil Mokae and returns to the US with the zombie powder.

An ambitious mix of pop anthropology, scientific exploration, political observation, and good old-fashioned Lewtonesque horror, THE SERPENT AND THE RAINBOW succeeds more often than it fails. Writer-director Craven presents Haiti as a vital, mysterious society where harsh economic reality and belief in the supernatural walk hand in hand. Craven's Haiti is a land in which the power elite have corrupted deep traditional religious beliefs to oppress the masses through fear of violence, death, or, even worse, zombification. Mokae, already the head of the vicious *Ton Ton Macout*, is equally feared as a sorcerer and it is this combination of the practical and spiritual that makes him so powerful. From this vivid sociopolitical morass emerges a chilling horror story in which the dead appear to walk and people are possessed by spirits regularly. To convey this sense of unease and dread, Craven combines the terrifying nightmare sequences of A NIGHTMARE ON ELM STREET with the subtle and evocative atmospherics of Lewton. The scene in which Pullman and Tyson meet with zombie Roberts in the graveyard is supremely chilling in the manner of Lewton, while Pullman's hallucinations that he has been zombified and buried alive recall the best moments of the "Elm Street" movies. Craven's work with the actors is impressive as well. Cathy Tyson is wonderfully mysterious and sexy, Brent Jennings strikes a tragic figure as the zombie who can recall his entire conversion to the undead, and Zakes Mokae, the veteran South African stage actor who appeared in "Master Harold and the Boys," is absolutely terrifying as the chief of the *Ton Ton Macout*. Only the casting of Bill Pullman as the ethnobotanist is questionable. Best known for his performance as Anita Morris' dim-witted lover in RUTHLESS PEOPLE, Pullman doesn't quite convince as the relatively unseasoned scientist who gets in over his head. There is no spark to his performance, and his decision to stay in Haiti despite brutal physical and psychological torture from Mokae doesn't ring true. Luckily, Craven's forceful direction disguises most of Pullman's shortcomings.

Reports from the set of THE SERPENT AND THE RAINBOW were just as bizarre as what goes on in the movie. Craven took his cast and crew to Haiti, where they were met by crippling poverty, disease, corrupt government officials, and a volatile populace that had to be kept at bay by the brutal Haitian army. When the thousands of Haitians employed as extras would become unruly, the military would take violent measures to quiet them. Before filming began, Craven was told to visit Haiti's most powerful *houngan*, who gave his approval to the project and performed a brief ceremony that guaranteed the crew's protection from harm, but not from voodoo. True to the *houngan's* prediction, several cast and crew members began dabbling in the local voodoo culture and found that it was more than they could handle. Pullman began seeing things after witnessing a voodoo ceremony, and screenwriter Richard Maxwell went temporarily mad and had to be sent home to Los Angeles immediately. Four days after his return to the States he snapped out of his malaise. After 12 weeks of shooting, Craven decided that it was becoming too dangerous to finish the film in Haiti and had the production moved to the safety of the Dominican Republic. Despite these hardships, Craven has delivered an adult horror film of depth and intelligence, which offers a rich image of a land and religion misunderstood in the US. *(Graphic violence, adult situations, sexual situations, nudity, profanity.)*

p, David Ladd, Doug Claybourne; d, Wes Craven; w, Richard Maxwell, A.R. Simoun (based on a book by Wade Davis); ph, John Lindley (Duart color); ed, Glenn Farr; m, Brad Fiedel; prod d, David Nichols; art d, David Brisbin; set d, Dawn Snyder; spec eff, Gary Gutierrez; cos, Peter Mitchell; makeup, Lance Anderson.

Horror **Cas.** **(PR:O MPAA:R)**

SEVEN HOURS TO JUDGEMENT zero (1988) 88m Sarlui-Diamant/Trans World c

Beau Bridges *(Judge John Eden)*, Ron Leibman *(David Reardon)*, Julianne Phillips *(Lisa Eden)*, Tiny Ron *(Ira)*, Al Freeman, Jr. *(Danny Larwin)*, Reggie Johnson *(Chino)*, Glen-Michael Jones *(Doctor)*, Chris Garcia *(Victor)*, Shawn Miller *(Doowa)*, Albert Ybarra *(Carlos)*, Tony Lee Troy *(Kiki)*, Nick Granado *(Jorges)*, Sandra Gimpel *(Ellen Reardon)*, Johnny S.B. Willis *(Officer Wilton)*, Harris Smith [Vaughn] *(Bailiff)*, John Billingsley *(Ed)*, Kurt Garfield *(Kaplan)*, David Wasman, Laurel Anne White, Tom Hammond *(Court Reporters)*, Jane Bray *(TV Reporter)*, Katherine Mesney-Hetter *(McKay)*, Gayle Bellows *(Lisa's Friend)*, John Aylward *(Taxi Driver)*, George Catalano *(Doowa's Cabbie)*, Don Creery *(John's Cabbie)*, Maxine Thompson *(Slinky Girl)*, Ruben Sierra *(Bartender)*, Lisa Pan *(Larwin's Friend)*, Michael Goodell, Creed Bratton *(Subway Workers)*, A.J. Michael *(Squatter)*, Tee Dennard, Johnny Hunter *(Bums)*, Casey Bridges *(Orderly)*, Coburn Sheldt *(Hospital Attendant in Morgue)*, Ann Ludlum *(Elderly Woman)*, Evelyn Perdue

(*Hag*), David McIntyre (*Cab Passenger*), Jordan Bridges, Dillon Bridges (*Two Young Boys*), Debbie Brown (*Reporter*), Gregory Noveck (*TV Announcer*), Steve Harris (*Reardon's Van Driver*), John Barttels (*Movie Announcer*).

After making an inauspicious directorial debut with 1987's THE WILD PAIR, Beau Bridges again directs himself in this wildly implausible thriller. Here he stars a judge who presides over the trial of a notorious street gang that has brutally robbed a woman on the subway, sending her to the hospital to fight for her life. As Bridges watches television in his chambers before the trial, a commercial featuring a "Crazy Eddie" -like electronics dealer comes on the screen. Moments later, the dealer himself (Leibman) appears; the husband of the woman who was attacked, he pleads with the judge to delay the trial because he has learned of evidence that will prove the gang's guilt. Bridges, however, informs Leibman that he can't talk with him and that he should present this information to the district attorney. The trial commences, but when the prosecution fails to present sufficient evidence, Bridges is forced to set the gang free. Meanwhile, Leibman's wife dies. That evening (all of this action ostensibly occurs during the course of one day), Leibman and his gigantic, addled henchman (Taylor) kidnap Bridges' wife (Phillips) and then the judge, taking him to a warehouse bedecked with video hardware that Leibman uses both to observe Bridges and to show him that Phillips is being held elsewhere. Leibman then gives Bridges seven hours to locate the evidence that would have convicted the gang. If the judge fails, Phillips will be killed. Deprived of his wallet and forbidden to contact the police, Bridges undertakes a journey through the city's sordid underbelly that brings him in contact with a surreal throng of subterranean homeless people and some tough Latino thugs before he finally wrests the incriminating evidence from another wacked-out character. But as Bridges races against the clock to return with the evidence, Leibman informs the gang of his whereabouts, and the judge leads them on a furious chase, eventually arriving at the warehouse, where, in the final showdown, he triumphs over Leibman and the high-tech trap he has set.

Bridges has occasionally shown himself to be a capable and convincing actor, but this is hardly one of his better performances, and, judging from this film and THE WILD PAIR, he still has a lot to learn about directing and choosing properties. His handling of the actors, camera, and pacing here is at best uneven, and frequently it is worse. Ron Leibman—a fine stage actor and generally a solid performer in films—is particularly badly served by Bridges' direction, and Julianne Phillips (one-time wife of Bruce Springsteen) is allowed to substitute dewy-eyed terror for character. But what really sinks SEVEN HOURS TO JUDGEMENT is its inept script—quite possibly 1988's implausibility champion. To begin with, there is Leibman's pretrial visit to Bridges' chambers. Even if we are willing to accept that the judge prepares to try a case by watching a little television, it's still an extraordinary coincidence that Leibman's commercial appears on the screen just before he walks through the door. Then there is the story's time frame: How exactly does Leibman manage to visit Bridges, be at his wife's side until she dies, kidnap both Bridges and Phillips, and rig up the warehouse's sophisticated video surveillance system in the course of one afternoon? The list of lapses in logic is endless, and those who enjoy cataloging such things may actually enjoy SEVEN HOURS TO JUDGEMENT as a continuous "What's Wrong with This Picture?" exercise. To Bridges' credit, his film does generate a fair amount of tension, but as a sort of would-be socially conscious AFTER HOURS, it means to be more than action-packed thriller; it also wants to be a message film. Apparently that message has something to do with the failure of those who administer justice to comprehend life on the streets. The problem is that in presenting a stereotypical, cartoon version of that street life, the filmmakers show that they are even farther removed from reality than the judicial system they condemn. Moreover, their hyperbolic portrait of city sleaze does nothing to elicit sympathy for the unfortunate denizens of this world. If, on the other hand, their intent was simply to portray the underclass as vile, malevolent monsters, then they have come closer to succeeding, but their reactionary motives are deplorable.

Set in New York (though this really becomes clear only in reading the film's press packet), SEVEN HOURS TO JUDGEMENT was actually filmed in Seattle, and although that they have failed to create a convincing Big Apple, the filmmakers have disguised their location effectively enough that the setting becomes a generic Big City. Unfortunately, that's not what they were going for, but then that's in keeping with the rest of this shoddy effort. (*Violence, adult situations, sexual situations, profanity.*)

p, Mort Abrahams; d, Beau Bridges; w, Walter Davis, Elliot Stephens; ph, Hanania

Baer (DeLuxe Color); ed, Bill Butler; m, John Debney; m/l, Tom Chase, Steve Rucker, John Massari, Douglas Fraser, S.A. Wylymz; prod d, Phedon Papamichael; set d, Geraldine Hofstatter; spec eff, Darrell D. Prichett; cos, Larry Lefler; stunts, Sandy Gimpel; makeup, Kathleen Hagen.

Thriller   Cas.   (PR:O MPAA:R)

SEVENTH SIGN, THE*   (1988) 97m Tri-Star-ML Delphi
                                 Premiere-Interscope/Tri-Star c

Demi Moore (*Abby Quinn*), Michael Biehn (*Russell Quinn*), Jurgen Prochnow (*David, the Boarder*), Peter Friedman (*Father Lucci*), Manny Jacobs (*Avi*), John Taylor (*Jimmy Zaragoza*), Lee Garlington (*Dr. Inness*), Akosua Busia (*Penny*), Harry W. Basil (*Kid's Korner Salesman*), Arnold Johnson (*Janitor*), John Walcutt (*Noviciate*), Michael Laskin (*Israeli Colonel*), Hugo L. Stanger (*Old Priest*), Patricia Allison (*Administrator*), Ian Buchanan (*Meterologist*), Glenn Edwards, Robin Groth, Dick Spangler (*Newscasters*), Darwyn Carson, Harry Bartron, Dale Butcher, Dorothy Sinclair, Larry Eisenberg (*Reporters*), Lisa Hestrin, Christiane Carman, Irene Fernicola, Karen Shaver, Kathryn Miller, Cornelia Whitcomb, Yuri Ogawa (*Nurses*), Mariko Tse (*Private Nurse*), Adam Nelson, David King (*Paramedics*), Sonny Santiago (*Medical Technician*), Fredric Arnold (*Surgeon*), Rabbi Baruch Cohon (*Cantor*), Leonardo Cimino (*Head Cardinal*), Richard Devon (*2nd Cardinal*), Rabbi William Kramer (*Rabbi Ornstein*), Blanche Rubin (*Mrs. Ornstein*), John Heard (*Reverend*), Joe Mays (*Motel Clerk*), Jane Frances (*Game Show Woman*), Robert Herron, J.N. Roberts, Hank Calia, Gary Epper, John Sherrod (*Jimmy's Guards*).

Willem Dafoe (THE LAST TEMPTATION OF CHRIST) wasn't the only actor to play Christ in a major motion picture in 1988. Jurgen Prochnow (DAS BOOT) had the same, this time dubious, honor in this truly odd—and truly terrible—biblical horror epic.

What makes THE SEVENTH SIGN so odd is that, this time out, Jesus isn't such a good guy. As he tells a terrified Moore, "I came as the lamb; I return as the lion." He's not kidding either. Calling himself David, for some unexplained reason, Prochnow wanders a troubled world cracking, one by one, the seals on seven ancient parchments, each describing biblical catastrophes leading up to—you guessed it—the Apocalypse. As each seal is broken, the described catastrophe occurs, usually in political hot spots like the Middle East, where a desert village is suddenly encased in ice. Prochnow shows up on pregnant Moore's doorstep—located in that other well-known global political hot spot, Venice, California—to rent her garage apartment and, since he's in the neighborhood, to claim her unborn child in fulfillment of the seventh, and final, catastrophe—the stillbirth of a baby without a soul. As if that were not enough to fill 97 minutes, Father Lucci (Friedman) is also following the progress of the Apocalypse with an unhealthy relish, just a step behind Prochnow. Meanwhile, Moore's husband (Biehn), a defense lawyer, is working nights to reverse the death penalty pronounced against his client, a mentally impaired youngster (effectively played by real-life impaired actor John Taylor) convicted of murdering his incestuous parents. Eventually, and amazingly, all four plots come together. It emerges through flashbacks (what's a bad movie without flashbacks?) that, in an earlier incarnation, Moore was offered the chance to give her own life in return for Christ's at the Crucifixion. Now she's given the chance, by Prochnow, to give her life to put off the Apocalypse. As a bonus, if she can also stop the condemned youngster's execution—the sixth sign—she can save her baby. As if they were needed, even more complications arise as the Roman soldier who offered Moore her past-life bargain turns out to be none other than Friedman, who can only be freed from eternal life on Earth by making sure the Apocalypse occurs. As a result, in the film's fire-and-brimstone climax, Moore, teetering on the verge of labor, battles both Friedman and the state of California (not to mention her bewildered husband) to stop the execution.

THE SEVENTH SIGN almost qualifies as a guilty pleasure. With its fast-moving profusion of subplots, it's frequently silly, but never boring. Gaping plot holes are abundant and add to the fun. There's even occasional evidence of intentional humor in the mishmash script, penned by Ellen and Clifford Green (under the credited, tongue-in-cheek pseudonyms W.W. Wicket and George Kaplan). Also, director Carl Schultz (CAREFUL, HE MIGHT HEAR YOU) and cinematographer Juan Ruiz Anchia pull out the stops when it comes to visual flourishes. Breathtaking special effects, gorgeous matte shots, stylish chiaroscuro lighting, and fluidly ominous camera movements abound to no great effect, but they're great fun to watch. Topping it all off is a typically eerie Jack Nitzche (STARMAN) music score. The valiant performances, with Demi Moore's being the most courageous of all, also include heroic star cameos by John Heard (THE TRIP TO BOUNTIFUL) and Akosua Busia (THE COLOR PURPLE). It's doubtful that anyone's career has been helped, but there is, nonetheless, something perversely entertaining about so many talented people coming together to make so exuberantly awful a film. Songs include "Mummies" (performed by J.S. Roberts), "Jenae" (David Kurt). (Violence, brief nudity.)

p, Ted Field, Robert W. Cort; d, Carl Schultz; w, W.W. Wicket [Ellen Green], George Kaplan [Clifford Green]; ph, Juan Ruiz Anchia (Panavision, Technicolor); ed, Caroline Biggerstaff; m, Jack Nitzche; m/l, David Kurt; prod d, Stephen Marsh; art d, Francesca Bartoccini; set d, Cricket Rowland; spec eff, Ray Svedin, Hans Metz; cos, Durinda Rice Wood; stunts, Gary Hymes; makeup, Robert Ryan, Greg Nelson, Kevin Yeager, Craig Reardon.

Horror	Cas.	(PR:C MPAA:R)

SEVERANCE †   (1988) 95m Euphoria/FOX-Lorber c

Lou Liotta (Ray Ponti), Lisa Nicole Wolpe (Cly Ponti), Linda Christian-Jones (P.J.), Carl Pistilli (Marty), Sandra Soehngen (Sonia), Martin Haber (Lyle), Lou Bonaki (Georgie).

An Air Force officer whose wife is killed in an automobile accident turns to the bottle and begins a downward slide. Having nowhere to go, he tries to reunite with his daughter, a go-go dancer who has just purchased the house in which she grew up. SEVERANCE received a festival release in late 1988.

p, Ann Bohrer, David Max Steinberg; d, David Max Steinberg; w, David Max Steinberg, Cynthia Hochman; ph, David Max Steinberg; ed, David Max Steinberg, Thomas R. Rodinella, Cecilia Zanuso; m, Daniel May.

Drama	Cas.	(PR:NR MPAA:NR)

SEXPOT †   (1988) 93m Platinum c

Ruth Collins (Ivy Barrington), Joyce Lyons (Boopsie), Frank Stewart (Jackson), Gregory Patrick (Damon), Jane Hamilton (Beth), Jennifer Delora (Barbara), Christina Veronica (Betty), Troy Donahue (Phillip), Jack Carter (Cal Farnsworth), Scott Bergold (Gorilla).

Chuck Vincent remakes his 1974 picture MRS. BARRINGTON, this time with Ruth Collins starring as the manipulative eight-time widow who marries old codgers and then murders them. Although their deaths all appear to be accidents, three disinherited daughters sense foul play. Vincent has some fun by letting some of his characters speak directly to the camera.

p, Chuck Vincent; d, Chuck Vincent; w, Craig Horrall (based on the film "Mrs. Barrington" by James Vidos, Chuck Vincent); ph, Larry Revene; ed, James Davalos; m, Joey Mennonna; art d, Edmond Ramage.

Comedy	Cas.	(PR:NR MPAA:R)

SHADOWS IN THE STORM †(1988) 81m Mediacom Filmworks/Vidmark Intl. c

Ned Beatty (Thelo), Mia Sara (Melanie), Michael Madsen (Earl), Donna Mitchell, James Widdoes, Joe Dorsey, William Bumiller.

In one of the most curious casting decisions of the year, Ned Beatty stars as a librarian-turned-poet who has a fondness for quoting John Donne (hence the title, taken from a Donne poem). After being fired for on-the-job drunkenness, the die-hard romantic retreats to the woods to live a poet's quiet existence. It's not long, however, before he meets the exotic young Sara (the beauty who appeared in LEGEND; FERRIS BUELLER'S DAY OFF; and this year's thriller APPRENTICE TO MURDER). The pair become lovers, Beatty murders Sara's abusive companion (or does he?), and then he becomes a blackmail victim, unaware that Sara is in on the scheme.

p, Strath Hamilton, J. Daniel Dusek; d, Terrell Tannen; w, Terrell Tannen; ph, John Connor; ed, Marcy Hamilton; m, Sasha Matson; art d, Elizabeth Moore; set d, Regina Puksar; spec eff, Tom Ryba; cos, Lesley Nikolson.

Thriller		(PR:NR MPAA:NR)

SHAKEDOWN**½   (1988) 105m Shapiro-Glickenhaus/UNIV c

Richard Brooks (Michael Jones), Jude Ciccolella (Patrick O'Leary), George Loros (Officer Varelli), Tom Waites (Officer Kelly), Daryl Edwards (Dr. Watson), Jos Laniado (Ruben), Peter Weller (Roland Dalton), Blanche Baker (Gail Feinberger), John McGinley (Sean Phillips), Patricia Charbonneau (Susan Cantrell), Shirley Stoler (Irma), Walter Flanagan (Prison Guard), Walter Bobbie (Dean Howland), Judd Henry Baker (Big Leroy), Sam Elliott (Richie Marks), Andrew Johns (Billy), Roy Milton Davis (Preacher), Kathryn Rossetter (Mrs. O'Leary), Larry Joshua (Rydel), Michael Medeiros (Bumpers), Bill Cwikowski (Collins), Everett Mendes III (Stevie), James Kruk, Kevin Ruskin (Teenage Boys), Kim Plumridge, Stacey Heinz (Teenage Girls), Karl Taylor, Kelly Rutherford (TV Watchers), Mary Beth Lee (Mary), Julia Mueller (Nancy), Bari K. Willerford (Monster), Antonio Fargas (Nicky Carr), Roy Thomas (Leon), Paul Bartel (Night Court Judge), James Eck-

house (Steve Rosen), Sheila Johnson (Carr's Lady), David Proval (Larry), John Finn (Bartender), Harold Perrineau, Jr. (Tommie), Rockets Redglare (Ira), Lisa Ann Poggi (Suzi), Buddy Van Horn (Police Officer), Augusta Dabney (Judge Maynard), Frank Colangelo (Jury Foreman), William Gleason (Court Clerk), William Prince (Mr. Feinberger), Dominic Marcus (Race Car Driver), Anthony Crivello (Julio), Richard Epper (Blade), Ronald Maccone (Mastrangelo), Dick Boccelli (Desk Sergeant), Tom Mardirosian (Cab Driver), Holt McCallany (Roadblock Officer), Dolores Garcia (Bailiff), Glenn C. Sadler (Captain), Leland J. Eller (1st Officer), Marie Marshall (Muffy), Frances Helm (Guest), Marya D. Dornya (Mrs. Feinberger), Vondie Curtis Hall (Speaker's Voice).

©MCA (UNIVERSAL)

SHAKEDOWN is a totally absurd crime film that also happens to be totally entertaining, thanks to some impressively mounted action scenes and strong performances from Peter Weller (ROBOCOP) and Sam Elliott (MASK). Veteran action film director James Glickenhaus (THE EXTERMINATOR; THE SOLDIER) juggles the various strands of his complicated plotline with aplomb and plows through the expository elements at breakneck speed in order to "cut to the chase." Those interested in realism shouldn't bother with this film, because SHAKEDOWN is a big, bawdy comic book of a movie in which plausibility doesn't exist. For the record, Weller is a 14-year veteran of the public defender's office who has just accepted a job with the Wall Street firm owned by his fiancee's (Baker) ultra-rich father. Although he loves being a public defender, he is convinced by Baker that the daily grind of murderers, rapists, and dope dealers is getting to him psychologically and that he would be much happier leading a sheltered yuppie existence with her. Old habits die hard, however, and in his last week on the job Weller becomes obsessed with his final case: that of a black drug dealer (Brooks) accused of murdering an undercover cop. Although Brooks freely admits to having shot the man, he claims that the cop never identified himself and shot him first to steal his cache of drugs. Convinced it was a matter of self-defense, Weller digs deeper and finds evidence of large-scale corruption within the New York City police department. Indeed, a great number of cops are working in cahoots with Manhattan drug kingpin Fargas, and the most venal of the cops, Waites, becomes determined to get rid of Weller before he blows the whistle on the entire operation. Enter Elliott, Weller's best friend and the only honest narcotics detective on the force. Surly, cynical, and unkempt, he could easily be mistaken for a bum by the average Manhattanite. A loner and man of few words, Elliott seems more a supernatural force than a human being and basically lives for the excitement of a good bust. He and Weller team up to expose the corruption in the police department. This, of course, leads to several outrageous action scenes, including a massive shoot-out/chase in Times Square, a Coney Island roller coaster careening off its tracks, and Elliott clinging to the landing gear of a Lear jet as it zooms over lower Manhattan. In the end the good guys win, justice is served, and Weller dumps his socialite fiancee (and the Wall Street job) for his ex-lover, assistant DA Charbonneau.

While most of SHAKEDOWN is extremely silly, director Glickenhaus and his actors invest the material with such verve as to make it all palatable. The characters are vivid, the plot serviceable, the humor amusing, and the action frequently stunning. Weller, who seems anxious to prove that he has a range beyond ROBOCOP, turns in a quirky, energetic performance. With a quick wit, sharp tongue, and a willingness to engage in some extremely dangerous physical activity, his public defender is part Perry Mason, part Indiana Jones. Weller's live-wire performance sets the pace for the film, as he races from courtroom to shoot-out to romance and back again with barely enough time to catch his breath. If Weller moves through the film like a zephyr, then Elliott is a steadily advancing typhoon that manages to destroy everything in its path as it descends upon the villains. At the same time his character is phantom-like, appearing just when needed and then vanishing just as quickly. An underrated and quite capable actor, Elliott even pulls off a lengthy and ultimately hilarious soliloquy about the only woman he ever loved. (Unfortunately, he accidentally killed his girl friend's dog when he was in her apartment playing fetch with the beast and tossed the ball out the open window of her high-rise. "The dog landed on the roof of a parked car. I looked down, threw up, and left. I never even told her she was the one.")

Weller and Elliott are an appealing buddy team, but Glickenhaus avoids much of the obligatory male-bonding exposition by letting his characters operate separately—so that the cop and the public defender don't spend the entire film on-screen at the same time and are only paired up when the action dictates. By structuring his narrative in this manner, Glickenhaus is able to pursue several plot strands at the same time and to cut back and forth between them, enabling the film to move along at a more rapid pace and heightening the tension. This is not to say that Glickenhaus' juggling of the complex structure is flawless—it isn't. Several aspects of the story are given a perfunctory treatment (especially Weller's relationship with Charbonneau) and occasionally Glickenhaus drops the ball entirely, which forces him to introduce a deus ex machina to bail himself out. Luckily, Glickenhaus establishes a movie universe in which just about anything can happen and horribly obvious plot devices simply don't matter. For those who like to spot inside jokes, pay attention during the Times Square sequences. When Elliott is first introduced he's asleep in a movie theater showing Glickenhaus' THE SOLDIER, and later, out on the street, Elliott walks past a theater showing FATAL BEAUTY—the film he starred in last year. *(Graphic violence, substance abuse, sexual situations, profanity.)*

p, J. Boyce Harman, Jr.; d, James Glickenhaus; w, James Glickenhaus; ph, John Lindley (TVC color); ed, Paul Fried; m, Jonathan Elias; prod d, Charles Bennett; set d, Guido DeCurtis; spec eff, Michael Wood; cos, Peggy Farrell Salten; stunts, Alan Gibbs, Jack Gill; makeup, Leslie Fuller.

Action/Crime   **Cas.**   **(PR:O MPAA:R)**

SHALLOW GRAVE †   (1988) 89m E.L.F./Intl. Film c

Tony March *(Sheriff Dean)*, Lisa Stahl *(Sue Ellen)*, Tom Law *(Deputy Scott)*, Carol Cadby *(Patty)*, Donna Baltron *(Rose)*, Just Kelly *(Cindy)*, Vince Tumeo *(Chad)*, Gregory Todd Davis *(Owen)*, Merry Rozelle, Roy Smart, Kimberly Johnson, Heidi Brown.

En route to Fort Lauderdale, four Catholic college girls make an unfortunate pit stop in Medley, Georgia. As in so many other films with similar plot contrivances (MACON COUNTY LINE; JACKSON COUNTY JAIL), the helpless visitors are then caught in a web of hellish violence. Two of them are gunned down after witnessing a man murder his girl friend, then buried in a *shallow grave* along with his first victim. True to genre conventions, the local authorities are Neanderthals who don't believe a word of the surviving girls' tall tale. The score is by Mason Daring, who has done the score for a number of John Sayles' films. After a brief, unnoticed 1987 theatrical release, this made-in-Florida thriller hit the video store shelves in 1988.

p, Barry H. Waldman; d, Richard Styles; w, George E. Fernandez (based on a story by George E. Fernandez, Carolyn J. Horton); ph, Orson Orchoa (Continental color); ed, Carolyn J. Horton; m, Mason Daring; art d, Alan Avchen; set d, Suzi Margolin.

Thriller   **Cas.**   **(PR:NR MPAA:R)**

SHAME*½   (1988, Aus.) 92m Barron/Hoyts-Skouras c

Deborra-Lee Furness *(Asta Cadell)*, Tony Barry *(Tim Curtis)*, Simone Buchanan *(Lizzie Curtis)*, Gillian Jones *(Tina Farrel)*, Peter Aanensen *(Sgt. Wal Cuddy)*, Margaret Ford *(Norma Curtis)*, David Franklin *(Danny Fiske)*, Bill McClusky *(Ross)*, Allison Taylor *(Penny)*, Phil Dean *(Gary)*, Graeme Wemyss *(Bobby)*, Douglas Walker *(Andrew)*.

After suffering a dry spell, with dull and predictable Hollywood-style output, the Australian film industry has finally put some spark back into its product with SHAME, a low-budget genre hybrid with an angry feminist perspective. The movie begins as a black-leather-clad, helmeted female motorcyclist (Furness) zooms through the deserted two-lane highways of rural Australia. A tough, independent barrister on holiday, Furness is forced to stop in the small, dusty town of Ginborak when her bike breaks down. She is treated like meat by the local lads gathered in front of the pub, but the attractive strawberry blonde ignores the loutish catcalls and stares of this Neanderthal bunch and asks for the nearest mechanic. Told to go to a service station at the outskirts of town, Furness meets the kindly owner, Barry, who allows her to borrow his tools and work on her bike. Finding she needs a spare part that must be ordered from Perth, Furness asks if she can sleep in the spare room off the garage, and Barry agrees, much to the dismay of his cantankerous elderly mother, Ford. During her stay, Furness realizes that Barry's teenage daughter, Buchanan, was recently gang raped. Unable to deal with the complexity of his emotions about the rape, Barry blames his daughter for what happened and seeks no legal recourse. On her trips into town, Furness discovers that the young men of Ginborak seem to have free run of the town and can sexually harass women with total impunity. Those men who have sisters, wives, and girl friends who have been attacked are bullied into silence and ostracized from the small community if they put up a fight. The fathers of the rapists adopt a boys-will-be-boys attitude, their mothers blame the victim and shame the girls into keeping their mouths shut, and Aanensen, the rotund sheriff, turns a blind eye to the boys' nocturnal activities. Furness, who is forced to fend off an attack herself, finds the situation intolerable and befriends Buchanan, urging her to press charges. Her gutsy stance helps bring Barry and Buchanan together and the family takes a stand against the code of silence. When six boys are rounded up and jailed, but then quickly bailed out, the outraged Furness slaps a restraining order on the rapists, forbidding them to go near the service station or Buchanan. After a bout of heavy drinking, the boys ignore the order and attack the station. In a siege that recalls STRAW DOGS, Furness manages to spirit Buchanan away on her motorcycle while Barry and Ford defend the house. Furness drops the girl off at the police station and rushes back to help Barry and Ford; however, unbeknownst to Furness, the police station is deserted and Buchanan is kidnaped by two of the boys. After a struggle in their car, Buchanan falls out of the speeding vehicle and down an embankment. Furness returns to the service station to find that Barry has been beaten to a pulp and Ford abducted. With most of the women in the community finally willing to take a stand, a small vigilante group led by Furness goes searching for Ford. She is found just as the teens are about to attack her, and the womenfolk are able to subdue the

creeps until the police arrive with Buchanan's abductors in tow. When it is learned that Buchanan is missing, Furness turns on the boy who was driving the car and strangles him until he confesses to the crime and tells her where the girl is. Furness rushes to the site on her motorcycle, but by the time the townsfolk catch up, they find her crying over Buchanan's lifeless body. The town is horrified by the event, and Buchanan's death may cause it to change its ways, but Furness is so devastated by the girl's death that one wonders if perhaps she took things too far.

Intelligently written by Beverley Blankenship and Michael Brindley and directed with flair by first-timer Steve Jodrell, SHAME is another astute genre hybrid film, echoing everything from the classic western SHANE to Australia's own MAD MAX films while retaining its own freshness and vitality. By tapping sources as familiar as the George Stevens western, the George Miller action films, the Marlon Brando biker movie THE WILD ONE, and even Sam Peckinpah's STRAW DOGS, director Jodrell is able to ensnare his audience through recognizable situations and characters before turning them on their heads and foiling expectations. This is a risky approach that might frustrate an audience, especially in a low-budget exploitation film, but Jodrell and his cast keep viewers engrossed in the complicated emotional, social, sexual, and even political maneuvering played out before them. For a film in which the central image is a beautiful woman clad in black leather and riding a motorcycle, SHAME is amazingly devoid of the kind of exploitative elements one would expect. There is no nudity, we are spared any voyeuristic rape scenes, and there are no guns fired. Jodrell has enough confidence in his material to allow the characters and situation to deliver the goods, and resists the temptation to toss in the odd explosion to liven things up.

SHAME is also surprisingly uncompromising in its characterizations. The men are a uniformly disgraceful lot, and while Jodrell allows them their humanity, he does not make them sympathetic. Even Barry, as the rape victim's confused father, is shown to have been willing to ostracize his own flesh and blood and go along with the town's refusal to acknowledge its hideous problem; only the intervention of Furness spurs Barry into recognizing the truth and doing something about it. While a handful of men are seen to become radicalized as events unfold, the film sticks to its guns and does not turn them into heroes. The *women* are the heroes here, for it is they who finally stand up for their rights and fight back—with or without help from the men. Blankenship, Brindley, and Jodrell don't simply paint all the women as victims, however; many of the towns women are shown to bear some implicit responsibility for the rapes when they make excuses for their sons and blame the female victims for their plight.

Part of what makes SHAME so compelling are the performances Jodrell elicits from his cast, all little-known actors with rugged, lived-in faces. Although she cuts a stunning screen presence, Deborra-Lee Furness is no glamor girl in black leather. Old enough to be convincing as an experienced lady lawyer, Furness conveys a tough, confident, mature, and dignified demeanor without suppressing her tenderness. She strikes a perfect balance between independence and vulnerability that keeps her character from becoming a kind of feminist Lone Ranger (while Jodrell does play with the mythic aspects of his material, he never allows his characters to become cartoons). Furness' astute performance is easily one of the best of the year and, with luck, she will soon break through to international stardom. Also excellent are young Simone Buchanan as the courageous rape victim and Tony Barry as her ineffectual father. Their sensitive performances add immeasurably to the emotional complexity of the material and help push this low-budget genre piece onto a higher plane. While SHAME's filmmakers are not afraid to make strong statements, they eschew the tiresome didactics often found in this sort of material. There is plenty of ambiguity here, and Jodrell does not avoid the complexity of his subject and all its various shadings. SHAME poses some difficult questions that may lack clear-cut answers, and makes the experience rewarding, powerful, and thought-provoking. *(Violence, sexual situations, adult situations, profanity.)*

p, Damien Parer, Paul D. Barron; d, Steve Jodrell; w, Beverly Blankenship, Michael Brindley; ph, Joseph Pickering; ed, Kerry Regan; m, Mario Millo; prod d, Phil Peters.

Drama   **(PR:O MPAA:R)**

SHE'S HAVING A BABY**   (1988) 106m PAR c

Kevin Bacon *(Jefferson "Jake" Briggs)*, Elizabeth McGovern *(Kristy Briggs)*, Alec Baldwin *(Davis McDonald)*, Isabel Lorca *(Fantasy Girl)*, William Windom *(Russ Bainbridge)*, Cathryn Damon *(Gayle Bainbridge)*, Holland Taylor *(Sarah Briggs)*, James Ray *(Jim Briggs)*, Dennis Dugan, Nancy Lenehan, John Ashton, Edie McClurg, Paul Gleason, Larry Hankin, Valeri Breiman, Bill Erwin, Reba McKinney.

Teenage *angst* specialist John Hughes' first foray into the adult universe (filmed before his PLANES, TRAINS, AND AUTOMOBILES) is a sporadically interesting effort that seems so personal to the writer-director as to be downright narcissistic. The film revolves around a sullen young man, Bacon, a would-be writer who passively blunders into every important decision of his life. Minutes before his wedding ceremony, Bacon sits in a sports car with his hedonistic best man, Baldwin, and worries that he is making a mistake. Baldwin warns him that the responsibilities of marriage will ruin him as a writer, and Bacon fears that his friend speaks the truth. But he does love his bride, McGovern, and is reluctant to disappoint their respective families. The wedding goes on as scheduled, and Bacon soon finds himself confronted with the constant carping of his wealthy father-in-law (Windom), who has no confidence that his new son can provide McGovern with the lifestyle to which she has become accustomed. Although his college degree in Romance languages has left Bacon just qualified to work on a loading dock, he eventually falls into a lucrative position as an advertising copywriter in Chicago. Before you can say "yuppie," Bacon finds himself the owner of a tastefully decorated home in an affluent suburb who commutes into the city on mass transit. While now outwardly successful, Bacon is bored with his job and alienated from his neighbors, and spends much of his time fantasizing about other women. Aware of her husband's impending wanderlust, McGovern goes off the pill in an attempt to get pregnant. When she discovers that they cannot conceive, McGovern has tests run, and the resulting verdict is that Bacon is infertile. Although he is ambivalent about parenthood, Bacon considers his infertility a challenge to his manhood and submits to several goofy schemes to correct the situation. Eventually the couple conceive and Bacon again drifts off into fantasy land as McGovern's womb begins to balloon. He is finally snapped out of his disaffected fog when McGovern goes into an extremely difficult labor that endangers her life. Suddenly faced with the loss of his wife, Bacon has a flood of flashbacks reminding him of all the good times they've had and realizes that his life isn't so bad after all. Luckily, McGovern survives the ordeal and gives birth successfully. Strengthened and matured by his brush with tragedy, Bacon finally accepts adulthood and funnels his experience into writing the great American novel.

While much of SHE'S HAVING A BABY is amusing on a purely superficial level, writer-director Hughes has yet to produce a film that is wholly satisfying. Part of the problem with this movie is its totally self-absorbed main character. Drifting through the film with a glazed look in his eye and spoiled brat's pout, Kevin Bacon comes across as an unsympathetic jerk vaguely dissatisfied with everything that happens to him. Even more infuriating is the character's extreme passivity—never once does he make his personal feelings known to his wife or, for that matter, assert himself with his pushy father-in-law. Instead, he opts to stare glumly into space, seeking refuge in fantasies. Even worse, Elizabeth McGovern's character, the object of all this loathing, is given no personality. Hughes presents her as a gently nagging, conniving, selfish, and humorless entity who drags Bacon kicking and screaming into maturity. Until the final flashbacks, Hughes never lets us see what it was about McGovern that Bacon fell in love with. He does a great disservice to his characters by hiding the positive aspects of the marriage from the audience this way. Although from the moment they are married McGovern is shown to be nothing but a badgering hausfrau who slowly picks away at her husband's real ambitions, it is Bacon who is the real culprit, for he never expresses his dissatisfaction and prefers instead to mope around and daydream of escape. (To her credit, McGovern tries hard with what little she is given and manages to bring some sympathy to a role that, as written, is nothing but an ignorant shrew.) In the end, Bacon finally decides to capitulate to what everyone expects from him, embracing suburban family life and finding a medium for his fantasies through his writing. What is Hughes is trying to say here? Is Bacon a sap for *not* liking a comfortable suburban existence, or is he a sap for *embracing* it? For much of the film Hughes seems to disdain the large house in the affluent suburb, the BMW in the driveway, the dull-but-stable job, the perfect wife and beautiful child. Bacon seems to be drowning in a sea of upper-middle-class values. Then, suddenly, Bacon snaps out of his malaise and realizes what a fool he's been. He agrees to play by the rules of the game, as Hughes opts for a happy ending that reaffirms traditional values instead of having Bacon ask for a divorce and move out to Hollywood to become a screenwriter—the direction in which his narrative really seemed to be heading. Because there is so much negativity prior to the happy ending, one is left with the distinct impression that Hughes doesn't even buy it himself.

SHE'S HAVING A BABY could have been a fascinating and funny look at the conflict between marriage and personal ambition had its writer-director probed more deeply into the subject. Instead, Hughes falls back on the easy jokes, hip music, and superficial character studies that have obscured the basic viability of all his work. It is not impossible to present frank, honest, and sometimes uncomfortable character observations through side-splitting humor—Albert Brooks does it all the time. But until Hughes becomes more honest with himself and his subjects, he will continue to produce unsatisfying, confused, and ambivalent films that evaporate from memory as soon as the credits roll. *(Adult situations, sexual situations, profanity.)*

p, John Hughes; d, John Hughes; w, John Hughes; ph, Don Peterman (Technicolor); ed, Alan Heim; m, Stewart Copeland, Nicky Holland; prod d, John W. Corso; set d, Louis M. Mann; cos, April Ferry; ch, Tony Stevens; stunts, Conrad E. Palmisano.

Comedy **Cas.** **(PR:C-O MPAA:PG-13)**

SHOOT TO KILL*** (1988) 106m Touchstone-Silver Screen Partners III/BV c

Sidney Poitier *(Warren Stantin)*, Tom Berenger *(Jonathan Knox)*, Kirstie Alley *(Sarah)*, Clancy Brown *(Steve)*, Richard Masur *(Norman)*, Andrew Robinson *(Harvey)*, Kevin Scannell *(Ben)*, Frederick Coffin *(Ralph)*, Michael MacRae *(Fournier)*, Robert Lesser *(Minelli)*, Les Lannom *(Sheriff Arnett)*, Frank C. Turner *(Crilly)*, Walter Marsh *(Sam Baker)*, Samuel Hiona *(Inspector Hsu)*, Michael Chapman *(Lawyer)*, Milton Selzer *(Mr. Berger)*, Janet Rotblatt *(Mrs. Berger)*, Ken Camroux *(Denham)*, Howard Storey *(Fisherman)*, Fred Henderson *(Agent Owenby)*, Robyn Masumi Gildemeester *(Maid)*, Jerry Wasserman, Gloria Lee *(FBI Agents)*, Freda Perry *(Computer Operator)*, Kevin McNulty *(San Francisco Policeman)*, William Taylor *(Police Captain)*, Ric Reid *(SWAT Sergeant)*, Claire Brown *(Mildred)*, Blu Mankuma *(Undercover Priest)*, Gary Hetherington *(Inspector)*, Allan Lysell *(Sergeant)*, Michele Goodger *(Woman with Stroller)*, Beatrice Boepple, Darcelle Chan *(Nuns)*, Maryanna Danguy, Craig Saunders *(Couple)*.

Sidney Poitier's long-awaited return to the silver screen is a fast-paced actioner, slickly directed by former Sam Peckinpah editor Roger Spottiswoode, which contains some of the most thrilling stunt work seen in quite some time. In the suspenseful opening sequence, veteran San Francisco FBI agent Poitier—a cool consummate professional—is grappling with a sticky situation. The wife of a prestigious jeweler is being held hostage by a homicidal maniac who demands a fortune in diamonds in exchange for the woman's life. The killer, a supremely clever villain who keeps his face obscured at all times, is holed up in the jeweler's home while the FBI sits stationed

© BUENA VISTA

around the property, waiting to get a clear shot. After the kidnaper cold-bloodedly kills the family maid, Poitier has no choice but to hand over the diamonds and try to catch the killer during his getaway. The heinous criminal proves too ingenious, however, and he makes off with the ransom, killing his hostage out of mere spite. Feeling he has failed, Poitier becomes obsessed with apprehending the killer and chases him into the rugged Pacific Northwest. In an attempt to cross the border into Canada, the killer happens upon an innocent businessman about to go on a weekend fishing trip in the wilderness with a group of strangers. He murders this man and assumes his identity, joining the group as they follow savvy guide Alley through the treacherous mountains. During the hike we see the killer's face for the first time, but since he is in the company of several familiar movie heavies (Robinson, Brown, and Masur among them), the audience doesn't yet know which man is the killer. Meanwhile, Poitier pieces together the few clues available and deduces exactly what his quarry has done. Determined to catch his man, Poitier demands to be taken up into the wilderness by Alley's mountain-man boy friend, Berenger. Berenger, desperate to rescue Alley, has nothing but contempt for the wilderness skills of city slicker Poitier ("Ain't no elevators out here, mister," he tells the FBI man) and refuses to take him along, claiming Poitier will only slow him down. When Poitier forces the issue, however, a reluctant Berenger saddles up a horse for the federal agent. Obviously out of his element but giving it a valiant try, Poitier struggles with the great outdoors, much to Berenger's annoyance; after several trials and tribulations, however, the FBI agent and the mountain man develop a grudging respect for each other. Suspecting the law may be on his trail, the killer lags behind and creates obstacles for those who may follow. Eventually the killer (Brown) is forced to reveal his identity and murders all his fellow hikers save Alley. Using her as a hostage, Brown forces Alley to guide him into Canada, where he plans to sell the fortune in diamonds. Poitier and Berenger remain one step behind, however, and when the scenery shifts from the imposing wilderness to the streets of Vancouver, it is the FBI man who becomes the guide for the mountaineer. Back on his own turf, Poitier launches into a swift and impressive display of modern investigative work and manages to catch up to Brown on a ferry boat. In a wild climax, Alley is saved by Berenger while Poitier and Brown plunge into the freezing waters for an underwater gunfight in which Poitier finally kills the evil Brown.

So what if the plot is full of holes and you think you've seen it all before? SHOOT TO KILL is a marvelously entertaining action-adventure that, through superior filmmaking skills and great central performances, rises above its mundane script—much like last year's LETHAL WEAPON. Director Spottiswoode, whose previous efforts include the interesting UNDER FIRE (1984) and the much-maligned THE BEST OF TIMES (1986), presents this material at an edge-of-your-seat pace that manages to be stylish without becoming pretentious (something rare in a genre dominated by the likes of Michael Mann and William Friedkin). Much of the credit goes to cinematographer Michael Chapman (RAGING BULL), whose skillful use of the widescreen format is impressive in both the urban setting and the gorgeous outdoor vistas of British Columbia. Although most of the film is a tightly constructed roller-coaster ride with several notable high points, the most gripping (and talked about) scene has to be that in which the Berenger character is forced to cross a deep gorge on a flimsy trolley cable while Poitier stands on the edge holding the safety line tied around Berenger's waist. Suddenly the trolley car (which was stuck on the other side) comes loose and rolls right at Berenger. Berenger is knocked off the cable and falls 150 feet straight down until the safety line snaps taut and he goes flying into the rock face with jarring force. Spottiswoode realizes the scene superbly and the fall, performed by 55-year-old stuntman David Jacox, will stun even the most jaded moviegoer.

Even more important than impressive technique, however, is the presence of Poitier, appearing on-screen for the first time in 11 years. Looking fit, trim, and virile, Poitier retains every iota of the commanding quality that made him a superstar. Most amazingly, this 60-year-old man looks as if he could whip Tom Berenger *and* Clancy Brown at the same time. Few actors can effortlessly dominate the screen the way Poitier does and it is his restrained acting style that gives this movie class. He handles even the most predictable bits of comedy relief with such aplomb as to make them seem new, fresh, and hilarious. Poitier's performance only serves to remind veteran moviegoers how few real stars there are left these days. Berenger, although outclassed (and that is not a criticism of his considerable talents), lends strong support and makes a good foil for Poitier. His role is a fairly thankless one and he makes the most of it. Kirstie Alley, in another nothing part, is quite convincing as a rugged outdoors type and wrests some nuance out of what could have been a typical struggle-and-scream woman's role. Last but not least is veteran baddie Brown (HIGHLANDER;

EXTREME PREJUDICE), who creates one of the more memorable and imposing movie villains of the 1980s. Although Spottiswoode misplays a few hands (the sudden revelation of Brown's identity could have been held off a bit longer) and script problems begin to overtake him shortly before the climax, SHOOT TO KILL remains one of the best actioners in recent memory. *(Graphic violence, profanity.)*

p, Ron Silverman, Daniel Petrie, Jr.; d, Roger Spottiswoode; w, Harv Zimmel, Michael Burton, Daniel Petrie, Jr. (based on a story by Harv Zimmel); ph, Michael Chapman (Widescreen, Alpha Cinecolor); ed, Garth Craven, George Bowers; m, John Scott; m/l, Harold Arlen, Ted Koehler; prod d, Richard Sylbert; art d, John Willett; set d, Jim Erickson; spec eff, John Thomas; cos, Richard Bruno; stunts, Fred Waugh; makeup, Joann Wabisca.

Crime	Cas.	(PR:O MPAA:R)

SHORT CIRCUIT 2*   (1988) 110m Turman-Foster Co./Tri-Star c

Fisher Stevens *(Ben Jahrvi)*, Michael McKean *(Fred Ritter)*, Cynthia Gibb *(Sandy Banatoni)*, Jack Weston *(Oscar Baldwin)*, Dee McCafferty *(Saunders)*, David Hemblen *(Jones)*, Tim Blaney *(Voice of Johnny Five)*, Don Lake *(Manic Mike)*, Damon D'Oliveira *(Bones)*, Tito Nunez *(Zorro)*, Jason Kuriloff *(Lil Man)*, Robert La Sardo *(Spooky)*, Lili Francks *(Officer Mendez)*, Wayne Best *(Officer O'Malley)*, Gerry Parkes *(Priest)*, Adam Ludwig *(Hans de Ruyter)*, Rex Hagon *(Dartmoor)*, Rummy Bishop *(News Vendor)*, Richard Comar *(Mr. Slater)*, Tony DeSantis *(Russian Taxi Driver)*, Eric Keenleyside *(Simpson's Truck Driver)*, Phil Jarrett *(Card Hustler)*, Jeremy Ratchford *(Bill)*, Kurt Reis *(Mr. Arnold)*, Garry Robbins *(Francis)*, Ric Sarabia *(Toy Robot Builder)*, Barry Flatman *(Robotic Company CEO)*, Jane Schoettle *(Robotic Executive)*, Carlton Watson *(Robotic Engineer)*, Eve Crawford *(Federal Judge)*, Craig Gardner, Micki Moore *(Art Lovers)*, Sam Moses *(Clothing Store Owner)*, Norwich Duff *(Paramedic)*, Claudette Roach *(Secretary)*, Frank Adamson *(Desk Sergeant)*, Chris Barker *(Bus Driver)*, Peter Shanne *(Entourage Leader)*, James Kileen *(Reporter)*, Patrick Greenwood *(Swat Team Officer)*.

© TRI-STAR

When last we saw No. 5—the Defense Department robot who came to life in SHORT CIRCUIT (1986)—he was escaping to the wide open spaces of Montana with Steve Guttenberg and Ally Sheedy, and the John Badham-directed film was on its way to becoming 1987's most popular home video rental. Little wonder, then, that producers Lawrence Turman and David Foster decided to bring the charming, wide-eyed robot back for this sequel, with veteran TV director Kenneth Johnson replacing Badham, who chose to direct STAKEOUT rather than SHORT CIRCUIT 2. Guttenberg and Sheedy are also absent, but Fisher Stevens, No. 5's East Indian cocreator, isn't. Sacked by Nova Industries for trying to protect the robot in the first film, Stevens now peddles pint-sized models of No. 5 on the streets of an unnamed American "big city." Gibb, a pretty assistant toy buyer for a department store, spots Stevens' high-tech toys and makes an agreement with him and McKean, the huckster who becomes Stevens' partner, to produce 1,000 of the little robots for $50,000. They set up shop in an abandoned warehouse that, unknown to them, also happens to be the starting point for a tunnel being dug by bank teller Weston and his nasty cohorts, who want to steal a valuable collection of diamonds kept in a bank across the street. In an attempt to scare off Stevens and McKean, Weston's henchmen destroy all of the robots they've already built. But just when all looks lost, a big crate arrives from Montana containing No. 5, now preferring to be called Johnny Five. In short order, Five builds the needed robot toys and secures the warehouse. Problems arise, however, when the input-hungry Five learns that he's in a big city. As if the curious Five's forays into the streets didn't get him into enough trouble, McKean decides that there's more money to be made by selling him, triggering a succession of misadventures that includes the robot's hang-gliding descent from the 34th floor of an office building. In the meantime, Stevens has fallen in love with Gibb and awkwardly woos her with Five's assistance. As the film builds to its climax, Weston's cronies lock Stevens and McKean in a freezer, Weston tricks Five into helping pull off the jewel heist, and the thieves then do their best to destroy him. Not too surprisingly, the "near-dead" Five, with some big help from McKean, refuses to give up, and a big chase hurtles the picture to its happy ending.

Despite its success at the box office and as a videocassette, many adults found SHORT CIRCUIT to be as insufferable as children found it enjoyable. The result is just about the same for SHORT CIRCUIT 2, except that the sequel lacks the charm and periodic wit of the original, and, sadly, those elements that grated most in SHORT CIRCUIT are piled on unrelentingly here. Stevens' gerund-speaking malaprops, occasionally funny the first time around, become tiresome very quickly. His inarticulate Indian scientist was mildly offensive as a supporting character; put now at the center of the film, Stevens' Ben becomes a ridiculous ethnic stereotype—cute, yes, and less randy than lovelorn, but unquestionably defaming. Likewise, No. 5's barrage of pop culture references—from commercials to his impression of John Wayne—were amusing in the original, but here they do nothing to develop Johnny Five's character and, worse, aren't funny. The story is strictly formulaic, the romance between Stevens and Gibb is uncompelling, and, in general, the acting is competent but unmemorable. Still, Five (voiced again by Tim Blaney), in those moments when he isn't involved in pop cultural regurgitation, manages to be endearing a la E.T.

What SHORT CIRCUIT 2 does have over its predecessor is the increased mobility and dexterity of Johnny Five, which truly give him a life of his own. Not truly a robot (which, strictly speaking, is a mechanism that interfaces with a computer to perform preprogrammed actions), Five is, in fact, a Remotely Operated Vehicle (ROV) manipulated by radio control transmitters. Designed by Syd Mead, Five was realized by mechanical effects wizard Eric Allard. In the first film, it took nine mechanical "puppeteers" to operate No. 5, but because Allard was able to employ a telemetry suit this time around, only five puppeteers were needed for the sequel. One of the operators wore the telemetry harness, and the movements he made with his upper body were transmitted to the robot and mirrored by it. The other four puppeteers controlled Five's head movements, facial expressions, and mobile base. The result is a stunningly realistic, surprisingly human robot.

Unfortunately, the filmmakers weren't as meticulous in conveying a sense of place. The metropolis in which the film is set remains nameless and the storyline demands only that it be an American city; however, few precautions appear to have been taken to disguise the fact that SHORT CIRCUIT 2 was filmed in Toronto—most notably, no one has bothered to change the Ontario license plates. In a better film, it's unlikely that one would notice (let alone be offended by) such an inconsistency, but the going gets mighty slow after a while in SHORT CIRCUIT 2. Still, younger kids are bound to enjoy this one, though it should be noted that it contains more violence than its predecessor. *(Violence, adult situations.)*

p, David Foster, Lawrence Turman, Gary Foster; d, Kenneth Johnson; w, S.S. Wilson, Brent Maddock; ph, John McPherson (Medallion color); ed, Conrad Buff; m, Charles Fox; prod d, Bill Brodie; art d, Alicia Keywan; set d, Steve Shewchuk; spec eff, Jeff Jarvis; cos, Larry Wells; tech, Eric Allard; stunts, Ken Bates; makeup, Patricia Green.

Comedy	Cas.	(PR:A MPAA:PG)

SHY PEOPLE*½   (1988) 119m Golan-Globus/Cannon c

Jill Clayburgh *(Diana Sullivan)*, Barbara Hershey *(Ruth Sullivan)*, Martha Plimpton *(Grace Sullivan)*, Merritt Butrick *(Mike Sullivan)*, John Philbin *(Tommy Sullivan)*, Don Swayze *(Mark Sullivan)*, Pruitt Taylor Vince *(Paul Sullivan)*, Mare Winningham *(Candy)*, Michael Audley *(Louie)*, Brad Leland *(Larry)*, Tony Epper *(Jake)*, Paul Landry *(Henry)*, Warren Battiste *(Dick)*, Edward Bunker *(Chuck)*, Vladimir Bibic *(Welder)*, Dominic Barto *(Chief)*, Dave Petitjean *(Sheriff)*, William Anderson, David Avne, Ronn Wright *(Policemen)*, Cheryl Starbuck, Claire Acerno *(Stewardesses)*, J. Larry McGill *(Black Man)*, Ernest Tan *(Vietnamese Pimp)*, Jack McGee *(Cab Driver)*, Jack Radosta *(1st Pal)*, Phyllis Guerrini *(Margo)*, Greg Guirard *(Man)*.

Released in Los Angeles for Oscar consideration during the final week of 1987, SHY PEOPLE was finally dumped into theaters in May 1988, a full year after earning Barbara Hershey the Best Actress award at the Cannes Film Festival. (Hershey would win the same honor at the 1988 Cannes festival, sharing her award with her two costars in Chris Menges' A WORLD APART.) A victim of a poor distribution deal made hastily by the financially floundering Cannon Group, SHY PEOPLE threatened to vanish from sight before it was even given a chance to find an audience. The fourth American film from Soviet emigre Andrei Konchalovsky (MARIA'S LOVERS; RUNAWAY TRAIN; and DUET FOR ONE preceded), SHY PEOPLE is about a meeting of two people, and two worlds, which initially appear to be diametrically opposed but which, we learn by the film's end, have more in common than we imagined. The wide-screen film opens with a magnificent panorama of the Manhattan skyline, finally settling in the high-rise apartment of Clayburgh, a reporter for *Cosmopolitan* who lives with Plimpton, her teenage, coke-sniffing daughter. Clayburgh, the very essence of the cosmopolitan Manhattanite, is having a tough time raising her seemingly apathetic daughter, a sexually budding youngster whose drug addiction is perpetuated by her involvement with a 40ish, drug-dealing Frenchman who used to be involved with Clayburgh. Clayburgh's latest journalistic assignment concerns family histories. At her editor's suggestion, she has traced her own roots back to the family black sheep—Uncle Joe, a Louisiana Bayou outlaw. She makes a plane reservation and manages to talk her bored daughter into accompanying her on a visit to her Bayou relatives. After a lengthy boat trip deep into the swamps, Clayburgh and Plimpton, both dressed in trendy, brightly colored, inappropriate Big Apple attire, are dropped off at the dock of the Sullivan family home—a moss-covered, dilapidated, Faulknerian mansion. Living there is Uncle Joe's widowed child-bride, Hershey; her three sons, the semi-retarded Vince ("He's got a button loose," says Hershey), Swayze, the man of the house, and Philbin, who is kept locked in an outdoor shed; and Swayze's very pregnant bride, Winningham. Although Clayburgh introduces herself to Hershey as her cousin, it takes a while for the Bayou woman to trust her, initially believing her to be an IRS agent. As Clayburgh and Plimpton reveal their metrocentricities (Plimpton is armed with a can of "Off" bug spray), their Cajun cousins reveal their backwoods, superstitious ways. Hershey informs her guests that the family is watched over by Joe, though he hasn't been seen for over 15 years. An eerie portrait of the patriarch hangs in the dining room, presiding over their every move. Hershey even keeps a chair for him at the head of the table in which Plimpton mistakenly seats herself. Vince sums up the fears of Bayou life when he produces a pet turtle with two heads—a mutation Hershey blames on the arrival of the oil companies. While Plimpton bops around the Bayou wearing flimsy clothes and exposing her cousins to fashion magazines and a Walkman that plays Elvis Costello, Clayburgh and Hershey flip through a photo album. One person, who appears in many of the pictures, is unidentifiable; his face his been scratched off of every picture. It is Hershey's "dead" son, Mike (Butrick)—a "sinner" who left the family and moved into town and is therefore thought of as dead. Hershey offers no parental forgiveness or "warmth," as Clayburgh suggests she should, countering with her belief that "warmth" is the problem with Yankees like her visitors—for religious fundamentalist Hershey, one must either be "hot or cold," as suggested in Revelations. As their short stay continues, Clayburgh and Plimpton are exposed to some very alien ways. Swayze heads out with gun in hand to take revenge on a local Vietnam vet who insists on poaching his crab traps. Instead of killing the man, Swayze, while drifting quietly in the foggy, late-night swamp, is bashed on the head by an unseen assailant. To avenge this attack on her boy, Hershey heads into the hated town with Clayburgh and Winningham (who wants her mother-in-law to buy her a battery-operated TV) and visits the local police. When police insist they cannot press charges against the vet, Hershey finds her man in a tavern/strip joint, shoots him in the hand, and nearly destroys the bar. She is arrested by police despite the pleas of the tavern owner—Butrick, her "dead" son. Meanwhile, Plimpton squeezes through the bars of the locked shed that imprisons Philbin. Flirting with the likable young man, she gets a kiss out of him, gives him some cocaine, and eventually has sex with him. She also offers some coke to Vince, who runs around with a Confederate flag and lets all the goats loose, and Swayze, who is so aroused by both Plimpton and her fashion magazines that he tries to rape her. She escapes by boat, paddling deep into the swamps. When the boat fills with water and sinks, the traumatized Plimpton is left clinging to a rotted, hollow tree trunk. Soon afterwards, Clayburgh, Hershey, and Winningham return. Clayburgh panics when she cannot find her daughter, but Hershey is more involved in the family battle now raging between Swayze and Philbin—the latter screaming that their father is dead and has been dead for years. At Hershey's orders, Swayze unlocks the shed and nearly beats Philbin to death. Meanwhile, Clayburgh has taken Hershey's boat into the swamps to find her daughter. Speeding along over the misty waters, she hits a partially submerged trunk, is thrown from the boat, and swims to the safety of a nearby tree. The boat continues on, wildly bouncing off the obstacle course of hollowed trunks that jut up through the water's surface. Clayburgh manages to find Plimpton and regain the boat, but not without the help of an ominous shadowed figure that may, or may not, be Uncle Joe's ghost. Later, while preparing to return home, the previously skeptical Clayburgh tells Hershey that she saw the ghost. Hershey explains that "in the swamp, you sees what you want to see." On their return flight home, mother and daughter reconcile as Clayburgh vows to lock Plimpton in a detox center and help her overcome her addiction. Back in the Louisiana, Hershey informs her reunited family that she is offering them the freedom to leave the Bayou if they so desire.

As in his 1985 RUNAWAY TRAIN, Konchalovsky here presents powerful characterizations, beautiful imagery, and philosophical content as entertainment that can appeal to the average filmgoer, but still has enough depth to stand up to critical analysis. SHY PEOPLE is an important, if occasionally heavy-handed, movie that serves simultaneously as an ethnographic film (an examination of cultures), a political film (an allegorical examination of the power held by Joseph Stalin, a very different "Uncle Joe," and the brutality of his tyranny), a religious film (a look at fundamentalism and the reasons people believe as they do), and a film about the power of the family (the strength of the bond between Hershey and Clayburgh). The one strain that is consistent in the film, regardless of how one views it as a whole, is the characters' quest for an unconditional love that is true and pure—a devotion that asks no questions and is built on faith. The Biblical quote from Revelations 3 with which the film ends, "I know thy works, that though art neither cold nor hot, I would thou wert cold or hot. So then because thou art lukewarm, and neither cold nor hot, I will spew thee out of my mouth," is central to the otherwise inexplicable actions of Hershey's character. It is precisely because Hershey's opposite number, Clayburgh, is "lukewarm" that her life has no direction. She must go back, not only to her roots, but to the roots of all humanity—the evolutionary primitivism of the swamps. Having removed herself far from reality by living far atop Manhattan, Clayburgh is no longer in touch with even the most basic human quality—motherhood. Her treatment of her daughter is therefore "lukewarm." She refuses to take a stand, simply allowing Plimpton to carry on without guidance. Plimpton, however, feels a need to be mothered, practically begging at one point for Clayburgh to take away her cocaine. Hershey's idea of motherhood is quite the opposite, never lukewarm. Her philosophy of life is shaped by an incident between her and her husband, Joe, that resulted in her first son's retardation. Pregnant during a flood that threatened to destroy their house, Hershey was ordered by her husband to help fight off the waters. In severe pain and unable to walk, she was punched twice in the stomach by her husband. Fearing that his purge would continue, Hershey rose up and helped fight off the flood. Now Hershey tells a shocked Clayburgh that had Joe not done that the flood would have killed them, destroyed their home, and prevented her three other children from being born. Like Clayburgh, however, Hershey's method of motherhood is only partially effective. What the children of both mothers desire is, if not actual freedom, the acknowledgment that they have freedom if they want it. It is by offering their children the freedom they desire that both Hershey and Clayburgh express their deepest love and reap their greatest reward—their children's love.

With SHY PEOPLE, Konchalovsky has made it clear that he is one of film's great directors of actors. MARIA'S LOVERS survived almost solely because of the fine performances of Nastassja Kinski, Robert Mitchum, Vincent Spano, and Keith Carradine. RUNAWAY TRAIN features some of the best acting seen anywhere, earning Oscar nominations for Jon Voight and Eric Roberts. DUET FOR ONE is watchable chiefly for Julie Andrews' virtuoso performance. Now, in SHY PEOPLE, Konchalovsky gives the already amazing Barbara Hershey a chance to impress once again and reaffirm her position as one of cinema's great actresses. Hershey, despite her false teeth, dingy clothes, and Cajun accent, never appears to be acting. It is as if a documentarian had managed to catch the Bayou child-bride simply going about her daily routine in front of the camera. (Interestingly, Konchalovsky's brother, director Nikita Mikhalkov, directed Marcello Mastroianni in DARK EYES in a role that earned him the Best Actor prize at the 1987 Cannes Festival where Hershey won Best Actress.) Jill Clayburgh, who has made a career out of playing grating characters, does so here to perfection, actually breathing some sympathy into what could have been a cold, cliched character. While the four Bayou sons and Mare Winningham are also all excellent, it is Martha Plimpton who proves the knockout. A wonderfully written child/woman character who bridges the gap between city girl and country girl (she does, after all, have sex with her own cousin), Plimpton is the catalyst for the action, exposing her cousins to aspects of modernity (drugs, rock'n'roll, television) that have been kept hidden from them. Plimpton, the 16-year-old daughter of actors Keith Carradine and Shelly Plimpton who has previously been seen in GOONIES and THE MOSQUITO COAST, is thoroughly enchanting in her role. (The Carradine connection extends also to Hershey, who was once married to David Carradine, thereby making Plimpton Hershey's niece by marriage.)

In addition to the high level of acting, SHY PEOPLE is excellently photographed by Chris Menges, who previously filmed such visually magnificent pictures as THE KILLING FIELDS and THE MISSION and this year cast Hershey in his directorial debut, A WORLD APART. Making great use of the wide-screen format, Menges is able to create some breathtaking compositions, which will, unfortunately, be bastardized on video. Mark Ulano's use of stereo sound is likewise astounding, creating an aural world that compliments Menges' visuals. The electronic score by Tangerine Dream, while not ranking with their best, does add a modern quality to the locales. For some ungodly reason, however, two Tangerine Dream songs (complete with lyrics, an oddity from this usually instrumental group), "Goin' Home" and "Shy People," are included, the latter of which is grossly out of place over the end credits. *(Violence, profanity, sexual situations, substance abuse).*

p, Menahem Golan, Yoram Globus; d, Andrei Konchalovsky; w, Gerard Brach, Andrei Konchalovsky, Marjorie David (based on a story by Andrei Konchalovsky); ph, Chris Menges (Rank color); ed, Alain Jakubowicz; md, Paula Erickson; m/l, Tangerine Dream, Michael Bishop, Gene Miller, Harold Bishop, Shelley Speck, Marvin Hamlisch, Alan Bergman, Marilyn Bergman; prod d, Stephen Marsh; art d, Leslie McDonald; set d, Leslie Morales; spec eff, Cal Acord; cos, Katherine Dover; tech, Greg Guirard; stunts, Michael Adams; makeup, Pat Gerhardt.

Drama **Cas.** **(PR:O MPAA:R)**

SILENCE AT BETHANY, THE † (1988) 90m American Playhouse c

Tom Dahlgren *(Phares Mitgang)*, Richard Fancy *(Elam Swope)*, Dakin Matthews *(Sam Mitgang)*, Mark Moses *(Ira Martin)*, Susan Wilder *(Pauline Mitgang Martin)*, Megan Bellwoar *(Phyllis Mitgang)*, Robert Billbrough *(Junior Mitgang)*, Ann Marie Breen *(Ella Brightbill)*, Faye Brenner *(Rosalie Swope)*, Alex Corcoran *(Levi Froch)*, Allen Fitzpatrick *(Gideon Maust)*, Ginny Graham *(Eunice Mitgang)*, Paul Hartel *(Jake Nissley)*, Duane Hespell *(Grady Mitgang)*, John Hunt *(Minister in Dream)*, Bob Lohrman *(Rowan Brightbill)*, Valerie Long *(Jonas)*, C. Nevin Miller *(Bishop Kleinfelter)*, Suzanne H. Smart *(Dorcas Nissley)*, Terri Treas *(Milly)*, Joe Walker *(Deacon Forney)*, Charlie Walnut *(Cyrus Wengert)*, Dolly Wheaton *(Mrs. Wengert)*, Ann Wilcox *(Ada Mitgang)*.

Set in a Mennonite farm community in Pennsylvania in 1939, this American Playhouse picture revolves around the doctrinal conflict between a liberal, newly ordained minister (Moses) and an older, orthodox bishop (Dahlgran), who also happens to be his wife's uncle. When a local dairy farmer's business faces bankruptcy because the tenets of the church prohibit him from delivering milk on Sunday, Moses is faced with a choice that may have serious consequences for him, his family, and his flock. Shown at several American film festivals in 1988, THE SILENCE AT BETHANY was helmed by Joel Oliansky, an Emmy award-winning scriptwriter who has directed episodes of "Kojak," "Emergency," "Quincy," and "Cagney and Lacey."

p, Tom Cherones, Fred Gerber; d, Joel Oliansky; w, Joyce Keener; ph, Charles Minsky (Foto-Kem color); ed, Pasquale Buba; m, Lalo Schifrin; prod d, Cletus Anderson; spec eff, Gene Grigg; cos, Barbara Anderson; makeup, Jeanee Josefczyk.

Drama **(PR:NR MPAA:NR)**

SILENT ASSASSINS** (1988) 92m Action Bros./Panache-Forum c

Sam J. Jones *(Sam Kettle)*, Linda Blair *(Sara)*, Jun Chong *(Jun Kim)*, Phillip Rhee *(Bernard)*, Bill Erwin *(Dr. London)*, Gustav Vintas *(Kendrick)*, Mako *(Oyama)*, Rebecca Ferrati *(Miss Amy)*, Peter Looney *(Dr. Thomas)*, Elise Briesette *(Betsey)*, Stuart Damon *(General)*, Bill "Superfoot" Wallace *(Colonel)*, Charles Young *(Capt. Cunningham)*, David Colette *(Hasbro)*, Joanna Chong *(Joanna)*, Greg Paik *(Jum Kim's Brother)*, Susan Rhee *(Joanna's Mother)*, Dan Beder *(Danny)*, Karen Witter *(Sushi Bar Girl)*, Ashley Ashton *(Art Gallery Girl)*, Simon Rhee, Tae Ill, Ken Nagayama, Max K., Clark Choi *(IGAs)*, Daniel Dvorsky, Kelly Clayton *(Dr. London's Bodyguards)*, Richard Shin, Frank Young, Howard Ng *(Oyama's Bodyguards)*, Lindsey Erwin *(Police Secretary)*, Eric Megason, Jon Sloan *(CBR Agents)*,

Kim Kahana (*Guard in Compound*), Steve Holin, Carlos Lloyd (*Terrorists in Kendo Studio*), Miriam Ezra, Mimi Yodney (*Girls in Kendo Studio*).

Jones stars as an LA cop who comes out of retirement to avenge his dead partners. The only surviving member of a stakeout team that was ambushed by ex-CIA agent Vintas, Jones steps back into action when Vintas strikes again, kidnaping a research scientist (Erwin) who holds half the formula for a deadly new biological weapon. Vintas' partners in crime are the *Iga*, a clan of ax-wielding Samurai who have fallen on hard times and become professional assassins. Jones is joined in his pursuit by Chong, an ex-South Korean Green Beret-turned-artist who is determined to avenge the death of his brother (hacked to pieces when Erwin was taken hostage) and rescue his six-year-old niece (abducted in the same incident). Meanwhile, Blair, Jones' long-suffering girl friend, tries to persuade him to quit and take a safer job in Colorado. With the *Iga* trying to kill them, Jones and Chong enlist the aid of Chong's family friend Mako, a retired yakuza leader, who promises to locate Vintas' secret hideout. They also try to get the help of Mako's son, Rhee, a kendo expert, but he remains unconvinced until his club is shot up and his girl friend poisoned at a sushi bar. Erwin stalls Vintas' attempts to gain the formula by sabotaging a computer and resisting torture, but when Chong's little niece is threatened, he relents and begins to spill the information. Vintas and his co-conspirators, on orders from their superior (a mysterious man who uses a leopard-shaped cigarette lighter), break into Mako's home and kill the entire household. Mako survives long enough, however, to hand over the location of Vintas' secret hideout to Jones and company, who destroy the base and rescue the hostages. The open-ended final scene has Jones presenting the formula to a pair of Army generals—one of whom uses a leopard-shaped lighter.

Made by a pair of transplanted South Korean filmmakers and released directly to video, this action picture is surprisingly entertaining. Jun Chong and Phillip Rhee produced, costarred, and handled the fight sequences, which are well done and exciting, most notably the melee at Mako's home. Rhee also provides comic relief, and Gustav Vintas makes a slimy villain. Other participants of note include Playmate model Rebecca Ferrati, as the statuesque assassin, and Linda Blair, who unfortunately disappears half way through the film. Director Lee Doo-yong keeps the film moving quickly along, pacing the action sequences nicely, aided by an excellent score. The picture's only real drawback is its production values, including the poorly recorded dialog. (*Violence, gore effects, profanity.*)

p, Jun Chong, Phillip Rhee; d, Lee Doo-yong, Scott Thomas; w, Will Gates, Ada Lin (based on a story by John Bruner); ph, Son Hyun-Chae (Foto-Kem color); ed, William Hoy; m, Paul Gilman; art d, John Nakayama; spec eff, Richard Johnson, John Eggett; cos, Liz Warner, Diana Smith; ch, Jun Chong; stunts, Phillip Rhee, Kim Kahana; makeup, Cida Ricciotti, Mel Slavick, Jeff Kirsch.

Action	Cas.	(PR:O MPAA:R)

SISTER SISTER★★   (1988) 91m Odyssey/NW c

Eric Stoltz (*Matt Rutledge*), Jennifer Jason Leigh (*Lucy Bonnard*), Judith Ivey (*Charlotte Bonnard*), Dennis Lipscomb (*Sheriff Cleve Doucet*), Anne Pitoniak (*Mrs. Bettleheim*), Benjamin Mouton (*Etienne LeViolette*), Natalia Nogulich (*Fran Steuben*), Richard Minchenberg (*Lenny Steuben*), Bobby Pickett (*Roger*), Jason Saucier (*Jud Nevins*), Jerry Leggio (*Mr. Bonnard*), Fay Cohn (*Mrs. Bonnard*), Ashley McMurry (*Young Lucy*), Ben Cook (*Young Matt*), Casey Levron (*Young Etienne*), Aggie the Dog (*Beau*).

© NEW WORLD

SISTER SISTER is pure southern gothic horror (in the tradition of HUSH . . . HUSH, SWEET CHARLOTTE) that begins promisingly enough, but then quickly disintegrates into a dull, predictable, and at times absurd chiller. The film, set in the Louisiana bayous, focuses on two sisters (Ivey and Leigh) who live together in a giant old plantation house left them by their parents. Having turned the old mansion into a bed-and-breakfast (which is failing), Ivey devotes much of her time to caring for the younger and more "delicate" Leigh. It is hinted that Leigh has had some emotional problems in the past, and because Ivey is afraid that separation from her sister will cause a relapse, she refuses the marriage proposals of kindly local sheriff Lipscomb. Leigh, a pale, lonely girl, spends much of her time fantasizing about ghosts and

dreaming up "Harlequin Romance" -style sexual scenarios with handyman Mouton, who she has known since they were children. All this sexual repression threatens to explode when handsome young Congressional aide Stoltz arrives on holiday. Leigh is very attracted to Stoltz, and he to her, much to the consternation of both Ivey and Mouton. With Ivey warning Leigh to stay away from Stoltz and Mouton warning Stoltz to keep clear of Leigh, the blossoming relationship seems doomed. But Stoltz persists, and Leigh begins to rebel against Ivey by insisting she feels fine and refusing to take her medicine. When Mouton sees the couple kiss, he appears to go over the edge, and when Leigh's beloved old dog is killed on that night the handyman is the prime suspect. While sheriff Lipscomb pursues Mouton, Stoltz and Leigh blatantly defy Ivey and make love. Ivey watches them through a hole drilled in the attic floor, and it quickly becomes apparent that she's the *true* loony. In a flashback, we see Ivey on her 18th birthday, about to be raped by her boy friend. Little Leigh happens upon the scene and the crazed rapist attacks her too. Ivey grabs a knife and accidentally kills him. Leigh notices the figure of a boy—who has witnessed the whole thing—standing in the shadows and assumes it's Mouton, keeping this a secret from Ivey until just recently in the story. After sex, Stoltz returns to his room. Shortly thereafter, Mouton is pursued through the bayous by an unseen attacker. When he is killed by several arrows shot into his body, we see that none other than Stoltz is the murderer. As it happens, Stoltz is the little brother of the rapist Ivey killed, and it was *he* who was standing in the shadows those many years before. Now it is left up to Ivey, who of course realizes the truth, to convince Leigh that her lover is the murderer. Leigh refuses to believe it, and Stoltz almost drowns her in the swamp, but suddenly, inexplicably, hands from beneath the bayou reach out and yank the evil Stoltz under. Leigh looks and sees that the ghosts of the bayou, led by Mouton, have protected her.

A handsomely mounted production, beautifully shot in widescreen format by cinematographer Stephen M. Katz, SISTER, SISTER is easy to look at, but hard to take. Directed and coscripted by STRANGE INVADERS writer Bill Condon in his feature directorial debut, the picture is all misty mood and little else. The twists and turns of the narrative, and the psychological complexities of the characters, are terribly cliched and painfully rudimentary. If anyone viewing the film hasn't figured out who the killer is after the first half-hour, he or she should be made to sit with a dunce cap on their heads and watch the entire Hitchcock *oeuvre* —as director Condon obviously has done. Luckily, Condon has cast two excellent actresses in the leads. Judith Ivey and Jennifer Jason Leigh are impressive here, striking all the right contrasts and similarities as two adult siblings sharing the same house. Both characters are full of strange contradictions, and Ivey and Leigh seize the opportunity to explore their ambiguous depths, with Leigh especially effective as a young woman struggling to free herself from her sister's domination. There are plenty of nice character touches as well, including Ivey's way of sneaking a smoke whenever Leigh and Lipscomb aren't looking. What little humorous relief there is is provided by a trio of obnoxious New Jersey tourists who show up at the mansion to stay the night; unfortunately, the characters are potentially offensive Jewish stereotypes and only the savvy, ultimately sympathetic performance of Anne Pitoniak as the matriarch of the tiny clan saves this misguided bit of comedy from going too far. Surprisingly, the weakest major performance comes from the usually excellent Eric Stoltz (MASK; SOME KIND OF WONDERFUL). Unconvincing as a southerner and rather bland to boot, even as the killer, Stoltz seem lost in his underwritten role. There is absolutely no hint of the sinister in his face, and when he is lit to appear scary and menacing the effect is almost comical. While Bill Condon should be commended for trying to steer the horror film away from the routine slasher fare that has nearly ruined the genre, he has failed to notice that he drove it right back into the ranks of boring gothic thrillers that slasher prototype HALLOWEEN rebelled against in the first place. (*Violence, nudity, sexual situations, profanity.*)

p, Walter Coblenz; d, Bill Condon; w, Bill Condon, Joel Cohen, Ginny Cerrella; ph, Stephen M. Katz (DeLuxe Color); ed, Marion Rothman; m, Richard Einhorn; m/l, Darrel Higginbotham, J.C. Phillips, Bob Boykin; prod d, Richard Sherman; art d, Philip Peters; set d, Cynthia Redman; spec eff, Wayne Beauchamp, Paul Hickerson; cos, Bruce Finlayson; stunts, Harry Wowchuk; makeup, Gabor Kernyaiszky.

Horror/Thriller	Cas.	(PR:O MPAA:R)

SISTERHOOD †   (1988) 76m Santa Fe/Concorde c

Rebecca Holden (*Alee*), Chuck Wagner (*Mikal*), Lynn-Holly Johnson (*Marya*), Barbara Hooper (*Vera*), Henry Strzalkowski (*Jon*), Robert Dryer (*Lord Barah*), David Light, Jim Moss, Anthony East, Tom McNeeley.

Here's yet another cheapo post-apocalyptic science-fiction film, this time centering on a group of female warriors with magical powers (led by Holden and Hooper) who are determined to fight against the warmongering males who survived the big bang and held many of their sisters captive. Faced with a trek across the deadly Forbidden Zone, the gals must fend off attacks by assorted mutants and other baddies before realizing their goal. B-movie queen Lynn-Holly Johnson plays a young lady who can communicate telepathically with her pet hawk and is eager to join the Sisterhood. This was given a fleeting theatrical bow before turning up on videocassette.

p, Cirio H. Santiago; d, Cirio H. Santiago; w, Thomas McKelvey Cleaver; ph, Ricardo Remias; ed, Edgar Viner; md, Jun Latonio; prod d, Avellana; art d, Ronnie Cruz.

Science Fiction	Cas.	(PR:NR MPAA:R)

'68*½ (1988) 98m Sixty-Eight/NW c

Eric Larson *(Peter Szabo)*, Robert Locke *(Sandy Szabo)*, Sandor Tecsi *(Zoltan Szabo)*, Anna Dukasz *(Zsuzsa Szabo)*, Miran Kwun *(Alana Chan)*, Terra Vandergaw *(Vera Kardos)*, Shony Alex Braun *(Tibor Kardos)*, Donna Pecora *(Piroska Kardos)*, Jan Nemec *(Dezso Horvath)*, Rusdi Lane *(Bela Csontos)*, Nike Doukas *(Beatrice)*, Neil Young *(Westy)*, Elizabeth De Charay *(Gizi Horvath)*, Sandy Bull *(Gang Leader)*, Anya Lem *(Isadora)*, Maureen McVerry *(Rusty)*, John Cippolina *(Rock Band Leader)*, Richard Butterfield *(Editor)*, Lee Carrau *(Professor)*, Roger Hart *(Percy Millard)*, Jim Russell *(Teamster)*, John Kovacs *(Bartender)*, Taylor Phelps *(Golfer)*, Cary Jay Silberman *(New Year's Eve Fat Man)*, Max Proudfoot *(Skinny)*, Paul Pedroli *(Client)*, Michael Sullivan *(Roosevelt)*, Ngaio Bealum *(Noah)*, Darrell Williams *(Leon)*, Tom Owens *(Induction Centre Physician)*, Joel Parker *(Protester)*.

Set during the watershed year of the turbulent 1960s, this low-budget, independently produced film presents its personal coming-of-age story against the backdrop of an America undergoing its own sociopolitical rite of passage. It begins with black-and-white footage of the 1956 Hungarian Revolution and then shifts to San Francisco in 1968, introducing the Szabo family. Patriarch Tecsi and his wife, Dukasz, who fled Hungary during the revolution, are in the process of opening a small restaurant with the help of their sons. Larson, the older of the two, is a student at the University of California-Berkeley, a fledgling journalist who is trying to make sense of the political upheaval that surrounds him. His younger brother, Locke, lives at home and is more involved with the running of the restaurant, though Tecsi considers him irresponsible. Impetuously, Locke becomes involved with Vandergaw, the pretty daughter of one of the Hungarian emigres who frequent the restaurant, and, over his father's initial objections, they become engaged. When Larson attempts to use an article he has written both as a campus newspaper piece and for a class assignment, he is bounced out of school for a semester (for what, illogically, amounts to self-plagiarism). Not wanting his father to find out, he takes a job in a motorcycle shop run by reactionary long-hair Young and continues his journalistic exploration of the movement, volunteering to do campaign work for Robert Kennedy and becoming involved with fellow RFK worker Kwun. In the course of events, he runs afoul of both Young and the Hell's Angels, who rob Young's store; meanwhile, Locke decides that he is gay, volunteers for the Army, and then decides that he wants no part of Vietnam, using a well-timed kiss at the induction center to make sure that Uncle Sam will have nothing to do with him. All of this is too much for Tecsi, whose life has already been complicated by the affair he is having with his waitress, and who cannot understand his sons' rejection of the society and values for which he and his wife fled their homeland. When he takes ill, his sons take over and transform Tecsi's struggling cafe into a hot spot, though Larson knows that he wants more out of life.

These personal dramas are interwoven with the larger drama unfolding on the national and international stage and, generally, witnessed by Larson on television (he always seems to be in front of a TV just as the big events are occurring). Lyndon Johnson's decision not to run for re-election, the assassinations of Martin Luther King, Jr., and Robert F. Kennedy, the street fighting outside the Democratic convention in Chicago, the Prague Spring (see THE UNBEARABLE LIGHTNESS OF BEING), and the civil rights struggle are interwoven with a portrayal of a burgeoning counterculture. '68 does an adequate job of evoking its period, but writer-director Steven Kovacs, who has based the film on his own experience as an immigrant's son during the 60s, has tried to cram so many events from that extraordinarily eventful year into the film, tried to touch so many bases in his portrait of a wildly diverse, rapidly shifting culture, that his characters never develop beyond caricatures. Arthur Penn's FOUR FRIENDS (1981) covered similar ground, but while his 60s backdrop was essential his film, it remained a context for the actions of the characters and never became a substitute for motivation or overwhelmed the characters. In '68, on the other hand, Kovacs relies too much on images of their time to explain the actions of his characters, and never really lets the audience see *where they are coming from* as people. Likewise, his portrayal of the Hungarian expatriate community is colorful and amusing, but never particularly insightful. The performances are adequate, though somewhat uneven, with no real standouts, and singer-songwriter Neil Young tackles a more ambitious role than his truck driver cameo in Alan Rudolph's MADE IN HEAVEN, but unfortunately delivers a kind of one-glare performance. Those interested 60s nostalgia will find plenty to interest them here, if little to aid their understanding the period; however, those looking for a profound exploration of generational struggles (immigrant or otherwise) or for a complex coming-of-age film will do better to look elsewhere. Songs include "For What It's Worth" (Stephen Stills, performed by Buffalo Springfield), "In the Midnight Hour" (Cropper, Pickett, performed by Wilson Pickett), "Somebody to Love" (Grace Slick, performed by Jefferson Airplane), "A Thing Called Love" (Joe McDonald), "I Wait for You at Seven" (Lajos Lajtai, Istvan Bekeffy), "Smouldering Cigarette" (Tamas Hegedus, Gyorgy G. Denes), "Green Onions" (Jones, Cropper, Jackson, Stineberg, performed by Booker T. and the MGs), "Stone Free", "Wind Cries Mary" (Jimi Hendrix, performed by Hendrix), "Piece of My Heart" (Berns, Ragavoy, performed by Janis Joplin), "Twin Fiddles" (John Gallagher, performed by Terra Vandergaw and Fly by Night), "I-Feel-Like-I'm-Fixin'-to-Die Rag" (MacDonald, performed by Country Joe and the Fish), "Susie Q (Dale Hawkins, Stan Lewis, Eleanor Broadwater, performed by Creedence Clearwater Revival). *(Nudity, profanity, sexual situations, violence.)*

p, Dale Djerassi, Isabel Maxwell, Steven Kovacs; d, Steven Kovacs; w, Steven Kovacs; ph, Daniel Lacambre (Monaco Color); ed, Cari Coughlin; m, John Cipollina, Shony Alex Braun, Johann Strauss; m/l, Stephen Stills, Steve Cropper, Wilson Pickett, Grace Slick, Joe McDonald, Lajos Lajtai, Istvan Bekeffy, Tamas Hegedus, Gyorgy G. Denes, Jimi Hendrix, John Gallagher, Dale Hawkins, Stan Lewis, Eleanor Broadwater; art d, Joshua Koral; set d, Kris Boxell; spec eff, Robert Kaiser; stunts, Rocky Capella.

Drama **Cas.** **(PR:O MPAA:R)**

SKELETON COAST † (1988) 98m Walanar-Breton/Silvertree c

Ernest Borgnine *(Col. Smith)*, Robert Vaughn *(Col. Schneider)*, Oliver Reed *(Capt. Simpson)*, Herbert Lom *(Elia)*, Daniel Greene *(Rick Weston)*, Leon Isaac Kennedy *(Chuck)*, Simon Sabela *(Gen. Sekatri)*, Nancy Mulford *(Sam)*, Peter Kwong, Robin Townsend, Arnold Vosloo, Larry Taylor.

Borgnine heads a commando squad battling Cuban and East German forces along the Angola-Namibia border, where Borgnine's son, a CIA operative, is being held and tortured by East German colonel Vaughn (presumably, because of *glasnost*, the Soviets are no longer marketable movie bad guys). Not suprisingly, since the film is set (and photographed) in Southwest Africa, there's a subplot about a diamond mine.

p, Harry Alan Towers; d, John "Bud" Cardos; w, Nadia Calliou (based on a story by Peter Welbeck [Harry Alan Towers]); ph, Hanro Mohr; ed, Allan Morrison, Mac Errington; m, Colin Shapiro, Barry Bekker; prod d, Leonardo Coen Cagli; stunts, Reo Ruiters.

Action/Adventure **Cas.** **(PR:NR MPAA:R)**

SLAUGHTERHOUSE*½ (1988) 85m American Artists-Slaughterhouse/Manson c

Sherry Bendorf *(Liz Borden)*, Don Barrett *(Lester Bacon)*, William Houck *(Sheriff)*, Joe Barton *(Buddy)*, Jane Higginson *(Annie)*, Eric Schwartz *(Skip)*, Jeff Grossi *(Buzz)*.

With SLAUGHTERHOUSE, director Rick Roessler has tried to capture the same mix of horror and humor that Tobe Hooper's classic TEXAS CHAINSAW MASSACRE (SLAUGHTERHOUSE's obvious role model) achieved, but delivers a film that falls far short of those high standards, despite some obvious talent behind the camera. Barrett plays the owner of a long-closed pig slaughterhouse. The land it sits on is valuable and when competitors offer to buy him out Barrett refuses. The businessmen are upset, as is Barrett, who, with the help of his obese son, Barton, begins to kill off his perceived enemies one by one. The typical subplot shows local teens Bendorf, Higginson, Schwartz, and Grossi living it up on a four-day weekend lark. They stumble upon the slaughterhouse and go exploring, eventually running into Barton, and the rest is pretty predictable.

Although a typical slasher film, SLAUGHTERHOUSE offers a few moments of genuine fright. Roessler presents Barton's character as an unstoppable killing monster who communicates only through pig grunts and groans. The result is unsettling, especially when the 370-pound Barton starts swinging his oversize mallet. The last 15 minutes are especially tense and well paced. It's obvious that Roessler has talent (his visual technique is quite good) but it's a shame that talent is invested in a movie that has little else to set it apart from the horde of slasher films available. *(Graphic violence, profanity.)*

p, Ron Matonak; d, Rick Roessler; w, Rick Roessler; ph, Richard Benda (Cinema Color); ed, Sergio Uribe; m, Joseph Garrison; m/l, Vantage Point; prod d, Michael Scaglione; spec eff, Barney Burman, Mark Lane; stunts, Mike Sharkey.

Horror **Cas.** **(PR:O MPAA:R)**

SLAUGHTERHOUSE ROCK* (1988) 90m First American-Arista/Arista c

Nicholas Celozzi *(Alex Gardner)*, Tom Reilly *(Richard Gardner)*, Donna Denton *(Carolyn Harding)*, Toni Basil *(Sammy Mitchell)*, Hope Marie Carlton *(Krista Halpern)*, Steven Brian Smith *(Jack)*, Ty Miller *(Marty)*, Al Fleming *(The Commandant)*.

Confused and at times incomprehensible, SLAUGHTERHOUSE ROCK tries so hard to include a little bit of everything that it ends up delivering nothing. This film is a wreck. Celozzi (son of the car dealer known to Chicago TV viewers) is a student having horrible dreams, dreams of a prison plagued by the dead in which he is an inmate. These visions grow so disturbing that they begin to interfere with his everyday life. With the help of his brother, Reilly, and his girl friend, Denton, Celozzi seeks the guidance of a local expert in the occult who deciphers that the place of his dreams is the abandoned island of Alcatraz. The instructor suggests that Celozzi go to the island and face his fear head on, whereupon his nightmares should cease. That night, backed up by a few wise-cracking friends, Celozzi heads out to the island and encounters the ghost of dead rock star Basil, who explains that Alcatraz is haunted by the evil spirit of US cavalry commandant Mordecai G. Langston, a good officer turned bad (it seems he had a thing for eating people raw). It is up to Celozzi to kill the demon and save his friends, who, one by one, are being killed and/or possessed by the rampaging beast. Eventually, Celozzi comes through by opening a door to a brilliant, blinding white light that torches the spirit and frees the island of its evil.

This movie is all over the place. One moment it is about a young man to deal with his terrifying nightmares, the next instant it is about a dead rock star chasing down evil spirits. For its first 20 minutes or so, SLAUGHTERHOUSE ROCK is a serious-minded horror tale (and a pretty promising one at that), then, when the group of kids arrives on Alcatraz, the film switches gears and decides it wants to be a comedy reminiscent of John Landis' AMERICAN WEREWOLF IN LONDON and Tim Burton's BEETLEJUICE. This switch is irritating and finally damaging to a film that asks its audience to take an already implausible story seriously. The overloaded premise doesn't help, either. Instead of a crisp, clean narrative, the filmmakers opt to bring in rock star Basil and her dead band to cloud matters up. The movie eventually becomes boring, then exhausting as it falls into the obvious patterns (traps?) of the genre. Not only is it muddled, SLAUGHTERHOUSE ROCK is not scary—quite a problem in a horror film. Songs include: "The Only One" (Mark Mothersbaugh, performed by Toni Basil), "Man Turned Inside Out," "Set Me Free" (Mothersbaugh, performed by Devo), "Part of You" (Mothersbaugh, Gerald V. Casale, performed by Devo). *(Graphic violence, sexual situations, profanity.)*

p, Louis George; d, Dimitri Logothetis; w, Ted Landon; ph, Nicholas Von Sternberg; ed, Daniel Gross; m/l, Mark Mothersbaugh, Gerald V. Castle; prod d, Peter Paul Raubertas.

Horror	Cas.	(PR:O MPAA:R)

SLEEPAWAY CAMP 2: UNHAPPY CAMPERS zero   (1988) 80m Double Helix c

Pamela Springsteen *(Angela Baker)*, Brian Patrick Clarke *(T.C.)*, Renee Estevez *(Molly)*, Walter Gotell *(Uncle John)*, Susan Marie Snyder *(Mare)*, Heather Binion *(Phoebe)*, Tony Higgins, Terry Hobbs, Kendall Bean, Valerie Hartman, Julie Murphy, Carol Chambers, Amy Fields.

Camp Rolling Hills has a problem. It seems that all of the organization's bad kids are being murdered in every grisly way imaginable: slashed, drilled, beaten, choked —and, on one occasion, drowned in an outhouse. But what exactly are "bad kids"? They are the ones who smoke, drink, swear, and fornicate at every opportunity, of course, and Rolling Hills is full of these brats. One by one, they are taught their lesson by Springsteen (yes, Bruce's younger sister), a harsh yet cheerful counselor who lives by the motto, "Keep your morals strong and you'll never go wrong." As the kids are murdered and the other counselors begin to wonder about their diminishing enrollment, Springsteen explains that she has sent the missing miscreants home for breaking the camp rules. Well, this gets her fired, and the film's nice couple (nice because they haven't "done it" yet) decide to comfort her. Following Springsteen into the woods, Estevez (yes, one of the famous clan) and Higgins discover the secret shed where Springsteen keeps the bodies and are then captured. Higgins eventually discovers that Springsteen is the killer from the previous film (after having had a sex-change operation), but, before he has time to pat himself on the back for that brilliant deduction, Springsteen cuts his head off. Estevez gets away and it's time for the big chase scene. Estevez finally loses her pursuer and, as she stumbles along a deserted road, she waves down an approaching pickup. Surprise! It's Springsteen driving the truck! She bellows, "Howdy Partner!" and Estevez screams. The End.

SLEEPAWAY CAMP 2 is a tired, lame excuse for a film—a shameless rip-off of FRIDAY THE 13TH (which in itself doesn't win any awards for originality) that is as exhausted as its title suggests. The acting is limp, the execution uninspired. This isn't a movie, it's a show reel for the special-effects man. Besides the numerous gallons of blood, the film has everything required of a typical slasher opus: promiscuous teens, bare breasts, loud music, and a panty raid—although the film does takes one step into originality in introducing the "jock raid." SLEEPAWAY CAMP 2 went straight to the home video market without a theatrical release. *(Graphic violence, nudity.)*

p, Jerry Silva, Michael A. Simpson; d, Michael A. Simpson; w, Fritz Gordon (based on a story idea by Robert Hiltzik); ph, Bill Mills (Cinefilm color); ed, John David Allen; m, James Oliverio; art d, Frank Galline; spec eff, Bill Johnson; stunts, Lonnie Smith.

Horror	Cas.	(PR:O MPAA:R)

SLIME CITY †   (1988) 85m Slime City/Slime City c

Robert C. Sabin *(Alex)*, Mary Huner *(Lori/Nicole)*, T.J. Merrick *(Jerry)*, Dick Biel *(Irish)*, Jane Reibel *(Lizzy)*, Bunny Levine *(Ruby)*, Dennis Embry *(Roman)*, Marilyn Oran *(Selina)*.

Shot on 16mm stock with a budget of $50,000, this ultra-cheap horror spoof turned up on the midnight show circuit in New York City and promptly vanished to await rebirth on the boob tube. Borrowing the rough concept from David Cronenberg's THEY CAME FROM WITHIN (1976), the film is set in an apartment building that becomes a living hell after a crazed cultist turned its inhabitants into prismatic slime monsters that ooze into humans and possess them. Unwitting college student Sabin signs the lease and moves in, to soon become one of "them."

p, Gregory Lamberson, Peter Clark, Marc Makowski; d, Gregory Lamberson; w, Gregory Lamberson; ph, Peter Clark (Lab-link Color); ed, Gregory Lamberson, Britton Petrucelly; m, Robert Tomaro; prod d, Bonnie Brinkley; spec eff, J. Scott Coulter, Tom Lauten.

Horror/Comedy		(PR:NR MPAA:NR)

SOMEONE TO LOVE**   (1988) 110m International Rainbow Picture/Rainbow-Castle Hill c

Orson Welles *(Danny's Friend)*, Henry Jaglom *(Danny Sapir)*, Andrea Marcovicci *(Helen Eugene)*, Michael Emil *(Mickey Sapir)*, Sally Kellerman *(Edith Helm)*, Oja Kodar *(Yelena)*, Stephen Bishop *(Blue)*, Dave Frishberg *(Harry)*, Geraldine Baron, Ronee Blakley, Barbara Flood, Pamela Goldblum, Robert Hallak, Kathryn Harrold, Monte Hellman, Jeremy Paul Kagan, Michael Kaye, Miles Kreuger, Amnon Meskin, Sunny Meyer, Peter Rafelson, Ora Rubens, Katherine Wallach.

Although painters' self-portraits and writers' autobiographies are greeted with enthusiasm and viewed as a way to better understand the artist, this has not been the

case in filmmaking. While there are exceptions (Jean Cocteau's THE TESTAMENT OF ORPHEUS, Woody Allen's STARDUST MEMORIES, and Federico Fellini's INTERVISTA), most filmmakers prefer to hide behind characters and drama. Even those directors who are viewed as being the most personal (Francois Truffaut, Martin Scorsese, Andrei Tarkovsky) veil their beliefs and philosophies with actors and fiction. It is precisely because of Henry Jaglom's refusal to hide himself in SOMEONE TO LOVE that this film is such a resounding success.

Written and directed by Jaglom, the film also stars him as a director named Danny who happens to make movies identical to Jaglom's own. (Jaglom's use of a character name here seems to be more for the benefit of the audience—who are still more comfortable with fiction than documentary—than as a mask for himself.) At the start of the film, he and his girl friend (played by Jaglom's longtime companion, Marcovicci) are beset with a romantic dilemma. He wants to spend the night at her place, but she refuses to submit to this symbol of commitment. Later, he meets with his brother (Emil, Jaglom's real-life brother and the film's executive producer), a talkative real estate developer who has never been married and is himself afraid to commit to anyone. Jaglom's own lack of fulfillment and his brother's loneliness prompt the director to throw a Valentine's Day party for all his lonely friends—those who are either divorced or have never been married. Without explaining the purpose of the gathering, he invites them to a beautiful old movie palace (Santa Monica's Mayfair) which is about to be shuttered as a result of Emil's real estate dealings. The guests arrive—a well-known movie star (Kellerman), a semi-famous pop singer (Bishop), a jazz pianist (Frishberg), an elegant European woman (Kodar, Orson Welles' longtime companion), and Marcovicci. Others who mingle about in the background are Ronee Blakely, Kathryn Harrold, Monte Hellman, and Jeremy Paul Kagan. There's also a mysterious presence that appears, seemingly at will, at the back of the movie theater—Welles. Armed with a camera crew, Jaglom asks his guests a number of questions: Why are you lonely? Do you mind being alone? Have you always been alone? Have your childhood dreams of adulthood materialized? Will you ever find someone to love? Mixed in with these personal testimonials is the characters' ongoing melodrama. One guest is attracted to Kodar, who, in turn, is attracted to Jaglom, who is still deeply in love with Marcovicci. A member of the camera crew is enamored of Kellerman, but she is preoccupied with her recent split with her husband. Bishop, who plays a baby blue guitar and sings "When Will the Right One Come Along?," asks Kellerman if she wants to have "major sex." By the end of the film, Jaglom and all his female guests have taken the stage; however, he is still no closer to answering his question than before. The camera cuts to the "cheap seats" where Welles is sitting in the last row, smoking a huge cigar. With Jaglom still on the stage, he and Welles converse about relationships, the role of woman in today's society and throughout history, the sexual revolution, and the view of women as slaves. Jaglom then asks Welles how to end his film. Finally, Welles just looks into the camera and says, "Cut!"

More than a film about making a film or a 109-minute group therapy session, SOMEONE TO LOVE is a brilliant example of a filmed diary. Despite the fact that one may not agree with the questions asked or the responses given, the structure and goal of the film are ones which have rarely been approached. Even if one hates Jaglom as a director, actor, and/or interviewer, the personal approach of his technique is undeniable. SOMEONE TO LOVE exists somewhere between the introspection of Woody Allen (a comparison which has no doubt overstayed its welcome with Jaglom) and the introspection of director Jean Rouch's documentary masterpiece CHRONIQUE D'UN ETE (Chronicle of a Summer). What it shares with Allen's films is self-examination, the overwhelming sense that the search for a perfect relationship is a hopeless one, and the adoration of women. What it shares with Rouch are its documentary explorations, its straightforward questioning (Rouch asked, "Are you happy?"; Jaglom asks, "Are you lonely?"), and its reflexivity (both films show us the audience and the theater).

There is much in SOMEONE TO LOVE that will turn away viewers. Some scenes are difficult to watch because they are unpolished. Some characters are embarrassing. Jaglom's probing is often abrasive and inconsiderate—a view which is best expressed by Kodar, who nevertheless manages to be the most honest of those interviewed. Most disturbing are the musical interludes, thrown into the film sporadically as entertaining morsels that help ease any audience tension. While most of the film distances the audience, these musical numbers reach out and try to soothe the viewer. Marcovicci's torch song is likable enough, but Jaglom could have done a service by leaving Bishop's on the cutting room floor.

Notwithstanding Jaglom's brilliance and honesty, the reason most viewers will see SOMEONE TO LOVE is the presence of Welles, in his final film appearance. Moreover, the film is " dedicated with love to Orson Welles,"the director whom many, including Jaglom, consider to be one of the greatest geniuses of the cinema. He sits in the back of the theater declaring his beliefs, serving as Jaglom's mentor, guiding him from the first frame of his film to the last. Like the theater which faces demolition, Welles is a part of the past. To Welles it is not a bad sign that the old theater is to be torn down and replaced, simply an evolutionary step no different than the sexual revolution. Throughout SOMEONE TO LOVE, Jaglom expresses and questions his loneliness. By the end of the film, we realize that he is not lonely because he faces losing Marcovicci, or because the grand old theater is facing the wrecking ball. He is lonely because Orson is dead—his friend and mentor is no longer in the cheap seats to shout his comments to the stage. Shown in 1987 at the Cannes Film Festival, released theatrically in 1988. Songs include " Someone to Love"(Diane Bulgarelli, performed by Andrea Marcovicci), " Looking For The Right One"(Stephen Bishop, performed by Bishop), " Listen Here"(Dave Frishberg, performed by Frishberg), " Sure Thing"- (Jerome Kern, Ira Gershwin, performed by Frishberg), " Long Ago and Far Away"(Kern, Gershwin). (Profanity).

p, M.H. Simonsons; d, Henry Jaglom; w, Henry Jaglom; ph, Hanania Baer (DeLuxe Color); ed, Ruth Wald; m/l, Diane Bulgarelli, Stephen Bishop, Dave Frishberg, Jerome Kern, Ira Gershwin.

Comedy/Drama   Cas.   (PR:A MPAA:R)

SORORITY BABES IN THE SLIMEBALL BOWL-O-RAMA † (1988) 78m Titan/Urban Classics c

Linnea Quigley (Spider), Michelle Bauer (Lisa), Andras Jones (Calvin), Robin Rochelle (Babs), Brinke Stevens (Taffy), Kathi Obrecht (Rhonda), Carla Baron (Frankie), Hal Havins (Jimmie), John Stuart Wildman (Keith), George (Buck) Flower (Janitor), Michael D. Sonye (The Imp's Voice).

One of the last gasps of the now-defunct Empire Pictures, this picture wound up being released through their subsidiary, Urban Classics, before beating a hasty retreat to the home video shelves. Originally titled THE IMP before Empire head Charles Band bestowed the current moniker, the story follows three college nerds who peek in on the kinky initiation rites of a sorority house. Caught by the girls, the lads are forced to do penance by accompanying pledges Bauer and Stevens to a local bowling alley, where they are to steal a trophy. When the thieves accidentally drop the trophy, a surly genie pops out and grants each of the kids a wish. The nasty little bugger tricks the girls, however, and turns them into monsters—whereupon the real fun begins. Female leads Michelle Bauer and Linnea Quigley also are featured in the similarly unforgettably titled, HOLLYWOOD CHAINSAW HOOKERS.

p, David DeCoteau, John Schouweiler; d, David DeCoteau; w, Sergei Hasenecz; ph, Stephen Ashley Blake (Foto-Kem Color); ed, Barry Zetlin, Tom Meshelski; m, Guy Moon; md, Jonathan Scott Bogner; prod d, Royce Mathew; spec eff, Craig Caton.

Comedy/Horror   Cas.   (PR:NR MPAA:R)

SOUS LE SOLEIL DE SATAN (SEE: UNDER SATAN'S SUN, 1988, Fr.)

SOUTH OF RENO † (1988) 94m Open Road-Pendulum/Castle Hill c

Jeffrey Osterhage (Martin Clark), Lisa Blount (Anette Clark), Joe Phelan (Hector), Lewis Van Bergen (Willard), Julia Montgomery (Susan), Brandis Kemp (Brenda), Danitza Kingsley (Louise), Mary Grace Canfield (Manager of Motel), Bert Remsen (Howard Stone).

SOUTH OF RENO is the low-budget, independent feature film debut of Polish-Canadian director Mark Rezyka—a veteran helmer of rock videos. Set in the American desert, the film follows dull-witted railroad employee Osterhage as he wastes his life away in his remote shack with his bored wife, Blount. Spending most of his time staring at his state-of-the-art Sony television, which only receives one channel—and poorly at that—Osterhage dreams with his buddy, Phelan, of taking a trip to the bright lights of Reno, 200 miles to the north. Osterhage gets so lonely that he frequently scatters glass and nails on the highway near his home in the hopes that hapless motorists with blown tires will be detained long enough for him to strike up conversations with them. Blount, meanwhile, is engaging in a rather flagrant affair with a surly auto mechanic, Van Bergen. When Phelan finally gets up enough nerve to go to Reno, Osterhage stays behind, content with the private Reno he has built in the desert out of thousands of Christmas lights. Trouble looms, however, when Osterhage and the mechanic decide to fight over Blount's affections. SOUTH OF RENO was given a short theatrical release in a few major markets and seems likely to turn up on videocassette soon.

p, Robert Tinnell; d, Mark Rezyka; w, Mark Rezyka, T.L. Lankford; ph, Bernard Auroux (CFI Color); ed, Marc Grossman; m, Nigel Holton, Clive Wright; prod d, Philip Duffin; art d, Elizabeth Moore.

Drama   (PR:NR MPAA:R)

SPELLBINDER † (1988) 98m MGM/UA c

Timothy Daly (Jeff Mills), Kelly Preston (Miranda Reed), Rick Rossovich (Derek Clayton), Audra Lindley (Mrs. White), Anthony Crivello (Aldys), Diana Bellamy (Grace Woods), Cary-Hiroyuki Tagawa (Lt. Lee), James Louis Watkins (Tim Weatherly), Kyle Heffner (Herbie Green), Roderick Cook (Ed Kennerle), M.C. Gainey (Brock), Sally Kemp (Marilyn De Witt), Stefan Gierasch (Edgar De Witt), Bob McCracken (Simmons), Karen Baldwin (Mona), Cynthia Steele (Receptionist), Richard Fancy (Sgt. Barry), John Finnegan (George), Peter Schreiner (Barry), John De Mita (Brad), Diane Racine (Woman in Coven), Alexandra Morgan (Pamela), Christopher Lawford (Phil), Dale Cummings (Frye), Harold Diamond (Man), Don Woodard (Steve).

A major studio (MGM) release that was in and out of theaters in the blink of an eye, SPELLBINDER taps into FATAL ATTRACTION's fear that a one-night stand may turn out to be more than a little bit weird. In this case, Daly (DINER), a yuppie lawyer, takes the advice of a friend (Rossovich, ROXANNE) and hits on the archetypal woman-in-distress, Preston (TWINS). What Daly eventually discovers is that Preston has a real reason to be distressed—she's a witch whose coven is trying to lure her back. This first feature from director Janet Greek was photographed by Adam Greenberg, the man behind the lens for THREE MEN AND A BABY; LA BAMBA; NEAR DARK; and THE TERMINATOR.

p, Joe Wizan, Brian Russell; d, Janet Greek; w, Tracey Torme; ph, Adam Greenberg; ed, Steve Mirkovich; m, Basil Poledouris; md, Lionel Newman; prod d, Rodger Maus; set d, Roland Hill, Tom Bugenhagen; spec eff, Burt Dalton, Pat Lee, William Klinger; cos, Libby Charlton; stunts, Douglas Coleman; makeup, Tony Lloyd, Rick Stratton.

Thriller   Cas.   (PR:NR MPAA:R)

SPIKE OF BENSONHURST**½ (1988) 101m Film Dallas c

Sasha Mitchell (Spike Fumo), Ernest Borgnine (Baldo Cacetti), Anne DeSalvo (Sylvia Cacetti), Sylvia Miles (Congresswoman), Geraldine Smith (Helen Fumo), Antonio Rey (Bandana's Mother), Rick Aviles (Bandana), Maria Pitillo (Angel), Talisa Soto (India), Chris Anthony Young, Mario Todisco, Rodney Harvey, Frank Adonis, Frankie Gio, Robert Compono, Tony Goodstone, Justin Lazard.

During a film year in which the virtues of Jonathan Demme's MARRIED TO THE MOB (and Dean Stockwell's wonderfully campy performance as Mafia boss "Tony the Tiger") were extolled, one would have thought that Paul Morrissey's SPIKE OF BENSONHURST might have at least latched onto THE MOB's box-office coat tails. It didn't. Morrissey, the former Andy Warhol associate who directed such 1970s cult classics as FLESH; TRASH; and HEAT, starring pretty boy Joe Dallesandro, has once again found a beefcake actor, male model Sasha Mitchell, on whom he relies to make his film look great. A mixture of Sylvester Stallone's Rocky Balboa and Matt Dillon's tough kid from RUMBLE FISH, Mitchell is the Spike of the title—a tough Italian street fighter from Brooklyn whose old man is a Mafia fall guy doing time in Sing Sing, and whose old lady is a spiteful lesbian. Since his father took the fall to cover for mob boss Baldo Cacetti (played with great energy and guts by Borgnine), the mobster has vowed to take care of Mitchell. Because Mitchell believes his future is in the ring, Borgnine gets him a few fights, complaining, however, that he left the boxing game because "it's too old . . . too ethnic." Most of the fights Mitchell wins, though, are those Borgnine has fixed. During one fight, Mitchell spots a pretty, tube-top-wearing young blonde (Patillo) in the crowd with her collegiate boy friend. Later he learns that Patillo is Borgnine's precious daughter—a Mafia princess who studies at a respected Catholic college and is planning, at her father's behest, to marry the clean-cut son of cocaine-snorting congresswoman Miles (whom Morrissey directed 16 years earlier in HEAT). Patillo wants Mitchell, however, and although the boxer doesn't balk at the idea, as something of a Neanderthal, he spends most of his time thinking about his fists and his future. He grows increasingly impatient with Borgnine, who, instead of backing him in the ring, tries to persuade him to take a "quality control" position in his video piracy operation. When Mitchell's thick head and loose mouth begin to cause problems for Borgnine and his operation, he is kicked out of New York neighborhood Bensonhurst. With nowhere to go, he is offered a place to stay and train in Red Hook, a poverty-stricken Puerto Rican neighborhood, where he is shocked at the poor living conditions. Patillo then devises a plan to help Mitchell regain admittance to Bensonhurst, letting him get her pregnant; however, Mitchell gets himself into a bind when he also impregnates the achingly beautiful Soto, sister of the Puerto Rican boxer who has befriended Mitchell. As happens in so many films like this, it all comes down to the big boxing match in which Mitchell must prove his stuff.

A likable, relatively accessible (for Morrissey) story, with photogenic leads, and a marketable combination of boxing and mobsters, SPIKE OF BENSONHURST somehow didn't make a dent at the box office. Although the film deals with all the predictable conflicts—the young delinquent wanting to marry the mobster's beloved daughter; the street kid battling not to be a loser like his father; and the guy juggling two romances at once—it manages to present them in an entertaining way. Since everything looks so pretty (like the Calvin Klein ads that grace Mitchell's resume), it's easy to watch the film without paying much attention to its content. It's what lies underneath the slick photography, flexed muscles, and pretty eyes that detracts from the film—a cynical Reagan-era story about family values and a bright new future. Like Stallone's Rocky, Mitchell's Spike Fumo achieves right through might. Although there's a cynical tone to Morrissey's direction, it's difficult to determine where the satire stops and the liberal posturing begins. If one ignores Morrissey's thematic concerns, however, SPIKE OF BENSONHURST not only supplies a few laughs (Mitchell's macho bantering with a Chicago opponent is hilarious, as is his vapid response when Patillo asks whether he wants to marry her or her father's mob—"Whatever"), but is also a showcase for some nice performances. Mitchell is a handsome male model who (surprise!) can actually act—or at least one hopes he's acting. (One hates to think that there are real-life characters like Spike who actually say, "Smatter witchew?") Maria Patillo is perfect as the freckled, sassy college girl-Mafia princess who asks her stud boxer, "Wanna have sex?" knowing that if he gets her pregnant her father can't continue to exile him from his "turf," Bensonhurst. Unforgettable, at least in terms of her looks, is Talisa Soto, whose feline, almost boyish appearance is reminiscent of a young Nastassia Kinski. Curiously, despite the fact that the young boxer gets both women pregnant and that much of the plot revolves around hormonal awakening, the film is downright chaste, barely showing even any kissing (another reflection of the film's conservatism, or a gutsy non-commercial risk—you be the judge). Providing the film with its most fun and biggest laughs is Ernest Borgnine, who plays his character on the razor's edge between parody and documentary. (*Violence, sexual situations, profanity.*)

p, David Weisman, Nelson Lyon, Mark Silverman; d, Paul Morrissey; w, Alan Bowne, Paul Morrissey; ph, Steven Fierberg; ed, Stan Salfas; m, Coati Mundi; prod d, Stephen McCabe; cos, Barbara Dente.

Comedy/Sports	Cas.	(PR:C MPAA:R)

SPLIT DECISIONS**   (1988) 95m Wizan/New Century-Vista c

Craig Sheffer (*Eddie McGuinn*), Jeff Fahey (*Ray McGuinn*), Gene Hackman (*Dan McGuinn*), John McLiam (*Pop McGuinn*), Jennifer Beals (*Barbara Uribe*), Eddie Velez (*Julian* "*Snake*" *Pedroza*), Carmine Caridi (*Lou Rubia*), James Tolkan (*Benny Platone*).

SPLIT DECISIONS is a tedious low-budget boxing film that contains yet another sensitive performance from Gene Hackman but is crippled by its predictable script and phony ROCKY-style ending. On the mean streets of New York City we meet young Sheffer, a Golden Gloves champ who has just been accepted into a prestigious university, where he hopes to train and qualify for the 1988 Olympics. His trainer father, Hackman, couldn't be prouder, for his young son's success helps soothe the anger and disappointment he feels toward his older boy, Fahey. Fahey, who is also a boxer, rejected his father's advice and went pro, signing with a sleazy fight manager. Now Fahey fights several small-time bouts a month, with little to show for it but an increasingly scarred face. Although Hackman has disinherited Fahey, Sheffer still keeps tabs on his brother, as do all their friends at the gym, and when Fahey comes back to town to promote a match with a dangerous Hispanic boxer nicknamed "Snake" (Velez), Sheffer accompanies his brother to the press conference against Hackman's wishes. There Sheffer meets mob-connected fight promotor Tolkan, and begins to realize that his brother has fallen in with a bad crowd. When his manager informs Fahey that he has to throw the fight with Velez, Fahey rebels and declares he won't do it. Feeling trapped, Fahey reaches out to his family and tries to make amends, and, although still stubborn, Hackman acknowledges his older son's efforts and things seem to be improving between them. Unfortunately, Tolkan will not accept Fahey's refusal to throw the fight. Fahey is taken to a deserted loft, where he is beaten up by a pair of mob goons. In the meantime, two young boxer friends of Fahey's have trailed him to the loft. One tries to watch the action while the other goes to call Sheffer. After breaking Fahey's right hand, Tolkan allows Velez to get in a few punches. To his manager's horror, Velez kills Fahey by knocking him out the window. When the hoods rush to the window to see if Fahey is still alive, they spot Fahey's friend and realize that he's witnessed the murder. Frightened, the boxer runs off, refusing to go to the police because he fears the mob's reprisal. When Sheffer learns what happened, he decides to avenge his brother by turning pro and taking the bout that Fahey was supposed to fight. Wanting to handle things his own way, Sheffer keeps the truth about his brother's death from his father, and when Hackman learns that Sheffer has turned pro, he kicks the boy out of the house; however, fearing that Sheffer will be killed in the ring by the bigger, faster, meaner Velez, Hackman swallows his pride and agrees to supervise Sheffer's training. After weeks of intensive workouts, the big day arrives. The fight is incredibly brutal and Sheffer gets the snot beat out of him in the first several rounds, while Velez takes his opponent so lightly that he frequently lets his guard down to taunt Sheffer. After losing round after round, the bloodied Sheffer finally manages to smack Velez in the chin after one of these taunts, then pulverizes him for a final knockout. As Sheffer is being crowned champion, the young boxer who witnessed Fahey's murder enters the auditorium with the police, having finally spilled his guts about what he saw.

With a plot straight out of an old Warner Bros. movie, SPLIT DECISIONS isn't terribly original. One wonders why it was made at all. Director David Drury (DEFENSE OF THE REALM), who was once an amateur boxer in England, brings nothing new to the hackneyed material except the kind of gritty realism that most low-budget movies rely on, because they have to shoot on actual locations. With the exception of Hackman's performance, most of the acting is unremarkable—not bad, but simply competent. An interesting family relationship begins to build between Hackman and his sons, but soon the melodramatic machinations of the plot take over and overwhelm the scant emotional nuance that had been established. The plot requires that logic be thrown to the wind and the last half of the film is filled with so many implausibilities and plot holes that any credible attempt at realism is lost. Furthermore, the script by David Fallon is vaguely sexist, and racist as well. The only woman in the film, Beals, has nothing to do but be dumped on by one brother and taken in by the other, serving only as an ornament for the men when they go out and to comfort them when they are depressed. She seems to have no life or purpose of her own, other than to wait around for these boxers. Even worse, the film, in its "Great White Hope" approach, tends to paint a more positive portrait of the working class Irish than of the dark-skinned minority boxers who have dominated the sport in the last 30 years. Although whites are shown to be the evildoers who actually control the events (suggesting that minorities are easily manipulated), minorities are shown to be more dangerous and less heroic than their white counterparts. Thus, the chief villain,

Velez, is Hispanic as well as psychotic; Sheffer's black and Hispanic friends are the only characters in the film shown to do illicit drugs (smoking a joint in a car); and the young boxer who witnessed the murder, also Hispanic, is too worried about his own safety to try and help Fahey when he is being beaten to death, or, subsequently, to go to the police. It is left up to the selfless Sheffer to sacrifice his Olympic aspirations and fight Velez in the ring, rather than the courts, because the young Hispanic is too scared to testify. There are also several short statements extolling the virtues of the Irish and predicting that they will soon reestablish themselves as a group to be reckoned with. There is nothing wrong with ethnic pride, but in SPLIT DECISIONS it comes at the expense of other groups. Although there is an attempt to balance the negative minority characters with positive ones—Hackman is seen training young minority fighters—it is a half-hearted effort, for none of the positive characters gets as much screen time as the negative ones. True, the racism inherent in this Great White Hope material seems to be more thoughtless than malicious, but it is nevertheless unfortunate.

Also unfortunate is the absurd ending, in which the much younger, lighter, less powerful, and inexperienced Sheffer takes a brutal beating from Velez, only to suddenly hit his opponent on the chin and turn the whole fight around in less than 10 seconds. Until this point, the film had been a fairly uncompromising look at the bleak realities of the boxing world, but ultimately realism is cavalierly tossed aside for the preposterous feel-good ending. Even Rocky himself, Sylvester Stallone, would be embarrassed by the inanities of SPLIT DECISIONS. (*Violence, profanity.*)

p, Joe Wizan, Michael Borofsky, Todd Black; d, David Drury; w, David Fallon; ph, Timothy Suhrstedt (CFI color); ed, John W. Wheeler, Jeff Freeman, Thomas Stanford; m, Basil Poledouris; art d, Michael Z. Hanan; set d, Kathe Klopp, Carol Nast; cos, Hilary Cochran; tech, Paul Stader.

Sports		(PR:O MPAA:R)

SPOOKIES †   (1988) 84m Twisted Souls/Safir c

Felix Ward (*Kreon*), Dan Scott (*Kreon's Servant*), Alec Nemser (*Billy*), Maria Pechukas (*Isabelle*).

Horror in the GREMLINS-GHOULIES-MUNCHIES mold, SPOOKIES places a group of youths in a scary old mansion and pits them against an ancient sorcerer seeking to revive his beloved wife—dead for 70 years—and in need of human sacrifices. The sorcerer conjures up a bevy of ghoulish monsters and sets them loose on the kids. Made back in 1986, this film won the Delirium Award for Best Entertainment at the 15th Annual International Science Fiction and Fantasy Film Festival in Paris, but failed to get a theatrical release and wound up on home video in 1988.

p, Eugenie Joseph, Thomas Doran, Brendan Faulkner, Frank M. Farel; d, Eugenie Joseph, Thomas Doran, Brendan Faulkner; w, Frank M. Farel, Thomas Doran, Brendan Faulkner, Joseph Burgund; ph, Robert Chappell, Ken Kelsch (Precision color); ed, Eugenie Joseph; m, Kenneth Higgins, James Calabrese; spec eff, Arnold Gargiulo II, Vincent J. Guastini, Gabriel Bartalos, Jennifer Aspinal, John Dods; stunts, Tony Guida, David Farkas.

Horror	Cas.	(PR:NR MPAA:R)

STAND AND DELIVER***½   (1988) 105m American Playhouse/WB c

Edward James Olmos (*Jaime Escalante*), Lou Diamond Phillips (*Angel*), Rosana De Soto (*Fabiola Escalante*), Andy Garcia (*Ramirez*), Ingrid Oliu (*Lupe*), Karla Montana (*Claudia*), Vanessa Marquez (*Ana*), Mark Eliot (*Tito*), Patrick Baca (*Javier*), Will Gotay (*Pancho*), Daniel Villarreal (*Chuco*), Carmen Argenziano (*Molina*), Virginia Paris (*Raquel Ortega*), Lydia Nicole (*Rafaela*), James Victor (*Ana's Father*), Rif Hutton (*Pearson*), Mark Everett (*Heavy Metal Boy*), Estelle Harris (*Secretary*), Mark Phelan (*Cop*), Adelaide Alvarez (*Sexy Girl*), Richard Martinez (*Heavy Metal Boy*), Tyde Kierney (*Joe Goodell*), Bodie Olmos (*Fernando Escalante*), Michael Goldfinger (*Coach*), Michael Yama (*Sanzaki*), Graham Galloway (*Craig*), Betty Carvahlo (*Angel's Grandmother*), Irene Olga Lopez (*Lupe's Mother*), Yvette Cruise (*Claudia's Mother*), Aixa Clemente (*Hospital Receptionist*), Victor Garron (*Jaime Escalante, Jr.*), Michael Adler (*Schloss*), Barbara Vera (*Proctor*), Star Frohman (*Female Cop*), Jessica Seynos, Dominic Lucero, Sonia Fuentes, David Brian Abalos, Irma Barrios, Henry Torres, Beatrice Giraldo, Richard Moreno, Phillip Elizalde (*Ganas Kids*).

STAND AND DELIVER is a powerful and enriching film about life in East Los Angeles that neatly contrasts with Dennis Hopper's gang picture COLORS. Opening on the same day as COLORS, STAND AND DELIVER expresses a different, more positive message about *ganas* —the Spanish word for desire. Based on a true story, the film stars Olmos as Jaime Escalante, an employee at an electronics firm who quits his job and becomes the computer science teacher at East LA's Garfield High. One day he is told he will be teaching mathematics, since the promised computers have not arrived. Olmos' class is filled with kids who have no desire to learn—they come late to class, can't do multiplication, talk and eat in class, and live in the fear of gang violence. After class he finds his car window smashed and his stereo stolen. Olmos is a special breed of teacher, however, who specializes in theatrics (he dresses as a chef and violently slices up apples to illustrate the concept of fractions) and refers to his class as a "show." Gradually the students come around to his side. Even gang banger Phillips (LA BAMBA) takes a liking to Olmos' class. In one of the film's finest scenes, Phillips asks Olmos, on the sly of course, for an extra book—one to keep at school and one to keep at home—so his friends won't see that he studies. While Olmos demands extra effort from his students, each must overcome certain obstacles.

The gifted Marquez is forced to quit school when her father demands she be a waitress at the family-owned *taqueria*. Gotay, the least intelligent and least motivated kid in class, fights Olmos all the way. He would prefer to drive a forklift and buy a new car than learn in school. All the young women in class must fight the stereotype that a man does not want an intelligent wife. Nonetheless, Olmos refuses to give up on his students. With his school facing a loss of accreditation, he makes a radical request to teach AP Calculus and therefore prepare his students for the Advanced Placement exams, a grueling test that only the top 2 percent of high schoolers take (even less receive college credit). Fearing that Olmos will do more harm than good if the students fail, the department chair, Paris, resigns her post. Olmos approaches his students with his idea, telling them that "calculus doesn't need to be made easy—it already is." He makes them sign contracts that bind them to their studies. They come to school early, stay late, and attend on Saturday mornings. After a full year at this pace, all 18 students take the AP test. All 18 receive credit. This scholastic miracle is debunked, however, by ETS, the Educational Testing Service, which claims that the students cheated. An ETS investigation headed by Garcia (THE UNTOUCHABLES) refuses to believe the credibility of either Olmos or his students. Another, more demanding, test is administered. Again all 18 students pass. Titles then appear on-screen that give the amazing statistics of AP scores at Garfield High over the last five years, culminating with 87 students receiving college credit in 1987.

Every now and again a film comes along which makes a minimal use of the art of film, its techniques, or its power as a visual medium, but still manages to have a powerful and profound effect on its viewers. STAND AND DELIVER is such a film—one which does more good for *people* than for *filmmaking*. It is the type of film that reinforces such cliched statements as "young people are the future of this country" or "you can be anything you want to be." Upon viewing STAND AND DELIVER, you can't help but become a believer. Begun in 1983 as a proposed PBS-TV special entitled "Walking on Water," STAND AND DELIVER was filmed on a $1.35 million budget with monies from American Playhouse, the ARCO Foundation (which also partially funded Escalante's teaching program), the Corporation for Public Broadcasting, the National Science Foundation, the Ford Foundation, and Atlantic Richfield. Shown in late 1987 at California's Mill Valley Film Festival under the title WALKING ON WATER, the film was picked up by Warner Brothers for $4 million ($1 million less than their original deal, because of a conflict between the American Playhouse PBS commitment and Warners' HBO deal). Carefully scripted and exceptionally acted, STAND AND DELIVER succeeds where many films fail in its ability to concentrate on numerous characters. First-time director Ramon Menendez, a Cuban UCLA graduate, takes the camera outside the classroom and into the students' own world. We see them at home, with other gang members, at work, etc., but it never seems extraneous. Instead, it gives each student a unique stamp. While everyone turns in a fine performance, Edward James Olmos is the standout. Best known to television viewers as the mustached, wavy-haired Lt. Castillo of *Miami Vice* and to some filmgoers as the title character in THE BALLAD OF GREGORIO CORTEZ, Olmos completely transforms himself physically for his role as Jaime Escalante. He has added 40 pounds, undergone treatments to thin his hair and add wisps over a balding top, and adopted a hunched posture with a shuffling walk. Don't let the subject scare you away (as it did most Hollywood studios, initially); STAND AND DELIVER isn't a film about math, but a film about overcoming obstacles and winning. Unlike most sports stories about winning (ROCKY, HOOSIERS), STAND AND DELIVER never overstates itself and instead concentrates on small, essentially nondramatic elements to make its point. Although there is some vulgarity and gang activity, STAND AND DELIVER should be seen by youngsters and, perhaps more importantly, by teachers who could learn a few things from Escalante's methods and philosophies.

An obtrusive, thoroughly out-of-place rock song by Mr. Mister was added by Warners over the final credits. It's a glaringly obvious move to bolster interest in the soundtrack album and whoever decided to include it should be publicly ridiculed. *(Profanity.)*

p, Tom Musca; d, Ramon Menendez; w, Ramon Menendez, Tom Musca; ph, Tom Richmond (Foto-Kem Color); ed, Nancy Richardson; m, Craig Safan; m/l, Richard Page, Steve George, John Lang; art d, Milo; cos, Kathryn Morrison; makeup, Dee Mansano, Vered Hochman.

Drama Cas. (PR:A MPAA:PG)

STAR SLAMMER: THE ESCAPE** (1988) 90m Jack H. Harris-Viking/Worldwide c

Sandy Brooke *(Taura)*, Susan Stokey *(Mike)*, Ross Hagen *(Bantor)*, Marya Gant *(Warden Exene)*, Aldo Ray *(The Inquisitor)*, Dawn Wildsmith *(Muffin)*, Richard Alan Hench *(Garth)*, Michael D. Sonye *(Krago)*, Lindy Skyles *(The Sovereign)*, Bobbi Bresee *(Marai)*, Danita Aljuwani *(Ruby)*, Dori Renee Crofts *(Scratch)*, Lial Mathias *(Stace)*, Mimi Monaco *(Squeeker)*, Vivian Louise Schilling *(Marni)*, Karen Stanton *(K.K.)*, Gwen Perlman *(Adriene)*, Jade Barrett *(Dr. Po)*, Johnny Legend *(Zaal)*, Christopher Ray *(Twizzle)*, John Carradine *(The Judge)*, Lee Forbes *(Joo Joo)*, Jerome L. Dennoe, Sandy Church *(Mogwarts)*, Joseph A. Lepera *(TV Wrestler)*, Robert Tinneli *(Zombie Alien)*, Steve Carter, Bob Ivey *(Troopers)*, Eric Caiden, Jimmy Skakel, Martin Nicholas *(Android Guards)*, Frank Bresee *(Game Show Announcer)*, Jack H. Harris *(Intercom Announcer)*, Fred Olen Ray *(Mouse Robot)*.

A few years ago, women-in-prison films made a surprising comeback, led by the camp hit REFORM SCHOOL GIRLS and fueled by cable and home video's endless need for exploitation titles. It was only natural that some enterprising producer would figure out a way to combine this genre with the other mainstay of the auxiliary markets, science fiction. The Cannes Film Festival issue of Variety a couple of years ago (where many projects are advertised as in production, never to be seen again) included several entries along this line. Leave it to director Fred Olen Ray to actually get it out, straight to the video store. The film opens as a pilgrim monk visits the Planet Arous camp of miner Brooke (who certainly doesn't look like she's been grubbing around in the dirt). They are soon set upon by Hagen, a tyrannical local magistrate for the "Empire," and his goons, who kill the monk for sport, then zap down Brooke's dwarf helpers. Brooke manages to kill a few of these assailants and horribly burn Hagen's hand before she is subdued and sentenced (by the late John Carradine) to a prison spaceship. After being threatened by the other inmates, led by Stokey, she is terrorized by head trustee Wildsmith and has a pass made at her by warden Gant. Back in the cells, the girls warm up to Brooke, and, after a huge mess-hall fight with Stokey, she is accepted as another leader. To complicate their lives, Hagen arrives on board, more deranged than ever thanks to the loss of his hand and looking for the opportunity to get even with Brooke. When he comes up with a way of lobotomizing the women, the inmates decide they have nothing to lose, plan a mutiny, and start killing guards, with Wildsmith the first to go. After a running battle through the ship in which most of the insurgents are killed, they make their way to a shuttle craft and take off, Hagen and a flotilla of fighters after them. What follows is a confusing rehash of the dogfight from STAR WARS by way of LAST STARFIGHTER, with lots of exploding ships and cheering women, who finally do away with Hagen then set course for a safe planet and a promised sequel.

Despite the film's sleazoid packaging and the title, this is actually more a comedy than anything, full of science-fiction in-jokes. Sandy Brooke is a serviceable heroine, while Dawn Wildsmith and Ross Hagen make memorable heavies. The most surprising thing about STAR SLAMMER, though, is simply the amount of money that appears to have been spent on it. Perhaps the sets are left over from something else, and the special effects dogfight sequence could have come out of any of dozens of movies of the last decade, but that doesn't detract from the fact that this thing looks amazingly good. *(Nudity, profanity, violence.)*

p, Jack H. Harris, Fred Olen Ray; d, Fred Olen Ray; w, Michael D. Sonye (based on a story by Michael D. Sonye, Miriam Preissel, Fred Olen Ray); ph, Paul Elliott (Fujicolor); ed, Miriam L. Preissel; m, Anthony Harris; prod d, Michael Novotny, Wayne Springfield; art d, Maxine Shepard; spec eff, Bret Mixon, Matt Rose, Mark Williams; cos, Jill Conner; stunts, John Stewart; makeup, Nancy De Turo.

Comedy/Science Fiction/Prison Cas. (PR:O MPAA:R)

STARS AND BARS* (1988) 94m COL c

Daniel Day Lewis *(Henderson Dores)*, Harry Dean Stanton *(Loomis Gage)*, Kent Broadhurst *(Sereno)*, Maury Chaykin *(Freeborn Gage)*, Matthew Cowles *(Beckman Gage)*, Joan Cusack *(Irene Stein)*, Keith David *(Teagarden)*, Spalding Gray *(Rev. Cardew)*, Glenne Headly *(Cora Gage)*, Laurie Metcalf *(Melissa)*, Bill Moor *(Beeby)*, Deirdre O'Connell *(Shanda Gage)*, Will Patton *(Duane Gage)*, Martha Plimpton *(Bryant)*, Rockets Redglare *(Gint)*, Celia Weston *(Monika)*, Beatrice Winde *(Alma-May)*, Steven Wright *(Pruitt)*, David Strathairn *(Charlie)*, Bruce C. Taylor *(General)*, Raynor Scheine *(Drunk)*, Bob Bost *(Auctioneer)*, Lit Conah *(Lady at Auction)*, J.J. Johnston *(Doorman)*, Peter Cherevas *(Hot-Dog Vendor)*, Tim Ware *(Bartender)*, Jeff Lewis, Matt Hoffman, Mark Heffernan *(Pursuers)*, Cameron Arnett, Victor Anthony Higgins, Jr. *(Cowboys)*, Robby Preddy, Allison Biggers *(Hotel Receptionists)*, Darlene Jamerson *(Indian Maiden)*, Ingrid Buxbaum *(Photographer)*, Danny Fendley *(Bellman)*, Scott Allan Christoffel *(Cavalry Bellman)*, Elaine Falone *(Waitress)*, Bill Cummings *(Waiter)*, Randy Cash, Susan Asher *(Diners)*, Sergio Aguirre *(Small Boy in Canoe)*, Jim Aycock *(Father in Canoe)*, Lisa Pastorino *(Woman in Canoe)*.

STARS AND BARS is a horribly miscalculated attempt at firing a satiric, slapstick zinger at the differences between the stiff, superior ways of the British and the boorish, combative ways of American Southerners. Day Lewis, a very proper young Englishman who has recently arrived in New York to take employment as an expert on 19th-century art, is in love with the US and believes anything is possible there. Despite his familiarity with big-city London, Day Lewis is completely lost in the Big Apple, but after earning the approval of his boss, he is sent to Georgia to purchase a long-thought-lost Renoir painting worth a cool $10 million. Before he leaves, Day Lewis meets and falls for Cusack, a likable computer expert. They promise to meet later in Atlanta after he closes the deal on the painting. A wrench is thrown into his carefully prepared itinerary, however, when Plimpton, the seductive 15-year-old daughter of Day Lewis' fiancee (Metcalf), surprises him and comes along on the trip. Day Lewis' fish-out-of-water existence becomes even more exaggerated than it was in New York when he arrives at the rural home of the painting's owner, Stanton, an accommodating sort whose family is a bit on the eccentric side. One overweight son, Chaykin, dresses like Elvis Presley and lives in a nearby trailer with his pregnant wife; another son, Patton, is a loony who claims to be a Vietnam War hero; and daughter Headly, who resembles Bette Davis, pretends to be blind. Although Stanton seems ready to sell his Renoir, which he claims to have paid $500 for as a soldier in France in 1946, Chaykin threatens to kill Day Lewis if he buys the painting. It seems Chaykin has already agreed to accept a $15-million offer from some shady, gun-toting art dealers. Gradually, Day Lewis' world comes apart at the seams. First, he incurs the wrath of his boss when he tells him that they are being outbid; then, as a result of a telephone mix-up, he books Cusack, whom he wants to see, and Metcalf, whom he doesn't, into the same luxurious hotel suite. Naturally, they arrive at the same time and simultaneously dump him. Locked out of his hotel room and wearing only a bath towel around his waist, Day Lewis chases Cusack through the hotel, passing the trees, rivers, and canoes that make up its adventure land decor. By the time he returns to Stanton's rural home, Plimpton has become engaged to Patton. It's not long after his return, though, that Stanton, angered that Patton is playing his rock 'n' roll too loud, dies of a heart attack. The events continue to spin wildly out of control: Patton tosses the Renoir onto a bonfire; Day Lewis drugs Plimpton and takes her home to New York; Patton follows and tries to forcibly reclaim his fiancee; and Chaykin and the art-dealing thugs apprehend Day Lewis. The frightened art expert is dragged along to a warehouse where art of all types is mass produced—from colorful Lichtenstein pop to Michelangelo nude sculptures. The thugs then force Day Lewis to strip and threaten to torture him unless he reveals the Renoir's whereabouts. However, he fools the thugs into thinking the painting is in his office and, during the commotion, manages to escape (nude again) through a warehouse window. Wandering through the streets in the pouring rain and wearing a pair of *overalls* made from a cardboard box, Day Lewis pairs up again with Cusack. Chaykin and company are finally defeated (in a fencing match, no less), but Day Lewis' troubles continue as he and Cusack are chased down the street by the crazed Patton. The camera cranes high over the street and the adventure continues . . . fortunately without us.

Embarrassingly unfunny, STARS AND BARS is the third theatrical feature directed by Irishman Pat O'Connor. After helming the intelligent and involving CAL and the sensitive drama A MONTH IN THE COUNTRY, O'Connor seemed to be one of the most promising directors working in the UK. STARS AND BARS and his 1989 feature, JANUARY MAN, however, raise serious doubts about his talents. At the very least, they prove that O'Connor and comedy don't mix. STARS AND BARS promises to be a madcap, slapstick assault on two wildly different cultures with only distinctive accents in common. Developed by David Puttnam (who turned the project over to producer Sandy Lieberson after Puttnam's move up at Columbia), the film is a satire of the ideals of Britons who come to America, as well as an attack on American ideals. Because Puttnam, O'Connor, and scriptwriter William Boyd (from whose novel the script is adapted) have all spent time in the US, one would think STARS AND BARS would have a ring of truth to it. It doesn't. Instead, STARS AND BARS' attempts at eliciting laughter are so pathetic that its gags probably couldn't provoke a response from a laugh track. And it's only a laugh track (and Day Lewis' unexpected full-frontal nudity) that separates this film from a mindless television sitcom. All the characters are, in varying degrees, cardboard cutouts that make the film's satirical attempts all the more ineffective. It's hard, however, to pinpoint the origin of the film's major fault; it just sort of cracks apart all over. This is most unfortunate since the cast—one of the finest collection of talent assembled this year—offers so much promise. Day Lewis, who agreed to do the role after finishing MY BEAUTIFUL LAUNDRETTE, proves that he is one of the most versatile actors around, despite his seeming discomfort at acting in so many ludicrous and embarrassing situations. Columbia Pictures, unmoved by the success of THE UNBEARABLE LIGHTNESS OF BEING (Day Lewis' follow-up to MY BEAUTIFUL LAUNDRETTE), still treated STARS AND BARS as a spoiled Puttnam leftover and dumped it into only a handful of theaters. For once, Columbia's despotic actions seem warranted. At least, there's a memorable theme song written and performed by Sting, "Englishman in New York." There's also a snippet of the George Jones country & western tune "A Picture of Me Without You" (Norris Wilson, George Richie). *(Nudity, profanity).*

p, Sandy Lieberson; d, Pat O'Connor; w, William Boyd (based on his novel); ph, Jerzy Zielinski; ed, Michael Bradsell; m, Stanley Myers; m/l, Sting, Norris Wilson, George Richie; prod d, Leslie Dilley, Stuart Craig; art d, Betty Block; set d, Anne Kuljian; cos, Ann Roth; stunts, Lonnie Smith; makeup, Lynn Barber.

Comedy **Cas.** **(PR:C-O MPAA:R)**

STEALING HOME* (1988) 98m Mount/WB c

Mark Harmon *(Billy Wyatt as an Adult)*, Blair Brown *(Ginny Wyatt)*, Jodie Foster *(Katie Chandler)*, Jonathan Silverman *(Alan Appleby as a Teen)*, Harold Ramis *(Alan Appleby as an Adult)*, John Shea *(Sam Wyatt)*, William McNamara *(Billy Wyatt as a Teen)*, Thatcher Goodwin *(Billy Wyatt as a Child)*, Judith Kahan *(Laura Appleby)*, Miriam Flynn *(Mrs. Parks)*, Christine Jones *(Grace Chandler)*, Richard Jenkins *(Hank Chandler)*.

The problems of STEALING HOME are too numerous to mention, but for starters, it's not really a film. Rather, it's a filmed screenplay—meaning there's nothing even remotely visually interesting about the movie. Everything exists for the words that the screenwriters put on the page. Fortunately for these screenwriters—Steven Kampmann and Will Aldis—they were also the directors. Any self-respecting director in touch with real people and emotions would have quickly tossed their script on the dung-heap. A two-headed monster of a film, STEALING HOME never seems to have any idea of what it wants to be. In one scene it's IRONWEED (Harmon is a derelict alcoholic living on the fringes of society), in another scene it's THE SUMMER OF '42 (Harmon's boyhood friend wants to get under the sheets with an older woman), then its DINER (heart-to-heart buddy talks), or PORKY'S (a teen's embarrassing first sexual encounter).

Structured in a series of confusing flashbacks, the film focuses on Harmon, a thirtysomething failure who could have been somebody—namely a star with the Philadelphia Phillies. In a bush league game, he steals home in the bottom of the ninth to give his team a victory, and is spotted by a Phillies scout, who promises him a big future. Mom and Dad (Brown and Shea) have been hoping for a college education for their boy, but the prospect of having a major leaguer in the family changes their minds. When Dad is killed in a car wreck, however, Harmon puts away his bat and glove. The film opens some 15 years later as the sleepy-eyed, unshaven Harmon gets a call from Brown informing him that his closest childhood friend, Foster, has just killed herself. "Come home," says Mom, and since stealing home was once his specialty, Harmon agrees. Along the way he smokes cigarettes and looks longingly out the train window at those delicate memories of his past, accompanied by some frightfully schmaltzy music. He sees his preteen self as enacted by 10-year-old Goodwin, who is understood only by his baby-sitter, the 16-year-old Foster. She teaches him how to smoke, takes him swimming, and tells him about girls. She also gives him a baseball-shaped pendant to always remind him that he's a ballplayer. After a few more shots of the glassy-eyed Harmon staring off into the distance, we meet him as a 16-year-old (McNamara). He and his best friend, Silverman, live for two things—baseball and, you guessed it, losing their virginity. McNamara loses "it" to a neighborhood girl whom Silverman has wanted to ask to the prom, while Silverman spends his evenings peering into the bedroom of an older woman who, conscious of her voyeur's presence, puts on teasing shows before flicking off the light. McNamara's favorite girl is still Foster, though. He loves her tough and free-spirited rebelliousness, and after years of reading Foster's signs, the ballplayer gets to home with her. But back to the mature Harmon, who, when we last left him, was smoking and staring off into space. By now his train has pulled into the station and his mother and Foster's parents are still stunned by her death. Harmon is equally stunned when he learns Foster has left him in charge of her ashes. He doesn't know what to do with them and, like a junior Sherlock Holmes, he pieces together their past friendship (he hasn't seen her in 10 years) to come up with Foster's final resting place. Now, judging from the title and the symbolic implications, one would guess that Harmon would sprinkle them on home plate. It would make perfect sense, especially given Harmon's return to semi-pro baseball at the end of the film, which finds him diving into home plate, in slow motion, his arms outstretched. Harmon, then, would be diving for both the plate *and* Foster—the only person who could bring him home again. But the writing and directing team of Kampmann and Aldis obviously have something else in mind, and Harmon tosses Foster's ashes off a pier. Big deal. We find out that Foster once stood at the pier's end and fantasized about being able to soar away from the earth, etc. By this finale it's hard to separate the audience's groans from the laughs.

Maybe if a great director of melodramas, say Douglas Sirk, had been in charge STEALING HOME might have been a great film. Even a mediocre director would have helped. In STEALING HOME, however, we get two subpar directors who make a mess of things. Almost all of their film plays like a poorly rehearsed script reading with simple, uninspired camerawork (there are a few ho-hum and very cliched crane shots), a treacly Muzak soundtrack, and some fine actors who are left in the lurch. Originally STEALING HOME was a David Puttnam project at Columbia, which just proves that *everything* Puttnam touched didn't turn to gold. After the changing of the guard at Columbia, Warner Brothers leapt for home plate and took over the $6.5 million film. With a pair of less-than-distinguished credits to their name (THE COUCH TRIP and BACK TO SCHOOL), Kampmann and Aldis were given the go-ahead, but even with the producer and cinematographer of BULL DURHAM on board, this picture is by far a minor-league effort.

The worst thing about STEALING HOME is that some fine actors are completely wasted and left to flail in front of the camera like a doomed man in quicksand. Harmon, who is no brilliant thespian but was once called "The Sexiest Man Alive," is given nothing to do. The extent of his direction probably sounded like this: "Okay Mark, make sure you don't shave . . . Now throw down your cigarette and look over there. Great. Let's try that again, but this time look more despondent." A one-time star quarterback at UCLA, Harmon isn't bad here, although he is less memorable than in his previous effort, THE PRESIDIO. However, somebody should help this guy find a script before it's too late. Again, as in THE PRESIDIO (in which he had almost no scenes with Meg Ryan, his supposed lover), Harmon is barely on-screen with the lead actress. This time he has no (count 'em, zero) scenes with Jodie Foster. The childhood incarnations of Harmon do, however, and both actors—Thacher Goodwin and William McNamara—survive the proceedings. John Shea is killed off too early to make an impression, while Harold Ramis clearly comes out as the winner in a wrestling match with the miserably mundane script. Foster, who is making something of a comeback, shines in a couple of scenes (her final one, specifically), but also falls victim to the pen of Kampmann and Aldis. *(Sexual situations, adult situations, substance abuse, profanity.)*

p, Thom Mount, Hank Moonjean; d, Steven Kampmann, Will Aldis; w, Steven Kampmann, Will Aldis; ph, Bobby Byrne (Technicolor); ed, Anthony Gibbs; m, David Foster; art d, Vaughan Edwards; set d, Robert Franco.

Drama/Sports **Cas.** **(PR:C MPAA:PG-13)**

STICKY FINGERS*½ (1988) 97m Hightop/Spectrafilm c

Helen Slater *(Hattie)*, Melanie Mayron *(Lolly)*, Danitra Vance *(Evanston)*, Eileen Brennan *(Stella)*, Carol Kane *(Kitty)*, Loretta Devine *(Diane)*, Stephen McHattie *(Eddie)*, Christopher Guest *(Sam)*, Gwen Welles *(Marcie)*, Shirley Stoller *(Reeba)*, Adam Shaw *(Jean-Marc)*, Elizabeth Kemp *(Nancy)*, Pierre Gautreau *(Jake)*, Katherine Cortez *(Leslie)*, Paul Brown *(Ray)*, Paul Hipp *(Michael)*, Erin Flannery *(Moura)*, Philip Moon *(Ike)*, Mung Ling *(Tina)*, Henry Yuk *(Joey)*, Paul Calderon *(Speed)*, Mini Friedman *(Poo Powell)*, Edward Bianchi *(Diamond Johnny)*, Jim Bearden *(Smokestack Sid)*, David Walden *(Tortellini Tony)*, Sylvia Kauders *(Francis)*, Francine Beers *(Gertie)*, Jeff Braunstin *(Music Salesman)*, Stuart Rudin *(Hippy)*, Zachary Bennett, T.J. Shimizu, Aaron Greenway *(Boys)*, Bob Lem *(Dealer)*, Wendy Lum *(Blackjack Dealer)*, By Mirano *(Spanish Woman)*, Chad Burton *(Counterman)*, Joe Maruzzo, Matt Carlson *(Hoods)*, George Buza *(Policeman)*, Hannah Cox, Bo Rucker, Fred Ephraim *(Cops)*, Richard Blackburn, Stephanie-Antorine Comtois, David Hurwith, Bill James, Mari-Jose Paradis, Roger Sinha, Sonia D'Orleans Juste *(Dancers)*.

One of the more disappointing offerings among 1988's welcome increase in films written and directed by women, this screwball affair focuses on a pair of female musicians trying to keep their heads above water as they scramble after success in the Big Apple. Slater and Mayron dress like Cindi Lauper but play violin and cello, busquing in the park to make ends meet—though as the film opens they aren't doing a very good job of it and their landlady, Brennan, is ready to evict them for failure to pay back rent. This problem is solved and a whole slew of others created when they learn that the suitcase left in their care by their friendly dope dealer (Devine) contains nearly a million ill-gotten bucks. What are two are avant-goofy but penniless girls to do? At first they just pay the rent, but after their apartment is burglarized they refurbish their digs into a high-tech pleasure palace and themselves into price-is-no-object fashion plates. As fast as you can say "Shop, buy, accumulate," they've spent nearly a quarter of a million dollars. Ah, but money doesn't buy happiness, and Slater is still overwhelmed with rejection and loneliness when she encounters her estranged husband at a party and learns that he plans to remarry as soon as their impending divorce becomes final. Mayron is similarly depressed by the behavior of her lover, Guest, a just-published first-time novelist who appears to be spending an inordinate amount of time with an obsessive old flame. To make matters worse, Devine tells them that she's on her way back to town. Desperate to recoup the squandered fortune, Mayron and Slater venture to a gambling parlor and, after some initial bad luck, win back even more money than they've spent; however, their winnings are stolen even before they can get home. All the while both the police and the mob have been keeping an eye on them. Devine returns, but, fearing that she has been followed, leaves the remaining money with Mayron and Slater and gives them a deadline to replace the missing hundreds of thousands. Yet again the hapless pair absentmindedly allow the bag of cash to disappear—this time on the back of a taxi—but everything turns out for the best when the police nab the drug dealers and the missing cash ends up in the hands of pair of elderly women.

STICKY FINGERS is presented with a certain panache, and, due in large part to its excellent costume and production design, it is frequently visually interesting. It fails, however, to create the kind of inspired zaniness that Jonathan Demme captured so well in SOMETHING WILD and that Susan Seidelman conveyed to as lesser extent in DESPERATELY SEEKING SUSAN and SMITHEREENS—the recent screwball comedies whose style and temperament this most closely resembles. Director Catlin Adams' pacing is uneven and her script, cowritten with Melanie Mayron (GIRLFRIENDS, TV's "thirtysomething"), holds few surprises. For the film to work, Mayron and Helen Slater needed to deliver charged performances and, to their credit, both actresses are believable when given the opportunity to demonstrate the genuine emotions surrounding their love lives; however, most of the dialog and actions they are handed are goofy without being particularly funny, and their relationship lacks the chemistry necessary to evoke viewer sympathy. Danitra Vance, a "Saturday Night Live" alumna who has had better luck with showing the fine work she is capable of doing onstage, is wasted here as the duo's slightly less frenetic friend. Eileen Brennan and Carol Kane also turn in forgettable cameo performances as the pair who watch over Mayron and Slater's building, but Christopher Guest (THIS IS SPINAL TAP, THE PRINCESS BRIDE), the film's only male character of any consequence, fares much better as Mayron's distracted, self-centered boy friend. The occasional visual flair that director Adams demonstrates seems to indicate that there are better films in her future, but not if she chooses material as familiar as this. Songs include "Opening Park Sonata", "Music Store Madness" (Gordon Minette), "Good Luck" (Allison Cornell, Dan Higgins, performed by Cornell), "Sticky Fingers" (Lisa Harlo, Jim Dyke, performed by Company B). (Profanity, substance abuse.)

p, Catlin Adams, Melanie Mayron; d, Catlin Adams; w, Catlin Adams, Melanie Mayron; ph, Gary Thieltges (DuArt Color); ed, Bob Reitano; m, Gary Chang; m/l, Gordon Minette, Allison Cornell, Dan Higgins, Lisa Harlo, Jim Dyke; prod d, Jessica Scott-Justice; art d, Susan Beeson, Reuben Freed; set d, Brendon Smith; cos, David Norbury, Cynthia Schumacher; ch, David Hurwith; stunts, Jery Hewitt, Shane Cardwell; makeup, Peggy Nicholson.

Comedy   Cas.   (PR:C MPAA:PG-13)

STORMY MONDAY* ½**   (1988, Brit.) 93m British Screen-Film Four Intl.-Moving Picture/Atlantic c

Melanie Griffith (Kate), Tommy Lee Jones (Cosmo), Sting (Finney), Sean Bean (Brendan), James Cosmo, Mark Long, Brian Lewis, Derek Hoxby, Heathcote Williams, Prunella Gee, Guy Manning, Alison Steadman, Al Matthews, Caroline Hutchison, Fiona Sloman, Roderic Leigh, Ying Tong John, Mick Hamer.

This feature debut from British writer-director-composer Mike Figgis is a tautly constructed, deftly executed crime thriller that replaces the kind of familiar slam-bang gangster pyrotechnics last seen in Brian DePalma's THE UNTOUCHABLES (1987) with a more realistic and reflective surface. The action is set in Newcastle, England, an economically depressed city so desperate for jobs that it has given itself up to American business interests to survive. Now the city is celebrating "America Week," a self-serving public relations gimmick engineered by American business magnate/gangster Jones, who is launching an ambitious money-laundering scheme by buying up lots of Newcastle real estate. Because of the city's dire economic crisis, local political and business leaders have been more than willing to cooperate with the oily Jones. One man, however, refuses all of Jones' lucrative offers: Sting, the owner of a successful jazz club. Caught up in the conflict are Griffith, an American woman from Minnesota who has worked for Jones as a call girl, and Bean, a young jazz enthusiast who has just landed a job as a janitor in Sting's club. Griffith and Bean meet and begin to fall in love, but she is ashamed of her past and is preparing for a potentially violent break with Jones. Bean, meanwhile, overhears two hired thugs from London discussing how best to "persuade" Sting to sell his club. With a warning from Bean, the undaunted Sting is able to turn the tables on Jones' thugs, and sends the head assassin back to London with a broken arm. At the same time, Griffith quits Jones by embarrassing him in public (she, ahem, viciously squeezes the genitalia of her amorous "john," a British politician, under the banquet table at a big bash thrown by her employer). Faced with these annoying and unanticipated setbacks, Jones decides it's time to get serious. Two of his men waylay Bean and Griffith on the highway and beat them up. While both men work on Griffith, Bean finds a gun and kills one of the assailants. Instead of simply having the couple gunned down in anger, Jones decides to fool Griffith and Bean by appearing to let them leave the country. Little do they

know, however, that he has planted a bomb in their car that is set to explode en route to the airport. Meanwhile, Jones meets with Sting in person and offers to make the club owner his partner in Newcastle. While driving to the airport, Bean smells a setup and he and Griffith return to the club just as Jones and his entourage arrive to close the deal with Sting. Upon seeing Griffith, Jones blurts, "Where's the car?" Having just lent the keys to the manager of a Polish jazz band playing at the club, a horrified Bean runs out to the street to stop him. He is too late, however, and the car explodes a block away. Bean pulls a gun and is about to kill the smug Jones, but he is dissuaded by Sting, who informs his employee that the American has decided to abandon his interests in Newcastle and return to the States. Before letting Jones leave, Sting warns the gangster that if any harm should come to Bean or Griffith there will be hell to pay. Jones confidently lights a cigar and asks Griffith if she would like to come along with him. "You're lucky he was holding the gun," she says, indicating Bean, and she, Bean, and Sting leave the gangsters and return to the club.

STORMY MONDAY is a surprisingly subdued gangster film that draws its strength from subtle shadings of character and a vivid evocation of its setting, Newcastle. Figgis' script is a tightly constructed, somewhat political work that at its core equates Reaganism with gangsterism and finds both pathetically impotent. His moody realization of the screenplay is quietly effective and brimming with visual nuance and irony. Newcastle itself is a main "character," as through Roger Deakins' superb cinematography the city becomes a noirish state of mind, all dark, oppressive, and drizzly. Taking a bevy of cliched characters and casting actors known for their distinctive quirks (specifically Tommy Lee Jones and Melanie Griffith), Figgis has his players underplay their roles and make their characters something more than they appear on the scripted page. The resulting performances by Griffith, Jones, and Sean Bean are excellent, but it is Sting (a native of Newcastle) who is the real revelation. After appearing in a series of movies that failed to tap into his considerable talents, Sting has finally been given a role that allows him the space to shine, and he delivers a tightly controlled and delicately balanced performance. In a further display of remarkable assurance for a first-time director, Figgis relates small character details visually, not through dialog. We know Sting's marriage is strained because we see him with a mistress and then later see his privately distraught wife. There is never any verbal explanation of the mistress or his marriage because the explicit, and yet at the same time ambiguous, visual details are much more evocative. Figgis is not the kind of director who dumps his film in the audience's lap; he provides the framework and it is up to the audience to fill in the backstory details. The movie contains several haunting and ambiguous moments, as when the Sting prepares to ritualistically break the arm of a hired thug with the thug's own crude equipment (two blocks of wood upon which the arm rests, and then a heavy bludgeon). As Sting lays out the tools, the thug begins quietly laughing through clenched teeth, both at the absurdity of the situation and in anticipation of the excruciating pain. At the point of impact, the action cuts to another location, sparing us from a predictable scene of gore and suffering. We don't need to see it in order to feel it. The little violent action there is takes place either very quickly or off-screen. What Figgis does show in detail is the aftermath of such actions, especially when the badly battered Griffith and Bean gingerly tend to their wounds and then make love for the first time.

There is an overwhelming sense of irony to STORMY MONDAY, most of it provided by the Polish jazz band, called the Kracow Jazz Ensemble, booked to appear in Sting's club. It is they who, by arriving for the gig a day early, instigate the series of coincidences that propel the plot. Because the band that Jones had booked for his luncheon was involved in a bad traffic accident (the aftermath of which is glimpsed during the credits sequence), he is forced to employ the Polish avant-gardists. After Jones gives his hackneyed, cynical speech about the imminent revival of Newcastle's economy, the band launches into a honking, squeaking, apocalyptic free-jazz rendition of "The Star-Spangled Banner" that totally undermines the bogus good-will address that precedes it. In addition to the Kracow group, Figgis' musical score and his choice of existing tunes is quite impressive overall. Derived mostly from classic jazz and R&B, the music makes for an effective addition to the visuals and is in perfect keeping with the melancholy atmosphere. One of the most memorable moments features Sting, alone in the club after hours, soloing on bass to sooth his nerves. His mournful playing provides exquisite background music for the scene that Figgis intercuts. (While showcasing the musicianship of this actor who was first known—and most famous—as a bass player may seem gratuitous, the scene is brief, perfectly in character, and very effective.) STORMY MONDAY is a remarkable and quite promising debut film that does not subscribe to audience expectations. While some may be put off by its apparent lack of action, STORMY MONDAY is a worthy addition to the fascinating British crime films (chiefly THE LONG GOOD FRIDAY and MONA LISA) that have recently made it to American shores. (Violence, sexual situations, nudity, profanity.)

p, Nigel Stafford-Clark; d, Mike Figgis; w, Mike Figgis; ph, Roger Deakins (Rank/Agfa Color); ed, David Martin; m, Mike Figgis; prod d, Andrew McAlpine; art d, Charmian Adams; cos, Sandy Powell; stunts, Denise Ryan.

Crime/Romance   Cas.   (PR:O MPAA:R)

STREET STORY †(1988) 90m Three Wise Monkeys/Films Around the World c

Angelo Lopez (Junior), Cookie (Joey), Lydia Ramirez (Cecilia), Melvin Muza (T.C.), Soraya Andrade (Rosa), Zerocks (Willie), Rena Zentner (Nadia), Edward W. Burrows (Father).

Given a festival release in late 1988, this low-budget American independent film shot in the South Bronx focuses on two brothers making a go of it in their depressed, drug-infested, violent neighborhood. The older brother is the local hero; his younger brother a smart kid who wants a college education. Together they fight the thugs who force their barber father to pay a monthly protection fee, and resist the influence of drug-pushing local gangs.

p, Joseph B. Vasquez; d, Joseph B. Vasquez; w, Joseph B. Vasquez; ph, Joseph B. Vasquez; ed, Joseph B. Vasquez; m, Edward W. Burrows.

Drama **(PR:NR MPAA:NR)**

STUDENT AFFAIRS † (1988) 94m Platinum c

Louie Bonanno *(Louie Balducci)*, Jim Abele *(Andy Armstrong)*, Deborah Blaisdell [Veronica Hart] *(Kelly)*, Beth Broderick *(Alexis)*, Alan Fisler *(Devon Wheler)*, Jane Hamilton *(Veronica Harper)*, Richard Parnes *(Rudy)*, Ron Sullivan *(B.C.)*, Janice Doskey, W.P. Dremak, John Fasano, Jeanne Marie, Andy Nichols, Molly O'Mara, David F. Friedman, Eddie Prevot, Adam Fried.

Low-budget sexploitation director Chuck Vincent undertakes another unusual approach as he tries again to crack the mainstream market. After having his actors address the camera directly in this year's SEXPOT, here he uses a film-within-a-film structure, with his mostly adult film vets playing both "real-life" actors and "on-screen" characters in a 1950s teen film. Featuring music by Flash Cadillac and the Continental Kids, STUDENT AFFAIRS was filmed in 1986, but didn't receive video distribution until this year.

p, Chuck Vincent; d, Chuck Vincent; w, Craig Horrall, Chuck Vincent (based on a story idea by John Weidner); ph, Larry Revene; ed, Chuck Vincent, James Davalos, Chip Lambert; art d, D. Gary Phelps.

Comedy **Cas.** **(PR:NR MPAA:R)**

SUICIDE CLUB, THE* (1988) 90m Suicide Prods./Angelika c

Mariel Hemingway *(Sasha Michaels)*, Robert Joy *(Michael Collins)*, Lenny Henry *(Cam)*, Madeleine Potter *(Nancy)*, Michael O'Donaghue *(Mervin)*, Anne Carlisle *(Catherine)*, Sullivan Brown *(Brian)*, Leta McCarty *(Cowgirl)*.

A living hell of baroque tedium, THE SUICIDE CLUB is the story of what happens when bored, drugged-out rich kids decide to dress up and play games. Hemingway stars as an heiress who has been teetering on the edge of a mental breakdown ever since the suicide of her brother. Because of her instability her relationship with boy friend Joy is falling apart. When the pair spend a night out at a posh (seemingly private) restaurant with a thoroughly obnoxious wealthy young couple, things start taking an odd turn. Waiter/friend Henry whisks Hemingway off, leaving Joy alone at the table without enough money to pay the bill. In a chauffeured limousine, Henry takes Hemingway to a private costume party in a gothic mansion. The guests are an under-thirty group of the idle rich who dress in elaborate costumes and assume pretentious poses. This is no ordinary party, however. When the guests get bored, *really* bored, they partake in a lethal card game in which the "winner" must swallow a poisonous drink. Naturally, Hemingway wants to play—apparently in a twisted effort to understand her dead brother's decision. Joy eventually tracks her down and almost everyone is killed off by the picture's end. Based on Robert Louis Stevenson's *The Suicide Club* short story collection, the film quickly becomes almost unwatchable because of director Bruce's peculiar decision to have his characters speak in a stilted Old English which is more suited to the period of Stevenson's story than to the present. Besides the leaden dialog, the direction is flat and uninspired. The restaurant scene is filmed in a continuous (sub-Di Palma) dolly shot which revolves nonstop around the four characters at their dinner table. It is so head-spinning it even gives one cocaine-sniffing character a nosebleed. A low-budget exercise in amateurish literary adaptation, THE SUICIDE CLUB rates attention only because it stars Hemingway in a less-than-noteworthy performance. Perhaps Hemingway and Crisman, her husband, the film's coproducer, should concentrate their efforts on running their New York restaurant. The Stevenson story was previously filmed in 1919 in Germany as UNHEIMLICHE GESCHICTEN and again in 1932 under the same title. In 1936, Robert Montgomery and Rosalind Russell starred in a 1936 MGM adaptation entitled TROUBLE FOR TWO. THE SUICIDE CLUB was shown at film festivals in Montreal and Chicago in 1987. *(Sexual situations, drug use, profanity, violence.)*

p, James Bruce; d, James Bruce; w, Matthew Gaddis, Suzan Kouguell, Carl Caportoto (based on a story by Robert Louis Stevenson); ph, Frank Prizzi (Du Art Color); ed, James Bruce, Keith Rouse; m, Joel Diamond; prod d, Steven McCabe; cos, Natasha Landau.

Drama **Cas.** **(PR:C MPAA:R)**

SUMMER STORY, A*½ (1988, US/Brit.) 96m ITC/Atlantic c

Imogen Stubbs *(Megan David)*, James Wilby *(Frank Ashton)*, Kenneth Colley *(Jim)*, Sophie Ward *(Stella Halliday)*, Susannah York *(Mrs. Narracombe)*, Jerome Flynn *(Joe Narracombe)*, Lee Billett *(Nick Narracombe)*, Oliver Perry *(Rick Narracombe)*, Harry Burton *(Robert Garton)*, John Savident *(Bank Clerk)*, John Elmes *(Phil Halliday)*, Camilla Power *(Sabina Halliday)*, Juliette Fleming *(Freda Halliday)*, Sukie Smith *(Betsy)*, Rachel Joyce *(Post Office Girl)*.

Based on John Galsworthy's novella *The Apple Tree*, this story of failed romance is set in the West Country of England in 1902. While hiking with a chum through picturesque Dartmoor, Wilby, a well-heeled London barrister and sometime poet, injures his ankle. As luck would have it, a comely, flaxen-haired farm lass (Stubbs) is on hand, and she escorts Wilby to her aunt's farmhouse, nestled in a beautiful valley, where he boards while his ankle heals. The glorious summer days pass, and Wilby and Stubbs fall for each other, making love on piled sheepskins after the community's post-shearing celebration, wandering the green and pleasant landscape together, stealing moments of midnight passion. Stubbs' aunt (York) and her loutish son (Flynn), to whom the beauty has been "promised," are mightily upset by this blossoming relationship. Soon they make it clear to Wilby that he has worn out his welcome. He leaves, but not before planning a rendezvous with Stubbs to take her away to London. He goes to Torquay, a coastal resort town, to get money to carry out his plan, but difficulties at the bank force him to stay on longer than he wants. In Torquay, Wilby runs into an old schoolmate (Elmes) who, when told about the romantic affair, asks if this country girl will really fit into Wilby's life. As class rears its hoary head, Wilby gradually becomes interested in Elmes' poised, suitably posh sister, Ward. He misses the train that was to have taken him to Stubbs, but she faithfully treks to Torquay, where she wanders the streets in lovelorn search of Wilby. He sees her, tries to go to her, but can't bring himself to do it. Twenty years later, Wilby, now married to Ward, returns to York's farm, where he learns of Stubbs' fate, the tragic end to his summer story.

Part TESS, part THE STORY OF ADELE H., part THE FRENCH LIEUTENANT'S WOMAN, and all "Masterpiece Theater," this would-be tearjerker is gorgeously produced, but disappointingly predictable and manipulative. Director Piers Haggard (VENOM, British TV's "Pennies from Heaven") and novelist-screenwriter Penelope Mortimer have invested Gallsworthy's story with precious little passion, presenting instead a tame melodrama, punctuated with tasteful but tepid love scenes and predictable confrontations, and complete with a cliched falling-in-love montage. Only after Stubbs begins her desperate journey does the film have any real impact, and then the viewer is left with the nagging sense of being dragged through the final reel with artificially seeded tear ducts. To be sure, film newcomer Imogen Stubbs, recent darling of the Royal Shakespeare Company, is an arresting screen presence, but, despite her earnestness, she and James Wilby (MAURICE) have little chemistry. Wilby, who is rapidly becoming the British cinema's designated weak-willed upper-class twit, is considerably more convincing in 1988's A HANDFUL OF DUST than he is here. His barrister poet cries out for an introspective portrayal, but Wilby's performance is much closer to the surface. The film's best performance—save for the magnificent Devon landscape, captured in the rich Constable-like photography of cinematographer Kenneth MacMillan—is by Jerome Flynn, as Stubbs' spurned suitor. Mixing jealousy with class rage, and undercutting his domineering cloddishness with heartfelt longing and need, he is the most believable character in a film that too often feels like something we've seen before. *(Nudity, sexual situations, adult situations.)*

p, Danton Rissner; d, Piers Haggard; w, Penelope Mortimer (based on the story *The Apple Tree* by John Galsworthy); ph, Kenneth MacMillan (Agfa-Gevaert color, Rank); ed, Ralph Sheldon; m, Georges Delerue; prod d, Leo Austin; art d, Diane Dancklefsen, Richard Elton; cos, Jenny Beavan; makeup, Nicholas Forder.

Romance **(PR:C-O MPAA:PG-13)**

SUNSET* (1988) 107m Tri-Star-ML-Delphi Premier/Tri-Star c

Bruce Willis *(Tom Mix)*, James Garner *(Wyatt Earp)*, Malcolm McDowell *(Alfie Alperin)*, Mariel Hemingway *(Cheryl King)*, Kathleen Quinlan *(Nancy Shoemaker)*, Jennifer Edwards *(Victoria Alperin)*, Patricia Hodge *(Christina Alperin)*, Richard Bradford *(Capt. Blackworth)*, M. Emmet Walsh *(Chief Dibner)*, Joe Dallesandro *(Dutch Kieffer)*, Andreas Katsulas *(Arthur)*, Dann Florek *(Marty Goldberg)*, Bill Marcus *(Hal Flynn)*, Michael C. Gwynne *(Mooch)*, Dermot Mulroney *(Michael Alperin)*, Miranda Garrison *(Spanish Dancer)*, Liz Torres *(Rosa)*, Castulo Guerra *(Pancho)*, Dakin Matthews *(William Singer)*, Vernon Wells *(Australian Houseman)*, Dennis Rucker *(Paul)*, John Dennis Johnston *(Ed)*, Kenny Call *(Cowboy Fred)*, Jack Garner *(Cowboy Henry)*, Jerry Tullos *(Leo Vogel)*, Steem Tanney *(Conductor)*, Peter Jason *(Frank Coe)*, Richard Fancy *(Academy Speaker)*, Glenn Shadix *(Roscoe Arbuckle)*, Lisa Alpert *(Michael's Secretary)*, Sonia Zimmer *(Dibner's Secretary)*, Marina Palmier, Tessa Taylor *(Candy Store Girls)*, John Van Ness *(Director)*, Randy Bowers *(Assistant Director)*, Maureen Teefy *(Stagecoach Lady)*, Arnold Johnson *(Mix Butler)*, Eric Harrison *(Alperin Butler)*, Amy Michelson *(Alfie's First Wife)*, James O'Connell *(Gate Guard)*, Bing Russell *(Studio Guard)*, C. James Lewis *(Jail Guard)*, Bill Applegate, Luis Contreras, Charles Noland, Robert Covarrubias *(Jail Inmates)*, Dolalin Patton, Kay Perry *(Girls at Lunch)*, Rod McCary *(Douglas Fairbanks)*, John Fountain *(John Gilbert)*, Irene Olga Lopez *(Asuncion Maria romero)*, Jeris Poindexter *(Cleaning Man)*, F. William Parker *(Mayor of Pasadena)*, Grant Heslov *(Car Attendant)*, Don Sparks, Melanie Jones, Darrah Meeley, Tom Tarpey, Krista Gray, Katie Morgan *(Reporters)*.

Here's an interesting idea for a movie: What if Wyatt Earp and Tom Mix teamed up to solve a murder in the late 1920s? Sounds like a "buddy movie" worth watching, right? Well, unfortunately, SUNSET falls short of its promising premise. The year is 1929 and Garner, playing Earp, is hired as a technical advisor for "The Lawman," a film about his life. In a brilliant casting stroke, McDowell, the sadistic head of Alperin Pictures, decides that silent film star Tom Mix (Willis) should play the legendary marshal in the biopic. After a day's shooting, Garner is summoned by Hodge, an old friend who also happens to be McDowell's wife. Amusingly disarming Katsulas, McDowell's chauffeur-body guard, before entering the mansion, Garner is asked by Hodge to look for her son (Mulroney), a typical Hollywood brat who may be in some kind of trouble. Later that evening, Garner and Willis visit the Candy Store, a house of ill repute. The Candy Store is run by Hemingway, who, unbeknownst to Garner and Willis, is actually the daughter of the bordello's owner, the original Candy, who, in order to prevent her daughter from "working," has Hemingway wear men's clothing. Hemingway leads Garner and Willis to the bar, where they encounter McDowell's sister (Edwards) and her gangster boy friend (Dallesandro). Instructed that Candy can be found in the bungalow out back, Willis and Garner go in search of the proprietor just in time to see a black Cadillac pull away from the bungalow. The

pair then discover Candy's dead body, the sight of which shocks Hemingway into a piercing scream, and also find Mulroney wandering around in a stupor. Willis calls a studio publicist friend, Quinlan, who agrees to let Mulroney hide from the police at her place, whereupon Garner and Mulroney head off in Willis' car, barely escaping the cops. In the course of the ensuing movie-making and the western heroes' investigation of Candy's death, Willis takes Garner under his wing and the two become friends, while Garner enjoys a brief romance with Hemingway. The film's finale occurs shortly after the first Academy Awards ceremony, when a car chase leads to the identification of the culprit.

SUNSET is a mystery without suspense and a comedy that just isn't funny, partly because of director-writer Blake Edwards' (the "Pink Panther" films; 10; S.O.B.; BLIND DATE—all much superior to this offering) burdensome script, which is loaded with plot twists that don't enhance the story. James Garner, however, is ideal as Wyatt Earp (who actually died in 1928, just before SUNSET's story takes place), maintaining the easygoing charm evident in everything he does, from MURPHY'S ROMANCE to "The Rockford Files." Bruce Willis turns up the star power as Mix and cuts an impressive figure in a cowboy suit; Malcolm McDowell is quite menacing as the evil head of Alperin Pictures. With so much talent wasted, this is truly one film that deserves to ride off into the sunset. (Violence, profanity, adult situations.)

p, Tony Adams; d, Blake Edwards; w, Blake Edwards (based on a story by Rod Amateau); ph, Anthony B. Richmond (Panavision, Technicolor); ed, Robert Pergament; m, Henry Mancini, Duke Ellington; prod d, Rodger Maus; art d, Richard Y. Haman; set d, Marvin March; spec eff, Dan Cangemi; cos, Patricia Norris; ch, Miranda Garrison, Miriam Nelson; stunts, Joe Dunne; makeup, Rick Sharp, Brad Wilder, Charlene Roberson, Dave Grayson.

Mystery/Western   **Cas.**   **(PR:C MPAA:R)**

SURVIVOR †   (1988, Brit.) 91m Matrix/Vestron c

Chip Mayer (Survivor), Richard Moll (Kragg), Sue Kiel, Richard Haines, John Carson, Rex Garner, Sandra Duncan, Sven Forsell, Bima Stagg.

The MAD MAX rip-offs just keep on coming. This one seems to have been filmed in South Africa. Chip Mayer stars as a NASA astronaut who returns to Earth after WW III has destroyed life as he knew it. Wandering the desert wasteland, he stumbles upon a subterranean society lorded over by crazed despot Moll (Bull on TV's "Night Court"), who has hoarded a bevy of beautiful women and plans to repopulate the planet in his image. Unfortunately, he can't keep up with the demand and he attempts to draft Mayer to aid the cause, but Mayer has other ideas and a pitched battle ensues. A direct-to-video release.

p, Martin Wragge; d, Michael Shackleton; w, Bima Stagg; ph, Fred Tammes; ed, Max Lemon; m, Andraan Strydom.

Science Fiction   **Cas.**   **(PR:NR MPAA:NR)**

SWEET HEART'S DANCE**   (1988) 101m Chestnut Hill/Tri-Star c

Don Johnson (Wiley Boon), Susan Sarandon (Sandra Boon), Jeff Daniels (Sam Manners), Elizabeth Perkins (Adie Nims), Kate Reid (Pearne Manners), Justin Henry (Kyle Boon), Holly Marie Combs (Debs Boon), Heather Coleman (BJ Boon), Matthew Wohl (Dick Merezini), Stephen Stabler (Wayne Rodemeyer), Laurie Corbin (Claire Norton), Lanie Conklin (Darielle Johnson), Jock MacDonald (Peter Barrett), Frits Momsen (Joe Canecki), Stephen Robert Moorhead (Robby Canecki), Paul Schnabel (Policeman), Jerrilyn Miller (Ellen Becker), Heather Driscoll (Sherry Rooney), Anna Groskin (Student), Mary Carol Maganzini (Lois Clarent), Meghan A. Brooks (Mouse), Mark Brooks (Tom Sechrist), Letitia Leahy (Eunice Wimert), Henry Haselton (Buzzy Barker), Jack Hughes (Rawson Mason), Samuel Kaufman, Jonathan Murad, Todd Ludy, Seth Feeley (Teenagers), Tyrone Shaw, Daniel Coane, Jerry Highter, Kathleen Coane (The Throbulators), Cecil Xavier, Juan Smith, Austin Bowen, Sinclair Hodge, Patrick Rogers (Late Hours), Al Cerullo (Helicopter Pilot).

Made watchable only by the efforts of its likable cast, SWEET HEART'S DANCE is a hopeless mess that plays more like a rough outline for a film than a finished

product. Set in a small town in Vermont, the movie follows the fortunes of two close buddies who have lived there their whole lives. Johnson is a contractor who married his high-school sweetheart, Sarandon, and quickly had three kids. His pal, Daniels, has become the principal of their former high school, is single, and still lives with his mother. Both are arrested adolescents and get along with each other better than they do with their families, constantly clowning around like a couple of teenagers—egging cars, ice-skating, sledding, and sailing. Although Johnson and Sarandon ostensibly have the perfect marriage, their relationship is dying due to lack of interest, and, feeling stifled, Johnson wants out and walks after a fight erupts between husband and wife during Thanksgiving dinner. Hired to build a new gymnasium at the high school, the contractor moves into a trailer on the work site. Meanwhile, Daniels has fallen for a young grade-school teacher, Perkins, and has to divide his attention among her and his lifelong friends. Emotional sparks fly for several weeks while Johnson and Sarandon try to adjust to life without each other and the children adapt to life without father. Teenager Henry is especially troubled, thinking his dad an immature jerk for wanting to change his life at the age of 35. With a community trip to the Caribbean in the offing, Sarandon decides she wants to go despite their marital problems and demands that Johnson take her, noting that "No parts of our bodies have to touch." Johnson gives in, and, flush with what he considers to be progress in his friends' marriage, Daniels goes off to propose to Perkins. Taken aback by the offer, Perkins declines, stating that marriage isn't really something she is considering at this point in her life. Crushed, Daniels goes to the Caribbean with his mother, but later receives a call from Perkins, who wants to continue the relationship. Things go from bad to worse between Johnson and Sarandon, with Sarandon so lonely that she climbs into bed with Daniels. He politely declines to make love with her, citing all the obvious reasons, but enfolds her in his comforting arms. Johnson then happens upon the scene and assumes the worst, but after much yelling and throwing of furniture, all is straightened out. The next day Johnson and Sarandon have a fight and then make love for the first time in over a year. However, this minor victory does not a marriage make and upon their return to Vermont, Johnson goes back to his trailer. In the end, though, he decides to make an effort to patch up their marriage by trying to recapture the romance of their youth.

Structured in a manner that prevents the scenes from flowing smoothly one into another, SWEET HEART'S DANCE jerks along at a sluggish pace and never really takes off. Each scene opens with a black-and-white freeze frame and a title card informing the viewer that it is Halloween, the first frost, Thanksgiving, Christmas, New Year's Eve, etc. The scenes themselves are short and perfunctory, as if created from mere notes rather than anything that has been thought through. Further, much of the key emotional action takes place off-screen, with the characters returning in the next scene to talk about what the viewer hasn't seen. As directed by Robert Greenwald, best known for the made-for-TV movie "The Burning Bed," the film is terribly unfocused and vague, leaving the audience to fill in the blanks. Is this a buddy film? Is it a domestic drama? Is it a small-town slice-of-life tale? Is it a romance? Is it a comedy? All of these elements are thrown together in SWEET HEART'S DANCE and none of them works. Just what the filmmakers are trying to say about these characters is anyone's guess. We are shown that Johnson and Daniels' basic immaturity is what prevents them from becoming responsible adults, and Johnson's childish high jinks and his nostalgia for the pranks of his youth are shown encouraging his son to behave irresponsibly. It is only through the heartbreak of the family's disintegrating that Henry begins to grow up and take on the mantle of adulthood—showing himself to be more mature than his own father. But if clinging to one's teenage years is meant to be seen as delusive and harmful, why does the film's conclusion seem to endorse an attempt to recapture the romance of youth? Are we to believe that it is Sarandon who is the real villain here because she has accepted her role as wife and mother—because she has grown up and left her husband behind? In the end the film seems to sanction emotional regression rather than mature growth.

ON GOLDEN POND writer Ernest Thompson wrote the screenplay but subsequently disowned SWEET HEART'S DANCE, citing a corruption of his concept. In addition, after the principal photography was completed it was decided that the film needed changes and the cast was called back for reshooting. This is especially apparent in the ending, wherein Don Johnson's hair suddenly becomes very "Miami Vice" like after the trip to the Caribbean. Despite the total chaos taking place on-screen, however, the viewer can cling to the somewhat engaging performances of Johnson, Susan Sarandon, Elizabeth Perkins, and especially Jeff Daniels. They are all pleasant people and, despite the fact that they behave like idiots, exude much warmth and humor. Moreover, the film does have a sense of community and friendship that is appealing, and the snowy Vermont scenery is certainly pretty. Unfortunately, the deficiencies of the material overwhelm the benefits of performance, crippling the film and making it an extremely frustrating experience. *(Profanity, adult situations, sexual situations, nudity.)*

p, Jeffrey Lurie; d, Robert Greenwald; w, Ernest Thompson; ph, Tak Fujimoto (Technicolor); ed, Robert Florio; m, Richard Gibbs; md, Debbie Gold; prod d, James Allen; set d, R. Lynn Smart; spec eff, Walter Wayne Walser; cos, Bobbie Read; stunts, Bobby Foxworth, Gary Hymes; makeup, Allan Apone, Allen Weisinger.

| Comedy/Drama | Cas. | (PR:C-O MPAA:R) |

SWITCHING CHANNELS**½   (1988) 105m Tri-Star c

Kathleen Turner *(Christy Colleran)*, Burt Reynolds *(John L. Sullivan IV)*, Christopher Reeve *(Blaine Bingham)*, Ned Beatty *(Roy Ridnitz)*, Henry Gibson *(Ike Roscoe)*, George Newbern *(Siegenthaler)*, Al Waxman *(Berger)*, Ken James *(Warden Terwilliger)*, Barry Flatman *(Zaks)*, Ted Simonett *(Tillinger)*, Anthony Sherwood *(Carvalho)*, Joe Silver *(Morosini)*, Charles Kimbrough *(Governor)*, Monica Parker *(Jessica)*, Allan Royal *(Obregon)*, Fiona Reid *(Pamela Farbrother)*, Andre Mayers *(Jesse)*, Bill Randolph *(Eric)*, Richard Comar *(Governor's Aide)*, Grant Cowan *(Crannock)*, Wayne Fleming *(Bryce)*, Laura Robinson *(Karen Ludlow)*, Angelo Rizacos *(Ridnitz's Sidekick)*, Tony Rosato *(Joker)*, Jackie Richardson *(Abigail)*, Laurie Paton, Warren Davis, Katya Ladan, Rex Hagon *(Reporters)*, Philip Akin, Patrick Patterson *(Guards)*, Jonathan Welsh *(Chaplain)*, Russell Gordon *(Jasper)*, Corrine Koslo *(Yvonne)*, Judah Katz *(Tillinger Sound Man)*, Jason Blicker *(Sound Man)*, Diane Douglass *(Upper-Class Woman)*, Ida Carnevali *(Poor "Yuppie" Mother)*, Noel Gray *(Nancy)*, Megan Smith, Jane Schoettle *(Booking Secretaries)*, Philip Malotte *(6'8" Cameraman)*, Chick Roberts *(Cop)*, Bill Cotterell *(Rusty)*, James Loxley *(Anchorman)*, Cheryl S. Wilson, Ray Landry *(SNN Anchorpersons)*, John Dee *(Old Man In Lobby)*, Peter Walachy *(Tattooee)*, John Davies *(Aide)*, Eric Fink *(Butler)*, Jack Duffy *(Emil, the Waiter)*, Robert Morelli *(Waiter)*, Arlene Mazerolle *(Hotel Receptionist)*.

© TRI-STAR

Sixty years after the Broadway opening of "The Front Page," that biting and expertly scripted Ben Hecht-Charles MacArthur comedy is still entertaining mass audiences. First filmed in 1931 as THE FRONT PAGE and starring Adolphe Menjou and Pat O'Brien, the story told of an escaped convict's surrender to a newsman and the comic events that followed as the story broke. A remake and revision came in 1940 as HIS GIRL FRIDAY. Under the direction of Howard Hawks and with the acting talents of Cary Grant, Rosalind Russell, and Ralph Bellamy, "The Front Page" became a newspaper *romantic* comedy simply by changing the sex of O'Brien's "Hildy Johnson." With a boiling sexual tension between Grant and Russell and Hawks' barrage of lightning-fast dialogue, HIS GIRL FRIDAY emerged as one the finest films ever made—a heralded example of the "screwball comedy" genre. The infallibility and timelessness of the Hecht-MacArthur story led to another adaptation in 1974—a tougher, more "realistic" version under Billy Wilder's cynical direction and with Walter Matthau and Jack Lemmon in the leads. Returning to the romantic triangle of HIS GIRL FRIDAY is this 1988 update starring Burt Reynolds, Kathleen Turner, and Christopher Reeve in the Grant, Russell, and Bellamy roles, respectively. SWITCHING CHANNELS is not so much a remake of HIS GIRL FRIDAY but a modernization that makes the story infinitely more palatable to today's media-minded audience.

The picture opens with Turner, a news reporter for fictional Chicago cable station SNN (Satellite News Network), working on a variety of tough assignments. She takes a much-needed vacation and ends up in love with Reeve, a smug, rich elitist who owns a gym equipment firm. Before running off with Reeve to a new life in New York as a personality on a morning talk show, Turner stops at the SNN offices to say farewell to news director Reynolds, her former husband and now former boss. Determined to keep the top-rated Turner on his station, Reynolds resorts to some unscrupulous means. He has his staff book all upcoming flights to New York so Turner can't leave. He sends the agoraphobic Reeve up 17 floors, and thereby into a panic, in a glass elevator. He strategically gives assignments that would have been handled by

Turner to a dizzy new reporter. Finally, by contracting for $150,000 of gym equipment from Reeve's company, he convinces Turner to do one last story. Turner secures a videotape interview with Gibson, a shy, reserved man about to be executed for killing his son's drug supplier without realizing that he was also a cop. The tape airs and convinces everyone that Gibson is merely a pawn in a political game to get corrupt DA Beatty elected governor. When Beatty is informed of a rumor that the present governor is going to pardon Gibson, he moves the execution up two hours and invites the press. (The governor is taking a nap, and apparently his staff, family, and friends have not heard about the televised execution—although every pressperson for miles around is in attendance.) Meanwhile, Turner has stood firm by her decision to quit. While on their way to the train station, Turner and Reeve drive by the prison. They see the prison lights go out. She then spots a panicked Gibson hurriedly zig-zagging away from the prison walls. Having performed a Houdini-inspired escape, Gibson managed to sneak away when the television equipment caused a power outage. Turner hides Gibson in the city news pressroom—not in a roll-top desk, as in the Hecht-MacArthur story, but in a copier machine. She then contacts Reynolds, who offers to buy the copier in order to sneak Gibson out of the packed room. They nearly escape by elevator but Beatty and a comic SWAT team corner them, filling the copier and, apparently, Gibson full of gunshot holes. Beatty opens the copier doors only to find that Gibson has pulled another Houdini trick. Beatty arrests Turner and Reynolds, but the governor arrives and Gibson comes out of hiding (from atop the elevator car). Pointing to Gibson, Reynolds, Turner, and Beatty, respectively, the governor says "You're pardoned, you're pardoned, you're pardoned, and you're not." Having rediscovered her love of the newsroom and of Reynolds, Turner gives Reeve the send-off and accepts Reynolds' proposal of remarriage.

It should come as no surprise that SWITCHING CHANNELS falters in comparison to all three previous Hecht-MacArthur adaptations, though it does provide some innocuous entertainment. Ted (FIRST BLOOD; FUN WITH DICK AND JANE; NORTH DALLAS FORTY) Kotcheff's direction is serviceable in its dependence on caricature and comic exaggeration, but his talents fall far short of those of Lewis Milestone, Howard Hawks, or Billy Wilder. As a result, the entire film feels forced—as if the biting pace and vitality of HIS GIRL FRIDAY had been replaced by a generic television quality. Looking more like a TV situation comedy than a film, nothing in SWITCHING CHANNELS reaches beyond the surface (which is probably appropriate for its TV station setting). The stars, however, do a great job within these limitations—Kathleen Turner makes up for the box-office dud JULIA AND JULIA; Christopher Reeve proves, as he did in STREET SMART, that he doesn't need his SUPERMAN cape; and Burt Reynolds (in a role originally set for Michael Caine, who went over schedule on JAWS: THE REVENGE, thereby also missing the acceptance of his HANNAH AND HER SISTERS Oscar) turns in his first "respectable" performance in some time. Working against them, however, is an empty-headed script which is so filled with extraneous situations (Turner's vacation travelog, Reeve's elevator trip) and plot implausibilities (the deux ex machina of Gibson's Houdini escapes, which simply let the screenwriter escape from his own impossible setups) that it's a wonder the film comes together by the finale. Destroying the film's atmosphere (something the previous pictures had plenty of) is its location—supposedly a gritty Chicago, it looks more like a generic suburb. (As in 1987's ADVENTURES IN BABYSITTING and THE BIG TOWN, Toronto is again the stand-in for the Midwestern metropolis.) There are, however, some genuinely funny moments, a few witty attacks on the insensitivity of the press, and a brilliant performance by Henry Gibson (one of the former stars of TV's "Laugh In" and a frequent member of Robert Altman's ensemble). By erasing the Grant-Russell sexual tension and making the Reynolds-Turner love relationship more akin to sibling rivalry, SWITCHING CHANNELS emerges as a squeaky clean comedy that (save for Beatty comically mouthing unheard obscenities) can safely be seen by youngsters.

p, Martin Ransohoff; d, Ted Kotcheff; w, Jonathan Reynolds (based on the play "The Front Page" by Ben Hecht, Charles MacArthur); ph, Francois Protat (Medallion Color); ed, Thom Noble; m, Michel Legrand; prod d, Anne Pritchard; art d, Charles Dunlop; set d, Mark Freeborn, Rose Marie McSherry; spec eff, Rory Cutler; cos, Mary McLeod; makeup, Katherine Southern.

| Comedy | Cas. | (PR:A MPAA:PG) |

T

TAFFIN* (1988, US/Brit.) 96m United British Artists-Rafford-MGM/MGM-UA c

Pierce Brosnan (*Mark Taffin*), Ray McAnally (*O'Rourke*), Alison Doody (*Charlotte*), Jeremy Child (*Martin*), Patrick Bergan (*Mo Taffin*), Ronan Wilmot (*The Deacon*), Alan Stanford (*Sprawley*), Gerard McSorley (*Ed*), Jim Bartley (*Conway*), Jonathan Ryan (*Gibson, Councilman*), Dearbhla Molloy (*Mrs. Martin*), Britta Smith (*Mrs. Taffin*), Liz Lloyd (*Valerie Gibson*), Liam O'Callaghan (*Henderson*), Frank Kelly (*Liam*), Catherine Byrne (*Shirley*), Sarah Carroll (*Maeve*), Connor Tallon (*Yellow Hat*), Sean Lawlor (*Seamus*), David Nolan (*Newton*), Margaret Fegan (*Sprawley's Secretary*), Stephen Ryan (*Mick*), Padraig O'Loinsig (*Kevin*), Andrew Roddy (*Chas*), Aiden Grenell (*Colonel Brain*), Clive Geraghty (*The Butcher*), Alec Doran (*Boat-shed Owner*), Dermot Morgan (*Micky Guest*), Robert Carrickford (*Alan Hart*), Fran Brennan (*Garda*), Peter Caffey (*Restaurant Owner*), Tina Shaw (*Lola*), Colette Dolan (*Stripper*), Dave Carey (*Car Dealer*), Bosco Hagan (*Builder*), Adele King (*Rosie*), Stanley Townsend (*Les*), Dave Duffy (*Dave*), Martin Dunne (*Harry*), Frank O'Sullivan (*Frank*).

TAFFIN is set in a small Irish town where the title character (Brosnan), an ex-seminarian, now earns his living as a debt collector. Brosnan is also a martial arts expert, as he proves when he visits a restaurant to collect money owed to a butcher, and easily defeats three burly employees who try to throw him out. Taffin goes to a pub to collect payment for a renovation done on the building, and there meets barmaid Doody. She asks him for a ride home, and before long he moves in with her. Upon learning that the local athletic field is threatened by road construction, Brosnan's brother, Mo (Bergan), encourages his sibling to help save it. Brosnan begins an investigation and finds that a councilman (Ryan) and farmer (O'Callaghan) have conspired to run the road through the playing field to protect O'Callaghan's land. Brosnan forces the pair to relent and the road is diverted. However, when it's learned that the road is going to serve a new chemical plant, a number of irate townspeople ask Brosnan to join their effort to block the plant. He declines, but after his former teacher (McAnally) is beaten by supporters of the plant, he gets involved, learning that corrupt businessman Stanford and another councilman (Child) are behind the plant construction. As Brosnan is about to expose Child, Stanford has the councilman murdered. Stanford then sends thugs to get rid of Brosnan, but he outwits the hired assassins, dispatching them and taking their car to meet Stanford, whom he also kills, insuring the plant will not be built.

Pierce Brosnan is sadly miscast as the hero of this turgid melodrama. In his battle scenes, his karate moves are amateurish and clumsy, and the rest of the time he's so mild-mannered and laid back it's impossible to understand why people fear him. Although it tries for depth, glancing over environmental issues, TAFFIN has little heart and less stomach for such heavy topics. It remains unsure whether it is an action film or a political tome, and becomes merely a confrontation between Irish townspeople and a big, bad conglomerate. Perhaps therein lies a lapsed Northern Ireland versus IRA fable. Perhaps not.

Technically the film is a mess. The burning down of a billboard proclaiming the wonders of the planned chemical plant occurs in broad daylight, but the next day, the vandalism is said to have been perpetrated under cover of darkness. Episodes with little or no bearing on one another take place on the same patch of countryside, and characters inexplicably come and go bearing little discernible relationship to the proceedings. Further, the confusing cast of villains is difficult to keep straight, and their acts of "violence" against the plant protesters are none too threatening, encompassing such mundane abuses as blowing up an outhouse and throwing one poor guy's laundry on a wet street. Horrors! As abysmal as this all is, it's easy to understand why this film received only a very limited release before turning up on video. (*Graphic violence, adult situations, sexual situations, nudity, profanity.*)

p, Peter Shaw; d, Francis Megahy; w, David Ambrose (based on the book by Lyndon Mallett); ph, Paul Beeson (Technicolor); ed, Rodney Holland; m, Stanley Myers, Hans Zimmer; prod d, William Alexander; art d, Martin Atkinson; set d, Jim Harken; spec eff, Kit West, David Watkins; cos, Imogen Magnus; stunts, Peter Brayham; makeup, Rosie Blackmore.

| Action/Political | Cas. | (PR:C MPAA:R) |

TAKE TWO † (1988) 100m Ronnie Hadar/TBJ c

Grant Goodeve (*Barry/Frank*), Robin Mattson (*Susan Bentley*), Frank Stallone (*Ted Marvin*), Nita Talbot (*Betty Griffith*), Warren Berlinger (*Apartment Manager*), Mickey Morton (*Det. Stratton*), Darwin Swalve (*Gun Dealer*), Suzee M. Slater (*Sherrie*), Karen Mayo-Chandler (*Dorothy*).

Yes, 1988 was definitely the year for movies about twins, and the direct-to-video releases are no exception. When a surrogate mother, Talbot, gives birth to twins, she keeps one named Barry for herself and hands the other, named Frank, over to the man who had paid for her to bear her *one* child. When the boys grow into adults, Talbot tells Barry (Goodeve) about his twin brother and encourages him to go to Los Angeles to collect his rightful share of his father's estate. Frank (also played by Goodeve) is now a successful businessman and has no time to listen to his twin's non-

sense. Seeking revenge, Barry poses as Frank and seduces his twin's bored and abused wife, Mattson. Since Mattson doesn't much care for her husband anyway, she is pleased to learn that Frank is really Barry, and teams up with the twin to murder the creep. Trouble looms, however, in the form of Mattson's other lover, Stallone, a brutish rock singer who wants a piece of the action.

p, Ronnie Hadar; d, Peter Rowe; w, Moshe Hadar; ph, James Mathers (Foto-Kem Color); ed, Terry Chiappe; m, Donald Hulette.

| Crime | Cas. | (PR:NR MPAA:R) |

TALK RADIO***½ (1988) 110m Cineplex Odeon-Edward R. Pressman-Ten Four/UNIV c

Eric Bogosian (*Barry Champlain*), Alec Baldwin (*Dan*), Ellen Greene (*Ellen*), Leslie Hope (*Laura*), John C. McGinley (*Stu*), John Pankow (*Chuck Dietz*), Michael Wincott (*Kent*), Zach Grenier (*Sid Greenberg*), Anna Levine (*Woman at Basketball Game*), Robert Trebor (*Jeffrey Fisher*), Linda Atkinson (*Sheila Fleming*), Allan Corduner (*Vince*).

Having positioned himself as the angry conscience of the American commercial cinema, writer-director Oliver Stone seems determined to point out the sickness he sees in American society, and does so with a single-minded fury and passion that sometimes threatens to overwhelm his films. In his latest effort, Stone has found a collaborator who shares his instincts, performance artist and writer Eric Bogosian. TALK RADIO is based on Bogosian's one-man play of the same name, which premiered in 1985 in Portland, Oregon, before moving to a sold-out engagement Off-Broadway in 1987. Stone and Bogosian decided to combine the play with material from the life and death of the controversial Denver radio talk show host Alan Berg, who was murdered by neo-fascists in 1984. A reflection of the warped American psyche, TALK RADIO is set in the conservative hotbed of Dallas, Texas, and presents us with loathsome radio talk show host Barry Champlain (Bogosian), a driven, self-loathing, Jewish liberal who actively antagonizes his listeners and ironically bills himself as "the man you love to love." Although his concerns seem humanistic, Bogosian enjoys mercilessly taunting both his detractors and supporters with a litany of hurtful words. A hopelessly optimistic wheelchair-bound listener or glad-handing black man are as likely to suffer Bogosian's wrath as the redneck, racist, anti-Semitic neo-Nazis who send him swastika flags and dead rats in the mail. Bogosian has a knack for quickly searching out his caller's vulnerabilities and then attacking them like a pit bull, humiliating his listeners. The biggest sin a caller can commit, however, is to bore the host, for he will immediately cut them off with a rude comment and hang up. In spite of Bogosian's repugnant demeanor, his show is a hit. During a set of commercials on his Friday night broadcast, Bogosian learns that his show is about to go national via a satellite feed on Monday. In the studio is Pankow, a radio network representative who has come to the station to observe Bogosian in action. Although station manager Baldwin has worked hard on the deal, Bogosian resents being judged, fears he will be asked to tone down his venom, and then goes out of his way to make his show even more scathing than usual. With the help of his loyal engineer McGinley, a parade of bizarre callers hits the air and Bogosian makes mincemeat of them. Although he is sleeping with his attractive female producer, Hope, Bogosian is still dependent on his ex-wife, Greene, and he asks her by phone to come to Dallas to lend moral support during the first national broadcast. Just as rude and insensitive away from the microphone as he is in front of it, Bogosian finds that his "fans" don't hesitate to abuse him in public when he makes a personal appearance at a basketball game and is booed out of the stadium. Picking up Greene at the airport on Sunday, Bogosian recalls how he got his start on radio while working as an outspoken suit salesman. A frequent guest on a local talk show, Bogosian's straight-shooting, acerbic style caught on with the listeners and soon he had his own program, during which, in order to keep the show interesting, Bogosian didn't hesitate to ask Greene to call in as the fictitious "Cheryl Ann" to spark some controversy. Succumbing to the temptations that come with fame, Bogosian destroyed the marriage when Greene caught him cheating on her. Back in the present, Bogosian confesses to Greene that he still loves her, but she claims that she is happy with her dull suburban existence and can't keep up with him any longer. Come Monday, Bogosian is shocked to learn that the deal for the national feed has been delayed, and the news seems to take him to the edge. Even more vicious than usual, Bogosian fends off several threats on his life from right-wing nuts and even invites an obviously unstable teenage caller (Wincott) to visit him at the studio, much to Baldwin's horror. Sensing that her ex-husband is on the brink of a nervous breakdown, Greene phones in as Cheryl Ann and confesses that she is bored with her safe suburban lifestyle and still in love with him. Bogosian responds to his ex-wife's heartfelt confession with an especially virulent tirade, which basically dismisses her as pathetic. Realizing that he is too far gone to save, Greene tearfully leaves the studio. When the teenager finally shows up, Bogosian interviews him live and is horrified by this moronic, drug-addled, amoral vision of America's future (actor Michael Wincott, a veteran of the stage production, nearly steals the film). When Wincott finally goes too far and is dragged out of the studio, he reaches into his jacket and pulls out a small camera, aiming it at Bogosian like a gun and flashing it in the talk-show host's face. Bogosian ends his show with a repudiation of his listeners, condemning them for turning their fear, hate, and suffering into their entertainment: "I tell you what you are. I have no choice, you frighten me . . . But I guess we're stuck with each other." When the exhausting show is over, Bogosian is certain that he has blown the national syndication deal and is surprised to hear from Pankow that all systems are still go. Walking to the parking lot with Hope, Bogosian bids her goodnight and goes to his car, where he is accosted by a man asking for an autograph. When Bogosian takes the pen and paper, the man—obviously a neo-Nazi—pulls a handgun and kills Bogosian. As the camera hovers above the city of Dallas, the airwaves are filled with callers lamenting Bogosian's death.

Fueled by a brilliant performance from Bogosian, TALK RADIO is an unrelentingly intense experience that will leave most audiences feeling drained. Director Stone took on the project to make some quick money after losing $50,000 on a bad stock tip he got while filming WALL STREET. Executive producer Ed Pressman, who had purchased the rights to Bogosian's play, gave the project to Stone, who filmed it on a $3.5 million budget in just 24 days. TALK RADIO is claustrophobic in the extreme, with Stone anchoring the vast majority of the film in the radio studio and leaving the camera focused on Bogosian's face as he provokes the excretion of American resentment, hatred, and fear. As in WALL STREET, Stone turns the workplace into a battleground, and his camera scurries into the trenches. The director transforms his rather static subject (man in front of microphone) into a dizzyingly mobile one by having the camera dance around Bogosian or Bogosian dance around it, aided by a headset-microphone combination with a long cord. This is the opposite approach to that taken by Jonathan Demme in SWIMMING TO CAMBODIA (which starred Spaulding Gray, often mentioned with Bogosian in discussions of contemporary "monologists"), wherein each camera move or cut was conducted with mathematic precision to enhance, not overwhelm, the performer. Stone's is a much more hysterical sensibility, and it is perfect for the material at hand. The camera—and sometimes the set itself—is always on the move, probing, swirling, searching, trying to break out of the tight space that confines it. What Stone does not do, thankfully, is take the route chosen by Barry Levinson in GOOD MORNING VIETNAM and cut to reaction shots of the radio listeners as the outrageous DJ struts his stuff. For Stone, the camera swooping in to a tight close-up of Bogosian is the listener substitute, a visual equivalent of the thousands of angry ghosts that haunt the airwaves of America.

Less successful is the expansion of the stageplay. Although the additional characters are well performed by the talented cast, they seem tacked on to give the audience a breather between tirades. Especially weak is the lengthy, overlit flashback sequence, which introduces some unnecessary background information and simplistic "psychological" motivation, thus cheapening the complicated Champlain. As a result, the flashback feels a bit too much like padding and serves to diffuse some of the tension built up by Stone in the first half. Overwrought lines of dialog like "He's all alone out there" and "He's going down in flames" also threaten to drive this dark, hard-edged material into melodramatics. Luckily, Stone seems to know just when to back off, and Bogosian's compelling performance effectively bulldozes over any minor annoyances in the screenplay. A distinctly unlikable character, Bogosian's Barry Champlain could be an extension of the James Woods role in Stone's SALVADOR, a self-confessed asshole who thrives on harsh, often violent, confrontation. But, whereas Woods' character is redeemed in the end, there is no such redemption for Champlain, only death at the hands of those he has provoked into revealing themselves. Although they raise far more questions about the state of things than they answer, Bogosian and Stone do a magnificent job drawing the viewer into Champlain's nocturnal world, encouraging our contempt for the callers. But then the filmmakers turn the tables on us in a chilling close-up, in which Champlain takes a slow, sidelong glance at the camera—implicating the movie audience along with himself and his sick callers. With the rise of shock radio, confrontational talk shows, and real-life crime exposes, Americans *have* turned all that is negative about their society into their entertainment—and that is the most frightening thought of all. Includes the song "Bad To The Bone" (performed by George Thorogood). *(Sexual situations, violence, adult situations, profanity.)*

p, Edward R. Pressman, A. Kitman Ho; d, Oliver Stone; w, Eric Bogosian, Oliver Stone (based on the play "Talk Radio" created by Eric Bogosian, Tad Savinar, written by Eric Bogosian, and the book *Talked to Death: The Life and Murder of Alan Berg* by Stephen Singular); ph, Robert Richardson (DeLuxe Color); ed, David Brenner, Joe Hutshing; m, Stewart Copeland; prod d, Bruno Rubeo; art d, Milo; set d, Derek R. Hill; cos, Ellen Mirojnick.

Drama **Cas.** **(PR:O MPAA:R)**

TALKING TO STRANGERS** (1988) 92m Baltimore Film Factory c

Ken Gruz *(Jesse)*, Dennis Jordan *(Red Coat)*, Marvin Hunter *(General)*, Caron Tate *(Ms. Taylor)*, Brian Constantini *(Angry Man)*, Bill Sanders *(Manager)*, Henry Strozier *(Priest)*, Richard Foster *(Slick)*, Linda Chambers *(Trigger)*, Sarah Rush *(Woman)*, Joanne Bauer, Lois Nettles, Sharri Valero, Lois Evans *(Taxi Passengers)*.

Technical fetishism and trite philosophy abound in TALKING TO STRANGERS, a relatively daring American independent film that, despite its strengths, only points out the creative plague in the rest of American independent cinema. Built around a simple gimmick—nine continuous takes arranged in random order and photographed with bravura camera moves and a one-to-one shooting ratio—the film is, metaphorically, about art and the struggle of the artist. Specifically, it is about a pompous, college-educated artiste who tries to find his material by "talking to strangers." His type, played by Gruz, is one of mankind's most despicable—a condescending, egocentric leech who preys on others in order to serve his own need to create art. Paradoxically and purposefully, however, the viewer is never really sure of the main character's identity. The film opens with an impressively photographed sequence in which Gruz, seen from overhead, wanders from street corner to street corner, trying to find the bus he wants. The next seven scenes, each photographed in one day and in one approximately ten-minute take (the maximum amount of film that fits into a camera magazine), are arranged in random order. As a result, the audience has no guide to the director's narrative intentions—an interesting but silly creative technique whereby chance is given more power than the creator. (Techniques of this sort are not particularly revolutionary and have been explored in other art forms—in the music of John Cage, the art of Marcel Duchamp, and the poetry of the Dadaists, for example.) In these sequences, Gruz's character (who is variously a writer, a student, a photographer, or a waiter) talks at, but rarely listens to, a number of strangers. In a soup kitchen, Gruz the writer is confronted by a regular (Hunter) who accuses the young man of being a "spy," someone who needs material more than he needs food and shelter. In another scene, Gruz the photographer meets a homeless but not hopeless young man (Jordan) who thinks he could be a fashion star like those the photographer supposedly knows. Gruz treats him with hip pomposity, promising to arrange a power lunch for the man. The next segment shows Gruz in a bank for a meeting about his school loan. While he waits, the loan officer (Tate), a young black woman, juggles an exchange with an irate customer and a personal and very traumatic phone conversation. Gruz intervenes and tries to come to the woman's aid (we eventually learn that she has had an abortion and that her mate has pretended to commit suicide). "What can you say to me?" she asks, with cynical honesty that Gruz cannot counter. A church visit and a conversation-confession with a Catholic priest (Strozier) comprise the next segment. Gruz, who has never been to confession before, questions the priest about the power of faith versus that of reason. Next, Gruz rides a water taxi that transports passengers around Baltimore. He mistakes three Catholic nuns for Mennonites and asks them if they dislike automobiles. Gruz is next seen on a bus, talking with an older woman who has come to town to visit her daughter. Suddenly a gang boards the bus, and a tough young woman (Chambers) pulls a gun as the main thug (Foster) leads an attack on the bus driver. They take the old woman to the back of the bus and gang rape her, while Chambers and Foster intimidate Gruz. The final stranger Gruz talks to is the potter he slept with the night before (played by Rush, she is the only person we do not see Gruz meet). When he learns that she has been a stripper and a whore, he wants out, claiming that he is looking for someone who is a virgin, at least spiritually. The final segment shows Gruz painting a nondescript area white, eventually turning the paint-sprayer on the camera lens.

TALKING TO STRANGERS can be, and has been, praised for its attention to form. It has taken narrative structure away from the Hollywood style of drama and placed it in the hands of chance. We are forced to fight our expectations and confront each scene on its own terms. The scenes have no obvious relation to one another other than the main character's "talking to strangers." The interest in form doesn't end there: writer-director Rob Tregenza, who also served as cameraperson, has placed much attention on the actual gathering of the image—the process of putting the image and sound on the screen. As his press material notes, Tregenza has used the Matthews Tulip Dolly, the Matthews CamRemote and Snorkel system, the Fisher Dolly, the Arri 35BL camera, 9,000 feet of Kodak 5294 film stock, and a Dolby compatible stereo mix (without CAT 22 cards). We also know that the scenes have been randomly sequenced and photographed in single takes, using only 9,000 feet of film—meaning that almost all the footage has made it into the final film. (Jon Jost, by now a veteran on the American independent scene, has similarly used a 1:1 shooting ratio.) Although nine scenes appear in the film, 12 were written. If one scene didn't work on its first take it was to be thrown out and replaced with a new scene (an event that never occurred, since all went off without a hitch except the potter scene, which was cut down to eight and one-half minutes). This technical gadgetry and data, combined with Tregenza's eye and imagination, have produced some beautifully choreographed camera moves, but it is only in the bus scene that the camerawork seems an integral part of the scene. Other scenes are impressively shot, especially in the logistics of moving through the crowded soup kitchen, but the camerawork is film-schoolish gimmickry. In the bus segment, on the other hand, the single take works to the scene's favor. At the edges of the frame we can glimpse the rape of the older woman in the back of the vehicle; our attention, however, is focused on Gruz's character. Here the viewer desperately wants to cut away from the violence occurring in the background, but is tied to it, unable to block it from sight or mind.

Because of its structure, some scenes in TALKING TO STRANGERS succeed better than others. However, the film must be taken as a whole (albeit a random whole), and, as a whole, it rarely rises above the conventions of American independent cinema—conventions that are just as prevalent in traditional Hollywood narrative cinema. It is cerebration in full force; every move exists to further the director's manifesto of film phenomenology. It is not a bad film, but a disappointing one—a daring, noble, and commercially suicidal attempt to push the envelope of narrative film structure that says everything with its form and nothing with its dialog. Where American independent film has failed in recent years is precisely where TALKING TO STRANGERS fails: It has attempted to create with equipment and technique (in all facets: preproduction, production, and postproduction) and not with ideas. But what is most unfortunate about TALKING TO STRANGERS is the reception it has received in the US, where it has been irresponsibly ignored by all American festivals to which it has been submitted (though it received some specialized screenings), including those that are supposedly supporters of American independent cinema. TALKING TO STRANGERS dares to be different and, though it may not be entirely successful, deserves to be seen and recognized as an alternative to today's Hollywood system. *(Violence.)*

p, J.K. Eareckson; d, Rob Tregenza; w, Rob Tregenza; ph, Rob Tregenza (DuArt color).

Drama **(PR:O MPAA:NR)**

TAPEHEADS*½ (1988) 97m NBC-Pacific Arts-Front Films/DEG-Avenue Pictures c

John Cusack *(Ivan Alexcov)*, Tim Robbins *(Josh Tager)*, Doug McClure *(Sidney Tager)*, Connie Stevens *(June Tager)*, Clu Gulager *(Norman Mart)*, Mary Crosby *(Samantha)*, Katy Boyer *(Belinda Mart)*, Lyle Alzado *(Thor Alexcov)*, King Cotton *(Roscoe)*, Don Cornelius *(Mo Fuzz)*, Jessica Walter *(Kay Mart)*, Sam Moore *(Billy*

Diamond), Junior Walker *(Lester Diamond)*, Susan Tyrrell.

This is one of those hipper-than-thou youth comedies that pack every frame with dozens of sophomoric bits in the hope that one or two of them may actually be funny. A satire on the music business, TAPEHEADS focuses on best pals Robbins and Cusack (good friends in real life), two security guards who dream of someday working in the rock video industry. The two are devoted to the music of a fictitious 1960s R & B duo, The Swanky Modes (Junior Walker and Sam Moore), and lament that such talents are no longer working in the music business. After they are fired from their jobs, Cusack—the business-minded brains of the duo—decides that the time is right to make their mark and break into the business. With him as the manager and Robbins as the creative genius, the boys set up their video production company and name it "Video Aces." Tossed out by Robbins' parents, McClure and Stevens, the guys move their facilities to a loft that they share with rich girl Boyer, whose dad owns the place. Working under the motto "You Do What You Gotta, So You Can Do What You Wanna," the boys take various bill-paying jobs including making a rap-style commercial for a local chicken-and-waffle emporium, videotaping a living will (a morbidly funny scene), a funeral, and a gala ball held at the home of Gulager, a fascist millionaire running for president. To fulfill their creative ambitions, the boys hook up with small record producer Cornelius (host of TV's "Soul Train") and make a couple of cheap videos "on spec" (for free). Through sexy rock critic Crosby, they get a chance to shoot a big-budget video for the fictitious heavy-metal band The Blender Children (played by real-life band The Lords of the New Church) featuring their song "Mr. MX-7." The shoot is a disaster, but when the band is killed the next day by a piece of Skylab that crashes onto the stage where they are playing, their video becomes a hit and Robbins and Cusack are hailed as geniuses. Meanwhile, it is learned that the boys accidentally took possession of a videotape exposing presidential hopeful Gulager's rather kinky sex life, and he sends Secret Service agents to retrieve it. Using their newfound fame to resurrect the careers of The Swanky Modes, Robbins and Cusack book them as the opening act for a Menudo concert that is being beamed by satellite to 30 countries. In a chaotic climax, Gulager's kinky sex tape is broadcast over the satellite feed, ruining his political career, and The Swanky Modes are the hit of the show.

The above synopsis fails to capture most of the hyperactive narrative of TAPEHEADS. Produced by Peter McCarthy, the man behind Alex Cox's REPO MAN and SID AND NANCY, the film tries to capture the same rebellious rock-culture attitude that the Cox films had, but former rock video director Bill Fishman crams so many giddy characters and subplots into his movie that one feels assaulted by the time it's over. Several set pieces, such as the living will, the scenes with Don Cornelius, and the filming of The Blender Children video work fairly well. But then the rest of the running time is made up of such unfunny material as urine-testing jokes, an extra in a restaurant scene with a straw up his nose, revolting puns, toilet humor, and other gags that will appeal to 12-year-olds. Significantly, the filmmakers think that the mere sight of a paneled station wagon—the stereotypical suburban mode of transportation—should draw a hearty, knowing laugh from the ultrahip audience. In addition, the dunderheaded characters played by Cusack and Robbins aren't the most likable guys with whom to spend nearly 100 minutes. Cusack, with his slick hair and seedy gigolo-style moustache, spends the entire movie running in circles and flailing his arms. By contrast, Robbins (who played the hot-shot pitcher in BULL DURHAM) looks like a quintessential nerd and acts catatonic. This is funny?

Another annoying characteristic that seems to be popping up both in films and on television lately is the embarrassing spectacle of white middle-class suburban kids desperately trying to attain some sort of hipness by mimicking the style of black 1960s soul singers (a trend that was probably initiated by John Belushi and Dan Aykroyd's Blues Brothers). One assumes that this wanna-be-black behavior is supposed to be a sign of love and respect for black artists, but the underlying message is more than a little racist, suggesting, first, that only young white kids truly appreciate the genius of these forgotten black artists, and, second, that through the savvy guidance of said white youths, these old black musicians can boost their sagging careers. Let's just call this notion . . . misguided. And it is at this kind of intelligence level that most of the social satire of TAPEHEADS is aimed. The Clu Gulager subplot is merely cynical and sophomoric, saying nothing of any interest or importance about how our presidents are chosen. Instead, everyone in the movie is shown to be a complete buffoon, only some more than others. These vain stabs at relevancy could have been titled "Things That Kind of Bug Us, But That We Really Haven't Thought Much About."

In the end, none of the above matters, for films like this usually find a small but rabid cult of admirers who thrill to cameos by people like Stiv Bators, Jello Biafra, ex-MTV veejay Martha Quinn, King Cotton, Ted Nugent, Weird Al Yankovic, Don Cornelius, Junior Walker, and Sam Moore. At the base of these movies is the belief that those who don't see the humor in them must be hopeless squares. Be that as it may, this sort of scattershot youth film has worked before, most notably those directed by Allan Arkush (ROCK AND ROLL HIGH SCHOOL and GET CRAZY). Arkush's films, while nutty and offbeat, are finely tuned and much funnier than the haphazard TAPEHEADS. Rent the Arkush films, avoid this. *(Sexual situations, comic violence, profanity.)*

p, Peter McCarthy; d, Bill Fishman; w, Bill Fishman, Peter McCarthy (based on a story by Fishman, McCarthy, Ryan Rowe, Jim Herzfeld); ph, Bojan Bazelli (DeLuxe Color); ed, Mondo Jenkins; m, Fishbone; md, Nigel Harrison; prod d, Catherine Hardwicke; art d, Don Diers; cos, Elizabeth McBride.

Comedy **Cas.** **(PR:O MPAA:R)**

TAXING WOMAN, A*½** (1988, Jap.) 127m Itami-New Century/Japanese Films c

Nobuko Miyamoto *(Ryoko Itakura, Tax Inspector)*, Tsutomu Yamazaki *(Hideki Gondo)*, Masahiko Tsugawa *(Assistant Chief Inspector Hanamura)*, Hideo Murota *(Ishii, Motel President)*, Shuji Otaki *(Tsuyuguchi, Tax Office Manager)*, Daisuke Yamashita *(Taro Gondo)*, Shinsuke Ashida, Keiju Kobayashi, Mariko Okada, Kiriko Shimizu, Kazuyo Matsui, Yasuo Daichi, Kinzo Sakura, Hajimeh Asoh, Shiro Ito, Eitaro Ozawa.

Continuing his series of energetic, incisive and very funny examinations of modern Japanese culture (burial rites in THE FUNERAL, food in TAMPOPO), director Juzo Itami now turns his unique cinematic gaze on that most sacred of current Nipponese obsessions—money. Part social satire, part procedural drama, A TAXING WOMAN takes its title from dedicated tax agent Miyamoto, a spunky, freckled woman with a Louise Brooks haircut and a cowlick her superiors continually remind her to tame. Capitalizing on her unassuming and demure looks, Miyamoto encourages tax cheats to let their guard down as she investigates their books. Well versed in the clever methods of tax evasion, she swiftly uncovers her quarry's secrets and suddenly bites like a pit bull, refusing to let go until the penalties are paid. One particularly vexing case involves the multimillion dollar empire of "adult motel" tycoon Yamazaki. Although cursed with a lame leg, Yamazaki is suave, cool, and very clever. Using his vast influence, Yamazaki launders his money through the *yakuza* (gangsters), phony corporations, real estate, and even his mistress, hoarding his booty in a huge safe hidden behind the bookcase in his house. When Miyamoto first begins her investigation, Yamazaki does not feel threatened, confident he can manipulate any woman to his will. Unfortunately for him, however, Miyamoto is even more clever and dedicated than he when it comes to the pursuit of money. Utilizing the expansive resources of the Japanese Tax Office, a raid involving more than 100 agents and state-of-the-art technology is launched against Yamazaki's home, offices, *yakuza* connections, and banks in an effort to expose all of his hidden income. Eventually the humbled Yamazaki admits defeat and in a fit of deep admiration, asks Miyamoto to become his wife. Although flattered, Miyamoto turns the handsome tax cheat down, for she is already married to the relentless pursuit of hidden income. In TAMPOPO, Itami relied heavily on an inventive Bunuelian structure that allowed him the freedom to suddenly shift gears and follow some delightfully vivid minor characters within the context of his main narrative. A TAXING WOMAN, however, is much more traditionally structured and is very reminiscent of such classic Akira Kurosawa procedural dramas as STRAY DOG, HIGH AND LOW, and THE BAD SLEEP WELL. We follow Miyamoto step by step as she meticulously investigates potential tax cheats, be they ma-and-pa grocers or bankers. While this approach makes for some fascinating drama, it also allows Itami to introduce his trademark bit players and biting satiric edge. Although not as out-and-out loopy as TAMPOPO, there are a few such moments, such as when Yamazaki seals a particularly lucrative deal and does a hilarious celebratory dance, and when Miyamoto finally outwits an arrogant *pachinko* parlor owner and his face suddenly turns beet red. What A TAXING WOMAN does best is examine the Japanese obsession with acquiring wealth and keeping as much of it as possible.Itami sees the entire society as money mad--everyone is a tax cheat—but even more manic than the populace are those sworn to expose them. The tax investigators are seen as zealous soldiers who live off the thrill of the hunt. Despite rain, sleet, or snow, the tax agents happily pick through garbage dumps, don disguises, spy, make secret videotapes, strip search, and launch invasions of military proportions. Both sides in the game are shown to be supremely clever, as the cheats invent new methods of deception as fast as the agents can uncover them. The boundless energy of the Japanese seems to be what really fascinates Itami, regardless of his subject matter. If the films of Yasujiro Ozu are revered for their portrayal of traditional Japanese family life, then Itami is well on his way to becoming the leading chronicler of life in modern-day Japan. In all his films there is a vibrant spark of wit, cleverness, and verve that makes his work unique and endearing. Again Itami presents a parade of lively characters who remain memorable whether on screen for one hour or one minute. Miyamoto (the director's wife) and Yamazaki continue to make a terrific team, as they did in THE FUNERAL and TAMPOPO, infusing their roles with detail and nuance rarely found in the films of any country. A TAXING WOMAN was a smash hit in Japan, and Itami has already gone into production on a sequel which once again features Miyamoto, this time pitting the plucky tax investigator against a religious cult. *(Nudity, sexual situations.)*

p, Yasushi Tamaoki, Seigo Hosoge; d, Juzo Itami; w, Juzo Itami; ph, Yonezo Maeda; ed, Akira Suzuki; m, Toshiyuki Honda.

Comedy/Drama **(PR:C-O MPAA:NR)**

TELEPHONE, THE* (1988) 82m NW-Odyssey/NW c

Whoopi Goldberg *(Vashti Blue)*, Severn Darden *(Max)*, Amy Wright*(Honey Boxe/ Irate Neighbor)*, Elliott Gould *(Rodney)*, John Heard *(Telephone Man)*, Ronald J. Stallings *(Saxophone Player)*.

Simply stated, THE TELEPHONE is a melange of Whoopi Goldberg monologs masquerading as a feature film. Other than the opening establishing shots and a brief scene in a cramped, dingy hallway, the entire film takes place in the eccentrically appointed apartment of struggling actress Vashti Blue (Goldberg), who spends the bulk of her time on the telephone. From the moment Goldberg enters her digs, we are furnished with a precis of her personal oddities: she owns an owl that she maintains resembles Herbert Marshall, allows her pet goldfish a few recreational laps in her bathtub, engages the recorded messages on her answering machine in sassy dialogs, etc. Much like the fortified apartment in Jules Feiffer's urban satire "Little Murders," Goldberg's place is a garrison isolating her from the shrill, callous universe just beyond her window. Once an initial battery of Goldberg's quirks are established, another dimension of her troubled "personality" surfaces: although she adroitly skirts the subject, she still suffers emotional aftershocks from her breakup with her boy friend. Retreating further and further from reality and into the safe confines of her apartment, her only conduit to a world that, in her vulnerability, she claims has forsaken her is her designer telephone. In a manner reminiscent of the character sketches that made her famous, Goldberg uses the phone—indeed the whole movie—as a vehicle to trot out a rogue's gallery of impersonations. A sequence of character takes is triggered by a call she makes to a friend to complain that a scene from a Capra movie she rented is missing. The "exchange" inspires a call to the police, which inspires a call to a local deli for delivery of cigarettes, which in turn inspires a call to the phone company to complain about harassment regarding an unpaid bill . . . one call follows another, as accent is piled upon accent—Indian, Irish, Oxbridge English, Chinese, Viennese, street black, and so on. Goldberg's phone performances are interspersed with parodies of pompous Shakespeare readings; she also, in a successful effort to annoy her understandably irritated neighbor, conjures a medley of voices skirmishing at an imaginary high-decibel cocktail party. Two thirds into the phone-a-thon, Gould appears as Vashti Blue's sleazy ex-agent and, after a brief, pointless turn, departs with his newest find, a talentless bimbo in the worst Hollywood tradition. After another interval of phone calls (to the inevitable accompaniment of her protesting neighbor), a man from the phone company (Heard) arrives to take away Goldberg's phone. In what would have been a stunning revelation in a film any less tedious, we learn that the phone has actually been disconnected for two months. The apologetic Heard confiscates the phone, but before he leaves Goldberg is seized by a paroxysm of rage and stabs him to death.

THE TELEPHONE (dimly recalling Rossellini's still-born short THE HUMAN VOICE) is from start to finish a vanity production, a bloated, self-serving showcase for the talents of the inarguably gifted Goldberg. Compounding the faults of a woefully weak, aimless script (an interminable filibuster by Terry Southern and Harry Nilsson) is an unresolved clash of interpretations: just as the film seems inclined to an investigation of alienation and incipient madness, it's subverted by Goldberg's yen for the easy laughs she's grown used to. Rip Torn's direction is flat, sluggish, and riddled with indecision (the claustrophobic camerawork is undermined by the overly lush cinematography). No one—least of all Torn—appears to be in charge. As for Goldberg, she appears in yet another inane role in an uninterrupted string of the same since her fine debut in THE COLOR PURPLE. THE TELEPHONE reinforces an impression Goldberg must do her best to dispel, namely that her talent is limited to short character takes and that she cannot create, develop, and sustain a role over the length of a project. Vashti Blue is not so much a character as she is many characters orbiting an indistinct core, cast adrift in a vapid and eminently forgettable film. *(Profanity.)*

p, Robert Katz, Moctesuma Esparza; d, Rip Torn; w, Harry Nilsson, Terry Southern; ph, David Claessen (Monaco Color); ed, Sandra Adair; m, Christopher Young; art d, Jim Pohl; set d, Antonio Vincent.

Comedy/Drama **Cas.** **(PR:C MPAA:R)**

TEQUILA SUNRISE**½ (1988) 116m Mount Co./WB c

Mel Gibson *(Dale McKussic)*, Kurt Russell *(Lt. Nick Frescia)*, Michelle Pfeiffer *(Jo Ann Vallenari)*, Raul Julia *(Escalante)*, J.T. Walsh *(Maguire)*, Arliss Howard *(Gregg Lindroff)*, Ann Magnuson *(Shaleen)*, Arye Gross *(Andy Leonard)*, Gabriel Damon *(Cody McKussic)*, Garret Pearson *(Arturo)*, Eric Thiele *(Vittorio)*, Tom Nolan *(Leland)*, Dawn Martel *(Sin Sister)*, Lala *(Sin Sister No. 2)*, Budd Boetticher *(Judge Nizetitch)*, Kenneth C. Moore *(Woody)*, Jason Randal *(Magician)*, Bob Swain *(Ralph Spudder)*, Jim Bentley *(Cop)*, Eric Waterhouse *(Steve)*, Geno Silva *(Mexican Cop)*, Daniel Addes *(Pepe)*, Efrain Figueroa, Tomas Goros *(Carlos' Men)*, Austin Hawk, Scott Harms *(Lifeguards)*, Sarah Davis *(Girl in Restaurant)*, John D. Steele, David Rees *(Men at Party)*, Oscar Abadia, Jim Ladd, Tom Schnabel *(Themselves)*.

As a screenwriter Robert Towne has few peers. He has written some of the great movies of the 1970s (CHINATOWN; THE LAST DETAIL; SHAMPOO) and performed uncredited "script doctor" duty on many others (THE GODFATHER; MARATHON MAN; HEAVEN CAN WAIT). His scripts are finely crafted works with intricate plots, multi-faceted characters, intelligence, wit, and precise, natural dialog that doesn't call attention to itself as the invention of a clever screenwriter. Regrettably, Towne has had few scripts produced in the 1980s, and in an effort to protect his writing from unsympathetic interpretation, he has begun to direct himself. The problem, however, is that while Towne is a superb screenwriter, he is not much of a director. His first directorial effort, PERSONAL BEST (1982), concentrated on dialog at the expense of the film's visuals and failed to completely engage the viewer. His latest film, TEQUILA SUNRISE, is beset with the same problem.

Plotted like an old Warner Bros. gangster picture, the film focuses two old high-school chums, Russell and Gibson, who have grown up on opposite sides of the law. The suavely confident Russell has become a cop in charge of Los Angeles County's drug task force, while the boyish Gibson is a wealthy cocaine dealer who has recently attempted to retire. Gibson, however, has found it difficult to go legit, for his old associates and customers continue to pester him. To make matters worse, his estranged wife threatens to take custody of their son if Gibson doesn't continue to fork over the tens of thousands of dollars she demands to maintain her opulent lifestyle. Faced with all these pressures, Gibson agrees to make one last score, which will also pay off a personal debt owed to a mysterious Mexican drug dealer known as "Carlos." Russell catches wind of this through pompous FBI agent Walsh, who has invaded Russell's office in an effort to nab the much-wanted Carlos. Russell tries to dissuade Gibson from making the deal lest he wind up in prison, but when his friend refuses, Russell goes all-out to nail him. He even goes so far as to romance Pfeiffer, the beautiful owner of Gibson's favorite restaurant, suspecting that she is involved with Gibson's drug operation and hoping to glean inside information from her. When Pfeiffer, who is innocent, realizes that she's being used by the tricky and charming Russell, she is driven into the arms of Gibson, who has been in love with her from afar but hasn't wanted to approach her until he was out of the cocaine racket. Once the couple's true feelings are revealed, their mutually repressed desire comes bubbling to the surface in Gibson's hot tub. Meanwhile, Russell and Walsh try to outmaneuver each other professionally, while Julia, an important Mexican police official who can identify Carlos, stakes out Gibson's home and waits for the drug dealer's arrival. Julia should know what Carlos looks like because *he is* Carlos. When the time is right, he turns up in Gibson's house and the old friends exchange warm greetings. Preparations are made to complete the deal, but while Gibson is away there is an unfortunate setback and Pfeiffer inadvertently witnesses Julia order the execution of an informant. Although he considers Gibson a friend, Julia cannot allow someone he does not trust to know his identity. During a drinking and coke-snorting get-together on Julia's yacht, the Mexican drug lord regretfully informs Gibson that Pfeiffer must be killed. Gibson plays along for a while, but then pulls a gun on Julia and escapes with Pfeiffer. Later, Gibson returns with his speed boat—filled with $15 million in cash—to complete his transaction with Julia, but he rigs the boat to explode. Julia expects this and pulls a gun. The two struggle and both are wounded. To make matters worse, crazed FBI agent Walsh, whose career is ruined because of his failure to recognize Julia as Carlos, arrives on the scene and starts blasting away at both men with a machine gun. Russell then turns up and tries to stop Walsh from murdering the unarmed Gibson, and when Walsh ignores him, Russell shots the FBI agent in the back. There is a massive explosion and it appears that Gibson is killed, but Russell has arranged for the coast patrol to rescue his pal and deliver him back to the grateful Pfeiffer.

Taking its title from the popular orange-red cocktail whose color resembles the early morning California sky, TEQUILA SUNRISE uses familiar genre trappings as a vehicle for ruminating on the nature of long friendships and whether they are possible, or even desirable, to maintain. Although seemingly inspired by Towne's personal experiences in the film industry (his close friendships with Jack Nicholson and Roman Polanski have been extremely rocky), his characters remain ambiguous and distant, manipulating each other as mercilessly as Towne manipulates the audience with his convoluted plot. This is not to say that ambiguity is inappropriate; indeed, most American films contain protagonists whose motivations are so obvious that it is hard to justify their existence as main characters at all. The characters in TEQULIA SUNRISE, however, are so obtuse and mysterious that when Towne finally reveals their supposedly poignant motivations, they seem trite and fall flat dramatically. Luckily, he has assembled a marvelous cast and they somehow manage to keep the film engaging, despite their obvious confusion over just what it is they're supposed to be feeling. Perhaps Towne kept them in the dark as well, preferring to let his actors flounder a little in the hope that their confusion would translate well on-screen as the characters struggle to make sense of their lives.

Gibson does a fine job as the boyish rogue finally attempting to grow up and accept genuine responsibility, and Russell is appropriately smooth as the coolly confident cop determined to crack the case (his appearance and mannerisms patterned after Los Angeles Lakers coach Pat Riley, a friend of Towne's who the writer hoped would play the part), but Pfeiffer, who is rapidly becoming one of this country's most interesting actresses, gives the most impressive performance as the tough, independent woman who finds herself caught in the middle. Towne has assembled a strong supporting cast as well, with Raul Julia nearly stealing the movie as the flamboyant Mexican drug dealer who has a fetish for ping-pong and who bursts into operatic song at inopportune moments. But while the actors do a good job of holding audience interest, Towne offers little to entertain the eye. Although impressively shot by veteran cinematographer Conrad Hall, the setups are dictated by the unending dialog of Towne's screenplay. TEQULIA SUNRISE is mostly talk, talk, talk, but at least it is wonderfully written talk, for Towne has a knack for sharp, telling dialog that is literate but unpretentious. Unfortunately, this is also one of those films written by a wealthy southern Californian *for* wealthy southern Californians, so much of Towne's nuance and irony will be lost on those living east of Los Angeles. TEQULIA SUNRISE is by no means a bad movie, just a terribly disappointing one from the man who wrote CHINATOWN. Songs include "Surrender To Me" (Richard Marx, Ross Vanelli, performed by Ann Wilson, Robin Zander); "Don't Worry Baby" (Brian Wilson, Roger Christian, performed by The Everly Bros. with The Beach Boys); "Do You Believe in Shame?" (John Taylor, Simon Lebon, Nick Rhodes, performed by Duran Duran); "Dead on the Money" (Steve Diamond, Todd Cerney, performed by Andy Taylor); "Recurring Dream" (Neil Finn, Nick Seymour, Paul Hester, Craig Hooper, performed by Crowded House); "Unsubstantiated" (Steven Kilbey, Peter Koppes, Marty Willson-Piper, Richard Ploog, performed by The Church); "Give a Little Love" (Albert Hammond, Diane Warren, performed by Ziggy Marley and The Melody Makers); "Beyond the Sea" (Jack Lawrence, Charles Trenet, performed by Bobby Darin); "Las Mananitas" (performed by El Mariachi Vargas).*(Violence, nudity, sexual situations, substance abuse, profanity)*

p, Thom Mount; d, Robert Towne; w, Robert Towne; ph, Conrad L. Hall (DeLuxe Color); ed, Claire Simpson; m, Dave Grusin; md, Danny Bramson; m/l, Richard Marx, Ross Vanelli, Brian Wilson, Roger Christian, John Taylor, Simon Lebon, Nick Rhodes, Steve Diamond, Todd Cerney, Neil Finn, Nick Seymour, Paul Hester, Craig Hooper, Steven Kilbey, Peter Koppes, Marty Willson-Piper, Richard Ploog, Albert Hammond, Diane Warren, Jack Lawrence, Charles Trenet; prod d, Richard Sylbert; art d, Peter Lansdown Smith; set d, Rick Simpson; spec eff, Jerry D. Williams; cos, Julie Weiss; tech, Bart A. Natisin; stunts, Bobby Bass, Dave Cass; makeup, Dorothy J. Pearl, Nadia DiPaolo.

Thriller **Cas.** **(PR:O MPAA:R)**

TERMINAL ENTRY † (1988) 95m TBA/Intercontinental c

Edward Albert *(Capt. Danny Jackson)*, Kabir Bedi *(Terrorist Commander)*, Heidi Helmer *(Chris)*, Mazhar Khan *(Abdul)*, Yaphet Kotto *(Styles)*, Patrick Labyorteaux

(Bob), Yvette Nipar (Tina), Kavi Raz (Mahaddi), Paul Smith (Stewart), Rob Stone (Tom), Tracy Brooks Swope (Dominique), Sam Temeles (Howie), Jill Terashita (Gwen), Barbara Edwards (Lady Electric), Terence Marinan (Communications Technician), Michael A. Saad (Hassan), Mario Piccirillo (Eyes), Robert Cervi (Mexican Bandit), Buddy Daniels (Bald Man), Reggie Demorton, Joseph L. Killinger, Chuck Wells, Bryan Utman (Military Men).

A group of college computer hackers get together at a remote location and accidentally tap into the command program of an Arab terrorist network led by Bedi. Thinking the system an elaborate computer game, the students begin to play and unknowingly assign terrorists based in Mexico to wreak havoc in the United States. National security advisor Smith thinks that Bedi and his terrorists have launched an all-out attack on the US, and he dispatches special agent Albert and his team of commandos to the border for a counter-offensive. The hackers, unaware that the "game" they are playing is actually getting people killed and putting their own lives in jeopardy, try to outsmart Albert and keep the deadly game going. This reportedly solid actioner was given a scant regional release in 1987, before mass distribution on home video in 1988.

p, Sharyon Reis Cobe; d, John Kincade; w, David Mickey Evans, Mark Sobel (based on a story by Mark Sobel); ph, James L. Carter (Foto-Kem color); ed, Dean Goodhill; m, Gene Hobson; m/l, Ken Brown, Jere Mendelsohn, Fredrick Lahmann, Jack Wride, Paul Martin; art d, Alexandra Kicenik; set d, Pamela Clouse; spec eff, Steve Galich; cos, Leslie Ballard; tech, Tom Jenssen; stunts, John Michael Stewart; makeup, Carlann Matz.

| Action | Cas. | (PR:NR MPAA:R) |

TERROR SQUAD †   (1988) 92m Matterhorn/Manson c

Chuck Connors (Chief Rawlings), Brodie Greer (Capt. Steiner), Bill Calvert (Johnny), Kerry Brennan (Jennifer), Kavi Raz (Yassir), Joseph Nasser (Gamel), Budge Threlkeld (Mr. Nero), Dennis Moynahan (Norman), Ken Foree, Nathan Dyer, Lisa Ross, Baggie Hardiman, Jill Sanders.

Chuck Connors plays a Kokomo, Indiana, police chief who gets more than he bargained for when Libyan terrorists attack a nuclear power plant in his jurisdiction. Cornered, the terrorists, led by Raz, invade a high school and hold the students hostage. The undaunted Connors hauls out a videocassette of DOG DAY AFTERNOON and uses it as a textbook for the delicate negotiations. Needless to say, this is another direct-to-video release. Reportedly, director Peter Maris has a flair for action scenes, especially a lengthy car chase that is supposedly worth the price of a rental.

p, Peter Maris; d, Peter Maris; w, Chuck Rose (based on a story by Mark Verheiden); ph, Peter Jensen (United Color); ed, Jack Tucker; m, Chuck Cirino; art d, Joe Dea.

| Action | Cas. | (PR:NR MPAA:NR) |

THEY LIVE*½**   (1988) 93m Alive/UNIV c

Roddy Piper (John Nada), Keith David (Frank), Meg Foster (Holly), George "Buck" Flower (Drifter), Peter Jason (Gilbert), Raymond St. Jacques (Street Preacher), Jason Robards, III (Family Man), John Lawrence (Bearded Man), Susan Barnes (Brown-Haired Woman), Sy Richardson (Black Revolutionary), Wendy Brainard (Family Man's Daughter), Lucille Meredith (Female Interviewer), Susan Blanchard (Ingenue), Norman Alden (Foreman), Dana Bratton (Black Junkie), John F. Goff (Well Dressed Customer), Norm Wilson (Vendor), Thelma Lee (Rich Lady), Stratton Leopold (Depressed Human), Rezza Shan (Arab Clerk), Norman Howell (Blond-Haired Cop), Larry Franco (Neighbor), Tom Searle (Biker), Robert Grasmere (Scruffy Blond Man), Vince Inneo, Bob Hudson (Passageway Guards), Jon Paul Jones (Manager), Dennis Michael (Male News Anchor), Nancy Gee (Female News Anchor), Claudia Stanlee (Young Female Executive), Christine Baur (Woman on Phone), Eileen Wesson (Pregnant Secretary), Gregory Barnett, Jim Nickerson (Security Guards), Kerry Rossall (2nd Unit Guard), Cibby Danyla (Naked Lady), Jeff Imada (Male Ghoul), Michelle Costello (Female Ghoul).

© MCA (UNIVERSAL)

The most vehemently anti-Reagan Hollywood film since Alex Cox's WALKER (1987), John Carpenter's THEY LIVE is a fun-filled throwback to the science-fiction paranoia films of the 1950s. Set in the very near future, the movie follows transient construction worker Piper as he drifts to Los Angeles. Although the media extol the virtues of the current administration and the economy seems to be booming, the fact of the matter is that the rich have gotten richer while the middle class has eroded and the ranks of the poor and homeless have swelled. Piper lands a job on a construction site, and after work fellow employee David takes him to a shanty town where most of the workers live. Although its residents are destitute, the camp has several television sets and the tired workers and their families sit before them like zombies watching popular cable station 54. Their viewing is interrupted, however, by another broadcast which jams the signal. A professorial-looking man appears on screen and urges the viewers to wake up and notice that things are not as they seem. The man claims that the working class is being oppressed by the rich, who control them through mass hypnosis. Piper, scoffing at the pirate broadcast and proclaiming that he still believes in America, notices some odd activity in a church across the street. An investigation reveals that the broadcast comes from the church and that a group of rebels is in charge. Shortly thereafter, the police launch a raid on the church and bulldoze the shanty town. The rebels and homeless scatter, and the next day Piper returns to retrieve a cardboard box he had seen concealed in the church. Hiding in an alley, he opens the box, thinking he will find something valuable. Instead he finds a box full of cheap sunglasses. Disappointed, he dumps the box in a garbage can and keeps one pair of the glasses. Donning the shades as he walks down Rodeo Drive, Piper is shocked to discover that the world appears in black and white, and that every sign, billboard, and magazine cover contains such subliminal messages as "Obey," "Consume," "Sleep," and "No Independent Thought." Most horrifying, however, is that most of the yuppies on the street have bug eyes and skull-like faces—they're not human. When these aliens realize that Piper is on to them, the police are dispatched to capture him. Cornered, Piper manages to waylay a human officer and take his weapons. He enters a bank and immediately begins blasting away at all the aliens he sees. On the run, Piper hides out in a parking garage and kidnaps a human Station 54 executive (Foster) and makes her take him to her house. Once there, he tries to convince her that America is being controlled by aliens and urges her to put on the glasses, but she refuses. When he lets his guard down she hits him in the head with a bottle and sends him crashing through a picture window onto the street below. Now a fugitive, Piper turns to David for help; David, however, wants nothing to do with Piper and warns him to stay away. Piper begs David to put on the sunglasses, and when David refuses, Piper initiates a hilariously long fistfight. Finally David puts on the sunglasses and is just as stunned as Piper has been when he sees the truth. The two men then track down the rebels and join in their effort to destroy the television signal that keeps the populace from seeing things clearly. To Piper's surprise, Foster appears at the meeting and offers to help, but again the meeting is broken up by the police. Piper and David escape and discover that the aliens are headquartered in an underground chamber where they recruit greedy humans to join their cause by offering them upper-class wealth and privilege. It seems that the aliens plan to exploit Earth as if it were a third-world country by exhausting its resources and then moving on to the next planet. Piper and David decide to launch an attack on the cable station by themselves, but are betrayed by Foster. David is killed and Piper mortally wounded as he makes it to the roof to destroy the transmitter. Piper succeeds in cutting off the signal, and shocked viewers throughout the country see the aliens for what they are. As Piper dies, he gives the "finger" to the aliens watching him from a helicopter.

Although a mess ideologically (indiscriminate slaughter of the "other" doesn't quite fit in with the populist message seemingly espoused by Carpenter), THEY LIVE is a whole lot of fun and well worth seeing—especially for those liberals in need of violent catharsis after suffering through the injustice of the Reagan administration and the disheartening absurdities of the 1988 presidential campaign. Carpenter seems to have his heart in the right place, but his thesis is terribly confused. He presents a jumble of challenging observations and damning accusations wrapped in intense moral indignation, but fails to come up with a solution any more thoughtful than a hysterical call to arms. Perhaps one can overlook the ideological flaws of THEY LIVE if one simply views it as a sudden, violent outpouring of one liberal's outrage and frustration at what has happened to the US during the 1980s. While the violence of the film may disturb some, Carpenter does make a loud plea for his fans to wake up and smell the political coffee, much as Spike Lee did in SCHOOL DAYS. But whereas Lee ended his film with that call, Carpenter comes out swinging from the outset, having his appropriately named everyman (the last name of Piper's character is Nada—Spanish for "nothing") don a pair of hipster's sunglasses and finally see the world for what it is. Carpenter seeks to expose the hypnotic influence capitalism has on its citizens by pointing out the subliminal influence of advertising. Because THEY LIVE never rises above the intellectual level of a comic book, Carpenter continually simplifies the complex and states the obvious—even going so far as to have "This is your God" as the subliminal message on American currency. This sort of ham-handedness is actually charming in a way, but it may alienate those who already consider themselves enlightened when it comes to the ins and outs of media manipulation.

The audience Carpenter seems to be aiming for is the same target group Michael Dukakis courted in the election—the so-called Reagan Democrats. By tapping into the blue-collar rage that DIE HARD similarly exploits, Carpenter attempts to bring those Reagan Democrats back into the populist fold by playing on their worst instincts—their delight at seeing yuppies exposed as evil creatures who deserve to be slaughtered with impunity. This of course assumes that the Reagan Democrats despise yuppies and skirts what may be the actual truth—that Reagan Democrats really want to be yuppies. Carpenter does concede this notion by showing a few heretofore disenfranchised citizens who willingly collaborate with the aliens for the opportunity of joining the ruling elite. Perhaps Carpenter thinks that by exposing the machinery used to seduce citizens into a nation of consumer cattle those who have been seduced will wake up, reject the manipulation, and fight to end the mass hypnosis. Maybe it will work, maybe it won't, but most Carpenter fans come to his films for the action payoff and the director, of course, delivers. Carpenter has few peers when it comes to smart visuals on a shoestring and once again he doesn't disappoint. One of the best wide-screen directors working today, he fashions compositions that are lean, uncluttered, and powerful. Again there are his usual *hommages* to cinema legends, especially to Howard Hawks and John Ford—most significantly during the lengthy fistfight between Piper and David, a scene that could have come from RED RIVER or THE SEARCHERS. While the scene works as an *hommage*, it is also a hilarious metaphor for the difficulty of making some people see what is right in front of them. As an actor, former pro wrestler Roddy Piper has potential, but his comic one-liners tend to mar the film and one wishes Kurt Russell had played the part. The supporting cast, headed up by the always-impressive Keith David, is excellent. As confused as THEY LIVE is, it is heartening to see a movie from a director who can still combine personal passion with genre thrills and make it work. *(Violence, profanity.)*

p, Larry Franco; d, John Carpenter; w, Frank Armitage [John Carpenter] (based on the short story *Eight O'Clock in the Morning* by Ray Nelson); ph, Gary B. Kibbe (Panavision, DeLuxe Color); ed, Frank E. Jimenez, Gib Jaffe; m, John Carpenter, Alan Howarth; art d, William J. Durrell, Jr., Daniel Lomino; set d, Marvin March; spec eff, Roy Arbogast; cos, Robin Bush; stunts, Jeff Imada; makeup, Frank Carrisosa.

Science Fiction **Cas.** **(PR:O MPAA:R)**

THINGS CHANGE*½** (1988) 105m Filmhaus/COL c

Don Ameche *(Gino)*, Joe Mantegna *(Jerry)*, Robert Prosky *(Joseph Vincent)*, J.J. Johnston *(Frankie)*, Ricky Jay *(Mr. Silver)*, Mike Nussbaum *(Mr. Green)*, Jack Wallace *(Repair Shop Owner)*, Dan Conway *(Butler)*, Willo Varsi Hausman *(Miss Bates)*, Gail Silver *(Housemaid)*, Len Hodera *(Ramone)*, Josh Conescu *(Bellenza)*, Merrill Holtzman *(No Pals)*, Adam Bitterman *(Marcotti)*, W.H. Macy *(Billy Drake)*, Steve Goldstein *(Randy)*, Sarah Ekhardt *(Cherry)*, Karen Kohlhaas *(Grace)*.

Described by its writer-director as a "mafia fable," THINGS CHANGE is a surprisingly light, upbeat follow-up to David Mamet's dark, psychological directorial debut, HOUSE OF GAMES. The picture opens in modern-day Chicago as two mafia goons take elderly Sicilian boot-black Ameche to see their boss, Nussbaum, one of the most powerful mafia dons in the country. It seems Nussbaum has murdered someone, and, since Ameche bears more than a passing resemblance to the don, it is "suggested" that he confess to the police and go to prison in Nussbaum's place. In return, Ameche will get a substantial amount of cash and his lifelong dream, a fishing boat in Sicily, upon his release from prison. Although he really has little choice in the matter, Ameche agrees to take the fall and is turned over to the custody of Mantegna, a problem mob goon who is "on probation." Understanding that this is his last chance to square himself with his bosses, Mantegna merely has to take Ameche to a downtown hotel room and help him memorize his "confession" in time for his court appearance on Monday. Although Ameche's rigid, moral, old-world demeanor is tough to crack, Mantegna feels sorry for the old guy and impulsively decides to take him to Lake Tahoe for a final fling before jail. In Tahoe, Mantegna's reticence about his charge's identity is taken for hush-hushness, and the mob-owned hotel treats Ameche as if he were an important mafia don. Mantegna milks this for all its worth, whispering that Ameche is the "guy behind the guy behind the *guy*," and gets wine, women, and song compliments of the house. Local mob boss Prosky, who just happens to be holding a bicoastal mob summit meeting that weekend, gets wind of the important visitor and invites Ameche to his estate. His scam spinning out of control, Mantegna sits helpless in the kitchen as Ameche and Prosky get acquainted. Although Ameche never says he is a don, Prosky assumes so and takes a liking to the philosophical Sicilian. That evening, when all the mob bigwigs show up, Mantegna is horrified to see his boss, Nussbaum, and other family cronies arrive. In a nerve-wracking scene, Mantegna manages to sneak Ameche out of the house—much to Ameche's annoyance, because he would like to say goodbye to his new friend Prosky. Mantegna steals a mob car and drives Ameche back to Chicago in record time. The pair are in the hotel barely long enough to change their clothes before mob goon Johnston shows up early to accompany them to court. While walking on the beach with Mantegna, Johnston informs the latter that the gang, rather than risking Ameche's talking in prison, has decided that Ameche must be killed and made to look like a suicide—and Mantegna has to pull the trigger. Mantegna is outraged that the mob would dare break their word to Ameche and renege on the deal, but is met with a shrug and a curt "Things change" from Johnston. Flipping out completely, Mantegna impulsively conks Johnston on the head with the gun, knocking him out. Now in deep trouble, Mantegna explains the situation to Ameche, who calmly goes to a public phone and uses the coin his friend Prosky had given him in case he was in any trouble and needed his help. True to his word, Prosky saves both Ameche and Mantegna, and when we last see the pair, they are both working in Ameche's little shoeshine shop under the elevated tracks in cold, blustery Chicago.

Fans of David Mamet's previous work, both on the stage and screen, may be surprised by the light sentimentality of this charming comedy coauthored by Shel Silverstein. THINGS CHANGE is a welcome throwback to the Ben Hecht-Charles MacArthur urban comedies of the 1930s and 40s. In an era in which most American comedies rely on big gags, blunt jokes, or elaborate slapstick for laughs, Mamet has taken audience expectations and played upon them brilliantly, without ever delivering the anticipated payoff. Every time a familiar plot contrivance kicks in, "things change" and the film shifts gears. What makes the movie funny is the buildup to—and then the avoidance of—the expected. (Eventually, however, Mamet must succumb to some plot devices in the last half-hour and begins to lose his grip on the material—many have complained about the amazingly quick drive from Tahoe to Chicago and the poor staging of the climactic beachfront scene.) More important, the charm of THINGS CHANGE lies in the characters. Mamet's dialog is crisp, the wit dry, and there are plenty of great lines in the film, most of which are delivered flawlessly. Much of the credit for this goes to the Don Ameche and Joe Mantegna. With his perfectly erect posture, deliberate demeanor, philosophical attitude, and heavy accent, Ameche oozes old-world honesty and pride. The veteran actor reportedly based his performance on his own father, an Italian immigrant, and the attention to detail pays off. Also superb is Mantegna, a longtime friend and collaborator of Mamet's. No actor on earth is better at delivering Mamet's trademark dialog than Mantegna. The two leads play well together and their rapport is crucial to the success of the film. Other Mamet veterans contribute solid support as well, including HOUSE OF GAMES familiars Mike Nussbaum, W.H. Macy, Ricky Jay, J.T. Walsh, Steven Goldstein, and especially Robert Prosky ("Glengarry Glen Ross") as the Lake Tahoe mafia don. Juan Ruiz Anchia, the excellent cinematographer who shot HOUSE OF GAMES, is also back and has toned down the sharp, icy look of Mamet's previous film to something lighter and warmer, while still retaining an edge. So what did the geniuses in Hollywood do with this charming, sentimental, light-hearted film? They tried to package it as a wacky situation comedy and cut trailers making it look like a geriatric version of FERRIS BUELLER'S DAY OFF. Predictably, the film flopped at the box office, thus dooming to obscurity one of the best comedies of the year. *(Adult situations, violence, profanity.)*

p, Michael Hausman; d, David Mamet; w, David Mamet, Shel Silverstein; ph, Juan Ruiz-Anchia; ed, Trudy Ship; m, Alaric Jans; prod d, Michael Merritt; cos, Nan Cibula.

Comedy/Crime **Cas.** **(PR:C MPAA:PG)**

THINKIN' BIG † (1988) 94m AFC/Arista c

Bruce Anderson *(Pud)*, Nancy Buechler *(Morgan)*, Darla Ralston *(Liz)*, Kenny Sargent *(The Chief)*, Randy Jandt *(Wong)*, Derek Hunter *(Barry)*, Regina Mikel *(Dee-Dee)*, Claudia Church *(Wendy)*, April Burrage *(Georgia)*.

More sophomoric student high jinks, this time from director S.F. Brownrigg, who is better known for his cheapo horror classics DON'T LOOK IN THE BASEMENT (1973) and KEEP MY GRAVE OPEN (1980). Basically a series of jokes involving the male sex organ, THINKIN' BIG takes its heroes, Pud (Anderson) and Wong (Jandt), down to the Texas shore for some fun in the sun. It seems that the Asian-American Wong, who has much success with the big-breasted, bikini-clad girls on the beach, is believed to have a 3-foot-long member—at least by Pud, who sets out to increase the size of his own penis to that of Wong's so that he too can get girls. Sounds like a laff riot. Filmed in Texas in 1985, THINKIN' BIG was shown theatrically only in California in 1986 before making its way to home video in 1988.

p, Jim C. Harris; d, S.F. Brownrigg; w, Robert Joseph Sterling, Loretta Yeargin; ph, Brian H. Hooper; ed, Brian H. Hooper; m, John Boy Cooke.

Comedy **Cas.** **(PR:NR MPAA:R)**

THRILLKILL † (1988, Can.) 87m Thrillkill-Manesco/Brightstar c

Robin Ward *(Frank)*, Gina Massey *(Bobbie)*, Laura Robinson *(Adrian)*, Diana Reis *(Carly)*, Colleen Embree *(Parrish)*, Kurt Reis *(Schofield)*, Eugene Clark *(Grissom)*, Frank Moore *(Caspar)*, Joy Boushel *(Maggie)*.

Filmed back in 1984 but unreleased in the US until its home video debut in 1988, THRILLKILL features Massey as a young woman who finds herself embroiled in violence and intrigue after her sister, Reis, disappears. As it turns out, Reis was involved in an embezzlement scheme in which $35 million was to be stolen from a bank through a computer. Apparently Reis hid the details of the heist in a computer game called Thrillkill, and the mob is desperate for the information. Although she's innocent, the mob holds Massey responsible and she is forced to turn to police detective Ward for help. Unfortunately for Massey, he too would like to get his hands on the $35 million.

p, Anthony Kramreither; d, Anthony Kramreither, Anthony D'Andrea; w, Anthony D'Andrea; ph, John Clement (Filmhouse Color); ed, Nick Rotundo; m, Tim McCauley; art d, Andrew Deskin.

Crime **Cas.** **(PR:NR MPAA:NR)**

TIGER WARSAW † (1988) 93m Continental/Sony c

Patrick Swayze *(Chuck "Tiger" Warsaw)*, Piper Laurie *(Frances Warsaw)*, Lee Richardson *(Mitchell Warsaw)*, Mary McDonnell *(Paula Warsaw)*, Barbara Williams *(Karen)*, Bobby DiCicco *(Tony)*, Jenny Chrisinger *(Val)*, James Patrick Gillis *(Roger)*, Michelle Glaven *(Emily)*, Kevin Bayer *(Robin)*, Beeson Carroll *(Uncle Gene)*, Sally-Jane Heit *(Aunt Barbara)*, Kaye Ballard *(Aunt Thelma)*, Thomas Mills Wood *(Lt. Fontana)*, Cynthia L Lammel *(Paula's Secretary)*, Sloane Shelton *(Patricia)*, Sylvia Davis *(Ms. Lily)*, Christopher Douglas *(Young Chuck)*, Aimee Dicks *(Young Paula)*, Tom Madden *(Basketball Snack-bar Customer)*, Kenneth Clarke *(Basketball Snack-bar Counterman)*, Socrates Kolitsos *(Stan)*, Don Brockett *(Carl)*, Hugo Washington *(Ernie)*, Lisa Cloud, Curt Debor, David J. Graban, Charles Barletto, Linda Weaver, Nick Mancuso *(Reunion Friends)*, Tommy Lauren *(Flashy Lady)*, Jeff Scott Yasko *(Police Officer)*, Frances Clause, Eric Frances *(Thugs)*, David Bruce Hinds *(Cab Driver)*, Keith Cunningham *(Sports Announcer)*, Bruce Wetzel *(St. Louis TV Announcer)*, Reverend Thomas Sebben *(TV Preacher)*.

This low-budget Patrick Swayze film, shot before DIRTY DANCING became so popular, was given an extremely limited theatrical release by Sony Pictures before showing up in the video stores. Set in a dreary western Pennsylvania steel town, the film follows Chuck "Tiger" Warsaw (Swayze) who has finally returned home after having run off 15 years before. A prodigal son now desperate to patch things up with his family, Swayze struggles to remember the incident that caused him to leave town and it is pieced together via flashbacks. It seems that Swayze once took a peek at his sister (McDonnell) undressing, and the uptight girl flipped out and cried incest. This led to a heated confrontation with dad (Richardson), which culminated with Swayze pulling a gun and plugging his pop. Swayze subsequently skipped town and headed to Miami where he has spent the last 15 years in a haze of drugs, booze, and other overindulgences. Now home, Swayze finds that the incident has left his dad a virtual catatonic whose only interest is high-school sports, his sister has become a ruthless real estate salesperson and is about to marry a dull yuppie type, and Mom (Laurie) simply doesn't want to talk about it. With no one to turn to except his high school sweetheart, Williams, Swayze tries to put his life back together and mend fences with his clan. Songs include "Dirty Water" (Ed Cobb, performed by The Standells), "House of the Rising Sun" (performed by Faz), "I'm Still Waiting" (Christopher Meredith, Jonathan Stuart, performed by Marge Raymond).

p, Amin Q. Chaudhri; d, Amin Q. Chaudhri; w, Roy London; ph, Robert Draper (Technicolor); ed, Brian Smedley-Aston; m, Ernest Troost; m/l, Ed Cobb, Christopher Meredith, Jonathan Stuart; prod d, Tom Targownik; set d, Chris O'Neal; cos, Sheila Kehoe; makeup, Gerald Gergely, Georgette Williams.

Drama **Cas.** **(PR:NR MPAA:R)**

TIGER'S TALE, A** (1988) 97m Vincent/Atlantic c

Ann-Margret *(Rose Butts)*, C. Thomas Howell *(Bubber Drumm)*, Charles Durning *(Charlie Drumm)*, Kelly Preston *(Shirley Butts)*, Ann Wedgeworth *(Claudine)*, William Zabka *(Randy)*, Tim Thomerson *(Lonny)*, Steven Kampmann *(Dr. Shorts)*, Traci Lin *(Penny)*, Angel Tompkins *(La Vonne)*, James Noble *(Sinclair)*, Linda Rae Favila *(Kiki Walker)*, Steve Farrell *(Dr. Frank)*, David Denney *(Tyronne)*, Jo Perkins *(Lucy)*, Scott Fults, Sean Flanery, Jimmy Pickens *(Buddies)*, Mike Marich *(Bob)*, Nik Hagler *(Deputy Dozel)*, Diane Perella *(Samantha)*, Barbara Collins *(Nurse)*, Charlotte Stanton *(Counsellor)*, Shannon Collins *(Girl at Clinic)*, James Cole *(Ronnie)*, Leigh Lombardi *(Marcia)*, Paul Menzel *(Husband)*, Sharon Menzel *(Wife)*, Amanda Goyen *(Girl with Dog)*, Ed Geldart *(Gamekeeper)*, Michael Bartula, Sumter Bruton, Jim Colgrove, Jim Milan, Johnny Reno, Craig Simecheck *(The Juke Jumpers)*, Valentino the Tiger.

Imagine THE GRADUATE with a Larry (*The Last Picture Show*) McMurtry script and directed by Robert Benton and the resulting vision will be what A TIGER'S TALE unsuccessfully tries to be. It's a younger man-older woman romance with hints of screwball comedy and the aura of a teen male fantasy, set in a dusty Texas town. C. Thomas Howell plays Bubber Drumm, a 19-year-old high-school senior who lives with his ex-veterinarian dad (Durning) in a roadside gas station. Their place is filled with an assortment of animals, including a very symbolic tiger named Valentino. Howell spends his nights with Preston, a bratty, sex-starved young woman who gets her thrills by teasing boys in front of her house, just hoping her mother will come along and find her in a compromising situation. One night, as Preston is baring her breasts to a flashlight-wielding Howell, Mom (Ann-Margret) wanders out in her bathrobe. Before long, Howell has shifted his attention to Ann-Margret, even though she's old enough to be *his* mother, too. At first, Ann-Margret seems merely to enjoy his flattery and coaxes him along. Things eventually get hot and heavy, however, and before long the whole town knows the score. The one who takes it worst is Preston, who demands that she be allowed to live with her daddy. After Preston moves out, Howell moves in. Ann-Margret has grown stubborn, however, and says he must pay room and board *and* sleep in Preston's old room. Howell demands that he be treated like her lover and not her son, but Ann-Margret has trouble adjusting. The relationship grows more troubled when Ann-Margret learns she is pregnant—her diaphragm having been punctured by her vindictive daughter. She has already had one family and won't start another, and she quickly decides that an abortion is the right course of action, despite Howell's pleas. After an argument with a self-centered working mother at the abortion clinic, Ann-Margret rethinks her strategy and agrees to keep the baby, but not Howell. She refuses to see him, or even read his letters. In the meantime, Howell symbolically sets his much-beloved tiger free at a wildlife refuge. He realizes that at some point in his life he must learn to let go of the things he loves. Ann-Margret thinks the same way, packs her bags, and heads for San Diego to have her baby. Along the way, she spots Howell sitting on the roadside, holding a sign that reads "Last Chance." She drives past, but when she encounters a series of "Last Chance" signs, she hits the brakes. Howell runs for the car and the two embrace.

Although it's difficult to tell from the above synopsis, A TIGER'S TALE is played, for the most part, as a comedy. Nevertheless, the problem with the film is that it never really seems to know what it wants to be. Its heart lies in the relationship between Ann-Margret and C. Thomas Howell. Played seriously, their romance is an often touching and heartfelt one, which doesn't seem to have a hope of surviving. This already rocky affair is made even more difficult, and thereby more believable, by the inclusion of a pregnancy. Although the happy conclusion seems tacked on to please audiences, the end result of the against-the-odds romance is a mature relationship. But the rest of A TIGER'S TALE is a muddled, poorly directed hodgepodge of quirky situations played by actors who deserve better. Charles Durning, Ann Wedgeworth, and James Noble all do fine work, but none of it seems particularly relevant to the rest of the film. Scenes which are supposed to be funny (Valentino eating a passer-by's Pekinese; the girl in the abortion clinic who claims her boy friend was possessed by an alien soul) fall flat. Scenes which are supposed to be suspenseful (Howell getting attacked by Valentino; Howell getting beat up by some local punks) are never very threatening. Unfortunately for Howell and Ann-Margret, the rest of the film keeps getting in the way of their story. As for their performances, neither Howell nor Ann-Margret sets the screen on fire with their supposed passion. It's all directed in a distant, almost clinical manner that doesn't leave much room for spontaneity or rapport—compared to the rest of the film, however, their romance is a ray of sunshine. Ann-Margret looks wonderful in A TIGER'S TALE and it's not hard to see why a 19-year-old kid would fall for her. What is peculiar, however, is the filmmakers' decision that her character should be somewhere in her mid- to late 30s. The actress was in her mid-40s when she made this film, and she looks incredible, so why not make her character an incredible-looking 45-year-old? *(Nudity, profanity, adult situations, sexual situations.)*

p, Peter Douglas; d, Peter Douglas; w, Peter Douglas (based on the novel *Love and Other Natural Disasters* by Allen Hannay III); ph, Tony Pierce-Roberts (CFI Color); ed, David Campling; m, Lee Holdridge; prod d, Shay Austin; art d, Lisa Roman; set d, Don L. Davis; cos, Elizabeth Palmer; ch, Glen Hunsucker; stunts, Greg Gault, Monty Cox; makeup, Pamela Peitzman, George Masters.

Comedy/Romance **Cas.** **(PR:C-O MPAA:R)**

TIME OF DESTINY, A* (1988) 118m Nelson-Alive/COL c

William Hurt *(Martin Larraneta)*, Timothy Hutton *(Jack McKenna)*, Melissa Leo *(Josie Larraneta)*, Francisco Rabal *(Jorge Larraneta)*, Concha Hidalgo *(Sebastiana Larraneta)*, Stockard Channing *(Margaret Larraneta)*, Megan Follows *(Irene Larraneta)*, Frederick Coffin *(Ed)*, Peter Palmer *(Policeman)*, Kelly Pacheco *(Young Josie Larraneta)*, Allan Chambers *(Gas Station Attendant)*, John O'Leary *(Father Basil)*, Darin Willis *(Bellboy)*, Charmaine Glennon *(Sister at Desk)*, Justin Gocke *(Young Martin Larraneta)*, John Thatcher *(Young George)*, Harriet Robinson *(Sister in Hall)*, Sam Vlahos *(Lawyer)*, Julie Philips *(WAC)*, Erik Holland *(Colonel in US)*, Jeff Harding *(Sergeant)*, Nancy Gair *(Army Nurse)*, Henry Bumstead *(Colonel in Italy)*, Robin Bennett *(Reporter)*, Predrag Pedja Petrovic *(Lieutenant)*, Jasmina Pasalic *(Italian Girl)*, David Gilliam *(Nelson)*, Mark Burton *(Bernotsky)*, Rolf Saxon *(Kentucky)*, Vjenceslav Kapural *(Basque Relative)*, Bill Luckey *(Cousin)*, Elizabeth Nava *(Aunt)*, Francisco Senosiain *(Eppie)*, Art Koustik *(Gabby)*, Joe Faust *(Rancher)*, Ron Davis *(Businessman)*, Mike Robelo *(Bonifacio)*, John Hawker *(Porter on Train)*, George Reel *(Man at the Train)*, Michael Miller *(Cement Truck Driver)*, Alan Tilvern *(Father Tony)*, Ralph Gallucci *(Priest at Funeral)*, Nicolasa Calvo *(Young Sebastiana)*, Felix Arcarazo *(Young Jorge Larraneta)*.

Despite its visual inventiveness, creative editing, and the presence of Oscar winners Timothy Hutton and William Hurt, A TIME OF DESTINY is a disappointingly overblown melodrama. Beginning at a battlefront in WW II Italy, where two American soldiers, Hutton and Hurt, appear to be closer than brothers, the story flashes back to San Diego. Rabal is a prosperous Basque immigrant, the Old World patriarch of a family that includes wife Hidalgo, married daughter Channing, youngest daughter Follows, and the apple of his eye, Leo, whose relationship with the boyishly handsome GI Hutton he has forbidden. Undaunted by Rabal's objections, Hutton and Leo elope, but when the strong-willed Basque learns of this, he coaxes his daughter from her honeymoon bed, and, in a driving rainstorm, Hutton follows them in his car. Rabal's vehicle fails to negotiate a curve and plunges into a lake, and though Hutton is able to rescue his wife, her father drowns. At the hospital, Hurt, the family's outcast son, arrives to visit the deathbed of the father who never loved or trusted him, but instead showered his affection on Leo and another son who died of tuberculosis. Unaware that Rabal has not even bothered to include him in his will, Hurt vows to gain vengeance on Hutton, whom he blames for Rabal's death. Hurt finagles a transfer so that he is shipped overseas with Hutton's unit, seemingly planning to do him in during the heat of battle; instead, the two become bosom buddies, though Hutton has no idea who Hurt is. Ironically, they save each other's lives and are awarded medals for their actions. On the eve of their return to the States at war's end, Hurt, whose demented nature has become increasingly obvious (to the audience if not to Hutton), tells his brother-in-law just who he really is and promises to kill Hutton if he tries to return to Leo. Hurt gets back to California first, and Leo and Hidalgo tell him that Rabal has left him in charge of the family ranch. Refusing to believe that his father would ever have welcomed him back into the fold, Hurt sells the ranch, as he had tried to do before and as Rabal had suspected he would do again. When Hutton returns, he and Leo head off to reaffirm their vows at the church where they were married. Hurt puts two and two together (things said in the past, information learned from reading one of Hutton's letters to Leo) and races to the church, where he tries to kill Hutton, finally chasing him to the church's bell tower for the film's climactic, VERTIGO-derived fight to the finish—in which Hurt stabs Hutton but then falls to his death. As the film ends, Hidalgo forgives Hutton and welcomes him into the family.

Writer-director Gregory Nava and writer-producer Anna Thomas, the husband-and-wife team responsible for the excellent EL NORTE (1984), have created a film here that intends to make a grand statement about love—both of the true and misguided variety—vengeance, and fate, but instead meanders ponderously to a conclusion that has less to do with destiny that predictability. With the exception of the well-realized performance of Stockard Channing, as the cynical older sister whose efforts to please failed to win her the kind of affection her father reserved for Leo, none of the characters are sympathetic enough that we ever really care what happens to them. Timothy Hutton and Melissa Leo are little more than cardboard cutouts to hang devotion on, and because their personalities are underdeveloped, it never becomes clear just exactly what it is that makes them love each other so damn much. Hurt is less one-dimensional, but the flashback psychological motivation provided for his strangely driven character is forced and his off-the-wall essay is brave but unconvincing. Some critics felt that A TIME OF DESTINY has an operatic quality characterized by sweeping emotions that don't rely on psychological realism for their impact; however, even if one applies this criterion, the film's characters still fail to intrigue, let alone sweep us up in the drama of their situation.

All of which is a shame, because director Nava has provided some stunning camerawork and memorable images that transcend his script's limitations. Most notable is his opening shot, the point-of-view journey of a shell through the barrel of an artillery piece, into its airborne trajectory, and ultimately to its explosive impact. The film is also intelligently edited, with symbolic, and only occasionally heavy-handed, juxtapositions and transitions, as between the outlines of mountains and human profiles. Yet, for all its visual inventiveness, A TIME OF DESTINY will leave those who become restless at the opera, and even those who don't, fidgeting in their seats long before the fat lady sings. (Sexual situations, violence, adult situations.)

p, Anna Thomas; d, Gregory Nava; w, Gregory Nava, Anna Thomas; ph, James Glennon (DeLuxe Color); ed, Betsy Blankett; m, Ennio Morricone; m/l, Giuseppe Verdi, Sol Selegna, Leonard Keller, Bob McCracken; prod d, Henry Bumstead; art d, Les Gobruegge; set d, Anne Kuljian; spec eff, David Watkins; cos, Amanda Chamberlin; stunts, Eddie Stacey; makeup, Karoly Balazs, Daniel Parker.

| Drama | Cas. | (PR:C MPAA:PG-13) |

TIN STAR VOID †   (1988) 95m Six-Shooter/Double Helix c

Daniel Chapman (Wade Holt), Ruth Collins (Annie), Loren Blackwell (Hawk), Karen Rizzo (Star), Phillip Nutman (Tough), John Pierce (Kid).

Such releases as 1987's STRAIGHT TO HELL and this year's THE BLUE IGUANA have paved the way for other hip, modern entries with a combination of futuristic, western, and film noir influences. TIN STAR VOID takes place in a town run by high-living criminals where punk cowboys drive slick 1950s roadsters. The film's guitar-playing hero lands in a seedy prison when he attempts to gain revenge for the murder of his brother, the town sheriff. After his release, he and a black prison mate return to the village to get the crime boss responsible for his brother's death. Shown on the festival circuit in late 1988.

p, Jean Bodon, Paul Falcone, Tom Gniazdowski, Leopold Wurm; d, Tom Gniazdowski; ph, Adam Goldfine; ed, Michael Lang; m, David Perlman; art d, David Perlman.

| Comedy/Crime/Western | | (PR:NR MPAA:NR) |

TOKYO POP*   (1988, Jap.) 97m Spectrafilm c

Carrie Hamilton (Wendy Reed), Yutaka Tadokoro (Hiro Yamaguchi), Taiji Tonoyoma (Grandfather), Tetsuro Tanba (Dota), Masumi Harukawa (Mother), Toki Shiozawa (Mama-san), Hiroshi Mikami (Seki), Miker Cerveris (Mike), Gina Belafonte (Holly), Daisuke Oyama (Yoji), Hiroshi Kobayashi (Kaz), Hiroshi Sugita (Taro), Satoshi Kanai (Shun).

Rock'n'roll is the Cupid that brings together East (Tadokoro), and West (Hamilton) in this light entertainment. Hamilton is a singer in a New York rock band whose career is going nowhere. When she receives a postcard saying "wish you were here" from a girl friend in Tokyo, she impulsively decides to visit—who knows, it might be a smart career move and it couldn't be worse than the New York scene. She arrives in Tokyo to find her friend has moved on to Thailand. This is only a minor setback for spunky Hamilton, however. She gets a room at an odd rooming house for down-on-their-luck westerners called Mickey House, and is able to make ends meet by working as a hostess in a bar where customers like to sing along with her on their favorite request, "Home on the Range." She meets Tadokoro, and is persuaded to join his struggling band. Her blonde, blue-eyed gaijin presence proves just the element needed to capture the young fans and, before long, the group is propelled to stardom. Along the way, a romance develops between Tadokoro and Hamilton—affording comic scenes of the expected clash of cultures variety—but as time goes by Hamilton grows dissatisfied with her Tokyo fame, which is based mainly on the novelty of her appearance, and decides to return to New York to try for real success based on her talents. Although heartbroken by her decision, Tadokoro is inspired to change direction in his music as well, and begins playing his own compositions instead of the formula pop tunes expected of him.

The first feature for director-cowriter Fran Rubel Kuzui, TOKYO POP manages to be entertaining despite its thin story line, mainly because of its striking visuals and the kooky charm of the leads. Imaginative use of locations and rich color photography result in memorable scenes, including the one shot in Yoyogi Park, where teens dress and dance in a bizarre replay of the 50s, or the view of Tadokoro's house—where each of the three resident generations expresses a different Japan, from kimonos and chop sticks to spiked hair and Kentucky Fried Chicken. Carrie Hamilton, the daughter of Carol Burnett, is engaging as the pixilated punker, and Yutaka Tadokoro, a real-life Japanese pop star, is thoroughly likable as the earnest rocker. (Sexual situations, nudity.)

p, Kaz Kuzui, Joel Tuber; d, Fran Rubel Kuzui; w, Fran Rubel Kuzui, Lynn Grossman (based on a story by Fran Rubel Kuzui); ph, James Hayman (TVC Color); ed, Camilla Toniolo; m, Alan Brewer; prod d, Terumi Hosoishi; cos, Asako Kobayashi.

| Comedy/Drama | Cas. | (PR:O MPAA:R) |

TORCH SONG TRILOGY½**   (1988) 120m Howard Gottfried/Ronald K. Fierstein/New Line c

Anne Bancroft (Ma), Matthew Broderick (Alan), Harvey Fierstein (Arnold Beckoff), Brian Kerwin (Ed), Karen Young (Laurel), Eddie Castrodad (David), Ken Page (Murray), Charles Pierce (Bertha Venation), Axel Vera (Marina Del Rey), Benji Schulman (Young Arnold), Nick Montgomery, Robert Neary (Chorus Boys), Kim Clark, Stephanie Penn (Female Bar Patrons), Geoffrey Harding (Man with Lighter), Michael Bond (Bar Patron), Michael Warga (Bartender), Phil Sky (Man in Back Room), Lorry Goldman (Phil Beckoff), Edgar Small (Arnold's Father), Harriet C. Leider (Maitre D'), Paul Joynt, Mitch David Carter (Hecklers in Club), Bob Minor (Gregory), Byron Deen (Roz), John Beckman (1st Cab Driver), Rabbi Elliott T. Spar (Rabbi), Alva Chinn (Photographer), Gregory Gilbert (Hustler), John Norman, Mark Zeisler (Bashers), Peter MacKenzie, Peter Nevargic (Young Men), Ted Hook (Old Man), Naill Gartlan (Boy in Fight), Catherine Blue, John Branagan (Teachers), Tracy Bogart (Secretary at School), Frits de Knegt (2nd Cab Driver).

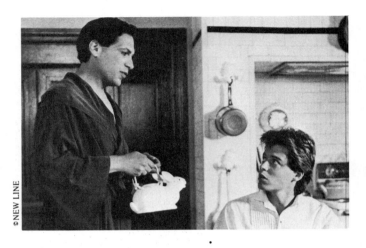

©NEW LINE

When Harvey Fierstein's "Torch Song Trilogy" premiered off-Broadway in the early 1980s, it became a word-of-mouth sensation for its caustically humorous homosexual script and performances, establishing a defiantly gay bill of rights within a context of piercingly witty melodrama. Fierstein captured theatergoers hearts with his naked sincerity, affectionately Jewish sensibility, and insight into what it means to be openly homosexual in a gay-bashing straight world. Now that the play is on film, moviegoers can see part of what the shouting was all about.

The story, taking place in New York City between 1971 and 1980, follows the roller-coaster love life of a gravel-voiced female impersonator (Fierstein). In Act One, Fierstein falls for a handsome and tender young hunk (Kerwin) whom he meets in a gay bar after work one night. They become intensely involved for a few weeks, but Kerwin, a bisexual, is soon put off by Fierstein's possessiveness and, yearning for acceptance in the straight world, starts dating a woman (Young). In Act Two, Fierstein connects with a 21-year-old fashion model (Broderick) who passes out drunk during Fierstein's cabaret act one night. This time, the relationship is a mutual, seemingly permanent one, but no matter how happy or at home Fierstein is with himself or his lovers, his parents, especially his mother (Bancroft), are ashamed of their son's lifestyle and profession. Just as Fierstein and Broderick are about to adopt a troubled gay teenager, the boy is beaten to death by a gang of gay bashers, leaving Fierstein grief-stricken and lonelier than ever. In Act Three, Fierstein is now a caring, concerned father to a precocious teenage son (Castrodad) and has resumed his long-dormant relationship with Kerwin, newly separated from wife Young for unexplained reasons. The movie ends with Fierstein sentimentally hugging a framed portrait of Broderick after angrily arguing with Bancroft about his way of life and the pain he has endured, telling her to accept and love him as he is or get out of his life. He will not hide what he is to please her bourgeois sensibility.

Above all else, TORCH SONG TRILOGY is Fierstein's showcase. He gives an emotional performance (some might call it mugging), hiding nothing of what he thinks or feels because it's his life he's dramatizing, after all. His script is loaded with sharp-tongued wit, warm humor, passion, and deeply felt conviction, but all the same, the movie as a whole has a dated feel to it, overemphasizing gayness and gay rights at the expense of all other human interests. It plays more like a preachy early 80s manifesto than a timeless drama showing us whole people from the inside out who also happen to be agonizingly gay. Indeed, Fierstein is the only actor here who is living his part, because he wears it on his sleeve, while Brian Kerwin and Matthew Broderick, though they both fit their roles physically, look uncomfortable espousing gay affections. And none of the three men ages one bit over the span of the story. Worst of all is Bancroft as Ma, clearly directed by Paul Bogart to act her role at a shrill pitch so we'll get the point instead of simply being the character and laying out for us why she is upset that her son is homosexual. She is Fierstein's mama because she is a star and because the script says so, not because we believe her. She is stereotyped and caricatured, whereas an actress like Lainie Kazan—excellent as the well-intentioned but intrusive Jewish mama on TV's "St. Elsewhere"—might have given the role more warmth and depth along with the maudlin angst.

Although Bogart, a TV sitcom veteran, brings some comedic touches to the movie, the show is Fierstein's. Whatever feelings or thoughts we take from it come from him rather than anything the director has imparted. But a great central performance doesn't make a great or even a good movie. This one is disjointed and fitful, coming to a sentimental, inclusive end instead of a satisfying, though-provoking finality that leaves one touched. *(Profanity, sexual situations, adult situations.)*

p, Howard Gottfried; d, Paul Bogart; w, Harvey Fierstein (based on the play by Harvey Fierstein); ph, Mikael Salomon (Metrocolor); ed, Nicholas C. Smith; m, Peter Matz; m/l, George Gershwin, Ira Gershwin, Harry Warren, Al Dubin, Kay Swift, Paul James, John Green, Edward Heyman, Robert Sour, Frank Eyton, Joseph Renard, Steve Cohen, Johnny Mercer, Hoagy Carmichael, DuBois Heyward, Bob Haggart, Johnny Burke, Cole Porter, Harold Arlen; prod d, Richard Hoover; art d, Michael Okowita, Marcie Dale; set d, Michael Warga, Marlene Marta; cos, Colleen Atwood; ch, Scott Salmon; makeup, Christa Reusch.

Drama **(PR:O MPAA:R)**

TOUGHER THAN LEATHER*½ (1988) 92m Def American/New Line c

Joseph Simmons *(Run)*, Darryl McDaniels *(DMC)*, Jason Mizell *(Jam Master Jay)*, Richard Edson *(Bernie)*, Jenny Lumet *(Pam)*, Rick Rubin *(Vic)*, Lois Ayer *(Charlotte)*, George Godfrey *(Nathan)*, Russell Simmons *(Russell)*, Ric Menello *(Arthur)*, Raymond White *(Runny Ray)*, Mickey Rubin *(Marty)*, Francesca Hodge, Daniel Simmons, Vic Noto, Nick D'Avolio, Carl Jordan, Russ Keehl, Larry Kase, Tim Summer, Will Rokos, Wayne Carisi.

©NEW LINE

After making their motion picture debut in 1985's KRUSH GROOVE, rap music's preeminent badasses, Run DMC, return to the screen with this self-produced actioner. While it contains concert footage not only of the stars but also of fellow rappers Slick Rick and the Beastie Boys, TOUGHER THAN LEATHER is cut from the mold of 1970s blaxploitation efforts, high in violence and macho heroics from Run DMC (Run aka Joseph Simmons, DMC aka Darryl McDaniels, and Jam Master Jay aka Jason Mizell). Beginning with Run's release from prison after doing time for an assault charge, the film follows the fellas as they sign to perform a concert tour for Strut Productions, the booking organization Rick Rubin (famed rap producer and the film's director) uses to launder his gangster father's drug money. But in order to get Run DMC to sign on the dotted line, Rubin also has to agree to put the Beastie Boys under contract, conveniently providing an opportunity for rap's nasty white boys to do their hip beer-swilling, rebellious thing, but adding absolutely nothing to the plot. More essential to the story is the plight of White, a Hollis (as in Queens, Run DMC's home turf) homeboy who has had trouble holding a job because his employers have been unwilling to see that, though he's a little slow in starting, he does good work when given the opportunity. Run gives him that chance, and White serves as the group's roadie as they undertake a zig-zagging cross-country tour, proving to be as invaluable as he is good-natured. Things start getting heavy, though, when Rubin's father tells him that one of his employees has been ripping him off. In the presence of lackeys Menello and Edson, and accompanied by his black enforcer, Godfrey, Rubin kills the transgressor backstage at a Run DMC gig. Unfortunately, White stumbles onto the proceedings, and he, too, is murdered; then both victims are littered with crack, prompting the police to decide that no further investigation into this drug-related incident is necessary. Determined to clear White's name, Run DMC put themselves on the case, endeavoring to find Edson so they can learn what actually went down and who the real murderer was. The search for Edson brings them into contact with a parade of racist white thugs who they coolly clobber in a bar brawl and alley assault. Eventually, the fellas catch up with Edson, he fingers Rubin, and Run DMC enlist the help of Rubin's not-so-loyal girl friend Ayer (the addition of an "s" to her last name may make her familiar to fans of adult films) in snaring Rubin. In the process, however, Rubin's henchmen nab Jam Master Jay, and an exchange of hostages in a warehouse turns into a bloodbath in which Jay is rescued and Rubin and several of his leather-jacketed cohorts are brutally dispatched by Run, DMC, and Jay.

Taken simply as an action film, TOUGHER THAN LEATHER is something of a sub-par effort, a long way from the heroics of Dirty Harry or John Shaft. The acting here is mediocre at best, the direction and script pedestrian, and the editing choppy; however, the film does fill the necessary quota of gut-bashing, gunplay, and gore (though not always very convincingly), throwing in a little sex and a smidgen of nudity as well. Director Rubin never manages create much in the way of tension, though, and while Run DMC (particularly Run) have a strong presence on film, it would difficult to call much of what they do on the screen acting. They are at their best in some of the film's quieter moments—their conversation in the car upon Run's release from prison, Run's job offer to White, DMC's bar-stool cool while all hell breaks loose around him—but in the scenes that call for emotional intensity it becomes clear that as actors these guys are great rappers. Moreover, the supporting performances are forgettable, and Richard Edson (STRANGER THAN PARADISE; EIGHT MEN OUT), one of the current cinema's most interesting faces and an engaging performer when in the right role and surrounded by the right actors, hits the mark only occasionally in his portrayal of Rubin's dim-witted lackey.

Violence and macho strutting (and sexism) are definitely at the center of TOUGHER THAN LEATHER, which, presumably, represents an extension of Run DMC's onstage pose and the attitude behind their records. Continually provoked by blatant white racists, they spend much of the film kicking Caucasian butts and blowing holes in white people, most of whom are drug-dealing criminals and all of whom deserve some kind of serious comeuppance. (It should also be noted that Godfrey, a mercenary black who sells his soul for the dollar, also gets his in the end.) Clearly, there is an important sociopolitical subtext here, and its message (beyond the problems that drugs have brought to the black community) is that white racism's ugly face is still pervasive and threatening. Nonetheless, it is disturbing to see violence depicted as so easy a response to racist harassment. At a time of great racial tension in many parts of the country, TOUGHER THAN LEATHER becomes more than an expression of black empowerment and pride; it is racially inflammatory, although no less so then the mainstream films with a penchant for black villains. It's somewhat surprising that Run DMC, the first black rap group to attract a large white following (the film's concert footage shows at least as many whites in the audience as blacks), would run the risk of alienating that audience with such a polarizing stance. More than that, it's disappointing that, given the opportunity to raise consciousness about racism, they have blunted their message by adopting a standard racist approach. *(Violence, excessive profanity, brief nudity, adult situations, sexual situations.)*

p, Vincent Giordano; d, Rick Rubin; w, Ric Menello, Rick Rubin (based on a story by Bill Adler, Lyor Cohen, Ric Menello); ph, Feliks Parnell; ed, Steven Brown.

Action **Cas.** **(PR:O MPAA:R)**

TRACK 29** (1988, Brit.) 90m HandMade/Island c

Theresa Russell *(Linda Henry)*, Gary Oldman *(Martin)*, Sandra Bernhard *(Nurse Stein)*, Christopher Lloyd *(Dr. Henry Henry)*, Colleen Camp *(Arlanda)*, Seymour Cassel *(Dr. Bernard Fairmont)*, Leon Rippy *(Trucker)*, Vance Colvig *(Mr. Ennis)*, Kathryn Tomlinson *(Receptionist)*, Jerry Rushing *(Redneck)*, Tommy Hull *(Counterman)*, J. Michael Hunter *(Waiter)*, Richard K. Olsen *(Delegate)*, Ted Barrow *(Old Man)*.

Nicolas Roeg's latest feature is a twisted family melodrama/thriller that expands the director's oft-stated premise "Nothing is what it seems." TRACK 29 (which could have been called "Don't Like Now," after Roeg's 1973 masterpiece, DON'T LOOK NOW) stars Russell as a North Carolina housewife who may or may not have just met her son, Oldman, at the local diner. There's a strange attraction between the pair that haunts Russell. Later, in the middle of the night, she looks out her second floor bedroom window and sees Oldman cosmically materialize on her front lawn. Oblivious to all of this, and everything else in his wife's life, is Russell's husband, Lloyd. Obsessed with model trains, he has constructed a sweeping miniature landscape throughout the top floor of their house, but, preoccupied with his "locos" (as he calls his locomotives), he fails to pay attention to his loco wife. Through Russell's daytime fantasies/memories, it is revealed that, at the age of 15, she lost her virginity to a trucker (who bears an uncanny resemblance to Oldman) and became pregnant. Her newborn son was immediately taken from the unmarried teen, and Oldman now pops into Russell's life, claiming to be that son. In his British accent, the leather-jacketed Oldman explains that he has spent all his time and money searching for his " mummy."Having been cheated out of 20 years of motherly affection, he decides to make up for lost time. In doing so, he regresses into childhood—pouting, indulging in baby talk, ogling mummy's breasts, wanting to be held and played with. It soon becomes clear, however, that Oldman exists only as a figment of Russell's imagination. He is the child Russell wishes she could have raised and, further, becomes the character through whom she vents her anger at her husband. Meanwhile, Lloyd, a geriatrician, is carrying on a perverse affair with his nurse (Bernhard), who spanks the naughty doctor while he listens to a cassette tape filled with chugging train sounds. When Lloyd and Bernhard are fired by their superior (Cassel), they spend the rest of their day at the "Trainorama,"a model train convention at which Lloyd is the keynote speaker. Back at home, Oldman is busy destroying (or so it seems) Lloyd's elaborate train setup, stomping on it Godzilla-like. Realizing she has been mentally derailed and fearing that Lloyd will be angry with her when he sees the damage that Oldman has done, Russell calls her best friend (Camp) and begs her to come over. Lloyd comes home and Camp eventually leaves, convinced by Russell that everything will be okay. As Lloyd proudly examines his train set (which seems again to be in proper order), a naked Oldman leaps out from a closet and stabs him to death. Russell is next seen dressed in a sporty white outfit, her long hair pinned up on her head. Looking every bit the elegant woman (as if this scene were an outtake from BLACK WIDOW), she hops into her car and leaves home. Meanwhile, a red blood stain soaks through the living room ceiling.

Nicolas Roeg seems to pride himself on making weird films. Is this his version of a Douglas Sirk melodrama—the tortured middle-class woman who does not fit in with the status quo because she is childless? Or is it his twisted version of PSYCHO, with Russell as Mrs. Bates, living her life through the imaginary incarnation of her son—Mommy doing naughty things and putting the blame on Baby? (One point in favor of this interpretation is screenwriter Dennis Potter's film BRIMSTONE AND TREACLE, wherein the mother's name is Norma Bates and her nemesis is called Martin, Oldman's character name in TRACK 29.) Or perhaps this is just another episode from the Theresa Russell thriller BLACK WIDOW, as she dons a new disguise (braces and a North Carolina accent) and spins her web around Lloyd, doing him in before FBI agent Debra Winger can arrive to save him? One thing is for sure about

Roeg: his pictures are overstated, heavily symbolic statements that pound the viewer over the head with a Big Theme. The road to Roeg's rather obvious ideas is paved with scenes that are alternately obnoxious and tedious. Yes, TRACK 29 is weird, and, yes, it must mean something, but one sure gets the feeling that it's not worth the time or effort to figure it out. TRACK 29 is a train ride you might enjoy for a few stops, but eventually you realize you're not going anywhere and would be obliged if the conductor would just let you off.

Set in North Carolina, USA, the film probes the American psyche, the power of the television, and the bond between mother and child. To drive his points home, Roeg gives us a television in nearly every scene (their screens offering the 1962 film CAPE FEAR, with its Bernard Herrmann score and its themes and setting similar to TRACK 29; a science-fiction program about the cosmos; and cartoon character Mr. Peabody discussing trains) and an overdose of maternal symbols ('Mom' tattoos, baby dolls, and two songs called 'Mother'). As the film opens over John Lennon's chilling song 'Mother,' a leather-jacketed Oldman hitchhikes on a bridge over the Cape Fear River. He then roars, 'Mummy!' The abandoned child wants his mommy and hitches a ride with a trucker, who may or may not be the man who raped Russell. Then again, Oldman himself may be the man who raped Russell. " Things are not what they seem."While daddy Lloyd is off playing with his toys, loco mommy Russell is going nutty because she has no toys of her own. She has a big collection of dolls, but she wants more—her own version of a train set, a toy that's also an obsession. Since her baby was taken away long ago, and since daddy Lloyd doesn't need any more toys (after all, he also has a nurse to play with), mommy Russell invents baby Oldman. When Russell feels naughty, Oldman is naughty. When Mommy wants to caress herself, Baby's hand is there. When Mommy wants to smash Daddy's toys, Baby does it for her. And, when Mommy wants to kill Daddy, Baby does the stabbing. Maybe Roeg is on to something interesting here, but the response that his methods tend to elicit is " So what."As a result, one begins to feel that TRACK 29 (the track at which one can catch the " Chattanooga Choo-Choo") is merely a filmmaking exercise for Roeg and screenwriter Potter.

Roeg and Potter toss a thesis onto the screen that never seems to go anywhere, not unlike some of Roeg's previous films—EUREKA; INSIGNIFICANCE; CASTAWAY; and his episode in this year's ARIA. The film's saving grace, besides Roeg's always lovely images, is the acting talent of Gary Oldman, whose performances in SID AND NANCY (as Sid Vicious) and PRICK UP YOUR EARS (as Joe Orton) are among the finest of any new young actor today. He is a powerful and frightening actor who pushes a performance to the edge, even though his little boy tantrums in TRACK 29 quickly grow irritating. Theresa Russell, while not Oldman's equal, does a fine job despite Roeg's continuously exploitative method of photographing her. Although Russell is Roeg's real-life wife, he photographs her with the same lack of respect that a sleazy movie mogul shows a young starlet. Supporting players Christopher Lloyd, Sandra Bernhard, Seymour Cassel, and Colleen Camp make good use of their screen time, but all their scenes are tangents that add little to the Oldman-Russell relationship. In addition to John Lennon's Mother, the soundtrack includes M-O-T-H-E-R (Theodore Morse, Fiske O'Hara), Chattanooga Choo-Choo (Harry Warren, Mack Gordon), When the Red Red Robin Comes Bob Bob Bobbin' Along (Harry Woods), and Young at Heart (John Richards, Carolyn Leigh, performed by Rosemary Clooney). *(Sexual situations, adult situations, profanity, nudity, violence.)*

p, Rick McCallum; d, Nicolas Roeg; w, Dennis Potter; ph, Alex Thomson (Technicolor); ed, Tony Lawson; m, Stanley Myers; m/l, Theodore Morse, Fiske O'Hara, John Lennon, Harry Woods, Harry Warren, Mack Gordon, John Richards, Carolyn Leigh; prod d, David Brockhurst; art d, Curtis Schnell, Francine Mercadante; set d, Douglas Mowat; spec eff, Dave Beavis, Dean Gates; cos, Shuna Harwood; makeup, Jeff Goodwyn.

Thriller **Cas.** **(PR:O MPAA:R)**

TRADING HEARTS † (1988) 88m Vista/Cineworld c

Raul Julia *(Vinnie)*, Beverly D'Angelo *(Donna)*, Jenny Lewis *(Yvonne)*, Parris Buckner *(Robert)*, Robert Gwaltney *(Ducky)*, Ruben Rabasa *(Pepe)*, Mark Harris *(Ralph)*, Robin Caldwell, Earleen Carey, Tom Kouchalakos, Edward L. Koch.

Although written by respected *Sports Illustrated* reporter Frank Deford and starring Raul Julia and Beverly D'Angelo, TRADING HEARTS (working title "Tweeners") never saw a theatrical release and went directly to home video. A romantic comedy set in 1957, the film features Julia as a washed-up pitcher for the Boston Red Sox who has just been cut from the roster during spring training in Florida. Feeling sorry for himself, Julia hits the bar circuit, where he meets D'Angelo, a not-getting-any-younger divorcee making a last-ditch attempt at a singing career in a local dive. Although Julia and D'Angelo do not get along at first, D'Angelo's precocious 11-year-old daughter, Lewis, who is a baseball nut and knows who Julia is, is determined to get her mom and the pitcher hitched. This doesn't seem likely, however, until D'Angelo's ex-husband (Buckner) succeeds in gaining custody of the child—an event which brings Julia and D'Angelo together.

p, Herb Jaffe, Mort Engelberg; d, Neil Leifer; w, Frank Deford; ph, Karen Grossman (DeLuxe Color); ed, Rick Shaine; m, Stanley Myers; prod d, George Goodridge; art d, James R. Bilz; set d, Regina McLarney; cos, Franco Caretti.

Comedy/Romance/Sports **Cas.** **(PR:NR MPAA:PG)**

TRAVELLING NORTH*** (1988, Aus.) 97m View Pictures-Australian Film Commission-Queensland

Leo McKern *(Frank)*, Julie Blake *(Frances)*, Graham Kennedy, Henri Szeps *(Saul)*, Michelle Fawdon *(Helen)*, Diane Craig *(Sophie)*, Andrea Moor *(Joan)*, Drew Forsythe *(Martin)*, John Gregg *(Jim)*, Rob Steele *(Syd)*, John Black *(Alan)*, Roger Oakley *(Stan)*, Joe MacColum *(Boat Owner)*, Nicholas Holland *(Waiter)*, Steve Shaw *(Estate Agent)*, Genevieve Mooy *(Gallery Attendant)*, Beavan Wilson *(Celebrant)*, Andrew McMahon, Mitchell McMahon, Jessica McMahon, Rebecca Fuller, Kim Herbert, Amy Fuller, Angie Thompson *(Children)*.

In TRAVELLING NORTH, McKern stars as a crusty engineer who reluctantly retires upon reaching the age of 70. Deciding he's had enough of life in Melbourne, McKern purchases a seaside cottage on the north coast of Australia, inviting a much younger divorcee (Blake) to join him. She is willing to do so, but her daughters (Fawdon and Craig) vehemently opposed their mother's moving hundreds of miles away with the brusque McKern. Blake gives in to McKern's persistence, however, and the two of them head for their home in northern Queensland. The tranquility of these new surroundings is soon shattered by the appearance of their neighbor, Kennedy, who, though friendly and well-meaning, is thoroughly exasperating in his nosiness and his nonstop chatter. Eventually, McKern, who has been experiencing chest pains for some time, visits a local doctor (Szeps) and is told he has a serious heart condition. In the meantime, Blake grows concerned about her daughters and talks Mckern into a trip to Melbourne to see the girls. During the journey McKern suffers a mild heart attack and they return to the cottage. As McKern recovers, Fawdon visits her mother and implores her to return to the city, after which Blake and McKern again head for Melbourne, where he suffers another heart attack and the pair returns to the North. Failing health has made McKern more disagreeable and demanding than ever, however, and his hostility finally drives Blake away and back to Melbourne. Filled with remorse, McKern calls and begs her to return, asking her to marry him. She accepts and they are wed in Sydney. McKern makes a valiant effort to be less cantankerous and more sensitive to Blake, but time soon runs out for him and he dies after suffering a massive coronary. Following his wishes, Blake, Kennedy, and Szeps share a bottle of champagne in McKern's memory.

Australia's leading playwright, David Williamson (screenwriter of PHAR LAP; GALLIPOLI; and THE YEAR OF LIVING DANGEROUSLY), adapted his own work for this film, and it does suffer from a stagebound quality. Nevertheless, Williamson has written some witty and insightful dialog and TRAVELLING NORTH works fairly well as a rumination on growing old. Its biggest asset is the blustery Leo McKern (LADYHAWKE; THE FRENCH LIEUTENANT'S WOMAN; TV's "Rumpole of the Bailey") as the bullying old man. Not surprisingly, he's terrific as the curmudgeon, but he also sensitively conveys the fear and sadness that overwhelm his character as he faces impending death. McKern's marvelous performance keeps the movie from slipping into tacky sentimentality. Good performances back him up: the lovely Julia Blake provides McKern with a sweet and delightful foil, artfully playing her character's love for this man who seems so intent on being unlovable; Henri Szeps and Graham Kennedy offer solid support as friends to McKern and potential suitors to Blake. Director Carl Schultz (CAREFUL, HE MIGHT HEAR YOU) keeps things moving along and the photography of the Australian scenery is often stunning. *(Profanity.)*

p, Ben Gannon; d, Carl Schultz; w, David Williamson (based on the play by David Williamson); ph, Julian Penney; ed, Henry Dangar; m, Alan John, Beethoven, Wolfgang Amadeus Mozart, Antonio Vivaldi; prod d, Owen Paterson; set d, Alethea Deane; cos, Jennie Tate; makeup, Violette Fontaine.

Drama **(PR:C MPAA:PG-13)**

TRAXX*½ (1988) 84m DEG c

Shadoe Stevens *(Traxx)*, Priscilla Barnes *(Mayor Alexandria Cray)*, Willard E. Pugh *(Deeter)*, John Hancock *(Chief Emmett Decker)*, Hugh Gillin *(Comm. R.B. Davis)*, Michael Kirk *(Mayhew)*, Raymond O'Connor *(Tibbs)*, Robert Davi *(Aldo Palucci)*, Hershal Sparber, Jonathan Lutz, Lucius Houghton *(Guziks)*, Darrow Igus *(Wendall)*, Arlene Lorre *(Celeste)*, Wally Amos *(Famous Amos)*, Wallace G. Merek *(Jerome)*, Jerry Colker *(Kent)*, Rick Overton *(Frank Williams)*, Robert Miano *(Arturo)*, Steve Boleo *(Lonnie)*, J. Michael Hunter *(Matt)*, Leon Rippy *(Killer)*, Stephen Ware *(Wesley)*, William Betts *(James)*, Derwin E. Luby *(James' Wife)*, Bev Appleton *(Morse)*, Graham F. Smith *(Ootz)*, Kim Weeks *(Nurse)*, Jon Thompson *(Dolan)*, James C. Gloster *(Eddie)*, James G. Martin, Jr. *(John)*, Suzanne Primeau, Karen L. Kristopher *(Hookers)*, Rodney Suiter *(Black Man)*, Michael Holowaty *(5-year-old kid)*, Tony Lea *(Cop)*, Michael W. Decker *(Miguel)*, Pat Miller *(Harold)*, William J. Arvay, Jr., Amanda Graham, Shirlene Foss, Martin Tucker, Richard Olsen, Irene Stewart, C.D. Roberts *(Reporters)*, Howard Kingkaid *(Paul)*, Art Kohn *(Newscaster)*, Martin Zehring, Domenic Secondo, G.B. Wallace, Lou Criscuolo, Richard Giachetti, Annamarie Smith *(Palucci's Gang)*, Mark R. Smith *(Limo Driver)*, George Lee *(Fletcher)*, Stephan MacDonald *(Hallis)*, Dorothy M. Craig *(Border Guard's Wife)*, David R. Greene, Sr. *(Officer)*, Chuck Kinlaw *(Coach)*, Gwendolyn Hajek *(Playmate)*, Tom Mason *(Old Man)*, Ruth Gottlieb Moore *(Old Woman)*, Janice Hart *(Therapist)*, Jim Simmons *(Carnival Barker)*, Colette Rubinson, Tammy Simpson Jones, Tina Renee Jackson *(Mocha Band Members)*, Ashley Woodman Hall *(Mocha Band Leader)*.

In this comic action film, Stevens plays Traxx, an ex-Texas state trooper-turned-mercenary. In El Salvador, the Middle East, and Nicaragua, we see him shooting up bad guys while admiring his own good looks and adjusting his hair. After a while he decides he's had enough, so he heads to Hadleyville, Texas, to take up his first love, baking cookies. At his riverside camp he makes like a muscular Betty Crocker, concocting strange crab cookies, tuna cookies, laxative and cough drop cookies—all without much success. In need of cash to open his business, he goes to work for town police chief Hancock and mayor Barnes as a "town tamer." Hadleyville is in desperate need of such a person, riddled as it is with murders, rapes, and explosions every 10 seconds, and with the town police beaten up regularly. Stevens sets right to work, roughing up the owners and patrons of the Stud Ranch and, in the process, picking up a sidekick, Igus. As he cleans up the sleazy porno strips of the town, Stevens continues to bake his inedible creations, prompting Igus to comment that he has two types of cookies: those that kill and those that don't. Stevens also starts a romance with Barnes, who becomes totally unglued at the mere sight of him. The local mob boss, Davi, so evil that he sends grams of coke to the members of Cocaine Anonymous, decides to call in the dreaded Guzik brothers to get rid of Stevens. The buffoonish brothers ride into town shooting Uzis out of the roof of their limo and take the town's little league team hostage. After getting rid of Davi—who eats one of Stevens' chili con carne cookies, breaks wind, lights a match, and blows up his car—our hero, though wounded, rescues the team and kills the Guziks in an Old West showdown. At a town celebration, his new store, "Snacks by Traxx", is unveiled and Wally Amos, of Famous Amos cookies, puts in a cameo appearance.

Despite its ludicrous plot TRAXX has some winning moments. Shadoe Stevens, best known as a West Coast DJ and Hollywood Square celeb, makes his film debut and has some genuinely funny scenes. With a deadpan smile, he delivers his lines with a nice, light, comic touch, helped along by the other good character performances. Director Jerome Gary keeps the action moving along at a fast clip, stumbling only in the last third of the film when the jokes turn stale. The straight-to-video release was filmed at DEG's North Carolina studio, and, unfortunately, too many of the scenes are set-bound and phony looking, detracting from the otherwise upbeat, lighthearted tone of the movie. Songs include: "Ain't Gonna Take It No More" (Jay Gruska, Paul Gordon, performed by Steve Donn), "Riggatoni Baloney" (Gruska, performed by Michele Gruska), "Everybody Knows It" (Gruska). *(Violence, nudity, profanity.)*

p, Gary De Vore, Richard McWhorter; d, Jerome Gary; w, Gary De Vore; ph, Giuseppe Maccari (Technicolor); ed, Michael Kahane; m, Jay Gruska; m/l, Jay Gruska, Paul Gordon; prod d, Jack Poplin; art d, Dennis Bradford; set d, Joseph Stone; spec eff, Robert Dawson; cos, Clifford Capone; makeup, June Pipkin.

Action/Comedy **Cas.** **(PR:O MPAA:R)**

TUCKER: THE MAN AND HIS DREAM**** (1988) 111m LFL/PAR c

Jeff Bridges *(Preston Tucker)*, Joan Allen *(Vera Tucker)*, Martin Landau *(Abe Karatz)*, Frederic Forrest *(Eddie Dean)*, Mako *(Jimmy Sakuyama)*, Lloyd Bridges *(Senator Homer Ferguson)*, Elias Koteas *(Alex Tremulis)*, Christian Slater *(Junior)*, Nina Siemaszko *(Marilyn Lee Tucker)*, Anders Johnson *(Johnny Tucker)*, Corky Nemec *(Noble Tucker)*, Marshall Bell *(Frank)*, Jay O. Sanders *(Kirby, Defense Attorney)*, Peter Donat *(Otto Kerner, Prosecutor)*, Dean Goodman *(Bennington)*, John X. Heart *(Ferguson's Agent)*, Don Novello *(Stan)*, Patti Austin *(Millie)*, Sandy Bull *(Stan's Assistant)*, Joseph Miksak *(Judge)*, Scott Beach *(Floyd Cerf)*, Roland Scrivner *(Oscar Beasley)*, Dean Stockwell *(Howard Hughes)*, Bob Safford *(Narrator)*, Larry Menkin *(Doc)*, Ron Close *(Fritz)*, Joe Flood *(Dutch)*, Leonard Gardner *(Gas Station Owner)*, Bill Bonham *(Garage Owner)*, Abigail Van Alyn, Taylor Gilbert *(Ferguson's Secretaries)*, David Booth *(Man in Hall)*, Jessie Nelson *(Woman on Steps)*, Al Hart *(Newscaster Voice)*, Cab Covay *(Security Guard)*, James Cranna *(Man in Audience)*, Bill Reddick *(Board Member)*, Ed Loerke *(Mayor)*, Jay Jacobus *(Head Engineer)*, Anne Lawder *(Bennington's Secretary)*, Jeanette Lana Sartain, Mary Buffett, Annie Stocking *(Singing Girls)*, Michael McShane *(Recording Engineer)*, Dean Goodman *(Drew Pearson's Voice)*, Hope Alexander-Willis, Taylor Young *(Tucker's Secretaries)*, Jim Giovanni *(Police Sergeant)*, Joe Lerer *(Reporter at Trial)*, Morgan Upton *(Ingram)*, Ken Grantham *(SEC Agent)*, Mark Anger *(Blue)*, Al Nalbandian *(Jury Foreman)*.

©LUCASFILM

A long-delayed dream project for director Francis Ford Coppola, TUCKER: THE MAN AND HIS DREAM may have its shortcomings as a character study—it is, in fact, much more dream than man—but on a purely visual level it is the most sumptuous American film of the year. Told in a hopelessly cheerful style that hearkens back to the boundless optimism of Frank Capra, the film tells the story of one Preston Tucker, part inventor, part con-man, who, in the late 1940s, attempted to buck the system and produce his own car—which he dubbed the Tucker Torpedo, "The Car of Tomorrow—Today!" The movie opens with a slick promotional film for the Torpedo that fills us in on background details. We learn that Tucker (played with boundless exuberance by Jeff Bridges) has worked his way up in the auto industry from the mail room to dealerships, finally designing a high-speed tank for the army. Although the army didn't care for the tank, they loved the rotating gun turret Bridges invented and decided to install them in airplanes. Flushed with success, Bridges turns his attention to his dream car, a futuristic automobile with such ahead-of-its-time features as aerodynamic design, seat belts, rear engine, fuel injection, disc brakes, pop-out windshield, and even a center headlight that would turn with the steering. Gathering together his extended family of actual kin, designers, grease monkeys, and test drivers, Bridges, with the help of old friend and New York financier Landau, starts up a company and begins taking out sensational advertising and issuing stock before the car is even built. Tossing together a prototype made from pieces of other cars, Bridges pushes his crew to the limit in an effort to get the car done before the scheduled unveiling at an important press conference. Scrambling to stop an oil leak backstage seconds before the car is to be shown, the mechanics manage to roll the car on stage just in time for Bridges to awe the anxious crowd. The premiere is a success, and enough stock and dealerships are sold to raise the necessary capital to begin assembly line production. Hoping to land the rights to a huge, deserted, government-owned factory on the southwest side of Chicago, Bridges allows Landau to bring in some credible businessmen to form a board of directors for the company. This, combined with Bridges' natural salesmanship, does the trick and production begins on the car—but slowly. Meanwhile, the big three auto manufacturers in Detroit get wind of Bridges' scheme and set out to quash the tiny interloper by cutting off his supply of steel, getting his board of directors to take over the company, and enlisting a powerful Michigan senator played by Lloyd Bridges (actor Jeff's father) to cook up a scheme to discredit Bridges and ruin the company. Exploiting Bridges' somewhat overenthusiastic love of hype and his association with Landau, who once served time for some shady business dealings, the senator pressures the Securities and Exchange Commission to bring fraud charges against Bridges. Although there isn't much rope to hang him with, the press gives the case hysterical treatment and paints Bridges as a hustler out to bilk the public. Much to his surprise, Bridges is summoned by Howard Hughes (Stockwell), who meets him in the hanger where the legendary Spruce Goose is stored. "They say it can't fly," mutters Stockwell, "but that's not the point." Sensing that he and Bridges are cut from the same cloth, Stockwell offers some advice and notes that he too will soon be facing a government inquisition. At his trial, Bridges himself makes the final summation in his defense and begs the jury to understand that big business in America is ruining little dreamers like himself, and, without the dreamers, someday Americans will be buying all their new products from the recently defeated Germany and Japan. Although the jury finds him innocent and Bridges is acquitted of all charges, the damage to his reputation is done and he loses his business, with only 51 Tucker Torpedos making it off the assembly line (46 of which are still on the road). Undaunted, Bridges enthusiastically begins dreaming about his next great invention.

Regardless of whether he sets out with this intention or not, some of Coppola's strongest films wind up being autobiographical. The trials and tribulations that drove him to the brink of madness while shooting APOCALYPSE NOW (1979) likened him to the character of Col. Kurtz in that film, while the sudden death of his beloved son Gio during the shooting of the vastly underrated GARDENS OF STONE added a personal, tragic air to a film about burying the nation's youth (TUCKER ends with the dedication, "For Gio, Who Loved Cars"). TUCKER, however, is Coppola's most overtly autobiographical film, even though it is about someone else's life. The parallels between the ambitions of Preston Tucker and Coppola's dreams of building his own studio were not lost on the director, and one can easily substitute "movies" for "cars" while watching TUCKER. The film is a glorious celebration of the creative process, reveling in the inspiration, the family-like atmosphere, the hard work, the long hours, and even the frustrations of trying to get the money men to have confidence in one's vision. From all accounts of Coppola's personal life, he and the Preston Tucker of his movie are very similar characters. Coppola's love for his family is legendary; he works with a close-knit extended family of actors and production people; at times he became the P.T. Barnum of Hollywood, making grandiose claims for what he could do; and he had absolutely no sense when it came to money. The forces that conspired to close down Tucker (at least in the film), are similar to what destroyed Coppola's Zoetrope Studios—stiff competition from entrenched companies who dominate the industry, overreaching ambitions, undercapitalization, and control by a visionary entrepreneur who was a lousy businessman.

What is genuinely surprising about the film is that, with material so ripe for a downbeat treatment—small dreamer mercilessly crushed by the inexorable forces of American big business—Coppola chooses to be remarkably upbeat and joyous. One cannot imagine such a perspective from the director who made THE CONVERSATION (1974), but as he has grown older, Coppola's anger has subsided and he seems to find more value in the act of dreaming than in making his dreams a success. Amazingly, he has designed such a gorgeous, fluid, wonderfully exhilarating movie—as beautiful as Tucker's car—that he just about persuades us to accept this view. Continuing and expanding upon the visual experiments he began in the notorious commercial flop ONE FROM THE HEART, Coppola fills TUCKER with some flawlessly executed transitions that will strike even the most jaded audience. Instead of employing the traditional split-screen technique during a phone conversation between Tucker and his wife, for example, Coppola uses the wide-screen format to place Tucker in the far back of the left side of the frame and his wife in huge close-up on the right side of the frame—all in the same shot with no optical trickery involved. Another striking moment occurs when Tucker and his men are in his living room planning the assembly line and Tucker suddenly bolts out of his seat, grabs his hat, and walks screen right into the giant, brightly lit warehouse—once again, all in one fluid shot without the benefit of special optical effects (obviously the living room set was built inside the warehouse and lit differently). The contributions of Oscar-winning cinematographer Vittorio Storaro, and of Coppola's loyal production design department headed by Dean and Alex Tavoularis, are immeasurable in assessing the beautiful look of this film, most of which, unless TUCKER is released on videocassette in the letterbox format, will be lost to VCR viewers.

As in all of Coppola's films, the acting is superior as well. Bridges—who may some-day receive the credit he is due as one of America's best young actors—is wonderful as Preston Tucker. Saddled with the task of being hopelessly cheerful and optimistic even when the chips are down, Bridges resorts to creating a series of smiles that convey different things. There is the genuine smile, the hustler smile, the bitter smile, and a host of others. Bridges wrestles the role from slipping into the idiotic with his unbridled energy. The supporting cast is also strong, with Frederic Forrest, Mako, Lloyd Bridges, and Joan Allen (a wonderful actress who is underutilized here) forming a team that would rival a supporting cast assembled in the golden days of Hollywood. Most impressive, however, are Martin Landau and Dean Stockwell, the latter in a fleeting appearance as Howard Hughes. A contemporary of James Dean who never seemed to get the right career break, Landau has finally landed a role in which he can showcase his considerable talent. Credible, funny, and very touching, his portrayal of Abe Karatz is the heart of the movie and adds a real edge to an otherwise bubbly film. Likewise, the brief scene with Stockwell's Hughes foreshadows Tucker's troubles and drives the film into darkness. In a scant amount of screen time, Stockwell is able to convey both the genius and madness of Hughes and turns him into a tragic figure. The scene is absolutely chilling and, as a result, threatens to throw the entire film off kilter, but Coppola is able to recover. With TUCKER announced as his last feature for a while (a short contained in NEW YORK STORIES follows), Coppola has gone to live in Rome, where he can make small films for himself without having to worry about commercial success. Luckily, he has left us with a reminder of the genuine joy he still feels for the process and it is to be hoped that he will return to the screen reinvigorated to do battle with the industry. Despite all its crowd-pleasing elements, TUCKER was a relative failure at the box office. Given Coppola's thesis—that dreaming is more important than success—this seems remarkably appropriate. Songs include "Rhythm Delivery" (Joe Jackson, performed by Jackson), "Tucker Jingle" (Carmine Coppola, Arnold Schulman), "When Johnny Comes Marching Home" (Patrick Gilmore, Mark Adler), "Tiger Rag" (Harry DeCosta, Edwin B. Edwards, D. James LaRocca, Anthony Sbarbaro, Larry Shields, performed by Jackson), "Tiger Rag" (Mills Brothers), "Song Of India" (Nikolay Rimsky-Korsakov, Bob Wilber).

p, Fred Roos, Fred Fuchs; d, Francis Ford Coppola; w, Arnold Schulman, David Seidler; ph, Vittorio Storaro (Technovision, Technicolor); ed, Priscilla Nedd; m, Joe Jackson; m/l, Joe Jackson, Arnold Schulman, Carmine Coppola, Patrick Gilmore, Harry DeCosta, Edwin B. Edwards, D. James LaRocca, Anthony Sbarbaro, Larry Shields, The Mills Brothers, Nikolay Rimsky-Korsakov, Edward Farley, Michael Riley, Ernest R. Ball, J.K. Brennan; prod d, Dean Tavoularis; art d, Alex Tavoularis; set d, Bob Goldstein, Jim Pohl; spec eff, David Pier; cos, Milena Canonero; ch, Paula Smuin; tech, Tom Sparks; stunts, Buddy Joe Hooker; makeup, Richard Dean.

Biography/Drama   **Cas.**   **(PR:A MPAA:PG)**

TWINS**   (1988) 112m UNIV c

Arnold Schwarzenegger (*Julius Benedict*), Danny DeVito (*Vincent Benedict*), Kelly Preston (*Marnie Mason*), Chloe Webb (*Linda Mason*), Bonnie Bartlett (*Mary Ann Benedict*), Marshall Bell (*Webster*), Trey Wilson (*Beetroot McKinley*), David Caruso (*Al Greco*), Hugh O'Brien (*Granger*), Tony Jay (*Werner*), Nehemiah Persoff (*Mitchell Traven*), Maury Chaykin (*Burt Klane*), Tom McCleister (*Bob Klane*), David Efron (*Morris Klane*), Peter Dvorsky (*Peter Garfield*), Robert Harper (*Gilbert Larsen*), Rosemary Dunamore (*Miss Busby*), Lora Milligan (*Stewardess*), Richard De Faut (*Custodian*), Richard Portnov (*Chop Shop Owner*), Billy D. Lucas, S.A. Griffin (*Hollywood Bikers*), Lew Hopson (*Cop*), Frances Bay (*Mother Superior*), Marvin J. McIntyre (*McKinley's Man*), Cary-Hiroyuki Tagawa (*Oriental Man*), Wayne Grace (*Cell Guard*), Thomas Wagner (*Visiting Room Guard*), Jay Arlen Jones, Tyrone Granderson Jones (*Movers*), Elizabeth Kaitan (*Secretary*), Tom Platz, Roger Callard (*Granger Sons*), Catherine Reitman (*Granger Granddaughter*), Jason Reitman (*Granger Grandson*), Dendrie Taylor (*Female Neighbor*), Sven-Ole Thorsen (*Sam Klane*), Gus Rethwisch (*Dave Klane*), Linda Porter (*Painter*), Bruce McBroom (*Handsome Father*), Joseph Medjuck (*Photographer*), Frank Davis, John Michael Bolger (*Security Guards*), Steve Reevis (*Indian*), Jeff Beck (*Lead Guitarist*), Nicolette Larson (*Singer*), Jill Avery (*Bass Player*), Tony Hymas (*Keyboards*), Terry Bozio (*Drums*).

As part of a government genetic experiment, scientists brought together six sperm donors to father a flawless human being, but instead of one baby, two were born. One, the perfect specimen, grew up on a faraway island acting as a scientist's assistant; the other was placed in an orphanage. Their mother was told by scientists that her offspring didn't survive, the perfect son that his mother was dead, and his less-than-perfect brother that he had been abandoned. What's more, neither brother knew of the other's existence. That's the back story. When TWINS gets going, many years later, Schwarzenegger, the perfect physical and intellectual specimen, is told about his twin (DeVito) and travels to Los Angeles to find him. DeVito is a corpulent, diminutive two-bit car thief and hustler who is in trouble with the police for some 200 overdue parking tickets and with loan sharks for the $20,000 he owes them. Nuns at the orphanage that was DeVito's home, suggest that Schwarzenegger look for his brother in jail, and Schwarzenegger bails out his disbelieving sibling only to be ditched by him. Later, after Schwarzenegger saves DeVito from the loan sharks, the two develop a tentative rapport; then DeVito inadvertently steals a car that harbors a $5 million booty in its trunk, payable upon delivery to a designated location in the southwestern US. Schwarzenegger, meanwhile, has tracked down one of the twins' fathers, who leads them to the scientist in charge of the genetic experiment. Reluctantly, the scientist tells them where they can find their mother, and the brothers, along with Devito's faithful girl friend (Preston) and her sister (Webb), head for New Mexico to both look up Mom and turn over the car. When they arrive, the woman

who was supposed to be the twins' mother not only refuses to believe their story but also claims that their mother is long dead. In short order, DeVito ditches his traveling companions to keep the illicit rendezvous and claim his money, forcing Schwarzenegger to save him from the gun-wielding killer who was supposed to have driven the car DeVito stole. Everything ends happily, however, when the twins' *real* mother reads of their adventures in the newspaper, tracks down the scientist in charge of the experiment, and is finally reunited with her sons.

Directed by Ivan Reitman, this sorry would-be comedy, which inexplicably became a huge hit during the 1988 holiday season, relies mainly on moviegoers' long-standing affection for its stars. Arnold Schwarzenegger proves to be mildly amusing in his first comedy role as the naive Julius, who delights in learning the ways of the world. But Danny DeVito, as Vincent, his low-down "twin" brother, seems to be coasting on his past reputation as an audience pleaser, contributing little to the comedy's middling laugh quotient. Nonetheless, a late-in-the-game pitch toward poignancy and sentimentality scores surprisingly well given the inherent shallowness of the script (which was credited to four writers). Viewers might want to compare the handling of the theme of brotherly love here with its treatment in two other 1988 releases, the Dustin Hoffman-Tom Cruise drama RAINMAN and DEAD RINGERS (also titled "Twins" until it surrendered the moniker to the Reitman comedy), which features a dual performance by Jeremy Irons. (*Violence, profanity, substance abuse, adult situations, sexual situations.*)

p, Ivan Reitman; d, Ivan Reitman; w, William Davies, William Osborne, Timothy Harris, Herschel Weingrod; ph, Andrzej Bartkowiak (DeLuxe Color); ed, Sheldon Kahn, Donn Cambern; m, Georges Delerue, Randy Edelman; md, Dave Williams, Peter Afterman; prod d, James D. Bissell; art d, Chris Burian-Mohr; set d, Nancy Patton, William J. Teegarden, Edward S. Verreaux; spec eff, Michael Lantieri; cos, Gloria Gresham; ch, Paula Smuin; stunts, Joel Kramer; makeup, Jeff Dawn, Leonard Engelman, Katherine Kotorakos.

Comedy   **Cas.**   **(PR:A MPAA:PG)**

TWISTED NIGHTMARE †   (1988) 94m United Filmmakers c

Rhonda Gray, Cleve Hall, Brad Bartrum, Robert Padillo, Heather Sullivan, Scott King, Juliet Martin.

Add another slice-and-dice epic to this year's list, this one set in a secluded backwoods camp where seven young couples are murdered one by one by an unseen killer (sound familiar?). As it turns out, the scourge may be the horribly scarred, retarded younger brother of one of the campers, who was accidentally set on fire and supposedly killed at the camp many moons ago. Then again, perhaps the angry ghosts of Indians are to blame, for the camp was built on a sacred burial ground. Who knows? Who cares?

p, Sandy Horowitz; d, Paul Hunt; w, Paul Hunt; ph, Paul Hunt, Gary Graver (Astral Bellevue Pathe color); ed, Allen Persselin; spec eff, Cleve Hall.

Horror   **(PR:NR MPAA:R)**

TWO MOON JUNCTION*½   (1988) 104m DDM/Lorimar c

Sherilyn Fenn (*April Delongpre*), Richard Tyson (*Perry*), Louise Fletcher (*Belle*), Kristy McNichol (*Patti-Jean*), Martin Hewitt (*Chad Douglas Fairchild*), Burl Ives (*Sheriff Earl Hawkins*), Juanita Moore (*Delilah*), Don Galloway (*Senator Delongpre*), Millie Perkins (*Mrs. Delongpre*), Milla (*Samantha*), Herve Villechaize (*Smiley*), Dabbs Greer (*Kyle*), Screamin' Jay Hawkins (*Black Club Singer*), Nicole Rosselle (*Judy*), Kerry Remsen (*Carolee*), Chris Pederson (*Speed*), Harry Cohn (*Buck*), Brad Logan (*Carny Vendor*), Lisa Peders (*Teenage Girl*), James Johnson (*Deputy*), Luisa Leshin (*Motel Maid*), Nancy Fish (*Ball M.C.*), Sharon Madden (*Caterer*), Robert Telford (*Gardener*), Jake (*Perry's dog*).

TWO MOON JUNCTION is a color-by-numbers soft-core picture from Zalman King (screenwriter of 9 1/2 WEEKS) that fills every frame from start to finish with passion. Not real-life passion, mind you, but the sort of MTV passion one sees in those embarrassing perfume ads and jeans commercials. Tyson plays a long-haired Conan type who works at a carnival and doesn't seem to own any shirts. He's wandering around bare-chested, like the king of the forest, when along comes Fenn, a blond Southern gal with more money than most Third World countries who is about

© LORIMAR

to be married off to Hewitt, a beautiful person just like herself. Of course, there's an animal attraction between the pair, but Fenn tries to control her desires. (We know she has desires because we've seen her spying on men, a la PORKY'S, as they shower in a local gym.) Since hubby-to-be Hewitt is out of town settling their condo deal, Fenn is free to be pounced upon by Tyson. She returns home one day and finds Tyson in her shower. He lathers up, while she threatens to call the police, but—big surprise—she can't resist him. She tries to break it off, but it's impossible. He just can't stand living without her. Then, his dog dies. Now he's really alone—but the wedding is tomorrow. Oh dear, what to do? Well, they decide to have one last fling at the "Two Moon Junction," a place that brings back loads of childhood memories for Fenn, most of which are related to the ways of the flesh. The wedding takes place as scheduled, but nothing can stop the bride's passion for her Neanderthal lover. Despite the huge rock on her wedding finger, Fenn surprises Tyson by sneaking into his shower, prepared to continue their (literally) steamy romance.

TWO MOON JUNCTION oozes sensuality. Its characters can't stay "hands off," nor can they keep their clothes on. They have no brains, thoughts (other than sexual), ideals, or common sense. They do, however, have glistening bodies, impressive muscles, and flowing manes of hair—all necessary for this type of film. (For some reason, they do not have any underwear. No one in this film has any underwear.) They do occasionally say some profound things ("I loved my dog"), but usually keep their remarks to the most mundane ("Don't ever take a Southern woman for granted," "She's come face to face with her libido"). In other words, if Louis Malle wanted to remake MY DINNER WITH ANDRE, he would not invite the characters April or Perry. TWO MOON JUNCTION does have a couple of points in its favor, however, which, while not completely redemptive, do help pass the time. Burl Ives and Kristy McNichol are both in the film and they haven't been on-screen together since Sam Fuller's superb film WHITE DOG. (Just thinking about WHITE DOG is more interesting than watching TWO MOON JUNCTION. There *are* two dogs in this film, though neither of them is as compelling as the one in WHITE DOG.) Louise Fletcher and Herve Villechaize are both in cameos, though this is probably the first time $g2they have ever been on-screen together. The same holds true for cult singer extraordinaire Screamin' Jay Hawkins and Oscar-winning actress Juanita Moore of Douglas Sirk's IMITATION OF LIFE. When it comes right down to it, TWO MOON JUNCTION could be far, far worse than it is, but, given the built-in limitations of this type of film, it can't be any better. Songs include "Never Tell No Lies" (Billy Bizeau, Michael Jonzun, performed by Bizeau), "Taken" (Jonzun, Loria Jonzun, performed Loria Jonzun), "Dig" (Screamin' Jay Hawkins, performed by Hawkins), "Lo, How a Rose E're Blooming" (Michael Practorius, performed by The Notre Dame Glee Club), "Who Do You Love" (E. McDaniel, performed by George Thorogood), "Man With a Gun" (Jerry Harrison, performed by Harrison), and "You Are So Beautiful" (Billy Preston, Bruce Fisher), "Roller Coaster" (PJ, performed by PJ and the Magic Bus). *(Nudity, sexual situations, adult situations, profanity.)*

p, Donald P. Borchers; d, Zalman King; w, Zalman King (based on a story by King, MacGregor Douglas); ph, Mark Plummer (CFI Color); ed, Marc Grossman; m, Jonathan Elias; m/l, Michael Practorius, E. McDaniel, Billy Bizeau, Michael Jonzun, PJ, Loria Jonzun, Billy Preston, Bruce Fisher, Screamin' Jay Hawkins, Jerry Harrison; prod d, Michelle Minch; art d, Sarah Burdick; set d, Susan Mina Eschelbach; cos, Maria Mancuso; ch, Russell Clark.

Drama   **Cas.**   **(PR:O MPAA:R)**

UV

UNBEARABLE LIGHTNESS OF BEING, THE½** (1988) 171m Orion c

Daniel Day Lewis *(Tomas)*, Juliette Binoche *(Tereza)*, Lena Olin *(Sabina)*, Derek de Lint *(Franz)*, Erland Josephson *(The Ambassador)*, Pavel Landovsky *(Pavel)*, Donald Moffat *(Chief Surgeon)*, Daniel Olbrychski *(Interior Ministry Official)*, Stellan Skarsgard *(The Engineer)*, Tomek Bork *(Jiri)*, Bruce Myers *(Czech Editor)*, Pavel Slaby *(Pavel's Nephew)*, Pascale Kalensky *(Nurse Katya)*, Jacques Ciron *(Swiss Restaurant Manager)*, Anne Lonnberg *(Swiss Photographer)*, Laszlo Szabo *(Russian Interrogator)*, Vladimir Valenta *(Mayor)*, Clovis Cornillac *(Boy in Bar)*, Leon Lissek *(Bald Man in Bar)*, Consuelo de Haviland *(Tall Brunette)*, Jacqueline Abraham-Vernier, Judith Atwell, Claudine Berg, Jean-Claude Bouillon, Miroslav Breuer, Niven Busch, Margot Capelier, Victor Chelkoff, Monica Constandache, Jean-Claude Dauphin, Dominique de Moncuit, Bernard Lepinaux, Josiane Leveque, Peter Majer, Charles Millot, Gerard Moulevrier, Jan Nemec, Charley Oleg, Syovie Plantard, Olga Baidar Poliakoff, Christine Pottier, Hana-Maria Pravda, Romano, Andre Sanfratello, Jiri Stanislav, Milos Svoboda, Helenka Verner, Marrian Walters.

Director Phil Kaufman's talent for bringing America to the screen is without equal among his contemporaries: THE GREAT NORTHFIELD, MINNESOTA RAID addressed the realities of the mythical Old West; his 1978 remake of INVASION OF THE BODY SNATCHERS brought science fiction to San Francisco; THE WANDERERS took a surrealistically nostalgic look at 1960s gangland teens in the Bronx; and THE RIGHT STUFF, Kaufman's masterpiece, is a breathtaking examination of that greatest of American heroes, the astronaut. Five years after the last film, in 1988, Kaufman has moved from "the right stuff" of American heroes to "the light stuff" of the Czechoslovakian lovers of Milan Kundera's critically acclaimed 1984 novel *The Unbearable Lightness of Being*. The film opens in Prague shortly before the Soviet invasion of 1968, with Day Lewis starring as a brilliant but cocky young brain surgeon. His outlook on life is so light that he cheerfully whistles a tune while sawing through the skull of a patient, and afterwards caddishly asks his nurse to undress for him. Nothing bothers Day Lewis, and his chief concern seems to be making love to Olin, a statuesque beauty who wears black lingerie and a matching bowler. On a medical trip to the country, Day Lewis meets the shy Binoche, a waitress who is thrilled finally to meet someone else familiar with Tolstoy's *Anna Karenina*. Day Lewis is very direct in his intentions, but returns to Prague before anything can happen between them. Later, Binoche unexpectedly arrives at his apartment, sneezing and sniffling from the snowy Czech winter. Day Lewis is only too glad to provide some medical attention, lifting her sweater and listening to her breathe. Moments later, they are entangled in a wild session of love-making—the shy country girl losing all control in the surgeon's arms. They soon marry, but Day Lewis finds himself still attracted to Olin, defending his occasional adultery by insisting that sex and love are not the same thing. When the Soviet tanks roll into Prague, their trouble-free and light lifestyle is threatened. Olin flees to Geneva, but Day Lewis and Binoche remain in the homeland. Binoche takes up photography, snapping pictures of the clampdown, riots, demonstrations, and resulting violence. When the Soviet presence proves too heavy even for Day Lewis and Binoche however, they also head for Geneva. There they lead a comfortable life—he as a top surgeon, she as an aspiring photographer. Thinking nothing of the consequences, Day Lewis again seeks out Olin, who is now an artist and involved with a married man, de Lint. Binoche is aware of his rendezvous with Olin and tries desperately to understand. When a magazine photo editor suggests she try fashion photography, Binoche knocks at Olin's door and asks to snap nude shots of the artist. After a few drinks, a playful game begins as Olin undresses before the watchful camera lens of the nervous Binoche. Binoche becomes increasingly more aggressive, while Olin grows more comfortable with the camera. Olin then turns the tables and has Binoche undress for her. Binoche switches instantaneously from aggressive viewer to bashful subject. Their session is interrupted by the arrival of de Lint, who bursts in with a suitcase in each hand to announce to Olin that he has left his wife. Faced with the potential commitment of marriage, Olin flees for the States. Binoche surprises Day Lewis by returning to Czechoslovakia, taking their faithful dog with her. Rather than live without Binoche, Day Lewis also returns to Prague, giving up his passport at the border. They reunite and live the life of lovers without feeling the weight of the Soviet influence. But authorities then discover that Day Lewis once wrote an anti-Communist article for a publisher friend that suggested that the Communist leaders, like Oedipus, poke out their own eyes. Although Day Lewis wrote the article on a whim, without real conviction, he now refuses to renounce it. Though relegated to a dingy public health clinic ("We cannot allow a politically suspicious man to operate on brains," he is told), Day Lewis refuses to surrender to the Party's weighty pressures. In the meantime, he continues to philander. Binoche, in an effort to understand his philosophy of sex versus love, gives herself to a man she meets in a bar. She, however, is not equipped for such "lightness of being" and suffers through the incident. A change of scenery takes the pair to the countryside, where they spend time with long-time friend Landovsky, a slobbish laborer with a Pilsner-guzzling pet pig named Mephistopheles. They live an idyllic life in the countryside until their dog dies a slow death. After one especially trying day, Day Lewis, Binoche, Landovsky, and Mephistopheles head to the local inn for some drinking and dancing. At dawn the following morning, Day Lewis and Binoche are returning home along a country road when their brakes fail, killing them both. In her California home, artist Olin receives word of the death of her two friends.

THE UNBEARABLE LIGHTNESS OF BEING is the quintessential European art film for American audiences who thirst for something more intellectual than the status quo, but not so intellectual that they can't understand it. It features an international cast (British Day Lewis; French Binoche; Swedish Olin, Josephson, and Skarsgard [all of Ingmar Bergman films]; Polish Olbrychski; Dutch de Lint), a distinguished technical crew (including Bergman's cinematographer, Sven Nykvist; Luis Bunuel's screenwriter, Jean-Claude Carriere; production designer Pierre Guffroy [a collaborator with Jean-Luc Godard, Francois Truffaut, Bunuel, and Roman Polanski]; and producer Saul Zaentz [AMADEUS; ONE FLEW OVER THE CUCKOO'S NEST]), a volatile political backdrop, and numerous scenes of sex and nudity, all of which are filtered through the American eye of director Kaufman. Unfortunately, however, for all its credentials the film doesn't add up to much, despite its length. At 172 minutes, it would seem that THE UNBEARABLE LIGHTNESS OF BEING would explore its themes—love and hedonism, freedom and commitment (political and sexual)—in depth. Instead, the film floats haphazardly from one scene to the next without any sort of emotional or intellectual development. Halfway through, it is as if everyone is repeating themselves. The viewer doesn't know the characters any better by the end than he does at the beginning.

Despite its ramblings, THE UNBEARABLE LIGHTNESS OF BEING is easy to watch, thanks to the virtuoso performances of the three leads. Daniel Day Lewis, familiar to audiences who have seen ROOM WITH A VIEW or MY BEAUTIFUL LAUNDRETTE, is remarkable as the conceited but charming Czech (his accent, like all the others', is convincing if not occasionally heavy). Although his attitude is often difficult to bear, one can see how Olin and Binoche become enamored of him. Lena Olin, of Ingmar Bergman's AFTER THE REHEARSAL, is a commanding and erotic screen presence whose part is unfortunately underwritten so as to practically ignore her vulnerability and insecurity. (Her tearful breakdown when de Lint announces he's left his wife is the only time she lets her real self show.) However, it is Juliette Binoche who is the film's standout. Unknown to American audiences, she has already been discovered by the French, having appeared in Godard's HAIL, MARY; Jacques Doillon's LA VIE DE FAMILLE; Andre Techine's RENDEZVOUS; and, in her finest role, BAD BLOOD (MAUVAIS SANG), the Leos Carax film of 1986. Under Kaufman's direction (as well as Carax's) the 23-year-old Binoche, with her radiant face, has the quality of a silent screen star, conveying more with her expression than Kaufman and Carriere do with their entire script. The most exciting European actress to grace the screen since Hanna Schygulla first appeared, Binoche alone is reason enough to see the film—again and again. The film became a minor success at the box office, though one suspects its audience attended only after being tantalized by a risque ad campaign. Without the numerous scenes of art-house sex and nudity (read: "respectable soft-core"), the filmmakers would have to have paid American viewers to come to see a picture about three Czechs during the Soviet invasion. The film was photographed in Geneva and Lyon, France, the latter town standing in for Prague. Any thoughts of shooting in Czechoslovakia were completely out of the question, as the Paris-based Kundera's novels are banned in his home country. Yugoslavia initially agreed to let the crew in, but backed off after learning of the Soviet invasion scene. In addition to the score by Czech composer Leos Janacek, the film includes a Czech version of the Beatles' "Hey Jude." (In English.) *(Nudity, sexual situations, adult situations, profanity, violence.)*

p, Saul Zaentz; d, Philip Kaufman; w, Jean-Claude Carriere, Philip Kaufman (based on the novel by Milan Kundera); ph, Sven Nykvist (Technicolor); ed, Walter Murch; m, Mark Adler, Keith Richards, Leos Janacek; prod d, Pierre Guffroy; art d, Gerard Viard; spec eff, Trielli Brothers; cos, Ann Roth; stunts, Remy Julienne; makeup, Suzanne Benoit.

Drama/Romance Cas. (PR:O MPAA:R)

UNDER SATAN'S SUN*** (1988, Fr.) 98m Erato-Films A2-Flach-Action-CNC-SOFICA/Gaumont-Cannon c

Gerard Depardieu *(Father Donissan)*, Sandrine Bonnaire *(Mouchette)*, Maurice Pialat *(Dean Menou-Segrais)*, Alain Artur *(Dr. Cadignan)*, Yann Dedet *(Gallet)*, Brigitte Legendre *(Mouchette's Mother)*, Jean-Claude Bourlat *(Malorthy)*, Jean-Christophe Bouvet *(Horse Trader)*, Philippe Pallut *(Quarryman)*, Marcel Anselin *(Monseigneur Gerbier)*, Yvette Lavogez *(Marthe)*, Pierre D'Hoffelize *(Havret)*, Corinne Bourdon *(Mother of Child)*, Thierry Der'Ven *(Sabroux)*, Marie-Antoinette Lorge *(Estelle)*, Bernard de Gouy *(Mons de Wamin)*, Yolene de Gouy *(Mme. de Wamin)*, Claudine Gauthier *(Worshipper)*, Thierry Artur *(Priest)*, Ghislain Boitrelle *(Coachman)*, Raymonde Jacquot *(Parishioner)*, Frederic Auburtin *(Young Priest)*, Edith Colnel *(Mme. Lambelin)*, Delphine Westrelin *(Farm Girl)*, Vincent Peignaux *(Child)*, Francoise Disle *(Fisherwoman)*, Fabienne Deleforge, Yolaine de Gelas, Anne Duquennoy, Karine Lambert, Carole Loth, Nathalie Lourtil, Sabrina Vervacke *(Marie's Children)*, Marie-Paule Vienne, Claudy Widczinski, Anne Cassagnou, Guillaume Dhoye, Jerome Dhoye, Franck Dhoye, David Dhoye *(Pilgrims)*.

A film of confrontations, UNDER SATAN'S SUN is a religious picture concerned with devotion and dilletantism, physical love and spiritual love, pure good and pure evil, and God and the Devil. Based on a 1926 novel by Catholic author Georges Bernanos (on whose writings Robert Bresson's DIARY OF A COUNTRY PRIEST and

MOUCHETTE were also based), the film stars Depardieu as a fanatically devoted young priest who firmly believes in the power of the Devil. Conscious of the weakness of the flesh, Depardieu brutally flagellates himself with chains, growing spiritually strong as his body deteriorates. Concerned by the unfaltering strength of Depardieu's devotion is his Father Superior, played by director Pialat, whom Depardieu considers a dilletante who only half-heartedly follows the ways of the Lord. As Depardieu goes about testing his spirit, a 16-year-old village girl, Bonnaire, is testing the power of her flesh. Pregnant by one man and mistress to others, Bonnaire murders the man who impregnated her and flees her town and parents. The killing is ruled a suicide. In the meantime, Depardieu must attend to matters in a neighboring village, walking eight miles through the peaceful countryside. Along the way, at nightfall, he is approached by a peasant horse trader (Bouvet), who, after gaining Depardieu's trust and leading him astray off the main road, plants a passionate kiss on the priest's mouth. Depardieu has confronted the Devil incarnate, and now knows the Devil will always be inside him. Unable to continue his journey, Depardieu returns to his own parish. Along this path he meets Bonnaire and has a vision of the girl's crime. He is determined to bring her back to God, but before he can do so she returns to her parents' home and slits her throat. In the film's most moving scene, the hulking Depardieu lifts her limp, bloodied body from the floor and carries her to the church's altar, returning this lost sheep to God's flock. In the haunting finale, Depardieu, driven half-mad by the spiritual pressures that weigh him down, is begged by villagers to cure a dying young boy. He enters the child's room to find the boy dead. Calling on the power of the Devil inside him, Depardieu breathes life back into the boy and is hailed by the villagers as a saint.

Named the winner of the Palme d'Or for Best Picture at the 1987 Cannes Film Festival, UNDER SATAN'S SUN became a center of controversy. The first French picture to win the top prize since 1966's A MAN AND A WOMAN, Maurice Pialat's film was, according to its opponents, chosen only because the French festival was celebrating its 40th year and wanted to be represented by a French entry, and when Pialat accepted his award he was greeted with a round of boos. In retaliation, he raised his fist in the air and lashed out, "You don't like me, well; I don't like you either." Regardless of its detractors' claims, however, UNDER SATAN'S SUN is a film of spiritual power and importance of subject. Strongly reverent, the film recalls the works of Bresson (especially through its Bernanos connection) in its attempts to transcend conventional religion. Slow, deliberate, static, and literal, the film itself induces spiritual introspection. Unfortunately, it's style lacks the inspiration to match the spiritual devotion of its characters. While the story is Depardieu's, and to a lesser degree Bonnaire's, its style is more in accord with that of the Father Superior (perhaps it's no coincidence that Pialat cast himself in this role)—a character who lacks spiritual passion. While Pialat's two previous films—A NOS AMOURS and POLICE—have been marked by a visually explosive camera style, UNDER SATAN'S SUN is solemn and meditative, filled with dark scenes, close-ups, and quiet moments. It is everything one would expect from a religious discourse on the nature of Man, God, and the Devil—nothing more, nothing less. It is a very great subject, and the film is beautifully written and acted, but almost wholly devoid of spiritual power. (By contrast, a film of a very different nature, Alain Cavalier's THERESE, the minimalist story of Carmelite nun Therese de Liseux, is in itself as spiritually moving as its subject matter.)

Despite the fact that it won the 1987 Palme d'Or, UNDER SATAN'S SUN fell victim to the politics of film distribution. Shown at the New York Film Festival in October 1987 without yet having a distribution deal, UNDER SATAN'S SUN never saw a US art-house release, and only occasionally surfaced in retrospectives or at film societies. Although more and more foreign directors are receiving attention in the US (the accolades heaped upon Bernardo Bertolucci's 1987 THE LAST EMPEROR testify to this), the lack of attention paid to UNDER SATAN'S SUN marks a disturbing trend in which only the most popular and commercial foreign films are distributed, while others are ignored. Besides Pialat (whose POLICE saw only a sparse art-house run), such directors as Raul Ruiz, Alain Resnais, Claude Chabrol, Jacques Doillon, Leos Carax, Jerzy Skolimowski, Keisuke Kinoshita, Nagisa Oshima, and even America's own expatriate director Sam Fuller often receive little or no distribution at all in America. (In French, English subtitles.) *(Adult situations, sexual situations.)*

p, Claude Abeille; d, Maurice Pialat; w, Sylvie Danton (based on the novel by Georges Bernanos); ph, Willy Kurant (Fujicolor); ed, Yann Dedet; m, Henri Dutilleux; art d, Katia Vischkof; set d, Alain Alexandre; cos, Gil Noir, Kirsten Morin; makeup, Thi Loan N'Guyen.

Religious **(PR:C-O MPAA:NR)**

UNDERACHIEVERS, THE † (1988) 90m PMS/Lightning c

Edward Albert *(Danny Warren)*, Barbara Carrera *(Katherine)*, Michael Pataki *(Murphy)*, Susan Tyrrell *(Mrs. Grant)*, Mark Blankfield *(Kline)*, Garrett Morris *(Dummont)*, Vic Tayback *(Coach)*, Jesse Aragon *(Carlos)*, Jewel Shepard, Lee Arenberg, Fox Harris, Judd Omen, Burton Gilliam, Roslyn Kind, Monte Landis.

Last year Jackie Kong directed BLOOD DINER, a horror film inspired by Herschell Gordon Lewis' 1963 gore classic, BLOOD FEAST. This year Kong updated the 1958 Albert Zugsmith-Jack Arnold camp favorite HIGH SCHOOL CONFIDENTIAL, revamping the classic adult-narc-posing-as-high-school-student plot. Albert stars as a failed baseball player who is hired by the cops to infiltrate a local night school suspected of harboring drug dealers. While trying to ingratiate himself with the student body, however, Albert is distracted by the very adult body of dedicated teacher Carrera and becomes involved in her battle with corrupt school official Tyrell. Another direct-to-video release.

p, Jackie Kong; d, Jackie Kong; w, Jackie Kong, Tony Rosato, Gary Thompson (based on a story by Rosato); ph, Chuck Colwell; ed, Tom Meshelski; m, Don Preston; prod d, Jay Burkhardt; art d, Woodward Romine, Jr.; set d, Jay Kaiwai.

Crime **Cas.** **(PR:NR MPAA:R)**

UNHOLY, THE* (1988) 100m Limelite-Team Effort/Vestron c

Ben Cross *(Father Michael)*, Ned Beatty *(Lt. Stern)*, Jill Carroll *(Millie)*, William Russ *(Luke)*, Hal Holbrook *(Archbishop Mosley)*, Trevor Howard *(Father Silva)*, Peter Frechette *(Claude)*, Claudia Robinson *(Teresa Montez)*, Nicole Fortier *(Demon)*, Ruben Rabasa *(Father Dennis)*, Phil Becker *(Doctor)*, Susan Bearden *(Hotel Manager)*, Xavier Barquet *(Bell Boy)*, Larl White *(Housekeeper)*, Jeff D'Onofrio *(Paramedic)*, Martha Hester *(Young Nun)*, John Boyland *(Dr. Valerio)*, Norma Donaldson *(Abby)*, Earleen Carey *(Lucille)*, Anthony Deans, Jr. *(Manolo)*, Frank Barnes, Selma Jones, Willemina Riley, Steven Hadley, Anthony Deans *(Parishoners)*, Laura Plyscco *(Lorna)*, Joshua Sussman, David Sanderson *(Bodyguards)*, Alan Warhaftig *(Intern)*, Sandy Queen *(Nurse)*, Ellen Cody *(Old Woman)*.

THE UNHOLY is another poor excuse for a horror film that once again pits a Catholic priest against the forces of darkness, this time in a poor New Orleans parish. It seems that, several years ago, not one, but two priests were horribly murdered while praying before the altar on Easter weekend. Although news of the crimes was kept quiet by the church, local police detective Beatty is determined to solve the killings. Meanwhile, stoic young priest Cross (CHARIOTS OF FIRE) accidentally takes a tumble out of an office building window while trying to save a suicidal jumper. Miraculously, Cross survives the fall without a scratch, a curiosity that convinces archbishop Holbrook and old blind priest Howard (in one of his last performances) that Cross is the one to fight whatever demons lurk in the killer parish. Aided by seen-it-all-before caretaker Robinson, Cross manages to clean up the church and entice parishioners back into the fold. While all seems well on the salvation front, Cross becomes obsessed with finding the killer of his two predecessors and begins digging for clues. This leads him to a local nightclub, owned by the seedy Russ, which specializes in titillating simulations of Satanic rituals. There he meets troubled club employee Carroll, a 19-year-old runaway who had turned to the previous priest, Fr. Dennis, for help shortly before his death. Carroll, who was sexually abused by her father and, therefore, shuns intimate contact (read: virgin), wants to escape the shameful club scene, but is afraid that Russ won't let her go. As Cross becomes more involved with Carroll's plight, strange things begin happening at the church. Unexplained gusts of wind, midnight phone calls from a man claiming to be Fr. Dennis, and bizarre Freudian nightmares plague Cross. Carroll also tempts Cross to deflower her, but he nobly declines. The priest assumes Russ is behind the hocus-pocus, but Holbrook and Howard know better and finally inform Cross that he has been chosen to do battle with Satan. They explain that only during the period between Ash Wednesday and the Feast of the Resurrection can Satan invade the church and sacrifice the power of good, etc.—consult your local parish for details. The upshot is that Satan will attempt to seduce the priest with what he most desires and then kill him. Armed with this knowledge, Cross goes back to his parish and, while praying, is confronted by a gorgeous naked redhead, Fortier, who attempts to seduce him (this is the very same demon who succeeded in seducing Fr. Dennis in the precredits sequence—apparently redheaded women with perfect breasts are what all priests most desire). Using all the intestinal fortitude he can muster, Cross rebukes the busty Fortier and begins mumbling some prayers. This does not sit well with the fiery succubus, who summons two silly-looking demons to accost the priest and nail him up on the altar. In the meantime, she transforms herself into a giant, four-legged, goopy monster with big teeth and a lapping tongue and begins slobbering over Cross. Then the still-virginal Carroll comes on the scene, and the monster turns its attention to her. In an effort to save Carroll, Cross summons up some truly impressive holy powers and is suddenly bathed in very bright light. He vaporizes Satan's little helpers and destroys the big demon with handy phrases: "Satan get thee behind me" and the like. Unfortunately, the strain of fighting evil saps Cross' strength and he collapses on the floor before the altar. Carroll rushes to his side and, when he comes to, we see that he is wearing the same milky contact lenses as Howard. Apparently fighting the devil will make you blind—which isn't exactly what the nuns used to tell you in school. Based on an old treatment that veteran screenwriter Phillip Yordan (JOHNNY GUITAR; KING OF KINGS; DAY OF THE TRIFFIDS) had lying around, THE UNHOLY is a dreadfully boring effort that wastes the considerable talents of its better-than-average-for-a-horror-movie cast. Cuban-born director Camilio Vila makes his Hollywood debut here, and it is less than impressive. Lots of fog, blue and red gels, and shadowy lighting pass for "mood" here; when that doesn't work, some jolting, bloody gore effects—a priest with his throat ripped out, an actor vomiting about 30 gallons of blood, the disemboweled Russ hanging upside down from a crucifix—are thrown in to wake viewers up (or send them running for the restroom, depending on their constitutions). However, no director could have salvaged the terribly clunky script by Yordan and Fernando Fonseca. The actors seem to have recognized this and turned in appropriately indifferent performances. While Cross' effort seems earnest, Holbrook, Beatty, and Howard sleepwalk through the material, and who can blame them? Those actors who really register are the lesser-known performers, with William Russ (DEAD OF WINTER) as the club owner and Claudia Robinson as the parish caretaker creating memorable characterizations.

Perhaps the most interesting thing about THE UNHOLY is its troubled production history. Shot in late 1986 and early 1987 at the Limelite Studios in Miami, the film was supposed to be released in time for Halloween 1987. The people at Vestron didn't like the original monster, however, and felt that the climax wasn't impressive enough. Vestron then put up the extra money to reshoot the entire end of the film with a redesigned monster. Having just seen WAXWORK, Vestron hired effects man Bob Keen (HELLRAISER) to rework the effects and direct the new ending. While the original demon was a tall, thin, toothless creature that stood upright, Keen's monster is a four-legged thing with rows of teeth and a more expressive face. Keen also added two smaller demons and integrated some of veteran optical man

John Dykstra's effects into the new ending. In addition, a really gratuitous montage of gore was added, showing a series of gruesome images that include eyes being poked out, front teeth being drilled, and lots of bare breasts and blood. The church set was broken down and shipped from Miami to Los Angeles for the shoot and Cross returned to play the end again—almost a year after he had thought the film finished. Since only a few photos of the original ending have been made available to the public, it is impossible to determine which was better. In any case, the existing ending is terribly ineffective. The shooting and editing are sloppy, the monsters laughable, and one must question whether it was really worth all the trouble. The film was finally released in spring 1988 and disappeared in a week, leaving it to languish on video store shelves by winter. And yes, THE UNHOLY contains far more blasphemous imagery than does Martin Scorsese's THE LAST TEMPTATION OF CHRIST, but zealous Christians didn't even notice, which is why it didn't make any money. (Violence, gore effects, sexual situations, nudity, profanity.)

p, Mathew Hayden; d, Camilio Vila; w, Philip Yordan, Fernando Fonseca; ph, Henry Vargas (CFI Color); ed, Mark Melnick; m, Roger Bellon; prod d, Fernando Fonseca; art d, Jose Duarte; set d, Carterlee Cullen; spec eff, John Dykstra, Bob Keen; cos, Beverly Safier.

Horror   **Cas.**   **(PR:O MPAA:R)**

UNINVITED, THE zero   (1988) 89m Heritage c

George Kennedy (Mike Harvey), Alex Cord (Walter Graham), Clu Gulager (Albert), Toni Hudson (Rachel), Eric Larson (Martin), Clare Carey (Bobbie), Rob Estes (Corey), Shari Shattuck (Suzanne), Austin Stoker (Carribean Officer), Greydon Clark (Lab Doctor), Michael Holden (Daryl Perkins), Cecile Callan (Girl in Pizza Parlor), Jack Heller (Concierge), Gina Schinasi (Bartender), Ron Presson (Man at Gas Station), Paul Martin (Lab Assistant), Trevor Clark (Boy on Beach), Beau Dremann.

A mutant cat that occasionally spits up a monster hand puppet from it's craw and gnaws people to death is the less-than-terrifying beastie in this straight-to-video release. Carey and Shattuck play college girls on spring break in Florida, where they meet Cord, a well-known financier whose fingers are in some less-than-legal pies. With the authorities closing in on him, Cord makes plans to sail his yacht to his bank in Bimini and retire to some beach without an extradition agreement. The girls are invited along as cover, and they bring along three guys (Estes, Dremann, and Larson) to help work as crew under female skipper Hudson. They also bring along a cat they found, which escaped from a secret government lab in the first scene. The feline infected with some sort of parasitic blood disease that allows the monster inside it to crawl out and kill with a single bite (which leads to exploding blood vessels) or simply to infect the food supply. Out at sea, problems develop with the engine. One of Cord's henchmen, Gulager, is the first to feel the puppet's fangs, and falls overboard in terror. More cast members follow in short order, henchman Kennedy most lingeringly. Cord refuses to call for help and destroys the radio. Eventually only he, Hudson, and Larson are alive as a hurricane sweeps over the foundering craft. They prepare to escape in a launch, but when Cord goes below to get his suitcase full of cash, he falls victim to the killer kitty. Larson and Shattuck retrieve the money and escape, watching the yacht sink, but they are suddenly attacked once again by the puppet. They fight him off twice, then realize that their only hope is to give him something else to float on. They empty the suitcase and toss it out, cheering when the cat climbs aboard and drifts away. Later, in Bimini, they tell police a much-simplified story and walk off with all the money. But wait . . . in the obligatory epilog, the briefcase drifts onto a beach and the bedraggled cat is picked up by a little boy who runs to show his family.

UNINVITED is a lousy film by any standards, made worse by the silliest monster since the moving rug in THE CREEPING TERROR. The thing is blatantly a hand puppet sticking out of the mouth of an obviously stuffed cat, and the sight of once-respectable actors like George Kennedy shrieking in pain and fear at this menace is too ridiculous for words. None of the performances are worth mentioning, save that of Clu Gulagher, who's become something of a fixture in horror films lately. His bespectacled, besotted henchman is the only memorable human here—too bad he's the first to die. That aside, the overall silliness allows one's mind to wander to the real, unanswered questions of this film, like, "When the monster is out of the cat, is the cat left limp like a flattened bag?" Or, "How does the monster get back into the cat, then turn around to face forward?" And, most urgently, "Who is most to blame for this waste of time and effort and what should happen to them?" Songs include: "Uninvited" (Chili Charles, Carl Galloway, Tom Gunn, performed by Charles Higgins, Jr.); "Seasons of Love" (Galloway, Charles); "Hard to Find" (Charles, Galloway, Gunn); "One More Try" (Gunn); "String Quartet in 6" (Dan Slider). (Violence, gore effects, adult situations, profanity.)

p, Greydon Clark; d, Greydon Clark; w, Greydon Clark; ph, Nicholas Von Sternberg; ed, Travis Clark; m, Dan Slider; m/l, Chili Charles, Tom Gunn; prod d, Peter Paul Raubertas; set d, Greg Maher; cos, Liz Warner; makeup, Mike Spatola.

Horror   **Cas.**   **(PR:O MPAA:PG-13)**

UNNAMABLE, THE †   (1988) 87m Yankee Classic/K.P. c

Charles King (Howard Damon), Mark Kinsey Stephenson (Randolph Carter), Alexandra Durrell (Tanya), Laura Albert (Wendy), Katrin Alexandre (Alyda Winthrop), Eben Ham (Bruce), Blane Wheatley (John Babcock), Mark Parra (Joel Manton).

Despite its RE-ANIMATOR-like appeal and interesting special make-up work, this low-budget adaptation of an H.P. Lovecraft short story went the direct-to-video

route. Updating Lovecraft's 1923 story, the film sets the action in a small college town where two young couples decide to spend the night in an ancient mansion. Rumor has it that in the 17th century, the house's owner, a warlock, was horribly murdered by an evil creature he kept chained in the attic. Looking to have some fun, the collegians enter the mansion and, to their horror, find the legend is true.

p, Dean Ramser, Jean-Paul Ouellette; d, Jean-Paul Ouellette; w, Jean-Paul Ouellette (based on a story by H.P. Lovecraft); ph, Tom Fraser (Foto-Kem Color); ed, Wendy J. Plump; m, David Bergeaud; prod d, Gene Abel; art d, Tim Keating; set d, Ann Job; spec eff, R. Christopher Biggs.

Horror   **Cas.**   **(PR:NR MPAA:R)**

VAMPIRE AT MIDNIGHT †   (1988) 93m Skouras c

Jason Williams (Det. Roger Sutter), Gustav Vintas (Victor Radkoff), Lesley Milne (Jenny Carlon), Jeanie Moore (Amalia), Esther Alise (Lucia), Ted Hamaguchi (Capt. Takato), Robert Random (Childress), Jonny Solomon (Lee), Barbara Hammond, Eddie, Jr., Christina Whitaker.

This straight-to-video release stars Jason Williams (best remembered as the title character in the X-rated comedy FLESH GORDON) as a Los Angeles police detective on the trail of a fiendishly clever serial killer who may be a vampire. The murderer, Vintas, is a brilliant-but-crazed hypnotherapist who puts his female victims into a trance before killing them and draining them of their blood. Reportedly, VAMPIRE AT MIDNIGHT is stylishly directed by Gregory McClatchy, with the emphasis on eroticism rather than gore.

p, Jason Williams, Tom Friedman; d, Gregory McClatchy; w, Dulhany Ross Clements (based on a story by Jason Williams, Tom Friedman); ph, Daniel Yarussi (United color); ed, Kaye Davis; m, Robert Etoll; art d, Beau Peterson; makeup, Mecki Heussen.

Crime/Horror   **Cas.**   **(PR:NR MPAA:R)**

VERNE MILLER*   (1988) 95m Three Aces/Alive c

Scott Glenn (Verne Miller), Barbara Stock (Vi Miles), Thomas G. Waites (Al Capone), Lucinda Jenney (Bobby), Sonny Carl Davis (Frank "Baldy" Nash), Diane Salinger (Mortician's Wife), Ed O'Ross (Ralph Capone), Vyto Rugins (Fitzsimmons), Andrew Robinson (Pretty Boy Floyd), Xander Berkley (Cardogan), Joseph Carberry (Hymie Ross), Richard Bright (Adam Richetti), Gil Boccaccio (Hoptoad Guinta), Kathy Brynner (1st Maid), Antonia Dauphin (Teacher), Rosebud Dixon Falana (Etta), Bruce Fischer (Harry Adler), Buck Ford (Elsworth Donaldson), Susan French (Bearded Lady), Tina Goetze (Capone's Nurse), Laura Harrington (Judge's Daughter), Danitza Kingsley (German Drink Girl), Sean Moran (Bugs Moran), Lisa Blake Richards (Judge's Wife), Armin Shimerman (Mortician), John Spencer (George Sally), Carl Spurlock (Judge), Gustav Vintas (Schiller), Henry Woessner (Herman), Jim Aycock (Cop No. 1), Fred Baldwin (Bald Policeman), Kerry Brennan (Debra), Kristal Brookliner (Girl Outside Tutwiler), J.B. Brown (Hoover's Secretary), Kenn Cooper (Perkins), Frank Costa (Jack McGurn), Tom Even (Pharmacist #1), Mark Gordon (Boyfriend/Tutwiler), Ray Reese (Cop in Diner), Roger LaPage (Bartender), Care Felix (Roadhouse Waitress), Michael Luther (Young Man in Roadster), Kenneth Scherr (Vinnie Caruso), Tom Preston (Uniformed Cop), Danny Nelson (Doctor), Dr. John Nixon (Pharmacist #2), John Oldach (Detective Leakling), Bob Penny (Real Estate Agent), Maureen Quinn (Fitzsimmon's Wife), Gary Shoemaker (Kidnapped Boy), James Newman (Dectective), Tom Stubblefield (German Card Player), Kim Hoyt (Cop #2), Paul Woods (Big Talker), Debbie Poe Sciandra (Maid), Tommy Manakides (Conferee), Paul Saveles (Caraldo), Tom Turbiville (Cop #3).

This wretched excuse for a gangster film floated around the market undistributed for nearly a year until Nelson Entertainment picked it up as a straight-to-video release. Ineptly directed by Rod Hewitt, the movie purports to be a factual biography of real-life gangster Verne Miller, a former South Dakota sheriff turned outlaw of the mid-

1920s. Played in a stoic manner by Glenn, Miller is presented as a dispassionate customer when it comes to murder, but sexually magnetic when it comes to women. Seemingly, every woman he meets, from the wife of a mortician to the bearded lady at a carnival, wants to go to bed with him. Although Glenn's transition from lawman to outlaw takes place before the movie begins, Stock's annoyingly vampish narration informs us that Glenn had decided that since lawmen and criminals were in the same business, he would go where the money was. After terrorizing St. Paul, Minnesota, and hooking up with Stock, a nightclub singer who would be his loyal, lifelong moll, Glenn travels to Chicago, where he offers his services to the infamous Al Capone (Waites). Glenn informs Waites that he doesn't want to work *for* him, but *with* him. Surprisingly, Waites is impressed by Glenn's bravado and, sensing that they are simpatico (both suffer from an advanced case of syphilis), gives the gunman an autonomy unheard of in the Capone organization. After Glenn performs a series of important hits, Waites makes him head of Waites' Kansas City organization. There Glenn lives in a palatial home staffed by gorgeous "maids" that cater to his carnal needs, and even joins a prestigious local country club where he can play golf. Eventually, Glenn gets too big for his britches and launches a move to rescue captured Waites henchman Davis against Waites' explicit orders. Aided by Pretty Boy Floyd (Robinson) and Adam Richetti (Bright), Glenn stages a daring rescue attempt at the Kanasas City train station. The plan is a botch, however, when the gangsters kill several police officers *and* intended escapee Davis. Waites is furious with Glenn over the rescue attempt and puts a contract out on him. Now pursued by both the mob and the police, Glenn takes it on the lam with Stock and Jenney, a young nurse who once tended his wounds and is now ensnared by his sexual dynamism. Unfortunately, Glenn's syphilis becomes terminal and begins affecting his motor abilities, eyesight, and mind. When the girls are cornered by the cops in a drugstore, the nearly blind Glenn takes off in the car, only to crash and be killed by either the cops or the mob—the culprits' identity remains ambiguous.

Whether VERNE MILLER sticks to the facts or not is really irrelevant; the film has many more severe problems than the degree of its historical accuracy. Rarely has a film that looks as nice as this one (good costumes, sets, and photography) been so incompetently scripted and directed. The movie has absolutely no sense of structure, development, or pace—to call it haphazard is an understatement—and plays like a series of blackout sketches with no real connection to one another. In fact, the camera coverage for some scenes is so bad that the editor has been forced to resort to quick dissolves or fade-outs *within the scene* to keep things moving logically. Plot holes and missing character motivations are filled in by the previously noted voice-over narration and lame songs sung by Stock, which only add to the embarrassingly clumsy feel of VERNE MILLER. As written by director Hewitt, Miller and Capone had insatiable appetites for guns and women, although this aspect of their personalities is not explored—only exploited. In fact, this view of the gangsters becomes utterly laughable: whenever there is a woman in the frame, the merest glance from either man will cause her to suddenly strike a sultry pose and purse her lips. In addition, Capone is shown to be a junkie whose habit is administered by a Playmate of the Month-type nurse. At this point the entire film veers into parody.

The casting is haphazard as well. Although Scott Glenn contributes a typically solid performance and Richard Bright and Andrew Robinson are memorable as the two gangsters who help out in the infamous Kansas City Massacre (by far the best scene in the movie), the rest of the cast is uniformly weak—especially the women. Admitted, any actor given the task of playing Al Capone after Robert DeNiro's definitive portrayal in THE UNTOUCHABLES (1987) is in for a tough assignment, but the casting of Thomas G. Waites is as misguided as the decision to cast Jason Robards as Capone in Roger Corman's THE ST. VALENTINE'S DAY MASSACRE (1967). Whereas the sheer force of Robards' bravura performance effectively bulldozed any doubts about the 1967 casting, however, Waites simply doesn't convince as Capone. His alternately brooding and blustery portrayal has no weight or authority. There is also absolutely no physical resemblance between the actor and Capone and he seems more Irish than Italian. Perhaps a bigger mistake was the selection of accomplished screen heavy Ed O'Ross to play Capone's brother Ralph. Whenever O'Ross is on-screen, one wishes that the casting had been the other way around, with O'Ross as Al and Waites as the lesser-known Ralph. Worst of all, however, is Barbara Stock as Glenn's dedicated moll. A former host of a television morning program, Stock lets her bland talk-show roots show in this hapless portrayal. Her attempts to act sultry and seductive but tough are simply embarrassing, as are her songs (which she cowrote) and singing. The most unfortunate aspect of her performance is the wholehearted seriousness of her approach to the material, which inadvertently becomes either pathetic or hilarious depending on your mood. The rest of the cast, mostly character actor veterans, treat the material with the lack of respect it deserves, while poor Stock seems to be striving for an Oscar.

Since he's not much of a writer and has no skill with actors, one would hope that Hewitt at least could put together some engaging scenes of violent action. Alas, he even bungles the shootouts, which are poorly staged and fairly tedious. Only the Kansas City Massacre sequence has any drama and suspense, but it is a fleetingly successful moment in a film filled with incompetence. For all the dramatic potential of its gangster tale set during the late 1920s and early 1930s, VERNE MILLER has to be one of the most uninteresting, unexciting, and unerotic gangster films ever made. Songs (performed by Stock) include "My Man's a Gambler" (Tom Chase, Steve Rucker, Barbara Stock, Red Hewitt), "Land of the River" (Roger Trefousse, Stock, Hewitt), "Verne's Blues" (Chase, Rucker, Stock), "Nighthawks" (Chase, Rucker, Stock). *(Violence, sexual situations, profanity, substance abuse.)*

p, Ann Broke Ashley; d, Rod Hewitt; w, Rod Hewitt; ph, Misha Suslov; ed, John O'Connor; m, Tom Chase, Steve Rucker; m/l, Tom Chase, Steve Rucker, Barbara Stock, Red Hewitt, Roger Trefousse; prod d, Victoria Paul; art d, Susan Raney; set d, Diana Williams; spec eff, Vern Hyde; cos, Leslie Ballard.

Biography/Crime **Cas.** **(PR:O MPAA:R)**

VIBES † (1988) 99m Imagine/COL c

Cyndi Lauper *(Sylvia Pickel)*, Jeff Goldblum *(Nick Deezy)*, Julian Sands *(Dr. Harrison Steele)*, Googy Gress *(Ingo Swedlin)*, Peter Falk *(Harry Buscafusco)*, Michael Lerner *(Burt Wilder)*, Ramon Bieri *(Eli Diamond)*, Elizabeth Pena *(Consuela)*, Ronald G. Joseph *(Carl)*, Susan Bugg *(Dr. Silver)*, Rodney Kageyama *(Dr. Harmon)*, Ahron Ipale *(Alejandro De La Vivar)*, John Kapelos *(Eugene)*, Karen Akers *(Hillary)*, Steve Buscemi *(Fred)*, Ray Stoddard *(Dr. Scott)*, Hercules Vilchez *(Juan)*, Jerry Vichi *(Baseball Man)*, Leo V. Finnie III *(Monty Man)*, Harvey J. Goldenberg *(Lyle)*, Tom Henschel *(Dr. Drake)*, Van Dyke Parks *(Dr. Weiner)*, Steven Scott *(Dr. Thompson)*, Joseph V. Perry *(Dave)*, Park Overall *(Jane)*, Max Perlich *(Busboy)*, Bruce MacVittie *(Tony)*, Don "Bubba" Bexley *(Lou)*, Bill McCutcheon *(Mr. Van Der Meer)*, Jennifer Balgobin *(Gloria)*, Fernando Verdugo *(Bellhop)*, Robert Covarrubias *(Waiter)*, Darryl Henriques *(Ricardo)*, Elvira Deval *(Nurse)*, Ronald Paul Ramirez *(Hotel Clerk)*.

Squeaky-voiced pop star Cyndi Lauper makes her film debut opposite Jeff Goldblum (in his first role since his virtuoso performance in THE FLY) in this comic adventure film. Despite the film's promise, however, it quickly disappeared from theaters after receiving mixed reviews—some critics despising it, others finding it a moderately entertaining summer diversion. Lauper plays Sylvia Pickel (accent on the last syllable), a psychic with an other-worldly connection named Louise who is able to help her with just about every facet of her life, except finding her a male companion. Although initially uninterested, Lauper is introduced to Goldblum, a psychometric—paranormal jargon for a person who can tell an object's entire history just by touching it. For example, he can pick up a relic on an archaeological dig and identify its age, place of origin, how it was used, and by whom. However, this talent also has its negative side. When Goldblum fondles his fiancee's panties, he learns they have passed through the paws of an entire football team. Because of their psychic powers, Lauper and Goldblum are recruited by the obviously shady Falk, who flies them to Ecuador, ostensibly to locate his missing son. His real intention, though, is to have them uncover a lost city of gold, buried deep in the Andes. Of course, they have to overcome the interference of a smarmy bad guy, Sands, a renowned scholar who wants all the riches and notoriety for himself.

VIBES' executive producer was Ron Howard, who financed the film under the banner of his Imagine Entertainment, and the script is by Lowell Ganz and Babaloo Mandel, whose previous credits include the Howard films NIGHT SHIFT; SPLASH; and GUNG HO! Songs include "I've Got a Hole in My Heart" (Richard Orange, performed by Lauper), "Berta," "Mona," and "Arturo" (Marcos Loya), and "Retango" (Osvaldo Barrios).

p, Deborah Blum, Tony Ganz; d, Ken Kwapis; w, Lowell Ganz (based on a story by Deborah Blum, Lowell Ganz, Babaloo Mandel), Babaloo Mandell; ph, John Bailey (DeLuxe Color), Daniel Ducovny; ed, Carol Littleton; m, James Horner; m/l, Richard Orange, Marcos Loya, Osvaldo Barrios; prod d, Richard Sawyer; art d, Gregory Pickrell, Eugene Gurlizt; set d, David Klassen; spec eff, Allen Hall; cos, Ruth Myers, John Boxer; ch, Miranda Garrison; stunts, John Branagan; makeup, Alan Friedman, Peter Wrona, Jr..

Adventure/Comedy **Cas.** **(PR:NR MPAA:PG)**

VICE VERSA**½ (1988) 98m COL c

Judge Reinhold *(Marshall Seymour)*, Fred Savage *(Charlie Seymour)*, Corinne Bohrer *(Sam)*, Swoosie Kurtz *(Tina)*, David Proval *(Turk)*, Jane Kaczmarek *(Robyn)*, Gloria Gifford *(Marcie)*, William Prince *(Avery)*, Beverly Archer *(Mrs. Luttrell)*, James Hong *(Kwo)*, Harry Murphy *(Larry)*, Richard Kind *(Floyd)*, Chip Lucia *(Cliff)*, Kevin O'Rourke *(Brad)*, Ajay Naidu *(Dale)*, Raymond Rosario *(Dooley)*, Elya Baskin *(Kerschner)*, Jane Lynch *(Ms. Lindstrom)*, Anuwat Tiernate, Surasri Klangsuwan *(Tomb Robbers)*, Penjit Prembudd *(Interpreter)*, Ram Waratum *(Government Spokesman)*, Sulaleewan Suwanatat *(Old Lady)*, Tuantone Kammesri *(Man in Warehouse)*, Danielle Kohl *(Lori)*, Jason Late *(Eric)*, Tom Crawford *(Judd)*, Christian Fitzpatrick *(Clipper)*, Joe Guastaferro *(Mr. Ferriera)*, Martyn S. David *(Rich Customer)*, Peggy Roeder *(Principal's Secretary)*, Paul Greatbatch *(Teacher)*, Robert Bundy *(Music Salesman)*, Jeff Kahn *(Music Kid)*, P.J. Brown *(Hockey Coach)*, Robert Petkoff *(Sporting Goods Salesman)*, Alan Shearman *(Security Salesman)*, Michelle Philpot *(Cosmetic Salesgirl)*, Harry Yorku *(Guru)*, Mike Bacarella *(Limo Driver)*, Bettina Wendt *(Babysitter)*, Bernie Landis *(Santa Claus)*, Ralph Foody *(Doorman)*, Steve Assad *(Waiter)*, Danny Goldring *(Motorcycle Cop)*, Rick Hall *(Shotgun Cop)*, Garrett Hohimer *(Kid Playing Football)*, Steve Cohen *(Burly Kid)*, Dayna O'Brien *(Receptionist)*, Albert Fields *(Band Singer)*, John T. Stibich *(Police Commander)*, Stella Vaicik *(Cafeteria Worker)*, Garrick Paul Axelrod *(Window Dresser)*, Darlene Anderson, Linda Jaffe, Cindy Legler, Kathleen B. Scott *(Salespeople)*, Mark Behn, Cliff Carothers, Michael Landauer, James Neal, Jay Reynolds *(Malice)*.

Though not the equal of the marvelous BIG, VICE VERSA is infinitely more entertaining than the other mind-and-body transference films Hollywood has coughed up in the last two years, LIKE FATHER, LIKE SON and 18 AGAIN. Reinhold is an ambitious, no-nonsense executive for Vigar and Avery, a Chicago department store (Marshall Field's in everything but name); Savage, his 11-year-old son, lives with Reinhold's ex-wife, Kaczmerek. Reinhold and his girl friend, Bohrer, another V and A executive, make a buying trip to Thailand, where smugglers hide a stolen jeweled skull among Reinhold's purchases before he returns to the States. When Savage comes to stay with his father, a off-hand wish to trade places is realized by the magical skull, and Reinhold suddenly finds himself bursting out of his son's clothing, while Savage is suddenly swimming in his father's. With his son's mind inhabiting his body, Reinhold goes off to face his jealous junior executive rivals, while Savage (his body, dad's mind) is off to school. Understandably bored in class, Savage frets over how Reinhold is handling the pressures at the department store. But while he's as worried about his pet frog as he is about the talking toy that's being returned en masse by dissatisfied V and A customers, Reinhold nonetheless manages to pull off his charade. Meanwhile, the smugglers (Proval and Kurtz) come to Chicago to try to get the skull back, but Reinhold and Savage have already taken it to an archeologist for study. Father and son continue to stumble through each others' lives, though not without some benefits for both. Reinhold, ironically now in a position to attend a parent-teacher conference to discuss himself, happens upon the older kids who have been bullying him all year, and, towering over them and pretending to be an authority figure, he forces them to clean toilets. The father-as-son is finally able to tell Bohrer how he really feels about her, but it takes the son-as-father to ask her to marry him. As the film builds to its climax, Reinhold is forced to defend an ambitious marketing scheme before a meeting of V and A bigwigs. With Savage relaying instructions via a hidden transistor radio receiver, Reinhold states his case, but Savage is nabbed by the smugglers before Reinhold can finish, and the sincere but affronted Reinhold walks out of the meeting. The smugglers make off with the skull, but Reinhold and Savage manage to get it back and use it to transmigrate back to their own bodies. The sentimental conclusion finds both father and son infinitely closer.

In 1987, LIKE FATHER, LIKE SON flip-flopped its way harmlessly but inanely across American movie screens, and although the critics generally had little positive to say about it, it was reasonably successful at the box office. In the succeeding months a bandwagon passed through Hollywood and no less than three productions jumped on board, presenting stories about men in boys' bodies and boys in men's bodies. The second of these films to be released, VICE VERSA, is based on the 1948 film of the same name, which was in turn adapted from an 1871 novel by F. Anstey, proving that the premise is hardly a new one. Yet somehow it isn't surprising that Hollywood would latch on to this particular concept, and not only because of the studios' proclivity for copy-cat attempts at box-office success. American culture has become increasingly youth-oriented and nowhere is growing old less fashionable than in southern California, which may, at least partly, explain Hollywood's fascination with a plot gimmick that provides a temporary fountain of youth for at least one character in these films and deals extensively with the confusion and discomfort felt with a dramatic change in one's age. Seemingly unable to address these issues head on without becoming overly sentimental or patronizing, Hollywood allows them to surface subconsciously.

Like BIG, VICE VERSA succeeds where LIKE FATHER, LIKE SON and 18 AGAIN fail because of its lead performances. When all is said and done, its story isn't any more believable than the others, and its walk-a-mile-in-my-shoes revelations no more profound, but its performances are. Reinhold makes his transformation from uptight, ambitious business executive to jittery, unpresuposing ll-year-old convincing and funny. His "get down" excitement as the boy in a big man's body after finally getting the best of his rivals in the toilet-cleaning incident is perfectly conveyed, as is his wide-eyed gyrating "spaz-out" at the heavy metal concert to which he takes Bohrer. VICE VERSA was something of an important film for Reinhold, who has scored big in the past in secondary roles (FAST TIMES AT RIDGEMONT HIGH; THE BEVERLY HILLS COP films) but failed to prove himself to be a solid box-office attraction in his previous two leads—HEAD OFFICE and OFFBEAT. He hoped this film would be different, but although he once again demonstrates his fine comedic range, VICE VERSA did not do big business. The other important "child" actor in the film, Savage (THE BOY WHO COULD FLY; THE PRINCESS BRIDE), is nearly as successful in his portrayal of the workaholic, self-centered father in his son's body. Whether he is demanding to use the phone in his grade school's office or giving orders to a chauffeur, Savage is every inch the little big man. Naturally, most of VICE VERSA's plentiful laughs come from the incongruities caused by the role reversal, but these situations are relatively predictable and it is the way they are milked by Reinhold and Savage that makes them work. A true family picture in the most entertaining sense, VICE VERSA provides laughs for both kids and adults. Songs include "Set the Night to Music" (Diane Warren, performed by Starship), "Crazy in the Night" (Mick Zane, Mark Behn, James Neal), "Vice Versa" (Zane, Behn, Paul Sabu, performed by Malice), "Bad to the Bone" (George Thorogoood), "Mony Mony" (Tommy James, Richie Cordell, Bo Gentry, Bobby Bloom, performed by Billy Idol). (Profanity.)

p, Dick Clement, Ian La Frenais; d, Brian Gilbert; w, Dick Clement, Ian La Frenais; ph, King Baggot (DeLuxe Color); ed, David Garfield; m, David Shire; m/l, Diane Warren, Mick Zane, Mark Behn, James Neal, Paul Sabu, George Thorogood, Tommy James, Richie Cordell, Bo Gentry, Bobby Bloom; prod d, Jim Schoppe; art d, Eva Anna Bohn; set d, Karen O'Hara; spec eff, Dennis Dion; cos, Jay Hurley; stunts, Max Kleven; makeup, Kimberly Phillips.

Comedy   Cas.   (PR:A-C MPAA:PG)

VOYAGE OF THE ROCK ALIENS †   (1988) 95m Inter Planetary Curb c

Pia Zadora (Dee Dee), Tom Nolan (Abed), Craig Sheffer (Frankie), Alison LaPiaca (Diane), Michael Berryman (Chainsaw), Ruth Gordon (Sheriff), Jermaine Jackson (Rain), Rhema Band, Jimmy and the Mustangs.

A tongue-in-cheek genre hybrid of science fiction, musicals, and beach party movies, VOYAGE OF THE ROCK ALIENS apparently exists primarily to showcase the singing of its star, Pia Zadora. Unfortunately for her, this 1984 production—which contains a Bob Giraldi-directed rock video featuring Zadora and Jermaine Jackson—went unreleased until 1988, when it quietly turned up on home video. The plot, such as it is, follows extraterrestrial Nolan and his cohorts (a rock band called

Rhema) as they search the universe for signs of intelligent life—that is, a planet that plays rock 'n' roll music. Of course, Earth fits the bill, and the aliens land at the small California beach town of Spielburg. Wanna-be singer Zadora hooks up with spaceman Nolan, and he agrees to make her an intergalactic star. This picture may appeal to the odd Zadora fan (like director John Waters) or those interested in seeing the late Ruth Gordon in one of her final roles, as, of all things, a sheriff.

p, Micheline H. Keller, Brian Russell; d, James Fargo, Bob Giraldi; w, S. James Guidotti, Edward Gold, Charles Hairston; ph, Gil Taylor (DeLuxe Color), Dante Spinotti; ed, Billy Williams, Malcolm Campbell; m, Jack White; prod d, Ninkey Dalton; spec eff, Image Engineering, Tony Tremblay; ch, Dennon Rawles, Sayhber Rawles.

Musical/Science Fiction   Cas.   (PR:NR MPAA:PG)

W

WALKING ON WATER **(SEE: STAND AND DELIVER, 1988)**

WAR † (1988) 99m Lloyd Kaufman/Michael Herz/Troma c

Carolyn Beauchamp *(Lydia)*, Sean Bowen *(Taylor)*, Michael Ryder *(Parker)*, Patrick Weathers *(Kirkland)*, Jessica Dublin *(Dottie)*, Steven Crossley *(Marshall)*, Charles Kay Hune *(Hardwick)*, Lorayn Lane DeLuca *(Maria)*, Ara Romanoff *(Cooney)*, Brenda Brock *(Kim)*, Lisbeth Kaufman, Lisa Patruno, Rick Collins, Burt Wright, Michael Lacascio.

This sounds like a typically vile epic from Troma, the infamous New York City-based, low-budget exploitation studio specializing in self-consciously sophomoric gross-out extravaganzas. When a plane-load of character stereotypes from Tromaville, New Jersey, crash-land on a remote tropical island, the travelers are dismayed to discover that the place is overrun with international terrorists preparing for an invasion of the good old U.S. of A. Patriotic souls, the crash survivors—a Jewish grandmother and an arrogant yuppie among them—band together to launch a bloody attack against the insidious foreign heathens. Sex and violence reign as the Troma gang go out of their way to offend everyone in this, their biggest-budget project yet.

p, Lloyd Kaufman, Michael Herz; d, Michael Herz, Samuel Weil; w, Mitchell Dana, Eric Hattler, Thomas Martinek, Lloyd Kaufman (based on story by Lloyd Kaufman); ph, James London; m, Christopher De Marco; spec eff, William Jennings, Pericles Lewnes; stunts, Scott Leva.

Action **(PR:NR MPAA:R)**

WATCHERS † (1988) 92m Concorde-Centaur-Rose & Ruby/UNIV c

Corey Haim *(Travis)*, Barbara Williams *(Nora)*, Michael Ironside *(Lem)*, Lala Sloatman *(Tracey)*, Duncan Fraser *(Sheriff Gaines)*, Blue Mankuma *(Cliff)*, Colleen Winton *(Deputy Porter)*, Norman Browning *(Hockney)*.

Based on a novel by Dean R. Koontz, who also penned the work that inspired THE DEMON SEED, WATCHERS deals with a top-secret government experiment gone haywire—prime Roger Corman material. This time the experiment involves a lovable dog that has been groomed to infiltrate enemy camps, paving the way for his partner, a nasty orange monster called Oxcom, to follow and literally devour the enemy. Together they are to be Our secret weapon for the next big war, but the little dog escapes and is befriended by Haim, a teenager whose small hometown isn't the same after Oxcom comes looking for his canine partner.

p, Damian Lee, David Mitchell, Mary Eilts; d, Jon Hess; w, Bill Freed, Damian Lee (based on the novel by Dean R. Koontz); ph, Richard Leiterman (Filmhouse color); ed, Bill Freda, Carolle Alain; m, Joel Goldsmith; prod d, Richard Wilcox Kent; art d, Tom Duquette; set d, Marti Wright; cos, Monique Stranan.

Horror **(PR:NR MPAA:R)**

WAXWORK † (1988) 97m Staffan Ahrenberg-Mario Sotela/Vestron c

Zach Galligan *(Mark)*, Deborah Foreman *(Sarah)*, Michelle Johnson *(China)*, David Warner *(Mr. Lincoln)*, Dana Ashbrook *(Tony)*, Patrick Macnee *(Sir Wilfred)*, Charles McCaughan *(Detective Roberts)*, J. Kenneth Campbell *(Marquis De Sade)*, Miles O'Keeffe *(Count Dracula)*, John Rhys-Davies *(Anton Weber)*, Eric Brown *(James)*, Micah Grant *(Johnathan)*, Clare Carey *(Gemma)*, Jack David Walker *(Junior)*.

Somewhat inspired by Paul Leni's classic 1924 silent horror film, WAXWORKS, this gory update is the feature film debut of 29-year-old writer-director Anthony Hickox, the son of director Douglas Hickox (THEATER OF BLOOD) and great-grandson of British film industry giant J. Arthur Rank. Boasting a cast whose assembled filmographies read like a list of tragic career moves, WAXWORK features Warner as the evil owner of a house of wax who invites dim-witted teens Foreman (VALLEY GIRL), Galligan (GREMLINS), Johnson (BLAME IT ON RIO), and Ashbrook (RETURN OF THE LIVING DEAD II) to a private showing of his special collection—an assembly of classic movie monsters and real-life historical nutcases. Of course, when the teens step beyond the velvet rope, they are instantly catapulted back in time and are stuck in the display with either Dracula (played by the oddly cast O'Keeffe), the wolfman (Rhys-Davies when human, a stuntman when monster), the Marquis De Sade (Campbell), or NIGHT OF THE LIVING DEAD land. It seems that Warner is going to use these revived evildoers to somehow conquer the world and it is up to the wheelchair-bound MacNee to save humankind. Sprinkled throughout the film are mini-*hommages* to such horror films as THE MUMMY; PHANTOM OF THE OPERA; ERASERHEAD; LITTLE SHOP OF HORRORS; and others. Judging from the production stills lovingly reproduced in such magazines as *Fangoria* and *Gorezone*, the gross-out effects in WAXWORK promise to be particularly disgusting. Given a fleeting release in a few major markets, this will no doubt make a quick transfer to videocassette.

p, Staffan Ahrenberg; d, Anthony Hickox; w, Anthony Hickox; ph, Gerry Lively (Foto-Kem color); ed, Christopher Cibelli; m, Roger Bellon; prod d, Gianni Quaranta; art d, Peter Marangoni; spec eff, Bob Keen; cos, Leonard Pollock.

Horror **Cas.** **(PR:NR MPAA:R)**

WEDDING IN GALILEE**** (1988, Bel./Fr.) 116m Marisa-LPA-French Ministry of Culture-French Community

Ali Mohammed El Akili *(Abu Adel, the Mukhtar)*, Bushra Karaman *(The Mother)*, Nazih Akleh *(Adel, the Groom)*, Makram Khouri *(Military General)*, Anna Achdian *(Samia, the Bride)*, Sonia Amar *(Sumaya, the Daughter)*, Youssef Abou Warda *(Baccum)*, Eyad Anis *(Hassan)*, Wael Barckouti *(Ziad)*, Juliano Mer Khamis, Ilan Chemi *(Officers)*, Tali Dorat *(Tali, Female Soldier)*, Tawfik Khleifi *(The Grandfather)*, Oum Fayez Deibes *(The Grandmother)*, Mohamed Daghach *(Uncle Khamis)*, Laila Warwar *(Zouhaira)*, Emtiaz Diab, Georges Khleifi, Hassan Diab, Abkas Himas.

©KINO INTERNATIONAL

WEDDING IN GALILEE is a moving and remarkable Belgian-French coproduction about Palestinian wedding customs, military and patriarchal dominance, and the quest for peace in the Middle East. Directed by the 36-year-old, Nazareth-born Michel Khleifi, who resides in Belgium, this film has not come to American shores without its share of accolades. It was awarded the 1987 Cannes Critic's Prize, named Best Film of the Year in Belgium, and took the Grand Prize at the San Sebastian Film Festival—where jury member Alain Tanner said to Khleifi, "Your film is greater than any prize we could give it." Filmed before the escalation in Palestinian-Israeli tensions of late 1987, WEDDING IN GALILEE is set (and was photographed) in the occupied West Bank, where the village *mukhtar*, or elder, played by Akili, has vowed to give his son a great wedding. The obstacle to this planned festivity is the imposed curfew that takes effect every evening at sundown. Akili appeals to the military governor, Khouri, to make an exception in this case, but to no avail. Khouri does propose that the wedding can take place on the condition that he and his Israeli aides are invited as guests of honor. Without pondering the consequences, Akili agrees and parts with the military governor on friendly terms. When he explains to his villagers that the Israelis will be in attendance there is an immediate split, with hostilities and insults hurled about at once. Even Akili's son, groom-to-be Akleh, disagrees with his father's decision. The wedding, however, *will* take place as Akili has promised. The villagers agree that they will attend out of respect for Akili, refusing to let the Israeli military presence divide them. Some even view the occasion as an opportunity to prove their unity to the Israeli guests. The daylong rituals then begin. The women prepare the robes and jewels for the beautiful young bride, Achdian, sensually bathing her with sponges, showering her with flower petals, singing traditional songs, and finally draping her in a pure white bridal robe with a veil that completely covers her face. For what appears to be hours the bride sits motionless in a bridal chair while the village women sing and dance in her honor. Meanwhile, the men prepare the groom, bathing him and showering him with flower petals as well. Dressed in a suit and covered in a white robe, he too is entertained by song and dance. Others prepare the huge wedding feast. A special table is set up for the military governor and his young associates, who are greeted with warmth by many of the villagers. One handsome young soldier is comically teased by a group of giddy teenage girls, led by Akili's sexually blossoming daughter, Amar. There are, however, three militant Palestinians who are wholly against the Israeli presence. Their credo is "No celebration without dignity, no dignity under the heel of the enemy." They concoct a half-baked plan to either kill the official or take him hostage, though the three are armed with only a couple of knives and a pistol—no match for automatic weapons. As the celebration wears on, the bride and groom are ceremoniously sent into a private bedroom to consummate their marriage. They are to then present the guests with the blood-stained nuptial bedsheet. The military governor has promised Akili that he and his guests will stay to the end and is determined to keep his promise, though the tensions between his party and some of the villagers are growing volatile. When it is discovered that a terrorist attack is being planned, albeit an unorganized one, the Israelis radio for more soldiers. The attack, however, is crushed, not by soldiers, but by a village elder who refuses to see Akili's celebration day end in bloodshed. The oppressive pressures from his father and the Israelis' presence prove too much for the young groom, who, as a result, cannot perform sexually. After some time in the bedroom, the bride and groom are visited by their parents, who try to offer advice. The groom feels more pressure, Akili grows ashamed, the Israelis grow impatient, and the villagers, who have by now consumed vast quantities of alcohol, are becoming uncontrollable. Still the groom cannot perform, despite his bride's efforts. Rather than see blood spilled in violence, the bride takes her own virginity, the nuptial sheet is presented, and the military leaves before a confrontation takes place.

A rich, lyrical film of many textures, WEDDING IN GALILEE presents Western audiences with a world rarely seen on-screen, familiar only from violent television news reports. As an anthropological film, it is educational and enlightening, presenting foreign locations and nonprofessional actors. But WEDDING IN GALILEE is much more than a film of cultural curiosity. It is a human drama, ranging in tone from comic to sad, from tense to sensual. Director Michel Khleifi is not afraid to let his camera linger on his locations, allowing it to move through the space and stare out an open window long after the characters have left and the action has ceased. Often the haunting musical score overpowers all other sounds until it is the only thing heard. At other times, however, Khleifi films with an economical sense of tension-filled storytelling. When two young village boys let Akili's beautiful thoroughbred racehorse out of its stall, they must call on their father and the soldiers to help coax it out of a mine field into which it has wandered. This harrowing scene is constructed in a commercial Western way to elicit an audience reaction, but its components are hardly typical—a mine field, a horse, Israeli soldiers, a Palestinian elder. Equally surprising is the sensuality and nudity present throughout WEDDING IN GALILEE. In this film steeped in tradition, the discovery of modern sexuality is jarring and, as a result, that much more effective. The three major women characters all experience a sexual awakening—the bride does so most literally as she loses her virginity (albeit in a nontraditional way); the younger daughter becomes aware of her own body and the power she has over men; and a female Israeli military aide, after fainting at dinner, is attended to by village women who massage her, undress her, and re-dress her in Palestinian robes. This burgeoning sexuality is contrasted with the impotence of the young Palestinian groom, who is powerless under the watchful eyes of his father and the Israeli oppressor. WEDDING IN GALILEE is thick with parallels to the political situation in the occupied West Bank and the relations between Jews and Arabs, but the film goes beyond these specific dimensions to present us with an all-encompassing view of the relations between all people, young and old, male and female. (In Arabic and Hebrew; English subtitles.) *(Nudity, sexual situations.)*

p, Michel Khleifi, Bernard Lorain; d, Michel Khleifi; w, Michel Khleifi; ph, Walther van de Ende; ed, Marie Castro Vasquez; m, Jean-Marie Senia; set d, Yves Brover, Rachid Michirawi; cos, Anne Verhoeven; makeup, Nancy Baudoux.

Drama   (PR:O MPAA:NR)

WELCOME IN VIENNA**   (1988, Aust./W. Ger.) 126m
                                             Thalia-ORF-ZDF-SSR-Austrian Federal Ministry of

Gabriel Barylli *(Freddy Wolff)*, Nicolas Brieger *(Sgt. Adler)*, Claudia Messner *(Claudia Schutte)*, Hubert Mann *(Capt. Karpeles)*, Karlheinz Hackl *(Treschensky)*, Liliana Nelska *(Russian Woman)*, Kurt Sowinetz *(Stodola)*.

WELCOME IN VIENNA is the first and only film made on the subject of Austrian and German emigres to the U.S. who joined the U.S. Army and then returned to their homeland in 1944 with the American liberating forces. Beautifully photographed in a grainy black-and-white (which gives a documentary visual quality), the film opens on Christmas Eve, 1944, as the American forces are holed up in a barn in the middle of a snowy field. The two main characters are Barylli, an Austrian Jew who has longed for this return home, and Brieger, a German intellectual who fled to the States in fear of the Nazis and has now become sympathetic to the Communists. Heading their command is a toughtalking, hard-drinking German-American, Kemmer, who has a firm belief in Teutonic anti-Semitism. In the battle that follows, a German deserter, Hackl, is captured—a man who, as it turns out, is an opportunistic Viennese and Nazi former friend of Barylli's. Time jumps ahead to May 1945 in Salzburg on the final day of the war as the liberating forces descend on the city. The first girl that Barylli lays eyes on is Messner, a pretty, bicycle-riding Austrian girl whose father is a colonel in the "Abwehr"—the Nazi counterintelligence. She informs U.S. authorities that her father is willing to surrender his information, but only if the U.S. receives him with full honors. Barylli has returned to Austria—his home—though he soon finds that things have changed. Thousands of Jews have disappeared, and as many buildings have been reduced to rubble. When he tries to locate his family's apartment, he finds it al-

most completely destroyed and learns that his family's possessions had been sold on the street. The "home" that he hoped to find no longer exists. He works his way up in the ranks of the new government, taking a cultural job because of his smattering knowledge of theater and literature. He falls in love with Messner, who is yet another representation of that Austria "home" that he cannot recapture. Although she loves him dearly she uses him as a means to further her career on the stage. Brieger, in the meantime, has become disillusioned in his admiration of Stalin's Communist rule, while Hackl, still the opportunist, has moved into a position of power in the black market. As the film ends, Barylli has lost Messner to the stage and must now decide whether or not to return to America. Funded by Austrian dollars, directed by Austrian Corti, and written by an Austrian expatriate living in Paris, Troller, WELCOME IN VIENNA is the first film, according to its filmmakers, that has accurately dealt with Austria's unflattering role during World War II. Labelled as the first innocent victim of Nazi aggression, Austria buckled under to Nazi forces with barely a struggle. From 1938 through the war years, there was no noticeable Resistance movement in Austria and anti-Semitism ran high, as it did in Germany. With a reported ten percent of its adult population members of the Nazi party, there existed little opposition to Hitler's aggression against the Jews. Rather than use these facts to condemn the population, Corti and Troller simply bring to light very real situations of the day. Accused of "behaving like a nest-fouler," Corti retaliates, "I feel that he who never looks down at what is underneath befouls his own nest." Describing his intentions further, Corti was quoted in an interview with film historian Francis Courtade as saying, "We did not want to make a movie about Good and Bad but intended to highlight facts and situations of a historic period of time and to display how everybody responds or, maybe, must respond to them, in his or her very special way." Echoing Jean Renoir's line of dialog that "Everybody has their reasons" from RULES OF THE GAME, Corti has presented an exceptional look at the human condition. Every element of the film rings of a desire to tell the truth—from the newsreel quality of the film stock to the locations to the unfaltering performances. Surprisingly, despite the political subject matter of the film and the general audience's distinct ignorance of world history, WELCOME IN VIENNA has received a brief US release. The film is, however, saddled with the inherent difficulty of distinguishing the Austrians from the Germans because of most audiences' unfamiliarity with the difference in dialects. To most American ears, they all sound German, adding some initial confusion, especially in the early battle sequences as German and Austrian soldiers in the American Army are fighting German troops. WELCOME IN VIENNA was shown on the festival circuit in 1987 earning a Best Director award at the San Sebastian film festival and the top honor of the Golden Hugo at the Chicago International Film Festival. (In Austrian and German, with English subtitles.)

d, Axel Corti; w, Axel Corti, Georg Stefan Troller; ph, Gernot Roll; ed, Ulrike Pahl, Claudia Rieneck; m, Hans Georg Koch, Franz Schubert; prod d, Matija Barl; set d, Fritz Hollergschwandtner; cos, Uli Fessler; makeup, Ellen Just, Adolf Uhrmacher.

War   (PR:O MPAA:NR)

WEST IS WEST †   (1988) 80m Rathod c

Ashotosh Gowariker *(Vikram)*, Heidi Carpenter *(Sue)*, Pearl Padamsee *(Mrs. Shah)*.

This low-budget independent film chronicles the difficulties of an Indian emigre (Gowariker) has in adjusting to life in the United States. Coming to America from Bombay, Gowariker is detained by US Customs officials, who cut his tourist visa from six months to just one. Next, Gowariker goes to the home of his sponsor, only to find that they have moved and not left a forwarding address. Gowariker then attempts to enroll at the University of California, but is denied. Unable to work or study and his visa about to expire, Gowariker must persuade an American woman to marry him or be deported.

p, David Rathod, Cristi Janaki Rathod; d, David Rathod; w, David Rathod; ph, Christopher Tufty; m, Sheila Chandra, Jai Uttal; art d, Cristi Janaki Rathod.

Drama   (PR:NR MPAA:NR)

WHEELS OF TERROR   (SEE: MISFIT BRIGADE, THE, 1988, It.)

WHEN THE WIND BLOWS**   (1988, Brit.) 85m Meltdown-British
                                             Screen-Film Four Intl.-TVC London-Penguin

Voices of: Peggy Ashcroft *(Hilda Bloggs)*, John Mills *(Jim Bloggs)*, Robin Houston *(Announcer)*, James Russell, Matt Irving, David Dundas.

With its striking simplicity, WHEN THE WIND BLOWS is a deeply moving parable of nuclear holocaust. Unlike the realistic television films "The Day After" or "Threads," this story is told through animation, following the story of a retired English couple who must deal with the post-nuclear winter. James Bloggs (voiced by John Mills) and his wife Hilda (voiced by Peggy Ashcroft) live in a small cottage located in the British countryside. While Hilda happily toils at her housework, James returns home from his daily trip into the nearby town. He brings with him some pamphlets printed by the government, designed to instruct citizens in proper home defense during a nuclear attack. World tensions have been building, according to radio reports, and war is imminent. James carefully builds a regulation shelter using household materials, while Hilda fusses about. She doesn't understand why her husband is going to all this bother and scolds him repeatedly. James responds by quoting her the facts as stated in the government pamphlets, and continues with his work. A few days later a bulletin comes over the radio announcing a nuclear strike has been launched. Hilda wants to bring in her washing off the line, but James angrily tells her there is not time for that. The bomb goes off, destroying the England James and Hilda love so dearly. After the atomic blast James and Hilda begin adjusting to the post-nuclear world. Hilda is surprised to see what a mess her house has been turned into, while James faithfully continues heeding the government instructions. Electricity, water, and all communications have been cut off, while their beloved vegetable garden has been completely destroyed. Still, James and Hilda are convinced this situation is merely a temporary crisis, and like WW II, one they can stick out until things get back to normal. Gradually, radiation begin taking its toll on the couple. Hilda grows sickly, but James tries to keep up her spirits, explaining her problems are typical for a woman her age. He too becomes ill, but still remains certain things will get better. Husband and wife decide to cuddle up together and James begins to pray. Not knowing any one prayer, his words are a mixture of various psalms, and Hilda is touched by what her dearest companion has said. The characters of James and Hilda are a comical pair, whose faith in everyday routine gives these catastrophic events a strong sense of pathos. The situation grows more desperate as the small, but important details of their lives slowly slip out of their control. These developments are handled with a gentle, sympathetic humor that subtly brings out the hopelessness in their plight. When James first tries to explain how they'll be unable to use the toilet in the days after the bomb, Hilda grows indignant. War or not, she intends on keeping a certain decorum. This becomes a running joke, until Hilda sees a rat climbing up the toilet bowl. A minor annoyance turns into personal tragedy as Hilda's vestiges of pride are shattered. James' staunch belief in the government pamphlets works in a similar way. He quotes Hilda passage after passage, convinced these instructions are their saving grace. They had listened to authorities during WW II with England emerging victorious, and James is convinced their leaders will guide them through a wartime crisis once more. Like Hilda's need for decorum, James' confidence in the pamphlets begins humorously before harsh reality settles in. Mills and Ashcroft are perfectly cast in their cartoon roles. Drawn as round, jovial caricatures, these two fine actors bring out the humanity in James and Hilda. They deliver their lines quietly, in an understated manner, with a rapport that could only exist between a long married couple. A variety of animation styles are used in WHEN THE WIND BLOWS with often striking visual effect. James and Hilda's house is a miniature set, while the characters are animated over this background by cels. This combination gives the film a slightly three dimensional look. At times the camera merely explores the destroyed set while Mills and Ashcroft are heard on the soundtrack discussing how to deal with their growing troubles. Other sequences, such as single shots depicting the war's buildup, use model animation and there's also stock footage of WW II employed during James and Hilda's reminiscing. WHEN THE WIND BLOWS marks the reuniting of an excellent creative team. Roland Briggs, on whose book this film is based, had previously written the popular children's story of innocence nurtured and lost, "The Snowman." This was made as a short film in 1982, with Jimmy T. Murakami serving as supervising director. He took over full directing chores for this work, while Briggs again supplied the screenplay (Briggs also adapted this story as a radio drama). David Bowie, who served as narrator for THE SNOWMAN, provided the title song here, while Roger Waters, of "Pink Floyd" fame, wrote the musical score and closing theme. Together this talented group has produced an eloquent work. Originally shown in England in 1986, WHEN THE WIND BLOWS was awarded the Getz World Peace Prize at the 1987 Chicago Film Festival. *(Adult situations.)*

p, John Coates; d, Jimmy T. Murakami; w, Raymond Briggs (based on the book by Raymond Briggs); ed, John Cary; m, Roger Waters; md, Ray Williams; m/l, David Bowie, Roger Waters, Genesis, Paul Hardcastle, Squeeze, Hugh Cornwall, Glenn Tilbrook, Pete Hammond, Erdal Kizilcay; spec eff, Stephen Weston.

Animation **Cas.** **(PR:C MPAA:NR)**

WHITE GHOST † (1988) 93m White Ghost/Gibraltar c

William Katt *(Steve Shepard)*, Rosalind Chao *(Thi Hau)*, Martin Hewitt *(Waco)*, Wayne Crawford *(Capt. Walker)*, Reb Brown *(Maj. Cross)*, Raymond Ma *(Camp Commander)*, Karl Johnson *(Brownie)*, Graham Clark *(Doc)*.

William Katt is a Rambo type who, dressed in Kabuki make-up, is still waging war against the Vietnamese. A squad of American soldiers, led by Katt's former Green Beret nemesis, is sent to Vietnam to find and stop the loose cannon.

p, Jay Davidson, William Fay; d, B.J. Davis; w, Gary Thompson; ph, Hans Kuhle (Kodak color); ed, Ettie Feldman; m, Parmer Fuller; art d, Dankert Guillaume; stunts, Paul Siebert.

Action/War **Cas.** **(PR:NR MPAA:R)**

WHITE MISCHIEF**½ (1988, Brit.) 107m Umbrella-Power Tower Investments-BBC/COL c

Sarah Miles *(Alice de Janze)*, Joss Ackland *(Sir John* "Jock" Delves Broughton), John Hurt *(Gilbert Colvile)*, Greta Scacchi *(Diana Caldwell)*, Charles Dance *(Josslyn Hay, Earl of Erroll)*, Susan Fleetwood *(Gwladys, Lady Delamere)*, Alan Dobie *(Harragin, Prosecutor)*, Hugh Grant *(Hugh Dickinson)*, Jacqueline Pearce *(Lady Idina Gordon)*, Catherine Neilson *(June Carberry)*, Murray Head *(Lizzie Lezard)*, Gregor Fisher *(McPherson)*, Ray McAnally *(Morris)*, Geraldine Chaplin *(Nina Soames)*, Trevor Howard *(Jack Soames)*, Tristram Jellinek *(Land Agent)*, Tim Myers *(Raymond de Trafford)*, Sean Mathias *(Gerald Portman)*, Ron Donachie *(Club Manager)*, Douglas Chege *(Kiptobe)*, Wensley Pithey *(Sheridan)*, Stephan Chase *(Carberry)*, Clare Travers-Deacon *(Muffin-Faced Woman)*, Seipal Ngojine, Pilip Saitoti *(Masai Warriors)*, Amanda Farkin *(Nancy Wirewater)*, Louis Mahoney *(Abdullah)*, Ilario Bisi-Pedro *(African Policeman)*, David Quilter *(Poppy)*, John Rees *(Baines)*, Olivier Pierre *(Kaplan)*, Anthony Benson *(Fox)*, Nigel Le Vaillant *(Handsome Reporter)*, Basil Whybray *(Spotty Reporter)*, John Darrell *(Registrar)*, Bill Moody *(Jury Foreman)*.

The scum of aristocratic decadence rises to the top in this film, which plays like an episode of "Masterpiece Theater" with a serious case of dementia. The year is 1941, and the "Happy Valley" set in the British colony of Nairobi is buzzing with its usual aphrodisiacs—drink, drugs, sex, sport, and general, all-purpose aristocratic posing. This is not your usual have-a-scotch-and-play-polo crowd, but one that's a bit more indulgent. The drug use is rampant and extends to the intravenous variety, the drinking is nonstop and far past the point of excess, and the sex is frank, open, and as socially accepted as teatime. The most exciting aspect of this "Happy Valley," however, is that it really existed and so did the characters and events of WHITE MISCHIEF. It was this aristocratic wildlife that led to the still-unsolved murder of playboy Josslyn Hay, the 22nd Earl of Erroll, a scandal that rocked Kenya and Great Britain. While the mischievous white aristocrats were frolicking about in Kenya, their countrymen at home were dodging nighttime German air raids in WW II. The film is set up as a basic love triangle—Ackland plays Sir "Jock" Broughton, a 59-year-old man who has squandered away his fortune and has relocated in "Happy Valley" with a new bride who is less than half his age, the lovely Scacchi as Diana Caldwell. As hormones would have it, Scacchi falls in love with the virile Dance, playing Joss Hay, a man whose motto is "To hell with husbands." Although they live in a society where all is permissable, there are certain rules to their game. It is all right to frolic under the covers with any partner you please, but things must be kept discreet. Dance, however, has no intention of keeping his relationship with Scacchi a secret. Worse yet, he *flaunts* it, publicly displaying his desire for Ackland's wife. When the gentlemanly Ackland requests that Dance end the affair, his request is matter-of-factly denied. Then, one morning, Dance is found slumped in his car, a bullet hole in his left ear. Scacchi becomes hysterical and Ackland is hauled in for questioning. The case comes to trial, but Ackland is acquitted. He tries to renew his romance with Scacchi, but she remains distant. She even doubts his innocence. Her trust is further shaken during a visit to the ranch of Hurt, the wealthiest man in Kenya and one who speaks as infrequently as possible. Upon seeing an old photo of Ackland, Scacchi becomes convinced her husband was the murderer. She returns home to confront her husband, only to have a distraught Ackland chase after her with a shotgun, eventually turning it on himself. Scacchi, however, survives the scandal and, as a title card informs us, weds Hurt shortly thereafter.

Although WHITE MISCHIEF revolves around a murder mystery, the murder is not the main concern of director Michael Radford, whose previous films are ANOTHER TIME, ANOTHER PLACE and 1984. Rather, the film is about the decadence of these wealthy whites living their amoral lives in a land and country that is not theirs. Living in their own world where there is no right or wrong, the "Happy Valley" crowd pays no attention to the Kenyan natives that surround them or the jury and media that judges them. Radford has explained that his is a film "about people who reduce everything to wit," and this description could hardly be more accurate. Despite the possibilities this observation has to offer, the film is a lifeless exercise that prefers to perform autopsies on its characters rather than bring them to life. Despite an occasionally satiric bite (a morbid morgue farewell to Dance from former lover Miles is unforgettable), WHITE MISCHIEF is a soap opera and not nearly as orgiastic as it pretends to be. It is the sort of material the Marquis de Sade would have thrown out on a bad day. Fortunately, the film offers some fine performances. Joss Ackland is a marvel as the man who has lost everything—money, love, youth, country, and respectability. The handsome Charles Dance, last seen as D.W. Griffith in the Taviani brothers' GOOD MORNING, BABYLON, seethes with a wily charm and is just the sort of man you wouldn't trust with your wife. Greta Scacchi (who also appeared in GOOD MORNING, BABYLON) is, as always, beautiful but has grown predictable in her frequent reliance on shedding her clothes before the camera. Here, more than ever, Scacchi looks as if she has stepped out of the pages of a 1940s glamour magazine. She is an actress who, unlike so many seen today, has created a larger-than-life aura on-screen. The rest of the cast is equally impressive, with special mention going to John Hurt—who again proves his stature as one of the greatest living actors, saying more with his face than with words—and to Trevor Howard in his final role as a sprightly friend of Ackland's.

The project's genesis dates back to 1969, when a pair of London journalists—Cyril Connolly and James Fox—printed their story about the Hay murder in *The Sunday Times Magazine.* Although Connolly died in 1974, Fox continued to investigate the mystery, traveling to Kenya in 1980 for an interview with a witness who claimed that "Jock" Broughton confessed his guilt to her on the night of the murder. Two years later, in 1982, Fox published his book *White Mischief,* in which the author points to the killer but fails to provide specific hows and whys, thereby leaving director Radford with poetic license. While much of the film is based in fact, at least in its spirit, the death of Broughton is neatly fictionalized. For the curious, instead of killing himself in front of his wife, he did so in 1942 in a Liverpool hotel room. Songs include "White Mischief" (Tom Finn), "Begin the Beguine" (Cole Porter), "The Alphabet Song" (performed by Sarah Miles). *(Nudity, substance abuse, sexual situations, adult situations, graphic violence, profanity.)*

p, Simon Perry; d, Michael Radford; w, Michael Radford, Jonathan Gems (based on the book by James Fox); ph, Roger Deakins (Agfa-Gevaert); ed, Tom Priestley;

m, George Fenton; m/l, Cole Porter, Tim Finn; prod d, Roger Hall; art d, Len Huntingford, Keith Pain; set d, Marianne Ford; cos, Marit Allen; ch, Stuart Hopps; makeup, Pat Hay.

Mystery/Romance	Cas.	(PR:O MPAA:R)

WHITE OF THE EYE***
(1988) 111m Cinema Group-Cannon c

David Keith (*Paul White*), Cathy Moriarty (*Joan White*), Art Evans (*Detective Charles Mendoza*), Alan Rosenberg (*Mike Desantos*), Michael Greene (*Phil Ross*), Danielle Smith (*Danielle White*), Alberta Watson (*Ann Mason*), William G. Schilling (*Harold Gideon*), David Chow (*Fred Hoy*), Marc Hayashi (*Stu*), Mimi Lieber (*Liza Manchester*), Pamela Seamon (*Caryanne*), Bob Zache (*Lucas Herman*), Danko Gurovich (*Arnold White*), China Cammell (*Ruby Hoy*).

After a succession of "safe" thrillers that prefer to provide a roller-coaster ride of thrills instead of genuinely disturbing ideas—films such as JAGGED EDGE; FATAL ATTRACTION; and SOMEONE TO WATCH OVER ME—it is refreshing to see a picture that makes the opposite choice. WHITE OF THE EYE, directed by Donald Cammell, who has made only two other pictures (as codirector with Nicolas Roeg of PERFORMANCE [1970], and director of 1977's DEMON SEED, his only other solo outing), begins in a small community outside Tucson, where an unseen killer stalks a young housewife in her clean, well-lit home. The camera glides through the hallway, sneaks up behind the woman, and proceeds to thrust her head through the door of her otherwise spotless microwave oven. This is, we learn, just one in a series of brutal murders that have plagued the community. When the police investigator, Evans, visits the crime scene, he realizes that this is the work of a psychologically disturbed person, and goes so far as to compare the scene—with its blood, shattered glass, and scattered groceries—to a work of Picasso. Meanwhile, seemingly unfazed by the events in the neighborhood, Moriarty and her husband, Keith, go about their daily routine. Keith, a sound-system wizard whose nasal cavity acts as a tuning fork, makes enough money to support his wife and young daughter by installing high-tech systems throughout Arizona. He and Moriarty have been married for some 10 years, ever since she and her then-lover, Rosenberg, left the Bronx for Malibu and met Keith in the desert. Keith took Rosenberg on hunting trips by day and became extra-friendly with Moriarty by night, and since that time Moriarty has not seen her former lover. One afternoon, however, she has a chance meeting with the Zen-philosophical Rosenberg, who works in a service station and makes peanut butter. Keith, meanwhile, is doing some repair work at the expensive home of bored housewife Watson. More than anything, the scantily clad Watson wants to bed Keith, who tries to fight his temptation. After a few clues, Moriarty gets wise to her husband's dalliance and, after discovering his van parked near the woman's house, pokes a hole in his expensive Baja tires. It is correspondingly revealed that the police investigation of the serial murders has turned up one important lead—a set of tire tracks outside the most recent victim's house. Naturally, the tread markings match those from Keith's van. After another murder (an exceptionally ruthless, though bloodless, killing of a local young woman who dresses like Watson), Keith is the prime suspect. Moriarty never even considers his guilt, assuming that he has done nothing more than bed Watson, but the disturbing discovery of some plastic-wrapped body parts in her bathroom changes Moriarty's mind. Instead of behaving like a B-movie scream-queen, however, loving but confused wife Moriarty confronts her husband. He responds matter-of-factly, then proceeds to launch into a tangential, demented philosophical theory that God is merely a middle-man for some cosmic black hole that controls the universe. For the rest of the evening, Moriarty tries to restore what is left of their marriage and makes love to her husband. Eventually, however, he clicks and turns into a raving madman, locking her in the attic and then wiring himself with dynamite. In the fashion mode of Travis Bickle, he then dons a flak jacket, shaves his head, and puts on some Indian makeup. In the apocalyptic finale, Keith pursues Moriarty through the Arizona wasteland, where Rosenberg—who is just as deranged as Keith—appears out of nowhere for a combative showdown. Keith and Rosenberg blow themselves to smithereens in a mushroom cloud of dust and dirt, while Moriarty is left to resume her never-completed journey to Malibu.

Far more sophisticated and complicated than a simple reading of the plot might suggest, WHITE OF THE EYE is a powerful, albeit flawed, portrait of a serial killer. The film is filled with stylish, hallucinogenic excesses that simultaneously weaken its emotional power and narrative drive and strengthen Cammell's visionary atmosphere. Making heavy use of flashbacks for the early meetings of Keith, Moriarty, and Rosenberg (all convincingly sporting hippie mannerisms), the film drifts back and forth between past and present without apparent reason. As frustrating as these constant diversions become, however, they succeed in raising the level of viewer curiosity. The film's biggest riddle concerns Keith's motives (since we never doubt that he is the killer). Cammell never tells us why Keith killed or how the character became so deranged, refusing even to provide any psychoanalytic excuses during the film's coda (a meeting between Moriarty and police investigator Evans)—a scene that gives the lie to PSYCHO's famous psychoanalytic mumbo-jumbo ending.

If Cammell is neither interested in providing explanations nor in the traditional exploitation of sex and violence (there is very little blood or gore and—more surprisingly—no nudity), that leaves the relationship between Moriarty and Keith as WHITE OF THE EYE'S main thrust. It is Moriarty's inability to see her husband's other self, and Keith's ability to completely fool his wife, that provide the film's most horrific, disturbing aspect. Early on, the viewer is witness to a curious piece of characterization: After the first murder, Keith drives down the highway listening to the famous "Pagliacci" opera theme, but when he arrives home to Moriarty, the music immediately cuts to a relaxed country tune. But although we are privileged with this view of Keith's dichotomy, Moriarty is less observant. She *thinks* she knows him—as she loudly states after she uncovers his affair with Watson. Her worst fears, or so she be-

lieves, are confirmed when she discovers that he is cheating on her. His sins, however, are infinitely worse, and she hasn't even begun to comprehend them. It is this aspect of Cammell's film that was both its most upsetting element and that which managed to anger its audience the most,

Given the film's themes and style, it's no surprise that WHITE OF THE EYE barely saw a theatrical release. Shown in England in 1987, it was acquired by Cannon Films when they purchased the library of Screen Entertainment Ltd., leaving the film without much chance for a US release. Despite some early press coverage pertaining to the disturbing nature of the film and the reappearance of Cathy Moriarty (after 1981's box-office flop NEIGHBORS, the Oscar-nominated lead actress of RAGING BULL hadn't been seen on the screen), WHITE OF THE EYE was a total box-office failure, but one which is destined to achieve cult status. Songs include "Vesti la Guibba" from I Pagliacci (Ruggiero Leoncavallo, performed by Luciano Pavarotti), "A Country Boy Can Survive" (Hank Williams, Jr., performed by Williams), "You Sexy Thing" (Errol Brown, performed by Hot Chocolate), "Slim Jenkin's Joint" (Booker T. Jones, Steve Cropper, Lewis Steenberg, Al Jackson, Jr.), "The Grand Tour" (Moras Wilson, Carmel Taylor, George Richey, performed by David Keith). Also includes "Second Symphony" (Gustav Mahler). (*Graphic violence, adult situations, sexual situations, profanity.*)

p, Cassian Elwes, Brad Wyman; d, Donald Cammell; w, China Cammell, Donald Cammell (based on the novel *Mrs. White* by Margaret Tracy); ph, Larry McConkey (Consolidated Color); ed, Terry Rawlings; m, Nick Mason, Rick Fenn; m/l, Ruggiero Leoncavallo, Hank Williams, Jr., Errol Brown, Booker T. Jones, Steve Cropper, Lewis Steenberg, Al Jackson, Jr., Moras Wilson, Carmel Taylor, George Richie, Gustav Mahler; prod d, Philip Thomas; set d, Richard Rutowski; spec eff, Thomas Ford; cos, Merril Greene; stunts, Dan Bradley; makeup, Jeanne Van Phue, Sharon Ilson Reed.

Thriller	Cas.	(PR:O MPAA:R)

WHO FRAMED ROGER RABBIT*****
(1988) 103m
Touchstone-Amblin-Silver Screen Partners III/BV c

Bob Hoskins (*Eddie Valiant*), Christopher Lloyd (*Judge Doom*), Joanna Cassidy (*Dolores*), Stubby Kaye (*Marvin Acme*), Alan Tilvern (*R.K. Maroon*), Richard Le Parmentier (*Lt. Santino*), Joel Silver (*Raoul Raoul, Director*), Betsy Brantley (*Jessica Performance Model*), Paul Springer (*Augie*), Richard Ridings (*Angelo*), Edwin Craig (*Arthritic Cowboy*), Linsday Holiday (*Soldier*), Mike Edmonds (*Midget*), Morgan Deare (*Editor*), Danny Capri, Christopher Hollosy, John-Paul Sipla (*Kids*), Laura Frances (*Blonde Starlet*), Joel Cutrara, Billy Mitchell (*Forensics*), Eric B. Sindon (*Mailman*), Ed Herlihy (*Newscaster*), James O'Connell (*Conductor*), Eugene Guirterrez (*Teddy Valiant*), April Winchell (*Mrs. Herman*), Charles Fleischer (*Roger Rabbit/Greasy/Psycho/Benny the Cab*), Lou Hirsch (*Baby Herman*), Kathleen Turner (*Jessica Rabbit*), Amy Irving (*Jessica Rabbit's Singing Voice*), Morgan Deare (*Gorilla*), Mae Questel (*Betty Boop*), Mel Blanc (*Daffy Duck/Tweety Bird/Bugs Bunny/Sylvester/Porky Pig*), Tony Anselmo (*Donald Duck*), Mary T. Radford (*Hippo*), Joe Alaskey (*Yosemite Sam*), David Lander (*Smart Ass*), Fred Newman (*Stupid*), June Foray (*Wheezy/Lena Hyena*), Russi Taylor (*Birds/Minnie Mouse*), Les Perkins (*Toad*), Richard Williams (*Droopy*), Wayne Allwine (*Mickey Mouse*), Pat Buttram, Jim Cummings, Jim Gallant (*Bullets*), Frank Sinatra (*Singing Sword*), Tony Pope (*Goofy/Wolf*), Peter Westy (*Pinocchio*), Cherry Davis (*Woody Woodpecker*).

© BUENA VISTA

Finally—a much-ballyhooed, big-budget, special-effects-filled, Hollywood epic from the auspices of Steven Spielberg that actually lives up to its hype. Thankfully, the complicated project was entrusted to director Robert Zemeckis—easily the most independent, interesting, and bright talent to have arisen from the stable of Spielberg's touted proteges. A magnificent entertainment, WHO FRAMED ROGER RABBIT is also a film that truly treads new ground. This is not merely so because the film boasts state-of-the-art movie technology that allows the filmmakers to wow audiences with images never before seen on the screen, but because the impressive technology is used to explore an incredibly rich and fertile premise, based on a simple, fanciful conceit: What if cartoon characters actually existed alongside human beings?

Zemeckis and company suspend our disbelief in the brilliant opening sequence, which begins with a classic 1940s-style cartoon—the kind that used to play before the feature in the old days—introducing us to Roger Rabbit, a lovable, hapless, goofy, stuttering bunny (voiced by comedian Fleischer), who has, as Zemeckis has put it, "a Disney body, a Warners head, and a Tex Avery attitude." Emulating the frenetic action of classic "Tom & Jerry" cartoons, the cartoon of the opening sequence shows Roger Rabbit being told by his female owner to watch little Baby Herman while she goes out. Of course, Baby Herman gets into all sorts of trouble, and Roger must frantically scurry about after the infant as it gets into one life-threatening situation after another. When a refrigerator winds up crashing on top of Roger and the door opens to reveal the stunned rabbit seeing little bluebirds circling his head, the command "Cut!" is suddenly heard, and the director—a human being (played by powerful Hollywood producer Silver)—begins shouting at the hapless rabbit for producing tweeting birds when the script called for *stars*. "Baby" Herman then turns out to be a foul-mouthed, cigar-chomping cartoon adult merely *playing* a baby, and he angrily stomps off to his trailer. You see, Roger Rabbit and Baby Herman are "Toons," a derogatory term used by humans to describe the wild, colorful animated characters who can do amazing things and suffer incredible violence without getting hurt. Driven by an insatiable desire to entertain, the Toons are resented and feared by humans because of their care-free attitude. Discrimination has forced them to live in a segregated neighborhood just outside of Hollywood called Toontown, an area most human policemen are loath to patrol. Sensing that Roger's lack of concentration on the job is due to marital troubles, the owner of Maroon Cartoons, R.K. Maroon (Tilvern), hires down-and-out detective Eddie Valiant (Hoskins) to get the goods on Roger's wife, Jessica (Turner, with Irving as Jessica's singing voice), an incredibly voluptuous, human-looking Toon, so that the rabbit will wise up and divorce her. Hoskins hates Toons because, when he was a cop, he and his brother had to patrol Toontown and his brother was killed by a Toon who dropped a safe on his head. Needing the work, however, Hoskins takes the case and traces Jessica to her job as a singer at the Ink and Paint, a popular nightclub that features Toon entertainers (such as Donald and Daffy Duck in a piano duet) but serves only humans. After Jessica's sexy number, Hoskins sneaks backstage to snap a few pictures of the femme fatale and a human, prop supplier Marvin Acme (Kaye), literally playing "patticake." The pictures are too much for poor Roger Rabbit, who goes crashing out the window of Tilvern's office and scurries off into the night when he sees them. The next day, Kaye is found dead—a safe was dropped on his head. Kaye's death is a tragedy for Toontown, for he owned the land on which Toontown sits, and was kind and generous to the Toons. Suspicion is thrown on the hapless Roger, who claims innocence and begs Hoskins to help him clear his name. Hoskins reluctantly agrees, but he must stay one step ahead of the villainous Judge Doom (Lloyd), a Toon-hating human who has developed a turpentine, acetone, and benzine combination known as "The Dip" that is the only thing that can kill a Toon—it virtually erases the ink-and-paint creatures. Aided by a pack of moronic cartoon weasels, Lloyd is hot on Roger's trail. As the mystery deepens, it is learned that Lloyd plans to scrap Los Angeles' clean, efficient trolley-car system and build a brand-new expressway for automobiles. Unfortunately for the Toons, Toontown sits where the off-ramp will go, and it was Lloyd who had Kaye killed. Hoskins' investigation takes him back into the dreaded Toontown, where he is the only human being in an entirely cartoon universe. Eventually there is a showdown between Hoskins and Lloyd, with the lives of Roger and Jessica hanging in the balance. During the battle, Lloyd is flattened like a pancake after being run over by the giant steamroller-type device that was ready to spray the Dip all over Toontown, but he gets up and pops back into shape—thus revealing himself as a turncoat Toon in disguise. Falling victim to his own insidious concoction, Lloyd melts like the Wicked Witch in THE WIZARD OF OZ and Toontown is saved.

The above synopsis is short on detail, for it's virtually impossible to convey accurately in words the bedazzling brilliance of this truly original work. A film that must be *seen* to be fully understood and appreciated, WHO FRAMED ROGER RABBIT is a movie-lover's feast that celebrates Hollywood studios, *film noir*, slapstick comedy, and—most importantly—animation. This film crosses boundaries heretofore unbroken in Hollywood moviemaking. Certainly, the boundary between human actors and animated characters has been breached before, but never with such amazing skill. More importantly, the mundane, but seemingly insurmountable, legal boundaries of copyright and trademark have been shattered through unheard-of cooperation between studios to make the film. This allowed such Disney icons as Mickey Mouse and Donald Duck to not only share screen space, but interact with, Warner Bros. characters like Bugs Bunny and Daffy Duck. And it isn't merely Disney and Warners figures who participate, but also Paramount's Betty Boop, MGM's Droopy Dog, Universal's Woody Woodpecker, and a host of other immediately recognizable characters that walk in and out of frame along with the human actors. The technical wizardry of the film, headed up by director of animation Richard Williams with assistance from Industrial Light and Magic and a small army of animators, cannot be praised enough. Filmmakers have been combining humans and cartoon characters since the beginning of filmmaking—in fact, the 1940 Warner Bros. cartoon, "You Ought to Be in Pictures" by Friz Freleng, is a direct precursor to WHO FRAMED ROGER RABBIT (in it, Porky Pig and Daffy Duck storm into the real office of Leon Schlesinger, the head of Warners' animation department, to demand better treatment)—but never before have live action and animation been combined so convincingly. Volumes have already been written detailing the complicated technical aspects of the production, but, simply put, WHO FRAMED ROGER RABBIT works by matching the play of light and shadow on the animated characters with the *film noir* lighting on the live-action set, by having the Toons interact with *real* props, by eliciting convincing performances from the actors who must imagine the presence of the Toons they are playing a scene with, and by actually moving the camera for optimum visual impact. In doing so—with a skill and verve never before seen—Zemeckis and company succeed in persuading the audience that the Toons actually exist alongside human beings. It is a testament to the skill of all involved that after a mere 10 minutes the gee-whiz quality of the effect wears off and the viewer has fully accepted this wholly unique movie universe. Although the most famous cartoon characters essentially make cameo appearances, the new faces—Roger Rabbit, Jessica, Baby Herman, Bennie the Cab, and the weasels—are fully realized, nuanced, interesting, endearing characters. Not only does this work to create audience empathy for the Toons, but Zemeckis and his wizards have also created a whole new set of lasting animated characters.

While the movie works brilliantly on the purely visual level, there are a few problems with the narrative. The pace of this feature-length film is that of a seven-minute vintage cartoon, and the action is almost relentless: one can be overwhelmed with the sheer amount of visual information bombarding from the screen, and may be left feeling assaulted. In addition, while the *film noir* plot elements, reminiscent of CHINATOWN, work just fine both as narrative and *hommage* (although the lament of the death of the trolley-car system will truly resonate only for residents of smog-choked Los Angeles), the exploitation and subsequent superficial treatment of racial issues—reflected in the discrimination against the Toons—is a bit dismaying if taken at more than face value. While WHO FRAMED ROGER RABBIT is the apex of Spielberg's brand of filmmaking, it still suffers from a distinctly shallow social and political viewpoint, one that says more about the filmmakers than it does about the serious topics occasionally broached. These problems, unfortunately, can be chalked up to the distressing lack of substance common to most Hollywood product of the 1980s.

Nevertheless, in the case of WHO FRAMED ROGER RABBIT thematic shortcomings can be forgiven, for the film's production stands as a monument to what can be done in Hollywood when there is heartfelt cooperation between studios, writers, technicians, animators, and actors to pitch in and work toward a shared vision. As critic Jonathan Rosenbaum asked in his review, who indeed *framed* Roger Rabbit? Filmmaking is an intensely collaborative art form in which the director is generally credited with authorship—it is his or her *vision* that dictates the process. But in WHO FRAMED ROGER RABBIT, how can one separate, evaluate, and judge the invaluable contributions of all who helped make it work? From the novel on which it was loosely based to the final cut, many, many "visions" contributed to the creation of this film. Who is to say that the vision of Zemeckis, the director of the live action, is more important than that of Williams, the director of the animation? Doesn't Charles Fleischer, whose incredible vocal talents gave speech to Roger Rabbit and a host of other characters in the film, share in the creation of the animated characters? Bob Hoskins must surely receive substantial credit for the film's success, for it is his vision—his ability literally to see the cartoon characters in the empty air around him—that persuades us to suspend our disbelief. And what of Spielberg himself, who not only gave director Zemeckis his start, but who personally negotiated with the various studios to secure the rights to the dozens of cartoon characters, an essential element that lends the film its unique vibrancy and very special charm? Once again, WHO FRAMED ROGER RABBIT crosses another boundary and forces us to look at the process afresh. With a hook that has been proven timeless (animation), dazzling technique, appealing characters, an interesting plot, and lots of humor and action, WHO FRAMED ROGER RABBIT is a movie that begs to be seen again and again. Cynics may argue, given the simplistic give-the-people-what-they-want quality of much of the Steven Spielberg-George Lucas output, that WHO FRAMED ROGER RABBIT is merely the latest in the line of expertly crafted, but ultimately empty, blockbusters designed for multiple viewings and maximum merchandising. But—while it's certainly a megahit ($150 million at the US box office alone and still rising) and the merchandising of it is pervasive (Roger Rabbit is already a staple at Disneyland and Disney World)—this is, finally, a film that warrants all the attention and deserves the success. WHO FRAMED ROGER RABBIT is the richest, most multifaceted Hollywood blockbuster in ages, and, most importantly, it has an age*less* quality, one which will thrill many generations to come. *(Comic violence.)*

p, Robert Watts, Frank Marshall; d, Robert Zemeckis; w, Jeffrey Price, Peter S. Seaman (based on the book *Who Censored Roger Rabbit?* by Gary K. Wolf); ph, Dean Cundey (Rank Color); ed, Arthur Schmidt; m, Alan Silvestri; prod d, Elliot Scott, Roger Cain; art d, Stephen Scott; set d, Peter Howitt; spec eff, Peter Biggs, Brian Morrison, Roger Nichols, David Watson, Brian Lince, Tony Dunsterville, Brian Warner; cos, Joanna Johnston; ch, Quinny Sacks, David Toguri; anim, Richard Williams; stunts, Peter Diamond; makeup, Peter Robb-King.

Animation/Comedy/Mystery **(PR:A MPAA:PG)**

WILDFIRE †(1988) 98m Jerry Tokofsky-Stanley R. Zupnik/Zupnik Cinema Group c

Steven Bauer *(Frank)*, Linda Fiorentino *(Kay)*, Will Patton *(Mike)*, Marshall Bell *(Lewis)*, Sandra Seacat, Richard Bradford, Alisha Byrd-Pena, Jonah Ellers-Issacs, Michelle Mayberry, William Hall, Sarah Luck Pearson, Jack Spratt.

This tragic tale of a romance begins when two children meet in an orphanage. As teenagers, the boy, Bauer (THE BEAST), and the girl, Fiorentino (THE MODERNS), bust out of the institution and hit the road together. Penniless, Bauer decides to rob a bank, but is caught and sent to prison, while Fiorentino is adopted by a nice, middle-class family and winds up marrying safe and stable yuppie Patton (NEAR DARK). All is more or less well until, predictably, Bauer is released from prison and shows up at Fiorentino's door with his cellmate, Bell. Fiorentino is not happy to see Bauer and tells him to forget the past, but when Patton goes out of town on business, she begins seeing Bauer again. Upon finding this out, Patton becomes insanely jealous, refusing to believe Fiorentino's protestations that the dates with Bauer have been strictly platonic. Patton's attitude drives Fiorentino back into the arms of Bauer, and she accompanies Bauer and Bell on a ride to San Diego, where Bauer has taken a job restoring vintage cars. The hot-headed Patton follows, of course, and violence ensues. Directed and cowritten by Zalman King, who wrote the screenplays to the execrable 9 1/2 WEEKS and TWO MOON JUNCTION, WILDFIRE was shown at the Montreal World Film Festival to negative reviews and seems unlikely to get a theatrical release.

p, Jerry Tokofsky, Hunt Lowry; d, Zalman King; w, Matthew Bright, Zalman King (based on a story by Matthew Bright); ph, Bill Butler; ed, Caroline Biggerstaff; m, Maurice Jarre; prod d, Geoffrey Kirkland.

Drama   **(PR:NR MPAA:PG)**

WILLOW**   (1988) 125m Lucasfilm-Imagine-MGM/MGM-UA c

Val Kilmer (*Madmartigan*), Joanne Whalley (*Sorsha, Bavmorda's Daughter*), Warwick Davis (*Willow*), Jean Marsh (*Queen Bavmorda*), Patricia Hayes (*Fin Raziel*), Billy Barty (*High Aldwin*), Pat Roach (*Gen. Kael*), Gavan O'Herlihy (*Airk Thaughbaer*), David Steinberg (*Meegosh*), Phil Fondacaro (*Vohnkar*), Tony Cox, Robert Gillibrand (*Vohnkar Warriors*), Mark Northover (*Burglekutt, Prefect*), Kevin Pollak (*Rool*), Rick Overton (*Franjean*), Maria Holvoe (*Cherlindrea*), Julie Peters (*Kiaya*), Mark Vande Brake (*Ranon*), Dawn Downing (*Mims*), Michael Cotterill (*Druid*), Zulema Dene (*Ethna*), Joanna Dickens (*Barmaid*), Jennifer Guy (*The Wench*), Ron Tarr (*Llug*), Sallyanne Law (*Mother*), Ruth Greenfield, Kate Greenfield (*Elora Danan*).

© MGM/UA

After 11 years of watching every nickel-and-dime outfit rip off STAR WARS, producer George Lucas finally decided to rip it off himself. The long-awaited WILLOW was shrouded in secrecy from its inception, and, as it turns out, for very good reason: the script is a blatant rewrite of STAR WARS. Every major character in WILLOW has a counterpart in STAR WARS, and the plot lines are almost exactly the same. The distressingly familiar story is set in a magical land sometime during prehistory, when trolls, brownies, fairies, and sorcerers are the order of the day. The kingdom is ruled by an evil empire controlled by a ruthless sorceress (Marsh, as a combination Darth Vader/Evil Emperor). Worried by a prophecy that proclaims that a baby girl will one day grow up to overthrow the empire, Marsh rounds up all the pregnant women and searches for a baby girl born with a special birthmark. When the child is born, however, a courageous midwife spirits the baby away, and when about to be slaughtered by Marsh's fearsome Death Dogs (canines in wart-hog costumes), she sends the child downriver like the baby Moses. The infant floats into the land of the Newlyns, a society of little people. Two Newlyn children discover the baby and call for their brave and compassionate father, Willow Ufgood (Davis, in the Luke Skywalker role). Davis and his family take the child and decide to raise it as their own, but the baby's presence causes trouble for the Newlyns and it is decided that Davis must return the child to the land of the Daikinis (regular-sized people). Davis, an aspiring sorcerer's apprentice, is told by the chief Newlyn sorcerer (Barty, as Yoda) to trust the magic (the force) and believe in himself. Thus begins a lengthy quest which takes Davis into the realm of the Daikinis. At a crossroads, he meets roguish thief and expert swordsman Madmartigan (Kilmer, in the Han Solo role), and after some initial bickering, the two team up. Davis learns the true destiny of the child from a fairy princess who assigns two brownies (Pollak and Overton, as C3PO and R2D2) to help guide them to the good castle of Tir Asleen, where the child will grow up to fulfill the prophecy. She also tells them to go to a remote island and contact a good sorceress (the Obi Wan Kenobi role) for help. Unfortunately, the sorceress has been turned into a muskrat and Davis fails in several attempts to transform her back into human form (she becomes a crow, and then a goat). Meanwhile, Marsh dispatches her beautiful and loyal daughter (Whalley, in the Princess Leia role) and her dark army led by the massive General Kael (Roach, *looking* like Darth Vader, but in a part too small to actually correspond to the role in STAR WARS) to find the child. The pursuit culminates in a huge battle scene at Tir Asleen between the forces of evil and the forces of good, the latter led by brave rebel warrior O'Herlihy. During the protracted conflict Davis and Kilmer must fend off a pair of obnoxious trolls, a giant two-headed monster called the Ebersisk (Ebert-Siskel, get it?), and a horde of soldiers. Also during the battle, Kilmer and Whalley fall in love and the evil queen's daughter joins the good guys. The bad guys, however, win this round and snatch the baby, taking it back to the imposing Nockmaar castle, where Marsh begins the ceremony that will eliminate the child and the prophecy. Davis, Kilmer, Whalley, and what's left of O'Herlihy's forces are in hot pursuit, however, and they mass outside the castle gates. Undaunted, Marsh uses her magic to turn the soldiers into pigs. Davis, however, finally manages to turn the good sorceress back into a woman, whereupon she transforms the pigs

back into soldiers. Eventually there is a special-effects showdown between the good sorceress (Obi Wan Kenobi) and Marsh (Darth Vader). With Davis' help the baby is saved, good triumphs over evil, the benevolent kingdom is restored, and Davis returns to the land of Newlyn a hero.

Even when Lucas penned STAR WARS this material was nothing new. The entire saga was inspired by a diversity of source materials ranging from the Bible and world mythology to FLASH GORDON serials and THE WIZARD OF OZ. What Lucas did with his conglomeration of ancient legends and modern pop icons was to realize it in such a grand, spectacular, and exciting way that this oft-told tale of good versus evil seemed fresh and new to millions of moviegoers. This, combined with a savvy merchandising campaign that saw the manufacture and sale of thousands of STAR WARS-related items—everything from toys to underwear—made Lucas' simple little morality play a multi*billion*-dollar industry. The incredible financial success of STAR WARS spawned a rash of imitations, each seeking to re-create the effective formula of the original. What had begun as an inspired retelling of ancient legends quickly became a boring and predictable movie cliche. Even the subsequent installments of the STAR WARS trilogy seemed to suffer from market overkill, each less effective than the one before it. By the time RETURN OF THE JEDI was released, more creative energy was funneled into the exploitation of the lucrative ancillary merchandizing and state-of-the-art special effects technique than simple storytelling. By the late 1980s the genre had sunk deep into self-parody.

Now, 11 years later, Lucas has tried to recapture the magic with WILLOW. Once again Lucas has tapped into the Bible, J.R.R. Tolkien, fairy tales, Jonathan Swift, PINOCCHIO, and many, many others, but this time he is content to merely parrot STAR WARS for his characters and plot, turning the patriarchal conflict in STAR WARS into a matriarchal conflict here. While the undiscriminating probably won't care about such obvious borrowing, WILLOW is just as uninspired on the cinematic level. Beautifully photographed on stunning locations in New Zealand and Wales, the film does not have many technical faults—although the usually flawless work of Industrial Light and Magic is surprisingly spotty. Poor Ron Howard—who, after two interesting adult fantasies, SPLASH and COCOON, has hitched his directorial wagon onto a Lucas train that is running in circles. Lucas' laziness seems to have infected Howard's direction, which is wholly uninspired. His camera placement is dictated by the special effects, his action scenes are unimaginatively staged, he continually cuts to cheap oh-so-cute reaction shots of the amazingly expressive infant, and he seems content to merely re-create tour-de-force sequences from other films. Every aspect of WILLOW seems as if it were written in stone before a shot was filmed, and the movie grinds on inescapably to its predictable climax, with the viewer fully aware of what awaits long before the film catches up to him. Where STAR WARS had great success in launching promising careers for a cast of virtual unknowns (although Harrison Ford is the only one to have gone on to what can be considered actual stardom), WILLOW's cast, with few exceptions, is unremarkable. Most of the performances are either hopelessly vague or over the top, with only 18-year-old Warwick Davis making any impression (not because of great acting ability, but because he becomes an ingratiating presence in an otherwise dull movie). The conventions have become so tired at this point that audiences need more than a change of setting and state-of-the-art special effects to enthrall them.

As with STAR WARS before it, the amount of pre-release WILLOW merchandizing is mind-boggling. Major corporations have jockeyed for position on the WILLOW bandwagon in the hopes of capitalizing on what they hope to be the next STAR WARS. General Foods, Kraft, Ziploc, Quaker Oats, Wendy's, Tonka, Parker Bros., Dow, Beatrice, Random House, and Ballantine are just a few of the corporations granted licensing agreements by Lucasfilm. Once again, more creative energy has gone into the ancillary merchandizing than into the making of the film. One would like to believe that George Lucas is a money-grubbing cynic hoping to bamboozle the public into committing their pocketbooks to another round of sequels and toys that will net him billions of dollars. Instead it appears, sadly, that he is merely a creatively burned-out filmmaker incapable of advancing beyond the concept that made his name a household word. (*Violence*.)

p, Nigel Wooll; d, Ron Howard; w, Bob Dolman (based on a story by George Lucas); ph, Adrian Biddle (Rank Color); ed, Daniel Hanley, Michael Hill; m, James Horner; prod d, Allan Cameron; art d, Tim Hutchinson, Tony Reading, Malcolm Stone; spec eff, John Richardson; cos, Barbara Lane; ch, Eleanor Fazan; stunts, Gerry Crampton; makeup, Nick Dudman, Alan Boyle.

Fantasy   **Cas.**   **(PR:AA MPAA:PG)**

WINGS OF DESIRE*****   (1988, Fr./W. Ger.) 130m Road-Argos-WDR/Orion Classics bw

Bruno Ganz (*Damiel*), Solveig Dommartin (*Marion*), Otto Sander (*Cassiel*), Curt Bois (*Homer*), Peter Falk (*Peter Falk*).

Wim Wenders' latest creation is a visual poem about the walls that exist in our world—those that separate fiction from reality, Heaven from Earth, history from the present, those who observe from those who feel, East Berlin from West Berlin, black and white from color, angels from mortals. Ganz and Sander play two of the angels that inhabit WINGS OF DESIRE. They are not your usual fairy-tale creatures, but middle-aged men in overcoats wearing their hair in small, fashionable ponytails. These heavenly bodies circulate in a black-and-white Berlin, the one part of the world that has seemed closest to hell in this century, where they "observe, collect, testify, and preserve" the world around them. Unseen by all but innocent children, the angels involve themselves in the lives of mortals, offering invisible comforts. When a wounded man lies on the street, the angels are nearby. As the troubled Berliners ride the bus, the angels are seated beside them, listening to their thoughts. Perched atop the Victory Column or the steeple of the Kaiser Wilhelm church, they keep a close watch over their city, and, like radio antennas, receive the signals—the voices and sounds—of their Berliners. But, while most mortals live in the hope of rising to the heavens for a peaceful afterlife, one of the angels—Ganz—desires the opposite. He longs to feel, not just emotionally but physically as well. To touch people *and* things, and to be touched in return, to see and be seen, to taste and smell coffee, to feel a rock. From above, angels Ganz and Sander zero in on three individuals—an octogenarian poet, Bois (the 86-year-old film veteran of CASABLANCA, among others); an American film and TV star, Falk (playing himself); and a French trapeze artist, Dommartin. It is Dommartin who sends thoughts of mortality into Ganz's head. Herself an angel of sorts, Dommartin soars through the air on her trapeze with a pair a manufactured wings attached to her back. For a moment Ganz sees her, as all mortals do, in color—a brief flash of human perception that further awakens his desire. The figure of Bois, on the other hand, represents something equally as important as Dommartin's symbolic synthesis of the mortal and the heavenly: a poet who remembers the old Berlin before the Wall, he is the physical embodiment of Germany's past and present. Bois walks through an empty, ruinous field and reflects on the life that once took place there, remembering the time when poets formed a community and would read their works to one another, instead of the present practice of being read from a private distance. This old Berlin is re-created when an American film crew comes to Berlin to make a WW II film. The streets of the film set are lined with Gestapo agents, Hitler youth, Jews, and Germans alike; there are no divisions now, as all of these characters are actors hired to reenact the past before the cameras. Playing the lead in the film is Falk, to whose aura Ganz is attracted for some reason yet unknown. While Sander is content with his existence as an angel, he is aware of Ganz's discontent. The two talk for the last time, and, at the dividing line between the physical and the ethereal (just a few yards from the border guards of the Wall), Ganz becomes mortal. He sees the world in colors. He is now free to pursue his romantic ideal of loving Dommartin. In the meantime, he visits the set of the WW II film. There, Falk reveals to Ganz that he, too, is a "fallen" angel, and that there are others all around the world. (Wenders has dedicated this film to "all former angels," including directors Francois Truffaut, Yasujiro Ozu, and Andrei Tarkovsky.) After Ganz meets Dommartin in the flesh, the two express, in the most purely romantic of terms, their eternal, undying love for one another—Ganz's final proof that Heaven exists on Earth. Ganz exclaims: "I know now what no angel knows." After his self-imposed exile in America, where he made HAMMETT; THE STATE OF THINGS; and PARIS, TEXAS; Wenders returned to his native West Germany to make WINGS OF DESIRE, his greatest film since 1976's KINGS OF THE ROAD. He has assembled a remarkable cast led by Bruno Ganz, a man whose face seems to have been created solely for the purpose of being filmed by Wenders. It is as if Ganz's face is emitting its own light and exposing the film. The truth, however, is that the face was lit and photographed by Henri Alekan, one of the foremost cinematographers of French film. Alekan, who filmed WINGS OF DESIRE at 79 years of age, is probably best remembered as the man who filmed Jean Cocteau's classic fairy tale BEAUTY AND THE BEAST, as well as Wenders' 1983 THE STATE OF THINGS. This film is as much an ode to Alekan's magic as it is to a city and romance—as noted by Wenders' playful naming of Dommartin's traveling circus troupe Cirque Alekan. Although much of the influence on WINGS OF DESIRE can be traced to Cocteau's filmic depiction of angels or to German poet Rainer Maria Rilke's writings, the film's roots are perhaps closest to Walter Ruttmann's classic 1927 silent documentary SYMPHONY OF A CITY. WINGS OF DESIRE, too, is a symphony on Berlin, though under Wenders' direction the city limits (which have been bisected by the Wall) become fantastic, extending far above to include those angels who keep a watchful eye on the world below. While so much of Wenders' early work (THE GOALIE'S ANXIETY AT THE PENALTY KICK; ALICE IN THE CITIES; KINGS OF THE ROAD; THE AMERICAN FRIEND; HAMMETT) shows a fascination with American culture, food, cars, films, and (most obviously) rock'n'roll, WINGS OF DESIRE concentrates far more on the particularly German Berlin.

The film fulfills the promise of the new directorial direction hinted at in PARIS, TEXAS. Where alienation and wanderlust were far more prevalent in early Wenders films, romance and emotion are now taking their place. Ganz's character, the angel Damiel, is the embodiment of all Wenders characters, and in just one two-hour-plus film he shows the development of the Wenders hero (and by extension Wenders himself) over the course of time. At the opening of WINGS OF DESIRE, Damiel is the archetypal alien—an observer who sees but is not seen, who wants to feel but cannot, and who wants to love but cannot. Like the goalie Bloch in THE GOALIE'S ANXIETY AT THE PENALTY KICK, Damiel the angel is able to stand motionless while the action on the playing field (or in this case all of Berlin) swirls around him. By the midpoint of WINGS OF DESIRE, Damiel has moved closer to Travis of PARIS, TEXAS, having found a person (in Travis' case his young son) who can pull him out of his alienated state and make him feel. By the end of WINGS OF DESIRE, Damiel has traveled further than any other Wenders character—he shares a declaration of love, purely romantic, poetic, everlasting (if, paradoxically, earthly) love. (It is perhaps relevant that Solveig Dommartin is Wenders' real-life companion; her character's presence is what transforms this alienated, director-like observer.)

One of the most curious aspects of WINGS OF DESIRE is the overwhelmingly positive reception it received. Far from the standard, mediocre, narrative art-house feature that has become the norm, Wenders' film is one of those few films which can rightly be called an essay film. It exists on a level that has almost nothing to do with the more popular forms of Hollywood-influenced art films. With its cadenced delivery of the weighty, Peter Handke-penned narration; the non-narrative structure of its opening half-hour (as the angels wander through Berlin); and the now-taboo use of black-and-white photography, one would think that WINGS OF DESIRE would alienate more audiences than it would seduce. But, like Damiel, the audience is attracted to the world Wenders parades before our eyes. Having torn down the wall (perhaps only temporarily) that exists between art film and commercial film, Wenders has, like Damiel, succeeded in touching his audience and crossing the dividing line between the fantastic and the real. His efforts were rewarded by the jury of the 1987 Cannes Film Festival, which named Wenders Best Director. Besides Jurgen Knieper's ethereal music, the score includes "The Carny," "From Her to Eternity" (Nick Cave and the Bad Seeds); "Six Bells Chime" (Crime and the City Solution); "Angel Fragments" (Laurie Anderson); "Les Filles du Calvaire" (Laurent Petitgand); "Pas Attendre" (Sprung aus den Wolken); "Some Guys" (Tuxedomoon) and "When I Go" (Minimal Compact). (In German; English subtitles.)

p, Wim Wenders, Anatole Dauman; d, Wim Wenders; w, Wim Wenders, Peter Handke; ph, Henri Alekan; ed, Peter Przygodda; m, Jurgen Knieper; prod d, Heidi Ludi; cos, Monika Jacobs.

Fantasy **(PR:C MPAA:PG-13)**

WITHOUT A CLUE**½ (1988) 106m ITC/Orion c

Michael Caine ("Sherlock Holmes" / Reginald Kinkaid), Ben Kingsley *(Dr. Watson)*, Jeffrey Jones *(Inspector Lestrade)*, Lysette Anthony *(Fake Leslie)*, Matthew Sim *(Real Leslie)*, Paul Freeman *(Dr. Moriarty)*, Nigel Davenport *(Lord Smithwick)*, Pat Keen *(Mrs. Hudson)*, Peter Cook *(Greenhough)*, Tim Killick *(Sebastian)*, Mathew Savage *(Wiggins)*, John Warner *(Peter Giles)*, Harold Innocent *(Mayor Johnson)*, George Sweeney *(John Clay)*, Murray Ewan *(Archie)*, Stephen Tiller, Michael O'Hagan, Ivor Roberts *(Reporters)*, Martin Pallot *(Photographer)*, Gregor Fisher *(Bobby at Warehouse)*, Caroline Milmoe *(Constance)*, Steven O'Donnell *(Bartender)*, James Bree *(Barrister)*, Sarah Parr-Byrne *(Singer)*, Clive Mantle, Dave Cooper *(Thugs)*, Richard Henry *(Hadlers)*, Lesley Daine *(Lady on Train)*, Jennifer Guy *(Christabel)*, John Tordoff *(Mr. Andrews)*, Alexandra Spencer *(Mrs. Andrews)*, Elizabeth Kelly *(Landlady)*, Sam Davies, Adam Kotz *(Locals)*, John Surman *(Constable at Lakes)*, Les White, Chris Webb *(Henchmen)*, Andy Bradford *(Dockworker)*, Evan Russell *(Sergeant at Docks)*, Alan Bodenham *(Driver)*, Prince the Dog *(The Duke)*.

There has been no shortage of revisionist film treatments of Arthur Conan Doyle's Sherlock Holmes in recent years. The 1975 comedy THE ADVENTURES OF SHERLOCK HOLMES' SMARTER BROTHER starred Gene Wilder (who also wrote and directed) as the famous sleuth's highly competitive sibling; in 1977, Nicholas Meyer penned THE SEVEN PER-CENT SOLUTION, which presented Holmes as a cocaine addict helped by a young Dr. Sigmund Freud; and 1988's YOUNG SHERLOCK HOLMES imagined the early school friendship between Holmes and Watson. WITHOUT A CLUE is an even greater departure from Conan Doyle's original stories and the familiar screen treatments that starred Basil Rathbone and Nigel Bruce. Its central premise is that Dr. John Watson (Kingsley) is the real crime solver and that Sherlock Holmes (Caine) is actually an undistinguished actor by the name of Reginald Kincaid, hired by Kingsley to portray the sleuth he'd made famous in his accounts for the *Strand* magazine. It seems that Kingsley had been up for a prestigious medical appointment and didn't want his moonlight sleuthing to work against his chances, so he invented Sherlock Holmes to take credit for the mysteries he continued to solve. Eventually the public became so hungry for a glimpse of Holmes that Caine, fresh from the stage disaster "Shadow of Death," was hired, given an Inverness cape, and presented to the world as the great sleuth. The problem is that Caine, an inveterate drunk totally lacking in the powers of deduction for which Holmes is so famous, has grown too big for his deerstalker hat and has taken to departing from the script when faced with the adoring press. Fed up, Kingsley gives Caine the sack, determined to make his own name as the Crime Doctor. Unfortunately, his *Strand* editor (Cook) doesn't want to hear of such things and no one seems to take Kingsley seriously as an investigator. The Chancellor of the Exchequer (Davenport), in a tizzy because the printing plate for the five-pound note has been stolen from the Royal Mint and replaced with a forgery, comes seeking Caine's help and isn't about to trust anyone else with a matter that could determine the fate of the empire. Kingsley is forced to rehire Caine for *one* more case, and, trailed by longtime Scotland Yard rival Jones, they go in search of Warner, a Royal Mint printer who has recently disappeared. The trail leads them to the Lake District, where an attempt is made on Kingsley's life, and the clever doctor deduces that the nefarious Prof. Moriarty (Freeman) is behind things. Caine and Kingsley have also taken into their protection Anthony, Warner's daughter, whom Freeman's goons try unsuccessfully to kidnap. Eventually, Caine and Kingsley confront Freeman and company on the docks at night and in the ensuing encounter the doctor is apparently killed. Caine becomes distraught and hits the bottle, but after deciding to redeem the honor of Kingsley, Caine uses his best deductive powers to determine . . . well, more or less nothing. Soon, however, one of the Baker Street Irregulars, Kingsley's street urchin assistants, arrives with a clue, a five-pound note printed on regular paper that has three serial numbers instead of the usual six. Caine determines that the serial number has been used by Warner as a clue to his location, and deduces that the number refers to the 23 Psalms and, by association, to the theater where "Shadow of Death" played. With housekeeper Keen providing backup, Caine heads for the theater, where the film reaches it rousing climax.

Beyond its clever role reversal, WITHOUT A CLUE doesn't offer many surprises (though the above synopsis leaves out a few, for the sake of those who aren't able to figure everything out before it happens). It does, however, feature fine comic performances by Michael Caine and Ben Kingsley. Directed by Thom Eberhardt (NIGHT OF THE COMET), this particular Sherlock Holmes film works much better as a buddy picture than as a mystery, and Kingsley and Caine have an engaging Laurel and Hardy-like chemistry. Kingsley, in his first film comedy role, vacillates wonderfully between logical equanimity and subtle exasperation (as usual, communicated mostly with his eyes) as the straight man who doesn't suffer Caine's foolishness easily. Caine, on the other hand, is a delightfully affable bumbler, boozer, and womanizer, the antithesis of everything that Sherlock Holmes has come to represent in the popular imagination.

Based on a screenplay by Gary Murphy and Larry Strawther (story editors for TV's "Night Court"), WITHOUT A CLUE is full of slapstick touches that will snowball for some viewers and become tedious for others. It's one of those movies: either one finds its one-joke premise endlessly amusing or one gets tired of it very quickly. The mystery itself, complicated by not particularly inventive twists and turns, is relatively predictable, and there isn't anything here that is going to put anybody on the edge of his seat, but even when the plot slows down or the slapstick becomes tiresome there are still the broad but amusing performances. In addition to the excellent work by Caine and Kingsley, Jeffrey Jones (Emperor Josef II in AMADEUS) contributes a brilliantly befuddled portrayal of Inspector Lestrade, Holmes' erstwhile Scotland Yard rival, and Pat Keen (CLOCKWISE) is properly loyal and bluff as Mrs. Hudson, 221-B Baker Street's housekeeper, who knows as well as Kingsley just how inept Caine really is. As with the other recent Holmes revisions, the production design for WITHOUT A CLUE is excellent, and cinematographer Alan Hume (A FISH CALLED WANDA) uses a variety of London locations—including the Camden Lock Canal, Clapham's Victoria Crescent, the Cambridge Theatre, and Hackney's Empire Theatre—to nicely evoke Victorian England. Made for $9 million, the film has already spawned a screenplay for a sequel, the production future of which will depend on WITHOUT A CLUE's long-term success at the box office and video stores. (Adult situations.)

p, Marc Stirdivant; d, Thom Eberhardt; w, Gary Murphy, Larry Strawther; ph, Alan Hume (Rank color); ed, Peter Tanner; m, Henry Mancini; prod d, Brian Ackland-Snow; art d, Terry Ackland-Snow, Tom Brown; set d, Peter James, Ian Whittaker; spec eff, Ian Wingrove; cos, Judy Moorcroft; stunts, Paul Weston; makeup, Peter Frampton, Lois Burwell.

Comedy   Cas.   (PR:A-C MPAA:PG)

WIZARD OF LONELINESS, THE**   (1988) 110m Virgin Vision-American
                                                          Playhouse/Skouras c

Lukas Haas (Wendall Olet), Lea Thompson (Sybil), Lance Guest (John T.), John Randolph (Doc), Dylan Baker (Duffy), Anne Pitoniak (Cornelia), Jeremiah Warner (Tom), Steve Hendrickson, Andrea Matheson.

Based on a novel by John Nichols, the author of The Milagro Beanfield War, THE WIZARD OF LONELINESS is an atmospheric coming-of-age tale set in a small Vermont town during WW II. Lukas Haas, best remembered for his wide-eyed performance in WITNESS, plays a precocious 12-year-old who is sent to live with his grandparents when his unloving mother dies and his father leaves to fight in the war. Sullen and fiercely independent, Haas makes little effort to fit in with either his family or the quaint New England community. He thinks himself to have great powers, and when angered imagines himself willing horrible fates on the offending parties. Grandfather Randolph, a kindly physician, tries to ease the boy's adjustment; grandmother Pitoniak is less understanding, particularly when she discovers that Haas has been stealing quarters in order to come up with train fare out of town. A leg injury has prevented Guest, Haas' young uncle, from entering the service, and he regales his unathletic nephew with stories of his father's prowess as a baseball player. Rounding out the household are Haas' pretty aunt, Thompson, a war widow, and Warner, her cute-as-a-button little son, who is Haas' frequent companion. Both Guest and Thompson mourn the death of Baker—his best friend, her former lover—who is thought to have been killed in the war. Actually, Baker has returned to the small town unnoticed. With his face transformed by a bushy beard, he sneaks around town, skittishly revealing himself to Thompson. His mind, however, has been warped by combat, and, given to fits of violence, he harms both Thompson and Warner—his son. Haas watches this drama unfold, and becomes inextricably involved with Baker's madness, until the boy becomes a participant in the film's violent, tragic climax.

Drenched in golden-hued nostalgia, THE WIZARD OF LONELINESS looks and often feels like it was directed by Norman Rockwell, but, seen from the perspective of Haas—the withdrawn, disdainful outsider—this close-knit small-town world is hardly idyllic. Moreover, something is askew in the little community. Its normal life has been interrupted by the war, and the battle-scarred Baker's haunting presence, which brings the tragedy of the war home, has as much to do with the ominous tone that pervades the film as does Haas' detachment. Unfortunately, the film's mood swings don't always work, primarily because the uneven screenplay is sabotaged by implausibilities. Just as the film begins to cast a magical spell, some inexplicable occurrence snaps the viewer back to self-consciousness. This is not merely a breakdown of willing suspension of disbelief, rather, it is a failure to create a consistent dramatic reality. The foremost offender is Baker's crucial presence. If the story were to take place over a matter of days or even weeks, it would be believable that Baker might roam the town unnoticed, but since the film covers more than a year, it is unthinkable that this man whose death has been commemorated with a plaque in the center of town would not have called more attention to himself. Part of the problem here is Dylan Baker's unconvincing performance in the difficult but pivotal role of the shattered veteran. Somehow, the blend of tenderness and terror with which he invests his character lacks the necessary weight. He seems too much like a character, too little like a real person. Similarly, the film's shocking ending has less to do with reality or dramatic necessity than it does with arriving at a convenient way to tie together thematic loose ends. Director Jenny Bowen (STREET MUSIC) and screenwriter Nancy Larson are more successful when dealing with Haas' interaction with his family and the world, but when the focus shifts to Baker, their film loses its impact. Lukas Haas contributes a fine performance as the odd, initially unsympathetic but ultimately endearing "wizard," and Lea Thompson, Lance Guest, and John Randolph also do nice turns. Many who see THE WIZARD OF LONELINESS, however, will remember the charming performance by 4-year-old Vermonter Jeremiah Warner better than anything else about the film, which is nice testimony to this first-time child actor's talents, but doesn't say much for this moody and disappointing film. (Violence, profanity, sexual situations, adult situations.)

p, Thom Tyson, Philip Porcella; d, Jenny Bowen; w, Nancy Larson (based on the novel by John Nichols); ph, Richard Bowen; ed, Lisa Day; m, Michel Colombier; prod d, Jeffrey Beecroft; cos, Stephanie Maslansky.

Drama   Cas.   (PR:C MPAA:PG-13)

WIZARD OF SPEED AND TIME, THE †   (1988) 98m Hollywood
                                          Wizard-Rochambeau-Shapiro Glickenhaus/Medusa c

Mike Jittlov (Mike/The Wizard/Torch Carrier), Richard Kaye (Harvey Bookman), Paige Moore (Cindy Lite/Dancer/Pretty Hitchhiker), David Conrad (Brian Lucas), Steve Brodie (Lucky Straeker), John Massari (Steve Shostakovich), Gary Schwartz (Geoff), Frank LaLoggia (Mutton), Philip Michael Thomas (Mick Polanko), Lynda Aldon (Minnie Smith), Baron (Pluto), Arnetia Walker (Tina Dream), Ben Kronen (C.C. de Schwartz), Angelique Pettyjohn (Dora Belair), Will Ryan (All the Union Clerks), Michelle Roth (Mary Lou Trew), Greg Jittlov (Greg Jittlov), Marie Jittlov (Mom Jittlov), Harvey Alperin (Harold de Schwartz), Missy Sauppe (Harold's Groupie), Paulette Breen (Virginia Slimm), Steven Stucker (S. Chesterfield), Lauri Riley (Girl Choreographer), Amy Rose (Sun Woman), Mark Conlon (Moon Man), Chuck McCollum (Meteor Man), Rob Reed (Studio Comedian), Patrick McGreal (Jupiter Man), Donovan Scott (Convict Actor), Paul Barselou (Angus MacTavish), David McCharren (Video Technician LSD), Joan Leizman (Muriel Bookman), Cynthia Frost (Paula Maul), Ward Kimball (IRS Chief), Christopher Barczak (Hollywood Tourist), Tim Frisbee (Studio Projectionist), Alan Lee Graf, Frank Davis, Jr. (Bookman's Guards), Rick Heebner (Bicycle Thief), Ben Lum (Studio Gateguard), Hal Etherington (Studio Director), Phil Boroff (Studio Writer), Steve Ecclesine (Video Editor), Doug Crepeau (Satellite Buyer), William Z. Ryan (Mr. President), Patricia Thomson (Girl on Suitcase), Bob Basso (Rollie), Annie Livingston (Skatelady), Pete Sorenson (Dancing Film Man), Patty Ryan (Bouncy Artiste), Evelyn Carpenter (Old Woman), Eddie Paul (Cycle Gang Leader), Slim E. Leatche (IRS Agent), Smokey Ochoa, Jeff Knoerle (Ying & Yang), Wilimeda Behanna, Anyavel Glynn, Jan Sayre (Prison Guards), The Unknown Producer (Ms. Belair's Playmate), Randi D. Cogert, Tery McPhie, Gwen Perlman, Monica B. Herzer (Girls in Avanti), Beth Sjogren, Galen Gorg (C.C.'s Groupies), Steve Mann (Boom Man/Captain Kung Fu), Laurie Rose (Laurie), Chris Coart (Blue Wizard), Christine Green (White Wizardess), William Hart, Jean Hart (Bearded Swordsman and Lady), Nick Worth, Frank Davis (Bouncers).

Mike Jittlov, a director of short films which concentrate on special effects and stop-motion animation, directed, wrote, edited, and stars in this film-within-a-film project about, appropriately enough, a special effect wiz. Jittlov plays himself (as well as a fantasy character known as the Wizard of Speed and Time), an aspiring filmmaker who visits a Hollywood studio to show his special effects reel to a producer. The producer is planning a television series on special effects and Jittlov hopes his film will be included. The show's director, convinced of the newcomer's talent, makes a $25,000 bet with the shady producer that Jittlov will deliver a great film. Since Jittlov has no cash he persuades his girl friend, family, and friends to take part—all of them lending a hand. When it becomes obvious that Jittlov will succeed and the show's director will win the bet, the producer hires some thugs to interfere with production. Naturally, good triumphs over evil, and Jittlov hits the big time. A curiously, self-congratulatory and self-deifying picture which saw a brief theatrical release in 1988. Songs include "Let's Not Get Married" (Diggy), "Carnivale Party Music" (Embra-Samba Band), "Creation" (The Riot Act).

p, Richard Kaye, Mike Jittlov, Deven Chierighino; d, Mike Jittlov; w, Mike Jittlov, Richard Kaye, Deven Chierighino; ph, Russell Carpenter (DeLuxe Color); ed, Mike Jittlov; m, John Massari; m/l, Diggy, Embra-Samba Band, The Riot Act; cos, Linda Booker, Ms. Pettyjohn; ch, Lauri Riley; makeup, Kristine Chadwick, Scott Maxon.

Comedy/Fantasy   (PR:NR MPAA:PG)

WORKING GIRL***½   (1988) 113m FOX c

Harrison Ford (Jack Trainer), Sigourney Weaver (Katharine Parker), Melanie Griffith (Tess McGill), Alec Baldwin (Mick Dugan), Joan Cusack (Cyn), Philip Bosco (Oren Trask), Nora Dunn (Ginny), Oliver Platt (Lutz), James Lally (Turkel), Kevin Spacey (Bob Speck), Robert Easton (Armbrister), Olympia Dukakis (Personnel Director), Jeffrey Nordling (Tim Rourke), Elizabeth Whitcraft (Doreen DiMucci), Maggie Wagner, Lou DiMaggio, David Cuchovny, Georgienne Millen (Tess's Birthday Party Friends), Caroline Aaron, Nancy Giles, Judy Milstein, Nicole Chevance, Kathleen Gray, Jane B. Harris, Sondra Hollander, Samantha Shane, Julie Silverman (Petty Marsh Secretaries), Gail Bearden, Melba LaRose (Secretaries in Ladies' Room), Jim Babchak (Junior Executive), Zach Grenier (Jim), Ken Larsen, Daniel B. Pollack, Pamela Lewis (Executives at Dim Sum Party), Ralph Byers, Leslie Ayvazian (Dewey Stone Reception Guests), Steve Cody (Cab Driver), Paige Matthews (Dewey Stone Receptionist), Lee Dalton (John Romano), Barbara Garrick (Phyllis Trask), Madolin B. Archer (Barbara Trask), Etain O'Malley (Hostess at Wedding), Ricki Lake (Bridesmaid), Marceline A. Hugot (Bitsy), Tom Rooney (Bridegroom), Peter Duchin (Trask Wedding Orchestra), Maeve McGuire (Trask Secretary), Tim Carhart (Tim Draper), Michael G. Chin (Delivery Man), Lloyd Lindsay Young (TV Weatherman), F.X. Vitolo (Bartender), Lily Froehlich (Clerk at Dry Cleaners), R.M. Haley (Heliport Attendant), Mario T. DeFelice, Jr., Anthony Mancini, Jr. (Helicopter Pilots), Suzanne Shepherd (Trask Receptionist), Amy Aquino (Baxter).

Plucky, ambitious businesswomen who finagle their way to success were staples of 1930s and 40s Hollywood fare, and in WORKING GIRL Mike Nichols dusts off that formula, infuses it with a 1980s sensibility, and lends it a feminist slant. Melanie Griffith, excellent in another strong 1988 film, STORMY MONDAY, gives an even more dazzling performance here as an industrious secretary for a brokerage firm who longs for a spot in the company's special entry program. The problem is that while she's taken enough night classes to earn a college degree, her blue-collar, Staten Island background doesn't satisfy the class requirements for a fast-track position on Wall Street. After being subjected to her boss' "pimping" yet again, Griffith humiliates him, quits in a huff, and finds herself in a last-chance opportunity as the secretary to Weaver, a female boss who *has* gone to all the right schools, wears the right clothes, and says all the right things. Yet Griffith is thrilled that Weaver thinks of them as a team and encourages her to share her ideas. When the astute secretary suggests to Weaver that a chain of radio stations might be of interest to a corporate bigwig (Bosco) who is interested in getting into the communications industry, Weaver takes the plan under advisement. Later, when Weaver is laid up in Switzerland as the result of a skiing accident, Griffith, while tending to her boss' house plants, learns that Weaver has been moving ahead on *her* idea with no apparent intention of giving the secretary any credit. Returning home, looking for solace, Griffith instead discovers her fisherman boy friend (Baldwin) sleeping with another woman. Determined to teach the world a lesson, Griffith transforms her wild mane into "serious hair," borrows Weaver's stylish clothes and accent, and undertakes to engineer the big deal herself, seeking out Ford, the outside deal-maker Weaver has slated for the project who also happens to be Weaver's lover. Not only does Ford—who is anxious for a success after a recent string of failures—believe Griffith when she claims to be Weaver's colleague, but he also falls in love with the stunning blonde, who has "a head for business and a body for sin." Through a series of bold maneuvers, including crashing a wedding, Griffith and Ford persuade Bosco to consider the radio deal, but just when an agreement is about to be reached, Weaver returns from Europe, claims the whole idea to be her own, and exposes Griffith. It appears as if Weaver is back in the driver's seat, until Griffith, with only an elevator ride's duration to do so, proves the takeover plan to be hers. Before the credits roll and Carly Simon's uplifting score swirls, Weaver has lost her man and reputation, and Griffith has gained Ford and her own office and secretary.

Just as he did earlier in the year in BILOXI BLUES, director Nichols (THE GRADUATE; CATCH-22) demonstrates again his assured command of the film medium—coaxing outstanding performances from lead and supporting players alike, using the camera to brilliant effect without calling undue attention to his careful visual choreography, and infusing the story with a measured blend of tension, romance, and good humor. Working from a well-crafted screenplay by actor-turned-playwright Kevin Wade ("Key Exchange"), Nichols carefully manipulates a smattering of plot twists and creates enough doubt that one is never quite sure what to expect from the narrative or the characters: Does Ford really care about Griffith, or is Weaver too good a "deal" to pass up? Is Weaver's rhetoric about Griffith being a part of the team just a smoke screen, or, as it appears at a crucial juncture during the film's climactic sequence, is she really sincere about trying to help her? That we aren't quite sure until the final reel makes the story's upbeat resolution all the more satisfying. Moreover, while there is an air of unreality that surrounds WORKING GIRL's "Luck and Pluck" plot, the sex- and class-based barriers that prevent Griffith from getting a foot up on the corporate ladder are given the same concreteness in the film that they have in the real world. Although Wade's screenplay seemingly views striving for capitalist success as a virtue, he nonetheless uses the story to identify the hurdles that keep working-class men and women from real access to the American Dream—and, significantly, he doesn't stop there. In placing Griffith at a boss' desk with Ford's blessing, WORKING GIRL not only goes beyond any kind of OFFICER AND A GENTLEMAN knight-on-a-white-horse ending, but also offers a feminist alternative to relations between coworkers: Griffith tells *her* secretary "never to get any coffee unless she wants some herself."

©20TH CENTURY FOX

By all indications, Griffith's wonderful work in WORKING GIRL has finally made her a star. Using her breathy, little-girl voice to its best advantage as the unreconstructed secretarial Tess, then softening it as when she apes Weaver, Griffith is sensual and sincere, radiating intelligence and determination as she goes for the brass ring. As in the past, more than a little of her flesh is on display, but what makes Griffith different from other actress renowned for their sexuality is her easy voluptuousness; slightly overweight, she seems more of the everyday world, not like an actress-goddess who she spends her life working out. Sigourney Weaver makes a wonderful foil for her, efficiently capturing the refined, confident, superior attitude that would have facilitated her rise in the male-dominated world of Wall Street. Yet beneath her calculated veneer she suggests a kernel of integrity that leaves us guessing about her intentions until the very end. In a nicely understated performance, Harrison Ford projects a confused vulnerability and an underlying decency, alternating quiet confidence with a more agitated lack thereof. The romance between him and Griffith may not exactly send off sparks, but their affection for each other at film's end is certainly believable. The supporting performances are also excellent, especially that of Joan Cusack as Griffith's teased-haired, rainbow eye makeup-wearing friend. Funny, touching, and ultimately tremendously buoyant, WORKING GIRL is a "feel good" movie with intelligence. *(Nudity, profanity, sexual situations.)*

p, Douglas Wick; d, Mike Nichols; w, Kevin Wade; ph, Michael Ballhaus (DeLuxe Color); ed, Sam O'Steen; m, Carly Simon; m/l, Anita Pointer, June Pointer, Ruth Pointer, Trevor Lawrence, Chris De Burgh, Richard Rodgers, Lorenz Hart, Sonny Rollins; prod d, Patrizia Von Brandenstein; art d, Doug Kraner; set d, George DeTitta; cos, Ann Roth; stunts, Frank Ferrara, Jim Dunn; makeup, J. Roy Helland.

Crime/Romance **Cas.** **(PR:O MPAA:R)**

WORLD APART, A**** (1988, Brit.) 113m Working Title-British Screen/Atlantic c

Barbara Hershey *(Diana Roth)*, Jodhi May *(Molly Roth)*, Jeroen Krabbe *(Gus Roth)*, Carolyn Clayton-Cragg *(Miriam Roth)*, Merav Gruer *(Jude Roth)*, Yvonne Bryceland *(Bertha)*, Albee Lesotho *(Solomon)*, Linda Mvusi *(Elsie)*, Rosalie Crutchley *(Mrs. Harris)*, Mackay Tickey *(Milius)*, Tim Roth *(Harold)*, Adrian Dunbar *(Le Roux)*, Paul Freeman *(Kruger)*, David Suchet *(Muller)*, Kate Fitzpatrick *(June Abelson)*, Toby Salaman *(Gerald Abelson)*, Nadine Chalmers *(Yvonne Abelson)*, Jude Akuwidike *(Priest)*, Maria Pilar *(Spanish Dance Teacher)*, Phyllis Naidoo *(Saeeda)*, Clement Muchachi *(Sipho)*, Esma Levend *(Whitworth)*, Theresa Memela *(Peggy)*, Stephen Williams *(Arresting Officer)*, Margaret Hogan *(History Teacher)*, Jo-Anne Huckle *(Debbie)*, Nomaziko Zondo *(Thandile)*, Andre Proctor *(Arresting Officer)*, Andrew Whaley *(Interrogating Officer)*, Cont Mhlanga *(Mtutuzeli Nzekwu)*, Henry Mlauzi, The Messias Choir, Lovemore Majaivana and the Zulu Band, The Jack Buckell Band.

Set in Johannesburg in 1963, three years after the banning of the African National Congress, A WORLD APART is based on a semiautobiographical screenplay by Shawn Slovo, the daughter of Joe Slovo, head of the South African Communist Party and one of two white members of the ANC executive council, and Ruth First, who was assassinated by a parcel bomb in Mozambique in 1982. May, playing the Slovo surrogate, is a 13-year-old whose world revolves around Spanish dancing lessons, hula-hooping, and swimming in the pool of her equally privileged best friend (Chalmers), that is, until her father (Krabbe), an ANC official, departs in the middle of the night on "business" not to return, leaving her journalist mother (Hershey) both to take care of May and her two younger sisters and to continue the struggle against apartheid. Much to May's confusion, Hershey's involvement with the movement makes her not a bad mother, but a distracted, inattentive one—distant because she fears she cannot trust her daughter with life-and-death secrets. Starved for attention, May grows close to Mvusi, the family's black live-in maid, and Lesotho, Mvusi's brother, a radical political leader. When the 90-Day Detention Act, permitting the government to incarcerate an individual without charge for three months, is enacted, Hershey is the first woman to be arrested. While Hershey is tortured mentally by Suchet, who taunts her with her failure as a mother, Bryceland comes to care for her granddaughters. Meanwhile, May, ostracized by her classmates, including Chalmers, begins boarding at school, mirroring her mother's isolated life. After 90 days, Hershey is released, only to be arrested again immediately while making a phone call outside of the prison. This time her resolve breaks down, and, fearing that she will begin naming names, she attempts suicide and is sent home under house arrest. During Hershey's recovery, May learns of her suicide attempt, protects her when the police search the house, and finally demands to be kept in the dark no longer. Later, when Lesotho is murdered, mother and daughter attend his funeral together, fellow travelers in the struggle. Amid the raised fists and green, gold, and black banners, they join in singing the stirring anthem "Nkosi Sikelel'i Afrika" ; the camera pulls back to reveal encroaching Army helicopters and armored cars; tear gas flies; the unarmed black demonstrators break formation; and, in slow motion, one man scoops up a canister and prepares to heave it back as the frame freezes.

The feature film directorial debut of Academy Award-winning cinematographer Chris Menges (THE KILLING FIELDS; THE MISSION), A WORLD APART is the second major film in the last two years to deal with South African issues. Richard Attenborough's 1987 effort, CRY FREEDOM, the story of the relationship between slain Black Consciousness leader Stephen Biko and Donald Woods, the white newspaperman he radicalized, met with mixed reviews, criticized in some corners both for deifying Biko and for shifting the focus of the story from Biko and the struggle of black South Africans to Woods and the experiences of sympathetic whites. But while CRY FREEDOM was neither a box-office nor a critical success in the US, in Britain it did contribute to a 30 percent increase in membership in the anti-apartheid movement. In A WORLD APART, Menges, too, has chosen to explore the abomination of apartheid primarily through the eyes of whites, but the black characters who do play a vital role in his film are considerably more developed than the black South Africans in Attenborough's film. More than symbols or mere background players, Mvusi and Lesotho are important participants in a drama that unfolds on several levels, with crucial intersections between events taking place in two cultures. May's growing intimacy with Mvusi and Lesotho finally allows her to understand her mother's commitment to the cause, but the scenes in the township, Lesotho's speech, and his death and funeral have a resonance of their own. It's true that A WORLD APART is first and foremost a story of misunderstanding, love, and reconciliation between a mother and daughter. But although it begins with the personal, it moves patiently toward the political—ultimately showing them to be interdependent. CRY FREEDOM, on the other hand, concentrates on the big picture and larger-than-life figures, leaving it to the actors (particularly to Denzel Washington as Biko) to try to personalize its story of courage in the face of indignity.

The performances in A WORLD APART are uniformly excellent, and the extraordinarily moving work of Barbara Hershey, Jodhi May, and Linda Mvusi garnered a shared Best Actress award at the Cannes Film Festival. Hershey, who also won the award last year for her performance in SHY PEOPLE, gives a stirring portrayal of determination and grace under pressure while always hinting at the tenderness underlying the tough veneer that ultimately buckles. Using her big, expressive eyes to great advantage, May—a London schoolgirl chosen from 3,000 would-be Mollies—involves the viewer deeply in her innocent confusion, disappointment, and anger. In an equally affecting performance, the nonprofessional Mvusi, an architect whose family left South Africa when she was 10, manages to convey a lifetime of suffering in her brief time on the screen. Jeroen Krabbe, David Suchet, Tim Roth, and Yvonne Bryceland (who has frequently appeared in the plays of Athol Fugard and helped found the first South African theater to break the ban on mixed casts and audiences), all contribute fine supporting work—but Albee Lesotho deserves special recognition, as he incorporates great joy, hope, sadness, compassion, and angry resolve in his portrayal of Soloman, the radical leader. Certainly Lesotho, a South African actor who was imprisoned for 18 months and released just prior to the beginning of filming, brought a wellspring of personal experience to his outstanding performance.

In interviews, Menges has cited his pursuit of Henri Cartier-Bresson's "decisive moment," and in A WORLD APART he sought the most honest, immediate performances he could get from his mixture of professional and nonprofessional actors. Determined to prevent the non-pros from losing their spontaneity or becoming self-conscious before the camera, Menges didn't allow any rehearsing, and often the first take of a scene was the one finally used (all of which reportedly was the cause of some friction between Hershey and the director). Not surprisingly, A WORLD APART is a beautifully photographed film, but, although Menges is one of the cinema's most accomplished masters of lighting (greatly influenced by British filmmaker Ken Loach), performance and plot never become subservient to striking images. Originally, Menges was approached to work as the cinematographer on the film, but when he learned that no director had been chosen, he lobbied hard for the position and got it. A veteran of documentary shoots in hot spots all around the world, Menges took a special interest in the story because, at 22, in 1963, the year of Ruth First's arrest, he was in South Africa filming a documentary on the 90-Day Detention Act for BBC-TV's "World in Action."

Obviously, though, no one is closer to the story than its author, Shawn Slovo, who wrote the screenplay as a response to her mother's murder in her office at the University of Mozambique on August 17, 1982. Using her own experiences, her father's recollections, and her mother's book *One Hundred and Seventeen Days* as the basis, Slovo wrote the screenplay while a student at Britain's National Film School and, after receiving a cool reception from American film producers, took it to Britain's Working Title, the risk-taking production company responsible for MY BEAUTIFUL LAUNDRETTE. The $5 million production was shot in 19 weeks in Bulawayo, Zimbabwe, which substitutes for suburban Johannesburg. Slovo was on hand for the shooting, but was forced to travel under a false name, with her hair dyed blonde, to protect her from South African reprisals. There is no doubt that the time has come for a black-made film about the South African struggle or at the very least a film that focuses fully on black South Africans, but until that time A WORLD APART is a most worthy substitute. Songs include "Nkosi Sikelela I-Afrika" (E.M. Sontonga), "Espani Cani" (Marquina-Narro, Marquina-Tallada), "Sway" (Molina, Ruiz, Gimbel, Hubert, Ithier), "Let's Twist Again" (Kal Mann, Dave Appel, performed by Chubby Checker), "The Girl from Ipanema" (Jobim, Moraes, Gimbel), "Happy Birthday to You" (Hill). Also includes the traditional songs "Zithulele Mama", "Ayanquikaza", "Amazing Grace". *(Adult situations, violence.)*

p, Sarah Radclyffe; d, Chris Menges; w, Shawn Slovo; ph, Peter Biziou (Eastmancolor); ed, Nicolas Gaster; m, Hans Zimmer; m/l, E.M. Sontonga, Marquina-Narro, Marquina-Tallada, Molina, Ruiz, Gimbel, Hubert, Ithier, Kal Mann, Dave Appel, Antonio Carlos Jobim, Moraes; prod d, Brian Morris; art d, Mike Philips; cos, Nic Ede; tech, Joyce Sikakane; makeup, Elaine Carew, Maureen Stephenson.

Biography **(PR:C-O MPAA:PG)**

WORLD GONE WILD** (1988) 94m Apollo/Lorimar c

Bruce Dern *(Ethan)*, Michael Pare *(George Landon)*, Catherine Mary Stewart *(Angie)*, Adam Ant *(Derek Abernathy)*, Anthony James *(Ten Watt)*, Rick Podell *(Exline)*, Julius Carry III *(Nitro)*, Alan Autry *(Hank)*.

It's 2087, it hasn't rained in 50 years, and water is the most precious commodity in the world. One surviving community is that of Lost Wells, an auto junkyard surrounding a spring that is one of the last remaining sources of water on earth. As WORLD GONE WILD opens, Stewart is holding a class for the young people in a school bus. Class is interrupted by shouts that visitors are coming, and a half-track towing a helicopter comes into view. Ant, dressed completely in white, emerges from the chopper, followed by a group of young men also clad in white. He greets the community, then tells his men to go to work. They produce automatic weapons and begin murdering all who cross their path. Once the carnage ends, Ant is ready to rape a woman while her child is forced to look on, but is interrupted when Dern appears and decapitates one of the invaders with a hubcap. Dern and Ant engage in a dialog, then Ant and his followers leave, taking with them some food, water, and a few inhabitants who will be indoctrinated into Ant's cult. Dern, warning that Ant will return, invites Stewart to join him on a two-day drive to the city to enlist the aid of ruffians in defending Lost Wells. In the city he finds Pare, his former protege, and the two of them are able to recruit sideshow cowboy Podell, explosives expert Carry, and motorcycle gang member Autry to help defend the junkyard town. On the way back, they meet James, who's a cannibal but also a friend of Pare's, and he joins the group. Back at Lost Wells, the mercenaries set about training the locals in defense tactics, while Pare and Stewart begin to fall in love. When Pare prevents Autry from raping Stewart, Autry takes off and finds Ant's camp, telling the cult leader about the secret spring at Lost Wells. Ant thanks him, then has him castrated and left hanging by his feet in a tree. The next day, Ant and his men attack Lost Wells, but are driven back by the defenders. That night they again attack, and are again defeated, with Ant killed in the fray.

An amalgam of "Mad Max" movies and THE MAGNIFICENT SEVEN (lest anyone fail to note the debt to the latter, Stewart sleeps with a photo of Steve McQueen next to her bed), WORLD GONE WILD is notable mainly for the eccentric performance turned in by Bruce Dern. He plays the leader of Lost Wells as a 1960s hippie, wearing a fringed leather vest and peace symbols, hanging posters of Jimi Hendrix and Janis Joplin in his trailer, and getting high while grooving to tunes on his Walkman. He seems to be having a ball, and if his casual approach to the role undermines whatever sense of drama there might be in the story, that's okay, because we've seen this kind of tale a hundred times before. Naturally, the film is high in camp content—Dern refers to Ant as a "corkscrew with legs" and calls his white minions "the men from Glad" ; seeing Lee Iacocca's biography among Stewart's books, Pare says, "Iacocca . . . I hear he was a great president" ; Ant reads to his followers from a book entitled *The Wit and Wisdom of Charles Manson*. Unfortunately, camp is all this film offers in the humor department, and that's not enough to save WORLD GONE WILD from mediocrity. It's a pity, because Dern and his offbeat band of mercenaries might well have been an amusing lot, had the script only provided them dialog spiced with a little more wit. *(Profanity, graphic violence.)*

p, Robert L. Rosen; d, Lee H. Katzin; w, Jorge Zamacona; ph, Don Burgess (Foto-Kem Color); ed, Gary A. Griffen; m, Laurence Juber; prod d, Donald L. Harris; set d, Andrew Bernard, Christian W. Russhon; spec eff, Cliff Wenger; cos, Dona Granata.

Action **Cas.** **(PR:O MPAA:R)**

WRONG GUYS, THE*½ (1988) 86m NW c

Louie Anderson *(Louie)*, Richard Lewis *(Richard)*, Richard Belzer *(Belz)*, Franklyn Ajaye *(Franklyn)*, Tim Thomerson *(Tim)*, Brion James *(Glen Grunski)*, Biff Manard *(Mark Grunski)*, John Goodman *(Duke Earl)*, Ernie Hudson *(Dawson)*, Timothy Van Patten *(J.T.)*, Bunny Summers, Carol Ita White, Garth Winsome, Dion Zamora.

THE WRONG GUYS opens in a suburban community in 1961, with a series of vignettes introducing us to the members of Cub Scout Den 7: Rich, a whining neurotic; Belz, a budding lothario; Franklyn, an aspiring counselor; Tim, an irresponsible airhead; and Louie, the portly leader of the group. Also on hand are the bullying Grunski brothers, angry because they were expelled from the Scouts and doing all they can to make life miserable for the den members. The film then flashes forward 17 years, where we find Louie (Anderson) still living in the same house with his mother, but distressed because construction of a new freeway means the old homestead will have to be torn down. For some reason, this prompts him to invite his old Cub Scout cronies back home for a reunion, and all show up: Rich (Lewis) now a whining, neurotic psychiatrist; Belz (Belzer) a womanizing belt designer; Franklyn (Ajaye) an advice-dispensing radio personality; and Tim (Thomerson) a surf bum. They assemble at Anderson's house and reluctantly agree to go camping at nearby Mt. Whitehead, where, years ago, they got lost during a campout and had to be rescued by their mothers. On the way to the mountain, they stop at a convenience store so that Lewis can load up on various medications. There they are spotted by the dreaded Grunski brothers (James and Manard), who also grow nostalgic for the good old days and follow the gang in hopes of again wreaking havoc upon them. In the meantime, convicted murderer Duke Earl (Goodman) has broken out of prison with two other convicts (Hudson and Van Patten), and the three decide Mt. Whitehead would make a great place to hide from the police. Also in the meantime, the wives of the Grunski brothers (White and Summers) are on their way to the same location, where they will attend a weekend seminar at a feminist retreat. Once all arrive at the mountain the fun begins, as the Grunski boys play nasty tricks on their former victims, Goodman and his gang mistake the aging Scouts for FBI agents and try to kill them, and Belzer and Thomerson find the distaff Grunskis to be as mean as their spouses when they invade the retreat in search of a little action. Of course, the boys of Den 7 eventually triumph over all, bringing the evil Goodman to justice, though their moms do have to put in another appearance to help out.

In fairness to THE WRONG GUYS, it must be said that this is probably the best movie ever made on the subject of Cub Scout reunions. But even with that seldom-tackled issue at its core and the presence of no less than five stand-up comics, THE WRONG GUYS is a pretty lame entry in the "zany bunch of guys" comedy category. Funny though these guys may be on the nightclub circuit, their comic abilities are nowhere in evidence here, largely due to the lackluster script. Richard Lewis' paranoid meanderings are worth a couple of laughs, but Richard Belzer's cynical aggressiveness makes him better suited to a villain's role. The others comedians (Louie Anderson, Franklyn Ajaye, and Tim Thomerson) and the reliable John Goodman (RAISING ARIZONA; TV's "Roseanne" ; and PUNCHLINE, which was *about* stand-up comics) do the best they can with a script that borrows heavily from the "Police Academy" series, as well as MEATBALLS and CADDYSHACK (a maniacal squirrel bears an uncanny resemblance to the gopher that bedeviled Bill Murray in the latter). It's all pretty lifeless, and it's easy to see why this film received only a limited theatrical release before playing on airlines and then turning up on video.

p, Chuck Gordon, Ronald E. Frazier; d, Danny Bilson; w, Danny Bilson, Paul de Meo; ph, Frank Byers (CFI Color); ed, Frank J. Jimenez; m, Joseph Conlan; prod d, George Costello; set d, Damon Medlen; cos, Jill Ohanneson.

Comedy **Cas.** **(PR:A MPAA:PG)**

XERO (SEE: HOME REMEDY, 1988)

YEAR MY VOICE BROKE, THE½** (1988, Aus.) 103m Avenue c

Noah Taylor (*Danny*), Loene Carmen (*Freya*), Ben Mendelsohn (*Trevor*), Graeme Blundell (*Nils Olson*), Lynette Curran (*Anne Olson*), Malcom Robertson (*Bruce Embling*), Judi Farr (*Sheila Embling*).

Set in a small town in New South Wales in 1962, this Australian coming-of-age tale focuses on the changing relationship between two teenagers who have been friends since they were "keeds." Pretty 16-year-old Carmen is in the midst of a confusing emergence into womanhood that seemingly leaves her younger friend (Taylor) behind, although he too is beginning to experience his first impulses of sexual desire. Unfortunately, his puppy lust is directed toward her, and though the affection is mutual, the attraction is not. Instead, Carmen is taken with Mendelsohn, a wild older boy whose "hyperactivity" includes starring at rugby and racing stolen automobiles around the local track until they run out of gas. When Taylor isn't busy jealously shadowing Carmen and Mendelsohn, he experiments with mental telepathy and hypnotism, both of which he tries to use to cause Carmen—whose photo and stolen panties he moons over—to be irresistibly attracted to him. Humoring Taylor, Carmen never makes light of his attentions, and above all else, she remains his friend. For his part, the mischievous Mendelsohn not only allows Taylor to tag along when he and Carmen are together, but also becomes Taylor's protector when Taylor is bullied by schoolmates who discover the poetry he's written. The trio visits a "haunted" house, and the mystery surrounding its former tenant intrigues Taylor, who learns that the promiscuous young woman who lived there died at the age of 17 from complications that arose during childbirth. Eventually, he also discovers that Carmen is actually her daughter (and it is implied that Taylor's father is also Carmen's). Before long history repeats, and Carmen learns that she is pregnant, scandalizing the town. Meanwhile, Mendelsohn, who has been sent off to reform school, escapes and returns to learn that he is a father. When the police corner the trio at the haunted house, Mendelsohn tries to escape and is killed in a car crash. Later, after being rejected by her "parents" (alcoholic Blundell and his wife, Curran), Carmen miscarries in the cold of the haunted house, but is rescued by Taylor, who is drawn there by kind of telepathy. At the film's end, Carmen boards a train that will take her to a new life elsewhere, and Taylor, her ever-loyal friend, sees her off, explaining in voice-over that this was the last time he saw her.

Though it covers familiar territory and is often overly precious, this well-acted, skillfully photographed film should satisfy most who enjoy examining the rites of passage. At its center are fine performances by the young leads. Loene Carmen is particularly right for her role, expressively capturing the burgeoning sensuality and increasingly complex emotions of a teen who, for most of the film, still hasn't completely let go of childhood. Disdainfully independent, rebellious, and coquettish, she also brings just the right mixture of consideration and unintentional adolescent insensitivity to her relationship with Taylor. Although she isn't a classic peaches-and-cream beauty, Carmen nonetheless glows on the screen. Noah Taylor, on the other hand, with his delicate features, is classically "movie cute"—but he is also appropriately soulful and goofy as the disappointed third wheel, who, one feels, will break more than his share of hearts when he is finally able to master his guitar. Ben Mendelsohn's performance as Carmen's live-wire boy friend is not quite as assured, but in some ways he has been handed the film's most difficult role, calling upon him to vacillate between moments of calm and frothy hyperactivity.

There are some wonderful, very real moments in THE YEAR MY VOICE BROKE, both humorous and touching, although occasionally, in aiming for the heart, writer-director John Duigan conjures up moments that are a little *too* wonderful. Still, the film's tone works more often than it doesn't, and the gentleness of its presentation should make this an especially involving picture for more introspective teenage viewers, who may be less acquainted with similarly themed films than are most adults—or who may have been exposed only to less patient Hollywood treatments. This is not to say that adults won't enjoy the film, only that they've probably been here before. (*Sexual situations.*)

p, Terry Hayes, Doug Mitchell, George Miller; d, John Duigan; w, John Duigan; ph, Geoff Burton; ed, Neil Thumpston; m, Christine Woodruff; prod d, Roger Ford.

Drama **Cas.** **(PR:C MPAA:PG-13)**

YOU CAN'T HURRY LOVE* (1988) 92m Lightning c

Charles Grodin (*Mr. Glerman*), Sally Kellerman (*Kelly Bones*), Kristy McNichol (*Rhonda Midnight*), David Leisure (*Peter Newcomb*), Lu Leonard (*Miss Frigget*), Anthony Geary (*Tony*), Luana Anders (*Macie Hayes*), Frank Bonner (*Chuck Hayes*), Judy Balduzzi (*Glenda "Madonna" Glerman*), Merete Van Kamp (*Monique*), Jake Steinfeld (*Sparky*), Danitza Kingsley (*Tracey*), Scott McGinnis (*Skip Dooley*), Bridget Fonda (*Peggy Kellogg*), David Packer (*Eddie Hayes*), Rudolph Laubscher (*Bus Driver*), Diz McNally (*Cab Driver*), Dan Golden (*Photographer*), Jean Poremba (*Model in Back*), Theresa Burrell (*Newcomb's Secretary*), Richard Perry (*Bruce*), Harry Perry (*Himself*), Tim Ryan (*Tim*), Kimber Sissions (*Brenda*), Jennifer Karr (*Girl from Ohio*), Kimberly Foster (*Girl Reading Book*),

Jean McNally (*Girl on Pier*), William Woff (*Delivery Man*), Catherine Lacy (*Sonya*), Kari Peyton (*Girl in Elevator*), Nancy Davis, Winnie Freedman, Jeanette Schwaba (*Sample Videotapes*), James Hoyt Kelley (*Sam*), Michael Peppe (*Performance Artist*), Michael Sorich (*Drug Dealer*), Simon R. Lewis (*Waiter*), Francesca Brenner (*Betty Newcomb*), Richard Martini, Lawrence Lanoff (*Party Men*), Tena Austin (*Party Woman*), Anson Downes (*Psychic Man*), Linda Rae Favila (*Psychic Woman*), Jonathan D. Krane (*Producer*), Nat Bernstein, Bill Evashwick (*Guys on Couch*), Eric Gardner (*Mr. Kaminsky*), Cal Gibson (*Aquarium Man*), Anthony Santa Croce (*Usher*), Marco Paul, Jr. (*Stuntman*), Alfie the Dog (*Spuds Lookalike*).

YOU CAN'T HURRY LOVE is a pretty awful comedy about dating in the 1980s that, underneath all of its trendy facade, tries to say something positive about romance. Packer stars as a 23-year-old kid from Akron who has just run off to LA after being left at the altar by both his bride-to-be and his best man. Armed with only a BA in advertising and the address of his too-hip cousin, McGinnis, Packer arrives in LA—without a girl, a car, a job, or a pick-up line. McGinnis lends him a car—a cute little two-tone Nash Rambler—and gives him a job lead at Vidiocity, a top ad agency. Ad exec Leisure (the "honest" Joe Isuzu from the auto commercials) promises him a bright future, but first he must start at the bottom, handing out fliers on the beach for Leisure's eccentric brother, Geary. On the beach, Packer meets Fonda, an employee of Video Valentine, a video dating service. Later, Packer agrees to make a dating video. First he pretends to be a hot TV commercial director, then a rock star, a race car driver, and a financial whiz. Along the way he meets a few winners—one practices "safe sex" by keeping all her clothes on; another forces him to wear a scuba suit and make love in a store window; a third (McNichol) is a performance artist-dominatrix who chases him around with a crossbow; and a fourth is a sultry sexpot who uses him to get her lover (Jake "Bodies by Jake" Steinfeld) jealous. After most of his dating misadventures, Packer meets Kellerman, the high-powered head of Vidiocity's New York branch. She takes a liking to him and offers him a position with the company. In the meantime, Packer finds himself falling for Fonda and realizing that he spends too much time trying to be someone he is not. He returns to Video Valentine and makes a new tape—an honest appeal to romance. The next day his answering machine is brimming with responses, including one from Fonda. Packer feels he has to see Fonda, but is told she is at a wedding. Apparently thinking he is Benjamin Braddock from THE GRADUATE (he's already worn the scuba outfit), Packer rushes to the church, interrupts the ceremony, rushes to Fonda at the altar, and makes a plea to go out with her. But wait—it's not Fonda's wedding, she's only a bridesmaid. As long as they're both at the altar, Packer and Fonda embrace and kiss in a romantic finale.

There's not much to say about YOU CAN'T HURRY LOVE that hasn't already been said about countless other "Life in LA" films. Fast cars and fast women are abundant, sleazy business people run the place, kooks are everywhere, and penis jokes get a lot of laughs. The big question viewers will find themselves asking is, "How does something like this get made?" A first feature from Richard Martini, YOU CAN'T HURRY LOVE reads like a textbook on how to make a first film. Hailing from suburban Chicago, working as Robert Towne's personal assistant, and scripting the 1987 film THREE FOR THE ROAD, Martini wrote and directed a low-budget, 30-minute short entitled VIDEO VALENTINE, casting friends from LA's Lembeck Workshop. The newly formed arm of Vestron Pictures, Lightning Films, found Martini's work impressive and gave him the green light to expand his short into a feature. He then managed to get a number of well-known performers cast, including Sally Kellerman (also in THREE FOR THE ROAD), Charles Grodin, and Kristy McNichol—each for one scene. Also recognizable are Anthony Geary (Luke of TV's "General Hospital"), Frank Bonner (TV's "WKRP in Cincinnati"), and a Spuds McKenzie impersonator named Alfie. As lame as the film is, David Packer (bearing a resemblance to Tom Hanks) and Bridget Fonda (daughter of Peter; also seen this year in ARIA) manage to make positive impressions, especially Fonda as the wholesome dating service employee who loves Packer for who he *really* is. The film includes some popular tunes from big names, including Phil Collins with You Can't Hurry Love (Edward Holland, Lamont Dozier, Brian Holland), Robert Palmer with Addicted to Love (Robert Palmer), The Rascals with Good Lovin', and Van Morrison with Wild Night. Sally Kellerman sings the closing song, To Lie to You for Your Love (Frankie Miller, Jeff Barry). Other songs are Headin' West/Cracked Crab (Andrew Todd, performed by Martini Ranch), Word Up (Larry Blackmon, Tomi Jenkins), "Uh Uh No No Casual Sex"(Willie Hutch, performed by Carrie McDowell), Invaders (Harry Perry, performed by Perry), Information Whiteout (Micheal Peppe, performed by Peppe), Obsession (Michelle Aller, Bob Esty). (*Nudity, substance abuse, sexual situations, excessive profanity.*)

p, Jonathan D. Krane; d, Richard Martini; w, Richard Martini; ph, Peter Lyons Collister, John Schwartzman (Duart Color); ed, Richard Candib; m, Bob Esty; md, Kevin Benson, Victor Levine; m/l, Andrew Todd, Larry Blackmon, Tomi Jenkins, Willie Hutch, Harry Perry, Robert Palmer, Michael Peppe, Edward Holland, Brian Holland, Lamont Dozier, Michelle Aller, Bob Esty, Frankie Miller, Jeff Barry; art d, Douglas A. Mowat; set d, Garreth Stover; cos, Colby Bart; makeup, Tena Austin.

Comedy **Cas.** **(PR:O MPAA:R)**

YOUNG GUNS** (1988) 97m FOX c

Emilio Estevez *(William H. Bonney aka* " Billy the Kid"), Kiefer Sutherland *(Josiah " Doc*"Scurlock), Lou Diamond Phillips *(Chevez Y Chavez)*, Charlie Sheen *(Dick Brewer)*, Dermot Mulroney (" Dirty Steve"Stephens), Casey Siemaszko *(Charley Bowdre)*, Terence Stamp *(John Henry Tunstall)*, Jack Palance *(Lawrence G. Murphy)*, Terrance O'Quinn *(Alex McSween)*, Sharon Thomas *(Susan McSween)*, Geoffrey Blake *(J. McCloskey)*, Alice Carter *(Yen Sun)*, Brian Keith *(Buckshot Roberts)*, Tom Callaway *(Texas Joe Grant)*, Patrick Wayne *(Pat Garrett)*, Lisa Banes *(Mallory)*, Sam Gauny *(Morton)*, Cody Palance *(Baker)*, Gadeek *(Henry Hill)*, Victor Izay *(Justice Wilson)*, Allen Robert Keller *(John Kinney)*, Craig M. Erikson *(Peppin)*, Jeremy H. Lepard *(Jimmy Dolan)*, Daniel Kamin *(Sheriff Brady)*, Richela Renkun *(Bar Girl)*, Pat Lee *(Janey)*, Gary Kanin *(Col. Dudley)*, Forrest Broadley *(Rynerson)*, Jeff Prettyman *(Judge Bristol)*, Randy Travis *(Ring Member)*, Alan Tobin *(Bartender)*, Joey Hanks *(Hindman)*, Loyd Lee Brown *(Soldier)*, Elena Parres *(Manuela's Mother)*.

In this latest attempt to rejuvenate the western genre, viewers are handed a film that is more like a hip fashion spread for *GQ* than a simple, straightforward oater. Haphazardly scripted by CROSSROADS (1986) writer John Fusco, YOUNG GUNS purports to be a study of the early days of William H. Bonney, a punk gunslinger soon to be known as Billy the Kid (played well by Emilio Estevez). The film opens in White Oaks, New Mexico, as Estevez is being chased through town by a group of angry citizens looking to hang him. Luckily, kindly British rancher Stamp happens along and hides Estevez in his buggy. It seems Stamp is a sagebrush Father Flanagan and has taken in a variety of scruffy young western ne'er-do-wells to work as the "Regulators" (hired guns) on his ranch in nearby Lincoln. In exchange for a job, food, and lodging, Stamp insists the boys learn to read, speak proper English, and maintain good table manners. Estevez is resistant to these controls at first, but he soon comes to respect Stamp and is very devoted to the rancher. The other boys (Sutherland, Phillips, Siemaszko, Mulroney, and Sheen) don't trust the stranger, however, and keep a close watch on him, especially foreman Sheen. Things soon change drastically when evil land baron Palance has Stamp killed because of a dispute over government beef contracts. The angry Regulators want revenge and with the help of Stamp's lawyer, O'Quinn, the boys are deputized and told to bring the killers in. Unfortunately, Estevez, who is a touch crazy, has no intention of arresting anybody and begins gunning down the guilty parties—much to the dismay of Sheen. Practically overnight, dime novels appear telling outlandish tales of the murderous Billy the Kid and Estevez delights in the publicity. When bounty hunter Keith kills Sheen in a shootout, Estevez becomes the leader of the gang and he decides Palance, his men, and the corrupt sheriff in Palance's pocket all have to die. Palance, however, has the government behind him and soon there are several ruthless bounty hunters *and* the US Cavalry out after the gang. When the boys' friend Pat Garrett (Wayne) tells them that Palance intends to kill O'Quinn and his wife, the boys come off the trail to Lincoln to defend the lawyer. To their surprise, the tip turns out to be a trap and the boys find themselves surrounded by all the factions that had been hunting them. After a long and bloody shootout, Estevez, Sutherland, and Phillips manage to escape. The latter two fade into obscurity while Estevez goes on to become one of the most infamous figures in the Old West.

This film must have been a Hollywood marketing mogul's dream project. Combine several of the most popular young actors in Hollywood in a wild shoot-em-up with a exploitable title like YOUNG GUNS and you cannot fail. Indeed, the movie was the number-one film at the box office the week it opened, knocking off some stiff competition, but it began fading quickly and was not the blockbuster everyone had hoped for (although it was a minor hit and a sequel cleverly titled YOUNG GUNS II has been announced). Part of the reason for this is that it is simply not a very good movie—western or otherwise. Although Fusco's script stays fairly close to the historical facts (although these are still much disputed), there is little character development and he muddles up the narrative with some unlikely supporting characters, including a Chinese girl (Carter) that Sutherland—who fancies himself a poet—falls in love with. Other incongruous moments include an extended and rather pointless peyote trip indulged in by the gang under half-breed Phillips' guidance, and the sudden decision by Carter to join the gang during the massive shootout at O'Quinn's house. While YOUNG GUNS tries hard to look like a good old-fashioned western, it seems very anachronistic—as if all these young Malibu actors got together to play dress-up on a lark. Christopher Cain, who directed the Estevez-scripted THAT WAS THEN, THIS IS NOW (1985), is an extremely unimaginative talent who seems content to let his stars strike poses, cut to gorgeous sunsets, and attempt to replicate the same kind of viscerally exciting slow-motion violence that only Sam Peckinpah could do properly. All in all, despite several shootouts, the film is overwhelmingly dull. Some of the blame can be pinned on the fact that the film was shot, edited, and released within six months—an incredibly fast schedule that sought to capitalize on a late summer release so that teens would still be out of school and more likely to see a film aimed at them. This does not excuse Fusco's chaotic script, however, which had been written years before the film went into production.

The performances are uneven as well. Visually, Emilio Estevez looks perfect as Billy the Kid and is probably one of the few actors to have played him who is close to the right height and age. He gives a true edge of madness to the character and seems very amoral, immature, and dangerous—but that's as far as it goes for character complexity. Kiefer Sutherland is given the unwieldy task of appearing sensitive and poetic while gunning down several men, and he struggles gamely with his part. Charlie Sheen (Estevez's real-life younger brother) is given a thankless role as the "square" of the bunch. Although they are mainly cast to provide colorful background, newcomer Dermot Mulroney and THREE O'CLOCK HIGH star Casey Siemaszko are quite good and look like the only two young guns who could have survived in the real Old West. Lou Diamond Phillips—a proven talent—is hopeless as the half-breed Indian. His supposedly impassioned speech about the plight of "his people" is badly written, hopelessly cliched, and given a perfunctory reading by Phillips that becomes embarrassing. Among the adults, Jack Palance gives his usual scenery-chewing performance, Terry O'Quinn is quite good, as is Terence Stamp, and Patrick Wayne as Pat Garrett is surprisingly solid given his scant amount of screen time. Best of all, however, is Brian Keith, virtually unrecognizable in a bear-skin coat and bushy moustache, as a no-nonsense bounty hunter who introduces himself and immediately starts blasting away at the young guns despite the fact that he is hopelessly outnumbered. His brief appearance is the best scene in the movie.

With Clint Eastwood's PALE RIDER (1985) and now YOUNG GUNS as the only westerns made in the 1980s to have been hits—both because of their stars and not because of the genre—the western remains in limbo. YOUNG GUNS could have been an admirable effort to introduce the American cinema's greatest genre to a whole new breed of moviegoers, but it simply was not good enough. For those interested in the best version of the Billy the Kid legend on film, rent Sam Peckinpah's masterful PAT GARRETT AND BILLY THE KID (1973), which, although cut to ribbons by insensitive studio moguls, remains a complicated, rich, and rewarding work that envisions the last three months of the Kid's life. *(Graphic violence, profanity, substance abuse.)*

p, Joe Roth, Christopher Cain; d, Christopher Cain; w, John Fusco; ph, Dean Semler (DeLuxe Color); ed, Jack Hofstra; m, Anthony Marinelli, Brian Banks; prod d, Jane Musky; art d, Harold Thrasher; set d, Robert Kracik; spec eff, Joe Quinlivan; cos, Richard Hornung; stunts, Everett Creach; makeup, Karoly Balazs.

Western **Cas.** **(PR:O MPAA:R)**

ZELLY AND ME*½** (1988) 87m Cypress/COL c

Alexandra Johnes *(Phoebe)*, Isabella Rossellini *(Joan,* "Zelly"), Glynis Johns *(Co-Co)*, Kaiulani Lee *(Nora)*, David Lynch *(Willie)*, Joe Morton *(Earl)*, Courtney Vickery *(Dora)*, Lindsay Dickon *(Kitty)*, Jason McCall *(Alexander)*, Aaron Boone *(David)*, Lee Lively *(Elegant Gentleman)*, John Raynes *(Bus Driver)*, Lynn Hallowell *(Waitress)*, Michael Stanton Kennedy *(Taxi Driver)*, Rick Warner *(Policeman)*, Julia Beale Williams *(Maid)*, Terrance Afer-Anderson *(Chauffeur)*, Jason Allen, Haley Curvin, Justin Grant, Andy Grimes, Jennifer Lee Harvey, Melissa Klein, Matt Laffler, Stephanie Malara, Sharon May, Katie McGinty, Kris Monson, David Norris, Abby Parker, Erika Ritter, Woody Sullender, Curtis Worth, Amy Young *(School Children on Bus)*.

This deceptively cuddly picture about the psychological violence inflicted by a pitiful grandmother on her saintly granddaughter is set against the idyllic backdrop of 1958 Virginia. Johnes plays Phoebe (the "Me" of the title), an orphaned eight-year-old whose parents were killed in a plane crash, leaving the child in the care of her grandmother, Johns (returning to the screen after a long absence). Johns is lonely woman in search of love who resides on an immaculate Virginia estate. Also living there is the gardener, Morton (the alien of THE BROTHER FROM ANOTHER PLANET); the housemaid, Lee; and the girl's nanny, Rossellini. Named Joan but called "Zelly" (short for "Mademoiselle-y"), Rossellini provides Johnes with all the love and affection any child could possibly need. The have heart-to-heart talks while swinging in the hammock, call each other by pet names, and create a fantasy world populated by Johnes' collection of stuffed animals. Johnes' favorite pastime is learning about St. Joan of Arc, the idol of both Johnes and Rossellini. She treasures a record album that narrates St. Joan's story and reads picture books that illustrate her burning at the stake, admiring the saint's inner strength and her refusal to denounce the voices that eventually led to her death. The child's problems are caused by Johns, who is determined to gain her granddaughter's love. Still feeling the loss of Johnes' parents, Johns tries to hang on to Johnes by separating the youngster from anyone who could possibly come between them. Johns is not wholly evil, however, as is indicated in a make-believe wedding ceremony for the girl's two favorite stuffed animals—Waddles the Bear and Queenie the Elephant—held on the mansion grounds. She is the perfect grandmother, even making flower wreaths for the occasion, until Morton presents Johnes with a handcrafted wooden honeymoon bed for the newlyweds and Johnes, with her eyes wide, exclaims that the bed is the most beautiful thing she's ever seen. Visibly disturbed that someone else has made her granddaughter happier than she, Johns fires Morton. Believing in Old World values by which women must be made tough in order to survive, Johns tries to "break" her granddaughter. Whenever the young girl does (or is perceived to do) something wrong, Johns orders her to get on her knees and apologize, forcing her to renounce her "willful and selfish" ways and repeatedly proclaim, "I love Co-co [Johns]." When Johns wrongly assumes that her granddaughter has told Rossellini about this forced apology, Rossellini is fired and told to leave in the middle of the night, without even speaking to the youngster. By now, however, Johnes has become obsessed with thoughts of St. Joan, and burns her skin with matches. Rossellini turns to a neighboring suitor, Lynch (director of BLUE VELVET and real-life companion to Rossellini), for help. Lynch, who lives alone in a large mansion, is Rossellini's Prince Charming, the man she believes will sweep her off her feet and return with her to Lyon, France. Unknown to her, however, Lynch is merely a servant who minds the house while the owner is away. Their plan to run away to France with Johnes eventually collapses when Lynch, his lowly status discovered, cannot bring himself to leave. In a taxi, Rossellini picks up Johnes at her school bus stop, but Johnes accepts the knowledge that she must return home—displaying a perfect understanding of her grandmother's need for love. Rossellini is nearly arrested for kidnaping, but is released when Johnes defends her. After everyone has left, Johns orders the remaining house servant, Lee, to take away all of Johnes' stuffed animals. Johnes is banished to her mother's former room (kept locked and treated as a shrine) with only her imagination, inner strength, and love of Rossellini to guide her.

A gentle and spiritual film, ZELLY AND ME may at first glance appear to be a sort of saccharine "Afterschool Special" about a misunderstood little girl, her overbearing grandmother, and the caring nanny who bridges the gap between the two. It is, however, more than that—a film directed with great grace, which succeeds on a higher level than most. Tina Rathborne here directs her first theatrical feature (she previously made an American Playhouse film called THE JOY THAT KILLS). In *Interview* magazine, Rathborne cited as two of her influences David Lynch and Brian De Palma (her real-life boyfriend): "I would say we are three very mild-mannered people with extremely violent and strange imaginations . . . Maybe mine is some kind of feminine vent—feminine violence comes out in a different way." This statement points to the heart of ZELLY AND ME. It is a film of unrelenting and discomforting violence—not of the physical sort but of a psychological and spiritual form. Rathborne is not concerned with drilling a woman into the floor, a la De Palma's BODY DOUBLE, or with cutting off a man's ear, a la BLUE VELVET. The treatment of ZELLY AND ME's young heroine by her grandmother is horrific enough, perhaps more so in its very real nature. The cruel grandmother (she, to paraphrase a saying of Jean Renoir's, "has her reasons" and, thereby, becomes a sympathetic figure) is a frightening example of a character who wants only to love and be loved, regardless of the consequences. Similarly, if Rathborne's violence, as she states, "is some kind of feminine vent," then so too is her young heroine's method of coping with that violence. Rather than fight back with outrage, or vengeance, little Phoebe follows the example of St. Joan of Arc. Envisioning herself as someone very different (a result of her nanny's encouragement), this young girl, because of her childhood experiences, is on the path to salvation—to one day become St. Phoebe of Virginia. Since her grandmother will prevent her from ever reaching out for love, Phoebe has no other choice than to listen to her own voice ("The voices are yourself," Zelly tells her). By the film's end she has retreated into a private world in which her only guidance will come from her two Joans—the saint from Arc, and the nanny from Lyon. Further demonstrating that there is more than meets the eye in ZELLY AND ME is the film's curious ending. Where a lesser director would sentimentally reconcile grandmother and granddaughter, Rathborne's solution is not so simple. In one sense the two *are* reconciled—they have come to terms with each other. The grandmother, however, does not change; in fact, she becomes even more venomous, separating her granddaughter from her stuffed animals and banishing her to a different bedroom. Since her grandmother will never change (she believes her discipline is right), Phoebe must, in essence, become a martyr who sacrifices herself to her grandmother's distorted ideas of loving.

Unfortunately for all involved, ZELLY AND ME is yet another victim of the changing of the guard at Columbia Pictures. Initiated by former Columbia CEO David Puttnam, the film was made for only $1.5 million, though it looks like it cost many times more. Before it could be released, however, Puttnam and Columbia parted ways, leaving ZELLY AND ME as a bastard child the new regime was not about to raise. Instead, it was dumped into a handful of theaters across the country, playing in out-of-the-way venues without the benefit of advertising. A victim of a self-fulfilling prophecy, ZELLY AND ME was a box-office bust, grossing only $200,000. Lost through Columbia's neglect, in addition to Rathborne's fine direction and some excellent technical credits (including the moving Pino Donaggio piano score), are some impeccable performances. Glynis Johns, last seen in the 1973 British horror film VAULT OF DEATH, makes a remarkable return to the screen, and the young Alexandra Johnes is a wonderful surprise who seems perfectly at ease with the camera. It is, however, Isabella Rossellini's film—featuring her best performance to date. After a trio of films in which her acting was purposely archetypical (WHITE NIGHTS; BLUE VELVET; and TOUGH GUYS DON'T DANCE), Rossellini finally gets a chance to act in a more natural, playful, and slightly goofy role. It is here, more than ever, that she bears an eerie resemblance to her mother, Ingrid Bergman. *(Adult situations.)*

p, Sue Jett, Tony Mark; d, Tina Rathborne; w, Tina Rathborne; ph, Mikael Salomon (Technicolor); ed, Cindy Kaplan Rooney; m, Pino Donaggio, Jeremiah Clarke; m/l, Leo Trombetta, Edward Mann; prod d, David Morong; art d, Dianna Freas; cos, Kathleen Detoro; makeup, Hiram Ortiz.

Drama   **Cas.**   **(PR:A MPAA:PG)**

THE MOTION PICTURE ANNUAL

1989

**People
to
Watch**

JULIETTE BINOCHE

The luminous face of 23–year–old Juliette Binoche is known throughout France, but until she appeared in THE UNBEARABLE LIGHTNESS OF BEING had only rarely been projected on US screens. As that film's shy country waitress who is liberated intellectually and sexually by the neurosurgeon she marries (played by Daniel Day Lewis), Binoche emerges as one of the most thoroughly riveting performers since Louise Brooks. Her first role, at 17, was a small part in the 1983 French film LIBERTY BELLE by Pascal Kane. Four more French films followed the next year—minor roles in Annick Laone's LES NANAS, Bob Decout's ADIEU BLAIREAU, and Jacques Doillon's LA VIE DE FAMILLE, and a supporting role in Jean–Luc Godard's HAIL, MARY. In the meantime, Binoche also performed on the stage, appearing in "Vera Gregh" with the Conservatoire National. By 1985, she had landed her first major film role, starring opposite Lambert Wilson and Jean–Louis Trintignant in Andre Techine's erotic and passionate RENDEZVOUS. The following year was even better to Binoche, who appeared in a pair of films with Michel Piccoli, MON BEAU–FRERE A TUE MA SOEUR and BAD BLOOD (MAUVAIS SANG), earning for the latter a Cesar nomination (the French Oscar equivalent) for Best Actress. In BAD BLOOD, under the direction of Leos Carax (her off–screen companion), Binoche glows with the same great qualities possessed by the great silent screen actresses. One can thank Saul Zaentz and Philip Kaufman, the producer and director of THE UNBEARABLE LIGHTNESS OF BEING, for casting Binoche and finally letting the US in on one of France's best–kept secrets.

ERIC BOGOSIAN

While Oliver Stone's hyperkinetic direction contributes much to the intensity of the film, TALK RADIO is Eric Bogosian's movie, for he wrote the play on which it was based and created his character on stage. As radio talk show host Barry Champlain, Bogosian acts as a lightning rod for America's darker impulses—for the paranoia, insecurity, resentment, hatred, and fear that bubbles and seethes just outside the studio and within Champlain himself. The 35–year–old Bogosian grew up in Woborun, Massachusetts, and would go on to study acting at Oberlin College. In 1975 he moved to New York City, where he quickly became a force in the artistic community, producing plays for The Kitchen, which specialized in performance art. Hanging out in punk clubs, Bogosian created a character called Ricky Paul, a loathesome and confrontational singer–comedian who would attempt to offend and antagonize everybody in the audience. Bogosian's stage persona and his real identity began to blur, however, and he adopted the mantle of bad boy, getting into fights and scuffles offstage. His life became more stable in 1980, when he met and married Australian graphic designer JoAnne Bonney (the couple now have a son, Harriss). In 1982, Broadway producer Joseph Papp presented Bogosian in two of Bogosian's performance pieces, "Men Inside" and "Fun House," at the Public Theater, and soon the actor was landing roles in movies (Larry Cohen's underrated SPECIAL EFFECTS) and television (guest shots on "Miami Vice," "Twilight Zone," and the TV version of "The Caine Mutiny Court Martial"). In 1986, Bogosian wrote and starred in "Drinking in America," a grim collection of monologs that reflected the incredible self–indulgence Bogosian saw in America during the 1980s. The play won him the Drama Desk and Obie awards. In 1987, Bogosian brought "Talk Radio" to New York, where it was seen by producer Ed Pressman, who asked the actor–playwright to collaborate with director–writer Oliver Stone on a movie version. Bogosian's next work is a one–man theater piece titled "Sex and Drugs & Rock'n'Roll."

EMMANUELLE CHAULET

Before meeting French director Eric Rohmer, Emmanuelle Chaulet was a stage actress, appearing in the plays of Moliere and Shakespeare and even a version of "The Rocky Horror Picture Show." Then she decided to invite the reclusive Rohmer to view one of her performances. He attended and, after the show, invited her to visit his home for tea. For months afterwards, director and actress drank tea, talked, took strolls, and went to films. Rohmer recorded their conversations and worked them into a screenplay, and offered Chaulet one of the leads in his BOYFRIENDS AND GIRLFRIENDS. Making her feature film debut at age 24 (the film was released in Paris in 1987), Chaulet continues Rohmer's long list of superb lead actresses. While the women Rohmer casts often have limited film careers (the naturalism he demands is often perceived by others as nonacting), Chaulet seems likely to break that barrier; her shift of character in BOYFRIENDS AND GIRLFRIENDS from a cautious and conservative young professional to an impulsive and radiant lover is not only a believable turn but a testament to her acting ability. Life outside Rohmer's film universe has already produced another role for Chaulet, a supporting part in the French picture CHOCOLAT, a feature film debut from Claire Denis.

NAVIN CHOWDHRY

Finding a 15–year–old actor to play opposite the great Shirley MacLaine is a difficult enough task on its own without also requiring that the actor be able to play piano convincingly, roller–skate, and seduce a woman more than twice his age in his character. After an exhaustive casting call and open auditions, Navin Chowdhry, an unknown 15–year–old of Indian heritage living in Bristol, England, was given the lead in MADAME SOUSATZKA. Although he had won various acting prizes at the Bristol grammar school, Chowdhry had no previous professional acting experience. Nor could he play the piano. After a week's training with the film's musical advisor, however, he could convincingly fake a rendition of a Scriabin piano etude, and after spending hundreds of hours in front of the keyboard, Chowdhry, with the help of editing and audio playback, mastered the piano. His talent, however, lies in more than an ability to fake a piano recital. His character—a child prodigy under the tutelage of the maniacal Madame Sousatzka (MacLaine)—must appear to be possessed by the internal fire of genius, and as an actor Chowdhry displays a magnetic charisma. While he appears to be a regular, roller–skating teenager away from the keyboard, he comes to life when playing, and Chowdhry's brilliance on the screen is most apparent in these moments—nearly fooling the viewer into believing they are watching documentary footage of a piano prodigy. On top of turning in a superb performance, Chowdhry is able to hold his own against the masterful MacLaine, which alone provides solid proof of his natural abilities.

DEBORRA–LEE FURNESS

At the beginning of SHAME, a lone motorcyclist wearing black leather and a dark helmet enters a dusty outback town in Australia and parks in front of the local pub, where most of the town's young men are gathered. The stranger dismounts and removes the helmet, revealing a mane of long, beautiful, strawberry blonde hair. The local lads—all slobbering sexists—are delighted to discover that the biker is a woman. Just when it seems the filmmakers have introduced yet another retrograde sexual icon to the screen, however, actress Deborra–Lee Furness and director Steve Jodrell turn the tables on the men. This isn't some teasing tart created to fulfill male fantasies, but a tough, intelligent, independent *feminist* lady barrister who won't take abuse from anybody—and she's got the will and the muscle to prove it. Reportedly as smart and independent as the character she plays, Furness first be-

JULIETTE BINOCHE

ERIC BOGOSIAN

NAVIN CHOWDHRY

VALERIA GOLINO

KEITH GORDON

DOUG HUTCHISON

gan pursuing an acting career at the age of 20, when she left Melbourne to study at the American Academy of Dramatic Arts in New York City. She landed a small role in CROSS-OVER DREAMS (1985), then returned to her native Australia for parts in JENNY KISSED ME (1985) and COOL CHANGE (1986) before finally getting her breakthrough role in SHAME, an admirable attempt to subvert the macho mentality of Australian men in an action film format. Furness also appeared in A CRY IN THE DARK, and will soon be seen in several European and/or Australian films, including ACT OF BE-TRAYAL; A MATTER OF CON-VENIENCE; TWO BROTHERS RUNNING; and THE HUMPTY DUMPTY MAN. Now back in America, Furness is determined to make it in Hollywood, and, based on her performance in SHAME, she should get her wish.

VALERIA GOLINO

Although she has been featured in eight European films—winning a Golden Lion from the Venice Film Festival and Italy's Nastro d'Argento award for her performance in Francesco Maselli's LOVE STORY and named Best Actress at the Italian Film Festival in Nice for FIGLIO MIO INFINTAMENTE CARO (My Son, Infinitely Beloved)—22-year-old Valeria Golino was virtually unknown in the United States until 1988, when she made her mark with supporting roles in BIG TOP PEE-WEE and RAIN MAN. Of Italian and Greek heritage (her father a journalist, her mother an artist), Golino was born in Naples and grew up in Athens. She had already modelled for two years when she was discovered for movies, at age 16, by director Lina Wertmuller (a friend of Golino's aunt and uncle's) who cast her in A JOKE OF DESTINY. Thereafter, she was featured in the aforementioned award-winning films, Peter Del Monte's LITTLE FLAMES, Alexandre Arkady's LAST SUM-MER IN TANGIERS, and several others. Despite the fact that the movie bombed and most critics failed to single out her performance, Golino received a lot of press in the US for her role in BIG TOP PEE-WEE, mainly because her character introduces Pee-Wee Herman to sex. Golino garnered far more attention for her performance as Tom Cruise's secretary and girl friend in Barry Levinson's RAIN MAN. Although the role was written for an American, Levinson cast Golino and added credibility in having Cruise's character, an importer of luxury cars, deal in Lamborghinis. Using her accent and foreign sensibility to supreme advantage, Golino brings a welcome spontaneity to the film and helps balance Dustin Hoffman's incredibly intense and tightly focused lead performance. Soon to be seen in TOR-RENTS OF SPRING opposite Timothy Hutton, the talented and beautiful Golino seems to have taken Hollywood by storm.

KEITH GORDON

The 27-year-old actor-turned-director Keith Gordon made a stunning debut behind the camera this year with THE CHOCOLATE WAR, his flawed but stylish adaptation of Robert Cormier's novel of the same name. The product of a theatrical family—his father acts, teaches, and directs—Gordon had his first professional role in a 1976 National Playwrights Conference production. That performance led to a part in JAWS 2, and soon thereafter the young actor had a featured role in the TV miniseries "Studs Lonigan," followed by several appearances in New York stage productions, including "Richard III," "Album," Israel Horovitz's "Sunday Runners in the Rain," and Michael Bennett's production of "Third Street." On-screen Gordon has appeared in Brian De Palma's HOME MOVIES; THE LEGEND OF BILLIE JEAN; and DRESSED TO KILL, but he is probably most recognizable as Arnie Cunningham, the high-school nerd possessed by a killer Plymouth Fury in CHRIS-TINE (1983), John Carpenter's adaptation of Stephen King's novel. Gordon also played Rodney Dangerfield's son in the 1987 comedy BACK TO SCHOOL. His off-camera involvement in filmmaking began with STATIC, an independently produced film that he co-wrote and coproduced, and in which he also starred. With THE CHOC-OLATE WAR, Gordon realized his long-held ambition to bring Cormier's novel to the screen. Working from his own script, employing an unusual narrative structure, flashy but effective camera movement, evocative lighting, and inventive editing, and coaxing excellent performances from his strong cast, Gordon has created a film that is occasionally overreaching, and hardly seamless, but unquestionably the work of a promising filmmaker.

MICHAEL HOFFMAN and RICK STEVENSON

PROMISED LAND, the third collaboration from writer-director Michael Hoffman and producer Rick Stevenson, met with mixed reviews this year, but though this earnest exploration of the downside of the American Dream doesn't live up to its ambitions, its mixture of arresting visuals, well-etched characters, and political insight serves notice that Hoffman and Stevenson are filmmakers to be reckoned with. Americans, they met at Oxford, where Rhodes scholar Hoffman was studying literature and Stevenson was reading for a doctorate in international relations. After watching Hoffman's innovative staging of "A Midsummer Night's Dream," Stevenson approached him with the idea of doing a film about Oxford. (The film bug had bitten Stevenson while making a documentary about the Youth Conservation Corps as part of his summer job with the US Department of the Interior.) The result was PRIVILEGED (1982), made with 17,000 pounds raised from the parents of Oxford under-

grads and featuring performances by three fellow students who have since distinguished themselves in other films: James Wilby (MAU-RICE; A HANDFUL OF DUST), Hugh Grant (MAURICE), and Imogen Stubbs (NANOU; A SUM-MER STORY, in which she costars with Wilby). RESTLESS NA-TIVES (1985), the second project of the Oxford Film Company (formed by Stevenson, Hoffman, Rupert Walters, and Andy Peterson), was a romantic comedy about two impoverished young Scots who make ends meet by robbing tour buses. Stevenson and Hoffman then returned to the US to make PROMISED LAND—written by Hoffman, based on an incident that occurred in his small Idaho hometown, and chosen as one of six films that were workshopped in 1984 at Robert Redford's Sundance Institute.

DOUG HUTCHISON

Every now and again a supporting actor in a truly awful movie is so exceptional that it somehow makes endurable the pain involved in watching the surrounding film. In the case of the Molly Ringwald–Andrew McCarthy feature FRESH HORSES, the redemptive bright new talent is Doug Hutchison, who plays a sleazy yet fascinating college kid. A newcomer to the screen who also had a supporting role this year in Keith Gordon's THE CHOCO-LATE WAR, Hutchison grew up in Detroit and Minneapolis, becoming involved in community theater after high school. After a short stint at Juilliard, Hutchison appeared onstage in the world premiere (in Minneapolis) of Garson Kanin's play "Time and Chance," and, with Kanin's help, found an agent. More stage credits followed, including "A-bandoned in Queens," "Fun," "Sparks in the Park," and "Brighton Beach Memoirs." What Hutchison shows in FRESH HORSES is a commanding screen presence and an uncanny gift for holding the audience's attention, even when appearing on-screen with such stars as Ringwald and McCarthy. Although he only appears in a few scenes in FRESH HORSES (ditto for THE CHOCOLATE WAR), he displays more energy and vitality than most other members of the cast. With just the few lines he is given in FRESH HORSES, he creates a fully developed personality, stirring audience interest and making us want to know more. If Doug Hutchison can carry a film as a minor character, one can only guess what will happen when he is given a lead role.

MARK ISHAM

It's difficult to imagine a better score for a 1988 release than the moody, romantic strains that composer Mark Isham provided for Alan Rudolph's THE MODERNS. Perhaps best known as a recording artist for the New Age music label Windham Hill, Isham (who has also recorded with an emsemble called Group 87) found himself in Rudolph's favor after the director heard Isham's album "Vapor Drawings." Although he also scored Gillian Armstrong's MRS. SOFFEL, Carroll Ballard's NEVER CRY WOLF, and the documentary THE LIFE AND TIMES OF HARVEY MILK, Isham's best work as a film composer can be heard in his collaborations with Rudolph: 1985's TROUBLE IN MIND; 1987's MADE IN HEAVEN; and THE MODERNS. As in his other 1988 score, that of THE BEAST (which saw only a brief theatrical release this year), Isham proves that he, more than most composers working today, understands the power of the film score. Most notably in THE MODERNS, his music contributes (along with some additional material by French singer CharElie Couture) a seductive atmosphere that not only complements Rudolph's romantic visuals, but lifts the film and the viewer to a higher, more ethereal level. After experiencing the film and music together just once, it becomes impossible to imagine one without the other.

RICKI LAKE

The most exuberant new face of the year belongs to Ricki Lake, the 19-year-old actress who starred in John Waters' wonderfully entertaining ode to his Baltimore adolescence, HAIRSPRAY. As Divine's daughter, Tracy Turnblad, Lake gave new meaning to the phrase, "Yeah, but she's got a great personality." Although overweight, Tracy makes herself the most popular teen in all of Baltimore with her sparkling character and phenomenal dancing ability, and Lake becomes a positive role model for everyone who has ever felt lonely and alienated because of their physical appearance. Growing up in Westchester County, New York, young Lake started out as a singer in cabaret shows, did some work in commercials, and had a guest shot on the television show "Kate and Allie" before landing the role in Waters' film. Her hair dyed and teased into an outrageous bouffant, Lake was ready to be taught the intricate dance steps of HAIRSPRAY's period (the early 60s) by none other than the late Divine (see Obituaries) and Waters—both of whom grew up in Baltimore in that era. Trouble arose on the set, however, when the 5-foot-3-inch, 150-pound Lake began losing weight during the shoot. A horrified Waters made the girl fatten back up until filming was over. Now slimmer, Lake can be seen in a small role dancing with Harrison Ford during the wedding scene in WORKING GIRL and will be featured opposite Emily Lloyd in the upcoming Susan Seidelman film COOKIE.

FRANK LaLOGGIA

Although he made his directorial debut in 1981 with the remarkably effective low-budget horror film FEAR NO EVIL, Frank LaLoggia didn't receive much attention until this year, when his second film, THE LADY IN WHITE, was released. Fiercely independent, La-Loggia waited seven years between pictures to ensure that he would have control of his next project. His experience with FEAR NO EVIL was not a happy one, for the studio, the now-defunct Avco-Embassy, took control of the project and denied the director final cut. For THE LADY IN WHITE, LaLoggia formed his own company, New Sky Communications, with his cousin Charley LaLoggia, and they raised 5 million independently. Inventively directed, highly personal, and quite haunting, THE LADY IN WHITE caught many critics who expected just another horror film by surprise. Within the frame of his gothic ghost story, LaLoggia draws a vivid picture of East Coast Italian family life in the early 1960s, including a suggestion of the social and political turmoil that would soon grip the nation. While at times LaLoggia's ambition seems to exceed his grasp, the young director did wonders on a low budget and managed to create one of the most memorable American independent features of the year. Despite LaLoggia's control of the final cut of THE LADY IN WHITE, he had little influence on the distribution of his film, which was quite haphazard and failed to capitalize on the generally favorable critical response, and the film did poorly at the box office. Fortunately, it has found new life on home video, and it is to be hoped that LaLoggia will make more films—without waiting seven years between them.

JOHDI MAY

The most remarkable acting debut of the year happens to come from the youngest of 1988's People to Watch, 12-year-old Londoner Johdi May, whose performance in Chris Menges' (see below) A WORLD APART won her the Best Actress award at the Cannes Film Festival, an honor she shared with costars Barbara Hershey and Linda Mvusi. As the daughter of the dedicated anti-apartheid activist played by Hershey, May beautifully conveys the pain, anger, and loneliness she feels when politics shut her out of her mother's life. Completely natural and unaffected on the screen, May delivers a wrenching performance that runs the gamut of emotions without ever falling back on easy sentiment or cloying mannerisms. Interested in acting since the age of seven, May began taking classes a few years ago at the Anna Scher Theatre School in London, and two weeks into her training was sent to eight auditions—one of which led to her role in A WORLD APART, a casting call in which 3,000 girls responded and 200 actually auditioned. Plunging into the material like a veteran, May researched her role and learned the history of South Africa. She also listened to a tape recording of a South African girl telling a story, took voice lessons from a coach, and attended school for two weeks in Zimbabwe, where the film was shot, to capture the proper accent. Despite her newfound fame, May intends to continue her education and worry about continuing her career once she's finished with school. She is already highly selective of her roles and will only interrupt her studies for something special. With her astounding natural talent and surprisingly mature attitude toward life and her career, May is an actress who promises to be around for quite a while.

RAMON MENENDEZ and TOM MUSCA

Every now and again a film comes along which makes minimal use of the art of film, its techniques, or its power as a visual medium, but still manages to have a powerful and profound effect on its viewers. This year's STAND AND DELIVER is such a film, and director Ramon Menendez and producer Tom Musca must be duly commended, not only for their filmic accomplishment, but also for their social vision. The film is based on the record of the remarkable East LA high-school calculus instructor Jaime Escalante, whose teaching ability helped change the lives of a number of students. Paralleling Escalante's course, with this film Menendez and Musca have reached and inspired audiences, teachers, and students across the country. Graduates of the UCLA film school, Menendez and Musca had previously collaborated on an American Film Institute project, and worked separately on a variety of other films: Menendez was first assistant director on Oliver Stone's SALVADOR; Musca had a bit part in Alex Cox's REPO MAN and did some writing on LITTLE NIKITA. After reading of Escalante's achievements in a 1983 newspaper article, Menendez and Musca optioned the rights to Escalante's story for 1, just enough to make it legal. With help from American Playhouse, PBS, and a variety of arts grants, they raised their 1.4 million budget and assembled an excellent cast of barely knowns—Edward James Olmos, Lou Diamond Phillips, and Andy Garcia. After a premiere at the Mill Valley Film Festival in Utah in late 1987, WALKING ON WATER (as it was then called) caught the attention of just about everyone in Hollywood before Warner Brothers snatched it up. When so many directors and producers in Hollywood are spending multimillions on insipid fluff, it is reassuring to see the emergence of these two filmmakers concerned with sociopolitical causes.

CHRIS MENGES

One of film's premier cinematographers, Oscar winner Chris Menges (THE KILLING FIELDS and THE MISSION) made an auspicious directorial debut this year with the incredibly powerful anti-apartheid drama A WORLD APART. Avoiding the strident didacticism that mars so many "socially relevant" films, A WORLD APART is a restrained, subtle, balanced, and sensitive work. Menges allows his subject to speak for itself, presenting his story through beautifully evocative visuals and eliciting

RICKI LAKE

FRANK LaLOGGIA

JOHDI MAY

CHRIS MENGES

PENELOPE ANN MILLER

ROCKY MORTON and ANNABEL JANKEL

JOHN PANKOW

CCH POUNDER

magnificent performances from his entire cast. This should be no surprise, for the 47–year–old filmmaker has been working in the medium since he was 17, when he began as a cutting room trainee. In 1963, at age 21, Menges was employed as an assistant cameraman for the BBC–TV documentary series "World in Action," and was sent on his first assignment to Johannesburg for a film about the 90–Day Law—the very same event with which A WORLD APART is concerned. In fact, Menges shot footage at this time of Ruth First—the prototype for Hershey's character—being sent to prison. Subsequently, Menges worked as a cameraman on dozens of important documentaries for such influential filmmakers as British Neorealist Ken Loach (KES; LOOKS AND SMILES; FAMILY LIFE) and Adrian Cowell (OPIUM WARLORDS; OPIUM TRAIL). This led to his work in narrative features, as Menges shot films for directors Stephen Frears (GUMSHOE), Bill Forsyth (LOCAL HERO), Neil Jordan (DANNY BOY), Andrei Konchalovsky (SHY PEOPLE), and Clare Peploe (HIGH SEASON), along with the aforementioned Oscar–winning Roland Joffe movies. Filmed on a relatively low budget of 4 million, A WORLD APART has garnered several awards and has established this great cinematographer as a director to be reckoned with as well.

PENELOPE ANN MILLER

This year she's played a Daisy, a Winnie, and a Sally, starring opposite Matthew Broderick, Pee–wee Herman, and Kevin Anderson in, respectively, BILOXI BLUES, BIG TOP PEE–WEE, and MILES FROM HOME. On the basis of just the diversity of these three roles, it's easy to guess that the 24–year–old Penelope Ann Miller has a promising future. Miller's first film role was in 1987's ADVENTURES IN BABYSITTING, but she attracted more attention in the stage version of Neil Simon's "Biloxi Blues," starring opposite Broderick. Cast by director Mike Nichols for the film version, Miller, dressed in mid–1940s attire, plays Daisy, a charmer who is the Broderick character's first love. In BIG TOP PEE–WEE, she is the peppy, platinum blonde schoolteacher Winnie, jilted by Pee–wee when a sexy Italian trapeze artist (Valeria Golino, see above) arrives on the scene. In MILES FROM HOME, Miller takes the role of Sally, an innocent but sexy young woman whose love–at–first–sight scene with a shy young farmer (Kevin Anderson) is warm and convincing. A Los Angeles native and the daughter of actor Mark Miller, Penelope Ann Miller went east to New York to study her trade, eventually working her way back to California to take small roles on a number of television shows. She appeared in such hits as "St. Elsewhere," "Family Ties," "The Facts of Life," "Tales from the Darkside," and the relatively unknown series "The Popcorn Kid," in which she had a lead role. It was her brief role in an epi-

sode of "Miami Vice," however, that has proved a turning point in her career. Having caught the attention of that show's star, Don Johnson, she was chosen to costar with him in the scheduled 1989 release of John Frankenheimer's DEAD BANG. Although the part was originally written for an older actress (both Faye Dunaway and Angelica Huston were considered), it was Miller who made the role hers.

ROCKY MORTON and ANNABEL JANKEL

With their first feature, D.O.A., the team of Rocky Morton and Annabel Jankel (a duo both professionally and personally) have become two of the most exciting and innovative film directors working within the confines of Hollywood studio filmmaking. Their D.O.A., while perhaps not an everlasting piece of great art, is one of the more visually arresting commercial pictures to come along in some time, and this combination of commercial appeal and creativity is the quality in Morton and Jankel's work that hold the most promise. Having met in London's West Surrey College of Art and Design in 1974 while both were animation students, Morton and Jankel eventually left art school, formed a production company, and began combining their animation background with live–action techniques. They gained acclaim as directors of television commercials and rock videos (The Tom–Tom Club and Elvis Costello), but it wasn't until 1982, with the creation of Britain's "Max Headroom" television series, that Morton and Jankel found true success. Collaborating with writer George Stone, Morton and Jankel directed an hour–long "Max Headroom" for Britain's Channel 4, followed by 13 half–hour episodes. When "Max Headroom" made its transatlantic crossing to ABC–TV and Coca–Cola ad campaigns, Morton and Jankel were out of the picture—and their cruel, satiric Max was transformed beyond their control into a harmless clown. Although their shows were later broadcast in the US on HBO's Cinemax channel, the duo didn't get a shot at Stateside success until they received an offer to direct United Artists' CHILD'S PLAY (then called BLOOD BUDDY). When it was in the end directed by Tom Holland), a film about a crazed doll with strange parallels to Max that, judging from D.O.A. and "Max Headroom," would have been far different in the hands of Morton and Jankel.

JOHN PANKOW

Chicago native John Pankow made an auspicious appearance in William Friedkin's TO LIVE AND DIE IN L.A. (1985), only to be overshadowed by costar and fellow Chicagoan William L. Petersen. After small supporting roles in BATTERIES NOT INCLUDED (1987) and THE SECRET OF MY SUCCESS (1987), Pankow has finally managed to get some long overdue recognition with two performances in 1988, as sardonic research scientist Geof-

frey Fisher in George Romero's unjustly neglected horror film MONKEY SHINES and as Chuck, the network executive eager to make Eric Bogosian's radio talk show national in Oliver Stone's powerful TALK RADIO. Pankow studied acting at Northeastern Illinois University and upon graduation joined Chicago's St. Nicholas Theatre (founded by David Mamet), appearing in several of their productions. Next he moved to Hollywood, where he found roles unforthcoming, then went on to Off–Broadway, where he landed a part in the critical and popular success "Slab Boys." This led to two more Off–Broadway roles (in "Forty Deuce" and "Hunting Scenes"), before the actor finally hit Broadway as Peter Firth's understudy in "Amadeus." Pankow made his Broadway debut in that play as Mozart to James Woods' Salieri; more Off–Broadway, New York Shakespeare Festival, movie, and television appearances were to follow before his featured roles in 1988. An extremely versatile actor, Pankow has played everything from uptight, by–the–book cops to drug–addled scientists to corporate executives—doing the character acting Hollywood has had trouble utilizing fully in recent years.

CLARE PEPLOE

From the looks of it one would think Clare Peploe, the director of HIGH SEASON, had success laid out for her on a silver platter—she is the former assistant to and companion of Michaelangelo Antonioni, the sister of screenwriter Mark Peploe (THE PASSENGER; THE LAST EMPEROR), a friend of Jack Nicholson's (who invested in HIGH SEASON), and the wife of Bernardo Bertolucci. To top it off, Clare Peploe is extremely beautiful. None of this helps, however, when one is cowriting (with Mark Peploe) and directing a first feature. What matters most is that Peploe, as she has proven with her debut feature and has already indicated in making the 1981 Oscar–winning short COUPLES AND ROBBERS, can direct a film. A witty satire on tourism and commerce that stylistically recalls both Preston Sturges and Jean Renoir, HIGH SEASON is directed with Peploe's talent for effectively juggling a number of story lines and characters. Loosely, almost casually constructed (a style that suits its "on holiday" theme), the film's scenes effortlessly shift, its characters drifting from one spot to the next and moving from one encounter to another. Not surprisingly, Peploe's efforts were attacked by a number of critics (both in America and her native England) who saw the film as nothing more than a picture postcard (set in Greece and photographed by the exceptional Chris Menges) with little to say.

CCH POUNDER

Looking as worn out and empty as the Mojave Desert that stretches out around her, CCH Pounder, as the proprietor of the truckstop/mini–Vegas in Percy Adlon's BAGDAD

CAFE, is the perfect counterpart to Marianne Sagebrecht's Bavarian *hausfrau* . Despite their very different outward appearances—Pounder seems wasted, Sagebrecht is formal in her suit and hat—both are similarly tough, earthy characters with rich cultural roots, be they in Bavaria or the deep South. While Sagebrecht's talents have already been showcased in Adlon's SUGAR-BABY, Pounder is a complete surprise in BAGDAD CAFE, turning a nasty and angry character into a warm, sympathetic one by the film's end. Born in South America and raised in British Guyana and England, Pounder began her acting career onstage, and, as early as 1982, appeared in the film I'M DANCING AS FAST AS I CAN. Another theatrical feature role came in 1984, in the Paul Winfield picture GO TELL IT ON THE MOUNTAIN. Since then Pounder's career has consisted of essentially bit parts, including a stint as a judge on TV's "L.A. Law" and roles in four television movies—1985's "The Atlanta Child Murders" and 1986's "As Summers Die," "If Tomorrow Comes," and "Resting Place," for which she received fourth billing. Her most memorable film role, before BAGDAD CAFE, came in 1985, when Pounder played the maid "Peaches Altamont" in John Huston's PRIZZI'S HONOR. After a long road of maid and welfare mother roles, Pounder has come into her own, her efforts rewarded by an NAACP Image Award nomination as best actress of the year.

TINA RATHBORNE

Although her first theatrical feature, ZELLY AND ME, was dumped into remote theaters like tossed–out leftovers, this was hardly the fault of director Tina Rathborne. A very personal, dark, and quiet psychological drama set in sunny Virginia in 1958, Rathborne's ZELLY AND ME was one of the most underrated Hollywood pictures in some time. It is the story of a misunderstood, orphaned eight–year–old girl, the overbearing grandmother with whom she is sent to live, and the caring nanny who bridges the gap between the two. In response to the grandmother's emotional abuse, the young girl comes to identify, at her nanny's urging, with the martyrdom of Joan of Arc. Directed with a sense of grace and spirituality that one usually associates with European cinema, ZELLY AND ME was caught in the David Puttnam–Dawn Steel changing of the guards at Columbia Pictures. As a result, the film was only barely released, despite its marketable cast—including the post–BLUE VELVET Isabella Rossellini and David Lynch. A 1973 Harvard graduate who received an MFA in film from Columbia University in 1983, Rathborne saw her education prove fruitful rather quickly. In 1984 she cowrote (with Nancy Dyer) and directed the acclaimed PBS "American Playhouse" film THE JOY THAT KILLS. Subsequently, with help from a former Columbia film instructor, Rathborne's script for ZELLY AND ME made it to David Puttnam's desk and in January 1987 a deal for the film's production was made. In an *Interview* magazine piece, Rathborne cited David Lynch and Brian De Palma (who is also her companion) as influences: "I would say we are three very mild–mannered people with extremely violent and strange imaginations . . . Maybe mine is some kind of feminine vent—feminine violence comes out in a different way." It is this violent underpinning to Rathborne's vision that makes her work so compelling and, apparently, so easy to misunderstand.

ALAN RICKMAN

As the terrorist Hans Gruber in this year's DIE HARD, Alan Rickman—in his movie debut—singlehandedly brought back to the screen the sort of suave, sophisticated, and thoroughly evil villain that used to pop up to torment Agent 007 in the early James Bond films. His deliciously nasty performance is the perfect counterpoint to the "blue–collar Joe" Bruce Willis persona, and the actors play off each other wonderfully. The British Rickman even gets a chance to employ an exaggerated American accent in a scene in which he is cornered by Willis—who only knows what his nemesis *sounds* like. Rickman didn't begin to study acting until he was in his late 20s, having trained as a graphic designer at the Chelsea School of Art for three years. At 26, he enrolled at the Royal Academy of Dramatic Art and was soon performing the classics at London's Royal Court, Hampstead, and Bush theatres. Rickman then joined the Royal Shakespeare Company, where, in 1985, he created the role of Le Vicomte de Valmont in the play "Les Liaisons Dangereuses." The play moved from London's West End to Broadway, where producer Joel Silver and director John McTiernan saw the actor in his Tony–nominated performance and immediately cast him as their villainous terrorist (ironically, John Malkovich would play Valmont in Stephen Frears' movie version, DANGEROUS LIAISONS). Although critical opinion of DIE HARD was mixed, even the negative reviews hailed Rickman's distinctive performance as Gruber. Rickman, whose success in Hollywood seems assured, walked off with his next film, playing Kevin Kline's eccentric artist friend in the 1989 release JANUARY MAN.

ROGER RABBIT

Though his wife, Jessica, has been getting all the attention lately—mainly from males who remain agog at her ample charms—Roger Rabbit has taken the world by storm. The first truly original cartoon character in years, Roger Rabbit owes his success to his many creators—from novelist Gary K. Wolf to director Robert Zemeckis to animator Richard Williams to vocal talent Charles Fleischer. The popularity of WHO FRAMED ROGER RABBIT, combined with a massive merchandising campaign, has made this cartoon bunny an instantly recognizable character. He is already a staple at Disneyland and Disney World, wandering the grounds along with Mickey Mouse, Donald Duck, and Goofy. Savvy merchandising alone cannot ensure success, however; does anyone really recall Gremlins or Ewoks with great fondness? Nope; you've got to have personality and Roger's got truckloads. With his stuttering speech, manic behavior, and wacky sense of humor, Roger managed to charm even Eddie Valiant—and he hated Toons. What does the future hold in store for Roger Rabbit? That seems to be a tightly held secret right now, so the public will have to be content with his appearances at Disney amusement parks and with his likeness on innumerable clothing items, bendable toys, paper plates, school supplies, and video games. Be it feature–length film or cartoon short, rest assured that the world has not seen the last of the inestimable Roger Rabbit.

MICHAEL ROOKER

Everybody loves a good villain, and actor Michael Rooker was happy to oblige in no less than four films this year. Although his roles in RENT–A–COP and ABOVE THE LAW were small, Rooker had a chance to prove what he could do as Chicago White Sox first baseman Arnold "Chick" Gandil in John Sayles' EIGHT MEN OUT and as a vicious Ku Klux Klansman in Alan Parker's controversial MISSISSIPPI BURNING. Born in Jasper, Alabama, Rooker moved with his family to Chicago in the mid–1960s and eventually enrolled at the Goodman School of Drama (at DePaul), earning an MFA. Upon graduation in 1982, he began working in Chicago's dynamic theater scene, appearing in productions at Wisdom Bridge, the Next Theatre Company, and Victory Gardens. Rooker also found regular movie work, with small parts in STREETS OF FIRE (1984) and LIGHT OF DAY (1987) and a starring role in HENRY, a low–budget independent film directed by John McNaughton. As the player who instigates the conspiracy to throw the game in EIGHT MEN OUT, Rooker perfectly captures Gandil's love of life in the fast lane and his bitterness toward the stingy team owner, Charles Comiskey. In MISSISSIPPI BURNING, Rooker is the embodiment of racism and audiences cheered at the powerful scene in which he finally gets his comeuppance at the hands of FBI man Gene Hackman. The busy actor recently completed a made–for–television movie titled "Gideon Oliver" with Lou Gossett, and is currently filming MUSIC BOX with Constantin Costa–Gavras, in which he will appear as Jessica Lange's brother—in his most challenging role to date and one that will allow him to demonstrate a much wider range of emotion.

TINA RATHBORNE

ALAN RICKMAN

ROGER RABBIT

MICHAEL ROOKER

UMA THURMAN

DIANE VENORA

GARY SINISE

Well known throughout the theater community as a cofounder and former artistic director of Chicago's Steppenwolf Theater Company, Gary Sinise arrived on the filmmaking scene in 1988 with his impressive and intelligent—albeit flawed—first feature, MILES FROM HOME. Although his only prior filmmaking experience was as director of an episode of the Michael Mann television series "Crime Story," Sinise brought with him to the set a reputation as one of the most intense stage directors and performers around. His Steppenwolf stagings of Sam Shepard's "True West" (with himself and John Malkovich in the leads), Lyle Kessler's "Orphans" (the costar of which, Kevin Anderson, brought the role to film in 1987 and appeared in MILES FROM HOME), and Lanford Wilson's "Balm in Gilead" helped bring the Chicago theater group international acclaim. After this measure of success, Sinise resigned as the company's artistic director and headed for Los Angeles (along with his wife, actress Moira Harris) with the hope of doing in film what he did in theater. On the strength of his confrontational acting and directing style, dubbed by some "the Chicago style," Sinise received an offer to direct Chris Gerolmo's screenplay about two brothers, one good and one bad. Placing the emphasis on acting, Sinise peppered his production with a number of Steppenwolf talents, including a co-starring role for Kevin Anderson and cameos for John Malkovich, Terry Kinney, Moira Harris, Randall Arney, Laurie Metcalf, and Francis Guinan. Sinise and his cast and crew received a moment of glory when MILES FROM HOME was shown in competition at the Cannes Film Festival. The film, however, received reviews ranging from unkind to lukewarm. Despite the poor box–office showing and the film's faults (the script's glossy, mythicizing view of the heartland), Sinise's career in film seems a promising one.

UMA THURMAN

Someone with the name "Uma" simply cannot be ignored, especially since the moniker refers to one of the mythical forms of the Hindu female divinity Siva–Shakti. Bestowing such a name to a young lady is a setup for great things, and there seems little doubt that Uma Thurman, the 18–year–old actress who appeared this year as the deflowered virgin Cecile de Volanges in Stephen Frears' DANGEROUS LIAISONS, will deliver on that promise. Born in Boston, raised in Woodstock, New York, and having spent time in Europe and India, Thurman left home at 15 to pursue an acting career in New York City. Although she temporarily did time as a dishwasher, Thurman eventually found work as a model and, at age 16, was given the lead in KISS DADDY GOOD NIGHT, an independent 16mm feature shot in New York. Early in 1988, Thurman had the misfortune to land a part in the pathetic "comedy" JOHNNY BE GOOD as Anthony Michael Hall's sweetheart. It was her appearance as Cecile de Volanges, however, that turned heads. If the typical initial reaction to Thurman's character is to stare and gasp at the heaving bosoms that threaten to burst from her 18th–century dresses (a costuming coup for the actress, perfectly symbolizing her character's sexual explosion), one is quick to realize that the rest of Thurman can act as well. Her comically delirious change from innocent virgin to insatiable teen is thoroughly enjoyable, and an indication of the talent and refreshing vitality that have made Thurman one of the fastest rising young actors of this year. Thurman makes her fourth film appearance costarring in a feature also filmed in 1988 but held up for a 1989 release, THE ADVENTURES OF BARON MUNCHAUSEN, Terry Gilliam's follow–up to BRAZIL.

DIANE VENORA

Although she first hit the screen in 1981 in the unusual horror film WOLFEN, actress Diane Venora really did not garner the attention she deserved until her virtuoso portrayal of Chan Parker in Clint Eastwood's magnificent biography of jazz musician Charlie Parker, BIRD. Not only does Venora bear a great physical resemblance to the character she plays (as does Forest Whitaker—who appeared in our People to Watch section in the 1987 annual), but she adroitly captures the spirit of the contradictory Chan Parker, a woman who was independent yet devoted, strong–willed yet vulnerable, and sophisticated yet childlike. It has taken Venora a long time to land a movie role as powerful as this one. Following WOLFEN she had supporting roles in THE COTTON CLUB (as Gloria Swanson); CRITICAL LIST; F/X; and IRONWEED, but her most significant work has been on the stage, where she has appeared in "The Seagull," "Peer Gynt," "Uncle Vanya," and "A Midsummer Night's Dream" and is one of the few women who have played the title role in "Hamlet" (at the New York Shakespeare Festival). To research her role in BIRD, Venora read Chan Parker's autobiography, *Life in E–Flat* (on which the film is based), spoke to Chan's friends and to jazz musicians, listened to Charlie Parker's music, and met with Chan herself, who had been flown to Hollywood from her home in France by director Eastwood. Venora made audiotapes of Chan's voice and observed the way she moved, using all the different bits and pieces to create a very vivid whole. The performances of Venora and Whitaker in BIRD are two of the finest pieces of acting this year, and that alone makes the film worth seeing, even if one isn't interested in jazz.

THE MOTION PICTURE ANNUAL

1989

Obituaries

Adams, Dorothy [Dorothy Adams Foulger]
Born 1910; died 16 March 1988, Woodland Hills, Calif.

Actress

Adams met her future husband, actor and director Byron Foulger, as a member of the touring Olsen Players. She and Foulger later joined the Pasadena Playhouse. The couple appeared together in several films; both were popular character actors specializing in timorous roles, with Adams most frequently playing downtrodden women. In the 1950s and 60s Adams became a lecturer on theater arts at UCLA. Her films include: BROADWAY MUSKETEERS; CONDEMNED WOMEN (1938); BACHELOR MOTHER; CALLING DR. KILDARE; DISPUTED PASSAGE; NINOTCHKA; THE WOMEN (1939); A CHILD IS BORN; CROSS–COUNTRY ROMANCE; THE GREAT MEDDLER; LUCKY PARTNERS; NOBODY'S CHILDREN; UNTAMED; WE WHO ARE YOUNG (1940); AFFECTIONATELY YOURS; THE DEVIL COMMANDS; THE FLAME OF NEW ORLEANS; MY LIFE WITH CAROLINE; PENNY SERENADE; THE SHEPHERD OF THE HILLS; TOBACCO ROAD; WHISTLING IN THE DARK (1941); BEDTIME STORY; HI NEIGHBOR!; LADY GANGSTER (1942); O MY DARLING CLEMENTINE; SO PROUDLY WE HAIL (1943); BATHING BEAUTY; LAURA; SINCE YOU WENT AWAY (1944); CAPTAIN EDDIE; CIRCUMSTANTIAL EVIDENCE; FALLEN ANGEL; MISS SUSIE SLAGLE'S; PHANTOM'S INC. (1945); THE BEST YEARS OF OUR LIVES; THE INNER CIRCLE; THE GANGSTER; NOCTURNE; O.S.S.; SENTIMENTAL JOURNEY (1946); THE FOXES OF HARROW; THAT'S MY MAN; THE TROUBLE WITH WOMEN; UNCONQUERED; WILL TOMORROW EVER COME? (1947); HE WALKED BY NIGHT; THE SAINTED SISTERS; SITTING PRETTY (1948); DOWN TO THE SEA IN SHIPS; NOT WANTED; SAMSON AND DELILAH (1949); THE CARIBOO TRAIL; THE JACKPOT; MONTANA; THE OUTRIDERS; PAID IN FULL (1950); THE FIRST LEGION (1951); CARRIE; FORT OSAGE; THE GREATEST SHOW ON EARTH; JET JOB; THE WINNING TEAM (1952); THE PRODIGAL (1955); THE BROKEN STAR; JOHNNY CONCHO; THE KILLING; THE MAN IN THE GREY FLANNEL SUIT; THE TEN COMMANDMENTS; THESE WILDER YEARS; THREE FOR JAMIE DAWN (1956); AN AFFAIR TO REMEMBER; THE BUCKSKIN LADY (1957); THE BIG COUNTRY; GUNMAN'S WALK; UNWED MOTHER (1958); FROM THE TERRACE (1960); THE GOOD GUYS AND THE BAD GUYS (1969); PEEPER (1975).

Ashby, Hal
Born Ogden, Utah, 1936; died 27 Dec. 1988, Malibu, Calif.

Director–Editor

A versatile and acclaimed director, Ashby first made his mark in film as an equally well-respected editor—notably in collaboration with Norman Jewison, whose IN THE HEAT OF THE NIGHT garnered Ashby a Best Editing Oscar and whose THE THOMAS CROWN AFFAIR and GAILY, GAILY Ashby associate produced. His directorial debut was 1970's THE LANDLORD; his next feature, 1971's HAROLD AND MAUDE (in which he appeared in a cameo, as he did in several of his films), became a favorite with innumerable revival house audiences. Ashby made a string of distinguished films in the 1970s, including THE LAST DETAIL; SHAMPOO; BOUND FOR GLORY; BEING THERE; and COMING HOME (earning a Best Director Oscar nomination for the last), but his more recent films have been critical and commercial disappointments. His films include: THE CINCINNATI KID (ed); THE LOVED ONE (ed) (1965); THE RUSSIANS ARE COMING, THE RUSSIANS ARE COMING (ed) (1966); IN THE HEAT OF THE NIGHT (ed) (1967); THE THOMAS CROWN AFFAIR (ed) (1968); THE LANDLORD (d) (1970); HAROLD AND MAUDE (a&d) (1971); THE LAST DETAIL (d) (1973); SHAMPOO (d) (1975); BOUND FOR GLORY (d) (1976); COMING HOME (a&d) (1978); BEING THERE (a&d); THE HAMPSTER OF HAPPINESS (d) (1979); SECOND–HAND HEARTS (d) (1981); LET'S SPEND THE NIGHT TOGETHER (d) (doc); LOOKIN' TO GET OUT (d) (1982); THE SLUGGER'S WIFE (a&d) (1985); 8 MILLION WAYS TO DIE (d) (1986); HAND CARVED COFFINS (d) (in preproduction, 1988).

Ballard, Lucien
Born 6 May 1904, Miami, Okla.; died 1 Oct. 1988, Rancho Mirage, Calif.

Cinematographer

Ballard began his career as a cutter and assistant cameraman at Paramount; he was reportedly seduced by the film world when a friend took him to a three-day party at Clara Bow's. After assisting on MOROCCO (1930), Ballard became a favorite of Josef von Sternberg, for whom he shot CRIME AND PUNISHMENT; THE DEVIL IS A WOMAN; and THE KING STEPS OUT in 1935–36. Hailed as a master of lighting and of both interior black–and–white and western color photography, Ballard was particularly associated with directors John Brahm (THE LODGER), Henry Hathaway (TRUE GRIT), Sam

Peckinpah (THE WILD BUNCH; RIDE THE HIGH COUNTRY) and Budd Boetticher (THE RISE AND FALL OF LEGS DIAMOND). He was briefly married to Merle Oberon, and shot five of her films. His films include: MOROCCO (1930); CRIME AND PUNISHMENT; THE DEVIL IS A WOMAN (1935); CRAIG'S WIFE; THE FINAL HOUR; THE KING STEPS OUT (1936); DEVIL'S PLAYGROUND; GIRLS CAN PLAY; I PROMISE TO PAY; LIFE BEGINS WITH LOVE; RACKETEERS IN EXILE; THE SHADOW; VENUS MAKES TROUBLE (1937); FLIGHT TO FAME; HIGHWAY PATROL; THE LONE WOLF IN PARIS; PENITENTIARY; SQUADRON OF HONOR (1938); BLIND ALLEY; COAST GUARD; LET US LIVE; OUTSIDE THESE WALLS; RIO GRANDE; TEXAS STAMPEDE; THE THUNDERING WEST (1939); THE VILLAIN STILL PURSUED HER (1940); MOONTIDE; ORCHESTRA WIVES; THE UNDYING MONSTER; WHISPERING GHOSTS; WILD GEESE CALLING (1942); BOMBER'S MOON; HOLY MATRIMONY; TONIGHT WE RAID CALAIS (1943); THE LODGER; SWEET AND LOWDOWN (1944); THIS LOVE OF OURS (1945); TEMPTATION (1946); NIGHT SONG (1947); BERLIN EXPRESS (1948); THE HOUSE ON TELEGRAPH HILL; FIXED BAYONETS; LET'S MAKE IT LEGAL (1951); DIPLOMATIC COURIER; DON'T BOTHER TO KNOCK; NIGHT WITHOUT SLEEP; O. HENRY'S FULL HOUSE; RETURN OF THE TEXAN (1952); THE DESERT RATS; THE GLORY BRIGADE; INFERNO (1953); NEW FACES; PRINCE VALIANT; THE RAID (1954); THE MAGNIFICENT MATADOR; SEVEN CITIES OF GOLD; WHITE FEATHER (1955); THE KILLER IS LOOSE; THE KILLING; THE KING AND FOUR QUEENS; A KISS BEFORE DYING; THE PROUD ONES (1956); BAND OF ANGELS; THE UNHOLY WIFE (1957); ANNA LUCASTA; BUCHANAN RIDES ALONE; I MARRIED A WOMAN; MURDER BY CONTRACT (1958); AL CAPONE; CITY OF FEAR (1959); THE BRAMBLE BUSH; DESIRE IN THE DUST; PAY OR DIE; THE RISE AND FALL OF LEGS DIAMOND (1960); MARINES, LET'S GO; THE PARENT TRAP; SUSAN SLADE (1961); RIDE THE HIGH COUNTRY (1962); THE CARETAKERS; TAKE HER, SHE'S MINE; WALL OF NOISE; WIVES AND LOVERS (1963); THE NEW INTERNS; ROUSTABOUT (1964); BOEING BOEING; DEAR BRIGETTE; THE SONS OF KATIE ELDER (1965); AN EYE FOR AN EYE; NEVADA SMITH (1966); HOUR OF THE GUN (1967); HOW SWEET IT IS; THE PARTY; WILL PENNY (1968); TRUE GRIT; THE WILD BUNCH (1969); THE BALLAD OF CABLE HOGUE; THE HAWAIIANS (1970); ARRUZA; A TIME FOR DYING; WHAT'S THE MATTER WITH HELEN? (1971); THE GETAWAY; JUNIOR BONNER (1972); LADY ICE (1973); THOMASINE AND BUSHROD; THREE THE HARD WAY (1974); BREAKOUT (1975); BREAKHEART PASS; DRUM; FROM NOON TO THREE; MIKEY AND NICKY; ST. IVES (1976); RABBIT TEST (1978).

Belasco

Belasco, Leon [Leonid Simeonovich Berladsky]
Born 11 Oct. 1902, Odessa [USSR]; died 1 June 1988, Orange, Calif.

Actor

Born in Odessa, educated in Manchuria and Japan, Belasco began a musical career in the early 1920s that led him from Tokyo (where he was first violinist with the symphony) to Los Angeles, where he appeared on radio, leading his own orchestra. He began acting in films in 1938 and continued to do so through the '70s, most often playing foreign or comic ethnic characters, especially excitable types. Belasco also acted on radio, most notably on "The Man Called X," and in TV programs and commercials. His films include: BROADWAY SERENADE; FISHERMAN'S WHARF; GOOD GIRLS GO TO PARIS; LEGION OF THE LOST FLYERS; TOPPER TAKES A TRIP (1939); COMRADE X; I TAKE THIS WOMAN; IT'S A DATE; THE LADY IN QUESTION; LUCKY PARTNERS; THE MUMMY'S HAND; MY FAVORITE WIFE; TUGBOAT ANNIE SAILS AGAIN (1940); THE CHOCOLATE SOLDIER; DESIGN FOR SCANDAL; A GIRL, A GUY, AND A GOB; I'LL WAIT FOR YOU; KISSES FOR BREAKFAST; NEVER GIVE A SUCKER AN EVEN BREAK; NOTHING BUT THE TRUTH; PLAYMATES; SKYLARK; TALL, DARK AND HANDSOME; WHERE DID YOU GET THAT GIRL? (1941); CASABLANCA; GIVE OUT, SISTERS; HOLIDAY INN; THE NIGHT BEFORE THE DIVORCE; OVER MY DEAD BODY; ROAD TO MOROCCO; ROXIE HART; THAT OTHER WOMAN; YANKEE DOODLE DANDY (1942); THE GANG'S ALL HERE; THE HEAT'S ON; HERS TO HOLD; IT COMES UP LOVE; SHE'S FOR ME (1943); AND THE ANGELS SING; THE CONSPIRATORS; MEET THE PEOPLE; NIGHT CLUB GIRL; PIN UP GIRL; SAN DIEGO, I LOVE YOU; STORM OVER LISBON (1944); EARL CARROLL'S VANITIES; EASY TO LOOK AT; HOLLYWOOD AND VINE; OUT OF THIS WORLD; WONDER MAN; YOLANDA AND THE THIEF (1945); LITTLE IODINE; SUSPENSE; SWING PARADE OF 1946 (1946); IT HAPPENED ON 5TH AVENUE; PHILO VANCE RETURNS (1947); EVERY GIRL SHOULD BE MARRIED; FOR THE LOVE OF MARY; I, JANE DOE; THREE DARING DAUGHTERS (1948); ADVENTURES OF DON JUAN; BAGDAD; EVERYBODY DOES IT; HOLIDAY IN HAVANA; LOVE

HAPPY (1949); ABBOTT AND COSTELLO IN THE FOREIGN LEGION; BOMBA AND THE HIDDEN CITY; LOVE THAT BRUTE; NANCY GOES TO RIO; PLEASE BELIEVE ME; THE TOAST OF NEW ORLEANS (1950); CUBAN FIREBALL; THE GOLDEN HORDE; HAVANA ROSE; LITTLE EGYPT (1951); THE FABULOUS SENORITA; GOBAS AND GALS; SON OF ALI BABA (1952); CALL ME MADAM; GERALDINE; JALOPY (1953); CAN–CAN (1960); MY SIX LOVES (1963); THE ART OF LOVE (1965); SUPERDAD (1974).

Berkeley, Ballard

Born 1904; died 16 Jan. 1988, London, England

Actor

Berkeley began in films playing leading roles that exploited his courtly, lanky military bearing. Early in his career, he also toured with the Fred and Adele Astaire revue "Stop Flirting." Berkeley later became known as a popular character actor of British films, theater, and television in such comic roles as the affable chap, the dogged policeman, the old lecher, and the retired military man—playing the last type most famously and recently as the dotty major of John Cleese's "Fawlty Towers" series. His films include: THE CHINESE BUNGALOW; LONDON MELODY (1930); TROUBLE (1933); WHITE ENSIGN (1934); EAST MEETS WEST (1936); JENNIFER HALE; THE LAST ADVENTURERS (1937); THE OUTSIDER (1938); THE SAINT IN LONDON (1939); IN WHICH WE SERVE; I BECAME A CRIMINAL (1947); QUIET WEEKEND (1948); BLACK-MAILED; STAGE FRIGHT; THIRD TIME LUCKY (1950); THE LONG DARK HALL (1951); THE NIGHT WON'T TALK (1952); THE BLUE PARROT; OPERATION DIPLOMAT; WHITE FIRE (1953); CHILD'S PLAY; CIRCUMSTANTIAL EVIDENCE; DANGEROUS CARGO; DELAYED ACTION (1954); SEE HOW THEY RUN (1955); PASSPORT TO TREASON (1956); AFTER THE BALL; BULLET FROM THE PAST; JUST MY LUCK; MEN OF SHERWOOD FOREST (1957); THE BETRAYAL; CHAIN OF EVENTS; FURTHER UP THE CREEK; LIFE IS A CIRCUS; THE MAN WHO WOULDN'T TALK (1958); TEENAGE BAD GIRL (1959); TROUBLE IN THE SKY (1961); THE STOLEN AIRLINER (1962); IMPACT; A MATTER OF CHOICE (1963); THE NIGHT CALLER (1965); THE MURDER GAME (1966); HOSTILE WITNESS; STAR! (1968); THE WEEKEND MURDERS (1972); CONFESSIONS OF A DRIVING INSTRUCTOR (1976); THE PLAYBIRDS (1978); CONFESSIONS FROM THE DAVID GALAXY AFFAIR; QUEEN OF THE BLUES (1979); THE WILDCATS OF ST. TRINIANS; LITTLE LORD FAUNTLEROY (1980); BULLSHOT (1983).

Besser, Joe

Besser

Born 1907; died 1 March 1988, Los Angeles, Calif.

Actor–Comedian

Besser was a member of the Three Stooges from 1955 to 1959, stepping into the role of third Stooge after Shemp Howard's death. He appeared in 19 shorts as Joe (the Stooge who whined "Ooh, you crazy" in response to Moe Howard's abuse), and specialized in playing obnoxious, bratty types, including the character Stinky on Abbott and Costello's TV show. Besser, who also became a regular on Joey Bishop's and Ken Murray's TV programs, left the Stooges to appear in the feature film SAY ONE FOR ME shortly before the television–aided explosion in the slapstick trio's popularity. His feature films include: HOT STEEL (1940); HEY, ROOKIE (1944); EADIE WAS A LADY (1945); TALK ABOUT A LADY (1946); FEUDIN', FUSSIN AND A–FIGHTIN (1948); AFRICA SCREAMS; WOMAN IN HIDING (1949); THE DESERT HAWK; JOE PALOOKA MEETS HUMPHREY; OUTSIDE THE WALL (1950); I THE JURY; SINS OF JEZEBEL (1953); ABBOTT AND COSTELLO MEET THE KEYSTONE KOPS; HEADLINE HUNTERS (1955); TWO–GUN LADY (1956); PLUNDERERS OF PAINTED FLATS; THE ROOKIE; SAY ONE FOR ME; THE STORY ON PAGE ONE; WOODCUTTER'S HOUSE (1959); LET'S MAKE LOVE (1960); THE ERRAND BOY (1961); THE SILENT CALL (1961); HAND OF DEATH (1962); WITH SIX YOU GET EGGROLL (1968); THE COMEBACK (1969); WHICH WAY TO THE FRONT? (1970).

Bodeen, DeWitt

Carey

Born 25 July 1908, Fresno, Calif.; died 12 March 1988, Woodland Hills Calif.

Stage/TV/Screenwriter–Journalist

A former stage actor with a productive career as a playwright already under way, Bodeen joined RKO as a reader in the late 30s and was Aldous Huxley's research assistant for JANE EYRE. In the next decade he wrote or cowrote several scripts for RKO, including the Val Lewton–produced chillers CAT PEOPLE; THE CURSE OF THE CAT PEOPLE; and THE SEVENTH VICTIM. After the 1940s Bodeen went on to write more than 50 teleplays, contribute frequently to film periodicals, author several books on film, and occasionally collaborate on film scripts. His films include: CAT PEOPLE (1942); THE SEVENTH VICTIM (1943); THE CURSE OF THE CAT PEOPLE; THE YELLOW CANARY (1944); THE ENCHANTED COTTAGE (1945); NIGHT SONG (1947); I REMEMBER MAMA; THE MIRACLE OF THE BELLS (1948); MRS. MIKE (1949); THE GIRL IN THE KREMLIN (1957); TWELVE TO THE MOON (1960); BILLY BUDD (1962).

Bozzuffi, Marcel

Born 28 Oct. 1929, Rennes, France; died 2 Feb. 1988, Paris, France

Actor–Writer–Director

Bozzuffi debuted on–screen as a truck driver in GAS–OIL (1955). He went on to a career in primarily French and Italian films marked by frequent portrayals of assorted criminal types, including several gangsters, the crazed gunman Gene Hackman chases in THE FRENCH CONNECTION, and the homosexual killer Vago in Z. Bozzuffi directed himself (from his own screenplay) in 1969 in L'AMERICAIN; his portrayal of a police inspector in Claude LeLouch's LIFE, LOVE, DEATH was one of his few screen roles on the right side of the law. His films include: GAS–OIL (1955); LA MEILLEURE PART; LE SALAIRE DU PECHE (1956); LE ROUGE EST MIS (1957); LE PIEGE (1958); ASPHALTE (1959); LE CAID (1960); TINTIN ET LE MYSTERE DE LA TOISON D'OR (1961); THE DAY AND THE HOUR; MAIGRET VOIT ROUGE (1963); SKY ABOVE HEAVEN (1964); LE DIEUXIEME SOUFFLE; THE SLEEPING CAR MURDER (1966); LE SAMOURAI; THE UPPER HAND (1967); L'AMERICAIN (a,d&w); LIFE, LOVE, DEATH; Z (1969); THE LADY IN THE CAR WITH GLASSES AND A GUN; LE VOYOU; LOVE IS A FUNNY THING; TIME OF THE WOLVES; VERTIGE POUR UN TUEUR (1970); COMPTES A REBOURS; THE FRENCH CONNECTION (1971); IMAGES; LES HOMMES; TROIS MILLIARDS SAN ASCENSEUR (1972); LES FILS (1973); CARAVAN TO VACCARES; THE DESTRUCTORS (1974); DRAMA OF THE RICH; LE GITAN (1975); CADAVERI ECCELLENTI; CHINO; LE DEUXIEME SOUFFLE (1976); LA GRANDE BOURGEOISIE; LE JUGE FAYARD DIT LE SHERIFF; MARCH OR DIE (1977); BLOODLINE; THE PASSAGE (1979); IL CAPPATTO DI ASTRAKAN (1980); LA CAGE AUX FOLLES II (1981); IDENTIFICATION OF A WOMAN (1983); LE OGRE (1987).

Butler, Lawrence W.

Born Akron, Ohio; died 19 Oct. 1988, Fallbrook, Calif., age 80

Special Effects Director

Butler began in films assisting his father, William Butler, a special and optical effects director at Warner Bros. He then worked for Alexander Korda in England, doing special effects on THE THIEF OF BAGHDAD (1940) and JUNGLE BOOK (1942), both of which won Butler Academy Awards. As the head of Columbia's special effects department after WW II, he also received Oscars for THAT HAMILTON WOMAN (1941) and A THOUSAND AND ONE NIGHTS (1945), as well as a special scientific and technical award in 1975. His films include: THINGS TO COME (1936); DARK JOURNEY; FIRE OVER ENGLAND; THE MAN WHO COULD WORK MIRACLES (1937); SOUTH RIDING (1938); THE THIEF OF BAGHDAD (1940); LYDIA; THAT HAMILTON WOMAN (1941); CASABLANCA; JUNGLE BOOK; TO BE OR NOT TO BE (1942); DESTINATION TOKYO; JANIE (1944); THE HORN BLOWS AT MIDNIGHT; SARATOGA TRUNK; A THOUSAND AND ONE NIGHTS; TONIGHT AND EVERY NIGHT (1945); THE LADY FROM SHANGHAI (1948); THE CAINE MUTINY (1954); THE DEVIL AT FOUR O CLOCK (1961); PANIC IN YEAR ZERO! (1962); ROBINSON CRUSOE ON MARS (1964); IN HARM'S WAY (1965); MAROONED; McKENNA'S GOLD (1969).

Cagney, William

Born 26 March 1905, New York, N.Y.; died 4 Jan. 1988, Newport Beach, Calif.

Producer–Actor

William Cagney was his brother James' closest confidante and adviser, first as an assistant producer at Warner Bros. (by the terms of James Cagney's contract) and later as head of William Cagney Productions, which sought to expand the star's commercial and artistic opportunities. William, who closely resembled his brother, had his own brief acting career in the 1930s; years later he played the brother to James' character in Cagney Productions' KISS TOMORROW GOODBYE (1950). His films include: ACE OF ACES (a) (1933); PALOOKA (a) (1934); FLIRTING WITH DANGER (a); LOST IN THE STRATOSPHERE (a); STOLEN HARMONY (a) (1935); THE TORRID ZONE (1940); THE BRIDE CAME C.O.D.; CITY FOR CONQUEST; THE STRAWBERRY BLONDE (1941); CAPTAINS OF THE CLOUDS; YANKEE DOODLE DANDY (1942) JOHNNY COME LATELY (1943); BLOOD ON THE SUN (1945); 13 RUE MADELEINE (1946); THE TIME OF YOUR LIFE (1948); KISS TOMORROW GOODBYE (p&a) (1950); ONLY THE VALIANT (1951); BUGLES IN THE AFTERNOON (1952); A LION IS IN THE STREETS (1953).

Carey, Olive [Olive Fuller Golden, Olive Deering]

Born 31 Jan. 1896; died 13 March 1988, Carpinteria, Calif.

Actress

The daughter of a founder of one of the first US actor's unions, Carey began her long career under the name Olive Golden on the silent screen. An original stock player for D.W. Griffith, she debuted in his THE SORROWFUL SHORE (1913). In 1916 she married cowboy star Harry Carey, later acting opposite him in many silent westerns, introducing him to John Ford (whose directorial career she reportedly helped launch), and managing his career. She emerged from semiretirement after her husband's death in 1947, acting under her married name, and is perhaps best known now for her appearances in the 1950s with John Wayne in THE SEARCHERS and THE ALAMO. Her films include: THE SORROWFUL SHORE (1913); TESS OF THE STORM COUNTRY (1914); JUST JIM (1915); LOVE'S LARIAT; A NIGHT ON THE RANGE (1916); THE SOUL HERDER (1917); TRADER HORN (1931); NAUGHTY MARIETTA (1935); ON DANGEROUS GROUND; THE WHIP HAND (1951); FACE TO FACE; MONKEY BUSINESS (1952); AFFAIR WITH A STRANGER (1953); ROGUE COP (1954); THE COBWEB; I DIED A THOUSAND TIMES (1955); PILLARS OF THE SKY; THE SEARCHERS (1956); GUNFIGHT AT THE O.K. CORRAL; NIGHT PASSAGE; RUN OF THE ARROW; THE WINGS OF EAGLES (1957); THE ALAMO; (1960); TWO RODE TOGETHER (1961); BILLY THE KID VS. DRACULA (1966).

Carradine, John [Richmond Reed Carradine, John Peter Richmond]
Born 5 Feb. 1906, New York, N.Y.; died 27 Nov. 1988, Milan, Italy
Actor

Carradine (born Richmond Reed Carradine) was both a painter and an actor when he came to Hollywood in 1928. Two years later he made his film debut in TOL'ABLE DAVID (billed as John Peter Richmond), embarking on a career that established him as one of filmdom's busiest, best-known, and most-respected character actors. His striking gaunt looks and deep voice served in a variety of offbeat characterizations, including bohemians and (most frequently) villains. He appeared in 10 films directed by John Ford (Casey in THE GRAPES OF WRATH is considered one of his best roles), and was frequently cast by Cecil B. De Mille, Henry King, and Richard Boleslawski, among others. As his career progressed, Carradine appeared with increasing frequency in low-budget, often low-quality horror movies, reportedly taking the roles to finance his stage career, in particular his lifelong devotion to Shakespearean performance. Like Carradine himself (whose father was an attorney, journalist, and poet), his sons have followed their father's artistic bent. David, Robert, Keith, and Bruce are all actors; Christopher Carradine is an architect. Carradine's films include: BRIGHT LIGHTS; TOL'ABLE DAVID (1930); HEAVEN ON EARTH (1931); FORGOTTEN COMMANDMENTS; SIGN OF THE CROSS (1932); THE INVISIBLE MAN; THE STORY OF TEMPLE DRAKE; THIS DAY AND AGE; TO THE LAST MAN (1933); THE BLACK CAT; CLEOPATRA; THE MEANEST GAL IN TOWN (1934); ALIAS MARY DOW; BAD BOY; THE BRIDE OF FRANKENSTEIN; CARDINAL RICHELIEU; CLIVE OF INDIA; THE CRUSADES; LES MISERABLES; THE MAN WHO BROKE THE BANK AT MONTE CARLO; SHE GETS HER MAN; TRANSIENT LADY (1935); ANYTHING GOES; DANIEL BOONE; DIMPLES; THE GARDEN OF ALLAH; MARY OF SCOTLAND; A MESSAGE TO GARCIA; THE PRISONER OF SHARK ISLAND; RAMONA; UNDER TWO FLAGS; WHITE FANG; WINTERSET (1936); ALI BABA GOES TO TOWN; CAPTAINS COURAGEOUS; DANGER--LOVE AT WORK; THE HURRICANE; THE LAST GANGSTER; LAUGHING AT TROUBLE; LOVE UNDER FIRE; NANCY STEELE IS MISSING; THANK YOU, MR. MOTO; THIS IS MY AFFAIR (1937); ALEXANDER'S RAGTIME BAND; FOUR MEN AND A PRAYER; GATEWAY; I'LL GIVE A MILLION; INTERNATIONAL SETTLEMENT; KENTUCKY MOONSHINE; KIDNAPPED; OF HUMAN HEARTS; SUBMARINE PATROL (1938); CAPTAIN FURY; DRUMS ALONG THE MOHAWK; FIVE CAME BACK; FRONTIER MARSHAL; THE HOUND OF THE BASKERVILLES; JESSE JAMES; MR. MOTO'S LAST WARNING; STAGECOACH; THE THREE MUSKETEERS (1939); BRIGHAM YOUNG--FRONTIERSMAN; CHAD HANNA; THE GRAPES OF WRATH; THE RETURN OF FRANK JAMES (1940); ALL THAT MONEY CAN BUY; BLOOD AND SAND; MAN HUNT; SWAMP WATER; WESTERN UNION (1941); NORTHWEST RANGERS; REUNION IN FRANCE; SON OF FURY; WHISPERING GHOSTS (1942); CAPTIVE WILD WOMAN; GANGWAY FOR TOMORROW; HITLER'S MADMAN; I ESCAPED FROM THE GESTAPO; ISLE OF FORGOTTEN SINS; REVENGE OF THE ZOMBIES; SILVER SPURS (1943); THE ADVENTURES OF MARK TWAIN; ALASKA; BARBARY COAST GENT; THE BLACK PARACHUTE; BLUEBEARD; HOUSE OF FRANKENSTEIN; INVISIBLE MAN'S REVENGE; JUNGLE WOMAN; THE MUMMY'S GHOST; RETURN OF THE APE MAN; VOODOO MAN; WATERFRONT (1944); CAPTAIN KIDD; FALLEN ANGEL; HOUSE OF DRACULA; IT'S IN THE BAG (1945); DOWN MISSOURI WAY; THE FACE OF MARBLE (1946); THE PRIVATE AFFAIRS OF BEL AMI (1947); C-MAN (1949); CASANOVA'S BIG NIGHT; THE EGYPTIAN; JOHNNY GUITAR; THUNDER PASS (1954); DESERT SANDS; THE FEMALE JUNGLE; HALF HUMAN; THE KENTUCKIAN; STRANGER ON HORSEBACK (1955); AROUND THE WORLD IN 80 DAYS; THE BLACK SLEEP; THE COURT JESTER; DARK VENTURE; HIDDEN GUNS; THE TEN COMMANDMENTS (1956); HELL SHIP MUTINY; THE STORY OF MANKIND; THE TRUE STORY OF JESSE JAMES; THE UNEARTHLY (1957); THE LAST HURRAH; THE PROUD REBEL; SHOWDOWN AT BOOT HILL (1958); THE COSMIC MAN; THE INCREDIBLE PETRIFIED WORLD; INVISIBLE INVADERS; THE OREGON TRAIL (1959); THE ADVENTURES OF HUCKLEBERRY FINN; SEX KITTENS GO TO COLLEGE; TARZAN THE MAGNIFICENT (1960); INVASION OF THE ANIMAL PEOPLE; THE MAN WHO SHOT LIBERTY VALANCE (1962); CHEYENNE AUTUMN; THE PATSY; WIZARD OF MARS (1964); CURSE OF THE STONE HAND; HOUSE OF THE BLACK DEATH; PSYCHO A GO-GO! (1965); BILLY THE KID VS. DRACULA; BROKEN SABRE; THE HOSTAGE; MUNSTER, GO HOME; NIGHT OF THE BEAST; NIGHT TRAIN TO MUNDO FINE (1966); BLOOD OF DRACULA'S CASTLE; CREATURES OF THE RED PLANET;

DR. TERROR'S GALLERY OF HORRORS; HILLBILLYS IN A HAUNTED HOUSE; LONELY MAN (1967); AUTOPSIA DE UN FANTASMA; GENESIS; THE HELICOPTER SPIES; MADAME DEATH; PACTO DIABOLICO; THEY RAN FOR THEIR LIVES (1968); THE ASTRO-ZOMBIES; CAIN'S WAY; THE GOOD GUYS AND THE BAD GUYS; THE GUN RIDERS; MAN WITH THE SYNTHETIC BRAIN; THE TROUBLE WITH GIRLS (AND HOW TO GET INTO IT); THE VAMPIRES (1969); BLOOD OF FRANKENSTEIN; HELL'S BLOODY DEVILS; HORROR OF THE BLOOD MONSTERS; IS THIS TRIP REALLY NECESSARY?; THE McMASTERS; MYRA BRECKINRIDGE (1970); THE SEVEN MINUTES; SHINBONE ALLEY (1971); BOXCAR BERTHA; BLOOD OF GHASTLY HORROR; EVERYTHING YOU ALWAYS WANTED TO KNOW ABOUT SEX BUT WERE AFRAID TO ASK; THE GATLING GUN; MOONCHILD; PORTNOY'S COMPLAINT; RICHARD; SHADOW HOUSE (1972); BAD CHARLESTON CHARLIE; BIG FOOT; HEX; HOUSE OF DRACULA'S DAUGHTER; LEGACY OF BLOOD; SUPERCHICK; TERROR IN THE WAX MUSEUM (1973); THE HOUSE OF SEVEN CORPSES; SILENT NIGHT, BLOODY NIGHT (1974); MARY, MARY, BLOODY MARY (1975); THE KILLER INSIDE ME; THE LAST TYCOON; THE SHOOTIST; WON TON TON, THE DOG WHO SAVED HOLLYWOOD (1976); CRASH; GOLDEN RENDEZVOUS; JOURNEY INTO THE BEYOND; THE MOUSE AND HIS CHILD; SATAN'S CHEERLEADERS; THE SENTINEL; SHOCK WAVES; THE WHITE BUFFALO (1977); THE BEES; SUNSET COVE (1978); THE MANDATE OF HEAVEN; MONSTER; NOCTURNA; TEHERAN INCIDENT; THE VAMPIRE HOOKERS (1979); THE BOOGEY MAN; PHOBIA (1980); FRANKENSTEIN ISLAND; THE HOWLING; THE MONSTER CLUB; THE NESTING (1981); SATAN'S MISTRESS; THE SCARECROW; THE SECRET OF NIMH (1982); BOOGEYMAN II; THE HOUSE OF LONG SHADOWS; THE IMMORAL MINORITY PICTURE SHOW (1983); THE ICE PIRATES (1984); EVILS OF THE NIGHT; THE TOMB; THE VALS (1985); BIGFOOT (doc); BOOGEYMAN III; CAPTAIN WILLOUGHBY; THE ICE KING; PEGGY SUE GOT MARRIED; REVENGE; SECRETS OF DR. TAVANER; WALDEN'S POND (doc) (1986); MONSTER IN THE CLOSET (1987); STAR SLAMMER (1988).

Carradine

Castellano, Richard
Born 4 Sept. 1933, Bronx, N.Y.; died 10 Dec. 1988, North Bergen, N.J.
Actor

Castellano took up acting in 1961; four years later he starred in the original off-Broadway production of Arthur Miller's "A View from the Bridge." He was highly regarded for his portrayals of Italian--Americans, including the mafioso Clemenza in THE GODFATHER; his Tony-and Oscar-nominated performance in the stage (1968) and film (1970) versions of LOVERS AND OTHER STRANGERS; and lead roles in TV's "The Super" and "Joe and Sons" series. With Ardell Sheridan, his wife, he was writing a history of method acting at the time of his death. His films include: A FINE MADNESS (1966); LOVERS AND OTHER STRANGERS (1970); THE GODFATHER (1972); NIGHT OF THE JUGGLER (1980).

Chandler, Chick
Born 18 Jan. 1905, Kingston, N.Y.; died 30 Sept. 1988, Laguna Beach, Calif
Actor

After beginning his career in legitimate theater and vaudeville, Chandler broke into films with RED LOVE in 1925. He had a long career in movies, taking both lead and supporting roles in a number of 1930s and 40s B films, often playing befuddled types. In 1955-56, Chandler costarred in the television series "Soldiers of Fortune"; in 1961 he was featured in "One Happy Family." His films include: RED LOVE (1925); BLOOD MONEY; MELODY CRUISE; SWEEPINGS (1933); HAROLD TEEN; THE PARTY'S OVER (1934); ALIAS MARY DOW; CIRCUMSTANTIAL EVIDENCE; LIGHTNING STRIKES TWICE; MURDER ON A HONEYMOON (1935); IN PARIS, A.W.O.L.; STAR FOR A NIGHT; STRAIGHT FROM THE SHOULDER; TANGO; THREE OF A KIND (1936); BORN RECKLESS; LADY FIGHTS BACK; LOVE AND HISSES; OFF TO THE RACES; ONE MILE FROM HEAVEN; PORTIA ON TRIAL; SING AND BE HAPPY; TIME OUT FOR ROMANCE; WOMAN-WISE (1937); CITY GIRL KENTUCKY; MR. MOTO TAKES A CHANCE; SPEED TO BURN; TIME OUT FOR MURDER; WHILE NEW YORK SLEEPS (1938); HOLLYWOOD CAVALCADE; HOTEL FOR WOMEN; INSIDE STORY; MISSING EVIDENCE; THE MYSTERIOUS MISS X; ROSE OF WASHINGTON SQUARE; SWANEE RIVER; TOO BUSY TO WORK (1939); CHARTER PILOT; FREE, BLONDE AND 21; HONEYMOON DEFERRED; ON THEIR OWN; PIER 13 (1940); BLONDIE IN SOCIETY; THE BRIDE CAME C.O.D.; CADET GIRL; THE PEOPLE VS. DR. KILDARE; PUDDIN' HEAD; REMEMBER THE DAY; RIDE, KELLY, RIDE; SAILORS ON LEAVE; TWO IN A TAXI (1941); BABY FACE MORGAN; THE BIG SHOT; A GENTLEMAN AT HEART; HOME IN WYOMIN'; I WAKE UP SCREAMING; SPRINGTIME IN THE ROCKIES (1942); ACTION IN THE NORTH ATLANTIC; HE HIRED THE BOSS; HI DIDDLE DIDDLE; MINESWEEPER; RHYTHM PARADE; SPY TRAIN; WEST SIDE KID; YOUTH ON PARADE (1943); IRISH EYES ARE SMILING; JOHNNY DOESN'T LIVE HERE ANY MORE; MAISIE GOES TO RENO; SEVEN DOORS TO DEATH (1944); CAPTAIN EDDIE; THE CHICAGO KID; LEAVE IT TO BLONDIE; NOB HILL (1945); DO YOU LOVE ME? (1946);

Day

Dean

Dell

MOTHER WORE TIGHTS (1947); BLONDIE'S REWARD; EVERY GIRL SHOULD BE MARRIED; FAMILY HONEYMOON; MUSIC MAN (1948); HOLIDAY AFFAIR (1949); CURTAIN CALL AT CACTUS CREEK; THE GREAT RUPERT (1950); LOST CONTINENT; MR. IMPERIUM; SHOW BOAT (1951); AARON SLICK FROM PUNKIN CRICK; STEEL TOWN (1952); PRIVATE EYES (1953); IT SHOULD HAPPEN TO YOU; A STAR IS BORN; THERE'S NO BUSINESS LIKE SHOW BUSINESS; THREE RING CIRCUS; UNTAMED HEIRESS (1954); BATTLE FLAME (1955); THE NAKED GUN (1956); DANGEROUS CHARTER (1962); IT'S A MAD, MAD, MAD, MAD WORLD (1963); NIGHTMARE IN THE SUN (1964); THE GIRL WHO KNEW TOO MUCH (1969).

Clements, John [Sir John Clements]

Born 25 April 1910, London, England; died 6 April 1988, Brighton, England

Actor–Director–Writer–Producer

Clements began his acting career onstage in 1930; he subsequently founded the Intimate Theatre in London in 1935. That year also marked his first screen appearance, in ONCE IN A NEW MOON. He played several leading roles in British films of the 1930s and 40s, and directed, produced, and scripted one film, CALL OF THE BLOOD (1948). Clements and his second wife, Kay Hammond, made up one of London's most popular theatrical duos. He was knighted in 1968 for his services to the British theater, including writing, producing, and directing as well as acting in plays. His films include: THE DIVINE SPARK; ONCE IN A NEW MOON (1935); REMBRANDT; THINGS TO COME; TICKET OF LEAVE (1936); I, CLAUDIUS; KNIGHT WITHOUT ARMOR (1937); SOUTH RIDING; STAR OF THE CIRCUS (1938); THE FOUR FEATHERS; THE HOUSEMASTER (1939); CONVOY; THE HIDDEN MENACE (1940); THIS ENGLAND (1941); SHIPS WITH WINGS (1942); AT DAWN WE DIE (1943); THEY CAME TO A CITY; UNDERGROUND GUERRILLAS (1944); CALL OF THE BLOOD (1948); TRAIN OF EVENTS (1952); THE SILENT ENEMY (1959); THE MIND BENDERS (1963); OH! WHAT A LOVELY WAR (1969); GANDHI (1982); THE JIGSAW MAN (1984).

Cohen, Nat [Nathan Cohen]

Born 23 Dec. 1905, London, England; died 10 Feb. 1988, London, England

Producer

Cohen entered the film industry as an exhibitor in 1930, moved into production and distribution in the 40s with Anglo Amalgamated Film Distributors, and eventually became the chairman and CEO of EMI. Under Cohen, Anglo Amalgamated produced a string of features based on Edgar Wallace's fiction and the first 13 of the popular "Carry On" comedies; with the British cinema's move toward greater realism in the 60s, its films included DARLING (for which Cohen has been credited with discovering Julie Christie); BILLY LIAR; A KIND OF LOVING; FAR FROM THE MADDING CROWD; and POOR COW. After a series of mergers absorbed Anglo Amalgamated into EMI (later Thorn EMI Screen Entertainment), Cohen became CEO, and under his chairmanship in the 70s and 80s the company released, among others, THE RAILWAY CHILDREN; LADY CAROLINE LAMB; STEPTOE AND SON; STARDUST; the big 1974 hit MURDER ON THE ORIENT EXPRESS; and its follow-ups, DEATH ON THE NILE (1978) and EVIL UNDER THE SUN (1982). CLOCKWISE (1985), starring John Cleese, was Cohen's last film as executive producer.

Cuthbertson, Allan

Born 1920, Perth, Australia; died 8 Feb. 1988, London, England

Actor

Cuthbertson left his native Australia to live in England in 1947, and made his debut in British films six years later. From the start he was cast in villainous or unsympathetic roles, portraying cold, ruthless, cowardly, or supercilious characters in many films, including ROOM AT THE TOP and its sequel, LIFE AT THE TOP. Cuthbertson's more endearing side was revealed in his British television performances—in which he played straight man to various comics and appeared in comedy series—and on the British stage. His films include: THE MILLION POUND NOTE (1953); COURT MARTIAL (1954); ANASTASIA; DICK TURPIN—HIGHWAYMAN; DOUBLE CROSS; EYEWITNESS; THE MAN WHO NEVER WAS; ON SUCH A NIGHT; POSTMARK FOR DANGER (1956); A NOVEL AFFAIR; OPERATION CONSPIRACY; YANGTSE INCIDENT (1957); DESERT ATTACK; HELL, HEAVEN OR HOBOKEN; LAW AND DISORDER (1958); THE CROWNING TOUCH; ROOM AT THE TOP; SHAKE HANDS WITH THE DEVIL (1959); KILLERS OF KILIMANJARO; THE STRANGLERS OF BOMBAY; TUNES OF GLORY (1960); THE GUNS OF NAVARONE; THE MALPAS MYSTERY; MAN AT THE CARLTON TOWER; ON THE DOUBLE (1961); THE BOYS; FREUD; TERM OF TRIAL (1962); BITTER HARVEST; THE FAST LADY; THE MOUSE ON THE MOON; NINE HOURS TO RAMA; THE RUNNING MAN (1963); THE SEVENTH DAWN; TAMAHINE (1964); THE BRAIN; GAME FOR THREE LOSERS; LIFE AT THE TOP; OPERATION CROSSBOW; UNDERWORLD INFORMERS (1965); CAST A GIANT SHADOW; PRESS FOR TIME; SOLO FOR SPARROW (1966); HALF A SIXPENCE; THE MALPAS MYSTERY; THOSE FANTASTIC FLYING FOOLS (1967); THE BODY STEALERS; CAPTAIN NEMO AND THE UNDERWA-

TER CITY; SINFUL DAVEY; THE TRYGON FACTOR (1969); THE ADVENTURERS; THE FIRECHASERS; ONE MORE TIME; PERFORMANCE (1970); THE RAILWAY CHILDREN (1971); DIAMONDS ON WHEELS (1972); IN THE DEVIL'S GARDEN (1974) HOPSCOTCH; THE MIRROR CRACK'D; THE OUTSIDER (1980); THE SEA WOLVES (1981); INVITATION TO THE WEDDING (1983).

Day, Dennis [Owen Patrick Eugene Denis McNulty]

Born 21 May 1917, Bronx, N.Y.; died 22 June 1988, Bel Air, Calif.

Singer–Actor–Comedian

Day got his first show–business job as a tenor on the CBS radio program "Varieties." In 1939 Mary Livingstone, wife of Jack Benny, added Day's name to the list of candidates for a slot on Benny's radio show. Day was chosen over 100 other tenors to join the troupe, and remained with Benny for 25 years—playing a long–winded but slow–witted teen (whose trademark line was "Gee, Mr. Benny!") on radio and an adult comic foil on television. Day also starred in his own TV show and in a number of films, including MUSIC IN MANHATTAN and GOLDEN GIRL. His films include: BUCK BENNY RIDES AGAIN (1940); THE POWERS GIRL (1942); SLEEPY LAGOON (1943); MUSIC IN MANHATTAN (1944); MELODY TIME (1948); I'LL GET BY (1950); GOLDEN GIRL (1951); THE GIRL NEXT DOOR (1953); WON TON TON, THE DOG WHO SAVED HOLLYWOOD (1976).

Dean, Priscilla

Born 25 Nov. 1896, New York, N.Y.; died 27 Dec. 1987

Actress

Dean was Universal Pictures' leading female star in the early 1920s, usually playing spitfires or wicked women who reformed at film's end. The daughter of actors, she began performing at the age of four in her parents' touring stock company and first appeared in films at 14. She became a lead actress in Universal's serial THE GRAY GHOST (1917). Among her most notable roles is that of Cigarette, the noble sweetheart of the French Foreign Legion in UNDER TWO FLAGS (1922); she costarred with future husband Wheeler Oakman in THE VIRGIN OF STAMBOUL (1920). Dean is considered one of the best dramatic actresses of the silent era. Her films include: MOTHER (1914); LOVE DYNAMITE AND BASEBALL (1916); BELOVED JIM; EVEN AS YOU AND I; THE HAND THAT ROCKS THE CRADLE (1917); BRAZEN BEAUTY; KISS OR KILL; THE TWO–SOUL WOMAN; WHICH WOMAN? (1918); THE EXQUISITE THIEF; PAID IN ADVANCE; PRETTY SMOOTH; SHE HIRED A HUSBAND; THE SILK–LINED BURGLAR; THE WICKED DARLING; THE WILD CAT OF PARIS (1919); THE VIRGIN OF STAMBOUL (1920); THE CONFLICT; OUTSIDE THE LAW; REPUTATION (1921); UNDER TWO FLAGS; WILD HONEY (1922); DRIFTING; THE FLAME OF LIFE; WHITE TIGER (1923); A CAFE IN CAIRO; THE SIREN OF SEVILLE; THE STORM DAUGHTER (1924); THE CRIMSON RUNNER (1925); THE DANGER GIRL; FORBIDDEN WATERS; THE SPEEDING VENUS; WEST OF BROADWAY (1926); BIRDS OF PREY; THE DICE WOMAN; JEWELS OF DESIRE (1927); TRAPPED (1931); BEHIND STONE WALLS; KLONDIKE; LAW OF THE SEA (1932).

Dell, Gabriel [Gabe Dell, Gabriel del Vecchio]

Born 7 Oct. 1919, Barbados; died 3 July 1988, Los Angeles, Calif.–

Actor

After his Broadway debut at age nine, the teenaged Dell appeared with Huntz Hall, Leo Gorcey, Bobby Jordan, and Billy Halop in the 1935 Broadway production of Sidney Kingsley's "Dead End." The play's success landed the young cast roles opposite Humphrey Bogart in William Wyler's 1937 filmed version of the play, and they became stars as the original members of the "Dead End Kids," later known as the "East Side Kids" and the "Bowery Boys." The long–running Bowery Boys series (1937–58) cleaned–up Kingsley's characters and lightened his social realism with a mix of action, melodrama, and especially comedy. After the series' heyday in the 1940s, Dell, unlike most other "Dead End" originals, successfully escaped his hooligan image to embark on a New York stage career, while occasionally appearing in character parts in films. One of his last movie roles was in THE MANCHU EAGLE MURDER CAPER MYSTERY (1975), a satire cowritten by Dell. His films include: DEAD END (1937); ANGELS WITH DIRTY FACES; CRIME SCHOOL; LITTLE TOUGH GUY (1938); ANGELS WASH THEIR FACES; DEAD END KIDS ON DRESS PARADE; HELL'S KITCHEN; THEY MADE ME A CRIMINAL (1939); GIVE US WINGS; YOU'RE NOT SO TOUGH (1940); HIT THE ROAD; MOB TOWN (1941); LET'S GET TOUGH; MR. WISE GUY; 'NEATH THE BROOKLYN BRIDGE; SMART ALECKS; TOUGH AS THEY COME (1942); KEEP 'EM SLUGGING; KID DYNAMITE; MR. MUGGS STEPS OUT; MUG TOWN (1943); BLOCK BUSTERS; BOWERY CHAMPS; FOLLOW THE LEADER; MILLION DOLLAR KID (1944); COME OUT FIGHTING (1945); MR. HEX; SPOOK BUSTERS (1946); BOWERY BUCKAROOS; HARD BOILED MAHONEY; NEWS HOUNDS (1947); ANGELS ALLEY; JINX MONEY; SMUGGLERS' COVE; TROUBLE MAKERS (1948); ANGELS IN DISGUISE; FIGHTING FOOLS; HOLD THAT BABY!; MASTER MINDS (1949); BLONDE DYNAMITE; BLUES BUSTERS; LUCKY LOSERS; TRIPLE TROUBLE (1950); ESCAPE FROM TERROR (1960); WHEN THE GIRLS TAKE OVER (1962); WHO IS HARRY KELLERMAN AND WHY IS HE SAYING THOSE

TERRIBLE THINGS ABOUT ME?; 300 YEAR WEEKEND (1971); EARTHQUAKE (1974); FRAMED; THE MANCHU EAGLE MURDER CAPER MYSTERY (1975); THE ESCAPE ARTIST (1982).

Diamond, I.A.L. [Itek Dommnici]
27 June 1920, Ungheni, Rumania; died 21 April 1988, Beverly Hills, Calif.

Screenwriter–Associate Producer

Diamond emigrated to Brooklyn in 1929 and began writing at Columbia University, where he majored in journalism, edited the paper, and wrote varsity shows. He went to Hollywood after graduation, receiving his first screen credit for MURDER IN THE BLUE ROOM (1944). Diamond and director–screenwriter Billy Wilder began their long creative partnership with the script for LOVE IN THE AFTERNOON (1957), and subsequently cowrote a total of 12 Wilder–directed films, sharing Oscar nominations for the scripts of SOME LIKE IT HOT and THE FORTUNE COOKIE and winning a Best Screenplay Oscar for THE APARTMENT. Diamond was also credited as associate producer for most of his films with Wilder. After 1957 Diamond wrote only two scripts, CACTUS FLOWER (under the name Abe Burrows) and MERRY ANDREW, independently of Wilder. His films include: MURDER IN THE BLUE ROOM (1944); NEVER SAY GOODBYE; TWO GUYS FROM MILWAUKEE (1946); ALWAYS TOGETHER; LOVE AND LEARN (1947); ROMANCE ON THE HIGH SEAS; TWO GUYS FROM TEXAS (1948); THE GIRL FROM JONES BEACH; IT'S A GREAT FEELING (1949); LET'S MAKE IT LEGAL; LOVE NEST (1951); MONKEY BUSINESS; SOMETHING FOR THE BIRDS (1952); THAT CERTAIN FEELING (1956); LOVE IN THE AFTERNOON (1957); MERRY ANDREW (1958); SOME LIKE IT HOT (1959); THE APARTMENT (1960); ONE, TWO, THREE (1961); IRMA LA DOUCE (1963); KISS ME, STUPID (1964); THE FORTUNE COOKIE (1966); CACTUS FLOWER (1969); THE PRIVATE LIFE OF SHERLOCK HOLMES (1970); AVANTI! (1972); THE FRONT PAGE (1974); FEDORA (1978).

Divine [Harris Glenn Milstead]
Born 1946, Lutherville, Md.; died 7 March 1988, Los Angeles, Calif.

Actor–Nightclub Performer

As Harris Glenn Milstead, Divine grew up in a suburb of Baltimore and became friends with John Waters, with whom his career remained closely linked. Waters and Milstead re-created the latter as the buxom, obnoxious, tawdry–glamorous Divine, and Milstead thereafter performed as Divine in such Waters' cult favorites-to-be as MONDO TRASHO; PINK FLAMINGOS (in which Divine was introduced as "the filthiest person alive"); and FEMALE TROUBLE. Divine continued in a career that included theater and nightclub appearances and a series of hit dance singles, in addition to growing popularity on–screen—finding his greatest audience to date in Waters' 1988 hit HAIRSPRAY, released 10 days before his death. In it Divine played the heroine's housewife mother as well as the racist (male) owner of a Baltimore TV station. His films include: MONDO TRASHO (1970); PINK FLAMINGOS (1972); FEMALE TROUBLE (1974); POLYESTER (1981); LUST IN THE DUST (1984); TROUBLE IN MIND (1985); HAIRSPRAY; OUT OF THE DARK (1988).

Dobbins, Bennie
Died 5 Feb. 1988, Schladming, Austria, age 56

Stuntman–Actor–Stunt Director

Dobbins performed bit roles and stunts in many films and was a three-time elected president of the Stuntman's Association of Motion Pictures. In recent years he directed the stunts in THE WHITE BUFFALO (1977); BREWSTER'S MILLIONS (1985); FERRIS BUELLER'S DAY OFF (1986); JUMPING JACK FLASH (1986); EXTREME PREJUDICE (1987); and THE RUNNING MAN (1987). Dobbins collapsed while staging a scene with Arnold Schwarzenegger for the 1988 release RED HEAT. His films include: RIDE LONESOME (1959); BARQUERO (1970); DIRTY HARRY; SOMETIMES A GREAT NOTION; WILD ROVERS (1971); THE LIFE AND TIMES OF JUDGE ROY BEAN (1972); 99 AND 44/100% DEAD (1974); THE DUCHESS AND THE DIRTWATER FOX (1976); THE WHITE BUFFALO (1977); THE MOUNTAIN MEN (1980); THE LEGEND OF THE LONE RANGER (1981); 48 HOURS (1982); BREWSTER'S MILLIONS (1985); FERRIS BUELLER'S DAY OFF; JUMPING JACK FLASH (1986); EXTREME PREJUDICE; THE RUNNING MAN (1987); RED HEAT (1988).

Donnell, Jeff [Jean Marie Donnell]
Born 10 July 1921, South Windham, Me.; died 11 April 1988, Hollywood, Calif.

Actress

After founding a New Hampshire playhouse with her first husband, Donnell moved to Hollywood under contract to Columbia Pictures at the age of 21. Her skills as a character actress and cheerful, youthful appearance were thereafter consistently employed—in the early 1940s in teenage roles, later in second leads (sometimes as the heroine's best friend), and finally in the portrayal of matronly characters. She may, however, be best known for her 1950s portrayal of Alice, George Gobel's TV wife on "The George Gobel Show." Her films include: THE BOOGIE MAN WILL GET YOU; MY SISTER EILEEN; A NIGHT TO REMEMBER (1942); CITY WITHOUT MEN;

DOUGHBOYS IN IRELAND; MR. SMUG; THERE'S SOMETHING ABOUT A SOLDIER; WHAT'S BUZZIN' COUSIN? (1943); CAROLINA BLUES; COWBOY CANTEEN; MR. WINKLE GOES TO WAR; NINE GIRLS; ONCE UPON A TIME; STARS ON PARADE; 3 IS A FAMILY (1944); DANCING IN MANHATTAN; EADIE WAS A LADY; HE'S MY GUY; OVER 21; THE POWER OF THE WHISTLER; SONG OF THE PRAIRIE (1945); COWBOY BLUES; IT'S GREAT TO BE YOUNG; MR. DISTRICT ATTORNEY; NIGHT EDITOR; THE PHANTOM THIEF; SINGING ON THE TRAIL; TARS AND SPARS; THAT TEXAS JAMBOREE; THROW A SADDLE ON A STAR; THE UNKNOWN (1946); MY PAL RINGEYE (1947); EASY LIVING; OUTCASTS OF THE TRAIL; POST OFFICE INVESTIGATOR; ROUGHSHOD; STAGECOACH KID (1949); BIG TIMBER; THE FULLER BRUSH GIRL; HOEDOWN; IN A LONELY PLACE; REDWOOD FOREST TRAIL; WALK SOFTLY, STRANGER (1950); THREE GUYS NAMED MIKE (1951); BECAUSE YOU'RE MINE; THE FIRST TIME; SKIRTS AHOY!; THIEF OF DAMASCUS (1952); THE BLUE GARDENIA; FLIGHT NURSE; SO THIS IS LOVE (1953); MASSACRE CANYON (1954); MAGNIFICENT ROUGHNECKS (1956); DESTINATION 60,000; THE GUNS OF FORT PETTICOAT; MY MAN GODFREY; SWEET SMELL OF SUCCESS (1957); FORCE OF IMPULSE; GIDGET GOES HAWAIIAN (1961); GIDGET GOES TO ROME; THE SWINGIN' MAIDEN (1963); THE COMIC (1969); TORA! TORA! TORA! (1970); STAND UP AND BE COUNTED (1972); McNAUGHTON'S DAUGHTER (1976).

Duggan, Andrew
Born 1923, Franklin, Ind.; died 15 May 1988, Westwood, Calif.

Actor

Though Duggan's voice and strong–jawed looks lent themselves admirably to the playing of authority figures, he was a versatile character actor who also essayed suave villains and occasional comic roles. He took up acting after WW II, at Melvyn Douglas' encouragement, beginning his career with a leading role onstage opposite Lucille Ball in "Dream Girl" and continuing with a series of starring roles on Broadway in the 1950s. He remained particularly active throughout his career on TV, where he was a frequent guest star on dramatic series and, after a 1978 operation on his throat that made his voice huskier, launched a new career in commercial voice–overs. His films include: PATTERNS (1956); DECISION AT SUNDOWN; DOMINO KID; THREE BRAVE MEN (1957); THE BRAVADOS; RETURN TO WARBOW; WESTBOUND;(1959); THE CHAPMAN REPORT; HOUSE OF WOMEN; MERRILL'S MARAUDERS (1962); PALM SPRINGS WEEKEND (1963); ALLIED DOLPHIN; FBI CODE 98; THE INCREDIBLE MR. LIMPET; SEVEN DAYS IN MAY (1964); THE GLORY GUYS (1965); IN LIKE FLINT (1967); THE SECRET WAR OF HARRY FRIGG (1968); SKIN GAME (1971); THE BEARS AND I; IT'S ALIVE (1974); IT LIVES AGAIN; THE PRIVATE FILES OF J. EDGAR HOOVER (1978); DR. DETROIT (1983).

Eldridge, Florence [Florence McKechnie]
Born 5 Sept. 1901, Brooklyn, N.Y.; died 1 Aug. 1988, Santa Barbara, Calif.

Actress

The talented Eldridge debuted onstage in 1918 and quickly became one of Broadway's brightest stars, gaining much as Daisy Buchanan in "The Great Gatsby." In 1927 she married Fredric March, a pairing that proved both personally and professionally successful. The couple acted together in numerous Broadway productions and in THE STUDIO MURDER MYSTERY; LES MISERABLES; INHERIT THE WIND; ANOTHER PART OF THE FOREST; and other films. In 1956, they appeared together in the original Broadway production of Eugene O'Neill's "Long Day's Journey into Night," with Eldridge in the role of the drug–addicted Mary Tyrone—a celebrated performance that still sets the standard for the part. Her films include: SIX CYLINDER LOVE (1923); CHARMING SINNERS; THE GREENE MURDER CASE; THE STUDIO MURDER MYSTERY (1929); THE DIVORCEE; THE MATRIMONIAL BED (1930); THIRTEEN WOMEN (1932) DANGEROUSLY YOURS; THE GREAT JASPER; THE STORY OF TEMPLE DRAKE (1933); A MODERN HERO (1934); LES MISERABLES (1935); MARY OF SCOTLAND (1936); AN ACT OF MURDER; ANOTHER PART OF THE FOREST (1948); CHRISTOPHER COLUMBUS (1949); INHERIT THE WIND (1960).

Evans, Gil [Ian Ernest Gilmore Green]
Born 13 May 1912, Toronto, Canada; died 20 March 1988, Cuernavaca, Mexico

Jazz Musician–Composer–Arranger

One of the most important orchestrators and composers in jazz, Evans, in collaboration with Miles Davis, produced some of the most influential recordings of postwar jazz. Evans' eclectic, vigorous, and exploratory artistic approach is exemplified in his musical direction of the score for ABSOLUTE BEGINNERS (1986), which features one Evans' composition, "The Naked and the Dead," along with music by everyone from Edward Tudorpole to Charles Mingus.

Fidler, Jimmie
Born 24 Aug. 1900, St. Louis, Mo.; died 9 Aug. 1988, Westlake, Calif.

Journalist–Broadcaster–Publicist

Divine

Donnell

Eldridge

Frobe

Fidler was the most durable, and perhaps the most dangerous, of a generation of Hollywood gossip columnists that included Hedda Hopper, Louella Parsons, and Walter Winchell. Failing to make it as a film actor, Fidler became an editor of the four–page *Hollywood News* in 1920, then worked as a publicist for Cecil B. DeMille and others. In the mid–1930s he began reporting on moviedom in print and on radio and—paying a network of spies among studio employees to supply him with the inside dirt. At the peak of his power, in 1950, Fidler was said to have had 40 million listeners on radio while his syndicated column was carried in 360 newspapers. In 1983, when Fidler stopped producing the radio show, he was still carried on about 100 stations. He appears, as himself, in GARDEN OF THE MOON (1938).

Fletcher, Bramwell

Born 20 Feb. 1904, Bradford, England; died 22 June 1988, Westmoreland, N.H.

Actor–Playwright

Fletcher first acted onstage at Stratford–on–Avon in 1927. He made his movie debut the following year, in time to appear in both the last silent and the first talking picture produced in Britain. In 1929 he moved to the US, and appeared in a number of pictures, including THE MUMMY and SVENGALI, before a contract dispute with Samuel Goldwyn led him to return to the New York stage, where he was particularly associated with Shavian roles. Fletcher starred in his own "The Bernard Shaw Story," touring with the one–man show in the 1960s and 70s. His films include: CHICK; S.O.S. (1928); TO WHAT RED HELL (1929); RAFFLES; SO THIS IS LONDON (1930); DAUGHTER OF THE DRAGON; MEN OF THE SKY; THE MILLIONAIRE; ONCE A LADY; SVENGALI (1931); A BILL OF DIVORCEMENT; THE FACE ON THE BARROOM FLOOR; THE MUMMY; THE SILENT WITNESS (1932); THE MONKEY'S PAW; ONLY YESTERDAY; RIGHT TO ROMANCE (1933); NANA (1934); LINE ENGAGED; THE SCARLET PIMPERNEL (1935); RANDOM HARVEST; THE UNDYING MONSTER; WHITE CARGO (1942); THE IMMORTAL SERGEANT (1943).

Folsey, George [George Folsey, Sr.]

Born 1898, New York, N.Y.; died 8 Nov. 1988, Santa Monica, Calif.

Cinematographer

Folsey became an assistant cameraman with Lasky Players in New York at age 15; four years later, he subbed for an absent director of photography and embarked on a career as one of film's most distinguished cinematographers. A 13–time Academy Award nominee and two–term president of the ASC, Folsey is credited with leading the transition from high–contrast to more subtly lit photography in black–and–white films, and was later well known for his use of Technicolor and a distinctive influence on the look of MGM films of the 30s, 40s, and 50s, collaborating with Vincente Minnelli (MEET ME IN ST. LOUIS), Frank Capra (STATE OF THE UNION), Rouben Mamoulian (APPLAUSE), George Cukor (ADAM'S RIB), Ernst Lubitsch, Busby Berkeley, and many others. His films include: HIS BRIDAL NIGHT (1919); THE FEAR MARKET; THE FRISKY MRS. JOHNSON; SINNERS; THE STOLEN KISS (1920); THE EDUCATION OF ELIZABETH; THE ROAD TO LONDON; THE PRICE OF POSSESSION; SHELTERED DAUGHTERS (1921); THE GAME CHICKEN; NANCY FROM NOWHERE; WHAT'S WRONG WITH THE WOMEN? (1922); THE BRIGHT SHAWL (1923); THE ENCHANTED COTTAGE (1924); THE HALF–WAY GIRL; THE NECESSARY EVIL; THE SCARLET SAINT (1925); LADIES AT PLAY; THE SAVAGE; TOO MUCH MONEY (1926); AMERICAN BEAUTY (1927); LADY BE GOOD (1928); APPLAUSE; THE BATTLE OF PARIS; THE COCOANUTS; GENTLEMEN OF THE PRESS; HOLE IN THE WALL; THE LETTER (1929); ANIMAL CRACKERS; THE BIG POND; DANGEROUS NAN McGREW; GLORIFYING THE AMERICAN GIRL; THE LAUGHING LADY; LAUGHTER; THE ROYAL FAMILY OF BROADWAY (1930); MY SIN; THE CHEAT; HONOR AMONG LOVERS; MY SIN; SECRETS OF A SECRETARY; THE SMILING LIEUTENANT; STOLEN HEAVEN (1931); THE ANIMAL KINGDOM; THE BIG BROADCAST; THE WISER SEX (1932); GOING HOLLYWOOD; MEN MUST FIGHT; REUNION IN VIENNA; STAGE MOTHER; STORM AT DAYBREAK (1933); CHAINED; MEN IN WHITE; OPERATOR 13 (1934); FORSAKING ALL OTHERS; I LIVE MY LIFE; KIND LADY; PAGE MISS GLORY; RECKLESS (1935); THE GORGEOUS HUSSY; THE GREAT ZIEGFELD; HEARTS DIVIDED (1936); THE BRIDE WORE RED; THE LAST OF MRS. CHEYNEY; MANNEQUIN (1937); ARSENE LUPIN RETURNS; HOLD THAT KISS; THE SHINING HOUR (1938); FAST AND LOOSE; LADY OF THE TROPICS; MILLION DOLLAR LEGS; REMEMBER?; SOCIETY LAWYER (1939); THIRD FINGER, LEFT HAND; TWO GIRLS ON BROADWAY (1940); COME LIVE WITH ME; DR. KILDARE'S WEDDING DAY; FREE AND EASY; LADY BE GOOD; MARRIED BACHELOR; THE TRIAL OF MARY DUGAN (1941); DR. GILLESPIE'S NEW ASSISTANT; GRAND CENTRAL MURDER; PANAMA HATTIE; RIO RITA; SEVEN SWEETHEARTS (1942); A GUY NAMED JOE; THOUSANDS CHEER; THREE HEARTS FOR JULIA (1943); MEET ME IN ST. LOUIS; THE WHITE CLIFFS OF DOVER (1944); THE CLOCK; ZIEGFELD FOLLIES (1945); THE GREEN YEARS; THE HARVEY GIRLS; THE SECRET HEART; TILL THE CLOUDS ROLL BY (1946); GREEN DOLPHIN STREET; IF WINTER COMES (1947); STATE OF THE UNION (1948); ADAM'S RIB; THE GREAT SINNER; TAKE ME OUT TO THE BALL GAME (1949); THE BIG HANGOVER; A LIFE OF HER OWN; MALAYA (1950); LAW AND THE LADY; THE MAN WITH A CLOAK;

MR. IMPERIUM; NIGHT INTO MORNING; SHADOW IN THE SKY; VENGEANCE VALLEY (1951); LOVELY TO LOOK AT; MILLION DOLLAR MERMAID (1952); ALL THE BROTHERS WERE VALIANT (1953); DEEP IN MY HEART; EXECUTIVE SUITE; MEN OF THE FIGHTING LADY; SEVEN BRIDES FOR SEVEN BROTHERS; TENNESSEE CHAMP (1954); THE COBWEB; HIT THE DECK (1955); FASTEST GUN ALIVE; FORBIDDEN PLANET; THE POWER AND THE PRIZE; THESE WILDER YEARS (1956); HOUSE OF NUMBERS; TIP ON A DEAD JOCKEY (1957); THE HIGH COST OF LOVING; IMITATION GENERAL; SADDLE THE WIND; TORPEDO RUN (1958); COUNT YOUR BLESSINGS (1959) CASH McCALL; I PASSED FOR WHITE (1960); THE BALCONY (1963); GLASS HOUSES (1972); THAT'S ENTERTAINMENT, PART II (new sequences) (1976).

Frank, Melvin

Born 13 Aug. 1913, Chicago, Ill.; died 13 Oct. 1988, Los Angeles.

Playwright–Director–Screenwriter–Producer

While students at the University of Chicago Frank and Norman Panama began their long, fruitful artistic partnership. Moving to Hollywood, they became writers for Bob Hope's radio show and, in 1942, collaborated on their first screenplay, MY FAVORITE BLONDE, for Hope. Throughout the 1940s they cowrote light features, mainly for Paramount, including the Hope–Crosby ROAD TO UTOPIA (1945). In 1948 they produced their script for MR. BLANDINGS BUILDS HIS DREAM HOUSE, and in the 50s regularly acted as director–producers (often alternating in these roles) of their own material, including STRICTLY DISHONORABLE (1951); THE COURT JESTER (1956); and LI'L ABNER (1959), the last from their stageplay. The partnership ended with THE ROAD TO HONG KONG (1962), after which Frank continued to produce, direct, and/or write such films as A FUNNY THING HAPPENED ON THE WAY TO THE FORUM (1966); A TOUCH OF CLASS (1973); and THE PRISONER OF SECOND AVENUE (1975). His films include: MY FAVORITE BLONDE (w); STAR SPANGLED RHYTHM (w) (1942); HAPPY GO LUCKY (w); THANK YOUR LUCKY STARS (w) (1943); AND THE ANGLES SING (w) (1944); DUFFY'S TAVERN (w); ROAD TO UTOPIA (w) (1945); MONSIEUR BEAUCAIRE (w); OUR HEARTS WERE GROWING UP (w) (1946); IT HAD TO BE YOU (w) (1947); MR. BLANDINGS BUILDS HIS DREAM HOUSE (p&w); THE RETURN OF OCTOBER (w); A SOUTHERN YANKEE (w) (1948); THE REFORMER AND THE REDHEAD (p,d&w) (1950); CALLAWAY WENT THATAWAY (p,d&w); STRICTLY DISHONORABLE (p,d&w) (1951); ABOVE AND BEYOND (p&d) (1953); KNOCK ON WOOD (p,d&w); WHITE CHRISTMAS (w) (1954); THE COURT JESTER (p,d&w); THAT CERTAIN FEELING (p,d&w) (1956); THE JAYHAWKERS (p,d&w); LI'L ABNER (d&w); THE TRAP (p) (1959); THE FACTS OF LIFE (p,d&w) (1960); THE ROAD TO HONG KONG (p&w) (1962); STRANGE BEDFELLOWS (p,d&w) (1965); A FUNNY THING HAPPENED ON THE WAY TO THE FORUM (p&w); NOT WITH MY WIFE, YOU DON'T! (w) (1966); BUONA SERA, MRS. CAMPBELL (p,d&w) (1968); A TOUCH OF CLASS (p,d&w) (1973); THE PRISONER OF SECOND AVENUE (p&d) (1975); THE DUCHESS AND THE DIRTWATER FOX (p,d&w) (1976); LOST AND FOUND (p,d&w) (1979); WALK LIKE A MAN (d) (1987).

Frey, Leonard

Born 4 Sept. 1938, Brooklyn, N.Y.; died 24 Aug. 1988, New York, N.Y.

Actor

Frey made his mark on Broadway as Harold in Mart Crowley's "The Boys in the Band," later reprising his role in the 1970 film based on the play. A skillful and stylish actor excelling in comedy, he earned a Best Supporting Actor Oscar nomination for his portrayal of Motel the tailor in FIDDLER ON THE ROOF (1970). Frey appeared frequently with the Lincoln Center and Yale repertory theaters and starred in the Broadway production of Peter Nichols' "National Health." At the end of his career he was increasingly visible on television. His films include: FINNEGAN'S WAKE (1965); THE BOYS IN THE BAND; THE MAGIC CHRISTIAN; TELL ME THAT YOU LOVE ME, JUNIE MOON (1970); FIDDLER ON THE ROOF (1970); UP THE ACADEMY; WHERE THE BUFFALO ROAM (1980); TATTOO (1981).

Frobe, Gert [Karl–Gerhard Frobe]

Born 25 Dec. 1912 (?), Planitz, [East]Ger.; died 5 Sept. 1988, Munich, W. Ger.

Actor

Frobe began working in theater as a stage decorator, then made his acting debut in 1937. His film career began after the end of WW II with a leading role in BERLINER BALLADE (1948). This first on–screen appearance was to be followed with roles in nearly 100 European and American films, a number featuring Frobe as a militaristic Prussian type, but he was most famous for his portrayal of the obnoxious title villain of the James Bond thriller GOLDFINGER (1964). (In Israel the film was banned, along with others featuring Frobe, after the actor's former membership in the German Nazi party became an issue, but the ban was lifted after a Jewish survivor of the Holocaust testified to Frobe's help in concealing his family.) His talents have been put to use in films by Fritz Lang (the DR. MABUSE films), Orson Welles (MR. ARKADIN), Jules Dassin, Rene Clement, Claude Chabrol, and

Ingmar Bergman, among many others. His films include: BERLINER BALLADE (1948); NACH REGEN SCHEINT SONNE (1949) DER TAG VOR DER HOCHZEIT; LES HEROS SONT FATIGUES (1952); ARLETTE EROBERT PARIS; EIN HERZ SPIELT FALSCH; HOCHZEIT AUF REISEN; MAN ON A TIGHTROPE; SALTO MORTALE (1953); DAS KREUZ AM JAGERSTIEG; DAS ZWEITE LEBEN; DIE KLEINE STADT WILL SCHLAFEN GEHN; EWIGER WALZER; MANNEQUINS FUR RIO; MORGENGRAUEN (1954); CONFIDENTIAL REPORT; DAS FORSTHAUS IN TIROL; DER DUNKLE STERN; DER POSTMEISTER; EIN MADCHEN AUS FLANDERN; THE HEROES ARE TIRED; ICH WEISS, WOFUR ICH LIEBE; THEY WERE SO YOUNG; VOM HIMMEL GEFALLEN (1955); CELUI QUI DOIT MOURIR; DAS HERZ VON ST. PAULI; DER TOLLE BOMBERG; EIN HERZ SCHLAGT FUR ERIKA; TYPHOON OVER NAGASAKI; WALDWINTER (1956); CHARMANTS GARCONS; ECHEC AU PORTEUR; EL HAKIM; (1957); DAS MADCHEN MIT DEM KATZENAUGEN; DER PAUKER; GRABENPLATZ 17; GRAFATIGUES; I BATELLIERI DE VOLGA; NASSE ASPHALT; NICK KNATTERTONS ABENTEUER (1958); AM TAG, ALS DER REGEN KAM; DOUZE HEURES D'HORLOGE; JONS UND ERDMAN; MENSCHEN IM HOTEL; OLD HEIDELBERG; SCHUSSE IM MORGENGRAUEN; UND EWIG SINGEN DIE WALDER (1959); BIS DASS DAS GELD EUCH SCHEIDET; DAS KUNSTEIDENE MADCHEN; DER GAUNER UND DER LIEBER GOTT; IT HAPPENED IN BROAD DAYLIGHT; LE BOIS D'AMANTS; ROSEMARY; SOLDATENSENDER CALAIS; THE THOUSAND EYES OF DR. MABUSE; 12 STUNDEN ANGST (1960); ES MUSS NICHT IMMER KAVIAR SEIN; THE GREEN ARCHER; THE RETURN OF DR. MABUSE; VIA MALA (1961); AUF WIEDERSEHEN; DIE ROTE; HEUTE KUNDIGT MIR MEIN MANN; THE LONGEST DAY; THE TESTAMENT OF DR. MABUSE (1962); KARUSSELL DER LEIDENSCHAFTEN; THREEPENNY OPERA (1963); GOLDFINGER (1964); BACK-FIRE; BANANA PEEL; DAS LIEBESKARUSSELL; GANOVERSEHRE; GREED IN THE SUN; A HIGH WIND IN JAMAICA; THE TERROR OF DR. MABUSE; THOSE MAGNIFICENT MEN IN THEIR FLYING MACHINES, OR, HOW I FLEW FROM LONDON TO PARIS IN 25 HOURS AND 11 MINUTES (1965); ENOUGH ROPE; THE GIRL AND THE LEGEND; IS PARIS BURNING? (1966); I KILLED RASPUTIN; THOSE FANTASTIC FLYING FOOLS; TRIPLE CROSS; THE UPPER HAND (1967); CAROLINE CHERIE; CHITTY CHITTY BANG BANG; TONIO KROGER (1968); THOSE DARING YOUNG MEN IN THEIR JAUNTY JALOPIES (1969); (1971); LUDWIG (1973); DER RAUBER HOTZENPLOTZ; L'HOMME SANS VISAGE; SHADOWMAN (1974); DR. JUSTICE; LES MAGICIENS; MEIN ONKEL THEODOR; PROFEZIA PER UN DELITTO; TEN LITTLE INDIANS (1975); FOLIES BOURGEOISES (1976); CASSANDRA CROSSING; DAS GESETZ DES CLANS; THE SERPENT'S EGG; TOD ODER FREIHEIT (1977); BLOODLINE (1979); THE FALCON; LE COUP DU PARAPLUIE (1980); THE DAISY CHAIN (1981).

Gibbs, Alan R.
Died 18 March 1988; Los Angeles, Calif., age 47
Stuntman–Stunt Coordinator–Second–Unit Director

Gibbs was stunt double for Jack Nicholson in several of the latter's films. He executed the famous car jump in SMOKEY AND THE BANDIT as a double for Burt Reynolds, directing the second unit for that film as well. In addition to doubling for Nicholson, Reynolds, and Charles Bronson, Gibbs coordinated stunts or directed second units on LEGAL EAGLES; ARMED AND DANGEROUS; THE RIVER; and other films. Gibbs worked on CROCODILE DUNDEE II and SHAKEDOWN (1988) shortly before his death. His films include: THE SAVAGE SEVEN (1968); SOMETIMES A GREAT NOTION (1971); THE MECHANIC (1972); ELECTRA GLIDE IN BLUE; SCORPIO; THE STONE KILLER (1973); CHINATOWN; DEATH WISH; THE MIDNIGHT MAN (1974); CRAZY MAMA; MITCHELL; ONE FLEW OVER THE CUCKOO'S NEST (1975); CANNONBALL; NICKELODEON (1976); SMOKEY AND THE BANDIT (1977); THE POSTMAN ALWAYS RINGS TWICE (1981); THE BORDER; FIGHTING BACK (1982); TERMS OF ENDEARMENT (1983); CANNONBALL RUN II; THE ICE PIRATES; THE RIVER (1984); ARMED AND DANGEROUS; LEGAL EAGLES (1986); BIG SHOTS; IRONWEED; THE WITCHES OF EASTWICK (1987); CROCODILE DUNDEE II; SHAKEDOWN (1988).

Gibney, Sheridan
Born 11 June 1893, New York, N.Y.; died 11 April 1988, Missoula, Mont.
Playwright–TV/Screenwriter

Gibney wrote literary criticism, librettos, and plays in the 1920s before going to work for Warner Bros., where he cowrote the script for I AM A FUGITIVE FROM A CHAIN GANG (1932). He subsequently wrote or collaborated on screenplays for several films, including ANTHONY ADVERSE and THE STORY OF LOUIS PASTEUR (both 1936), winning Oscars for Best Original Story and Best Screenplay for the latter. He produced as well as wrote OUR HEARTS WERE YOUNG AND GAY. Gibney was president of the Screen Writers Guild from 1930 to 1941 and again in 1947–48. His films include: I AM A FUGITIVE FROM A CHAIN GANG; TWO AGAINST THE WORLD; WEEKEND MARRIAGE (1932); THE HOUSE ON 56TH STREET; THE WORLD CHANGES (1933);

MASSACRE (1934); ANTHONY ADVERSE; GREEN PASTURES; THE STORY OF LOUIS PASTEUR (1936); LETTER OF INTRODUCTION (1938); DISPUTED PASSAGE (1939); SOUTH OF SUEZ (1940); CHEERS FOR MISS BISHOP (1941); ONCE UPON A HONEYMOON (1942); OUR HEARTS WERE YOUNG AND GAY (p&w) (1944); THE LOCKET (1946); EVERYTHING BUT THE TRUTH (1956).

Graham, Sheilah [Lily Sheil]
Born London, England; died 17 Nov. 1988, West Palm Beach, Calif., age 84
Author–Gossip Columnist

After a rags–to–riches youth in which she moved from an orphanage to marriage to an industrialist and a career as a London model, show girl, and journalist, Graham came to the US in 1933, and two years later began writing a syndicated Hollywood column that established her—with Hedda Hopper and Louella Parsons—as part of a powerful gossip triumvirate. Shortly thereafter she began an affair with F. Scott Fitzgerald, recalled in *Beloved Infidel* , her best–selling account of the writer's last years (he based the heroine of his unfinished *The Last Tycoon* on Graham) made into a film starring Gregory Peck and Deborah Kerr in 1959. Her popularity as a columnist peaked in the mid–1950s and early 60s, when she was syndicated in 178 papers and hosted radio and TV shows. Graham's books include further remembrances of Fitzgerald; the autobiography *A State of Heat* ; *Confessions of a Gossip Columnist* ; and *Hollywood Revisited* . Her films include: THAT'S RIGHT—YOU'RE WRONG (1939); JIGGS AND MAGGIE IN SOCIETY (1948); IMPACT (1949); BELOVED INFIDEL (w); GIRL'S TOWN (1959); COLLEGE CONFIDENTIAL (1960).

Guido, Beatriz
Born Rosario, Argentina; died 4 March 1988, Madrid, Spain, age 63
Screenwriter–Novelist

Novelist Guido cowrote numerous screenplays with her husband, Argentinian director Leopoldo Torre Nilsson, who adapted her novels *La casa del angel* , *La Caida* , and *La mano en la trampa* for the screen. Torre Nilsson's version of *La casa del angel* (released in the US as END OF INNOCENCE in 1960), with its portrayal of a corrupt, repressed Argentinian bourgeoisie, gained him an international reputation, influenced the development of Argentinian cinema, and set the tone and style for many of his and Guido's subsequent scripts. Their films include: DIAS DE ODIO (1954); EL SECUESTRADOR (1958); LA CAIDA (1959); END OF INNOCENCE; FIN DE FIESTA; UN GUAPO DEL 900 (1960); HOMENAJA A LA HORA DE LA SIESTA; SETENTA VECES SIETE; SUMMERSKIN (1962); THE HAND IN THE TRAP (1963); THE TERRACE (1964); CAVAR UN FOSO; THE EAVESDROPPER (1966); LOS TRAIDORES DE SAN ANGEL; MONDAY'S CHILD (1967); MARTIN FIERRO (1968); EL SANTO DE LA ESPADA (1970); GUEMES—LA TIERRA EN ARMAS; THE MAFIA (1972); LOS SIETE LOCOS (1973); BOQUITAS PINTADAS (1974); DIARIO DE LA GUERRA DEL CERDO (1975); EL PIBE CABEZA; PIEDRA LIBRA (1976).

Hawtrey, Charles [George Hartree]
Born in England; died 27 Oct. 1988, Walmer, England, age 73
Actor

A boy soprano, Hawtrey sung on several recordings before making his acting debut onstage in 1925. Entering films in the 1930s, he appeared in many movies before establishing himself as a bespectacled scapegoat among the regular cast of the campy "Carry On" comedy series. A popular comic performer on radio, the stage, and television throughout his long career, Hawtrey also produced theatrical shows. His films include: THE MELODY MAKER (1933); WELL DONE, HENRY (1936); SABOTAGE; WHERE THERE'S A WILL (1937); JAILBIRDS; WHERE'S THAT FIRE? (1939); THE GHOST OF ST. MICHAEL'S (1941); THE GOOSE STEPS OUT; LET THE PEOPLE SING (1942); A CANTERBURY TALE (1944); WHAT DO WE DO NOW? (1945); THE END OF THE RIVER; MEET ME AT DAWN (1947); THE STORY OF SHIRLEY YORKE (1948); DARK SECRET; PASSPORT TO PIMLICO; ROOM TO LET (1949); THE GALLOPING MAJOR; SMART ALEC (1951); BRANDY FOR THE PARSON; HAMMER THE TOFF; YOU'RE ONLY YOUNG TWICE (1952); PAID TO KILL (1954); THE ATOMIC MAN; MAN OF THE MOMENT (1955); JUMPING FOR JOY; THE MARCH HARE; SIMON AND LAURA; WHO DONE IT? (1956); I ONLY ASKED! (1958); CARRY ON NURSE; CARRY ON SERGEANT (1959); CARRY ON CONSTABLE; INN FOR TROUBLE; PLEASE TURN OVER (1960); CARRY ON REGARDLESS; WHAT A WHOPPER (1961); CARRY ON TEACHER (1962); CARRY ON CABBIE; CARRY ON JACK (1963); CARRY ON CLEO; CARRY ON SPYING (1964); CARRY ON COWBOY; CARRY ON SCREAMING (1966); DON'T LOSE YOUR HEAD; FOLLOW THAT CAMEL; THE TERRORNAUTS (1967); CARRY ON DOCTOR; CARRY ON, UP THE KHYBER (1968); CARRY ON AGAIN, DOCTOR; CARRY ON CAMPING; ZETA ONE (1969); CARRY ON HENRY VIII; CARRY ON LOVING; CARRY ON UP THE JUNGLE (1970); CARRY ON 'ROUND THE BEND (1972).

Herman, Woody [Woodrow Charles Herman]

Born 16 May 1913, Milwaukee, Wis.; died 29 Oct. 1987, Los Angeles, Calif.

Jazz Musician–Composer–Arranger

Houseman

Herman's long musical career began with his childhood vaudeville appearances as "The Boy Wonder of the Clarinet." In 1936, after performing in a number of bands as a singer and saxophonist, he formed the ensemble that hit it big with the jazz standard–to–be "Woodchopper's Ball" in 1939. Through the next four decades Herman led a succession of bands called the "Thundering Herds," whose frequently changing personnel often featured young unknowns. Herman and orchestra appeared in NEW ORLEANS with Louis Armstrong and Billie Holiday; it was the latter's only feature film. WHAT'S COOKIN'? featured the band playing "Woodchopper's Ball." Herman's films include: WHAT'S COOKIN'? (1942); WINTERTIME (1943); EARL SENSATIONS OF 1945 (1944); EARL CARROLL'S VANITIES (1945); HIT PARADE OF 1947; NEW ORLEANS (1947).

Higgins, Colin

Born 28 July 1941, Noumea, New Caledonia; died 5 Aug. 1988, Beverly Hills, Calif.

Director–Screenwriter

A former actor, Higgins began his professional filmmaking career when his master's thesis for the UCLA graduate film program, a screenplay about a love affair between a suicidal teenager and an 80–year–old woman, was picked up by Paramount in 1971. HAROLD AND MAUDE flopped upon its initial release but later became an enduring cult hit. Higgins' next filmed screenplay, SILVER STREAK (1976), was an instant hit, a pattern of popular success repeated in his subsequent films—on all of which he served as writer–director—and TV work. His films include: HAROLD AND MAUDE (p&w) (1971); SILVER STREAK (w) (1976); FOUL PLAY (d&w) 1978); NINE TO FIVE (d&w) (1980); THE BEST LITTLE WHOREHOUSE IN TEXAS (d&w) (1982); INTO THE NIGHT (a) (1984).

Houseman, John [Jacques Haussmann]

Born 22 Sept. 1902, Bucharest, Rumania; died 31 Oct. 1988, Malibu, Calif.

Radio/Stage Director–Radio/Stage/Film Writer–Actor–Producer

Howard

Houseman first made his mark in theater as director of the Virgil Thomson–Gertrude Stein opera "Four Saints in Three Acts" in 1934. He soon began his legendary collaboration with Orson Welles through the Federal Theater Project, producing Welles' avant garde stagings of "Macbeth," "Doctor Faustus," and "The Cradle Will Rock." They then founded the Mercury Theater, which eventually became radio's Mercury Theater of the Air and broadcast the famous "War of the Worlds" that panicked the nation in 1938. After Mercury disbanded, Houseman joined Welles in Hollywood, producing Welles' uncompleted first film and collaborating on the story (without credit) for CITIZEN KANE before the two parted unamiably in 1941. After WW II, Houseman divided his time among TV production, stage direction, and producing films for Paramount, Universal, and MGM. After his Oscar–winning role as the formidable Prof. Kingsfield in THE PAPER CHASE (1973), Houseman added acting fame to his list of distinctions, becoming rich as a performer and commercial spokesman. Houseman traced his protean career in an autobiography in three parts, *Run–Through*, *Front and Center*, and *Final Dress*. His films include: TOO MUCH JOHNSON (p&a) (uncompleted) (1938); CITIZEN KANE (w, uncredited) (1941); JANE EYRE (w) (1944); MISS SUSIE SLAGLE'S (p); THE UNSEEN (1945) (p); THE BLUE DAHLIA (p) (1946); LETTER FROM AN UNKNOWN WOMAN (p) (1948); THEY LIVE BY NIGHT (p) (1949); THE COMPANY SHE KEEPS (p) (1950); ON DANGEROUS GROUND (p) (1951); THE BAD AND THE BEAUTIFUL (p); HOLIDAY FOR SINNERS (p) (1952); JULIUS CAESAR (p) (1953); EXECUTIVE SUITE (p) (1954); THE COBWEB (p); MOONFLEET (p) (1955); LUST FOR LIFE (p) (1956); ILL MET BY MOONLIGHT (1957); NIGHT AMBUSH (p) (1958); ALL FALL DOWN (p); TWO WEEKS IN ANOTHER TOWN (p) (1962); IN THE COOL OF THE DAY (p) (1963); SEVEN DAYS IN MAY (a) (1964); THIS PROPERTY IS CONDEMNED (p) (1966); THE PAPER CHASE (a) (1973); ROLLERBALL (a); THREE DAYS OF THE CONDOR (a) (1975); ST. IVES (a) (1976); THE CHEAP DETECTIVE (a) (1978); OLD BOYFRIENDS (a) (1979); THE FOG (a); MY BODYGUARD (a); WHOLLY MOSES (a) (1980); BELLS (a); GHOST STORY (a) (1981); ANOTHER WOMAN (a); BRIGHT LIGHTS, BIG CITY (a); THE NAKED GUN: FROM THE FILES OF POLICE SQUAD (a); SCROOGED (a) (1988).

Howard, Trevor

Born 29 Sept. 1916, Cliftonville, England; died 7 Jan. 1988, Bushey, England

Actor

Howard made his stage debut in 1934, while still studying at the Royal Academy of Dramatic Art. He made his film debut a decade later, with a small part in Carol Reed's THE WAY AHEAD. His appearance marked the beginning of a fruitful cinematic association with Reed (whose THE THIRD MAN; THE OUTCAST OF THE ISLANDS; and THE KEY all featured fine Howard performances) and attracted the notice of Noel Coward, who picked him for the male lead in BRIEF ENCOUNTER, David Lean's film version of Coward's play. Howard's portrayal in that film of a fundamentally decent man whose honor is imperiled by circumstances was to influence the actor's future

screen persona, leading, as he grew older, to a string of characterizations of stalwart Englishmen and strict military types, such as Captain Bligh in the 1962 MUTINY ON THE BOUNTY. Ranked among the best and most versatile British actors, Howard received his only Academy Award nomination playing against type as Walter Morel in SONS AND LOVERS (1960). He made his last film appearance in THE UNHOLY. His films include: THE WAY AHEAD (1944); BRIEF ENCOUNTER; JOHNNY IN THE CLOUDS (1945); THE ADVENTURESS; GREEN FOR DANGER (1946); I BECAME A CRIMINAL; SO WELL REMEMBERED (1947); ONE WOMAN'S STORY (1949); THE CLOUDED YELLOW; GOLDEN SALAMANDER; THE THIRD MAN (1950); ODETTE (1951); GLORY AT SEA; OUTCAST OF THE ISLANDS (1952); THE HEART OF THE MATTER (1954); THE COCKLESHELL HEROES; LADY GODIVA RIDES AGAIN; THE STRANGER'S HAND (1955); AROUND THE WORLD IN 80 DAYS; RUN FOR THE SUN (1956); LOVER'S NET; PICKUP ALLEY; STOWAWAY GIRL (1957); THE KEY; THE ROOTS OF HEAVEN (1958); SONS AND LOVERS (1960); THE LION; MALAGA; MUTINY ON THE BOUNTY (1962); FATHER GOOSE; MAN IN THE MIDDLE (1964); MORITURI; OPERATION CROSSBOW; VON RYAN'S EXPRESS (1965); THE LIQUIDATOR; THE POPPY IS ALSO A FLOWER (1966); THE LONG DUEL; TRIPLE CROSS (1967); THE CHARGE OF THE LIGHT BRIGADE; A MATTER OF INNOCENCE (1968); THE BATTLE OF BRITAIN (1969); THE NIGHT VISITOR; RYAN'S DAUGHTER (1970); CATCH ME A SPY; KIDNAPPED; LOLA; MARY, QUEEN OF SCOTS (1971); POPE JOAN; SOMETHING LIKE THE TRUTH (1972); A DOLL'S HOUSE; LUDWIG; THE OFFENSE (1973); CRAZE; PERSECUTION; 11 HARROWHOUSE (1974); CONDUCT UNBECOMING; HENNESSY; WHO? (1975); THE BAWDY ADVENTURES OF TOM JONES; COUNT OF MONTE CRISTO; ELIZA FRASER; WHISPERING DEATH (1976); ACES HIGH; THE LAST REMAKE OF BEAU GESTE; SLAVERS (1977); NIGHT OF THE ASKARI; STEVIE; SUPERMAN (1978); HURRICANE; METEOR (1979); ALBINO; THE SHILLINGBURY BLOWERS; SIR HENRY AT RAWLINSON END; WINDWALKER (1980); THE SEA WOLVES (1981); DEADLY GAMES; GANDHI; LIGHT YEARS AWAY; THE MISSIONARY (1982); SWORD OF THE VALIANT (1984); DUST; TIME AFTER TIME (1985); FOREIGN BODY (1986); THE UNHOLY (1988).

Hubbell, Carl

Born 22 June 1903, Carthage, Mo.; died 21 Nov. 1988, Scottsdale, Ariz.

Baseball Pitcher

Dubbed "The Meal Ticket" by New York Giants players and fans during the Depression, two–time National League MVP Hubbell was one of the greatest pitchers in baseball. In addition to leading the Giants to three World Series (1933, 1936, and 1937) and establishing the screwball, he accomplished the legendary feat of striking out Hall of Famers Babe Ruth, Lou Gehrig, Jimmie Foxx, Al Simmons, and Joe Cronin in succession in the 1934 All–Star Game. Developing elbow trouble in 1938, Hubbell retired in 1943. Ten years later he appeared, as himself, in the film BIG LEAGUER.

Jones, Duane

Born Duquesne, Pa.; died 22 July 1988, Mineola, N.Y., age 51

Actor–Stage Director

Jones was director of the Maguire Theater at SUNY–Old Westbury and artistic director at New York's Richard Allen Center. He was particularly active with black theater companies, both as actor and director, and was also a former English teacher and professor. Jones sometimes appeared on TV and in films; he was the hero in George Romero's NIGHT OF THE LIVING DEAD (1968) who is mistaken for a zombie and shot at the movie's end, and starred in GANJA AND HESS. His films include: NIGHT OF THE LIVING DEAD (1968); GANJA AND HESS (1973); BLOOD COUPLE (1974); LOSING GROUND (1982); BEAT STREET (1984); TAROT (aka VAMPIRES, unreleased); TO DIE FOR (forthcoming).

Jordan, Jim

Died 1 April 1988, Los Angeles, Calif., age 91

Actor

Jordan and Marian Driscoll met in Peoria, Ill., and married in 1918. Over the next several years, in radio and vaudeville appearances, the couple developed the characters that eventually became "Fibber McGee and Molly" and charmed Americans for over 20 years on NBC radio. The Jordans appeared as the McGees in four films, two of which, LOOK WHO'S LAUGHING and HERE WE GO AGAIN, paired them with fellow radio star Edgar Bergen. Later Jim Jordan provided one of the voices in the 1977 animated film THE RESCUERS. His films include: THIS WAY PLEASE (1937); LOOK WHO'S LAUGHING (1941); HERE WE GO AGAIN (1942); HEAVENLY DAYS (1944); THE RESCUERS (1977).

Kapoor, Raj

Born 4 Dec. 1924, Bombay, India; died 2 June 1988, New Delhi, India

Actor–Director–Producer

Kapoor began in films as an assistant to his father, Prithvi Raj Kapoor, an actor and later exhibitor and producer of Indian films. Raj Kapoor went on to become the most popular Indian actor in that country and throughout the Middle East, China and the USSR, establishing his on–screen personality in portrayals of a Chaplinesque naif who suffers and eventually triumphs over a series of ordeals. Kapoor, who produced and directed many of his films, has been credited with addressing social issues in romantic films and with introducing greater eroticism to popular Indian cinema, despite struggles with censors. His films include: CHITTOR VIJAY; DIL KI RANI; JAIL YATRA; NEEL KAMAL (1947); AAG (FIRE) (a,p&d); AMAR PREM; GOPINATH (1948); ANDAZ; BARSAAT (a,p&d); SUNAHRE DIN (1949); BAWRA; BANWRE NAIN, DASTAN; JAAN PEH-CHAN; PAYR; SARGAM (1950); AWARA (THE VAGABOND) (a,p&d) (1951); AMBER; ANHONEE; ASHIANA; BEWAFA (1952); AAH (p&a); DHOON, PAPI (1953); BOOT POLISH (p) (1954); SHREE 420 (a,p&d) (1955); CHORI CHORI; JAGTE RAHO (p&a) (1956); AB DILLI DOOR NAHIN (p); SHARDA (1957); PARVARISH; PHIR SUBAH HOGI (1958); ANARI; CHAR DIL CHAR RAHEN; DO USTAD; KANHAIYA; MAIN NASHE MEN HOON (1959); CHHALIA; JIS DESH MEN GANGA BEHTI HAI (p&a); SHREEMAN SATYAWADI (1960); NAZRANA (1961); AASHIQ (1962); DIL HI TO HAI; EK DIL SAU AFSANE (1963); DULHA DULHAN; SANGAM (a,p&d) (1964); TEESRI KASAM (1966); AROUND THE WORLD; DIWANA (1967); SAPNON KA SAUDAGAR (1968); MERA NAAM JOKER (a,p&d) (1970); KAL AAJ AUR KAL (p&a) (1972); BOBBY (p&d) (1973); DO JASOOS (1975); DHARAM KARAM (p&a) (1976); SATYAM SHIVAM SUNDARAM (p&d) (1978); AB-DULLAH (1980); BIWI–O–BIWI (p) (1981); GOPICHAND JASOOS; PREM ROG (p&d) (1982); CHOR MANDALA (1983); RAM TERI GANGA MAILI (p) (1984).

Kinnear, Roy
Born 8 Jan. 1934, Wigan, England; died 20 Sept. 1988, Toledo, Spain
Actor

Kinnear died during filming of Richard Lester's THE LAST RE-TURN OF THE THREE MUSKETEERS, in which he plays d'Artagnan's servant Planchet, a role he originated in Lester's 1974 THE THREE MUSKETEERS. A favorite of Lester's and a specialist in satiric befuddlement, Kinnear appeared in HELP!; A FUNNY THING HAPPENED ON THE WAY TO THE FORUM; HOW I WON THE WAR and other Lester films after gaining fame on BBC–TV's popular "That Was the Week That Was." Kinnear was also popular on the British stage, appearing with the Royal Shakespeare Company and the National Theater. His films include: THE MILLIONAIRESS (1960); THE BOYS; TIARA TAHITI (1962); HEAVENS ABOVE!; THE SMALL WORLD OF SAMMY LEE; SPARROWS CAN'T SING (1963); FRENCH DRESSING; A PLACE TO GO (1964); HELP!; THE HILL; UNDERWORLD INFORMERS (1965); A FUNNY THING HAPPENED ON THE WAY TO THE FORUM (1966); THE DEADLY AFFAIR; HOW I WON THE WAR (1967); THE MINI–AFFAIR (1968); THE BED SITTING ROOM; LOCK UP YOUR DAUGHTERS (1969); EGGHEAD'S ROBOT; THE FIRECHASERS; ON A CLEAR DAY YOU CAN SEE FOREVER; SCROOGE; TASTE THE BLOOD OF DRACULA (1970); MELODY; RAISING THE ROOF; WILLY WONKA AND THE CHOCOLATE FACTORY (1971); THE ALF GARNETT SAGA; ALICE'S ADVENTURES IN WONDERLAND; THE PIED PIPER; RENTADICK; THAT'S YOUR FUNERAL (1972); THE AMOROUS MILKMAN; ESKIMO NELL; THREE FOR ALL (1974); JUGGERNAUT; THE THREE MUSKETEERS (1974); THE ADVENTURE OF SHERLOCK HOLMES' SMARTER BROTHER; BARRY McKENZIE HOLDS HIS OWN; THE FOUR MUSKETEERS; ONE OF OUR DINOSAURS IS MISSING; ROYAL FLASH (1975); NOT NOW, COMRADE (1976); HERBIE GOES TO MONTE CARLO; THE LAST REMAKE OF BEAU GESTE (1977); CANDLESHOE; WATERSHIP DOWN (1978); MAD DOGS AND CRICKETERS; THE OMEGA CONNECTION (1979); A FAIR WAY TO PLAY; DICK TURPIN; HAWK THE SLAYER; HIGH RISE DONKEY; THE HOUND OF THE BASK-ERVILLES (1980); HAMMETT (1982); THE BOYS IN BLUE (1973); PAVLOVA—A WOMAN FOR ALL TIME; SQUARING THE CIRCLE (1985); PIRATES (1986); JUST ASK FOR DIAMOND; THE LAST RETURN OF THE THREE MUSKE-TEERS (forthcoming).

Kjellin, Alf [Christopher Kent]
Born 28 Feb. 1920, Lund, Sweden; died 5 April 1988, Los Angeles, Calif.
Actor–Director–Screenwriter

A popular leading man in Swedish films in the early 1940s, Kjellin received international recognition when he starred in Alf Sjoberg's HETS (US title TORMENT, 1947), written by Ingmar Bergman. Kjellin's performance caught the attention of David O. Selznick, who gave him a major role (under the pseudonym Christopher Kent) in Vincente Minnelli's MADAME BOVARY (1949). Thereafter, Kjellin continued acting under his real name in Swedish and American films (including Bergman's ILLICIT INTERLUDE), and directed films and television shows in both countries in the 1950s, 60s, and 70s. His films include: JOHN ERICSSON, THE VICTOR AT HAMPTON ROADS (1937); FELLOW CADETS; REJOICE WHILE YOU'RE YOUNG (1939); HIS GRACE'S WILL; A NIGHT IN JUNE (1940); NIGHT IN THE HARBOR (1943); WANDERING WITH THE MOON (1945); APPASSIONATA; IRIS AND THE LIEUTEN-ANT; SUNSHINE FOLLOWS RAIN (1946); A GIRL FROM THE MARSH CROFT; TORMENT; WOMAN WITHOUT A FACE (1947); MADAME BOVARY (1949); SINGOALLA; THIS CAN'T HAPPEN HERE; THE WHITE CAT (1950); ROLLING SEA; DI-

VORCED (1951); AFFAIRS OF A MODEL; THE IRON MIS-TRESS; MY SIX CONVICTS (1952); THE JUGGLER; NO MAN'S WOMAN (1953); ILLICIT INTERLUDE (1954); GIRL IN THE RAIN (a,d&w); SEVENTEEN YEARS OLD (d&w); ENCOUN-TERS AT DUSK (d) (1957); PLAYING ON A RAINBOW (1958); SWINGING AT THE CASTLE (p) (1959); ONLY A WAITER (d) (1960); PLEASURE GARDEN (d) (1961); SISKA (d) (1962); MY LOVE IS A ROSE; THE VICTORS (1963); TWO LIVING, ONE DEAD (1964); THE SHIP OF FOOLS (1965); ASSAULT ON A QUEEN (1966); ICE STATION ZEBRA (1968); MIDAS RUN (d) (1969); THE McMASTERS (d) (1970); ZANDY'S BRIDE (1974).

Kohner, Paul
Born Teplice–Sanov, Czech.; died 16 March 1988, Los Angeles, Calif., at 85
Producer–Agent

Kohner was invited in 1920 by Universal president Carl Laemmle to work for the studio after Kohner interviewed him for a Prague–based film newspaper. Kohner produced THE HUNCHBACK OF NOTRE DAME (1923) and THE PHANTOM OF THE OPERA (1925) for Universal, then became head of its European division in late 1920s. Returning to the US in the 30s, he continued producing pictures, including more than 50 foreign–language films. In 1938 he opened the Paul Kohner talent agency, which represented many stars, including a number European emigres who came to the US with the help of the European Relief Fund, which he helped organize. Over 50 years his clients included Marlene Dietrich, Greta Garbo, Maurice Chevalier, John Huston, Liv Ullmann, Billy Wilder, Henry Fonda, Erich von Stroheim, David Niven, and Ingmar Bergman. His films include: THE HUNCHBACK OF NOTRE DAME (1923); THE PHANTOM OF THE OPERA (1925); THE CHINESE PARROT (1927); LOVE ME AND THE WORLD IS MINE (1928); A HOUSE DIVIDED (1932); EAST OF JAVA; THE PRODIGAL SON (1935); NEXT TIME WE LOVE (1936).

Koster, Henry [Hermann Kosterlitz]
Born 1 May 1905, Berlin, Germany; died 21 Sept. 1988, Camarillo, Calif.
Director–Screenwriter

After working in a variety of jobs that included writing film criticism, Koster became a screenwriter for UFA in 1925, directing his first film seven years later. With the Nazis' rise to power he emigrated, working in Austria, Hungary, and Italy before going to Hollywood in 1936—where, changing his name to Henry Koster, he directed a string of films starring ingenue Deanna Durbin that are said to have saved Universal from bankruptcy. Koster was particularly adept at making such light, charming films as HARVEY; THE INSPECTOR GEN-ERAL; MR. HOBBS TAKES A VACATION; and THE BISHOP'S WIFE (for which he received a Best Director Oscar nomination), but his reputation for technical excellence and adherence to schedule also garnered him such dramatic projects as THE ROBE (1953), the first film made in CinemaScope. His films include: DAS ABENTEUR DER THEA ROLAND; THE JAZZBAND FIVE (w) (1932); DAS HASSLICHE MADCHEN (d&w); THERE GOES THE BRIDE (w) (1933); PETER; KLEINE MUTTI (1934); KATHARINA DIE LETZTE (1935); DAS TAGEBUCH DER GELIEBTEN (1936); THREE SMART GIRLS; 100 MEN AND A GIRL (1937); AF-FAIRS OF MAUPASSANT; THE RAGE OF PARIS (1938); FIRST LOVE; THREE SMART GIRLS GROW UP (1939); SPRING PA-RADE (1940); IT STARTED WITH EVE (p&d) (1941); BETWEEN US GIRLS (p&d) (1942); MUSIC FOR MILLIONS (1944); TWO SISTERS FROM BOSTON (1946); THE BISHOP'S WIFE; THE UNFINISHED DANCE (1947); LUCK OF THE IRISH (1948); COME TO THE STABLE; THE INSPECTOR GENERAL (1949); HARVEY; MY BLUE HEAVEN; WABASH AVENUE (1950); ELOPEMENT; MR. BELVEDERE RINGS THE BELL; NO HIGHWAY IN THE SKY (1951); MY COUSIN RACHEL; O. HENRY'S FULL HOUSE ("The Cop and the Anthem" episode); STARS AND STRIPES FOREVER (1952); THE ROBE (1953); DE-SIREE (1954); GOOD MORNING, MISS DOVE; THE MAN CALLED PETER; THE VIRGIN QUEEN (1955); D–DAY, THE SIXTH OF JUNE; THE POWER AND THE PRIZE (1956); MY MAN GODFREY (1957); FRAULEIN (1958); THE NAKED MAJA (1959); THE STORY OF RUTH (1960); FLOWER DRUM SONG (1961); MR. HOBBS TAKES A VACATION (1962); TAKE HER, SHE'S MINE (p&d) (1963); DEAR BRIGETTE (p&d) (1965); THE SINGING NUN (1966).

Krasner, Milton
Born 17 Feb. 1904, Philadelphia, Pa.; died 16 July 1988, Woodland Hills, Calif.
Cinematographer

Krasner came to Hollywood in 1925 after beginning his career with New York's Vitagraph and Biograph studios. He worked as an assistant cameraman until given his first director of photography assignment for Paramount's GOLDEN HARVEST in 1933. For the next 10 years Krasner filmed primarily B pictures, but by the mid–1940s he had been nominated for an Academy Award (for 1942's ARABIAN NIGHTS) and won such major assignments as Fritz Lang's SCAR-LET STREET and THE WOMAN IN THE WINDOW (1945) on the strength of his dramatic black–and–white photography. Later, with Fox in the 50s, he became known as a specialist in CinemaScope and other widescreen color processes. Krasner received Academy Award nominations for ALL ABOUT EVE; AN AFFAIR TO REMEM-

Kinnear

Livingston

BER; HOW THE WEST WAS WON; LOVE WITH THE PROPER STRANGER; and FATE IS THE HUNTER in addition to ARABIAN NIGHTS; in 1954 he won the Oscar for THREE COINS IN THE FOUNTAIN. His films include: GOLDEN HARVEST; I LOVE THAT MAN; SITTING PRETTY; STRICTLY PERSONAL (1933); DEATH ON THE DIAMOND; THE GREAT FLIRTATION; PARIS INTERLUDE; PRIVATE SCANDAL; SHE MADE HER BED (1934); GREAT GOD GOLD; THE GREAT IMPERSONATION; MAKE A MILLION; MURDER IN THE FLEET; THE VIRGINIA JUDGE; WOMEN MUST DRESS (1935); CHEERS OF THE CROWD; CRASH DONOVAN; FORBIDDEN HEAVEN; THE GIRL ON THE FRONT PAGE; HONEYMOON LIMITED; LAUGHING IRISH EYES; LOVE LETTERS OF A STAR; MISTER CINDERELLA; YELLOWSTONE (1936); A GIRL WITH IDEAS; LADY FIGHTS BACK; LOVE IN A BUNGALOW; MYSTERIOUS CROSSING; OH DOCTOR; PRESCRIPTION FOR ROMANCE; SHE'S DANGEROUS; THERE GOES THE GROOM; WE HAVE OUR MOMENTS (1937); CRIME OF DR. HALLET; THE DEVIL'S PARTY; THE JURY'S SECRET; MIDNIGHT INTRUDER; THE MISSING GUEST; NURSE FROM BROOKLYN; THE STORM (1938); THE FAMILY NEXT DOOR; THE HOUSE OF FEAR; I STOLE A MILLION; LITTLE ACCIDENT; MISSING EVIDENCE; NEWSBOY'S HOME; YOU CAN'T CHEAT AN HONEST MAN (1939); THE BANK DICK; DIAMOND FRONTIER; HIRED WIFE; THE HOUSE OF THE SEVEN GABLES; THE INVISIBLE MAN RETURNS; THE MAN FROM MONTREAL; OH JOHNNY, HOW YOU CAN LOVE!; PRIVATE AFFAIRS; SANDY IS A LADY; SKI PATROL; TRAIL OF THE VIGILANTES; ZANZIBAR (1940); BACHELOR DADDY; BUCK PRIVATES; LADY FROM CHEYENNE; PARIS CALLING; THIS WOMAN IS MINE; TOO MANY BLONDES (1941); ARABIAN NIGHTS; A GENTLEMAN AFTER DARK; THE GHOST OF FRANKENSTEIN; MEN OF TEXAS; PARDON MY SARONG; THE SPOILERS (1942); GUNG HO!; THE MAD GHOUL; SO'S YOUR UNCLE; TWO TICKETS TO LONDON; WE'VE NEVER BEEN LICKED (1943); HAT CHECK HONEY; INVISIBLE MAN'S REVENGE (1944); ALONG CAME JONES; DELIGHTFULLY DANGEROUS; SCARLET STREET; THE WOMAN IN THE WINDOW (1945); THE DARK MIRROR; WITHOUT RESERVATIONS (1946); A DOUBLE LIFE; THE EGG AND I; THE FARMER'S DAUGHTER; SOMETHING IN THE WIND (1947); THE SAXON CHARM; UP IN CENTRAL PARK (1948); THE ACCUSED; HOLIDAY AFFAIR; HOUSE OF STRANGERS; THE SET-UP (1949); ALL ABOUT EVE; NO WAY OUT; THREE CAME HOME (1950); HALF ANGEL; I CAN GET IT FOR YOU WHOLESALE; THE MODEL AND THE MARRIAGE BROKER; PEOPLE WILL TALK; RAWHIDE (1951); DEADLINE—U.S.A.; DREAMBOAT; MONKEY BUSINESS; O. HENRY'S FULL HOUSE; PHONE CALL FROM A STRANGER (1952); DREAM WIFE; TAXI; VICKI (1953); DEMETRIUS AND THE GLADIATORS; DESIREE; GARDEN OF EVIL; THREE COINS IN THE FOUNTAIN (1954); THE GIRL IN THE RED VELVET SWING; HOW TO BE VERY, VERY POPULAR; THE RAINS OF RANCHIPUR; THE SEVEN YEAR ITCH (1955); BUS STOP; 23 PACES TO BAKER STREET (1956); AN AFFAIR TO REMEMBER; BOY ON A DOLPHIN; KISS THEM FOR ME (1957); A CERTAIN SMILE; THE GIFT OF LOVE (1958); COUNT YOUR BLESSINGS; THE MAN WHO UNDERSTOOD WOMEN; THE REMARKABLE MR. PENNYPACKER (1959); BELLS ARE RINGING; HOME FROM THE HILL (1960); GO NAKED IN THE WORLD; KING OF KINGS (1961); THE FOUR HORSEMEN OF THE APOCALYPSE; HOW THE WEST WAS WON; SWEET BIRD OF YOUTH; TWO WEEKS IN ANOTHER TOWN (1962); THE COURTSHIP OF EDDY'S FATHER; LOVE WITH THE PROPER STRANGER (1963); A TICKLISH AFFAIR; ADVANCE TO THE REAR; FATE IS THE HUNTER; GOODBYE CHARLIE; LOOKING FOR LOVE (1964); RED LINE 7000; THE SANDPIPER (1965); MADE IN PARIS; THE SINGING NUN (1966); HURRY SUNDOWN; THE ST. VALENTINE'S DAY MASSACRE; THE VENETIAN AFFAIR (1967); BALLAD OF JOSIE; DON'T JUST STAND THERE (1968); THE STERILE CUCKOO (1969); BENEATH THE PLANET OF THE APES (1970).

L'Amour, Louis

Born 22 March 1908, Jamestown, N.D.; died 10 June 1988, Los Angeles, Calif.

Novelist

The author of 101 books (86 of them novels), L'Amour was one of the century's best-selling authors, defining the American West for readers around the world. This popularity carried into films: more than 45 of his works were adapted for such film and television features as the John Wayne–starring HONDO (1953). L'Amour began writing novels in 1951, after working as a journalist, boxer, lumberjack, gold prospector, and cattle skinner, among other jobs. He was completing an autobiography at the time of his death. Films based on his works include: EAST OF SUMATRA; HONDO (1953); FOUR GUNS TO THE BORDER (1954); TREASURE OF RUBY HILLS (1955); BLACKJACK KETCHUM, DESPERADO; THE BURNING HILLS (1956); THE TALL STRANGER; UTAH BLAINE (1957); GUNS OF THE TIMBERLAND; HELLER IN PINK TIGHTS (1960); TAGGART (1964); KID RODELO (1966); CATLOW (1971); CANCEL MY RESERVATION (1972); THE MAN CALLED NOON (1973).

Larson, Eric

Born Cleveland, Utah; died 25 Oct. 1988, La Canada–Flintridge, Calif., at 83

Animator–Animation Director

After moving to Los Angeles to work as a reporter in 1933, Larson was hired by Walt Disney as an animator for SNOW WHITE AND THE SEVEN DWARFS—making him one of Disney's original "nine old men." Thereafter Larson worked as an animator or animation director on classic Disney films for four decades, ending his career as an animation consultant on THE GREAT MOUSE DETECTIVE (1986). His films include: SNOW WHITE AND THE SEVEN DWARFS (anim) (1937); FANTASIA (anim); PINOCCHIO (anim d) (1940); BAMBI (anim) (1942); THE THREE CABALLEROS (anim) (1944); MAKE MINE MUSIC (anim); SONG OF THE SOUTH (anim) (1946); MELODY TIME (1948); SO DEAR TO MY HEART (anim) (1949); CINDERELLA (1950); ALICE IN WONDERLAND (anim d) (1951); PETER PAN (anim) (1953); LADY AND THE TRAMP (anim d) (1955); SLEEPING BEAUTY (d) (1959); ONE HUNDRED AND ONE DALMATIANS (anim) (1961); THE SWORD IN THE STONE (anim) (1963); MARY POPPINS (anim) (1964); THE JUNGLE BOOK (anim) (1967); THE ARISTOCATS (anim) (1970); BEDKNOBS AND BROOMSTICKS (1971); ROBIN HOOD (anim) (1973).

Lasky, Jr., Jesse L.

Born 19 Sept. 1908, New York, N.Y.; died 11 April 1988, London, England

TV/Screenwriter–Playwright–Author

Jesse L. Lasky, Jr., son of production executive Jesse L. Lasky, collaborated on the scripts of seven films by his father's associate Cecil B. DeMille, including REAP THE WILD WIND; SAMSON AND DELILAH; and the 1956 THE TEN COMMANDMENTS. During WW II he wrote scripts for documentaries and organized the Army School of Film Training at the Signal Corps Photographic Center. Lasky also wrote novels, TV shows, and plays (often cowriting with his wife, Pat Silver), and the autobiographical *Whatever Happened to Hollywood?* His films include: COMING OUT PARTY; RED HEAD; THE WHITE PARADE (1934); THE GAY DECEPTION; MUSIC IS MAGIC (1935); SECRET AGENT (1936); LAND OF LIBERTY; UNION PACIFIC (1939); NORTHWEST MOUNTED POLICE (1940); BACK IN THE SADDLE; THE SINGING HILLS; STEEL AGAINST THE SKY (1941); THE OMAHA TRAIL; REAP THE WILD WIND (1942); ATTACK!—THE BATTLE OF NEW BRITAIN (1944); APPOINTMENT IN TOKYO (1945); UNCONQUERED (1947); SAMSON AND DELILAH (1949); LORNA DOONE; MASK OF THE AVENGER; NEVER TRUST A GAMBLER (1951); THE BRIGAND; THE THIEF OF VENICE (1952); MISSION OVER KOREA; SALOME; THE SILVER WHIP (1953); HELL AND HIGH WATER; THE IRON GLOVE (1954); PEARL OF THE SOUTH PACIFIC (1955); HOT BLOOD; THE TEN COMMANDMENTS (1956); THE BUCCANEER (1958); JOHN PAUL JONES (1959); THE WIZARD OF BAGHDAD (1960); PIRATES OF TORTUGA; SEVEN WOMEN FROM HELL (1961); LAND RAIDERS (1969); AN ACE UP MY SLEEVE (1975); CRIME AND PASSION (1976).

Legg, Stuart

Born 31 Aug. 1910, London, England; died 23 July 1988, Wiltshire, England

Writer–Documentary Producer–Director–Editor

Legg was among the young men who joined John Grierson's pioneer British documentary movement in the early 1930s. He continued to work primarily as a producer with Grierson, creating with him a series of wartime propaganda films for Canada's National Film Board that included the 1942 Oscar winner, CHURCHILL'S ISLAND. In Britain, Legg became chairman of Film Centre International in 1957, after producing such documentaries as POWERED FLIGHT and SONG OF THE CLOUDS. The author of several distinguished books on varied subjects, Legg also directed the fictional silent VARSITY (1930). His documentary films include: THE NEW GENERATION; THE NEW OPERATOR (1932); TELEPHONE WORKERS; TELEPHONE SHIP; THE COMING OF THE DIAL (1953); BBC—THE VOICE OF BRITAIN (1934); MONEY BEHIND THE SCREEN (w) (1937); POWERED FLIGHT (1953); SONG OF THE CLOUDS (1956).

Livingston, Robert [Bob Livingston, Robert E. Randall]

Born 9 Dec. 1908, Quincy, Ill.; died 7 March 1988, Tarzana, Calif.

Actor

In the 1930s Livingston played Stoney Brooke in Republic's popular "Three Mesquiteers" series (costarring Max Terhune and Ray "Crash" Corrigan), and in 1939 he became the only Lone Ranger to take off his mask in Republic's THE LONE RANGER RIDES AGAIN. He was eventually replaced in the "Mesquiteers" series by the young John Wayne, but he remained one of the screen's top cowboys in the 40s as the star of PRC's "Lone Rider" series, this time paired with sidekick Al "Fuzzy" St. John. In later years he appeared principally in character roles. His brother was the singing cowboy Addison "Jack" Randall. Livingston's films include: DANCE, FOOLS, DANCE (1931); THE BAND PLAYS ON; DEATH ON THE DIAMOND; ENLIGHTEN YOUR DAUGHTER (1934); BABY FACE HARRINGTON; MUTINY ON THE BOUNTY; MURDER IN THE FLEET; WEST

POINT OF THE AIR; THE WINNING TICKET (1935); ABSO-LUTE QUIET; BOLD CABALLERO; SMALL TOWN GIRL; SPEED; SUZY; THREE GODFATHERS; THE THREE MES-QUITEERS; THE VIGILANTES ARE COMING (serial) (1936); CIRCUS GIRL; COME ON, COWBOYS; GHOST TOWN GOLD; GUNSMOKE RANCH; HEART OF THE ROCKIES; HIT THE SADDLE; LARCENY ON THE AIR; RANGE DEFENDERS; RENFREW OF THE ROYAL MOUNTED; ROARIN' LEAD (1937); ARSON GANG BUSTERS; ARSON RACKET SQUAD; CALL THE MESQUITEERS; HEROES OF THE HILLS; KING OF THE NEWSBOYS; LADIES IN DISTRESS; THE NIGHT HAWK; OUTLAWS OF SONORA; THE PURPLE VIGILANTES; RIDERS OF THE BLACK HILLS; WILD HORSE RODEO (1938); COWBOYS FROM TEXAS; FEDERAL MANHUNT; THE KAN-SAS TERRORS; THE LONE RANGER RIDES AGAIN (serial); ORPHANS OF THE STREET (1939); COVERED WAGON DAYS; HEROES OF THE SADDLE; LONE STAR RAIDERS; OKLA-HOMA RENEGADES; PIONEERS OF THE WEST; ROCKY MOUNTAIN RANGERS; THE TRAIL BLAZERS; UNDER TEXAS SKIES (1940); GANGS OF SONORA; PALS OF THE PE-COS; PRAIRIE PIONEERS; SADDLEMATES (1941); COWBOYS FROM TEXAS; OVERLAND STAGECOACH (1942); LONE RIDER IN DEATH RIDES THE PLAINS; PISTOL PACKIN' MAMA; WILD HORSE RUSTLERS; WOLVES OF THE RANGE (1943); BENEATH WESTERN SKIES; THE BIG BONANZA; BRAZIL; DEATH RIDES THE PLAINS; GOODNIGHT, SWEET-HEART; LAKE PLACID SERENADE; THE LARAMIE TRAIL; LAW OF THE SADDLE; PRIDE OF THE PLAINS; RAIDERS OF RED GAP; STORM OVER LISBON (1944); BELLS OF ROSARITA; THE CHEATERS; DAKOTA; DON'T FENCE ME IN; STEPPIN' IN SOCIETY; TELL IT TO A STAR (1945); THE UNDERCOVER WOMAN; VALLEY OF THE ZOMBIES (1946); DAREDEVILS OF THE CLOUDS; THE FEATHERED SER-PENT; GRAND CANYON TRAIL (1948); THE MYSTERIOUS DESPERADO; RIDERS IN THE SKY (1949); LAW OF THE BADLANDS; MULE TRAIN (1950); SADDLE LEGION (1951); NIGHT STAGE TO GALVESTON; SOMETHING FOR THE BIRDS (1952); WINNING OF THE WEST (1953); ONCE UPON A HORSE (1958); GIRLS FOR RENT (1974); THE NAUGHTY STE-WARDESSES; BLAZING STEWARDESSES (1975).

Loder, John [John Muir Lowe]
Born 3 Jan. 1898, York, England; died December 1988
Actor

A Gallipoli veteran and general's son, the tall, aristocratic-looking Loder played movie leads on both sides of the Atlantic, but was most popular in British films of the 1930s. After his screen debut in 1926, Loder appeared in silents, then in Paramount's first talkie, THE DOC-TOR'S SECRET (1929). At the height of his UK fame, he starred in Hitchcock's SABOTAGE, the 1937 KING SOLOMON'S MINES, and LORNA DOONE, among others. Back in Hollywood (and later on Broadway), Loder's roles included that of Ianto in HOW GREEN WAS MY VALLEY and the widower rejected by Bette Davis in NOW, VOYAGER. DISHONORED LADY (1947) cast Loder with Hedy Lamarr, the third of his five wives. In 1977 he published an auto-biography, *Hollywood Hussar* . His films include: MADAME WUNSCHT KEINE KINDER (1926); THE FIRST BORN (1928); BLACK WATERS; THE DOCTOR'S SECRET; THE RACKE-TEER; RICH PEOPLE; SUNSET PASS; THE UNHOLY NIGHT (1929); HER PRIVATE AFFAIR; LILIES OF THE FIELD; THE MAN HUNTER; ONE NIGHT AT SUSIE'S; THE SECOND FLOOR MYSTERY; SWEETHEARTS AND WIVES (1930); THE SEAS BENEATH (1931); MONEY MEANS NOTHING; WED-DING REHEARSAL (1932); MONEY FOR SPEED; PARIS PLANE; THE PRIVATE LIFE OF HENRY VIII (1933); THE BATTLE; LOVE, LIFE, AND LAUGHTER; MY SONG GOES ROUND THE WORLD; ROLLING IN MONEY; SING AS WE GO; WARN LONDON!; YOU MADE ME LOVE YOU (1934); IT HAPPENED IN PARIS; JAVA HEAD; LORNA DOONE; THE SI-LENT PASSENGER; 18 MINUTES (1935); DAREDEVILS OF EARTH; GUILTY MELODY; THE MAN WHO LIVED AGAIN; QUEEN OF HEARTS (1936); DOCTOR SYN; KING SOLO-MON'S MINES; MADEMOISELLE DOCTEUR; NON-STOP NEW YORK; RIVER OF UNREST; SABOTAGE (1937); KATIA; TO THE VICTOR (1938); CONTINENTAL EXPRESS; MURDER WILL OUT (1939); ADVENTURE IN DIAMONDS; DIAMOND FRONTIER; MOZART; TIN PAN ALLEY (1940); CONFIRM OR DENY; HOW GREEN WAS MY VALLEY; ONE NIGHT IN LIS-BON; SCOTLAND YARD (1941); EAGLE SQUADRON; GEN-TLEMAN JIM; GORILLA MAN; MAXWELL ARCHER, DE-TECTIVE; NOW, VOYAGER (1942); ADVENTURES IN IRAQ; MURDER ON THE WATERFRONT; THE MYSTERIOUS DOC-TOR; OLD ACQUAINTANCE; UNDER SECRET ORDERS (1943); ABROAD WITH TWO YANKS; THE HAIRY APE; PAS-SAGE TO MARSEILLE (1944); THE BRIGHTON STRANGLER; THE FIGHTING GUARDSMAN; A GAME OF DEATH; JEAL-OUSY; WOMAN WHO CAME BACK (1945); ONE MORE TO-MORROW; THE WIFE OF MONTE CRISTO (1946); DISHON-ORED LADY (1947); SMALL HOTEL; THE STORY OF ESTHER COSTELLO; THE WOMAN AND THE HUNTER (1957); THE SECRET MAN (1958); GIDEON OF SCOTLAND YARD (1959); ESQUIU (1965); FIRECHASERS (1970).

Loewe, Frederick
Born 10 June 1901, Vienna, Austria; died 14 Feb. 1988, Palm Springs, Calif.
Composer

Loewe, the son of a well-known Viennese tenor, was a youthful prod-igy as a pianist and composer. At 15 he wrote the song "Katrina," which was a hit throughout Europe. Spurred by his early successes to try his luck in the US, Loewe came to New York in 1924, but his career sputtered until his meeting with fellow Lambs Club member Alan Jay Lerner in 1942. The two began collaborating on scores for musicals, finding their first big Broadway success with "Brigadoon" (1947). Their next production together was "Paint Your Wagon" in 1951, fol-lowed by "My Fair Lady," starring Rex Harrison and Julie Andrews, in 1956. Hailed by critics as a masterpiece, the production ran for 2,717 performances and grossed nearly 12 million in its first two years. Ler-ner and Loewe next collaborated on the film musical GIGI (1958)—the first film to win nine Academy Awards—and the 1960 stage production of "Camelot," but their relationship deteriorated dur-ing work on the latter and the partnership broke up, with Loewe going into retirement. The two reunited once more, however, to create the score for THE LITTLE PRINCE (1974). Films featuring Loewe's lyri-cal, Old World-tinged melodies include: BRIGADOON (1954); GIGI (1958); MY FAIR LADY (1964); CAMELOT (1967); PAINT YOUR WAGON (1969); THE LITTLE PRINCE (1974).

Logan, Joshua
Born 5 Oct. 1908, Texarkana, Tex.; died 12 July 1988, New York, N.Y.
Director–Producer–Playwright–Actor

Logan

Interested in drama as a teen, Logan attended Princeton (in 1927) be-cause of the university's Triangle Club, and became involved with the intercollegiate University Players, a troupe that included Margaret Sullavan, James Stewart, and Henry Fonda. After studying in Moscow with Stanislavsky, Logan made his first Broadway appearance in 1932 and his Broadway directorial debut in 1935. He then went to Holly-wood as a dialog director, and in 1938 both directed his first film, I MET MY LOVE AGAIN (codirected by Arthur Ripley), and achieved his first Broadway hit, "I Married and Angel" (beginning his long collaboration with composer Richard Rodgers). Included among Logan's many subsequent Broadway successes (several of which he co-authored) were "Annie Get Your Gun," "South Pacific," "Mister Roberts," "Picnic," and "Fanny." Logan's films were mostly movie versions of his stage hits. He received Best Director Oscar nominations for PICNIC (1955) and SAYONARA (1957), but his last films, CAM-ELOT (1967) and PAINT YOUR WAGON (1969), were critical fail-ures and among the last of the big-budget Hollywood musicals. His films include: I MET MY LOVE AGAIN (1938); HIGHER AND HIGHER (w) (1943); MAIN STREET TO BROADWAY (a) (1953); MISTER ROBERTS (w); PICNIC (1955); BUS STOP; SAYONARA (1957); SOUTH PACIFIC (d&w) (1958); TALL STORY (p&d) (1960); FANNY (p,d,&w) (1961); ENSIGN PULVER (p,d,&w) (1964); CAMELOT (1967); PAINT YOUR WAGON (1969).

Lummis, Dayton
Born 1903, Summit, N.J.; died 23 June, Santa Monica, Calif.
Actor

Character actor Lummis appeared in about 50 films and 400 TV pro-grams. In 1936, after acting in stock companies in the American West and Canada, he began a radio career in New York City that eventually included acting, announcing, directing, and producing. He began per-forming on Broadway in the 1940s, then moved to Los Angeles in 1950, where his screen credits included roles in PRINCE OF PLAY-ERS; HOW TO MARRY A MILLIONAIRE; THE COURT MAR-TIAL OF BILLY MITCHELL; HIGH SOCIETY; SPARTACUS and many others. His films include: ANDROCLES AND THE LION; LES MISERABLES; RUBY GENTRY (1952); ALL I DE-SIRE; CHINA VENTURE; THE GLENN MILLER STORY; THE GOLDEN BLADE; HOW TO MARRY A MILLIONAIRE; JULIUS CAESAR; MAN IN THE DARK; THE MISSISSIPPI GAMBLER; PORT SINISTER; THE PRESIDENT'S LADY; TANGIER INCIDENT (1953); DEMETRIUS AND THE GLADI-ATORS; DRAGON'S GOLD; LOOPHOLE; RETURN TO TREA-SURE ISLAND; 20,000 LEAGUES UNDER THE SEA; THE YELLOW MOUNTAIN (1954); THE COBWEB; THE COURT–MARTIAL OF BILLY MITCHELL; HIGH SOCIETY; A MAN CALLED PETER; MY SISTER EILEEN; PRINCE OF PLAYERS; THE PRODIGAL; THE SPOILERS; SUDDEN DANGER; THE VIEW FROM POMPEY'S HEAD (1955); THE BAD SEED; A DAY OF FURY; THE FIRST TEXAN; OVER–EXPOSED; SHOW-DOWN AT ABILENE; THE WRONG MAN (1956); MONKEY ON MY BACK (1957); FROM HELL TO TEXAS (1958); COM-PULSION (1959); ELMER GANTRY; THE MUSIC BOX KID; SPARTACUS (1960); THE FLIGHT THAT DISAPPEARED (1961); DEADLY DUO; JACK THE GIANT KILLER (1962); BEAUTY AND THE BEAST (1963); MOONFIRE (1970).

Meeker, Ralph [Ralph Rathgeber]
Born 21 Nov. 1920, Minneapolis, Minn.; died 5 Aug. 1988, Woodland Hills Calif.
Actor

Meeker

Meeker broke into films on the strength of his Broadway performances in "Picnic" and "A Streetcar Named Desire" (successfully replacing Marlon Brando in the latter), and appeared as well in "Mr. Roberts," "Strange Fruit," and others. In films, Meeker was a respected per-former in both lead and character roles, often playing macho—sometimes also mean or cowardly—men in such films as KISS ME DEADLY (as Mickey Spillane's Mike Hammer); PATHS OF GLORY; THE DIRTY DOZEN; and SOMETHING WILD (1961). In 1960-61 he also starred in his own TV series, "Not for Hire." His films include: FOUR IN A JEEP; SHADOW IN THE SKY; TERESA (1951); GLORY ALLEY; SOMEBODY LOVES ME (1952); CODE TWO; JEOPARDY; THE NAKED SPUR (1953); BIG HOUSE, U.S.A.; DESERT SANDS; KISS ME DEADLY (1955); A WOMAN'S DEVOTION (1956); THE FUZZY PINK NIGHTGOWN; PATHS OF GLORY; RUN OF THE ARROW (1957); ADA; SOMETHING WILD (1961); WALL OF NOISE (1963); THE DIRTY DOZEN; GENTLE GIANT; THE ST. VALENTINE'S DAY MASSACRE (1967); THE DETECTIVE (1968); THE DEVIL'S 8 (1969); I WALK THE LINE (1970); THE ANDERSON TAPES (1971); THE HAPPINESS CAGE (1972); LOVE COMES QUIETLY (1974); BRANNIGAN; JOHNNY FIRECLOUD (1975); THE ALPHA INCIDENT; THE FOOD OF THE GODS (1976); HI-RIDERS; MY BOYS ARE GOOD BOYS (1978); WINTER KILLS (1979); WITHOUT WARNING (1980); MY BOYS ARE GOOD BOYS (p&a) (1986).

Moore

Mitry, Jean

Born 7 Nov. 1907, Soissons, France; died 18 Jan. 1988, Paris, France

Film Historian–Theoretician–Director

As a young film enthusiast and cofounder of France's first film society, Mitry worked with Abel Gance, Marcel L'Herbier, and Jean Renoir before founding the Cinematheque Francaise with Henri Langlois and Georges Franju in 1936. Among his critical, theoretical, and historical works on film are studies of Ford, Clair, Eisenstein, and Chaplin; the *Larousse Dictionary of the Cinema*; *Aesthetic and Psychology of the Cinema*; and the massive *Filmographic universelle*, a compilation of international film credits and filmographies spanning cinematic history. Mitry directed several short films, including visualizations of the music of Honegger, Debussy, and Boulez; he made one feature–length fiction film, ENIGME AUX FOLIES–BERGERE (1959). His films include: PARIS CINEMA (1929); PACIFIC 231 (1949); LE PAQUEBOT LIBERTE (1950); IMAGES POUR DEBUSSY (1951); SYMPHONIE MECANIQUE (1955); LE MIRACLE DES AILES (1956); CHOPIN (1957); ENIGME AUX FOLIES–BERGERE (1959); RENCONTRES (1960); LA MACHINE ET L'HOMME (1962).

Murray

Moore, Colleen [Kathleen Morrison]

Born 19 Aug. 1902, Port Huron, Mich.; died 25 Jan. 1988, Paso Robles, Calif.

Actress

Moore came to Hollywood at age 16, hired by D.W. Griffith as repayment for a favor done him by her uncle, Chicago newspaperman Walter Howey (the prototype for Walter Burns in "The Front Page"). She appeared for several years in B pictures and westerns, including several Tom Mix films, but became an "overnight" star as the heroine of the silent FLAMING YOUTH in 1923. Moore's distinctive look—Dutch boy–bobbed hair (newly cut for the role), gamine eyes (one brown, one blue), small bosom, low waistline, above–the–knee skirt—established the emerging flapper as a nationwide phenomenon, presented an urbane antitype to previous silent film heroines, and made Moore one of the highest paid stars in movies. She continued to play variations of the flapper role throughout the 20s (often in pictures produced by her first husband, John McCormick), although she attempted to buck typecasting in SO BIG (1924). She made a few sound films, including THE POWER AND THE GLORY, before retiring. She was the author of an autobiography, *Silent Star*, *How Women Can Make Money in the Stock Market*, and *Colleen Moore's Doll House*, about her elaborate miniature house, now on permanent display in Chicago. Her films include: THE BAD BOY; HANDS UP; AN OLD FASHIONED YOUNG MAN; THE SAVAGE (1917); A HOOSIER ROMANCE (1918); THE BUSHER; COMMON PROPERTY; THE EGG CRATE WALLOP; LITTLE ORPHAN ANNIE; THE MAN IN THE MOONLIGHT; THE WILDERNESS TRAIL (1919); THE CYCLONE; THE DEVIL'S CLAIM; DINTY; SO LONG LETTY; WHEN DAWN CAME (1920); HIS NIBS; THE LOTUS EATER; THE SKY PILOT (1921); AFFINITIES; BROKEN CHAINS; COME ON OVER; FORSAKING ALL OTHERS; THE NINETY AND NINE; THE WALL FLOWER (1922); APRIL SHOWERS; THE BROKEN HEARTS OF BROADWAY; FLAMING YOUTH; THE HUNTRESS; LOOK YOUR BEST; THE NTH COMMANDMENT; SLIPPY McGEE (1923); FLIRTING WITH LOVE; PAINTED PEOPLE; THE PERFECT FLAPPER; SO BIG; THROUGH THE DARK (1924); THE DESERT FLOWER; SALLY; WE MODERNS (1925); ELLA CINDERS; IRENE; IT MUST BE LOVE; TWINKLETOES (1926); HER WILD OAT; NAUGHTY BUT NICE; ORCHIDS AND ERMINE (1927); HAPPINESS AHEAD; LILAC TIME; OH, KAY (1928); FOOTLIGHTS AND FOOLS; SMILING IRISH EYES; SYNTHETIC SIN; WHY BE GOOD? (1929); THE POWER AND THE GLORY (1933); THE SCARLET LETTER; SOCIAL REGISTER; SUCCESS AT ANY PRICE (1934).

Murray, Ken [Kenneth Abner Doncourt]

Born 14 July 1903, New York, N.Y.; died 12 Oct. 1988, Burbank, Calif.

Vaudevillian–Film/TV Actor

Veteran vaudevillian Murray made his film debut in HALF–MARRIAGE in 1929, and continued to appear intermittently on–screen until the mid–1970s. His diverse career included a seven–year run on the Hollywood stage in "Ken Murray's Blackouts," a bawdy revue featuring numerous guest stars and Marie Wilson as Murray's airhead straight woman. BILL AND COO (1947), a fantasy about birds starring, written, and produced by Murray, earned him a

special Academy Award for "novel and entertaining use" of the film medium. Murray's "home movies" of movie stars in their daily lives have been internationally distributed and shown on TV, where he also starred on 1950s hit "Ken Murray Show." His films include: HALF–MARRIAGE (1929); LEATHERNECKING (1930); CROONER; LADIES OF THE JURY (1932); DISGRACED; FROM HEADQUARTERS (1933); YOU'RE A SWEETHEART (1937); SWING, SISTER, SWING (1938); A NIGHT AT EARL CARROLL'S (1940); SWING IT SOLDIER (1941); JUKE BOX JENNY (1942); BILL AND COO (a,p&w) (1947); THE MARSHAL'S DAUGHTER (a&p) (1953); THE MAN WHO SHOT LIBERTY VALANCE (1962); SON OF FLUBBER (1963); FOLLOW ME, BOYS! (1966); THE WAY WEST (1967); THE POWER (1968); WON TON TON, THE DOG WHO SAVED HOLLYWOOD (1976).

Napier, Alan [Alan Napier–Clavering]

Born 7 Jan. 1903, Birmingham, England; died 8 Aug. 1988, Santa Monica, Calif.

Actor

Though best known to recent generations as Alfred, the butler on TV's "Batman," Napier's distinguished career in fact spanned six decades. After debuting in the 1920s at the Oxford Repertory with fellow students Laurence Olivier and John Gielgud, Napier went on to a successful stage career in London that culminated in the original production of Noel Coward's "Bittersweet." He entered British films in 1930, working steadily until emigrating to the US in 1939. There the tall, suave character actor found steady employment in such films as CAT PEOPLE; THE SONG OF BERNADETTE; MINISTRY OF FEAR; LASSIE, COME HOME; and JULIUS CAESAR. Napier appeared with John Houseman, a longtime associate, in his last film, THE PAPER CHASE, in 1973. His films include: CASTE (1930); STAMBOUL (1931); LOYALTIES (1934); IN A MONASTERY GARDEN (1935); FOR VALOR (1937); THE WIFE OF GENERAL LING (1938); WE ARE NOT ALONE; WINGS OVER AFRICA (1939); THE HOUSE OF THE SEVEN GABLES; THE INVISIBLE MAN RETURNS; THE SECRET FOUR (1940); CONFIRM OR DENY (1941); CAT PEOPLE; EAGLE SQUADRON; RANDOM HARVEST; WE WERE DANCING; A YANK AT ETON (1942); APPOINTMENT IN BERLIN; LASSIE, COME HOME; MADAME CURIE; THE SONG OF BERNADETTE (1943); ACTION IN ARABIA; DARK WATERS; THE HAIRY APE; LOST ANGEL; MADEMOISELLE FIFI; THIRTY SECONDS OVER TOKYO; THE UNINVITED (1944); HANGOVER SQUARE; ISLE OF THE DEAD; MINISTRY OF FEAR (1945); HOUSE OF HORRORS; A SCANDAL IN PARIS; THE STRANGE WOMAN; THREE STRANGERS (1946); ADVENTURE ISLAND; DRIFTWOOD; FIESTA; FOREVER AMBER; HIGH CONQUEST; IVY; LONE WOLF IN LONDON; LURED; SINBAD THE SAILOR; UNCONQUERED (1947); HILLS OF HOME; JOAN OF ARC; JOHNNY BELINDA; MACBETH; MY OWN TRUE LOVE (1948); CHALLENGE TO LASSIE; A CONNECTICUT YANKEE IN KING ARTHUR'S COURT; CRISS CROSS; MANHANDLED; MASTER MINDS; THE RED DANUBE; TARZAN'S MAGIC FOUNTAIN (1949); DOUBLE CROSSBONES; TRIPOLI (1950); ACROSS THE WIDE MISSOURI; THE BLUE VEIL; THE GREAT CARUSO; THE HIGHWAYMAN; THE STRANGE DOOR; TARZAN'S PERIL (1951); BIG JIM McLAIN (1952); JULIUS CAESAR; YOUNG BESS (1953); DESIREE (1954); MOONFLEET (1955); THE COURT JESTER; MIAMI EXPOSE; THE MOLE PEOPLE (1956); UNTIL THEY SAIL (1957); ISLAND OF LOST WOMEN; JOURNEY TO THE CENTER OF THE EARTH (1959); TENDER IS THE NIGHT; WILD IN THE COUNTRY (1961); THE PREMATURE BURIAL (1962); THE SWORD IN THE STONE (1963); MARNIE; MY FAIR LADY; SIGNPOST TO MURDER (1964); THE LOVED ONE; 36 HOURS (1965); BATMAN (1966); THE PAPER CHASE (1973).

Nelson, Ralph

Born 12 Aug. 1916, New York, N.Y.; died 21 Dec. 1987, Santa Monica, Calif.

Director–Producer–Screenwriter–Playwright–Actor

Nelson began acting onstage at the age of 17, and went on to write and direct plays on Broadway. After WW II he began directing television dramas, including Rod Serling's teleplay "Requiem for a Heavyweight." He directed the film version of "Requiem" in 1962, followed by his hit adaptation of LILIES OF THE FIELD, which he produced and directed on a shoestring budget. Nelson made several films with his own Rainbow Productions, including SOLDIER IN THE RAIN; FATE IS THE HUNTER; and CHARLY, playing minor roles in a number of them. His films include: REQUIEM FOR A HEAVYWEIGHT (1962); LILIES OF THE FIELD; SOLDIER IN THE RAIN (1963); FATE IS THE HUNTER; FATHER GOOSE (1964); ONCE A THIEF (1965); DUEL AT DIABLO (1966); COUNTERPOINT (1967); CHARLY (1968); SOLDIER BLUE; . . . TICK . . . TICK . . . TICK . . . (1970); FLIGHT OF THE DOVES (1971); THE WRATH OF GOD (1972); THE WILBY CONSPIRACY (1975); EMBRYO (1976); A HERO AIN'T NOTHIN' BUT A SANDWICH (1977).

Nico [Christa Paffgen, Christa Pavlovski, Nico Ozsak]

Born 16 Oct. 1938, Cologne, [West]Germany; died 25 June 1988, Ibiza, Spain

Actress–Singer–Composer

Nico worked as a teenage model in Europe before getting a minor role in LA DOLCE VITA in 1960. After emigrating to New York, she became one of Andy Warhol's Factory–associate "superstars," appearing in his 1967 THE CHELSEA GIRLS and later films and becoming lead singer (with Lou Reed) of the Velvet Underground. Tall, gravely beautiful, with long blond hair and a heavily accented, deadpan singing voice, Nico presented the New York scene's perfect answer to the California flower child. In the 70s and 80s she recorded and performed fairly infrequently, producing four solo albums and appearing in films by Philippe Garrel, but her reputation as avant–garde *chanteuse* remained indelible. Her films include: LA DOLCE VITA (1960); FOUR STARS (1967); IMITATION OF CHRIST (1970); THE INNER SCAR (1972); L'ATHANOR (1973); BALLHAUS BARMBEK (1988).

Novak, Eva
Born St. Louis, Mo.; died 17 April 1988, Woodland Hills, Calif., age 90
Actress

Novak followed her sister Jane, who was acting for Hal Roach, to California shortly after WW I. After appearing as a Mack Sennett bathing beauty, she became Tom Mix's leading lady in several of the cowboy star's movies. With Mix's advice, she began to do her own stunts, and continued to do so in subsequent westerns with William S. Hart. She married stuntman and director William Reed in 1921 and the couple made films in Australia. Returning to the US in the 30s, Novak continued to perform in talkies, including movies directed by her brother–in–law Alfred E. Green and by her friend John Ford. Her films include: THE FEUD; THE SPEED MANIAC (1919); THE DAREDEVIL; DESERT LOVE; THE TESTING BLOCK; UP IN MARY'S ATTIC; WANTED AT HEADQUARTERS (1920); LAST TRAIL; O'-MALLEY OF THE MOUNTED; THE ROUGH DIAMOND; THE SMART SEX; SOCIETY'S SECRETS; THE TORRENT; TRAILIN'; WOLVES OF THE NORTH (1921); BARRIERS OF FOLLY; CHASING THE MOON; THE GREAT NIGHT; MAKING A MAN; THE MAN FROM HELL'S RIVER; THE MAN WHO SAW TOMORROW; SKY HIGH; UP AND GOING (1922); BOSTON BLACKIE; DOLLAR DEVILS; THE MAN LIFE PASSED BY; A NOISE IN NEWBORO; TEMPTATION; THE TIGER'S CLAW (1923); THE BATTLING FOOL; BATTLING MASON; THE BEAUTIFUL SINNER; THE FATAL MISTAKE; A FIGHT FOR HONOR; LAUGHING AT DANGER; LISTEN LESTER; LURE OF THE YUKON; MISSING DAUGHTERS; RACING FOR LIFE; SAFE GUARDED; TAINTED MONKEY; WOMEN FIRST (1924); THE FEARLESS LOVER; NORTHERN CODE; SALLY (1925); THE DIXIE FLYER; IRENE; THE MILLIONAIRE POLICEMAN; NO MAN'S GOLD; 30 BELOW ZERO (1926); DUTY'S REWARD; RED SIGNALS (1927); THE MEDICINE MAN; PHANTOM OF THE DESERT (1930); STAGECOACH (1939); APOLOGY FOR MURDER; THE BELLS OF ST. MARY'S (1945); BLACKMAIL (1947); FORT APACHE; FOUR FACES WEST; I, JANE DOE (1948); HELLFIRE; SHE WORE A YELLOW RIBBON (1949); THE BLONDE BANDIT; SUNSET BOULEVARD (1950); TALL MAN RIDING (1955); THE KETTLES ON OLD MacDONALD'S FARM (1957); SERGEANT RUTLEDGE (1960); THE MAN WHO SHOT LIBERTY VALANCE (1962); WILD SEED (1965).

O'Rourke, Heather
Born 27 Dec. 1975, Chicago, Ill.; died 1 Feb. 1988, San Diego, Calif.
Actress

The sweetly blonde–haired, blue–eyed O'Rourke was discovered in classic movie fashion by POLTERGEIST cowriter–coproducer Stephen Spielberg when he spied her in an MGM commissary. As the child snatched into the beyond by ghosts inhabiting her family's house, O'Rourke warned, "They're heeeere" and "They're baaaaack" —national catchphrases–to–be—in an eerie, cool voice in the first two "Poltergeist" films, and had completed work on POLTERGEIST III at the time of her death. She appeared frequently on TV after her film debut. Her films were POLTERGEIST (1982); POLTERGEIST II (1986); and POLTERGEIST III (1988).

Orbison, Roy
Born 23 April 1936, Vernon, Tex.; died 6 Dec. 1988, Hendersonville, Tenn.
Rock Musician–Composer

Known for his eerie tenor–falsetto voice; sunglasses, black leather, and pompadour; and solid compositions, from uptempo rockabilly to heart–rending ballads, Orbison scored his first hit, "Ooby Dooby," with Sun Records in 1956. A string of hits followed—including "Only the Lonely," "Crying," "Dream Baby," and "Oh, Pretty Woman" —until family tragedies in the mid–1960s crippled Orbison's career. His popularity revived, however, first as a composer, when such stars as Linda Ronstadt covered his songs in the 70s, later as a performer, including a stint as a member of the pseudonymous rock 'n' roll supergroup the Traveling Wilburys. He recorded a solo album, "Mystery Girl," just before his death. Orbison stars in the Civil War drama THE FASTEST GUITAR ALIVE (1967) and appears in ROADIE (1980); his songs can be heard in INSIGNIFICANCE (1985); BLUE VELVET (1986, with Dean Stockwell lip–syncing "In Dreams"); LESS THAN ZERO (1987); and HIDING OUT (1987).

Paton, Alan
Born 11 Jan. 1913, Pietermaritzburg, S. Afr.; died 12 April 1988, Durban, S. Afr.
Novelist

One of South Africa's foremost writers and political figures, Paton was head of a reformatory for black juveniles when he began writing *Cry, the Beloved Country*. The novel's appearance in 1948 directed worldwide attention to the effects of South African apartheid as represented in Paton's portrayal of a Zulu minister's experiences; it has since sold more than 15 million copies in 20 languages. Kurt Weill and Maxwell Anderson's musical version, "Lost in the Stars," opened on Broadway in 1949, and the film CRY, THE BELOVED COUNTRY, written and coproduced by Paton and starring Canada Lee, appeared in 1952. Paton was a founder (in 1953) and first president South Africa's Liberal Party, disbanded in 1969 when the government banned interracial parties. His writings include three novels, a two tobiography, and many political essays.

Pinero, Miguel
Died 16 June 1988, New York, N.Y., age 41
Playwright–Actor–Poet

Pinero claimed, at age 25, that he had already spent seven years in prison. He was in Sing Sing when he began writing "Short Eyes," which was named the New York Drama Critics best American play of 1974. A view of prison life focusing on the treatment of a newly incarcerated child molester, "Short Eyes" was filmed in 1976 by Robert M. Young from Pinero's script; the author also played "Go Go" in the film. Pinero continued to act in several other films and on TV, often playing addicts and criminals. He was, in fact, in frequent legal trouble after his literary success, but continued writing plays and poetry as a leading voice of the "Nuyorican" community. His films include: LOOKING UP; SHORT EYES (a&w) (1977); TIMES SQUARE (1980); FORT APACHE, THE BRONX (1981); BREATHLESS; DEAL OF THE CENTURY; EXPOSED (1983); ALMOST YOU; ALPHABET CITY (1984); THE PICK–UP ARTIST (1987).

Pressburger, Emeric
Born 5 Dec. 1902, Miskolc, Hungary; died 5 Feb. 1988, Saxstead, England
Screenwriter–Director–Producer–Novelist

Pressburger joined UFA studio in 1926, but after Hitler's rise, emigrated to Paris and, in 1936, to London, where fellow Hungarian Alexander Korda hired him at London Films. Korda introduced Pressburger to director Michael Powell, and the two began their long creative collaboration with U–BOAT 29 (THE SPY IN BLACK in Great Britain). The partnership went on to produce such films as THE INVADERS, for which Pressburger received an Academy Award; ONE OF OUR AIRCRAFT IS MISSING; COLONEL BLIMP; BLACK NARCISSUS; and their greatest success, THE RED SHOES. Between 1942 and 1956 Pressburger and Powell were listed as coproducers, codirectors, and cowriters of all the team's films with their own production company, Archers Film Producing Co., but Pressburger's contribution is generally assumed to have been confined principally to the writing and originating of screenplays, while Powell was in full charge of direction. Pressburger wrote, produced, and directed TWICE UPON A TIME (1953) independently of Powell; MIRACLE IN SOHO (1957) was also a solo project. Fred Zinnemann's 1964 film BEHOLD A PALE HORSE is based on a Pressburger novel. Pressburger's films include: BEAUTIFUL ADVENTURE (1932); ONE RAINY AFTERNOON (1936); THE CHALLENGE; SPY FOR A DAY; U–BOAT 29 (1939); BLACKOUT (1940); ATLANTIC FERRY; THE INVADERS (1941); ONE OF OUR AIRCRAFT IS MISSING; ADVENTURE IN BLACKMAIL; SQUADRON LEADER X (1943); A CANTERBURY TALE; COLONEL BLIMP; THE SILVER FLEET (1945); STAIRWAY TO HEAVEN; WAITING FOR MURDER (1946); BLACK NARCISSUS; THE END OF THE RIVER; I KNOW WHERE I'M GOING (1947); THE RED SHOES; HOUR OF GLORY (1949); THE FIGHTING PIMPERNEL (1950); THE TALES OF HOFFMANN (1951); THE WILD HEART (1952); TWICE UPON A TIME (1953); OH ROSALINDA (1956); MIRACLE IN SOHO; PURSUIT OF THE GRAF SPEE (1957); NIGHT AMBUSH (1958); BEHOLD A PALE HORSE (1964); THEY'RE A WEIRD MOB (1966); THE BOY WHO TURNED YELLOW (1972).

Prevert, Pierre
Born 26 May 1906, Paris, France; died 6 April 1988, Paris, France
Director–Actor–Screenwriter

Prevert began in films as an assistant director to Alberto Cavalcanti and Jean Renoir before directing the irreverent surrealist burlesque L'AFFAIRE EST DANS LE SAC in 1932. The film's screenplay was written by his more famous brother, poet, surrealist, and screenwriter Jacques Prevert. The Preverts collaborated similarly on Pierre's ADIEU LEONARD and VOYAGE SURPRISE. Pierre also directed films for French television and acted in supporting roles in several films, including Buñuel's 1930 L'AGE D'OR; the Prevert brothers can be seen as extras at the station in Jean Vigo's L'ATALANTE (1947). Pierre Prevert's films (as director) include: SOUVENIRS DE PARIS (co–d) (1928 doc.); L'AFFAIRE EST DANS LE SAC (a&d) (1932); LE COMMISSAIRE EST BON ENFANT (co–d) (1934 short); ADIEU LEONARD (a,d&w) (1943); VOYAGE SURPRISE (a,d&w) (1946); PARIS MANGE SON PAIN (1958 short); PARIS, LA BELLE (1959 doc.).

Novak

O'Rourke

Ramsey

Rich

Rogell

Raab, Kurt

Born 20 July 1941, Czech.; died 28 June 1988, Hamburg, W. Ger.

Actor–Screenwriter–Art/Production Director–Director

Raab met Rainer Werner Fassbinder through Munich's Action–Theater (Hanna Schygulla was also a member) in the late 1960s; the two formed a close association until their rancorous 1977 parting. He appeared in many of Fassbinder's films (including the title role in WHY DOES HERR R. RUN AMOK?)—serving also as art or production director on several—and directed the experimental Theater am Turm with Fassbinder and Roland Petri in 1974–75. After Fassbinder's death in 1982, Raab cowrote an insider's description of the Fassbinder circle that accused the director of casting Raab in roles that harmed the actor's career and enhanced Fassbinder's; Raab nonetheless appeared frequently in films by other German directors, notably Reinhard Hauff. Raab directed and scripted one film himself, INSEL DER BLUTIGEN PLANTAGE, in which he also performed. His films include: LIEBE IST KALTER ALS DER TOD (1969); DIE NIKLASHAUSEN FAHRT; RIO DAS MORTES; WHITY (1970); DER HANDLER DER VIER JAHRESZEITEN; MATTHIAS KNEISSL; PIONIERE IN INGOLSTADT (art d) (1971); ACHT STUNDEN SIND KEIN TAG; THE AMERICAN SOLDIER (a&prod d); THE BITTER TEARS OF PETRA VON KANT (art d) (1972); MARTHA; WELT AM DRAHT; THE TENDERNESS OF WOLVES (a&w) (1973); DIE VERROHUNG DES FRANZ BLUMS; EFFI BRIEST (art d) (1974); ANGST VOR DER ANGST (a&art d) (1975); GRUPPENBILD MIT DAME; ICH WILL DOCH NUR, DASS IHR MICH LIEBT (art d); FOX AND HIS FRIENDS; MOTHER KUSTERS GOES TO HEAVEN (a,w&art d); SATANSBRATEN (1976); ADOLF UND MARLENE; BOLWEISER; JAIL BAIT (a&art d); LEIDENSCHAFTLICHE BLUMEN; WHY DOES HERR R. RUN AMOK? (a&prod d) (1977); BELCANTO, ODER, DARF EINE NUTTE SCHLUCHZEN?; BILDNIS EINER TRINKERIN; WARUM DIE UFOS UNSER SALAT KLAUEN (1979); ENDSTATION FREIHEIT; UNTER VERSCHLUSS (1980); DAS LIEBESKONZIL; DIE ZAUBERBERG; FRANKFURT "KAISERSTRASSE"; HEUTE SPIELEN WIR DEN BOSS—WO GEHT'S DENN HIER ZUM FILM?; WIE DIE WELTMEISTER (1981); DAS GESPENST; INSEL DER BLUTIGEN PLANTAGE (a,d&w) (1982); BELLA DONNA; LES TRICHEURS (1983); ABWARTS; ENGEL AUS EISEN (1984); DER REKORD; PARKER (1985); ANGRY HARVEST; MOTTEN IM LICHT; TRANSITTRAUME (1986); WOHIN? (1988).

Ramsey, Anne

Born 1929, Omaha, Neb.; died 11 Aug. 1988, Los Angeles, Calif.

Actress

Ramsey and fellow actor Logan Ramsey married in 1954 and cofounded Philadelphia's Theater of the Living Arts in 1959. Ramsey acted on the New York stage and wrote for the *New York Times* before she and Logan moved to Los Angeles in the 1960s, and made her film debut as Logan's wife in THE SPORTING CLUB (they were spouses again in 1971's ANY WHICH WAY YOU CAN). Although Ramsey had part of her tongue removed in 1985 due to throat cancer, her speech impediment did nothing to hinder her Oscar–nominated performance as Danny DeVito's obnoxious, wildly domineering mother in 1987's THROW MAMMA FROM THE TRAIN—the role that, briefly, made her a star. Her films include: THE SPORTING CLUB (1971); THE NEW CENTURIONS; UP THE SANDBOX (1972); FOR PETE'S SAKE; FUN WITH DICK AND JANE (1977); GOIN' SOUTH (1978); WHEN YOU COMIN' BACK, RED RYDER? (1979); ANY WHICH WAY YOU CAN; THE BLACK MARBLE (1980); NATIONAL LAMPOON'S CLASS REUNION (1982); THE KILLERS (1984); THE GOONIES (1985); DEADLY FRIEND; SAY YES (1986); THROW MAMMA FROM THE TRAIN; WEEDS (1987); DR. HACKENSTEIN; HOMER AND EDDIE; LIFE ON THE EDGE.

Rich, Irene

Born 13 Oct. 1891, Buffalo, N.Y.; died 22 April 1988, Santa Barbara, Calif.

Actress

Rich was in her mid–20s and a successful seller of real estate when she first appeared as an extra on–screen in 1918; she was subsequently cast in melodramatic leading roles that played off her aristocratic image. Rich also appeared in silent comedies opposite Will Rogers and continued to act with him into the sound era, playing his nagging and pretentious wife in such films as THEY HAD TO SEE PARIS (1929). Her many notable performances of the 20s and 30s also included roles in Ernst Lubitsch's LADY WINDERMERE'S FAN (1925); CRAIG'S WIFE (1928); and THE CHAMP (1931). Her career shifted to radio in the 1930s, and she starred in the WW II "Dear John" radio drama. Onstage she performed nearly 5,000 times in the vaudeville sketch "Ask the Wife" and appeared on Broadway from 1948 to 1950 in the long–running "As the Girls Go." Rich occasionally played matronly character parts in movies of the late 30s and 40s, last appearing on–screen in 1948 in FORT APACHE and JOAN OF ARC. Her films include: THE GIRL IN HIS HOUSE; A LAW UNTO HERSELF; OLD WIVES FOR NEW; STELLA MARIS (1918); A MAN IN THE OPEN; CASTLES IN THE AIR; HER PURCHASE PRICE; THE LONE STAR RANGER; TODD OF THE TIMES; WOLVES OF THE NIGHT (1919); THE BLUE BONNET; JES' CALL ME JIM; THE STAR ROVER; STOP THIEF; THE STRANGE BOARDER; THE STREET CALLED STRAIGHT; WATER, WATER, EVERYWHERE (1920); BOYS WILL BE BOYS; DESPER-

ATE TRAILS; THE INVISIBLE POWER; JUST OUT OF COLLEGE; ONE MAN IN A MILLION; THE POVERTY OF RICHES; SUNSET JONES; A TALE OF TWO WORLDS; A VOICE IN THE DARK (1921); BRAWN OF THE NORTH; THE CALL OF HOME; A FOOL THERE WAS; THE FRUITS OF EARTH; THE MARRIAGE CHANCE; ONE CLEAR CALL; THE ROPIN' FOOL; STRENGTH OF THE PINES; THE TRAP; WHILE JUSTICE WAITS; THE YOSEMITE TRAIL (1922); BOY OF MINE; BRASS; DANGEROUS TRAILS; DEFYING DESTINY; LUCRETIA LOMBARD; MICHAEL O'HALLORAN; ROSITA; SNOW DRIFT; YESTERDAY'S WIFE (1923); BEAU BRUMMEL; BEHOLD THE WOMAN; BEING RESPECTABLE; CAPTAIN JANUARY; CYTHEREA; A LOST LADY; PAL O'MINE; THIS WOMAN; WHAT THE BUTLER SAW (1924); COMPROMISE; EVE'S LOVER; LADY WINDERMERE'S FAN; THE MAN WITHOUT A CONSCIENCE; MY WIFE AND I; THE PLEASURE BUYERS; THE WIFE WHO WASN'T WANTED; A WOMAN WHO SINNED (1925); THE HONEYMOON EXPRESS; MY OFFICIAL WIFE; SILKEN SHACKLES (1926); THE CLIMBERS; DEARIE; THE DESIRED WOMAN; DON'T TELL THE WIFE; THE SILVER SLAVE (1927); BEWARE OF MARRIED MEN; CRAIG'S WIFE; THE PERFECT CRIME; POWDER MY BACK; WOMEN THEY TALK ABOUT (1928); DAUGHTERS OF DESIRE; THE EXALTED FLAPPER; NED McCOBB'S DAUGHTER; SHANGHAI ROSE; THEY HAD TO SEE PARIS (1929); AMOS 'N' ANDY; ON YOUR BACK; SO THIS IS LONDON (1930); BEAU IDEAL; THE CHAMP; FATHER'S SON; FIVE AND TEN; THE MAD PARADE; STRANGERS MAY KISS; WICKED (1931); DOWN TO EARTH; HER MAD NIGHT; MANHATTAN TOWER (1932); THAT CERTAIN AGE (1938); EVERYBODY'S HOBBY (1939); THE LADY IN QUESTION; THE MORTAL STORM; QUEEN OF THE YUKON (1940); KEEPING COMPANY; THREE SONS O'GUNS (1941); THIS TIME FOR KEEPS (1942); ANGEL AND THE BADMAN; CALENDAR GIRL; NEW ORLEANS (1947); FORT APACHE; JOAN OF ARC (1948).

Roberson, Chuck [Charles H. Roberson]

Born Joy, Tex.; died 8 June 1988, Bakersfield, Calif., age 69

Actor–Stuntman

After working on ranches and serving in WW II, Roberson joined Republic as a stunt rider. Not long thereafter he did John Wayne's stunts in THE FIGHTING KENTUCKIAN (1949); he subsequently continued to double for Wayne, to whom he bore a strong resemblance, in nearly all of the actor's movies. Roberson also doubled for Clark Gable, Jeff Chandler, Gregory Peck, and Ronald Reagan, among others, and was the subject of Bodie Thoene's book *The Fall Guy*, the basis of the Lee Majors TV series of the same name. His films include: PLAINSMAN AND THE LADY (1946); SONG OF SCHEHERAZADE (1947); THE FIGHTING KENTUCKIAN; I SHOT JESSE JAMES; STAMPEDE; WESTERN RENEGADES (1949); BANDIT QUEEN; COW TOWN; FRONTIER OUTPOST; LIGHTNING GUNS; OUTCAST OF BLACK MESA; RIO GRANDE (1950); FORT DODGE STAMPEDE; RIDIN' THE OUTLAW TRAIL (1951); THE LUSTY MEN (1952); GUN BELT (1953); SIGN OF THE PAGAN (1954); THE FAR COUNTRY; THE PRODIGAL (1955); THE RAWHIDE YEARS; THE SEARCHERS; SEVEN MEN FROM NOW (1956); FORTY GUNS; NIGHT PASSAGE; RUN OF THE ARROW; THE WINGS OF EAGLES (1957); THE BIG COUNTRY; MAN OF THE WEST (1958); THE WONDERFUL COUNTRY (1959); THE ALAMO; SERGEANT RUTLEDGE; SPARTACUS (1960); THE MISFITS; TWO RODE TOGETHER (1961); HOW THE WEST WAS WON; THE MAN WHO SHOT LIBERTY VALANCE; MERRILL'S MARAUDERS (1962); DONOVAN'S REEF; McLINTOCK!; SHOCK CORRIDOR (1963); ADVANCE TO THE REAR; CHEYENNE AUTUMN (1964); BLACK SPURS; CAT BALLOU (1965); SMOKY (1966); EL DORADO; THE WAR WAGON (1967); THE GREEN BERETS; HELLFIGHTERS; THE SCALPHUNTERS (1968); THE UNDEFEATED (1969); THE HAWAIIANS; RIO LOBO (1970); McQ; 99 AND 44/100% DEAD (1974); THE SHOOTIST (1976); BLUE THUNDER (1983); COBRA (1986).

Rogell, Albert S.

Born 1 Aug. 1901, Oklahoma City, Okla.; died 7 April 1987, Los Angeles, Calif.

Director

Rogell began working in 1916 as an assistant cameraman for the Washington Motion Picture Company in Spokane. The next year he moved to Hollywood, where he worked various jobs at studios and eventually became assistant director to George Loane Tucker at Paramount. He shot several two-reel westerns in the early 1920s and was eventually hired to direct a series of westerns starring Fred Thompson for Monogram in 1924. For the next few years he directed westerns for First National and Universal that starred Ken Maynard and Jack Hoxie. By the advent of sound Rogell was a well–established B movie director known for his quick, efficient, effective filmmaking. He continued to make westerns (with Tom Mix and the young John Wayne, among others) and filmed one of the first Technicolor movies, MAMBA, in 1930. Rogell directed a string of secondary features in all genres into the 1950s, when he began directing for television. His films include: THE GREATEST MENACE (1923); THE DANGEROUS COWARD; THE FIGHTING SAP; GALLOPING GALLAGHER; GEARED TO GO; LIGHTNING ROMANCE; THE MASK OF LOPEZ; NORTH OF NEVADA; THE SILENT STRANGER; THUNDERING HOOFS (1924); THE CIRCUS CYCLONE; CRACK O'-

DAWN; CYCLONE CAVALIER; EASY MONEY; THE FEAR FIGHTER; FIGHTING FATE; GOAT GETTER; THE KNOCK-OUT KID; THE SNOB BUSTER; SUPER SPEED; YOUTH'S GAMBLE (1925); THE MAN FROM THE WEST; MEN OF THE NIGHT; THE PATENT LEATHER PUG; RED HOT LEATHER; SENOR DAREDEVIL; THE UNKNOWN CAVALIER; THE WILD HORSE STAMPEDE (1926); THE DESERT'S SADDLE; THE FIGHTING THREE; GRINNING GUNS; MEN OF DARING; THE OVERLAND STAGE; THE RED RAIDERS; ROUGH AND READY; SOMEWHERE IN SONORA; THE SUNSET DERBY; THE WESTERN ROVER; THE WESTERN WHIRL-WIND (1927); THE CANYON OF ADVENTURE; THE GLORIOUS TRAIL; THE PHANTOM CITY; THE SHEPHERD OF THE HILL; THE UPLAND RIDER (1928); THE CALIFORNIA MAIL; CHEYENNE; THE FLYING MARINE; THE LONE WOLF'S DAUGHTER; PAINTED FACES (1929); MAMBA (1930); ALOHA; SUICIDE FLEET; SWEEPSTAKES; THE TIP-OFF (1931); CARNIVAL BOAT; RIDER OF DEATH VALLEY (1932); AIR HOSTESS; BELOW THE SEA; EAST OF FIFTH AVE.; THE WRECKER (1933); AMONG THE MISSING; FOG; FUGITIVE LADY; THE HELL CAT; NAME THE WOMAN; NO MORE WOMEN (1934); AIR HAWKS; ATLANTIC ADVENTURE; ESCAPE FROM DEVIL'S ISLAND; UNKNOWN WOMAN (1935); GRAND JURY; ROAMING LADY; YOU MAY BE NEXT (1936); MURDER IN GREENWICH VILLAGE (1937); CITY STREETS; THE LAST WARNING; THE LONE WOLF IN PARIS; START CHEERING (1938); FOR LOVE OR MONEY; HAWAIIAN NIGHTS; LAUGH IT OFF (1939); ARGENTINE NIGHTS; I CAN'T GIVE YOU ANYTHING BUT LOVE, BABY; LI'L ABNER; PRIVATE AFFAIRS (1940); THE BLACK CAT; PUBLIC ENEMIES; SAILORS ON LEAVE; TIGHT SHOES (1941); BUTCH MINDS THE BABY; JAIL HOUSE BLUES; PRIORITIES ON PARADE; SLEEPYTIME GAL; TRUE TO THE ARMY (1942); HIT PARADE OF 1943; IN OLD OKLAHOMA; YOUTH ON PARADE (1943); LOVE, HONOR AND GOODBYE (1945); EARL CARROLL SKETCHBOOK; THE MAGNIFICENT ROGUE (1946); HEAVEN ONLY KNOWS (1947); NORTHWEST STAMPEDE (1948); SONG OF INDIA (1949); THE ADMIRAL WAS A LADY (1950); SHADOW OF FEAR (1956).

Rose, George

Born 19 Feb. 1920, Bicester, England; died 5 May 1988, Sosua, Dominican Republic

Actor

Rose joined London's Old Vic Theater for four seasons after serving in WW II. He was a popular supporting player in West End productions and in British films during the 1940s and 50s, and established a reputation as a fine comic actor with the Royal Shakespeare Company. In 1961 he originated the role of the Common Man in "A Man for All Seasons" in London and in the American touring production. Rose then settled in New York and became one of Broadway's most beloved and versatile performers, receiving Tony Awards in 1976 for "My Fair Lady" and in 1985 for "The Mystery of Edwin Drood." Rose played the First Gravedigger in John Gielgud's 1964 staging of Hamlet and in the filmed version of the production; more recent on-screen parts include that of Walter Matthau's canny butler in A NEW LEAF (1971) and the Major-General in THE PIRATES OF PENZANCE (1983). His films include: THE PICKWICK PAPERS (1952); THE BEGGAR'S OPERA (1953); DEVIL ON HORSEBACK; THE GOOD DIE YOUNG (1954); THE NIGHT MY NUMBER CAME UP; PORT OF ESCAPE; THE SEA SHALL NOT HAVE THEM; THE SQUARE RING; WICKED WIFE (1955); THE LAST WAGON; SAILOR BEWARE!; TRACK THE MAN DOWN (1956); BROTHERS IN LAW; THE GOOD COMPANIONS; NO TIME FOR TEARS; THE SHIRALEE; THE THIRD KEY (1957); ALL AT SEA; CAT AND MOUSE; A NIGHT TO REMEMBER (1958); THE DEVIL'S DISCIPLE; THE HEART OF A MAN; JACK THE RIPPER (1959); DESERT MICE (1960); JET STORM; MANIA (1961); MACBETH (1963); HAMLET (1964); HAWAII (1966); THE PINK JUNGLE (1968); THE TREE (1969); A NEW LEAF (1971); FROM THE MIXED-UP FILES OF MRS. BASIL E. FRANKWEILER (1973); THE PIRATES OF PENZANCE (1983).

Rosson, Hal [Harold Rosson]

Born 1895, New York City, N.Y.; died 6 Sept. 1988, Palm Beach, Fla.

Cinematographer

The brother of directors Arthur and Richard Rosson and silent screen actress Helene Rosson, Hal Rosson began his screen career as a bit player with Vitagraph Studios in 1908, then trained in various capacities before becoming a camera operator on Allan Dwan's DAVID HARUM in 1915 and a cameraman on Dwan's PANTHEA two years later. Rosson went on to form long-standing collaborations with directors Dwan, Cecil B. DeMille, Josef Von Sternberg, Victor Fleming (for whom he shot THE WIZARD OF OZ), Howard Hawks (including EL DORADO, Rosson's last film), and Jack Conway, among others. Rosson also shot several films featuring Jean Harlow, to whom he was briefly married; he was also a favorite cameraman of Gloria Swanson's and Spencer Tracy's. Rosson received Oscar nominations for his work on BOOM TOWN; THIRTY SECONDS OVER TOKYO (with Robert Surtees); THE ASPHALT JUNGLE; and THE BAD SEED. He shared a special Academy Award with W. Howard Greene for their pioneering work in Technicolor in THE GARDEN OF ALLAH (1936). His films include: DAVID HARUM (1915); PANTHEA (co-p) (1917); THE CINEMA MURDER; HELIOTROPE; POLLY OF THE STORM COUNTRY (1920); BURIED TREASURE (1921); THE CRADLE; FOR THE DEFENSE; A HOMESPUN

VAMP (1922); DARK SECRETS; GARRISON'S FINISH; THE GLIMPSES OF THE MOON; QUICKSANDS (co-ph); LAWFUL LARCENY; ZAZA (1923); MANHANDLED; MANHATTAN; A SOCIETY SCANDAL; STORY WITHOUT A NAME (1924); INFATUATION; A MAN MUST LIVE; THE STREET OF FORGOTTEN MEN (1925); ALMOST A LADY; INFATUATION; MAN BAIT; UP IN MABEL'S ROOM (co-ph) (1926); A GENTLEMAN OF PARIS; GETTING GERTIE'S GARTER; JIM THE CONQUEROR; ROUGH HOUSE ROSIE; SERVICE FOR LADIES (1927); ABIE'S IRISH ROSE; THE DOCKS OF NEW YORK; THE DRAGNET; GENTLEMEN PREFER BLONDES; THREE WEEK-ENDS (1928); THE CASE OF LENA SMITH; THE FAR CALL; FROZEN JUSTICE; SOUTH SEA ROSE; TRENT'S LAST CASE (1929); MADAME SATAN; PASSION FLOWER; THIS MAD WORLD (1930); THE CUBAN LOVE SONG; MEN CALL IT LOVE; THE PRODIGAL; SON OF INDIA; SPORTING BLOOD; THE SQUAW MAN (1931); ARE YOU LISTENING?; DOWNSTAIRS; FELLER NEEDS A FRIEND; KONGO; RED DUST; RED HEADED WOMAN; TARZAN, THE APE MAN (co-ph) (1932); THE BARBARIAN; BOMBSHELL; HELL BELOW; HOLD YOUR MAN; PENTHOUSE (co-ph); TURN BACK THE CLOCK (ed&ph); CAT AND THE FIDDLE; THIS SIDE OF HEAVEN; TREASURE ISLAND (co-ph) (1934); THE SCARLET PIMPERNEL (1935); AS YOU LIKE IT; THE DEVIL IS A SISSY; THE GARDEN OF ALLAH; THE GHOST GOES WEST (1936); CAPTAINS COURAGEOUS; THE EMPEROR'S CANDLESTICKS; THE MAN WHO COULD WORK MIRACLES; THEY GAVE HIM A GUN (1937); TOO HOT TO HANDLE; A YANK A OXFORD (1938); THE WIZARD OF OZ (1939); BOOM TOWN; DR. KILDARE GOES HOME; EDISON THE MAN; FLIGHT COMMAND; I TAKE THIS WOMAN (1940); HONKY TONK; MEN OF BOYS TOWN; THE PENALTY; WASHINGTON MELODRAMA (1941); JOHNNY EAGER; SOMEWHERE I'LL FIND YOU; TENNESSEE JOHNSON (1942); SLIGHTLY DANGEROUS (1943); AN AMERICAN ROMANCE; THIRTY SECONDS OVER TOKYO (co-ph) (1944); DUEL IN THE SUN (co-ph); MY BROTHER TALKS TO HORSES; NO LEAVE, NO LOVE (co-ph); THREE WISE FOOLS (1946); THE HUCKSTERS; LIVING IN A BIG WAY (1947); COMMAND DECISION; HOMECOMING (1948); ANY NUMBER CAN PLAY; ON THE TOWN; THE STRATTON STORY (1949); THE ASPHALT JUNGLE; KEY TO THE CITY; TO PLEASE A LADY (1950); THE RED BADGE OF COURAGE (1951); LONE STAR; LOVE IS BETTER THAN EVER; SINGIN' IN THE RAIN (1952); THE ACTRESS; DANGEROUS WHEN WET; I LOVE MELVIN; THE STORY OF THREE LOVES (co-ph) (1953); MAMBO; PETE KELLY'S BLUES; STRANGE LADY IN TOWN; ULYSSES (co-ph) (1955); THE BAD SEED; TOWARD THE UNKNOWN (1956); THE ENEMY BELOW (1957); NO TIME FOR SERGEANTS; ONIONHEAD (1958); EL DORADO (1967).

Salvatori, Renato

Born 20 March 1933, Porte dei Marmi, Italy; died 27 March 1988, Rome, Italy

Actor

Salvatori was reportedly discovered working as a lifeguard by Italian director Luciano Emmer in 1951. He debuted the following year in Emmer's LE RAGAZZE DI PIAZZA DI SPAGNA, and steadily gained recognition through the next 10 years in Dino Risi's POVERI MA BELLI; Rossellini's ERA NOTTE A ROMA; Monicelli's THE BIG DEAL ON MADONNA STREET; and (as the ambitious boxer) Visconti's ROCCO AND HIS BROTHERS (1961). That film also featured Salvatori's wife, Annie Girardot, and Alain Delon, both of whom Salvatori would act with several times in his career. He appeared in films by Costa-Gavras (Z; STAGE OF SIEGE), De Sica (TWO WOMEN; A BRIEF VACATION), and Bertolucci (LA LUNA; TRAGEDY OF A RIDICULOUS MAN), among other distinguished filmmakers. His films include: LE RAGAZZE DI PIAZZA DI SPAGNA (1952); LA CICALA (1955); POVERI MA BELLI (1956); BELLA MA POVERE; MARISA LA CIVETTA; MARITI IN CITTA; LE NONNA SABELLA (1957); NELLA CITTA L'INFERNO; POVERI MILIONARI (1959); THE BIG DEAL ON MADONNA STREET; ERA NOTTE A ROMA; VENTO DEL SUD (1960); AND THE WILD, WILD WOMEN; ROCCO AND HIS BROTHERS; TWO WOMEN (1961); SMOG (1962); FIASCO IN MILAN; OMICRON; THE ORGANIZER (1963); DISORDER; OF FLESH AND BLOOD; TWO ARE GUILTY (1964); EXTRACONJUGALE; UNA BELLA GRINTA (1965); L'HAREM (1968); HOW TO SEDUCE A PLAYBOY; THREE NIGHTS OF LOVE; Z (1969); BURN; THE LIGHT AT THE EDGE OF THE WORLD (1971); THE BURGLARS; LE PROFESSEUR (1972); LES GRANGES BRULEES; STATE OF SIEGE (1973); A BRIEF VACATION; FLIC STORY; IL SOSPETTO; LE GITAN (1975); CADAVERI ECCELLENTI; LE DERNIERE FEMME; TODO MODO (1976); ARMAGUEDON; LE SOUPCON (1977); ERNESTO; LUNA (1979); ASO (1981); THE TRAGEDY OF A RIDICULOUS MAN (1982).

Seymour, Anne [Anne Seymour Eckert]

Born 11 Sept. 1909, New York, N.Y.; died 8 Dec. 1988, Los Angeles, Calif.

Actress

Descending from a line of thespians that began in 1740 with Irish comedian Jack Johnstone (her great-great-grandfather), Seymour first trod the boards in 1928 and made her screen debut in 1949, as Lucy Stark in ALL THE KING'S MEN. In addition to her distinguished stage career and numerous film appearances, principally in comedic

Silva

and character roles, Seymour performed on more than 5,000 radio programs (some of which she wrote or directed) and many TV shows, from "Studio One" to "Gunsmoke" to "Cagney and Lacey." Her films include: ALL THE KING'S MEN (1949); WHISTLE AT EATON FALLS (1951); FOUR BOYS AND A GUN; MAN ON FIRE (1957); DESIRE UNDER THE ELMS; THE GIFT OF LOVE; HANDLE WITH CARE (1958); ALL THE FINE YOUNG CANNIBALS; HOME FROM THE HILL; POLLYANNA; THE SUBTERRANEANS; SUNRISE AT CAMPOBELLO (1960); MISTY (1961); GOOD NEIGHBOR SAM; STAGE TO THUNDER ROCK; WHERE LOVE HAS GONE (1964); MIRAGE (1965); BLINDFOLD; WACO (1966); FITZWILLY (1967); STAY AWAY, JOE (1968); THE MAN (1972); SO LONG, BLUE BOY (1973); GEMINI AFFAIR; HEARTS OF THE WEST (1975); HOW TO SUCCEED IN BUSINESS WITHOUT REALLY TRYING (1976); NEVER NEVER LAND (1982); TRIUMPHS OF A MAN CALLED HORSE (1983); TRANCERS (1985); BIG TOP PEE-WEE (1988); SHOELESS JOE (forthcoming).

Silva, Jr., Trinidad

Born Mission, Tex.; died 31 July 1988, Whittier, Calif., age 38
Actor

Silva's two best-known performances found him cast as gang leaders. As Jesus Martinez on TV's "Hill Street Blues" he regularly taunted police captain Frank Furillo by calling him "Frankie boy," and he appeared as senior gang leader "Frog" in COLORS, Dennis Hopper's controversial depiction of gang warfare in Los Angeles. At the time of his death, Silva had just costarred in a TV pilot with fellow "Hill Street Blues" alumnus Michael Warren and had recently started his own production company. His films include: ALAMBRISTA! (1977); WALK PROUD (1979); SECOND THOUGHTS (1983); CRACKERS; EL NORTE (1984); JOCKS (1987); COLORS; THE MILAGRO BEANFIELD WAR; THE NIGHT BEFORE (1988).

Sofaer, Abraham

Born 1 Oct. 1896, Rangoon, Burma; died 21 Jan. 1988, Woodland Hills, Calif.
Actor

Sofaer's acting career began with a Shakespearean debut in 1921. He appeared regularly on the British stage and radio after 1925, and after 1930 performed frequently on Broadway. In the 30s he began acting in British films, including THE DREYFUS CASE; NELL GWYN; QUO VADIS; and REMBRANDT. The Burmese actor moved to Hollywood in the 50s, playing sinister, exotic and foreign characters on TV and in such films as THE NAKED JUNGLE; ELEPHANT WALK; BHOWANI JUNCTION; CAPTAIN SINDBAD; and his last film, CHISUM, in which he played a native American. His films include: THE DREYFUS CASE; THE HOUSE OPPOSITE; STAMBOUL (1931); THE FLAG LIEUTENANT; THE FLYING SQUAD; INSULT (1932); ASK BECCLES; HIGH FINANCE; KARMA; LITTLE MISS NOBODY; TROUBLE (1933); THE ADMIRAL'S SECRET; OH NO DOCTOR!; THE PRIVATE LIFE OF DON JUAN (1934); NELL GWYN; THE WANDERING JEW (1935); REMBRANDT; THINGS TO COME (1936); CROOKS TOUR (1940); A VOICE IN THE NIGHT (1941); STAIRWAY TO HEAVEN (1946); DUAL ALIBI; GHOSTS OF BERKELEY SQUARE (1947); CALLING PAUL TEMPLE (1948); CHRISTOPHER COLUMBUS; THE GREEN PROMISE (1949); CAIRO ROAD (1950); PANDORA AND THE FLYING DUTCHMAN; QUO VADIS (1951); JUDGMENT DEFERRED (1952); HIS MAJESTY O'KEEFE; THE NAKED JUNGLE (1953); ELEPHANT WALK (1954); BHOWANI JUNCTION; THE FIRST TEXAN (1956); OMAR KHAYYAM; OUT OF THE CLOUDS; THE SAD SACK; THE STORY OF MANKIND (1957); KING OF KINGS (1961); TARAS BULBA (1962); CAPTAIN SINDBAD; TWICE TOLD TALES (1963); THE GREATEST STORY EVER TOLD (1965); JOURNEY TO THE CENTER OF TIME (1967); HEAD (1968); CHE!; JUSTINE (1969); CHISUM (1970).

Sperling, Milton

Born New York, N.Y.; died August 1988, Beverly Hills, Calif., age 76
Screenwriter–Producer

A founding member of the Writers Guild of America, Sperling started out at Paramount's studios in Long Island City. Later, in Hollywood, he was secretary to Darryl Zanuck and Hal B. Wallis and an associate producer before moving to screenwriting with SING, BABY, SING in 1936. After WW II, he formed the independent production company United States Pictures. One of the company's top films was 1955's THE COURT–MARTIAL OF BILLY MITCHELL, which Sperling produced and cowrote with Emmet Lavery, earning an Oscar nomination for the screenplay. His films include: SING, BABY, SING (w) (1936); THIN ICE (w) (1937); HAPPY LANDING (w); I'LL GIVE A MILLION (w) (1938); HERE I AM A STRANGER (w); RETURN OF THE CISCO KID (w) (1939); FOUR SONS (w); THE GREAT PROFILE (w) (1940); SUN VALLEY SERENADE (p) (1941); I WAKE UP SCREAMING (p); RINGS ON HER FINGERS (1942) (p); CRASH DIVE (p); HELLO, FRISCO, HELLO (p) (1943); CLOAK AND DAGGER (p) (1946); PURSUED (p) (1947); MY GIRL TISA (p) (1948); SOUTH OF ST. LOUIS (p) (1949); THREE SECRETS (p) (1950); DISTANT DRUMS (p); THE ENFORCER (p) (1951); BLOWING WILD (p) (1953); THE COURT–MARTIAL OF BILLY MITCHELL (p&w) (1955); MARJORIE MORNINGSTAR (p) (1958); THE BRAMBLE BUSH (p&w); THE RISE AND FALL OF LEGS DIAMOND (p) (1960); MERRILL'S

MARAUDERS (p&w) (1962); BATTLE OF THE BULGE (p&w) (1965); CAPTAIN APACHE (p&w) (1971).

St. Johns, Adela Rogers

Born 20 May 1894, Los Angeles, Calif.; died 10 Aug. 1988, Arroyo Grande, Calif.
Journalist–Novelist–Screenwriter

A criminal lawyer's daughter, St. Johns claimed her real "education" came in observing the shady types that passed through his office. Her father was friendly with newspaper czar William Randolph Hearst, whose *San Francisco Examiner* hired the 19–year–old St. Johns as a cub reporter at 7 per week. In her long association with the Hearst papers, during which she covered the top stories of her day and achieved many "firsts" for women journalists, St. Johns became known as "the world's greatest girl reporter." Her work with *Photoplay*, on the other hand, caused her to be dubbed "Mother Confessor of Hollywood." She also *wrote* for Hollywood, scripting silents and, later, serving as an MGM story consultant and script doctor, while several of her stories served as the basis for films by other studios. The probable prototype for the spunky female reporters of 1930s films, St. Johns also appeared in Warren Beatty's REDS (1981), his portrait of her fellow reporter John Reed. Her films include: RED KIMONO (1925); THE SKYROCKET (1926); SINGED (1927); THE HEART OF A FOLLIES GIRL (1928); THE SINGLE STANDARD (1929); THE GREAT MAN'S LADY (1942); GOVERNMENT GIRL (1943); THAT BRENNAN GIRL (1946); SMART WOMAN (1948); THE GIRL WHO HAD EVERYTHING (1953); REDS (a) (1981).

Steele, Bob [Bob Bradbury, Jr.; Robert North Bradbury, Jr.]1988, Burbank, Calif.

Born 23 Jan. 1906, Pendleton, Ore.; died 22 Dec. 1988, Burbank, Calif.
Actor

Western hero Steele apprenticed under the direction of his father, silent action director Robert N. Bradbury, who cast Steele (as Bob Bradbury, Jr.) in juvenile parts in westerns and earlier directed a series of nature shorts, THE ADVENTURES OF BOB AND BILL, featuring his twin sons. He had his first starring role (as Bob Steele) at age 20, in his father's THE MOJAVE KID. Through the 1930s the young, relatively diminutive but dynamic Steele appeared in scores of oaters, many directed by his father, becoming one of the most favored stars of the genre. His popularity reached its height during the 40s, when he starred in six PRC "Billy the Kid" films and made some 20 appearances as Tucson Smith in Republic's "Three Mesquiteers" series. After WW II he appeared in primarily villainous character roles in films and on TV, where Steele was best-known as Trooper Duffy from the "F Troop" series. His films include: THE BORDER SHERIFF; THE COLLEGE BOOB; WITH DANIEL BOONE THRU THE WILDERNESS; WITH DAVY CROCKETT AT THE FALL OF THE ALAMO (1926); THE BANDIT'S SON; THE MOJAVE KID; WITH SITTING BULL AT THE SPIRIT LAKE MASSACRE (1927); BREED OF THE SUNSETS; CAPTAIN CARELESS (a&w); DRIFTIN' SANDS; HEADIN' FOR DANGER; LIGHTNING SPEED; MAN IN THE ROUGH; THE RIDING RENEGADE; THE TRAIL OF COURAGE (1928); AMAZING VAGABOND; COME AND GET IT; THE COWBOY AND THE OUTLAW; THE INVADERS; LAUGHING AT DEATH; A TEXAS COWBOY (1929); BREEZY BILL; HEADIN' NORTH; HUNTED MEN; THE LAND OF MISSING MEN; THE MAN FROM NOWHERE; NEAR THE RAINBOW'S END; OKLAHOMA CYCLONE; THE OKLAHOMA SHERIFF (1930); AT THE RIDGE; NEAR THE TRAIL'S END; THE NEVADA BUCKAROO; THE RIDIN' FOOL; SUNRISE TRAIL (1931); HIDDEN VALLEY; LAW OF THE WEST; MAN FROM HELL'S EDGES; RIDERS OF THE DESERT; SON OF OKLAHOMA; SOUTH OF SANTA FE; TEXAS BUDDIES; YOUNG BLOOD (1932); BREED OF THE BORDER; THE CALIFORNIA TRAIL; FIGHTING CHAMP; THE GALLANT FOOL; GALLOPING ROMEO; MYSTERY SQUADRON (serial); THE RANGER'S CODE; TRAILING NORTH (1933); BRAND OF HATE; A DEMON FOR TROUBLE (1934); ALIAS JOHN LAW; BIG CALIBRE; KID COURAGEOUS; NO MAN'S RANGE; POWDERSMOKE RANGE; THE RIDER OF THE LAW; SMOKEY SMITH; TOMBSTONE TERROR; TRAIL OF TERROR; WESTERN JUSTICE (1935); BRAND OF THE OUTLAWS; CAVALRY; THE KID RANGER; THE LAST OF THE WARRENS; THE LAW RIDES (1936); ARIZONA GUNFIGHTER; BORDER PHANTOM; DOOMED AT SUNDOWN; GUN LORDS OF STIRRUP BASIN; THE GUN RANGER; LIGHTNIN' CRANDALL; THE RED ROPE; RIDIN' THE LONE TRAIL; SUNDOWN SAUNDERS; THE TRUSTED OUTLAW (1937); COLORADO KID; DESERT PATROL; DURANGO VALLEY RAIDERS; FEUD MAKER; PAROLED—TO DIE; THUNDER IN THE DESERT (1938); EL DIABLO RIDES; FEUD OF THE RANGE; MESQUITE BUCKAROO; OF MICE AND MEN; THE PAL FROM TEXAS; RIDERS OF THE SAGE; SMOKY TRAILS (1939); BILLY THE KID IN TEXAS; BILLY THE KID OUTLAWED; BILLY THE KID'S JUSTICE; CARSON CITY KID; LONE STAR RAIDERS; PINTO CANYON; THE TRAIL BLAZERS; UNDER TEXAS SKIES; WILD HORSE VALLEY (1940); BILLY THE KID IN SANTA FE; BILLY THE KID'S FIGHTING PALS; BILLY THE KID'S RANGE WAR; CITY FOR CONQUEST; GANGS OF SONORA; GAUCHOS OF EL DORADO; THE GREAT TRAIN ROBBERY; OUTLAWS OF THE CHEROKEE TRAIL; PALS OF THE PECOS; PRAIRIE PIONEERS; SADDLEMATES; WEST OF CIMARRON (1941); CODE OF THE OUTLAW; THE PHANTOM PLAINSMEN; RAIDERS OF THE RANGE; SHADOWS ON THE SAGE; VALLEY OF

HUNTED MEN; WESTWARD HO (1942); THE BLOCKED TRAIL; REVENGE OF THE ZOMBIES; RIDERS OF THE RIO GRANDE; SANTA FE SCOUTS; THUNDERING TRAILS (1943); ARIZONA WHIRLWIND; DEATH VALLEY RANGERS; MARKED TRAILS; OUTLAW TRAIL; SONORA STAGECOACH; TRIGGER LAW; THE UTAH KID; WESTWARD BOUND (1944); NORTHWEST TRAIL; WILDFIRE (1945); AMBUSH TRAIL; THE BIG SLEEP; THE NAVAJO KID; RIO GRANDE RAIDERS; SHERIFF OF REDWOOD VALLEY; SIX GUN MAN; THUNDER TOWN (1946); BANDITS OF DARK CANYON; CHEYENNE; EXPOSED; KILLER McCOY; TWILIGHT ON THE RIO GRANDE (1947); SOUTH OF ST. LOUIS (1949); THE SAVAGE HORDE (1950); CATTLE DRIVE; THE ENFORCER; FORT WORTH; SILVER CANYON (1951); BUGLES IN THE AFTERNOON; THE LION AND THE HORSE; ROSE OF CIMARRON (1952); COLUMN SOUTH; ISLAND IN THE SKY; SAN ANTONE; SAVAGE FRONTIER (1953); DRUMS ACROSS THE RIVER; THE OUTCAST (1954); THE FIGHTING CHANCE; THE SPOILERS (1955); LAST OF THE DESPERADOES; PARDNERS; THE STEEL JUNGLE (1956); BAND OF ANGELS; DECISION AT SUNDOWN; DUEL AT APACHE WELLS; GUN FOR A COWARD; THE PARSON AND THE OUTLAW (1957); GIANT FROM THE UNKNOWN; ONCE UPON A HORSE (1958); PORK CHOP HILL; RIO BRAVO (1959); THE ATOMIC SUBMARINE; HELL BENT FOR LEATHER (1960); SIX BLACK HORSES (1961); THE WILD WESTERNERS (1962); THE COMMANCHEROS; HE RIDES TALL; McLINTOCK! (1963); CHEYENNE AUTUMN (uncredited); MAJOR DUNDEE (uncredited); TAGGART (1964); THE BOUNTY KILLER; REQUIEM FOR A GUNFIGHTER; SHENANDOAH; TOWN TAMER (1965); HANG'EM HIGH (1968); THE GREAT BANK ROBBERY (1969); RIO LOBO (1970); SKIN GAME; SOMETHING BIG (1971).

Steno [Stefano Vanzina]

Born 19 Jan. 1915, Rome, Italy; died 12 March 1988, Rome, Italy
Director–Screenwriter

Steno (born Stefano Vanzina) studied filmmaking, then worked briefly as a writer and cartoonist before beginning professionally as an assistant director and screenwriter in 1939. He directed his first eight films, most starring the Italian comedian Toto, in collaboration with Mario Monicelli before making his solo debut with L'UOMO, LA BESTIA, E LA VIRTU (featuring Orson Welles) in 1953. His subsequent films (several with Toto) have generally been slapstick or satirical comedies coscripted by Steno and starring many of Italy's top comic actors, although the 1972 thriller LA POLIZIA RINGRAZIA was one of his biggest successes. His films include: LA SCUOLA DI TIMIDI (w) (1941); TUTTA LA CITTA CANTA (w) (1943); AQUILA NEGRA (w) (1946); I MISERABILE (w); LA FIGLIA DEL CAPITANO (w); L'EBREO ERRANTE (w) (1947); IL CAVALIERE MISTERIOSO (w) 1948); AL DIAVOLO LA CELEBRITA (co–d) (1949); E ARRIVATO IL CAVALIERE (co–d); TOTO CERCA CASA (co–d); VITA DA CANI (co–d) (1950); GUARDIE E LADRI (co–d) (1951); TOTO E I RE DI ROMA (co–d) (1952); L'UOMO LA BESTIA E LA VIRTU; TOTO A COLORI (co–d); TOTO E LE DONNE (co–d); UN GIORNO IN PRETURA (1953); CINEMA D'ALTRI TEMPI; LE AVVENTURE DI GIACOMO CASANOVA; UN AMERICANO A ROMA (1954); PICCOLA POSTA (1956); FEMMINE TRE VOLTE; SUSANNA TUTTA PANNA (1957); GUARDIO, LADRO E CAMERIERA; MI NONNA POLIZZIOTO (1958); I TARTASSATI; TEMPE DURI PER I VAMPIRI; TOTO, EVA E IL PENNELLO PROIBITO; TOTO IN THE MOON (1959); A NOI PIACE FREDDO; IL LETTO A TRE PIAZZE; UN MILITARE E MEZZO; THE UNFAITHFULS (co–d&w) (1960); COPACABANA PALACE; I MOSCHETTIERI DEL MARE; LA RAGAZZA DI MILLE MESI; NERO'S MISTRESS; PSYCOSISSIMO; TOTO DIABOLICUS (1962); THE TWO COLONELS; TOTO CONTRO I QUATTRO (1963); GLI EROI DEL WEST; I GEMELLI DEL TEXAS (1964); A DAY IN COURT; LETTI SBAGLIATI (1965); AMORE ALL'ITALIANA; ROSE ROSSE PER ANGELICA (1966); ARRIVA DORELLIK (1967); GIRL GAME; CAPRICCIO ALL'ITALIANA ("Il Mostra della Domenica" episode); LA FELDMARESCIALLA (1968); I TRAPIANTO (1969); COSE DE COSA NOSTRA; IL VICHINGO VENUTO DAL SUD (1971); IL TERRORE CON GLI OCCHI STORTI; LA POLIZIA RINGRAZIA; L'UCCELLO MIGRATORE (1972); FLATFOOT (1974); FEBBRE DA CAVALLO; TRE TIGRI CONTRO TRE TIGRI (1977); AMORI MIEI; DOPPIO DELITTO; FLATFOOT ON THE NILE (1978); IL DOTTORE JEKILL JR. (1979); A TANGO OF JEALOUSY (1985); MI FACCIA CAUSA (1985); METROPOLITAN ANIMALS (forthcoming).

Stoppa, Paolo

Born 16 June 1906, Rome, Italy; died 1 May 1988, Rome, Italy
Actor

Stoppa debuted in a Pirandello play in 1925, then acted with various theater companies before cofounding, in 1938, the Teatro Eliseo in Rome. Among the directors he worked with at the Eliseo was Luchino Visconti, in whose ROCCO AND HIS SEVEN BROTHERS and THE LEOPARD Stoppa later appeared. One of Italy's foremost character actors, Stoppa performed in many Italian and international films—including MIRACLE IN MILAN; LES BELLES–DE–NUI; BECKET; BEHOLD A PALE HORSE; and ONCE UPON A TIME IN THE WEST—while continuing his stage career. His films include: RE BURLONE (1935); MARCELLA (1937); FRENESIA (1939); AN ADVENTURE OF SALVATOR ROSA; LA CORONA DI

FERRO (1940); DON GIOVANNI (1942); AQUILA NERA (1946); ETERNAL MELODIES; ROSSINI (1948); FABIOLA; RETURN OF THE BLACK EAGLE (1949); DONNE E BRIGANTI; MIRACLE IN MILAN (1951); BEAUTY AND THE DEVIL; LES BELLES–DE–NUIT (1952); LE RETOUR DE DON CAMILLO; PUCCINI; RING AROUND THE CLOCK; THE SEVEN DEADLY SINS; TIMES GONE BY (1953); CASA RICORDI; DAUGHTERS OF DESTINY; INDISCRETION OF AN AMERICAN WIFE; PANE AMORE E GELOSIA (1954); MY SEVEN LITTLE SINS; PEPOTE (1956); GOLD OF NAPLES; THE MILLER'S WIFE (1957); VACANZE A ISCHIA; WHERE THE HOT WIND BLOWS (1960); CARTHAGE IN FLAMES; FROM A ROMAN BALCONY; NEOPOLITAN CAROUSEL; ROCCO AND HIS BROTHERS (1961); BOCCACCIO '70; THE MOST WANTED MAN (1962); THE LEOPARD (1963); BECKET; BEHOLD A PALE HORSE; THE VISIT (1964); MALE COMPANION (1965); AFTER THE FOX (1966); DROP DEAD, MY LOVE; LA MATRIARCA (1968); ONCE UPON A TIME IN THE WEST (1969); THE ADVENTURES OF GERARD (1970); JUS PRIMAE NOCTIS (1972); IL CASOTTO (1977); LA MAZETTA (1978); SUOR OMICIDI (1979).

Sundberg

Sundberg, Clinton

Born 7 Dec. 1906, Appleton, Minn.; died 14 Dec. 1987, Santa Monica, Calif.
Actor

Sundberg began acting in stock theater and later appeared on the London and New York stage, but in 1946 he began acting in films as a contract player with MGM. The character actor typically played fussy worriers, sympathetic butlers, and the like; one of his best roles was as J. Scott Smart's right–hand man in THE FAT MAN (1951). Sundberg appeared almost exclusively on TV towards the end of his career. His films include: LOVE LAUGHS AT ANDY HARDY; THE MIGHTY McGURK; UNDERCURRENT (1946); DESIRE ME; GOOD NEWS; THE HUCKSTERS; LIVING IN A BIG WAY; SONG OF LOVE; UNDERCOVER MAISIE (1947); COMMAND DECISION; A DATE WITH JUDY; EASTER PARADE; GOOD SAM; THE KISSING BANDIT; MR. PEABODY AND THE MERMAID; WORDS AND MUSIC (1948); THE BARKLEYS OF BROADWAY; BIG JACK; IN THE GOOD OLD SUMMERTIME (1949); ANNIE GET YOUR GUN; THE DUCHESS OF IDAHO; FATHER IS A BACHELOR; KEY TO THE CITY; MRS. O'MALLEY AND MR. MALONE; THE TOAST OF NEW ORLEANS; TWO WEEKS WITH LOVE (1950); AS YOUNG AS YOU FEEL; THE FAT MAN; ON THE RIVIERA (1951); THE BELLE OF NEW YORK (1952); THE CADDY; THE GIRL NEXT DOOR; MAIN STREET TO BROADWAY; SWEETHEARTS ON PARADE (1953); BACHELOR IN PARADISE (1961); HOW THE WEST WAS WON; THE WONDERFUL WORLD OF THE BROTHERS GRIMM (1962); THE BIRDS AND THE BEES (1965); HOTEL (1967).

Tonti, Aldo

Born 2 March 1910, Rome, Italy; died 7 July 1988, Italy
Cinematographer

Tonti started in Italian films as a camera assistant in 1934, then became a lighting cameraman and director of photography. His camerawork on Luchino Visconti's OSSESSIONE, released in Italy in 1942, contributed to one of the major statements of the emerging Neo–Realist movement. Among his many credits are major films by Fellini, Rossellini, Lattuada, Huston, Ray, and Vidor. Tonti also occasionally appeared in films, playing comic roles. His films include: SEI BAMBINE E IL PERSEO (1939); CARAVAGGIO (1940); NOZZI DI SANGUE (1941); BENGASI (1942); LA PORTA DEL CIELO; ROMA CITTA LIBERA (1946); IL DELITTO DI GIOVANNI EPISCOPO; LA FIGLIA DEL CAPITANO (1947); AMORE; MOLTI SOGNI PER LE STRADE; PROIBITO RUBARE (1948); THE BANDIT; IL LUPO DELLA SILA; IL MULINO DEL PO; MERCHANT OF SLAVES; OUTCRY; PEDDLIN' IN SOCIETY; WITHOUT PITY (1949); IL BRIGANTE MUSOLINO; NAPOLI MILIONARIA; SIDE STREET STORY; SIGNORINELLA (1950); ROMANTICISMO (1951); EUROPA '51 (1952); ANNI FACILI; DOV'E LA LIBERTA?; LA LUPA (1953); CENTO ANNI D'AMORE; THE GREATEST LOVE; HELLO ELEPHANT; PROIBITO, ULISSE; SENSUALITA (1954); WAR AND PEACE (1956); NIGHTS OF CABIRIA (1957); ATTILA; FORTUNELLA; INDIA (documentary); TEMPEST (1958); FOR THE FIRST TIME; IT HAPPENED IN ROME; OSSESSIONE (1959); THE SAVAGE INNOCENTS; UNDER TEN FLAGS; THE UNFAITHFULS (1960); LOST SOULS (1961); AGOSTINO; BARABBAS (1962); THE DEVIL; THE HUNCHBACK OF ROME; THE SHIP OF CONDEMNED WOMEN; (1963); THE APE WOMAN (1964); CASANOVA '70 (1965); CAST A GIANT SHADOW (1966); KISS THE GIRLS AND MAKE THEM DIE; REFLECTIONS IN A GOLDEN EYE (1967); THE DEVIL IN LOVE; THE MAN WITH THE BALLOONS; TREASURE OF SAN GENNARO (1968); CITTA VIOLENTA (1970); THE BIG AND THE BAD; THE DESERTER (1971); THE VALACHI PAPERS (1972); CRAZY JOE; THE FAMILY; THREE TOUGH GUYS (1974); THE COUNT OF MONTE CRISTO; UN FEMME A SA FENETRE (1976); RENE LA CANNE; QUELLE STRANE OCCASIONI (1977); ASHANTI (1979).

Wilson

Williams, Kenneth

Born 22 Feb. 1926, London, England; died 15 April 1988, London, England

A revue veteran who entertained the troops in WW II, Williams was featured in most of the popular British "Carry On" comedies, including the first of the series, CARRY ON SERGEANT (1959). His distinctively campy delivery of smutty lines and sharp caricature of English snobbery made him perennially popular on the British stage, television, and radio. He rarely appeared in dramatic roles and, according to his 1975 autobiography, never desired to do so. His films include: THE BEGGAR'S OPERA; MEN ARE CHILDREN TWICE; TRENT'S LAST CASE (1953); INNOCENTS IN PARIS; LAND OF FURY (1955); CARRY ON NURSE; CARRY ON SERGEANT (1959); CARRY ON CONSTABLE; MAKE MINE MINK; TOMMY THE TOREADOR (1960); CARRY ON REGARDLESS; HIS AND HERS (1961); CARRY ON CRUISING; CARRY ON TEACHER; ROOMMATES; TWICE AROUND THE DAFFODILS (1962); CARRY ON JACK (1963); CARRY ON CLEO; CARRY ON SPYING (1964); CARRY ON COWBOY; CARRY ON SCREAMING (1966); DON'T LOSE YOUR HEAD; FOLLOW THAT CAMEL (1967); CARRY ON DOCTOR; CARRY ON, UP THE KHYBER (1968); CARRY ON AGAIN, DOCTOR; CARRY ON CAMPING (1969); CARRY ON HENRY VIII; CARRY ON LOVING (1970); CARRY ON 'ROUND THE BEND (1972); CARRY ON MATRON (1973); CARRY ON EMANUELLE (1978); THE HOUND OF THE BASKERVILLES (1980).

Wilson, Lois

Born 28 June 1894 (?), Pittsburgh, Pa.; died 3 March 1988, Reno, Nev.

Actress

Wilson went to Hollywood in 1915, after winning a statewide beauty contest in Alabama. She was cast in a small part in THE DUMB GIRL OF PORTICI, starring Anna Pavlova, and subsequently got a contract with Paramount. She played the leading lady in several films starring J. Warren Kerrigan, most notably THE COVERED WAGON (1923), the first epic movie western. Wilson also had leading roles in, among many others, THE GREAT GATSBY (1926), in which she played Daisy Buchanan; the Rudolph Valentino picture MONSIEUR BEAUCAIRE; and THE VANISHING AMERICAN. In 1924 Paramount selected her to represent motion pictures at a British exposition as "a typical example of the American girl in character, culture, and beauty." After retiring from films she continued to appear onstage and on television soap operas. Her films include: THE BECKONING TRAIL; THE DUMB GIRL OF PORTICI; THE GAY LORD WARING; LANDON'S LEGACY; THE MORALS OF HILDA; THE POOL OF FLAME; THE SILENT BATTLE; A SON OF THE IMMORTALS (1916); A MAN'S MAN; TREASON (1917); THE BELLS; HIS ROBE OF HONOR; PRISONER OF THE PINES; THREE X GORDON; THE TURN OF THE CARD (1918); THE END OF THE GAME; GATES OF BRASS; IT PAYS TO ADVERTISE; THE PRICE WOMAN PAYS; WHY SMITH LEFT HOME (1919); BURGLARPROOF; THE CITY OF MASKS; A FULL HOUSE; LOVE INSURANCE; MIDSUMMER MADNESS; TOO MUCH JOHNSON; THOU ART THE MAN; WHAT'S YOUR HURRY?; WHO'S YOUR SERVANT? (1920); CITY OF SILENT MEN; THE HELL DIGGERS; THE LOST ROMANCE; MISS LULU BETT; WHAT EVERY WOMAN KNOWS (1921); BROAD DAYLIGHT; IS MATRIMONY A FAILURE?; MANSLAUGHTER; OUR LEADING CITIZEN; WITHOUT COMPROMISE; THE WORLD'S CHAMPION (1922); THE CALL OF THE CANYON; THE COVERED WAGON; ONLY 38; RUGGLES OF RED GAP; TO THE LAST MAN (1923); ANOTHER SCANDAL; ICEBOUND; THE MAN WHO FIGHTS ALONE; MONSIEUR BEAUCAIRE; NORTH OF 36; PIED PIPER MALONE (1924); CONTRABAND; IRISH LUCK; RUGGED WATER; THE THUNDERING HERD; THE VANISHING AMERICAN; WELCOME HOME (1925); BLUEBEARD'S SEVEN WIVES; THE GREAT GATSBY; LET'S GET MARRIED; THE SHOW OFF (1926); ALIAS THE LONE WOLF; BROADWAY NIGHTS; FRENCH DRESSING; THE GINGHAM GIRL; NEW YORK (1927); CONEY ISLAND; ON TRIAL; RANSOM; SALLY'S SHOULDERS (1928); CONQUEST; THE GAMBLERS; KID GLOVES; OBJECT—ALIMONY (1929); THE FURIES; LOVIN' THE LADIES; ONCE A GENTLEMAN; TEMPTATION; WEDDING RINGS (1930); THE AGE FOR LOVE; SEED (1931); THE DEVIL IS DRIVING; DIVORCE IN THE FAMILY; DRIFTING SOULS; THE EXPERT; LAW AND ORDER; RIDER OF DEATH VALLEY; SECRETS OF WU SIN; THE CRASH (1932); DELUGE; FEMALE; LAUGHING AT LIFE; OBEY THE LAW (1933); BRIGHT EYES; IN THE MONEY; NO GREATER GLORY; THE SHOW-OFF; TICKET TO CRIME (1934); BORN TO GAMBLE; CAPPY RICKS RETURNS; PUBLIC OPINION; SCHOOL FOR GIRLS; SOCIETY FEVER; YOUR UNCLE DUDLEY (1935); THE RETURN OF JIMMY VALENTINE; WEDDING PRESENT (1936); LAUGHING AT TROUBLE (1937); BAD LITTLE ANGEL; LIFE RETURNS (1939); NOBODY'S CHILDREN (1940); FOR BEAUTY'S SAKE (1941); THE GIRL FROM JONES BEACH (1949).

Wright, Basil

Born 12 June 1907, London, England; died 14 Oct. 1987

Documentary Director–Producer

Wright was the first of the inexperienced filmmakers (others were Edgar Anstey, Arthur Elton, and Stuart Legg) recruited in the late 1920s to the British documentary movement by its founder, John Grierson. With Grierson's GPO film unit, Wright directed two of the social reformist movement's best–known and most lyrical works, SONG OF CEYLON (1934) and NIGHT MAIL (1936), collaborating on the latter's direction with Harry Watt. Shortly thereafter, Wright founded Realist Films with John Taylor and Alberto Calvalcanti; after WW II he formed the International Realist, Ltd. production company. More recently he made films for UNESCO and lectured and wrote on film. His films (as director) include: THE COUNTRY COMES TO TOWN (d&w) (1931); O'ER HILL AND DALE (d,w&ph); GIBRALTAR (d,w&ph) (1932); WINDMILL IN BARBADOS (d,w&ph); CARGO FROM JAMAICA (d&ph); LINER CRUISING SOUTH (d,w&ph); SONG OF CEYLON (d,w&ph) (1934); NIGHT MAIL (co–d) (1936); CHILDREN AT SCHOOL (d&w) (1937); THE FACE OF SCOTLAND (d&w) (1938); HARVEST HELP (1940); THIS WAS JAPAN (1945); BERNARD MILES ON GUN DOGS (p,d&w) (1948); WATERS OF TIME (p,co–d&w) (1950); WORLD WITHOUT END (p&co–d) (1953); THE STAINED GLASS AT FAIRFORD (p&d) (1955); THE IMMORTAL LAND (co–p&d) (1958); GREEK SCULPTURE (co–p&co–d) (1959); A PLACE FOR GOLD (p&d).

THE MOTION PICTURE ANNUAL 1989

Awards

AWARDS INDEX

This section covers the major awards given to films released in 1988. Awards included are those given by: Academy of Motion Picture Arts & Sciences; American Society of Cinematographers; British Academy of Film and Television; Directors Guild of America; Academy of Canadian Cinema & TV; Hollywood Foreign Press Assn. (Golden Globes); London Film Critics; Los Angeles Film Critics; National Board of Review; National Society of Film Critics Awards; New York Film Critics; Writers Guild of America.

61ST AWARDS OF THE ACADEMY OF MOTION PICTURE ARTS AND SCIENCES

Best Picture
THE ACCIDENTAL TOURIST, produced by Lawrence Kasdan, Charles Okun, Michael Grillo.
DANGEROUS LIAISONS, produced by Norma Heyman, Hank Moonjean.
MISSISSIPPI BURNING, produced by Frederick Zollo, Robert F. Colesberry.
RAIN MAN, produced by Mark Johnson.*
WORKING GIRL, produced by Douglas Wick.

Best Actor
Gene Hackman for MISSISSIPPI BURNING.
Tom Hanks for BIG.
Dustin Hoffman for RAIN MAN.*
Edward James Olmos for STAND AND DELIVER.
Max von Sydow for PELLE THE CONQUEROR.

Best Actress
Glenn Close for DANGEROUS LIAISONS.
Jodie Foster for THE ACCUSED.*
Melanie Griffith for WORKING GIRL.
Meryl Streep for A CRY IN THE DARK.
Sigourney Weaver for GORILLAS IN THE MIST.

Best Supporting Actor
Alec Guinness for LITTLE DORRIT.
Kevin Kline for A FISH CALLED WANDA.*
Martin Landau for TUCKER: THE MAN AND HIS DREAM.
River Phoenix for RUNNING ON EMPTY.
Dean Stockwell for MARRIED TO THE MOB.

Best Supporting Actress
Joan Cusack for WORKING GIRL.
Geena Davis for THE ACCIDENTAL TOURIST.*
Frances McDormand for MISSISSIPPI BURNING.
Michelle Pfeiffer for DANGEROUS LIAISONS.
Sigourney Weaver for WORKING GIRL.

Best Direction
Charles Crichton for A FISH CALLED WANDA.
Barry Levinson for RAIN MAN.*
Mike Nichols for WORKING GIRL.
Alan Parker for MISSISSIPPI BURNING.
Martin Scorsese for THE LAST TEMPTATION OF CHRIST.

Best Adapted Screenplay
Frank Galati, Lawrence Kasdan for THE ACCIDENTAL TOURIST.
Christopher Hampton for DANGEROUS LIAISONS.*
Anna Hamilton Phelan for GORILLAS IN THE MIST.
Christine Edzard for LITTLE DORRIT.
Jean-Claude Carriere, Philip Kaufman for THE UNBEARABLE LIGHTNESS OF BEING.

Best Original Screenplay
Gary Ross, Anne Spielberg for BIG.
Ron Shelton for BULL DURHAM.
John Cleese, Charles Crichton for A FISH CALLED WANDA.
Ronald Bass, Barry Morrow for RAIN MAN.*
Naomi Foner for RUNNING ON EMPTY.

Best Foreign Film
HANUSSEN (Hung.).
THE MUSIC TEACHER (Bel.).
PELLE THE CONQUEROR (Den.).*
SALAAM BOMBAY! (India).
WOMEN ON THE VERGE OF A NERVOUS BREAKDOWN (Sp.).

Best Cinematography
Peter Biziou for MISSISSSPI BURNING.*
John Seale for RAIN MAN.
Conrad L. Hall for TEQUILA SUNRISE.
Sven Nykvist for THE UNBEARABLE LIGHTNESS OF BEING.
Dean Cundey for WHO FRAMED ROGER RABBIT.

Best Film Editing
Frank J. Urioste, John F. Link for DIE HARD.
Stuart Baird for GORILLAS IN THE MIST.
Gerry Hambling for MISSISSIPPI BURNING.
Stu Linder for RAIN MAN.
Arthur Schmidt for WHO FRAMED ROGER RABBIT.*

Best Art Direction/Set Decoration
Albert Brenner, Garrett Lewis for BEACHES.
Stuart Craig, Gerard James for DANGEROUS LIAISONS.*
Ida Random, Linda DeScenna for RAIN MAN.
Dean Tavoularis, Armin Ganz for TUCKER: THE MAN AND HIS DREAM.
Elliot Scott, Peter Howitt for WHO FRAMED ROGER RABBIT

Best Costume Design
Deborah Nadoolman for COMING TO AMERICA.
James Acheson for DANGEROUS LIAISONS.*
Jane Robinson for A HANDFUL OF DUST.
Patricia Norris for SUNSET.
Milena Canonero for TUCKER: THE MAN AND HIS DREAM.

Best Makeup
Ve Neill, Steve LaPorte, Robert Short for BEETLEJUICE.*
Rick Baker for COMING TO AMERICA.
Tom Burman, Bari Drieband-Burman for SCROOGED.

Best Original Score
John Williams for THE ACCIDENTAL TOURIST.
George Fenton for DANGEROUS LIAISONS.
Maurice Jarre for GORILLAS IN THE MIST.
Dave Grusin for THE MILAGRO BEANFIELD WAR.*
Hans Zimmer for RAIN MAN.

Best Song
Bob Telson for "Calling You" from BAGDAD CAFE.
Carly Simon for "Let The River Run" from WORKING GIRL.*
Lamont Dozier, Phil Collins for "Two Hearts" from BUSTER.

Documentaries
Best Short Documentary
THE CHILDREN'S STOREFRONT, Karen Goodman.
FAMILY GATHERING, Lise Yasul, Ann Tegnell.
GANG COPS, Thomas B. Fleming, Daniel J. Marks.
PORTRAIT OF IMOGEN, Nancy Hale, Meg Partridge.
YOU DON'T HAVE TO DIE, William Guttentag, Malcolm Clarke.*
Best Feature Documentary
THE CRY OF REASON—BEYERS NAUDE: AN AFRIKANER SPEAKS OUT, Robert Bilhelmer, Ronald Mix.
HOTEL TERMINUS: THE LIFE AND TIMES OF KLAUS BARBIE, Marcel Ophuls.*
LET'S GET LOST, Bruce Weber, Nan Bush.
PROMISES TO KEEP, Ginny Durrin.
WHO KILLED VINCENT CHIN? Renee Tajima, Christine Choy.

Short Subjects
Best Animated Film
THE CAT CAME BACK, Cordell Barker.
TECHNOLOGICAL THREAT, Bill Kroyer.
TIN TOY, John Lasseter.*
Best Live Action Film
THE APPOINTMENT OF DENNIS JENNINGS, Dean Parisot, Steven Wright.*
CADILLAC DREAMS, Matia Karrel.
GULLAH TALES, Gary Moss.

Best Sound
Les Frescholtz, Dick Alexander, Vern Poore, Willie D. Burton for BIRD.*
Don Bassman, Kevin F. Cleary, Richard Overton, Al Overton for DIE HARD.
Andy Nelson, Brian Saunders, Peter Handford for GORILLAS IN THE MIST.
Robert Litt, Elliot Tyson, Richard C. Kline, Danny Michael for MISSISSIPPI BURNING.
Robert Knudson, John Boyd, Don Digirolamo, Tony Dawe for WHO FRAMED ROGER RABBIT.

Best Sound Effects Editing
Stephen H. Flick, Richard Shorr for DIE HARD.
Charles L. Campbell, Louis L. Edemann for WHO FRAMED ROGER RABBIT.*
Ben Burtt, Richard Hymns for WILLOW.

Best Visual Effects
Richard Edlund, Al DiSarro, Brent Boates, Thaine Morris for DIE HARD.
Ken Ralston, Richard Williams, Edward Jones, George Gibbs for WHO FRAMED ROGER RABBIT.*
Dennis Muren, Michael McAlister, Phil Tippett, Chris Evans for WILLOW.

3RD AMERICAN SOCIETY OF CINEMATOGRAPHERS AWARDS
Peter Biziou, BSC, for MISSISSIPPI BURNING.
Conrad Hall, ASC for TEQUILA SUNRISE.*
Sven Nykvist, ASC for THE UNBEARABLE LIGHTNESS OF BEING.
Philippe Rousselot for DANGEROUS LIAISONS.
John Seale, ASC for RAIN MAN.

BRITISH ACADEMY OF FILM AND TELEVISION AWARDS
Best Film
JEAN DE FLORETTE (Fr.), Claude Berri.

Best Direction
Oliver Stone for PLATOON (US).

Best Original Screenplay
David Leland for WISH YOU WERE HERE (Brit.).

Best Adapted Screenplay
Claude Berri, Gerard Brach for JEAN DE FLORETTE (Fr.).

Best Actress
Anne Bancroft for '84 CHARING CROSS ROAD (US).

Best Actor
Sean Connery for THE NAME OF THE ROSE (US).

Best Supporting Actress
Susan Wooldridge for HOPE AND GLORY (Brit.).

Best Supporting Actor
Daniel Auteuil for JEAN DE FLORETTE (Fr.)

Best Score
Ennio Morricone for THE UNTOUCHABLES (US).

Best Foreign Language Film
THE SACRIFICE (Swed./Fr.), Andrei Tarkovsky.

Best Cinematography
Bruno Nuytten for JEAN DE FLORETTE (Fr.).

Best Makeup
Hasso von Hugo for THE NAME OF THE ROSE (US).

Best Sound
Jonathan Bates, Simon Kay, Gerry Humphreys for CRY FREEDOM (Brit.).

Best Production Design
Santo Loquasto for RADIO DAYS (US).

Best Costume Design
Jeffrey Kurland for RADIO DAYS (US).

Best Visual Effects
Michael Owens for THE WITCHES OF EASTWICK (US).

Best Editing
Claire Simpson for PLATOON (US).

40TH DIRECTORS GUILD OF AMERICA AWARDS
Charles Crichton for A FISH CALLED WANDA.
Alan Parker for MISSISSIPPI BURNING.
Barry Levinson for RAIN MAN.*
Robert Zemeckis for WHO FRAMED ROGER RABBIT.
Mike Nichols for WORKING GIRL.

15TH GENIE AWARDS OF THE ACADEMY OF CANADIAN CINEMA AND TELEVISION

Best Picture
A CORPS PERDU, produced by Denise Robert, Robin Spry.
DEAD RINGERS, produced by David Cronenberg, Marc Boyman.*
THE OUTSIDE CHANCE OF MAXIMILIAN GLICK, produced by Stephen Foster.
LES PORTES TOURNANTES, produced by Francyne Morin, Rene Malo.
A WINTER TAN, produced by Jackie Burroughs, Louise Clark, John Frizzell, John Walker, Aerlyn Weissman.

Best Actor
Zachary Ansley for COWBOYS DON'T CRY.
Jeremy Irons for DEAD RINGERS.*
Elias Koteas for MALAREK.
Jan Rubes for SOMETHING ABOUT LOVE.
Saul Rubinek for THE OUTSIDE CHANCE OF MAXIMILIAN GLICK.
Ron White for COWBOYS DON'T CRY.

Best Actress
Jackie Burroughs for A WINTER TAN.*
Genevieve Bujold for DEAD RINGERS.
Kerrie Keane for OBSESSED.
Josette Simon for MILK AND HONEY.
Monique Spaziani for LES PORTES TOURNANTES.

Best Supporting Actor
Maury Chaykin for IRON EAGLE II.
Remy Girard for LES PORTES TOURNANTES.*
Ron James for SOMETHING ABOUT LOVE.
Michael Rudder for BUYING TIME.

Best Supporting Actress
Colleen Dewhurst for OBSESSED.*
Janet-Laine Green for COWBOYS DON'T CRY.
Helen Hughes for MARTHA, RUTH & EDIE.
Miou Miou for LES PORTES TOURNANTES.
Susan Douglas Rubes for THE OUTSIDE CHANCE OF MAXIMILIAN GLICK.

Best Direction
Jackie Burroughs, Louise Clark, John Frizzell, John Walker, Aerlyn Weissman for A WINTER TAN.
Roger Cardinal for MALAREK.
David Cronenberg for DEAD RINGERS.*
Francis Mankiewicz for LES PORTES TOURNANTES.

Anne Wheeler for COWBOYS DON'T CRY.

Best Original Screenplay
Jacques Bobet, Andre Melancon for LA GRENOUILLE ET LA BALEINE.
Michel Cournot, Claude Fournier, Marie-Jose Raymond for LE TISSERANDS DU POUVOIR.
Guy Maddin for TALES FROM THE GIMLI HOSPITAL.
Trevor Rhone, Glen Salzman for MILK AND HONEY.*
Michael Rubbo for TOMMY TRICKER AND THE STAMP TRAVELLER.

Best Adapted Screenplay
Douglas Bowie, Robin Spry for OBSESSED.
Jackie Burroughs for A WINTER TAN.
David Cronenberg, Norman Snider for DEAD RINGERS.*
Francis Mankiewicz, Jacques Savoie for LES PORTES TOURNANTES.
Phil Savath for THE OUTSIDE CHANCE OF MAXIMILIAN GLICK.

Best Cinematography
Tom Burstyn for LA GRENOUILLE ET LA BALEINE.
Karol Ike for MALAREK.
Pierre Mignot for A CORPS PERDU.
Rene Ohashi for SHADOW DANCING.
Peter Suschitzky for DEAD RINGERS.*
Thomas Vamos for LES PORTES TOURNANTES.

Best Art Direction/Production Design
Vianney Guathier for A CORPS PERDU.
Anne Pritchard for LES PORTES TOURNANTES.
Carol Spier for DEAD RINGERS.*

Best Film Editing
Michel Arcand for A CORPS PERDU.
Alan Lee, Susan Martin for A WINTER TAN.
Ronald Sanders for DEAD RINGERS.*

Best Costume Design
Renee April for THE KISS.
Francois Barbeau for LES PORTES TOURNANTES.*
Christiane Cost, Michele Hamel for LES TISSERANDS DU POUVOIR.
Denise Cronenberg for DEAD RINGERS.
Maya Mani for SHADOW DANCING.
Charlotte Penner for THE OUTSIDE CHANCE OF MAXIMILIAN GLICK.

Best Score
Billy Bryans, Aaron Davis for OFFICE PARTY.
Francois Dompierre for LES PORTES TOURNANTES.
Micky Erbe, Maribeth Solomon for MILK AND HONEY.
Richard Gregoire for LA LIGNE DE CHALEUR.
Osvaldo Montes for A CORPS PERDU.
Howard Shore for DEAD RINGERS.*

Best Song
Louise Bennett for "You're Going Home" from MILK AND HONEY.
Nathalie Carson, Normand Dube, Guy Trepanier for "We Are The One" from LA GRENOUILLE ET LA BALEINE.
Jay Gruska, Marc Jordan for "Shadow Dance" from SHADOW DANCING.
Louis Natale, Anne Wheeler for "Cowboys Don't Cry" from COWBOYS DON'T CRY.*
Rufus Wainwright for "I'm Running" from TOMMY TRICKER AND THE STAMP TRAVELLER.

Best Sound
Don Cohen, Keith Elliott, Austin Grimaldi, Dino Pigat for THE KISS.
Brian Day, Andy Nelson, Don White for DEAD RINGERS.*
Joe Grimaldi, Michael Liotta, Dino Pigat, Eli Yarkoni for IRON EAGLE II.
Joe Grimaldi, Michael Liotta, Gabor Vadnay, Don White for OBSESSED.
Michael Liotta, Aerlynn Weissman, Don White for A WINTER TAN.

Best Sound Editing
Terry Burke, Richard Cadger, David Evans, David Giammarco, Wayne Griffen for DEAD RINGERS.*
Terry Burke, Tony Currie, Wayne Griffin, Marta Sternberg, Jane Tattersall for BUYING TIME.
Richard Cadger, David Evans, Ken Heeley-Ray, Drew King, Robin Leigh for IRON EAGLE II.
Alison Clark, Alison Grace, Greg Glynn, Andrew Malcolm, Denise McCormick for A WINTER TAN.
Alison Grace, Penny Hozy, Andy Malcolm, Mike O'Farrell, Peter Thillaye for THE KISS.

Documentaries
Best Feature Documentary
CALLING THE SHOTS, produced by Janis Cole, Holly Dale.
COMIC BOOK CONFIDENTIAL, produced by Ron Mann.*
GROWING UP IN AMERICA, produced by Morley Markson.
A RUSTLING OF LEAVES; INSIDE THE PHILIPPINE REVOLUTION, produced by Nettie Wild.
WITNESSES, produced by Martyn Burke, David M. Ostriker.
Best Short Documentary
DYING TO BE PERFECT, produced by Eileen Hoeter.
SPACE PIONEERS, A CANADIAN STORY, produced by Rudy Buttignol.
THE WORLD IS WATCHING, produced by Harold Crooks, Jim Munro, Peter Raymont.*

Short Subjects
  Best Animated Short
    THE CAT CAME BACK, produced Cordell Barker, Richard Condie.*
    NOCTURNES, produced by Yves Leduc.

  Best Live Action Short
    INSIDE/OUT, produced by Lori Spring.
    THE JOB, produced by Donald Scott.
    THE MILKMAN COMETH, produced by Lorne Bailey.
    THE MYSTERIOUS MOON MEN OF CANADA, produced by Colin Brunton, Bruce McDonald.*
    LE PIED TENDRE, produced by Viateur Castonguay, Roger Boire.

46TH GOLDEN GLOBE AWARDS

Best Motion Picture-Drama
  RAIN MAN, UA/MGM-UA.

Best Motion Picture-Comedy/Musical
  WORKING GIRL.

Best Foreign Language Film
  PELLE THE CONQUEROR, (Den.).

Best Actor-Drama
  Dustin Hoffman for RAINMAN.

Best Actress-Drama (tie)
  Jodie Foster for THE ACCUSED.
  Shirley MacLaine for MADAME SOUSATZKA.

Best Actor-Comedy/Musical
  Tom Hanks for BIG.

Best Actress-Comedy/Musical
  Melanie Griffith for WORKING GIRL.

Best Supporting Actor
  Martin Landau for TUCKER: THE MAN AND HIS DREAM

Best Supporting Actress
  Sigourney Weaver for WORKING GIRL.

Best Director
  Clint Eastwood for BIRD.

Best Screenplay
  Naomi Foner for RUNNING ON EMPTY.

Best Original Score
  Maurice Jarre for GORILLAS IN THE MIST.

Best Original Song (tie)
  Carly Simon for "Let The River Run," WORKING GIRL.
  Lamont Dozier, Phil Collins for "Two Hearts," BUSTER.

Cecil B. DeMille Award
  Doris Day.

LONDON FILM CRITICS AWARDS

Best Film
  HOUSE OF GAMES, David Mamet.

Best Director
  John Huston for THE DEAD.

Best Actors
  Leo McKern for TRAVELLING NORTH (Aus.).
  Stephane Audran for BABETTE'S FEAST (Den.).

Best Screenplay
  David Mamet for HOUSE OF GAMES.

Best Foreign Language Film
  BABETTE'S FEAST (Den.), Gabriel Axel.

Best Music
  Miklos Rozsa for career achievement.

LOS ANGELES FILM CRITICS ASSOCIATION AWARDS

Best Film
  LITTLE DORRIT (Brit.), Christine Edzard.

Best Director
  David Cronenberg for DEAD RINGERS (Can.).

Best Actor
  Tom Hanks for BIG and PUNCHLINE.

Best Actress
  Christine Lahti for RUNNING ON EMPTY.

Best Foreign Film
  WINGS OF DESIRE (Ger.), Wim Wenders.

Best Supporting Actor
  Alec Guinness for LITTLE DORRIT (Brit.).

Best Supporting Actress
  Genevieve Bujold for DEAD RINGERS (Can.) and THE MODERNS.

Best Cinematography
  Henri Alekan for WINGS OF DESIRE (Ger.).

Best Screenplay
  Ron Shelton for BULL DURHAM.

Best Music
  Mark Isham for THE MODERNS.

Best Documentary
  HOTEL TERMINUS: THE LIFE AND TIMES OF KLAUS BARBIE, Marcel Ophuls.

Independent/Experimental Film
  THE LAST OF ENGLAND, Derek Jarman (Brit.).
  AMERIKA, Al Razutis.

Career Achievement Award
  Donald Siegel.

New Generation Award
  Mira Nair, director, SALAAM BOMBAY (India).

NATIONAL BOARD OF REVIEW D.W. GRIFFITH AWARDS

Best Picture
  MISSISSIPPI BURNING, Alan Parker.

Best Foreign Language Film
  WOMEN ON THE VERGE OF A NERVOUS BREAKDOWN (Sp.), Pedro Almodovar.

Best Director
  Alan Parker for MISSISSIPPI BURNING.

Best Actor
  Gene Hackman for MISSISSIPPI BURNING.

Best Actress
  Jodie Foster for THE ACCUSED.

Best Supporting Actor
  River Phoenix for RUNNING ON EMPTY.

Best Supporting Actress
  Frances McDormand for MISSISSIPPI BURNING.

Special Award for Best Documentary
  THE THIN BLUE LINE, Errol Morris.

NATIONAL SOCIETY OF FILM CRITICS

Best Picture
  THE UNBEARABLE LIGHTNESS OF BEING, Philip Kaufman.

Best Director
  Philip Kaufman for THE UNBEARABLE LIGHTNESS OF BEING.

Best Actor
  Michael Keaton

Best Actress
  Judy Davis

Best Supporting Actor
  Dean Stockwell

Best Supporting Actress
  Mercedes Ruehl

Best Screenplay
  Ron Shelton for BULL DURHAM.

Best Cinematography
  Henri Alekan for WINGS OF DESIRE.

Best Documentary
  THE THIN BLUE LINE, Errol Morris.

Special Award
  Pedro Almodovar for originality; WOMEN ON THE VERGE OF A NERVOUS BREAKDOWN, MATADOR.

54TH NEW YORK FILM CRITICS CIRCLE AWARDS

Best Picture
  THE ACCIDENTAL TOURIST, Lawrence Kasdan.

Best Director
  Chris Menges for A WORLD APART.

Best Actor
  Jeremy Irons for DEAD RINGERS.

Best Actress
  Meryl Streep for A CRY IN THE DARK.

Best Supporting Actor
  Dean Stockwell for MARRIED TO THE MOB and TUCKER.

Best Supporting Actress
  Diane Venora for BIRD.

Best Foreign Film
WOMEN ON THE VERGE OF A NERVOUS BREAKDOWN (Sp.), Pedro Almodovar.

Best Screenplay
Ron Shelton for BULL DURHAM.

Best Cinematography
Henri Alekan for WINGS OF DESIRE (Ger.).

Best Documentary
THE THIN BLUE LINE, Errol Morris.

41ST WRITERS GUILD OF AMERICA AWARDS

Best Screenplay Written Directly for the Screen
Gary Ross, Anne Spielberg for BIG.
Ron Shelton for BULL DURHAM.*
John Cleese for A FISH CALLED WANDA.
Ronald Bass, Barry Morrow for RAIN MAN.
Kevin Wade for WORKING GIRL.

Best Screenplay Adapted from Another Medium
Christopher Hampton for DANGEROUS LIAISONS.*
Frank Galati, Lawrence Kasdan for THE ACCIDENTAL TOURIST.
Jean-Claude Carriere, Philip Kaufman for THE UNBEARABLE LIGHTNESS OF BEING.
Anna Hamilton Phelan for GORILLAS IN THE MIST.
Jeffrey Price, Peter Seaman for WHO FRAMED ROGER RABBIT.

PHOTO CREDITS

All photos run with the permission of, and with all rights reserved by, the studios listed below.

ALIVE FILMS: VERNE MILLER

ATLANTIC ENTERTAINMENT: COP

BUENA VISTA: BIG BUSINESS; HEARTBREAK HOTEL; THE RESCUE; RETURN TO SNOWY RIVER, PART II; SHOOT TO KILL; WHO FRAMED ROGER RABBIT

CANNON GROUP: BRADDOCK: MISSING IN ACTION III

CINECOM: JULIA AND JULIA

CINETEL: BULLETPROOF

COLUMBIA: LITTLE NIKITA; THE NEW ADVENTURES OF PIPPI LONGSTOCKING; PUNCHLINE; SCHOOL DAZE

20TH CENTURY FOX: ALIEN NATION; BIG; DIE HARD; WORKING GIRL

KINO INTERNATIONAL: WEDDING IN GALILEE

LORIMAR: RETURN OF THE LIVING DEAD: PART II; TWO MOON JUNCTION

LUCASFILM: TUCKER: A MAN AND HIS DREAM

METROPOLIS: CANDY MOUNTAIN

MGM/UA: A FISH CALED WANDA; MASQUERADE; POLTERGIEST III; WILLOW; RAINMAN

MIRAMAX: RIDERS OF THE STORM

NEW CENTURY/VISTA: PASS THE AMMO; THE PENITENT

NEW LINE: HAIRSPRAY; CRITTERS 2: THE MAIN COURSE; A HANDFUL OF DUST; JUDGMENT IN BERLIN; TORCH SONG TRILOGY; TOUGHER THAN LEATHER

NEW STAR ENTERTAINMENT: FRANKENSTEIN GENERAL HOSPITAL

NEW WORLD: 18 AGAIN; SISTER SISTER

ORION: BULL DURHAM; COLORS; DIRTY ROTTEN SCOUNDRELS; EIGHT MEN OUT; MARRIED TO THE MOB; MISSISSIPPI BURNING; MONKEY SHINES: AN EXPERIMENT IN FEAR; AU REVOIR LES ENFANTS

PARAMOUNT: BIG TOP PEE WEE; COMING TO AMERICA; FRIDAY THE 13TH: PART VII—THE NEW BLOOD; PERMANENT RECORD; THE PRESIDIO; SCROOGED; THE NAKED GUN

RAINBOW/CASTLE HILL: SOMEONE TO LOVE

TRANS WORLD: FULL MOON IN BLUE WATER; KANSAS; SEVEN HOURS TO JUDGMENT

TRI-STAR: BAT 21; THE BLOB; FOR KEEPS; HIGH SPIRITS; IRON EAGLE II; THE SEVENTH SIGN; SHORT CIRCUIT 2; SUNSET; SWEETHEARTS DANCE; SWITCHING CHANNELS; THE KISS; RED HEAT

UNITED FILM: RETRIBUTION

MCA (UNIVERSAL): CASUAL SEX; THE GREAT OUTDOORS; THE LAND BEFORE TIME; THE LAST TEMPTATION OF CHRIST; MIDNIGHT RUN; MILAGRO BEANFIELD WAR; MOON OVER PARADOR; PHANTASM II; SHAKEDOWN; THEY LIVE; TWINS; GORILLAS IN THE MIST

WARNER BROS.: RUNNING ON EMPTY

WEINTRAUB ENTERTAINMENT: MY STEPMOTHER IS AN ALIEN